W9-CLD-571

Literature to Go

FOURTH EDITION

MICHAEL MEYER

University of Connecticut

D. QUENTIN MILLER

Suffolk University

bedford/st.martin's
Macmillan Learning
Boston | New York

For Bedford/St. Martin's

Vice President, Editorial, Macmillan Learning Humanities: Leasa Burton
Program Director for English: Stacey Purviance
Senior Program Manager: John E. Sullivan, III
Marketing Manager: Lauren Arrant
Director of Content Development, Humanities: Jane Knetzger
Executive Developmental Editor: Christina Gerogiannis
Associate Editor: Lexi DeConti
Senior Content Project Manager: Kendra LeFleur
Workflow Project Manager: Lisa McDowell
Production Supervisor: Robin Besofsky
Media Project Manager: Allison Hart
Assistant Editor: Cari Goldfine
Editorial Assistant: Samantha Storms
Project Management: Lumina Datamatics, Inc.
Composition: Lumina Datamatics, Inc.
Text Permissions Manager: Kalina Ingham
Text Permissions Researcher: Arthur Johnson
Photo Permissions Editor: Angela Boehler
Photo Researcher: Brittani Morgan
Director of Design, Content Management: Diana Blume
Text Design: Lumina Datamatics, Inc.
Cover Design: William Boardman
Cover Image: Phoebe Beasley, *Flowers For My Soul To Keep*/Education Images/UIG/ Getty Images
Printing and Binding: LSC Communications

Manufactured in the United States of America.

1 2 3 4 5 6   23 22 21 20 19

For information, write: Bedford/St. Martin's, 75 Arlington Street, Boston, MA 02116

ISBN 978-1-319-19592-2 *(paperback)*

Acknowledgments

Text acknowledgments and copyrights appear at the back of the book on pages 1174–1180, which constitute an extension of the copyright page. Art acknowledgments and copyrights appear on the same page as the art selections they cover.

For My Wife
Regina Barreca
—M. M.

For Michael:
Mentor, Guide, Friend.
—D. Q. M.

About Michael Meyer

Michael Meyer, Emeritus Professor of English, taught writing and literature courses for more than thirty years — since 1981 at the University of Connecticut and before that at the University of North Carolina at Charlotte and the College of William and Mary. In addition to being an experienced teacher, Meyer is a highly regarded literary scholar. His scholarly articles have appeared in distinguished journals such as *American Literature, Studies in the American Renaissance,* and *Virginia Quarterly Review.* An internationally recognized authority on Henry David Thoreau, Meyer is a former president of the Thoreau Society and coauthor (with Walter Harding) of *The New Thoreau Handbook,* a standard reference source. His first book, *Several More Lives to Live: Thoreau's Political Reputation in America,* was awarded the Ralph Henry Gabriel Prize by the American Studies Association. He is also the editor of *Frederick Douglass: The Narrative and Selected Writings.* He has lectured on a variety of American literary topics from Cambridge University to Peking University. His other books for Bedford/St. Martin's include *The Bedford Introduction to Literature, The Compact Bedford Introduction to Literature, Thinking and Writing about Poetry, Poetry: An Introduction,* and *Thinking and Writing about Literature.*

About D. Quentin Miller

D. Quentin Miller, Professor of English, has taught literature and writing at Suffolk University in Boston since 2000. Prior to that he taught at Gustavus Adolphus College in Minnesota, at the University of Connecticut (where he wrote his dissertation under the direction of Michael Meyer), and in a variety of other settings, including prisons. Miller is the author, editor, or coeditor of a dozen books and over two dozen critical essays in collections and in scholarly journals such as *American Literature, African American Review,* and *The James Baldwin Review.* He is an internationally renowned scholar on the works of James Baldwin and has also published original fiction and reviews in publications such as *TLS.* His most recent books are *James Baldwin in Context* (2019), *Understanding John Edgar Wideman* (2018), *American Literature in Transition: 1980–1990* (2018), and *The Routledge Introduction to African American Literature* (2016).

Preface for Instructors

Like its predecessors, the fourth edition of *Literature to Go* assumes that reading and understanding literature offers a valuable means of apprehending life in its richness and diversity. This book also reflects the hope that its selections will inspire students to become lifelong readers of imaginative literature, as well as more thoughtful and skillful writers.

As before, the text is flexibly organized into four parts focusing on fiction, poetry, drama, and critical thinking and writing. The first three parts explain the literary elements of each genre. These three parts also explore several additional approaches to reading literature and conclude with an anthology of literary works. The fourth part provides detailed instruction on thinking, reading, and writing about literature that can be assigned selectively throughout the course. Sample student papers and hundreds of assignments appear in the text, offering students the support they need to read and write about literature.

Literature to Go accommodates many different teaching styles. New to the fourth edition are 131 carefully chosen stories, poems, and plays — as well as thematic case studies on privacy and on war and its aftermath in the fiction section, a case study on song lyrics in the poetry section, and streamlined and up-to-date support for critical thinking, reading, and writing.

FEATURES OF *LITERATURE TO GO*, FOURTH EDITION

A wide and well-balanced selection of literature

36 stories, 227 poems, and 8 plays represent a variety of periods, nationalities, cultures, styles, and voices — from the serious to the humorous, and from the traditional to the contemporary. Each selection has been chosen for its appeal to students and for its effectiveness in demonstrating the elements, significance, and pleasures of literature. As in previous editions, canonical works by Ernest Hemingway, John Keats, Susan Glaspell, Oscar Wilde, and many others are generously represented. In addition, there are many contemporary selections from well-regarded writers including T. C. Boyle, Martín Espada, ZZ Packer, and Lynn Nottage. This edition also includes a selection of song lyrics as poetry, a topic that should generate considerable interest for both instructors and students.

Many options for teaching and learning about literature

In an effort to make literature come to life for students and the course a pleasure to teach for instructors, *Literature to Go* offers these innovative features:

PERSPECTIVES ON LITERATURE Intriguing documents — including letters, critical essays, interviews, and contextual images — appear throughout the book to stimulate class discussion and writing.

CONNECTIONS BETWEEN "POPULAR" AND "LITERARY" CULTURE The fiction, poetry, and drama introductions incorporate examples from popular culture, effectively introducing students to the literary elements of a given genre through what they already know, such as song lyrics as a close relative of poetry. Lively visuals throughout the anthology demonstrate how literature is woven into the fabric of popular culture and art. These images help students recognize the imprint of literature on their everyday lives.

CASE STUDIES THAT TREAT AUTHORS IN DEPTH Each genre section includes a chapter that focuses closely on at least one major figure. There are three stories by Flannery O'Connor; an extensive selection of poems by Emily Dickinson; and a play each by Sophocles and Shakespeare with background information to help students engage with these master works. Complementing the literature in these chapters are biographical introductions (with author photographs); critical perspectives (including complementary critical readings where writers argue for different interpretations of the same texts); cultural documents (such as letters and draft manuscript pages); and a generous collection of images that serve to contextualize the works. A variety of critical thinking and writing questions follow the selections to stimulate student responses. All these supplementary materials engage students more fully with the writers and their works. In addition, a case study created in collaboration with contemporary poet Billy Collins presents the author's own works alongside rare photographs, manuscript pages, and his insights (written specifically for this book) into each work, giving students a unique opportunity to have a major writer speak directly to them.

ACCESSIBLE COVERAGE OF LITERARY THEORY For instructors who wish to incorporate literary theory into their courses, Chapter 30, "Critical Strategies for Reading," introduces students to a variety of critical strategies, ranging from formalism to cultural criticism. In brief examples the approaches are applied in analyzing Kate Chopin's "The Story of an Hour" as well as other works, so that students will develop a sense of how to use these strategies in their own reading and writing.

Plenty of help with reading, writing, and research

CRITICAL READING[1]   Advice on how to read literature appears at the beginning of each genre section. Sample close readings of selections including Kate Chopin's "The Story of an Hour" and Susan Glaspell's *Trifles* provide analyses of the language, images, and other literary elements at work in these selections. Interpretive annotations in the Chopin and Glaspell selections clearly show students the process of close reading and provide examples of the kind of critical thinking that leads to strong academic writing.

Later in the book, Chapter 31, "Writing about Literature," provides more instruction on how to read a work closely, annotate a text, take notes, keep a reading journal, and develop a topic into a thesis, with a section on arguing persuasively about literature. An Index of Terms appears at the back of the book, and a glossary provides thorough explanations of more than two hundred terms central to the study of literature.

THE WRITING AND RESEARCH PROCESS   The fourth part of the anthology, the newly streamlined "Strategies for Reading and Writing," covers every step of the writing process — from generating topics to documenting sources — while sample student papers model the results.

Chapter 31, "Writing about Literature," offers models of the types of papers most frequently assigned in the introductory course and contains sections on the particular demands of writing about fiction, poetry, and drama.

Sample student papers — all in up-to-date MLA style — model how to analyze and argue about literature and how to support ideas by citing examples. The papers are integrated throughout the book, as are "Questions for Writing" units that guide students through particular writing tasks: reading and writing responsively; developing a topic into a revised thesis; incorporating secondary sources; applying a critical approach to a work; and writing about multiple works by an author.

Chapter 32, "The Literary Research Paper," offers detailed advice for finding, evaluating, and incorporating sources in a paper and includes current, detailed MLA documentation guidelines.

QUESTIONS FOR CRITICAL READING AND WRITING   Hundreds of questions and assignments — "Considerations for Critical Thinking and Writing," "Connections to Other Selections," "First Response" prompts, "Critical Strategies" questions, and "Creative Response" assignments — spark students' interest, sharpen their thinking, and improve their reading, discussion, and writing skills.

---

[1] A reference chart on the book's inside front cover outlines all of the book's help for reading and writing about literature.

NEW TO THIS EDITION

131 classic and contemporary selections

24 STORIES, 103 POEMS, AND 4 PLAYS representing canonical, multicultural, contemporary, and popular literature are new to this edition. Complementing the addition of several classic literary works are numerous stories, poems, and plays not frequently anthologized. These include stories by Judith Ortiz Cofer, Edwidge Danticat, James Baldwin, and Ursula K. Le Guin; poems by Charles Bukowski, Kwame Dawes, and Patricia Smith; and plays by Lynn Nottage, David Auburn, and Oscar Wilde. The stories, poems, and plays new to this edition are a rich collection of traditional, contemporary, and multicultural literature — works that will make classroom discussion come alive.

A thematic case study on the natural world

This chapter offers literature as rich, varied, and often personal as the subject itself — with such works as Gail White's "Dead Armadillos" (on beauty, scarcity, and what we choose to save) and Dave Lucas's "November" (a vivid description of how quickly and dramatically our surroundings can change).

A case study on song lyrics as poetry

In 2016 the Nobel Prize in Literature was awarded to a songwriter — Bob Dylan — for the first time, and the Pulitzer Prize in Music was awarded to Kendrick Lamar in 2018, the first time the award was given to a hip-hop artist. The association between music and poetry is ancient, but now is an excellent time to acknowledge the connection and to invite students to further explore the possibilities it affords.

Reimagined and up-to-date support for critical thinking, reading, and writing

Three streamlined chapters now appear as a single grouping at the end of the book. The accessible, relatable, and realistic advice in these chapters gives students the help they need to write thoughtfully and critically about literature.

ACKNOWLEDGMENTS

This book has benefited from the ideas, suggestions, and corrections of scores of careful readers who helped transform various stages of an evolving manuscript into a finished book and into subsequent editions. We remain grateful to those we have thanked in previous prefaces, particularly the late Robert Wallace of Case Western Reserve University. In addition, many instructors who have used these anthologies responded to a questionnaire. For their valuable comments and advice, we are grateful to Sandra Cooper, College of Central Florida; Andrea Dickinson, Muskegon Community College; Laurie Dickinson, Lord Fairfax Community College; Jennifer Eble, Cleveland State Community College; Paul Edwards, Lord Fairfax Community College; Peter Eliopoulos, North Shore Community College; Bryna Siegel Finer, Indiana University of Pennsylvania; Megan Fischer, Angelina College; Charity Freeman, Hillsborough Community College; Jeannie Gauthier, Louisiana College; Neil Johnston, Louisiana College; Susan Meyer, Harford Community College; Tony Perrello, California State University at Stanislaus; Marc Pietrzykowski, Niagara County Community College; Meredyth Puller, Harford Community College; and Kathleen Smith, University of South Carolina at Aiken.

We would also like to give special thanks to the following instructors who contributed teaching tips to *Resources for Teaching Literature to Go*: Sandra Adickes, Helen J. Aling, Sr. Anne Denise Brenann, Robin Calitri, James H. Clemmer, Robert Croft, Thomas Edwards, Elizabeth Kleinfeld, Olga Lyles, Timothy Peters, Catherine Rusco, Robert M. St. John, Richard Stoner, Nancy Veiga, Karla Walters, and Joseph Zeppetello.

We are also indebted to those who cheerfully answered questions and generously provided miscellaneous bits of information. What might have seemed to them like inconsequential conversations turned out to be important leads. Among these friends and colleagues are Raymond Anselment, Barbara Campbell, Ann Charters, Karen Chow, John Christie, Eleni Coundouriotis, Irving Cummings, William Curtin, Patrick Hogan, Lee Jacobus, Thomas Jambeck, Bonnie Januszewski-Ytuarte, Greta Little, George Monteiro, Brenda Murphy, Joel Myerson, Rose Quiello, Thomas Recchio, William Sheidley, Stephanie Smith, Milton Stern, Kenneth Wilson, and the dedicated reference librarians at the Homer Babbidge Library, University of Connecticut. We are particularly happy to acknowledge the tactful help of Roxanne Cody, owner of R. J. Julia Booksellers in Madison, Connecticut, whose passion for books authorizes her as the consummate matchmaker for writers, readers, and titles.

We continue to be grateful for what we have learned from teaching our students and for the many student papers we have received over the years that have served as good and accessible models of student writing.

At Bedford/St. Martin's, our debts require more time to acknowledge than the deadline allows. This edition has benefited from the savvy insights of Leasa Burton, Jane Knetzger, John Sullivan, and Maura Shea. As our development editor, Christina Gerogiannis expertly kept the book on track and made the journey a pleasure to the end; her valuable contributions richly remind us of how fortunate we are to be Bedford/St. Martin's authors. Lexi DeConti, associate editor; Cari Goldfine, assistant editor; and Samantha Storms, editorial assistant, gracefully handled a variety of important editorial tasks. Permissions were deftly arranged by Hilary Newman, Kalina Ingham, Arthur Johnson, Angela Boehler, and Brittani Morgan Grimes. The difficult tasks of production were skillfully managed by Kendra LeFleur and Aravinda Doss, whose attention to details and deadlines was essential to the completion of this project. We thank all of the people at Bedford/St. Martin's — including William Boardman, who designed the cover, and Lauren Arrant, the marketing manager — who helped to make this formidable project a manageable one. And we thank Bedford/St. Martin's founders Charles H. Christensen and Joan E. Feinberg for initiating the first edition and launching it with their intelligence, energy, and sound advice.

Finally, we are grateful for our families: Michael for his sons, Timothy and Matthew, for all kinds of help, but mostly he's just grateful they're his sons. And for making all the difference, Michael thanks his wife, Regina Barreca. Quentin is grateful for his sons, Brennan and Owen, for helping him rediscover the pleasures of reading and teaching all over again, and for his wife, Julie Nash, his first and best reader.

— Michael Meyer
— D. Quentin Miller

BEDFORD/ST. MARTIN'S PUTS YOU FIRST

From day one, our goal has been simple: to provide inspiring resources that are grounded in best practices for teaching reading and writing. For more than 35 years, Bedford/St. Martin's has partnered with the field, listening to teachers, scholars, and students about the support writers need. We are committed to helping every writing instructor make the most of our resources.

How can we help you?

- Our editors can align our resources to your outcomes through correlation and transition guides for your syllabus. Just ask us.
- Our sales representatives specialize in helping you find the right materials to support your course goals.
- Our *Bits* blog on the Bedford/St. Martin's English Community (**community.macmillan.com**) publishes fresh teaching ideas weekly. You'll also find easily downloadable professional resources and links to author webinars on our community site.

Contact your Bedford/St. Martin's sales representative or visit **macmillanlearning.com** to learn more.

Print and Digital Options for Literature to Go

Choose the format that works best for your course, and ask about our packaging options that offer savings for students.

Print

- To order the paperback edition, use ISBN 978-1-319-19592-2.

Digital

- *Innovative digital learning space.* Bedford/St. Martin's suite of digital tools makes it easy to get everyone on the same page by putting student writers at the center. For details, visit **macmillanlearning.com/englishdigital**.
- *Popular e-book formats.* For details about our e-book partners, visit **macmillanlearning.com/ebooks**.
- *Inclusive Access.* Enable every student to receive their course materials through your LMS on the first day of class. Macmillan Learning's Inclusive Access program is the easiest, most affordable way to ensure

all students have access to quality educational resources. Find out more at **macmillanlearning.com/inclusiveaccess**.

Your Course, Your Way

No two writing programs or classrooms are exactly alike. Our Curriculum Solutions team works with you to design custom options that provide the resources your students need. (Options below require enrollment minimums.)

- *ForeWords for English.* Customize any print resource to fit the focus of your course or program by choosing from a range of prepared topics, such as Sentence Guides for Academic Writers.
- *Macmillan Author Program (MAP).* Add excerpts or package acclaimed works from Macmillan's trade imprints to connect students with prominent authors and public conversations. A list of popular examples or academic themes is available upon request.
- *Bedford Select.* Build your own print handbook or anthology from a database of more than 800 selections, and add your own materials to create your ideal text. Package with any Bedford/St. Martin's text for additional savings. Visit **macmillanlearning.com/bedfordselect**.

Instructor Resources

You have a lot to do in your course. We want to make it easy for you to find the support you need — and to get it quickly.

Resources for Teaching Literature to Go is available as a PDF that can be downloaded from **macmillanlearning.com**. In addition to chapter overviews and teaching tips, the instructor's manual includes sample syllabi, suggested responses to questions throughout the text, and classroom activities.

Brief Contents

STRATEGIES FOR READING AND WRITING 1067

Contents

FICTION IN DEPTH 231

A COLLECTION OF STORIES 287

POETRY   359

THE ELEMENTS OF POETRY   361

11. Reading Poetry   363

A COLLECTION OF POEMS 641

Developing a Draft, Integrating Sources, and Organizing the Paper

Documenting Sources and Avoiding Plagiarism

Glossary of Literary Terms

INTRODUCTION

Reading
Imaginative Literature

To seek the source, the impulse of a
story is like tearing a flower to pieces
for wantonness.
— KATE CHOPIN

Missouri Historical Society,
St. Louis.

THE NATURE OF LITERATURE

Literature does not lend itself to a single tidy definition because the making
of it over the centuries has been as complex, unwieldy, and natural as life
itself. Is literature everything that has been written, from ancient prayers to
graffiti? Does it include songs and stories that were not written down until
many years after they were recited? Does literature include the television
scripts from *The Simpsons* as well as Shakespeare's *King Lear*? Is literature
only writing that has permanent value and continues to move people? Must
literature be true or beautiful or moral? Should it be socially useful?

Although these kinds of questions are not conclusively answered in this
book, they are implicitly raised by the stories, poems, and plays included

1

here. No definition of literature, particularly a brief one, is likely to satisfy everyone because definitions tend to weaken and require qualification when confronted by the uniqueness of individual works. In this context it is worth recalling Herman Melville's humorous use of a definition of a whale in *Moby-Dick* (1851). In the course of the novel Melville presents his imaginative and symbolic whale as inscrutable, but he begins with a quotation from Georges Cuvier, a French naturalist who defines a whale in his nineteenth-century study *The Animal Kingdom* this way: "The whale is a mammiferous animal without hind feet." Cuvier's description is technically correct, of course, but there is little wisdom in it. Melville understood that the reality of the whale (which he describes as the "ungraspable phantom of life") cannot be caught by isolated facts. If the full meaning of the whale is to be understood, it must be sought on the open sea of experience, where the whale itself is, rather than in exclusionary definitions. Facts and definitions are helpful; however, they do not always reveal the whole truth.

Despite Melville's reminder that a definition can be too limiting and even comical, it is useful for our purposes to describe literature as a fiction consisting of carefully arranged words designed to stir the imagination. Stories, poems, and plays are fictional. They are made up — imagined — even when based on actual historic events. Such imaginative writing differs from other kinds of writing because its purpose is not primarily to transmit facts or ideas. Imaginative literature is a source more of pleasure than of information, and we read it for basically the same reasons we listen to music or view a dance: enjoyment, delight, and satisfaction. Like other art forms, imaginative literature offers pleasure and usually attempts to convey a perspective, mood, feeling, or experience. Writers transform the facts the world provides — people, places, and objects — into experiences that suggest meanings.

Consider, for example, the difference between the following factual description of a snake and a poem on the same subject. Here is *Merriam-Webster's Eleventh New Collegiate Dictionary*'s definition:

> any of numerous limbless scaled reptiles (suborder Serpentes syn. Ophidia) with a long tapering body and with salivary glands often modified to produce venom which is injected through grooved or tubular fangs.

Contrast this matter-of-fact definition with Emily Dickinson's poetic evocation of a snake in "A narrow Fellow in the Grass":

A narrow Fellow in the Grass
Occasionally rides —
You may have met Him — did you not
His notice sudden is —

The Grass divides as with a Comb —   5
A spotted shaft is seen —
And then it closes at your feet
And opens further on —

He likes a Boggy Acre
A floor too cool for Corn —
Yet when a Boy, and Barefoot —
I more than once at Noon

Have passed, I thought, a Whip lash
Unbraiding in the Sun
When stooping to secure it
It wrinkled, and was gone —

Several of Nature's People
I know, and they know me —
I feel for them a transport
Of cordiality —

But never met this Fellow
Attended, or alone
Without a tighter breathing
And Zero at the Bone —

10

15

20

The dictionary provides a succinct, anatomical description of what a snake is, while Dickinson's poem suggests what a snake can mean, or how it might be perceived by someone with a keen creative sensibility. The definition offers facts; the poem offers an experience. The dictionary would probably allow someone who had never seen a snake to sketch one with reasonable accuracy. The poem also provides some vivid subjective descriptions — for example, the snake dividing the grass "as with a Comb" — yet it offers more than a picture of serpentine movements. The poem conveys the ambivalence many people have about snakes — the kind of feeling, for example, so evident on the faces of visitors viewing the snakes at a zoo. In the poem there is both a fascination with and a horror of what might be called snakehood; this combination of feelings has been coiled in most of us since Adam and Eve.

That "narrow Fellow" so cordially introduced by way of a riddle (the word *snake* is never used in the poem) is, by the final stanza, revealed as a snake in the grass. In between, Dickinson uses language expressively to convey her meaning. For instance, in the line "His notice sudden is," listen to the *s* sound in each word and note how the verb *is* unexpectedly appears at the end, making the snake's hissing presence all the more "sudden." And anyone who has ever been surprised by a snake knows the "tighter breathing / And Zero at the Bone" that Dickinson evokes so successfully by the rhythm of her word choices and line breaks. Perhaps even more significant, Dickinson's poem allows those who have never encountered a snake to imagine such an experience.

A good deal more could be said about the numbing fear that undercuts the affection for nature at the beginning of this poem, but the point here is that imaginative literature gives us not so much the full, factual proportions of the world as some of its experiences and meanings. Instead of defining the world, literature encourages us to try it out in our imaginations.

THE VALUE OF LITERATURE

Mark Twain once shrewdly observed that a person who chooses not to read has no advantage over a person who is unable to read. In industrialized societies today, however, the question is not who reads, because nearly everyone can and does, but what is read. Why should anyone spend precious time with literature when there is so much informational reading material available on our smart phones? Why should a literary artist's imagination compete for attention that could be spent on the firm realities that constitute everyday life? In fact, national best-seller lists much less often include collections of stories, poems, or plays than they do cookbooks, and not surprisingly, diet books. Although such fare may be filling, it doesn't stay with you. Most people have other appetites too.

Certainly one of the most important values of literature is that it nourishes our emotional lives. An effective literary work may seem to speak directly to us, especially if we are ripe for it. The inner life that good writers reveal in their characters often gives us glimpses of some portion of ourselves. We can be moved to laugh, cry, tremble, dream, ponder, shriek, or rage with a character by simply turning a page instead of turning our lives upside down. Although the experience itself is imagined, the emotion is real. That's why the final chapters of a good adventure novel can make a reader's heart race as much as a 100-yard dash or why the repressed love of Hester Prynne in Nathaniel Hawthorne's novel *The Scarlet Letter* (1850) is painful to a sympathetic reader. Human emotions speak a universal language regardless of when or where a work was written.

In addition to appealing to our emotions, literature broadens our perspectives on the world. Most of the people we meet tend to be like ourselves, and what we can see of the world even over the course of a lifetime is astonishingly limited. Literature allows us to move beyond the inevitable boundaries of our own lives and culture because it introduces us to people different from ourselves, places remote from our neighborhoods, and times other than our own. Reading makes us more aware of life's possibilities as well as its subtleties and ambiguities. Put simply, people who read literature experience more life and have a keener sense of a common human identity than those who do not. It is true, of course, that many people go through life without reading imaginative literature, but they are missing out on an essential human experience. They may find themselves troubled by the same kinds of questions that reveal Daisy Buchanan's restless, vague discontentment in F. Scott Fitzgerald's *The Great Gatsby* (1925): "What'll we do with ourselves this afternoon?" cried Daisy, "and the day after that, and the next thirty years?"

Sometimes students mistakenly associate literature more with school than with life. Accustomed to reading it in order to write a paper or pass an examination, students may perceive such reading as a chore instead of a pleasurable opportunity, something considerably less important than studying for the "practical" courses that prepare them in obvious ways for a career. The study of literature, however, is also practical because it engages readers in the kinds of problem solving important in a variety of fields, from philosophy to science and technology. The interpretation of literary texts demands an engagement with ambiguity, morality, and emotional volatility, all of which are unavoidable aspects of life.

Because it pushes the boundaries of language, literature embraces the complexity of human experience. People who make the most significant contributions to their professions — whether in business, engineering, teaching, or some other area — tend to become excited about the existence of multiple possibilities. Instead of retreating to the way things have always been done, they bring freshness and creativity to their work. F. Scott Fitzgerald once astutely described the "test of a first-rate intelligence" as "the ability to hold two opposed ideas in the mind at the same time, and still retain the ability to function." People with such intelligence know how to read situations, shape questions, interpret details, and evaluate competing points of view. Equipped with a healthy respect for facts, they also understand the value of pursuing hunches and exercising their imaginations. They are interested as much in "problem finding" as "problem solving." Reading literature encourages a suppleness of mind that is helpful in any discipline or work.

Once the requirements for your degree are completed, what ultimately matters are not the courses listed on your transcript but the sensibilities and habits of mind that you bring to your work, friends, family, and every other dimension of your life. A healthy economy changes and grows with the times; people do too, but only if they are prepared for more than simply filling a job description, or solving a problem that someone else has identified. The range and variety of life that literature affords can help you to interpret your own experiences and the world in which you live.

To discover the insights that literature reveals requires careful reading and sensitivity. One of the purposes of a college introduction to literature class is to cultivate the analytic skills necessary for reading well. Class discussions often help establish an understanding of a work that might not be available if you were reading in solitude. You can also develop interpretive skills by writing about what you read. Writing is an effective means of clarifying and deepening your responses and ideas because it requires you to account for the author's use of language as well as your own. This book is based on two premises: that reading literature is pleasurable and that reading and understanding a work sensitively by thinking, talking, or writing about it increases the pleasure of the experience of it.

Understanding literature's basic elements — such as point of view, symbol, theme, tone, irony, and so on — is a prerequisite to an informed appreciation of it. This kind of understanding allows you to perceive more in a literary work in much the same way that a spectator at a tennis match sees more if he or she understands the rules and conventions of the game. But rules and conventions are just the beginning. It might take many years of watching tennis to understand the unique gifts of Rafael Nadal or Serena Williams even if you see them dominate (or even lose) an individual match. The more literature you read, the richer the experience becomes as you understand how every poem, play, or story is a unique contribution to the ever-growing literary landscape even though all of them are basically rear-rangements of the same twenty-six letters of the alphabet. The analytic skills that open up literature also have their uses when you listen to music, or watch a television program or film and, more important, when you attempt to sort out the significance of the people, places, and events that constitute your own life. Literature enhances and sharpens your perceptions. What could be more lastingly practical as well as satisfying?

THE CHANGING LITERARY CANON

Perhaps the best reading creates some kind of change in us: we see more clearly; we're alert to nuances; we ask questions that previously didn't occur to us. Henry David Thoreau had that sort of reading in mind when he remarked in *Walden* (1854) that the books he valued most were those that caused him to date "a new era in his life from the reading." Readers are sometimes changed by literature, but it is also worth noting that the life of a literary work can also be affected by the ways books are distributed, reviewed, and recommended (as well as assigned in courses like the one you are taking). Fitzgerald's *The Great Gatsby*, for instance, really achieved the status of an accepted classic not when it was first published, but a quar-ter-century later during World War II, when the American military distrib-uted tens of thousands of copies of the book to G.I.s who needed to pass the time. This is not to take away from the book's greatness, but rather to suggest that a huge number of readers help a book's reputation. Around the turn of the twenty-first century Oprah Winfrey's televised book club could instantly turn an obscure writer into a household name. Today book reviews on Amazon or on social media sites such as Goodreads have weak-ened the power of traditional professional literary reviewers in venues like the *New York Times Book Review* or the *Times Literary Supplement*.

Such changes have steadily accelerated as the literary **canon** — those works considered by scholars, critics, and teachers to be the most import-ant to read and study — has undergone a significant series of shifts. The importance of certain canonical writers such as William Shakespeare or Charles Dickens has rarely been questioned, but other writers that your great-grandparents would likely have heard of such as Anthony Trollope or Sherwood Anderson are probably not in your field of reference. There has also been a widespread effort to scrutinize whether the establishment of an agreed-upon list of "great books" excluded writers whose voices, per-spectives, and backgrounds were marginal to society's mainstream. In the nineteenth and twentieth centuries, the people who established the canon were almost uniformly wealthy, educated, white, and male, and the authors they canonized were as well. Writers who previously were overlooked, undervalued, neglected, or studiously ignored have been brought into focus in an effort to create a more diverse literary canon, one that recognizes the contributions of many cultures and a wide range of individual perspectives. In the 1980s, for example, the famous novelist Alice Walker argued convincingly that American readers had been neglecting the work of Zora Neale Hurston, a folklorist and fiction writer who died in poverty and obscurity in 1960 after achieving some fame during the Harlem Renaissance in the 1920s. Walker argued that Hurston was neglected partially because of her race, gender, and refusal to conform to standard literary tastes. Walker's argument was convincing: at least for a time, Hurston's novel *Their Eyes Were Watching God* (1937) was widely taught in high schools and colleges alongside canonical works like J. D. Salinger's *The Catcher in the Rye* (1951). This kind of enlargement of the canon resulted from reform movements of the 1960s and 1970s. The civil rights, feminist, and gay pride movements of that era sensitized literary critics to the political, moral, and esthetic necessity of reevaluating women writers and African American literature. More recently, LGBTQ+, Native American, Asian, and Latinx writers have been making their way into the American literary canon. Moreover, on a broader scale, the canon is being revised and enlarged to include the works of writers from parts of the world other than the West, a development that reflects the changing values, concerns, and complexities of recent decades, when literary landscapes have shifted as dramatically as the political boundaries of much of the world.

No semester's reading list — or anthology — can adequately or accurately echo all the new voices competing to be heard as part of the mainstream literary canon, but recent efforts to open up the canon attempt to sensitize readers to a plurality of writers from all over the world. This development has not occurred without its urgent advocates or passionate dissenters. It's no surprise that issues about race, gender, and class often get people off the fence and on their feet. (These controversies are discussed further in Chapter 30, "Critical Strategies for Reading.") Although what we regard as literature — whether it's called great, classic, or canonical — continues to generate debate, there is no question that such controversy will continue to reflect readers' values as well as the writers they admire.

FICTION

The Elements
of Fiction

1

Reading Fiction

When you're writing, you're trying to find out something which you don't know. The whole language of writing for me is finding out what you don't want to know, what you don't want to find out. But something forces you to anyway.

— JAMES BALDWIN

READING FICTION RESPONSIVELY

Reading a literary work responsively can be an intensely demanding activity. Henry David Thoreau — about as intense and demanding a reader and writer as they come — insists that "books must be read as deliberately and reservedly as they were written." Thoreau is right about the necessity for a conscious, sustained involvement with a literary work. Imaginative literature does demand more from us than, say, browsing through *People* magazine in a dentist's waiting room, but Thoreau makes the process sound a little more daunting than it really is. For when we respond to the demands of responsive reading, our efforts are usually rewarded with pleasure as well as understanding. Careful, deliberate reading — the kind that engages a reader's imagination as it calls forth the writer's — is a means of exploration that can take a reader outside whatever circumstance or experience previously defined his or her world. Just as we respond moment by moment to people and situations in our lives, we also respond to literary works as we read them, though we may not be fully aware of how we are affected at each point along the way. The more conscious we are of how and why we respond to works in particular ways, the more likely we are to be imaginatively engaged in our reading.

In a very real sense both the reader and the author create the literary work. How a reader responds to a story, poem, or play will help to determine its meaning. The author arranges the various elements that constitute his or her craft — elements such as plot, character, setting, point of view, symbolism, theme, and style, which you will be examining in subsequent chapters and which are defined in the Glossary of Literary Terms (p. 1152) — but the author cannot completely control the reader's response any more than a person can absolutely predict how a remark or action will be received by a stranger, a friend, or even a family member. Few authors *tell* readers how to respond. Our sympathy, anger, confusion, laughter, sadness, or whatever the feeling might be is left up to us to experience. Writers may have the talent to evoke such feelings, but they don't have the power and authority to enforce them. Because of the range of possible responses produced by imaginative literature, there is no single, correct, definitive response or interpretation. There can be readings that are wrongheaded or foolish, and some readings are better than others — that is, more responsive to a work's details and more persuasive — but that doesn't mean there is only one possible reading of a work (see Chapter 31, "Writing about Literature").

Experience tells us that different people respond differently to the same work. Consider, for example, how often you've heard Melville's *Moby-Dick* described as one of the greatest American novels. This, however, is how a reviewer in *New Monthly Magazine* described the book when it was published in 1851: it is "a huge dose of hyperbolical slang, maudlin sentimentalism and tragic-comic bubble and squeak." Melville surely did not intend or desire this response; but there it is, and it was not a singular, isolated reaction. This reading — like any other reading — was influenced by the values, assumptions, and expectations that the readers brought to the novel from both previous readings and life experiences. The reviewer's refusal to take the book seriously may have caused him to miss the boat from the perspective of many other readers of *Moby-Dick,* but it indicates that even "classics" (perhaps especially those kinds of works) can generate disparate readings.

Consider the following brief story by Kate Chopin, a writer whose fiction (like Melville's) sometimes met with indifference or hostility in her own time. As you read, keep track of your responses to the central character, Mrs. Mallard. Write down your feelings about her in a substantial paragraph when you finish the story. Think, for example, about how you respond to the emotions she expresses concerning news of her husband's death. What do you think of her feelings about marriage? Do you think you would react the way she does under similar circumstances?

KATE CHOPIN (1851–1904)

The Story of an Hour 1894

Knowing that Mrs. Mallard was afflicted with a heart trouble, great care was taken to break to her as gently as possible the news of her husband's death.

Missouri Historical Society, St. Louis.

It was her sister Josephine who told her, in broken sentences; veiled hints that revealed in half concealing. Her husband's friend Richards was there, too, near her. It was he who had been in the newspaper office when intelligence of the railroad disaster was received, with Brently Mallard's name leading the list of "killed." He had only taken the time to assure himself of its truth by a second telegram, and had hastened to forestall any less careful, less tender friend in bearing the sad message.

She did not hear the story as many women have heard the same, with a paralyzed inability to accept its significance. She wept at once, with sudden, wild abandonment, in her sister's arms. When the storm of grief had spent itself she went away to her room alone. She would have no one follow her.

There stood, facing the open window, a comfortable, roomy armchair. Into this she sank, pressed down by a physical exhaustion that haunted her body and seemed to reach into her soul.

She could see in the open square before her house the tops of trees that were all aquiver with the new spring life. The delicious breath of rain was in the air. In the street below a peddler was crying his wares. The notes of a distant song which some one was singing reached her faintly, and countless sparrows were twittering in the eaves.

There were patches of blue sky showing here and there through the clouds that had met and piled one above the other in the west facing her window.

She sat with her head thrown back upon the cushion of the chair, quite motionless, except when a sob came up into her throat and shook her, as a child who has cried itself to sleep continues to sob in its dreams.

She was young, with a fair, calm face, whose lines bespoke repression and even a certain strength. But now there was a dull stare in her eyes, whose gaze was fixed away off yonder on one of those patches of blue sky. It was not a glance of reflection, but rather indicated a suspension of intelligent thought.

There was something coming to her and she was waiting for it, fearfully. What was it? She did not know; it was too subtle and elusive to name. But she felt it, creeping out of the sky, reaching toward her through the sounds, the scents, the color that filled the air.

Now her bosom rose and fell tumultuously. She was beginning to recognize this thing that was approaching to possess her, and she was striving to beat it back with her will — as powerless as her two white slender hands would have been.

When she abandoned herself a little whispered word escaped her slightly parted lips. She said it over and over under her breath: "free, free, free!" The vacant stare and the look of terror that had followed it went from her eyes. They stayed keen and bright. Her pulses beat fast, and the coursing blood warmed and relaxed every inch of her body.

She did not stop to ask if it were or were not a monstrous joy that held her. A clear and exalted perception enabled her to dismiss the suggestion as trivial.

She knew that she would weep again when she saw the kind, tender hands folded in death; the face that had never looked save with love upon her, fixed and gray and dead. But she saw beyond that bitter moment a long procession of years to come that would belong to her absolutely. And she opened and spread her arms out to them in welcome.

There would be no one to live for her during those coming years; she would live for herself. There would be no powerful will bending hers in that blind persistence with which men and women believe they have a right to impose a private will upon a fellow-creature. A kind intention or a cruel intention made the act seem no less a crime as she looked upon it in that brief moment of illumination.

And yet she had loved him — sometimes. Often she had not. What did 15 it matter! What could love, the unsolved mystery, count for in face of this possession of self-assertion which she suddenly recognized as the strongest impulse of her being!

"Free! Body and soul free!" she kept whispering.

Josephine was kneeling before the closed door with her lips to the keyhole, imploring for admission. "Louise, open the door! I beg; open the door — you will make yourself ill. What are you doing, Louise? For heaven's sake open the door."

"Go away. I am not making myself ill." No; she was drinking in a very elixir of life through that open window.

Her fancy was running riot along those days ahead of her. Spring days, and summer days, and all sorts of days that would be her own. She breathed a quick prayer that life might be long. It was only yesterday she had thought with a shudder that life might be long.

She arose at length and opened the door to her sister's importunities. 20 There was a feverish triumph in her eyes, and she carried herself unwittingly like a goddess of Victory. She clasped her sister's waist, and together they descended the stairs. Richards stood waiting for them at the bottom.

Some one was opening the front door with a latchkey. It was Brently Mallard who entered, a little travel-stained, composedly carrying his grip-sack and umbrella. He had been far from the scene of accident, and did not even know there had been one. He stood amazed at Josephine's piercing cry; at Richards' quick motion to screen him from the view of his wife.

But Richards was too late.

When the doctors came they said she had died of heart disease — of joy that kills.

A SAMPLE CLOSE READING

An Annotated Section of "The Story of an Hour"

Even as you read a story for the first time, you can highlight passages, circle or underline words, and write responses in the margins. Subsequent readings will yield more insights once you begin to understand how various elements such as plot, characterization, and word choice build toward the conclusion and what you perceive to be the story's central ideas. The following annotations for the first eleven paragraphs of "The Story of an Hour" provide a perspective written by someone who had read the work several times. Your own approach might, of course, be quite different — as the sample paper that follows the annotated passage amply demonstrates.

KATE CHOPIN (1851–1904)

The Story of an Hour   1894

Knowing that Mrs. Mallard was afflicted with a heart trouble, great care was taken to break to her as gently as possible the news of her husband's death.

It was her sister Josephine who told her, in broken sentences; veiled hints that revealed in half concealing. Her husband's friend Richards was there, too, near her. It was he who had been in the newspaper office when intelligence of the railroad disaster was received, with Brently Mallard's name leading the list of "killed." He had only taken the time to assure himself of its truth by a second telegram, and had hastened to forestall any less careful, less tender friend in bearing the sad message.

She did not hear the story as many women have heard the same, with a paralyzed inability to accept its significance. She wept at once, with sudden, wild abandonment, in her sister's arms. When the storm of grief had spent itself she went away to her room alone. She would have no one follow her.

There stood, facing the open window, a comfortable, roomy armchair. Into this she sank, pressed down by a physical exhaustion that haunted her body and seemed to reach into her soul.

She could see in the open square before her house the 5 tops of trees that were all aquiver with the new spring life. The delicious breath of rain was in the air. In the street below a peddler was crying his wares. The notes of a distant song which some one was singing reached her faintly, and countless sparrows were twittering in the eaves.

The title could point to the brevity of the story — only 23 short paragraphs — or to the decisive nature of what happens in very short period of time. Or both.

Mrs. Mallard's first name (Louise) is not given until paragraph 17, yet h sister Josephine is named immediatel. This emphasizes Mrs. Mallard's married identity.

Given the nature of the cause of Mrs. Mallard's death at the story's end, it's worth noting the ambiguous description that sh "was afflicted with a heart trouble." Is this one of Chopin' (rather than Josephine's) "veiled hints"?

When Mrs. Mallard weeps with "wild abandonment," the reader is again confronted with an ambiguous phrase: she grieves in an overwhelming manner yet seems to express relief at being abandoned by Brently's death.

ese 3 paragraphs
eate an
creasingly "open"
mosphere
at leads to the
elicious" outside
here there are
viting sounds
d "patches of
ue sky." There's
definite tension
etween the inside
d outside worlds.

nough still stunned
y grief, Mrs. Mallard
egins to feel a
nange come over
er owing to her
owing awareness
 a world outside
er room. What that
nange is remains
oo subtle and
usive to name."

rs. Mallard's
nflicted struggle
described in
assionate, physical
rms as if she
"possess[ed]"
y a lover she is
owerless" to resist.

nce she has
bandoned"
erself (see the
bandonment" in
aragraph 3), the
ader realizes that
er love is to be
ree, free, free." Her
ecognition is evident
 the "coursing blood
hat] warmed and
elaxed every inch of
er body."

There were patches of blue sky showing here and there through the clouds that had met and piled one above the other in the west facing her window.

She sat with her head thrown back upon the cushion of the chair, quite motionless, except when a sob came up into her throat and shook her, as a child who has cried itself to sleep continues to sob in its dreams.

She was young, with a fair, calm face, whose lines bespoke repression and even a certain strength. But now there was a dull stare in her eyes, whose gaze was fixed away off yonder on one of those patches of blue sky. It was not a glance of reflection, but rather indicated a suspension of intelligent thought.

There was something coming to her and she was waiting for it, fearfully. What was it? She did not know; it was too subtle and elusive to name. But she felt it, creeping out of the sky, reaching toward her through the sounds, the scents, the color that filled the air.

Now her bosom rose and fell tumultuously. She was 10 beginning to recognize this thing that was approaching to possess her, and she was striving to beat it back with her will — as powerless as her two white slender hands would have been.

When she abandoned herself a little whispered word escaped her slightly parted lips. She said it over and over under her breath: "free, free, free!" The vacant stare and the look of terror that had followed it went from her eyes. They stayed keen and bright. Her pulses beat fast, and the coursing blood warmed and relaxed every inch of her body. . . .

Do you find Mrs. Mallard a sympathetic character? Some readers think that she is callous, selfish, and unnatural — even monstrous — because she ecstatically revels in her newly discovered sense of freedom so soon after learning of her husband's presumed death. Others read her as a victim of her inability to control her own life in a repressive, male-dominated society. Is it possible to hold both views simultaneously, or are they mutually exclusive? Are your views in any way influenced by your being male or female? Does your age affect your perception? What about your social and economic background? Does your nationality, race, or religion in any way shape your attitudes? Do you have particular views about the institution of marriage that inform your assessment of Mrs. Mallard's character? Have other reading experiences — perhaps a familiarity with some of Chopin's other stories — predisposed you one way or another to Mrs. Mallard?

Understanding potential influences might be useful in determining whether a particular response to Mrs. Mallard is based primarily on the story's details and their arrangement or on an overt or a subtle bias that is brought to the story. If you unconsciously project your beliefs and assumptions onto a literary work, you run the risk of distorting it to accommodate your prejudice. Your feelings can be a reliable guide to interpretation, but you should be aware of what those feelings are based on.

Often specific questions about literary works cannot be answered definitively. For example, Chopin does not explain why Mrs. Mallard suffers a heart attack at the end of this story. Is the shock of seeing her "dead" husband simply too much for this woman "afflicted with a heart trouble"? Does she die of what the doctors call a "joy that kills" because she is so glad to see her husband? Is she so profoundly guilty about feeling "free" at her husband's expense that she has a heart attack? Is her death a kind of willed suicide in reaction to her loss of freedom? Your answers to these questions will depend on which details you emphasize in your interpretation of the story and the kinds of perspectives and values you bring to it. If, for example, you read the story from a feminist perspective, you would be likely to pay close attention to Chopin's comments about marriage in paragraph 14. Or if you read the story as an oblique attack on the insensitivity of physicians of the period, you might want to find out whether Chopin wrote elsewhere about doctors (she did) and compare her comments with historic sources. (A number of critical strategies for reading, including feminist and historical approaches, appear in Chapter 30.)

Reading responsively makes you an active participant in the process of creating meaning in a literary work. The experience that you and the author create will most likely not be identical to another reader's encounter with the same work, but then that's true of nearly any experience you'll have, and it is part of the pleasure of reading. Indeed, talking and writing about literature is a way of sharing responses so that they can be enriched and deepened.

A SAMPLE PAPER

Differences in Responses to Kate Chopin's "The Story of an Hour"

The following paper was written in response to an assignment that called for a three- to four-page discussion of how different readers might interpret Mrs. Mallard's character. The paper is based on the story as well as on the discussion of reader-response criticism (pp. 1083) in Chapter 30, "Critical Strategies for Reading." As that discussion indicates, reader-response criticism is a critical approach that focuses on the reader rather than on the work itself in order to describe how the reader creates meaning from the text.

Wally Villa

Professor Brian

English 210

12 January 2019

Differences in Responses to

Kate Chopin's "The Story of an Hour"

Kate Chopin's "The Story of an Hour" appears merely to explore a woman's unpredictable reaction to her husband's assumed death and reappearance, but actually Chopin offers Mrs. Mallard's bizarre story to reveal problems that are inherent in the institution of marriage. By offering this depiction of a marriage that stifles the woman to the point that she celebrates the death of her kind and loving husband, Chopin challenges her readers to examine their own views of marriage and relationships between men and women. Each reader's judgment of Mrs. Mallard and her behavior inevitably stems from his or her own personal feelings about marriage and the influences of societal expectations. Readers of differing genders, ages, and marital experiences are, therefore, likely to react differently to Chopin's startling portrayal of the Mallards' marriage, and that certainly is true of my response to the story compared to my father's and grandmother's responses.

Marriage often establishes boundaries between people that make them unable to communicate with each other. The Mallards' marriage was evidently crippled by both their inability to talk to one another and Mrs. Mallard's conviction that her marriage was defined by a "powerful will bending hers in that blind persistence with which men and women believe they have a right to impose a private will upon a fellow-creature" (16). Yet she does not recognize that it is not just men who impose their will upon women and that the problems inherent in marriage affect men and women equally. To me, Mrs. Mallard is a somewhat sympathetic character, and I appreciate

Margin annotations:

Thesis providing writer's interpretation of story's purpose

Introduction setting up other reader responses discussed later in paper

Analysis of story's portrayal of marriage, with textual evidence her longing to live out the "years to come that would belong to her absolutely" (16). However, I also believe that she could have tried to improve her own situation somehow, either by reaching out to her husband or by abandoning the marriage altogether. Chopin uses Mrs. Mallard's tragedy to illuminate aspects of marriage that are harmful and, in this case, even deadly. Perhaps the Mallards' relationship should be taken as a warning to others: sacrificing one's own happiness in order to satisfy societal expectations can poison one's life and even destroy entire families.

Analysis of character and plot, connecting with story's purpose

When my father read "The Story of an Hour," his reaction to Mrs. Mallard was more antagonistic than my own. He sees Chopin's story as a timeless "battle of the sexes," serving as further proof that men will never really be able to understand what it is that women want. Mrs. Mallard endures an obviously unsatisfying marriage without ever explaining to her husband that she feels trapped and unfulfilled. Mrs. Mallard dismisses the question of whether or not she is experiencing a "monstrous joy" (16) as trivial, but my father does not think that this is a trivial question. He believes Mrs. Mallard is guilty of a monstrous joy because she selfishly celebrates the death of her husband without ever having allowed him the opportunity to understand her feelings. He believes that, above all, Brently Mallard should be seen as the most victimized character in the story. Mr. Mallard is a good, kind man, with friends who care about him and a marriage that he thinks he can depend on. He "never looked save with love" (16) upon his wife, his only "crime" (16) was his presence in the house, and yet he is the one who is bereaved at the end of the story, for reasons he will never understand. Mrs. Mallard's passion for her newly discovered freedom is perhaps understandable, but according to my father, Mr. Mallard is the character most deserving of sympathy.

Contrasting summary and analysis of another reader's response

Maybe not surprisingly, my grandmother's interpretation of "The Story of an Hour" was radically different from both mine and my father's.

Villa 3

Contrasting summary and analysis of another reader's response

My grandmother was married in 1936 and widowed in 1959 and therefore can identify with Chopin's characters, who live at the turn of the twentieth century. Her first reaction, aside from her unwavering support for Mrs. Mallard and her predicament, was that this story demonstrates the differences between the ways men and women related to each other a century ago and the way they relate today. Unlike my father, who thinks Mrs. Mallard is too passive, my grandmother believes that Mrs. Mallard doesn't even know that she is feeling repressed until after she is told that Brently is dead. In 1894, divorce was so scandalous and stigmatized that it simply wouldn't have been an option for Mrs. Mallard, and so her only way out of the marriage would have been one of their deaths. Being relatively young, Mrs. Mallard probably considered herself doomed to a long life in an unhappy marriage. My grandmother also feels that, in spite of all we know of Mrs. Mallard's feelings about her husband and her marriage, she still manages to live up to everyone's expectations of her as a woman both in life and in death. She is a dutiful wife to Brently, as she is expected to be. She weeps "with sudden, wild abandonment" when she hears the news of his death; she locks herself in her room to cope with her new situation, and she has a fatal heart attack upon seeing her husband arrive home. Naturally the male doctors would think that she died of the "joy that kills" (16) — nobody could have guessed that she was unhappy with her life, and she would never have wanted them to know.

Cultural and historical background providing context for response and story itself

Analysis supported with textual evidence

Conclusion summarizing reader responses explored in the paper

Interpretations of "The Story of an Hour" seem to vary according to the gender, age, and experience of the reader. While both male and female readers can certainly sympathize with Mrs. Mallard's plight, female readers — as was evident in our class discussions — seem to relate more easily to her predicament and more quickly exonerate her of any responsibility for her unhappy situation. Conversely, male readers are more likely to feel compassion for Mr. Mallard, who loses his wife for reasons that will always remain entirely unknown to him.

Villa 4

Older readers probably understand more readily the strength of social forces
and the difficulty of trying to deny societal expectations concerning gender
roles in general and marriage in particular. Younger readers seem to feel that
Mrs. Mallard is too passive and that she could have improved her domestic
life immeasurably if she had taken the initiative to either improve or end her
relationship with her husband. Ultimately, how each individual reader responds
to Mrs. Mallard's story reveals his or her own ideas about marriage, society, and
how men and women communicate with each other.

Villa 5

Work Cited

Chopin, Kate. "The Story of an Hour." *Literature to Go*, edited by Michael
    Meyer and D. Quentin Miller, 4th ed., Bedford/St. Martin's, 2020,
    p. 16.

Before beginning your own writing assignment on fiction, you should
review Chapter 31, "Writing about Literature," which provides a step-by-
step explanation of how to choose a topic, develop a thesis, and organize
various types of writing assignments. If you use outside sources, you should
also be familiar with the conventional documentation procedures described
in Chapter 32, "The Literary Research Paper."

EXPLORATIONS AND FORMULAS

Each time we pick up a work of fiction, go to the theater, or turn on the
television, we have a trace of the same magical expectation that can be
heard in the voice of a child who begs, "Tell me a story." Human beings have
enjoyed stories ever since they learned to speak. Whatever the motive for

creating stories — even if simply to delight or instruct — the basic human impulse to tell and hear stories existed long before the development of written language. Myths about the origins of the world and legends about the heroic exploits of demigods were among the earliest forms of storytelling to develop into oral traditions, which were eventually written down. These narratives are the ancestors of the stories we read on the printed page today. Unlike the early listeners to ancient myths and legends, we tend to read our stories silently, but the pleasure derived from the mysterious power of someone else's artfully arranged words remains largely the same. Every one of us likes a good story.

The stories that appear in anthologies for college students are generally chosen for their high literary quality. Such stories can affect us at the deepest emotional level, reveal new insights into ourselves or the world, and stretch us to exercise our imaginations. They warrant careful reading and close study to appreciate the art that has gone into creating them. The following chapters on plot, character, setting, and the other elements of literature are designed to provide the terms and concepts that can help you understand how a work of fiction achieves its effects and meanings. It is worth acknowledging, however, that many people buy and read fiction that is quite different from the stories usually anthologized in college texts. What about all those paperbacks with exciting, colorful covers near the cash registers in shopping malls and airports?

These books, known as *formula fiction*, are the adventure, western, mystery, science fiction, horror, and romance novels that entertain millions of readers annually. What makes them so popular? What do their characters, plots, and themes offer readers that accounts for the tremendous sales of stories with titles like *Caves of Doom, My Knight, My Lover, Range Riders,* and *Slay Ride*? Many of the writers included in this book have enjoyed wide popularity and written best-sellers, but there are more readers of formula fiction than there are readers of Ernest Hemingway, William Faulkner, or Joyce Carol Oates, to name only a few. Formula novels do provide entertainment, of course, but that makes them no different from serious stories, if entertainment means pleasure. Any of the stories in this or any other anthology can be read for pleasure.

Formula fiction, though, is usually characterized as escape literature. There are sensible reasons for this description. Adventure stories about soldiers of fortune are eagerly read by men who live pretty average lives doing ordinary jobs. Romance novels about attractive young women falling in love with tall, dark, handsome men are read mostly by women who dream themselves out of their familiar existences. The excitement, violence, and passion that such stories provide are a kind of reprieve from everyday experience.

And yet readers of serious fiction may also use it as a refuge, a liberation from monotony and boredom. Mark Twain's humorous stories have, for example, given countless hours of pleasurable relief to readers who would rather spend time in Twain's light and funny world than in their own.

Others might prefer the terror of Edgar Allan Poe's fiction or the painful predicament of two lovers in a Joyce Carol Oates story.

Thus, to get at some of the differences between formula fiction and serious literature, it is necessary to go beyond the motives of the reader to the motives of the writer and the qualities of the work itself.

Unlike serious fiction, the books displayed next to the cash registers (and their short story equivalents on the magazine racks) are written with essentially one goal: to be sold. They are aimed at specific consumer markets that can be counted on to buy them. This does not mean that all serious writers must live in cold garrets writing for audiences who have not yet discovered their work. No one writes to make a career of poverty. It does mean, however, that if a writer's primary purpose is to anticipate readers' generic expectations about when the next torrid love scene, bloody gunfight, or thrilling chase is due, there is little room to be original or to have something significant to say. There is little if any chance to explore seriously a character, idea, or incident if the major focus is not on the integrity of the work itself.

Although the specific elements of formula fiction differ depending on the type of story, some basic ingredients go into all westerns, mysteries, adventures, and romances. From the very start, a reader can anticipate a happy ending for the central character, with whom he or she will identify. There may be suspense, but no matter what or how many the obstacles, complications, or near defeats, the hero or heroine succeeds and reaffirms the values and attitudes the reader brings to the story. Virtue triumphs, love conquers all, honesty is the best policy, and hard work guarantees success. Hence, the villains are corralled, the wedding vows are exchanged, the butler confesses, and gold is discovered at the last moment. The visual equivalents of such formula stories are readily available at movie theaters and in television series. Some are better than others, but all are relatively limited by the writer's goal of giving an audience what will sell.

While formula fiction may not offer many surprises, it provides pleasure to a wide variety of readers. College professors, for example, are just as likely to be charmed by formula stories as anyone else. Readers of serious fiction who revel in exploring more challenging imaginative worlds can also enjoy formulaic stories, which offer little more than an image of the world as a simple place in which our assumptions and desires are confirmed. The familiarity of a given formula is emotionally satisfying because we are secure in our expectations of it. We know at the start of a Sherlock Holmes story that the mystery will be solved by that famous detective's relentless scientific analysis of the clues, but we take pleasure in seeing how Holmes unravels the mystery before us. Similarly, we know that James Bond's wit, grace, charm, courage, and skill will ultimately prevail over the diabolic schemes of eccentric villains, but we volunteer for the mission anyway.

Although it is useful to recognize the conventions of genre fiction and to know that they are in place for a certain kind of reader's expectations, there are limitations to any classification system. A novel doesn't have to have dragons and trolls to be considered "high fantasy," for example. The emphasis on plot in adventure novels doesn't mean that they can't also have compelling characters. Also, literary fiction (as we've been calling it) is not necessarily free from conventions, although it might be said that the best literary fiction is comprised of the works that are willing to push those conventions to their limits, or to break them, or at least to reveal a keen awareness of how they provide the framework for a story that is distinctive and important. Literary fiction is an art as well as a craft, and its practitioners experience the freedom that excites artists even if they are somewhat aware of the marketplace that will provide them with readers — and a living.

As you read the following stories, "Wants" by Grace Paley and "Volar" by Judith Ortiz Cofer, consider the way they are both like and unlike other stories you have read, perhaps beginning with a comparison to Chopin's "The Story of an Hour" earlier in this chapter.

GRACE PALEY   (1922–2007)

Wants   1994

I saw my ex-husband in the street. I was sitting on the steps of the new library.

Hello, my life, I said. We had once been married for twenty-seven years, so I felt justified.

He said, What? What life? No life of mine.

I said, O.K. I don't argue when there's real disagreement. I got up and went into the library to see how much I owed them.

The librarian said $32 even and you've owed it for eighteen years. I didn't deny anything. Because I don't understand how time passes. I have had those books. I have often thought of them. The library is only two blocks away.

My ex-husband followed me to the Books Returned desk. He interrupted the librarian, who had more to tell. In many ways, he said, as I look back, I attribute the dissolution of our marriage to the fact that you never invited the Bertrams to dinner.

That's possible, I said. But really, if you remember: first, my father was sick that Friday, then the children were born, then I had those Tuesday-night meetings, then the war began. Then we didn't seem to know them any more. But you're right. I should have had them to dinner.

I gave the librarian a check for $32. Immediately she trusted me, put my past behind her, wiped the record clean, which is just what most other municipal and/or state bureaucracies will *not* do.

I checked out the two Edith Wharton books I had just returned because I'd read them so long ago and they are more apropos now than ever. They were *The House of Mirth* and *The Children,* which is about how life in the United States in New York changed in twenty-seven years fifty years ago. A nice thing I do remember is breakfast, my ex-husband said. I was surprised. All we ever had was coffee. Then I remembered there was a hole in the back of the kitchen closet which opened into the apartment next door. There, they always ate sugar-cured smoked bacon. It gave us a very grand feeling about breakfast, but we never got stuffed and sluggish.

That was when we were poor, I said.

When were we ever rich? he asked.

Oh, as time went on, as our responsibilities increased, we didn't go in need. You took adequate financial care, I reminded him. The children went to camp four weeks a year and in decent ponchos with sleeping bags and boots, just like everyone else. They looked very nice. Our place was warm in winter, and we had nice red pillows and things.

I wanted a sailboat, he said. But you didn't want anything.

Don't be bitter, I said. It's never too late.

No, he said with a great deal of bitterness. I may get a sailboat. As a matter of fact I have money down on an eighteen-foot two-rigger. I'm doing well this year and can look forward to better. But as for you, it's too late. You'll always want nothing.

He had had a habit throughout the twenty-seven years of making a narrow remark which, like a plumber's snake, could work its way through the ear down the throat, halfway to my heart. He would then disappear, leaving me choking with equipment. What I mean is, I sat down on the library steps and he went away.

I looked through *The House of Mirth,* but lost interest. I felt extremely accused. Now, it's true, I'm short of requests and absolute requirements. But I do want *something.*

I want, for instance, to be a different person. I want to be the woman who brings these two books back in two weeks. I want to be the effective citizen who changes the school system and addresses and Board of Estimate on the troubles of this dear urban center.

I *had* promised my children to end the war before they grew up.

I wanted to have been married forever to one person, my ex-husband or my present one. Either has enough character for a whole life, which as it turns out is really not such a long time. You couldn't exhaust either man's qualities or get under the rock of his reasons in one short life.

Just this morning I looked out the window to watch the street for a while and saw that the little sycamores the city had dreamily planted a couple of years before the kids were born had come that day to the prime of their lives.

Well! I decided to bring those two books back to the library. Which proves that when a person or an event comes along to jolt or appraise me I *can* take some appropriate action, although I am better known for my hospitable remarks.

Considerations for Critical Thinking and Discussion

1. **FIRST RESPONSE.** There are many details about the narrator's past life included in a relatively short space. Which ones seem most significant to you?

2. How would you describe your emotional connection to the narrator: sympathy, pity, indifference, affection, or something more complex than any of those words?

3. Does the narrator present herself differently to her ex-husband, to the librarian, and to us, the reader? The librarian is said to trust the narrator after she pays her overdue fine; do you trust her?

4. Consider the significance of the story's title. Some wants are expressed explicitly in the story; are there some that aren't?

5. Note all references to time and money in the story. How do these two motifs frame what might be story's theme, or central focus and meaning?

Judith Ortiz Cofer (1952–2016)

Volar° 1993

At twelve I was an avid consumer of comic books — *Supergirl* being my favorite. I spent my allowance of a quarter a day on two twelve-cent comic books or a double issue for twenty-five. I had a stack of *Legion of Super Heroes* and *Supergirl* comic books in my bedroom closet that was as tall as I am. I had a recurring dream in those days: that I had long blond hair and could fly. In my dream I climbed the stairs to the top of our apartment building as myself, but as I went up each flight, changes would be taking place. Step by step I would fill out: My legs would grow

long, my arms harden into steel, and my hair would magically go straight and turn a golden color. Of course I would add the bonus of breasts, but not too large; Supergirl had to be aerodynamic. Sleek and hard as a super-sonic missile. Once on the roof, my parents safely asleep in their beds, I would get on tiptoe, arms outstretched in the position for flight, and jump out my fifty-story-high window into the black lake of the sky. From up there, over the rooftops, I could see everything, even beyond the few blocks of our barrio;° with my X-ray vision I could look inside the homes of people who interested me. Once I saw our landlord, whom I knew my parents feared, sitting in a treasure-room dressed in an ermine coat and a large gold crown. He sat on the floor counting his dollar bills. I played a trick on him. Going up to his building's chimney, I blew a little puff of my superbreath into his fire-place, scattering his stacks of money so that he had to start counting all over again. I could more or less program my Supergirl dreams in those days by focusing on the object of my current obsession. This way I "saw" into the private lives

Volar: To fly (Spanish).
barrio: Spanish-speaking neighborhood.

of my neighbors, my teachers, and in the last days of my childish fantasy and the beginning of adolescence, into the secret room of the boys I liked. In the mornings I'd wake up in my tiny bedroom with the incongruous — at least in our tiny apartment — white "princess" furniture my mother had chosen for me, and find myself back in my body: my tight curls still clinging to my head, skinny arms and legs and flat chest unchanged.

In the kitchen my mother and father would be talking softly over a café con leche.° She would come "wake me" exactly forty-five minutes after they had gotten up. It was their time together at the beginning of each day and even at an early age I could feel their disappointment if I interrupted them by getting up too early. So I would stay in my bed recalling my dreams of flight, perhaps planning my next flight. In the kitchen they would be discussing events in the barrio, Actually, he would be carrying that part of the conversation; when it was her turn to speak she would, more often than not, try shifting the topic toward her desire to see her *familia* on the Island: *How about a vacation in Puerto Rico together this year, Querido?°* We could rent a car, go to the beach. We could . . . And he would answer patiently, gently, Mi amor,° do you know how much it would cost for all of us to fly there? It is not possible for me to take the time off . . . Mi vida,° please understand. . . . And I knew that soon she would rise from the table. Not abruptly. She would light a cigarette and look out the kitchen window. The view was of a dismal alley that was littered with refuse thrown from windows. The space was too narrow for anyone larger than a skinny child to enter safely, so it was never cleaned. My mother would check the time on the clock over her sink, the one with a prayer for patience and grace written in Spanish. A birthday gift. She would see that it was time to wake me. She'd sigh deeply and say the same thing the view from her kitchen window always inspired her to say: *Ay, si yo pudiera volar.°*

1993

leche: Coffee with milk.
Querido: Beloved, dear.
Mi amor: My love.
Mi vida: My life.
Ah, si. . . volar: Oh, if only I could fly.

CONSIDERATIONS FOR CRITICAL THINKING AND DISCUSSION

1. FIRST RESPONSE. Like Grace Paley's "Wants," this is a story told in the first person: that is, the narrator is a character in the story. Does the story seem to be more about her or her mother?

2. The comic books the narrator reads are a version of the formula fiction we describe above. What role do they have in her life?

3. The narrator's superhero fantasies begin when she is twelve and end as she is entering adolescence. How does her understanding of her own body coincide with intellectual and emotional changes during those years?'

4. What is the specific connection between the narrator's desire to fly and her mother's? What idea does the story advance through that implied connection?

CONNECTIONS TO ANOTHER SELECTION

1. Neither story names any of its characters. Is that fact significant?

2. Both stories are explicitly about desires: one is even titled "Wants." Consider carefully the nature of those desires and the factors that impede those desires. Do the stories have the exact same message about the function of desire in the lives of humans? Put differently, is desire a foolish fantasy that leaves us feeling dissatisfied or is it the very thing that makes us work to improve our lives?

3. How do both stories control the passage of time? How significant is time as a key thematic element within them? (A further comparison to "The Story of an Hour" might be interesting with regard to this question.)

4. Both stories pay attention to money within the lives of their characters. How does money factor into the lives of both narrators?

5. Are the stories essentially different because one describes the childish fantasies of a young teen and the other the lengthy marriage of an adult woman?

6. How does reading influence the lives of both narrators?

7. Discuss the idea of life changes in both stories. How much control do both narrators have over the changes in their lives? What factors limit their control over their lives?

2

Plot

Ermeni Studio, Milan.
Courtesy of the Ernest
Hemingway Photographic
Collection, John Fitzgerald
Kennedy Library, Boston.

Never mistake motion for action.
— ERNEST HEMINGWAY

Created by a writer's imagination, a work of fiction need not be factual or historically accurate. Although actual people, places, and events may be included in fiction, facts are not as important as is the writer's use of them. We can learn much about Russian life in the early part of the nineteenth century from Leo Tolstoy's *War and Peace* (1867), but that historical information is incidental to Tolstoy's exploration of human nature. Tolstoy, like most successful writers, makes us accept as real the world in his novel no matter how foreign it may be to our own reality. One of the ways a writer achieves this acceptance and engagement — and one of a writer's few obligations — is to interest us in what is happening in the story. We are carried into the writer's fictional world by the plot.

Plot is the author's arrangement of incidents in a story. It is the organizing principle that controls the order of events. This structure is, in a sense, what remains after a writer edits out what is irrelevant to the story being told. We don't need to know, for example, what happens to Rip Van Winkle's faithful dog, Wolf, during his amiable master's twenty-year nap in the Catskill Mountains in order to be enchanted by Washington Irving's story of a henpecked husband. Instead, what is told takes on meaning as it is brought into focus by a skillful writer who selects and orders the events that constitute the story's plot.

Events can be presented in a variety of orders. A chronological arrangement begins with what happens first, then second, and so on, until the last incident is related. That is how "John Updike's 'A & P'" is told. The events in William Faulkner's "A Rose for Emily," however, are not arranged in chronological order because that would give away the story's surprise ending; instead, Faulkner moves back and forth between the past and present to provide information that leads up to the final startling moment (which won't be given away here either; the story begins on p. 40).

Some stories begin at the end and then lead up to why or how events worked out as they did. Stories can also begin in the middle of things (the Latin term for this common plot strategy is *in medias res*). In this kind of plot we enter the story on the verge of some important moment. John Updike's "A & P" (p. 138) begins with the narrator, a teenager working at a checkout counter in a supermarket, telling us: "In walks these three girls in nothing but bathing suits." Right away we are brought into the middle of a situation that will ultimately create the conflict in the story.

Another common strategy is the *flashback*, a device that informs us about events that happened before the opening scene of a work. James Baldwin's masterful story "Sonny's Blues" (p. 76) begins with news of the character Sonny's arrest, but much of the rest of the story returns to incidents earlier in his life that might have changed the way the narrator (and the reader) respond to that arrest. Whatever the plot arrangement, you should be aware of how the writer's conscious ordering of events affects your responses to the action.

T. C. BOYLE (B. 1948)

Sueddeutsche Zeitung Photo/Alamy Stock Photo.

T. C. Boyle (b. 1948) is a prolific author of literary fiction, much of it darkly comic. The author of sixteen novels and over one hundred short stories, Boyle often concerns himself with eccentric figures from American history (such as the nutritionist, cereal inventor and purveyor of pseudo-science John Harvey Kellogg or the psychologist Alfred Kinsey who studied the sex habits of Americans in the mid-twentieth century). His concerns include the human destruction of the environment, the dangers of ideology and hypocrisy, and the forces of fate in the context of ancestry.

A great many stories share a standard plot pattern that might best be described as cause and effect. Even stories that rely heavily on very detailed plots leave out as much as they include. Incidents or episodes in stories are significant because the author has chosen to include them and thus emphasize their potential meaning, but plot does not mean "everything that happened." We don't necessarily need to know that a character brushed her teeth and flossed before going to bed, but if that detail is included in a story, the author must have felt there was a reason to do so. The following short story, "The Hit Man," is a darkly humorous attempt to tell the story of a character's entire life through a series of incidents, complete with section titles for those incidents. In one sense, this story is all about character, but he is a character type whose only function, as the title suggests, is to assassinate people.

The Hit Man   1977

Early Years

The Hit Man's early years are complicated by the black bag that he wears over his head. Teachers correct his pronunciation, the coach criticizes his attitude, the principal dresses him down for branding preschoolers with a lit cigarette. He is a poor student. At lunch he sits alone, feeding bell peppers and salami into the dark slot of his mouth. In the hallways, wiry young athletes snatch at the black hood and slap the back of his head. When he is thirteen he is approached by the captain of the football team, who pins him down and attempts to remove the hood. The Hit Man wastes him. Five years, says the judge.

Back on the Street

The Hit Man is back on the street in two months.

First Date

The girl's name is Cynthia. The Hit Man pulls up in front of her apartment in his father's hearse. (The Hit Man's father, whom he loathes and abominates, is a mortician. At breakfast the Hit Man's father had slapped the cornflakes from his son's bowl. The son threatened to waste his father. He did not, restrained no doubt by considerations of filial loyalty and the deepseated taboos against patricide that permeate the universal unconscious.)

Cynthia's father has silver sideburns and plays tennis. He responds to the Hit Man's knock, expresses surprise at the Hit Man's appearance. The Hit Man takes Cynthia by the elbow, presses a twenty into her father's palm, and disappears into the night.

Father's Death

At breakfast the Hit Man slaps the cornflakes from his father's bowl. Then 5 wastes him.

Mother's Death

The Hit Man is in his early twenties. He shoots pool, lifts weights, and drinks milk from the carton. His mother is in the hospital, dying of cancer or heart disease. The priest wears black. So does the Hit Man.

First Job

Porfirio Buñoz, a Cuban financier, invites the Hit Man to lunch. I hear you're looking for work, says Buñoz.

That's right, says the Hit Man.

Peas

The Hit Man does not like peas. They are too difficult to balance on the fork.

Talk Show

The Hit Man waits in the wings, the white slash of a cigarette scarring the 10 midnight black of his head and upper torso. The makeup girl has done his mouth and eyes, brushed the nap of his hood. He has been briefed. The guest who precedes him is a pediatrician. A planetary glow washes the stage where the host and the pediatrician, separated by a potted palm, cross their legs and discuss the little disturbances of infants and toddlers.

After the station break the Hit Man finds himself squeezed into a director's chair, white lights in his eyes. The talk-show host is a baby-faced man in his early forties. He smiles like God and all His Angels. Well, he says. So you're a hit man. Tell me — I've always wanted to know — what does it feel like to hit someone?

Death of Mateo María Buñoz

The body of Mateo María Buñoz, the cousin and business associate of a prominent financier, is discovered down by the docks on a hot summer morning. Mist rises from the water like steam, there is the smell of fish. A large black bird perches on the dead man's forehead.

Marriage

Cynthia and the Hit Man stand at the altar, side by side. She is wearing a white satin gown and lace veil. The Hit Man has rented a tuxedo, extra-large, and a silk-lined black-velvet hood.

. . . Till death do you part, says the priest.

Moods

The Hit Man is moody, unpredictable. Once, in a luncheonette, the waitress   1
brought him the meatloaf special but forgot to eliminate the peas. There
was a spot of gravy on the Hit Man's hood, about where his chin should be.
He looked up at the waitress, his eyes like pins behind the triangular slots,
and wasted her.

Another time he went to the track with $25, came back with $1,800.
He stopped at a cigar shop. As he stepped out of the shop a wino tugged
at his sleeve and solicited a quarter. The Hit Man reached into his pocket,
extracted the $1,800 and handed it to the wino. Then wasted him.

First Child

A boy. The Hit Man is delighted. He leans over the edge of the playpen and
molds the tiny fingers around the grip of a nickel-plated derringer. The gun
is loaded with blanks — the Hit Man wants the boy to get used to the noise.
By the time he is four the boy has mastered the rudiments of Tae Kwon Do,
can stick a knife in the wall from a distance of ten feet and shoot a moving target with either hand. The Hit Man rests his broad palm on the boy's
head. You're going to make the Big Leagues, Tiger, he says.

Work

He flies to Cincinnati. To L.A. To Boston. To London. The stewardesses get
to know him.

Half an Acre and a Garage

The Hit Man is raking leaves, amassing great brittle piles of them. He is
wearing a black T-shirt, cut off at the shoulders, and a cotton work hood,
also black. Cynthia is edging the flower bed, his son playing in the grass.
The Hit Man waves to his neighbors as they drive by. The neighbors wave
back.

When he has scoured the lawn to his satisfaction, the Hit Man draws   20
the smaller leaf-hummocks together in a single mound the size of a pickup
truck. Then he bends to ignite it with his lighter. Immediately, flames leap
back from the leaves, cut channels through the pile, engulf it in a ball of fire.
The Hit Man stands back, hands folded beneath the great meaty biceps. At
his side is the three-headed dog. He bends to pat each of the heads, smoke
and sparks raging against the sky.

Stalking the Streets of the City

He is stalking the streets of the city, collar up, brim down. It is late at night.
He stalks past department stores, small businesses, parks, and gas stations.
Past apartments, picket fences, picture windows. Dogs growl in the shad-
ows, then slink away. He could hit any of us.

Retirement

A group of businessman-types — sixtyish, seventyish, portly, diamond rings, cigars, liver spots — throws him a party. Porfirio Buñoz, now in his eighties, makes a speech and presents the Hit Man with a gilded scythe. The Hit Man thanks him, then retires to the lake, where he can be seen in his speedboat, skating out over the blue, hood rippling in the breeze.

Death

He is stricken, shrunken, half his former self. He lies propped against the pillows at Mercy Hospital, a bank of gentians drooping round the bed. Tubes run into the hood at the nostril openings, his eyes are clouded and red, sunk deep behind the triangular slots. The priest wears black. So does the Hit Man.

On the other side of town the Hit Man's son is standing before the mirror of a shop that specializes in Hit Man attire. Trying on his first hood.

This story begins with **exposition**, the background information the reader needs to make sense of the situation in which the characters are placed. Like everything in the story, the intent is parody: we learn that the Hit Man had a "complicated" childhood because, like an executioner, he wore a black hood on his head, but Boyle thwarts our desire to know *why* he wore the hood. The fact of the hood is the salient detail that separates the main character from everyone else, and it may even be read as a **symbol** of that difference and alienation, but the point is that the reader has to accept that detail in order to move on. The poet Samuel Taylor Coleridge in 1817 spoke of the "willing suspension of disbelief": a reader has to be somewhat willing to go along with what a writer posits even if the writer pushes the boundaries of plausibility. Other details in the first paragraph seem less important than the black hood: why are we told that his lunch consisted of bell peppers and salami? If we dismiss that detail as insignificant, we are also likely to dismiss the detail later in the story that he doesn't like peas . . . but the story forces us to reconsider that dismissal a few paragraphs later when he murders a waitress for bringing him peas.

Once this exposition supplies a context for the main character's difference, the plot gains momentum with the **rising action**, a complication that intensifies the situation: the Hit Man, having more or less gotten away with murder in high school, determines that there are no consequences for his actions, so he continues to kill at will. We might assume that the main plot points of the rest of the story occur every time he "wastes" someone, but these moments gradually vanish. We are told that he flies to various cities for work, but we don't actually see him doing his work in those places: he might as well be a travelling salesman by that point in the story. In fact, many of what we might consider to be the details we most want to hear — like *how* does he "waste" people? — are omitted. Even his first lunch meeting to arrange his first professional "hit" is far from complete: his future boss says, "I hear you're looking for work," and he replies, "That's right." That's it.

All stories must have a *conflict*, or a problem that must be addressed if not solved. This story makes us work a bit to identify the conflict. Since the murders are described in a matter-of-fact way, it could be said that the conflict is not in the episodes when the Hit Man kills someone, but in the difference between those and the episodes when he courts his future wife, or gets married, or is delighted by the birth of his child, or rakes leaves in his yard. These sound like the details of a very common, boring middle-class life, difficult to reconcile with the fact that our *protagonist* or *hero* is a cold-blooded killer. (*Protagonist* is often a better term for the central character of a story than *hero* or *heroine* because heroism is also associated with positive moral behavior: Can a man who mows down his father, a waitress who serves him peas, and a wino be considered heroic?)

Related to the *conflict*, then, is often an *antagonist*, a character who represents a force that opposes the protagonist. Just as we are not told why the Hit Man wears a black hood, we are not told why he "loathes and abominates" his father, but we should also notice that he doesn't seem to have any emotions whatsoever toward his other victims. We know little about his father except that he is a mortician who drives a hearse, and that he behaves violently toward his son. The conflict between fathers and sons is a familiar one, and in this case it is briefly complicated by the protagonist's sense of morality: he doesn't want to kill his father because of "filial loyalty and the deep-seated taboos against patricide that permeate the universal unconscious." A writer who was not trafficking in dark humor would perhaps use the tension between a murderous urge and moral restraint to create *suspense*: over time there might be a series of episodes that make the Hit Man feel ever more conflicted about what to do with his negative feelings. In this story, though, Boyle deprives us of the pleasures of suspense: impulsively, the Hit Man "wastes" his father. The author gives us all of the elements of plot in a very short space: the *conflict* between the Hit Man and his father reaches an immediate *climax* when he slaps the cornflakes out of his father's bowl just as his father had done to him, and it reaches a seeming *resolution* when he then sends his father to the great beyond.

Is that true, though? Generally, the arc of a story builds to a *resolution* that occurs toward the story's end. The *resolution* is a dramatic moment that addresses if not fully resolves the conflict. In most stories, the resolution is followed by a *dénouement* (a French word meaning the "untying of the knot"), which is sometimes referred to as the falling action or, in tragedy, catastrophe. The *dénouement* promises to clear up all the mysteries of the story, but that doesn't happen here, not if we are only looking at plot. If we look at it another way, the Hit Man's father's sudden and unremarkable death can be seen as a suggestion of what's to come, also known as *foreshadowing*, in this case of the protagonist's sudden and unremarkable death at the story's conclusion.

In a story this playful in terms of *plot* — meaning the selection, development, and arrangement of significant episodes — we might have to reframe what the conflict actually is. We know that the protagonist is the Hit Man — there aren't any other candidates — and that the antagonist must be his father, the only person toward whom he shows any emotion. There is the mystery about why he wears a black hood that seems to simply be a fact we must accept, but consider that his father was a mortician who drove a hearse. The Hit Man's executioner's hood and executioner's behavior suggests that he is, on some level, just like his father. This connection is reinforced when he slaps his father's cereal bowl just like his father had done to him. It could be said that the story is about the way sons have no choice but to repeat their fathers' behaviors, even if they hate their fathers. Looking at the story this way, the true *conflict* is not what we do with negative emotions, but whether or not we have control over our destiny. When the Hit Man's son is born, he is "delighted" and does what every good father would do: he hands his infant boy a gun and wraps his tiny fingers around its grip. That moment could properly be identified as the *climax*. When the boy tries on his first Hit Man hood at the end of the story, we should not be surprised. The story tells us that we can't control our destiny, that we are doomed to repeat the sins of our parents. The absurd plot is merely a structure for that **theme**. The story is funny, but its intent is dead serious.

Although the classic pattern of exposition, rising action, conflict, suspense, climax, and resolution provides a useful outline of many plots that emphasize physical action, a greater value of this pattern is that it helps us to see how innovative artists move beyond formula fiction by manipulating and changing the pattern for their own purposes. At the furthest extreme are those modern storytellers like Boyle who reject or manipulate traditional plotting techniques in favor of experimental approaches. Instead of including fully developed characters who wrestle with conflicts, experimental fiction frequently may remove traditional identity markers: note that "the Hit Man" doesn't have a name. Rather than ordering experience, such writers disrupt it by insisting that meanings in fiction are as elusive — or nonexistent — as meanings in life; they are likely to question both traditional values and traditional forms of writing. More traditional writers, however, use conflicts in their plots to reveal characters and convey meanings. The nature of those conflicts can help determine how important physical action is to the plot.

The primary conflict that the Hit Man experiences in his interactions with society is external. External conflicts may place the protagonist in opposition to another individual, nature, or society. The Hit Man's battle with societal values begins the moment he wears his executioner's hood to school and faces pressure to conform. He will learn that an individual's conflict with society can be as frustrating as it is complex, which is why so many plots in serious fiction focus on this conflict. It can be seen, to cite only two examples, in a repressive society's insistence on absolute control in Ursula K. Le Guin's "The Ones Who Walk Away from Omelas" (p. 111) and in the need for a young man to play jazz music despite his brother's demands for a more stable career path in James Baldwin's "Sonny's Blues" (p. 76).

Conflict may also be internal; in such a case, some moral or psychological issue must be resolved within the protagonist. Inner conflicts frequently accompany external ones, as in Manuel Muñoz's "Zigzagger" (p. 143). The conflict, though puzzling, is more significant in "Zigzagger" because that story subtly explores some troubling issues that cannot be resolved simply through action. The protagonist struggles with both internal and external forces. His parents and friends know he is sick and try to cure him with typical remedies, but they are unaware of (as is the reader, initially) what caused the sickness. It is only through telling the story through multiple points of view with significant flashbacks that the internal and external conflicts can be resolved. Muñoz creates questions for the reader rather than suspense. We are compelled to keep asking why the protagonist in his story is ill instead of what is going to happen next. The meaning of the action is not self-evident as it would be in a conventionally arranged story in which plot follows chronology. Instead, meaning must be drawn from a careful reading of the interrelated details and dialogues that constitute this story's action.

"The Hit Man" plays with plot conventions partly to amuse the reader who might be expecting something different, but partly to lull us into thinking that the story is only meant to delight; then it offers the possibility that it has an important instructional function as well. This kind of reading is more demanding, but ultimately more satisfying, because as we confront conflicts in serious fiction we read not only absorbing stories but also ourselves. We are invited not to escape life but to look long and hard at it. Although serious fiction can be as diverting and pleasurable as most standard action-packed plots, serious fiction offers an additional important element: a perspective on experience that reflects rather than deflects life.

The following two stories, William Faulkner's "A Rose for Emily" and Joyce Carol Oates's "Tick" — are remarkable for the tension produced by a subtle use of plot.

WILLIAM FAULKNER (1897–1962)

Born into an old Mississippi family that had lost its influence and wealth during the Civil War, William Faulkner lived nearly all his life in the South writing about Yoknapatawpha County, an imagined Mississippi county similar to his home in Oxford. Among his novels based on this fictional location are *The Sound and the Fury* (1929), *As I Lay Dying* (1930), *Light in August* (1932), and *Absalom, Absalom!* (1936). Although his writings are regional

Cofield Collection, Archives and Special Collections, University of Mississippi Libraries.

in their emphasis on local social history, his concerns are broader. In his 1950 acceptance speech for the Nobel Prize for Literature, he insisted that the "problems of the human heart in conflict with itself . . . alone can make good writing because only that is worth writing about, worth the agony and the sweat." This commitment is evident in his novels and in *The Collected Stories of William Faulkner* (1950). "A Rose for Emily," about the mysterious life of Emily Grierson, presents a personal conflict rooted in her southern identity. It also contains a grim surprise.

A Rose for Emily 1931

I

When Miss Emily Grierson died, our whole town went to her funeral: the men through a sort of respectful affection for a fallen monument, the women mostly out of curiosity to see the inside of her house, which no one save an old manservant — a combined gardener and cook — had seen in at least ten years.

It was a big, squarish frame house that had once been white, decorated with cupolas and spires and scrolled balconies in the heavily lightsome style of the seventies, set on what had once been our most select street. But garages and cotton gins had encroached and obliterated even the august names of that neighborhood; only Miss Emily's house was left, lifting its stubborn and coquettish decay above the cotton wagons and the gasoline pumps — an eyesore among eyesores. And now Miss Emily had gone to join the representatives of those august names where they lay in the cedar-bemused cemetery among the ranked and anonymous graves of Union and Confederate soldiers who fell at the battle of Jefferson.

Alive, Miss Emily had been a tradition, a duty, and a care; a sort of hereditary obligation upon the town, dating from that day in 1894 when Colonel Sartoris, the mayor — he who fathered the edict that no Negro woman should appear on the streets without an apron — remitted her taxes, the dispensation dating from the death of her father on into perpetuity. Not that Miss Emily would have accepted charity. Colonel Sartoris invented an involved tale to the effect that Miss Emily's father had loaned money to the town, which the town, as a matter of business, preferred this way of repaying. Only a man of Colonel Sartoris' generation and thought could have invented it, and only a woman could have believed it.

When the next generation, with its more modern ideas, became mayors and aldermen, this arrangement created some little dissatisfaction. On the first of the year they mailed her a tax notice. February came, and there was no reply. They wrote her a formal letter, asking her to call at the sheriff's office at her convenience. A week later the mayor wrote her himself, offering to call or to send his car for her, and received in reply a note on paper of an archaic shape, in a thin, flowing calligraphy in faded ink, to the effect that she no longer went out at all. The tax notice was also enclosed, without comment.

They called a special meeting of the Board of Aldermen. A deputation waited upon her, knocked at the door through which no visitor had passed since she ceased giving china-painting lessons eight or ten years earlier. They were admitted by the old Negro into a dim hall from which a stairway mounted into still more shadow. It smelled of dust and disuse — a close, dank smell. The Negro led them into the parlor. It was furnished in heavy, leather-covered furniture. When the Negro opened the blinds of one window, they could see that the leather was cracked; and when they sat down, a faint dust rose sluggishly about their thighs, spinning with slow motes in the single sun-ray. On a tarnished gilt easel before the fireplace stood a crayon portrait of Miss Emily's father.

They rose when she entered — a small, fat woman in black, with a thin gold chain descending to her waist and vanishing into her belt, leaning on an ebony cane with a tarnished gold head. Her skeleton was small and spare; perhaps that was why what would have been merely plumpness in another was obesity in her. She looked bloated, like a body long submerged in motionless water, and of that pallid hue. Her eyes, lost in the fatty ridges of her face, looked like two small pieces of coal pressed into a lump of dough as they moved from one face to another while the visitors stated their errand.

She did not ask them to sit. She just stood in the door and listened quietly until the spokesman came to a stumbling halt. Then they could hear the invisible watch ticking at the end of the gold chain.

Her voice was dry and cold. "I have no taxes in Jefferson. Colonel Sartoris explained it to me. Perhaps one of you can gain access to the city records and satisfy yourselves."

"But we have. We are the city authorities, Miss Emily. Didn't you get a notice from the sheriff, signed by him?"

"I received a paper, yes," Miss Emily said. "Perhaps he considers himself the sheriff . . . I have no taxes in Jefferson."

"But there is nothing on the books to show that, you see. We must go by the —"

"See Colonel Sartoris. I have no taxes in Jefferson."

"But, Miss Emily —"

"See Colonel Sartoris." (Colonel Sartoris had been dead almost ten years.) "I have no taxes in Jefferson. Tobe!" The Negro appeared. "Show these gentlemen out."

II

So she vanquished them, horse and foot, just as she had vanquished their fathers thirty years before about the smell. That was two years after her father's death and a short time after her sweetheart — the one we believed would marry her — had deserted her. After her father's death she went out very little; after her sweetheart went away, people hardly saw her at all. A few of the ladies had the temerity to call, but were not received, and the only sign of life about the place was the Negro man — a young man then — going in and out with a market basket.

"Just as if a man — any man — could keep a kitchen properly," the ladies said; so they were not surprised when the smell developed. It was another link between the gross, teeming world and the high and mighty Griersons.

A neighbor, a woman, complained to the mayor, Judge Stevens, eighty years old.

"But what will you have me do about it, madam?" he said.

"Why, send her word to stop it," the woman said. "Isn't there a law?"

"I'm sure that won't be necessary," Judge Stevens said. "It's probably just a snake or a rat that nigger of hers killed in the yard. I'll speak to him about it." 20

The next day he received two more complaints, one from a man who came in diffident deprecation. "We really must do something about it, Judge. I'd be the last one in the world to bother Miss Emily, but we've got to do something." That night the Board of Aldermen met — three graybeards and one younger man, a member of the rising generation.

"It's simple enough," he said. "Send her word to have her place cleaned up. Give her a certain time to do it in, and if she don't . . ."

"Dammit, sir," Judge Stevens said, "will you accuse a lady to her face of smelling bad?"

So the next night, after midnight, four men crossed Miss Emily's lawn and slunk about the house like burglars, sniffing along the base of the brick-work and at the cellar openings while one of them performed a regular sow-ing motion with his hand out of a sack slung from his shoulder. They broke open the cellar door and sprinkled lime there, and in all the outbuildings. As they recrossed the lawn, a window that had been dark was lighted and Miss Emily sat in it, the light behind her, and her upright torso motionless as that of an idol. They crept quietly across the lawn and into the shadow of the locusts that lined the street. After a week or two the smell went away.

That was when people had begun to feel really sorry for her. People 25 in our town, remembering how old lady Wyatt, her great-aunt, had gone completely crazy at last, believed that the Griersons held themselves a little too high for what they really were. None of the young men were quite good enough for Miss Emily and such. We had long thought of them as a tableau, Miss Emily a slender figure in white in the background, her father a sprad-dled silhouette in the foreground, his back to her and clutching a horse-whip, the two of them framed by the back-flung front door. So when she got to be thirty and was still single, we were not pleased exactly, but vindicated; even with insanity in the family she wouldn't have turned down all of her chances if they had really materialized.

When her father died, it got about that the house was all that was left to her; and in a way, people were glad. At last they could pity Miss Emily. Being left alone, and a pauper, she had become humanized. Now she too would know the old thrill and the old despair of a penny more or less.

The day after his death all the ladies prepared to call at the house and offer condolence and aid, as is our custom. Miss Emily met them at the door, dressed as usual and with no trace of grief on her face. She told them that her father was not dead. She did that for three days, with the ministers calling on her, and the doctors, trying to persuade her to let them dispose of the body. Just as they were about to resort to law and force, she broke down, and they buried her father quickly.

We did not say she was crazy then. We believed she had to do that. We remembered all the young men her father had driven away, and we knew that with nothing left, she would have to cling to that which had robbed her, as people will.

III

She was sick for a long time. When we saw her again, her hair was cut short, making her look like a girl, with a vague resemblance to those angels in colored church windows — sort of tragic and serene.

The town had just let the contracts for paving the sidewalks, and in the summer after her father's death they began the work. The construction company came with niggers and mules and machinery, and a foreman named Homer Barron, a Yankee — a big, dark, ready man, with a big voice and eyes lighter than his face. The little boys would follow in groups to hear him cuss the niggers, and the niggers singing in time to the rise and fall of picks. Pretty soon he knew everybody in town. Whenever you heard a lot of laughing anywhere about the square, Homer Barron would be in the center of the group. Presently we began to see him and Miss Emily on Sunday afternoons driving in the yellow-wheeled buggy and the matched team of bays from the livery stable.

At first we were glad that Miss Emily would have an interest, because the ladies all said, "Of course a Grierson would not think seriously of a Northerner, a day laborer." But there were still others, older people, who said that even grief could not cause a real lady to forget *noblesse oblige*° — without calling it *noblesse oblige*. They just said, "Poor Emily. Her kinsfolk should come to her." She had some kin in Alabama; but years ago her father had fallen out with them over the estate of old lady Wyatt, the crazy woman, and there was no communication between the two families. They had not even been represented at the funeral.

And as soon as the old people said, "Poor Emily," the whispering began. "Do you suppose it's really so?" they said to one another. "Of course it is. What else could . . ." This behind their hands; rustling of craned silk and

---

noblesse oblige: The obligation of people of high social position.

satin behind jalousies closed upon the sun of Sunday afternoon as the thin, swift clop-clop-clop of the matched team passed: "Poor Emily."

She carried her head high enough — even when we believed that she was fallen. It was as if she demanded more than ever the recognition of her dignity as the last Grierson; as if it had wanted that touch of earthiness to reaffirm her imperviousness. Like when she bought the rat poison, the arsenic. That was over a year after they had begun to say "Poor Emily," and while the two female cousins were visiting her.

"I want some poison," she said to the druggist. She was over thirty then, still a slight woman, though thinner than usual, with cold, haughty black eyes in a face the flesh of which was strained across the temples and about the eye-sockets as you imagine a lighthouse-keeper's face ought to look. "I want some poison," she said.

"Yes, Miss Emily. What kind? For rats and such? I'd recom — " 35

"I want the best you have. I don't care what kind."

The druggist named several. "They'll kill anything up to an elephant. But what you want is — "

"Arsenic," Miss Emily said. "Is that a good one?"

"Is . . . arsenic? Yes, ma'am. But what you want — "

"I want arsenic." 40

The druggist looked down at her. She looked back at him, erect, her face like a strained flag. "Why, of course," the druggist said. "If that's what you want. But the law requires you to tell what you are going to use it for."

Miss Emily just stared at him, her head tilted back in order to look him eye for eye, until he looked away and went and got the arsenic and wrapped it up. The Negro delivery boy brought her the package; the druggist didn't come back. When she opened the package at home there was written on the box, under the skull and bones: "For rats."

IV

So the next day we all said, "She will kill herself"; and we said it would be the best thing. When she had first begun to be seen with Homer Barron, we had said, "She will marry him." Then we said, "She will persuade him yet," because Homer himself had remarked — he liked men, and it was known that he drank with the younger men in the Elks' Club — that he was not a marrying man. Later we said, "Poor Emily" behind the jalousies as they passed on Sunday afternoon in the glittering buggy, Miss Emily with her head high and Homer Barron with his hat cocked and a cigar in his teeth, reins and whip in a yellow glove.

Then some of the ladies began to say that it was a disgrace to the town and a bad example to the young people. The men did not want to inter-fere, but at last the ladies forced the Baptist minister — Miss Emily's people were Episcopal — to call upon her. He would never divulge what happened during that interview, but he refused to go back again. The next Sunday they again drove about the streets, and the following day the minister's wife wrote to Miss Emily's relations in Alabama.

So she had blood-kin under her roof again and we sat back to watch developments. At first nothing happened. Then we were sure that they were to be married. We learned that Miss Emily had been to the jeweler's and ordered a man's toilet set in silver, with the letters H. B. on each piece. Two days later we learned that she had bought a complete outfit of men's clothing, including a nightshirt, and we said, "They are married." We were really glad. We were glad because the two female cousins were even more Grierson than Miss Emily had ever been.

So we were not surprised when Homer Barron — the streets had been finished some time since — was gone. We were a little disappointed that there was not a public blowing-off, but we believed that he had gone on to prepare for Miss Emily's coming, or to give her a chance to get rid of the cousins. (By that time it was a cabal, and we were all Miss Emily's allies to help circumvent the cousins.) Sure enough, after another week they departed. And, as we had expected all along, within three days Homer Barron was back in town. A neighbor saw the Negro man admit him at the kitchen door at dusk one evening.

And that was the last we saw of Homer Barron. And of Miss Emily for some time. The Negro man went in and out with the market basket, but the front door remained closed. Now and then we would see her at a window for a moment, as the men did that night when they sprinkled the lime, but for almost six months she did not appear on the streets. Then we knew that this was to be expected too; as if that quality of her father which had thwarted her woman's life so many times had been too virulent and too furious to die.

When we next saw Miss Emily, she had grown fat and her hair was turning gray. During the next few years it grew grayer and grayer until it attained an even pepper-and-salt iron-gray, when it ceased turning. Up to the day of her death at seventy-four it was still that vigorous iron-gray, like the hair of an active man.

From that time on her front door remained closed, save for a period of six or seven years, when she was about forty, during which she gave lessons in china-painting. She fitted up a studio in one of the downstairs rooms, where the daughters and granddaughters of Colonel Sartoris' contemporaries were sent to her with the same regularity and in the same spirit that they were sent to church on Sundays with a twenty-five-cent piece for the collection plate. Meanwhile her taxes had been remitted.

Then the newer generation became the backbone and the spirit of the town, and the painting pupils grew up and fell away and did not send their children to her with boxes of color and tedious brushes and pictures cut from the ladies' magazines. The front door closed upon the last one and remained closed for good. When the town got free postal delivery, Miss Emily alone refused to let them fasten the metal numbers above her door and attach a mailbox to it. She would not listen to them.

Daily, monthly, yearly we watched the Negro grow grayer and more stooped, going in and out with the market basket. Each December we sent her a tax notice, which would be returned by the post office a week later, unclaimed. Now and then we would see her in one of the downstairs windows — she had evidently shut up the top floor of the house — like the carven torso of an idol in a niche, looking or not looking at us, we could never tell which. Thus she passed from generation to generation — dear, inescapable, impervious, tranquil, and perverse.

And so she died. Fell ill in the house filled with dust and shadows, with only a doddering Negro man to wait on her. We did not even know she was sick; we had long since given up trying to get information from the Negro. He talked to no one, probably not even to her, for his voice had grown harsh and rusty, as if from disuse.

She died in one of the downstairs rooms, in a heavy walnut bed with a curtain, her gray head propped on a pillow yellow and moldy with age and lack of sunlight.

V

The Negro met the first of the ladies at the front door and let them in, with their hushed, sibilant voices and their quick, curious glances, and then he disappeared. He walked right through the house and out the back and was not seen again.

The two female cousins came at once. They held the funeral on the 55 second day, with the town coming to look at Miss Emily beneath a mass of bought flowers, with the crayon face of her father musing profoundly above the bier and the ladies sibilant and macabre; and the very old men — some in their brushed Confederate uniforms — on the porch and the lawn, talking of Miss Emily as if she had been a contemporary of theirs, believing that they had danced with her and courted her perhaps, confusing time with its mathematical progression, as the old do, to whom all the past is not a diminishing road but, instead, a huge meadow which no winter ever quite touches, divided from them now by the narrow bottle-neck of the most recent decade of years.

Already we knew that there was one room in that region above stairs which no one had seen in forty years, and which would have to be forced. They waited until Miss Emily was decently in the ground before they opened it.

The violence of breaking down the door seemed to fill this room with pervading dust. A thin, acrid pall as of the tomb seemed to lie everywhere upon this room decked and furnished as for a bridal: upon the valance curtains of faded rose color, upon the rose-shaded lights, upon the dressing table, upon the delicate array of crystal and the man's toilet things backed with tarnished silver, silver so tarnished that the monogram was obscured. Among them lay a collar and tie, as if they had just been removed, which, lifted, left upon the surface a pale crescent in the dust. Upon a chair hung the suit, carefully folded; beneath it the two mute shoes and the discarded socks.

The man himself lay in the bed.

For a long while we just stood there, looking down at the profound and fleshless grin. The body had apparently once lain in the attitude of an embrace, but now the long sleep that outlasts love, that conquers even the grimace of love, had cuckolded him. What was left of him, rotted beneath what was left of the nightshirt, had become inextricable from the bed in which he lay; and upon him and upon the pillow beside him lay that even coating of the patient and biding dust.

Then we noticed that in the second pillow was the indentation of a head. One of us lifted something from it, and leaning forward, that faint and invisible dust dry and acrid in the nostrils, we saw a long strand of iron-gray hair.

Considerations for Critical Thinking and Writing

1. **FIRST RESPONSE.** The story has five numbered sections. If you were to give them titles as in T. C. Boyle's story "The Hit Man," what would those titles be? What effect would each have on the reader?

2. What is the effect of the final paragraph of the story? How does it contribute to your understanding of Emily? Why is it important that we get this information last rather than at the beginning of the story?

3. What details foreshadow the conclusion of the story? Did you anticipate the ending?

4. Contrast the order of events as they happen in the story with the order in which they are told. How does this plotting create interest and suspense?

5. Faulkner uses a number of gothic elements in this plot: the imposing decrepit house, the decayed corpse, and the mysterious secret horrors connected with Emily's life. How do these elements forward the plot and establish the atmosphere?

6. How does the information provided by the exposition indicate the nature of the conflict in the story? What does Emily's southern heritage contribute to the story?

7. Who or what is the antagonist of the story? Why is it significant that Homer Barron is a construction foreman and a northerner?

8. In what sense does the narrator's telling of the story serve as "A Rose for Emily"? Why do you think the narrator uses *we* rather than *I*?

9. Explain how Emily's reasons for murdering Homer are related to her personal history and to the ways she handled previous conflicts.

10. Discuss how Faulkner's treatment of the North and the South contributes to the meaning of the story.

11. Provide an alternative title and explain how the emphasis in your title is reflected in the story.

A SAMPLE CLOSE READING

An Annotated Section of "A Rose for Emily"

Even as you read a story for the first time, you can highlight passages, circle or underline words, and write responses in the margins. Subsequent readings will yield more insights once you begin to understand how various elements such as plot, character, and wording build toward the conclusion and what you perceive to be the story's central ideas. The following annotations for the first five paragraphs of "A Rose for Emily" provide a perspective written by someone who had read the work several times.

WILLIAM FAULKNER (1897–1962)

From *A Rose for Emily*   1931

> The title suggests that the story is an expression of affection and mourning, as well as a tribute, for Emily — despite her bizarre behavior.

I

When Miss Emily Grierson died, our whole town went to her funeral: the men through a sort of respectful affection for a fallen monument, the women mostly out of curiosity to see the inside of her house, which no one save an old manservant — a combined gardener and cook — had seen in at least ten years.

> The story begins (and ends) with death, and the "fallen monument" signals Emily's special meaning to the narrator and the community.

It was a big, squarish frame house that had once been white, decorated with cupolas and spires and scrolled balconies in the heavily lightsome style of the seventies, set on what had once been our most select street. But garages and cotton gins had encroached and obliterated even the august names of that neighborhood; only Miss Emily's house was left, lifting its stubborn and coquettish decay above the cotton wagons and the gasoline pumps — an eyesore among eyesores. And now Miss Emily had gone to join the representatives of those august names where they lay in the cedar-bemused cemetery among the ranked and anonymous graves of Union and Confederate soldiers who fell at the battle of Jefferson.

> The importance of the decayed old South setting is emphasized by being detailed even before Emily is described. The lingering conflict between the North and South is implicitly linked to the garages and gas pumps (the modern) that overtake the old southern neighborhood.

Alive, Miss Emily had been a tradition, a duty, and a care; a sort of hereditary obligation upon the town, dating from that day in 1894 when Colonel Sartoris, the mayor — he who fathered the edict that no Negro woman should appear on the streets without an apron — remitted her taxes, the dispensation dating from the death of her father on into perpetuity. Not that Miss Emily would have accepted charity. Colonel Sartoris invented an involved tale

> Emily is associated with southern tradition, duty, and privilege that require protection. This helps explain why the townspeople attend her funeral.

to the effect that Miss Emily's father had loaned money to the town, which the town, as a matter of business, preferred this way of repaying. Only a man of Colonel Sartoris' generation and thought could have invented it, and only a woman could have believed it.

When the next generation, with its more modern ideas, became mayors and aldermen, this arrangement created some little dissatisfaction. On the first of the year they mailed her a tax notice. February came, and there was no reply. They wrote her a formal letter, asking her to call at the sheriff's office at her convenience. A week later the mayor wrote her himself, offering to call or to send his car for her, and received in reply a note on paper of an archaic shape, in a thin, flowing calligraphy in faded ink, to the effect that she no longer went out at all. The tax notice was also enclosed, without comment.

They called a special meeting of the Board of Aldermen. A deputation waited upon her, knocked at the door through which no visitor had passed since she ceased giving china-painting lessons eight or ten years earlier. They were admitted by the old Negro into a dim hall from which a stairway mounted into still more shadow. It smelled of dust and disuse — a close, dank smell. The Negro led them into the parlor. It was furnished in heavy, leather-covered furniture. When the Negro opened the blinds of one window, they could see that the leather was cracked; and when they sat down, a faint dust rose sluggishly about their thighs, spinning with slow motes in the single sun-ray. On a tarnished gilt easel before the fireplace stood a crayon portrait of Miss Emily's father.

Margin notes:

Like Emily, her "archaic," "thin," and "faded" note resists change and "modern ideas." She dismisses any attempts by the town to assess her for taxes or for anything else. She won't even leave the house.

The description of the "dank" house smelling of "dust and disuse" reinforces Emily's connection with the past and her refusal to let go of it. As the men sat down, "a faint dust rose" around them. The passage of time is alluded to in each of these paragraphs and ultimately emerges as a kind of antagonist.

A SAMPLE STUDENT RESPONSE

Josiah Parker

Professor Altschuler

English 200-A

14 December 2018

Conflict in the Plot of William Faulkner's "A Rose for Emily"

The conflict of William Faulkner's "A Rose for Emily" is the driving force of the story's plot. However, the conflict is not the act of murder, nor is it Miss Emily's bizarre, reclusive lifestyle. The conflict is located instead in Miss Emily's background, her history. She is portrayed as a hardened, bitter old woman, but we soon realize she herself is a victim. She has been oppressed her entire life by her domineering father, unable to take a suitor and marry, which is what she desires most. This lifelong oppression becomes the central conflict, and is what drives Miss Emily, causing her "to cling to that which had robbed her" (Faulkner, "Rose" 43).

After her father's death, Miss Emily immediately takes a lover, then poisons him when he tries to leave her. She has been taught her whole life not to take a lover, certainly not to take a life. Her willingness to go against what she has always known to be moral and right creates dramatic tension and advances the story. In this way, the act of murder is nothing more than a portion of the plot, "the author's arrangement of incidents in a story," rather than the conflict itself (Meyer and Miller 31). . . .

Works Cited

Faulkner, William. "A Rose for Emily." Meyer, pp. 40–47.

Meyer, Michael and D. Quentin Miller, editors. *Literature to Go*. 4th ed., Bedford/St. Martin's, 2020.

Joyce Carol Oates (b. 1938)

The sheer volume of Joyce Carol Oates's writing is almost hard to fathom. Since the publication of her first story collection in 1963, she has published fifty-seven novels, eleven novellas, and forty-two collections of short stories, and those numbers don't include an almost equal number of works in other genres: essay collections, memoirs, poetry, young adult fiction, and children's fiction. She has received dozens of awards, including the Rea Award for Short Fiction and the National Book Award, and she has been a finalist for the Pulitzer Prize for Fiction on five occasions. Although it is impossible to generalize about a body of work as varied and as wide-ranging as hers, the passionate emotional and psychological intensity evident in the following story, "Tick," is one hallmark of her work.

Tick 1988

She said, I can't live with you under these conditions, and her husband said, But these *are* the conditions. And moved out. And did not telephone her for several days. And when he did call she told him quickly, I'm happy here alone — I've gotten through the worst of it. Don't spoil my happiness again.

Since then the telephone rings at odd hours and she never answers. She will never answer — it's that simple. She does her work in the apartment spreading her books and papers out on the dining room table and she is working well, better than she has in years but it's all precarious, she knows it's precarious, not the temptation to kill herself — she understands this is an adolescent fantasy and would never act upon it — but the temptation to succumb to thoughts of despair, self-hatred. Easier, she thinks, to hate yourself than to respect yourself: it involves less imagination.

Tonight, contemplating these matters, she runs her fingers through her hair and comes upon a small bump on her head, the very crown of her head. A pimple, except it isn't a pimple. A mysterious hardness, shell-like. Could it be a tiny pebble embedded in her scalp? But how? She tries gently to dislodge it with her fingernails but it is stuck fast. What can it be? — she's fastidious about grooming, shampooing her hair every morning when she showers.

She tries to comb the thing out of her hair first with a plastic comb and then with a fine-toothed steel comb her husband left behind. It won't budge. Perhaps it is a tiny wound, a tiny scab, she thinks, and then she thinks, It's alive, it has its jaws in me. And she realizes it must be a tick.

Since her husband moved out and it is possible for her to go for days with- 5 out seeing anyone she has made a conscientious effort to be better groomed than she has ever been in her life. Shaves her underarms before the harsh stubble appears, keeps her legs smooth and hairless. Always dresses no matter the black rain falling against the windows in the early morning and the faint odors of garbage and wet ashes pervading the apartment building. Puts on lipstick, sometimes even a touch of cologne on her wrist, behind her ear. Pride! she thinks, winking in the mirror. Self-reliance! There you go!

She's in the bathroom trying desperately to inspect the top of her head in the medicine cabinet mirror. Roughly parting her hair, stooping, her eyes rolling up in their sockets. But she can't see — it's impossible. She runs for a hand mirror and holds it at such an angle that she can see into the cabinet mirror where she parts her hair clumsily with the fingers of one hand and she gives a little scream and nearly drops the mirror: it *is* a tick, bloated and purplish-black, stuck fast in her scalp.

She instructs herself to be calm. Not to panic. Not to give in to nausea, gagging. It's only an insect after all, one of those tiny black spiderlike things, parasites that suck animal and human blood, it's said the woods and fields are filled with them because of the rain this spring, and the heat, or is it because of the dryness and the heat, they're remarkably quick, darting and leaping and flying, raining from the trees onto unknowing human heads which is how she must have picked this one up — walking through the park the other morning, forcing herself to look and to really *see* the beauty of the natural world which she'd lost these past several months or has it been these past several years, embarked upon the precarious enterprise of adulthood, wifehood, loneliness.

She recalls that ticks secrete an anesthetic when they bite so you can't feel the bite. She recalls they're so hardy they can't be killed by ordinary methods, can't be squashed — the most practical method is to flush them down the toilet.

She is digging furiously at her scalp with her nails and the sink is flecked with blood, her blood, and a number of hairs. No reason to panic but she can't stop the frantic digging, she's bent low over the sink, panting, cursing, blood beating in her eyeballs and rivulets of sweat running down her back.

She feels a sensation of nausea, a taste of something hot and acid at the back of her mouth but she manages to swallow it down. She thinks of the book she'd been planning to read this evening and the piano pieces by a contemporary composer whose work she admires she'd planned to study and work out though she hasn't a piano in the apartment yet (she intends to buy one, or rent one, soon, now that she'll have more time for it, and more energy) and these activities strike her suddenly as remote, preposterous.

Her husband once had a medical handbook, she goes to look for it in the bedroom in a pile of books he left behind but can't find it, she tries the bookshelves in the living room then the stack of books in the kitchen beside the refrigerator, mostly paperbacks and shamelessly dusty, and when she's about to give up she discovers it, *The Family Medical Companion,* thank God her husband was so angry and hurt, so eager to get away from her, he'd left it behind. With trembling fingers she opens it to the section "Insects" that begins, "Insects are both friends and enemies of man. Some simply annoy by their bites and stings, but a few carry disease-bearing microbes."

The paragraph on ticks is disappointingly brief. She reads that she should not try to yank the tick out of her skin since ticks embed themselves so snugly, part of its body will very likely remain and there's the chance of infection. She has her choice of several procedures: she can hold a lighted match or cigarette against the tick's back until it wriggles free; she can coat it with Vaseline, gasoline, kerosene, or turpentine; she can pick the tick off gently with a tweezers.

She tries the tweezers. Tries repeatedly, a dozen times or more, at the bathroom sink, until the tweezers slips from her numbed fingers. She's crying. Her face is flushed as if with sunstroke, her eyes in the mirror are those of a deranged woman. To her horror she feels, or believes she feels, the tick stirring in her scalp — enlivened, enraged, burrowing more deeply into her flesh. She wonders if it has the power to pierce the bone, to embed itself in her very brain.

She jams her knuckles into her mouth to muffle her screaming.

She's close to hysteria so she leaves the bathroom and paces about the apartment, from one room to another, one room to another, in an effort to calm herself. Minutes pass: she has no idea how many. She beats her hands softly together, the fleshy parts of the palms, she tries to breathe deeply and rhythmically, after all this is such a minor problem, hardly a matter of life and death, if worse comes to worst she can take a taxi to a hospital to an emergency room but what if they laugh at her there? — what if they're furious with her there? — her with her face like death, trembling and panting as if she'd been physically assaulted, *a mere tick embedded in her scalp.* More plausibly, she might go next door and ask for help from her neighbor — but when she envisions knocking at the door, handing the astonished young woman the tweezers and begging her to extricate the thing in her head, she knows she can't do it. She isn't acquainted with the woman even casually — she's a shy cold girl very like herself. When they meet in the foyer or in the elevator each smiles faintly and pointedly looks away thinking, *Don't talk to me. Please. Not right now.*

Perhaps she should kill herself after all — it would be the easiest solution   15 to all her problems.

By this time she's walking fast, on the verge of breaking into a run, can't stop! can't sit down! her heart beating wildly and her breath audible. At the crown of her head there's a hot piercing throbbing pain. Her fingernails are edged with blood. She's rushing from room to room, pacing, turning in tight corners like a trapped animal, hardly seeing where she's careening, her eyes filled with tears of hurt, rage, frustration, shame — this is what it comes to, she's thinking, this is all it comes to, and she's leaning in a doorway trying to get her breath trying to stave off an attack of faintness when she hears the telephone ring and understands it has been ringing for some time.

She heads for it like a sleepwalker, propelled by a rough shove. She foresees a reconciliation, lovemaking both anguished and tender. She foresees starting a child. It's time.

CONSIDERATIONS FOR CRITICAL THINKING AND WRITING

1. FIRST RESPONSE. The marital separation at the beginning of the story is not explained: the wife and husband break up because of "these conditions." Are we supposed to speculate about the reasons for the breakup or is this detail unimportant?

2. Neither the protagonist of this story nor her husband is given a name: what is the effect of that choice?

3. How does the narrator's personality type explain her reaction to the tick? What details from the story that are not specifically about the tick help you to understand her character?

4. List as many details as you can find in the story that have to do with the protagonist's body: why is it emphasized?

5. Summarize the plot of the story in three sentences. What important features of the story does this plot summary fail to capture?

6. What would you identify as the story's climactic moment in terms of plot?

7. How does the story comment on the condition of being alone?

8. In the final paragraph, when the protagonist is contemplating reuniting with her husband, she mentions that they are ready to have a child. How important is this detail? Does it have anything to do with the tick that precipitates her panicky crisis?

CONNECTIONS TO ANOTHER SELECTION

1. Compare the depiction of marriage in "Tick" and Charlotte Perkins Gilman's "The Yellow Wallpaper" (p. 117).

3

Character

Bettmann/Getty Images.

When I find a well-drawn character in fiction or biography, I generally take a warm personal interest in him, for the reason that I have known him before — met him on the river.
— MARK TWAIN

Character is essential to plot. Without characters, Grace Paley's "Wants" would be a list of the cost of overdue library books and Faulkner's "A Rose for Emily" little more than a faded history of a sleepy town in the South. If stories were depopulated, the plots would disappear because characters and plots are interrelated. A library fee is important only because we care what effect it has on a character. Characters are influenced by events just as events are shaped by characters. The protagonist of Paley's story is someone who is intellectually curious and often unwilling to conform to society's guidelines: the fact that she has kept library books for a very long time, and that she returns them and cheerfully pays what she owes, comprise the basic plot of "Wants," but they are also strong indications of the type of person she is.

The methods by which a writer creates people in a story so that they seem actually to exist are called ***characterization***. Huck Finn never lived, yet those who have read Mark Twain's novel about Huck's adventures along the Mississippi River feel as if they know him. A good writer gives us the illusion that a character is real, but we should also remember that a character is not an actual person but instead has been created by the author. Though we might walk out of a room in which Huck Finn's Pap talks racist nonsense, we would not throw away the book in a similar fit of anger. This illusion of reality is the magic that allows us to move beyond the circumstances of our own lives into a writer's fictional world, where we can encounter everyone from royalty to paupers, murderers, lovers, cheaters, martyrs, artists, destroyers, and nearly always, some part of ourselves. The life that a writer breathes into a character adds to our own experiences and enlarges our view of the world.

A character is usually but not always a person. In Jack London's *Call of the Wild*, the protagonist is a devoted sled dog; in Ernest Hemingway's "The Short, Happy Life of Francis Macomber," the story's point of view occasionally enters the mind of a wounded lion. Perhaps the only possible qualification to be placed on character is that whatever it is — whether an animal or even an inanimate object, such as a robot — it must have some recognizable human qualities. The action of the plot interests us primarily because we care about what happens to people and what they do. We may identify with a character's desires and aspirations, or we may be disgusted by his or her viciousness and selfishness. To understand our response to a story, we should be able to recognize the methods of characterization the author uses.

TOBIAS WOLFF (B. 1945)

Known as much for his memoirs (*This Boy's Life* in 1989 and *In Pharaoh's Army* in 1994) as his award-winning fiction, Tobias Wolff's prose is clean and honest. He deals with the gritty realities of experience, sometimes relying on his own years as a soldier and sometimes on his upbringing, including the often strained relationships among family members, as in the following story, "Powder," about a boy and his father navigating a hazardous winter road.

ZUMA Press, Inc./Alamy Stock Photo.

Powder   1996

Just before Christmas my father took me skiing at Mount Baker. He'd had to fight for the privilege of my company, because my mother was still angry with him for sneaking me into a nightclub during his last visit, to see Thelonious Monk.

He wouldn't give up. He promised, hand on heart, to take good care of me and have me home for dinner on Christmas Eve, and she relented. But as we were checking out of the lodge that morning it began to snow, and in this snow he observed some rare quality that made it necessary for us to get in one last run. We got in several last runs. He was indifferent to my fretting. Snow whirled around us in bitter, blinding squalls, hissing like sand, and still we skied. As the lift bore us to the peak yet again, my father looked at his watch and said, "Criminy. This'll have to be a fast one."

By now I couldn't see the trail. There was no point in trying. I stuck to him like white on rice and did what he did and somehow made it to the bottom without sailing off a cliff. We returned our skis and my father put chains on the Austin-Healey while I swayed from foot to foot, clapping my mittens and wishing I was home. I could see everything. The green tablecloth, the plates with the holly pattern, the red candles waiting to be lit.

We passed a diner on our way out. "You want some soup?" my father asked. I shook my head. "Buck up," he said. "I'll get you there. Right, doctor?"

I was supposed to say, "Right, doctor," but I didn't say anything.   5

A state trooper waved us down outside the resort. A pair of sawhorses were blocking the road. The trooper came up to our car and bent down to my father's window. His face was bleached by the cold. Snowflakes clung to his eyebrows and to the fur trim of his jacket and cap.

"Don't tell me," my father said.

The trooper told him. The road was closed. It might get cleared, it might not. Storm took everyone by surprise. So much, so fast. Hard to get people moving. Christmas Eve. What can you do.

My father said, "Look. We're talking about five, six inches. I've taken this car through worse than that."

The trooper straightened up. His face was out of sight but I could hear   10
him. "The road is closed."

My father sat with both hands on the wheel, rubbing the wood with his thumbs. He looked at the barricade for a long time. He seemed to be trying to master the idea of it. Then he thanked the trooper, and with a weird, old-maidy show of caution turned the car around. "Your mother will never forgive me for this," he said.

"We should have left before," I said. "Doctor."

He didn't speak to me again until we were in a booth at the diner, waiting for our burgers. "She won't forgive me," he said. "Do you understand? Never."

"I guess," I said, but no guesswork was required; she wouldn't forgive him.

"I can't let that happen." He bent toward me. "I'll tell you what I want. I   15
want us all to be together again. Is that what you want?"

"Yes, sir."

He bumped my chin with his knuckles. "That's all I needed to hear."

When we finished eating he went to the pay phone in the back of the diner, then joined me in the booth again. I figured he'd called my mother, but he didn't give a report. He sipped at his coffee and stared out the window at the empty road. "Come on, come on," he said, though not to me. A little while later he said it again. When the trooper's car went past, lights flashing, he got up and dropped some money on the check. "Okay. Vamanos."

The wind had died. The snow was falling straight down, less of it now and lighter. We drove away from the resort, right up to the barricade. "Move it," my father told me. When I looked at him he said, "What are you waiting for?" I got out and dragged one of the sawhorses aside, then put it back after he drove through. He pushed the door open for me. "Now you're an accomplice," he said. "We go down together." He put the car into gear and gave me a look. "Joke, son."

Down the first long stretch I watched the road behind us, to see if the 20 trooper was on our tail. The barricade vanished. Then there was nothing but snow: snow on the road, snow kicking up from the chains, snow on the trees, snow in the sky; and our trail in the snow. Then I faced forward and had a shock. The lay of the road behind us had been marked by our own tracks, but there were no tracks ahead of us. My father was breaking virgin snow between a line of tall trees. He was humming "Stars Fell on Alabama." I felt snow brush along the floorboards under my feet. To keep my hands from shaking I clamped them between my knees.

My father grunted in a thoughtful way and said, "Don't ever try this yourself."

"I won't."

"That's what you say now, but someday you'll get your license and then you'll think you can do anything. Only you won't be able to do this. You need, I don't know — a certain instinct."

"Maybe I have it."

"You don't. You have your strong points, but not this. I only mention it 25 because I don't want you to get the idea this is something just anybody can do. I'm a great driver. That's not a virtue, okay? It's just a fact, and one you should be aware of. Of course you have to give the old heap some credit, too. There aren't many cars I'd try this with. Listen!"

I did listen. I heard the slap of the chains, the stiff, jerky rasp of the wipers, the purr of the engine. It really did purr. The old heap was almost new. My father couldn't afford it, and kept promising to sell it, but here it was.

I said, "Where do you think that policeman went to?"

"Are you warm enough?" He reached over and cranked up the blower. Then he turned off the wipers. We didn't need them. The clouds had brightened. A few sparse, feathery flakes drifted into our slipstream and were swept away. We left the trees and entered a broad field of snow that ran level for a while and then tilted sharply downward. Orange stakes had been planted at intervals in two parallel lines and my father steered a course between them, though they were far enough apart to leave considerable doubt in my mind as to exactly where the road lay. He was humming again, doing little scat riffs around the melody.

"Okay then. What are my strong points?"

"Don't get me started," he said. "It'd take all day."

"Oh, right. Name one."

"Easy. You always think ahead."

True. I always thought ahead. I was a boy who kept his clothes on numbered hangers to insure proper rotation. I bothered my teachers for homework assignments far ahead of their due dates so I could draw up schedules. I thought ahead, and that was why I knew that there would be other troopers waiting for us at the end of our ride, if we even got there. What I did not know was that my father would wheedle and plead his way past them — he didn't sing "O Tannenbaum," but just about — and get me home for dinner, buying a little more time before my mother decided to make the split final. I knew we'd get caught; I was resigned to it. And maybe for this reason I stopped moping and began to enjoy myself.

Why not? This was one for the books. Like being in a speedboat, only better. You can't go downhill in a boat. And it was all ours. And it kept coming, the laden trees, the unbroken surface of snow, the sudden white vistas. Here and there I saw hints of the road, ditches, fences, stakes, but not so many that I could have found my way. But then I didn't have to. My father was driving. My father in his forty-eighth year, rumpled, kind, bankrupt of honor, flushed with certainty. He was a great driver. All persuasion, no coercion. Such subtlety at the wheel, such tactful pedalwork. I actually trusted him. And the best was yet to come — switchbacks and hairpins impossible to describe. Except maybe to say this: if you haven't driven fresh powder, you haven't driven.

If this story were included in the chapter that explains *plot*, you might scratch your head a bit. The plot? A man and his son get caught in a snowstorm, drive down a harrowing road in defiance of the police, and survive, maybe even enjoy the ride. In a plot-heavy story, we would expect a car crash, perhaps followed by a full-throated argument between father and son, maybe even an arrest for driving on a forbidden road. The restrained plot in "Powder" gives the author ample room to develop rich and full characters in a relatively small space. There are a total of four characters in this story: the narrator, his father, his mother (who is not technically in the story, but whose invisible presence is significant), and the trooper. The mother and the trooper are minor characters who both represent the same oppositional force: they set the rules and parameters that the narrator's father breaks. The story wouldn't be the same without them: it might not even exist. They are minor, but significant in that the guidelines they set highlight the salient points of contact between the two main characters.

We evaluate fictional characters in much the same way we understand people in our own lives. By piecing together bits of information, we create a context that allows us to interpret their behavior. We can predict, for instance, that an acquaintance who is a chronic complainer is not likely to have anything good to say about a roommate. Complaints can be verbal or nonverbal: a rant and an eye-roll can convey similar gripes. One of the most crucial techniques to pay attention to in determining character is to observe the balance between *dialogue* and ***description***. *Dialogue* simply refers to the words people speak in a story. Plays, as we discuss in Chapter 25 and beyond, are comprised almost entirely of dialogue, and yet an actor's job on stage is rarely to stand stock still and recite dialogue: actors also wring their hands, run, slap each other, or stab each other while reciting their lines. When a character speaks in a short story, it is generally as part of a conversation, in reaction to something someone else has said. We can't always control what we say in such situations: emotions, fatigue, drunkenness, or being caught off guard are all circumstances that might alter our expected words. In "Powder" the narrator and his father have some sort of in-joke: the narrator is supposed to respond, "Right, doctor" when his father says "Right, doctor?" When he does not fill in this formula, we can assume that his father understands that his silence indicates extreme displeasure. Later on, he chides his father by adding "Doctor" to the stern sentence, "We should have left earlier," probably after a measured pause. His choice to omit "doctor" from their conversation and then to include it when it isn't called for are important clues to their relationship at this particular moment. We interpret words and actions in the light of what we already know about someone, and that is why keeping track of what characters say (and how they say it) along with what they do (and don't do) is important. Characters have histories, habits, quirks, and psychological responses to their environments, all of which combine to tell us who they are.

In addition to dialogue, authors reveal characters by a wide variety of means. It should be noted that some stories are all description and some are all dialogue, but these cases are rare: most authors blend them, and in a very particular way. Try highlighting all the dialogue in two or three stories: do you notice any patterns about where it tends to be most prevalent?

Physical descriptions can indicate important inner qualities; disheveled hair, a crafty smile, or a blush might communicate as much as or more than what a character says. Even clothing matters: in the parodic story "The Hit Man" by T. C. Boyle (p. 33), the protagonist is always wearing black, especially his executioner's hood: he wouldn't be "the Hit Man" without this costume. Sometimes clothing can be an obvious indicator of character: in classic Western movies the good guys wore white hats and the bad guys wore black hats. More often, we are encouraged to attend to subtler traits based on context. If a character wears a bright, flowery dress to a somber funeral where everyone else is dressed in traditional black, is she clueless? Does she care little for convention? Is she ecstatic at the death of the deceased because she always hated him? Is she the type of person who believes we should celebrate someone's life rather than mourn their passing? We would have to learn a little more about the character and the context for the funeral to decide. Characters can also be revealed by the words and actions of others who respond to them. In literature, moreover, we have one great advantage that life cannot offer; a work of fiction can give us access to a person's thoughts, which may come in the form of fully formed sentences that look like dialogue or in incoherent partial sentences or word jumbles known as **stream of consciousness**. "Joyce Carol Oates's story 'Tick' is narrated by a third-person narrator, but we are given ample access to her thoughts as her panic grows about the parasite in her scalp, and those thoughts become less and less like fully formed thoughts, culminating with this phrase: 'this is what it comes to, she's thinking, this is all it comes to.' The stream-of-consciousness technique allows words to come out as they might appear in our private thoughts rather than expressing them in complete, grammatically perfect sentences." Jamaica Kincaid's "Girl" (p. 316) is all dialogue, but it's actually snippets of many conversations that have occurred over a period of time, and it's certainly one-sided as dialogues go.

Authors have two major methods of presenting characters: **showing** and **telling**. Characters shown in dramatic situations reveal themselves indirectly by what they say and do. The general preference in modern fiction is to choose showing over telling when there is a choice. The art of fiction involves exercising the imagination, so fiction writers (like poets) gravitate toward images, or mental pictures. The narrator of Wolff's story has the option of telling you the type of person his father is; he might say, "My father was a jazz enthusiast who loved me and my mom, but who was bad at fulfilling his duties to the point of reckless irresponsibility." Instead, the author *shows* the father's love of jazz: he once got in trouble for sneaking his son into a club to see the legendary Thelonious Monk, he hums "Stars Fell on Alabama" as they barrel through the virgin snow, he does "little scat riffs around the melody" as the drive continues. There are many illustrations of his love for his wife and son, but also of his irresponsibility. We detect a little clownishness in the story's second paragraph when the father "promised, hand on heart, to take good care" of his son: the hand on heart is an insincere gesture, and we can almost picture his mother scowling in response, knowing how hollow the promise is after a lifetime of such behavior. In that same paragraph the father consults his watch after they take "several last runs" and is surprised by the time. The narrator isn't. He's been aware of the time all day, and worried about it.

By showing us the father's character rather than telling it, the author is able to reveal a character patiently and subtly, and to offer some ambiguity as a result. If the narrator merely proclaimed his father "reckless and irresponsible," we might be less likely to see his charms: his obvious joy in life, his confidence, his willingness to take risks. When he hums jazz tunes at a time that might seem stressful, we understand that he is a man bursting with positive energy: if the narrator just told us his father liked jazz, we might not intuit that trait. There are times, though, when telling is the most efficient or only possible way to communicate. The first sentence of the story — "Just before Christmas my father took me skiing at Mount Baker" — is all telling, and it's necessary information for us to have. It doesn't require interpretation: it's simply a fact that the narrator must establish before the story can continue. In a ***first-person narrative*** like this one, we should always be wary of perspective, though, because the storyteller is also a character whose perspective might be limited or distorted by his or her involvement in the story. For example, late in the story the narrator asks his father to list the narrator's "strong points." If we were evaluating the narrator's character at that moment, we might assume he's a little insecure. His father initially deflects the question, saying, "Don't get me started. . . . It'd take all day," and the narrator responds, "Oh, right. Name one." This response indicates either that possible insecurity or a scepticism that his father really values what he considers his strong points: their values are different. They seem to agree that one of the narrator's strong points is that he "always think[s] ahead," but the illustrations of this thinking ahead border on obsession or anxiety: do you know anyone who keeps their "clothes on numbered hangers to ensure proper rotation"? That's a fairly extreme version of "thinking ahead," to be generous. The narrator and his father tell us one thing but show us something slightly different. In this way, telling and showing complement each other.

Characters can be convincing whether they are presented by telling or showing, provided their actions are ***motivated***. There must be reasons for how they behave and what they say. If adequate motivation is offered, we can understand and find ***plausible*** their actions no matter how bizarre. In "A Rose for Emily" (p. 40), Faulkner makes Emily Grierson's intimacy with a corpse credible by preparing us with information about her father's death along with her inability to leave the past and live in the present. Emily turns out to be ***consistent***. Although we are surprised by the ending of the story, the behavior it reveals is compatible with her temperament. Sometimes a character is motivated but unsure how best to achieve his or her goals and desires. The father in "Powder" says plainly, "I'll tell you what I want. I want us all to be together again." We are likely to believe him, but we also must question if he's going about that goal the right way. He seems less concerned with considering his wife's and son's desires for a punctual Christmas Eve dinner than he is with his own need for adventure.

Some kinds of fiction consciously break away from our expectations of traditional realistic stories. Consistency, plausibility, and motivation are not very useful concepts for understanding and evaluating characterizations in modern ***absurdist literature***, for instance, in which characters are often alienated from themselves and their environment in an irrational world. In this world there is no possibility for traditional heroic action; instead we find an ***antihero*** who has little control over events. T. C. Boyle's protagonist in "The Hit Man" is petting a three-headed dog toward the story's end. Gregor Samsa, the protagonist of Franz Kafka's "The Metamorphosis" (1915), wakes up as a bug one morning and has to deal with the human world as an insect would. The narrator of John Barth's story "Night-Sea Journey" is a sperm swimming toward an egg among millions of sperm just like him. These works force us to consider the notion of character in terms that derive less from our experience than from our capacity for imaginative understanding.

In most realistic stories we expect characters to act plausibly and in ways consistent with their personalities, but that does not mean that characters cannot develop and change. A ***dynamic*** character undergoes some kind of change because of the action of the plot. Huck Finn's view of Jim, the runaway slave in Mark Twain's novel, develops during their experiences on the raft. Huck discovers Jim's humanity and, therefore, cannot betray him because Huck no longer sees his companion as merely the property of a white owner. On the other hand, Huck's friend, Tom Sawyer, is a ***static*** character because he does not change. He remains interested only in high adventure, even at the risk of Jim's life. As static characters often do, Tom serves as a *foil* to Huck; his frivolous concerns are contrasted with Huck's serious development. A ***foil*** helps to reveal by contrast the distinctive qualities of another character. We can see a similar dynamic in "Powder." The narrator's father is *static* in the sense that he cannot or is not willing to change. It would seem that the narrator is also static in that it appears as if he is doomed to worry, perhaps as a way of compensating for his father's tendency to break rules, but for a brief, important moment in the crucial final two paragraphs of the story he relaxes: "I stopped moping and began to enjoy myself." Even if it's a temporary change, we have to be a little relieved by this response. The easygoing, joyful final sentence of the story sounds more like his father than like him.

The protagonist in a story is usually a dynamic character who experiences some conflict that makes an impact on his or her life. Less commonly, static characters can also be protagonists. Rip Van Winkle wakes up from his twenty-year sleep in Washington Irving's story to discover his family dramatically changed and his country no longer a British colony, but none of these important events has an impact on his character; he continues to be the same shiftless and idle man that he was before he fell asleep. The protagonist in Faulkner's "A Rose for Emily" is also a static character; indeed, she rejects all change. The reader's understanding of her changes, but she does not. Ordinarily, however, a plot contains one or two dynamic characters with any number of static characters in supporting roles. This is especially true of short stories, in which brevity limits the possibilities of character development.

The extent to which a character is developed is another means by which character can be analyzed. The novelist E. M. Forster coined the terms *flat* and *round* to distinguish degrees of character development. A ***flat character*** embodies one or two qualities, ideas, or traits that can be readily described in a brief summary. For instance, the trooper in "Powder" might be a fascinating guy at home with an extensive collection of rare artwork and the ability to juggle running chainsaws, but in this story his role is to say, "The road is closed," and to haunt the narrator's worried mind thereafter. He's just a cop, doing his job. Flat characters tend to be one-dimensional. They are readily accessible because their characteristics are few and simple; they are not created to be psychologically complex.

Some flat characters are immediately recognizable as ***stock characters***. These stereotypes are particularly popular in formula fiction, television programs, and action movies. Stock characters are types rather than individuals. The poor but dedicated writer falls in love with a hard-working understudy, who gets nowhere because the corrupt producer favors his boozy, pampered mistress for the leading role. Characters such as these — the loyal servant, the mean stepfather, the henpecked husband, the dumb blonde, the sadistic army officer, the dotty grandmother — are pre-packaged; they lack individuality because their authors have, in a sense, not imaginatively created them but simply summoned them from a warehouse of clichés and social prejudices. Stock characters can become fresh if a good writer makes them vivid, interesting, or memorable, but too often a writer's use of these stereotypes is simply weak characterization.

Round characters are more complex than flat or stock characters. Round characters have more depth and require more attention. They may surprise us or puzzle us. Although they are more fully developed, round characters are also more difficult to summarize because we are aware of competing ideas, values, and possibilities in their lives. As a flat character, Huck Finn's alcoholic, bigoted father is clear to us; we know that Pap is the embodiment of racism and irrationality. But Huck is considerably less predictable because he struggles with what Twain calls a "sound heart and a deformed conscience."

An author's use of a flat character — even as a protagonist — does not necessarily represent an artistic flaw. It might be a conscious choice so that we pay even closer attention to the dynamic, round characters in the story, particularly as they interact with flat characters. Moreover, both flat and round characters can be either dynamic or static. Each plot can be made most effective by its own special kind of characterization. Terms such as *round* and *flat* are helpful tools to use to determine what we know about a character, but they are not an infallible measurement of the quality of a story.

The next two stories — Xu Xi's "Famine" and James Baldwin's "Sonny's Blues" — offer character studies worthy of close analysis. As you read them, notice the methods of characterization used to bring each to life.

Xu Xi (B. 1954)

Raised in Hong Kong and a resident there until her mid-twenties, Xu Xi graduated from the M.F.A. Program for Poets and Writers at the University of Massachusetts and has taught at the City University of Hong Kong. Among her published fictions are *Chinese Walls* (1994), *Hong Kong Rose* (1997), *The Unwalled City* (2001), *Habit of a Foreign Sky* (2010), and *That Man in Our Lives* (2016) and five collections of stories and essays — *Daughters of Hui* (1996), *History's Fiction* (2001), *Overleaf Hong Kong* (2004), *Access: Thirteen Tales* (2011), and *Insignificance: Hong Kong Stories* (2018). "Famine" was chosen for the *O. Henry Prize Stories 2006*.

ANDREW ROSS/AFP/Getty Images.

Famine   2004

I escape. I board Northwest 18 to New York, via Tokyo. The engine starts, there is no going back. Yesterday, I taught the last English class and left my job of thirty-two years. Five weeks earlier, A-Ma died of heartbreak, within days of my father's sudden death. He was ninety-five, she ninety. Unlike A-Ba, who saw the world by crewing on tankers, neither my mother nor I ever left Hong Kong.

Their deaths rid me of responsibility at last, and I could forfeit my pension and that dreary existence. I am fifty-one and an only child, unmarried.

I never expected my parents to take so long to die.

This meal is *luxurious,* better than anything I imagined.

My colleagues who fly every summer complain of the indignities of travel. Cardboard food, cramped seats, long lines, and these days, too much security nonsense, they say. They fly Cathay, our "national" carrier. This makes me laugh. We have never been a nation; "national" isn't our adjective. *Semantics,* they say, dismissive, just as they dismiss what I say of debt, that it is not an inevitable state, or that children exist to be taught, not spoilt. My colleagues live in overpriced, new, mortgaged flats and indulge 1 to 2.5 children. Most of my students are uneducable.

Back, though, to this in-flight meal. Smoked salmon and cold shrimp, endive salad, strawberries and melon to clean the palate. Then, steak with mushrooms, potatoes *au gratin,* a choice between a shiraz or cabernet sauvignon. Three cheeses, white chocolate mousse, coffee, and port or a liqueur or brandy. Foods from the pages of a novel, perhaps.

My parents ate sparingly, long after we were no longer impoverished, and disdained "unhealthy" Western diets. A-Ba often said that the only thing he really discovered from travel was that the world was hungry, and that there would never be enough food for everyone. It was why, he said, he did not miss the travel when he retired.

I have no complaints of my travels so far.

My complaining colleagues do not fly business. This seat is an *island* of a bed, surrounded by air. I did not mean to fly in dignity, but having never traveled in summer, or at all, I didn't plan months ahead, long before flights filled up. I simply rang the airlines and booked Northwest, the first one that had a seat, only in business class.

Friends and former students, who do fly business when their companies 10 foot the bill, were horrified. *You* paid *full fare? No one does!* I have money, I replied, why shouldn't I? *But you've given up your "rice bowl." Think of the future.*

I hate rice, always have, even though I never left a single grain, because under my father's watchful glare, A-Ma inspected my bowl. Every meal, even after her eyes dimmed.

The Plaza Suite is nine hundred square feet, over three times the size of home. I had wanted the Vanderbilt or Ambassador and would have settled for the Louis XV, but they were all booked, by those more important than I, no doubt. Anyway, this will have to do. "Nothing unimportant" happens here at the Plaza is what their website literature claims.

The porter arrives, and wheels my bags in on a trolley.

My father bought our tiny flat in a village in Shatin with his disability settlement. When he was forty-five and I one, a falling crane crushed his left leg and groin, thus ending his sailing and procreating career. Shatin isn't very rural anymore, but our home has denied progress its due. We didn't get a phone till I was in my thirties.

I tip the porter five dollars and begin unpacking the leather luggage set. 15 There is too much space for my things.

Right about now, you're probably wondering, along with my colleagues, former students, and friends, *What on earth does she think she's doing?* It was what my parents shouted when I was twelve and went on my first hunger strike.

My parents were illiterate, both refugees from China's rural poverty. A-Ma fried tofu at Shatin market. Once A-Ba recovered from his accident, he worked there also as a cleaner, cursing his fate. They expected me to support them as soon as possible, which should have been after six years of primary school, the only compulsory education required by law in the sixties.

As you see, I clearly had no choice but to strike, since my exam results proved I was smart enough for secondary school. My father beat me, threatened to starve me. *How dare I*, when others were genuinely hungry, unlike me, the only child of a tofu seller who always ate. *Did I want him and A-Ma to die of hunger just to send me to school? How dare I risk their longevity and old age?*

But I was unpacking a Spanish leather suitcase when the past, that country bumpkin's territory, so rudely interrupted.

Veronica, whom I met years ago at university while taking a literature course, foisted this luggage on me. She runs her family's garment enterprise, and is married to a banker. Between them and their three children, they own four flats, three cars, and at least a dozen sets of luggage. Veronica invites me out to dinner (she always pays) whenever she wants to complain about her family. Lately, we've dined often.

"Kids," she groaned over our rice porridge, two days before my trip. "My daughter won't use her brand-new Loewe set because, she says, that's *passé*. All her friends at Stanford sling these canvas bags with one fat strap. Canvas, imagine. Not even leather."

"Ergonomics," I told her, annoyed at this bland and inexpensive meal. "It's all about weight and balance." And cost, I knew, because the young overspend to conform, just as Veronica eats rice porridge because she's overweight and no longer complains that I'm thin.

She continued. "You're welcome to take the set if you like."

"Don't worry yourself. I can use an old school bag."

"But that's barely a cabin bag! Surely not enough to travel with."

In the end, I let her nag me into taking this set, which is more bag than clothing.

Veronica sounded worried when I left her that evening. "Are you *sure* you'll be okay?"

And would she worry, I wonder, if she could see me now, here, in this suite, this enormous space where one night's bill would have taken my parents years, no, *decades,* to earn and even for me, four years' pay, at least when I first started teaching in my rural enclave (though you're thinking, of course, quite correctly, *Well, what about inflation,* the thing economists cite to dismiss these longings of an English teacher who has spent her life instructing those who care not a whit for our "official language," the one they never speak, at least not if they can choose, especially not now when there is, increasingly, a choice).

My unpacking is done; the past need not intrude. I draw a bath, as one does in English literature, to wash away the heat and grime of both cities in summer. *Why New York?* Veronica asked, at the end of our last evening together. Because, I told her, it will be like nothing I've ever known. For the first time since we've known each other, Veronica actually seemed to envy *me,* although perhaps it was my imagination.

The phone rings, and it's "Guest Relations" wishing to welcome me and offer hospitality. The hotel must wonder, since I grace no social register. I ask for a table at Lutèce tonight. Afterwards, I tip the concierge ten dollars for successfully making the reservation. As you can see, I am no longer an ignorant bumpkin, even though I never left the schools in the New Territories, our urban countryside now that no one farms anymore. Besides, Hong Kong magazines detail lives of the rich and richer so I've read of the famous restaurant and know about the greasy palms of New Yorkers.

I order tea and scones from Room Service. It will hold me till dinner at eight.

The first time I ever tasted tea and scones was at the home of my private student. To supplement income when I enrolled in Teacher Training, I tutored Form V students who needed to pass the School Certificate English exam. This was the compromise I agreed to with my parents before they would allow me to qualify as a teacher. Oh yes, there was a second hunger strike two years prior, before they would let me continue into Form IV. That time, I promised to keep working in the markets after school with A-Ma, which I did.

Actually, my learning English at all was a stroke of luck, since I was *hardly* at a "name school" of the elite. An American priest taught at my secondary school, so I heard a native speaker. He wasn't a very good teacher, but he paid attention to me because I was the only student who liked the subject. A little attention goes a long way.

Tea and scones! I am *supposed* to be eating, not dwelling on the ancient past. The opulence of the tray Room Service brings far surpasses what that pretentious woman served, mother of the hopeless boy, my first private student of many, who only passed his English exam because he cheated (he paid a friend to sit the exam for him), not that I'd ever tell since he's now a wealthy international businessman of some repute who can hire staff to communicate in English with the rest of the world, since he still cannot, at least not with any credibility. That scone ("from Cherikoff," she bragged) was cold and dry, hard as a rock.

Hot scones, oozing with butter. To ooze. I like the lasciviousness of that 35 word, with its excess of vowels, the way an excess of wealth allows people to waste kindness on me, as my former student still does, every lunar new year, by sending me a *laisee* packet with a generous check which I deposit in my parents' bank account, the way I surrender all my earnings, as any filial and responsible unmarried child should, or so they said.

I eat two scones oozing with butter and savor tea enriched by cream and sugar, here at this "greatest hotel in the world," to vanquish, once and for all, my parents' fear of death and opulence.

Eight does not come soon enough. In the taxi on the way to Lutèce, I ponder the question of pork.

When we were poor but not impoverished, A-Ma once dared to make pork for dinner. It was meant to be a treat, to give me a taste of meat, because I complained that tofu was bland. A-Ba became a vegetarian after his accident and prohibited meat at home; eunuchs are angry people. She dared because he was not eating with us that night, a rare event in our family (I think some sailors he used to know invited him out).

I shat a tapeworm the next morning — almost ten inches long — and she never cooked pork again.

I have since tasted properly cooked pork, naturally, since it's unavoidable in Chinese cuisine. In my twenties, I dined out with friends, despite my parents' objections. But friends marry and scatter; the truth is that there is no one but family in the end, so over time, I submitted to their way of being and seldom took meals away from home, meals my mother cooked virtually till the day she died.

I am distracted. The real question, of course, is whether or not I should order pork tonight.

I did not expect this trip to be fraught with pork!

At Lutèce, I have the distinct impression that the two couples at the next table are talking about me. Perhaps they pity me. People often pitied me my life. *Starved of affection,* they whispered, although why they felt the need to whisper what everyone could hear I failed to understand. All I desired was greater gastronomic variety, but my parents couldn't bear the idea of my eating without them. I ate our plain diet and endured their perpetual skimping because they did eventually learn to leave me alone. That much filial propriety was reasonable payment. I just didn't expect them to *stop* complaining, to fear for what little fortune they had, because somewhere someone was less fortunate than they. That fear made them cling hard to life, forcing me to suffer their fortitude, their good health, and their longevity.

I should walk over to those overdressed people and tell them how things are, about famine, I mean, the way I tried to tell my students, the way my parents dinned it into me as long as they were alive.

Famine has no menu! The waiter waits as I take too long to study the menu. He does not seem patient, making him an oxymoron in his profession. My students would no more learn the oxymoron than they would learn about famine. *Daughter, did you lecture your charges today about famine?* A-Ba would ask every night before dinner. *Yes,* I learned to lie, giving him the answer he needed. This waiter could take a lesson in patience from me.

Finally, I look up at this man who twitches, and do not order pork. *Very good,* he says, as if I should be graded for my literacy in menus. He returns shortly with a bottle of the most expensive red available, and now I *know* the people at the next table are staring. The minute he leaves, the taller of the two men from that table comes over.

"Excuse me, but I believe we met in March? At the U.S. Consulate cocktail in Hong Kong? You're Kwai-sin Ho, aren't you?" He extends his hand. "Peter Martin."

Insulted, it's my turn to stare at this total stranger. I look *nothing* like that simpering socialite who designs wildly fashionable hats that are all the rage in Asia. Hats! We don't have the weather for hats, especially not those things, which are good for neither warmth nor shelter from the sun.

Besides, what use are hats for the hungry?

I do not accept his hand. "I'm her twin sister," I lie. "Kwai-sin and I are estranged."

He looks like he's about to protest, but retreats. After that, they don't stare, although I am sure they discuss me now that I've contributed new gossip for those who are nurtured by the crumbs of the rich and famous. But at least I can eat in peace.

It's my outfit, probably. Kwai-sin Ho is famous for her *cheongsams,* which is all she ever wears, the way I do. It was my idea. When we were girls together in school, I said the only thing I'd ever wear when I grew up was the *cheongsam,* the shapely dress with side slits and a neck-strangling collar. She grimaced and said they weren't fashionable, that only spinster schoolteachers and prostitutes wore them, which, back in the sixties, wasn't exactly true, but Kwai-sin was never too bright or imaginative.

That was long ago, before she became Kwai-sin in the *cheongsam* once these turned fashionable again, long before her father died and her mother became the mistress of a prominent businessman who whisked them into the stratosphere high above mine. For a little while, she remained my friend, but then we grew up, she married one of the shipping Hos, and became the socialite who refused, albeit politely, to recognize me the one time we bumped into each other at some function in Hong Kong.

So now, vengeance is mine. I will not entertain the people who fawn over her and possess no powers of recognition.

Food is getting sidelined by memory. This is unacceptable. I cannot allow 55 all these intrusions. I must get back to the food, which is, after all, the point of famine.

This is due to a lack of diligence, as A-Ma would say, this lazy meandering from what's important, this succumbing to sloth. My mother was terrified of sloth, almost as much as she was terrified of my father.

She used to tell me an old legend about sloth.

There once was a man so lazy he wouldn't even lift food to his mouth. When he was young, his mother fed him, but as his mother aged, she couldn't. So he marries a woman who will feed him as his mother did. For a time, life is bliss.

Then one day, his wife must return to her village to visit her dying mother. "How will I eat?" he exclaims in fright. The wife conjures this plan. She bakes a gigantic cookie and hangs it on a string around his neck. All the lazy man must do is bend forward and eat. "Wonderful!" he says, and off she goes, promising to return.

On the first day, the man nibbles the edge of the cookie. Each day, he 60 nibbles further. By the fourth day, he's eaten so far down there's no more cookie unless he turns it, which his wife expected he would since he could do this with his mouth.

However, the man's so lazy he lies down instead and waits for his wife's return. As the days pass, his stomach growls and begins to eat itself. Yet the man still won't turn the cookie. By the time his wife comes home, the lazy man has starved to death.

Memory causes such unaccountable digressions! There I was in Lutèce, noticing that people pitied me. Pity made my father livid, which he took out on A-Ma and me. Anger was his one escape from timidity. He wanted no sympathy for either his dead limb or useless genitals.

Perhaps people find me odd rather than pitiful. I will describe my appearance and let you judge. I am thin but not emaciated and have strong teeth. This latter feature is most unusual for a Hong Kong person of my generation. Many years ago, a dentist courted me. He taught me well about oral hygiene, trained as he had been at an American university. Unfortunately, he was slightly rotund, which offended A-Ba. I think A-Ma wouldn't have minded the marriage, but she always sided with my father, who believed it wise to marry one's own physical type (illiteracy did not prevent him from developing philosophies, as you've already witnessed). I was then in my mid-thirties. After the dentist, there were no other men and as a result, I never left home, which is our custom for unmarried women and men, a loathsome custom but difficult to overthrow. We all must pick our battles, and my acquiring English, which my parents naturally knew not a word, was a sufficiently drastic defiance to last a lifetime, or at least till they expired.

This dinner at Lutèce has come and gone, and you haven't tasted a thing. It's what happens when we converse overmuch and do not concentrate on the food. At home, we ate in the silence of A-Ba's rage.

What a shame, but never mind, I promise to share the bounty next time. This meal must have been good because the bill is in the thousands. I pay by traveler's checks because, not believing in debt, I own no credit cards.

Last night's dinner weighs badly, despite my excellent digestion, so I take a long walk late in the afternoon and end up in Chelsea. New York streets are dirtier than I imagined. Although I did not really expect pavements of gold, in my deepest fantasies, there did reign a glitter and sheen.

No one talks to me here.

The air is fetid with the day's leftover heat and odors. Under a humid, darkening sky, I almost trip over a body on the corner of Twenty-fourth and Seventh. It cannot be a corpse! Surely cadavers aren't left to rot in the streets.

A-Ma used to tell of a childhood occurrence in her village. An itinerant had stolen food from the local pig trough. The villagers caught him, beat him senseless, cut off his tongue and arms, and left him to bleed to death behind the rubbish heap. In the morning, my mother was at play, and while running, tripped over the body. She fell into a blood pool beside him. The corpse's eyes were open.

He surely didn't mean to steal, she always said in the telling, her eyes burning from the memory. *Try to forget,* my father would say. My parents specialized in memory. They both remained lucid and clearheaded till they died.

But this body moves. It's a man awakening from sleep. He mumbles something. Startled, I move away. He is still speaking. I think he's saying he's hungry.

I escape. A taxi whisks me back to my hotel, where my table is reserved at the restaurant.

The ceiling at the Oak Room is roughly four times the height of an average basketball player. The ambience is not as seductive as promised by the Plaza's literature. The problem with reading the wrong kind of literature is that you are bound to be disappointed.

This is a man's restaurant, with a menu of many steaks. Hemingway and Fitzgerald used to eat here. Few of my students have heard of these two, and none of them will have read a single book by either author.

As an English teacher, especially one who was not employed at a "name 75 school" of the elite, I became increasingly marginal. Colleagues and friends converse in Cantonese, the only official language out of our three that people live as well as speak. The last time any student read an entire novel was well over twenty years ago. English literature is not on anyone's exam roster anymore; to desire it in a Chinese colony is as irresponsible as it was of me to master it in our former British one.

Teaching English is little else than a linguistic requirement. Once, it was my passion and flight away from home. Now it is merely my entrée to this former men's club.

But I must order dinner and stop thinking about literature.

The entrées make my head spin, so I turn to the desserts. There is no gooseberry tart! Ever since *David Copperfield,* I have wanted to taste a gooseberry tart (or perhaps it was another book, I don't remember). I tell the boy with the water jug this.

He says. "The magician, madam?"

"The orphan," I reply.   80

He stands, openmouthed, without pouring water. What is this imbecility of the young? They neither serve nor wait.

The waiter appears. "Can I help with the menu?"

"Why?" I snap. "It isn't heavy."

But what upsets me is the memory of my mother's story, which I'd long forgotten until this afternoon, just as I hoped to forget about the teaching of English literature, about the uselessness of the life I prepared so hard for.

The waiter hovers. "Are you feeling okay?"   85

I look up at the sound of his voice and realize my hands are shaking. Calming myself, I say, "*Au jus.* The prime rib, please, and escargots to start," and on and on I go, ordering in the manner of a man who retreats to a segregated club, who indulges in oblivion because he can, who shuts out the stirrings of the groin and the heart.

I wake to a ringing phone. Housekeeping wants to know if they may clean. It's already past noon. This must be jet lag. I tell Housekeeping, Later.

It's so *comfortable* here that I believe it is possible to forget.

I order brunch from Room Service. Five-star hotels in Hong Kong serve brunch buffets on weekends. The first time I went to one, Veronica paid. We were both students at university. She wasn't wealthy, but her parents gave her spending money, whereas my entire salary (I was already a working teacher by then) belonged to my parents. The array of food made my mouth water.

Pace yourself, Veronica said. *It's all you can eat.* I wanted to try everything, but gluttony frightened me.

Meanwhile, A-Ba's voice. *After four or more days without food, your stomach begins to eat itself,* and his laugh, dry and caustic.

But I was choosing brunch.

Mimosa. Smoked salmon. Omelet with Swiss cheese and chives. And salad, the expensive kind that's imported back home, crisp Romaine in a Caesar. Room Service asks what I'd like for dessert, so I say chocolate ice-cream sundae. Perhaps I'm more of a bumpkin than I care to admit. My colleagues, former students, and friends would consider my choices boring, unsophisticated, lacking in culinary imagination. They're right, I suppose, since everything I've eaten since coming to New York I could just as easily have obtained back home. They can't understand, though. It's not *what* but *how much.* How opulent. The opulence is what counts to stop the cannibalism of internal organs.

Will that be all?

I am tempted to say, Bring me an endless buffet, whatever your chef concocts, whatever your tongues desire.

How long till my money runs out, my finite account, ending this sweet exile?

Guest Relations knocks, insistent. I have not let anyone in for three days. I open the door wide to show the manager that everything is fine, that their room is not wrecked, that I am not crazy even if I'm not on the social register. If you read the news, as I do, you know it's necessary to allay fears. So I do, because I do not wish to give the wrong impression. I am not a diva or an excessively famous person who trashes hotel rooms because she can.

I say, politely, that I've been a little unwell, nothing serious, and to please have Housekeeping stop in now. The "please" is significant; it shows I am not odd, that I am, in fact, cognizant of civilized language in English. The manager withdraws, relieved.

For dinner tonight, I decide on two dozen oysters, lobster, and filet mignon. I select a champagne and the wines, one white and one red. Then, it occurs to me that since this is a suite, I can order enough food for a party, so I tell Room Service that there will be a dozen guests for dinner, possibly more. *Very good,* he says, and asks how many extra bottles of champagne and wine, to which I reply, As many as needed.

My students will be my guests. They more or less were visitors during those years I tried to teach. You mustn't think I was always disillusioned, though I seem so now. To prove it to you I'll invite all my colleagues, the few friends I have, like Veronica, the dentist who courted me and his wife and two children, even Kwai-sin and my parents. I bear no grudges; I am not bitter towards them. What I'm uncertain of is whether or not they will come to my supper.

This room, this endless meal, can save me. I feel it. I am vanquishing my fear of death and opulence.

There was a time we did not care about opulence and we dared to speak of death. You spoke of famine because everyone knew the stories from China were true. Now, even in this country, people more or less know. You could educate students about starvation in China or Africa or India because they knew it to be true, because they saw the hunger around them, among the beggars in our streets, and for some, even in their own homes. There was a time it was better *not* to have space, or things to put in that space, and to dream of having instead, because no one had much, except royalty and movie stars and they were *meant* to be fantasy — untouchable, unreal — somewhere in a dream of manna and celluloid.

But you can't speak of famine anymore. Anorexia's fashionable and desirably profitable on runways, so students simply *can't see the hunger.* My colleagues and friends also can't, and refuse to speak of it, changing the subject to what they prefer to see. Even our journalists can't seem to see, preferring the reality they fashion rather than the reality that is. I get angry, but then, when I'm calm, I am simply baffled. Perhaps my parents, and friends and colleagues and memory, are right, that I *am* too stubborn, perhaps even too slothful because instead of *seeing* reality, I've hidden in my parents' home, in my life as a teacher, even though the years were dreary and long, when what I truly wanted, what I desired, was to embrace the opulence, forsake the hunger, but was too lazy to turn the cookie instead.

I mustn't be angry at them, by which I mean all the "thems" I know and don't know, the big impersonal "they." Like a good English teacher I tell my students, you *must* define the "they." Students are students and continue to make the same mistakes, and all I can do is remind them that "they" are you and to please, please, try to remember because language is a root of life.

Most of the people can't be wrong all the time. Besides, whose fault is it if the dream came true? Postdream is like postmodern; no one understands it, but everyone condones its existence.

Furthermore, what you can't, or won't see, *doesn't* exist.   105

Comfort, like food, exists, *surrounds* me here.

Not wishing to let anger get the better of me, I eat. Like the Romans, I disgorge and continue. It takes hours to eat three lobsters and three steaks, plus consume five glasses of champagne and six of wine, yet still the food is not enough.

The guests arrive and more keep coming. Who would have thought all these people would show up, all these people I thought I left behind. Where do they come from? My students, colleagues, the dentist and his family, a horde of strangers. Even Kwai-sin and her silly hats, and do you know something, we *do* look a little alike, so Peter Martin wasn't completely wrong. I changed my language to change my life, but still the past throngs, bringing all these people and their Cantonese chatter. The food is not enough, the food is never enough.

Room Service obliges round the clock.

Veronica arrives and I feel a great relief, because the truth is, I no longer   110
cared for her anymore when all we ate was rice porridge. It was mean-spirited,

I was ungrateful, forgetting that once she fed me my first buffet, teasing my appetite. *Come out, travel,* she urged over the years. It's not her fault I stayed at home, afraid to abandon my responsibility, traveling only in my mind.

Finally, my parents arrive. My father sits down first to the feast. His leg is whole, and sperm gushes out from between his legs. *It's not so bad here,* he says, and gestures for my mother to join him. This is good. A-Ma will eat if A-Ba does, they're like that, those two. My friends don't understand, not even Veronica. She repeats now what she often has said, that my parents are "controlling." Perhaps, I say, but that's unimportant. I'm only interested in not being responsible anymore.

The noise in the room is deafening. We can barely hear each other above the din. Cantonese is a noisy language, unlike Mandarin or English, but it is alive. This suite that was too empty is stuffed with people, all needing to be fed.

I gaze at the platters of food, piled in this space with largesse. What does it matter if there *are* too many mouths to feed? A phone call is all it takes to get more food, and more. I am fifty-one and have waited too long to eat. They're right, they're all right. If I give in, if I let go, I will vanquish my fears. *This* is bliss, truly.

A-Ma smiles at the vast quantities of food. This pleases me because she so rarely smiles. She says, *Not like lazy cookie man, hah?*

Feeling benevolent, I smile at my parents. *No, not like him,* I say. *Now, eat.* 1

CONSIDERATIONS FOR CRITICAL THINKING AND WRITING

1. FIRST RESPONSE. How does Xu Xi engage the reader in the first three paragraphs of the story?

2. Explain how the narrator's parents' values and sensibilities are revealed through exposition.

3. How do Veronica and Kwai-sin function as foils to the narrator?

4. What is the relevance of the narrator's having been an English teacher for her entire career?

5. Do you find any humor in "Famine"? Describe the story's tone. Is it consistent?

6. Choose a paragraph in which Xu Xi uses details particularly well to create a mood, set a scene, or unify the plot, and discuss how that effect is achieved through her carefully chosen language.

7. Can you find the story's theme (or themes) stated directly in a specific paragraph, or is it developed implicitly through the plot, characters, symbols, or some other literary element?

CONNECTION TO ANOTHER SELECTION

1. Discuss the narrator's symbolic relationship to food in "Famine" and in Sally Croft's poem "Home-Baked Bread" (p. 428).

JAMES BALDWIN (1924–1987)

The most prominent African American writer of the Civil Rights Era of the 1950s and 1960s, James Baldwin wrote prolifically and passionately in many styles and genres. His book-length essay *The Fire Next Time* (1963) was a groundbreaking meditation on race relations and religion that ended on a note of fiery prophecy about America's possible future. His novels *Go Tell It on the Mountain* (1953) and *Giovanni's Room* (1956) demonstrated early in his career the range of his topics and interests, anticipating topics that writers would deal with in even more depth after his premature death in 1987 — topics such as racial mythology, bisexuality, and gender identity. As an expatriate who lived for

Everett Collection Inc/Alamy Stock Photo.

extended periods in Paris, the south of France, and Turkey, Baldwin gained a global perspective that is only now being fully appreciated. His works have recently been made into acclaimed films: *I Am Not Your Negro* (2016) and *If Beale Street Could Talk* (2018). The following short story, "Sonny's Blues," is one of the finest in the English language.

Sonny's Blues   1957

I read about it in the paper, in the subway, on my way to work. I read it, and I couldn't believe it, and I read it again. Then perhaps I just stared at it, at the newsprint spelling out his name, spelling out the story. I stared at it in the swinging lights of the subway car, and in the faces and bodies of the people, and in my own face, trapped in the darkness which roared outside.

It was not to be believed and I kept telling myself that, as I walked from the subway station to the high school. And at the same time I couldn't doubt it. I was scared, scared for Sonny. He became real to me again. A great block of ice got settled in my belly and kept melting there slowly all day long, while I taught my classes algebra. It was a special kind of ice. It kept melting, sending trickles of ice water all up and down my veins, but it never got less. Sometimes it hardened and seemed to expand until I felt my guts were going to come spilling out or that I was going to choke or scream. This would always be at a moment when I was remembering some specific thing Sonny had once said or done.

When he was about as old as the boys in my classes his face had been bright and open, there was a lot of copper in it; and he'd had wonderfully direct brown eyes, and great gentleness and privacy. I wondered what he looked like now. He had been picked up, the evening before, in a raid on an apartment downtown, for peddling and using heroin.

I couldn't believe it: but what I mean by that is that I couldn't find any room for it anywhere inside me. I had kept it outside me for a long time. I hadn't wanted to know. I had had suspicions, but I didn't name them, I kept putting them away. I told myself that Sonny was wild, but he wasn't crazy. And he'd always been a good boy, he hadn't ever turned hard or evil or disrespectful, the way kids can, so quick, so quick, especially in Harlem. I didn't want to believe that I'd ever see my brother going down, coming to nothing, all that light in his face gone out, in the condition I'd already seen so many others. Yet it had happened and here I was, talking about algebra to a lot of boys who might, every one of them for all I knew, be popping off needles every time they went to the head. Maybe it did more for them than algebra could.

I was sure that the first time Sonny had ever had horse, he couldn't have been much older than these boys were now. These boys, now, were living as we'd been living then, they were growing up with a rush and their heads bumped abruptly against the low ceiling of their actual possibilities. They were filled with rage. All they really knew were two darknesses, the darkness of their lives, which was now closing in on them, and the darkness of the movies, which had blinded them to that other darkness, and in which they now, vindictively, dreamed, at once more together than they were at any other time, and more alone. 5

When the last bell rang, the last class ended, I let out my breath. It seemed I'd been holding it for all that time. My clothes were wet — I may have looked as though I'd been sitting in a steam bath, all dressed up, all afternoon. I sat alone in the classroom a long time. I listened to the boys outside, downstairs, shouting and cursing and laughing. Their laughter struck me for perhaps the first time. It was not the joyous laughter which — God knows why — one associates with children. It was mocking and insular, its intent was to denigrate. It was disenchanted, and in this, also, lay the authority of their curses. Perhaps I was listening to them because I was thinking about my brother and in them I heard my brother. And myself.

One boy was whistling a tune, at once very complicated and very simple, it seemed to be pouring out of him as though he were a bird, and it sounded very cool and moving through all that harsh, bright air, only just holding its own through all those other sounds.

I stood up and walked over to the window and looked down into the courtyard. It was the beginning of the spring and the sap was rising in the boys. A teacher passed through them every now and again, quickly, as though he or she couldn't wait to get out of that courtyard, to get those boys out of their sight and off their minds. I started collecting my stuff. I thought I'd better get home and talk to Isabel.

The courtyard was almost deserted by the time I got downstairs. I saw this boy standing in the shadow of a doorway, looking just like Sonny. I almost called his name. Then I saw that it wasn't Sonny, but somebody we used to know, a boy from around our block. He'd been Sonny's friend. He'd never been mine, having been too young for me, and, anyway, I'd never liked him. And now, even though he was a grown-up man, he still hung around that block, still spent hours on the street corners, was always high and raggy. I used to run into him from time to time and he'd often work around to asking me for a quarter or fifty cents. He always had some real good excuse, too, and I always gave it to him, I don't know why.

But now, abruptly, I hated him. I couldn't stand the way he looked at me, 10 partly like a dog, partly like a cunning child. I wanted to ask him what the hell he was doing in the school courtyard.

He sort of shuffled over to me, and he said, "I see you got the papers. So you already know about it."

"You mean about Sonny? Yes, I already know about it. How come they didn't get you?"

He grinned. It made him repulsive and it also brought to mind what he'd looked like as a kid. "I wasn't there. I stay away from them people."

"Good for you." I offered him a cigarette and I watched him through the smoke. "You come all the way down here just to tell me about Sonny?"

"That's right." He was sort of shaking his head and his eyes looked 15 strange, as though they were about to cross. The bright sun deadened his damp dark brown skin and it made his eyes look yellow and showed up the dirt in his kinked hair. He smelled funky. I moved a little away from him and I said, "Well, thanks. But I already know about it and I got to get home."

"I'll walk you a little ways," he said. We started walking. There were a couple of kids still loitering in the courtyard and one of them said goodnight to me and looked strangely at the boy beside me.

"What're you going to do?" he asked me. "I mean, about Sonny?"

"Look. I haven't seen Sonny for over a year, I'm not sure I'm going to do anything. Anyway, what the hell *can* I do?"

"That's right," he said quickly, "ain't nothing you can do. Can't much help old Sonny no more, I guess."

It was what I was thinking and so it seemed to me he had no right to say it. 20

"I'm surprised at Sonny, though," he went on — he had a funny way of talking, he looked straight ahead as though he were talking to himself — "I thought Sonny was a smart boy, I thought he was too smart to get hung."

"I guess he thought so too," I said sharply, "and that's how he got hung. And how about you? You're pretty goddamn smart, I bet."

Then he looked directly at me, just for a minute. "I ain't smart," he said. "If I smart, I'd have reached for a pistol a long time ago."

"Look. Don't tell *me* your sad story, if it was up to me, I'd give you one." Then I felt guilty — guilty, probably, for never having supposed that the poor bastard *had* a story of his own, much less a sad one, and I asked, quickly, "What's going to happen to him now?"

He didn't answer this. He was off by himself some place. "Funny thing," he said, and from his tone we might have been discussing the quickest way to get to Brooklyn, "when I saw the papers this morning, the first thing I asked myself was if I had anything to do with it. I felt sort of responsible."

I began to listen more carefully. The subway station was on the corner, just before us, and I stopped. He stopped, too. We were in front of a bar and he ducked slightly, peering in, but whoever he was looking for didn't seem to be there. The juke box was blasting away with something black and bouncy and I half watched the barmaid as she danced her way from the juke box to her place behind the bar. And I watched her face as she laughingly responded to something someone said to her, still keeping time to the music. When she smiled one saw the little girl, one sensed the doomed, still-struggling woman beneath the battered face of the semi-whore.

"I never *give* Sonny nothing," the boy said finally, "but a long time ago I come to school high and Sonny asked me how it felt." He paused, I couldn't bear to watch him, I watched the barmaid, and I listened to the music which seemed to be causing the pavement to shake. "I told him it felt great." The music stopped, the barmaid paused and watched the juke box until the music began again. "It did."

All this was carrying me some place I didn't want to go. I certainly didn't want to know how it felt. It filled everything, the people, the houses, the music, the dark, quicksilver barmaid, with menace; and this menace was their reality.

"What's going to happen to him now?" I asked again.

"They'll send him away some place and they'll try to cure him." He shook his head. "Maybe he'll even think he's kicked the habit. Then they'll let him loose" — he gestured, throwing his cigarette into the gutter. "That's all."

"What do you mean, that's *all?*"

But I knew what he meant.

"I *mean,* that's *all.*" He turned his head and looked at me, pulling down the corners of his mouth. "Don't you know what I mean?" he asked, softly.

"How the hell *would* I know what you mean?" I almost whispered it, I don't know why.

"That's right," he said to the air, "how would *he* know what I mean?" He turned toward me again, patient and calm, and yet I somehow felt him shaking, shaking as though he were going to fall apart. I felt that ice in my guts again, the dread I'd felt all afternoon; and again I watched the barmaid, moving about the bar, washing glasses, and singing. "Listen. They'll let him out and then it'll just start all over again. That's what I mean."

"You mean — they'll let him out. And then he'll just start working his way back in again. You mean he'll never kick the habit. Is that what you mean?"

"That's right," he said, cheerfully. "*You* see what I mean."

"Tell me," I said at last, "why does he want to die? He must want to die, he's killing himself, why does he want to die?"

He looked at me in surprise. He licked his lips. "He don't want to die. He wants to live. Don't nobody want to die, ever."

Then I wanted to ask him — too many things. He could not have 40
answered, or if he had, I could not have borne the answers. I started walking.
"Well, I guess it's none of my business."

"It's going to be rough on old Sonny," he said. We reached the subway
station. "This is your station?" he asked. I nodded. I took one step down.
"Damn!" he said, suddenly. I looked up at him. He grinned again. "Damn it
if I didn't leave all my money home. You ain't got a dollar on you, have you?
Just for a couple of days, is all."

All at once something inside gave and threatened to come pouring out
of me. I didn't hate him any more. I felt that in another moment I'd start crying like a child.

"Sure," I said. "Don't sweat." I looked in my wallet and didn't have a dollar, I only had a five. "Here," I said. "That hold you?"

He didn't look at it — he didn't want to look at it. A terrible, closed look
came over his face, as though he were keeping the number on the bill a secret
from him and me. "Thanks," he said, and now he was dying to see me go.
"Don't worry about Sonny. Maybe I'll write him or something."

"Sure," I said. "You do that. So long." 45

"Be seeing you," he said. I went on down the steps.

And I didn't write Sonny or send him anything for a long time. When I
finally did, it was just after my little girl died, he wrote me back a letter which
made me feel like a bastard.

Here's what he said:

> Dear brother,
> You don't know how much I needed to hear from you. I wanted to
> write you many a time but I dug how much I must have hurt you and so I
> didn't write. But now I feel like a man who's been trying to climb up out of
> some deep, real deep and funky hole and just saw the sun up there, outside.
> I got to get outside.
> I can't tell you much about how I got here. I mean I don't know how
> to tell you. I guess I was afraid of something or I was trying to escape
> from something and you know I have never been very strong in the head
> (smile). I'm glad Mama and Daddy are dead and can't see what's happened
> to their son and I swear if I'd known what I was doing I would never have
> hurt you so, you and a lot of other fine people who were nice to me and
> who believed in me.
> I don't want you to think it had anything to do with me being a musi-
> cian. It's more than that. Or maybe less than that. I can't get anything
> straight in my head down here and I try not to think about what's going
> to happen to me when I get outside again. Sometime I think I'm going to
> flip and *never* get outside and sometime I think I'll come straight back. I
> tell you one thing, though, I'd rather blow my brains out than go through
> this again. But that's what they all say, so they tell me. If I tell you when I'm
> coming to New York and if you could meet me, I sure would appreciate it.

Give my love to Isabel and the kids and I was sure sorry to hear about little Gracie. I wish I could be like Mama and say the Lord's will be done, but I don't know it seems to me that trouble is the one thing that never does get stopped and I don't know what good it does to blame it on the Lord. But maybe it does some good if you believe it.

> Your brother,
> Sonny

Then I kept in constant touch with him and I sent him whatever I could and I went to meet him when he came back to New York. When I saw him many things I thought I had forgotten came flooding back to me. This was because I had begun, finally, to wonder about Sonny, about the life that Sonny lived inside. This life, whatever it was, had made him older and thinner and it had deepened the distant stillness in which he had always moved. He looked very unlike my baby brother. Yet, when he smiled, when we shook hands, the baby brother I'd never known looked out from the depths of his private life, like an animal waiting to be coaxed into the light.

"How you been keeping?" he asked me.   5

"All right. And you?"

"Just fine." He was smiling all over his face. "It's good to see you again."

"It's good to see you."

The seven years' difference in our ages lay between us like a chasm: I wondered if these years would ever operate between us as a bridge. I was remembering, and it made it hard to catch my breath, that I had been there when he was born; and I had heard the first words he had ever spoken. When he started to walk, he walked from our mother straight to me. I caught him just before he fell when he took the first steps he ever took in this world.

"How's Isabel?"   5

"Just fine. She's dying to see you."

"And the boys?"

"They're fine, too. They're anxious to see their uncle."

"Oh, come on. You know they don't remember me."

"Are you kidding? Of course they remember you."   6(

He grinned again. We got into a taxi. We had a lot to say to each other, far too much to know how to begin.

As the taxi began to move, I asked, "You still want to go to India?"

He laughed. "You still remember that. Hell, no. This place is Indian enough for me."

"It used to belong to them," I said.

And he laughed again. "They damn sure knew what they were doing   65 when they got rid of it."

Years ago, when he was around fourteen, he'd been all hipped on the idea of going to India. He read books about people sitting on rocks, naked, in all kinds of weather, but mostly bad, naturally, and walking barefoot through hot coals and arriving at wisdom. I used to say that it sounded to me as though they were getting away from wisdom as fast as they could. I think he sort of looked down on me for that.

"Do you mind," he asked, "if we have the driver drive alongside the park? On the west side — I haven't seen the city in so long."

"Of course not," I said. I was afraid that I might sound as though I were humoring him, but I hoped he wouldn't take it that way.

So we drove along, between the green of the park and the stony, lifeless elegance of hotels and apartment buildings, toward the vivid, killing streets of our childhood. These streets hadn't changed, though housing projects jutted up out of them now like rocks in the middle of a boiling sea. Most of the houses in which we had grown up had vanished, as had the stores from which we had stolen, the basements in which we had first tried sex, the rooftops from which we had hurled tin cans and bricks. But houses exactly like the houses of our past yet dominated the landscape, boys exactly like the boys we once had been found themselves smothering in these houses, came down into the streets for light and air and found themselves encircled by disaster. Some escaped the trap, most didn't. Those who got out always left something of themselves behind, as some animals amputate a leg and leave it in the trap. It might be said, perhaps, that I had escaped, after all, I was a school teacher; or that Sonny had, he hadn't lived in Harlem for years. Yet, as the cab moved uptown through streets which seemed, with a rush, to darken with dark people, and as I covertly studied Sonny's face, it came to me that what we both were seeking through our separate cab windows was that part of ourselves which had been left behind. It's always at the hour of trouble and confrontation that the missing member aches.

We hit 110th Street and started rolling up Lenox Avenue. And I'd 70 known this avenue all my life, but it seemed to me again, as it had seemed on the day I'd first heard about Sonny's trouble, filled with a hidden menace which was its very breath of life.

"We almost there," said Sonny.

"Almost." We were both too nervous to say anything more.

We live in a housing project. It hasn't been up long. A few days after it was up it seemed uninhabitably new, now, of course, it's already rundown. It looks like a parody of the good, clean, faceless life — God knows the people who live in it do their best to make it a parody. The beat-looking grass lying around isn't enough to make their lives green, the hedges will never hold out the streets, and they know it. The big windows fool no one, they aren't big enough to make space out of no space. They don't bother with the windows, they watch the TV screen instead. The playground is most popular with the children who don't play at jacks, or skip rope, or roller skate, or swing, and they can be found in it after dark. We moved in partly because it's not too far from where I teach, and partly for the kids; but it's really just like the houses in which Sonny and I grew up. The same things happen, they'll have the same things to remember. The moment Sonny and I started into the house I had the feeling that I was simply bringing him back into the danger he had almost died trying to escape.

Sonny has never been talkative. So I don't know why I was sure he'd be dying to talk to me when supper was over the first night. Everything went fine, the oldest boy remembered him, and the youngest boy liked him, and Sonny had remembered to bring something for each of them; and Isabel, who is really much nicer than I am, more open and giving, had gone to a lot of trouble about dinner and was genuinely glad to see him. And she's always been able to tease Sonny in a way that I haven't. It was nice to see her face so vivid again and to hear her laugh and watch her make Sonny laugh. She wasn't, or, anyway, she didn't seem to be, at all uneasy or embarrassed. She chatted as though there were no subject which had to be avoided and she got Sonny past his first, faint stiffness. And thank God she was there, for I was filled with that icy dread again. Everything I did seemed awkward to me, and everything I said sounded freighted with hidden meaning. I was trying to remember everything I'd heard about dope addiction and I couldn't help watching Sonny for signs. I wasn't doing it out of malice. I was trying to find out some-thing about my brother. I was dying to hear him tell me he was safe.

"Safe!" my father grunted, whenever Mama suggested trying to move to a neighborhood which might be safer for children. "Safe, hell! Ain't no place safe for kids, nor nobody."

He always went on like this, but he wasn't, ever, really as bad as he sounded, not even on weekends, when he got drunk. As a matter of fact, he was always on the lookout for "something a little better," but he died before he found it. He died suddenly, during a drunken weekend in the middle of the war, when Sonny was fifteen. He and Sonny hadn't ever got on too well. And this was partly because Sonny was the apple of his father's eye. It was because he loved Sonny so much and was frightened for him, that he was always fighting with him. It doesn't do any good to fight with Sonny. Sonny just moves back, inside himself, where he can't be reached. But the principal reason that they never hit it off is that they were so much alike. Daddy was big and rough and loud-talking, just the opposite of Sonny, but they both had — that same privacy.

Mama tried to tell me something about this, just after Daddy died. I was home on leave from the army.

This was the last time I ever saw my mother alive. Just the same, this picture gets all mixed up in my mind with pictures I had of her when she was younger. The way I always see her is the way she used to be on a Sunday afternoon, say, when the old folks were talking after the big Sunday dinner. I always see her wearing pale blue. She'd be sitting on the sofa. And my father would be sitting in the easy chair, not far from her. And the living room would be full of church folks and relatives. There they sit, in chairs all around the living room, and the night is creeping up outside, but nobody knows it yet. You can see the darkness growing against the windowpanes and you hear the street noises every now and again, or maybe the jangling beat of a tambourine from one of the churches close by, but it's real quiet in the room. For a moment nobody's talking, but every face looks darkening, like the sky outside. And my mother rocks a little from the waist, and my father's eyes are closed. Everyone is looking at something a child can't see. For a minute they've forgotten the children. Maybe a kid is lying on the rug, half asleep. Maybe somebody's got a kid in his lap and is absent-mindedly stroking the kid's head. Maybe there's a kid, quiet and big-eyed, curled up in a big chair in the corner. The silence, the darkness coming, and the darkness in the faces frightens the child obscurely. He hopes that the hand which strokes his forehead will never stop — will never die. He hopes that there will never come a time when the old folks won't be sitting around the living room, talking about where they've come from, and what they've seen, and what's happened to them and their kinfolk.

But something deep and watchful in the child knows that this is bound to end, is already ending. In a moment someone will get up and turn on the light. Then the old folks will remember the children and they won't talk any more that day. And when light fills the room, the child is filled with darkness. He knows that every time this happens he's moved just a little closer to that darkness outside. The darkness outside is what the old folks have been talking about. It's what they've come from. It's what they endure. The child knows that they won't talk any more because if he knows too much about what's happened to *them*, he'll know too much too soon, about what's going to happen to *him*.

The last time I talked to my mother, I remember I was restless. I wanted to get out and see Isabel. We weren't married then and we had a lot to straighten out between us.

There Mama sat, in black, by the window. She was humming an old church song. *Lord, you brought me from a long ways off.* Sonny was out somewhere. Mama kept watching the streets.

"I don't know," she said, "if I'll ever see you again, after you go off from here. But I hope you'll remember the things I tried to teach you."

"Don't talk like that," I said, and smiled. "You'll be here a long time yet."

She smiled, too, but she said nothing. She was quiet for a long time. And I said, "Mama, don't you worry about nothing. I'll be writing all the time, and you be getting the checks. . . ."

"I want to talk to you about your brother," she said, suddenly. "If anything happens to me he ain't going to have nobody to look out for him."

"Mama," I said, "ain't nothing going to happen to you *or* Sonny. Sonny's all right. He's a good boy and he's got good sense."

"It ain't a question of his being a good boy," Mama said, "nor of his having good sense. It ain't only the bad ones, nor yet the dumb ones that gets sucked under." She stopped, looking at me. "Your Daddy once had a brother," she said, and she smiled in a way that made me feel she was in pain. "You didn't never know that, did you?"

"No," I said, "I never knew that," and I watched her face.

"Oh, yes," she said, "your Daddy had a brother." She looked out of the window again. "I know you never saw your Daddy cry. But *I* did — many a time, through all these years."

I asked her, "What happened to his brother? How come nobody's ever talked about him?"

80

85

90

This was the first time I ever saw my mother look old.

"His brother got killed," she said, "when he was just a little younger than you are now. I knew him. He was a fine boy. He was maybe a little full of the devil, but he didn't mean nobody no harm."

Then she stopped and the room was silent, exactly as it had sometimes been on those Sunday afternoons. Mama kept looking out into the streets.

"He used to have a job in the mill," she said, "and, like all young folks, he just liked to perform on Saturday nights. Saturday nights, him and your father would drift around to different place, go to dances and things like that, or just sit around with people they knew, and your father's brother would sing, he had a fine voice, and play along with himself on his guitar. Well, this particular Saturday night, him and your father was coming home from some place, and they were both a little drunk and there was a moon that night, it was bright like day. Your father's brother was feeling kind of good, and he was whistling to himself, and he had his guitar slung over his shoulder. They was coming down a hill and beneath them was a road that turned off from the highway. Well, your father's brother, being always kind of frisky, decided to run down this hill, and he did, with that guitar banging and clanging behind him, and he ran across the road, and he was making water behind a tree. And your father was sort of amused at him and he was still coming down the hill, kind of slow. Then he heard a car motor and that same minute his brother stepped from behind the tree, into the road, in the moonlight. And he started to cross the road. And your father started to run down the hill, he says he don't know why. This car was full of white men. They was all drunk, and when they seen your father's brother they let out a great whoop and holler and they aimed the car straight at him. They was having fun, they just wanted to scare him, the way they do sometimes, you know. But they was drunk. And I guess the boy, being drunk, too, and scared, kind of lost his head. By the time he jumped it was too late. Your father says he heard his brother scream when the car rolled over him, and he heard the wood of that guitar when it give, and he heard them strings go flying, and he heard them white men shouting, and the car kept on a-going and it ain't stopped till this day. And, time your father got down the hill, his brother weren't nothing but blood and pulp."

Tears were gleaming on my mother's face. There wasn't anything I could say.   95

"He never mentioned it," she said, "because I never let him mention it before you children. Your Daddy was like a crazy man that night and for many a night thereafter. He says he never in his life seen anything as dark as that road after the lights of that car had gone away. Weren't nothing, weren't nobody on that road, just your Daddy and his brother and that busted guitar. Oh, yes. Your Daddy never did really get right again. Till the day he died he weren't sure but that every white man he saw was the man that killed his brother."

She stopped and took out her handkerchief and dried her eyes and looked at me.

"I ain't telling you all this," she said, "to make you scared or bitter or to make you hate nobody. I'm telling you this because you got a brother. And the world ain't changed."

I guess I didn't want to believe this. I guess she saw this in my face. She turned away from me, toward the window again, searching those streets.

"But I praise my Redeemer," she said at last, "that He called your Daddy 100 home before me. I ain't saying it to throw no flowers at myself, but, I declare, it keeps me from feeling too cast down to know I helped your father get safely through this world. Your father always acted like he was the roughest, strongest man on earth. And everybody took him to be like that. But if he hadn't had *me* there — to see his tears!"

She was crying again. Still, I couldn't move. I said, "Lord, Lord, Mama, I didn't know it was like that."

"Oh, honey," she said, "there's a lot that you don't know. But you are going to find it out." She stood up from the window and came over to me. "You got to hold on to your brother," she said, "and don't let him fall, no matter what it looks like is happening to him and no matter how evil you gets with him. You going to be evil with him many a time. But don't you forget what I told you, you hear?"

"I won't forget," I said. "Don't you worry, I won't forget. I won't let nothing happen to Sonny."

My mother smiled as though she were amused at something she saw in my face. Then, "You may not be able to stop nothing from happening. But you got to let him know you's *there*."

Two days later I was married, and then I was gone. And I had a lot of 105 things on my mind and I pretty well forgot my promise to Mama until I got shipped home on a special furlough for her funeral.

And, after the funeral, with just Sonny and me alone in the empty kitchen, I tried to find out something about him.

"What do you want to do?" I asked him.

"I'm going to be a musician," he said.

For he had graduated, in the time I had been away, from dancing to the juke box to finding out who was playing what, and what they were doing with it, and he had bought himself a set of drums.

"You mean, you want to be a drummer?" I somehow had the feeling 110 that being a drummer might be all right for other people but not for my brother Sonny.

"I don't think," he said, looking at me very gravely, "that I'll ever be a good drummer. But I think I can play a piano."

I frowned. I'd never played the role of the older brother quite so seriously before, had scarcely ever, in fact, *asked* Sonny a damn thing. I sensed myself in the presence of something I didn't really know how to handle, didn't understand. So I made my frown a little deeper as I asked: "What kind of musician do you want to be?"

He grinned. "How many kinds do you think there are?"

"Be *serious*," I said.

He laughed, throwing his head back, and then looked at me. "I *am* serious."

"Well, then, for Christ's sake, stop kidding around and answer a serious question. I mean, do you want to be a concert pianist, you want to play classical music and all that, or — or what?" Long before I finished he was laughing again. "For Christ's *sake*, Sonny!"

He sobered, but with difficulty. "I'm sorry. But you sound so — *scared!*" and he was off again.

"Well, you may think it's funny now, baby, but it's not going to be so funny when you have to make your living at it, let me tell you *that.*" I was furious because I knew he was laughing at me and I didn't know why.

"No," he said, very sober now, and afraid, perhaps, that he'd hurt me, "I don't want to be a classical pianist. That isn't what interests me. I mean" — he paused, looking hard at me, as though his eyes would help me to understand, and then gestured helplessly, as though perhaps his hand would help — "I mean, I'll have a lot of studying to do, and I'll have to study *everything*, but, I mean, I want to play *with* — jazz musicians." He stopped. "I want to play jazz," he said.

Well, the word had never before sounded as heavy, as real, as it sounded that afternoon in Sonny's mouth. I just looked at him and I was probably frowning a real frown by this time. I simply couldn't see why on earth he'd want to spend his time hanging around nightclubs, clowning around on bandstands, while people pushed each other around a dance floor. It seemed — beneath him, somehow. I had never thought about it before, had never been forced to, but I suppose I had always put jazz musicians in a class with what Daddy called "good-time people."

"Are you *serious*?"

"Hell, *yes,* I'm serious."

He looked more helpless than ever, and annoyed, and deeply hurt.

I suggested, helpfully: "You mean — like Louis Armstrong?"

His face closed as though I'd struck him. "No. I'm not talking about none of that old-time, down home crap."

"Well, look, Sonny, I'm sorry, don't get mad. I just don't altogether get it, that's all. Name somebody — you know, a jazz musician you admire."

"Bird."

"Who?"

"Bird! Charlie Parker! Don't they teach you nothing in the goddamn army?"

I lit a cigarette. I was surprised and then a little amused to discover that I was trembling. "I've been out of touch," I said, "You'll have to be patient with me. Now. Who's this Parker character?"

"He's just one of the greatest jazz musicians alive," said Sonny, sullenly, his hands in his pockets, his back to me. "Maybe *the* greatest," he added, bitterly, "that's probably why *you* never heard of him."

"All right," I said, "I'm ignorant. I'm sorry. I'll go out and buy all the cat's records right away, all right?"

"It don't," said Sonny, with dignity, "make any difference to me. I don't care what you listen to. Don't do me no favors."

I was beginning to realize that I'd never seen him so upset before. With another part of my mind I was thinking that this would probably turn out to be one of those things kids go through and that I shouldn't make it seem important by pushing it too hard. Still, I didn't think it would do any harm to ask: "Doesn't all this take a lot of time? Can you make a living at it?"

He turned back to me and half leaned, half sat, on the kitchen table. 135 "Everything takes time," he said, "and — well, yes, sure, I can make a living at it. But what I don't seem to be able to make you understand is that it's the only thing I want to do."

"Well, Sonny," I said, gently, "you know people can't always do exactly what they *want* to do —"

"*No,* I don't know that," said Sonny, surprising me. "I think people *ought* to do what they want to do, what else are they alive for?"

"You getting to be a big boy," I said desperately, "it's time you started thinking about your future."

"I'm thinking about my future," said Sonny, grimly. "I think about it all the time."

I gave up. I decided, if he didn't change his mind, that we could always 140 talk about it later. "In the meantime," I said, "you got to finish school." We had already decided that he'd have to move in with Isabel and her folks. I knew this wasn't the ideal arrangement because Isabel's folks are inclined to be dicty and they hadn't especially wanted Isabel to marry me. But I didn't know what else to do. "And we have to get you fixed up at Isabel's."

There was a long silence. He moved from the kitchen table to the window. "That's a terrible idea. You know it yourself."

"Do you have a *better* idea?"

He just walked up and down the kitchen for a minute. He was as tall as I was. He had started to shave. I suddenly had the feeling that I didn't know him at all.

He stopped at the kitchen table and picked up my cigarettes. Looking at me with a kind of mocking, amused defiance, he put one between his lips. "You mind?"

"You smoking already?" 145

He lit the cigarette and nodded, watching me through the smoke. "I just wanted to see if I'd have the courage to smoke in front of you." He grinned and blew a great cloud of smoke to the ceiling. "It was easy." He looked at my face. "Come on, now. I bet you was smoking at my age, tell the truth."

I didn't say anything but the truth was on my face, and he laughed. But now there was something very strained in his laugh. "Sure. And I bet that ain't all you was doing."

He was frightening me a little. "Cut the crap," I said. "We already decided that you was going to go and live at Isabel's. Now what's got into you all of a sudden?"

"*You* decided it," he pointed out. "*I* didn't decide nothing." He stopped in front of me, leaning against the stove, arms loosely folded. "Look, brother.

I don't want to stay in Harlem no more, I really don't." He was very earnest. He looked at me, then over toward the kitchen window. There was something in his eyes I'd never seen before, some thoughtfulness, some worry all his own. He rubbed the muscle of one arm. "It's time I was getting out of here."

"Where do you want to *go*, Sonny?"

"I want to join the army. Or the navy, I don't care. If I say I'm old enough, they'll believe me."

Then I got mad. It was because I was so scared. "You must be crazy. You goddamn fool, what the hell do you want to go and join the *army* for?"

"I just told you. To get out of Harlem."

"Sonny, you haven't even finished *school*. And if you really want to be a musician, how do you expect to study if you're in the *army?*"

He looked at me, trapped, and in anguish. "There's ways. I might be able to work out some kind of deal. Anyway, I'll have the G.I. Bill when I come out."

"*If* you come out." We stared at each other. "Sonny, please. Be reasonable. I know the setup is far from perfect. But we got to do the best we can."

"I ain't learning nothing in school," he said. "Even when I go." He turned away from me and opened the window and threw his cigarette out into the narrow alley. I watched his back. "At least, I ain't learning nothing you'd want me to learn." He slammed the window so hard I thought the glass would fly out, and turned back to me. "And I'm sick of the stink of these garbage cans!"

"Sonny," I said, "I know how you feel. But if you don't finish school now, you're going to be sorry later that you didn't." I grabbed him by the shoulders. "And you only got another year. It ain't so bad. And I'll come back and I swear I'll help you do *whatever* you want to do. Just try to put up with it till I come back. Will you please do that? For me?"

He didn't answer and he wouldn't look at me.

"Sonny. You hear me?"

He pulled away. "I hear you. But you never hear anything *I* say."

I didn't know what to say to that. He looked out of the window and then back at me. "OK," he said, and sighed. "I'll try."

Then I said, trying to cheer him up a little, "They got a piano at Isabel's. You can practice on it."

And as a matter of fact, it did cheer him up for a minute. "That's right," he said to himself. "I forgot that." His face relaxed a little. But the worry, the thoughtfulness, played on it still, the way shadows play on a face which is staring into the fire.

But I thought I'd never hear the end of that piano. At first, Isabel would write me, saying how nice it was that Sonny was so serious about his music and how, as soon as he came in from school, or wherever he had been when he was supposed to be at school, he went straight to that piano and stayed there until suppertime. And, after supper, he went back to that piano and stayed there until everybody went to bed. He was at the piano all day Saturday and all day Sunday. Then he bought a record player and started playing records. He'd play one record over and over again, all day long sometimes, and he'd improvise along with it on the piano. Or he'd play one section of the record, one chord, one change, one progression, then he'd do it on the piano. Then back to the record. Then back to the piano.

Well, I really don't know how they stood it. Isabel finally confessed that it wasn't like living with a person at all, it was like living with sound. And the sound didn't make any sense to her, didn't make any sense to any of them — naturally. They began, in a way, to be afflicted by this presence that was living in their home. It was as though Sonny were some sort of god, or monster. He moved in an atmosphere which wasn't like theirs at all. They fed him and he ate, he washed himself, he walked in and out of their door; he certainly wasn't nasty or unpleasant or rude, Sonny isn't any of those things; but it was as though he were all wrapped up in some cloud, some fire, some vision all his own; and there wasn't any way to reach him.

At the same time, he wasn't really a man yet, he was still a child, and they had to watch out for him in all kinds of ways. They certainly couldn't throw him out. Neither did they dare to make a great scene about that piano because even they dimly sensed, as I sensed, from so many thousands of miles away, that Sonny was at that piano playing for his life.

But he hadn't been going to school. One day a letter came from the school board and Isabel's mother got it — there had, apparently, been other letters but Sonny had torn them up. This day, when Sonny came in, Isabel's mother showed him the letter and asked where he'd been spending his time. And she finally got it out of him that he'd been down in Greenwich Village, with musicians and other characters, in a white girl's apartment. And this scared her and she started to scream at him and what came up, once she began — though she denies it to this day — was what sacrifices they were making to give Sonny a decent home and how little he appreciated it.

Sonny didn't play the piano that day. By evening, Isabel's mother had calmed down but then there was the old man to deal with, and Isabel herself. Isabel says she did her best to be calm but she broke down and started crying. She says she just watched Sonny's face. She could tell, by watching him, what was happening with him. And what was happening was that they penetrated his cloud, they had reached him. Even if their fingers had been a thousand times more gentle than human fingers ever are, he could hardly help feeling that they had stripped him naked and were spitting on that nakedness. For he also had to see that his presence, that music, which was life or death to him, had been torture for them and that they had endured it, not at all for his sake, but only for mine. And Sonny couldn't take that. He can take it a little better today than he could then but he's still not very good at it and, frankly, I don't know anybody who is.

The silence of the next few days must have been louder than the sound **170** of all the music ever played since time began. One morning, before she went to work, Isabel was in his room for something and she suddenly realized that all of his records were gone. And she knew for certain that he was gone. And he was. He went as far as the navy would carry him. He finally sent me a postcard from some place in Greece and that was the first I knew that Sonny was still alive. I didn't see him any more until we were both back in New York and the war had long been over.

He was a man by then, of course, but I wasn't willing to see it. He came by the house from time to time, but we fought almost every time we met. I didn't like the way he carried himself, loose and dreamlike all the time, and I didn't like his friends, and his music seemed to be merely an excuse for the life he led. It sounded just that weird and disordered.

Then we had a fight, a pretty awful fight, and I didn't see him for months. By and by I looked him up, where he was living, in a furnished room in the Village, and I tried to make it up. But there were lots of other people in the room and Sonny just lay on his bed, and he wouldn't come downstairs with me, and he treated these other people as though they were his family and I weren't. So I got mad and then he got mad, and then I told him that he might just as well be dead as live the way he was living. Then he stood up and he told me not to worry about him any more in life, that he *was* dead as far as I was concerned. Then he pushed me to the door and the other people looked on as though nothing were happening, and he slammed the door behind me. I stood in the hallway, staring at the door. I heard somebody laugh in the room and then the tears came to my eyes. I started down the steps, whistling to keep from crying, I kept whistling to myself, *You going to need me, baby, one of these cold, rainy days.*

I read about Sonny's trouble in the spring. Little Grace died in the fall. She was a beautiful little girl. But she only lived a little over two years. She died of polio and she suffered. She had a slight fever for a couple of days, but it didn't seem like anything and we just kept her in bed. And we would certainly have called the doctor, but the fever dropped, she seemed to be all right. So we thought it had just been a cold. Then, one day, she was up, playing, Isabel was in the kitchen fixing lunch for the two boys when they'd come in from school, and she heard Grace fall down in the living room. When you have a lot of children you don't always start running when one of them falls, unless they start screaming or something. And, this time, Grace was quiet. Yet, Isabel says that when she heard that *thump* and then that silence, something happened in her to make her afraid. And she ran to the living room and there was little Grace on the floor, all twisted up, and the reason she hadn't screamed was that she couldn't get her breath. And when she did scream, it was the worst sound, Isabel says, that she'd ever heard in all her life, and she still hears it sometimes in her dreams. Isabel will sometimes wake me up with a low, moaning, strangled sound and I have to be quick to awaken her and hold her to me and where Isabel is weeping against me seems a mortal wound.

I think I may have written Sonny the very day that little Grace was buried. I was sitting in the living room in the dark, by myself, and I suddenly thought of Sonny. My trouble made his real.

One Saturday afternoon, when Sonny had been living with us, or, anyway, been in our house, for nearly two weeks, I found myself wandering aimlessly about the living room, drinking from a can of beer, and trying to work up the courage to search Sonny's room. He was out, he was usually out whenever I was home, and Isabel had taken the children to see their grandparents. Suddenly I was standing still in front of the living room window, watching Seventh Avenue. The idea of searching Sonny's room made me still. I scarcely dared to admit to myself what I'd be searching for. I didn't know what I'd do if I found it. Or if I didn't.

On the sidewalk across from me, near the entrance to a barbecue joint, some people were holding an old-fashioned revival meeting. The barbecue cook, wearing a dirty white apron, his conked hair reddish and metallic in the pale sun, and a cigarette between his lips, stood in the doorway, watching them. Kids and older people paused in their errands and stood there, along with some older men and a couple of very tough-looking women who watched everything that happened on the avenue, as though they owned it, or were maybe owned by it. Well, they were watching this, too. The revival was being carried on by three sisters in black, and a brother. All they had were their voices and their Bibles and a tambourine. The brother was testifying and while he testified two of the sisters stood together, seeming to say, amen, and the third sister walked around with the tambourine outstretched and a couple of people dropped coins into it. Then the brother's testimony ended and the sister who had been taking up the collection dumped the coins into her palm and transferred them to the pocket of her long black robe. Then she raised both hands, striking the tambourine against the air, and then against one hand, and she started to sing. And the two other sisters and the brother joined in.

It was strange, suddenly, to watch, though I had been seeing these street meetings all my life. So, of course, had everybody else down there. Yet, they paused and watched and listened and I stood still at the window. *"Tis the old ship of Zion,"* they sang, and the sister with the tambourine kept a steady, jangling beat, *"it has rescued many a thousand!"* Not a soul under the sound of their voices was hearing this song for the first time, not one of them had been rescued. Nor had they seen much in the way of rescue work being done around them. Neither did they especially believe in the holiness of the three sisters and the brother, they knew too much about them, knew where they lived, and how. The woman with the tambourine, whose voice dominated the air, whose face was bright with joy, was divided by very little from the woman who stood watching her, a cigarette between her heavy, chapped lips, her hair a cuckoo's nest, her face scarred and swollen from many beatings, and her black eyes glittering like coal. Perhaps they both knew this, which was why, when, as rarely, they addressed each other, they addressed each other as Sister. As the singing filled the air the watching, listening faces underwent a change, the eyes focusing on something within; the music seemed to soothe a poison out of them; and time seemed, nearly, to fall away from the sullen, belligerent, battered faces, as though they were fleeing back to their first condition, while dreaming of their last. The barbecue cook half shook his head and smiled, and dropped his cigarette and disappeared into his joint. A man fumbled in his pockets for change and stood holding it in his hand impatiently, as though he had just remembered a pressing appointment further up the avenue. He looked furious. Then I saw Sonny, standing on the edge of the crowd. He was carrying a wide, flat notebook with a green cover, and it made him look, from where I was standing, almost like a schoolboy. The coppery sun brought out the copper in his skin, he was very faintly smiling, standing very still. Then the singing stopped, the tambourine turned into a collection plate again. The furious man dropped in his coins and vanished, so did a couple of the women, and Sonny dropped some change in the plate, looking directly at the woman with a little smile. He started across the avenue, toward the house. He has a slow, loping walk, something like the way Harlem hipsters walk, only he's imposed on this his own half-beat. I had never really noticed it before.

I stayed at the window, both relieved and apprehensive. As Sonny disappeared from my sight, they began singing again. And they were still singing when his key turned in the lock.

"Hey," he said.

"Hey, yourself. You want some beer?"

"No. Well, maybe." But he came up to the window and stood beside me, looking out. "What a warm voice," he said.

They were singing *If I could only hear my mother pray again!*

"Yes," I said, "and she can sure beat that tambourine."

"But what a terrible song," he said, and laughed. He dropped his notebook on the sofa and disappeared into the kitchen. "Where's Isabel and the kids?"

"I think they went to see their grandparents. You hungry?"

"No." He came back into the living room with his can of beer. "You want to come some place with me tonight?"

I sensed, I don't know how, that I couldn't possibly say no. "Sure. Where?"

He sat down on the sofa and picked up his notebook and started leafing through it. "I'm going to sit in with some fellows in a joint in the Village."

"You mean, you're going to play, tonight?"

"That's right." He took a swallow of his beer and moved back to the window. He gave me a sidelong look. "If you can stand it."

"I'll try," I said.

He smiled to himself and we both watched as the meeting across the way broke up. The three sisters and the brother, heads bowed, were singing *God be with you till we meet again.* The faces around them were very quiet. Then the song ended. The small crowd dispersed. We watched the three women and the lone man walk slowly up the avenue.

"When she was singing before," said Sonny, abruptly, "her voice reminded me for a minute of what heroin feels like sometimes — when it's in your veins. It makes you feel sort of warm and cool at the same time. And distant. And — and sure." He sipped his beer, very deliberately not looking at me. I watched his face. "It makes you feel — in control. Sometimes you've got to have that feeling."

"Do you?" I sat down slowly in the easy chair.

"Sometimes." He went to the sofa and picked up his notebook again. 195
"Some people do."

"In order," I asked, "to play?" And my voice was very ugly, full of contempt and anger.

"Well" — he looked at me with great, troubled eyes, as though, in fact, he hoped his eyes would tell me things he could never otherwise say — "they *think* so. And *if* they think so —!"

"And what do *you* think?" I asked.

He sat on the sofa and put his can of beer on the floor. "I don't know," he said, and I couldn't be sure if he were answering my question or pursuing his thoughts. His face didn't tell me. "It's not so much to *play*. It's to *stand* it, to be able to make it at all. On any level." He frowned and smiled: "In order to keep from shaking to pieces."

"But these friends of yours," I said, "they seem to shake themselves to 200 pieces pretty goddamn fast."

"Maybe." He played with the notebook. And something told me that I should curb my tongue, that Sonny was doing his best to talk, that I should listen. "But of course you only know the ones that've gone to pieces. Some don't — or at least they haven't *yet* and that's just about all *any* of us can say." He paused. "And then there are some who just live, really, in hell, and they know it and they see what's happening and they go right on. I don't know." He sighed, dropped the notebook, folded his arms. "Some guys, you can tell from the way they play, they on something *all* the time. And you can see that, well, it makes something real for them. But of course," he picked up his beer from the floor and sipped it and put the can down again, "they *want* to, too, you've got to see that. Even some of them that say they don't — *some*, not all."

"And what about you?" I asked — I couldn't help it. "What about you? Do *you* want to?"

He stood up and walked to the window and remained silent for a long time. Then he sighed. "Me," he said. Then: "While I was downstairs before, on my way here, listening to that woman sing, it struck me all of a sudden how much suffering she must have had to go through — to sing like that. It's *repulsive* to think you have to suffer that much."

I said: "But there's no way not to suffer — is there, Sonny?"

"I believe not," he said and smiled, "but that's never stopped anyone from 205 trying." He looked at me. "Has it?" I realized, with this mocking look, that there stood between us, forever, beyond the power of time or forgiveness, the fact that I had held silence — so long! — when he had needed human speech to help him. He turned back to the window. "No, there's no way not to suffer. But you try all kinds of ways to keep from drowning in it, to keep on top of it, and to make it seem — well, like *you*. Like you did something, all right, and now you're suffering for it. You know?" I said nothing. "Well you know," he said, impatiently, "why *do* people suffer? Maybe it's better to do something to give it a reason, *any* reason."

"But we just agreed," I said, "that there's no way not to suffer. Isn't it better, then, just to — take it?"

"But nobody just takes it," Sonny cried, "that's what I'm telling you! *Everybody* tries not to. You're just hung up on the *way* some people try — it's not *your* way!"

The hair on my face began to itch, my face felt wet. "That's not true," I said, "that's not true. I don't give a damn what other people do, I don't even care how they suffer. I just care how *you* suffer." And he looked at me. "Please believe me," I said, "I don't want to see you — die — trying not to suffer."

"I won't," he said, flatly, "die trying not to suffer. At least, not any faster than anybody else."

"But there's no need," I said, trying to laugh, "is there? in killing yourself."

I wanted to say more, but I couldn't. I wanted to talk about will power and how life could be — well, beautiful. I wanted to say that it was all within; but was it? or, rather, wasn't that exactly the trouble? And I wanted to promise that I would never fail him again. But it would all have sounded — empty words and lies.

So I made the promise to myself and prayed that I would keep it.

"It's terrible sometimes, inside," he said, "that's what's the trouble. You walk these streets, black and funky and cold, and there's not really a living ass to talk to, and there's nothing shaking, and there's no way of getting it out — that storm inside. You can't talk it and you can't make love with it, and when you finally try to get with it and play it, you realize *nobody's* listening. So *you've* got to listen. You got to find a way to listen."

And then he walked away from the window and sat on the sofa again, as though all the wind had suddenly been knocked out of him. "Sometimes you'll do *anything* to play, even cut your mother's throat." He laughed and looked at me. "Or your brother's." Then he sobered, "Or your own." Then: "Don't worry. I'm all right now and I think I'll *be* all right. But I can't forget — where I've been. I don't mean just the physical place I've been, I mean where I've *been*. And *what* I've been."

"What have you been, Sonny?" I asked.

He smiled — but sat sideways on the sofa, his elbow resting on the back, his fingers playing with his mouth and chin, not looking at me. "I've been something I didn't recognize, didn't know I could be. Didn't know anybody could be." He stopped, looking inward, looking helplessly young, looking old. "I'm not talking about it now because I feel *guilty* or anything like that — maybe it would be better if I did, I don't know. Anyway, I can't really talk about it. Not to you, not to anybody," and now he turned and faced me. "Sometimes, you know, and it was actually when I was most *out* of the world, I felt that I was in it, that I was *with* it, really, and I could play or I didn't really have to *play*, it just came out of me, it was there. And I don't know how I played, thinking about it now, but I know I did awful things, those times, sometimes, to people. Or it wasn't that I *did* anything to them — it was that they weren't real." He picked up the beer can; it was empty; he rolled it between his palms: "And other times — well, I needed a fix, I needed to find a place to lean, I needed to clear a space to *listen*—and I couldn't find it, and I—went crazy, I did terrible things to *me*, I was terrible *for* me." He began pressing the beer can between his hands, I watched the metal begin to give. It glittered, as he played with it, like a knife, and I was afraid he would cut himself, but I said nothing. "Oh well. I can never tell you. I was all by myself at the bottom of something, stinking and sweating and crying and shaking, and I smelled it, you know? *my* stink, and I thought I'd die if I couldn't get away from it and yet, all the same, I knew that everything I was doing was just locking me in with it. And I didn't know," he paused, still flattening the beer can, "I didn't know, I still *don't* know, something kept telling me that maybe it was good to smell your own stink, but I didn't think that *that* was what I'd been trying to do—and—who can stand it?" and he abruptly dropped the ruined beer can, looking at me with a small, still smile, and then rose, walking to the window as though it were the lodestone rock. I watched his face, he watched the avenue. "I couldn't tell you when Mama died—but the reason I wanted to leave Harlem so bad was to get away from drugs. And then, when I ran away, that's what I was running from—really. When I came back, nothing had changed, I hadn't changed, I was just—older." And he stopped, drumming with his fingers on the windowpane. The sun had vanished, soon darkness would fall. I watched his face. "It can come again," he said, almost as though speaking to himself. Then he turned to me. "It can come again," he repeated. "I just want you to know that."

"All right," I said, at last. "So it can come again. All right."

He smiled, but the smile was sorrowful. "I had to try to tell you," he said.

"Yes," I said. "I understand that."

"You're my brother," he said, looking straight at me, and not smiling at all. 220

"Yes," I repeated, "yes. I understand that."

He turned back to the window, looking out. "All that hatred down there," he said, "all that hatred and misery and love. It's a wonder it doesn't blow the avenue apart."

We went to the only nightclub on a short, dark street, downtown. We squeezed through the narrow, chattering, jam-packed bar to the entrance of the big room, where the bandstand was. And we stood there for a moment, for the lights were very dim in this room and we couldn't see. Then, "Hello, boy," said a voice and an enormous black man, much older than Sonny or myself, erupted out of all that atmospheric lighting and put an arm around Sonny's shoulder. "I been sitting right here," he said, "waiting for you."

He had a big voice, too, and heads in the darkness turned toward us.

Sonny grinned and pulled a little away, and said, "Creole, this is my 225 brother. I told you about him."

Creole shook my hand. "I'm glad to meet you, son," he said, and it was clear that he was glad to meet me *there*, for Sonny's sake. And he smiled, "You got a real musician in *your* family," and he took his arm from Sonny's shoulder and slapped him, lightly, affectionately, with the back of his hand.

"Well. Now I've heard it all," said a voice behind us. This was another musician, and a friend of Sonny's, a coal-black, cheerful-looking man, built close to the ground. He immediately began confiding to me, at the top of his lungs, the most terrible things about Sonny, his teeth gleaming like a light-house and his laugh coming up out of him like the beginning of an earth-quake. And it turned out that everyone at the bar knew Sonny, or almost everyone; some were musicians, working there, or nearby, or not working, some were simply hangers-on, and some were there to hear Sonny play. I was introduced to all of them and they were all very polite to me. Yet, it was clear that, for them, I was only Sonny's brother. Here, I was in Sonny's world. Or, rather: his kingdom. Here, it was not even a question that his veins bore royal blood.

They were going to play soon and Creole installed me, by myself, at a table in a dark corner. Then I watched them, Creole, and the little black man, and Sonny, and the others, while they horsed around, standing just below the bandstand. The light from the bandstand spilled just a little short of them and, watching them laughing and gesturing and moving about, I had the feeling that they, nevertheless, were being most careful not to step into that circle of light too suddenly: that if they moved into the light too suddenly, without thinking, they would perish in flame. Then, while I watched, one of them, the small, black man, moved into the light and crossed the bandstand and started fooling around with his drums. Then — being funny and being, also, extremely ceremonious — Creole took Sonny by the arm and led him to the piano. A woman's voice called Sonny's name and a few hands started clapping. And Sonny, also being funny and being ceremonious, and so touched, I think, that he could have cried, but neither hiding it nor showing it, riding it like a man, grinned, and put both hands to his heart and bowed from the waist.

Creole then went to the bass fiddle and a lean, very bright-skinned brown man jumped up on the bandstand and picked up his horn. So there they were, and the atmosphere on the bandstand and in the room began to change and tighten. Someone stepped up to the microphone and announced them. Then there were all kinds of murmurs. Some people at the bar shushed others. The waitress ran around, frantically getting in the last orders, guys and chicks got closer to each other, and the lights on the bandstand, on the quartet, turned to a kind of indigo. Then they all looked different there. Creole looked about him for the last time, as though he were making certain that all his chickens were in the coop, and then he — jumped and struck the fiddle. And there they were.

All I know about music is that not many people ever really hear it. And 230 even then, on the rare occasions when something opens within, and the music enters, what we mainly hear, or hear corroborated, are personal, pri-vate, vanishing evocations. But the man who creates the music is hearing something else, is dealing with the roar rising from the void and impos-ing order on it as it hits the air. What is evoked in him, then, is of another order, more terrible because it has no words, and triumphant, too, for that same reason. And his triumph, when he triumphs, is ours. I just watched Sonny's face. His face was troubled, he was working hard, but he wasn't with it. And I had the feeling that, in a way, everyone on the bandstand was waiting for him, both waiting for him and pushing him along. But as I began to watch Creole, I realized that it was Creole who held them all back. He had them on a short rein. Up there, keeping the beat with his whole body, wailing on the fiddle, with his eyes half closed, he was listening to everything, but he was listening to Sonny. He was having a dialogue with Sonny. He wanted Sonny to leave the shoreline and strike out for the deep water. He was Sonny's witness that deep water and drowning were not the same thing—he had been there, and he knew. And he wanted Sonny to know. He was waiting for Sonny to do the things on the keys which would let Creole know that Sonny was in the water.

And, while Creole listened, Sonny moved, deep within, exactly like someone in torment. I had never before thought of how awful the relationship must be between the musician and his instrument. He has to fill it, this instrument, with the breath of life, his own. He has to make it do what he wants it to do. And a piano is just a piano. It's made out of so much wood and wires and little hammers and big ones, and ivory. While there's only so much you can do with it, the only way to find this out is to try; to try and make it do everything.

And Sonny hadn't been near a piano for over a year. And he wasn't on much better terms with his life, not the life that stretched before him now. He and the piano stammered, started one way, got scared, stopped; started another way, panicked, marked time, started again; then seemed to have found a direction, panicked again, got stuck. And the face I saw on Sonny I'd never seen before. Everything had been burned out of it, and, at the same time, things usually hidden were being burned in, by the fire and fury of the battle which was occurring in him up there.

Yet, watching Creole's face as they neared the end of the first set, I had the feeling that something had happened, something I hadn't heard. Then they finished, there was scattered applause, and then, without an instant's warning, Creole started into something else, it was almost sardonic, it was *Am I Blue*. And, as though he commanded, Sonny began to play. Something began to happen. And Creole let out the reins. The dry, low, black man said something awful on the drums, Creole answered, and the drums talked back. Then the horn insisted, sweet and high, slightly detached perhaps, and Creole listened, commenting now and then, dry, and driving, beautiful and calm and old. Then they all came together again, and Sonny was part of the family again. I could tell this from his face. He seemed to have found, right there beneath his fingers, a damn brand-new piano. It seemed that he couldn't get over it. Then, for awhile, just being happy with Sonny, they seemed to be agreeing with him that brand-new pianos certainly were a gas.

Then Creole stepped forward to remind them that what they were playing was the blues. He hit something in all of them, he hit something in me, myself, and the music tightened and deepened, apprehension began to beat the air. Creole began to tell us what the blues were all about. They were not about anything very new. He and his boys up there were keeping it new, at the risk of ruin, destruction, madness, and death, in order to find new ways to make us listen. For, while the tale of how we suffer, and how we are delighted, and how we may triumph is never new, it always must be heard. There isn't any other tale to tell, it's the only light we've got in all this darkness.

And this tale, according to that face, that body, those strong hands on those strings, has another aspect in every country, and a new depth in every generation. Listen, Creole seemed to be saying, listen. Now these are Sonny's blues. He made the little black man on the drums know it, and the bright, brown man on the horn. Creole wasn't trying any longer to get Sonny in the water. He was wishing him Godspeed. Then he stepped back, very slowly, filling the air with the immense suggestion that Sonny speak for himself.

Then they all gathered around Sonny and Sonny played. Every now and again one of them seemed to say, amen. Sonny's fingers filled the air with life, his life. But that life contained so many others. And Sonny went all the way back, he really began with the spare, flat statement of the opening phrase of the song. Then he began to make it his. It was very beautiful because it wasn't hurried and it was no longer a lament. I seemed to hear with what burning he had made it his, with what burning we had yet to make it ours, how we could cease lamenting. Freedom lurked around us and I understood, at last, that he could help us to be free if we would listen, that he would never be free until we did. Yet, there was no battle in his face now. I heard what he had gone through, and would continue to go through until he came to rest in earth. He had made it his: that long line, of which we knew only Mama and Daddy. And he was giving it back, as everything must be given back, so that, passing through death, it can live forever. I saw my mother's face again, and felt, for the first time, how the stones of the road she had walked on must have bruised her feet. I saw the moonlit road where my father's brother died. And it brought something else back to me, and carried me past it, I saw my little girl again and felt Isabel's tears again, and I felt my own tears begin to rise. And I was yet aware that this was only a moment, that the world waited outside, as hungry as a tiger, and that trouble stretched above us, longer than the sky.

Then it was over. Creole and Sonny let out their breath, both soaking wet, and grinning. There was a lot of applause and some of it was real. In the dark, the girl came by and I asked her to take drinks to the bandstand. There was a long pause, while they talked up there in the indigo light and after awhile I saw the girl put a Scotch and milk on top of the piano for Sonny. He didn't seem to notice it, but just before they started playing again, he sipped from it and looked toward me, and nodded. Then he put it back on top of the piano. For me, then, as they began to play again, it glowed and shook above my brother's head like the very cup of trembling.

Considerations for Critical Thinking and Writing

1. **First Response.** Do you share the narrator's fear for his brother's life? Does your response change over the course of the story?

2. Why is it significant that the narrator encounters the news of what happened to Sonny first in a newspaper and then through one of Sonny's friends?

3. One important factor in gaining insight into a character is their chosen profession. Compare the professions of math teacher and jazz musician. To what degree do those careers outline other important features of the narrator's and Sonny's characters?

4. The narrator is an educator, and yet he seems to be the one who has something to learn in the story. What does he learn, when does he learn it, and what are the significant steps that lead to his learning it?

5. Sonny claims that the main difference between him and his brother is the way they try to avoid suffering. How do their two methods of avoiding suffering compare?

6. The story is titled after Sonny, but is he the protagonist?

7. The primary relationship examined in the story is obviously between the narrator and Sonny. How many other significant characters populate the story? (These might include characters who are not technically in the story.) How does each of them affect the way the relationship between Sonny and his brother unfolds?

8. What motivates the narrator?

9. If there is growth in either of the main characters, is it emotional, intellectual, or spiritual?

10. From the title onward, the story is largely about music. What are the various ways music helps to define these two characters?

11. The narrator has always wanted to change Sonny, but Sonny is resistant to those efforts. Does that make Sonny a static character as defined earlier in this chapter?

12. Is the narrator's character revealed more in his conversations with Sonny or in his "private" admissions to the reader?

13. How is the story framed in terms of the tension between private and public selves?

Connections to Other Selections

1. Compare the way "Sonny's Blues" and Charlotte Perkins Gilman's story "The Yellow Wallpaper" (p. 117) examine relationships and the will to control the behavior of a loved one, sometimes as a result of societal conventions.

2. Louise Erdrich's story "The Red Convertible" (p. 161) is also a story of two brothers, one of whom is evidently damaged by his past experiences. Compare the two stories in terms of the way the narrators both reveal and conceal their own motivation for telling stories about their brothers.

4

Setting

One of the troubles with our culture is we do not respect and train the imagination. It needs exercise. It needs practice. You can't tell a story unless you've listened to a lot of stories and then learned how to do it.

— URSULA K. LE GUIN

Setting is the context in which the action of a story occurs. The major elements of setting are time, place, and the social environment that frames the characters. These elements establish the world in which the characters act. In most stories they also serve as more than backgrounds and furnishings. If we are sensitive to the contexts provided by setting, we are better able to understand the behavior of the characters and the significance of their actions. It may be tempting to read quickly through a writer's descriptions and ignore the details of the setting once a geographic location and a historic period are established. But if you read a story so impatiently, the significance of the setting may slip by you. That kind of reading is similar to traveling on interstate highways: a lot of ground gets covered, but very little is seen along the way.

Settings can be used to evoke a mood or atmosphere that will prepare the reader for what is to come. In "Young Goodman Brown," Nathaniel

Hawthorne has his pious protagonist leave his wife and village one night to keep an appointment in a New England forest near the site of the seventeenth-century witch trials. This is Hawthorne's description of Brown entering the forest:

> He had taken a dreary road, darkened by all the gloomiest trees of the forest, which barely stood aside to let the narrow path creep through, and closed immediately behind. It was all as lonely as could be; and there is this peculiarity in such a solitude, that the traveler knows not who may be concealed by the innumerable trunks and the thick boughs overhead; so that with lonely footsteps he may yet be passing through an unseen multitude.

The atmosphere established in this descriptive setting is somber and threatening. Careful reading reveals that the forest is not simply the woods; it is a moral wilderness, where anything can happen.

If we ask why a writer chooses to include certain details in a work, then we are likely to make connections that relate the details to some larger purpose, such as the story's meaning. John Updike's story "A & P" takes place, as the title indicates, in the grocery store where the protagonist works. The story confronts the opposing forces of conformity and rebellion, so it is fitting that it takes place in a supermarket chain where every store is the same, from the Atlantic to the Pacific (which is what A & P stands for). There is usually a reason for placing a story in a particular time or location. Katherine Mansfield has the protagonist in "Miss Brill" discover her loneliness and old age in a French vacation town, a lively atmosphere that serves as a cruel contrast to an elderly (and foreign) lady's painful realization.

Time, location, and the physical features of a setting can all be relevant to the overall purpose of a story. So too is the social environment in which the characters are developed. In Faulkner's "A Rose for Emily" (p. 40) the changes in Emily's southern town serve as a foil for her tenacious hold on a lost past. She is regarded as a "fallen monument," as old-fashioned and peculiar as the "stubborn and coquettish decay" of her house. Neither she nor her house fits into the modern changes that are paving and transforming the town. Without the social context, this story would be mostly an account of a bizarre murder rather than an exploration of the conflicts Faulkner associated with the changing South. Setting enlarges the meaning of Emily's actions.

Some settings have traditional associations that are closely related to the action of a story. Adventure and romance, for example, flourish in the fertile soil of most exotic settings: the film version of Isak Dinesen's novel *Out of Africa* is a lush visual demonstration of how setting can play a significant role in generating the audience's expectations of love and excitement.

Sometimes writers reverse traditional expectations. When a tranquil garden is the scene for a horrendously bloody murder, we are as much taken by surprise as the victim is. In John Updike's "A & P" (p. 138) there seems to be little possibility for heroic action in so mundane a place as a supermarket, but the setting turns out to be appropriate for the important, unexpected decision the protagonist makes about life. Traditional associations are also disrupted in Tobias Wolff's "Powder" (p. 56) by making a blizzard a place of excitement and father-son bonding rather than a site of danger and peril. By drawing on traditional associations, a writer can fulfill or disrupt a reader's expectations about a setting in order to complement the elements of the story.

Not every story uses setting as a means of revealing mood, idea, meaning, or characters' actions. Some stories have no particularly significant setting. It is entirely possible to envision a story in which two characters speak to each other about a conflict between them and little or no mention is made of the time or place they inhabit. If, however, a shift in setting would make a serious difference to our understanding of a story, then the setting is probably an important element in the work. The story "Famine" (p. 65) by Xu Xi takes place in Manhattan, mostly in a luxury hotel, but when the narrator wanders south of midtown she is confronted with abject poverty. In a story that confronts so deliberately the disparity between wealth and poverty, no American city illustrates this disparity as clearly as New York City does. The setting is integral to that story.

The following three stories — Ernest Hemingway's "Soldier's Home," Ursula K. Le Guin's "The Ones Who Walk Away from Omelas," and Charlotte Perkins Gilman's "The Yellow Wallpaper" — include settings that serve to shape their meanings.

ERNEST HEMINGWAY (1899–1961)

Because of his writing's stylistic innovations, Ernest Hemingway was considered one of the most influential writers of his time and was awarded the Nobel Prize in Literature in 1954, one of only eleven Americans in history to earn that honor. In 1918, a year after graduating from high school in Oak Park, Illinois, Ernest Hemingway volunteered as an ambulance driver in World War I. At the Italian front, he was seriously wounded. This experience haunted him and many of the characters in his short stories and novels. *In Our Time* (1925) is a collection of short stories, including "Soldier's Home," that reflect some of Hemingway's own attempts

Ermeni Studio, Milan. Courtesy of the Ernest Hemingway Photographic Collection, John Fitzgerald Kennedy Library, Boston.

to readjust to life back home after the war. *The Sun Also Rises* (1926), *A Farewell to Arms* (1929), and *For Whom the Bell Tolls* (1940) are also about war and its impact on people's lives. Hemingway courted violence all his life in war, the bullring, the boxing ring, and big game hunting. When he was sixty-two years old and terminally ill with cancer, he committed suicide by shooting himself with a shotgun. "Soldier's Home" takes place in a small town in Oklahoma; the war, however, is never distant from the protagonist's mind as he struggles to come home again.

Soldier's Home   1925

Krebs went to the war from a Methodist college in Kansas. There is a picture which shows him among his fraternity brothers, all of them wearing exactly the same height and style collar. He enlisted in the Marines in 1917 and did not return to the United States until the second division returned from the Rhine in the summer of 1919.

There is a picture which shows him on the Rhine with two German girls and another corporal. Krebs and the corporal look too big for their uniforms. The German girls are not beautiful. The Rhine does not show in the picture.

By the time Krebs returned to his home town in Oklahoma the greeting of heroes was over. He came back much too late. The men from the town who had been drafted had all been welcomed elaborately on their return. There had been a great deal of hysteria. Now the reaction had set in. People seemed to think it was rather ridiculous for Krebs to be getting back so late, years after the war was over.

At first Krebs, who had been at Belleau Wood, Soissons, the Champagne, St. Mihiel, and in the Argonne° did not want to talk about the war at all. Later he felt the need to talk but no one wanted to hear about it. His town had heard too many atrocity stories to be thrilled by actualities. Krebs found that to be listened to at all he had to lie, and after he had done this twice he, too, had a reaction against the war and against talking about it. A distaste for everything that had happened to him in the war set in because of the lies he had told. All of the times that had been able to make him feel cool and clear inside himself when he thought of them; the times so long back when he had done the one thing, the only thing for a man to do, easily and naturally, when he might have done something else, now lost their cool, valuable quality and then were lost themselves.

His lies were quite unimportant lies and consisted in attributing to   5 himself things other men had seen, done, or heard of, and stating as facts certain apocryphal incidents familiar to all soldiers. Even his lies were not

---

Belleau Wood . . . Argonne: Sites of battles in World War I in which American troops were instrumental in pushing back the Germans.

sensational at the pool room. His acquaintances, who had heard detailed accounts of German women found chained to machine guns in the Argonne forest and who could not comprehend, or were barred by their patriotism from interest in, any German machine gunners who were not chained, were not thrilled by his stories.

Krebs acquired the nausea in regard to experience that is the result of untruth or exaggeration, and when he occasionally met another man who had really been a soldier and they talked a few minutes in the dressing room at a dance he fell into the easy pose of the old soldier among other soldiers: that he had been badly, sickeningly frightened all the time. In this way he lost everything.

During this time, it was late summer, he was sleeping late in bed, getting up to walk down town to the library to get a book, eating lunch at home, reading on the front porch until he became bored, and then walking down through the town to spend the hottest hours of the day in the cool dark of the pool room. He loved to play pool.

In the evening he practiced on his clarinet, strolled down town, read, and went to bed. He was still a hero to his two young sisters. His mother would have given him breakfast in bed if he had wanted it. She often came in when he was in bed and asked him to tell her about the war, but her attention always wandered. His father was noncommittal.

Before Krebs went away to the war he had never been allowed to drive the family motor car. His father was in the real estate business and always wanted the car to be at his command when he required it to take clients out into the country to show them a piece of farm property. The car always stood outside the First National Bank building where his father had an office on the second floor. Now, after the war, it was still the same car.

Nothing was changed in the town except that the young girls had grown up. But they lived in such a complicated world of already defined alliances and shifting feuds that Krebs did not feel the energy or the courage to break into it. He liked to look at them, though. There were so many good-looking young girls. Most of them had their hair cut short. When he went away only little girls wore their hair like that or girls that were fast. They all wore sweaters and shirt waists with round Dutch collars. It was a pattern. He liked to look at them from the front porch as they walked on the other side of the street. He liked to watch them walking under the shade of the trees. He liked the round Dutch collars above their sweaters. He liked their silk stockings and flat shoes. He liked their bobbed hair and the way they walked.

When he was in town their appeal to him was not very strong. He did not like them when he saw them in the Greek's ice cream parlor. He did not want them themselves really. They were too complicated. There was something else. Vaguely he wanted a girl but he did not want to have to work to get her. He would have liked to have a girl but he did not want to have to spend a long time getting her. He did not want to get into the intrigue and the politics. He did not want to have to do any courting. He did not want to tell any more lies. It wasn't worth it.

He did not want any consequences. He did not want any consequences ever again. He wanted to live alone without consequences. Besides he did not really need a girl. The army had taught him that. It was all right to pose as though you had to have a girl. Nearly everybody did that. But it wasn't true. You did not need a girl. That was the funny thing. First a fellow boasted how girls meant nothing to him, that he never thought of them, that they could not touch him. Then a fellow boasted that he could not get along without girls, that he had to have them all the time, that he could not go to sleep without them.

That was all a lie. It was all a lie both ways. You did not need a girl unless you thought about them. He learned that in the army. Then sooner or later you always got one. When you were really ripe for a girl you always got one. You did not have to think about it. Sooner or later it would come. He had learned that in the army.

Now he would have liked a girl if she had come to him and not wanted to talk. But here at home it was all too complicated. He knew he could never get through it all again. It was not worth the trouble. That was the thing about French girls and German girls. There was not all this talking. You couldn't talk much and you did not need to talk. It was simple and you were friends. He thought about France and then he began to think about Germany. On the whole he had liked Germany better. He did not want to leave Germany. He did not want to come home. Still, he had come home. He sat on the front porch.

He liked the girls that were walking along the other side of the street. 15 He liked the look of them much better than the French girls or the German girls. But the world they were in was not the world he was in. He would like to have one of them. But it was not worth it. They were such a nice pattern. He liked the pattern. It was exciting. But he would not go through all the talking. He did not want one badly enough. He liked to look at them all, though. It was not worth it. Not now when things were getting good again.

He sat there on the porch reading a book on the war. It was a history and he was reading about all the engagements he had been in. It was the most interesting reading he had ever done. He wished there were more maps. He looked forward with a good feeling to reading all the really good histories when they would come out with good detail maps. Now he was really learning about the war. He had been a good soldier. That made a difference.

One morning after he had been home about a month his mother came into his bedroom and sat on the bed. She smoothed her apron.

"I had a talk with your father last night, Harold," she said, "and he is willing for you to take the car out in the evenings."

"Yeah?" said Krebs, who was not fully awake. "Take the car out? Yeah?"

"Yes. Your father has felt for some time that you should be able to take 20 the car out in the evenings whenever you wished but we only talked it over last night."

"I'll bet you made him," Krebs said.

"No. It was your father's suggestion that we talk the matter over."

"Yeah. I'll bet you made him," Krebs sat up in bed.

"Will you come down to breakfast, Harold?" his mother said.

"As soon as I get my clothes on," Krebs said.

His mother went out of the room and he could hear her frying something downstairs while he washed, shaved, and dressed to go down into the dining-room for breakfast. While he was eating breakfast his sister brought in the mail.

"Well, Hare," she said. "You old sleepyhead. What do you ever get up for?"

Krebs looked at her. He liked her. She was his best sister.

"Have you got the paper?" he asked.

She handed him the Kansas City *Star* and he shucked off its brown wrapper and opened it to the sporting page. He folded the *Star* open and propped it against the water pitcher with his cereal dish to steady it, so he could read while he ate.

"Harold," his mother stood in the kitchen doorway, "Harold, please don't muss up the paper. Your father can't read his *Star* if it's been mussed."

"I won't muss it," Krebs said.

His sister sat down at the table and watched him while he read.

"We're playing indoor over at school this afternoon," she said. "I'm going to pitch."

"Good," said Krebs. "How's the old wing?"

"I can pitch better than lots of the boys. I tell them all you taught me. The other girls aren't much good."

"Yeah?" said Krebs.

"I tell them all you're my beau. Aren't you my beau, Hare?"

"You bet."

"Couldn't your brother really be your beau just because he's your brother?"

"I don't know."

"Sure you know. Couldn't you be my beau, Hare, if I was old enough and if you wanted to?"

"Sure. You're my girl now."

"Am I really your girl?"

"Sure."

"Do you love me?"

"Uh, huh."

"Will you love me always?"

"Sure."

"Will you come over and watch me play indoor?"

"Maybe."

"Aw, Hare, you don't love me. If you loved me, you'd want to come over and watch me play indoor."

Krebs's mother came into the dining-room from the kitchen. She carried a plate with two fried eggs and some crisp bacon on it and a plate of buckwheat cakes.

"You run along, Helen," she said. "I want to talk to Harold."

She put the eggs and bacon down in front of him and brought in a jug 55
of maple syrup for the buckwheat cakes. Then she sat down across the table
from Krebs.

"I wish you'd put down the paper a minute, Harold," she said.

Krebs took down the paper and folded it.

"Have you decided what you are going to do yet, Harold?" his mother
said, taking off her glasses.

"No," said Krebs.

"Don't you think it's about time?" His mother did not say this in a mean 60
way. She seemed worried.

"I hadn't thought about it," Krebs said.

"God has some work for everyone to do," his mother said. "There can
be no idle hands in His Kingdom."

"I'm not in His Kingdom," Krebs said.

"We are all of us in His Kingdom."

Krebs felt embarrassed and resentful as always. 65

"I've worried about you so much, Harold," his mother went on. "I know
the temptations you must have been exposed to. I know how weak men are.
I know what your own dear grandfather, my own father, told us about the
Civil War and I have prayed for you. I pray for you all day long, Harold."

Krebs looked at the bacon fat hardening on his plate.

"Your father is worried, too," his mother went on. "He thinks you have
lost your ambition, that you haven't got a definite aim in life. Charley Simmons, who is just your age, has a good job and is going to be married. The
boys are all settling down; they're all determined to get somewhere; you can
see that boys like Charley Simmons are on their way to being really a credit
to the community."

Krebs said nothing.

"Don't look that way, Harold," his mother said. "You know we love you and 70
I want to tell you for your own good how matters stand. Your father does not
want to hamper your freedom. He thinks you should be allowed to drive the
car. If you want to take some of the nice girls out riding with you, we are only
too pleased. We want you to enjoy yourself. But you are going to have to settle
down to work, Harold. Your father doesn't care what you start in at. All work is
honorable as he says. But you've got to make a start at something. He asked me
to speak to you this morning and then you can stop in and see him at his office."

"Is that all?" Krebs said.

"Yes. Don't you love your mother, dear boy?"

"No," Krebs said.

His mother looked at him across the table. Her eyes were shiny. She
started crying.

"I don't love anybody," Krebs said. 75

It wasn't any good. He couldn't tell her, he couldn't make her see it. It
was silly to have said it. He had only hurt her. He went over and took hold
of her arm. She was crying with her head in her hands.

"I didn't mean it," he said. "I was just angry at something. I didn't mean I didn't love you."

His mother went on crying. Krebs put his arm on her shoulder.

"Can't you believe me, mother?"

His mother shook her head.

"Please, please, mother. Please believe me."

"All right," his mother said chokily. She looked up at him. "I believe you, Harold."

Krebs kissed her hair. She put her face up to him.

"I'm your mother," she said. "I held you next to my heart when you were a tiny baby."

Krebs felt sick and vaguely nauseated.

"I know, Mummy," he said. "I'll try and be a good boy for you."

"Would you kneel and pray with me, Harold?" his mother asked.

They knelt down beside the dining-room table and Krebs's mother prayed.

"Now, you pray, Harold," she said.

"I can't," Krebs said.

"Try, Harold."

"I can't."

"Do you want me to pray for you?"

"Yes."

So his mother prayed for him and then they stood up and Krebs kissed his mother and went out of the house. He had tried so to keep his life from being complicated. Still, none of it had touched him. He had felt sorry for his mother and she had made him lie. He would go to Kansas City and get a job and she would feel all right about it. There would be one more scene maybe before he got away. He would not go down to his father's office. He would miss that one. He wanted his life to go smoothly. It had just gotten going that way. Well, that was all over now, anyway. He would go over to the schoolyard and watch Helen play indoor baseball.

CONSIDERATIONS FOR CRITICAL THINKING AND WRITING

1. **FIRST RESPONSE.** The title, "Soldier's Home," focuses on the setting. Do you have a clear picture of Krebs's home? Describe it, filling in missing details from your associations of home, Krebs's routine, or anything else you can use.

2. What does the photograph of Krebs, the corporal, and the German girls reveal?

3. Belleau Wood, Soissons, the Champagne, St. Mihiel, and the Argonne were the sites of fierce and bloody fighting. What effect have these battles had on Krebs? Why do you think he won't talk about them to the people at home?

4. Why does Krebs avoid complications and consequences? How has the war changed his attitudes toward work and women? How is his

hometown different from Germany and France? What is the conflict in the story?

5. Why do you think Hemingway refers to the protagonist as Krebs rather than Harold? What is the significance of his sister calling him "Hare"?

6. How does Krebs's mother embody the community's values? What does Krebs think of those values?

7. Why can't Krebs pray with his mother?

8. What is the resolution to Krebs's conflict?

9. Comment on the appropriateness of the story's title.

10. Explain how Krebs's war experiences are present throughout the story even though we get no details about them.

11. CRITICAL STRATEGIES. Read the section on reader-response criticism (pp. 1083–85) in Chapter 30, "Critical Strategies for Reading," and consider the following: Perhaps, after having been away from home for a time, you have returned to find yourself alienated from your family or friends. Describe your experience. What caused the change? How does this experience affect your understanding of Krebs? Alternately, if alienation hasn't been your experience, how does that difference affect your reading of Krebs?

CONNECTION TO ANOTHER SELECTION

1. How might Krebs's rejection of his community's values be related to Sammy's relationship to his supermarket job in John Updike's "A & P" (p. 138)? What details does Updike use to make the setting in "A & P" a comic, though nonetheless serious, version of Krebs's hometown?

Perspective

ERNEST HEMINGWAY (1899–1961)

On What Every Writer Needs   1954

The most essential gift for a good writer is a built-in, shock-proof, shit detector. This is the writer's radar and all great writers have had it.

From *Writers at Work: The Paris Review Interviews* (Second Series)

CONSIDERATIONS FOR CRITICAL THINKING AND WRITING

1. Hemingway is typically forthright here, but it is tempting to dismiss his point as simply humorous. Take him seriously. What does he insist a good writer must be able to do?

2. How might Krebs in Hemingway's "Soldier's Home" (p. 104) be seen as having a similar kind of "shit detector" and "radar"?

3. Try writing a pithy, quotable statement that makes an observation about reading or writing.

Ursula K. Le Guin (1929–2018)

Ursula K. Le Guin is most strongly associated with the genres of fantasy and science fiction, though she resisted such labels. The daughter of an anthropologist and a writer, Le Guin combined those sensibilities in her work, which constructs fabulous landscapes to address social interactions familiar to late twentieth- and early twenty-first-century Americans, such as the challenges of cultural contact, environmental destruction, and feminist activism. A prolific writer, she is perhaps best remembered for her Earthsea fantasy novels (1968–2001) and for her Hainish series of science fiction

Beth Gwinn/Michael Ochs Archives/ Getty Images.

works (1966–2000). The following story, "The Ones Who Walk Away from Omelas," is a good starting point into the rest of Le Guin's work in terms of her themes and style.

The Ones Who Walk Away from Omelas   1973

(Variations on a theme by William James)

With a clamor of bells that set the swallows soaring, the Festival of Summer came to the city Omelas, bright-towered by the sea. The rigging of the boats in harbor sparkled with flags. In the streets between houses with red roofs and painted walls, between old moss-grown gardens and under avenues of trees, past great parks and public buildings, processions moved. Some were decorous: old people in long stiff robes of mauve and grey, grave master workmen, quiet, merry women carrying their babies and chatting as they walked. In other streets the music beat faster, a shimmering of gong and tambourine, and the people went dancing, the procession was a dance. Children dodged in and out, their high calls rising like the swallows' crossing flights over the music and the singing. All the processions wound towards the north side of the city, where on the great water-meadow called the Green Fields boys and girls, naked in the bright air, with mud-stained feet and ankles and long, lithe arms, exercised their restive horses before the race. The horses wore no gear at all but a halter without bit. Their manes were braided with streamers of silver, gold, and green. They flared their nostrils and pranced and boasted to one another; they were vastly excited, the horse being the only animal who has adopted our ceremonies as his own. Far off to the north and west the mountains stood up half encircling Omelas on her bay. The air of morning was so clear that the snow still crowning the Eighteen Peaks burned with white-gold fire across the miles of sunlit air, under the dark blue of the sky. There was just enough wind to make the banners that marked the racecourse snap and flutter now and then. In the silence of the broad green meadows one could hear the music winding through the city streets, farther and nearer and ever approaching, a cheerful faint sweetness of the air that from time to time trembled and gathered together and broke out into the great joyous clanging of the bells.

Joyous! How is one to tell about joy? How describe the citizens of Omelas?

They were not simple folk, you see, though they were happy. But we do not say the words of cheer much any more. All smiles have become archaic. Given a description such as this one tends to make certain assumptions. Given a description such as this one tends to look next for the King, mounted on a splendid stallion and surrounded by his noble knights, or perhaps in a golden litter borne by a great-muscled slave. But there was no king. They did not use swords, or keep slaves. They were not barbarians. I do not know the rules and laws of their society, but I suspect that they were singularly few. As they did without monarchy and slavery, so they also got on without the stock exchange, the advertisement, the secret police, and the bomb. Yet I repeat that these were not simple folk, not dulcet shepherds, noble savages, bland utopians. They were not less complex than us. The trouble is that we have a bad habit, encouraged by pedants and sophisticates, of considering happiness as something rather stupid. Only pain is intellectual, only evil interesting. This is the treason of the artist: a refusal to admit the banality of evil and the terrible boredom of pain. If you can't lick 'em, join 'em. If it hurts, repeat it. But to praise despair is to condemn delight, to embrace violence is to lose hold of everything else. We have almost lost hold; we can no longer describe a happy man, nor make any celebration of joy. How can I tell you about the people of Omelas? They were not naïve and happy children — though their children were, in fact, happy. They were mature, intelligent, passionate adults whose lives were not wretched. O miracle! but I wish I could describe it better. I wish I could convince you. Omelas sounds in my words like a city in a fairy tale, long ago and far away, once upon a time. Perhaps it would be best if you imagined it as your own fancy bids, assuming it will rise to the occasion, for certainly I cannot suit you all. For instance, how about technology? I think that there would be no cars or helicopters in and above the streets; this follows from the fact that the people of Omelas are happy people. Happiness is based on a just discrimination of what is necessary, what is neither necessary nor destructive, and what is destructive. In the middle category, however — that of the unnecessary but undestructive, that of comfort, luxury, exuberance, etc. — they could perfectly well have central heating, subway trains, washing machines, and all kinds of marvelous devices not yet invented here, floating light-sources, fuelless power, a cure for the common cold. Or they could have none of that: it doesn't matter. As you like it. I incline to think that people from towns up and down the coast have been coming in to Omelas during the last days before the Festival on very fast little trains and double-decked trams, and that the train station of Omelas is actually the handsomest building in town, though plainer than the magnificent Farmers' Market. But even granted trains, I fear that Omelas so far strikes some of you as goody-goody. Smiles, bells, parades, horses, bleh. If so, please add an orgy. If an orgy would help, don't hesitate. Let us not, however, have temples from which issue beautiful nude priests and priestesses already half in ecstasy and ready to copulate with any man or woman, lover or stranger, who desires union with the deep godhead of the blood, although that was my first idea. But really it would be better not to have temples in Omelas — at least, not manned temples. Religion yes, clergy no. Surely the beautiful nudes can just wander about, offering themselves like divine soufflés to the hunger of the needy and the rapture of the flesh. Let them join the processions. Let tambourines be struck above the copulations, and the glory of desire be proclaimed upon the gongs, and (a not unimportant point) let the offspring of these delightful rituals be beloved and looked after by all. One thing I know there is none of in Omelas is guilt. But what else should there be? I thought at first there were no drugs, but that is puritanical. For those who like it, the faint insistent sweetness of *drooz* may perfume the ways of the city, *drooz* which first brings a great lightness and brilliance to the mind and limbs, and then after some hours a dreamy langour, and wonderful visions at last of the very arcana and inmost secrets of the Universe, as well as exciting the pleasure of sex beyond all belief; and it is not habit-forming. For more modest tastes I think there ought to be beer. What else, what else belongs in the joyous city? The sense of victory, surely, the celebration of courage. But as we did without clergy, let us do without soldiers. The joy built upon successful slaughter is not the right kind of joy; it will not do; it is fearful and it is trivial. A boundless and generous contentment, a magnanimous triumph felt not against some outer enemy but in communion with the finest and fairest in the souls of all men everywhere and the splendor of the world's summer: this is what swells the hearts of the people of Omelas, and the victory they celebrate is that of life. I really don't think many of them need to take *drooz*.

Most of the processions have reached the Green Fields by now. A marvelous smell of cooking goes forth from the red and blue tents of the provisioners. The faces of small children are amiably sticky; in the benign grey beard of a man a couple of crumbs of rich pastry are entangled. The youths and girls have mounted their horses and are beginning to group around the starting line of the course. An old woman, small, fat, and laughing, is passing out flowers from a basket, and tall young men wear her flowers in their shining hair. A child of nine or ten sits at the edge of the crowd, alone, playing on a wooden flute. People pause to listen, and they smile, but they do not speak to him, for he never ceases playing and never sees them, his dark eyes wholly rapt in the sweet, thin magic of the tune.

He finishes, and slowly lowers his hands holding the wooden flute. 5

As if that little private silence were the signal, all at once a trumpet sounds from the pavilion near the starting line: imperious, melancholy, piercing. The horses rear on their slender legs, and some of them neigh in answer. Sober-faced, the young riders stroke the horses' necks and soothe them, whispering, "Quiet, quiet, there my beauty, my hope. . . ." They begin to form in rank along the starting line. The crowds along the racecourse are like a field of grass and flowers in the wind. The Festival of Summer has begun.

Do you believe? Do you accept the festival, the city, the joy? No? Then let me describe one more thing.

In a basement under one of the beautiful public buildings of Omelas, or perhaps in the cellar of one of its spacious private homes, there is a room. It has one locked door, and no window. A little light seeps in dustily between cracks in the boards, secondhand from a cobwebbed window somewhere across the cellar. In one corner of the little room a couple of mops, with stiff, clotted, foul-smelling heads, stand near a rusty bucket. The floor is dirt, a little damp to the touch, as cellar dirt usually is. The room is about three paces long and two wide: a mere broom closet or disused tool room. In the room a child is sitting. It could be a boy or a girl. It looks about six, but actually is nearly ten. It is feebleminded. Perhaps it was born defective, or perhaps it has become imbecile through fear, malnutrition, and neglect. It picks its nose and occasionally fumbles vaguely with its toes or genitals, as it sits hunched in the corner farthest from the bucket and the two mops. It is afraid of the mops. It finds them horrible. It shuts its eyes, but it knows the mops are still standing there; and the door is locked; and nobody will come. The door is always locked; and nobody ever comes, except that sometimes — the child has no understanding of time or interval — sometimes the door rattles terribly and opens, and a person, or several people, are there. One of them may come in and kick the child to make it stand up. The others never come close, but peer in at it with frightened, disgusted eyes. The food bowl and the water jug are hastily filled, the door is locked, the eyes disappear. The people at the door never say anything, but the child, who has not always lived in the tool room, and can remember sunlight and its mother's voice, sometimes speaks. "I will be good," it says. "Please let me out. I will be good!" They never answer. The child used to scream for help at night, and cry a good deal, but now it only makes a kind of whining, "eh-haa, eh-haa," and it speaks less and less often: It is so thin there are no calves to its legs; its belly protrudes; it lives on a half-bowl of corn meal and grease a day. It is naked. Its buttocks and thighs are a mass of festered sores, as it sits in its own excrement continually.

They all know it is there, all the people of Omelas. Some of them have come to see it, others are content merely to know it is there. They all know that it has to be there. Some of them understand why, and some do not, but they all understand that their happiness, the beauty of their city, the tenderness of their friendships, the health of their children, the wisdom of their scholars, the skill of their makers, even the abundance of their harvest and the kindly weathers of their skies, depend wholly on this child's abominable misery.

This is usually explained to children when they are between eight and twelve, whenever they seem capable of understanding; and most of those who come to see the child are young people, though often enough an adult comes, or comes back, to see the child. No matter how well the matter has been explained to them, these young spectators are always shocked and sickened at the sight. They feel disgust, which they had thought themselves superior to. They feel anger, outrage, impotence, despite all the explanations. They would like to do something for the child. But there is nothing they can do. If the child were brought up into the sunlight out of that vile place, if it were cleaned and fed and comforted, that would be a good thing, indeed; but if it were done, in that day and hour all the prosperity and beauty and delight of Omelas would wither and be destroyed. Those are the terms. To exchange all the goodness and grace of every life in Omelas for that single, small improvement: to throw away the happiness of thousands for the chance of the happiness of one: that would be to let guilt within the walls indeed.

The terms are strict and absolute; there may not even be a kind word spoken to the child.

Often the young people go home in tears, or in a tearless rage, when they have seen the child and faced this terrible paradox. They may brood over it for weeks or years. But as time goes on they begin to realize that even if the child could be released, it would not get much good of its freedom: a little vague pleasure of warmth and food, no doubt, but little more. It is too degraded and imbecile to know any real joy. It has been afraid too long ever to be free of fear. Its habits are too uncouth for it to respond to humane treatment. Indeed, after so long it would probably be wretched without walls about it to protect it, and darkness for its eyes, and its own excrement to sit in. Their tears at the bitter injustice dry when they begin to perceive the terrible justice of reality, and to accept it. Yet it is their tears and anger, the trying of their generosity and the acceptance of their helplessness, which are perhaps the true source of the splendor of their lives. Theirs is no vapid, irresponsible happiness. They know that they, like the child, are not free. They know compassion. It is the existence of the child, and their knowledge of its existence, that makes possible the nobility of their architecture, the poignancy of their music, the profundity of their science. It is because of the child that they are so gentle with children. They know that if the wretched one were not there snivelling in the dark, the other one, the flute-player, could make no joyful music as the young riders line up in their beauty for the race in the sunlight of the first morning of summer.

Now do you believe in them? Are they not more credible? But there is one more thing to tell, and this is quite incredible.

At times one of the adolescent girls or boys who go to see the child does not go home to weep or rage, does not, in fact, go home at all. Sometimes also a man or woman much older falls silent for a day or two, and then leaves home. These people go out into the street, and walk down the street alone. They keep walking, and walk straight out of the city of Omelas, through the beautiful gates. They keep walking across the farmlands of Omelas. Each one goes alone, youth or girl, man or woman. Night falls; the traveler must pass down village streets, between the houses with yellow-lit windows, and on out into the darkness of the fields. Each alone, they go west or north, towards the mountains. They go on. They leave Omelas, they walk ahead into the darkness, and they do not come back. The place they go towards is a place even less imaginable to most of us than the city of happiness. I cannot describe it at all. It is possible that it does not exist. But they seem to know where they are going, the ones who walk away from Omelas.

CONSIDERATIONS FOR CRITICAL THINKING AND WRITING

1. **FIRST RESPONSE.** In paragraph 1 the narrator describes Omelas in very familiar, fairy tale–like terms, but in the third paragraph she alters her description to counter some of our expectations, and even criticizes her own powers of description: "Omelas sounds in my words like a city in a fairy tale, long ago and far away, once upon a time." What is the effect of the initial description followed by the later correction?

2. Note all of the adjectives in the story's first paragraph. Which are the most significant and what is their overall effect in terms of enabling you to "see" Omelas?

3. Toward the end of paragraph three the narrator invites the reader to help create the world. Orgies and drugs are permissible, but clergy and soldiers are not. Do these qualifications to the initial description — which is quite vivid and definite — make the picture of Omelas clearer or fuzzier?

4. The story discusses joy and happiness at length. How are those concepts related to Omelas as a setting?

5. The setting is not only the city of Omelas in general, but the Festival of Summer in particular. How does a momentous occasion associated with a particular place affect your sense of setting? (Consider, for instance, Mardi Gras in New Orleans or New Year's Eve in New York's Times Square.)

6. What is the effect on you as a reader when the narrator asks you if you believe her description, and even voices your scepticism for you? ("Do you believe? . . . No?")

7. Compare the details of the description of the cellar room where the child is locked to the descriptions of the public spaces in Omelas. Are they parallel? Is one easier to picture than the other? Why?

8. How would the story be changed if Le Guin had described the cellar room with the abused child first and the descriptions of the Festival of Summer second?

9 The narrator abandons the description of the Festival of Summer at a crucial moment, just as it is about to begin, with horses lining up and crowds gathering around them. Why does the narrator not return to this scene after introducing the miserable child in the cellar?

10. The descriptions of both Omelas and the cellar room are fairly detailed, and they appeal to multiple senses. Given the narrator's powers of description, why is it significant when her powers of description abandon her with regard to the place where the exiles are going: "I cannot describe it at all"?

CONNECTIONS TO OTHER SELECTIONS

1. Consider the importance of ritual and the relationship between an individual and a community in this story and in Shirley Jackson's "The Lottery" (p. 188).

2. Discuss attitudes toward wealth/luxury/indulgence and suffering/poverty/sacrifice in this story and in "Famine" by Xu Xi (p. 65).

CHARLOTTE PERKINS GILMAN (1860–1935)

At the intersection of a number of reform movements in the late nineteenth century, Charlotte Perkins Gilman was an activist and lecturer as well as a professional writer of poems, essays, and fiction. Suffering from what we now understand to be postpartum depression after the birth of her daughter, Gilman was prescribed a "rest cure" by one Dr. Silas Weir Mitchell. It involved nearly complete isolation and a severe reduction in intellectual and creative activities, and, of course, it worsened her symptoms rather than curing them. This misguided "treatment" provided the basis for what is by far Gilman's most renowned work, "The Yellow Wallpaper."

Everett Collection Inc/Alamy Stock Photo.

The Yellow Wallpaper 1892

It is very seldom that mere ordinary people like John and myself secure ancestral halls for the summer.

A colonial mansion, a hereditary estate, I would say a haunted house, and reach the height of romantic felicity — but that would be asking too much of fate!

Still I will proudly declare that there is something queer about it.

Else, why should it be let so cheaply? And why have stood so long untenanted?

John laughs at me, of course, but one expects that in marriage.   5

John is practical in the extreme. He has no patience with faith, an intense horror of superstition, and he scoffs openly at any talk of things not to be felt and seen and put down in figures.

John is a physician, and *perhaps* — (I would not say it to a living soul, of course, but this is dead paper and a great relief to my mind) — *perhaps* that is one reason I do not get well faster.

You see he does not believe I am sick!

And what can one do?

If a physician of high standing, and one's own husband, assures friends   10
and relatives that there is really nothing the matter with one but temporary nervous depression — a slight hysterical tendency° — what is one to do?

My brother is also a physician, and also of high standing, and he says the same thing.

So I take phosphates or phosphites° — whichever it is, and tonics, and journeys, and air, and exercise, and am absolutely forbidden to "work" until I am well again.

Personally, I disagree with their ideas.

Personally, I believe that congenial work, with excitement and change, would do me good.   15

But what is one to do?

I did write for a while in spite of them; but it *does* exhaust me a good deal — having to be so sly about it, or else meet with heavy opposition.

I sometimes fancy that in my condition if I had less opposition and more society and stimulus — but John says the very worst thing I can do is to think about my condition, and I confess it always makes me feel bad.

So I will let it alone and talk about the house.

The most beautiful place! It is quite alone, standing well back from the road, quite three miles from the village. It makes me think of English places that you read about, for there are hedges and walls and gates that lock, and lots of separate little houses for the gardeners and people.

There is a *delicious* garden! I never saw such a garden — large and   20
shady, full of box-bordered paths, and lined with long grape-covered arbors with seats under them.

There were greenhouses, too, but they are all broken now.

There was some legal trouble, I believe, something about the heirs and co-heirs; anyhow, the place has been empty for years.

hysterical tendency: In the nineteenth century, women's illnesses of all sorts were gener-ally characterized as "hysteria," although the symptoms might range from pain to anxiety, fatigue to depression. These symptoms were presumed to have a somatic origin.
phosphates or phosphites: Any salt or ester of phosphoric acid, used during the nineteenth century to cure exhaustion of the nerve centers, neuralgia, mania, melancholia, and often sexual exhaustion.

That spoils my ghostliness, I am afraid, but I don't care — there is something strange about the house — I can feel it.

I even said so to John one moonlight evening, but he said what I felt was a *draught,* and shut the window.

I get unreasonably angry with John sometimes. I'm sure I never used to be so sensitive. I think it is due to this nervous condition.

But John says if I feel so, I shall neglect proper self-control; so I take pains to control myself — before him, at least, and that makes me very tired.

I don't like our room a bit. I wanted one downstairs that opened on the piazza and had roses all over the window, and such pretty old-fashioned chintz hangings! but John would not hear of it.

He said there was only one window and not room for two beds, and no near room for him if he took another.

He is very careful and loving, and hardly lets me stir without special direction.

I have a schedule prescription for each hour in the day; he takes all care from me, and so I feel basely ungrateful not to value it more.

He said we came here solely on my account, that I was to have perfect rest and all the air I could get. "Your exercise depends on your strength, my dear," said he, "and your food somewhat on your appetite; but air you can absorb all the time." So we took the nursery at the top of the house.

It is a big, airy room, the whole floor nearly, with windows that look all ways, and air and sunshine galore. It was nursery first and then playroom and gymnasium, I should judge; for the windows are barred for little children, and there are rings and things in the walls.

The paint and paper look as if a boys' school had used it. It is stripped off — the paper — in great patches all around the head of my bed, about as far as I can reach, and in a great place on the other side of the room low down. I never saw a worse paper in my life.

One of those sprawling flamboyant patterns committing every artistic sin.

It is dull enough to confuse the eye in following, pronounced enough to constantly irritate and provoke study, and when you follow the lame uncertain curves for a little distance they suddenly commit suicide — plunge off at outrageous angles, destroy themselves in unheard of contradictions.

The color is repellant, almost revolting; a smouldering unclean yellow, strangely faded by the slow-turning sunlight.

It is a dull yet lurid orange in some places, a sickly sulphur tint in others.

No wonder the children hated it! I should hate it myself if I had to live in this room long.

There comes John, and I must put this away, — he hates to have me write a word.

We have been here two weeks, and I haven't felt like writing before, since that first day.

I am sitting by the window now, up in this atrocious nursery, and there is nothing to hinder my writing as much as I please, save lack of strength.

John is away all day, and even some nights when his cases are serious.

I am glad my case is not serious!

But these nervous troubles are dreadfully depressing.

John does not know how much I really suffer. He knows there is no 45 *reason* to suffer, and that satisfies him.

Of course it is only nervousness. It does weigh on me so not to do my duty in any way!

I meant to be such a help to John, such a real rest and comfort, and here I am a comparative burden already!

Nobody would believe what an effort it is to do what little I am able, — to dress and entertain, and order things.

It is fortunate Mary is so good with the baby. Such a dear baby!

And yet I *cannot* be with him, it makes me so nervous. 50

I suppose John never was nervous in his life. He laughs at me so about this wall-paper!

At first he meant to repaper the room, but afterwards he said that I was letting it get the better of me, and that nothing was worse for a nervous patient than to give way to such fancies.

He said that after the wall-paper was changed it would be the heavy bedstead, and then the barred windows, and then that gate at the head of the stairs, and so on.

"You know the place is doing you good," he said, "and really, dear, I don't care to renovate the house just for a three months' rental."

"Then do let us go downstairs," I said, "there are such pretty rooms there." 55

Then he took me in his arms and called me a blessed little goose, and said he would go down cellar, if I wished, and have it whitewashed into the bargain.

But he is right enough about the beds and windows and things.

It is an airy and comfortable room as any one need wish, and, of course, I would not be so silly as to make him uncomfortable just for a whim.

I'm really getting quite fond of the big room, all but that horrid paper.

Out of one window I can see the garden, those mysterious deep-shaded 60 arbors, the riotous old-fashioned flowers, and bushes and gnarly trees.

Out of another I get a lovely view of the bay and a little private wharf belonging to the estate. There is a beautiful shaded lane that runs down there from the house. I always fancy I see people walking in these numerous paths and arbors, but John has cautioned me not to give way to fancy in the least. He says that with my imaginative power and habit of story-making, a nervous weakness like mine is sure to lead to all manner of excited fancies, and that I ought to use my will and good sense to check the tendency. So I try.

I think sometimes that if I were only well enough to write a little it would relieve the press of ideas and rest me.

But I find I get pretty tired when I try.

It is so discouraging not to have any advice and companionship about my work. When I get really well, John says we will ask Cousin Henry and

Julia down for a long visit; but he says he would as soon put fireworks in my pillow-case as to let me have those stimulating people about now.

I wish I could get well faster.

But I must not think about that. This paper looks to me as if it *knew* what a vicious influence it had!

There is a recurrent spot where the pattern lolls like a broken neck and two bulbous eyes stare at you upside down.

I get positively angry with the impertinence of it and the everlastingness. Up and down and sideways they crawl, and those absurd, unblinking eyes are everywhere. There is one place where two breadths didn't match, and the eyes go all up and down the line, one a little higher than the other.

I never saw so much expression in an inanimate thing before, and we all know how much expression they have! I used to lie awake as a child and get more entertainment and terror out of blank walls and plain furniture than most children could find in a toy-store.

I remember what a kindly wink the knobs of our big, old bureau used to have, and there was one chair that always seemed like a strong friend.

I used to feel that if any of the other things looked too fierce I could always hop into that chair and be safe.

The furniture in this room is no worse than inharmonious, however, for we had to bring it all from downstairs. I suppose when this was used as a playroom they had to take the nursery things out, and no wonder! I never saw such ravages as the children have made here.

The wall-paper, as I said before, is torn off in spots, and it sticketh closer than a brother — they must have had perseverance as well as hatred.

Then the floor is scratched and gouged and splintered, the plaster itself is dug out here and there, and this great heavy bed which is all we found in the room, looks as if it had been through the wars.

But I don't mind it a bit — only the paper.

There comes John's sister. Such a dear girl as she is, and so careful of me! I must not let her find me writing.

She is a perfect and enthusiastic housekeeper, and hopes for no better profession. I verily believe she thinks it is the writing which made me sick!

But I can write when she is out, and see her a long way off from these windows.

There is one that commands the road, a lovely shaded winding road, and one that just looks off over the country. A lovely country, too, full of great elms and velvet meadows.

This wallpaper has a kind of sub-pattern in a different shade, a particularly irritating one, for you can only see it in certain lights, and not clearly then.

But in the places where it isn't faded and where the sun is just so — I can see a strange, provoking, formless sort of figure, that seems to skulk about behind that silly and conspicuous front design.

There's sister on the stairs!

———

Well, the Fourth of July is over! The people are all gone and I am tired out. John thought it might do me good to see a little company, so we just had mother and Nellie and the children down for a week.

Of course I didn't do a thing. Jennie sees to everything now.

But it tired me all the same. 85

John says if I don't pick up faster he shall send me to Weir Mitchell° in the fall.

But I don't want to go there at all. I had a friend who was in his hands once, and she says he is just like John and my brother, only more so!

Besides, it is such an undertaking to go so far.

I don't feel as if it was worth while to turn my hand over for anything, and I'm getting dreadfully fretful and querulous.

I cry at nothing, and cry most of the time. 90

Of course I don't when John is here, or anybody else, but when I am alone.

And I am alone a good deal just now. John is kept in town very often by serious cases, and Jennie is good and lets me alone when I want her to.

So I walk a little in the garden or down that lovely lane, sit on the porch under the roses, and lie down up here a good deal.

I'm getting really fond of the room in spite of the wallpaper. Perhaps *because* of the wallpaper.

It dwells in my mind so! 95

I lie here on this great immovable bed — it is nailed down, I believe — and follow that pattern about by the hour. It is as good as gymnastics, I assure you. I start, we'll say, at the bottom, down in the corner over there where it has not been touched, and I determine for the thousandth time that I *will* follow that pointless pattern to some sort of a conclusion.

I know a little of the principle of design, and I know this thing was not arranged on any laws of radiation, or alternation, or repetition, or symmetry, or anything else that I ever heard of.

It is repeated, of course, by the breadths, but not otherwise.

Looked at in one way each breadth stands alone, the bloated curves and flourishes — a kind of "debased Romanesque"° with *delirium tremens* — go waddling up and down in isolated columns of fatuity.

But, on the other hand, they connect diagonally, and the sprawling out- 100 lines run off in great slanting waves of optic horror, like a lot of wallowing seaweeds in full chase.

The whole thing goes horizontally, too, at least it seems so, and I exhaust myself in trying to distinguish the order of its going in that direction.

They have used a horizontal breadth for a frieze,° and that adds wonderfully to the confusion.

S. Weir Mitchell: Mitchell (1829–1914) was a famous Civil War doctor and later novelist, who treated shell shock during and after the Civil War. Later, he developed a "rest cure" for women and men suffering from neurasthenia.
debased Romanesque: European architectural style with elaborate ornamentation and complexity, as well as repeated motifs.
frieze: A decorative band used as a border around a room or mantle.

There is one end of the room where it is almost intact, and there, when the crosslights fade and the low sun shines directly upon it, I can almost fancy radiation after all, — the interminable grotesques seem to form around a common centre and rush off in headlong plunges of equal distraction.

It makes me tired to follow it. I will take a nap I guess.

I don't know why I should write this.

I don't want to.

I don't feel able.

And I know John would think it absurd. But I *must* say what I feel and think in some way — it is such a relief!

But the effort is getting to be greater than the relief.

Half the time now I am awfully lazy, and lie down ever so much.

John says I mustn't lose my strength, and has me take cod liver oil and lots of tonics and things, to say nothing of ale and wine and rare meat.

Dear John! He loves me very dearly, and hates to have me sick. I tried to have a real earnest reasonable talk with him the other day, and tell him how I wish he would let me go and make a visit to Cousin Henry and Julia.

But he said I wasn't able to go, nor able to stand it after I got there; and I did not make out a very good case for myself, for I was crying before I had finished.

It is getting to be a great effort for me to think straight. Just this nervous weakness I suppose.

And dear John gathered me up in his arms, and just carried me upstairs and laid me on the bed, and sat by me and read to me till it tired my head.

He said I was his darling and his comfort and all he had, and that I must take care of myself for his sake, and keep well.

He says no one but myself can help me out of it, that I must use my will and self-control and not let any silly fancies run away with me.

There's one comfort, the baby is well and happy, and does not have to occupy this nursery with the horrid wallpaper.

If we had not used it, that blessed child would have! What a fortunate escape! Why, I wouldn't have a child of mine, an impressionable little thing, live in such a room for worlds.

I never thought of it before, but it is lucky that John kept me here after all, I can stand it so much easier than a baby, you see.

Of course I never mention it to them any more — I am too wise, — but I keep watch of it all the same.

There are things in that paper that nobody knows but me, or ever will.

Behind that outside pattern the dim shapes get clearer every day.

It is always the same shape, only very numerous.

And it is like a woman stooping down and creeping about behind that pattern. I don't like it a bit. I wonder — I begin to think — I wish John would take me away from here!

It is so hard to talk to John about my case, because he is so wise, and because he loves me so.

But I tried it last night.

It was moonlight. The moon shines in all around just as the sun does.

I hate to see it sometimes, it creeps so slowly, and always comes in by one window or another.

John was asleep and I hated to waken him, so I kept still and watched ¹³⁰ the moonlight on that undulating wallpaper till I felt creepy.

The faint figure behind seemed to shake the pattern, just as if she wanted to get out.

I got up softly and went to feel and see if the paper *did* move, and when I came back John was awake.

"What is it, little girl?" he said. "Don't go walking about like that — you'll get cold."

I thought it was a good time to talk, so I told him that I really was not gaining here, and that I wished he would take me away.

"Why, darling!" said he, "our lease will be up in three weeks, and I can't ¹³⁵ see how to leave before.

"The repairs are not done at home, and I cannot possibly leave town just now. Of course if you were in any danger, I could and would, but you really are better, dear, whether you can see it or not. I am a doctor, dear, and I know. You are gaining flesh and color, your appetite is better, I feel really much easier about you."

"I don't weigh a bit more," said I, "nor as much; and my appetite may be better in the evening when you are here, but it is worse in the morning when you are away!"

"Bless her little heart!" said he with a big hug, "she shall be as sick as she pleases! But now let's improve the shining hours° by going to sleep, and talk about it in the morning!"

"And you won't go away?" I asked gloomily.

"Why, how can I, dear? It is only three weeks more and then we will ¹⁴⁰ take a nice little trip of a few days while Jennie is getting the house ready. Really dear you are better!"

"Better in body perhaps —" I began, and stopped short, for he sat up straight and looked at me with such a stern, reproachful look that I could not say another word.

"My darling," said he, "I beg of you, for my sake and for our child's sake, as well as for your own, that you will never for one instant let that idea enter your mind! There is nothing so dangerous, so fascinating, to a temperament like yours. It is a false and foolish fancy. Can you not trust me as a physician when I tell you so?"

---

improve the shining hours: These lines are adapted from "Song XX" by English hymnist Isaac Watts (1674–1748): "How doth the little busy bee / Improve each shining hour, / And gather honey all the day / From every opening flower!"

So of course I said no more on that score, and we went to sleep before long. He thought I was asleep first, but I wasn't, and lay there for hours trying to decide whether that front pattern and the back pattern really did move together or separately.

———

On a pattern like this, by daylight, there is a lack of sequence, a defiance of law, that is a constant irritant to a normal mind.

The color is hideous enough, and unreliable enough, and infuriating enough, but the pattern is torturing.

You think you have mastered it, but just as you get well underway in following, it turns a back-somersault and there you are. It slaps you in the face, knocks you down, and tramples upon you. It is like a bad dream.

The outside pattern is a florid arabesque, reminding one of a fungus. If you can imagine a toadstool in joints, an interminable string of toadstools, budding and sprouting in endless convolutions — why, that is something like it.

That is, sometimes!

There is one marked peculiarity about this paper, a thing nobody seems to notice but myself, and that is that it changes as the light changes.

When the sun shoots in through the east window — I always watch for that first long, straight ray — it changes so quickly that I never can quite believe it.

That is why I watch it always.

By moonlight — the moon shines in all night when there is a moon — I wouldn't know it was the same paper.

At night in any kind of light, in twilight, candlelight, lamplight, and worst of all by moonlight, it becomes bars! The outside pattern I mean, and the woman behind it is as plain as can be.

I didn't realize for a long time what the thing was that showed behind, that dim sub-pattern, but now I am quite sure it is a woman.

By daylight she is subdued, quiet. I fancy it is the pattern that keeps her so still. It is so puzzling. It keeps me quiet by the hour.

I lie down ever so much now. John says it is good for me, and to sleep all I can.

Indeed he started the habit by making me lie down for an hour after each meal.

It is a very bad habit I am convinced, for you see I don't sleep.

And that cultivates deceit, for I don't tell them I'm awake — O no!

The fact is I am getting a little afraid of John.

He seems very queer sometimes, and even Jennie has an inexplicable look.

It strikes me occasionally, just as a scientific hypothesis, — that perhaps it is the paper!

I have watched John when he did not know I was looking, and come into the room suddenly on the most innocent excuses, and I've caught him several times *looking at the paper!* And Jennie too. I caught Jennie with her hand on it once.

She didn't know I was in the room, and when I asked her in a quiet, a very quiet voice, with the most restrained manner possible, what she was doing with the paper — she turned around as if she had been caught stealing, and looked quite angry — asked me why I should frighten her so!

Then she said that the paper stained everything it touched, that she had found yellow smooches on all my clothes and John's, and she wished we would be more careful! 165

Did not that sound innocent? But I know she was studying that pattern, and I am determined that nobody shall find it out but myself!

———

Life is very much more exciting now than it used to be. You see I have something more to expect, to look forward to, to watch. I really do eat better, and am more quiet than I was.

John is so pleased to see me improve! He laughed a little the other day, and said I seemed to be flourishing in spite of my wall-paper.

I turned it off with a laugh. I had no intention of telling him it was *because* of the wall-paper — he would make fun of me. He might even want to take me away.

I don't want to leave now until I have found it out. There is a week 170 more, and I think that will be enough.

———

I'm feeling ever so much better! I don't sleep much at night, for it is so interesting to watch developments; but I sleep a good deal in the daytime.

In the daytime it is tiresome and perplexing.

There are always new shoots on the fungus, and new shades of yellow all over it. I cannot keep count of them, though I have tried conscientiously.

It is the strangest yellow, that wall-paper! It makes me think of all the yellow things I ever saw — not beautiful ones like buttercups, but old foul, bad yellow things.

But there is something else about that paper — the smell! I noticed it 175 the moment we came into the room, but with so much air and sun it was not bad. Now we have had a week of fog and rain, and whether the windows are open or not, the smell is here.

It creeps all over the house.

I find it hovering in the dining-room, skulking in the parlor, hiding in the hall, lying in wait for me on the stairs.

It gets into my hair.

Even when I go to ride, if I turn my head suddenly and surprise it — there is that smell!

Such a peculiar odor, too! I have spent hours in trying to analyze it, to 180 find what it smelled like.

It is not bad — at first, and very gentle, but quite the subtlest, most enduring odor I ever met.

In this damp weather it is awful, I wake up in the night and find it hanging over me.

It used to disturb me at first. I thought seriously of burning the house — to reach the smell.

But now I am used to it. The only thing I can think of that it is like is the *color* of the paper! A yellow smell.

There is a very funny mark on this wall, low down, near the mop-board. A streak that runs round the room. It goes behind every piece of furniture, except the bed, a long, straight, even *smooch*, as if it had been rubbed over and over.

I wonder how it was done and who did it, and what they did it for. Round and round and round — round and round and round — it makes me dizzy!

———

I really have discovered something at last.

Through watching so much at night, when it changes so, I have finally found out.

The front pattern *does* move — and no wonder! The woman behind shakes it!

Sometimes I think there are a great many women behind, and sometimes only one, and she crawls around fast, and her crawling shakes it all over.

Then in the very bright spots she keeps still, and in the very shady spots she just takes hold of the bars and shakes them hard.

And she is all the time trying to climb through. But nobody could climb through that pattern — it strangles so; I think that is why it has so many heads.

They get through, and then the pattern strangles them off and turns them upside down, and makes their eyes white!

If those heads were covered or taken off it would not be half so bad.

———

I think that woman gets out in the daytime!

And I'll tell you why — privately — I've seen her!

I can see her out of every one of my windows!

It is the same woman, I know, for she is always creeping, and most women do not creep by daylight.

I see her in that long shaded lane, creeping up and down. I see her in those dark grape arbors, creeping all around the garden.

I see her on that long road under the trees, creeping along, and when a carriage comes she hides under the blackberry vines.

I don't blame her a bit. It must be very humiliating to be caught creeping by daylight!

I always lock the door when I creep by daylight. I can't do it at night, for I know John would suspect something at once.

And John is so queer now, that I don't want to irritate him. I wish he would take another room! Besides, I don't want anybody to get that woman out at night but myself.

I often wonder if I could see her out of all the windows at once.

But, turn as fast as I can, I can only see out of one at one time.

And though I always see her, she *may* be able to creep faster than I can turn!

I have watched her sometimes away off in the open country, creeping as fast as a cloud shadow in a high wind.

———

If only that top pattern could be gotten off from the under one! I mean to try it, little by little.

I have found out another funny thing, but I shan't tell it this time! It does not do to trust people too much.

There are only two more days to get this paper off, and I believe John is 210 beginning to notice. I don't like the look in his eyes.

And I heard him ask Jennie a lot of professional questions about me. She had a very good report to give.

She said I slept a good deal in the daytime.

John knows I don't sleep very well at night, for all I'm so quiet!

He asked me all sorts of questions, too, and pretended to be very loving and kind.

As if I couldn't see through him! 215

Still, I don't wonder he acts so, sleeping under this paper for three months.

It only interests me, but I feel sure John and Jennie are secretly affected by it.

———

Hurrah! This is the last day, but it is enough. John to stay in town over night, and won't be out until this evening.

Jennie wanted to sleep with me — the sly thing! But I told her I should undoubtedly rest better for a night all alone.

That was clever, for really I wasn't alone a bit! As soon as it was moon- 220 light and that poor thing began to crawl and shake the pattern, I got up and ran to help her.

I pulled and she shook, I shook and she pulled, and before morning we had peeled off yards of that paper.

A strip about as high as my head and half around the room.

And then when the sun came and that awful pattern began to laugh at me, I declared I would finish it to-day!

We go away to-morrow, and they are moving all my furniture down again to leave things as they were before.

Jennie looked at the wall in amazement, but I told her merrily that I did 225 it out of pure spite at the vicious thing.

She laughed and said she wouldn't mind doing it herself, but I must not get tired.

How she betrayed herself that time!

But I am here, and no person touches this paper but me, — not *alive!*

She tried to get me out of the room — it was too patent! But I said it was so quiet and empty and clean now that I believed I would lie down again and sleep all I could; and not to wake me even for dinner — I would call when I woke.

So now she is gone, and the servants are gone, and the things are gone, and there is nothing left but that great bedstead nailed down, with the canvas mattress we found on it.

We shall sleep downstairs to-night, and take the boat home tomorrow.

I quite enjoy the room, now it is bare again.

How those children did tear about here!

This bedstead is fairly gnawed!

But I must get to work.

I have locked the door and thrown the key down into the front path.

I don't want to go out, and I don't want to have anybody come in, till John comes.

I want to astonish him.

I've got a rope up here that even Jennie did not find. If that woman does get out, and tries to get away, I can tie her!

But I forgot I could not reach far without anything to stand on!

This bed will *not* move!

I tried to lift and push it until I was lame, and then I got so angry I bit off a little piece at one corner — but it hurt my teeth.

Then I peeled off all the paper I could reach standing on the floor. It sticks horribly and the pattern just enjoys it! All those strangled heads and bulbous eyes and waddling fungus growths just shriek with derision!

I am getting angry enough to do something desperate. To jump out of the window would be admirable exercise, but the bars are too strong even to try.

Besides I wouldn't do it. Of course not. I know well enough that a step like that is improper and might be misconstrued.

I don't like to *look* out of the windows even — there are so many of those creeping women, and they creep so fast.

I wonder if they all come out of that wall-paper as I did?

But I am securely fastened now by my well-hidden rope — you don't get *me* out in the road there!

I suppose I shall have to get back behind the pattern when it comes night, and that is hard!

It is so pleasant to be out in this great room and creep around as I please!

I don't want to go outside. I won't, even if Jennie asks me to.

For outside you have to creep on the ground, and everything is green instead of yellow.

But here I can creep smoothly on the floor, and my shoulder just fits in that long smooch around the wall, so I cannot lose my way.

Why there's John at the door!

It is no use, young man, you can't open it!

How he does call and pound!

Now he's crying for an axe.

It would be a shame to break down that beautiful door!

"John dear!" said I in the gentlest voice, "the key is down by the front steps, under a plaintain leaf!"

260

That silenced him for a few moments.

Then he said — very quietly indeed, "Open the door, my darling!"

"I can't," said I. "The key is down by the front door under a plantain leaf!"

And then I said it again, several times, very gently and slowly, and said it so often that he had to go and see, and he got it of course, and came in. He stopped short by the door.

"What is the matter?" he cried. "For God's sake, what are you doing!"

I kept on creeping just the same, but I looked at him over my shoulder. 265

"I've got out at last," said I, "in spite of you and Jane. And I've pulled off most of the paper, so you can't put me back!"

Now why should that man have fainted? But he did, and right across my path by the wall, so that I had to creep over him every time!

CONSIDERATIONS FOR CRITICAL THINKING AND WRITING

1. **FIRST RESPONSE.** How would you describe the narrator based on her voice? Do the paragraphs — which are often notably short — contribute to your impression?

2. The narrator describes the house she inhabits as "the most beautiful place!" Are there elements of the description that initially cause you to question its beauty or do we take her words at face value at that point in the story?

3. Look again at the initial description of the yellow wallpaper (paras. 33–37). How does the description take on new significance after you have completed the story?

4. Aside from the wallpaper, what details does the narrator share about her room that help us to picture it, and what do these details collectively tell us?

5. How is John's character developed through his words and/or through summaries of his words? Would your impression be different, do you imagine, if you encountered him directly rather than through the narrator's writing?

6. The narrator's descriptions of the wallpaper become increasingly fanciful as the story continues. She is clearly equipped to describe it in terms of the principles of design (frieze, arabesque, etc.), but are you ever really able to picture it? If so, which details are the most vivid?

7. Whether or not the yellow wallpaper is visible to you, what feelings do the narrator's descriptions of it evoke?

8. How does John attempt to assert and reinforce his control over the narrator? What words or phrases would you use to describe their relationship?

9. Discuss attitudes toward the imagination in "The Yellow Wallpaper." Is imagination dangerous or liberating? Regardless of your answer, what factors make it so?

10. Jennie is a less central figure in the story than either the narrator or John, but she is mentioned frequently. What makes Jennie important to the story overall?

11. The wallpaper is personified repeatedly. Could it be considered a character in the story or are its human characteristics just the narrator's projections?

12. CRITICAL STRATEGIES. Read the section on feminist criticism (pp. 1079–80) in Chapter 30, "Critical Strategies for Reading." How do you think a feminist critic might interpret the gender dynamics in "The Yellow Wallpaper"?

CONNECTIONS TO OTHER SELECTIONS

1. Compare the way the narrator of "Sonny's Blues" (p. 76) attempts to control his brother to the way John attempts to control the narrator in this story. Are the narrator of "Sonny's Blues" and John similarly motivated? Are their methods of control similar in significant ways?

2. The narrator of ZZ Packer's "Drinking Coffee Elsewhere" (p. 335) and the narrator of this story are both sceptical of the "treatments" they are subjected to. Describe their resistance to these treatments, and discuss the way their resistance helps shape their characterization.

5

Point of View

I think it's important to have faith in your idea — to believe that it's really important, truly worthwhile.
— MAGGIE MITCHELL

Photo courtesy of Jill Sutton.

Because one of the pleasures of reading fiction consists of seeing the world through someone else's eyes, it is easy to overlook the eyes that control our view of the plot, characters, and setting. *Point of view* refers to who tells us the story and how it is told. What we know and how we feel about the events in a story are shaped by the author's choice of a point of view. The teller of a story, the *narrator*, inevitably affects our understanding of the characters' actions by filtering what is told through his or her own perspective. The narrator should not be confused with the author who has created the narrative voice because the two are usually distinct (more on this point later).

If the narrative voice is changed, the story will change. Consider, for example, how different "The Yellow Wallpaper" (p. 117) would be if Gilman had chosen to tell the story from John's point of view. Your opinion of his wife would undoubtedly change. You would see her, to some degree, as John sees her: as a mentally ill woman who will only get better if she sticks to the "rest cure" he has prescribed. Your sympathy for her wretched situation would likely be diminished, and you would probably see John more as a frustrated, dutiful husband than as a condescending oppressor.

The possible ways of telling a story are many, and the point of view can shift within a single story (as you will see in Manuel Muñoz's "Zigzagger," p. 143, later in this chapter). However, the various points of view that storytellers draw on can be conveniently grouped into two broad categories: (1) the third-person narrator and (2) the first-person narrator. The third-person narrator uses *he, she,* or *they* to tell the story and does not participate in the action. The first-person narrator uses *I* and is a major or minor participant in the action. A second-person narrator, *you,* is possible but is rarely used because of the awkwardness in thrusting the reader into the story, as in "You are minding your own business on a park bench when a drunk steps out of the bushes and demands your lunch bag." This technique can even be sustained over the course of a novel, as in Jay McInerney's *Bright Lights, Big City* (1984), but writers generally tend to choose one of the other two points of view. A first-person narrator will sometimes address the reader directly: the most famous example comes from Charlotte Brontë's *Jane Eyre* (1847) when Jane states, simply, "Reader, I married him." In "The Ones Who Walk Away from Omelas" (p. 111), Le Guin's narrator also addresses the reader directly, asking if we find her description of Omelas plausible. These examples of addressing the reader are not the same thing as a second-person narrative: in the second person, "you" is a character, not just a reader.

Let's look now at the most important and most often used variations within first- and third-person narrations.

THIRD-PERSON NARRATOR (Nonparticipant)

1. Omniscient (the narrator takes us inside multiple characters' minds)
2. Limited omniscient (the narrator takes us inside one or two characters' minds)
3. Objective (the narrator is outside the consciousness of all the characters)

No type of third-person narrator appears as a character in a story. The **omniscient narrator** is all-knowing. From this point of view, the narrator can move from place to place and pass back and forth through time, slipping into and out of characters as no human being possibly could in real life. This narrator can report the characters' thoughts and feelings as well as what they say and do. In Nathaniel Hawthorne's "The Minister's Black Veil," the narrator can move deftly into the minds of the minister (Mr. Hooper), his wife, and all the members of his church. When Hooper dies, the narrator proclaims, "awful is still the thought that [his face] moldered beneath the Black Veil!" This kind of intrusion is called **editorial omniscience**. In contrast, narration that allows characters' actions and thoughts to speak for themselves is known as **neutral omniscience**. Most modern writers use neutral omniscience so that readers can reach their own conclusions.

The **limited omniscient narrator** is much more confined than the omniscient narrator. With limited omniscience the author very often restricts the narrator to the single perspective of either a major or a minor character. Sometimes a narrator can see into more than one character, particularly in a longer work that focuses, for example, on two characters alternately from one chapter to the next. Short stories, however, frequently are restricted by length to a single character's point of view. The way people, places, and events appear to that character is the way they appear to the reader. The reader has access to the thoughts and feelings of the characters revealed by the narrator, but neither the reader nor the character has access to the inner lives of any of the other characters in the story. The events in Katherine Mansfield's "Miss Brill" are viewed entirely through the protagonist's eyes; we see a French vacation town as an elderly woman does. Miss Brill represents the central consciousness of the story. She unifies the story by being present through all the action. We are not told of anything that happens away from the character because the narration is based on her perception of things.

In Hemingway's "Soldier's Home" (p. 104), a limited omniscient narrator is the predominant point of view. Krebs's thoughts and reaction to being home from the war are made available to the reader by the narrator, who tells us that Krebs "felt embarrassed and resentful" or "sick and vaguely nauseated" by the small-town life he has reentered. (Phrases like "He thought," "She felt," "She remembered," and so forth should clue you in to the fact that this narrative is filtered through a character's consciousness.) Occasionally, however, Hemingway uses an objective point of view when he dramatizes particularly tense moments between Krebs and his mother. In the following excerpt, Hemingway's narrator shows us Krebs's feelings instead of telling us what they are. Krebs's response to his mother's concerns is presented without comment. The external details of the scene reveal his inner feelings.

> "I've worried about you so much, Harold," his mother went on. "I know the temptations you must have been exposed to. I know how weak men are. I know what your own dear grandfather, my own father, told us about the Civil War and I have prayed for you. I pray for you all day long, Harold."
>
> Krebs looked at the bacon fat hardening on his plate.
>
> "Your father is worried, too," his mother went on. "He thinks you have lost your ambition, that you haven't got a definite aim in life. Charley Simmons, who is just your age, has a good job and is going to be married. The boys are all settling down; they're all determined to get somewhere; you can see that boys like Charley Simmons are on their way to being really a credit to the community."
>
> Krebs said nothing.
>
> "Don't look that way, Harold. . . ."

When Krebs looks at the bacon fat, we can see him cooling and hardening too. Hemingway does not describe the expression on Krebs's face, yet we know it is a look that disturbs his mother as she goes on about what she thinks she knows. Krebs and his mother are clearly tense and upset; the details, action, and dialogue reveal that without the narrator telling the reader how each character feels.

The most intense use of a central consciousness in narration can be seen in the ***stream-of-consciousness technique*** developed by modern writers such as James Joyce, Virginia Woolf, and William Faulkner. This technique takes a reader inside a character's mind to reveal perceptions, thoughts, and feelings on a conscious or unconscious level. A stream of consciousness suggests the flow of thought as well as its content; hence complete sentences may give way to fragments as the character's mind makes rapid associations free of conventional logic or transitions.

The following passage is from Joyce's *Ulysses* (1922), a novel famous for its extended use of this technique. In this paragraph Joyce takes us inside the mind of a character who is describing a funeral:

> Coffin now. Got here before us, dead as he is. Horse looking round at it with his plume skeowways [askew]. Dull eye: collar tight on his neck, pressing on a blood-vessel or something. Do they know what they cart out of here every day? Must be twenty or thirty funerals every day. Then Mount Jerome for the protestants. Funerals all over the world everywhere every minute. Shovelling them under by the cartload doublequick. Thousands every hour. Too many in the world.

The character's thoughts range from specific observations to speculations about death. Joyce creates the illusion that we are reading the character's thoughts as they occur. The stream-of-consciousness technique provides an intimate perspective on a character's thoughts.

In contrast, the ***objective point of view*** employs a narrator who does not see into the mind of any character. From this detached and impersonal perspective, the narrator reports action and dialogue without telling us directly what the character feels and thinks. We observe the characters in much the same way we would perceive events in a film or play: we supply the meanings; no analysis or interpretation is provided by the narrator. This point of view places a heavy premium on dialogue, actions, and details to reveal character. Shirley Jackson's "The Lottery" (p. 188) is a good example of this type of narration. Note how the narrator of that story is factual, like a reporter. Instead of telling us "Mrs. Delacroix felt dread as she anticipated what would happen next," the objective narrator says, "She held her breath while her husband went forward." We feel more removed from the characters in this story than we might in another story in which we are permitted to enter their minds.

FIRST-PERSON NARRATOR (Participant)

1. Major character
2. Minor character

With a ***first-person narrator***, the *I* presents the point of view of only one character's consciousness. The reader is restricted to the perceptions, thoughts, and feelings of that single character. This is Baldwin's technique with the narrator of "Sonny's Blues" (p. 76). Everything learned about the characters, action, and plot comes from the unnamed teacher. He knows Sonny well — he is his brother, after all — but the story is largely about the limits of his knowledge. He first reads about Sonny's arrest in the newspaper, a fact that indicates right away that they do not communicate well. There are huge swaths of Sonny's life that are unavailable to the narrator, as the two men lead separate lives. The story reveals how our understanding of another person is always limited, yet communication — sometimes through nonverbal means such as music — is essential to our humanity.

The narrator of "Sonny's Blues" is a major character; indeed, many readers may consider him the protagonist, or the character most in need of positive change. A first-person narrator can, however, also be a minor character (imagine how different the story would be if it were told by, say, the bandleader named Creole or by an observer who had little or nothing to do with the action). Faulkner uses an observer in "A Rose for Emily" (p. 40).

His *we*, though plural and representative of the town's view of Emily, is nonetheless a first-person narrator.

One of the primary reasons for identifying the point of view in a story is to determine where the author stands in relation to the story. Behind the narrative voice of any story is the author, manipulating events and providing or withholding information. It is a mistake to assume that the narrative voice of a story is the author. The narrator, whether a first-person participant or a third-person nonparticipant, is a creation of the writer. To return to "Sonny's Blues," James Baldwin was the oldest brother in his family, but the similarities between him and the narrator end there: he was not a math teacher, was never married, did not have a child who died of polio, and loved jazz music. A narrator's perceptions may be accepted, rejected, or modified by an author, depending on how the narrative voice is articulated.

The narrator of Charlotte Perkins Gilman's "The Yellow Wallpaper" (p. 117) is an **unreliable narrator**, whose interpretation of events is dependent on a subjective perspective that perhaps does not coincide with objective reality. As her mental illness intensifies over the course of the story, we become more sceptical of her version of events. At the story's beginning we are likely to accept her assessment of the wallpaper as ugly, but later we are not likely to go along with her account of a woman crawling around behind it. She interprets bars on the window, a bed nailed to the floor, metal rings on the wall, and scratch marks all around the room as evidence that children had played there with excitement and vigor, but we begin to understand that the room had been more prison than playroom, and it still is.

Narrators can be unreliable for a variety of reasons: they might lack self-knowledge, like Sonny's brother, or they might be innocent and inexperienced, like John Updike's narrator in "A & P" (p. 138). Youthful innocence frequently characterizes a **naive narrator** such as Mark Twain's Huck Finn or Holden Caulfield, J. D. Salinger's twentieth-century version of Huck in *The Catcher in the Rye* (1951). These narrators lack the sophistication to interpret accurately what they see; they are unreliable because the reader must go beyond their understanding of events to comprehend the situations described. Huck and Holden describe their respective social environments, but the reader, with more experience, supplies the critical perspective that each boy lacks. In "A & P" the narrator is actually in the process of maturing during the course of the story, leading him to question the consequences of his actions by the end of the story rather than to view them as pure heroism.

Few generalizations can be made about the advantages or disadvantages of using a specific point of view. What can be said with confidence, however, is that writers choose a point of view to achieve particular effects because point of view determines what we know about the characters and events in a story. We should, therefore, be aware of who is telling the story and whether the narrator sees things clearly and reliably.

The next three works warrant a careful examination of their points of view. In John Updike's "A & P," the youthful narrator makes a crucial decision that will change his sensibilities. In Manuel Muñoz's "Zigzagger," a boy falls ill after a sexual encounter at a local dance. And in Maggie Mitchell's "It Would Be Different If," a woman reflects upon an early rejection in her life.

JOHN UPDIKE (1932–2009)

John Updike grew up in the small town of Shillington, Pennsylvania, and on a family farm nearby. Academic success in school earned him a scholarship to Harvard, where he studied English and graduated in 1954. He soon sold his first story and poem to the *New Yorker,* to which he contributed regularly through his career. Updike's second novel *Rabbit, Run* (1960), about a discontented young father who struggles to find meaning after peaking in high school, solidified his reputation as one of the most important American writers of his time. It was to be the first of a series of novels he published at roughly

Joanne Rathe/Boston Globe/Getty Images.

ten-year intervals which together constitute a chronicle of American history in the latter twentieth century. The prolific Updike — he published more than sixty books — lived in Massachusetts the rest of his life and continued to publish essays, poems, a novel, or a book of stories nearly every year, including *The Centaur* (1963), winner of the National Book Award; *Rabbit Is Rich* (1981) and *Rabbit at Rest* (1990), both Pulitzer Prize winners; and *The Witches of Eastwick* (1984), which was made into a major motion picture (Warner Bros., 1987). He was also a prolific book reviewer, and his astonishing number of essay collections reveal only a fraction of what he managed to read when he was not writing. Updike's fiction is noted for its exemplary use of storytelling conventions, its unique prose style, and its engaging picture of middle-class American life, although he also ranged considerably into other landscapes (like Brazil, eastern Europe, and sub-Saharan Africa) and other time periods (as in the time-travelling novel *Toward the End of Time* [1997] and *Gertrude and Claudius* [2000], a rewritten version of Shakespeare's *Hamlet*).

A & P   1961

In walks these three girls in nothing but bathing suits. I'm in the third checkout slot, with my back to the door, so I don't see them until they're over by the bread. The one that caught my eye first was the one in the plaid green two-piece. She was a chunky kid, with a good tan and a sweet broad soft-looking can with those two crescents of white just under it, where the sun never seems to hit, at the top of the backs of her legs. I stood there with my hand on a box of HiHo crackers trying to remember if I rang it up or not. I ring it up again and the customer starts giving me hell. She's one of these cash-register-watchers, a witch about fifty with rouge on her cheekbones and no eyebrows, and I know it made her day to trip me up. She'd been watching cash registers for fifty years and probably never seen a mistake before.

By the time I got her feathers smoothed and her goodies into a bag—she gives me a little snort in passing, if she'd been born at the right time they would have burned her over in Salem—by the time I get her on her way the girls had circled around the bread and were coming back, without a pushcart, back my way along the counters, in the aisle between the checkouts and the Special bins. They didn't even have shoes on. There was this chunky one, with the two-piece—it was bright green and the seams on the bra were still sharp and her belly was still pretty pale so I guessed she just got it (the suit)—there was this one, with one of those chubby berry-faces, the lips all bunched together under her nose, this one, and a tall one, with black hair that hadn't quite frizzed right, and one of these sunburns right across under the eyes, and a chin that was too long—you know, the kind of girl other girls think is very "striking" and "attractive" but never quite makes it, as they very well know, which is why they like her so much—and then the third one, that wasn't quite so tall. She was the queen. She kind of led them, the other two peeking around and making their shoulders round. She didn't look around, not this queen, she just walked straight on slowly, on these long white prima-donna legs. She came down a little hard on her heels, as if she didn't walk in her bare feet that much, putting down her heels and then letting the weight move along to her toes as if she was testing the floor with every step, putting a little deliberate extra action into it. You never know for sure how girls' minds work (do you really think it's a mind in there or just a little buzz like a bee in a glass jar?) but you got the idea she had talked the other two into coming in here with her, and now she was showing them how to do it, walk slow and hold yourself straight.

She had on a kind of dirty-pink — beige maybe, I don't know — bathing suit with a little nubble all over it and, what got me, the straps were down. They were off her shoulders looped loose around the cool tops of her arms, and I guess as a result the suit had slipped a little on her, so all around the top of the cloth there was this shining rim. If it hadn't been there you wouldn't have known there could have been anything whiter than those shoulders. With the straps pushed off, there was nothing between the top of the suit and the top of her head except just *her,* this clean bare plane of the top of her chest down from the shoulder bones like a dented sheet of metal tilted in the light. I mean, it was more than pretty.

She had sort of oaky hair that the sun and salt had bleached, done up in a bun that was unraveling, and a kind of prim face. Walking into the A & P with your straps down, I suppose it's the only kind of face you *can* have. She held her head so high her neck, coming up out of those white shoulders, looked kind of stretched, but I didn't mind. The longer her neck was, the more of her there was.

She must have felt in the corner of her eye me and over my shoulder 5 Stokesie in the second slot watching, but she didn't tip. Not this queen. She kept her eyes moving across the racks, and stopped, and turned so slow it made my stomach rub the inside of my apron, and buzzed to the other two, who kind of huddled against her for relief, and then they all three of them went up the cat-and-dogfood-breakfast-cereal-macaroni-rice-raisins-seasonings-spreads-spaghetti-soft-drinks-crackers-and-cookies aisle. From the third slot I look straight up this aisle to the meat counter, and I watched them all the way. The fat one with the tan sort of fumbled with the cookies, but on second thought she put the package back. The sheep pushing their carts down the aisle — the girls were walking against the usual traffic (not that we have one-way signs or anything) — were pretty hilarious. You could see them, when Queenie's white shoulders dawned on them, kind of jerk, or hop, or hiccup, but their eyes snapped back to their own baskets and on they pushed. I bet you could set off dynamite in an A & P and the people would by and large keep reaching and checking oatmeal off their lists and muttering "Let me see, there was a third thing, began with A, asparagus, no, ah, yes, applesauce!" or whatever it is they do mutter. But there was no doubt, this jiggled them. A few houseslaves in pin curlers even looked around after pushing their carts past to make sure what they had seen was correct.

You know, it's one thing to have a girl in a bathing suit down on the beach, where what with the glare nobody can look at each other much anyway, and another thing in the cool of the A & P, under the fluorescent lights, against all those stacked packages, with her feet paddling along naked over our checker-board green-and-cream rubber-tile floor.

"Oh Daddy," Stokesie said beside me. "I feel so faint."

"Darling," I said. "Hold me tight." Stokesie's married, with two babies chalked up on his fuselage already, but as far as I can tell that's the only difference. He's twenty-two, and I was nineteen this April.

"Is it done?" he asks, the responsible married man finding his voice. I forgot to say he thinks he's going to be manager some sunny day, maybe in 1990 when it's called the Great Alexandrov and Petrooshki Tea Company or something.

What he meant was, our town is five miles from a beach, with a big summer colony out on the Point, but we're right in the middle of town, and the women generally put on a shirt or shorts or something before they get out of the car into the street. And anyway these are usually women with six children and varicose veins mapping their legs and nobody, including them, could care less. As I say, we're right in the middle of town, and if you stand at our front doors you can see two banks and the Congregational church and the newspaper store and three real-estate offices and about twenty-seven old freeloaders tearing up Central Street because the sewer broke again. It's not as if we're on the Cape, we're north of Boston and there's people in this town haven't seen the ocean for twenty years.

The girls had reached the meat counter and were asking McMahon something. He pointed, they pointed, and they shuffled out of sight behind a pyramid of Diet Delight peaches. All that was left for us to see was old McMahon patting his mouth and looking after them sizing up their joints. Poor kids, I began to feel sorry for them, they couldn't help it.

Now here comes the sad part of the story, at least my family says it's sad, but I don't think it's so sad myself. The store's pretty empty, it being Thursday afternoon, so there was nothing much to do except lean on the register and wait for the girls to show up again. The whole store was like a pinball machine and I didn't know which tunnel they'd come out of. After a while they come around out of the far aisle, around the light bulbs, records at discount of the Caribbean Six or Tony Martin Sings or some such gunk you wonder they waste the wax on, sixpacks of candy bars, and plastic toys done up in cellophane that fall apart when a kid looks at them anyway. Around they come, Queenie still leading the way, and holding a little gray jar in her hands. Slots Three through Seven are unmanned and I could see her wondering between Stokes and me, but Stokesie with his usual luck draws an old party in baggy gray pants who stumbles up with four giant cans of pineapple juice (what do these bums *do* with all that pineapple juice? I've often asked myself). So the girls come to me. Queenie puts down the jar and I take it into my fingers icy cold. Kingfish Fancy Herring Snacks in Pure Sour Cream: 49¢. Now her hands are empty, not a ring or a bracelet, bare as God made them, and I wonder where the money's coming from. Still with that prim look she lifts a folded dollar bill out of the hollow at the center of her nubbled pink top. The jar went heavy in my hand. Really, I thought that was so cute.

Then everybody's luck begins to run out. Lengel comes in from haggling with a truck full of cabbages on the lot and is about to scuttle into that door marked MANAGER behind which he hides all day when the girls touch his eye. Lengel's pretty dreary, teaches Sunday school and the rest, but he doesn't miss that much. He comes over and says, "Girls, this isn't the beach."

Queenie blushes, though maybe it's just a brush of sunburn I was noticing for the first time, now that she was so close. "My mother asked me to pick up a jar of herring snacks." Her voice kind of startled me, the way voices do when you see the people first, coming out so flat and dumb yet kind of tony, too, the way it ticked over "pick up" and "snacks." All of a sudden I slid right down her voice into the living room. Her father and the other men were standing around in ice-cream coats and bow ties and the women were in sandals picking up herring snacks on toothpicks off a big glass plate and they were all holding drinks the color of water with olives and sprigs of mint in them. When my parents have somebody over they get lemonade and if it's a real racy affair Schlitz in tall glasses with "They'll Do It Every Time" cartoons stenciled on.

"That's all right," Lengel said. "But this isn't the beach." His repeating this struck me as funny, as if it had just occurred to him, and he had been thinking all these years the A & P was a great big dune and he was the head lifeguard. He didn't like my smiling — as I say he doesn't miss much — but he concentrates on giving the girls that sad Sunday-school-superintendent stare.

Queenie's blush is no sunburn now, and the plump one in plaid, that I liked better from the back — a really sweet can — pipes up, "We weren't doing any shopping. We just came in for the one thing."

"That makes no difference," Lengel tells her, and I could see from the way his eyes went that he hadn't noticed she was wearing a two-piece before. "We want you decently dressed when you come in here."

"We *are* decent," Queenie says suddenly, her lower lip pushing, getting sore now that she remembers her place, a place from which the crowd that runs the A & P must look pretty crummy. Fancy Herring Snacks flashed in her very blue eyes.

"Girls, I don't want to argue with you. After this come in here with your shoulders covered. It's our policy." He turns his back. That's policy for you. Policy is what the kingpins want. What the others want is juvenile delinquency.

All this while, the customers had been showing up with their carts but, you know, sheep, seeing a scene, they had all bunched up on Stokesie, who shook open a paper bag as gently as peeling a peach, not wanting to miss a word. I could feel in the silence everybody getting nervous, most of all Lengel, who asks me, "Sammy, have you rung up their purchase?"

I thought and said "No" but it wasn't about that I was thinking. I go through the punches, 4, 9, GROC. TOT — it's more complicated than you think, and after you do it often enough, it begins to make a little song, that you hear words to, in my case "Hello (*bing*) there, you (*gung*) hap-py *pee*-pul (*splat*)!" — the *splat* being the drawer flying out. I uncrease the bill, tenderly as you may imagine, it just having come from between the two smoothest scoops of vanilla I had ever known were there, and pass a half and a penny into her narrow pink palm, and nestle the herrings in a bag and twist its neck and hand it over, all the time thinking.

The girls, and who'd blame them, are in a hurry to get out, so I say "I quit" to Lengel quick enough for them to hear, hoping they'll stop and watch me, their unsuspected hero. They keep right on going, into the electric eye; the door flies open and they flicker across the lot to their car, Queenie and Plaid and Big Tall Goony-Goony (not that as raw material she was so bad), leaving me with Lengel and a kink in his eyebrow.

"Did you say something, Sammy?"

"I said I quit."

"I thought you did."   25

"You didn't have to embarrass them."

"It was they who were embarrassing us."

I started to say something that came out "Fiddle-de-doo." It's a saying of my grandmother's, and I know she would have been pleased.

"I don't think you know what you're saying," Lengel said.

"I know you don't," I said. "But I do." I pull the bow at the back of my   30 apron and start shrugging it off my shoulders. A couple customers that had been heading for my slot begin to knock against each other, like scared pigs in a chute.

Lengel sighs and begins to look very patient and old and gray. He's been a friend of my parents for years. "Sammy, you don't want to do this to your Mom and Dad," he tells me. It's true, I don't. But it seems to me that once you begin a gesture it's fatal not to go through with it. I fold the apron, "Sammy" stitched in red on the pocket, and put it on the counter, and drop the bow tie on top of it. The bow tie is theirs, if you've ever wondered. "You'll feel this for the rest of your life," Lengel says, and I know that's true, too, but remembering how he made the pretty girl blush makes me so scrunchy inside I punch the No Sale tab and the machine whirs "pee-pul" and the drawer splats out. One advantage to this scene taking place in summer, I can follow this up with a clean exit, there's no fumbling around getting your coat and galoshes, I just saunter into the electric eye in my white shirt that my mother ironed the night before, and the door heaves itself open, and outside the sunshine is skating around on the asphalt.

I look around for my girls, but they're gone, of course. There wasn't anybody but some young married screaming with her children about some candy they didn't get by the door of a powder-blue Falcon station wagon. Looking back in the big windows, over the bags of peat moss and aluminum lawn furniture stacked on the pavement, I could see Lengel in my place in the slot, checking the sheep through. His face was dark gray and his back stiff, as if he'd just had an injection of iron, and my stomach kind of fell as I felt how hard the world was going to be to me hereafter.

CONSIDERATIONS FOR CRITICAL THINKING AND WRITING

1. **FIRST RESPONSE.** Describe the setting. How accurate do you think Updike's treatment of the A & P is?

2. What kind of person is Sammy? How do his actions and speech constitute his own individual style?

3. Analyze the style of the first paragraph. How does it set the tone for the rest of the story?

4. What is the story's central conflict? Does it seem to be a serious or trivial conflict to you?

5. With what kind of values is Lengel associated? Do you feel any sympathy for him?

6. What do you think is Stokesie's function in the story?

7. Consider Sammy's treatment of the three girls. Do you think his account of them is sexist? Explain why or why not.

8. Locate the climax of the story. How does the climax affect your attitude toward Sammy?

9. How do you think the story would be different if it were told from another character's point of view instead of Sammy's?

10. Discuss the thematic significance of the story's final paragraph. Would you read the story differently if this last paragraph were eliminated?

CONNECTION TO ANOTHER SELECTION

1. Compare the tone established by the point of view in this story and in Maggie Mitchell's "It Would Be Different If" (p. 154).

MANUEL MUÑOZ (b. 1972)

Born and raised in a small farming town in central California, Manuel Muñoz was educated at Harvard and Cornell universities and now teaches at the University of Arizona. He is the author of two collections of short fiction set in the Central Valley of his upbringing and of one novel, *What You See in the Dark* (2011). This novel begins in the second person to draw the reader in, though much of it is narrated in the more conventional third person. Note the way the point of view shifts in the following story, "Zigzagger," the title story of Muñoz's first collection.

Zigzagger   2003

By six in the morning, the boy's convulsions have stopped. The light is graying in the window, allowing the boy's bedroom a shadowy calm — they can see without the lamp; and the father rises to turn it out. The boy's mother moves to stop him and the father realizes that she is still afraid, so he leaves it on. The sun seems slow to rise, and the room cannot brighten as quickly as they would like — it will be cloudy today.

The father is a bold man, but even he could not touch his teenage son several hours ago, when his jerking body was at its worst. The father makes the doorways in their house look narrow and small, his shoulders threatening to brush the jambs, yet even he had trouble controlling the boy and his violent sleep. And it was the father who first noticed how the room had become strangely cold to them, and they put on sweaters in the middle of July — the boy's body glistening, his legs kicking away the blankets as he moaned. The mother had been afraid to touch him at all and, even as the sun began rising, still made no move toward the boy.

In the morning light, the boy seems to have returned to health. He is sleeping peacefully now; he has not pushed away the quilts. His face has come back to a dark brown, the swelling around the eyes gone.

"I'll check his temperature," the father tells the mother, and she does not shake her head at the suggestion. She watches her husband closely as he moves to the bed and reaches for the edge of the quilt. She holds her breath. He pulls the quilt back slowly and reveals their son's brown legs, his bare feet. He puts out his hand to touch the boy's calf but doesn't pull away his fingers once he makes contact with the skin. The father turns to the mother, his fingers moving to the boy's hands and face. "I think he's okay now."

The mother sighs and, for the first time in hours, looks away from the   5 bed. She remembers that today is Sunday and, with the encouragement of the coming morning, she rises from her chair to see for herself.

Saturdays in this town are for dancing. The churchgoers think it is a vile day, and when they drive by the fields on their way to morning services, they sometimes claim to see workers swaying their hips as they pick tomatoes or grapes. They say that nothing gets done on Saturday afternoons because the workers go home too early in order to prepare for a long night of dancing. It is not just evenings, but the stretch of day — a whole cycle of temptation — and the churchgoers feel thwarted in their pleadings to bring back the ones who have strayed. They see them in town at the dry cleaners or waxing their cars. They see them buying food that isn't necessary.

The churchgoers have war veterans among them, some of whom serve as administrators for the town's Veterans Hall. They argue with each other about the moral questions of renting out their hall for Saturday's recklessness. The war veterans tell them that theirs is a public building and that the banquet room, the ballroom, and the wing of tidy classrooms are for all sorts of uses. Sometimes the veterans toss out angry stories about Korea, and the more civil of the lot mention how they converted villagers while fighting.° But others claim freedom, including their hall, and to mortify the churchgoers, they tell tales of Korean girls spreading their legs for soldiers and the relief it brought. The churchgoers end the conversation there.

By Saturday afternoon, there is always a bus from Texas or Arizona parked in back of the Veterans Hall, and sometimes workers on their way

fighting: I.e., in the Korean War (1950–53).

home will catch a glimpse of the musicians descending from the vehicle with accordions and sequined suits and sombreros in tow. Some days it is simply a chartered bus. But other times, it is a bus with the band's name painted along the side — CONJUNTO ALVAREZ, BENNIE JIMÉNEZ Y FUEGO — and the rumor of a more popular group coming through town will start the weekend much earlier than usual. It means people from towns on the other side of the Valley will make the trek. It means new and eager faces.

The churchgoers smart at the sight of young girls walking downtown toward the hall, their arms crossed in front of their breasts and holding themselves, as if the July evening breeze were capable of giving them a chill. For some of them, these young girls with arm-crossed breasts remind them of their own daughters who no longer live in town. They have moved away with babies to live alone in Los Angeles. All over town, the churchgoers know, young girls sneak from their homes to visit the friends their parents already dislike. There, they know, the girls put on skirts that twirl and makeup that might glisten against the dull lights of the makeshift dance floor. These girls practice walking on high heels, dance with each other in their bedrooms to get the feel in case a man asks them to do a *cumbia*.° The churchgoers remember when they were parents and listening to the closed doors and the girls too silent. Or their teenage boys, just as quiet, then leaving with their pockets full of things hidden craftily in their rooms.

And much of this starts early in the day: the general movement of the town, the activity in the streets and shops — women buying panty hose at the last minute, twisting lipsticks at the pharmacy in search of a plum color. Men carry cases of beer home to drink in their front yards. Pumpkin seeds and beef jerky. Taking showers only minutes before it is time to go.

Saturdays in this town are for dancing, have always been. This town is only slightly bigger than the ones around it, but it is the only one with a Veterans Hall, big enough to hold hundreds. By evening, those other little towns are left with bare streets, their lone gas stations shutting down for the night, a stream of cars heading away to the bigger town. They leave only the churchgoers and the old people already in their beds. They leave parents awake, listening for the slide of a window or too many footsteps. They leave the slow blink atop the height of the water tower, a red glow that dulls and then brightens again as if it were any other day of the week.

For a moment, the mother does not know whether to go to the kitchen herself or to send her husband. She does not want to take her eyes away from her son and yet at the same time is afraid to be alone with him. She says to her husband, *"Una crema"*° but doesn't move toward getting the items she needs to make a lotion for the boy. She needs crushed mint leaves from the kitchen. She needs oil and water, rose petals from the yard.

---

cumbia: A Latin American Dance.
Una crema: A cream.

"Do you want me to go?" her husband asks her. On the bed, the boy is sound asleep, and the sight of him in such a peaceful state almost makes her say yes. But she resists.

"No," she tells her husband. "I'll go."

She is sore from so much sitting, and the tension of having stayed awake   15 makes movement all the worse. The rest of the house seems strangely pleasant: the living room bright because it faces east, the large clock ticking contentedly. She wishes she could tell her husband what to do, but she knows they cannot call a doctor and have him witness this. She has considered a priest, but her husband does not go to church. In the face of this indecision, the calm rooms in the rest of the house frustrate her. She wants to make noise, even from simple activity. From the kitchen, she takes a large bowl and searches her windowsill for a few sprigs of mint. She sets out a bottle of olive oil and a cup of cold water from the faucet.

In the front yard, where the roses line the skinny walkway to their door, the day is brighter than it appeared through the windows. It is overcast, but not a ceiling of low clouds, only large ones with spaces in between, and she can see how the sun will be able to shine through them. They appear to be fast-racing clouds, and, once the sun is high enough, they will plummet the town into gray before giving way to light again. Though slight, the day erases the fear in her.

She notices the skinny walkway and the open gate where their son stumbled home, the place where he vomited into the grass. She had watched from the living room window, his friends behind him at a far distance, dark forms in the street, and she had waited for them to go away as her son entered the house, cursing terribly. From her rosebushes, she notices a gathering of flies buzzing around the mess, some of it on the gray stone of their walkway. There's a streak of red in it, she can see. She quickens her pace with the rose petals when the breeze comes up and the smell of the vomit in the grass lifts, reminding her of how ill her son was only hours ago. Dropping the petals into the bowl, she hurries back into the house, trying to get away from that smell.

She is crying in the kitchen, mixing the mint and the oil and the water, and to make it froth, she adds a bit of milk and egg. The concoction doesn't seem right to her anymore, doesn't match what she recalls as a young girl, her grandmother taking down everyday bottles from the cabinets and blessing their cuts and coughs. The mother does it without any knowledge, only guessing, but it makes her feel better despite feeling lost in her inability to remember. She takes the bowl into the bathroom and dumps half a bottle of hand lotion into the bowl, and the mix turns softer and creamy.

Back in the bedroom, her husband is still at their son's bedside, but the boy has not moved. The stale odor of the room reminds her again of outside and the earlier hours and her son's vile language and her husband's frantic struggle to keep the boy in bed, wild as he was. The boy tore off his own clothes, his thin hands ripping through his shirt and even his pants, shredding them, and he stalked into his bedroom naked and growling and strong.

Her husband came to tower over him, beat him for coming home this way. The fear crept into her when the boy fought back and challenged and then, only by exhaustion, collapsed on the bed. He was quiet. And then the odor came. The smell was of liquor at first, but then a heavy urine. Then of something rotting. Her husband had yelled at her to open the windows. Even now, the smell lingers in the air.

"He's still sleeping," her husband whispers. "What do you have there?"

"A cure my grandmother used to give us," she says, half expecting her husband to ignore her and the bowl.

"You want to put it on him?" he offers, and she knows that her husband is asking whether or not she is still afraid.

She does not answer him but moves to the bed, setting the bowl on the floor. With her fingertips, she dips into the concoction and then, resisting an impulse to hold her breath, rubs it on her son's bare legs. They are remarkably smooth, and she looks at her husband as if to have him reassure her that what she had seen last night had not been an illusion. Her son's legs are hairless and cool to the touch. There are no raised veins. They are not reddened with welts. They are not laced with deep scratches made with terrible fingers.

The boy spent the early part of Saturday evening with a group of friends, all of them drinking in the backyard at the house of a girl whose parents were visiting relatives in another town. Even before the sun had set, most or the boy's friends had already had enough to drink, and they tried to convince some of the older boys to go back out and buy beer. But by then, the girls put a stop to all of it, saying the hall wouldn't let them in if they smelled beer on them.

The boy liked being with these friends because he did not have to do much. He laughed at other people when the joke was on them, and it made him feel more comfortable about himself. He smoked cigarettes and watched the orange tips get brighter and brighter as the sun went down. He looked at the girls coming in and out of the back door as they got ready for the dance. He did not drink, because he did not like the acrid taste of beer, yet he liked being here with them, knowing that every sip was what their own parents had done at their age. He did not mind seeing the others drunk—after a certain point, he knew that the drunker boys would sit next to him and talk. He would not respond except to smile, because he didn't know what else to do, what to make of their joking, their arms heavy around his shoulders.

They gathered themselves after the girls were ready and they walked to the hall, twos and threes along the sidewalk, some of them chewing big wads of hard pink gum and then spitting them into the grass. He was not as crass as the other boys, who waited to spit until they saw the dark figures of the churchgoers scowling from their porches. They divided mints between them when the hall came into view: the taillights of cars easing into the parking lot, women sitting in passenger seats waiting for their doors to be opened.

The boy got in line with the rest of them, watching as a pair of older women at the ticket table looked disapprovingly at the girls and motioned with their fingers for each of them to extend their arms. They fastened pink plastic bracelets around their wrists, ignoring the odor of alcohol. When the boy made it to them, he tried to move as close as possible, to show he was not like the rest of them, but one of the women only said, "No beer," strapping the pink bracelet tightly and taking his dollar bills.

Inside, his friends had already fractured. A flurry of kids their age milled around the edge of the dance floor while the older couples swayed gently to the band's ballad of horns and *bandeneón.*° All he saw were bodies pressed together, light coming through in the spaces cleared for the dance steps of other couples, hips and fake jewelry catching. He saw the smoke blue in the air around the hanging lights; the cigarettes, which he felt contributed to the heat; the men with unbuttoned shirt collars, their hands around the backs of laughing women.

When the song ended, with a long and mournful note on a single horn, the couples separated to applaud, and some of the women went back to their own tables. He saw that people of every situation were there — older, single women sitting at the circular tables, men his father's age with shiny belt buckles and boots. Of his own age, the boys were pestering some of the older men to buy them beer, hiding the telltale pink bands that showed their age, sneaking sips in the darker shadows of the hall's great room.

As the next song began — a wild, brash *ranchera* complete with accor- 30 dion at full expansion — the milling began again, people alone, people together. He put his hands in his pockets while men removed their hats and cornered women for a dance. Couples with joined hands pushed their way to the floor that had only just settled its dust. Some alone, some together. The music roared its way through the hall, and the boy reasoned that everyone felt the way he did at the moment — lost and unnoticed, standing in place as he was.

The boy's mother spreads the concoction more vigorously, her son's legs giving way where the flesh is soft, reminding her that he is not fully grown, not a man yet. She believes her rubbing will wake him, and when he doesn't respond, she looks at her husband, who does nothing but look back.

She speaks to her son. "Are you awake?" she asks him, her hands grasping his legs quickly to shake him, but he only stirs, his head moving to one side and then stopping. "Are you in pain?"

Her husband stands up to look closely at their son's face and says to her, "His eyes are open." He waves his hand slowly in front of the boy, but still he will not speak. "I don't think he sees me."

"Are you awake?" she says again, rising to see for herself. His eyes are open, just as her husband said, but they don't seem to stare back at her. She

---

bandeneón: A South American reed instrument.

thinks for a moment that his open eyes will begin to water and she waits for him to blink, but he only closes his eyes once more.

"It's early still," the father says. "Don't worry."

The boy felt as if he had been the only person to notice the man with the plain silver buckle, a belt that shimmered against the glow of the yellow bulbs strung across the hall's high rafters. A plain silver buckle that gleamed like a cold eye, open and watching. Even from a distance, the boy knew it was plain, that it had no etchings, no tarnish, no scratches. He watched it tilt at the waist as the man put his boot up on the leg of a stool, leaning down to one of the girls who had come with the boy, whispering to her.

He felt as if he were the only one watching how the girl flicked her hair deliberately with her left wrist, as if to show the pink bracelet in a polite gesture to move on: she was too young.

The boy pictured himself with the same kind of arrogance, the posture that cocked the man's hips, the offering he suggested to this girl, and he wondered if he would ever grow into that kind of superiority, being capable of seducing and tempting. He watched the silver buckle blink at him, as if it watched back, as if it knew where the boy was looking.

The man finally left the girl alone, but the boy watched him, circling the dance floor, sometimes losing him between songs as the hall dimmed the lighting to invite a slow dance. Or losing him when one of the other boys distracted him with a stolen beer. But he would quickly find him again, the belt buckle gleaming and catching—a circle of silver light moving through the dark tables.

The girl from before came up to the boy and said, "That man kept bugging me," as if she expected the boy to do something about it. He turned to look at her—she was one of the girls who regularly went to church, didn't know how to behave at a dance, put up her hair because her girlfriends told her to. And now, with that strange man, she wanted trouble for its own sake, he thought. He could hear in her voice that she wanted the attention in some form—his defense, or that man's proposal—so no one would look at her as the girl with the straight dark hair, a Sunday girl.

So the boy moved, without looking at the girl, keeping his eye on the silver buckle and followed the man, catching up to him toward the back of the hall, where only the couples who could not wait to get home were kissing, leaning against each other, backing into the wall. The man stood next to a woman, facing her and talking among all the bodies rubbing against each other, his silver buckle the only still thing, and the boy noticed that the man wore nothing but black, down to his boots. The man's teeth gleamed as he smiled, watching the boy approach. He smiled as if he expected him and ignored the woman, who disappeared into the dark bodies.

Before the boy could say anything about the girl, the man extended his hand, offering a beer. "My apologies," he said to the boy, his voice clear and strong, and the boy noticed his face—what a handsome man he was, his skin as dark as anyone's in town — but his voice not anchored by the heaviness of accent. He was not like them, the boy knew instantly.

The mother opens all the doors in the house, though the sky doesn't look as if it will break one way or the other. She draws more curtains, all the rooms filled with the muted daylight. Even the closet doors are open, flush against the walls, and she pushes the clothes apart to allow the light in the tight spaces. She thinks of the kitchen cabinets and the drawers, the small knobs that pull out of tables and nightstands, the blankets hiding the dust motes under the beds. The husband lets her do this and then says nothing as she sits in the living room all by herself with her head in her hands.

Because the front door is wide open, she hears the footsteps on the sidewalk long before they approach the house, and she looks to the porch to see a group of her son's friends coming. They walk so close together; they seem afraid and apologetic at the same time. All of them have their heads bowed, the girls and the boys in fresh Sunday church clothes, and she knows they see the mess her son made on the front lawn.

It is odd for her to be sitting on her living room couch and seeing not the 45 television but her own front yard, and she can do nothing but watch as the boys and girls stop at the porch, almost startled that they do not have to knock.

"What do you want?" she hears her husband say, and she turns to see him in the archway to the kitchen, where he must have heard them coming. "What did you give him last night?"

Her husband's voice is filled with rage, but she can see that her son's friends have come out of concern. And she knows they will tell her that her son had not been drinking, that they will deny that he took any drugs, and she will believe them. But she knots her fingers and her hands, trying to build up a false anger, because she is too ashamed and afraid to let them know what she and her husband saw on her boy's body, the things he said in a voice that was not his, how the house seemed to swell and breathe as if it were living itself, the whole space filling out in the same terrible way that her chest wanted to burst forth.

"We didn't give him anything," one of the boys says. "He wouldn't even take one beer."

"He's sick now!" her husband yells at them. "You understand that? *¿Entienden?*"

"Let them go home," the mother says. "They don't need to know anything." 50

The boys and girls still stand on the porch, because they see she has been talking to her husband and not them, waiting for him to order them away. But the husband does not say anything, and then one of the boys speaks up and says, "I brought him home because we found him sick. Outside the hall. He was just sick. We don't know how."

No one responds, no one asks questions. Not the husband, not the mother. And just when the mother is about to rise from the couch to point her finger to the street, to show them away from the porch, they all know to look in the hall archway leading to the bedroom. There, clad only in his underwear, his skin pale and the dampness of the day swimming through the house, stands the boy.

He is aware of himself in a way that is unsettling, as if he has escaped his body once and for all and yet, exhausted as he feels, knows that his body is his own again. He is aware that the window to his bedroom is open and the day is overcast; the curtains move in a breeze that is chilly and has made the sheets underneath him cold. He shivers.

He hears the voices in the front of the house, the sound of his father's anger, the way only his father can sound, and his mother's hesitations. He hears the sounds of his friends but can't tell how many.

He feels the cold on his legs and he rises from the bed slowly, putting his feet on the floor, and the act of moving — like water, like the leaves outside his bedroom window today — startles him, the ease of it. Looking at his thin legs, the hollow of his own chest, he does not feel ashamed of himself as he once did.

The boy knows what he has done, what has happened, and yet, deep inside, he believes it could not have been. He thinks back to the man in the black clothes and the silver buckle, the offered beer, and the few words they spoke. The man had asked him if he spoke Spanish and when he had said no, the man had looked almost pleased. He does not remember what else they might have spoken of, only that the hall seemed to tilt and sway, the *ranchera* amplified to ten times as loud as he has ever heard, so that the man's voice came from within him. It came from the darkness when he closed his eyes to the hall's dipping and sinking, and when he opened them, it was still dark and he felt the nip of the outside air, the summer night cool compared to the pushed-together bodies of the dance inside. The cool of the sheets beneath him this morning makes him recall that outside air, how he had felt it not against his face but the bare skin of his chest, then his belly, and the metallic touch of the silver belt buckle pressing close. The music was distant — they were away from the hall, away from the cars in the parking lot, where couples were leaving, the engines starting. He recalls now the rough edges of a tree against his back, the bark and the summer sap, the branches a canopy that hid the stars, because he looked up and saw nothing but the spaces between leaves, small stars peeking through to see him.

He had said nothing to this man, remembers how he allowed the man's hands to grab his waist, his entire arm wrapped around, lifting the boy's feet from the ground, the feeling of rising, almost levitating. He felt as if the man rose with him because he felt the hot press of the man's belly, the rough texture of hair, and now he remembers how he had let his hands run down the man's back, the knots on his spine, the fine-worked furrow, their feet on air. He kept looking up, searching for the stars between the branches.

The man, his back broad, grunted heavily. The sound frightens the boy now as he recalls it in broad daylight. The man's sound made him grow, pushing the boy up higher and higher, to where the boy could see himself in the arms of the man who glowed in the darkness of the canopy of branches, his skin a dull red, the pants and boots gone. And though he felt he was in air, he saw a flash of the man's feet entrenched fast in the ground — long, hard hooves digging into the soil, the height of horses when they charge — it was then that the boy remembers seeing and feeling at the same time — the hooves, then a piercing in the depth of his belly that made his eyes flash a whole battalion of stars, shooting and brilliant, more and more of them, until he had no choice but to scream out.

And now, at midmorning, his father and mother in the front of the house, his skin smelling of mint and roses, he knows enough to go forward and send his friends away. He wonders if he will sound different; he wonders if they will see how he carries himself now; he remembers how feeling the furrow of the man's back reminded him of the hard work of picking grapes in the summer months — his father will punish him with it. The hard work and the rattlers under the vines, their forked tongues brushing the air, and the boy remembers that the man's tongue pushed into his with the same vigor, searching him with the same kind of terrible flick.

He rises from the bed and steps, with an unfamiliar grace, to the wide- 60 open door of his bedroom and down the hall.

The mother sees him, the look in his eye, and she wants to say nothing at all. She believes, as she always has, that talking aloud brings moments to light, and she has refused to speak of her mother's death, of her husband's cheating, of the hatred of her brothers and sisters. She sees her son at the doorway and wants to tell him not to speak.

They all stand and wait for the boy to talk, the doors and windows open as wide as possible and every last secret of their home ready to make an easy break to the outside. The curtains swell with a passing breeze.

"You're awake," the father says, and walks toward the boy, and the mother hopes that he will not speak and reveal his voice. She wonders if her husband knows now, if he can tell how the side-to-side swivel of the dancers at the hall and the zigzag of their steps have invited an ancient trouble, if her husband knows the countless stories of midnight goings-on, of women with broken blood vessels streaming underneath their skin from the touch of every strange man.

She keeps wondering, even when her husband turns to the boy's friends and tells them, "See? He's fine. Now go home," and motions them away from the porch and they leave without asking her son anything at all. She wonders now if her husband has ever awakened at night, dreaming of dances where bags of church-blessed rattlesnakes have been opened in the darkness of the place, the mad slithering between feet and the screams, the rightness of that punishment, the snakes that spoke in human voices, the rushed side-to-side movement of the snakes before they coiled underneath tables to strike at ankles.

When her husband turns his back to walk to the porch, watching 65 the boy's friends walk off warily, she takes her chance and rushes to her underwear-clad son in the archway and grabs him by his arms — his flesh cold — and says, under her breath, "I know, I know," and then bravely, without waiting to hear what his voice might sound like, tries to pry open his mouth and check for herself.

Considerations for Critical Thinking and Writing

1. **FIRST RESPONSE.** No one in this story is named. How does that choice affect your emotional response to the story? Would you feel differently about the story if at least the protagonist ("the boy") had a name?

2. There are two basic groups of people in town: the field workers and the churchgoers. How does this division frame the story's main conflict? What is that conflict?

3. The point of view in the story shifts not only from the mother to the son, but from the present to the preceding night. How does the author control this movement without confusing the reader?

4. The boy is fascinated by the man with the silver buckle because he can tell he is somehow different from everyone else in the dance hall. What are some of the factors that indicate the boy's own difference from his friend group?

5. In question 1 we identify the boy as the story's protagonist, but the story's shifting point of view essentially begins and ends with his mother. Is she actually the story's protagonist? If so, does the meaning of the story shift?

6. Leaving aside for a moment the boy's sexual encounter with the man at the dance, discuss the opposition between his group of friends and his family as a way of articulating his central conflict.

7. How do you interpret the story's title?

8. The story could be described as a rite of passage story involving the loss of innocence that accompanies sexual initiation. Is there a sense that his experience will bring about a permanent change in his life or does it seem random and isolated?

9. Discuss the passages in the story that are most abstract, or least realistic. How do these passages interact with the more straightforward or realistic passages?

10. Consider the way gender roles are reinforced in this town. What is the boy's reaction to these roles? How does he both uphold and resist them?

Connections to Other Selections

1. Discuss the treatment of parental expectations in this story and in Jamaica Kincaid's "Girl" (p. 316). What important similarities and differences do you see?

2. Consider the relationship between home towns and individual transformations in this story and in Hemingway's "Soldier's Home" (p. 104).

MAGGIE MITCHELL (B. 1970)

Maggie Mitchell grew up in a small town in the northernmost part of New York State, on the Canadian border. She received an undergraduate degree in English from Cornell University and a Ph.D. from the University of Connecticut, and she now teaches English at the University of West Georgia. Her first novel, *Pretty Is* (2015), has been widely translated. Mitchell's short fiction has appeared in a number of literary magazines, including *New Ohio Review, American Literary Review,* and *Green Mountains Review.* The stark landscape of her childhood often finds its way into her short stories, as it does in "It Would Be Different If," which originally appeared in *New South.*

Photo courtesy of Jill Sutton.

It Would Be Different If 2011

Here's what I remember. If I could hate you, this is what I would hate you for. It's a summer night, humid, starry. It's already pretty late but we're all heading over to Canada, to a bar called the Shipyard. She is there, which surprises me, because the Shipyard is the kind of place where people crack beer bottles over each other's heads, and I wouldn't have thought it was her scene. But she's been hanging out with your sister Megan all summer, working down at the restaurant, back when it was still the Riverside. She's always around. She annoys me, but I don't suspect anything yet. There are two boats; we're splitting into groups. I'm standing on the dock, a beer in my hand. I've had a little too much to drink already, probably, because everything seems very dark, slightly confused. I'm trying to figure out which boat you're in so I don't get stuck in the other one. Just then a car happens to go by on Water Street and its headlights flicker across us. You're already in the first boat, and you're reaching your hand up toward the dock, smiling. I move blindly in your direction, thinking you're reaching for me, when another flash of light shows me that she is grabbing for your hand, you're swinging her down, the smile is for her, it's not a mistake. I stand on the dock in a miniskirt and a very skimpy cropped top, my hair sprayed into a sort of stiff gold cloud because it is the 80s. I feel, for the first time in my life, completely ridiculous. There's no turning back, though. I can't just announce, like a little kid, that I'm going home, I don't want to play anymore, though that's exactly what I feel.

The first boat is full. The headlights veer away: everything is dark again. I tumble somehow into the second boat, wishing I had something to cover myself with: I feel naked, although back then I always dressed like that, we all did. At the Shipyard I mostly stay in the bathroom, drinking and crying. I don't remember the boat ride home. But that's it, that's the end of it. That much I remember.

I've heard variations on this story from everyone, over the years. I'm always the victim, the one people feel sorry for. Maybe there are other versions where I get what's coming to me, where I've always needed to be put in my place, something like that, but I doubt it. People have never liked Amber much; they tend to be on my side. Or at least they did: as the years go by, I notice, that's less true. It's so long ago that people can't get too worked up about it anymore. Now they talk as if it was somehow inevitable, and we just didn't know it yet — you know, isn't life funny, but look how it all works out in the end. Except when it doesn't.

It would be different if we lived in the kind of place where people can disappear, never see each other again. It would be different if I could pretend you didn't exist. But there you are: you are at the post office, peering into your mailbox, pulling out a stack of envelopes and catalogues while I drop my electric bill in the mail slot; I wait till you turn around, to make sure you see me. You would rather not see me. You're at the table on the other side of the restaurant, bending forward to speak to her, or wiping food off your kid's face. You're getting gas, staring off into the distance, forgetting what you are doing. You don't notice that I'm driving by. What are you thinking of? You're everywhere. I think you have ruined my life.

And now she's the one they feel sorry for. Yes, of course I know what you've been up to. Everyone knows. I see your truck in the parking lot at Jude's every night, and they say you don't tend to leave alone. I see her sometimes: Amber. She looks smaller, paler, less pretty. I could almost feel sorry for her myself, to tell you the truth. I don't blame you, of course. It's just because it's all wrong. I could have told you it would happen. 5

I wasn't supposed to be one of those people, the unmarryable ones. I never expected to be. I had you, and we had plans, ever since our junior year: Nikki and Jeff. Nikki Gilbert. It sounded right. We joked about getting old, how you would go bald and I'd go pure white, and we'd go fishing in the summer, cross-country skiing in the winter, with our dog. It was a beagle. I had a bit of a stoop; you had put on some weight. You can't cancel that out.

It wasn't fair. She had gone away — to college, the city, whatever. She was the kind of person who goes away, doesn't come back: that's what everyone expected. But she did come back and she chose you, of all people. Why you? You're not like her. You are like us.

Well. Here's what I imagine. It's the best I can do. I am working, finishing up someone's hair. It's late afternoon — that quiet time when the sun starts to come in sideways. Whose hair? Someone like Deb White, not much of a talker, but lots of hair, complicated hair, ever since Don got his job back and they gave up on that hippie phase. I'm finished with the cut and now I'm styling it, taking my time because I don't have any more appointments that day, blowing it out section by section, working through the layers. Her eyes are half closed, I hum a little. It's nice.

Then I hear the door clang as it swings shut behind someone. I glance over and it's you. I am calm; we say nothing. I just nod, and you pick up a magazine and sit down on the couch to wait. Like anyone else. I don't rush Deb. If anything I slow down, taking extra time with each wave, making it perfect. You're just sitting there but somehow you fill the air, you're everywhere and invisible. I breathe you, I walk on you, I curl you into Deb's frosted waves. But I don't shake, or sweat. I'm not nervous. You're like a birthday, a red X on the calendar. Sooner or later you'll happen, one way or the other: it doesn't matter what I do. Eventually Deb rises to her feet, admires herself in the mirror. She writes a check; I don't take credit cards. It seems to take her forever, like one of those women in line at the grocery store. In the meantime I sweep up the heap of doll-like hair around the chair, straighten up the station. She makes an appointment for the next month. Finally she drifts toward the door and I follow her, because she is chatting about something, telling me a story about one of her daughters; she always does this. I wave as she maneuvers herself into her car, careful not to disturb her hair.

When I return to the shop you have seated yourself in the chair that is 10 probably still warm from its contact with Deb White's bony behind. I think of this, for some reason. I see myself smile in the mirror and our eyes, for the first time, meet each other's reflections. I drape a hunter green smock across you, attach it behind your neck with velcro straps.

I cut your hair. I use four different kinds of scissors, a razor, two combs, a touch of mousse. I used to cut your hair in high school, for practice. Now I do it better. Mostly I keep my eyes focused on your head, like an artist putting the final touches on some life-sized sculpture, but every now and then I look up, and there you are in the mirror. We always look at the same moment. We know exactly how long to wait between looks; we know not to overdo it. Your eyes are still the same blue as always but there are crinkles, now, at the corners. I think you are better looking than ever. My work does you justice: this is the best haircut you will ever, ever get.

I remove the smock when it's over. You do not pay. You don't speak. You look at me one more time, and you touch my hand — so far, given the circumstances, I have been the one to do all the touching — and then you leave. I wait until your truck has pulled away to sweep up the short brown hairs. I can't throw them away, so I tilt the contents of the dustpan into one of the nice creamy envelopes I use for gift certificates.

I don't know what happens after that. Probably you don't leave her right away. But sooner or later I know you'll come. I'll be waiting. For now I'll settle for the trimmings, glossy and shampoo-scented, and for the traces of your reflection that you seem to have left in the mirror. You flicker endlessly between the stiff curls of middle-aged ladies in pastel pantsuits, the long doomed locks of small terrified boys, the towering, glittery updos of girls on their way to the prom. You remind me to wait, promise that things will be different. I believe you.

CONSIDERATIONS FOR CRITICAL THINKING AND WRITING

1. **FIRST RESPONSE.** What actually happens in this story? What is the status of the present in relation to memory and imagination?

2. How does the narrator invite the reader's sympathy? Is it important that we sympathize with her?

3. How trustworthy is the narrator's version of events? What specific lines or passages reinforce or undermine her perspective?

4. What kind of resolution does this story offer? Would you say that the conflict has been resolved, in any sense?

5. What does the narrator's way of relating this story — not *what* she says, but the way she says it — reveal about her world or about her character?

6. What sense do you get of the town in which this story is set? How important is the setting to your understanding of the story and the characters?

7. What is the significance of the final line of the story?

8. **CREATIVE RESPONSE.** Use what you think you can infer about the narrator from this story to craft a paragraph from a third-person point of view in which Nikki is portrayed unsympathetically.

CONNECTION TO ANOTHER SELECTION

1. Compare the accounts of long-term relationships that have ended in this story and in Grace Paley's "Wants" (p. 26): what do both of them tell us and not tell us about the reasons these relationships did not last permanently? What difference does point of view make, if any?

6

Symbolism

Everett Collection/Newscom.

Now mind, I recognize no dichotomy
between art and protest.

—RALPH ELLISON

A *symbol* is a person, object, or event that suggests more than its literal meaning. This basic definition is simple enough, but the use of symbol in literature makes some students slightly nervous because they tend to regard it as a booby trap, a hidden device that can go off during a seemingly harmless class discussion. "I didn't see that when I was reading the story" is a frequently heard comment. This sort of surprise and recognition is both natural and common. Most readers go through a story for the first time getting their bearings, figuring out what is happening to whom and so on. Patterns and significant details often require a second or third reading before they become evident — before a symbol sheds light on a story. Then the details of a work may suddenly fit together, and its meaning may be reinforced, clarified, or enlarged by the symbol. Symbolic meanings are usually embedded in the texture of a story, but they are not "hidden"; instead, they are carefully placed. Reading between the lines (where there is only space) is unnecessary. What is needed is a careful consideration of the elements of the story, a sensitivity to its language, and some common sense.

Common sense is a good place to begin. Symbols appear all around us; anything can be given symbolic significance. Without symbols our lives would be stark and vacant. Awareness of a writer's use of symbols is not all that different from the kinds of perceptions and interpretations that allow us to make sense of our daily lives. We know, for example, that a ring used in a wedding is more than just a piece of jewelry because it suggests the unity and intimacy of a closed circle. The bride's gown may be white because we tend to associate innocence and purity with that color. Or consider the meaning of a small polo pony sewn on a shirt or some other article of clothing. What started as a company trademark has gathered around it a range of meanings suggesting everything from quality and money to preppiness and silliness. The ring, the white gown, and the polo pony trademark are symbolic because each has meanings that go beyond its specific qualities and functions.

Symbols such as these that are widely recognized by a society or culture are called ***conventional symbols***. The Christian cross, the Star of David, or a nation's flag all have meanings understood by large groups of people. Certain kinds of experiences also have traditional meanings in Western cultures. Winter, the setting sun, and the color black suggest death, while spring, the rising sun, and the color green evoke images of youth and new beginnings. (It is worth noting, however, that individual cultures sometimes have their own conventions; some Eastern cultures associate white rather than black with death and mourning. And obviously the polo pony trademark would mean nothing to anyone totally unfamiliar with American culture.) These broadly shared symbolic meanings are second nature to us.

Writers use conventional symbols to reinforce meanings. Kate Chopin, for example, emphasizes the spring setting in "The Story of an Hour" (p. 15) as a way of suggesting the renewed sense of life that Mrs. Mallard feels when she thinks herself free from her husband.

A ***literary symbol*** can include traditional, conventional, or public meanings, but it may also be established internally by the total context of the work in which it appears. In "Soldier's Home" (p. 104), Hemingway does not use Krebs's family home as a conventional symbol of safety, comfort, and refuge from the war. Instead, Krebs's home becomes symbolic of provincial, erroneous presuppositions compounded by blind innocence, sentimentality, and smug middle-class respectability. The symbolic meaning of his home reveals that Krebs no longer shares his family's and town's view of the world. Their notions of love, the value of a respectable job, and a belief in God seem to him petty, complicated, and meaningless. The significance of Krebs's home is determined by the events within the story, which reverse and subvert the traditional associations readers might bring to it. Krebs's interactions with his family and the people in town reveal what home has come to mean to him.

A literary symbol can be a setting, character, action, object, name, or anything else in a work that maintains its literal significance while suggesting other meanings. Symbols cannot be restricted to a single meaning; they are suggestive rather than definitive. Their evocation of multiple meanings allows a writer to say more with less. Symbols are economical devices for evoking complex ideas without having to resort to painstaking explanations that would make a story more like an essay than an experience. In Gilman's "The Yellow Wallpaper" (p. 117), the symbol is named in the title, and it suggests multiple meanings that unify the story. Wallpaper covers up a wall, hiding its imperfections with a decorative surface. This story is about revealing the truth, though, so the narrator finds the wallpaper not pleasing, but menacing. Like the rest cure her husband enforces, the wallpaper suffocates her. She not only rejects its hideous color and chaotic patterns, but she sees it as a living thing that oppresses a woman hiding behind it. Her action of tearing it off the wall represents much more than just a desire to redecorate.

When a character, object, or incident indicates a single, fixed meaning, the writer is using **allegory** rather than symbol. Whereas symbols have literal functions as well as multiple meanings, the primary focus in allegory is on the abstract idea called forth by the concrete object. John Bunyan's *Pilgrim's Progress,* published during the seventeenth century, is a classic example of allegory because the characters, action, and setting have no existence beyond their abstract meanings. Bunyan's purpose is to teach his readers the exemplary way to salvation and heaven. The protagonist, named Christian, flees the City of Destruction in search of the Celestial City. Along the way he encounters characters who either help or hinder his spiritual journey. Among them are Mr. Worldly Wiseman, Faithful, Prudence, Piety, and a host of others named after the virtues or vices they display. These characters, places, and actions exist solely to illustrate religious doctrine. Allegory tends to be definitive rather than suggestive. It drives meaning into a corner and keeps it there. Most modern writers prefer the exploratory nature of symbol to the reductive nature of pure allegory.

Stories often include symbols that you may or may not perceive on a first reading. Their subtle use is a sign of a writer's skill in weaving symbols into the fabric of the characters' lives. Symbols may sometimes escape you, but that is probably better than finding symbols where only literal meanings are intended. Allow the text to help you determine whether a symbolic reading is appropriate. Once you are clear about what literally happens, read carefully and notice the placement of details that are emphasized. The pervasive references to time in Faulkner's "A Rose for Emily" (p. 40) and the glass of scotch whiskey and milk that the narrator sends to his brother at the conclusion of Baldwin's "Sonny's Blues" (p. 76) call attention to themselves and warrant symbolic readings. A symbol, however, need not be repeated to have an important purpose in a story. The drink that Sonny accepts is only mentioned at the end of the story and is accompanied by an **allusion** to the Bible, the "cup of trembling." The unpleasant-sounding cocktail also represents a blend of the dangerous or self-destructive — whiskey, representing Sonny's experiences — and his need for nurturing (milk). It was also the preferred drink of Charlie Parker, the jazz musician who is Sonny's hero, and who died at a very young age from drug addiction, which is exactly what the narrator fears will happen to Sonny.

By keeping track of the total context of the story, you should be able to decide whether your reading is reasonable and consistent with the other facts; plenty of lemons in literature yield no symbolic meaning even if they are squeezed. Be sensitive to the meanings that the author associates with people, places, objects, and actions. You may not associate home with provincial innocence as Hemingway does in "Soldier's Home," but a close reading of the story will permit you to see how and why he constructs that symbolic meaning. If you treat stories like people — with tact and care — they ordinarily are accessible and enjoyable.

The next three stories — Louise Erdrich's "The Red Convertible," Cynthia Ozick's "The Shawl," and Ann Beattie's "Janus" — rely on symbols to convey meanings that go far beyond the specific incidents described in their plots.

LOUISE ERDRICH (B. 1954)

Louise Erdrich's poetry and fiction deals mainly with the experiences of Native Americans of the Great Plains and upper Midwest. Born in Minnesota to a father of German heritage and a Chippewa mother, Erdrich is best known for a series of novels begun in 1984 with *Love Medicine*. This novel, which some would argue is more a story sequence, traces the intertwined stories of a number of families who connect and clash over

Agence Opale/Alamy Stock Photo.

a long period of history on an Ojibwe reservation in North Dakota. Subsequent books such as *The Beet Queen* (1986) and *Tracks* (1988) continue and deepen this saga. The following story, "The Red Convertible," is taken from *Love Medicine*. It takes place in 1974 toward the end of the U.S. war in Vietnam.

The Red Convertible   1984

I was the first one to drive a convertible on my reservation. And of course it was red, a red Olds. I owned that car along with my brother Henry Junior. We owned it together until his boots filled with water on a windy night and he bought out my share. Now Henry owns the whole car, and his younger brother Lyman (that's myself), Lyman walks everywhere he goes.

How did I earn enough money to buy my share in the first place? My one talent was I could always make money. I had a touch for it, unusual in a

Chippewa. From the first I was different that way, and everyone recognized it. I was the only kid they let in the American Legion Hall to shine shoes, for example, and one Christmas I sold spiritual bouquets for the mission door to door. The nuns let me keep a percentage. Once I started, it seemed the more money I made the easier the money came. Everyone encouraged it. When I was fifteen I got a job washing dishes at the Joliet Café, and that was where my first big break happened.

It wasn't long before I was promoted to busing tables, and then the short-order cook quit and I was hired to take her place. No sooner than you know it I was managing the Joliet. The rest is history. I went on managing. I soon became part owner, and of course there was no stopping me then. It wasn't long before the whole thing was mine.

After I'd owned the Joliet for one year, it blew over in the worst tornado ever seen around here. The whole operation was smashed to bits. A total loss. The fryalator was up in a tree, the grill torn in half like it was paper. I was only sixteen. I had it all in my mother's name, and I lost it quick, but before I lost it I had every one of my relatives, and their relatives, to dinner, and I also bought that red Olds I mentioned, along with Henry.

The first time we saw it! I'll tell you when we first saw it. We had gotten a ride up to Winnipeg, and both of us had money. Don't ask me why, because we never mentioned a car or anything, we just had all our money. Mine was cash, a big bankroll from the Joliet's insurance. Henry had two checks — a week's extra pay for being laid off, and his regular check from the Jewel Bearing Plant.

We were walking down Portage anyway, seeing the sights, when we saw it. There it was, parked, large as life. Really as *if* it was alive. I thought of the word *repose*, because the car wasn't simply stopped, parked, or whatever. That car reposed, calm and gleaming, a FOR SALE sign in its left front window. Then, before we had thought it over at all, the car belonged to us and our pockets were empty. We had just enough money for gas back home.

We went places in that car, me and Henry. We took off driving all one whole summer. We started off toward the Little Knife River and Mandaree in Fort Berthold and then we found ourselves down in Wakpala somehow, and then suddenly we were over in Montana on the Rocky Boy, and yet the summer was not even half over. Some people hang on to details when they travel, but we didn't let them bother us and just lived our everyday lives here to there.

I do remember this one place with willows. I remember I laid under those trees and it was comfortable. So comfortable. The branches bent down all around me like a tent or a stable. And quiet, it was quiet, even though there was a powwow close enough so I could see it going on. The air was not too still, not too windy either. When the dust rises up and hangs in the air around the dancers like that, I feel good. Henry was asleep with his arms thrown wide. Later on, he woke up and we started driving again. We were somewhere in Montana, or maybe on the Blood Reserve — it could have been anywhere. Anyway it was where we met the girl.

All her hair was in buns around her ears, that's the first thing I noticed about her. She was posed alongside the road with her arm out, so we stopped. That girl was short, so short her lumber shirt looked comical on her, like a nightgown. She had jeans on and fancy moccasins and she carried a little suitcase.

"Hop on in," says Henry. So she climbs in between us.

"We'll take you home," I says. "Where do you live?"

"Chicken," she says.

"Where the hell's that?" I ask her.

"Alaska."

"Okay," says Henry, and we drive.

We got up there and never wanted to leave. The sun doesn't truly set there in summer, and the night is more a soft dusk. You might doze off, sometimes, but before you know it you're up again, like an animal in nature. You never feel like you have to sleep hard or put away the world. And things would grow up there. One day just dirt or moss, the next day flowers and long grass. The girl's name was Susy. Her family really took to us. They fed us and put us up. We had our own tent to live in by their house, and the kids would be in and out of there all day and night. They couldn't get over me and Henry being brothers, we looked so different. We told them we knew we had the same mother, anyway.

One night Susy came in to visit us. We sat around in the tent talking of this and that. The season was changing. It was getting darker by that time, and the cold was even getting just a little mean. I told her it was time for us to go. She stood up on a chair.

"You never seen my hair," Susy said.

That was true. She was standing on a chair, but still, when she unclipped her buns the hair reached all the way to the ground. Our eyes opened. You couldn't tell how much hair she had when it was rolled up so neatly. Then my brother Henry did something funny. He went up to the chair and said, "Jump on my shoulders." So she did that, and her hair reached down past his waist, and he started twirling, this way and that, so her hair was flung out from side to side.

"I always wondered what it was like to have long pretty hair," Henry says. Well we laughed. It was a funny sight, the way he did it. The next morning we got up and took leave of those people.

On to greener pastures, as they say. It was down through Spokane and across Idaho then Montana and very soon we were racing the weather right along under the Canadian border through Columbus, Des Lacs, and then we were in Bottineau County and soon home. We'd made most of the trip, that summer, without putting up the car hood at all. We got home just in time, it turned out, for the army to remember Henry had signed up to join it.

I don't wonder that the army was so glad to get my brother that they turned him into a Marine. He was built like a brick outhouse anyway. We liked to tease him that they really wanted him for his Indian nose. He had a nose big and sharp as a hatchet, like the nose on Red Tomahawk, the Indian who killed Sitting Bull, whose profile is on signs all along the North Dakota highways. Henry went off to training camp, came home once during Christmas, then the next thing you know we got an overseas letter from him. It was 1970, and he said he was stationed up in the northern hill country. Whereabouts I did not know. He wasn't such a hot letter writer, and only got off two before the enemy caught him. I could never keep it straight, which direction those good Vietnam soldiers were from.

I wrote him back several times, even though I didn't know if those letters would get through. I kept him informed all about the car. Most of the time I had it up on blocks in the yard or half taken apart, because that long trip did a hard job on it under the hood.

I always had good luck with numbers, and never worried about the draft myself. I never even had to think about what my number was. But Henry was never lucky in the same way as me. It was at least three years before Henry came home. By then I guess the whole war was solved in the government's mind, but for him it would keep on going. In those years I'd put his car into almost perfect shape. I always thought of it as his car while he was gone, even though when he left he said, "Now it's yours," and threw me his key.

"Thanks for the extra key," I'd said. "I'll put it up in your drawer just in case I need it." He laughed. 25

When he came home, though, Henry was very different, and I'll say this: the change was no good. You could hardly expect him to change for the better, I know. But he was quiet, so quiet, and never comfortable sitting still anywhere but always up and moving around. I thought back to times we'd sat still for whole afternoons, never moving a muscle, just shifting our weight along the ground, talking to whoever sat with us, watching things. He'd always had a joke, then, too, and now you couldn't get him to laugh, or when he did it was more the sound of a man choking, a sound that stopped up the throats of other people around him. They got to leaving him alone most of the time, and I didn't blame them. It was a fact: Henry was jumpy and mean.

I'd bought a color TV set for my mom and the rest of us while Henry was away. Money still came very easy. I was sorry I'd ever bought it though, because of Henry. I was also sorry I'd bought color, because with black-and-white the pictures seem older and farther away. But what are you going to do? He sat in front of it, watching it, and that was the only time he was completely still. But it was the kind of stillness that you see in a rabbit when it freezes and before it will bolt. He was not easy. He sat in his chair gripping the armrests with all his might, as if the chair itself was moving at a high speed and if he let go at all he would rocket forward and maybe crash right through the set.

Once I was in the room watching TV with Henry and I heard his teeth click at something. I looked over, and he'd bitten through his lip. Blood was going down his chin. I tell you right then I wanted to smash that tube to pieces. I went over to it but Henry must have known what I was up to. He rushed from his chair and shoved me out of the way, against the wall. I told myself he didn't know what he was doing.

My mom came in, turned the set off real quiet, and told us she had made something for supper. So we went and sat down. There was still blood going down Henry's chin, but he didn't notice it and no one said anything, even though every time he took a bite of his bread his blood fell onto it until he was eating his own blood mixed in with the food.

While Henry was not around we talked about what was going to happen to him. There were no Indian doctors on the reservation, and my mom couldn't come around to trusting the old man, Moses Pillager, because he courted her long ago and was jealous of her husbands. He might take revenge through her son. We were afraid that if we brought Henry to a regular hospital they would keep him.

"They don't fix them in those places," Mom said; "they just give them drugs."

"We wouldn't get him there in the first place," I agreed, "so let's just forget about it."

Then I thought about the car.

Henry had not even looked at the car since he'd gotten home, though like I said, it was in tip-top condition and ready to drive. I thought the car might bring the old Henry back somehow. So I bided my time and waited for my chance to interest him in the vehicle.

One night Henry was off somewhere. I took myself a hammer. I went out to that car and I did a number on its underside. Whacked it up. Bent the tail pipe double. Ripped the muffler loose. By the time I was done with the car it looked worse than any typical Indian car that has been driven all its life on reservation roads, which they always say are like government promises — full of holes. It just about hurt me, I'll tell you that! I threw dirt in the carburetor and I ripped all the electric tape off the seats. I made it look just as beat up as I could. Then I sat back and waited for Henry to find it.

Still, it took him over a month. That was all right, because it was just getting warm enough, not melting, but warm enough to work outside.

"Lyman," he says, walking in one day, "that red car looks like shit."

"Well it's old," I says. "You got to expect that."

"No way!" says Henry. "That car's a classic! But you went and ran the piss right out of it, Lyman, and you know it don't deserve that. I kept that car in A-one shape. You don't remember. You're too young. But when I left, that car was running like a watch. Now I don't even know if I can get it to start again, let alone get it anywhere near its old condition."

"Well you try," I said, like I was getting mad, "but I say it's a piece of junk."

Then I walked out before he could realize I knew he'd strung together more than six words at once.

After that I thought he'd freeze himself to death working on that car. He was out there all day, and at night he rigged up a little lamp, ran a cord out the window, and had himself some light to see by while he worked. He was better than he had been before, but that's still not saying much. It was easier for him to do the things the rest of us did. He ate more slowly and didn't jump up and down during the meal to get this or that or look out the window. I put my hand in the back of the TV set, I admit, and fiddled around with it good, so that it was almost impossible now to get a clear picture. He didn't look at it very often anyway. He was always out with that car or going off to get parts for it. By the time it was really melting outside, he had it fixed.

I had been feeling down in the dumps about Henry around this time. We had always been together before. Henry and Lyman. But he was such a loner now that I didn't know how to take it. So I jumped at the chance one day when Henry seemed friendly. It's not that he smiled or anything. He just said, "Let's take that old shitbox for a spin." Just the way he said it made me think he could be coming around.

We went out to the car. It was spring. The sun was shining very bright. My only sister, Bonita, who was just eleven years old, came out and made us stand together for a picture. Henry leaned his elbow on the red car's wind-shield, and he took his other arm and put it over my shoulder, very care-fully, as though it was heavy for him to lift and he didn't want to bring the weight down all at once.

"Smile," Bonita said, and he did.   45

That picture. I never look at it anymore. A few months ago, I don't know why, I got his picture out and tacked it on the wall. I felt good about Henry at the time, close to him. I felt good having his picture on the wall, until one night when I was looking at television. I was a little drunk and stoned. I looked up at the wall and Henry was staring at me. I don't know what it was, but his smile had changed, or maybe it was gone. All I know is I couldn't stay in the same room with that picture. I was shaking. I got up, closed the door, and went into the kitchen. A little later my friend Ray came over and we both went back into that room. We put the picture in a brown bag, folded the bag over and over tightly, then put it way back in a closet.

I still see that picture now, as if it tugs at me, whenever I pass that closet door. The picture is very clear in my mind. It was so sunny that day Henry had to squint against the glare. Or maybe the camera Bonita held flashed like a mirror, blinding him, before she snapped the picture. My face is right out in the sun, big and round. But he might have drawn back, because the shadows on his face are deep as holes. There are two shadows curved like little hooks around the ends of his smile, as if to frame it and try to keep it there — that one, first smile that looked like it might have hurt his face. He has his field jacket on and the worn-in clothes he'd come back in and kept wearing ever since. After Bonita took the picture, she went into the house and we got into the car. There was a full cooler in the trunk. We started off, east, toward Pembina and the Red River because Henry said he wanted to see the high water.

The trip over there was beautiful. When everything starts changing, dry-ing up, clearing off, you feel like your whole life is starting. Henry felt it, too. The top was down and the car hummed like a top. He'd really put it back in shape, even the tape on the seats was very carefully put down and glued back in layers. It's not that he smiled again or even joked, but his face looked to me as if it was clear, more peaceful. It looked as though he wasn't thinking of anything in particular except the bare fields and windbreaks and houses we were passing.

The river was high and full of winter trash when we got there. The sun was still out, but it was colder by the river. There were still little clumps of dirty snow here and there on the banks. The water hadn't gone over the banks yet, but it would, you could tell. It was just at its limit, hard swollen, glossy like an old gray scar. We made ourselves a fire, and we sat down and watched the current go. As I watched it I felt something squeezing inside me and tightening and trying to let go all at the same time. I knew I was not just feeling it myself; I knew I was feeling what Henry was going through at that moment. Except that I couldn't stand it, the closing and opening. I jumped to my feet. I took Henry by the shoulders and I started shaking him. "Wake up," I says, "wake up, wake up, wake up!" I didn't know what had come over me. I sat down beside him again.

His face was totally white and hard. Then it broke, like stones break all   50 of a sudden when water boils up inside them.

"I know it," he says. "I know it. I can't help it. It's no use."

We start talking. He said he knew what I'd done with the car. It was obvious it had been whacked out of shape and not just neglected. He said he wanted to give the car to me for good now, it was no use. He said he'd fixed it just to give it back and I should take it.

"No way," I says. "I don't want it."

"That's okay," he says, "you take it."

"I don't want it, though," I says back to him, and then to emphasize, just   55 to emphasize, you understand, I touch his shoulder. He slaps my hand off.

"Take that car," he says.

"No," I say. "Make me," I say, and then he grabs my jacket and rips the arm loose. That jacket is a class act, suede with tags and zippers. I push Henry backwards, off the log. He jumps up and bowls me over. We go down in a clinch and come up swinging hard, for all we're worth, with our fists. He socks my jaw so hard I feel like it swings loose. Then I'm at his rib cage and land a good one under his chin so his head snaps back. He's dazzled. He looks at me and I look at him and then his eyes are full of tears and blood and at first I think he's crying. But no, he's laughing. "Ha! Ha!" he says. "Ha! Ha! Take good care of it."

"Okay," I says. "Okay, no problem. Ha! Ha!"

I can't help it, and I start laughing, too. My face feels fat and strange, and after a while I get a beer from the cooler in the trunk, and when I hand it to Henry he takes his shirt and wipes my germs off. "Hoof-and-mouth disease," he says. For some reason this cracks me up, and so we're really laughing for a while, and then we drink all the rest of the beers one by one and throw them in the river and see how far, how fast, the current takes them before they fill up and sink.

"You want to go on back?" I ask after a while. "Maybe we could snag a 60
couple nice Kashpaw girls."

He says nothing. But I can tell his mood is turning again.

"They're all crazy, the girls up here, every damn one of them."

"You're crazy too," I say, to jolly him up. "Crazy Lamartine boys!"

He looks as though he will take this wrong at first. His face twists, then
clears, and he jumps up on his feet. "That's right!" he says. "Crazier 'n hell.
Crazy Indians!"

I think it's the old Henry again. He throws off his jacket and starts 65
springing his legs up from the knees like a fancy dancer. He's down doing
something between a grass dance and a bunny hop, no kind of dance I ever
saw before, but neither has anyone else on all this green growing earth. He's
wild. He wants to pitch whoopee! He's up and at me and all over. All this
time I'm laughing so hard, so hard my belly is getting tied up in a knot.

"Got to cool me off!" he shouts all of a sudden. Then he runs over to
the river and jumps in.

There's boards and other things in the current. It's so high. No sound
comes from the river after the splash he makes, so I run right over. I look
around. It's getting dark. I see he's halfway across the water already, and I
know he didn't swim there but the current took him. It's far. I hear his voice,
though, very clearly across it.

"My boots are filling," he says.

He says this in a normal voice, like he just noticed and he doesn't know
what to think of it. Then he's gone. A branch comes by. Another branch.
And I go in.

By the time I get out of the river, off the snag I pulled myself onto, the sun 70
is down. I walk back to the car, turn on the high beams, and drive it up the
bank. I put it in first gear and then I take my foot off the clutch. I get out,
close the door, and watch it plow softly into the water. The headlights reach
in as they go down, searching, still lighted even after the water swirls over
the back end. I wait. The wires short out. It is all finally dark. And then
there is only the water, the sound of it going and running and going and
running and running.

Considerations for Critical Thinking and Writing

1. FIRST RESPONSE. The way Lyman describes his brother's death and the
   fate of the car in the first paragraph is abstract: the reader would have
   no way of knowing what he means by "his boots filled with water" or
   "Now Henry owns the whole car." What is the effect of this indirect
   description at the beginning of the story?

2. Why does Lyman emphasize money? What is his attitude toward it?

3. Based on Lyman's initial description of the car, what is its importance?
   What can you tell about Lyman's and Henry's lives that makes sense of
   their attraction to the car?

4. Compare the scenes when Lyman describes lying under willow trees and when the Alaskan girl they temporarily live with lets her hair down all the way to the ground. Can you make sense of these two parallel scenes within the context of the story as a whole?

5. Discuss the tension between motion and stillness in the story.

6. If Henry needs to be healed after his war experience, why does Lyman damage the red convertible (which is strongly associated with Henry)?

7. From the moment Lyman describes a fryolator in a tree after a tornado, we are aware that nature and mechanical objects have a strange relationship in this story. Locate descriptions of both and discuss their relationship to one another as a way of sharpening your sense of the story's theme.

8. Look again at the section of the story where Lyman discusses the last photograph taken of his brother, and of his reaction to having that photo in his house. What is the significance of this section to the story overall?

9. The red convertible is obviously meaningful to the story: it is the title, after all. As a symbol, how do you interpret it? Bear in mind its color as you respond, since its redness is emphasized.

CONNECTION TO ANOTHER SELECTION

1. Discuss the relationship between brothers in this story and in James Baldwin's "Sonny's Blues" (p. 76).

CYNTHIA OZICK (B. 1928)

Born in New York City, Cynthia Ozick was raised by parents who had emigrated from Russia. She was educated at New York University and the Ohio State University. Ozick's work has garnered many prestigious awards, including the National Book Award, the PEN/Nabokov Award, and the PEN/Malamud Award. Most of her two dozen books are novels and story collections, though she has also published eight essay collections and a play. Her work engages deeply with Jewish identity, particularly with the trauma in the aftermath of the Holocaust. Such is the case in the following short story, "The Shawl," first published in 1980 and widely studied since.

Ulf Andersen/Getty Images Entertainment/ Getty Images.

The Shawl   1980

Stella, cold, cold, the coldness of hell. How they walked on the roads together, Rosa with Magda curled up between sore breasts, Magda wound up in the shawl. Sometimes Stella carried Magda. But she was jealous of Magda. A thin girl of fourteen, too small, with thin breasts of her own, Stella wanted to be wrapped in a shawl, hidden away, asleep, rocked by the march, a baby, a round infant in arms. Magda took Rosa's nipple, and Rosa never stopped walking, a walking cradle. There was not enough milk; sometimes Magda sucked air; then she screamed. Stella was ravenous. Her knees were tumors on sticks, her elbows chicken bones.

Rosa did not feel hunger; she felt light, not like someone walking but like someone in a faint, in trance, arrested in a fit, someone who is already a floating angel, alert and seeing everything, but in the air, not there, not touching the road. As if teetering on the tips of her fingernails. She looked into Magda's face through a gap in the shawl: a squirrel in a nest, safe, no one could reach her inside the little house of the shawl's windings. The face, very round, a pocket mirror of a face: but it was not Rosa's bleak complexion, dark like cholera, it was another kind of face altogether, eyes blue as air, smooth feathers of hair nearly as yellow as the Star sewn into Rosa's coat. You could think she was one of *their* babies.

Rosa, floating, dreamed of giving Magda away in one of the villages. She could leave the line for a minute and push Magda into the hands of any woman on the side of the road. But if she moved out of line they might shoot. And even if she fled the line for half a second and pushed the shawl-bundle at a stranger, would the woman take it? She might be surprised, or afraid; she might drop the shawl, and Magda would fall out and strike her head and die. The little round head. Such a good child, she gave up screaming, and sucked now only for the taste of the drying nipple itself. The neat grip of the tiny gums. One mite of a tooth tip sticking up in the bottom gum, how shining, an elfin tombstone of white marble gleaming there. Without complaining, Magda relinquished Rosa's teats, first the left, then the right; both were cracked, not a sniff of milk. The duct-crevice extinct, a dead volcano, blind eye, chill hole, so Magda took the corner of the shawl and milked it instead. She sucked and sucked, flooding the threads with wetness. The shawl's good flavor, milk of linen.

It was a magic shawl, it could nourish an infant for three days and three nights. Magda did not die, she stayed alive, although very quiet. A peculiar smell, of cinnamon and almonds, lifted out of her mouth. She held her eyes open every moment, forgetting how to blink or nap, and Rosa and sometimes Stella studied their blueness. On the road they raised one burden of a leg after another and studied Magda's face. "Aryan," Stella said, in a voice grown as thin as a string; and Rosa thought how Stella gazed at Magda like a young cannibal. And the time that Stella said "Aryan," it sounded to Rosa as if Stella had really said "Let us devour her."

But Magda lived to walk. She lived that long, but she did not walk very   5
well, partly because she was only fifteen months old, and partly because
the spindles of her legs could not hold up her fat belly. It was fat with air,
full and round. Rosa gave almost all her food to Magda, Stella gave nothing; Stella was ravenous, a growing child herself, but not growing much.
Stella did not menstruate. Rosa did not menstruate. Rosa was ravenous, but
also not; she learned from Magda how to drink the taste of a finger in one's
mouth. They were in a place without pity, all pity was annihilated in Rosa,
she looked at Stella's bones without pity. She was sure that Stella was waiting
for Magda to die so she could put her teeth into the little thighs.

Rosa knew Magda was going to die very soon; she should have been
dead already, but she had been buried away deep inside the magic shawl,
mistaken there for the shivering mound of Rosa's breasts; Rosa clung to the
shawl as if it covered only herself. No one took it away from her. Magda was
mute. She never cried. Rosa hid her in the barracks, under the shawl, but she
knew that one day someone would inform; or one day someone, not even
Stella, would steal Magda to eat her. When Magda began to walk, Rosa knew
that Magda was going to die very soon, something would happen. She was
afraid to fall asleep; she slept with the weight of her thigh on Magda's body;
she was afraid she would smother Magda under her thigh. The weight of
Rosa was becoming less and less; Rosa and Stella were slowly turning into air.

Magda was quiet, but her eyes were horribly alive, like blue tigers. She
watched. Sometimes she laughed — it seemed a laugh, but how could it
be? Magda had never seen anyone laugh. Still, Magda laughed at her shawl
when the wind blew its corners, the bad wind with pieces of black in it, that
made Stella's and Rosa's eyes tear. Magda's eyes were always clear and tearless. She watched like a tiger. She guarded her shawl. No one could touch
it; only Rosa could touch it. Stella was not allowed. The shawl was Magda's
own baby, her pet, her little sister. She tangled herself up in it and sucked on
one of the corners when she wanted to be very still.

Then Stella took the shawl away and made Magda die.

Afterward Stella said: "I was cold."

And afterward she was always cold, always. The cold went into her   10
heart: Rosa saw that Stella's heart was cold. Magda flopped onward with her
little pencil legs scribbling this way and that, in search of the shawl; the pen-
cils faltered at the barracks opening, where the light began. Rosa saw and
pursued. But already Magda was in the square outside the barracks, in the
jolly light. It was the roll-call arena. Every morning Rosa had to conceal
Magda under the shawl against a wall of the barracks and go out and stand
in the arena with Stella and hundreds of others, sometimes for hours, and
Magda, deserted, was quiet under the shawl, sucking on her corner. Every
day Magda was silent, and so she did not die. Rosa saw that today Magda
was going to die, and at the same time a fearful joy ran in Rosa's two palms,
her fingers were on fire, she was astonished, febrile:° Magda, in the sunlight,

---

febrile: Feverish, excited.

swaying on her pencil legs, was howling. Ever since the drying up of Rosa's nipples, ever since Magda's last scream on the road, Magda had been devoid of any syllable; Magda was a mute. Rosa believed that something had gone wrong with her vocal cords, with her windpipe, with the cave of her larynx; Magda was defective, without a voice; perhaps she was deaf; there might be something amiss with her intelligence; Magda was dumb. Even the laugh that came when the ash-stippled wind made a clown out of Magda's shawl was only the air-blown showing of her teeth. Even when the lice, head lice and body lice, crazed her so that she became as wild as one of the big rats that plundered the barracks at daybreak looking for carrion, she rubbed and scratched and kicked and bit and rolled without a whimper. But now Magda's mouth was spilling a long viscous rope of clamor.

"Maaaa —"

It was the first noise Magda had ever sent out from her throat since the drying up of Rosa's nipples.

"Maaaa . . . aaa!"

Again! Magda was wavering in the perilous sunlight of the arena, scribbling on such pitiful little bent shins. Rosa saw. She saw that Magda was grieving for the loss of her shawl, she saw that Magda was going to die. A tide of commands hammered in Rosa's nipples: Fetch, get, bring! But she did not know which to go after first, Magda or the shawl. If she jumped out into the arena to snatch Magda up, the howling would not stop, because Magda would still not have the shawl; but if she ran back into the barracks to find the shawl, and if she found it, and if she came after Magda holding it and shaking it, then she would get Magda back, Magda would put the shawl in her mouth and turn dumb again.

Rosa entered the dark. It was easy to discover the shawl. Stella was   15
heaped under it, asleep in her thin bones. Rosa tore the shawl free and flew — she could fly, she was only air — into the arena. The sunheat murmured of another life, of butterflies in summer. The light was placid, mellow. On the other side of the steel fence, far away, there were green meadows speckled with dandelions and deep-colored violets; beyond them, even farther, innocent tiger lilies, tall, lifting their orange bonnets. In the barracks they spoke of "flowers," of "rain": excrement, thick turd-braids, and the slow stinking maroon waterfall that slunk down from the upper bunks, the stink mixed with a bitter fatty floating smoke that greased Rosa's skin. She stood for an instant at the margin of the arena. Sometimes the electricity inside the fence would seem to hum; even Stella said it was only an imagining, but Rosa heard real sounds in the wire: grainy sad voices. The farther she was from the fence, the more clearly the voices crowded at her. The lamenting voices strummed so convincingly, so passionately, it was impossible to suspect them of being phantoms. The voices told her to hold up the shawl, high; the voices told her to shake it, to whip with it, to unfurl it like a flag. Rosa lifted, shook, whipped, unfurled. Far off, very far, Magda leaned across her air-fed belly, reaching out with the rods of her arms. She was high up,

elevated, riding someone's shoulder. But the shoulder that carried Magda was not coming toward Rosa and the shawl, it was drifting away, the speck of Magda was moving more and more into the smoky distance. Above the shoulder a helmet glinted. The light tapped the helmet and sparkled it into a goblet. Below the helmet a black body like a domino and a pair of black boots hurled themselves in the direction of the electrified fence. The electric voices began to chatter wildly. "Maamaa, maaamaaa," they all hummed together. How far Magda was from Rosa now, across the whole square, past a dozen barracks, all the way on the other side! She was no bigger than a moth.

All at once Magda was swimming through the air. The whole of Magda traveled through loftiness. She looked like a butterfly touching a silver vine. And the moment Magda's feathered round head and her pencil legs and balloonish belly and zigzag arms splashed against the fence, the steel voices went mad in their growling, urging Rosa to run and run to the spot where Magda had fallen from her flight against the electrified fence; but of course Rosa did not obey them. She only stood, because if she ran they would shoot, and if she tried to pick up the sticks of Magda's body they would shoot, and if she let the wolf's screech ascending now through the ladder of her skeleton break out, they would shoot; so she took Magda's shawl and filled her own mouth with it, stuffed it in and stuffed it in, until she was swallowing up the wolf's screech and tasting the cinnamon and almond depth of Magda's saliva; and Rosa drank Magda's shawl until it dried.

CONSIDERATIONS FOR CRITICAL THINKING AND WRITING

1. **FIRST RESPONSE.** The shawl is twice described as "a magic shawl." Which other elements in the story are in the realm of the unrealistic, otherworldly, or abstract? What is the effect of a story about one of the harshest events in history employing imagery of this nature?

2. The shawl is a complex symbol. What are its primary associations? What are its less obvious associations? Ultimately, what do you think it symbolizes?

3. In addition to symbolism, the story relies on the figurative language common in poetry (metaphor and simile). For example, in the first paragraph, Stella's body is described this way: "Her knees were tumors on sticks, her elbows chicken bones." List other examples of figurative language in the story and consider how they contribute to its overall effect on the reader.

4. Discuss the motifs of hunger and eating throughout the story.

5. In the arresting eighth paragraph, the baby Magda's death is blamed on the fact that Stella took the shawl away from her. It is clear that her death and her miserable existence are the fault of the Nazis who created the concentration camps. What is the effect of blaming Stella, who is also a victim?

6. What other images of predators and prey do you see in the story? What is their significance in terms of its theme?

7. Why do you think Ozick chose to refer to the three characters in the story by their first names instead of by their relationships (mother, daughter, sister, etc.)?

8. How do you interpret the voices Rosa hears toward the end of the story?

9. Although the story's setting is clearly a Nazi concentration camp, the story does not name that setting explicitly. How does Ozick evoke that setting without naming it?

10. How would you characterize the story's point of view (see Chapter 5)? Is it consistent throughout?

11. The story presents its characters' bodies in an unusual way: How does it present them and why is this presentation effective in terms of the story's broader aims?

12. Appropriate to its subject matter, the story is gruesome and horrifying. Is there anything to balance its horrifying imagery? Is the shawl, in fact, that balancing force or does it ultimately become part of the horror?

CONNECTION TO ANOTHER SELECTION

1. Compare human suffering in "The Shawl" and in Ursula K. Le Guin's "The Ones Who Walk Away from Omelas" (p. 111). Does the fact that one story is rooted in grim reality and the other in fantasy affect your comparison?

A SAMPLE STUDENT RESPONSE

Aria Sergany

Professor Curtis

English 101

1 January 2019

Layers of Symbol in Cynthia Ozick's "The Shawl"

Although it is a profound and unsettling depiction of life in the barracks during the Holocaust, "The Shawl" never directly states the nature of the conflict, the surrounding events, or anything substantial about the characters. The story introduces Rosa and her two daughters: Magda, a baby wrapped in a shawl, and Stella, a fourteen-year-old who is "jealous of Magda" and the special treatment the shawl provides her (Ozick, 170). The shawl immediately becomes representative of a one-sided conflict in the daughters' relationship: "Stella [is] not allowed" to even touch the shawl (171). The sparse information given about character, setting, and time period forces the reader to focus all of their attention on this symbol. The weight given to the shawl makes it a magical object to the reader, as it is for the family in the story. The careful unpacking of this symbol reveals a contradiction: the shawl is representative of not only what the reader expects it to be (like safety, life, and food), but also of the failure to speak out for people who have had these rights taken away. By so successfully utilizing the symbol of the shawl, Cynthia Ozick captures the core of the Holocaust and the struggle of each individual in it through the story of one family and their personal tragedy. The shawl comes to represent not only comfort in life, but the phenomenon in which humanity looks the other way in times of tragedy and the cost of that silence.

The shawl, at first, seems an uncomplicated symbol to analyze. Ozick says outright that it is "a magic shawl, it [can] nourish an infant for three days and three nights" (170). Without the shawl "Stella [is] ravenous" the story repeats (170, 171). The imaginary world of the shawl works in contrast with the horrors of reality outside of it; "Stella want[s] to be wrapped in a shawl, hidden away, asleep, rocked by the march, a baby, a round infant in arms" (170). On this march where Rosa and Stella cannot attain simple means of survival, the physical object of the shawl comes to represent a much larger, metaphorical, magical meaning. Rosa considers giving Magda away because "you could think [Magda is] one of *their* babies" (170). Part of the magic is that the shawl makes one passably Aryan: the one thing they cannot be, and the only thing that could save them. This chance at survival, along with the façade of Magda's present health and safety, is what drives Stella's jealousy: when Stella says "'Aryan,' it sound[s] to Rosa as if Stella had really said 'Let us devour [Magda]'" (170). Rosa is driven by saving Magda, which leaves Stella to fend for herself. Stella makes a choice; she takes "the shawl away and [makes] Magda die" (171). It is easy to blame Stella for this choice, but Ozick reminds the reader that this family is "in a place without pity" (p. 171).

Stella has lost her compassion for Magda. From the very start, Stella is "cold, cold, the coldness of hell" (170). Stella sees Magda living in relative bliss and not sharing any of it with her sister. Stella looks "into Magda's face through a gap in the shawl: a squirrel in a nest, safe, no one could reach her inside the little house of the shawl's windings" (170). When Stella takes the shawl, the symbol expands to include the tendency that humans have to be unwilling to help others when their own lives are comfortable, or because they are afraid of what will happen to them. This aspect of the symbol is what makes the story universal. People can relate to the fear or reality of being ignored in times of distress, as well as the desire not to get involved in what are considered other's problems. The shawl is not only representative of comfort, but of the psychological effect that having or not having that comfort can have on an individual. Stella, with no comfort of her own in a horrible situation, starts to look at Magda "like a young cannibal" (170). Rosa is sure that Stella is "waiting for Magda to die so she [can] put her teeth into the little thighs" (171). Stella's decision to take the shawl away from Magda only makes Stella even colder. After, Stella is "always cold, always. The cold went into her heart" (171). Rosa is old enough to understand the consequences of taking the shawl from Magda: Rosa sees "that Magda [is] grieving for the loss of her shawl, she [sees] that Magda [is] going to die" (172). Stella fails to comprehend that without the shawl Magda's fate is set. She does not realize this until it is too late.

Stella's ignorance allows her to become apathetic toward Magda. Apathy, in many ways, exacerbated the Holocaust. While the average person did not start the Holocaust, by doing and saying nothing to stop it they allowed it to continue. It is easy to choose the wellbeing of oneself over someone else, as in the case of Stella and Magda. However, there is another issue at play here: silence. No one in this story speaks out against the many atrocities that are happening: the exception being Magda's cries right at the end. In fact, there is little sound in the story at all. Stella says "I was cold" as her reasoning for taking the shawl (171). The sound of Magda's laughter: "sometimes she laughed — it seemed a laugh, but how could it be? Magda had never seen anyone laugh" (171). But mostly, it is just Magda's silence; it is brought up over and over again. "Every day Magda was silent, and so she did not die" (171). "Magda was quiet" (171). "Magda had been devoid of any syllable: Magda was a mute" (172). Magda's silence when in the shawl is emphasized to dramatize her screams at the end. Without the comfort of the shawl, Magda's "mouth [is] spilling a long viscous rope of clamor," she is pushed to speak out, to yell, and eventually to be seen by a guard and taken to her death (172). Fear keeps Rosa and Stella from speaking even without the shawl, but Magda is too young to have developed that fear. Magda still has a chance to speak out, and she briefly gets to have her voice heard.

Ozick uses symbol so effectively that the reader is pulled into the story and forced to live through the impossible choices that the characters have to make. Rosa makes a very difficult decision in the final moments of the story: she can either snatch up Madga and try to get her to safety although she will be noticed, or she can go get the shawl to quiet Magda. She chooses the shawl. Returning to Magda with the shawl, Rosa realizes it is already too late. Rosa hears "real sounds in the wire: grainy sad voices" coming from the electric fence (172). These voices represent the victims of the past and all of Rosa's personal history telling her that she needs to do something. To speak. To stop this from ever happening again. To act in Magda's memory despite that she would certainly die as well. "The steel voices went mad in their growling, urging Rosa to run and run to the spot where Magda had fallen" (173). Rosa stays quiet in her fear; she shoves the shawl into her mouth to keep from screaming. With the loss of Magda (and the silence of her family in the face of her loss) the potential for change dies and the fear lives on. Then "Rosa [drinks] Magda's shawl until it drie[s]" in an attempt to mitigate her pain (173). The last bit of the shawl's magic is used up, and Rosa and Stella are left with nothing. Without the shawl and without Magda there is nothing to look forward to, there is no hope for any sort of future. There is not even anything for Stella to be jealous of any-more. In Stella's selfishness and Rosa's silence, they lose themselves to the war. The shawl now symbolizes what the constant fear and oppression can do to a person. In the same way the shawl shifts from seemingly comforting to horrifying, Stella shifts from her expected role as a loving sister to a selfish person able to commit indirect murder. Stella's heart turns cold like the rest of her, and the last of her humanity is lost. The shawl can give us a blissful life, but it is up to us to use that privilege to speak out for those who cannot speak for themselves.

Works Cited

Meyer, Michael and D. Quentin Miller, editors. Literature to Go. 4th ed., Bedford/St. Martin's, 2020.

Ozick, Cynthia. "The Shawl." Meyer and Miller, pp. 170–73.

ANN BEATTIE (B. 1947)

Ann Beattie published her first novel and first story collection the same year, 1976, to great acclaim. Since then she has produced a steady stream of novels and stories; like other authors in this book (John Cheever, John Updike, and Raymond Carver, for example), many of her stories were published in the *New Yorker*, one of the premier literary magazines. Beattie has been recognized with the Rea Award, which recognizes authors for their significant achievements in the short story genre. She is often associated with a literary movement that flourished in the 1970s and 1980s known as minimalism, a style that portrays the emotionally stark lives

Ulf Andersen/Getty Images Entertainment/Getty Images.

of its characters in prose that is straightforward and stripped down, and that maintains a certain narrative distance.

Janus 1986

The bowl was perfect. Perhaps it was not what you'd select if you faced a shelf of bowls, and not the sort of thing that would inevitably attract a lot of attention at a crafts fair, yet it had real presence. It was as predictably admired as a mutt who has no reason to suspect he might be funny. Just such a dog, in fact, was often brought out (and in) along with the bowl.

Andrea was a real estate agent, and when she thought that some prospective buyers might be dog lovers, she would drop off her dog at the same time she placed the bowl in the house that was up for sale. She would put a dish of water in the kitchen for Mondo, take his squeaking plastic frog out of her purse and drop it on the floor. He would pounce delightedly, just as he did every day at home, batting around his favorite toy. The bowl usually sat on a coffee table, though recently she had displayed it on top of a pine blanket chest and on a lacquered table. It was once placed on a cherry table beneath a Bonnard° still life, where it held its own.

Everyone who has purchased a house or who has wanted to sell a house must be familiar with some of the tricks used to convince a buyer that the house is quite special: a fire in the fireplace in early evening; jonquils in a pitcher on the kitchen counter, where no one ordinarily has space to put flowers; perhaps the slight aroma of spring, made by a single drop of scent vaporizing from a lamp bulb.

The wonderful thing about the bowl, Andrea thought, was that it was both subtle and noticeable — a paradox of a bowl. Its glaze was the color of cream and seemed to glow no matter what light it was placed in. There were

Bonnard: A French painter active in the early to mid-twentieth century.

a few bits of color in it — tiny geometric flashes — and some of these were tinged with flecks of silver. They were as mysterious as cells seen under a microscope; it was difficult not to study them, because they shimmered, flashing for a split second, and then resumed their shape. Something about the colors and their random placement suggested motion. People who liked country furniture always commented on the bowl, but then it turned out that people who felt comfortable with Biedermeier° loved it just as much. But the bowl was not at all ostentatious, or even so noticeable that anyone would suspect that it had been put in place deliberately. They might notice the height of the ceiling on first entering a room, and only when their eye moved down from that, or away from the refraction of sunlight on a pale wall, would they see the bowl. Then they would go immediately to it and comment. Yet they always faltered when they tried to say something. Perhaps it was because they were in the house for a serious reason, not to notice some object.

Once, Andrea got a call from a woman who had not put in an offer on a   5 house she had shown her. That bowl, she said — would it be possible to find out where the owners had bought that beautiful bowl? Andrea pretended that she did not know what the woman was referring to. A bowl, somewhere in the house? Oh, on a table under the window. Yes, she would ask, of course. She let a couple of days pass, then called back to say that the bowl had been a present and the people did not know where it had been purchased.

When the bowl was not being taken from house to house, it sat on Andrea's coffee table at home. She didn't keep it carefully wrapped (although she transported it that way, in a box); she kept it on the table, because she liked to see it. It was large enough so that it didn't seem fragile, or particularly vulnerable if anyone sideswiped the table or Mondo blundered into it at play. She had asked her husband to please not drop his house key in it. It was meant to be empty.

When her husband first noticed the bowl, he had peered into it and smiled briefly. He always urged her to buy things she liked. In recent years, both of them had acquired many things to make up for all the lean years when they were graduate students, but now that they had been comfortable for quite a while, the pleasure of new possessions dwindled. Her husband had pronounced the bowl "pretty," and he had turned away without picking it up to examine it. He had no more interest in the bowl than she had in his new Leica°.

She was sure that the bowl brought her luck. Bids were often put in on houses where she had displayed the bowl. Sometimes the owners, who were always asked to be away or to step outside when the house was being shown, didn't even know that the bowl had been in their house. Once — she could not imagine how — she left it behind, and then she was so afraid that something might have happened to it that she rushed back to the house and sighed with relief when the woman owner opened the door. The bowl, Andrea explained — she had purchased a bowl and set it on the chest for safekeeping while she toured the house with the prospective buyers, and

Biedermeier: A style of German furniture design from the mid-nineteenth century; elegant but simple.
Leica: An expensive camera.

she . . . She felt like rushing past the frowning woman and seizing her bowl. The owner stepped aside, and it was only when Andrea ran to the chest that the lady glanced at her a little strangely. In the few seconds before Andrea picked up the bowl, she realized that the owner must have just seen that it had been perfectly placed, that the sunlight struck the bluer part of it. Her pitcher had been moved to the far side of the chest, and the bowl predominated. All the way home, Andrea wondered how she could have left the bowl behind. It was like leaving a friend at an outing — just walking off. Sometimes there were stories in the paper about families forgetting a child somewhere and driving to the next city. Andrea had only gone a mile down the road before she remembered.

In time, she dreamed of the bowl. Twice, in a waking dream — early in the morning, between sleep and a last nap before rising — she had a clear vision of it. It came into sharp focus and startled her for a moment — the same bowl she looked at every day.

She had a very profitable year selling real estate. Word spread, and she had more clients than she felt comfortable with. She had the foolish thought that if only the bowl were an animate object she could thank it. There were times when she wanted to talk to her husband about the bowl. He was a stockbroker, and sometimes told people that he was fortunate to be married to a woman who had such a fine aesthetic sense and yet could also function in the real world. They were a lot alike, really — they had agreed on that. They were both quiet people — reflective, slow to make value judgments, but almost intractable once they had come to a conclusion. They both liked details, but while ironies attracted her, he was more impatient and dismissive when matters became many sided or unclear. But they both knew this; it was the kind of thing they could talk about when they were alone in the car together, coming home from a party or after a weekend with friends. But she never talked to him about the bowl. When they were at dinner, exchanging their news of the day, or while they lay in bed at night listening to the stereo and murmuring sleepy disconnections, she was often tempted to come right out and say that she thought that the bowl in the living room, the cream-colored bowl, was responsible for her success. But she didn't say it. She couldn't begin to explain it. Sometimes in the morning, she would look at him and feel guilty that she had such a constant secret.

Could it be that she had some deeper connection with the bowl — a relationship of some kind? She corrected her thinking: how could she imagine such a thing, when she was a human being and it was a bowl? It was ridiculous. Just think of how people lived together and loved each other . . . But was that always so clear, always a relationship? She was confused by these thoughts, but they remained in her mind. There was something within her now, something real, that she never talked about.

The bowl was a mystery, even to her. It was frustrating, because her involvement with the bowl contained a steady sense of unrequited good fortune; it would have been easier to respond if some sort of demand were made in return. But that only happened in fairy tales. The bowl was just a bowl. She did not believe that for one second. What she believed was that it was something she loved.

In the past, she had sometimes talked to her husband about a new property she was about to buy or sell — confiding some clever strategy she had devised to persuade owners who seemed ready to sell. Now she stopped doing that, for all her strategies involved the bowl. She became more deliberate with the bowl, and more possessive. She put it in houses only when no one was there, and removed it when she left the house. Instead of just moving a pitcher or a dish, she would remove all the other objects from a table. She had to force herself to handle them carefully, because she didn't really care about them. She just wanted them out of sight.

She wondered how the situation would end. As with a lover, there was no exact scenario of how matters would come to a close. Anxiety became the operative force. It would be irrelevant if the lover rushed into someone else's arms, or wrote her a note and departed to another city. The horror was the possibility of the disappearance. That was what mattered.

She would get up at night and look at the bowl. It never occurred to 15 her that she might break it. She washed and dried it without anxiety, and she moved it often, from coffee table to mahogany corner table or wherever, without fearing an accident. It was clear that she would not be the one who would do anything to the bowl. The bowl was only handled by her, set safely on one surface or another; it was not very likely that anyone would break it. A bowl was a poor conductor of electricity: it would not be hit by lightning. Yet the idea of damage persisted. She did not think beyond that — to what her life would be without the bowl. She only continued to fear that some accident would happen. Why not, in a world where people set plants where they did not belong, so that visitors touring a house would be fooled into thinking that dark corners got sunlight — a world full of tricks?

She had first seen the bowl several years earlier, at a crafts fair she had visited half in secret, with her lover. He had urged her to buy the bowl. She didn't *need* any more things, she told him. But she had been drawn to the bowl, and they had lingered near it. Then she went on to the next booth, and he came up behind her, tapping the rim against her shoulder as she ran her fingers over a wood carving. "You're still insisting that I buy that?" she said. "No," he said. "I bought it for you." He had bought her other things before this — things she liked more, at first — the child's ebony-and-turquoise ring that fitted her little finger; the wooden box, long and thin, beautifully dovetailed, that she used to hold paper clips; the soft gray sweater with a pouch pocket. It was his idea that when he could not be there to hold her hand she could hold her own — clasp her hands inside the lone pocket that stretched across the front. But in time she became more attached to the bowl than to any of his other presents. She tried to talk herself out of it. She owned other things that were more striking or valuable. It wasn't an object whose beauty jumped out at you; a lot of people must have passed it by before the two of them saw it that day.

Her lover had said that she was always too slow to know what she really loved. Why continue with her life the way it was? Why be two-faced, he asked her. He had made the first move toward her. When she would not decide in his favor, would not change her life and come to him, he asked her what made her think she could have it both ways. And then he made the last move and left. It was a decision meant to break her will, to shatter her intransigent ideas about honoring previous commitments.

Time passed. Alone in the living room at night, she often looked at the bowl sitting on the table, still and safe, unilluminated. In its way, it was perfect: the world cut in half, deep and smoothly empty. Near the rim, even in dim light, the eye moved toward one small flash of blue, a vanishing point on the horizon.

CONSIDERATIONS FOR CRITICAL THINKING AND WRITING

1. FIRST RESPONSE. At what point in the story did you first realize that the bowl has a symbolic meaning that goes beyond its function as a household object?

2. In paragraph 11 Andrea begins to wonder about her attachment to the bowl: "Could it be that she had some deeper connection with the bowl — a relationship of some kind?" If you were to describe her connection as a human relationship, how would you characterize that relationship? For starters, is it healthy?

3. How does Beattie characterize Andrea's husband (who is never named)?

4. The story initially seems to be more about the bowl than about Andrea: At what point does that emphasis shift?

5. Do we learn anything meaningful about Andrea that does *not* involve her relationship with the bowl?

6. What are the physical properties of the bowl that make it a potent symbol?

7. Discuss the balance of dialogue and narrative description in the story, and speculate about why the author chose this particular balance.

8. Why is Andrea's profession appropriate to her character?

9. The story's title refers to a Roman god who has two faces. Conduct some Internet research to understand how the allusion to Janus might enhance your understanding of the story.

10. In paragraph 6 there is a striking line: "The bowl was meant to be empty." The very purpose of a bowl is to be filled. How do you understand this line in conjunction with what you take to be the story's theme?

CONNECTIONS TO OTHER SELECTIONS

1. Consider the way human relationships and inanimate objects function in conversation with one another in this story and in Tobias Wolff's "Powder" (p. 56).

2. Louise Erdrich's story "The Red Convertible" (p. 161) and Cynthia Ozick's "The Shawl" (p. 170), also in this chapter on "symbolism," both name their central symbols in their titles. Discuss the choices one or both of these authors make to identify their primary symbol in the story's title in contrast to "Janus" (which could have been titled "The Bowl"). How do these choices affect your understanding of the stories in terms of emphasis, theme, and the reader's emotional response?

7

Theme

Nothing ever really ends. That's the horrible part of being in the short-story business — you have to be a real expert on ends. Nothing in real life ends. "Millicent at last understands." Nobody ever understands.

— KURT VONNEGUT

GL Archive/Alamy Stock Photo.

Theme is the central idea or meaning of a story. It provides a unifying point around which the plot, characters, setting, point of view, symbols, and other elements of a story are organized. In some works the theme is explicitly stated. Nathaniel Hawthorne's "Wakefield," for example, begins with the author telling the reader that the point of his story is "done up neatly, and condensed into the final sentence." Most modern writers, however, present their themes implicitly (as Hawthorne does in the majority of his stories), so determining the underlying meaning of a work often requires more effort than it does from the reader of "Wakefield." One reason for the difficulty is that the theme is fused into the elements of the story, and these must be carefully examined in relation to one another as well as to the work as a whole. But then that's the value of determining the theme, for it requires a close analysis of all the elements of a work. Such a close reading often results in sharper insights into this overlooked character or that seemingly unrelated incident. Accounting for the details and seeing how they fit together result in greater understanding of the story. Such familiarity creates pleasure in much the same way that a musical piece heard more than once becomes a rich experience rather than simply a repetitive one.

Themes are not always easy to express, but some principles can aid you in articulating the central meaning of a work. First distinguish between the theme of a story and its subject. They are not equivalents. Many stories share identical subjects, such as fate, death, innocence, youth, loneliness, racial prejudice, and disillusionment. T. C. Boyle's "The Hit Man" (p. 33) and John Updike's "A & P" (p. 138) both focus on the connection between the main character and his job. Yet each story usually makes its own statement about the subject and expresses a different view of life.

People have different responses to life, and so it is hardly surprising that responses to literature are not identical. When theme is considered, the possibilities for meaning are usually expanded and not reduced to categories such as "right" or "wrong." Although readers may differ in their interpretations of a story, that does not mean that *any* interpretation is valid. If we were to assert that the soldier's dissatisfactions in Ernest Hemingway's "Soldier's Home" (p. 104) could be readily eliminated by his settling down to marriage and a decent job (his mother's solution), we would have missed Hemingway's purposes in writing the story; we would have failed to see how Krebs's war experiences have caused him to reexamine the assumptions and beliefs that previously nurtured him but now seem unreal to him. We would have to ignore much in the story in order to arrive at such a reading. To be valid, the statement of the theme should be responsive to the details of the story. It must be based on evidence within the story rather than solely on experiences, attitudes, or values the reader brings to the work — such as personally knowing a war veteran who successfully adjusted to civilian life after getting a good job and marrying. Familiarity with the subject matter of a story can certainly be an aid to interpretation, but it should not get in the way of seeing the author's perspective.

Sometimes readers too hastily conclude that a story's theme always consists of a moral, some kind of lesson that is dramatized by the various elements of the work. There are stories that do this — Hawthorne's "Wakefield," for example. Here are the final sentences in his story about a middle-aged man who drops out of life for twenty years:

> He has left us much food for thought, a portion of which shall lend its wisdom to a moral, and be shaped into a figure. Amid the seeming confusion of our mysterious world, individuals are so nicely adjusted to a system, and systems to one another and to a whole, that, by stepping aside for a moment, a man exposes himself to a fearful risk of losing his place forever. Like Wakefield, he may become, as it were, the Outcast of the Universe.

Most stories, however, do not include such direct caveats about the conduct of life. A tendency to look for a lesson in a story can produce a reductive and inaccurate formulation of its theme. Consider the damage done to Ursula K. Le Guin's "The Ones Who Walk Away from Omelas" (p. 111) if its theme is described this way: "People who imprison and torment children are bad and should not be allowed to enjoy their lives if they do so." Note that even the title focuses not on the people of Omelas who sanction the suffering of a child, but rather on the ones who walk away from a society who would do that. We don't know much about those people — who they are, where they go, whether or not they live or die — but their reaction to the situation is significant in determining the story's theme. In fact, a good many stories go beyond traditional social values to explore human behavior instead of condemning or endorsing it.

Determining the theme of a story can be a difficult task because all the story's elements may contribute to its central idea. Indeed, you may discover that finding the theme is more challenging than coming to grips with the author's values as they are revealed in the story. There is no precise formula that can take you to the center of a story's meaning and help you to articulate it. However, several strategies are practical and useful once you have read the story. Apply these pointers during a second or third reading:

1. Pay attention to the title of the story. It often provides a lead to a major symbol (Ernest Hemingway's "Soldier's Home," p. 104) or to the subject around which the theme develops (Grace Paley's "Wants," p. 26).

2. Look for details in the story that have potential for symbolic meanings. Careful consideration of names, places, objects, minor characters, and incidents can lead you to the central meaning — for example, think of the narrator's daughter Grace in Baldwin's "Sonny's Blues" (p. 76). Be especially attentive to elements you did not understand on the first reading.

3. Decide whether the protagonist changes or develops some important insight as a result of the action. Carefully examine any generalizations the protagonist or narrator makes about the events in the story.

4. When you formulate the theme of the story in your own words, write it down in one or two complete sentences that make some point about the subject matter. Revenge may be the subject of a story, but its theme should make a statement about revenge: "Instead of providing satisfaction, revenge defeats the best in one's self" is one possibility.

5. Be certain that your expression of the theme is a generalized statement rather than a specific description of particular people, places, and incidents in the story. Contrast the preceding statement of a theme on revenge with this too-specific one: "In Nathaniel Hawthorne's *The Scarlet Letter,* Roger Chillingworth loses his humanity owing to his single-minded attempts to punish Arthur Dimmesdale for fathering a child with Chillingworth's wife, Hester." Hawthorne's theme is not restricted to a single fictional character named Chillingworth but to anyone whose life is ruined by revenge. Be certain that your statement of theme does not focus on only part of the story. The theme just cited

for *The Scarlet Letter,* for example, relegates Hester to the status of a minor character. What it says about Chillingworth is true, but the statement is incomplete as a generalization about the novel.

6. Be wary of using clichés as a way of stating theme. They tend to short-circuit ideas instead of generating them. It may be tempting to resort to something like "money is the root of all evil" as a statement of the theme of Xu Xi's story "Famine" (p. 65); however, even the slightest second thought reveals how much more ambiguous that story is.

7. Be aware that some stories emphasize theme less than others. Stories that have as their major purpose adventure, humor, mystery, or terror may have little or no theme. In Edgar Allan Poe's "The Pit and the Pendulum," for example, the protagonist is not used to condemn torture; instead, he becomes a sensitive gauge to measure the pain and horror he endures at the hands of his captors.

What is most valuable about articulating the theme of a work is the process by which the theme is determined. Ultimately, the theme is expressed by the story itself and is inseparable from the experience of reading the story. Tim O'Brien's explanation of "How to Tell a True War Story" is probably true of most kinds of stories: "In a true war story, if there's a moral [or theme] at all, it's like the thread that makes the cloth. You can't tease it out. You can't extract the meaning without unraveling the deeper meaning." Describing the theme should not be a way to consume a story, to be done with it. It is a means of clarifying our thinking about what we've read and probably felt intuitively.

Shirley Jackson's "The Lottery," Edgar Allan Poe's "The Cask of Amontillado," and Zora Neale Hurston's "Sweat" are three stories whose respective themes emerge from the authors' skillful use of plot, character, setting, and symbol.

SHIRLEY JACKSON (1916–1965)

Although she published more than 200 stories in her relatively short lifetime, Shirley Jackson is undoubtedly best remembered for the following story, "The Lottery," published in the *New Yorker* in 1948. A native of San Francisco, Jackson relocated with her family to upstate New York when she was a senior in high school. She graduated from Syracuse University, where she published her first short story and where she met her future husband, Stanley Edgar Hyman, a prominent literary critic. They moved to Vermont where they raised four children, although biographers have described their domestic

Walter Oleksy/Alamy Stock Photo.

situation as far from the mid-twentieth century stereotype of prosperity and harmony. Jackson earned a good living through publishing her stories and six novels, including the challenging, inventive horror novel *The Haunting of Hill House* (1959), but she became increasingly reclusive and her health declined precipitously, leading to her death of heart failure at the age of forty-eight. Her works are known for their explorations of psychological horror and what might be termed the dark side of human experience, as you will clearly see in "The Lottery."

The Lottery   1948

The morning of June 27th was clear and sunny, with the fresh warmth of a full-summer day; the flowers were blossoming profusely and the grass was richly green. The people of the village began to gather in the square, between the post office and the bank, around ten o'clock; in some towns there were so many people that the lottery took two days and had to be started on June 26th, but in this village, where there were only about three hundred people, the whole lottery took less than two hours, so it could begin at ten o'clock in the morning and still be through in time to allow the villagers to get home for noon dinner.

The children assembled first, of course. School was recently over for the summer, and the feeling of liberty sat uneasily on most of them; they tended to gather together quietly for a while before they broke into boisterous play, and their talk was still of the classroom and the teacher, of books and reprimands. Bobby Martin had already stuffed his pockets full of stones, and the other boys soon followed his example, selecting the smoothest and roundest stones; Bobby and Harry Jones and Dickie Delacroix — the villagers pronounced this name "Dellacroy" — eventually made a great pile of stones in one corner of the square and guarded it against the raids of the other boys. The girls stood aside, talking among themselves, looking over their shoulders at the boys, and the very small children rolled in the dust or clung to the hands of their older brothers or sisters.

Soon the men began to gather, surveying their own children, speaking of planting and rain, tractors and taxes. They stood together, away from the pile of stones in the corner, and their jokes were quiet and they smiled rather than laughed. The women, wearing faded house dresses and sweaters, came shortly after their menfolk. They greeted one another and exchanged bits of gossip as they went to join their husbands. Soon the women, standing by their husbands, began to call to their children, and the children came reluctantly, having to be called four or five times. Bobby Martin ducked under his mother's grasping hand and ran, laughing, back to the pile of stones. His father spoke up sharply, and Bobby came quickly and took his place between his father and his oldest brother.

The lottery was conducted — as were the square dances, the teenage club, the Halloween program — by Mr. Summers, who had time and energy to devote to civic activities. He was a roundfaced, jovial man and he ran the coal business, and people were sorry for him, because he had no children and his wife was a scold. When he arrived in the square, carrying the black wooden box, there was a murmur of conversation among the villagers and he waved and called, "Little late today, folks." The postmaster, Mr. Graves, followed him, carrying a three-legged stool, and the stool was put in the center of the square and Mr. Summers set the black box down on it. The villagers kept their distance, leaving a space between themselves and the stool, and when Mr. Summers said, "Some of you fellows want to give me a hand?" there was a hesitation before two men, Mr. Martin and his oldest son, Baxter, came forward to hold the box steady on the stool while Mr. Summers stirred up the papers inside it.

The original paraphernalia for the lottery had been lost long ago, and the black box now resting on the stool had been put into use even before Old Man Warner, the oldest man in town, was born. Mr. Summers spoke frequently to the villagers about making a new box, but no one liked to upset even as much tradition as was represented by the black box. There was a story that the present box had been made with some pieces of the box that had preceded it, the one that had been constructed when the first people settled down to make a village here. Every year, after the lottery, Mr. Summers began talking again about a new box, but every year the subject was allowed to fade off without anything's being done. The black box grew shabbier each year; by now it was no longer completely black but splintered badly along one side to show the original wood color, and in some places faded or stained.

Mr. Martin and his oldest son, Baxter, held the black box securely on the stool until Mr. Summers had stirred the papers thoroughly with his hand. Because so much of the ritual had been forgotten or discarded, Mr. Summers had been successful in having slips of paper substituted for the chips of wood that had been used for generations. Chips of wood, Mr. Summers had argued, had been all very well when the village was tiny, but now that the population was more than three hundred and likely to keep on growing, it was necessary to use something that would fit more easily into the black box. The night before the lottery, Mr. Summers and Mr. Graves made up the slips of paper and put them in the box, and it was then taken to the safe of Mr. Summers's coal company and locked up until Mr. Summers was ready to take it to the square next morning. The rest of the year, the box was put away, sometimes one place, sometimes another; it had spent one year in Mr. Graves's barn and another year underfoot in the post office, and sometimes it was set on a shelf in the Martin grocery and left there.

There was a great deal of fussing to be done before Mr. Summers declared the lottery open. There were lists to make up — of heads of families, heads of households in each family, members of each household in each family. There was the proper swearing-in of Mr. Summers by the postmaster, as the official of the lottery; at one time, some people remembered, there had been a recital of some sort, performed by the official of the lottery, a perfunctory, tuneless chant that had been rattled off duly each year; some people believed that the official of the lottery used to stand just so when he said or sang it, others believed that he was supposed to walk among the people, but years and years ago this part of the ritual had been allowed to lapse. There had been, also, a ritual salute, which the official of the lottery had had to use in addressing each person who came up to draw from the box, but this also had changed with time, until now it was felt necessary only for the official to speak to each person approaching. Mr. Summers was very good at all this; in his clean white shirt and blue jeans, with one hand resting carelessly on the black box, he seemed very proper and important as he talked interminably to Mr. Graves and the Martins.

Just as Mr. Summers finally left off talking and turned to the assembled villagers, Mrs. Hutchinson came hurriedly along the path to the square, her sweater thrown over her shoulders, and slid into place in the back of the crowd. "Clean forgot what day it was," she said to Mrs. Delacroix, who stood next to her, and they both laughed softly. "Thought my old man was out back stacking wood," Mrs. Hutchinson went on, "and then I looked out the window and the kids were gone, and then I remembered it was the twenty-seventh and came a-running." She dried her hands on her apron, and Mrs. Delacroix said, "You're in time, though. They're still talking away up there."

Mrs. Hutchinson craned her neck to see through the crowd and found her husband and children standing near the front. She tapped Mrs. Delacroix on the arm as a farewell and began to make her way through the crowd. The people separated good-humoredly to let her through; two or three people said, in voices just loud enough to be heard across the crowd, "Here comes your Missus, Hutchinson," and "Bill, she made it after all." Mrs. Hutchinson reached her husband, and Mr. Summers, who had been waiting, said cheerfully, "Thought we were going to have to get on without you, Tessie." Mrs. Hutchinson said, grinning, "Wouldn't have me leave m'dishes in the sink, now would you, Joe?" and soft laughter ran through the crowd as the people stirred back into position after Mrs. Hutchinson's arrival.

"Well, now," Mr. Summers said soberly, "guess we better get started, get 10 this over with, so's we can go back to work. Anybody ain't here?"

"Dunbar," several people said. "Dunbar, Dunbar."

Mr. Summers consulted his list. "Clyde Dunbar," he said. "That's right. He's broke his leg, hasn't he? Who's drawing for him?"

"Me, I guess," a woman said, and Mr. Summers turned to look at her. "Wife draws for her husband," Mr. Summers said. "Don't you have a grown boy to do it for you, Janey?" Although Mr. Summers and everyone else in the village knew the answer perfectly well, it was the business of the official of the lottery to ask such questions formally. Mr. Summers waited with an expression of polite interest while Mrs. Dunbar answered.

"Horace's not but sixteen yet," Mrs. Dunbar said regretfully. "Guess I gotta fill in for the old man this year."

"Right," Mr. Summers said. He made a note on the list he was holding. 15 Then he asked, "Watson boy drawing this year?"

A tall boy in the crowd raised his hand. "Here," he said. "I'm drawing for m'mother and me." He blinked his eyes nervously and ducked his head as several voices in the crowd said things like "Good fellow, Jack," and "Glad to see your mother's got a man to do it."

"Well," Mr. Summers said, "guess that's everyone. Old Man Warner make it?"

"Here," a voice said, and Mr. Summers nodded.

A sudden hush fell on the crowd as Mr. Summers cleared his throat and looked at the list. "All ready?" he called. "Now, I'll read the names — heads of families first — and the men come up and take a paper out of the box. Keep the paper folded in your hand without looking at it until everyone has had a turn. Everything clear?"

The people had done it so many times that they only half listened to the 20 directions; most of them were quiet, wetting their lips, not looking around. Then Mr. Summers raised one hand high and said, "Adams." A man disengaged himself from the crowd and came forward. "Hi, Steve," Mr. Summers said, and Mr. Adams said, "Hi, Joe." They grinned at one another humorlessly and nervously. Then Mr. Adams reached into the black box and took out a folded paper. He held it firmly by one corner as he turned and went hastily back to his place in the crowd, where he stood a little apart from his family, not looking down at his hand.

"Allen," Mr. Summers said. "Anderson. . . . Bentham."

"Seems like there's no time at all between lotteries any more," Mrs. Delacroix said to Mrs. Graves in the back row. "Seems like we got through with the last one only last week."

"Time sure goes fast," Mrs. Graves said.

"Clark. . . . Delacroix."

"There goes my old man," Mrs. Delacroix said. She held her breath 25 while her husband went forward.

"Dunbar," Mr. Summers said, and Mrs. Dunbar went steadily to the box while one of the women said, "Go on, Janey," and another said, "There she goes."

"We're next," Mrs. Graves said. She watched while Mr. Graves came around from the side of the box, greeted Mr. Summers gravely, and selected a slip of paper from the box. By now, all through the crowd there were men holding the small folded papers in their large hands, turning them over and over nervously. Mrs. Dunbar and her two sons stood together, Mrs. Dunbar holding the slip of paper.

"Harburt. . . . Hutchinson."

"Get up there, Bill," Mrs. Hutchinson said, and the people near her laughed.

"Jones."

"They do say," Mr. Adams said to Old Man Warner, who stood next to 30 him, "that over in the north village they're talking of giving up the lottery."

Old Man Warner snorted. "Pack of crazy fools," he said. "Listening to the young folks, nothing's good enough for *them*. Next thing you know, they'll be wanting to go back to living in caves, nobody work any more, live *that* way for a while. Used to be a saying about 'Lottery in June, corn be heavy soon.' First thing you know, we'd all be eating stewed chickweed and acorns. There's *always* been a lottery," he added petulantly. "Bad enough to see young Joe Summers up there joking with everybody."

"Some places have already quit lotteries," Mrs. Adams said.

"Nothing but trouble in *that*," Old Man Warner said stoutly. "Pack of young fools."

"Martin." And Bobby Martin watched his father go forward. "Over- 35 dyke.... Percy."

"I wish they'd hurry," Mrs. Dunbar said to her older son. "I wish they'd hurry."

"They're almost through," her son said.

"You get ready to run tell Dad," Mrs. Dunbar said.

Mr. Summers called his own name and then stepped forward precisely and selected a slip from the box. Then he called, "Warner."

"Seventy-seventh year I been in the lottery," Old Man Warner said as he 40 went through the crowd. "Seventy-seventh time."

"Watson." The tall boy came awkwardly through the crowd. Someone said, "Don't be nervous, Jack," and Mr. Summers said, "Take your time, son."

"Zanini."

After that, there was a long pause, a breathless pause, until Mr. Summers, holding his slip of paper in the air, said, "All right, fellows." For a minute, no one moved, and then all the slips of paper were opened. Suddenly, all women began to speak at once, saying, "Who is it?" "Who's got it?" "Is it the Dunbars?" "Is it the Watsons?" Then the voices began to say, "It's Hutchinson. It's Bill." "Bill Hutchinson's got it."

"Go tell your father," Mrs. Dunbar said to her older son.

People began to look around to see the Hutchinsons. Bill Hutchinson 45 was standing quiet, staring down at the paper in his hand. Suddenly, Tessie Hutchinson shouted to Mr. Summers, "You didn't give him time enough to take any paper he wanted. I saw you. It wasn't fair!"

"Be a good sport, Tessie," Mrs. Delacroix called, and Mrs. Graves said, "All of us took the same chance."

"Shut up, Tessie," Bill Hutchinson said.

"Well, everyone," Mr. Summers said, "that was done pretty fast, and now we've got to be hurrying a little more to get done in time." He consulted his next list. "Bill," he said, "you draw for the Hutchinson family. You got any other households in the Hutchinsons?"

"There's Don and Eva," Mrs. Hutchinson yelled. "Make *them* take their chance!"

"Daughters draw with their husbands' families, Tessie," Mr. Summers 50 said gently. "You know that as well as anyone else."

"It wasn't fair," Tessie said.

"I guess not, Joe," Bill Hutchinson said regretfully. "My daughter draws with her husband's family, that's only fair. And I've got no other family except the kids."

"Then, as far as drawing for families is concerned, it's you," Mr. Summers said in explanation, "and as far as drawing for households is concerned, that's you, too. Right?"

"Right," Bill Hutchinson said.

"How many kids, Bill?" Mr. Summers asked formally. 55

"Three," Bill Hutchinson said. "There's Bill, Jr., and Nancy, and little Dave. And Tessie and me."

"All right, then," Mr. Summers said. "Harry, you got their tickets back?"

Mr. Graves nodded and held up the slips of paper. "Put them in the box, then," Mr. Summers directed. "Take Bill's and put it in."

"I think we ought to start over," Mrs. Hutchinson said, as quietly as she could. "I tell you it wasn't *fair*. You didn't give him time enough to choose. *Every*body saw that."

Mr. Graves had selected the five slips and put them in the box, and he 60 dropped all the papers but those onto the ground, where the breeze caught them and lifted them off.

"Listen, everybody," Mrs. Hutchinson was saying to the people around her.

"Ready, Bill?" Mr. Summers asked, and Bill Hutchinson, with one quick glance around at his wife and children, nodded.

"Remember," Mr. Summers said, "take the slips and keep them folded until each person has taken one. Harry, you help little Dave." Mr. Graves took the hand of the little boy, who came willingly with him up to the box. "Take a paper out of the box, Davy," Mr. Summers said. Davy put his hand into the box and laughed. "Take just *one* paper," Mr. Summers said. "Harry, you hold it for him." Mr. Graves took the child's hand and removed the folded paper from the tight fist and held it while little Dave stood next to him and looked up at him wonderingly.

"Nancy next," Mr. Summers said. Nancy was twelve, and her school friends breathed heavily as she went forward, switching her skirt, and took a slip daintily from the box. "Bill, Jr.," Mr. Summers said, and Billy, his face red and his feet over-large, nearly knocked the box over as he got a paper out. "Tessie," Mr. Summers said. She hesitated for a minute, looking around defiantly, and then set her lips and went up to the box. She snatched a paper out and held it behind her.

"Bill," Mr. Summers said, and Bill Hutchinson reached into the box and 65 felt around, bringing his hand out at last with the slip of paper in it.

The crowd was quiet. A girl whispered, "I hope it's not Nancy," and the sound of the whisper reached the edges of the crowd.

"It's not the way it used to be," Old Man Warner said clearly. "People ain't the way they used to be."

"All right," Mr. Summers said. "Open the papers. Harry, you open little Dave's."

Mr. Graves opened the slip of paper and there was a general sigh through the crowd as he held it up and everyone could see that it was blank. Nancy and Bill, Jr., opened theirs at the same time, and both beamed and laughed, turning around to the crowd and holding their slips of paper above their heads.

"Tessie," Mr. Summers said. There was a pause, and then Mr. Summers 70 looked at Bill Hutchinson, and Bill unfolded his paper and showed it. It was blank.

"It's Tessie," Mr. Summers said, and his voice was hushed. "Show us her paper, Bill."

Bill Hutchinson went over to his wife and forced the slip of paper out of her hand. It had a black spot on it, the black spot Mr. Summers had made the night before with the heavy pencil in the coal-company office. Bill Hutchinson held it up, and there was a stir in the crowd.

"All right, folks," Mr. Summers said, "let's finish quickly."

Although the villagers had forgotten the ritual and lost the original black box, they still remembered to use stones. The pile of stones the boys had made earlier was ready; there were stones on the ground with the blowing scraps of paper that had come out of the box. Mrs. Delacroix selected a stone so large she had to pick it up with both hands and turned to Mrs. Dunbar. "Come on," she said. "Hurry up."

Mrs. Dunbar had small stones in both hands, and she said, gasping for 75 breath, "I can't run at all. You'll have to go ahead and I'll catch up with you."

The children had stones already, and someone gave little Davy Hutchinson a few pebbles.

Tessie Hutchinson was in the center of a cleared space by now, and she held her hands out desperately as the villagers moved in on her. "It isn't fair," she said. A stone hit her on the side of the head.

Old Man Warner was saying, "Come on, come on, everyone." Steve Adams was in the front of the crowd of villagers, with Mrs. Graves beside him.

"It isn't fair, it isn't right," Mrs. Hutchinson screamed, and then they were upon her.

CONSIDERATIONS FOR CRITICAL THINKING AND WRITING

1. FIRST RESPONSE. Would you have a different emotional response to the story if the character selected in the lottery was someone other than Tessie Hutchinson? Put differently, do individual characters matter in this story?

2. The village in which the story takes place is contrasted with other towns in the first paragraph and they are brought up again later in the narrative. Why is it important to know about these other towns if they are not part of the story?

3. Is it significant that the story takes place in summer (and, further, that the man who oversees the lottery is Mr. Summers)? Why does the narrator emphasize the behavior of the out-of-school children in the second paragraph?

4. How might the black box described in paragraphs 4–6 be interpreted as a symbol?

5. The lottery is obviously a ritual that the author has imagined as opposed to something that happened historically, but how is it connected to actual rituals? Do these connections help you to articulate the story's theme?

6. The narrator emphasizes that certain aspects of the ritual have changed over time. Why is that fact important?

7. Husbands and wives seem to have what we would now call traditional roles in this story: How is that observation significant to your understanding of its theme?

8. How does the story frame a conflict between younger and older generations?

9. Why is it significant that children as well as adults take part in the ritual?

10. The story does not indicate why the ritual sacrifice takes place, or why it began in the first place. Would your understanding of the story's theme change if you were given this information?

CONNECTION TO ANOTHER SELECTION

1. Consider ritual as a major thematic component of this story and of Ursula K. Le Guin's "The Ones Who Walk Away from Omelas" (p. 111).

EDGAR ALLAN POE (1809–1849)

Edgar Allan Poe grew up in the home of John Allan, in Richmond, Virginia, after his mother died in 1811, and he was educated in Scotland and England for five years before completing his classical education in Richmond. After a short stint at the University of Virginia, Poe went to Boston, where he began publishing his poetry. His foster father sent him to West Point Military Academy, but Poe was expelled and moved on to New York, where he published a book of poems inspired by the Romantic movement. Moving among editorial jobs

Library of Congress, Prints and Photographs Division.

in Baltimore, Richmond, and New York, Poe married his thirteen-year-old cousin Virginia Clemm. Early in his story-writing career, Poe published his only novel-length piece, *The Narrative of Arthur Gordon Pym* (1838), and the following year, he began to work in the genre of the supernatural and horrible, with the stories "William Wilson" and "The Fall of the House of Usher." He gained publicity with the detective story "The Murders in the Rue Morgue," became nationally famous with the publication of his poem "The Raven" in 1845, and died four years later in Baltimore after a drinking binge. Poe theorized that the short story writer should plan every word toward the achievement of a certain effect, and that stories should be read in a single sitting. Morbidity and dreamlike flights of fancy, for which Poe is often recognized, do not detract from his lucid crafting of suspense and his erudite control of language and symbol.

The Cask of Amontillado   1846

The thousand injuries of Fortunato I had borne as I best could; but when he ventured upon insult, I vowed revenge. You, who so well know the nature of my soul, will not suppose, however, that I gave utterance to a threat. *At length* I would be avenged; this was a point definitely settled — but the very definitiveness with which it was resolved precluded the idea of risk. I must not only punish, but punish with impunity. A wrong is unredressed when retribution overtakes its redresser. It is equally unredressed when the avenger fails to make himself felt as such to him who has done the wrong.

It must be understood, that neither by word nor deed had I given Fortunato cause to doubt my goodwill. I continued, as was my wont, to smile in his face, and he did not perceive that my smile *now* was at the thought of his immolation.

He had a weak point — this Fortunato — although in other regards he was a man to be respected and even feared. He prided himself on his connoisseurship in wine. Few Italians have the true virtuoso spirit. For the most part their enthusiasm is adopted to suit the time and opportunity — to practice imposture upon the British and Austrian *millionnaires*. In painting and gemmary Fortunato, like his countrymen, was a quack — but in the matter of old wines he was sincere. In this respect I did not differ from him materially: I was skilful in the Italian vintages myself, and bought largely whenever I could.

It was about dusk, one evening during the supreme madness of the carnival season, that I encountered my friend. He accosted me with excessive warmth, for he had been drinking much. The man wore motley. He had on a tight-fitting parti-striped dress, and his head was surmounted by the conical cap and bells. I was so pleased to see him, that I thought I should never have done wringing his hand.

I said to him: "My dear Fortunato, you are luckily met. How remarkably 5 well you are looking to-day! But I have received a pipe° of what passes for Amontillado, and I have my doubts."

"How?" said he. "Amontillado? A pipe? Impossible! And in the middle of the carnival!"

"I have my doubts," I replied; "and I was silly enough to pay the full Amontillado price without consulting you in the matter. You were not to be found, and I was fearful of losing a bargain."

pipe: A large keg.

"Amontillado!"

"I have my doubts."

"Amontillado!"

"And I must satisfy them."

"Amontillado!"

"As you are engaged, I am on my way to Luchesi. If any one has a critical turn, it is he. He will tell me —— "

"Luchesi cannot tell Amontillado from Sherry."

"And yet some fools will have it that his taste is a match for your own."

"Come, let us go."

"Whither?"

"To your vaults."

"My friend, no; I will not impose upon your good nature. I perceive you have an engagement. Luchesi —— "

"I have no engagement; — come."

"My friend, no. It is not the engagement, but the severe cold with which I perceive you are afflicted. The vaults are insufferably damp. They are encrusted with nitre."

"Let us go, nevertheless. The cold is merely nothing. Amontillado! You have been imposed upon. And as for Luchesi, he cannot distinguish Sherry from Amontillado."

Thus speaking, Fortunato possessed himself of my arm. Putting on a mask of black silk, and drawing a *roquelaire*° closely about my person, I suffered him to hurry me to my palazzo.

There were no attendants at home; they had absconded to make merry in honor of the time. I had told them that I should not return until the morning, and had given them explicit orders not to stir from the house. These orders were sufficient, I well knew, to insure their immediate disappearance, one and all, as soon as my back was turned.

I took from their sconces two flambeaux, and giving one to Fortunato, bowed him through several suites of rooms to the archway that led into the vaults. I passed down a long and winding staircase, requesting him to be cautious as he followed. We came at length to the foot of the descent, and stood together on the damp ground of the catacombs of the Montresors.

The gait of my friend was unsteady, and the bells upon his cap jingled as he strode.

"The pipe?" said he.

"It is farther on," said I; "but observe the white web-work which gleams from these cavern walls."

He turned toward me, and looked into my eyes with two filmy orbs that distilled the rheum of intoxication.

"Nitre?" he asked, at length.

"Nitre," I replied. "How long have you had that cough?"

roquelaire: A short cloak.

"Ugh! ugh! ugh! — ugh! ugh! ugh! — ugh! ugh! ugh! — ugh! ugh! ugh! — ugh! ugh! ugh!"

My poor friend found it impossible to reply for many minutes.

"It is nothing," he said, at last.

"Come," I said, with decision, "we will go back; your health is precious. 35 You are rich, respected, admired, beloved; you are happy, as once I was. You are a man to be missed. For me it is no matter. We will go back; you will be ill, and I cannot be responsible. Besides, there is Luchesi—"

"Enough," he said; "the cough is a mere nothing; it will not kill me. I shall not die of a cough."

"True — true," I replied; "and, indeed, I had no intention of alarming you unnecessarily; but you should use all proper caution. A draught of this Medoc will defend us from the damps."

Here I knocked off the neck of a bottle which I drew from a long row of its fellows that lay upon the mould.

"Drink," I said, presenting him the wine.

He raised it to his lips with a leer. He paused and nodded to me famil- 40 iarly, while his bells jingled.

"I drink," he said, "to the buried that repose around us."

"And I to your long life."

He again took my arm, and we proceeded.

"These vaults," he said, "are extensive."

"The Montresors," I replied, "were a great and numerous family." 45

"I forget your arms."

"A huge human foot d'or,° in a field azure; the foot crushes a serpent rampant whose fangs are imbedded in the heel."

"And the motto?"

"*Nemo me impune lacessit.*"°

"Good!" he said. 50

The wine sparkled in his eyes and the bells jingled. My own fancy grew warm with the Medoc. We had passed through walls of piled bones, with casks and puncheons intermingling into the inmost recesses of the catacombs. I paused again, and this time I made bold to seize Fortunato by an arm above the elbow.

"The nitre!" I said; "see, it increases. It hangs like moss upon the vaults. We are below the river's bed. The drops of moisture trickle among the bones. Come, we will go back ere it is too late. Your cough—"

"It is nothing," he said; "let us go on. But first, another draught of the Medoc."

I broke and reached him a flagon of De Grâve. He emptied it at a breath. His eyes flashed with a fierce light. He laughed and threw the bottle upward with a gesticulation I did not understand.

---

d'or: Of gold.
Nemo . . . lacessit (Latin): No one wounds me with impunity.

I looked at him in surprise. He repeated the movement — a grotesque one. 55

"You do not comprehend?" he said.

"Not I," I replied.

"Then you are not of the brotherhood."

"How?"

"You are not of the masons." 60

"Yes, yes," I said; "yes, yes."

"You? Impossible! A mason?"

"A mason," I replied.

"A sign," he said.

"It is this," I answered, producing a trowel from beneath the folds of my 65 *roquelaire.*

"You jest," he exclaimed, recoiling a few paces. "But let us proceed to the Amontillado."

"Be it so," I said, replacing the tool beneath the cloak, and again offering him my arm. He leaned upon it heavily. We continued our route in search of the Amontillado. We passed through a range of low arches, descended, passed on, and descending again, arrived at a deep crypt, in which the foulness of the air caused our flambeaux rather to glow than flame.

At the most remote end of the crypt there appeared another less spacious. Its walls had been lined with human remains, piled to the vault overhead, in the fashion of the great catacombs of Paris. Three sides of this interior crypt were still ornamented in this manner. From the fourth the bones had been thrown down, and lay promiscuously upon the earth, forming at one point a mound of some size. Within the wall thus exposed by the displacing of the bones, we perceived a still interior recess, in depth about four feet, in width three, in height six or seven. It seemed to have been constructed for no especial use within itself, but formed merely the interval between two of the colossal supports of the roof of the catacombs, and was backed by one of their circumscribing walls of solid granite.

It was in vain that Fortunato, uplifting his dull torch, endeavored to pry into the depth of the recess. Its termination the feeble light did not enable us to see.

"Proceed," I said; "herein is the Amontillado. As for Luchesi —" 70

"He is an ignoramus," interrupted my friend, as he stepped unsteadily forward, while I followed immediately at his heels. In an instant he had reached the extremity of the niche, and finding his progress arrested by the rock, stood stupidly bewildered. A moment more and I had fettered him to the granite. In its surface were two iron staples, distant from each other about two feet, horizontally. From one of these depended a short chain, from the other a padlock. Throwing the links about his waist, it was but the work of a few seconds to secure it. He was too much astounded to resist. Withdrawing the key I stepped back from the recess.

"Pass your hand," I said, "over the wall; you cannot help feeling the nitre. Indeed it is *very* damp. Once more let me *implore* you to return. No? Then I must positively leave you. But I must first render you all the little attentions in my power."

"The Amontillado!" ejaculated my friend, not yet recovered from his astonishment.

"True," I replied; "the Amontillado."

As I said these words I busied myself among the pile of bones of which 75 I have before spoken. Throwing them aside, I soon uncovered a quantity of building stone and mortar. With these materials and with the aid of my trowel, I began vigorously to wall up the entrance of the niche.

I had scarcely laid the first tier of the masonry when I discovered that the intoxication of Fortunato had in a great measure worn off. The earliest indication I had of this was a low moaning cry from the depth of the recess. It was *not* the cry of a drunken man. There was then a long and obstinate silence. I laid the second tier, and the third, and the fourth; and then I heard the furious vibrations of the chain. The noise lasted for several minutes, during which, that I might hearken to it with the more satisfaction, I ceased my labors and sat down upon the bones. When at last the clanking subsided, I resumed the trowel, and finished without interruption the fifth, the sixth, and the seventh tier. The wall was now nearly upon a level with my breast. I again paused, and holding the flambeaux over the masonwork, threw a few feeble rays upon the figure within.

A succession of loud and shrill screams, bursting suddenly from the throat of the chained form, seemed to thrust me violently back. For a brief moment I hesitated — I trembled. Unsheathing my rapier, I began to grope with it about the recess; but the thought of an instant reassured me. I placed my hand upon the solid fabric of the catacombs, and felt satisfied. I reapproached the wall. I replied to the yells of him who clamored. I reechoed — I aided — I surpassed them in volume and in strength. I did this, and the clamorer grew still.

It was now midnight, and my task was drawing to a close. I had completed the eighth, the ninth, and the tenth tier. I had finished a portion of the last and the eleventh; there remained but a single stone to be fitted and plastered in. I struggled with its weight; I placed it partially in its destined position. But now there came from out the niche a low laugh that erected the hairs upon my head. It was succeeded by a sad voice, which I had difficulty in recognizing as that of the noble Fortunato. The voice said —

"Ha! ha! ha! — he! he! — a very good joke indeed — an excellent jest. We will have many a rich laugh about it at the palazzo — he! he! he! — over our wine — he! he! he!"

"The Amontillado!" I said. 80

"He! he! he! — he! he! he! — yes, the Amontillado. But is it not getting late? Will not they be awaiting us at the palazzo, the Lady Fortunato and the rest? Let us be gone."

"Yes," I said, "let us be gone."

"*For the love of God, Montresor!*"

"Yes," I said, "for the love of God!"

But to these words I hearkened in vain for a reply. I grew impatient. 85 I called aloud:

"Fortunato!"

No answer. I called again:

"Fortunato!"

No answer still, I thrust a torch through the remaining aperture and let it fall within. There came forth in return only a jingling of the bells. My heart grew sick — on account of the dampness of the catacombs. I hastened to make an end of my labor. I forced the last stone into its position; I plastered it up. Against the new masonry I re-erected the old rampart of bones. For the half of a century no mortal has disturbed them. *In pace requiescat!*°

In pace requiescat! (Latin): In peace may he rest!

CONSIDERATIONS FOR CRITICAL THINKING AND WRITING

1. **FIRST RESPONSE.** In the second sentence of the story Montresor addresses the reader directly: "You, who so well know the nature of my soul . . . " How do you imagine he understands the identity of his auditor? Is it an actual person?

2. The name "Montresor" translates from French as "my treasure" and the name Fortunato translates from Italian as "lucky." How do you interpret the use of these names in the context of this story?

3. Montresor undertakes his ghastly revenge based on a "thousand injuries" followed by "insult." What is the effect of his withholding the specific nature of these injuries and insult?

4. The story takes place during "the supreme madness of the carnival season." Carnival is the feast before the somber season of Lent, related to Mardi Gras in the American South. This explains the costumes the men are wearing, but why are these costumes or disguises also fitting to the story's theme?

5. How does the Montresor family coat of arms — both the image and the motto — enhance the theme of the story?

6. What is the effect of titling the story "The Cask of Amontillado" — a desired object that does not exist — rather than involving the story's central action (live burial) or after one of its characters?

7. Montresor has clearly plotted his revenge carefully. Is there any evidence that he hesitates in his purpose or that he feels guilt?

8. Fortunato is fairly drunk by the time Montresor chains him to the wall. Is that the only factor that explains why he is so easily led to his demise?

9. How does Poe create and sustain suspense in the story?

CONNECTIONS TO ANOTHER SELECTION

1. Consider the reliability of the narrator in this story and compare it to the reliability of the narrator of Charlotte Perkins Gilman's "The Yellow Wallpaper" (p. 117).

ZORA NEALE HURSTON (1891–1960)

Zora Neale Hurston was one of the central
figures of the Harlem Renaissance. Born
in Alabama and raised in the incorporated
all-black town of Eatonville, Florida, she
eventually moved to New York to attend
Barnard College and Columbia University,
where she was trained as an anthropologist, a field that would greatly influence
her fiction. Hurston also published books
of nonfiction based on her anthropologi-
cal field studies in the American South and
the Caribbean (especially Haiti), but most

Library of Congress.

readers today know her as the author of *Their Eyes Were Watching God*,
a 1937 novel. Although she was one of the most celebrated writers of the
Harlem Renaissance through the end of the 1930s, the end of Hurston's
life was marked by financial and medical difficulties. She died in relative obscurity and was buried in an unmarked grave, but novelist Alice
Walker led a campaign to reconsider the importance of her life and leg-
acy, and she is now widely read, studied, and appreciated. The following
story, "Sweat," demonstrates two hallmarks of Hurston's writing: sensitivity to the powerless and an emphasis on beauty and hope in a world that
can be cruel.

Sweat   1926

It was eleven o'clock of a Spring night in Florida. It was Sunday. Any other
night, Delia Jones would have been in bed for two hours by this time. But
she was a washwoman, and Monday morning meant a great deal to her.
So she collected the soiled clothes on Saturday when she returned the clean
things. Sunday night after church, she sorted them and put the white things
to soak. It saved her almost a half day's start. A great hamper in the bedroom held the clothes that she brought home. It was so much neater than a
number of bundles lying around.

She squatted in the kitchen floor beside the great pile of clothes, sorting
them into small heaps according to color, and humming a song in a mournful key, but wondering through it all where Sykes, her husband, had gone
with her horse and buckboard.

Just then something long, round, limp and black fell upon her shoulders and slithered to the floor beside her. A great terror took hold of her. It
softened her knees and dried her mouth so that it was a full minute before
she could cry out or move. Then she saw that it was the big bull whip her
husband liked to carry when he drove.

She lifted her eyes to the door and saw him standing there bent over with laughter at her fright. She screamed at him.

"Sykes, what you throw dat whip on me like dat? You know it would skeer 5
me — looks just like a snake, an' you knows how skeered Ah is of snakes."

"Course Ah knowed it! That's how come Ah done it." He slapped his leg with his hand and almost rolled on the ground in his mirth. "If you such a big fool dat you got to have a fit over a earth worm or a string, Ah don't keer how bad Ah skeer you."

"You aint got no business doing it. Gawd knows it's a sin. Some day Ah'm gointuh drop dead from some of yo' foolishness. 'Nother thing, where you been wid mah rig? Ah feeds dat pony. He aint fuh you to be drivin' wid no bull whip."

"You sho is one aggravatin' nigger woman!" he declared and stepped into the room. She resumed her work and did not answer him at once. "Ah done tole you time and again to keep them white folks' clothes outa dis house."

He picked up the whip and glared down at her. Delia went on with her work. She went out into the yard and returned with a galvanized tub and set it on the washbench. She saw that Sykes had kicked all of the clothes together again, and now stood in her way truculently, his whole manner hoping, *praying,* for an argument. But she walked calmly around him and commenced to re-sort the things.

"Next time, Ah'm gointer kick 'em outdoors," he threatened as he struck 10
a match along the leg of his corduroy breeches.

Delia never looked up from her work, and her thin, stooped shoulders sagged further.

"Ah aint for no fuss t'night Sykes. Ah just come from taking sacrament at the church house."

He snorted scornfully. "Yeah, you just come from de church house on a Sunday night, but heah you is gone to work on them clothes. You ain't nothing but a hypocrite. One of them amen-corner Christians — sing, whoop, and shout; then come home and wash white folks clothes on the Sabbath."

He stepped roughly upon the whitest pile of things, kicking them helter-skelter as he crossed the room. His wife gave a little scream of dismay, and quickly gathered them together again.

"Sykes, you quit grindin' dirt into these clothes! How can Ah git 15
through by Sat'day if Ah don't start on Sunday?"

"Ah don't keer if you never git through. Anyhow, Ah done promised Gawd and a couple of other men, Ah aint gointer have it in mah house. Don't gimme no lip neither, else Ah'll throw 'em out and put mah fist up side yo' head to boot."

Delia's habitual meekness seemed to slip from her shoulders like a blown scarf. She was on her feet; her poor little body, her bare knuckly hands bravely defying the strapping hulk before her.

"Looka heah, Sykes, you done gone too fur. Ah been married to you fur fifteen years, and Ah been takin' in washin' fur fifteen years. Sweat, sweat, sweat! Work and sweat, cry and sweat, pray and sweat!"

"What's that got to do with me?" he asked brutally.

"What's it got to do with you, Sykes? Mah tub of suds is filled yo' belly 20 with vittles more times than yo' hands is filled it. Mah sweat is done paid for this house and Ah reckon Ah kin keep on sweatin' in it."

She seized the iron skillet from the stove and struck a defensive pose, which act surprised him greatly, coming from her. It cowed him and he did not strike her as he usually did.

"Naw you won't," she panted, "that ole snaggle-toothed black woman you runnin' with aint comin' heah to pile up on *mah* sweat and blood. You aint paid for nothin' on this place, and Ah'm gointer stay right heah till Ah'm toted out foot foremost."

"Well, you better quit gittin' me riled up, else they'll be totin' you out sooner than you expect. Ah'm so tired of you Ah don't know whut to do. Gawd! how Ah hates skinny wimmen!"

A little awed by this new Delia, he sidled out of the door and slammed the back gate after him. He did not say where he had gone, but she knew too well. She knew very well that he would not return until nearly daybreak also. Her work over, she went on to bed but not to sleep at once. Things had come to a pretty pass!

She lay awake, gazing upon the debris that cluttered their matrimonial 25 trail. Not an image left standing along the way. Anything like flowers had long ago been drowned in the salty stream that had been pressed from her heart. Her tears, her sweat, her blood. She had brought love to the union and he had brought a longing after the flesh. Two months after the wedding, he had given her the first brutal beating. She had the memory of his numerous trips to Orlando with all of his wages when he had returned to her penniless, even before the first year had passed. She was young and soft then, but now she thought of her knotty, muscled limbs, her harsh knuckly hands, and drew herself up into an unhappy little ball in the middle of the big feather bed. Too late now to hope for love, even if it were not Bertha it would be someone else. This case differed from the others only in that she was bolder than the others. Too late for everything except her little home. She had built it for her old days, and planted one by one the trees and flowers there. It was lovely to her, lovely.

Somehow, before sleep came, she found herself saying aloud: "Oh well, whatever goes over the Devil's back, is got to come under his belly. Sometime or ruther, Sykes, like everybody else, is gointer reap his sowing." After that she was able to build a spiritual earthworks against her husband. His shells could no longer reach her. *Amen*. She went to sleep and slept until he announced his presence in bed by kicking her feet and rudely snatching the covers away.

"Gimme some kivah heah, an' git yo' damn foots over on yo' own side! Ah oughter mash you in yo' mouf fuh drawing dat skillet on me."

Delia went clear to the rail without answering him. A triumphant indifference to all that he was or did.

The week was as full of work for Delia as all other weeks, and Saturday found her behind her little pony, collecting and delivering clothes.

It was a hot, hot day near the end of July. The village men on Joe Clarke's 3
porch even chewed cane listlessly. They did not hurl the cane-knots° as
usual. They let them dribble over the edge of the porch. Even conversation
had collapsed under the heat.

"Heah come Delia Jones," Jim Merchant said, as the shaggy pony came
'round the bend of the road toward them. The rusty buckboard was heaped
with baskets of crisp, clean laundry.

"Yep," Joe Lindsay agreed. "Hot or col', rain or shine, jes ez reg'lar ez de
weeks roll roun' Delia carries 'em an' fetches 'em on Sat'day."

"She better if she wanter eat," said Moss. "Syke Jones aint wuth de shot
an' powder hit would tek tuh kill 'em. Not to *huh* he aint."

"He sho' aint," Walter Thomas chimed in. "It's too bad, too, cause she
wuz a right pritty lil trick when he got huh. Ah'd uh mah'ied huh mahseff if
he hadnter beat me to it."

Delia nodded briefly at the men as she drove past.   35

"Too much knockin' will ruin *any* 'oman. He done beat huh 'nough tuh
kill three women, let 'lone change they looks," said Elijah Moseley. "How
Syke kin stommuck dat big black greasy Mogul he's layin' roun' wid, gits me.
Ah swear dat eight-rock° couldn't kiss a sardine can Ah done thowed out de
back do' 'way las' yeah."

"Aw, she's fat, thass how come. He's allus been crazy 'bout fat women,"
put in Merchant. "He'd a' been tied up wid one long time ago if he could a'
found one tuh have him. Did Ah tell yuh 'bout him come sidlin' roun' *mah*
wife — bringin' her a basket uh peecans outa his yard fuh a present? Yeah,
mah wife! She tol' him tuh take 'em right straight back home, cause Delia
works so hard ovah dat washtub she reckon everything on de place taste lak
sweat an' soapsuds. Ah jus' wisht Ah'd a' caught 'im 'roun' dere! Ah'd a' made
his hips ketch on fiah down dat shell road."

"Ah know he done it, too. Ah sees 'im grinnin' at every 'oman dat passes,"
Walter Thomas said. "But even so, he useter eat some mighty big hunks uh
humble pie tuh git dat lil' 'oman he got. She wuz ez pritty ez a speckled pup! Dat
wuz fifteen yeahs ago. He useter be so skeered uh losin' huh, she could make
him do some parts of a husband's duty. Dey never wuz de same in de mind."

"There oughter be a law about him," said Lindsay. "He aint fit tuh carry
guts tuh a bear."

Clarke spoke for the first time. "Taint no law on earth dat kin make a man 40
be decent if it aint in 'im. There's plenty men dat takes a wife lak dey do a joint
uh sugar-cane. It's round, juicy an' sweet when dey gits it. But dey squeeze an'
grind, squeeze an' grind an' wring tell dey wring every drop uh pleasure dat's
in 'em out. When dey's satisfied dat dey is wrung dry, dey treats 'em jes lak dey
do a cane-chew. Dey thows 'em away. Dey knows whut dey is doin' while dey
is at it, an' hates theirselves fuh it but they keeps on hangin' after huh tell she's
empty. Den dey hates huh fuh bein' a cane-chew an' in de way."

---

cane-knots: pieces of sugar cane to be chewed and discarded.
eight-rock: person with very dark skin.

"We oughter take Syke an' dat stray 'oman uh his'n down in Lake How-
ell swamp an' lay on de rawhide till they cain't say Lawd a' mussy. He allus
wuz uh ovahbearin' niggah, but since dat white 'oman from up north done
teached 'im how to run a automobile, he done got too biggety to live — an'
we oughter kill 'im," Old Man Anderson advised.

A grunt of approval went around the porch. But the heat was melting
their civic virtue and Elijah Moseley began to bait Joe Clarke.

"Come on, Joe, git a melon outa dere an' slice it up for yo' customers.
We'se all sufferin' wid de heat. De bear's done got *me!*"

"Thass right, Joe, a watermelon is jes' whut Ah needs tuh cure de eppizudicks,"° Walter Thomas joined forces with Moseley. "Come on dere, Joe.
We all is steady customers an' you aint set us up in a long time. Ah chooses
dat long, bowlegged Floridy favorite."

"A god, an' be dough. You all gimme twenty cents and slice way," Clarke   45
retorted. "Ah needs a col' slice m'self. Heah, everybody chip in. Ah'll lend
y'll mah meat knife."

The money was quickly subscribed and the huge melon brought forth.
At that moment, Sykes and Bertha arrived. A determined silence fell on the
porch and the melon was put away again.

Merchant snapped down the blade of his jackknife and moved toward
the store door.

"Come on in, Joe, an' gimme a slab uh sow belly an' uh pound uh coffee —
almost fuhgot 'twas Sat'day. Got to git on home." Most of the men left also.

Just then Delia drove past on her way home, as Sykes was ordering
magnificently for Bertha. It pleased him for Delia to see.

"Git whutsoever yo' heart desires, Honey. Wait a minute, Joe. Give huh   50
two botles uh strawberry soda-water, uh quart uh parched ground-peas, an'
a block uh chewin' gum."

With all this they left the store, with Sykes reminding Bertha that this
was his town and she could have it if she wanted it.

The men returned soon after they left, and held their watermelon feast.

"Where did Syke Jones git da 'oman from nohow?" Lindsay asked.

"Ovah Apopka. Guess dey musta been cleanin' out de town when she
lef'. She don't look lak a thing but a hunk uh liver wid hair on it."

"Well, she sho' kin squall," Dave Carter contributed. "When she gits   55
ready tuh laff, she jes' opens huh mouf an' latches it back tuh de las' notch.
No ole grandpa alligator down in Lake Bell ain't got nothin' on huh."

Bertha had been in town three months now. Sykes was still paying her room
rent at Della Lewis' — the only house in town that would have taken her in.
Sykes took her frequently to Winter Park to "stomps."° He still assured her
that he was the swellest man in the state.

"Sho' you kin have dat lil' ole house soon's Ah kin git dat 'oman outa
dere. Everything b'longs tuh me an' you sho' kin have it. Ah sho' 'bominates

eppizudicks: some form of disease or illness, related to "epidemic," but in a playful colloquial way.
stomps: dance parties.

uh skinny 'oman. Lawdy, you sho' is got one portly shape on you! You kin git *anything* you wants. Dis is *mah* town an' you sho' kin have it."

Delia's work-worn knees crawled over the earth in Gethsemane° and up the rocks of Calvary many, many times during these months. She avoided the villagers and meeting places in her efforts to be blind and deaf. But Bertha nullified this to a degree, by coming to Delia's house to call Sykes out to her at the gate.

Delia and Sykes fought all the time now with no peaceful interludes. They slept and ate in silence. Two or three times Delia had attempted a timid friendliness, but she was repulsed each time. It was plain that the breaches must remain agape.

The sun had burned July to August. The heat streamed down like a 60 million hot arrows, smiting all things living upon the earth. Grass withered, leaves browned, snakes went blind in shedding and men and dogs went mad. Dog days!

Delia came home one day and found Sykes there before her. She wondered, but started to go on into the house without speaking, even though he was standing in the kitchen door and she must either stoop under his arm or ask him to move. He made no room for her. She noticed a soap box beside the steps, but paid no particular attention to it, knowing that he must have brought it there. As she was stooping to pass under his outstretched arm, he suddenly pushed her backward, laughingly.

"Look in de box dere Delia, Ah done brung yuh somethin'!"

She nearly fell upon the box in her stumbling, and when she saw what it held, she all but fainted outright.

"Syke! Syke, mah Gawd! You take dat rattlesnake 'way from heah! You *gottuh*. Oh, Jesus, have mussy!"

"Ah aint gut tuh do nuthin' uh de kin' — fact is Ah aint got tuh do 65 nothin' but die. Taint no use uh you puttin' on airs makin' out lak you skeered uh dat snake — he's gointer stay right heah tell he die. He wouldn't bite me cause Ah knows how tuh handle 'im. Nohow he wouldn't risk breakin' out his fangs 'gin yo' skinny laigs."

"Naw, now Syke, don't keep dat thing 'roun' heah tuh skeer me tuh death. You knows Ah'm even feared uh earth worms. Thass de biggest snake Ah evah did see. Kill 'im Syke, please."

"Doan ast me tuh do nothin' fuh yuh. Goin' 'roun' tryin' tuh be so damn asterperious.° Naw, Ah aint gonna kill it. Ah think uh damn sight mo' uh him dan you! Dat's a nice snake an' anybody doan lak 'im kin jes' hit de grit."

The village soon heard that Sykes had the snake, and came to see and ask questions.

"How de hen-fire did you ketch dat six-foot rattler, Syke?" Thomas asked.

"He's full uh frogs so he caint hardly move, thass how Ah eased up on 'm. 70 But Ah'm a snake charmer an' knows how tuh handle 'em. Shux, dat aint nothin'. Ah could ketch one eve'y day if Ah so wanted tuh."

Gethsemane: The garden outside Jerusalem where Jesus was arrested the night before his crucifixion.
asterperious: uppity.

"Whut he needs is a heavy hick'ry club leaned real heavy on his head. Dat's de bes' way tuh charm a rattlesnake."

"Naw, Walt, y'll jes' don't understand dese diamon' backs lak Ah do," said Sykes in a superior tone of voice.

The village agreed with Walter, but the snake stayed on. His box remained by the kitchen door with its screen wire covering. Two or three days later it had digested its meal of frogs and literally came to life. It rattled at every movement in the kitchen or the yard. One day as Delia came down the kitchen steps she saw his chalky-white fangs curved like scimitars hung in the wire meshes. This time she did not run away with averted eyes as usual. She stood for a long time in the doorway in a red fury that grew bloodier for every second that she regarded the creature that was her torment.

That night she broached the subject as soon as Sykes sat down to the table.

"Syke, Ah wants you tuh take dat snake 'way fum heah. You done 75 starved me an' Ah put up widcher, you done beat me an Ah took dat, but you done kilt all mah insides bringin' dat varmint heah."

Sykes poured out a saucer full of coffee and drank it deliberately before he answered her.

"A whole lot Ah keer 'bout how you feels inside uh out. Dat snake aint goin' no damn wheah till Ah gits ready fuh 'im tuh go. So fur as beatin' is concerned, yuh aint took near all dat you gointer take ef yuh stay' roun' *me*."

Delia pushed back her plate and got up from the table. "Ah hates you, Sykes," she said calmly. "Ah hates you tuh de same degree dat Ah useter love yuh. Ah done took an' took till mah belly is full up tuh mah neck. Dat's de reason Ah got mah letter fum de church an' moved mah membership tuh Woodbridge—so Ah don't haftuh take no sacrament wid yuh. Ah don't wantuh see yuh 'roun' me atall. Lay 'roun' wid dat 'oman all yuh wants tuh, but gwan 'way fum me an' mah house. Ah hates yuh lak uh suck-egg dog."

Sykes almost let the huge wad of corn bread and collard greens he was chewing fall out of his mouth in amazement. He had a hard time whipping himself up to the proper fury to try to answer Delia.

"Well, Ah'm glad you does hate me. Ah'm sho' tiahed uh you hangin' 80 ontuh me. Ah don't want yuh. Look at yuh stringey ole neck! Yo' rawbony laigs an' arms is enough tuh cut uh man tuh death. You looks jes' lak de devvul's doll-baby tuh *me*. You cain't hate me no worse dan Ah hates you. Ah been hatin' *you* fuh years."

"Yo' ole black hide don't look lak nothin' tuh me, but uh passle uh wrinkled up rubber, wid yo' big ole yeahs flappin' on each side lak uh paih uh buzzard wings. Don't think Ah'm gointuh be run 'way fum mah house neither. Ah'm goin' tuh de white folks about *you*, mah young man, de very nex' time you lay yo' han's on me. Mah cup is done run ovah."° Delia said this with no signs of fear and Sykes departed from the house, threatening her, but made not the slightest move to carry out any of them.

That night he did not return at all, and the next day being Sunday, Delia was glad she did not have to quarrel before she hitched up her pony and drove the four miles to Woodbridge.

She stayed to the night service — "love feast" — which was very warm and full of spirit. In the emotional winds her domestic trials were borne far and wide so that she sang as she drove homeward,

"Jurden° water, black an' col'
Chills de body, not de soul
An' Ah wantah cross Jurden in uh calm time."

She came from the barn to the kitchen door and stopped.

"Whut's de mattah, ol' satan, you aint kickin' up yo' racket?" She addressed the snake's box. Complete silence. She went on into the house with a new hope in its birth struggles. Perhaps her threat to go to the white folks had frightened Sykes! Perhaps he was sorry! Fifteen years of misery and suppression had brought Delia to the place where she would hope *anything* that looked towards a way over or through her wall of inhibitions.

She felt in the match safe behind the stove at once for a match. There was only one there.

"Dat niggah wouldn't fetch nothin' heah tuh save his rotten neck, but he kin run thew whut Ah brings quick enough. Now he done toted off nigh on tuh haff uh box uh matches. He done had dat 'oman heah in mah house, too."

Nobody but a woman could tell how she knew this even before she struck the match. But she did and it put her into a new fury.

Presently she brought in the tubs to put the white things to soak. This time she decided she need not bring the hamper out of the bedroom; she would go in there and do the sorting. She picked up the pot-bellied lamp and went in. The room was small and the hamper stood hard by the foot of the white iron bed. She could sit and reach through the bedposts — resting as she worked.

"Ah wantah cross Jurden in uh calm time." She was singing again. The mood of the "love feast" had returned. She threw back the lid of the basket almost gaily. Then, moved by both horror and terror, she sprang back toward the door. *There lay the snake in the basket!* He moved sluggishly at first, but even as she turned round and round, jumped up and down in an insanity of fear, he began to stir vigorously. She saw him pouring his awful beauty from the basket upon the bed, then she seized the lamp and ran as fast as she could to the kitchen. The wind from the open door blew out the light and the darkness added to her terror. She sped to the darkness of the yard, slamming the door after her before she thought to set down the lamp. She did not feel safe even on the ground, so she climbed up in the hay barn.

There for an hour or more she lay sprawled upon the hay a gibbering wreck.

Finally she grew quiet, and after that, coherent thought. With this, stalked through her a cold, bloody rage. Hours of this. A period of introspection, a space of retrospection, then a mixture of both. Out of this an awful calm.

"Well, Ah done de bes' Ah could. If things aint right, Gawd knows taint mah fault."

Jurden: the biblical river Jordan; the site of Jesus's baptism.

She went to sleep—a twitch sleep—and woke up to a faint gray sky. There was a loud hollow sound below. She peered out. Sykes was at the wood-pile, demolishing a wire-covered box.

He hurried to the kitchen door, but hung outside there some minutes before 95 he entered, and stood some minutes more inside before he closed it after him.

The gray in the sky was spreading. Delia descended without fear now, and crouched beneath the low bedroom window. The drawn shade shut out the dawn, shut in the night. But the thin walls held back no sound.

"Dat ol' scratch° is woke up now!" She mused at the tremendous whirr inside, which every woodsman knows, is one of the sound illusions. The rattler is a ventriloquist. His whirr sounds to the right, to the left, straight ahead, behind, close under foot—everywhere but where it is. Woe to him who guesses wrong unless he is prepared to hold up his end of the argument! Sometimes he strikes without rattling at all.

Inside, Sykes heard nothing until he knocked a pot lid off the stove while trying to reach the match safe in the dark. He had emptied his pockets at Bertha's.

The snake seemed to wake up under the stove and Sykes made a quick leap into the bedroom. In spite of the gin he had had, his head was clearing now.

"Mah Gawd!" he chattered, "ef Ah could on'y strack uh light!" 100

The rattling ceased for a moment as he stood paralyzed. He waited. It seemed that the snake waited also.

"Oh, fuh de light! Ah thought he'd be too sick"—Sykes was muttering to himself when the whirr began again, closer, right underfoot this time. Long before this, Sykes' ability to think had been flattened down to primitive instinct and he leaped—onto the bed.

Outside Delia heard a cry that might have come from a maddened chimpanzee, a stricken gorilla. All the terror, all the horror, all the rage that man possibly could express, without a recognizable human sound.

A tremendous stir inside there, another series of animal screams, the intermittent whirr of the reptile. The shade torn violently down from the window, letting in the red dawn, a huge brown hand seizing the window stick, great dull blows upon the wooden floor punctuating the gibberish of sound long after the rattle of the snake had abruptly subsided. All this Delia could see and hear from her place beneath the window, and it made her ill. She crept over to the four-o'clocks and stretched herself on the cool earth to recover.

She lay there. "Delia, Delia!" She could hear Sykes calling in a most 105 despairing tone as one who expected no answer. The sun crept on up, and he called. Delia could not move—her legs were gone flabby. She never moved, he called, and the sun kept rising.

"Mah Gawd!" She heard him moan, "Mah Gawd fum Heben!" She heard him stumbling about and got up from her flower-bed. The sun was growing warm. As she approached the door she heard him call out hopefully, "Delia, is dat you Ah heah?"

She saw him on his hands and knees as soon as she reached the door. He crept an inch or two toward her—all that he was able, and she saw his

Scratch: Satan; the devil.

horribly swollen neck and his one open eye shining with hope. A surge of pity too strong to support bore her away from that eye that must, could not, fail to see the tubs. He would see the lamp. Orlando with its doctors was too far. She could scarcely reach the Chinaberry tree, where she waited in the growing heat while inside she knew the cold river was creeping up and up to extinguish that eye which must know by now that she knew.

CONSIDERATIONS FOR CRITICAL THINKING AND WRITING

1. FIRST RESPONSE. Sykes is one of the least likable characters in literature. How did you feel about his death when you first read about it, and how do you now feel about your response?

2. Delia is characterized by her "habitual meekness" (para. 17). Do her words and actions more often reinforce that description or refute it?

3. Name all the ways Sykes attempts to control, manipulate, bully, or abuse Delia. Which of those verbs would you say best describes his behavior?

4. In paragraph 25 Delia reflects back on her fifteen years of marriage and thinks of "the salty stream that had been pressed from her heart. Her tears, her sweat, her blood." Of these three salty excretions, why do you suppose Hurston chooses "sweat" as the story's title?

5. Find examples of the beauty of nature in "Sweat." How do they lead to your understanding of its possible theme?

6. How do the men on Joe Clarke's porch fit into the themes of the story? Why are they essential to it?

7. Sykes and Delia's relationship is more war than marriage, and we would probably describe it as abusive, but they are not the only man and woman in the story. How does their story connect to the relationship between the sexes more generally as it is depicted in "Sweat"?

8. Can the rattlesnake be read as a symbol or is it just a tool for Sykes to torment Delia?

9. Discuss the function of religion in "Sweat."

10. There are no white people in the story, yet they are mentioned at key points: How does their invisible presence affect the story's theme?

11. Is Delia's inaction when it comes to warning or helping Sykes at the end of the story murder, self-defense or neither?

12. CRITICAL STRATEGIES. Read the section on feminist criticism (pp. 1079–80) in Chapter 30, "Critical Strategies for Reading" and consider what a feminist critic might choose to focus on when interpreting "Sweat."

CONNECTION TO ANOTHER SELECTION

1. Both Sykes and Delia in this story and the narrator and her husband John in "The Yellow Wallpaper" (p. 117) are in unhealthy marriages. Are the endings of both stories inevitable? What is the range of choices each woman has, and what limits that range?

8

Style, Tone, and Irony

Rose Lincoln/Harvard Staff Photographer.

> We writers may see, observe, care and feel, but language is the medium by which that all comes across. Language is the transom of thought and feeling.
>
> — ZZ PACKER

STYLE

Style is a concept that everyone understands on some level because in its broadest sense it refers to the particular way in which anything is made or done. Style is everywhere around us. The world is saturated with styles in cars, clothing, buildings, teaching, dancing, music, politics — in anything that reflects a distinctive manner of expression or design. Consider, for example, how a tune sung by the Beatles differs from the same tune performed by a string orchestra. There's no mistaking the two styles.

Authors also have different characteristic styles. *Style* refers to the distinctive manner in which a writer arranges words to achieve particular effects. That arrangement includes individual word choices and matters such as the length of sentences, their structure and tone, and the use of irony.

Diction refers to a writer's choice of words. Because different words evoke different associations in a reader's mind, the writer's choice of words is crucial in controlling a reader's response. The diction must be appropriate for the characters and the situations in which the author places them. In T. C. Boyle's story "The Hit Man" (p. 33), the protagonist repeatedly "wastes" people around him, from his classmate, to his father, to a waitress who serves him peas. The word is slang for "murders," and it is a particular type of slang. To understand it, we probably have to have some familiarity with the popular culture lore of a hired assassin, and we would probably have access to it through movies or TV shows. Although it refers to murder, the word is humorous in the context of the story, especially since it is repeated so often, and so factually. If Boyle had chosen the flatter word *murders* or a specific description of how the murder took place (*shoots, strangles* etc.), the effect would be different.

Sentence structure is another element of a writer's style. Hemingway's terse, economical sentences are frequently noted and readily perceived. Here are the concluding sentences of Hemingway's "Soldier's Home" (p. 104), in which Krebs decides to leave home:

> He had tried so to keep his life from being complicated. Still, none of it had touched him. He had felt sorry for his mother and she had made him lie. He would go to Kansas City and get a job and she would feel all right about it. There would be one more scene maybe before he got away. He would not go down to his father's office. He would miss that one. He wanted his life to go smoothly. It had just gotten going that way. Well, that was all over now, anyway. He would go over to the schoolyard and watch Helen play indoor baseball.

Hemingway expresses Krebs's thought the way Krebs thinks. The style avoids any "complicated" sentence structures. Seven of the eleven sentences begin with the word *He*. There are no abstractions or qualifications. We feel as if we are listening not only to *what* Krebs thinks but to *how* he thinks. The style reflects his firm determination to make, one step at a time, a clean, unobstructed break from his family and the entangling complications they would impose on him.

Contrast this straightforward style with the first paragraph of James Baldwin's story "Sonny's Blues" (p. 76):

> I read about it in the paper, in the subway, on my way to work. I read it, and I couldn't believe it, and I read it again. Then perhaps I just stared at it, at the newsprint spelling out his name, spelling out the story. I stared at it in the swinging lights of the subway car, and in the faces and bodies of the people, and in my own face, trapped in the darkness which roared outside.

The cadence of Baldwin's sentences, the rhythmic repetitions, are striking here. It is like a relay race with each sentence passing a baton to the next one: "I read it" joins the first two sentences and is repeated within the second. That phrase slides into "I stared at it" in the third sentence, which is urged ahead by the repetition of the word *spelling* within that sentence. The final sentence begins again with "I stared at it" and leads us to the final image: the narrator looks outward at the subway window and it becomes a mirror, leading him back to his own face and a feeling of being trapped. This image sets up contrasts that recur throughout the story: of darkness and light, interiors and exteriors, others and selves. We are lulled by these repetitions, drawn into the mystery of the narrator's words, which flow without giving us the same factual details that typify Hemingway's work. The word *it* is in each of these four initial sentences, but we haven't yet been told what it is. We trust that the flowing river of Baldwin's sentences will eventually carry us there.

Hemingway's and Baldwin's uses of language are very different, yet each style successfully fuses what is said with how it is said. We could write summaries of both passages, but our summaries, owing to their styles, would not have the same effect as the originals. And that makes all the difference.

TONE

Style reveals **tone**, the author's implicit attitude toward the people, places, and events in a story. When we speak, tone is conveyed by our voice inflections, our wink of an eye, or some other gesture. A professor who says "You're going to fail the next exam" may be indicating concern, frustration, sympathy, alarm, humor, or indifference, depending on the tone of voice. In a literary work that spoken voice is unavailable; instead we must rely on the context surrounding a statement in order to interpret it correctly.

In Chopin's "The Story of an Hour" (p. 15), for example, we can determine that the author sympathizes with Mrs. Mallard despite the fact that her grief over her husband's assumed death is mixed with joy. Though Mrs. Mallard thinks she's lost her husband, she experiences relief because she feels liberated from an oppressive male-dominated life. That's why she collapses when she sees her husband alive at the end of the story. Chopin makes clear by the tone of the final line ("When the doctors came they said she had died of heart disease — of joy that kills") that the men misinterpret both her grief and joy, for in the larger context of Mrs. Mallard's emotions we see, unlike the doctors, that her death may well have been caused not by a shock of joy but by an overwhelming recognition of her lost freedom.

If we are sensitive to tone, we can get behind a character and see him or her from the author's perspective. In John Updike's "A & P" (p. 138), the narrator clues us into his perspective right away: "In walks these three girls," he begins. This sounds like the beginning of an anecdote someone might tell at a party, maybe even a joke. Sammy, we learn, is a teenaged worker in a grocery store. His casual tone is meant to lull us into the false sense that this story is not monumental, just something that happened at work.

Yet the story builds subtly in intensity to the point that Sammy's dramatic, almost impulsive decision to quit takes on the weight of self-definition. A teen quits a dead-end job: no big deal, happens all the time. But the story's final line reveals that this decision has profound consequences in terms of his life's trajectory. He may not realize that, but his author — a Harvard-educated professional writer with a tremendous command of the English language and a boundless vocabulary, as the reader of his other works will quickly see — is well aware of the difference between his character's voice and his own. An insensitivity to tone can lead a reader astray in determining the theme of a work. Regardless of who is speaking in a story, it is wise to listen for the author's voice too.

IRONY

One of the enduring themes in literature is that things are not always what they seem to be. What we see — or think we see — is not always what we get. The unexpected complexity that often surprises us in life — what Herman Melville in *Moby-Dick* called the "universal thump" — is fertile ground for writers of imaginative literature. They cultivate that ground through the use of *irony*, a device that reveals a reality different from what appears to be true.

Verbal irony consists of a person saying one thing but meaning the opposite. If a student driver smashes into a parked car and the angry instructor turns to say " Great job," the statement is an example of verbal irony. What is meant is not what is said. Verbal irony that is calculated to hurt someone by false praise is commonly known as **sarcasm**. In literature, however, verbal irony is usually not openly aggressive; instead, it is more subtle and restrained though no less intense.

In Gilman's "The Yellow Wallpaper" (p. 117), the narrator says, "John laughs at me, of course, but one expects that in marriage." Does "one"? If there were no irony intended in the statement, the reader would chuckle and say, "One sure does! That's marriage for you! Lots of mockery makes everyone happy." We know immediately that we're not supposed to agree. We scowl at John and wonder to what degree the narrator believes her own statement. Is she conditioned to believe she should be laughed at or is she burying feelings of resentment and even anger that might come out as the story progresses?

Situational irony exists when there is an incongruity between what is expected to happen and what actually happens. For instance, at the end of Chopin's "The Story of an Hour," we expect Mrs. Mallard to hug her husband and shed tears of joy when he returns, not to die. In Ellison's "King of the Bingo Game," we expect that the protagonist will be handed a check when the bingo wheel lands on double zero, the only number that signifies a win, but he is instead clubbed and hauled off stage. In each of these instances the ironic situation creates a distinction between appearances and realities and brings the reader closer to the central meaning of the story.

Another form of irony occurs when an author allows the reader to know more about a situation than a character knows. **Dramatic irony** creates a discrepancy between what a character believes or says and what the reader understands to be true. In Flannery O'Connor's "Revelation" (p. 266), the insecure Mrs. Turpin, as a member of "the home-and-land owner" class, believes herself to be superior to "niggers," "white-trash," and mere "home owners." She takes pride in her position in the community and in what she perceives to be her privileged position in relation to God. The reader, however, knows that her remarks underscore her failings rather than any superiority. Dramatic irony can be an effective way for an author to have a character unwittingly reveal himself or herself.

As you read Raymond Carver's "Popular Mechanics," George Saunders's "I Can Speak™," and Mark Twain's "The Story of the Good Little Boy," pay attention to the author's artful use of style, tone, and irony to convey meanings.

RAYMOND CARVER (1938–1988)

Born in 1938 in Clatskanie, Oregon, to working-class parents, Raymond Carver grew up in Yakima, Washington, was educated at Humboldt State College in California, and did graduate work at the University of Iowa. He married at age nineteen and during his college years worked at a series of low-paying jobs to help support his family. These difficult years eventually ended in divorce. He taught at a number of universities, among them the University of California, Berkeley; the University of Iowa; the University of Texas, El Paso; and Syracuse University. Carver's collections of stories include *Will You Please Be Quiet, Please?* (1976); *What We Talk about When We Talk about Love* (1981), from which "Popular Mechanics" is taken; *Cathedral* (1984); and *Where I'm Calling From: New and Selected Stories* (1988). Though extremely brief, "Popular Mechanics" describes a stark domestic situation with a startling conclusion.

Sophie Bassouls/Sygma/Getty Images.

Popular Mechanics   1981

Early that day the weather turned and the snow was melting into dirty water. Streaks of it ran down from the little shoulder-high window that faced the backyard. Cars slushed by on the street outside, where it was getting dark. But it was getting dark on the inside too.

He was in the bedroom pushing clothes into a suitcase when she came to the door.

I'm glad you're leaving! I'm glad you're leaving! she said. Do you hear?

He kept on putting his things into the suitcase.

Son of a bitch! I'm so glad you're leaving! She began to cry. You can't   5 even look me in the face, can you?

Then she noticed the baby's picture on the bed and picked it up.

He looked at her and she wiped her eyes and stared at him before turning and going back to the living room.

Bring that back, he said.

Just get your things and get out, she said.

He did not answer. He fastened the suitcase, put on his coat, looked   10 around the bedroom before turning off the light. Then he went out to the living room.

She stood in the doorway of the little kitchen, holding the baby.

I want the baby, he said.

Are you crazy?

No, but I want the baby. I'll get someone to come by for his things.

You're not touching this baby, she said.   15

The baby had begun to cry and she uncovered the blanket from around his head.

Oh, oh, she said, looking at the baby.

He moved toward her.

For God's sake! she said. She took a step back into the kitchen.

I want the baby.

Get out of here!   20

She turned and tried to hold the baby over in a corner behind the stove.

But he came up. He reached across the stove and tightened his hands on the baby.

Let go of him, he said.

Get away, get away! she cried.

The baby was red-faced and screaming. In the scuffle they knocked   25 down a flowerpot that hung behind the stove.

He crowded her into the wall then, trying to break her grip. He held on to the baby and pushed with all his weight.

Let go of him, he said.

Don't, she said. You're hurting the baby, she said.

I'm not hurting the baby, he said.   30

The kitchen window gave no light. In the near-dark he worked on her fisted fingers with one hand and with the other hand he gripped the screaming baby up under an arm near the shoulder.

She felt her fingers being forced open. She felt the baby going from her.

No! she screamed just as her hands came loose.

She would have it, this baby. She grabbed for the baby's other arm. She caught the baby around the wrist and leaned back.

But he would not let go. He felt the baby slipping out of his hands and   35 he pulled back very hard.

In this manner, the issue was decided.

CONSIDERATIONS FOR CRITICAL THINKING AND WRITING

1. FIRST RESPONSE. Discuss the story's final lines. What is the "issue" that is "decided"?

2. Though there is little description of the setting in this story, how do the few details that are provided help to establish the tone?

3. How do small actions take on larger significance in the story? Consider the woman picking up the baby's picture and the knocked-down flowerpot.

4. Why is this couple splitting up? Do we know? Does it matter? Explain your response.

5. Discuss the title of the story. The original title was "Mine." Which do you think is more effective?

6. What is the conflict? How is it resolved?

7. Read 1 Kings 3 in the Bible for the story of Solomon. How might "Popular Mechanics" be read as a retelling of this story? What significant differences do you find in the endings of each?

8. Explain how Carver uses irony to convey theme.

CONNECTION TO ANOTHER SELECTION

1. Compare Carver's style with Ernest Hemingway's in "Soldier's Home" (p. 104).

A SAMPLE STUDENT RESPONSE

Skyler Hansen

Professor Ríos

English 200

6 November 2018

The Minimalist Style of Raymond Carver's "Popular Mechanics"

Raymond Carver provides little information in the story "Popular Mechanics." We are not given a complete background of the characters or vivid descriptions of setting. Even the dialogue is limited, and we are thrown into a scene already in progress. However, even though Carver does not tell us "a word more than [he] absolutely need[s] to" (Barth 265), all the necessary elements of a story are right there in front of us. Despite the minimalist style, we understand the characters and their motives by reading closely.

The plot of the story is simple: in the wake of a bitter fight, a man packs his suitcase and is about to leave the mother of his child. Many seemingly important details are missing. We're not certain whether the couple is married or what they are arguing about. We don't even know their names. However, all the story's complexities are there. The main conflict emerges when the man decides that he wants the baby. And while we might initially assume this has always been his intention, we realize that's not the case. He first plans to take a picture of the baby, and when the woman won't let him, he suddenly decides to raise the stakes:

>He did not answer. He fastened the suitcase, put on his coat, looked around the bedroom before turning off the light. Then he went out to the living room.
>
>She stood in the doorway of the little kitchen, holding the baby.
>
>I want the baby, he said. (217)

Here, we are practically able to watch the man's thought process. He feels so much anger toward the woman that he wants to hurt her before he leaves. As he packs, he searches for something he can take from her, and finally decides on the baby. His motive has little (perhaps nothing) to do with the child. He seeks only to devastate the child's mother.

Though the story appears to be open-ended, the resolution is clear. The two struggle for the baby, forcefully, violently, unwilling to give in to the other:

> She caught the baby around the wrist and leaned back.
>
> But he would not let go. He felt the baby slipping out of his hands and he pulled back very hard.
>
> In this manner, the issue was decided. (218)

While we do not know the extent of the damage, or what will become of these people, we do know that the baby suffers most as a result of the altercation, a theme Carver makes clear. . . .

Works Cited

Barth, John. "On Minimalist Fiction." in Michael Meyer and D. Quentin Miller, eds., *The Compact Bedford Introduction to Literature*, 12th ed., Bedford/St. Martin's, 2020, p. 218.

Carver, Raymond. "Popular Mechanics." Meyer and Miller, pp. 217-218.

Meyer, Michael, and D. Quentin Miller, editors. *Literature to Go*, 4th ed., Bedford/St. Martin's, 2020.

GEORGE SAUNDERS (B. 1958)

A native of Amarillo, Texas, George Saunders earned his bachelor's degree at the Colorado School of Mines and his master's degree at Syracuse University, where he has taught since 1997. Most of his publications have been short stories, often with absurdist or comic overtones. He has won many prestigious awards, including the National Magazine Award for Fiction four times, and he is the recipient of both a Guggenheim Fellowship and a MacArthur "genius" grant. Breaking the pattern of many fiction writers, Saunders published his only novel, *Lincoln in the Bardo* (2017), after many years as a short story writer. That novel was published to

Eamonn McCabe/Getty Images.

great critical acclaim, including Britain's prestigious Man Booker prize. He is only the second American author to win that prize. He cites as influences many short story authors included in this anthology — Ernest Hemingway, Raymond Carver, Mark Twain, and Tobias Wolff — and critics have compared him to another: Kurt Vonnegut Jr. All of their selections would make interesting stylistic and thematic comparisons to the following story.

I Can Speak™ *1999*

Mrs. Ruth Faniglia
210 Lester Street
Rochester, N.Y. 14623

DEAR MRS. FANIGLIA,

We were very sorry to receive your letter of 23 Feb., which accompanied the I CAN SPEAK!™ you returned, much to our disappointment. We here at KidLuv believe that the I CAN SPEAK!™ is an innovative and essential educational tool that, used with proper parental guidance, offers a rare early-development opportunity for babies and toddlers alike. And so I thought I would take some of my personal time (I am on lunch) and try to address the questions you raised in your letter, which is here in front of me on my (cluttered!) desk.

First, may I be so bold as to suggest that your disappointment may stem from your own, perhaps unreasonable, expectations? Because in your letter, what you indicated, when I read it, was that you think and/or thought that somehow the product can read your baby's mind? Our product cannot read your baby's mind, Mrs. Faniglia. No one can read a baby's mind, at least not yet. Although believe me, we are probably working on it! All the I CAN SPEAK!™ can do, however, is respond to aural patterns in a way that makes baby seem older. Say baby sees a peach. If you or Mr. Faniglia (I hope I do not presume) were to loudly say something like "What a delicious peach!" the I CAN SPEAK!™, hearing this, through that little slotted hole near the neck, would respond by saying something like "I LIKE PEACH." Or "I WANT PEACH." Or, if you had chosen the ICS2000 (you chose the ICS1900, which is fine, perfectly good for most babies), the I CAN SPEAK!™ might even respond by saying something like "FRUIT, ISN'T THAT ONE OF THE MAJOR FOOD GROUPS?" Which would be pretty good, for a six-month-old like Derek, your son, don't you think?

But here I must reiterate: That would not in reality be Derek speaking. Derek would not in reality know that a peach is fruit, or that fruit is a major food group. The I CAN SPEAK!™ knows, however, and, from its position on Derek's face, it will give the illusion that Derek knows, by giving the illusion that Derek is speaking out of the twin moving SimuLips. But that is it. That is all we claim.

Furthermore, in your letter, Mrs. Faniglia, you state that the I CAN   5 SPEAK!™ "mask" (your terminology) takes on a "stressed-out look when talking that is not what a real baby's talking face appears like but is more like some nervous middle-aged woman." Well, maybe that is so, but, with all due respect, you try it! You try making a latex face look and talk and move like the real face of an actual live baby! Inside are over 5000 separate circuits and 390 moving parts. And as far as looking like a middle-aged woman, we beg to differ: we do not feel that a middle-aged stressed-out woman has (1) no hair on head and (2) chubby cheeks and (3) fine downy facial hair. The ICS1900 unit is definitely the face of a baby, Mrs. Faniglia. We took over twenty-five hundred photos of different babies and using a computer combined them to make this face, this face we call Male Composite 37 or, affectionately, Little Roger. But what you possibly seem to be unhappy about is that Little Roger's face is not Derek's face? To be frank, Mrs. Faniglia, many of you, our customers, have found it disconcerting that their baby looks different with the I CAN SPEAK!™ on. Which we find so surprising. Did you, we often wonder, not look at the cover of the box? On that cover the ICS1900 is very plainly shown, situated on a sort of rack, looking facewise like Little Roger, albeit Little Roger is a bit crumpled and has a forehead furrow of sorts.

But this is why we came up with the ICS2100. With the ICS2100, your baby looks just like your baby. And, because we do not want anyone to be unhappy with us, we would like to give you a complimentary ICS2100 upgrade! We would like to come to your house on Lester Street and make a personalized plaster cast of Derek's real, actual face! And soon, via FedEx, here will come Derek's face in a box, and when you slip that ICS2100 over Derek's head and Velcro the Velcro, he will look so very much like himself! Plus we have another free surprise, which is that, while at your house, we will tape his actual voice and use it to make our phrases, the phrases Derek will subsequently say. So not only will he look like himself, he will sound like himself, as he crawls around your house appearing to speak!

Plus we will throw in several other personalizing options. Say you call Derek "Lovemeister." (I am using this example from my own personal home, as my wife, Ann, and I call our son Billy "Lovemeister," because he is so sweet.) With the ICS2100, you might choose to have Derek say, upon crawling into a room, "HERE COMES THE LOVEMEISTER!" or "STOP TALKING DIRTY, THE LOVEMEISTER HAS ARRIVED!" How we do this is, laser beams coming out of the earlobes, which sense the doorframe. So the I CAN SPEAK!™ knows it has just entered a room, from its position on Derek's head! And also you will have over one hundred Discretionary Phrases to more highly personalize Derek. For instance, you might choose to have him say, on his birthday, "MOMMY AND DADDY, REMEMBER THAT TIME YOU CONCEIVED ME IN ARUBA?" Although probably you did not in fact conceive Derek in Aruba. That we do not know. (Our research is not that extensive!) Or say your dog comes up and gives Derek a lick. You could make Derek say (if your dog's name is Queenie), "QUEENIE, GIVE IT A REST!" Which, you know what? It makes you love him more. Because suddenly he is articulate. Suddenly he is not just sitting there going glub glub glub while examining a piece of his own feces on his own thumb, which is something we recently found Billy doing! Sometimes we have felt that our childless friends think badly of us for having a kid who just goes glub glub glub in the corner while looking at his feces on his thumb. But now when childless friends are over, what we have found, my wife, Ann, and I, is that it's great to have your kid say something witty and self-possessed years before he or she would actually in reality be able to say something witty or self-possessed. The bottom line is that it's just *fun* when you and your childless friends are playing cards, and your baby suddenly blurts out (in his *very own probable future voice*), "IT IS LIKELY THAT WE STILL DON'T FULLY UNDERSTAND THE IMPORT OF ALL OF EINSTEIN'S FINDINGS!"

Here I must admit that we have several times seen a sort of softening in the eyes of our resolute childless friends, as if they, too, would suddenly like to have a baby.

And as far as Derek flinching whenever that voice issues forth from him? When that speaker near his mouth sort of buzzes his lips? May I say this is not unusual? What I suggest? Try putting the ICS on Derek for a short time at first, maybe ten minutes a day, then gradually building up his Wearing Time. That is what we did. And it worked super. Now Billy wears his even while sleeping. In fact, if we forget to put it back on after his bath, he pitches a fit. Kind of begs for it! He starts to say, you know, "Mak! Mak!" Which we think is his word for mask. And when we put the mask on and Velcro the Velcro, he says, or rather it says, "GUTEN MORGEN, PAPA!" because we are trying to teach him German, and have installed the German Learning module in our ICS2100. Or for example, if his pants are not yet on, he'll say, "HOW ABOUT SLAPPING ON MY ROMPERS SO I CAN GET ON WITH MY DAY!" (I wrote that one.)

My point is, with the ICS2100 Billy is much, much cleverer than he ever 10
was with the ICS1900. He has recently learned, for example, that if he spills a
little milk on his chin, his SimuLips will issue a MOO sound. Which he really
seems to get a kick out of! I'll be in the living room doing a little evening paperwork and from the kitchen I'll hear, you know, "MOO! MOO! MOO!" And I'll
rush in, and there'll be this sort of lake of milk on the floor. And there'll be Billy,
pouring milk on his chin until I yank the milk away, at which point he bellows,
"DON'T FENCE ME IN." (Ann's contribution — she was raised in Wyoming!)

I, for one, Mrs. Faniglia, do not believe that any baby wants to sit around
all day going glub glub glub. My feeling is that a baby, sitting in its diaper,
looking around at the world, thinks to itself, albeit in some crude nonverbal
way, What the heck is wrong with me, why am I the only one going glub glub
glub while all these other folks are talking in whole complete sentences? And
hence, possibly, lifelong psychological damage may result. Now, am I saying that your Derek runs the risk of feeling bad about himself as a grownup
because as a baby he felt he didn't know how to talk right? No, it is not for me
to say that, Mrs. Faniglia, I am only in Sales. But I will say that I am certainly
not taking any chances with our Billy. My belief is that when Billy hears a
competent, intelligent voice issuing from the area near his mouth, he feels
excellent about himself. And I feel excellent about him. Not that I didn't feel
excellent about him before. But now we can actually have a sort of conversation! And also — and most importantly — when that voice issues from his
SimuLips he learns something invaluable; namely, that when he finally does
begin speaking, he will be speaking via using his mouth.

Now, Mrs. Faniglia, you may be thinking, Hold on a sec, of course this
guy loves his I CAN SPEAK!™ He probably gets his for free! But not so, Mrs.
Faniglia, I get mine for two grand, just like you. We get no discounts, so much
in demand is the I CAN SPEAK!™, and in addition we are strongly encouraged
by our management to purchase and use the I CAN SPEAK!™ at home, on our
own kids. (Or even, in one case, on an elderly senile mom! Suffice it to say
that, though she looks sort of funny with the Little Roger head on her somewhat frail frame, the family takes great comfort in hearing all the witty things
she has to say. Just like her old self!) Not that I wouldn't use it otherwise.
Believe me, I would. Since we upgraded to the ICS2100, things have been
great, Billy looks almost identical to himself; and is not nearly so, you know,
boring as before, when we had the ICS1900, which (frankly) says some
rather predictable things, which I expect is partly why you were so unhappy
with it, Mrs. Faniglia, you seem like a very intelligent woman. When people
come over now, sometimes we just gather around Billy and wait for his next
howler, and last weekend my supervisor, Mr. Ted Ames, stopped by (a super
guy, he has really given me support, please let him know if you've found this
letter at all helpful) and boy did we all crack up laughing when Billy began
rubbing his face very rapidly across the carpet in order to make his ICS2100
shout, "FRICTION IS A COMMON AND USEFUL SOURCE OF HEAT!"

Mrs. Faniglia, it is nearing the end of my lunch, and so I must wrap this
up, but I hope I have been of service. On a personal note, I did not have the

greatest of pasts when I came here, having been in a few scrapes and even rehab situations, but now, wow, the commissions roll in, and I have made a nice life for me and Ann and Billy. Not that the possible loss of my commission is the reason for my concern. Please do not think so. While it is true that, if you decline my upgrade offer and persist in your desire to return your ICS1900, my commission must be refunded, by me, to Mr. Ames, it is no big deal, I have certainly refunded commissions to Mr. Ames before, especially lately. I don't quite know what I'm doing wrong. But that is not your concern, Mrs. Faniglia. Your concern is Derek. My real reason for writing this letter, on my lunch break, is that, hard as we all work at KidLuv to provide innovative and essential development tools for families like yours, Mrs. Faniglia, it is always sort of a heartbreak when our products are misapprehended. Please do accept our offer of a free ICS2100 upgrade. We at KidLuv really love what kids are, Mrs. Faniglia, which is why we want them to become something better as soon as possible! Baby's early years are so precious, and must not be wasted, as we are finding out, as our Billy grows and grows, learning new skills every day.

> Sincerely yours,
> Rick Sminks
> Product Service Representative
> KidLuv, Inc.

CONSIDERATIONS FOR CRITICAL THINKING AND WRITING

1. **FIRST RESPONSE.** There is a long tradition (called the "epistolary tradition") of fiction comprised of letters, but stories or novels in this tradition often contain a series of letters rather than just one. What makes this single letter a story?

2. How does the narrator subtly evoke setting? Why does it matter to this story?

3. List all of the corporate branding terms the narrator uses in his letter to Ruth Faniglia and consider how they contribute to its humor.

4. Analyze the way the narrator, Rick Sminks, treads the line between politeness and rudeness in his letter. Is the story funnier when he crosses that line, or when he tries especially hard to restrain himself?

5. Consider how the narrator's use of exclamation points is a factor in making the story humorous.

6. How is the very notion of a mask that talks for a baby humorous? What are the cultural factors that make it so?

7. Rick Sminks conjures many scenarios of either his child or Ruth's saying odd or inappropriate things. Which is the funniest? Why?

8. Humor often crosses a line between the harmless and the distasteful. When Rick applies the I Can Speak!™ technology to "an elderly senile mom" (para. 12) does the story cross that line, or does this example just amplify the humor?

9. Read the definition of satire in the introduction to this chapter (and feel free to do more research: our definition is brief, and satire is a deep, rich field). Assume that this is a satire: Would you say that its primary target is overzealous parenting, the way corporations take over our domestic lives, or something else? Cite evidence.

MARK TWAIN (1835–1910)

Bettmann/Getty Images.

Mark Twain is the pen name of Samuel Clemens, born in Missouri in 1835. Twain spent most of his childhood in Hannibal, Missouri, on the Mississippi River, and after the death of his father when he was eleven, he worked at a series of jobs to help support his family. A newspaper job prepared him to wander east working for papers and exploring St. Louis, New York, and Philadelphia. Later he trained as a steamboat pilot on the Mississippi and piloted boats professionally until the onset of the Civil War. Clemens had used a couple of different pseudonyms for minor publications before this point, but in 1863 he signed a travel narrative "Mark Twain," from a boating term that means "two fathoms deep," and the name for the great American humorist was created. Twain gained fame in 1865 with his story "The Celebrated Jumping Frog of Calaveras County," which appeared in the New York–based *Saturday Press*. He then became a traveling correspondent, writing pieces on his travels to Europe and the Middle East, and returned to the United States in 1870, when he married and moved to Connecticut. Twain produced *Roughing It* (1872) and *The Gilded Age* (1873) while he toured the country lecturing, and in 1876 published *The Adventures of Tom Sawyer*, an instant hit. His subsequent publications include *A Tramp Abroad* (1880), *The Prince and the Pauper* (1881), and the masterpiece *Adventures of Huckleberry Finn* (1884). Often traveling and lecturing, Twain wrote several more books, including story collections, *The Tragedy of Pudd'nhead Wilson* (1894), and *Tom Sawyer, Detective* (1896), before he died in Italy in 1910. His work is noted for the combination of rough humor and vernacular language it often uses to convey keen social insights.

The Story of the Good Little Boy   1870

Once there was a good little boy by the name of Jacob Blivens. He always obeyed his parents, no matter how absurd and unreasonable their demands were; and he always learned his book, and never was late at Sabbath-school.

He would not play hookey, even when his sober judgment told him it was the most profitable thing he could do. None of the other boys could ever make that boy out, he acted so strangely. He wouldn't lie, no matter how convenient it was. He just said it was wrong to lie, and that was sufficient for him. And he was so honest that he was simply ridiculous. The curious ways that that Jacob had, surpassed everything. He wouldn't play marbles on Sunday, he wouldn't rob birds' nests, he wouldn't give hot pennies to organ-grinders' monkeys; he didn't seem to take any interest in any kind of rational amusement. So the other boys used to try to reason it out and come to an understanding of him, but they couldn't arrive at any satisfactory conclusion. As I said before, they could only figure out a sort of vague idea that he was "afflicted," and so they took him under their protection, and never allowed any harm to come to him.

This good little boy read all the Sunday-school books; they were his greatest delight. This was the whole secret of it. He believed in the good little boys they put in the Sunday-school books; he had every confidence in them. He longed to come across one of them alive once; but he never did. They all died before his time, maybe. Whenever he read about a particularly good one he turned over quickly to the end to see what became of him, because he wanted to travel thousands of miles and gaze on him; but it wasn't any use; that good little boy always died in the last chapter, and there was a picture of the funeral, with all his relations and the Sunday-school children standing around the grave in pantaloons that were too short, and bonnets that were too large, and everybody crying into handkerchiefs that had as much as a yard and a half of stuff in them. He was always headed off in this way. He never could see one of those good little boys on account of his always dying in the last chapter.

Jacob had a noble ambition to be put in a Sunday-school book. He wanted to be put in, with pictures representing him gloriously declining to lie to his mother, and her weeping for joy about it; and pictures representing him standing on the doorstep giving a penny to a poor beggar-woman with six children, and telling her to spend it freely, but not to be extravagant, because extravagance is a sin; and pictures of him magnanimously refusing to tell on the bad boy who always lay in wait for him around the corner as he came from school, and welted him over the head with a lath, and then chased him home, saying, "Hi! hi!" as he proceeded. That was the ambition of young Jacob Blivens. He wished to be put in a Sunday-school book. It made him feel a little uncomfortable sometimes when he reflected that the good little boys always died. He loved to live, you know, and this was the most unpleasant feature about being a Sunday-school-book boy. He knew it was not healthy to be good. He knew it was more fatal than consumption to be so supernaturally good as the boys in the books were; he knew that none of them had ever been able to stand it long, and it pained him to think that if they put him in a book he wouldn't ever see it, or even if they did get the book out before he died it wouldn't be popular without any picture of his funeral in the back part of it. It couldn't be much of a Sunday-school book that couldn't tell about the advice he gave to the community when he was dying. So at last, of course, he had to make up his mind to do the best he could under the circumstances — to live right, and hang on as long as he could, and have his dying speech all ready when his time came.

But somehow nothing ever went right with this good little boy; nothing ever turned out with him the way it turned out with the good little boys in the books. They always had a good time, and the bad boys had the broken legs; but in his case there was a screw loose somewhere, and it all happened just the other way. When he found Jim Blake stealing apples, and went under the tree to read to him about the bad little boy who fell out of a neighbor's apple tree and broke his arm, Jim fell out of the tree, too, but he fell on *him* and broke *his* arm, and Jim wasn't hurt at all. Jacob couldn't understand that. There wasn't anything in the books like it.

And once, when some bad boys pushed a blind man over in the mud,   5 and Jacob ran to help him up and receive his blessing, the blind man did not give him any blessing at all, but whacked him over the head with his stick and said he would like to catch him shoving *him* again, and then pretending to help him up. This was not in accordance with any of the books. Jacob looked them all over to see.

One thing that Jacob wanted to do was to find a lame dog that hadn't any place to stay, and was hungry and persecuted, and bring him home and pet him and have that dog's imperishable gratitude. And at last he found one and was happy; and he brought him home and fed him, but when he was going to pet him the dog flew at him and tore all the clothes off him except those that were in front, and made a spectacle of him that was astonishing. He examined authorities, but he could not understand the matter. It was of the same breed of dogs that was in the books, but it acted very differently. Whatever this boy did he got into trouble. The very things the boys in the books got rewarded for turned out to be about the most unprofitable things he could invest in.

Once, when he was on his way to Sunday-school, he saw some bad boys starting off pleasuring in a sailboat. He was filled with consternation, because he knew from his reading that boys who went sailing on Sunday invariably got drowned. So he ran out on a raft to warn them, but a log turned with him and slid him into the river. A man got him out pretty soon, and the doctor pumped the water out of him, and gave him a fresh start with his bellows, but he caught cold and lay sick abed nine weeks. But the most unaccountable thing about it was that the bad boys in the boat had a good time all day, and then reached home alive and well in the most surprising manner. Jacob Blivens said there was nothing like these things in the books. He was perfectly dumbfounded.

When he got well he was a little discouraged, but he resolved to keep on trying anyhow. He knew that so far his experiences wouldn't do to go in a book, but he hadn't yet reached the allotted term of life for good little boys, and he hoped to be able to make a record yet if he could hold on till his time was fully up. If everything else failed he had his dying speech to fall back on.

He examined his authorities, and found that it was now time for him to go to sea as a cabin-boy. He called on a ship-captain and made his application, and when the captain asked for his recommendations he proudly drew out a tract and pointed to the word, "To Jacob Blivens, from his affectionate teacher." But the captain was a coarse, vulgar man, and he said, "Oh, that be blowed! *that* wasn't any proof that he knew how to wash dishes or handle a slush-bucket, and he guessed he didn't want him." This was altogether the most extraordinary thing that ever happened to Jacob in all his life. A compliment from a teacher, on a tract, had never failed to move the tenderest emotions of ship-captains, and open the way to all offices of honor and profit in their gift — it never had in any book that ever *he* had read. He could hardly believe his senses.

This boy always had a hard time of it. Nothing ever came out according to the authorities with him. At last, one day, when he was around hunting up bad little boys to admonish, he found a lot of them in the old iron-foundry fixing up a little joke on fourteen or fifteen dogs, which they had tied together in long procession, and were going to ornament with empty nitroglycerin cans made fast to their tails. Jacob's heart was touched. He sat down on one of those cans (for he never minded grease when duty was before him), and he took hold of the foremost dog by the collar, and turned his reproving eye upon wicked Tom Jones. But just at that moment Alderman McWelter, full of wrath, stepped in. All the bad boys ran away, but Jacob Blivens rose in conscious innocence and began one of those stately little Sunday-school-book speeches which always commence with "Oh, sir!" in dead opposition to the fact that no boy, good or bad, ever starts a remark with "Oh, sir." But the alderman never waited to hear the rest. He took Jacob Blivens by the ear and turned him around, and hit him a whack in the rear with the flat of his hand; and in an instant that good little boy shot out through the roof and soared away toward the sun, with the fragments of those fifteen dogs stringing after him like the tail of a kite. And there wasn't a sign of that alderman or that old iron-foundry left on the face of the earth; and, as for young Jacob Blivens, he never got a chance to make his last dying speech after all his trouble fixing it up, unless he made it to the birds; because, although the bulk of him came down all right in a tree-top in an adjoining county, the rest of him was apportioned around among four townships, and so they had to hold five inquests on him to find out whether he was dead or not, and how it occurred. You never saw a boy scattered so.°

Thus perished the good little boy who did the best he could, but didn't come out according to the books. Every boy who ever did as he did prospered except him. His case is truly remarkable. It will probably never be accounted for.

This glycerin catastrophe is borrowed from a floating newspaper item, whose author's name I would give if I knew it. M.T.

CONSIDERATIONS FOR CRITICAL THINKING AND WRITING

1. FIRST RESPONSE. This story is about the death of a child. What's so funny about that?

2. What is the story's central irony?

3. Which sentences are particularly effective in imitating the style of Sunday-school books? Which sentences are clearly Twain's style? What is the effect of having both styles side by side?

4. How does the story's irony reveal Twain's attitude toward Jacob? Find specific passages to support your points.

5. What sort of lesson does Twain's version of Sunday-school instruction teach?

6. Is there a serious point to the humor here? What is the theme of the story?

7. It might be tempting to sum up this story with something like "Nice guys finish last." Discuss the adequacy of this as a statement of theme.

8. Characterize the tone of voice that tells the story. Is it indignant, amused, cynical, bitter, disinterested, or what?

CONNECTION TO ANOTHER SELECTION

1. Write an essay comparing notions of goodness and obedience in this story and in John Updike's "A & P" (p. 138).

Fiction in Depth

9

A Study of Flannery O'Connor

In most English classes the short story has become a kind of literary specimen to be dissected. Every time a story of mine appears in a Freshman anthology, I have a vision of it, with its little organs laid open, like a frog in a bottle.

— FLANNERY O'CONNOR

I am always having it pointed out to me that life in Georgia is not at all the way I picture it, that escaped criminals do not roam the roads exterminating families, nor Bible salesmen prowl about looking for girls with wooden legs.

— FLANNERY O'CONNOR

Apic/Getty Images.

When Flannery O'Connor (1925–1964) died of lupus before her fortieth birthday, her work was cruelly cut short. Nevertheless, she had completed two novels, *Wise Blood* (1952) and *The Violent Bear It Away* (1960), as well as thirty-one short stories. Despite her brief life and relatively modest output, her work is regarded as among the most distinguished American fiction of the mid-twentieth century. Her two collections of short stories, *A Good Man Is Hard to Find* (1955) and *Everything That Rises Must Converge* (1965), were included in *The Complete Stories of Flannery O'Connor* (1971), which won the National Book Award. The stories included in this chapter offer a glimpse into the work of this important twentieth-century writer.

Cheers,
F. Lannery

A BRIEF BIOGRAPHY AND INTRODUCTION

O'Connor's fiction grapples with living a spiritual life in a secular world. Although this major concern is worked into each of her stories, she takes a broad approach to spiritual issues by providing moral, social, and psychological contexts that offer a wealth of insights and passion that her readers have found both startling and absorbing. Her stories are challenging because her characters, who initially seem radically different from people we know, turn out to be, by the end of each story, somehow familiar — somehow connected to us.

O'Connor inhabited simultaneously two radically different worlds. The world she created in her stories is populated with bratty children, malcontents, incompetents, pious frauds, bewildered intellectuals, deformed cynics, rednecks, hucksters, racists, perverts, and murderers who experience dramatically intense moments that surprise and shock readers. Her personal life, however, was largely uneventful. She humorously acknowledged its quiet nature in 1958 when she claimed that "there won't be any biographies of me because, for only one reason, lives spent between the house and the chicken yard do not make exciting copy."

A broad outline of O'Connor's life may not offer very much "exciting copy," but it does provide clues about why she wrote such powerful fiction. The only child of Catholic parents, O'Connor was born in Savannah, Georgia, where she attended a parochial grammar school and high school. When she was thirteen, her father became ill with disseminated lupus, a rare, incurable blood disease, and had to abandon his real-estate business. The family moved to Milledgeville in central Georgia, where her mother's family had lived for generations. Because there were no Catholic schools in Milledgeville, O'Connor attended a public high school. In 1942, the year after her father died of lupus, O'Connor graduated from high school and enrolled in Georgia State College for Women. There she wrote for the literary magazine until receiving her diploma in 1945. Her stories earned her a fellowship to the Writers' Workshop at the University of Iowa, and for two years she learned to write steadily and seriously. She sold her first story to *Accent* in 1946 and earned her Master of Fine Arts degree in 1947. She wrote stories about life in the rural South, and this subject matter, along with her devout Catholic perspective, became central to her fiction.

With her formal education behind her, O'Connor was ready to begin her professional career at the age of twenty-two. Equipped with determination ("No one can convince me that I shouldn't rewrite as much as I do") and offered the opportunity to be around other practicing writers, she moved to New York, where she worked on her first novel, *Wise Blood*. In 1950, however, she was diagnosed as having lupus, and returning to Georgia for treatment, she took up permanent residence on her mother's farm in Milledgeville. There she lived a severely restricted but productive life, writing stories and raising peacocks.

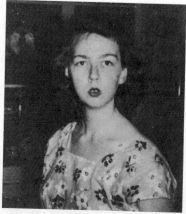

Flannery O'Connor (above left) as a child and (above right) in her teens (age sixteen or seventeen). O'Connor, whose youth was marked by the declining health and death of her father, once wrote, "[A]nybody who has survived childhood has enough information about life to last him the rest of the days."

Flannery O'Connor poses with her book *Wise Blood* in 1952.

The *Corinthian* Staff. Flannery O'Connor (seated, center) as editor of the *Corinthian*, the literary magazine at Georgia State College for Women (now Georgia College and State University). O'Connor attended the college from 1942 through 1945 and earned a B.A. in social science.

Courtesy of Ina Dillard Russell Library Special Collections, Georgia College and State University.

With the exception of O'Connor's early years in Iowa and New York and some short lecture trips to other states, she traveled little. Although she made a pilgrimage to Lourdes (apparently more for her mother's sake than for her own) and then to Rome for an audience with the pope, her life was centered in the South. Like those of William Faulkner and many other southern writers, O'Connor's stories evoke the rhythms of rural southern speech and manners in insulated settings where widely diverse characters mingle. Also like Faulkner, she created works whose meanings go beyond their settings. She did not want her fiction to be seen in the context of narrowly defined regionalism: she complained that "in almost every hamlet you'll find at least one old lady writing epics in Negro dialect and probably two or three old gentlemen who have impossible historical novels on the way." Refusing to be caricatured, she knew that "the woods are full of regional writers, and it is the great horror of every serious Southern writer that he will become one of them." O'Connor's stories are rooted in rural southern culture, but in a larger sense they are set within the psychological and spiritual landscapes of the human soul. This interior setting universalizes local materials in much the same way that Nathaniel Hawthorne's New England stories do. Indeed, O'Connor once described herself as "one of his descendants": "I feel more of a kinship with him than any other American."

O'Connor's deep spiritual convictions coincide with the traditional emphasis on religion in the South, where, she said, there is still the belief "that man has fallen and that he is only perfectible by God's grace, not by his own unaided efforts." Although O'Connor's Catholicism differs from the prevailing Protestant fundamentalism of the South, the religious ethos so pervasive even in rural southern areas provided fertile ground for the spiritual crises her characters experience. In a posthumous collection of her articles, essays, and reviews aptly titled *Mystery and Manners* (1969), she summarized her basic religious convictions:

> I am no disbeliever in spiritual purpose and no vague believer. I see from the standpoint of Christian orthodoxy. This means that for me the meaning of life is centered in our Redemption by Christ and what I see in the world I see in its relation to that. I don't think that this is a position that can be taken halfway or one that is particularly easy in these times to make transparent in fiction.

O'Connor realized that she was writing against the grain of the readers who discovered her stories in the *Partisan Review, Sewanee Review, Mademoiselle,* or *Harper's Bazaar.* Many readers thought that Christian dogma would make her writing doctrinaire, but she insisted that the perspective of Christianity allowed her to interpret the details of life and guaranteed her "respect for [life's] mystery." O'Connor's stories contain no prepackaged prescriptions for living, no catechisms that lay out all the answers. Instead, her characters struggle with spiritual questions in bizarre, incongruous situations. Their lives are grotesque — even comic — precisely because they do not understand their own spiritual natures. Their actions are extreme and abnormal. O'Connor explains the reasons for this in *Mystery and Manners;* she says she sought to expose the "distortions" of "modern life" that appear "normal" to her audience. Hence, she used "violent means" to convey her vision to a "hostile audience." "When you can assume that your audience holds the same beliefs you do, you can relax a little and use more normal means of talking to it." But when the audience holds different values, "you have to make your vision apparent by shock — to the hard of hearing you shout, and for the almost-blind you draw large and startling figures." O'Connor's characters lose or find their soul-saving grace in painful, chaotic circumstances that bear little or no resemblance to the slow but sure progress to the Celestial City of repentant pilgrims in traditional religious stories.

Because her characters are powerful creations who live convincing, even if ugly, lives, O'Connor's religious beliefs never supersede her storytelling. One need not be either Christian or Catholic to appreciate her concerns about human failure and degradation and her artistic ability to render fictional lives that are alternately absurdly comic and tragic. The ironies that abound in her work leave plenty of room for readers of all persuasions. O'Connor's work is narrow in the sense that her concerns are emphatically spiritual, but her compassion and her belief in human possibilities — even among the most unlikely characters — afford her fictions a capacity for wonder that is exhilarating. Her precise, deft use of language always reveals more than it seems to tell.

Like Hawthorne's fiction, O'Connor's stories present complex experiences that cannot be tidily summarized; it takes the entire story to suggest the meanings. Read the following three stories for the pleasure of entering the remarkable world O'Connor creates. You're in for some surprises.

A Good Man Is Hard to Find   1953

The grandmother didn't want to go to Florida. She wanted to visit some of her connections in east Tennessee and she was seizing at every chance to change Bailey's mind. Bailey was the son she lived with, her only boy. He was sitting on the edge of his chair at the table, bent over the orange sports section of the *Journal.* "Now look here, Bailey," she said, "see here, read this," and she stood with one hand on her thin hip and the other rattling the newspaper at his bald head. "Here this fellow that calls himself The Misfit is aloose from the Federal Pen and headed toward Florida and you read here what it says he did to these people. Just you read it. I wouldn't take my children in any direction with a criminal like that aloose in it. I couldn't answer to my conscience if I did."

Bailey didn't look up from his reading so she wheeled around then and faced the children's mother, a young woman in slacks, whose face was as broad and innocent as a cabbage and was tied around with a green headkerchief that had two points on the top like a rabbit's ears. She was sitting on the sofa, feeding the baby his apricots out of a jar. "The children have been to Florida before," the old lady said. "You all ought to take them somewhere else for a change so they would see different parts of the world and be broad. They never have been to east Tennessee."

The children's mother didn't seem to hear her but the eight-year-old boy, John Wesley, a stocky child with glasses, said, "If you don't want to go to Florida, why dontcha stay at home?" He and the little girl, June Star, were reading the funny papers on the floor.

"She wouldn't stay at home to be queen for a day," June Star said without raising her yellow head.

"Yes and what would you do if this fellow, The Misfit, caught you?" the grandmother asked.   5

"I'd smack his face," John Wesley said.

"She wouldn't stay at home for a million bucks," June Star said. "Afraid she'd miss something. She has to go everywhere we go."

"All right, Miss," the grandmother said. "Just remember that the next time you want me to curl your hair."

June Star said her hair was naturally curly.

The next morning the grandmother was the first one in the car, ready to go. She had her big black valise that looked like the head of a hippopotamus in one corner, and underneath it she was hiding a basket with Pitty Sing, the cat, in it. She didn't intend for the cat to be left alone in the house for three days because he would miss her too much and she was afraid he might brush against one of the gas burners and accidentally asphyxiate himself. Her son, Bailey, didn't like to arrive at a motel with a cat.

She sat in the middle of the back seat with John Wesley and June Star on either side of her. Bailey and the children's mother and the baby sat in front and they left Atlanta at eight forty-five with the mileage on the car at 55890. The grandmother wrote this down because she thought it would be interesting to say how many miles they had been when they got back. It took them twenty minutes to reach the outskirts of the city.

The old lady settled herself comfortably, removing her white cotton gloves and putting them up with her purse on the shelf in front of the back window. The children's mother still had on slacks and still had her head tied up in a green kerchief, but the grandmother had on a navy blue straw sailor hat with a bunch of white violets on the brim and a navy blue dress with a small white dot in the print. Her collars and cuffs were white organdy trimmed with lace and at her neckline she had pinned a purple spray of cloth violets containing a sachet. In case of an accident, anyone seeing her dead on the highway would know at once that she was a lady.

She said she thought it was going to be a good day for driving, neither too hot nor too cold, and she cautioned Bailey that the speed limit was fifty-five miles an hour and that the patrolmen hid themselves behind billboards and small clumps of trees and sped out after you before you had a chance to slow down. She pointed out interesting details of the scenery: Stone Mountain; the blue granite that in some places came up to both sides of the highway; the brilliant red clay banks slightly streaked with purple; and the various crops that made rows of green lace-work on the ground. The trees were full of silver-white sunlight and the meanest of them sparkled. The children were reading comic magazines and their mother had gone back to sleep.

"Let's go through Georgia fast so we won't have to look at it much," John Wesley said.

"If I were a little boy," said the grandmother, "I wouldn't talk about my native state that way. Tennessee has the mountains and Georgia has the hills."

"Tennessee is just a hillbilly dumping ground," John Wesley said, "and Georgia is a lousy state too."

"You said it," June Star said.

"In my time," said the grandmother, folding her thin veined fingers, "children were more respectful of their native states and their parents and everything else. People did right then. Oh look at the cute little pickaninny!" she said and pointed to a Negro child standing in the door of a shack. "Wouldn't that make a picture, now?" she asked and they all turned and looked at the little Negro out of the back window. He waved.

"He didn't have any britches on," June Star said.

"He probably didn't have any," the grandmother explained. "Little niggers in the country don't have things like we do. If I could paint, I'd paint that picture," she said.

The children exchanged comic books.

The grandmother offered to hold the baby and the children's mother passed him over the front seat to her. She set him on her knee and bounced him and told him about the things they were passing. She rolled her eyes and screwed up her mouth and stuck her leathery thin face into his smooth bland one. Occasionally he gave her a faraway smile. They passed a large cotton field with five or six graves fenced in the middle of it, like a small island. "Look at the graveyard!" the grandmother said, pointing it out. "That was the old family burying ground. That belonged to the plantation."

"Where's the plantation?" John Wesley asked.

"Gone With the Wind," said the grandmother. "Ha. Ha."

When the children finished all the comic books they had brought, they opened the lunch and ate it. The grandmother ate a peanut butter sandwich and an olive and would not let the children throw the box and the paper napkins out the window. When there was nothing else to do they played a game by choosing a cloud and making the other two guess what shape it suggested. John Wesley took one the shape of a cow and June Star guessed a cow and John Wesley said, no, an automobile, and June Star said he didn't play fair, and they began to slap each other over the grandmother.

The grandmother said she would tell them a story if they would keep quiet. When she told a story, she rolled her eyes and waved her head and was very dramatic. She said once when she was a maiden lady she had been courted by a Mr. Edgar Atkins Teagarden from Jasper, Georgia. She said he was a very good-looking man and a gentleman and that he brought her a watermelon every Saturday afternoon with his initials cut in it, E.A.T. Well, one Saturday, she said, Mr. Teagarden brought the watermelon and there was nobody at home and he left it on the front porch and returned in his buggy to Jasper, but she never got the watermelon, she said, because a nigger boy ate it when he saw the initials, E.A.T.! This story tickled John Wesley's funny bone and he giggled and giggled but June Star didn't think it was any good. She said she wouldn't marry a man that just brought her a watermelon on Saturday. The grandmother said she would have done well to marry Mr. Teagarden because he was a gentleman and had bought Coca-Cola stock when it first came out and that he had died only a few years ago, a very wealthy man.

They stopped at The Tower for barbecued sandwiches. The Tower was a part stucco and part wood filling station and dance hall set in a clearing outside of Timothy. A fat man named Red Sammy Butts ran it and there were signs stuck here and there on the building and for miles up and down the highway saying, TRY RED SAMMY'S FAMOUS BARBECUE. NONE LIKE FAMOUS RED SAMMY'S! RED SAM! THE FAT BOY WITH THE HAPPY LAUGH. A VETERAN! RED SAMMY'S YOUR MAN!

Red Sammy was lying on the bare ground outside The Tower with his head under a truck while a gray monkey about a foot high, chained to a small chinaberry tree, chattered nearby. The monkey sprang back into the tree and got on the highest limb as soon as he saw the children jump out of the car and run toward him.

Inside, The Tower was a long dark room with a counter at one end and tables at the other and dancing space in the middle. They all sat down at a board table next to the nickelodeon and Red Sam's wife, a tall burnt-brown woman with hair and eyes lighter than her skin, came and took their order. The children's mother put a dime in the machine and played "The Tennessee Waltz," and the grandmother said that tune always made her want to dance. She asked Bailey if he would like to dance but he only glared at her. He didn't have a naturally sunny disposition like she did and trips made him nervous. The grandmother's brown eyes were very bright. She swayed her head from side to side and pretended she was dancing in her chair. June Star said play something she could tap to so the children's mother put in another dime and played a fast number and June Star stepped out onto the dance floor and did her tap routine.

"Ain't she cute?" Red Sam's wife said, leaning over the counter. "Would you like to come be my little girl?"

"No I certainly wouldn't," June Star said. "I wouldn't live in a broken-down place like this for a million bucks!" and she ran back to the table.

"Ain't she cute?" the woman repeated, stretching her mouth politely.

"Aren't you ashamed?" hissed the grandmother.

Red Sam came in and told his wife to quit lounging on the counter and hurry up with these people's order. His khaki trousers reached just to his hip bones and his stomach hung over them like a sack of meal swaying under his shirt. He came over and sat down at a table nearby and let out a combination sigh and yodel. "You can't win," he said. "You can't win," and he wiped his sweating red face off with a gray handkerchief. "These days you don't know who to trust," he said. "Ain't that the truth?"

"People are certainly not nice like they used to be," said the grandmother.

"Two fellers come in here last week," Red Sammy said, "driving a Chrysler. It was a old beat-up car but it was a good one and these boys looked all right to me. Said they worked at the mill and you know I let them fellers charge the gas they bought? Now why did I do that?"

"Because you're a good man!" the grandmother said at once.

"Yes'm, I suppose so," Red Sam said as if he were struck with this answer.

His wife brought the orders, carrying the five plates all at once without a tray, two in each hand and one balanced on her arm. "It isn't a soul in this green world of God's that you can trust," she said. "And I don't count nobody out of that, not nobody," she repeated, looking at Red Sammy.

"Did you read about that criminal, The Misfit, that's escaped?" asked   40
the grandmother.

"I wouldn't be a bit surprised if he didn't attack this place right here," said the woman. "If he hears about it being here, I wouldn't be none surprised to see him. If he hears it's two cent in the cash register, I wouldn't be a tall surprised if he. . . ."

"That'll do," Red Sam said. "Go bring these people their Co'-Colas," and the woman went off to get the rest of the order.

"A good man is hard to find," Red Sammy said. "Everything is getting terrible. I remember the day you could go off and leave your screen door unlatched. Not no more."

He and the grandmother discussed better times. The old lady said that in her opinion Europe was entirely to blame for the way things were now. She said the way Europe acted you would think we were made of money and Red Sam said it was no use talking about it, she was exactly right. The children ran outside into the white sunlight and looked at the monkey in the lacy chinaberry tree. He was busy catching fleas on himself and biting each one carefully between his teeth as if it were a delicacy.

They drove off again into the hot afternoon. The grandmother took   45
cat naps and woke up every few minutes with her own snoring. Outside of Toombsboro she woke up and recalled an old plantation that she had visited in this neighborhood once when she was a young lady. She said the house had six white columns across the front and that there was an avenue of oaks leading up to it and two little wooden trellis arbors on either side in front where you sat down with your suitor after a stroll in the garden. She recalled exactly which road to turn off to get to it. She knew that Bailey would not be willing to lose any time looking at an old house, but the more she talked about it, the more she wanted to see it once again and find out if the little twin arbors were still standing. "There was a secret panel in this house," she said craftily, not telling the truth but wishing that she were, "and the story went that all the family silver was hidden in it when Sherman° came through but it was never found. . . ."

"Hey!" John Wesley said. "Let's go see it! We'll find it! We'll poke all the woodwork and find it! Who lives there? Where do you turn off at? Hey Pop, can't we turn off there?"

"We never have seen a house with a secret panel!" June Star shrieked. "Let's go to the house with the secret panel! Hey Pop, can't we go see the house with the secret panel!"

Sherman: William Tecumseh Sherman (1820–1891), Union Army commander who led infamous marches through the South during the Civil War.

"It's not far from here, I know," the grandmother said. "It won't take over twenty minutes."

Bailey was looking straight ahead. His jaw was as rigid as a horseshoe. "No," he said.

The children began to yell and scream that they wanted to see the house with the secret panel. John Wesley kicked the back of the front seat and June Star hung over her mother's shoulder and whined desperately into her ear that they never had any fun even on their vacation, that they could never do what THEY wanted to do. The baby began to scream and John Wesley kicked the back of the seat so hard that his father could feel the blows in his kidney.

"All right!" he shouted and drew the car to a stop at the side of the road. "Will you all shut up? Will you all just shut up for one second? If you don't shut up, we won't go anywhere."

"It would be very educational for them," the grandmother murmured.

"All right," Bailey said, "but get this: this is the only time we're going to stop for anything like this. This is the one and only time."

"The dirt road that you have to turn down is about a mile back," the grandmother directed. "I marked it when we passed."

"A dirt road," Bailey groaned.

After they had turned around and were headed toward the dirt road, the grandmother recalled other points about the house, the beautiful glass over the front doorway and the candle-lamp in the hall. John Wesley said that the secret panel was probably in the fireplace.

"You can't go inside this house," Bailey said. "You don't know who lives there."

"While you all talk to the people in front, I'll run around behind and get in a window," John Wesley suggested.

"We'll all stay in the car," his mother said.

They turned onto the dirt road and the car raced roughly along in a swirl of pink dust. The grandmother recalled the times when there were no paved roads and thirty miles was a day's journey. The dirt road was hilly and there were sudden washes in it and sharp curves on dangerous embankments. All at once they would be on a hill, looking down over the blue tops of trees for miles around, then the next minute, they would be in a red depression with the dust-coated trees looking down on them.

"This place had better turn up in a minute," Bailey said, "or I'm going to turn around."

The road looked as if no one had traveled on it for months.

"It's not much farther," the grandmother said and just as she said it, a horrible thought came to her. The thought was so embarrassing that she turned red in the face and her eyes dilated and her feet jumped up, upsetting her valise in the corner. The instant the valise moved, the newspaper top she had over the basket under it rose with a snarl and Pitty Sing, the cat, sprang onto Bailey's shoulder.

The children were thrown to the floor and their mother, clutching the baby, was thrown out the door onto the ground; the old lady was thrown into the front seat. The car turned over once and landed right-side-up in a gulch off the side of the road. Bailey remained in the driver's seat with the cat — gray-striped with a broad white face and an orange nose — clinging to his neck like a caterpillar.

As soon as the children saw they could move their arms and legs, they 65 scrambled out of the car, shouting, "We've had an ACCIDENT!" The grandmother was curled up under the dashboard, hoping she was injured so that Bailey's wrath would not come down on her all at once. The horrible thought she had before the accident was that the house she had remembered so vividly was not in Georgia but in Tennessee.

Bailey removed the cat from his neck with both hands and flung it out the window against the side of a pine tree. Then he got out of the car and started looking for the children's mother. She was sitting against the side of the red gutted ditch, holding the screaming baby, but she only had a cut down her face and a broken shoulder. "We've had an ACCIDENT!" the children screamed in a frenzy of delight.

"But nobody's killed," June Star said with disappointment as the grandmother limped out of the car, her hat still pinned to her head but the broken front brim standing up at a jaunty angle and the violet spray hanging off the side. They all sat down in the ditch, except the children, to recover from the shock. They were all shaking.

"Maybe a car will come along," said the children's mother hoarsely.

"I believe I have injured an organ," said the grandmother, pressing her side, but no one answered her. Bailey's teeth were clattering. He had on a yellow sport shirt with bright blue parrots designed in it and his face was as yellow as the shirt. The grandmother decided that she would not mention that the house was in Tennessee.

The road was about ten feet above and they could see only the tops of 70 the trees on the other side of it. Behind the ditch they were sitting in there were more woods, tall and dark and deep. In a few minutes they saw a car some distance away on top of a hill, coming slowly as if the occupants were watching them. The grandmother stood up and waved both arms dramatically to attract their attention. The car continued to come on slowly, disappeared around a bend and appeared again, moving even slower, on top of the hill they had gone over. It was a big black battered hearse-like automobile. There were three men in it.

It came to a stop just over them and for some minutes, the driver looked down with a steady expressionless gaze to where they were sitting, and didn't speak. Then he turned his head and muttered something to the other two and they got out. One was a fat boy in black trousers and a red sweat shirt with a silver stallion embossed on the front of it. He moved around on the right side of them and stood staring, his mouth partly open in a kind of loose grin. The other had on khaki pants and a blue striped coat and a gray hat pulled down very low, hiding most of his face. He came around slowly on the left side. Neither spoke.

The driver got out of the car and stood by the side of it, looking down at them. He was an older man than the other two. His hair was just beginning to gray and he wore silver-rimmed spectacles that gave him a scholarly look. He had a long creased face and didn't have on any shirt or undershirt. He had on blue jeans that were too tight for him and was holding a black hat and a gun. The two boys also had guns.

"We've had an ACCIDENT!" the children screamed.

The grandmother had the peculiar feeling that the bespectacled man was someone she knew. His face was as familiar to her as if she had known him all her life but she could not recall who he was. He moved away from the car and began to come down the embankment, placing his feet carefully so that he wouldn't slip. He had on tan and white shoes and no socks, and his ankles were red and thin. "Good afternoon," he said. "I see you all had you a little spill."

"We turned over twice!" said the grandmother.

"Oncet," he corrected. "We seen it happen. Try their car and see will it run, Hiram," he said quietly to the boy with the gray hat.

"What you got that gun for?" John Wesley asked. "Whatcha gonna do with that gun?"

"Lady," the man said to the children's mother, "would you mind calling them children to sit down by you? Children make me nervous. I want all you all to sit down right together there where you're at."

"What are you telling US what to do for?" June Star asked.

Behind them the line of woods gaped like a dark open mouth. "Come here," said their mother.

"Look here now," Bailey said suddenly, "we're in a predicament! We're in. . . ."

The grandmother shrieked. She scrambled to her feet and stood staring. "You're The Misfit!" she said. "I recognized you at once!"

"Yes'm," the man said, smiling slightly as if he were pleased in spite of himself to be known, "but it would have been better for all of you, lady, if you hadn't of reckernized me."

Bailey turned his head sharply and said something to his mother that shocked even the children. The old lady began to cry and The Misfit reddened.

"Lady," he said, "don't you get upset. Sometimes a man says things he don't mean. I don't reckon he meant to talk to you thataway."

"You wouldn't shoot a lady, would you?" the grandmother said and removed a clean handkerchief from her cuff and began to slap at her eyes with it.

The Misfit pointed the toe of his shoe into the ground and made a little hole and then covered it up again. "I would hate to have to," he said.

"Listen," the grandmother almost screamed, "I know you're a good man. You don't look a bit like you have common blood. I know you must come from nice people!"

"Yes mam," he said, "finest people in the world." When he smiled he showed a row of strong white teeth. "God never made a finer woman than my mother and my daddy's heart was pure gold," he said. The boy with the red sweat shirt had come around behind them and was standing with his gun at his hip. The Misfit squatted down on the ground. "Watch them children, Bobby Lee," he said. "You know they make me nervous." He looked at the six of them huddled together in front of him and he seemed to be embarrassed as if he couldn't think of anything to say. "Ain't a cloud in the sky," he remarked, looking up at it. "Don't see no sun but don't see no cloud neither."

"Yes, it's a beautiful day," said the grandmother. "Listen," she said, "you 90 shouldn't call yourself The Misfit because I know you're a good man at heart. I can just look at you and tell."

"Hush!" Bailey yelled. "Hush! Everybody shut up and let me handle this!" He was squatting in the position of a runner about to sprint forward but he didn't move.

"I pre-chate that, lady," The Misfit said and drew a little circle in the ground with the butt of his gun.

"It'll take a half a hour to fix this here car," Hiram called, looking over the raised hood of it.

"Well, first you and Bobby Lee get him and that little boy to step over yonder with you," The Misfit said, pointing to Bailey and John Wesley. "The boys want to ast you something," he said to Bailey. "Would you mind stepping back in them woods there with them?"

"Listen," Bailey began, "we're in a terrible predicament! Nobody real- 95 izes what this is," and his voice cracked. His eyes were as blue and intense as the parrots in his shirt and he remained perfectly still.

The grandmother reached up to adjust her hat brim as if she were going to the woods with him but it came off in her hand. She stood staring at it and after a second she let it fall to the ground. Hiram pulled Bailey up by the arm as if he were assisting an old man. John Wesley caught hold of his father's hand and Bobby Lee followed. They went off toward the woods and just as they reached the dark edge, Bailey turned and supporting himself against a gray naked pine trunk, he shouted, "I'll be back in a minute, Mamma, wait on me!"

"Come back this instant!" his mother shrilled but they all disappeared into the woods.

"Bailey Boy!" the grandmother called in a tragic voice but she found she was looking at The Misfit squatting on the ground in front of her. "I just know you're a good man," she said desperately. "You're not a bit common!"

"Nome, I ain't a good man," The Misfit said after a second as if he had considered her statement carefully, "but I ain't the worst in the world neither. My daddy said I was a different breed of dog from my brothers and sisters. 'You know,' Daddy said, 'it's some that can live their whole life out without asking about it and it's others has to know why it is, and this boy is one of the latters. He's going to be into everything!'" He put on his black hat and looked up suddenly and then away deep into the woods as if he were embarrassed again. "I'm sorry I don't have on a shirt before you ladies," he said, hunching his shoulders slightly. "We buried our clothes that we had on when we escaped and we're just making do until we can get better. We borrowed these from some folks we met," he explained.

"That's perfectly all right," the grandmother said. "Maybe Bailey has an extra shirt in his suitcase."

"I'll look and see terrectly," The Misfit said.

"Where are they taking him?" the children's mother screamed.

"Daddy was a card himself," The Misfit said. "You couldn't put anything over on him. He never got in trouble with the Authorities though. Just had the knack of handling them."

"You could be honest too if you'd only try," said the grandmother. "Think how wonderful it would be to settle down and live a comfortable life and not have to think about somebody chasing you all the time."

The Misfit kept scratching in the ground with the butt of his gun as if he were thinking about it. "Yes'm, somebody is always after you," he murmured.

The grandmother noticed how thin his shoulder blades were just behind his hat because she was standing up looking down on him. "Do you ever pray?" she asked.

He shook his head. All she saw was the black hat wiggle between his shoulder blades. "Nome," he said.

There was a pistol shot from the woods, followed closely by another. Then silence. The old lady's head jerked around. She could hear the wind move through the tree tops like a long satisfied insuck of breath. "Bailey Boy!" she called.

"I was a gospel singer for a while," The Misfit said. "I been most everything. Been in the arm service, both land and sea, at home and abroad, been twict married, been an undertaker, been with the railroads, plowed Mother Earth, been in a tornado, seen a man burnt alive oncet," and he looked up at the children's mother and the little girl who were sitting close together, their faces white and their eyes glassy; "I even seen a woman flogged," he said.

"Pray, pray," the grandmother began, "pray, pray. . . ."

"I never was a bad boy that I remember of," The Misfit said in an almost dreamy voice, "but somewheres along the line I done something wrong and got sent to the penitentiary. I was buried alive," and he looked up and held her attention to him by a steady stare.

"That's when you should have started to pray," she said. "What did you do to get sent to the penitentiary that first time?"

"Turn to the right, it was a wall," The Misfit said, looking up again at the cloudless sky. "Turn to the left, it was a wall. Look up it was a ceiling, look down it was a floor. I forget what I done, lady. I set there and set there, trying to remember what it was I done and I ain't recalled it to this day. Oncet in a while, I would think it was coming to me, but it never come."

"Maybe they put you in by mistake," the old lady said vaguely.

"Nome," he said. "It wasn't no mistake. They had the papers on me."

"You must have stolen something," she said.

The Misfit sneered slightly. "Nobody had nothing I wanted," he said. "It was a head-doctor at the penitentiary said what I had done was kill my daddy but I known that for a lie. My daddy died in nineteen ought nineteen of the epidemic flu and I never had a thing to do with it. He was buried in the Mount Hopewell Baptist churchyard and you can see for yourself."

"If you would pray," the old lady said, "Jesus would help you."

"That's right," The Misfit said.

"Well then, why don't you pray?" she asked trembling with delight suddenly.   120

"I don't want no hep," he said. "I'm doing all right by myself."

Bobby Lee and Hiram came ambling back from the woods. Bobby Lee was dragging a yellow shirt with bright blue parrots in it.

"Throw me that shirt, Bobby Lee," The Misfit said. The shirt came flying at him and landed on his shoulder and he put it on. The grandmother couldn't name what the shirt reminded her of. "No, lady," The Misfit said while he was buttoning it up, "I found out the crime don't matter. You can do one thing or you can do another, kill a man or take a tire off his car, because sooner or later you're going to forget what it was you done and just be punished for it."

The children's mother had begun to make heaving noises as if she couldn't get her breath. "Lady," he asked, "would you and that little girl like to step off yonder with Bobby Lee and Hiram and join your husband?"

"Yes, thank you," the mother said faintly. Her left arm dangled help-   125 lessly and she was holding the baby, who had gone to sleep, in the other. "Hep that lady up, Hiram," The Misfit said as she struggled to climb out of the ditch, "and Bobby Lee, you hold onto that little girl's hand."

"I don't want to hold hands with him," June Star said. "He reminds me of a pig."

The fat boy blushed and laughed and caught her by the arm and pulled her off into the woods after Hiram and her mother.

Alone with The Misfit, the grandmother found that she had lost her voice. There was not a cloud in the sky nor any sun. There was nothing around her but woods. She wanted to tell him that he must pray. She opened and closed her mouth several times before anything came out. Finally she found herself saying, "Jesus, Jesus," meaning Jesus will help you, but the way she was saying it, it sounded as if she might be cursing.

"Yes'm," The Misfit said as if he agreed. "Jesus thown everything off balance. It was the same case with Him as with me except He hadn't committed any crime and they could prove I had committed one because they had the papers on me. Of course," he said, "they never shown me my papers. That's why I sign myself now. I said long ago, you get your signature and sign everything you do and keep a copy of it. Then you'll know what you done and you can hold up the crime to the punishment and see do they match and in the end you'll have something to prove you ain't been treated right. I call myself The Misfit," he said, "because I can't make what all I done wrong fit what all I gone through in punishment."

There was a piercing scream from the woods, followed closely by a pistol report. "Does it seem right to you, lady, that one is punished a heap and another ain't punished at all?"

"Jesus!" the old lady cried. "You've got good blood! I know you wouldn't shoot a lady! I know you come from nice people! Pray! Jesus, you ought not to shoot a lady. I'll give you all the money I've got!"

"Lady," The Misfit said, looking beyond her far into the woods, "there never was a body that give the undertaker a tip."

There were two more pistol reports and the grandmother raised her head like a parched old turkey hen crying for water and called, "Bailey Boy, Bailey Boy!" as if her heart would break.

"Jesus was the only One that ever raised the dead," The Misfit continued, "and He shouldn't have done it. He thown everything off balance. If He did what He said, then it's nothing for you to do but thow away everything and follow Him, and if He didn't, then it's nothing for you to do but enjoy the few minutes you got left the best way you can — by killing somebody or burning down his house or doing some other meanness to him. No pleasure but meanness," he said and his voice had become almost a snarl.

"Maybe He didn't raise the dead," the old lady mumbled, not knowing what she was saying and feeling so dizzy that she sank down in the ditch with her legs twisted under her.

"I wasn't there so I can't say He didn't," The Misfit said. "I wisht I had of been there," he said, hitting the ground with his fist. "It ain't right I wasn't there because if I had of been there I would of known. Listen lady," he said in a high voice, "if I had of been there I would of known and I wouldn't be like I am now." His voice seemed about to crack and the grandmother's head cleared for an instant. She saw the man's face twisted close to her own as if he were going to cry and she murmured, "Why you're one of my babies. You're one of my own children!" She reached out and touched him on the shoulder. The Misfit sprang back as if a snake had bitten him and shot her three times through the chest. Then he put his gun down on the ground and took off his glasses and began to clean them.

Hiram and Bobby Lee returned from the woods and stood over the ditch, looking down at the grandmother who half sat and half lay in a puddle of blood with her legs crossed under her like a child's and her face smiling up at the cloudless sky.

Without his glasses, The Misfit's eyes were red-rimmed and pale and defenseless-looking. "Take her off and thow her where you thown the others," he said, picking up the cat that was rubbing itself against his leg.

"She was a talker, wasn't she?" Bobby Lee said, sliding down the ditch with a yodel.

"She would of been a good woman," The Misfit said, "if it had been somebody there to shoot her every minute of her life."

"Some fun!" Bobby Lee said.

"Shut up, Bobby Lee," The Misfit said. "It's no real pleasure in life."

CONSIDERATIONS FOR CRITICAL THINKING AND WRITING

1. FIRST RESPONSE. How does O'Connor portray the family? What is comic about them? What qualities about them are we meant to take seriously? Are you shocked by what happens to them? Does your attitude toward them remain constant during the course of the story?

2. How do the grandmother's concerns about the trip to Florida foreshadow events in the story?

3. Describe the grandmother. How does O'Connor make her the central character?

4. What is Red Sammy's purpose in the story? Relate his view of life to the story's conflicts.

5. Characterize The Misfit. What makes him so? Can he be written off as simply insane? How does the grandmother respond to him?

6. Why does The Misfit say that "Jesus thown everything off balance" (para. 129)? What does religion have to do with the brutal action of this story?

7. What does The Misfit mean at the end when he says about the grandmother, "She would of been a good woman . . . if it had been somebody there to shoot her every minute of her life"?

8. Describe the story's tone. Is it consistent? What is the effect of O'Connor's use of tone?

9. How is coincidence used to advance the plot? How do coincidences lead to ironies in the story?

10. Explain how the title points to the story's theme.

Good Country People   1955

Besides the neutral expression that she wore when she was alone, Mrs. Freeman had two others, forward and reverse, that she used for all her human dealings. Her forward expression was steady and driving like the advance of a heavy truck. Her eyes never swerved to left or right but turned as the story turned as if they followed a yellow line down the center of it. She seldom used the other expression because it was not often necessary for her to retract a statement, but when she did, her face came to a complete stop, there was an almost imperceptible movement of her black eyes, during which they seemed to be receding, and then the observer would see that Mrs. Freeman, though she might stand there as real as several grain sacks thrown on top of each other, was no longer there in spirit. As for getting anything across to her when this was the case, Mrs. Hopewell had given it up. She might talk her head off. Mrs. Freeman could never be brought to admit herself wrong on any point. She would stand there and if she could be brought to say anything, it was something like, "Well, I wouldn't of said it was and I wouldn't of said it wasn't," or letting her gaze range over the top kitchen shelf where there was an assortment of dusty bottles, she might remark, "I see you ain't ate many of them figs you put up last summer."

They carried on their most important business in the kitchen at breakfast. Every morning Mrs. Hopewell got up at seven o'clock and lit her gas heater and Joy's. Joy was her daughter, a large blonde girl who had an artificial leg. Mrs. Hopewell thought of her as a child though she was thirty-two years old and highly educated. Joy would get up while her mother was eating and lumber into the bathroom and slam the door, and before long, Mrs. Freeman would arrive at the back door. Joy would hear her mother call, "Come on in," and then they would talk for a while in low voices that were indistinguishable in the bathroom. By the time Joy came in, they had usually finished the weather report and were on one or the other of Mrs. Freeman's daughters, Glynese or Carramae, Joy called them Glycerin and Caramel. Glynese, a redhead, was eighteen and had many admirers; Carramae, a blonde, was only fifteen but already married and pregnant. She could not keep anything in her stomach. Every morning Mrs. Freeman told Mrs. Hopewell how many times she had vomited since the last report.

Mrs. Hopewell liked to tell people that Glynese and Carramae were two of the finest girls she knew and that Mrs. Freeman was a *lady* and that she was never ashamed to take her anywhere or introduce her to anybody they might meet. Then she would tell how she had happened to hire the Freemans in the first place and how they were a godsend to her and how she had had them four years. The reason for her keeping them so long was that they were not trash. They were good country people. She had telephoned the man whose name they had given as a reference and he had told her that Mr. Freeman was a good farmer but that his wife was the nosiest woman ever to walk the earth. "She's got to be into everything," the man said. "If she don't get there before the dust settles, you can bet she's dead, that's all. She'll want to know all your business. I can stand him real good," he had said, "but me nor my wife neither could have stood that woman one more minute on this place." That had put Mrs. Hopewell off for a few days.

She had hired them in the end because there were no other applicants but she had made up her mind beforehand exactly how she would handle the woman. Since she was the type who had to be into everything, then, Mrs. Hopewell decided, she would not only let her be into everything, she would *see to it* that she was into everything — she would give her the responsibility of everything, she would put her in charge. Mrs. Hopewell had no bad qualities of her own but she was able to use other people's in such a constructive way that she never felt the lack. She had hired the Freemans and she had kept them four years.

Nothing is perfect. This was one of Mrs. Hopewell's favorite sayings. Another was: that is life! And still another, the most important, was: well, other people have their opinions too. She would make these statements, usually at the table, in a tone of gentle insistence as if no one held them but her, and the large hulking Joy, whose constant outrage had obliterated every expression from her face, would stare just a little to the side of her, her eyes icy blue, with the look of someone who has achieved blindness by an act of will and means to keep it.

When Mrs. Hopewell said to Mrs. Freeman that life was like that, Mrs. Freeman would say, "I always said so myself." Nothing had been arrived at by anyone that had not first been arrived at by her. She was quicker than Mr. Freeman. When Mrs. Hopewell said to her after they had been on the place a while, "You know, you're the wheel behind the wheel," and winked, Mrs. Freeman had said, "I know it. I've always been quick. It's some that are quicker than others."

"Everybody is different," Mrs. Hopewell said.

"Yes, most people is," Mrs. Freeman said.

"It takes all kinds to make the world."

"I always said it did myself."

10

The girl was used to this kind of dialogue for breakfast and more of it for dinner; sometimes they had it for supper too. When they had no guest they ate in the kitchen because that was easier. Mrs. Freeman always managed to arrive at some point during the meal and to watch them finish it. She would stand in the doorway if it were summer but in the winter she would stand with one elbow on top of the refrigerator and look down on them, or she would stand by the gas heater, lifting the back of her skirt slightly. Occasionally she would stand against the wall and roll her head from side to side. At no time was she in any hurry to leave. All this was very trying on Mrs. Hopewell but she was a woman of great patience. She realized that nothing is perfect and that in the Freemans she had good country people and that if, in this day and age, you get good country people, you had better hang onto them.

She had had plenty of experience with trash. Before the Freemans she had averaged one tenant family a year. The wives of these farmers were not the kind you would want to be around you for very long. Mrs. Hopewell, who had divorced her husband long ago, needed someone to walk over the fields with her; and when Joy had to be impressed for these services, her remarks were usually so ugly and her face so glum that Mrs. Hopewell would say, "If you can't come pleasantly, I don't want you at all," to which the girl, standing square and rigid-shouldered with her neck thrust slightly forward, would reply, "If you want me, here I am—LIKE I AM."

Mrs. Hopewell excused this attitude because of the leg (which had been shot off in a hunting accident when Joy was ten). It was hard for Mrs. Hopewell to realize that her child was thirty-two now and that for more than twenty years she had had only one leg. She thought of her still as a child because it tore her heart to think instead of the poor stout girl in her thirties who had never danced a step or had any *normal* good times. Her name was really Joy but as soon as she was twenty-one and away from home, she had had it legally changed. Mrs. Hopewell was certain that she had thought and thought until she had hit upon the ugliest name in any language. Then she had gone and had the beautiful name,

Joy, changed without telling her mother until after she had done it. Her legal name was Hulga.

When Mrs. Hopewell thought the name, Hulga, she thought of the broad blank hull of a battleship. She would not use it. She continued to call her Joy to which the girl responded but in a purely mechanical way.

Hulga had learned to tolerate Mrs. Freeman who saved her from taking walks with her mother. Even Glynese and Carramae were useful when they occupied attention that might otherwise have been directed at her. At first she had thought she could not stand Mrs. Freeman for she had found that it was not possible to be rude to her. Mrs. Freeman would take on strange resentments and for days together she would be sullen but the source of her displeasure was always obscure; a direct attack, a positive leer, blatant ugliness to her face — these never touched her. And without warning one day, she began calling her Hulga.

She did not call her that in front of Mrs. Hopewell who would have been incensed but when she and the girl happened to be out of the house together, she would say something and add the name Hulga to the end of it, and the big spectacled Joy-Hulga would scowl and redden as if her privacy had been intruded upon. She considered the name her personal affair. She had arrived at it first purely on the basis of its ugly sound and then the full genius of its fitness had struck her. She had a vision of the name working like the ugly sweating Vulcan° who stayed in the furnace and to whom, presumably, the goddess had to come when called. She saw it as the name of her highest creative act. One of her major triumphs was that her mother had not been able to turn her dust into Joy, but the greater one was that she had been able to turn it herself into Hulga. However, Mrs. Freeman's relish for using the name only irritated her. It was as if Mrs. Freeman's beady steel-pointed eyes had penetrated far enough behind her face to reach some secret fact. Something about her seemed to fascinate Mrs. Freeman and then one day Hulga realized that it was the artificial leg. Mrs. Freeman had a special fondness for the details of secret infections, hidden deformities, assaults upon children. Of diseases, she preferred the lingering or incurable. Hulga had heard Mrs. Hopewell give her the details of the hunting accident, how the leg had been literally blasted off, how she had never lost consciousness. Mrs. Freeman could listen to it any time as if it had happened an hour ago.

When Hulga stumped into the kitchen in the morning (she could walk without making the awful noise but she made it — Mrs. Hopewell was certain — because it was ugly-sounding), she glanced at them and did not speak. Mrs. Hopewell would be in her red kimono with her hair tied around her head in rags. She would be sitting at the table, finishing her breakfast and Mrs. Freeman would be hanging by her elbow outward from the refrigerator, looking down at the table. Hulga always put her eggs on the stove to boil and then stood over them with her arms folded, and Mrs. Hopewell would look at her — a kind of indirect gaze divided between her and Mrs. Freeman — and

---

Vulcan: Roman god of fire.

would think that if she would only keep herself up a little, she wouldn't be so bad looking. There was nothing wrong with her face that a pleasant expression wouldn't help. Mrs. Hopewell said that people who looked on the bright side of things would be beautiful even if they were not.

Whenever she looked at Joy this way, she could not help but feel that it would have been better if the child had not taken the Ph.D. It had certainly not brought her out any and now that she had it, there was no more excuse for her to go to school again. Mrs. Hopewell thought it was nice for girls to go to school to have a good time but Joy had "gone through." Anyhow, she would not have been strong enough to go again. The doctors had told Mrs. Hopewell that with the best of care, Joy might see forty-five. She had a weak heart. Joy had made it plain that if it had not been for this condition, she would be far from these red hills and good country people. She would be in a university lecturing to people who knew what she was talking about. And Mrs. Hopewell could very well picture her there, looking like a scarecrow and lecturing to more of the same. Here she went about all day in a six-year-old skirt and a yellow sweat shirt with a faded cowboy on a horse embossed on it. She thought this was funny; Mrs. Hopewell thought it was idiotic and showed simply that she was still a child. She was brilliant but she didn't have a grain of sense. It seemed to Mrs. Hopewell that every year she grew less like other people and more like herself — bloated, rude, and squint-eyed. And she said such strange things! To her own mother she had said — without warning, without excuse, standing up in the middle of a meal with her face purple and her mouth half full — "Woman! do you ever look inside? Do you ever look inside and see what you are *not*? God!" she had cried sinking down again and staring at her plate, "Malebranche° was right: we are not our own light. We are not our own light!" Mrs. Hopewell had no idea to this day what brought that on. She had only made the remark, hoping Joy would take it in, that a smile never hurt anyone.

The girl had taken the Ph.D. in philosophy and this left Mrs. Hopewell at a complete loss. You could say, "My daughter is a nurse," or "My daughter is a schoolteacher," or even, "My daughter is a chemical engineer." You could not say, "My daughter is a philosopher." That was something that had ended with the Greeks and Romans. All day Joy sat on her neck in a deep chair, reading. Sometimes she went for walks but she didn't like dogs or cats or birds or f lowers or nature or nice young men. She looked at nice young men as if she could smell their stupidity.

One day Mrs. Hopewell had picked up one of the books the girl had 20 just put down and opening it at random, she read, "Science, on the other hand, has to assert its soberness and seriousness afresh and declare that it is concerned solely with what-is. Nothing — how can it be for science anything but a horror and a phantasm? If science is right, then one thing stands firm: science wishes to know nothing of nothing. Such is after all the strictly scientific approach to Nothing. We know it by wishing to know nothing of

Malebranche: Nicolas Malebranche (1638–1715), a French philosopher.

Nothing." These words had been underlined with a blue pencil and they worked on Mrs. Hopewell like some evil incantation in gibberish. She shut the book quickly and went out of the room as if she were having a chill.

This morning when the girl came in, Mrs. Freeman was on Carramae. "She thrown up four times after supper," she said, "and was up twict in the night after three o'clock. Yesterday she didn't do nothing but ramble in the bureau drawer. All she did. Stand up there and see what she could run up on."

"She's got to eat," Mrs. Hopewell muttered, sipping her coffee, while she watched Joy's back at the stove. She was wondering what the child had said to the Bible salesman. She could not imagine what kind of a conversation she could possibly have had with him.

He was a tall gaunt hatless youth who had called yesterday to sell them a Bible. He had appeared at the door, carrying a large black suitcase that weighted him so heavily on one side that he had to brace himself against the door facing. He seemed on the point of collapse but he said in a cheerful voice, "Good morning, Mrs. Cedars!" and set the suitcase down on the mat. He was not a bad-looking young man though he had on a bright blue suit and yellow socks that were not pulled up far enough. He had prominent face bones and a streak of sticky-looking brown hair falling across his forehead.

"I'm Mrs. Hopewell," she said.

"Oh!" he said, pretending to look puzzled but with his eyes sparkling, "I 25 saw it said 'The Cedars' on the mailbox so I thought you was Mrs. Cedars!" and he burst out in a pleasant laugh. He picked up the satchel and under cover of a pant, he fell forward into her hall. It was rather as if the suitcase had moved first, jerking him after it. "Mrs. Hopewell!" he said and grabbed her hand. "I hope you are well!" and he laughed again and then all at once his face sobered completely. He paused and gave her a straight earnest look and said, "Lady, I've come to speak of serious things."

"Well, come in," she muttered, none too pleased because her dinner was almost ready. He came into the parlor and sat down on the edge of a straight chair and put the suitcase between his feet and glanced around the room as if he were sizing her up by it. Her silver gleamed on the two sideboards; she decided he had never been in a room as elegant as this.

"Mrs. Hopewell," he began, using her name in a way that sounded almost intimate, "I know you believe in Chrustian service."

"Well yes," she murmured.

"I know," he said and paused, looking very wise with his head cocked on one side, "that you're a good woman. Friends have told me."

Mrs. Hopewell never liked to be taken for a fool. "What are you sell- 30 ing?" she asked.

"Bibles," the young man said and his eye raced around the room before he added, "I see you have no family Bible in your parlor, I see that is the one lack you got!"

Mrs. Hopewell could not say, "My daughter is an atheist and won't let me keep the Bible in the parlor." She said, stiffening slightly, "I keep my Bible by my bedside." This was not the truth. It was in the attic somewhere.

"Lady," he said, "the word of God ought to be in the parlor."

"Well, I think that's a matter of taste," she began. "I think . . ."

"Lady," he said, "for a Chrustian, the word of God ought to be in every 35 room in the house besides in his heart. I know you're a Chrustian because I can see it in every line of your face."

She stood up and said, "Well, young man, I don't want to buy a Bible and I smell my dinner burning."

He didn't get up. He began to twist his hands and looking down at them, he said softly, "Well lady, I'll tell you the truth — not many people want to buy one nowadays and besides, I know I'm real simple. I don't know how to say a thing but to say it. I'm just a country boy." He glanced up into her unfriendly face. "People like you don't like to fool with country people like me!"

"Why!" she cried, "good country people are the salt of the earth! Besides, we all have different ways of doing, it takes all kinds to make the world go 'round. That's life!"

"You said a mouthful," he said.

"Why, I think there aren't enough good people in the world!" she said, 40 stirred. "I think that's what's wrong with it!"

His face had brightened. "I didn't introduce myself," he said. "I'm Manley Pointer from out in the country around Willohobie, not even from a place, just from near a place."

"You wait a minute," she said. "I have to see about my dinner." She went out to the kitchen and found Joy standing near the door where she had been listening.

"Get rid of the salt of the earth," she said, "and let's eat."

Mrs. Hopewell gave her a pained look and turned the heat down under the vegetables. "I can't be rude to anybody," she murmured and went back into the parlor.

He had opened the suitcase and was sitting with a Bible on each knee. 45

"You might as well put those up," she told him. "I don't want one."

"I appreciate your honesty," he said. "You don't see any more real honest people unless you go way out in the country."

"I know," she said, "real genuine folks!" Through the crack in the door she heard a groan.

"I guess a lot of boys come telling you they're working their way through college," he said, "but I'm not going to tell you that. Somehow," he said, "I don't want to go to college. I want to devote my life to Chrustian service. See," he said, lowering his voice, "I got this heart condition. I may not live long. When you know it's something wrong with you and you may not live long, well then, lady . . ." He paused, with his mouth open, and stared at her.

He and Joy had the same condition! She knew that her eyes were fill- 50 ing with tears but she collected herself quickly and murmured, "Won't you stay for dinner? We'd love to have you!" and was sorry the instant she heard herself say it.

"Yes mam," he said in an abashed voice, "I would sher love to do that!"

Joy had given him one look on being introduced to him and then throughout the meal had not glanced at him again. He had addressed several remarks to her, which she had pretended not to hear. Mrs. Hopewell could not understand deliberate rudeness, although she lived with it, and she felt she had always to overflow with hospitality to make up for Joy's lack of courtesy. She urged him to talk about himself and he did. He said he was the seventh child of twelve and that his father had been crushed under a tree when he himself was eight years old. He had been crushed very badly, in fact, almost cut in two and was practically not recognizable. His mother had got along the best she could by hard working and she had always seen that her children went to Sunday School and that they read the Bible every evening. He was now nineteen years old and he had been selling Bibles for four months. In that time he had sold seventy-seven Bibles and had the promise of two more sales. He wanted to become a missionary because he thought that was the way you could do most for people. "He who losest his life shall find it," he said simply and he was so sincere, so genuine and earnest that Mrs. Hopewell would not for the world have smiled. He prevented his peas from sliding onto the table by blocking them with a piece of bread which he later cleaned his plate with. She could see Joy observing sidewise how he handled his knife and fork and she saw too that every few minutes, the boy would dart a keen appraising glance at the girl as if he were trying to attract her attention.

After dinner Joy cleared the dishes off the table and disappeared and Mrs. Hopewell was left to talk with him. He told her again about his childhood and his father's accident and about various things that had happened to him. Every five minutes or so she would stifle a yawn. He sat for two hours until finally she told him she must go because she had an appointment in town. He packed his Bibles and thanked her and prepared to leave, but in the doorway he stopped and wrung her hand and said that not on any of his trips had he met a lady as nice as her and he asked if he could come again. She had said she would always be happy to see him.

Joy had been standing in the road, apparently looking at something in the distance, when he came down the steps toward her, bent to the side with his heavy valise. He stopped where she was standing and confronted her directly. Mrs. Hopewell could not hear what he said but she trembled to think what Joy would say to him. She could see that after a minute Joy said something and that then the boy began to speak again, making an excited gesture with his free hand. After a minute Joy said something else at which the boy began to speak once more. Then to her amazement, Mrs. Hopewell saw the two of them walk off together, toward the gate. Joy had walked all the way to the gate with him and Mrs. Hopewell could not imagine what they had said to each other, and she had not yet dared to ask.

Mrs. Freeman was insisting upon her attention. She had moved from the refrigerator to the heater so that Mrs. Hopewell had to turn and face her in order to seem to be listening. "Glynese gone out with Harvey Hill again last night," she said. "She had this sty." 55

"Hill," Mrs. Hopewell said absently, "is the one who works in the garage?"

"Nome, he's the one that goes to chiropractor school," Mrs. Freeman said. "She had this sty. Been had it two days. So she says when he brought her in the other night he says, 'Lemme get rid of that sty for you,' and she says, 'How?' and he says, 'You just lay yourself down acrost the seat of that car and I'll show you.' So she done it and he popped her neck. Kept on a-popping it several times until she made him quit. This morning," Mrs. Freeman said, "she ain't got no sty. She ain't got no traces of a sty."

"I never heard of that before," Mrs. Hopewell said.

"He ast her to marry him before the Ordinary,° " Mrs. Freeman went on, "and she told him she wasn't going to be married in no *office*."

"Well, Glynese is a fine girl," Mrs. Hopewell said. "Glynese and Carramae are both fine girls." ⁶⁰

"Carramae said when her and Lyman was married Lyman said it sure felt sacred to him. She said he said he wouldn't take five hundred dollars for being married by a preacher."

"How much would he take?" the girl asked from the stove.

"He said he wouldn't take five hundred dollars," Mrs. Freeman repeated.

"Well we all have work to do," Mrs. Hopewell said.

"Lyman said it just felt more sacred to him," Mrs. Freeman said. "The doctor wants Carramae to eat prunes. Says instead of medicine. Says them cramps is coming from pressure. You know where I think it is?" ⁶⁵

"She'll be better in a few weeks," Mrs. Hopewell said.

"In the tube," Mrs. Freeman said. "Else she wouldn't be as sick as she is."

Hulga had cracked her two eggs into a saucer and was bringing them to the table along with a cup of coffee that she had filled too full. She sat down carefully and began to eat, meaning to keep Mrs. Freeman there by questions if for any reason she showed an inclination to leave. She could perceive her mother's eye on her. The first round-about question would be about the Bible salesman and she did not wish to bring it on. "How did he pop her neck?" she asked.

Mrs. Freeman went into a description of how he had popped her neck. She said he owned a '55 Mercury but that Glynese said she would rather marry a man with only a '36 Plymouth who would be married by a preacher. The girl asked what if he had a '32 Plymouth and Mrs. Freeman said what Glynese had said was a '36 Plymouth.

Mrs. Hopewell said there were not many girls with Glynese's common sense. She said what she admired in those girls was their common sense. She said that reminded her that they had had a nice visitor yesterday, a young man selling Bibles. "Lord," she said, "he bored me to death but he was so sincere and genuine I couldn't be rude to him. He was just good country people, you know," she said, "— just the salt of the earth." ⁷⁰

Ordinary: Justice of the peace.

"I seen him walk up," Mrs. Freeman said, "and then later — I seen him walk off," and Hulga could feel the slight shift in her voice, the slight insinuation, that he had not walked off alone, had he? Her face remained expressionless but the color rose into her neck and she seemed to swallow it down with the next spoonful of egg. Mrs. Freeman was looking at her as if they had a secret together.

"Well, it takes all kinds of people to make the world go 'round," Mrs. Hopewell said. "It's very good we aren't all alike."

"Some people are more alike than others," Mrs. Freeman said.

Hulga got up and stumped, with about twice the noise that was necessary, into her room and locked the door. She was to meet the Bible salesman at ten o'clock at the gate. She had thought about it half the night. She had started thinking of it as a great joke and then she had begun to see profound implications in it. She had lain in bed imagining dialogues for them that were insane on the surface but that reached below to depths that no Bible salesman would be aware of. Their conversation yesterday had been of this kind.

He had stopped in front of her and had simply stood there. His face 75 was bony and sweaty and bright, with a little pointed nose in the center of it, and his look was different from what it had been at the dinner table. He was gazing at her with open curiosity, with fascination, like a child watching a new fantastic animal at the zoo, and he was breathing as if he had run a great distance to reach her. His gaze seemed somehow familiar but she could not think where she had been regarded with it before. For almost a minute he didn't say anything. Then on what seemed an insuck of breath, he whispered, "You ever ate a chicken that was two days old?"

The girl looked at him stonily. He might have just put this question up for consideration at the meeting of a philosophical association. "Yes," she presently replied as if she had considered it from all angles.

"It must have been mighty small!" he said triumphantly and shook all over with little nervous giggles, getting very red in the face, and subsiding finally into his gaze of complete admiration, while the girl's expression remained exactly the same.

"How old are you?" he asked softly.

She waited some time before she answered. Then in a flat voice she said, "Seventeen."

His smiles came in succession like waves breaking on the surface of a 80 little lake. "I see you got a wooden leg," he said. "I think you're brave. I think you're real sweet."

The girl stood blank and solid and silent.

"Walk to the gate with me," he said. "You're a brave sweet little thing and I liked you the minute I seen you walk in the door."

Hulga began to move forward.

"What's your name?" he asked, smiling down on the top of her head.

"Hulga," she said.

"Hulga," he murmured, "Hulga. Hulga. I never heard of anybody name 85 Hulga before. You're shy, aren't you, Hulga?" he asked.

She nodded, watching his large red hand on the handle of the giant valise.

"I like girls that wear glasses," he said. "I think a lot. I'm not like these people that a serious thought don't ever enter their heads. It's because I may die."

"I may die too," she said suddenly and looked up at him. His eyes were very small and brown, glittering feverishly.

"Listen," he said, "don't you think some people was meant to meet on 90 account of what all they got in common and all? Like they both think serious thoughts and all?" He shifted the valise to his other hand so that the hand nearest her was free. He caught hold of her elbow and shook it a little. "I don't work on Saturday," he said. "I like to walk in the woods and see what Mother Nature is wearing. O'er the hills and far away. Pic-nics and things. Couldn't we go on a pic-nic tomorrow? Say yes, Hulga," he said and gave her a dying look as if he felt his insides about to drop out of him. He had even seemed to sway slightly toward her.

During the night she had imagined that she seduced him. She imagined that the two of them walked on the place until they came to the storage barn beyond the two back fields and there, she imagined, that things came to such a pass that she very easily seduced him and that then, of course, she had to reckon with his remorse. True genius can get an idea across even to an inferior mind. She imagined that she took his remorse in hand and changed it into a deeper understanding of life. She took all his shame away and turned it into something useful.

She set off for the gate at exactly ten o'clock, escaping without drawing Mrs. Hopewell's attention. She didn't take anything to eat, forgetting that food is usually taken on a picnic. She wore a pair of slacks and a dirty white shirt, and as an afterthought, she had put some Vapex° on the collar of it since she did not own any perfume. When she reached the gate no one was there.

She looked up and down the empty highway and had the furious feeling that she had been tricked, that he had only meant to make her walk to the gate after the idea of him. Then suddenly he stood up, very tall, from behind a bush on the opposite embankment. Smiling, he lifted his hat which was new and wide-brimmed. He had not worn it yesterday and she wondered if he had bought it for the occasion. It was toast-colored with a red and white band around it and was slightly too large for him. He stepped from behind the bush still carrying the black valise. He had on the same suit and the same yellow socks sucked down in his shoes from walking. He crossed the highway and said, "I knew you'd come!"

The girl wondered acidly how he had known this. She pointed to the valise and asked, "Why did you bring your Bibles?"

He took her elbow, smiling down on her as if he could not stop. "You 95 can never tell when you'll need the word of God, Hulga," he said. She had a moment in which she doubted that this was actually happening and then they began to climb the embankment. They went down into the pasture

---

Vapex: Trade name for a nasal spray.

toward the woods. The boy walked lightly by her side, bouncing on his toes. The valise did not seem to be heavy today; he even swung it. They crossed half the pasture without saying anything and then, putting his hand easily on the small of her back, he asked softly, "Where does your wooden leg join on?"

She turned an ugly red and glared at him and for an instant the boy looked abashed. "I didn't mean you no harm," he said. "I only meant you're so brave and all. I guess God takes care of you."

"No," she said, looking forward and walking fast, "I don't even believe in God."

At this he stopped and whistled. "No!" he exclaimed as if he were too astonished to say anything else.

She walked on and in a second he was bouncing at her side, fanning with his hat. "That's very unusual for a girl," he remarked, watching her out of the corner of his eye. When they reached the edge of the wood, he put his hand on her back again and drew her against him without a word and kissed her heavily.

The kiss, which had more pressure than feeling behind it, produced   10 that extra surge of adrenaline in the girl that enables one to carry a packed trunk out of a burning house, but in her, the power went at once to the brain. Even before he released her, her mind, clear and detached and ironic anyway, was regarding him from a great distance, with amusement but with pity. She had never been kissed before and she was pleased to discover that it was an unexceptional experience and all a matter of the mind's control. Some people might enjoy drain water if they were told it was vodka. When the boy, looking expectant but uncertain, pushed her gently away, she turned and walked on, saying nothing as if such business, for her, were common enough.

He came along panting at her side, trying to help her when he saw a root that she might trip over. He caught and held back the long swaying blades of thorn vine until she had passed beyond them. She led the way and he came breathing heavily behind her. Then they came out on a sunlit hillside, sloping softly into another one a little smaller. Beyond, they could see the rusted top of the old barn where the extra hay was stored.

The hill was sprinkled with small pink weeds. "Then you ain't saved?" he asked suddenly, stopping.

The girl smiled. It was the first time she had smiled at him at all. "In my economy," she said, "I'm saved and you are damned but I told you I didn't believe in God."

Nothing seemed to destroy the boy's look of admiration. He gazed at her now as if the fantastic animal at the zoo had put its paw through the bars and given him a loving poke. She thought he looked as if he wanted to kiss her again and she walked on before he had the chance.

"Ain't there somewheres we can sit down sometime?" he murmured,   105 his voice softening toward the end of the sentence.

"In that barn," she said.

They made for it rapidly as if it might slide away like a train. It was a large two-story barn, cool and dark inside. The boy pointed up the ladder that led into the loft and said, "It's too bad we can't go up there."

"Why can't we?" she asked.

"Yer leg," he said reverently.

The girl gave him a contemptuous look and putting both hands on 110 the ladder, she climbed it while he stood below, apparently awestruck. She pulled herself expertly through the opening and then looked down at him and said, "Well, come on if you're coming," and he began to climb the ladder, awkwardly bringing the suitcase with him.

"We won't need the Bible," she observed.

"You never can tell," he said, panting. After he had got into the loft, he was a few seconds catching his breath. She had sat down in a pile of straw. A wide sheath of sunlight, filled with dust particles, slanted over her. She lay back against a bale, her face turned away, looking out the front opening of the barn where hay was thrown from a wagon into the loft. The two pink-speckled hillsides lay back against a dark ridge of woods. The sky was cloudless and cold blue. The boy dropped down by her side and put one arm under her and the other over her and began methodically kissing her face, making little noises like a fish. He did not remove his hat but it was pushed far enough back not to interfere. When her glasses got in his way, he took them off of her and slipped them into his pocket.

The girl at first did not return any of the kisses but presently she began to and after she had put several on his cheek, she reached his lips and remained there, kissing him again and again as if she were trying to draw all the breath out of him. His breath was clear and sweet like a child's and the kisses were sticky like a child's. He mumbled about loving her and about knowing when he first seen her that he loved her, but the mumbling was like the sleepy fretting of a child being put to sleep by his mother. Her mind, throughout this, never stopped or lost itself for a second to her feelings. "You ain't said you loved me none," he whispered finally, pulling back from her. "You got to say that."

She looked away from him off into the hollow sky and then down at a black ridge and then down farther into what appeared to be two green swelling lakes. She didn't realize he had taken her glasses but this landscape could not seem exceptional to her for she seldom paid any close attention to her surroundings.

"You got to say it," he repeated. "You got to say you love me." 115

She was always careful how she committed herself. "In a sense," she began, "if you use the word loosely, you might say that. But it's not a word I use. I don't have illusions. I'm one of those people who see *through* to nothing."

The boy was frowning. "You got to say it. I said it and you got to say it," he said.

The girl looked at him almost tenderly. "You poor baby," she murmured. "It's just as well you don't understand," and she pulled him by the neck, face-down, against her. "We are all damned," she said, "but some of us have taken off our blindfolds and see that there's nothing to see. It's a kind of salvation."

The boy's astonished eyes looked blankly through the ends of her hair. "Okay," he almost whined, "but do you love me or don'tcher?"

"Yes," she said and added, "in a sense. But I must tell you something. There mustn't be anything dishonest between us." She lifted his head and looked him in the eye. "I am thirty years old," she said. "I have a number of degrees."

The boy's look was irritated but dogged. "I don't care," he said. "I don't care a thing about what all you done. I just want to know if you love me or don'tcher?" and he caught her to him and wildly planted her face with kisses until she said, "Yes, yes."

"Okay then," he said, letting her go. "Prove it."

She smiled, looking dreamily out on the shifty landscape. She had seduced him without even making up her mind to try. "How?" she asked, feeling that he should be delayed a little.

He leaned over and put his lips to her ear. "Show me where your wooden leg joins on," he whispered.

The girl uttered a sharp little cry and her face instantly drained of color. The obscenity of the suggestion was not what shocked her. As a child she had sometimes been subject to feelings of shame but education had removed the last traces of that as a good surgeon scrapes for cancer; she would no more have felt it over what he was asking than she would have believed in his Bible. But she was as sensitive about the artificial leg as a peacock about his tail. No one ever touched it but her. She took care of it as someone else would his soul, in private and almost with her own eyes turned away. "No," she said.

"I known it," he muttered, sitting up. "You're just playing me for a sucker."

"Oh no no!" she cried. "It joins on at the knee. Only at the knee. Why do you want to see it?"

The boy gave her a long penetrating look. "Because," he said, "it's what makes you different. You ain't like anybody else."

She sat staring at him. There was nothing about her face or her round freezing-blue eyes to indicate that this had moved her; but she felt as if her heart had stopped and left her mind to pump her blood. She decided that for the first time in her life she was face to face with real innocence. This boy, with an instinct that came from beyond wisdom, had touched the truth about her. When after a minute, she said in a hoarse high voice, "All right," it was like surrendering to him completely. It was like losing her own life and finding it again, miraculously, in his.

Very gently he began to roll the slack leg up. The artificial limb, in a white sock and brown flat shoe, was bound in a heavy material like canvas and ended in an ugly jointure where it was attached to the stump. The boy's face and his voice were entirely reverent as he uncovered it and said, "Now show me how to take it off and on."

She took it off for him and put it back on again and then he took it off himself, handling it as tenderly as if it were a real one. "See!" he said with a delighted child's face. "Now I can do it myself!"

"Put it back on," she said. She was thinking that she would run away with him and that every night he would take the leg off and every morning put it back on again. "Put it back on," she said.

"Not yet," he murmured, setting it on its foot out of her reach. "Leave it off for a while. You got me instead."

She gave a little cry of alarm but he pushed her down and began to kiss her again. Without the leg she felt entirely dependent on him. Her brain seemed to have stopped thinking altogether and to be about some other function that it was not very good at. Different expressions raced back and forth over her face. Every now and then the boy, his eyes like two steel spikes, would glance behind him where the leg stood. Finally she pushed him off and said, "Put it back on me now."

"Wait," he said. He leaned the other way and pulled the valise toward   135 him and opened it. It had a pale blue spotted lining and there were only two Bibles in it. He took one of these out and opened the cover of it. It was hollow and contained a pocket flask of whiskey, a pack of cards, and a small blue box with printing on it. He laid these out in front of her one at a time in an evenly-spaced row, like one presenting offerings at the shrine of a goddess. He put the blue box in her hand. THIS PRODUCT TO BE USED ONLY FOR THE PREVENTION OF DISEASE, she read, and dropped it. The boy was unscrewing the top of the flask. He stopped and pointed, with a smile, to the deck of cards. It was not an ordinary deck but one with an obscene picture on the back of each card. "Take a swig," he said, offering her the bottle first. He held it in front of her, but like one mesmerized, she did not move.

Her voice when she spoke had an almost pleading sound. "Aren't you," she murmured, "aren't you just good country people?"

The boy cocked his head. He looked as if he were just beginning to understand that she might be trying to insult him. "Yeah," he said, curling his lip slightly, "but it ain't held me back none. I'm as good as you any day in the week."

"Give me my leg," she said.

He pushed it farther away with his foot. "Come on now, let's begin to have us a good time," he said coaxingly. "We ain't got to know one another good yet."

"Give me my leg!" she screamed and tried to lunge for it but he pushed   140 her down easily.

"What's the matter with you all of a sudden?" he asked, frowning as he screwed the top on the flask and put it quickly back inside the Bible. "You just a while ago said you didn't believe in nothing. I thought you was some girl!"

Her face was almost purple. "You're a Christian!" she hissed. "You're a fine Christian! You're just like them all — say one thing and do another. You're a perfect Christian, you're . . ."

The boy's mouth was set angrily. "I hope you don't think," he said in a lofty indignant tone, "that I believe in that crap! I may sell Bibles but I know which end is up and I wasn't born yesterday and I know where I'm going!"

"Give me my leg!" she screeched. He jumped up so quickly that she barely saw him sweep the cards and the blue box into the Bible and throw the Bible into his valise. She saw him grab the leg and then she saw it for an instant slanted forlornly across the inside of the suitcase with a Bible at either side of its opposite ends. He slammed the lid shut and snatched up the valise and swung it down the hole and then stepped through himself.

When all of him had passed but his head, he turned and regarded her with a look that no longer had any admiration in it. "I've gotten a lot of interesting things," he said. "One time I got a woman's glass eye this way. And you needn't to think you'll catch me because Pointer ain't really my name. I use a different name at every house I call at and don't stay nowhere long. And I'll tell you another thing, Hulga," he said, using the name as if he didn't think much of it, "you ain't so smart. I been believing in nothing ever since I was born!" and then the toast-colored hat disappeared down the hole and the girl was left, sitting on the straw in the dusty sunlight. When she turned her churning face toward the opening, she saw his blue figure struggling successfully over the green speckled lake.

Mrs. Hopewell and Mrs. Freeman, who were in the back pasture, digging up onions, saw him emerge a little later from the woods and head across the meadow toward the highway. "Why, that looks like that nice dull young man that tried to sell me a Bible yesterday," Mrs. Hopewell said, squinting. "He must have been selling them to the Negroes back in there. He was so simple," she said, "but I guess the world would be better off if we were all that simple."

Mrs. Freeman's gaze drove forward and just touched him before he disappeared under the hill. Then she returned her attention to the evil-smelling onion shoot she was lifting from the ground. "Some can't be that simple," she said. "I know I never could."

CONSIDERATIONS FOR CRITICAL THINKING AND WRITING

1. FIRST RESPONSE. What do you think of Hulga's conviction that intelligence and education are incompatible with religious faith?

2. Why is it significant that Mrs. Hopewell's daughter has two names? How do the other characters' names serve to characterize them?

3. Why do you think Mrs. Freeman and Mrs. Hopewell are introduced before Hulga? What do they contribute to Hulga's story?

4. Identify the conflict in this story. How is it resolved?

5. Hulga and the Bible salesman play a series of jokes on each other. How are these deceptions related to the theme?

6. What is the effect of O'Connor's use of the phrase "good country people" throughout the story? Why is it an appropriate title?

7. The Bible salesman's final words to Hulga are "You ain't so smart. I been believing in nothing ever since I was born!" What religious values are expressed in the story?

8. After the Bible salesman leaves Hulga at the end of the story, O'Connor adds two more paragraphs concerning Mrs. Hopewell and Mrs. Freeman. What is the purpose of these final paragraphs?

9. Hulga's perspective on life is ironic, but she is also the subject of O'Connor's irony. Explain how O'Connor uses irony to reveal Hulga's character.

10. This story would be different if told from Hulga's point of view. Describe how the use of a limited omniscient narrator contributes to the story's effects.

CONNECTION TO ANOTHER SELECTION

1. How do Mrs. Hopewell's assumptions about life compare with those of Krebs's mother in Hemingway's "Soldier's Home" (p. 104)? Explain how the conflict in each story is related to what the mothers come to represent in the eyes of the central characters.

Revelation 1964

The doctor's waiting room, which was very small, was almost full when the Turpins entered and Mrs. Turpin, who was very large, made it look even smaller by her presence. She stood looming at the head of the magazine table set in the center of it, a living demonstration that the room was inadequate and ridiculous. Her little bright black eyes took in all the patients as she sized up the seating situation. There was one vacant chair and a place on the sofa occupied by a blond child in a dirty blue romper who should have been told to move over and make room for the lady. He was five or six, but Mrs. Turpin saw at once that no one was going to tell him to move over. He was slumped down in the seat, his arms idle at his sides and his eyes idle in his head; his nose ran unchecked.

Mrs. Turpin put a firm hand on Claud's shoulder and said in a voice that included anyone who wanted to listen, "Claud, you sit in that chair there," and gave him a push down into the vacant one. Claud was florid and bald and sturdy, somewhat shorter than Mrs. Turpin, but he sat down as if he were accustomed to doing what she told him to.

Mrs. Turpin remained standing. The only man in the room besides Claud was a lean stringy old fellow with a rusty hand spread out on each knee, whose eyes were closed as if he were asleep or dead or pretending to be so as not to get up and offer her his seat. Her gaze settled agreeably on a well-dressed gray-haired lady whose eyes met hers and whose expression said: if that child belonged to me, he would have some manners and move over — there's plenty of room there for you and him too.

Claud looked up with a sigh and made as if to rise.

"Sit down," Mrs. Turpin said. "You know you're not supposed to stand on that leg. He has an ulcer on his leg," she explained. 5

Claud lifted his foot onto the magazine table and rolled his trouser leg up to reveal a purple swelling on a plump marble-white calf.

"My!" the pleasant lady said. "How did you do that?"

"A cow kicked him," Mrs. Turpin said.

"Goodness!" said the lady.

Claud rolled his trouser leg down.

"Maybe the little boy would move over," the lady suggested, but the child did not stir. 10

"Somebody will be leaving in a minute," Mrs. Turpin said. She could not understand why a doctor — with as much money as they made charging five dollars a day to just stick their head in the hospital door and look at you — couldn't afford a decent-sized waiting room. This one was hardly bigger than a garage. The table was cluttered with limp-looking magazines and at one end of it there was a big green glass ash tray full of cigarette butts and cotton wads with little blood spots on them. If she had had anything to do with the running of the place, that would have been emptied every so often. There were no chairs against the wall at the head of the room. It had a rectangular-shaped panel in it that permitted a view of the office where the nurse came and went and the secretary listened to the radio. A plastic fern in a gold pot sat in the opening and trailed its fronds down almost to the floor. The radio was softly playing gospel music.

Just then the inner door opened and a nurse with the highest stack of yellow hair Mrs. Turpin had ever seen put her face in the crack and called for the next patient. The woman sitting beside Claud grasped the two arms of her chair and hoisted herself up; she pulled her dress free from her legs and lumbered through the door where the nurse had disappeared.

Mrs. Turpin eased into the vacant chair, which held her tight as a corset. "I wish I could reduce," she said, and rolled her eyes and gave a comic sigh.

"Oh, *you* aren't fat," the stylish lady said. 15

"Ooooo I am too," Mrs. Turpin said. "Claud he eats all he wants to and never weighs over one hundred and seventy-five pounds, but me I just look at something good to eat and I gain some weight," and her stomach and shoulders shook with laughter. "You can eat all you want to, can't you, Claud?" she asked, turning to him.

Claud only grinned.

"Well, as long as you have such a good disposition," the stylish lady said, "I don't think it makes a bit of difference what size you are. You just can't beat a good disposition."

Next to her was a fat girl of eighteen or nineteen, scowling into a thick blue book which Mrs. Turpin saw was entitled *Human Development.* The girl raised her head and directed her scowl at Mrs. Turpin as if she did not like her looks. She appeared annoyed that anyone should speak while she tried to read. The poor girl's face was blue with acne and Mrs. Turpin thought how pitiful it was to have a face like that at that age. She gave the girl a friendly smile but the girl only scowled the harder. Mrs. Turpin herself was fat but she had always had good skin, and though she was forty-seven years old, there was not a wrinkle in her face except around her eyes from laughing too much.

Next to the ugly girl was the child, still in exactly the same position, 20 and next to him was a thin leathery old woman in a cotton print dress. She and Claud had three sacks of chicken feed in their pump house that was in the same print. She had seen from the first that the child belonged with the old woman. She could tell by the way they sat — kind of vacant and white-trashy, as if they would sit there until Doomsday if nobody called and told them to get up. And at right angles but next to the well-dressed pleasant lady was a lank-faced woman who was certainly the child's mother. She had on a yellow sweat shirt and wine-colored slacks, both gritty-looking, and the rims of her lips were stained with snuff. Her dirty yellow hair was tied behind with a little piece of red paper ribbon. Worse than niggers any day, Mrs. Turpin thought.

The gospel hymn playing was, "When I looked up and He looked down," and Mrs. Turpin, who knew it, supplied the last line mentally, "And wona these days I know I'll we-eara crown."

Without appearing to, Mrs. Turpin always noticed people's feet. The well-dressed lady had on red and gray suede shoes to match her dress. Mrs. Turpin had on her good black patent leather pumps. The ugly girl had on Girl Scout shoes and heavy socks. The old woman had on tennis shoes and the white-trashy mother had on what appeared to be bedroom slippers, black straw with gold braid threaded through them — exactly what you would have expected her to have on.

Sometimes at night when she couldn't go to sleep, Mrs. Turpin would occupy herself with the question of who she would have chosen to be if she couldn't have been herself. If Jesus had said to her before he made her, "There's only two places available for you. You can either be a nigger or white-trash," what would she have said? "Please, Jesus, please," she would have said, "just let me wait until there's another place available," and he would have said, "No, you have to go right now and I have only those two places so make up your mind." She would have wiggled and squirmed and begged and pleaded but it would have been no use and finally she would have said, "All right, make me a nigger then — but that don't mean a trashy one." And he would have made her a neat clean respectable Negro woman, herself but black.

Next to the child's mother was a red-headed youngish woman, reading one of the magazines and working a piece of chewing gum, hell for leather, as Claud would say. Mrs. Turpin could not see the woman's feet. She was not white-trash, just common. Sometimes Mrs. Turpin occupied herself at night naming the classes of people. On the bottom of the heap were most colored people, not the kind she would have been if she had been one, but most of them; then next to them — not above, just away from — were the white-trash; then above them were the homeowners, and above them the home-and-land owners, to which she and Claud belonged. Above she and Claud were people with a lot of money and much bigger houses and much more land. But here the complexity of it would begin to bear in on her, for some of the people with a lot of money were common and ought to be below she and Claud and some of the people who had good blood had lost their money and had to rent and then there were colored people who owned their homes and land as well. There was a colored dentist in town who had two red Lincolns and a swimming pool and a farm with registered white-face cattle on it. Usually by the time she had fallen asleep all the classes of people were moiling and roiling around in her head, and she would dream they were all crammed in together in a box car, being ridden off to be put in a gas oven.

"That's a beautiful clock," she said and nodded to her right. It was a big wall clock, the face encased in a brass sunburst. 25

"Yes, it's very pretty," the stylish lady said agreeably. "And right on the dot too," she added, glancing at her watch.

The ugly girl beside her cast an eye upward at the clock, smirked, then looked directly at Mrs. Turpin and smirked again. Then she returned her eyes to her book. She was obviously the lady's daughter because, although they didn't look anything alike as to disposition, they both had the same shape of face and the same blue eyes. On the lady they sparkled pleasantly but in the girl's seared face they appeared alternately to smolder and to blaze.

What if Jesus had said, "All right, you can be white-trash or a nigger or ugly"!

Mrs. Turpin felt an awful pity for the girl, though she thought it was one thing to be ugly and another to act ugly.

The woman with the snuff-stained lips turned around in her chair and looked up at the clock. Then she turned back and appeared to look a little to the side of Mrs. Turpin. There was a cast in one of her eyes. "You want to know wher you can get you one of themther clocks?" she asked in a loud voice. 30

"No, I already have a nice clock," Mrs. Turpin said. Once somebody like her got a leg in the conversation, she would be all over it.

"You can get you one with green stamps," the woman said. "That's most likely wher he got hisn. Save you up enough, you can get you most anythang. I got me some joo'ry."

Ought to have got you a wash rag and some soap, Mrs. Turpin thought.

"I get contour sheets with mine," the pleasant lady said.

The daughter slammed her book shut. She looked straight in front of her, directly through Mrs. Turpin and on through the yellow curtain and the plate glass window which made the wall behind her. The girl's eyes seemed lit all of a sudden with a peculiar light, an unnatural light like night road signs give. Mrs. Turpin turned her head to see if there was anything going 35 on outside that she should see, but she could not see anything. Figures passing cast only a pale shadow through the curtain. There was no reason the girl should single her out for her ugly looks.

"Miss Finley," the nurse said, cracking the door. The gum-chewing woman got up and passed in front of her and Claud and went into the office. She had on red high-heeled shoes.

Directly across the table, the ugly girl's eyes were fixed on Mrs. Turpin as if she had some very special reason for disliking her.

"This is wonderful weather, isn't it?" the girl's mother said.

"It's good weather for cotton if you can get the niggers to pick it," Mrs. Turpin said, "but niggers don't want to pick cotton any more. You can't get the white folks to pick it and now you can't get the niggers — because they got to be right up there with the white folks."

"They gonna *try* anyways," the white-trash woman said, leaning forward. 40

"Do you have one of the cotton-picking machines?" the pleasant lady asked.

"No," Mrs. Turpin said, "they leave half the cotton in the field. We don't have much cotton anyway. If you want to make it farming now, you have to have a little of everything. We got a couple of acres of cotton and a few hogs and chickens and just enough white-face that Claud can look after them himself."

"One thang I don't want," the white-trash woman said, wiping her mouth with the back of her hand. "Hogs. Nasty stinking things, a-gruntin and a-rootin all over the place."

Mrs. Turpin gave her the merest edge of her attention. "Our hogs are not dirty and they don't stink," she said. "They're cleaner than some children I've seen. Their feet never touch the ground. We have a pig parlor — that's where you raise them on concrete," she explained to the pleasant lady, "and Claud scoots them down with the hose every afternoon and washes off the floor." Cleaner by far than that child right there, she thought. Poor nasty little thing. He had not moved except to put the thumb of his dirty hand into his mouth.

The woman turned her face away from Mrs. Turpin. "I know I wouldn't 45 scoot down no hog with no hose," she said to the wall.

You wouldn't have no hog to scoot down, Mrs. Turpin said to herself.

"A-gruntin and a-rootin and a-groanin," the woman muttered.

"We got a little of everything," Mrs. Turpin said to the pleasant lady. "It's no use in having more than you can handle yourself with help like it is. We found enough niggers to pick our cotton this year but Claud he has to go after them and take them home again in the evening. They can't walk that half a mile. No they can't. I tell you," she said and laughed merrily, "I sure am tired of buttering up niggers, but you got to love em if you want em to work for you. When they come in the morning, I run out and I say, 'Hi yawl this morning?' and when Claud drives them off to the field I just wave to beat the band and they just wave back." And she waved her hand rapidly to illustrate.

"Like you read out of the same book," the lady said, showing she understood perfectly.

"Child, yes," Mrs. Turpin said. "And when they come in from the field, I run out with a bucket of icewater. That's the way it's going to be from now on," she said. "You may as well face it."

"One thang I know," the white-trash woman said. "Two thangs I ain't going to do: love no niggers or scoot down no hog with no hose." And she let out a bark of contempt.

The look that Mrs. Turpin and the pleasant lady exchanged indicated they both understood that you had to *have* certain things before you could *know* certain things. But every time Mrs. Turpin exchanged a look with the lady, she was aware that the ugly girl's peculiar eyes were still on her, and she had trouble bringing her attention back to the conversation.

"When you got something," she said, "you got to look after it." And when you ain't got a thing but breath and britches, she added to herself, you can afford to come to town every morning and just sit on the Court House coping and spit.

A grotesque revolving shadow passed across the curtain behind her and was thrown palely on the opposite wall. Then a bicycle clattered down against the outside of the building. The door opened and a colored boy glided in with a tray from the drugstore. It had two large red and white paper cups on it with tops on them. He was a tall, very black boy in discolored white pants and a green nylon shirt. He was chewing gum slowly, as if to music. He set the tray down in the office opening next to the fern and stuck his head through to look for the secretary. She was not in there. He rested his arms on the ledge and waited, his narrow bottom stuck out, swaying to the left and right. He raised a hand over his head and scratched the base of his skull.

"You see that button there, boy?" Mrs. Turpin said. "You can punch that and she'll come. She's probably in the back somewhere."

"Is that right?" the boy said agreeably, as if he had never seen the button before. He leaned to the right and put his finger on it. "She sometime out," he said and twisted around to face his audience, his elbows behind him on the counter. The nurse appeared and he twisted back again. She handed him a dollar and he rooted in his pocket and made the change and counted it out to her. She gave him fifteen cents for a tip and he went out with the empty tray. The heavy door swung to slowly and closed at length with the sound of suction. For a moment no one spoke.

"They ought to send all them niggers back to Africa," the white-trash woman said. "That's wher they come from in the first place."

"Oh, I couldn't do without my good colored friends," the pleasant lady said.

"There's a heap of things worse than a nigger," Mrs. Turpin agreed. "It's all kinds of them just like it's all kinds of us."

"Yes, and it takes all kinds to make the world go round," the lady said in her musical voice.

As she said it, the raw-complexioned girl snapped her teeth together. Her lower lip turned downwards and inside out, revealing the pale pink inside of her mouth. After a second it rolled back up. It was the ugliest face Mrs. Turpin had ever seen anyone make and for a moment she was certain that the girl had made it at her. She was looking at her as if she had known and disliked her all her life — all of Mrs. Turpin's life, it seemed too, not just all the girl's life. Why, girl, I don't even know you, Mrs. Turpin said silently.

She forced her attention back to the discussion. "It wouldn't be practical to send them back to Africa," she said. "They wouldn't want to go. They got it too good here."

"Wouldn't be what they wanted — if I had anythang to do with it," the woman said.

"It wouldn't be a way in the world you could get all the niggers back over there," Mrs. Turpin said. "They'd be hiding out and lying down and turning sick on you and wailing and hollering and raring and pitching. It wouldn't be a way in the world to get them over there."

"They got over here," the trashy woman said. "Get back like they got 65 over."

"It wasn't so many of them then," Mrs. Turpin explained.

The woman looked at Mrs. Turpin as if here was an idiot indeed but Mrs. Turpin was not bothered by the look, considering where it came from.

"Nooo," she said, "they're going to stay here where they can go to New York and marry white folks and improve their color. That's what they all want to do, every one of them, improve their color."

"You know what comes of that, don't you?" Claud asked.

"No, Claud, what?" Mrs. Turpin said.   70

Claud's eyes twinkled. "White-faced niggers," he said with never a smile.

Everybody in the office laughed except the white-trash and the ugly girl. The girl gripped the book in her lap with white fingers. The trashy woman looked around her from face to face as if she thought they were all idiots. The old woman in the feed sack dress continued to gaze expressionless across the floor at the high-top shoes of the man opposite her, the one who had been pretending to be asleep when the Turpins came in. He was laughing heartily, his hands still spread out on his knees. The child had fallen to the side and was lying now almost face down in the old woman's lap.

While they recovered from their laughter, the nasal chorus on the radio kept the room from silence.

"You go to blank blank
And I'll go to mine
But we'll all blank along
To-geth-ther,
And all along the blank
We'll hep each other out
Smile-ling in any kind of
Weath-ther!"

Mrs. Turpin didn't catch every word but she caught enough to agree with the spirit of the song and it turned her thoughts sober. To help anybody out that needed it was her philosophy of life. She never spared herself when she found somebody in need, whether they were white or black, trash or decent. And of all she had to be thankful for, she was most thankful that this was so. If Jesus had said, "You can be high society and have all the money you want and be thin and svelte-like, but you can't be a good woman with it," she would have had to say, "Well don't make me that then. Make me a good woman and it don't matter what else, how fat or how ugly or how poor!" Her heart rose. He had not made her a nigger or white-trash or ugly! He had made her herself and given her a little of everything. Jesus, thank you! she said. Thank you thank you thank you! Whenever she counted her blessings she felt as buoyant as if she weighed one hundred and twenty-five pounds instead of one hundred and eighty.

"What's wrong with your little boy?" the pleasant lady asked the white- 75 trashy woman.

"He has a ulcer," the woman said proudly. "He ain't give me a minute's peace since he was born. Him and her are just alike," she said, nodding at the old woman, who was running her leathery fingers through the child's pale hair. "Look like I can't get nothing down them two but Co' Cola and candy."

That's all you try to get down em, Mrs. Turpin said to herself. Too lazy to light the fire. There was nothing you could tell her about people like them that she didn't know already. And it was not just that they didn't have anything. Because if you gave them everything, in two weeks it would all be broken or filthy or they would have chopped it up for lightwood. She knew all this from her own experience. Help them you must, but help them you couldn't.

All at once the ugly girl turned her lips inside out again. Her eyes fixed like two drills on Mrs. Turpin. This time there was no mistaking that there was something urgent behind them.

Girl, Mrs. Turpin exclaimed silently, I haven't done a thing to you! The girl might be confusing her with somebody else. There was no need to sit by and let herself be intimidated. "You must be in college," she said boldly, looking directly at the girl. "I see you reading a book there."

The girl continued to stare and pointedly did not answer. 80

Her mother blushed at this rudeness. "The lady asked you a question, Mary Grace," she said under her breath.

"I have ears," Mary Grace said.

The poor mother blushed again. "Mary Grace goes to Wellesley College," she explained. She twisted one of the buttons on her dress. "In Massachusetts," she added with a grimace. "And in the summer she just keeps right on studying. Just reads all the time, a real book worm. She's done real well at Wellesley; she's taking English and Math and History and Psychology and Social Studies," she rattled on, "and I think it's too much. I think she ought to get out and have fun."

The girl looked as if she would like to hurl them all through the plate glass window.

"Way up north," Mrs. Turpin murmured and thought, well, it hasn't 85 done much for her manners.

"I'd almost rather to have him sick," the white-trash woman said, wrenching the attention back to herself. "He's so mean when he ain't. Look like some children just take natural to meanness. It's some gets bad when they get sick but he was the opposite. Took sick and turned good. He don't give me no trouble now. It's me waitin to see the doctor," she said.

If I was going to send anybody back to Africa, Mrs. Turpin thought, it would be your kind, woman. "Yes, indeed," she said aloud, but looking up at the ceiling, "it's a heap of things worse than a nigger." And dirtier than a hog, she added to herself.

"I think people with bad dispositions are more to be pitied than anyone on earth," the pleasant lady said in a voice that was decidedly thin.

"I thank the Lord he has blessed me with a good one," Mrs. Turpin said. "The day has never dawned that I couldn't find something to laugh at."

"Not since she married me anyways," Claud said with a comical straight 90 face.

Everybody laughed except the girl and the white-trash.

Mrs. Turpin's stomach shook. "He's such a caution," she said, "that I can't help but laugh at him."

The girl made a loud ugly noise through her teeth.

Her mother's mouth grew thin and tight. "I think the worst thing in the world," she said, "is an ungrateful person. To have everything and not appreciate it. I know a girl," she said, "who has parents who would give her anything, a little brother who loves her dearly, who is getting a good education, who wears the best clothes, but who can never say a kind word to anyone, who never smiles, who just criticizes and complains all day long."

"Is she too old to paddle?" Claud asked. 95

The girl's face was almost purple.

"Yes," the lady said, "I'm afraid there's nothing to do but leave her to her folly. Some day she'll wake up and it'll be too late."

"It never hurt anyone to smile," Mrs. Turpin said. "It just makes you feel better all over."

"Of course," the lady said sadly, "but there are just some people you can't tell anything to. They can't take criticism."

"If it's one thing I am," Mrs. Turpin said with feeling, "it's grateful. 100 When I think who all I could have been besides myself and what all I got, a little of everything, and a good disposition besides, I just feel like shouting, 'Thank you, Jesus, for making everything the way it is!' It could have been different!" For one thing, somebody else could have got Claud. At the thought of this, she was flooded with gratitude and a terrible pang of joy ran through her. "Oh thank you, Jesus, Jesus, thank you!" she cried aloud.

The book struck her directly over her left eye. It struck almost at the same instant that she realized the girl was about to hurl it. Before she could utter a sound, the raw face came crashing across the table toward her, howling. The girl's fingers sank like clamps into the soft flesh of her neck. She heard the mother cry out and Claud shout, "Whoa!" There was an instant when she was certain that she was about to be in an earthquake.

All at once her vision narrowed and she saw everything as if it were happening in a small room far away, or as if she were looking at it through the wrong end of a telescope. Claud's face crumpled and fell out of sight. The nurse ran in, then out, then in again. Then the gangling figure of the doctor rushed out of the inner door. Magazines flew this way and that as the table turned over. The girl fell with a thud and Mrs. Turpin's vision suddenly reversed itself and she saw everything large instead of small. The eyes of the white-trashy woman were staring hugely at the floor. There the girl, held down on one side by the nurse and on the other by her mother, was wrenching and turning in their grasp. The doctor was kneeling astride her, trying to hold her arm down. He managed after a second to sink a long needle into it.

Mrs. Turpin felt entirely hollow except for her heart which swung from side to side as if it were agitated in a great empty drum of flesh.

"Somebody that's not busy call for the ambulance," the doctor said in the off-hand voice young doctors adopt for terrible occasions.

Mrs. Turpin could not have moved a finger. The old man who had been sitting next to her skipped nimbly into the office and made the call, for the secretary still seemed to be gone.

"Claud!" Mrs. Turpin called.

He was not in his chair. She knew she must jump up and find him but she felt like some one trying to catch a train in a dream, when everything moves in slow motion and the faster you try to run the slower you go.

"Here I am," a suffocated voice, very unlike Claud's, said.

He was doubled up in the corner on the floor, pale as paper, holding his leg. She wanted to get up and go to him but she could not move. Instead, her gaze was drawn slowly downward to the churning face on the floor, which she could see over the doctor's shoulder.

The girl's eyes stopped rolling and focused on her. They seemed a much lighter blue than before, as if a door that had been tightly closed behind them was now open to admit light and air.

Mrs. Turpin's head cleared and her power of motion returned. She leaned forward until she was looking directly into the fierce brilliant eyes. There was no doubt in her mind that the girl did know her, knew her in some intense and personal way, beyond time and place and condition. "What you got to say to me?" she asked hoarsely and held her breath, waiting, as for a revelation.

The girl raised her head. Her gaze locked with Mrs. Turpin's. "Go back to hell where you came from, you old wart hog," she whispered. Her voice was low but clear. Her eyes burned for a moment as if she saw with pleasure that her message had struck its target.

Mrs. Turpin sank back in her chair.

After a moment the girl's eyes closed and she turned her head wearily to the side.

The doctor rose and handed the nurse the empty syringe. He leaned   115
over and put both hands for a moment on the mother's shoulders, which
were shaking. She was sitting on the floor, her lips pressed together, holding
Mary Grace's hand in her lap. The girl's fingers were gripped like a baby's
around her thumb. "Go on to the hospital," he said. "I'll call and make the
arrangements."

"Now let's see that neck," he said in a jovial voice to Mrs. Turpin. He
began to inspect her neck with his first two fingers. Two little moon-shaped
lines like pink fish bones were indented over her windpipe. There was the
beginning of an angry red swelling above her eye. His fingers passed over
this also.

"Lea' me be," she said thickly and shook him off. "See about Claud. She
kicked him."

"I'll see about him in a minute," he said and felt her pulse. He was a thin
gray-haired man, given to pleasantries. "Go home and have yourself a vacation the rest of the day," he said and patted her on the shoulder.

Quit your pattin me, Mrs. Turpin growled to herself.

"And put an ice pack over that eye," he said. Then he went and squatted   120
down beside Claud and looked at his leg. After a moment he pulled him up
and Claud limped after him into the office.

Until the ambulance came, the only sounds in the room were the tremulous moans of the girl's mother, who continued to sit on the floor. The
white-trash woman did not take her eyes off the girl. Mrs. Turpin looked
straight ahead at nothing. Presently the ambulance drew up, a long dark
shadow, behind the curtain. The attendants came in and set the stretcher
down beside the girl and lifted her expertly onto it and carried her out. The
nurse helped the mother gather up her things. The shadow of the ambulance moved silently away and the nurse came back in the office.

"That ther girl is going to be a lunatic, ain't she?" the white-trash woman
asked the nurse, but the nurse kept on to the back and never answered her.

"Yes, she's going to be a lunatic," the white-trash woman said to the rest
of them.

"Po' critter," the old woman murmured. The child's face was still in her
lap. His eyes looked idly out over her knees. He had not moved during the
disturbance except to draw one leg up under him.

"I thank Gawd," the white-trash woman said fervently, "I ain't a lunatic."   125
Claud came limping out and the Turpins went home.

As their pick-up truck turned into their own dirt road and made the
crest of the hill, Mrs. Turpin gripped the window ledge and looked out sus-
piciously. The land sloped gracefully down through a field dotted with lavender weeds and at the start of the rise their small yellow frame house, with
its little flower beds spread out around it like a fancy apron, sat primly in
its accustomed place between two giant hickory trees. She would not have
been startled to see a burnt wound between two blackened chimneys.

Neither of them felt like eating so they put on their house clothes and
lowered the shade in the bedroom and lay down, Claud with his leg on a

pillow and herself with a damp washcloth over her eye. The instant she was flat on her back, the image of a razor-backed hog with warts on its face and horns coming out behind its ears snorted into her head. She moaned, a low quiet moan.

"I am not," she said tearfully, "a wart hog. From hell." But the denial had no force. The girl's eyes and her words, even the tone of her voice, low but clear, directed only to her, brooked no repudiation. She had been singled out for the message, though there was trash in the room to whom it might justly have been applied. The full force of this fact struck her only now. There was a woman there who was neglecting her own child but she had been overlooked. The message had been given to Ruby Turpin, a respectable, hard-working, church-going woman. The tears dried. Her eyes began to burn instead with wrath.

She rose on her elbow and the washcloth fell into her hand. Claud was lying on his back, snoring. She wanted to tell him what the girl had said. At the same time, she did not wish to put the image of herself as a wart hog from hell into his mind.

"Hey, Claud," she muttered and pushed his shoulder.

Claud opened one pale baby blue eye.

She looked into it warily. He did not think about anything. He just went his way.

"Wha, whasit?" he said and closed the eye again.

"Nothing," she said. "Does your leg pain you?"

"Hurts like hell," Claud said.

"It'll quit terreckly," she said and lay back down. In a moment Claud was snoring again. For the rest of the afternoon they lay there. Claud slept. She scowled at the ceiling. Occasionally she raised her fist and made a small stabbing motion over her chest as if she was defending her innocence to invisible guests who were like the comforters of Job, reasonable-seeming but wrong.

About five-thirty Claud stirred. "Got to go after those niggers," he sighed, not moving.

She was looking straight up as if there were unintelligible handwriting on the ceiling. The protuberance over her eye had turned a greenish-blue. "Listen here," she said.

"What?"

"Kiss me."

Claud leaned over and kissed her loudly on the mouth. He pinched her side and their hands interlocked. Her expression of ferocious concentration did not change. Claud got up, groaning and growling, and limped off. She continued to study the ceiling.

She did not get up until she heard the pick-up truck coming back with the Negroes. Then she rose and thrust her feet in her brown oxfords, which she did not bother to lace, and stumped out onto the back porch and got her red plastic bucket. She emptied a tray of ice cubes into it and filled it half full of water and went out into the back yard. Every afternoon after Claud brought the hands in, one of the boys helped him put out hay and the rest waited in the back of the truck until he was ready to take them home. The truck was parked in the shade under one of the hickory trees.

"Hi yawl this evening?" Mrs. Turpin asked grimly, appearing with the bucket and the dipper. There were three women and a boy in the truck.

"Us doin nicely," the oldest woman said. "Hi you doin?" and her gaze 145 struck immediately on the dark lump on Mrs. Turpin's forehead. "You done fell down, ain't you?" she asked in a solicitous voice. The old woman was dark and almost toothless. She had on an old felt hat of Claud's set back on her head. The other two women were younger and lighter and they both had new bright green sunhats. One of them had hers on her head; the other had taken hers off and the boy was grinning beneath it.

Mrs. Turpin set the bucket down on the floor of the truck. "Yawl hep yourselves," she said. She looked around to make sure Claud had gone. "No, I didn't fall down," she said, folding her arms. "It was something worse than that."

"Ain't nothing bad happen to you!" the old woman said. She said it as if they all knew that Mrs. Turpin was protected in some special way by Divine Providence. "You just had you a little fall."

"We were in town at the doctor's office for where the cow kicked Mr. Turpin," Mrs. Turpin said in a flat tone that indicated they could leave off their foolishness. "And there was this girl there. A big fat girl with her face all broke out. I could look at that girl and tell she was peculiar but I couldn't tell how. And me and her mama was just talking and going along and all of a sudden WHAM! She throws this big book she was reading at me and . . ."

"Naw!" the old woman cried out.

"And then she jumps over the table and commences to choke me." 150

"Naw!" they all exclaimed, "naw!"

"Hi come she do that?" the old woman asked. "What ail her?"

Mrs. Turpin only glared in front of her.

"Somethin ail her," the old woman said.

"They carried her off in an ambulance," Mrs. Turpin continued, "but 155 before she went she was rolling on the floor and they were trying to hold her down to give her a shot and she said something to me." She paused. "You know what she said to me?"

"What she say?" they asked.

"She said," Mrs. Turpin began, and stopped, her face very dark and heavy. The sun was getting whiter and whiter, blanching the sky overhead so that the leaves of the hickory tree were black in the face of it. She could not bring forth the words. "Something real ugly," she muttered.

"She sho shouldn't said nothin ugly to you," the old woman said. "You so sweet. You the sweetest lady I know."

"She pretty too," the one with the hat on said.

"And stout," the other one said. "I never knowed no sweeter white lady." 160

"That's the truth befo' Jesus," the old woman said. "Amen! You des as sweet and pretty as you can be."

Mrs. Turpin knew exactly how much Negro flattery was worth and it added to her rage. "She said," she began again and finished this time with a fierce rush of breath, "that I was an old wart hog from hell."

There was an astounded silence.

"Where she at?" the youngest woman cried in a piercing voice.

"Lemme see her. I'll kill her!"

"I'll kill her with you!" the other one cried.

"She b'long in the sylum," the old woman said emphatically. "You the sweetest white lady I know."

"She pretty too," the other two said. "Stout as she can be and sweet. Jesus satisfied with her!"

"Deed he is," the woman declared.

Idiots! Mrs. Turpin growled to herself. You could never say anything intelligent to a nigger. You could talk at them but not with them. "Yawl ain't drunk your water," she said shortly. "Leave the bucket in the truck when you're finished with it. I got more to do than just stand around and pass the time of day," and she moved off and into the house.

She stood for a moment in the middle of the kitchen. The dark protuberance over her eye looked like a miniature tornado cloud which might any moment sweep across the horizon of her brow. Her lower lip protruded dangerously. She squared her massive shoulders. Then she marched into the front of the house and out the side door and started down the road to the pig parlor. She had the look of a woman going single-handed, weaponless, into battle.

The sun was deep yellow now like a harvest moon and was riding westward very fast over the far tree line as if it meant to reach the hogs before she did. The road was rutted and she kicked several good-sized stones out of her path as she strode along. The pig parlor was on a little knoll at the end of a lane that ran off from the side of the barn. It was a square of concrete as large as a small room, with a board fence about four feet high around it. The concrete floor sloped slightly so that the hog wash could drain off into a trench where it was carried to the field for fertilizer. Claud was standing on the outside, on the edge of the concrete, hanging onto the top board, hosing down the floor inside. The hose was connected to the faucet of a water trough nearby.

Mrs. Turpin climbed up beside him and glowered down at the hogs inside. There were seven long-snouted bristly shoats in it — tan with liver-colored spots — and an old sow a few weeks off from farrowing. She was lying on her side grunting. The shoats were running about shaking themselves like idiot children, their little slit pig eyes searching the floor for anything left. She had read that pigs were the most intelligent animal. She doubted it. They were supposed to be smarter than dogs. There had even been a pig astronaut. He had performed his assignment perfectly but died of a heart attack afterwards because they left him in his electric suit, sitting upright throughout his examination when naturally a hog should be on all fours.

A-gruntin and a-rootin and a-groanin.

"Gimme that hose," she said, yanking it away from Claud. "Go on and 175 carry them niggers home and then get off that leg."

"You look like you might have swallowed a mad dog," Claud observed, but he got down and limped off. He paid no attention to her humors.

Until he was out of earshot, Mrs. Turpin stood on the side of the pen, holding the hose and pointing the stream of water at the hind quarters of any shoat that looked as if it might try to lie down. When he had had time to get over the hill, she turned her head slightly and her wrathful eyes scanned the path. He was nowhere in sight. She turned back again and seemed to gather herself up. Her shoulders rose and she drew in her breath.

"What do you send me a message like that for?" she said in a low fierce voice, barely above a whisper but with the force of a shout in its concentrated fury. "How am I a hog and me both? How am I saved and from hell too?" Her free fist was knotted and with the other she gripped the hose, blindly pointing the stream of water in and out of the eye of the old sow whose outraged squeal she did not hear.

The pig parlor commanded a view of the back pasture where their twenty beef cows were gathered around the hay-bales Claud and the boy had put out. The freshly cut pasture sloped down to the highway. Across it was their cotton field and beyond that a dark green dusty wood which they owned as well. The sun was behind the wood, very red, looking over the paling of the trees like a farmer inspecting his own hogs.

"Why me?" she rumbled. "It's no trash around here, black or white, that 180 I haven't given to. And break my back to the bone every day working. And do for the church."

She appeared to be the right size woman to command the arena before her. "How am I a hog?" she demanded. "Exactly how am I like them?" and she jabbed the stream of water at the shoats. "There was plenty of trash there. It didn't have to be me.

"If you like trash better, go get yourself some trash then," she railed. "You could have made me trash. Or a nigger. If trash is what you wanted why didn't you make me trash?" She shook her fist with the hose in it and a watery snake appeared momentarily in the air. "I could quit working and take it easy and be filthy," she growled. "Lounge about the sidewalks all day drinking root beer. Dip snuff and spit in every puddle and have it all over my face. I could be nasty.

"Or you could have made me a nigger. It's too late for me to be a nigger," she said with deep sarcasm, "but I could act like one. Lay down in the middle of the road and stop traffic. Roll on the ground."

In the deepening light everything was taking on a mysterious hue. The pasture was growing a peculiar glassy green and the streak of highway had turned lavender. She braced herself for a final assault and this time her voice rolled out over the pasture. "Go on," she yelled, "call me a hog! Call me a hog again. From hell. Call me a wart hog from hell. Put that bottom rail on top. There'll still be a top and bottom!"

A garbled echo returned to her.

A final surge of fury shook her and she roared, "Who do you think you are?"

The color of everything, field and crimson sky, burned for a moment with a transparent intensity. The question carried over the pasture and across the highway and the cotton field and returned to her clearly like an answer from beyond the wood.

She opened her mouth but no sound came out of it.

A tiny truck, Claud's, appeared on the highway, heading rapidly out of sight. Its gears scraped thinly. It looked like a child's toy. At any moment a bigger truck might smash into it and scatter Claud's and the niggers' brains all over the road.

Mrs. Turpin stood there, her gaze fixed on the highway, all her muscles rigid, until in five or six minutes the truck reappeared, returning. She waited until it had had time to turn into their own road. Then like a monumental statue coming to life, she bent her head slowly and gazed, as if through the very heart of mystery, down into the pig parlor at the hogs. They had settled all in one corner around the old sow who was grunting softly. A red glow suffused them. They appeared to pant with a secret life.

Until the sun slipped finally behind the tree line, Mrs. Turpin remained there with her gaze bent to them as if she were absorbing some abysmal life-giving knowledge. At last she lifted her head. There was only a purple streak in the sky, cutting through a field of crimson and leading, like an extension of the highway, into the descending dusk. She raised her hands from the side of the pen in a gesture hieratic and profound. A visionary light settled in her eyes. She saw the streak as a vast swinging bridge extending upward from the earth through a field of living fire. Upon it a vast horde of souls were rumbling toward heaven. There were whole companies of white-trash, clean for the first time in their lives, and bands of black niggers in white robes, and battalions of freaks and lunatics shouting and clapping and leaping like frogs. And bringing up the end of the procession was a tribe of people whom she recognized at once as those who, like herself and Claud, had always had a little of everything and the God-given wit to use it right. She leaned forward to observe them closer. They were marching behind the others with great dignity, accountable as they had always been for good order and common sense and respectable behavior. They alone were on key. Yet she could see by their shocked and altered faces that even their virtues were being burned away. She lowered her hands and gripped the rail of the hog pen, her eyes small but fixed unblinkingly on what lay ahead. In a moment the vision faded but she remained where she was, immobile.

At length she got down and turned off the faucet and made her slow way on the darkening path to the house. In the woods around her the invisible cricket choruses had struck up, but what she heard were the voices of the souls climbing upward into the starry field and shouting hallelujah.

Considerations for Critical Thinking and Writing

1. FIRST RESPONSE. Does your attitude toward Mrs. Turpin change or remain the same during the story? Do you *like* her more at some points than at others? Explain why.

2. Why is it appropriate that the two major settings for the action in this story are a doctor's waiting room and a "pig parlor"?

3. How does Mrs. Turpin's treatment of her husband help to characterize her?

4. Mrs. Turpin notices people's shoes. What does this and her thoughts about "classes of people" (para. 24) reveal about her? How does she see herself in relation to other people?

5. Why does Mary Grace attack Mrs. Turpin?

6. Why is it significant that the book Mary Grace reads is *Human Development*? What is the significance of her name?

7. What does the background music played on the radio contribute to the story?

8. To whom does Mrs. Turpin address this anguished question: "What do you send me a message [Mary Grace's whispered words telling her "Go back to hell where you came from, you old wart hog"] like that for?" (para. 112). Why is Mrs. Turpin so angry and bewildered?

9. What is the "abysmal life-giving knowledge" that Mrs. Turpin discovers in the next to the last paragraph? Why is it "abysmal"? How is it "life-giving"?

10. Given the serious theme, consider whether the story's humor is appropriate.

11. When Mrs. Turpin returns home bruised, a hired African American woman tells her that nothing really "bad" happened: "You just had you a little fall" (para. 147). Pay particular attention to the suggestive language of this sentence, and discuss its significance in relation to the rest of the story.

12. CRITICAL STRATEGIES. Choose a critical approach from Chapter 30, "Critical Strategies for Reading," that you think is particularly useful for explaining the themes of this story.

Connections to Other Selections

1. Compare and contrast Mary Grace with Hulga of "Good Country People."

2. Explain how "Revelation" could be used as a title for any of the O'Connor stories you have read.

3. Explore the nature of the "revelation" in O'Connor's story and in John Updike's "A & P" (p. 138).

Perspectives on O'Connor

FLANNERY O'CONNOR (1925–1964)
On the Use of Exaggeration and Distortion   1969

When I write a novel in which the central action is a baptism, I am very well aware that for a majority of my readers, baptism is a meaningless rite, and so in my novel I have to see that this baptism carries enough awe and mystery to jar the reader into some kind of emotional recognition of its significance. To this end I have to bend the whole novel — its language, its structure, its action. I have to make the reader feel, in his bones if nowhere else, that something is going on here that counts. Distortion in this case is an instrument; exaggeration has a purpose, and the whole structure of the story or novel has been made what it is because of belief. This is not the kind of distortion that destroys; it is the kind that reveals, or should reveal.

From "Novelist and Believer" in *Mystery and Manners*

CONSIDERATIONS FOR CRITICAL THINKING AND WRITING

1. It has been observed that in many of O'Connor's works the central action takes the form of some kind of "baptism" that initiates, tests, or purifies a character. Select an O'Connor story that illustrates this generalization, and explain how the conflict results in a kind of baptism.

2. O'Connor says that exaggeration and distortion reveal something in her stories. What is the effect of such exaggeration and distortion? Typically, what is revealed? Focus your comments on a single story to illustrate your points.

3. Do you think that O'Connor's stories have anything to offer a reader who has no religious faith? Explain why or why not.

JOSEPHINE HENDIN (B. 1946)
On O'Connor's Refusal to "Do Pretty"   1970

There is, in the memory of one Milledgeville matron, the image of O'Connor at nineteen or twenty who, when invited to a wedding shower for an old family friend, remained standing, her back pressed against the wall, scowling at the group of women who had sat down to lunch. Neither the devil nor her mother could make her say yes to this fiercely gracious female society, but Flannery O'Connor could not say no even in a whisper. She could not refuse the invitation but she would not accept it either. She did not exactly "fuss" but neither did she "do pretty."

From *The World of Flannery O'Connor*

CONSIDERATIONS FOR CRITICAL THINKING AND WRITING

1. How is O'Connor's personality revealed in this anecdote about her ambivalent response to society? Allow the description to be suggestive for you, and flesh out a brief portrait of her.

2. Consider how this personality makes itself apparent in any one of O'Connor's stories you have read. How does the anecdote help to characterize the narrator's voice in the story?

3. To what extent do you think biographical details such as this — assuming the Milledgeville matron's memory to be accurate — can shed light on a writer's works?

CLAIRE KATZ (B. 1935)

The Function of Violence in O'Connor's Fiction   1974

From the moment the reader enters O'Connor's backwoods, he is poised on the edge of a pervasive violence. Characters barely contain their rage; images reflect a hostile nature; and even the Christ to whom the characters are ultimately driven is a threatening figure . . . full of the apocalyptic wrath of the Old Testament.

O'Connor's conscious purpose is evident enough . . . : to reveal the need for grace in a world grotesque without a transcendent context. "I have found that my subject in fiction is the action of grace in territory largely held by the devil," she wrote [in *Mystery and Manners*], and she was not vague about what the devil is: "an evil intelligence determined on its own supremacy." It would seem that for O'Connor, given the fact of original Sin, any intelligence determined on its own supremacy was intrinsically evil. For in each work, it is the impulse toward secular autonomy, the smug confidence that human nature is perfectible by its own efforts, that she sets out to destroy, through an act of violence so intense that the character is rendered helpless, a passive victim of a superior power. Again and again she creates a fiction in which a character attempts to live autonomously, to define himself and his values, only to be jarred back to what she calls "reality" — the recognition of helplessness in the face of contingency, and the need for absolute submission to the power of Christ.

From "Flannery O'Connor's Rage of Vision" in *American Literature*

CONSIDERATIONS FOR CRITICAL THINKING AND WRITING

1. Choose an O'Connor story, and explain how grace — the divine influence from God that redeems a person — is used in it to transform a character.

2. Which O'Connor characters can be accurately described as having an "evil intelligence determined on its own supremacy" (para. 2)? Choose one character, and write an essay explaining how this description is central to the conflict of the story.

Time *Magazine, on* A Good Man Is Hard to Find and Other Stories 1962

Highly unladylike . . . a brutal irony, a slam-bang humor, and a style of writing as balefully direct as a death sentence.

From a *Time* magazine blurb quoted on the cover of the second American edition of *A Good Man Is Hard to Find and Other Stories*

CONSIDERATIONS FOR CRITICAL THINKING AND WRITING

1. How accurate do you think this blurb is in characterizing the three O'Connor stories in this chapter?

2. CREATIVE RESPONSE. Write your own blurb for the three stories and be prepared to justify your pithy description.

A Collection of Stories

10

Stories for Further Reading

Drama, situation, is made out of the conflicts thus produced between social order and individual appetites, and the art of rendering life in fiction can never, in the last analysis, be anything, or need to be anything, but the disengaging of crucial moments from the welter of existence.

— EDITH WHARTON

Everett Collection Inc/Alamy Stock Photo.

JOHN CHEEVER (1912–1982)

A native of Quincy, Massachusetts, John Cheever's work is mostly associated with New York City and its suburbs, where he lived after a stint in the army during World War II. During the 1940s and 1950s his short stories were frequently published in *the New Yorker*. Dissatisfied with being too closely associated with that magazine, Cheever began to publish novels in the late 1950s and continued to write short fiction, which began to take some experimental risks. His final novel, *Falconer* (1977), which takes place mostly in prison, was a noted departure and enjoyed both critical and popular acclaim, yet Cheever is

David Lees/Corbis Historical/Getty Images.

remembered more as a master of the short story form than as a novelist. His collection *The Stories of John Cheever*, published in 1979, won the Pulitzer Prize that year. The following is the title story from his first collection.

The Enormous Radio   1947

Jim and Irene Westcott were the kind of people who seem to strike that satisfactory average of income, endeavor, and respectability that is reached by the statistical reports in college alumni bulletins. They were the parents of two young children, they had been married nine years, they lived on the twelfth floor of an apartment house near Sutton Place, they went to the theatre on an average of 10.3 times a year, and they hoped someday to live in Westchester. Irene Westcott was a pleasant, rather plain girl with soft brown hair and a wide, fine forehead upon which nothing at all had been written, and in the cold weather she wore a coat of fitch skins dyed to resemble mink. You could not say that Jim Westcott looked younger than he was, but you could at least say of him that he seemed to feel younger. He wore his graying hair cut very short, he dressed in the kind of clothes his class had worn at Andover, and his manner was earnest, vehement, and intentionally naïve. The Westcotts differed from their friends, their classmates, and their neighbors only in an interest they shared in serious music. They went to a great many concerts — although they seldom mentioned this to anyone — and they spent a good deal of time listening to music on the radio.

Their radio was an old instrument, sensitive, unpredictable, and beyond repair. Neither of them understood the mechanics of radio — or of any of the other appliances that surrounded them — and when the instrument faltered, Jim would strike the side of the cabinet with his hand. This sometimes helped. One Sunday afternoon, in the middle of a Schubert quartet, the music faded away altogether. Jim struck the cabinet repeatedly, but there was no response; the Schubert was lost to them forever. He promised to buy Irene a new radio, and on Monday when he came home from work he told her that he had got one. He refused to describe it, and said it would be a surprise for her when it came.

The radio was delivered at the kitchen door the following afternoon, and with the assistance of her maid and the handyman Irene uncrated it and brought it into the living room. She was struck at once with the physical ugliness of the large gumwood cabinet. Irene was proud of her living room, she had chosen its furnishings and colors as carefully as she chose her clothes, and now it seemed to her that the new radio stood among her intimate possessions like an aggressive intruder. She was confounded by the number of dials and switches on the instrument panel, and she studied them thoroughly before she put the plug into a wall socket and turned the radio on. The dials flooded with a malevolent green light, and in the distance she heard the music of a piano quintet. The quintet was in the distance for only an instant; it bore down upon her with a speed greater than light and filled the apartment with the noise of music amplified so mightily that it knocked a china ornament from a table to the floor. She rushed to the instrument and reduced the volume. The violent forces that were snared in the ugly gumwood cabinet made her uneasy. Her children came home from school then, and she took them to the Park. It was not until later in the afternoon that she was able to return to the radio.

The maid had given the children their suppers and was supervising their baths when Irene turned on the radio, reduced the volume, and sat down to listen to a Mozart quintet that she knew and enjoyed. The music came through clearly. The new instrument had a much purer tone, she thought, than the old one. She decided that tone was most important and that she could conceal the cabinet behind a sofa. But as soon as she had made her peace with the radio, the interference began. A crackling sound like the noise of a burning powder fuse began to accompany the singing of the strings. Beyond the music, there was a rustling that reminded Irene unpleasantly of the sea, and as the quintet progressed, these noises were joined by many others. She tried all the dials and switches but nothing dimmed the interference, and she sat down, disappointed and bewildered, and tried to trace the flight of the melody. The elevator shaft in her building ran beside the living-room wall, and it was the noise of the elevator that gave her a clue to the character of the static. The rattling of the elevator cables and the opening and closing of the elevator doors were reproduced in her loudspeaker, and, realizing that the radio was sensitive to electrical currents of all sorts, she began to discern through the Mozart the ringing of telephone bells, the dialing of phones, and the lamentation of a vacuum cleaner. By listening more carefully, she was able to distinguish doorbells, elevator bells, electric razors, and Waring mixers, whose sounds had been picked up from the apartments that surrounded hers and transmitted through her loudspeaker. The powerful and ugly instrument, with its mistaken sensitivity to discord, was more than she could hope to master, so she turned the thing off and went into the nursery to see her children.

When Jim Westcott came home that night, he went to the radio confidently and worked the controls. He had the same sort of experience Irene had had. A man was speaking on the station Jim had chosen, and his voice swung instantly from the distance into a force so powerful that it shook the apartment. Jim turned the volume control and reduced the voice. Then, a minute or two later, the interference began. The ringing of telephones and doorbells set in, joined by the rasp of the elevator doors and the whir of cooking appliances. The character of the noise had changed since Irene had tried the radio earlier; the last of the electric razors was being unplugged, the vacuum cleaners had all been returned to their closets, and the static reflected that change in pace that overtakes the city after the sun goes down. He fiddled with the knobs but couldn't get rid of the noises, so he turned the radio off and told Irene that in the morning he'd call the people who had sold it to him and give them hell.

The following afternoon, when Irene returned to the apartment from a luncheon date, the maid told her that a man had come and fixed the radio. Irene went into the living loom before she took off her hat or her furs and tried the instrument. From the loudspeaker came a recording of the "Missouri Waltz." It reminded her of the thin, scratchy music from an old-fashioned phonograph that she sometimes heard across the lake where she spent her summers. She waited until the waltz had finished, expecting an explanation of the recording, but there was none. The music was followed by silence, and then the plaintive and scratchy record was repeated. She turned the dial and got a satisfactory burst of Caucasian° music — the thump of bare feet in the dust and the rattle of coin jewelry — but in the background she could hear the ringing of bells and a confusion of voices. Her children came home from school then, and she turned off the radio and went to the nursery.

When Jim came home that night, he was tired, and he took a bath and changed his clothes. Then he joined Irene in the living room. He had just turned on the radio when the maid announced dinner, so he left it on, and he and Irene went to the table.

Jim was too tired to make even a pretense of sociability, and there was nothing about the dinner to hold Irene's interest, so her attention wandered from the food to the deposits of silver polish on the candlesticks and from there to the music in the other room. She listened for a few minutes to a Chopin prelude and then was surprised to hear a man's voice break in. "For Christ's sake, Kathy," he said, "do you always have to play the piano when I get home?" The music stopped abruptly. "It's the only chance I have," a woman said. "I'm at the office all day." "So am I," the man said. He added something obscene about an upright piano, and slammed a door. The passionate and melancholy music began again.

"Did you hear that?" Irene asked.

"What?" Jim was eating his dessert.   10

"The radio. A man said something while the music was still going on — something dirty."

"It's probably a play."

"I don't think it *is* a play," Irene said.

They left the table and took their coffee into the living room. Irene asked Jim to try another station. He turned the knob. "Have you seen my garters?" a man asked. "Button me up," a woman said. "Have you seen my garters?" the man said again. "Just button me up and I'll find your garters," the woman said. Jim shifted to another station. "I wish you wouldn't leave apple cores in the ashtrays," a man said. "I hate the smell."

"This is strange," Jim said.   15

"Isn't it?" Irene said.

Jim turned the knob again. "'On the coast of Coromandel where the early pumpkins blow,'" a woman with a pronounced English accent said,

Caucasian: Refers to the Caucasus region of eastern Europe.

"'in the middle of the woods lived the Yonghy-Bonghy-Bò. Two old chairs, and half a candle, one old jug without a handle . . .'"

"My God!" Irene cried. "That's the Sweeneys' nurse."

"'These were all his worldly goods,'" the British voice continued.

"Turn that thing off," Irene said. "Maybe they can hear *us*." Jim switched the radio off. "That was Miss Armstrong, the Sweeneys' nurse," Irene said. "She must be reading to the little girl. They live in 17-B. I've talked with Miss Armstrong in the Park. I know her voice very well. We must be getting other people's apartments."

"That's impossible," Jim said.

"Well, that was the Sweeneys' nurse," Irene said hotly. "I know her voice. I know it very well. I'm wondering if they can hear us."

Jim turned the switch. First from a distance and then nearer, nearer, as if borne on the wind, came the pure accents of the Sweeneys' nurse again: "'*Lady Jingly! Lady Jingly!*'" she said, "'*sitting where the pumpkins blow, will you come and be my wife*? said the Yonghy-Bonghy-Bò . . .'"

Jim went over to the radio and said "Hello" loudly into the speaker.

"'*I am tired of living singly,*'" the nurse went on, "'*on this coast so wild and shingly, I'm a-weary of my life; if you'll come and be my wife, quite serene would be my life . . .*'"

"I guess she can't hear us," Irene said. "Try something else."

Jim turned to another station, and the living room was filled with the uproar of a cocktail party that had overshot its mark. Someone was playing the piano and singing the "Whiffenpoof Song," and the voices that surrounded the piano were vehement and happy. "Eat some more sandwiches," a woman shrieked. There were screams of laughter and a dish of some sort crashed to the floor.

"Those must be the Fullers, in 11-E," Irene said. "I knew they were giving a party this afternoon. I saw her in the liquor store. Isn't this too divine? Try something else. See if you can get those people in 18-C."

The Westcotts overheard that evening a monologue on salmon fishing in Canada, a bridge game, running comments on home movies of what had apparently been a fortnight at Sea Island, and a bitter family quarrel about an overdraft at the bank. They turned off their radio at midnight and went to bed, weak with laughter. Sometime in the night, their son began to call for a glass of water and Irene got one and took it to his room. It was very early. All the lights in the neighborhood were extinguished, and from the boy's window she could see the empty street. She went into the living room and tried the radio. There was some faint coughing, a moan, and then a man spoke. "Are you all right, darling?" he asked. "Yes," a woman said wearily. "Yes, I'm all right, I guess," and then she added with great feeling, "But, you know, Charlie, I don't feel like myself any more. Sometimes there are about fifteen or twenty minutes in the week when I feel like myself. I don't like to go to another doctor, because the doctor's bills are so awful already, but I just don't feel like myself, Charlie. I just never feel like myself." They were not young, Irene thought. She guessed from the timbre of their voices that they were middle-aged. The restrained melancholy of the dialogue and the draft from the bedroom window made her shiver, and she went back to bed.

The following morning, Irene cooked breakfast for the family — the maid 30 didn't come up from her room in the basement until ten — braided her daughter's hair, and waited at the door until her children and her husband had been carried away in the elevator. Then she went into the living room and tried the radio. "I don't want to go to school," a child screamed. "I hate school. I won't go to school. I hate school." "You will go to school," an enraged woman said. "We paid eight hundred dollars to get you into that school and you'll go if it kills you." The next number on the dial produced the worn record of the "Missouri Waltz." Irene shifted the control and invaded the privacy of several breakfast tables. She overheard demonstrations of indigestion, carnal love, abysmal vanity, faith, and despair. Irene's life was nearly as simple and sheltered as it appeared to be, and the forthright and sometimes brutal language that came from the loudspeaker that morning astonished and troubled her. She continued to listen until her maid came in. Then she turned off the radio quickly, since this insight, she realized, was a furtive one.

Irene had a luncheon date with a friend that day, and she left her apartment at a little after twelve. There were a number of women in the elevator when it stopped at her floor. She stared at their handsome and impassive faces, their furs, and the cloth flowers in their hats. Which one of them had been to Sea Island? she wondered. Which one had overdrawn her bank account? The elevator stopped at the tenth floor and a woman with a pair of Skye terriers joined them. Her hair was rigged high on her head and she wore a mink cape. She was humming the "Missouri Waltz."

Irene had two Martinis at lunch, and she looked searchingly at her friend and wondered what her secrets were. They had intended to go shopping after lunch, but Irene excused herself and went home. She told the maid that she was not to be disturbed; then she went into the living room, closed the doors, and switched on the radio. She heard, in the course of the afternoon, the halting conversation of a woman entertaining her aunt, the hysterical conclusion of a luncheon party, and a hostess briefing her maid about some cocktail guests. "Don't give the best Scotch to anyone who hasn't white hair," the hostess said. "See if you can get rid of that liver paste before you pass those hot things, and could you lend me five dollars? I want to tip the elevator man."

As the afternoon waned, the conversations increased in intensity. From where Irene sat, she could see the open sky above the East River. There were hundreds of clouds in the sky, as though the south wind had broken the winter into pieces and were blowing it north, and on her radio she could hear the arrival of cocktail guests and the return of children and businessmen from their schools and offices. "I found a good-sized diamond on the bathroom floor this morning," a woman said. "It must have fallen out of that bracelet Mrs. Dunston was wearing last night." "We'll sell it," a man said. "Take it down to the jeweler on Madison Avenue and sell it. Mrs. Dunston won't know the difference, and we could use a couple of hundred bucks . . ." " 'Oranges and lemons, say the bells of St. Clement's,' " the Sweeneys' nurse sang. " 'Halfpence and farthings, say the bells of St. Martin's. When will you pay me? say the bells at old Bailey . . .' " "It's not a hat," a woman cried, and at her back roared a cocktail party. "It's not a hat, it's a love affair. That's what Walter Florell said. He said it's not a hat, it's a love affair," and then, in a lower voice, the same woman added, "Talk to somebody, for Christ's sake, honey, talk to somebody. If she catches you standing here not talking to anybody, she'll take us off her invitation list, and I love these parties."

The Westcotts were going out for dinner that night, and when Jim came home, Irene was dressing. She seemed sad and vague, and he brought her a drink. They were dining with friends in the neighborhood, and they walked to where they were going. The sky was broad and filled with light. It was one of those splendid spring evenings that excite memory and desire, and the air that touched their hands and faces felt very soft. A Salvation Army band was on the corner playing "Jesus Is Sweeter." Irene drew on her husband's arm and held him there for a minute, to hear the music. "They're really such nice people, aren't they?" she said. "They have such nice faces. Actually, they're so much nicer than a lot of the people we know." She took a bill from her purse and walked over and dropped it into the tambourine. There was in her face, when she returned to her husband, a look of radiant melancholy that he was not familiar with. And her conduct at the dinner party that night seemed strange to him, too. She interrupted her hostess rudely and stared at the people across the table from her with an intensity for which she would have punished her children.

It was still mild when they walked home from the party, and Irene   35 looked up at the spring stars. " 'How far that little candle throws its beams,' " she exclaimed. " 'So shines a good deed in a naughty world.' " She waited that night until Jim had fallen asleep, and then went into the living room and turned on the radio.

Jim came home at about six the next night. Emma, the maid, let him in, and he had taken off his hat and was taking off his coat when Irene ran into the hall. Her face was shining with tears and her hair was disordered. "Go up to 16-C, Jim!" she screamed. "Don't take off your coat. Go up to 16-C. Mr. Osborn's beating his wife. They've been quarreling since four o'clock, and now he's hitting her. Go up there and stop him."

From the radio in the living room, Jim heard screams, obscenities, and thuds. "You know you don't have to listen to this sort of thing," he said. He strode into the living room and turned the switch. "It's indecent," he said. "It's like looking in windows. You know you don't have to listen to this sort of thing. You can turn it off."

"Oh, it's so horrible, it's so dreadful," Irene was sobbing. "I've been listening all day, and it's so depressing."

"Well, if it's so depressing, why do you listen to it? I bought this damned radio to give you some pleasure," he said. "I paid a great deal of money for it. I thought it might make you happy. I wanted to make you happy."

"Don't, don't, don't, don't quarrel with me," she moaned, and laid her 40 head on his shoulder. "All the others have been quarreling all day. Everybody's been quarreling. They're all worried about money. Mrs. Hutchinson's mother is dying of cancer in Florida and they don't have enough money to send her to the Mayo Clinic. At least, Mr. Hutchinson says they don't have enough money. And some woman in this building is having an affair with the handyman — with that hideous handyman. It's too disgusting. And Mrs. Melville has heart trouble and Mr. Hendricks is going to lose his job in April and Mrs. Hendricks is horrid about the whole thing and that girl who plays the 'Missouri Waltz' is a whore, a common whore, and the elevator man has tuberculosis and Mr. Osborn has been beating Mrs. Osborn." She wailed, she trembled with grief and checked the stream of tears down her face with the heel of her palm.

"Well, why do you have to listen?" Jim asked again. "Why do you have to listen to this stuff if it makes you so miserable?"

"Oh, don't, don't, don't," she cried. "Life is too terrible, too sordid and awful. But we've never been like that, have we, darling? Have we? I mean, we've always been good and decent and loving to one another, haven't we? And we have two children, two beautiful children. Our lives aren't sordid, are they, darling? Are they?" She flung her arms around his neck and drew his face down to hers. "We're happy, aren't we, darling? We are happy, aren't we?"

"Of course we're happy," he said tiredly. He began to surrender his resentment. "Of course we're happy. I'll have that damned radio fixed or taken away tomorrow." He stroked her soft hair. "My poor girl," he said.

"You love me, don't you?" she asked. "And we're not hypercritical or worried about money or dishonest, are we?"

"No, darling," he said. 45

A man came in the morning and fixed the radio. Irene turned it on cautiously and was happy to hear a California-wine commercial and a recording of Beethoven's Ninth Symphony, including Schiller's "Ode to Joy." She kept the radio on all day and nothing untoward came from the speaker.

A Spanish suite was being played when Jim came home. "Is everything all right?" he asked. His face was pale, she thought. They had some cocktails and went in to dinner to the "Anvil Chorus" from *Il Trovatore*. This was followed by Debussy's "La Mer."

"I paid the bill for the radio today," Jim said. "It cost four hundred dollars. I hope you'll get some enjoyment out of it."

"Oh, I'm sure I will," Irene said.

"Four hundred dollars is a good deal more than I can afford," he went 50 on. "I wanted to get something that you'd enjoy. It's the last extravagance we'll be able to indulge in this year. I see that you haven't paid your clothing bills yet. I saw them on your dressing table," He looked directly at her. "Why did you tell me you'd paid them? Why did you lie to me?"

"I just didn't want you to worry, Jim," she said. She drank some water. "I'll be able to pay my bills out of this month's allowance. There were the slipcovers last month, and that party."

"You've got to learn to handle the money I give you a little more intelligently, Irene," he said. "You've got to understand that we won't have as much money this year as we had last. I had a very sobering talk with Mitchell today. No one is buying anything. We're spending all our time promoting new issues, and you know how long that takes. I'm not getting any younger, you know. I'm thirty-seven. My hair will be gray next year. I haven't done as well as I'd hoped to do. And I don't suppose things will get any better."

"Yes, dear," she said.

"We've got to start cutting down," Jim said. "We've got to think of the children. To be perfectly frank with you, I worry about money a great deal. I'm not at all sure of the future. No one is. If anything should happen to me, there's the insurance, but that wouldn't go very far today. I've worked awfully hard to give you and the children a comfortable life," he said bitterly. "I don't like to see all of my energies, all of my youth, wasted in fur coats and radios and slipcovers and —"

"Please, Jim," she said. "Please. They'll hear us."   55

"*Who'll hear us?* Emma can't hear us."

"The radio."

"Oh, I'm sick!" he shouted. "I'm sick to death of your apprehensiveness. The radio can't hear us. Nobody can hear us. And what if they can hear us? Who cares?"

Irene got up from the table and went into the living room. Jim went to the door and shouted at her from there. "Why are you so Christly all of a sudden? What's turned you overnight into a convent girl? You stole your mother's jewelry before they probated her will. You never gave your sister a cent of that money that was intended for her — not even when she needed it. You made Grace Howland's life miserable, and where was all your piety and your virtue when you went to that abortionist? I'll never forget how cool you were. You packed your bag and went off to have that child murdered as if you were going to Nassau. If you'd had any reasons, if you'd had any good reasons —"

Irene stood for a minute before the hideous cabinet, disgraced and   60 sickened, but she held her hand on the switch before she extinguished the music and the voices, hoping that the instrument might speak to her kindly, that she might hear the Sweeneys' nurse. Jim continued to shout at her from the door. The voice on the radio was suave and noncommittal. "An early-morning railroad disaster in Tokyo," the loudspeaker said, "killed twenty-nine people. A fire in a Catholic hospital near Buffalo for the care of blind children was extinguished early this morning by nuns. The temperature is forty-seven. The humidity is eighty-nine."

CONSIDERATIONS FOR CRITICAL THINKING AND WRITING

1. FIRST RESPONSE. The story was published in 1947, long before the Internet Age. What parallels can you see between the enormous radio and contemporary technology (and average Americans' responses to it)?

2. The Westcotts are initially described in terms of their averageness. Why is that detail important to the story?

3. How is the radio described physically? What are the connotations of this description?

4. Examine the differences between the way Irene and Jim react to the radio as a way of scrutinizing 1940s gender roles and expectations.

5. When the Westcotts first figure out that they can hear the conversations of their neighbors through the radio, they are wary of it and Irene wants to turn it off. What causes them to change?

6. The maid (Emma) never speaks. Why is she integral to the story?

7. If the sordid stories of her neighbors' private lives depress Irene, why do you suppose she continues to listen to them?

8. What would you describe as the story's climax? Does it resolve the conflict? How?

SUGGESTION FOR CRITICAL ANALYSIS

1. Read the section on cultural criticism in Chapter 30, Critical Strategies for Reading (p. 1078). The immediate aftermath of World War II is often considered a time of tranquility and domestic harmony in the United States. Research the cultural history of the decade following the end of the war. How might the story be read as a critique of that era?

EDWIDGE DANTICAT (B. 1969)

Born in Port-au-Prince, Haiti, Edwige Danticat immigrated to the United States when she was twelve. She was influenced by Haitian storytelling as a youth and showed an interest in writing from a young age. She published her first work in English while still a teenager and went on to study

Agence Opale/Alamy Stock Photo.

writing as an undergraduate at Barnard College and to earn her M.F.A. at Brown University. Danticat is the author of over a dozen books, including story collections, young adult novels, novels, a memoir, and travel writing, and she has won many prestigious literary awards including the National Book Critics Circle Award. The following story is from her first collection, *Krik? Krak!* (1996), the title of which refers to the call a Haitian storyteller uses to get the audience's attention ("Krik?") and the audience's attentive response ("Krak!").

The Missing Peace 1996

We were playing with leaves shaped like butterflies. Raymond limped from the ashes of the old schoolhouse and threw himself on top of a high pile of dirt. The dust rose in clouds around him, clinging to the lapels of his khaki uniform.

"You should see the sunset from here." He grabbed my legs and pulled me down on top of him. The rusty grass brushed against my chin as I slipped out of his grasp.

I got up and tried to run to the other side of the field, but he caught both my legs and yanked me down again.

"Don't you feel like a woman when you are with me?" He tickled my neck. "Don't you feel beautiful?"

He let go of my waist as I turned over and laid flat on my back. The 5 sun was sliding behind the hills, and the glare made the rocks shimmer like chunks of gold.

"I know I can make you feel like a woman," he said, "so why don't you let me?"

"My grandmother says I can have babies."

"Forget your grandmother."

"Would you tell me again how you got your limp?" I asked to distract him.

It was a question he liked to answer, a chance for him to show his bravery. 10

"If I tell you, will you let me touch your breasts?"

"It is an insult that you are even asking."

"Will you let me do it?"

"You will never know unless you tell me the story."

He closed his eyes as though the details were never any farther than a 15 stage behind his eyelids.

I already knew the story very well.

"I was on guard one night," he said, taking a deep theatrical breath. "No one told me that there had been a coup in Port-au-Prince. I was still wearing my old régime uniform. My friend Toto from the youth corps says he didn't know if I was old régime or new régime. So he shot a warning at the uniform. Not at me, but at the uniform.

"The shots were coming fast. I was afraid. I forgot the password. Then one of Toto's bullets hit me on my leg and I remembered. I yelled out the password and he stopped shooting."

"Why didn't you take off your uniform?" I asked, laughing.

He ignored the question, letting his hand wander between the buttons 20 of my blouse.

"Do you remember the password?" he asked.

"Yes."

"I don't tell it to just anyone. Lean closer and whisper it in my ear."

I leaned real close and whispered the word in his ear.

"Don't ever forget it if you're in trouble. It could save your life," he said. 25

"I will remember."

"Tell me again what it is."

I swallowed a gulp of dusty air and said, "Peace."

A round of gunshots rang through the air, signaling that curfew was about to begin.

"I should go back now," I said.   30

He made no effort to get up, but raised his hand to his lips and blew me a kiss.

"Look after yourself tonight," I said.

"Peace."

On the way home, I cut through a line of skeletal houses that had been torched the night of the coup. A lot of the old régime followers died that night. Others fled to the hills or took boats to Miami.

I rushed past a churchyard, where the security officers sometimes bur-   35
ied the bodies of old régime people. The yard was bordered with a chain link fence. But every once in a while, if you looked very closely, you could see a bushy head of hair poking through the ground.

There was a bed of red hibiscus on the footpath behind the yard. Covering my nose, I pulled up a few stems and ran all the way home with them.

My grandmother was sitting in the rocking chair in front of our house, making knots in the sisal rope around her waist. She grabbed the hibiscus from my hand and threw them on the ground.

"How many times must I tell you?" she said. "Those things grow with blood on them." Pulling a leaf from my hair, she slapped me on the shoulder and shoved me inside the house.

"Somebody rented the two rooms in the yellow house," she said, saliva flying out from between her front teeth. "I want you to bring the lady some needles and thread."

My grandmother had fixed up the yellow house very nicely so that   40
many visitors who passed through Ville Rose came to stay in it. Sometimes our boarders were French and American journalists who wanted to take pictures of the churchyard where you could see the bodies.

I rushed out to my grandmother's garden, hoping to catch a glimpse of our new guest. Then I went over to the basin of rainwater in the yard and took off my clothes. My grandmother scrubbed a handful of mint leaves up and down my back as she ran a comb through my hair.

"It's a lady," said my grandmother. "Don't give her a headful of things to worry about. Things you say, thoughts you have, will decide how people treat you."

"Is the lady alone?"

"She is like all those foreign women. She feels she can be alone. And she smokes too." My grandmother giggled. "She smokes just like an old woman when life gets hard."

"She smokes a pipe?"

"Ladies her age don't smoke pipes."

"Cigarettes, then?"

"I don't want you to ask her to let you smoke any."

"Is she a journalist?" I asked.

"That is no concern of mine," my grandmother said.

"Is she intelligent?"

"Intelligence is not only in reading and writing."

"Is she old régime or new régime?"

"She is like us. The only régime she believe in is God's régime. She says she wants to write things down for posterity."

"What did you tell her when she said that?"

"That I already have posterity. I was once a baby and now I am an old woman. That is posterity."

"If she asks me questions, I am going to answer them," I said.

"One day you will stick your hand in a stew that will burn your fingers. I told her to watch her mouth as to how she talks to people. I told her to watch out for vagabonds like Toto and Raymond."

"Never look them in the eye."

"I told her that too," my grandmother said as she discarded the mint leaves.

My whole body felt taut and taint-free. My grandmother's face softened as she noticed the sheen of cleanliness.

"See, you can be a pretty girl," she said, handing me her precious pouch of needles, thimbles, and thread. "You can be a very pretty girl. Just like your mother used to be."

A burst of evening air chilled my face as I walked across to the yellow house. I was wearing my only Sunday outfit, a white lace dress that I had worn to my confirmation two years before.

The lady poked her head through the door after my first knock.

"Mademoiselle Gallant?"

"How do you know my name?"

"My grandmother sent me."

She was wearing a pair of *abakos,* American blue jeans.

"It looks as though your grandmother has put you to some inconvenience," she said. Then she led me into the front room, with its oversized mahogany chairs and a desk that my grandmother had bought especially for the journalists to use when they were working there.

"My name is really Emilie," she said in Creole, with a very heavy American accent. "What do people call you?"

"Lamort."

"How did your name come to be 'death'?"

"My mother died while I was being born," I explained. "My grandmother was really mad at me for that."

"They should have given you your mother's name," she said, taking the pouch of needles, thread, and thimbles from me. "That is the way it should have been done."

She walked over to the table in the corner and picked up a pitcher of lem- 75 onade that my grandmother made for all her guests when they first arrived.

"Would you like some?" she said, already pouring the lemonade.

"*Oui*, Madame. Please."

She held a small carton box of butter cookies in front of me. I took one, only one, just as my grandmother would have done.

"Are you a journalist?" I asked her.

"Why do you ask that?" 80

"The people who stay here in this house usually are, journalists."

She lit a cigarette. The smoke breezed in and out of her mouth, just like her own breath.

"I am not a journalist," she said. "I have come here to pay a little visit."

"Who are you visiting?"

"Just people." 85

"Why don't you stay with the people you are visiting?"

"I didn't want to bother them."

"Are they old régime or new régime?"

"Who?"

"Your people?" 90

"Why do you ask?"

"Because things you say, thoughts you have, will decide how people treat you."

"It seems to me, *you* are the journalist," she said.

"What do you believe in? Old régime or new régime?"

"Your grandmother told me to say to anyone who is interested, 'The 95 only régime I believe in is God's régime.' I would wager that you are a very good source for the journalists. Do you have any schooling?"

"A little."

Once again, she held the box of cookies in front of me. I took another cookie, but she kept the box there, in the same place. I took yet another cookie, and another, until the whole box was empty.

"Can you read what it says there?" she asked, pointing at a line of red letters.

"I cannot read American," I said. Though many of the journalists who came to stay at the yellow house had tried to teach me, I had not learned.

"It is not American," she said. "They are French cookies. That says *Le* 100 *Petit Ecolier*."

I stuffed my mouth in shame.

"Intelligence is not only in reading and writing," I said.

"I did not mean to make you feel ashamed," she said, dropping her cigarette into the half glass of lemonade in her hand. "I want to ask you a question."

"I will answer if I can."

"My mother was old régime," she said. "*She* was a journalist. For a newspaper called *Libèté* in Port-au-Prince."

"She came to Ville Rose?"

"Maybe. Or some other town. I don't know. The people who worked with her in Port-au-Prince think she might be in this region. Do you remember any shootings the night of the coup?"

"There were many shootings," I said.

"Did you see any of the bodies?"

"My grandmother and me, we stayed inside."

"Did a woman come to your door? Did anyone ever say that a woman in a purple dress came to their door?"

"No."

"I hear there is a mass burial site," she said. "Do you know it?"

"Yes. I have taken journalists there."

"I would like to go there. Can you take me?"

"Now?"

"Yes."

She pulled some coins from her purse and placed them on the table.

"I have more," she said.

From the back pocket of her jeans, she took out an envelope full of pictures. I ran my fingers over the glossy paper that froze her mother into all kinds of smiling poses: a skinny brown woman with shiny black hair in short spiral curls.

"I have never seen her," I admitted.

"It is possible that she arrived in the evening, and then the coup took place in the middle of the night. Do you know if they found any dead women the day after the coup?"

"There were no bodies," I said, "That is to say no funerals."

I heard my grandmother's footsteps even before she reached the door to the yellow house.

"If you tell her that I'm here, I can't go with you," I said.

"Go into the next room and stay there until I come for you."

My grandmother knocked once and then a second time. I rushed to the next room and crouched in a corner.

The plain white sheets that we usually covered the bed with had been replaced by a large piece of purple cloth. On the cement floor were many small pieces of cloth lined up in squares, one next to the other.

"Thank you for sending me the needles," I heard Emilie say to my grandmother. "I thought I had packed some in my suitcase, but I must have forgotten them."

"My old eyes are not what they used to be," my grandmother said, in the shy humble voice she reserved for prayers and for total strangers. "But if you need some mending, I can do it for you."

"Thank you," said Emilie, "but I can do the mending myself."

"Very well then. Is my granddaughter here?"

"She had to run off," Emilie said.

"Do you know where she went?"

"I don't know. She was dressed for a very fancy affair."   135

My grandmother was silent for a minute as her knuckles tapped the wood on the front door.

"I will let you rest now," said my grandmother.

"Thank you for the needles," said Emilie.

Emilie bolted the door after my grandmother had left.

"Is there a way we can leave without her seeing you?" She came into the   140
room with a flashlight and her American passport. "You might get a little beating when you go home."

"What are all these small pieces of cloth for?" I asked.

"I am going to sew them onto that purple blanket," she said. "All her life, my mother's wanted to sew some old things together onto that piece of purple cloth."

She raised a piece of white lace above her head. "That's from my mother's wedding dress."

Grabbing a piece of pink terry cloth, she said, "That's an old baby bib."

Tears were beginning to cloud her eyes. She fought them away fast by   145
pushing her head back.

"Purple," she said, "was Mama's favorite color."

"I can ask my grandmother if she saw your mother," I said.

"When I first came, this afternoon," she said, "I showed her the pictures and, like you, she said no."

"We would tell you if we had seen her."

"I want to go to the churchyard," she said. "You say you have already   150
taken other people there."

"I walk by it every day."

"Let's go then."

"Sometimes the yard's guarded at night," I warned her.

"I have an American passport. Maybe that will help."

"The soldiers don't know the difference. Most of them are like me.   155
They would not be able to identify your cookies either."

"How old are you?" she asked.

"Fourteen."

"At your age, you already have a wide reputation. I have a journalist friend who has stayed in this house. He told me you are the only person who would take me to the yard."

I could not think which particular journalist would have given me such a high recommendation, there had been so many.

"Better to be known for good than bad," I said to her.   160

"I am ready to go," she announced.

"If she is there, will you take her away?"

"Who?"

"Your mother?"

"I have not thought that far."   165

"And if you see them carrying her, what will you do? She will belong to them and not you."

"They say a girl becomes a woman when she loses her mother," she said. "You, child, were born a woman."

We walked through the footpath in my grandmother's garden, toward the main road.

"I have been having these awful dreams," Emilie whispered as she plucked some leaves off my grandmother's pumpkin vines. "I see my mother sinking into a river, and she keeps calling my name."

A round of gunshots echoed in the distance, signals from the night guards who had no other ways of speaking to one another.

We stopped on the side of the road and waited for a while and then continued on our way.

The night air blew the smell of rotting flesh to my nose. We circled the churchyard carefully before finding an entrance route. There was a rustle in the yard, like pieces of tin scraping the moist dirt.

"Who is there?"

I thought she stopped breathing when the voice echoed in the night air.

"I am an American journalist," Emilie said in breathless Creole.

She pulled out her passport and raised it toward a blinding flashlight beam. The guard moved the light away from our faces.

It was Raymond's friend, Toto, the one who had shot at him. He was tall and skinny and looked barely sixteen. He was staring at me as though he was possessed by a spirit. In the night, he did not know me.

He took Emilie's passport and flipped through it quickly.

"What are you doing here?" he asked, handing the passport back to her. "It is after curfew."

"The lady was not feeling well," I said. "So she asked me to take her for a walk."

"Didn't you hear the signals?" asked Toto. "The curfew has already started. You would not want to have blood on your nice communion dress."

Two other soldiers passed us on their way to the field. They were dragging the blood-soaked body of a bearded man with an old election slogan written on a T-shirt across his chest: ALONE WE ARE WEAK. TOGETHER WE ARE A FLOOD. The guards were carrying him, feet first, like a breech birth.

Emilie moved toward the body as though she wanted to see it better.

"You see nothing," Toto said, reaching up to turn Emilie's face. Her eyes twitched from Toto's touch on her cheek.

"Under God's sky, you do this to people!" she hollered in a brazen Creole.

Toto laughed loudly.

"We are doing that poor indigent a favor burying him," he said.

Emilie moved forward, trying to follow the guards taking the body into the yard.

"You see nothing," Toto said again, grabbing her face. She raised her arm as if to strike him. He seized her wrist in midair and whisked her hand behind her back.

"You see nothing," he said, his voice hissing between his teeth. "Repeat 190 after me. You see nothing."

"I see nothing," I said in her place. "The lady does not understand."

"I see you," she said in Creole. "How can that be nothing?"

"Peace, let her go," I said.

"You are a coward," she told him.

He lowered his head so he was staring directly into her eyes. He twisted 195 her arm like a wet rag.

"Peace, have mercy on her," I said.

"Let her ask for herself," he said.

She stamped her feet on his boots. He let go of her hand and tapped his rifle on her shoulder. Emilie looked up at him, angry and stunned. He moved back, aiming his rifle at her head, squinting as though he was going to shoot.

"Peace!" I hollered.

My eyes fell on Raymond's as he walked out of the field. I mouthed the 200 word, pleading for help. *Peace. Peace. Peace.*

"They'll go," Raymond said to Toto.

"Then go!" Toto shouted. "Let me watch you go."

"Let's go," I said to Emilie. "My grandmother will be mad at me if I get killed."

Raymond walked behind us as we went back to the road.

"The password has changed," he said. "Stop saying 'peace.'" 205

By the time I turned around to look at his face, he was already gone.

Emilie and I said nothing to each other on the way back. The sound of bullets continued to ring through the night.

"You never look them in the eye," I told her when we got to the yellow house doorstep.

"Is that how you do it?"

I helped her up the steps and into the house. 210

"I am going to sew these old pieces of cloth onto my mother's blanket tonight," she said.

She took a needle from my grandmother's bundle and began sewing. Her fingers moved quickly as she stitched the pieces together.

"I should go," I said, eyeing the money still on the table.

"Please, stay. I will pay you more if you stay with me until the morning."

"My grandmother will worry." 215

"What was your mother's name?" she asked.

"Marie Magdalène," I said.

"They should have given you that name instead of the one you got. Was your mother pretty?"

"I don't know. She never took portraits like the ones you have of yours."

"Did you know those men who were in the yard tonight?"

"Yes."

"I didn't fight them because I didn't want to make trouble for you later," she said. "We should write down their names. For posterity."

"We have already had posterity," I said.

"When?"

"We were babies and we grew old."

"You're still young," she said. "You're not old."

"My grandmother is old for me."

"If she is old for you, then doesn't it matter if you get old? You can't say that. You can't just say what she wants for you to say. I didn't get in a fight with them because I did not want them to hurt you," she said.

"I will stay with you," I said, "because I know you are afraid."

I curled my body on the floor next to her and went to sleep.

She had the patches sewn together on the purple blanket when I woke up that morning. On the floor, scattered around her, were the pictures of her mother.

"I became a woman last night," she said. "I lost my mother and all my other dreams."

Her voice was weighed down with pain and fatigue. She picked up the coins from the table, added a dollar from her purse, and pressed the money into my palm.

"Will you whisper their names in my ear?" she asked. "I will write them down."

"There is Toto," I said. "He is the one that hit you."

"And the one who followed us?"

"That is Raymond who loves leaves shaped like butterflies."

She jotted their names on the back of one of her mother's pictures and gave it to me.

"My mother's name was Isabelle," she said, "keep this for posterity."

Outside, the morning sun was coming out to meet the day. Emilie sat on the porch and watched me go to my grandmother's house. Loosely sewn, the pieces on the purple blanket around her shoulders were coming apart.

My grandmother was sitting in front of the house waiting for me. She did not move when she saw me. Nor did she make a sound.

"Today, I want you to call me by another name," I said.

"Haughty girls don't get far," she said, rising from the chair.

"I want you to call me by her name," I said.

She looked pained as she watched me moving closer to her.

"Marie Magdalène?"

"Yes, Marie Magdalène," I said. "I want you to call me Marie Magdalène." I liked the sound of that.

CONSIDERATIONS FOR CRITICAL THINKING AND WRITING

1. FIRST RESPONSE. Explore Danticat's use of the word *Peace* both in the title and throughout the story.

2. Lamort has Raymond tell his war story even though she has heard it before: Why?

3. Characterize the relationship between *Raymond and Lamort.*

4. Describe the relationship between nature and the war-torn landscape in this story.

5. Lamort's grandmother speaks in proverbs. How do you understand the fact that Lamort repeats some of them?

6. Lamort's name means "death" in French, as Emilie points out, and yet it can also sound like *l'amour,* which means "love." How does this paradox complicate her character?

7. What do gunshots signify at different points in the story?

8. Why is it significant that Lamort compares the blood-soaked body of a dead man being dragged by soldiers to a "breach birth?"

9. What are the various definitions of womanhood in the story? Is it possible to reconcile them?

10. Lamort concludes the story by asking to be renamed. What is the significance of names and naming throughout the story?

11. Emilie claims that she has lost her dreams after her confrontation with the soldier Toto. Is she defeated or does the phrase mean something else in the context of the story?

CONNECTION TO ANOTHER SELECTION

1. Discuss growth and maturity in the context of war in this story and in Kurt Vonnegut's "Happy Birthday, 1951" (p. 353).

DAGOBERTO GILB

Love in L.A. 1993

Jake slouched in a clot of near motionless traffic, in the peculiar gray of concrete, smog, and early morning beneath the overpass of the Hollywood Freeway on Alvarado Street. He didn't really mind because he knew how much worse it could be trying to make a left onto the onramp. He certainly didn't do that every day of his life, and he'd assure anyone who'd ask that he never would either. A steady occupation had its advantages and he couldn't deny thinking about that too. He needed an FM radio in something better than this '58 Buick he drove. It would have crushed velvet interior with electric controls for the L.A. summer, a nice warm heater and defroster for the winter drives at the beach, a cruise control for those longer trips, mellow speakers front and rear of course, windows that hum closed, snuffing out that nasty exterior noise of freeways. The fact was that he'd probably have to change his whole style. Exotic colognes, plush, dark nightclubs, maitais and daiquiris, necklaced ladies in satin gowns, misty and sexy like in a tequila ad. Jake could imagine lots of possibilities when he let himself, but none that ended up with him pressed onto a stalled freeway.

Jake was thinking about this freedom of his so much that when he glimpsed its green light he just went ahead and stared bye bye to the steadily employed. When he turned his head the same direction his windshield faced, it was maybe one second too late. He pounced the brake pedal and steered the front wheels away from the tiny brakelights but the smack was unavoidable. Just one second sooner and it would only have been close. One second more and he'd be crawling up the Toyota's trunk. As it was, it seemed like only a harmless smack, much less solid than the one against his back bumper.

Jake considered driving past the Toyota but was afraid the traffic ahead would make it too difficult. As he pulled up against the curb a few carlengths ahead, it occurred to him that the traffic might have helped him get away too. He slammed the car door twice to make sure it was closed fully and to give himself another second more, then toured front and rear of his Buick for damage on or near the bumpers. Not an impressionable scratch even in the chrome. He perked up. Though the car's beauty was secondary to its ability to start and move, the body and paint were clean except for a few minor dings. This stood out as one of his few clearcut accomplishments over the years.

Before he spoke to the driver of the Toyota, whose looks he could see might present him with an added complication, he signaled to the driver of the car that hit him, still in his car and stopped behind the Toyota, and waved his hands and shook his head to let the man know there was no problem as far as he was concerned. The driver waved back and started his engine.

"It didn't even scratch my paint," Jake told her in that way of his. "So ⁵ how you doin? Any damage to the car? I'm kinda hoping so, just so it takes a little more time and we can talk some. Or else you can give me your phone number now and I won't have to lay my regular b.s. on you to get it later."

He took her smile as a good sign and relaxed. He inhaled her scent like it was clean air and straightened out his less than new but not unhip clothes.

"You've got Florida plates. You look like you must be Cuban."

"My parents are from Venezuela."

"My name's Jake." He held out his hand.

"Mariana."   10

They shook hands like she'd never done it before in her life.

"I really am sorry about hitting you like that." He sounded genuine. He fondled the wide dimple near the cracked taillight. "It's amazing how easy it is to put a dent in these new cars. They're so soft they might replace waterbeds soon." Jake was confused about how to proceed with this. So much seemed so unlikely, but there was always possibility. "So maybe we should go out to breakfast somewhere and talk it over."

"I don't eat breakfast."

"Some coffee then."

"Thanks, but I really can't."   15

"You're not married, are you? Not that that would matter that much to me. I'm an openminded kinda guy."

She was smiling. "I have to get to work."

"That sounds boring."

"I better get your driver's license," she said.

Jake nodded, disappointed. "One little problem," he said. "I didn't bring   20 it. I just forgot it this morning. I'm a musician," he exaggerated greatly, "and, well, I dunno, I left my wallet in the pants I was wearing last night. If you have some paper and a pen I'll give you my address and all that."

He followed her to the glove compartment side of her car.

"What if we don't report it to the insurance companies? I'll just get it fixed for you."

"I don't think my dad would let me do that."

"Your dad? It's not your car?"

"He bought it for me. And I live at home."   25

"Right." She was slipping away from him. He went back around to the back of her new Toyota and looked over the damage again. There was the trunk lid, the bumper, a rear panel, a taillight.

"You do have insurance?" she asked, suspicious, as she came around the back of the car.

"Oh yeah," he lied.

"I guess you better write the name of that down too."

He made up a last name and address and wrote down the name of   30 an insurance company an old girlfriend once belonged to. He considered giving a real phone number but went against that idea and made one up.

"I act too," he lied to enhance the effect more. "Been in a couple of movies."

She smiled like a fan.

"So how about your phone number?" He was rebounding maturely.

She gave it to him.

"Mariana, you are beautiful," he said in his most sincere voice.   35

"Call me," she said timidly.

Jake beamed. "We'll see you, Mariana," he said holding out his hand. Her hand felt so warm and soft he felt like he'd been kissed.

Back in his car he took a moment or two to feel both proud and sad about his performance. Then he watched the rear view mirror as Mariana pulled up behind him. She was writing down the license plate numbers on his Buick, ones that he'd taken off a junk because the ones that belonged to his had expired so long ago. He turned the ignition key and revved the big engine and clicked into drive. His sense of freedom swelled as he drove into the now moving street traffic, though he couldn't stop the thought about that FM stereo radio and crushed velvet interior and the new car smell that would even make it better.

CONSIDERATIONS FOR CRITICAL THINKING AND WRITING

1. FIRST RESPONSE. From the title on, the setting (Los Angeles) seems important. In what specific ways does the setting frame the story's themes?

2. How would you describe the story's conflict? Is there more than one?

3. Jake's fantasy about a better car with an FM radio and crushed velvet interior exists both at the beginning and end of the story. How does it guide you toward understanding the story's main concerns?

4. Why does Mariana trust Jake? Are there significant details that indicate that her trust in him is not absolute?

5. At what specific point does your trust in Jake falter?

6. Jake lies, he has put fake license plates on his car, he is a cad, and he is generally only concerned about himself. Is there anything about him that invites your sympathy as a reader?

7. Discuss the length of the story as a component of the way it achieves its effects.

8. How do you understand the word "love" in the title?

9. Jake seems observant and able to size up situations quickly. How do those qualities connect to the central action of the story — a car accident that is caused by his inattention?

CONNECTION TO ANOTHER SELECTION

1. Compare your level of sympathy between Jake in this story and the father in Tobias Wolff's "Powder" (p. 56). What factors contribute most to your assessment?

JAMES JOYCE

Eveline 1914

James Joyce (1882–1941) is considered one of the most important and most challenging writers of the twentieth century. Born in Dublin at a time when the literary/artistic movement known as Modernism was about to change radically the possibilities of art in modern society, Joyce was keenly aware of how traditional Irish culture and the Catholic church that underpinned it were a threat to individual freedom and national progress. His fiction — beginning with the story collection *Dubliners* in 1914, which contains the following story "Eveline" — takes place exclusively in Ireland, but all of it was written during his exile abroad which began in 1904 in European cities like Zurich, Trieste, and Paris and lasted the rest of his life. His most important work is the novel *Ulysses* (1922), a narrative tour-de-force that takes place over the course of an ordinary day in the life of Dubliner Leopold Bloom, but understands the small motions of that life in the context of Homer's epic *Odysseus*. Much of his fiction, including the following story, can be viewed as a variation on the theme of flight and return that governs Homer's epic and that was replicated in Joyce's life.

She sat at the window watching the evening invade the avenue. Her head was leaned against the window curtains and in her nostrils was the odor of dusty cretonne. She was tired.

Few people passed. The man out of the last house passed on his way home; she heard his footsteps clacking along the concrete pavement and afterwards crunching on the cinder path before the new red houses. One time there used to be a field there in which they used to play every evening with other people's children. Then a man from Belfast bought the field and built houses in it — not like their little brown houses but bright brick houses with shining roofs. The children of the avenue used to play together in that field — the Devines, the Waters, the Dunns, little Keogh the cripple, she and her brothers and sisters. Ernest, however, never played: he was too grown up. Her father was not so bad then; and besides, her mother was alive. That thorn stick; but usually little Keogh used to keep *nix* and call out when he saw her father coming. Still they seemed to have been rather happy then. Her father was not so bad then; and besides, her mother was alive. That was a long time ago; she and her brothers and sisters were all grown up; her mother was dead. Tizzie Dunn was dead, too, and the Waters had gone back to England. Everything changes. Now she was going to go away like the others, to leave her home.

Home! She looked round the room, reviewing all its familiar objects which she had dusted once a week for so many years, wondering where on earth all the dust came from. Perhaps she would never see again those familiar objects from which she had never dreamed of being divided. And yet during all those years she had never found out the name of the priest whose yellowing photograph hung on the wall above the broken harmonium beside the colored print of the promises made to Blessed Margaret Mary Alacoque. He had been a school friend of her father. Whenever he showed the photograph to a visitor her father used to pass it with a casual word:

— He is in Melbourne now.

She had consented to go away, to leave her home. Was that wise? She 5
tried to weigh each side of the question. In her home anyway she had shelter and food; she had those whom she had known all her life about her. Of course she had to work hard both in the house and at business. What would they say of her in the Stores when they found out that she had run away with a fellow? Say she was a fool, perhaps; and her place would be filled up by advertisement. Miss Gavan would be glad. She had always had an edge on her, especially whenever there were people listening.

— Miss Hill, don't you see these ladies are waiting?

— Look lively, Miss Hill, please.

She would not cry many tears at leaving the Stores.

But in her new home, in a distant unknown country, it would not be like that. Then she would be married — she, Eveline. People would treat her with respect then. She would not be treated as her mother had been. Even now, though she was over nineteen, she sometimes felt herself in danger of her father's violence. She knew it was that that had given her the palpitations. When they were growing up he had never gone for her, like he used to go for Harry and Ernest, because she was a girl; but latterly he had begun to threaten her and say what he would do to her only for her dead mother's sake. And now she had nobody to protect her. Ernest was dead and Harry, who was in the church decorating business, was nearly always down somewhere in the country. Besides, the invariable squabble for money on Saturday nights had begun to weary her unspeakably. She always gave her entire wages — seven shillings — and Harry always sent up what he could but the trouble was to get any money from her father. He said she used to squander the money, that she had no head, that he wasn't going to give her his hard-earned money to throw about the streets, and much more, for he was usually fairly bad of a Saturday night. In the end he would give her the money and ask her had she any intention of buying Sunday's dinner. Then she had to rush out as quickly as she could and do her marketing, holding her black leather purse tightly in her hand as she elbowed her way through the crowds and returning home late under her load of provisions. She had hard work to keep the house together and to see that the two young children who had been left to her charge went to school regularly and got their meals regularly. It was hard work — a hard life — but now that she was about to leave it she did not find it a wholly undesirable life.

She was about to explore another life with Frank. Frank was very kind, manly, open-hearted. She was to go away with him by the night-boat to be his wife and to live with him in Buenos Aires where he had a home waiting for her. How well she remembered the first time she had seen him; he was lodging in a house on the main road where she used to visit. It seemed a few weeks ago. He was standing at the gate, his peaked cap pushed back on his head and his hair tumbled forward over a face of bronze. Then they had come to know each other. He used to meet her outside the Stores every evening and see her home. He took her to see *The Bohemian Girl* and she felt elated as she sat in an unaccustomed part of the theater with him. He was awfully fond of music and sang a little. People knew that they were courting and, when he sang about the lass that loves a sailor, she always felt pleasantly confused. He used to call her Poppens out of fun. First of all it had been an excitement for her to have a fellow and then she had begun to like him. He had tales of distant countries. He had started as a deck boy at a pound a month on a ship of the Allan Line going out to Canada. He told her the names of the ships he had been on and the names of the different services. He had sailed through the Straits of Magellan and he told her stories of the terrible Patagonians. He had fallen on his feet in Buenos Aires, he said, and had come over to the old country just for a holiday. Of course, her father had found out the affair and had forbidden her to have anything to say to him.

—I know these sailor chaps, he said.

One day he had quarreled with Frank and after that she had to meet her lover secretly.

The evening deepened in the avenue. The white of two letters in her lap grew indistinct. One was to Harry; the other was to her father. Ernest had been her favorite but she liked Harry too. Her father was becoming old lately, she noticed; he would miss her. Sometimes he could be very nice. Not long before, when she had been laid up for a day, he had read her out a ghost story and made toast for her at the fire. Another day, when their mother was alive, they had all gone for a picnic to the Hill of Howth. She remembered her father putting on her mother's bonnet to make the children laugh.

Her time was running out but she continued to sit by the window, leaning her head against the window curtain, inhaling the odor of dusty cretonne. Down far in the avenue she could hear a street organ playing. She knew the air. Strange that it should come that very night to remind her of the promise to her mother, her promise to keep the home together as long as she could. She remembered the last night of her mother's illness; she was again in the close dark room at the other side of the hall and outside she heard a melancholy air of Italy. The organ-player had been ordered to go away and given sixpence. She remembered her father strutting back into the sickroom saying:

—Damned Italians! coming over here!   15

As she mused the pitiful vision of her mother's life laid its spell on the very quick of her being — that life of commonplace sacrifices closing in final craziness. She trembled as she heard again her mother's voice saying constantly with foolish insistence:

—Derevaun Seraun! Derevaun Seraun!°

She stood up in a sudden impulse of terror. Escape! She must escape! Frank would save her. He would give her life, perhaps love, too. But she wanted to live. Why should she be unhappy? She had a right to happiness. Frank would take her in his arms, fold her in his arms. He would save her.

She stood among the swaying crowd in the station at the North Wall. He held her hand and she knew that he was speaking to her, saying something about the passage over and over again. The station was full of soldiers with brown baggages. Through the wide doors of the sheds she caught a glimpse of the black mass of the boat, lying in beside the quay wall, with illumined portholes. She answered nothing. She felt her cheek pale and cold and, out of a maze of distress, she prayed to God to direct her, to show her what was her duty. The boat blew a long mournful whistle into the mist. If she went, tomorrow she would be on the sea with Frank, steaming toward Buenos Aires. Their passage had been booked. Could she still draw back after all he had done for her? Her distress awoke a nausea in her body and she kept moving her lips in silent fervent prayer.

A bell clanged upon her heart. She felt him seize her hand: 20

—Come!

Derevaun Seraun!: "The end of pleasure is pain!" (Gaelic).

All the seas of the world tumbled about her heart. He was drawing her into them: he would drown her. She gripped with both hands at the iron railing.

— Come!

No! No! No! It was impossible. Her hands clutched the iron in frenzy. Amid the seas she sent a cry of anguish!

— Eveline! Evvy!

He rushed beyond the barrier and called to her to follow. He was shouted at to go on but he still called to her. She set her white face to him, passive, like a helpless animal. Her eyes gave him no sign of love or farewell or recognition.

CONSIDERATIONS FOR CRITICAL THINKING AND WRITING

1. FIRST RESPONSE. Explain why you approve or disapprove of Eveline's decision.

2. Describe the character of Eveline. What do you think she looks like? Though there are no physical details about her in the story, write a one-page description of her as you think she would appear at the beginning of the story looking out the window.

3. Describe the physical setting of Eveline's home. How does she feel about living at home?

4. What sort of relationship does Eveline have with her father? Describe the range of her feelings toward him.

5. How is Frank characterized? Why does Eveline's father forbid them to see each other?

6. Why does thinking of her mother make Eveline want to "escape"?

7. Before she meets him at the dock, how does Eveline expect Frank to change her life?

8. Why doesn't she go with Frank to Buenos Aires?

9. What associations do you have about Buenos Aires and Dublin? What symbolic value does this Argentine city have in the story from the vantage point of Ireland?

10. Read carefully the water imagery in the final paragraphs of the story. How does this imagery help to suggest Eveline's reasons for not leaving with Frank?

CONNECTIONS TO OTHER SELECTIONS

1. How does Eveline's response to her life at home compare with that of the young man in Manuel Muñoz's "Zigzagger" (p. 143)? Write an essay that explores the similarities and differences in their efforts to escape to something better.

2. Write an essay about the meaning of "home" to the protagonists in "Eveline" and Ernest Hemingway's "Soldier's Home" (p. 104).

JAMAICA KINCAID (B. 1949)

Trix Rosen.

Jamaica Kincaid was born Elaine Potter Richardson on the Caribbean island of Antigua. She moved to New York in 1965 to work as an au pair, studied photography at both the New School for Social Research and Franconia College, and changed her name to Jamaica Kincaid in 1973 with her first publication, "When I Was 17," a series of interviews. Over the next few years, she wrote for the *New Yorker* magazine, first as a free-lancer and then as a staff writer. In 1978, Kincaid wrote her first piece of fiction, "Girl," published in the *New Yorker* and included in her debut short story collection, *At the Bottom of the River* (1983), which won an award from the Academy and Institute of Arts and Letters and was nominated for the PEN/Faulkner Award. Her other work includes *Annie John* (1985), *Lucy* (1990), *Autobiography of My Mother* (1994), *See Now Then* (2013), *Mr. Potter* (2002), and three nonfiction books, *A Small Place* (1988), *My Brother* (1997), and *Among Flowers: A Walk in the Himalaya* (2005). Whether autobiographical fiction or nonfiction, her work usually focuses on the perils of postcolonial society, paralleled by an examination of rifts in mother-daughter relationships.

Girl   1978

Wash the white clothes on Monday and put them on the stone heap; wash the color clothes on Tuesday and put them on the clothesline to dry; don't walk barehead in the hot sun; cook pumpkin fritters in very hot sweet oil; soak your little cloths right after you take them off; when buying cotton to make yourself a nice blouse, be sure that it doesn't have gum on it, because that way it won't hold up well after a wash; soak salt fish overnight before you cook it; is it true that you sing benna° in Sunday school?; always eat your food in such a way that it won't turn someone else's stomach; on Sundays try to walk like a lady and not like the slut you are so bent on becoming; don't sing benna in Sunday school; you mustn't speak to wharf-rat boys, not even to give directions; don't eat fruits on the street — flies will follow you; *but I don't sing benna on Sundays at all and never in Sunday school*; this is how to sew on a button; this is how to make a buttonhole for the button you have just sewed on; this is how to hem a dress when you see the hem coming down and so to prevent yourself from looking like the slut I know you are so bent on

benna: Calypso music.

becoming; this is how you iron your father's khaki shirt so that it doesn't have a crease; this is how you iron your father's khaki pants so that they don't have a crease; this is how you grow okra — far from the house, because okra tree harbors red ants; when you are growing dasheen,° make sure it gets plenty of water or else it makes your throat itch when you are eating it; this is how you sweep a corner; this is how you sweep a whole house; this is how you sweep a yard; this is how you smile to someone you don't like too much; this is how you smile to someone you don't like at all; this is how you smile to someone you like completely; this is how you set a table for tea; this is how you set a table for dinner; this is how you set a table for dinner with an important guest; this is how you set a table for lunch; this is how you set a table for breakfast; this is how to behave in the presence of men who don't know you very well, and this way they won't recognize immediately the slut I have warned you against becoming; be sure to wash every day, even if it is with your own spit; don't squat down to play marbles — you are not a boy, you know; don't pick people's flowers — you might catch something; don't throw stones at blackbirds, because it might not be a blackbird at all; this is how to make a bread pudding; this is how to make doukona;° this is how to make pepper pot;° this is how to make a good medicine for a cold; this is how to make a good medicine to throw away a child before it even becomes a child; this is how to catch a fish; this is how to throw back a fish you don't like, and that way something bad won't fall on you; this is how to bully a man; this is how a man bullies you; this is how to love a man, and if this doesn't work there are other ways, and if they don't work don't feel too bad about giving up; this is how to spit up in the air if you feel like it, and this is how to move quick so that it doesn't fall on you; this is how to make ends meet; always squeeze bread to make sure it's fresh; *but what if the baker won't let me feel the bread?*; you mean to say that after all you are really going to be the kind of woman who the baker won't let near the bread?

dasheen: The edible rootstock of taro, a tropical plant.
doukona: A spicy plantain pudding.
pepper pot: A stew.

CONSIDERATIONS FOR CRITICAL THINKING AND WRITING

1. FIRST RESPONSE. Explain whether or not the "Girl" is the protagonist or antagonist in this story.
2. Consider whether the mother is a stock or round character.
3. What details indicate the nature of the mother's advice? How would you describe her perceptions of her daughter?
4. How does the mother inadvertently reveal and characterize herself?
5. Describe the daughter's responses to the mother's admonitions.
6. CREATIVE RESPONSE. Write a one-paragraph response to the mother from the daughter's perspective.

CONNECTION TO ANOTHER SELECTION

1. Compare the teenager's relationship to authority in Kincaid's story and in John Updike's "A & P" (p. 138).

JHUMPA LAHIRI (B. 1967)

Born in London to Indian emigrant parents, Jhumpa Lahiri moved to the United States when she was two, and has since moved to Rome. She still spends part of her time in the United States as a professor of creative writing at Princeton University. Not surprisingly, her fiction is often about the experience of adapting to new cultures and situations. Lahiri is rare, if not unique, in American literary history in that her first book won the Pulitzer Prize for fiction. That book, the story collection *Interpreter of Maladies* (1999), included the following story, "Sexy." Lahiri has since published another collection of stories (*Unaccustomed Earth*, 2008) and three novels, the most recent (*Dove mi Trovo*, 2018) in Italian. She has also published two works of nonfiction in Italian and has translated multiple Italian works.

Sexy 1999

It was a wife's worst nightmare. After nine years of marriage, Laxmi told Miranda, her cousin's husband had fallen in love with another woman. He sat next to her on a plane, on a flight from Delhi to Montreal, and instead of flying home to his wife and son, he got off with the woman at Heathrow. He called his wife, and told her he'd had a conversation that had changed his life, and that he needed time to figure things out. Laxmi's cousin had taken to her bed.

"Not that I blame her," Laxmi said. She reached for the Hot Mix she munched throughout the day, which looked to Miranda like dusty orange cereal. "Imagine. An English girl, half his age." Laxmi was only a few years older than Miranda, but she was already married, and kept a photo of herself and her husband, seated on a white stone bench in front of the Taj Mahal, tacked to the inside of her cubicle, which was next to Miranda's. Laxmi had been on the phone for at least an hour, trying to calm her cousin down. No one noticed; they worked for a public radio station, in the fund-raising department, and were surrounded by people who spent all day on the phone, soliciting pledges.

"I feel worst for the boy," Laxmi added. "He's been at home for days. My cousin said she can't even take him to school."

"It sounds awful," Miranda said. Normally Laxmi's phone conversations — mainly to her husband, about what to cook for dinner — distracted Miranda as she typed letters, asking members of the radio station to increase their annual pledge in exchange for a tote bag or an umbrella. She could hear Laxmi clearly, her sentences peppered every now and then with an Indian word, through the laminated wall between their desks. But that afternoon Miranda hadn't been listening. She'd been on the phone herself, with Dev, deciding where to meet later that evening.

"Then again, a few days at home won't hurt him." Laxmi ate some more 5 Hot Mix, then put it away in a drawer, "He's something of a genius. He has a Punjabi mother and a Bengali father, and because he learns French and English at school he already speaks four languages. I think he skipped two grades."

Dev was Bengali, too. At first Miranda thought it was a religion. But then he pointed it out to her, a place in India called Bengal, in a map printed in an issue of *The Economist*. He had brought the magazine specially to her apartment, for she did not own an atlas, or any other books with maps in them. He'd pointed to the city where he'd been born, and another city where his father had been born. One of the cities had a box around it, intended to attract the reader's eye. When Miranda asked what the box indicated, Dev rolled up the magazine, and said, "Nothing you'll ever need to worry about," and he tapped her playfully on the head.

Before leaving her apartment he'd tossed the magazine in the garbage, along with the ends of the three cigarettes he always smoked in the course of his visits. But after she watched his car disappear down Commonwealth Avenue, back to his house in the suburbs, where he lived with his wife, Miranda retrieved it, and brushed the ashes off the cover, and rolled it in the opposite direction to get it to lie flat. She got into bed, still rumpled from their lovemaking, and studied the borders of Bengal. There was a bay below and mountains above. The map was connected to an article about something called the Gramin Bank. She turned the page, hoping for a photograph of the city where Dev was born, but all she found were graphs and grids. Still, she stared at them, thinking the whole while about Dev, about how only fifteen minutes ago he'd propped her feet on top of his shoulders, and pressed her knees to her chest, and told her that he couldn't get enough of her.

She'd met him a week ago, at Filene's. She was there on her lunch break, buying discounted pantyhose in the Basement. Afterward she took the escalator to the main part of the store, to the cosmetics department, where soaps and creams were displayed like jewels, and eye shadows and powders shimmered like butterflies pinned behind protective glass. Though Miranda had never bought anything other than a lipstick, she liked walking through the cramped, confined maze, which was familiar to her in a way the rest of Boston still was not. She liked negotiating her way past the women planted at every turn, who sprayed cards with perfume and waved them in the air; sometimes she would find a card days afterward, folded in her coat pocket, and the rich aroma, still faintly preserved, would warm her as she waited on cold mornings for the T.

That day, stopping to smell one of the more pleasing cards, Miranda noticed a man standing at one of the counters. He held a slip of paper covered in a precise, feminine hand. A saleswoman took one look at the paper and began to open drawers. She produced an oblong cake of soap in a black case, a hydrating mask, a vial of cell renewal drops, and two tubes of face cream. The man was tanned, with black hair that was visible on his knuckles. He wore a flamingo pink shirt, a navy blue suit, a camel overcoat with gleaming leather buttons. In order to pay he had taken off pigskin gloves. Crisp bills emerged from a burgundy wallet. He didn't wear a wedding ring.

"What can I get you, honey?" the saleswoman asked Miranda. She looked 10 over the tops of her tortoiseshell glasses, assessing Miranda's complexion.

Miranda didn't know what she wanted. All she knew was that she didn't want the man to walk away. He seemed to be lingering, waiting, along with the saleswoman, for her to say something. She stared at some bottles, some short, others tall, arranged on an oval tray, like a family posing for a photograph.

"A cream," Miranda said eventually.

"How old are you?"

"Twenty-two."

The saleswoman nodded, opening a frosted bottle. "This may seem a 15 bit heavier than what you're used to, but I'd start now. All your wrinkles are going to form by twenty-five. After that they just start showing."

While the saleswoman dabbed the cream on Miranda's face, the man stood and watched. While Miranda was told the proper way to apply it, in swift upward strokes beginning at the base of her throat, he spun the lipstick carousel. He pressed a pump that dispensed cellulite gel and massaged it into the back of his ungloved hand. He opened a jar, leaned over, and drew so close that a drop of cream flecked his nose.

Miranda smiled, but her mouth was obscured by a large brush that the saleswoman was sweeping over her face. "This is blusher Number Two," the woman said. "Gives you some color."

Miranda nodded, glancing at her reflection in one of the angled mirrors that lined the counter. She had silver eyes and skin as pale as paper, and the contrast with her hair, as dark and glossy as an espresso bean, caused people to describe her as striking, if not pretty. She had a narrow, egg-shaped head that rose to a prominent point. Her features, too, were narrow, with nostrils so slim that they appeared to have been pinched with a clothespin. Now her face glowed, rosy at the cheeks, smoky below the brow bone. Her lips glistened.

The man was glancing in a mirror, too, quickly wiping the cream from his nose. Miranda wondered where he was from. She thought he might be Spanish, or Lebanese. When he opened another jar, and said, to no one in particular, "This one smells like pineapple," she detected only the hint of an accent.

"Anything else for you today?" the saleswoman asked, accepting Miran- 20 da's credit card.

"No thanks."

The woman wrapped the cream in several layers of red tissue. "You'll be very happy with this product." Miranda's hand was unsteady as she signed the receipt. The man hadn't budged.

"I threw in a sample of our new eye gel," the saleswoman added, handing Miranda a small shopping bag. She looked at Miranda's credit card before sliding it across the counter, "Bye-bye, Miranda."

Miranda began walking. At first she sped up. Then, noticing the doors that led to Downtown Crossing, she slowed down.

"Part of your name is Indian," the man said, pacing his steps with hers. 25

She stopped, as did he, at a circular table piled with sweaters, flanked with pinecones and velvet bows. "Miranda?"

"Mira. I have an aunt named Mira."

His name was Dev. He worked in an investment bank back that way, he said, tilting his head in the direction of South Station, He was the first man with a mustache, Miranda decided, she found handsome.

They walked together toward Park Street station, past the kiosks that sold cheap belts and handbags. A fierce January wind spoiled the part in her hair. As she fished for a token in her coat pocket, her eyes fell to his shopping bag. "And those are for her?"

"Who?"

"Your Aunt Mira."

"They're for my wife." He uttered the words slowly, holding Miranda's gaze. "She's going to India for a few weeks." He rolled his eyes. "She's addicted to this stuff."

30

Somehow, without the wife there, it didn't seem so wrong. At first Miranda and Dev spent every night together, almost. He explained that he couldn't spend the whole night at her place, because his wife called every day at six in the morning, from India, where it was four in the afternoon. And so he left her apartment at two, three, often as late as four in the morning, driving back to his house in the suburbs. During the day he called her every hour, it seemed, from work, or from his cell phone. Once he learned Miranda's schedule he left her a message each evening at five-thirty, when she was on the T coming back to her apartment, just so, he said, she could hear his voice as soon as she walked through the door. "I'm thinking about you," he'd say on the tape. "I can't wait to see you." He told her he liked spending time in her apartment, with its kitchen counter no wider than a breadbox, and scratchy floors that sloped, and a buzzer in the lobby that always made a slightly embarrassing sound when he pressed it. He said he admired her for moving to Boston, where he knew no one, instead of remaining in Michigan, where she'd grown up and gone to college. When Miranda told him it was nothing to admire, that she'd moved to Boston precisely for that reason, he shook his head. "I know what it's like to be lonely," he said, suddenly serious, and at that moment Miranda felt that he understood her — understood how she felt some nights on the T, after seeing a movie on her own, or going to a bookstore to read magazines, or having drinks with Laxmi, who always had to meet her husband at Alewife station in an hour or two. In less serious moments Dev said he liked that her legs were longer than her torso, something he'd observed the first time she walked across a room naked. "You're the first," he told her, admiring her from the bed. "The first woman I've known with legs this long."

Dev was the first to tell her that. Unlike the boys she dated in college, who were simply taller, heavier versions of the ones she dated in high school, Dev was the first always to pay for things, and hold doors open, and reach across a table in a restaurant to kiss her hand. He was the first to bring her a bouquet of flowers so immense she'd had to split it up into all six of her drinking glasses, and the first to whisper her name again and again when they made love. Within days of meeting him, when she was at work, Miranda began to wish that there were a picture of her and Dev tacked to the inside of her cubicle, like the one of Laxmi and her husband in front of the Taj Mahal. She didn't tell Laxmi about Dev. She didn't tell anyone. Part of her wanted to tell Laxmi, if only because Laxmi was Indian, too. But Laxmi was always on the phone with her cousin these days, who was still in bed, whose husband was still in London, and whose son still wasn't going to school. "You must eat something," Laxmi would urge. "You mustn't lose your health." When she wasn't speaking to her cousin, she spoke to her husband, shorter conversations, in which she ended up arguing about whether to have chicken or lamb for dinner. "I'm sorry," Miranda heard her apologize at one point. "This whole thing just makes me a little paranoid."

Miranda and Dev didn't argue. They went to movies at the Nickelodeon 35 and kissed the whole time. They ate pulled pork and cornbread in Davis Square, a paper napkin tucked like a cravat into the collar of Dev's shirt. They sipped sangria at the bar of a Spanish restaurant, a grinning pig's head presiding over their conversation. They went to the MFA and picked out a poster of water lilies for her bedroom. One Saturday, following an afternoon concert at Symphony Hall, he showed her his favorite place in the city, the Mapparium at the Christian Science center, where they stood inside a room made of glowing stained-glass panels, which was shaped like the inside of a globe, but looked like the outside of one. In the middle of the room was a transparent bridge, so that they felt as if they were standing in the center of the world. Dev pointed to India, which was red, and far more detailed than the map in *The Economist*. He explained that many of the countries, like Siam and Italian Somaliland, no longer existed in the same way; the names had changed by now. The ocean, as blue as a peacock's breast, appeared in two shades, depending on the depth of the water. He showed her the deepest spot on earth, seven miles deep, above the Mariana Islands. They peered over the bridge and saw the Antarctic archipelago at their feet, craned their necks and saw a giant metal star overhead. As Dev spoke, his voice bounced wildly off the glass, sometimes loud, sometimes soft, sometimes seeming to land in Miranda's chest, sometimes eluding her ear altogether. When a group of tourists walked onto the bridge, she could hear them clearing their throats, as if through microphones. Dev explained that it was because of the acoustics.

Miranda found London, where Laxmi's cousin's husband was, with the woman he'd met on the plane. She wondered which of the cities in India Dev's wife was in. The farthest Miranda had ever been was to the Bahamas once when she was a child. She searched but couldn't find it on the glass panels. When the tourists left and she and Dev were alone again, he told her to stand at one end of the bridge. Even though they were thirty feet apart, Dev said, they'd be able to hear each other whisper.

"I don't believe you," Miranda said. It was the first time she'd spoken since they'd entered. She felt as if speakers were embedded in her ears.

"Go ahead," he urged, walking backward to his end of the bridge. His voice dropped to a whisper. "Say something." She watched his lips forming the words; at the same time she heard them so clearly that she felt them under her skin, under her winter coat, so near and full of warmth that she felt herself go hot.

"Hi," she whispered, unsure of what else to say.

"You're sexy," he whispered back.   40

At work the following week, Laxmi told Miranda that it wasn't the first time her cousin's husband had had an affair. "She's decided to let him come to his senses," Laxmi said one evening as they were getting ready to leave the office. "She says it's for the boy. She's willing to forgive him for the boy." Miranda waited as Laxmi shut off her computer. "He'll come crawling back, and she'll let him," Laxmi said, shaking her head. "Not me. If my husband so much as looked at another woman I'd change the locks." She studied the picture tacked to her cubicle. Laxmi's husband had his arm draped over her shoulder, his knees leaning in toward her on the bench. She turned to Miranda. "Wouldn't you?"

She nodded. Dev's wife was coming back from India the next day. That afternoon he'd called Miranda at work, to say he had to go to the airport to pick her up. He promised he'd call as soon as he could.

"What's the Taj Mahal like?" she asked Laxmi.

"The most romantic spot on earth." Laxmi's face brightened at the memory. "An everlasting monument to love."

While Dev was at the airport, Miranda went to Filene's Basement to buy   45
herself things she thought a mistress should have. She found a pair of black high heels with buckles smaller than a baby's teeth. She found a satin slip with scalloped edges and a knee-length silk robe. Instead of the pantyhose she normally wore to work, she found sheer stockings with a seam. She searched through piles and wandered through racks, pressing back hanger after hanger, until she found a cocktail dress made of a slinky silvery material that matched her eyes, with little chains for straps. As she shopped she thought about Dev, and about what he'd told her in the Mapparium. It was the first time a man had called her sexy, and when she closed her eyes she could still feel his whisper drifting through her body, under her skin. In the fitting room, which was just one big room with mirrors on the walls, she found a spot next to an older woman with a shiny face and coarse frosted hair. The woman stood barefoot in her underwear, pulling the black net of a body stocking taut between her fingers.

"Always check for snags," the woman advised.

Miranda pulled out the satin slip with scalloped edges. She held it to her chest.

The woman nodded with approval. "Oh yes."

"And this?" She held up the silver cocktail dress.

"Absolutely," the woman said. "He'll want to rip it right off you."   50

Miranda pictured the two of them at a restaurant in the South End they'd been to, where Dev had ordered foie gras and a soup made with champagne and raspberries. She pictured herself in the cocktail dress, and Dev in one of his suits, kissing her hand across the table. Only the next time Dev came to visit her, on a Sunday afternoon several days since the last time they'd seen each other, he was in gym clothes. After his wife came back, that was his excuse: on Sundays he drove into Boston and went running along the Charles. The first Sunday she opened the door in the knee-length robe, but Dev didn't even notice it; he carried her over to the bed, wearing sweatpants and sneakers, and entered her without a word. Later, she slipped on the robe when she walked across the room to get him a saucer for his cigarette ashes, but he complained that she was depriving him of the sight of her long legs, and demanded that she remove it. So the next Sunday she didn't bother. She wore jeans. She kept the lingerie at the back of a drawer, behind her socks and everyday underwear. The silver cocktail dress hung in her closet, the tag dangling from the seam. Often, in the morning, the dress would be in a heap on the floor; the chain straps always slipped off the metal hanger.

Still, Miranda looked forward to Sundays. In the mornings she went to a deli and bought a baguette and little containers of things Dev liked to eat, like pickled herring, and potato salad, and tortes of pesto and mascarpone cheese. They ate in bed, picking up the herring with their fingers and ripping the baguette with their hands. Dev told her stories about his childhood, when he would come home from school and drink mango juice served to him on a tray, and then play cricket by a lake, dressed all in white. He told her about how, at eighteen, he'd been sent to a college in upstate New York during something called the Emergency, and about how it took him years to be able to follow American accents in movies, in spite of the fact that he'd had an English-medium education. As he talked he smoked three cigarettes, crushing them in a saucer by the side of her bed. Sometimes he asked her questions, like how many lovers she'd had (three) and how old she'd been the first time (nineteen). After lunch they made love, on sheets covered with crumbs, and then Dev took a nap for twelve minutes. Miranda had never known an adult who took naps, but Dev said it was something he'd grown up doing in India, where it was so hot that people didn't leave their homes until the sun went down. "Plus it allows us to sleep together," he murmured mischievously, curving his arm like a big bracelet around her body.

Only Miranda never slept. She watched the clock on her bedside table, or pressed her face against Dev's fingers, intertwined with hers, each with its half-dozen hairs at the knuckle. After six minutes she turned to face him, sighing and stretching, to test if he was really sleeping. He always was. His ribs were visible through his skin as he breathed, and yet he was beginning to develop a paunch. He complained about the hair on his shoulders, but Miranda thought him perfect, and refused to imagine him any other way.

At the end of twelve minutes Dev would open his eyes as if he'd been awake all along, smiling at her, full of a contentment she wished she felt herself. "The best twelve minutes of the week." He'd sigh, running a hand along the backs of her calves. Then he'd spring out of bed, pulling on his sweatpants and lacing up his sneakers. He would go to the bathroom and brush his teeth with his index finger, something he told her all Indians knew how to do, to get rid of the smoke in his mouth. When she kissed him good-bye she smelled herself sometimes in his hair. But she knew that his excuse, that he'd spent the afternoon jogging, allowed him to take a shower when he got home, first thing.

Apart from Laxmi and Dev, the only Indians whom Miranda had known 55 were a family in the neighborhood where she'd grown up, named the Dixits. Much to the amusement of the neighborhood children, including Miranda, but not including the Dixit children, Mr. Dixit would jog each evening along the flat winding streets of their development in his everyday shirt and trousers, his only concession to athletic apparel a pair of cheap Keds. Every weekend, the family — mother, father, two boys, and a girl — piled into their car and went away, to where nobody knew. The fathers complained that Mr. Dixit did not fertilize his lawn properly, did not rake his leaves on time, and agreed that the Dixits' house, the only one with vinyl siding, detracted from the neighborhood's charm. The mothers never invited Mrs. Dixit to join them around the Armstrongs' swimming pool. Waiting for the school bus with the Dixit children standing to one side, the other children would say "The Dixits dig shit," under their breath, and then burst into laughter.

One year, all the neighborhood children were invited to the birthday party of the Dixit girl. Miranda remembered a heavy aroma of incense and onions in the house, and a pile of shoes heaped by the front door. But most of all she remembered a piece of fabric, about the size of a pillowcase, which hung from a wooden dowel at the bottom of the stairs. It was a painting of a naked woman with a red face shaped like a knight's shield. She had enormous white eyes that tilted toward her temples, and mere dots for pupils. Two circles, with the same dots at their centers, indicated her breasts. In one hand she brandished a dagger. With one foot she crushed a struggling man on the ground. Around her body was a necklace composed of bleeding heads, strung together like a popcorn chain. She stuck her tongue out at Miranda.

"It is the goddess Kali," Mrs. Dixit explained brightly, shifting the dowel slightly in order to straighten the image. Mrs. Dixit's hands were painted with henna, an intricate pattern of zigzags and stars. "Come please, time for cake."

Miranda, then nine years old, had been too frightened to eat the cake. For months afterward she'd been too frightened even to walk on the same side of the street as the Dixits' house, which she had to pass twice daily, once to get to the bus stop, and once again to come home. For a while she even held her breath until she reached the next lawn, just as she did when the school bus passed a cemetery.

It shamed her now. Now, when she and Dev made love, Miranda closed her eyes and saw deserts and elephants, and marble pavilions floating on lakes beneath a full moon. One Saturday, having nothing else to do, she walked all the way to Central Square, to an Indian restaurant, and ordered a plate of tandoori chicken. As she ate she tried to memorize phrases printed at the bottom of the menu, for things like "delicious" and "water" and "check, please." The phrases didn't stick in her mind, and so she began to stop from time to time in the foreign-language section of a bookstore in Kenmore Square, where she studied the Bengali alphabet in the Teach Yourself series. Once she went so far as to try to transcribe the Indian part of her name, "Mira," into her Filofax, her hand moving in unfamiliar directions, stopping and turning and picking up her pen when she least expected to. Following the arrows in the book, she drew a bar from left to right from which the letters hung; one looked more like a number than a letter, another looked like a triangle on its side. It had taken her several tries to get the letters of her name to resemble the sample letters in the book, and even then she wasn't sure if she'd written Mira or Mara. It was a scribble to her, but somewhere in the world, she realized with a shock, it meant something.

During the week it wasn't so bad. Work kept her busy, and she and Laxmi 60
had begun having lunch together at a new Indian restaurant around the corner, during which Laxmi reported the latest status of her cousin's marriage. Sometimes Miranda tried to change the topic; it made her feel the way she once felt in college, when she and her boyfriend at the time had walked away from a crowded house of pancakes without paying for their food, just to see if they could get away with it. But Laxmi spoke of nothing else. "If I were her I'd fly straight to London and shoot them both," she announced one day. She snapped a papadum in half and dipped it into chutney. "I don't know how she can just wait this way."

Miranda knew how to wait. In the evenings she sat at her dining table and coated her nails with clear nail polish, and ate salad straight from the salad bowl, and watched television, and waited for Sunday. Saturdays were the worst because by Saturday it seemed that Sunday would never come. One Saturday when Dev called, late at night, she heard people laughing and talking in the background, so many that she asked him if he was at a concert hall. But he was only calling from his house in the suburbs. "I can't hear you that well," he said. "We have guests. Miss me?" She looked at the television screen, a sitcom that she'd muted with the remote control when the phone rang. She pictured him whispering into his cell phone, in a room upstairs, a hand on the doorknob, the hallway filled with guests. "Miranda, do you miss me?" he asked again. She told him that she did.

The next day, when Dev came to visit, Miranda asked him what his wife looked like. She was nervous to ask, waiting until he'd smoked the last of his cigarettes, crushing it with a firm twist into the saucer. She wondered if they'd quarrel. But Dev wasn't surprised by the question. He told her, spreading some smoked whitefish on a cracker, that his wife resembled an actress in Bombay named Madhuri Dixit.

For an instant Miranda's heart stopped. But no, the Dixit girl had been named something else, something that began with P. Still, she wondered if the actress and the Dixit girl were related. She'd been plain, wearing her hair in two braids all through high school.

A few days later Miranda went to an Indian grocery in Central Square which also rented videos. The door opened to a complicated tinkling of bells. It was dinnertime, and she was the only customer. A video was playing on a television hooked up in a corner of the store: a row of young women in harem pants were thrusting their hips in synchrony on a beach.

"Can I help you?" the man standing at the cash register asked. He was eating a samosa, dipping it into some dark brown sauce on a paper plate. Below the glass counter at his waist were trays of more plump samosas, and what looked like pale, diamond-shaped pieces of fudge covered with foil, and some bright orange pastries floating in syrup. "You like some video?"

Miranda opened up her Filofax, where she had written "Mottery Dixit." She looked up at the videos on the shelves behind the counter. She saw women wearing skirts that sat low on the hips and tops that tied like bandannas between their breasts. Some leaned back against a stone wall, or a tree. They were beautiful, the way the women dancing on the beach were beautiful, with kohl-rimmed eyes and long black hair. She knew then that Madhuri Dixit was beautiful, too.

"We have subtitled versions, miss," the man continued. He wiped his fingertips quickly on his shirt and pulled out three titles.

"No," Miranda said. "Thank you, no." She wandered through the store, studying shelves lined with unlabeled packets and tins. The freezer case was stuffed with bags of pita bread and vegetables she didn't recognize. The only thing she recognized was a rack lined with bags and bags of the Hot Mix that Laxmi was always eating. She thought about buying some for Laxmi, then hesitated, wondering how to explain what she'd been doing in an Indian grocery.

"Very spicy," the man said, shaking his head, his eyes traveling across Miranda's body. "Too spicy for you."

By February, Laxmi's cousin's husband still hadn't come to his senses. He had returned to Montreal, argued bitterly with his wife for two weeks, packed two suitcases, and flown back to London. He wanted a divorce.

Miranda sat in her cubicle and listened as Laxmi kept telling her cousin that there were better men in the world, just waiting to come out of the woodwork. The next day the cousin said she and her son were going to her parents' house in California, to try to recuperate. Laxmi convinced her to arrange a weekend layover in Boston. "A quick change of place will do you good," Laxmi insisted gently, "besides which, I haven't seen you in years."

Miranda stared at her own phone, wishing Dev would call. It had been four days since their last conversation. She heard Laxmi dialing directory assistance, asking for the number of a beauty salon. "Something soothing," Laxmi requested. She scheduled massages, facials, manicures, and pedicures. Then she reserved a table for lunch at the Four Seasons. In her determination to cheer up her cousin, Laxmi had forgotten about the boy. She rapped her knuckles on the laminated wall.

"Are you busy Saturday?"

The boy was thin. He wore a yellow knapsack strapped across his back, gray herringbone trousers, a red V-necked sweater, and black leather shoes. His hair was cut in a thick fringe over his eyes, which had dark circles under them. They were the first thing Miranda noticed. They made him look haggard, as if he smoked a great deal and slept very little, in spite of the fact that he was only seven years old. He clasped a large sketch pad with a spiral binding. His name was Rohin.

"Ask me a capital," he said, staring up at Miranda. 75

She stared back at him. It was eight-thirty on a Saturday morning. She took a sip of coffee. "A what?"

"It's a game he's been playing," Laxmi's cousin explained. She was thin like her son, with a long face and the same dark circles under her eyes. A rust-colored coat hung heavy on her shoulders. Her black hair, with a few strands of gray at the temples, was pulled back like a ballerina's. "You ask him a country and he tells you the capital."

"You should have heard him in the car," Laxmi said. "He's already memorized all of Europe."

"It's not a game," Rohin said. "I'm having a competition with a boy at school. We're competing to memorize all the capitals. I'm going to beat him."

Miranda nodded. "Okay. What's the capital of India?" 80

"That's no good." He marched away, his arms swinging like a toy soldier. Then he marched back to Laxmi's cousin and tugged at a pocket of her overcoat. "Ask me a hard one."

"Senegal," she said.

"Dakar!" Rohin exclaimed triumphantly, and began running in larger and larger circles. Eventually he ran into the kitchen. Miranda could hear him opening and closing the fridge.

"Rohin, don't touch without asking," Laxmi's cousin called out wearily. She managed a smile for Miranda. "Don't worry, he'll fall asleep in a few hours. And thanks for watching him."

"Back at three," Laxmi said, disappearing with her cousin down the 85 hallway. "We're double-parked."

Miranda fastened the chain on the door. She went to the kitchen to find Rohin, but he was now in the living room, at the dining table, kneeling on one of the director's chairs. He unzipped his knapsack, pushed Miranda's basket of manicure supplies to one side of the table, and spread his crayons over the surface. Miranda stood over his shoulder. She watched as he gripped a blue crayon and drew the outline of an airplane.

"It's lovely," she said. When he didn't reply, she went to the kitchen to pour herself more coffee.

"Some for me, please," Rohin called out.

She returned to the living room. "Some what?"

"Some coffee. There's enough in the pot. I saw," 90

She walked over to the table and sat opposite him. At times he nearly stood up to reach for a new crayon. He barely made a dent in the director's chair.

"You're too young for coffee."

Rohin leaned over the sketch pad, so that his tiny chest and shoulders almost touched it, his head tilted to one side. "The stewardess let me have coffee," he said. "She made it with milk and lots of sugar." He straightened, revealing a woman's face beside the plane, with long wavy hair and eyes like asterisks. "Her hair was more shiny," he decided, adding, "My father met a pretty woman on a plane, too." He looked at Miranda. His face darkened as he watched her sip. "Can't I have just a little coffee? Please?"

She wondered, in spite of his composed, brooding expression, if he were the type to throw a tantrum. She imagined his kicking her with his leather shoes, screaming for coffee, screaming and crying until his mother and Laxmi came back to fetch him. She went to the kitchen and prepared a cup for him as he'd requested. She selected a mug she didn't care for, in case he dropped it.

"Thank you," he said when she put it on the table. He took short sips, 95 holding the mug securely with both hands.

Miranda sat with him while he drew, but when she attempted to put a coat of clear polish on her nails he protested. Instead he pulled out a paperback world almanac from his knapsack and asked her to quiz him. The countries were arranged by continent, six to a page, with the capitals in boldface, followed by a short entry on the population, government, and other statistics. Miranda turned to a page in the Africa section and went down the list.

"Mali," she asked him.

"Bamako," he replied instantly.

"Malawi."

"Lilongwe." 100

She remembered looking at Africa in the Mapparium. She remembered the fat part of it was green.

"Go on," Rohin said.

"Mauritania."

"Nouakchott."

"Mauritius."

He paused, squeezed his eyes shut, then opened them, defeated. "I can't remember."

"Port Louis," she told him.

"Port Louis." He began to say it again and again, like a chant under his breath.

When they reached the last of the countries in Africa, Rohin said he wanted to watch cartoons, telling Miranda to watch them with him. When the cartoons ended, he followed her to the kitchen, and stood by her side as she made more coffee. He didn't follow her when she went to the bathroom a few minutes later, but when she opened the door she was startled to find him standing outside.

"Do you need to go?" 110

He shook his head but walked into the bathroom anyway. He put the cover of the toilet down, climbed on top of it, and surveyed the narrow glass shelf over the sink which held Miranda's toothbrush and makeup.

"What's this for?" he asked, picking up the sample of eye gel she'd gotten the day she met Dev.

"Puffiness."

"What's puffiness?"

"Here," she explained, pointing. 115

"After you've been crying?"

"I guess so."

Rohin opened the tube and smelled it. He squeezed a drop of it onto a finger, then rubbed it on his hand. "It stings." He inspected the back of his hand closely, as if expecting it to change color. "My mother has puffiness. She says it's a cold, but really she cries, sometimes for hours. Sometimes straight through dinner. Sometimes she cries so hard her eyes puff up like bullfrogs."

Miranda wondered if she ought to feed him. In the kitchen she discovered a bag of rice cakes and some lettuce. She offered to go out, to buy something from the deli, but Rohin said he wasn't very hungry, and accepted one of the rice cakes. "You eat one too," he said. They sat at the table, the rice cakes between them. He turned to a fresh page in his sketch pad. "You draw."

She selected a blue crayon. "What should I draw?" 120

He thought for a moment. "I know," he said. He asked her to draw things in the living room: the sofa, the director's chairs, the television, the telephone. "This way I can memorize it."

"Memorize what?"

"Our day together." He reached for another rice cake.

"Why do you want to memorize it?" 125

"Because we're never going to see each other, ever again."

The precision of the phrase startled her. She looked at him, feeling slightly depressed. Rohin didn't look depressed. He tapped the page. "Go on."

And so she drew the items as best as she could — the sofa, the director's chairs, the television, the telephone. He sidled up to her, so close that it was sometimes difficult to see what she was doing. He put his small brown hand over hers. "Now me."

She handed him the crayon.

He shook his head, "No, now draw me."

"I can't," she said. "It won't look like you." 130

The brooding look began to spread across Rohin's face again, just as it had when she'd refused him coffee. "Please?"

She drew his face, outlining his head and the thick fringe of hair. He sat perfectly still, with a formal, melancholy expression, his gaze fixed to one side. Miranda wished she could draw a good likeness. Her hand moved in conjunction with her eyes, in unknown ways, just as it had that day in the bookstore when she'd transcribed her name in Bengali letters. It looked nothing like him. She was in the middle of drawing his nose when he wriggled away from the table.

"I'm bored," he announced, heading toward her bedroom. She heard him opening the door, opening the drawers of her bureau and closing them.

When she joined him he was inside the closet. After a moment he emerged, his hair disheveled, holding the silver cocktail dress. "This was on the floor."

"It falls off the hanger."

Rohin looked at the dress and then at Miranda's body. "Put it on."

"Excuse me?"

"Put it on."

There was no reason to put it on. Apart from in the fitting room at Filene's she had never worn it, and as long as she was with Dev she knew she never would. She knew they would never go to restaurants, where he would reach across a table and kiss her hand. They would meet in her apartment, on Sundays, he in his sweatpants, she in her jeans. She took the dress from Rohin and shook it out, even though the slinky fabric never wrinkled. She reached into the closet for a free hanger.

"Please put it on," Rohin asked, suddenly standing behind her. He pressed his face against her, clasping her waist with both his thin arms. "Please?"

"All right," she said, surprised by the strength of his grip.

He smiled, satisfied, and sat on the edge of her bed.

"You have to wait out there," she said, pointing to the door. "I'll come out when I'm ready."

"But my mother always takes her clothes off in front of me."

"She does?"

Rohin nodded. "She doesn't even pick them up afterward. She leaves them all on the floor by the bed, all tangled.

"One day she slept in my room," he continued. "She said it felt better than her bed, now that my father's gone."

"I'm not your mother," Miranda said, lifting him by the armpits off her bed. When he refused to stand, she picked him up. He was heavier than she expected, and he clung to her, his legs wrapped firmly around her hips, his head resting against her chest. She set him down in the hallway and shut the door. As an extra precaution she fastened the latch. She changed into the dress, glancing into the full-length mirror nailed to the back of the door. Her ankle socks looked silly, and so she opened a drawer and found the stockings. She searched through the back of the closet and slipped on the high heels with the tiny buckles. The chain straps of the dress were as light as paper clips against her collarbone. It was a bit loose on her. She could not zip it herself.

Rohin began knocking. "May I come in now?"

She opened the door. Rohin was holding his almanac in his hands, muttering something under his breath. His eyes opened wide at the sight of her. "I need help with the zipper," she said. She sat on the edge of the bed.

Rohin fastened the zipper to the top, and then Miranda stood up and twirled. Rohin put down the almanac. "You're sexy," he declared.

"What did you say?"

"You're sexy."

Miranda sat down again. Though she knew it meant nothing, her heart skipped a beat. Rohin probably referred to all women as sexy. He'd probably heard the word on television, or seen it on the cover of a magazine. She remembered the day in the Mapparium, standing across the bridge from Dev. At the time she thought she knew what his words meant. At the time they'd made sense.

Miranda folded her arms across her chest and looked Rohin in the eyes. "Tell me something." 155

He was silent.

"What does it mean?"

"What?"

"That word. 'Sexy.' What does it mean?"

He looked down, suddenly shy. "I can't tell you." 160

"Why not?"

"It's a secret." He pressed his lips together, so hard that a bit of them went white.

"Tell me the secret. I want to know."

Rohin sat on the bed beside Miranda and began to kick the edge of the mattress with the backs of his shoes. He giggled nervously, his thin body flinching as if it were being tickled.

"Tell me," Miranda demanded. She leaned over and gripped his ankles, holding his feet still. 165

Rohin looked at her, his eyes like slits. He struggled to kick the mattress again, but Miranda pressed against him. He fell back on the bed, his back straight as a board. He cupped his hands around his mouth, and then he whispered, "It means loving someone you don't know."

Miranda felt Rohin's words under her skin, the same way she'd felt Dev's. But instead of going hot she felt numb. It reminded her of the way she'd felt at the Indian grocery, the moment she knew, without even looking at a picture, that Madhuri Dixit, whom Dev's wife resembled, was beautiful.

"That's what my father did," Rohin continued. "He sat next to someone he didn't know, someone sexy, and now he loves her instead of my mother."

He took off his shoes and placed them side by side on the floor. Then he peeled back the comforter and crawled into Miranda's bed with the almanac. A minute later the book dropped from his hands, and he closed his eyes. Miranda watched him sleep, the comforter rising and falling as he breathed. He didn't wake up after twelve minutes like Dev, or even twenty. He didn't open his eyes as she stepped out of the silver cocktail dress and back into her jeans, and put the high-heeled shoes in the back of the closet, and rolled up the stockings and put them back in her drawer.

When she had put everything away she sat on the bed. She leaned toward him, close enough to see some white powder from the rice cakes stuck to the corners of his mouth, and picked up the almanac. As she turned the pages she imagined the quarrels Rohin had overheard in his house in Montreal. "Is she pretty?" his mother would have asked his father, wearing the same bathrobe she'd worn for weeks, her own pretty face turning 170 spiteful. "Is she sexy?" His father would deny it at first, try to change the subject. "Tell me," Rohin's mother would shriek, "tell me if she's sexy." In the end his father would admit that she was, and his mother would cry and cry, in a bed surrounded by a tangle of clothes, her eyes puffing up like bullfrogs. "How could you," she'd ask, sobbing, "how could you love a woman you don't even know?"

As Miranda imagined the scene she began to cry a little herself. In the Mapparium that day, all the countries had seemed close enough to touch, and Dev's voice had bounced wildly off the glass. From across the bridge, thirty feet away, his words had reached her ears, so near and full of warmth that they'd drifted for days under her skin. Miranda cried harder, unable to stop. But Rohin still slept. She guessed that he was used to it now, to the sound of a woman crying.

On Sunday, Dev called to tell Miranda he was on his way. "I'm almost ready. I'll be there at two."

She was watching a cooking show on television. A woman pointed to a row of apples, explaining which were best for baking. "You shouldn't come today."

"Why not?"

"I have a cold," she lied. It wasn't far from the truth; crying had left her congested. "I've been in bed all morning."

"You do sound stuffed up." There was a pause. "Do you need anything?"

"I'm all set."

"Drink lots of fluids."

"Dev?"

"Yes, Miranda?"

"Do you remember that day we went to the Mapparium?"

"Of course."

"Do you remember how we whispered to each other?"

"I remember," Dev whispered playfully.

"Do you remember what you said?"

There was a pause. "'Let's go back to your place.'" He laughed quietly. "Next Sunday, then?"

The day before, as she'd cried, Miranda had believed she would never forget anything — not even the way her name looked written in Bengali. She'd fallen asleep beside Rohin and when she woke up he was drawing an airplane on the copy of *The Economist* she'd saved, hidden under the bed. "Who's Deva-jit Mitra?" he had asked, looking at the address label.

Miranda pictured Dev, in his sweatpants and sneakers, laughing into the phone. In a moment he'd join his wife downstairs, and tell her he wasn't going jogging. He'd pulled a muscle while stretching, he'd say, settling down to read the paper. In spite of herself, she longed for him. She would see him one more Sunday, she decided, perhaps two. Then she would tell him the things she had known all along: that it wasn't fair to her, or to his wife, that they both deserved better, that there was no point in it dragging on.

But the next Sunday it snowed, so much so that Dev couldn't tell his wife he was going running along the Charles. The Sunday after that, the snow had melted, but Miranda made plans to go to the movies with Laxmi, and when she told Dev this over the phone, he didn't ask her to cancel them. The third Sunday she got up early and went out for a walk. It was cold but sunny, and so she walked all the way down Commonwealth Avenue, past the restaurants where Dev had kissed her, and then she walked all the way to the Christian Science center. The Mapparium was closed, but she bought a cup of coffee nearby and sat on one of the benches in the plaza outside the church, gazing at its giant pillars and its massive dome, and at the clear-blue sky spread over the city.

Considerations for Critical Thinking and Writing

1. **FIRST RESPONSE.** What is your emotional response to Miranda's difficult situation as the lover of a married man? Setting aside your general feelings about infidelity or monogamy, what factors within the story help to frame your response?

2. What three adjectives would you choose to describe Dev, Miranda's married lover? What details in the story help to illustrate those qualities?

3. Maps, globes, and geography are recurrent features of this story. Locate as many references to them as you can, then consider their importance in terms of your understanding of the story's theme.

4. How does the meaning of the word "sexy" change over the course of the story? Why do you suppose Lahiri chose that word as the title?

5. Discuss the importance of scenes in the story that take place in retail stores.

6. The story emphasizes Miranda's encounters with the people and cultures of India. How important is this cultural encounter to the story's main concerns as you understand them? (Or is cultural encounter in fact the story's main concern?)

7. The scene in which Miranda volunteers to look after Rohin is clearly a turning point. Would you describe it as the story's climax? Why or why not?

8. Does Miranda grow or learn anything about herself over the course of the story? If so, what is it, precisely?

Connection to Another Selection

1. Compare the way relationships begin, evolve, and end in this story and in ZZ Packer's "Drinking Coffee Elsewhere" (p. 335). To what degree are these relationships affected by factors internal to and external to the stories' protagonists?

ZZ PACKER (b. 1973)

Born in Chicago and raised in Georgia and Kentucky, ZZ Packer earned her undergraduate degree from Yale, a master's degree from Johns Hopkins, and an M.F.A. in creative writing from the University of Iowa. She has also taught creative writing at a variety of prestigious American universities. Her collection *Drinking Coffee Elsewhere*, the title story of which is included below, was one of the most celebrated publications of 2003. She has not published anything else to date, though she has spoken of a novel set in the aftermath of the Civil War, and its publication is much anticipated.

Rose Lincoln/Harvard Staff Photographer.

Drinking Coffee Elsewhere 2000

Orientation games began the day I arrived at Yale from Baltimore. In my group we played heady, frustrating games for smart people. One game appeared to be charades reinterpreted by existentialists; another involved listening to rocks. Then a freshman counselor made everyone play Trust. The idea was that if you had the faith to fall backward and wait for four scrawny former high school geniuses to catch you, just before your head cracked on the slate sidewalk, then you might learn to trust your fellow students. Russian roulette sounded like a better way to go.

"No way," I said. The white boys were waiting for me to fall, holding their arms out for me, sincerely, gallantly. "No fucking way."

"It's all cool, it's all cool," the counselor said. Her hair was a shade of blond I'd seen only on *Playboy* covers, and she raised her hands as though backing away from a growling dog. "Sister," she said, in an I'm-down-with-the-struggle voice, "you don't have to play this game. As a person of color, you shouldn't have to fit into any white, patriarchal system."

I said, "It's a bit too late for that."

In the next game, all I had to do was wait in a circle until it was my turn to say what inanimate object I wanted to be. One guy said he'd like to be a gadfly, like Socrates. "Stop me if I wax Platonic," he said. I didn't bother mentioning that gadflies weren't inanimate — it didn't seem to make a difference. The girl next to him was eating a rice cake. She wanted to be the Earth, she said. Earth with a capital E.

There was one other black person in the circle. He wore an Exeter T-shirt and his overly elastic expressions resembled a series of facial exercises. At the end of each person's turn, he smiled and bobbed his head with unfettered enthusiasm. "Oh, that was good," he said, as if the game were an experiment he'd set up and the results were turning out better than he'd expected. "Good, good, good!"

When it was my turn I said, "My name is Dina, and if I had to be any object, I guess I'd be a revolver." The sunlight dulled as if on cue. Clouds passed rapidly overhead, presaging rain. I don't know why I said it. Until that moment I'd been good in all the ways that were meant to matter. I was an honor roll student—though I'd learned long ago not to mention it in the part of Baltimore where I lived. Suddenly I was hard-bitten and recalcitrant, the kind of kid who took pleasure in sticking pins into cats; the kind who chased down smart kids to spray them with Mace.

"A revolver," a counselor said, stroking his chin, as if it had grown a rabbinical beard. "Could you please elaborate?"

The black guy cocked his head and frowned, as if the beakers and Erlenmeyer flasks of his experiment had grown legs and scurried off.

"You were just kidding," the dean said, "about wiping out all of mankind. That, I suppose, was a joke." She squinted at me. One of her hands curved atop the other to form a pink, freckled molehill on her desk. 10

"Well," I said, "maybe I meant it at the time." I quickly saw that this was not the answer she wanted. "I don't know. I think it's the architecture."

Through the dimming light of the dean's office window, I could see the fortress of the old campus. On my ride from the bus station to the campus, I'd barely glimpsed New Haven—a flash of crumpled building here, a trio of straggly kids there. A lot like Baltimore. But everything had changed when we reached those streets hooded by gothic buildings. I imagined how the college must have looked when it was founded, when most of the students owned slaves. I pictured men wearing tights and knickers, smoking pipes.

"The architecture," the dean repeated. She bit her lip and seemed to be making a calculation of some sort. I noticed that she blinked less often than most people. I sat there, intrigued, waiting to see how long it would be before she blinked again.

My revolver comment won me a year's worth of psychiatric counseling, weekly meetings with Dean Guest, and—since the parents of the roommate I'd never met weren't too hip on the idea of their Amy sharing a bunk bed with a budding homicidal loony—my very own room.

Shortly after getting my first C ever, I also received the first knock on my door. The female counselors never knocked. The dean had spoken to them; I was a priority. Every other day, right before dinnertime, they'd look in on me, unannounced. "Just checking up," a counselor would say. It was the voice of a suburban mother in training. By the second week, I had made a point of sitting in a chair in front of the door, just when I expected a counselor to pop her head around. This was intended to startle them. I also made a point of being naked. The unannounced visits ended. 15

The knocking persisted. Through the peephole I saw a white face, distorted and balloonish.

"Let me in." The person looked like a boy but it sounded like a girl. "Let me in," the voice repeated.

"Not a chance," I said. I had a suicide single, and I wanted to keep it that way. No roommates, no visitors.

Then the person began to sob, and I heard a back slump against the door. If I hadn't known the person was white from the peephole, I'd have known it from a display like this. Black people didn't knock on strangers' doors, crying. Not that I understood the black people at Yale. Most of them were from New York and tried hard to pretend that they hadn't gone to prep schools. And there was something pitiful in how cool they were. Occasionally one would reach out to me with missionary zeal, but I'd rebuff the person with haughty silence.

"I don't have anyone to talk to!" the person on the other side of the door cried.

"That is correct."

"When I was a child," the person said, "I played by myself in a corner of the schoolyard all alone. I hated dolls and I hated games, animals were not friendly and birds flew away. If anyone was looking for me I hid behind a tree and cried out 'I am an orphan —' "

I opened the door. It was a she.

"Plagiarist!" I yelled. She had just recited a Frank O'Hara poem as though she'd thought it up herself. I knew the poem because it was one of the few things I'd been forced to read that I wished I'd written myself.

The girl turned to face me, smiling weakly, as though her triumph was not in getting me to open the door but in the fact that she was able to smile at all when she was so accustomed to crying. She was large but not obese, and crying had turned her face the color of raw chicken. She blew her nose into the waist end of her T-shirt, revealing a pale belly.

"How do you know that poem?"

She sniffed. "I'm in your Contemporary Poetry class."

She said she was Canadian and her name was Heidi, although she said she wanted people to call her Henrik. "That's a guy's name," I said. "What do you want? A sex change?"

She looked at me with so little surprise that I suspected she hadn't discounted this as an option. Then her story came out in teary, hiccup-like bursts. She had sucked some "cute guy's dick" and he'd told everybody and now people thought she was "a slut."

"Why'd you suck his dick? Aren't you a lesbian?"

She fit the bill. Short hair, hard, roach-stomping shoes. Dressed like an aspiring plumber. And then there was the name Henrik. The lesbians I'd seen on TV were wiry, thin strips of muscle, but Heidi was round and soft and had a moonlike face. Drab henna-colored hair. And lesbians had cats. "Do you have a cat?" I asked.

Her eyes turned glossy with new tears. "No," she said, her voice quavering, "and I'm not a lesbian. Are you?"

"Do I look like one?" I said.

She didn't answer.

"O.K.," I said. "I could suck a guy's dick, too, if I wanted. But I don't. 35 The human penis is one of the most germ-ridden objects there is." Heidi looked at me, unconvinced. "What I meant to say," I began again, "is that I don't like anybody. Period. Guys or girls. I'm a misanthrope."

"I am, too."

"No," I said, guiding her back through my door and out into the hall-way. "You're not."

"Have you had dinner?" she asked. "Let's go to Commons."

I pointed to a pyramid of ramen noodle packages on my windowsill. "See that? That means I never have to go to Commons. Aside from class, I have contact with no one."

"I hate it here, too," she said. "I should have gone to McGill, eh." 40

"The way to feel better," I said, "is to get some ramen and lock yourself in your room. Everyone will forget about you and that guy's dick and you won't have to see anyone ever again. If anyone looks for you—"

"I'll hide behind a tree."

"A revolver?" Dr. Raeburn said, flipping through a manila folder. He looked up at me as if to ask another question, but he didn't.

Dr. Raeburn was the psychiatrist. He had the gray hair and whiskers of a Civil War general. He was also a chain smoker with beige teeth and a navy wool jacket smeared with ash. He asked about the revolver at the beginning of my first visit. When I was unable to explain myself, he smiled, as if this were perfectly reasonable.

"Tell me about your parents." 45

I wondered what he already had on file. The folder was thick, though I hadn't said a thing of significance since Day One.

"My father was a dick and my mother seemed to like him."

He patted his pockets for his cigarettes. "That's some heavy stuff," he said. "How do you feel about Dad?" The man couldn't say the word "father." "Is Dad someone you see often?"

"I hate my father almost as much as I hate the word 'Dad.'"

He started tapping his cigarette. 50

"You can't smoke in here."

"That's right," he said, and slipped the cigarette back into the packet. He smiled, widening his eyes brightly. "Don't ever start."

I thought that that first encounter would be the last of Heidi or Henrik, or whatever, but then her head appeared in a window of Linsly-Chit during my Chaucer class. A few days later, she swooped down a flight of stairs in Harkness, following me. She hailed me from across Elm Street and found me in the Ster-ling Library stacks. After one of my meetings with Dr. Raeburn, she was wait-ing for me outside Health Services, legs crossed, cleaning her fingernails.

"You know," she said, as we walked through Old Campus, "you've got to stop eating ramen. Not only does it lack a single nutrient but it's full of MSG."

I wondered why she even bothered, and was vaguely flattered she cared,
but I said, "I like eating chemicals. It keeps the skin radiant."

"There's also hepatitis." She knew how to get my attention — mention a
disease.

"You get hepatitis from unwashed lettuce," I said. "If there's anything
safe from the perils of the food chain, it's ramen."

"But do you refrigerate what you don't eat? Each time you reheat it,
you're killing good bacteria, which then can't keep the bad bacteria in check.
A guy got sick from reheating Chinese noodles, and his son died from it. I
read it in the *Times*." With this, she put a jovial arm around my neck. I continued walking, a little stunned. Then, just as quickly, she dropped her arm
and stopped walking. I stopped, too.

"Did you notice that I put my arm around you?"

"Yes," I said. "Next time, I'll have to chop it off."

"I don't want you to get sick," she said. "Let's eat at Commons."

In the cold air, her arm had felt good.

The problem with Commons was that it was too big; its ceiling was as high
as a cathedral's, but below it there were no awestruck worshippers, only
eighteen-year-olds at heavy wooden tables, chatting over veal patties and
Jell-O.

We got our food, tacos stuffed with meat substitute, and made our way
through the maze of tables. The Koreans had a table. Each singing group
had a table. The crew team sat at a long table of its own. We passed the
black table. Heidi was so plump and moonfaced that the sheer quantity of
her flesh accentuated just how white she was. The black students gave me a
long, hard stare.

"How you doing, sista?" a guy asked, his voice full of accusation, eye-
balling me as though I were clad in a Klansman's sheet and hood. "I guess we
won't see you till graduation."

"If," I said, "you graduate."

The remark was not well received. As I walked past, I heard protests,
angry and loud as if they'd discovered a cheat at their poker game. Heidi
and I found an unoccupied table along the periphery, which was isolated and
dark. We sat down. Heidi prayed over her tacos.

"I thought you didn't believe in God," I said.

"Not in the God depicted in the Judeo-Christian Bible, but I do believe
that nature's essence is a spirit that —"

"All right," I said. I had begun to eat, and cubes of diced tomato fell from
my mouth when I spoke. "Stop right there. Tacos and spirits don't mix."

"You've always got to be so flip," she said. "I'm going to apply for another
friend."

"There's always Mr. Dick," I said. "Slurp, slurp."

"You are so lame. So unbelievably lame. I'm going out with Mr. Dick.
Thursday night at Atticus. His name is Keith."

Heidi hadn't mentioned Mr. Dick since the day I'd met her. That was
more than a month ago and we'd spent a lot of that time together. I checked

for signs that she was lying; her habit of smiling too much, her eyes bright and cheeks full so that she looked like a chipmunk. But she looked normal. Pleased, even, to see me so flustered.

"You're insane! What are you going to do this time?" I asked. "Sleep with 75 him? Then when he makes fun of you, what? Come pound your head on my door reciting the collected poems of Sylvia Plath?"

"He's going to apologize for before. And don't call me insane. You're the one going to the psychiatrist."

"Well, I'm not going to suck his dick, that's for sure."

She put her arm around me in mock comfort, but I pushed it off, and ignored her. She touched my shoulder again, and I turned, annoyed, but it wasn't Heidi after all; a sepia-toned boy dressed in khakis and a crisp plaid shirt was standing behind me. He thrust a hot-pink square of paper toward me without a word, then briskly made his way toward the other end of Commons, where the crowds blossomed. Heidi leaned over and read it: "Wear Black Leather — the Less, the Better."

"It's a gay party," I said, crumpling the card. "He thinks we're fucking gay."

Heidi and I signed on to work at the Saybrook dining hall as dishwashers. 80 The job consisted of dumping food from plates and trays into a vat of rushing water. It seemed straightforward, but then I learned better. You wouldn't believe what people could do with food until you worked in a dish room. Lettuce and crackers and soup would be bullied into a pulp in the bowl of some bored anorexic; ziti would be mixed with honey and granola; trays would appear heaped with mashed potato snow women with melted chocolate ice cream for hair. Frat boys arrived at the dish-room window, en masse. They liked to fill glasses with food, then seal them, airtight, onto their trays. If you tried to prize them off, milk, Worcestershire sauce, peas, chunks of bread vomited onto your dish-room uniform.

When this happened one day in the middle of the lunch rush, for what seemed like the hundredth time, I tipped the tray toward one of the frat boys as he turned to walk away, popping the glasses off so that the mess spurted onto his Shetland sweater.

He looked down at his sweater. "Lesbo bitch!"

"No," I said, "that would be your mother."

Heidi, next to me, clenched my arm in support, but I remained motionless, waiting to see what the frat boy would do. He glared at me for a minute, then walked away.

"Let's take a smoke break," Heidi said. 85

I didn't smoke, but Heidi had begun to, because she thought it would help her lose weight. As I hefted a stack of glasses through the steamer, she lit up.

"Soft packs remind me of you," she said. "Just when you've smoked them all and you think there's none left, there's always one more, hiding in that little crushed corner." Before I could respond she said, "Oh, God. Not another mouse. You know whose job that is."

By the end of the rush, the floor mats got full and slippery with food. This was when mice tended to appear, scurrying over our shoes; more often than not, a mouse got caught in the grating that covered the drains in the floor. Sometimes the mouse was already dead by the time we noticed it. This one was alive.

"No way," I said. "This time you're going to help. Get some gloves and a trash bag."

"That's all I'm getting. I'm not getting that mouse out of there."

"Put on the gloves," I ordered. She winced, but put them on. "Reach down," I said. "At an angle, so you get at its middle. Otherwise, if you try to get it by its tail, the tail will break off."

"This is filthy, eh."

"That's why we're here," I said. "To clean up filth. Eh."

She reached down, but would not touch the mouse. I put my hand around her arm and pushed it till her hand made contact. The cries from the mouse were soft, songlike. "Oh, my God," she said. "Oh, my God, ohmigod." She wrestled it out of the grating and turned her head away.

"Don't you let it go," I said.

"Where's the food bag? It'll smother itself if I drop it in the food bag. Quick," she said, her head still turned away, her eyes closed. "Lead me to it."

"No. We are not going to smother this mouse. We've got to break its neck."

"You're one heartless bitch."

I wondered how to explain that if death is unavoidable it should be quick and painless. My mother had died slowly. At the hospital, they'd said it was kidney failure, but I knew, in the end, it was my father. He made her so scared to live in her own home that she was finally driven away from it in an ambulance.

"Breaking its neck will save it the pain of smothering," I said. "Breaking its neck is more humane. Take the trash bag and cover it so you won't get any blood on you, then crush."

The loud jets of the steamer had shut off automatically and the dish room grew quiet. Heidi breathed in deeply, then crushed the mouse. She shuddered, disgusted. "Now what?"

"What do you mean, 'now what?' Throw the little bastard in the trash."

At our third session, I told Dr. Raeburn I didn't mind if he smoked. He sat on the sill of his open window, smoking behind a jungle screen of office plants.

We spent the first ten minutes discussing the Iliad, and whether or not the text actually states that Achilles had been dipped in the River Styx. He said it did, and I said it didn't. After we'd finished with the Iliad, and with my new job in what he called "the scullery," he asked questions about my parents. I told him nothing. It was none of his business. Instead, I talked about Heidi. I told him about that day in Commons, Heidi's plan to go on a date with Mr. Dick, and the invitation we'd been given to the gay party.

"You seem preoccupied by this soirée." He arched his eyebrows at the word "soirée."

"Wouldn't you be?"

"Dina," he said slowly, in a way that made my name seem like a song title, "have you ever had a romantic interest?"

"You want to know if I've ever had a boyfriend?" I said. "Just go ahead and ask if I've ever fucked anybody."

This appeared to surprise him. "I think that you are having a crisis of identity," he said.

"Oh, is that what this is?"   110

His profession had taught him not to roll his eyes. Instead, his exasperation revealed itself in a tiny pursing of his lips, as though he'd just tasted something awful and was trying very hard not to offend the cook.

"It doesn't have to be, as you say, someone you've fucked, it doesn't have to be a boyfriend," he said.

"Well, what are you trying to say? If it's not a boy, then you're saying it's a girl —"

"Calm down. It could be a crush, Dina." He lit one cigarette off another. "A crush on a male teacher, a crush on a dog, for heaven's sake. An interest. Not necessarily a relationship."

It was sacrifice time. If I could spend the next half hour talking about   115
some boy, then I'd have given him what he wanted.

So I told him about the boy with the nice shoes.

I was sixteen and had spent the last few coins in my pocket on bus fare to buy groceries. I didn't like going to the Super Fresh two blocks away from my house, plunking government food stamps into the hands of the cashiers.

"There she go reading," one of them once said, even though I was only carrying a book. "Don't your eyes get tired?"

On Greenmount Avenue you could read schoolbooks — that was understandable. The government and your teachers forced you to read them. But anything else was antisocial. It meant you'd rather submit to the words of some white dude than shoot the breeze with your neighbors.

I hated those cashiers, and I hated them seeing me with food stamps, so   120
I took the bus and shopped elsewhere. That day, I got off the bus at Govans, and though the neighborhood was black like my own — hair salon after hair salon of airbrushed signs promising arabesque hair styles and inch-long fingernails — the houses were neat and orderly, nothing at all like Greenmount, where every other house had at least one shattered window. The store was well swept, and people quietly checked long grocery lists — no screaming kids, no loud cashier-customer altercations. I got the groceries and left the store.

I decided to walk back. It was a fall day, and I walked for blocks. Then I sensed someone following me. I walked more quickly, my arms around the sack, the leafy lettuce tickling my nose. I didn't want to hold the sack so close that it would break the eggs or squash the hamburger buns, but it was slipping, and as I looked behind me a boy my age, maybe older, rushed toward me.

"Let me help you," he said.

"That's all right." I set the bag on the sidewalk. Maybe I saw his face, maybe it was handsome enough, but what I noticed first, splayed on either side of the bag, were his shoes. They were nice shoes, real leather, a stitched design like a widow's peak on each one, or like birds' wings, and for the first time in my life I understood what people meant when they said "wing-tip shoes."

"I watched you carry them groceries out that store, then you look around, like you're lost, but like you liked being lost, then you walk down the sidewalk for blocks and blocks. Rearranging that bag, it almost gone to slip, then hefting it back up again."

"Uh-huh," I said.

"And then I passed my own house and was still following you. And then your bag really look like it was gone crash and everything. So I just thought I'd help." He sucked in his bottom lip, as if to keep it from making a smile. "What's your name?" When I told him, he said, "Dina, my name is Cecil." Then he said, "D comes right after C."

"Yes," I said, "it does, doesn't it."

Then, half question, half statement, he said, "I could carry your groceries for you? And walk you home?"

I stopped the story there. Dr. Raeburn kept looking at me. "Then what happened?"

I couldn't tell him the rest: that I had not wanted the boy to walk me home, that I didn't want someone with such nice shoes to see where I lived.

Dr. Raeburn would only have pitied me if I'd told him that I ran down the sidewalk after I told the boy no, that I fell, the bag slipped, and the eggs cracked, their yolks running all over the lettuce. Clear amniotic fluid coated the can of cinnamon rolls. I left the bag there on the sidewalk, the groceries spilled out randomly like cards loosed from a deck. When I returned home, I told my mother that I'd lost the food stamps.

"Lost?" she said. I'd expected her to get angry, I'd wanted her to get angry, but she hadn't. "Lost?" she repeated. Why had I been so clumsy and nervous around a harmless boy? I could have brought the groceries home and washed off the egg yolk, but instead I'd just left them there. "Come on," Mama said, snuffing her tears, pulling my arm, trying to get me to join her and start yanking cushions off the couch. "We'll find enough change here. We got to get something for dinner before your father gets back."

We'd already searched the couch for money the previous week, and I knew there'd be nothing now, but I began to push my fingers into the couch's boniest corners, pretending that it was only a matter of time before I'd find some change or a lost watch or an earring. Something pawnable, perhaps.

"What happened next?" Dr. Raeburn asked again. "Did you let the boy walk you home?"

"My house was far, so we went to his house instead." Though I was sure Dr. Raeburn knew that I was making this part up, I continued. "We made out on his sofa. He kissed me."

Dr. Raeburn lit his next cigarette like a detective. Cool, suspicious. "How did it feel?"

"You know," I said. "Like a kiss feels. It felt nice. The kiss felt very, very nice."

Raeburn smiled gently, though he seemed unconvinced. When he called time on our session, his cigarette had become one long pole of ash. I left his office, walking quickly down the corridor, afraid to look back. It would be like him to trot after me, his navy blazer flapping, just to get the truth out of me. *You never kissed anyone.* The words slid from my brain, and knotted in my stomach.

When I reached my dorm, I found an old record player blocking my door and a Charles Mingus LP propped beside it. I carried them inside and then, lying on the floor, I played the Mingus over and over again until I fell asleep. I slept feeling as though Dr. Raeburn had attached electrodes to my head, willing into my mind a dream about my mother. I saw the lemon meringue of her skin, the long bone of her arm as she reached down to clip her toenails. I'd come home from a school trip to an aquarium, and I was explaining the differences between baleen and sperm whales according to the size of their heads, the range of their habitats, their feeding patterns.

I awoke remembering the expression on her face after I'd finished my 140 dizzying whale lecture. She looked like a tourist who'd asked for directions to a place she thought was simple enough to get to only to hear a series of hypothetical turns, alleys, one-way streets. Her response was to nod politely at the perilous elaborateness of it all; to nod and save herself from the knowledge that she would never be able to get where she wanted to go.

The dishwashers always closed down the dining hall. One night, after everyone else had punched out, Heidi and I took a break, and though I wasn't a smoker, we set two milk crates upside down on the floor and smoked cigarettes.

The dishwashing machines were off, but steam still rose from them like a jungle mist. Outside in the winter air, students were singing carols in their groomed and tailored singing-group voices. The Whiffenpoofs were back in New Haven after a tour around the world, and I guess their return was a huge deal. Heidi and I craned our necks to watch the year's first snow through an open window.

"What are you going to do when you're finished?" Heidi asked. Sexy question marks of smoke drifted up to the windows before vanishing.

"Take a bath."

She swatted me with her free hand. "No, silly. Three years from now. 145 When you leave Yale."

"I don't know. Open up a library. Somewhere where no one comes in for books. A library in a desert."

She looked at me as though she'd expected this sort of answer and didn't know why she'd asked in the first place.

"What are you going to do?" I asked her.

"Open up a psych clinic. In a desert. And my only patient will be some wacko who runs a library."

"Ha," I said. "Whatever you do, don't work in a dish room ever again. 150 You're no good." I got up from the crate. "C'mon. Let's hose the place down."

We put out our cigarettes on the floor, since it was our job to clean it anyway. We held squirt guns in one hand and used the other to douse the floors with the standard-issue, eye-burning cleaning solution. We hosed the dish room, the kitchen, the serving line, sending the water and crud and suds into the drains. Then we hosed them again so the solution wouldn't eat holes in our shoes as we left. Then I had an idea. I unbuckled my belt.

"What the hell are you doing?" Heidi said.

"Listen, it's too cold to go outside with our uniforms all wet. We could just take a shower right here. There's nobody but us."

"What the fuck, eh?"

I let my pants drop, then took off my shirt and panties. I didn't wear a bra, since I didn't have much to fill one. I took off my shoes and hung my clothes on the stepladder.

"You've flipped," Heidi said. "I mean, really, psych-ward flipped."

I soaped up with the liquid hand soap until I felt as glazed as a ham. "Stand back and spray me."

"Oh, my God," she said. I didn't know whether she was confused or delighted, but she picked up the squirt gun and sprayed me. She was laughing. Then she got too close and the water started to sting.

"God damn it!" I said. "That hurt!"

"I was wondering what it would take to make you say that."

When all the soap had been rinsed off, I put on my regular clothes and said, "O.K. You're up next."

"No way," she said.

"Yes way."

She started to take off her uniform shirt, then stopped.

"What?"

"I'm too fat."

"You goddam right." She always said she was fat. One time I'd told her that she should shut up about it, that large black women wore their fat like mink coats. "You're big as a house," I said now. "Frozen yogurt may be low in calories, but not if you eat five tubs of it. Take your clothes off. I want to get out of here."

She began taking off her uniform, then stood there, hands cupped over her breasts, crouching at the pubic bone.

"Open up," I said, "or we'll never get done."

Her hands remained where they were. I threw the bottle of liquid soap at her, and she had to catch it, revealing herself as she did.

I turned on the squirt gun, and she stood there, stiff, arms at her side, eyes closed, as though awaiting mummification. I began with the water on low, and she turned around in a full circle, hesitantly, letting the droplets from the spray fall on her as if she were submitting to a death by stoning.

When I increased the water pressure, she slipped and fell on the sudsy floor. She stood up and then slipped again. This time she laughed and remained on the floor, rolling around on it as I sprayed.

I think I began to love Heidi that night in the dish room, but who is to say that I hadn't begun to love her the first time I met her? I sprayed her and sprayed her, and she turned over and over like a large beautiful dolphin, lolling about in the sun.

Heidi started sleeping at my place. Sometimes she slept on the floor; sometimes we slept sardinelike, my feet at her head, until she complained that my
feet were "taunting" her. When we finally slept head to head, she said, "Much
better." She was so close I could smell her toothpaste. "I like your hair," she told
me, touching it through the darkness. "You should wear it out more often."

"White people always say that about black people's hair. The worse it   175
looks, the more they say they like it."

I'd expected her to disagree, but she kept touching my hair, her hands
passing through it till my scalp tingled. When she began to touch the hair
around the edge of my face, I felt myself quake. Her fingertips stopped for a
moment, as if checking my pulse, then resumed.

"I like how it feels right here. See, mine just starts with the same old
texture as the rest of my hair." She found my hand under the blanket and
brought it to her hairline. "See," she said.

It was dark. As I touched her hair, it seemed as though I could smell it,
too. Not a shampoo smell. Something richer, murkier. A bit dead, but sweet,
like the decaying wood of a ship. She guided my hand.

"I see," I said. The record she'd given me was playing in my mind, and I
kept trying to shut it off. I could also hear my mother saying that this is what
happens when you've been around white people: things get weird. So weird
I could hear the stylus etching its way into the flat vinyl of the record. "Listen," I said finally, when the bass and saxes started up. I heard Heidi breathe
deeply, but she said nothing.

We spent the winter and some of the spring in my room — never   180
hers — missing tests, listening to music, looking out my window to comment on people who wouldn't have given us a second thought. We read
books related to none of our classes. I got riled up by *The Autobiography of
Malcolm X* and *The Chomsky Reader*; Heidi read aloud passages from *The
Anxiety of Influence*. We guiltily read mysteries and *Clan of the Cave Bear*,
then immediately threw them away. Once we looked up from our books at
exactly the same moment, as though trapped at a dinner table with nothing
to say. A pleasant trap of silence.

Then one weekend I went back to Baltimore and stayed with my father. He
asked me how school was going, but besides that, we didn't talk much. He
knew what I thought of him. I stopped by the Enoch Pratt Library, where my
favorite librarian, Mrs. Ardelia, cornered me into giving a little talk to the after-
school kids, telling them to stay in school. They just looked at me like I was
crazy; they were only nine or ten, and it hadn't even occurred to them to bail.

When I returned to Yale — to a sleepy, tree-scented spring — a group
of students were holding what was called "Coming Out Day." I watched it
from my room.

The emcee was the sepia boy who'd given us the invitation months back.
His speech was strident but still smooth and peppered with jokes. There was
a speech about AIDS, with lots of statistics: nothing that seemed to make
"coming out" worth it. Then the women spoke. One girl pronounced herself

"out" as casually as if she'd announced the time. Another said nothing at all: she came to the microphone with a woman who began cutting off her waist-length, bleached-blond hair. The woman doing the cutting tossed the shorn hair in every direction as she cut. People were clapping and cheering and catching the locks of hair.

And then there was Heidi. She was proud that she liked girls, she said when she reached the microphone. She loved them, wanted to sleep with them. She was a dyke, she said repeatedly, stabbing her finger to her chest in case anyone was unsure to whom she was referring. She could not have seen me. I was across the street, three stories up. And yet, when everyone clapped for her, she seemed to be looking straight at me.

Heidi knocked. "Let me in."

It was like the first time I met her. The tears, the raw pink of her face.

We hadn't spoken in weeks. Outside, pink-and-white blossoms hung from the Old Campus trees. Students played Hacky Sack in T-shirts and shorts. Though I was the one who'd broken away after she went up to that podium, I still half expected her to poke her head out a window in Linsly-Chit, or tap on my back in Harkness, or even join me in the Commons dining hall, where I'd asked for my dish-room shift to be transferred. She did none of these.

"Well," I said, "what is it?"

She looked at me. "My mother," she said.

She continued to cry, but seemed to have grown so silent in my room I wondered if I could hear the numbers change on my digital clock.

"When my parents were getting divorced," she said, "my mother bought a car. A used one. An El Dorado. It was filthy. It looked like a huge crushed can coming up the street. She kept trying to clean it out. I mean—"

I nodded and tried to think what to say in the pause she left behind. Finally I said, "We had one of those," though I was sure ours was an Impala.

She looked at me, eyes steely from trying not to cry. "Anyway, she'd drive me around in it and although she didn't like me to eat in it, I always did. One day I was eating cantaloupe slices, spitting the seeds on the floor. Maybe a month later, I saw this little sprout, growing right up from the car floor. I just started laughing and she kept saying what, what? I was laughing and then I saw she was so—"

She didn't finish. So what? So sad? So awful? Heidi looked at me with what seemed to be a renewed vigor. "We could have gotten a better car, eh?"

"It's all right. It's not a big deal," I said.

Of course, that was the wrong thing to say. And I really didn't mean it to sound the way it had come out.

I told Dr. Raeburn about Heidi's mother having cancer and how I'd said it wasn't a big deal, though I'd wanted to say the opposite. I told Dr. Raeburn how I meant to tell Heidi that my mother had died, that I knew how one eventually accustoms oneself to the physical world's lack of sympathy: the buses that are still running late, the kids who still play in the street, the clocks that won't stop ticking for the person who's gone.

"You're pretending," Dr. Raeburn said, not sage or professional, but a little shocked by the discovery, as if I'd been trying to hide a pack of his cigarettes behind my back.

"I'm pretending?" I shook my head. "All those years of psych grad," I said. "And to tell me *that*?"

"What I mean is that you construct stories about yourself and dish them   200
out — one for you, one for you — " Here he reenacted this process, showing me handing out lies as if they were apples.

"Pretending. I believe the professional name for it might be denial," I said. "Are you calling me gay?"

He pursed his lips noncommittally, then finally said, "No, Dina. I don't think you're gay."

I checked his eyes. I couldn't read them.

"No. Not at all," he said, sounding as it he were telling a subtle joke. "But maybe you'll finally understand."

"Understand what?"   205

"Oh, just that constantly saying what one doesn't mean accustoms the mouth to meaningless phrases." His eyes narrowed. "Maybe you'll understand that when you finally need to express something truly significant your mouth will revert to the insignificant nonsense it knows so well." He looked at me, his hands sputtering in the air in a gesture of defeat. "Who knows?" he asked with a glib, psychiatric smile I'd never seen before. "Maybe it's your survival mechanism. Black living in a white world."

I heard him, but only vaguely. I'd hooked on to that one word, pretending. Dr. Raeburn would never realize that "pretending" was what had got me this far. I remembered the morning of my mother's funeral. I'd been given milk to settle my stomach; I'd pretended it was coffee. I imagined I was drinking coffee elsewhere. Some Arabic-speaking country where the thick coffee served in little cups was so strong it could keep you awake for days.

Heidi wanted me to go with her to the funeral. She'd sent this message through the dean. "We'll pay for your ticket to Vancouver," the dean said.

These people wanted you to owe them for everything. "What about my return ticket?" I asked the dean. "Maybe the shrink will chip in for that."

The dean looked at me as though I were an insect she'd like to squash.   210
"We'll pay for the whole thing. We might even pay for some lessons in manners."

So I packed my suitcase and walked from my suicide single dorm to Heidi's room. A thin wispy girl in ragged cutoffs and a shirt that read "LSBN!" answered the door. A group of short-haired girls in thick black leather jackets, bundled up despite the summer heat, encircled Heidi in a protective fairy ring. They looked at me critically, clearly wondering if Heidi was too fragile for my company.

"You've got our numbers," one said, holding on to Heidi's shoulder. "And Vancouver's got a great gay community."

"Oh, God," I said, "She's going to a funeral, not a Save the Dykes rally."
One of the girls stepped in front of me.

"It's O.K., Cynthia," Heidi said. Then she ushered me into her bedroom
and closed the door. A suitcase was on her bed, half packed.

"I could just uninvite you," Heidi said. "How about that? You want
that?" She folded a polka-dotted T-shirt that was wrong for any occasion and put it in her suitcase. "Why haven't you talked to me?" she said,
looking at the shirt instead of me. "Why haven't you talked to me in two
months?"

"I don't know," I said.

"*You don't know,*" she said, each syllable steeped in sarcasm. "You don't
know. Well, *I* know. You thought I was going to try to sleep with you."

"Try to? We slept together all winter!"

"If you call smelling your feet sleeping together, you've got a lot to learn."
She seemed thinner and meaner; every line of her body held me at bay.

"So tell me," I said. "What can you show me that I need to learn?" But
as soon as I said it I somehow knew she still hadn't slept with anyone. "Am
I supposed to come over there and sweep your enraged self into my arms?"
I said. "Like in the movies? Is this the part where we're both so mad we kiss
each other?"

She shook her head and smiled weakly. "You don't get it," she said. "My
mother is dead." She closed her suitcase, clicking shut the old-fashioned
locks. "My mother is dead," she said again, this time reminding herself. She
set her suitcase upright on the floor and sat on it. She looked like someone
waiting for a train.

"Fine," I said. "And she's going to be dead for a long time." Though it
sounded stupid, I felt good saying it. As though I had my own locks to click
shut.

Heidi went to Vancouver for her mother's funeral. I didn't go with her.
Instead, I went back to Baltimore and moved in with an aunt I barely knew.
Every day was the same: I read and smoked outside my aunt's apartment,
studying the row of hair salons across the street, where girls in denim cutoffs and tank tops would troop in and come out hours later, a flash of neon
nails, coifs the color and sheen of patent leather. And every day I imagined Heidi's house in Vancouver. Her place would not be large, but it would
be clean. Flowery shrubs would line the walks. The Canadian wind would
whip us about like pennants. I'd be visiting her in some vague time in the
future, deliberately vague, for people like me, who realign past events to
suit themselves. In that future time, you always have a chance to catch the
groceries before they fall; your words can always be rewound and erased,
rewritten and revised.

Then I'd imagine Heidi visiting me. There are no psychiatrists or deans,
no boys with nice shoes or flip cashiers. Just me in my single room. She
knocks on the door and says, "Open up."

CONSIDERATIONS FOR CRITICAL THINKING AND WRITING

1. FIRST RESPONSE. Dina is obviously plagued by a lack of trust. Do you think she trusts us, her readers? Why or why not?

2. How does Dina's response to the initial orientation exercises at Yale set up key aspects of her character that develop throughout the story?

3. Dina is in the minority at Yale for multiple reasons: she is black, she comes from a poor background, and she has homosexual yearnings. Do any of these factors seem to explain her feelings of alienation more than the others or do they all operate equally together? Are there other factors as well?

4. Dina is often the smartest person in the room. Does her intelligence contribute to her difficult relationships or is it the one attribute that connects her to other people who are like her?

5. What is the narrative function of Dina's school-assigned therapist Dr. Raeburn? Does he help her in any way?

6. When Dina encourages Heidi to crush a mouse, Heidi calls her "heartless," but Dina claims she is being "humane." Who is right?

7. Why is the anecdote about "the boy with the nice shoes" crucial to understanding Dina's mindset?

8. Find examples of Dina rejecting identity labels. Can you speculate about why she rejects them?

9. How does Dina's room function as a symbol within the story?

10. Explain the title, at first only using Dina's association and then building on that to offer your own assessment of her character.

11. Analyze the final line of the story. Where else is that line repeated?

CONNECTIONS TO OTHER SELECTIONS

1. Compare this story to John Updike's "A & P" (p. 138) in terms of maturity. Who makes more progress toward growing up: Sammy or Dina?

2. Contrast attitudes toward same-sex desire in this story and in Manuel Muñoz's "Zigzagger" (p. 143).

ANNIE PROULX (B. 1935)

Annie Proulx was born in 1935 and did not finish her first book until 1988. She received a B.A. from the University of Vermont in 1969 and a master's degree from Sir George Williams University, both in history, and later became a freelance writer of articles for magazines in the United States. She published short stories occasionally until she had enough to make her first collection, *Heart Songs*

John Harding/The LIFE Images Collection/Getty Images.

and Other Stories (1988), which she followed with the novel *Postcards* in 1992. Her breakthrough novel was *The Shipping News* (1993), which won both the Pulitzer Prize and the National Book Award, and she has since produced three novels, *Accordion Crimes* (1996), *The Old Ace in the Hole* (2003), and *Barkskins* (2016), and three books of short stories, *Close Range: Wyoming Stories* (1999), *Bad Dirt: Wyoming Stories 2* (2004), and *Fine Just the Way It Is: Wyoming Stories 3* (2008). Setting her works in places as distant as Newfoundland and Wyoming, Proulx conveys her dark, comic stories by creating a strong sense of place, using her talent for keen detail and for reproducing the peculiarities of local speech. *The Shipping News* and the short story "Brokeback Mountain" from *Close Range* were made into popular films. In 2011, Proulx published *Bird Cloud: A Memoir,* about her life in Wyoming.

55 Miles to the Gas Pump   1999

Rancher Croom in handmade boots and filthy hat, that walleyed cattleman, stray hairs like curling fiddle string ends, that warm-handed, quick-foot dancer on splintery boards or down the cellar stairs to a rack of bottles of his own strange beer, yeasty, cloudy, bursting out in garlands of foam, Rancher Croom at night galloping drunk over the dark plain, turning off at a place he knows to arrive at a canyon brink where he dismounts and looks down on tumbled rock, waits, then steps out, parting the air with his last roar, sleeves surging up windmill arms, jeans riding over boot tops, but before he hits he rises again to the top of the cliff like a cork in a bucket of milk.

Mrs. Croom on the roof with a saw cutting a hole into the attic where she has not been for twelve years thanks to old Croom's padlocks and warnings, whets to her desire, and the sweat flies as she exchanges the saw for a chisel and hammer until a ragged slab of peak is free and she can see inside: just as she thought: the corpses of Mr. Croom's paramours — she recognizes them from their photographs in the paper: MISSING WOMAN — some desiccated as jerky and much the same color, some moldy from lying beneath roof leaks, and all of them used hard, covered with tarry handprints, the marks of boot heels, some bright blue with the remnants of paint used on the shutters years ago, one wrapped in newspaper nipple to knee.

When you live a long way out you make your own fun.

CONSIDERATIONS FOR CRITICAL THINKING AND WRITING

1. FIRST RESPONSE. Do you think this story is humorous? Why or why not?

2. What kinds of assumptions about rural and urban life are made in the story? To what extent does Proulx challenge or endorse conventional views of rural and urban values?

3. Consider whether Mr. and Mrs. Croom are round, flat, or stock characters.

4. Is there a resolution to the conflict(s) in the plot?

5. How important is the setting?

6. Write a sentence that expresses your reading of the theme.

7. Describe the style and tone of each paragraph. How do they contribute to the theme?

8. CREATIVE RESPONSE. Substitute Proulx's title and final paragraph with your own. How do these changes affect your interpretation of the entire work?

CONNECTIONS TO OTHER SELECTIONS

1. Despite their brevity, how do "55 Miles to the Gas Pump" and Raymond Carver's "Popular Mechanics" (p. 217) manage to create compelling fictional worlds?

2. Kurt Vonnegut Jr. is also considered a humorist who addresses dark themes. Compare his "Happy Birthday, 1951" (p. 353) to this story. Which is funnier? Why?

3. Consider the use of irony in Proulx's story and in Mark Twain's "The Story of the Good Little Boy" (p. 226). Explain why you find the endings of the stories similar or different in tone.

KURT VONNEGUT JR. (1922–2007)

The author of fourteen novels and nearly two hundred short stories as well as several volumes of nonfiction, Kurt Vonnegut Jr. remains as popular among college-aged readers today as he was during his heyday in the 1960s. Vonnegut left college to enlist in the army in 1943, during the second World War. He was captured by the German army and witnessed the allied forces' attack on the city of Dresden. He survived by taking shelter in a slaughterhouse. This experience became the basis for his most enduring novel, *Slaughterhouse Five* (1969). The mode of his most popular novels is absurd satire, but his collected stories, many of which were written

GL Archive/Alamy Stock Photo.

before his novels (though some were published posthumously, including the following story), tend to be closer to a traditional realist mode.

Happy Birthday, 1951　2008

"Summer is a fine time for a birthday," said the old man. "And, as long as you have a choice, why not choose a summer day?" He wet his thumb on his tongue, and leafed through the sheaf of documents the soldiers had ordered him to fill out. No document could be complete without a birthdate, and, for the boy, one had to be chosen.

"Today can be your birthday, if you like it," said the old man.

"It rained in the morning," said the boy.

"All right, then — tomorrow. The clouds are blowing off to the south. The sun should shine all day tomorrow."

Looking for shelter from the morning rainstorm, the soldiers had found   5
the hiding place where, miracle of miracles, the old man and the boy had lived in the ruins for seven years without documents — without, as it were, official permission to be alive. They said no person could get food or shelter or clothing without documents. But the old man and the boy had found all three for the digging in the catacombs of cellars beneath the shattered city, for the filching at night.

"Why are you shaking?" said the boy.

"Because I'm old. Because soldiers frighten old men."

"They don't frighten me," said the boy. He was excited by the sudden intrusion into their underground world. He held something shiny, golden in the narrow shaft of light from the cellar window. "See? One of them gave me a brass button."

There had been nothing frightening about the soldiers. Since the man was so old and the child so young, the military took a playful view of the pair — who, of all the people in the city, alone had recorded their presence nowhere, had been inoculated against nothing, had sworn allegiance to nothing, renounced or apologized for nothing, voted or marched for nothing, since the war.

"I meant no harm," the old man had told the soldiers with a pretense of   10
senility. "I didn't know." He told them how, on the day the war ended, a refugee woman had left a baby in his arms and never returned. That was how he got the boy. The child's nationality? Name? Birthdate? He didn't know.

The old man rolled potatoes from the stove's wood fire with a stick, knocked the embers from their blackened skins. "I haven't been a very good father, letting you go without birthdays this long," he said. "You're entitled to one every year, you know, and I've let six years go by without a birthday. And presents, too. You're supposed to get presents." He picked up a potato gingerly, and tossed it to the boy, who caught it and laughed. "So you've decided tomorrow's the day, eh?"

"Yes, I think so."

"All right. That doesn't give me much time to get you a present, but there'll be something."

"What?"

"Birthday presents are better if they're a surprise." He thought of the 15
wheels he had seen on a pile of rubble down the street. When the boy fell
asleep, he would make some sort of cart.

"Listen!" said the boy.

As at every sunset, over the ruins from a distant street came the sound
of marching.

"Don't listen," said the old man. He held up a finger for attention. "And
you know what we'll do on your birthday?"

"Steal cakes from the bakery?"

"Maybe — but that isn't what I was thinking of. You know what I'd like 20
to do tomorrow? I'd like to take you where you've never been in all your
life — where I haven't been for years." The thought made the old man
excited and happy. This would be *the* gift. The cart would be nothing.
"Tomorrow I'll take you away from war."

He didn't see that the boy looked puzzled, and a little disappointed.

———

It was the birthday the boy had chosen for himself, and the sky, as the old
man had promised, was clear. They ate breakfast in the twilight of their cellar. The cart the old man had made late at night sat on the table. The boy ate
with one hand, his other hand resting on the cart. Occasionally, he paused
in eating to move the cart back and forth a few inches, and to imitate the
sound of a motor.

"That's a nice truck you've got there, Mister," said the old man. "Bringing animals to the market, are you?"

"Brummmaaaa, brummmaaaa. Out of my way! Brummmaaaa. Out of
the way of my tank."

"Sorry," sighed the old man, "thought you were a truck. You like it 25
anyway, and that's what counts." He dropped his tin plate into the bucket
of water simmering on the stove. "And this is only the beginning, only the
beginning," he said expansively. "The best is yet to come."

"Another present?"

"In a way. Remember what I promised? We'll get away from war today.
We'll go to the woods."

"Brummmaaaa, brummmaaaa. Can I take my tank?"

"If you'll let it be a truck, just for today."

The boy shrugged. "I'll leave it, and play with it when I get back." 30

———

Blinking in the bright morning, the two walked down their deserted street,
turned into a busy boulevard lined with brave new façades. It was as though
the world had suddenly become fresh and clean and whole again. The people didn't seem to know that desolation began a block on either side of the
fine boulevard, and stretched for miles. The two, with lunches under their
arms, walked toward the pine-covered hills to the south, toward which the
boulevard lifted in a gentle grade.

Four young soldiers came down the sidewalk abreast. The old man stepped into the street, out of their way. The boy saluted, and held his ground. The soldiers smiled, returned his salute, and parted their ranks to let him pass.

"Armored infantry," said the boy to the old man.

"Hmmmm?" said the old man absently, his eyes on the green hills. "Really? How did you know that?"

"Didn't you see the green braid?"

"Yes, but those things change. I can remember when armored infantry was black and red, and green was — " He cut the sentence short, "It's all non-sense," he said, almost sharply. "It's all meaningless, and today we're going to forget all about it. Of all days, on your birthday, you shouldn't be thinking about — "

"Black and red is the engineers," interrupted the boy seriously. "Plain black is the military police, and red is the artillery, and blue and red is the medical corps, and black and orange is . . ."

The pine forest was very still. The centuries-old carpet of needles and green roof deadened the sounds floating up from the city. Infinite colonnades of thick brown trunks surrounded the old man and the boy. The sun, directly overhead, showed itself to them only as a cluster of bright pinpoints through the fat, dense blanket of needles and boughs above.

"Here?" said the boy.

The old man looked about himself. "No — just a little farther." He pointed. "There — see through there? We can see the church from here," The black skeleton of a burned steeple was framed against a square of sky between two trunks on the edge of the forest. "But listen — hear that? Water. There's a brook up above, and we can get down in its little valley and see nothing but treetops and sky."

"All right," said the boy. "I like this place, but all right." He looked at the steeple, then at the old man, and raised his eyebrows questioningly.

"You'll see — you'll see how much better," said the old man.

As they reached the top of the ridge, he gestured happily at the brook below. "There! And what do you think of this? Eden! As it was in the beginning — trees, sky, and water. This is the world you should have had, and today, at least, you can have it."

"And look!" said the boy, pointing to the ridge on the other side.

A huge tank, rusted to the color of the fallen pine needles, squatted on shattered treads on the ridge, with scabs of corrosion about the black hole where its gun had once been.

"How can we cross the water to get to it?" said the boy.

"We don't want to get to it," said the old man irritably. He held the boy's hand tightly. "Not today. Some other day we can come out here, maybe. But not today."

The boy was crestfallen. His small hand grew limp in the old man's.

"Here's a bend up ahead, and around that we'll find exactly what we want."

The boy said nothing. He snatched up a rock, and threw it at the tank. 50
As the little missile fell toward the target, he tensed, as though the whole
world were about to explode. A faint click came from the turret, and he
relaxed, somehow satisfied. Docilely, he followed the old man.

Around the bend, they found what the old man had been looking for:
a smooth, dry table of rock, out by the stream, walled in by high banks. The
old man stretched out on the moss, affectionately patted the spot beside him,
where he wanted the boy to sit. He unwrapped his lunch.

After lunch, the boy fidgeted. "It's very quiet," he said at last.

"It's as it should be," said the old man. "One corner of the world — as it
should be."

"It's lonely."

"That's its beauty," 55

"I like it better in the city, with the soldiers and — "

The old man seized his arm roughly, squeezed it hard. "No you don't.
You just don't know. You're too young, too young to know what this is, what
I'm trying to give you. But, when you're older, you'll remember, and want to
come back here — long after your little cart is broken."

"I don't want my cart to be broken," said the boy.

"It won't, it won't. But just lie here, close your eyes and listen, and forget
about everything. This much I can give you — a few hours away from war."
He closed his eyes.

The boy lay down beside him, and dutifully closed his eyes, too. 60

The sun was low in the sky when the old man awakened. He ached and felt
damp from his long nap by the brook. He yawned and stretched. "Time to
go," he said, his eyes still closed. "Our day of peace is over." And then he
saw that the boy was gone. He called the boy's name unconcernedly at first;
and then, getting no answer but the wind's, he stood and shouted.

Panic welled up in him. The boy had never been in the woods before,
could easily get lost if he were to wander north, deeper into the hills and forest. He climbed onto higher ground and shouted again. No answer.

Perhaps the boy had gone down to the tank again, and tried to cross the
stream. He couldn't swim. The old man hurried downstream, around the
bend to where he could see the tank. The ugly relic gaped at him balefully
from across the cut. Nothing moved, and there was only the sound of wind
and the water.

"Bang!" cried a small voice.

The boy raised his head from the turret triumphantly. "Gotcha!" he said. 65

CONSIDERATIONS FOR CRITICAL THINKING AND WRITING

1. FIRST RESPONSE. Parents sometimes forbid their children to play with
   violent toys such as fake swords or guns, or even toy soldiers, and will
   also later in life restrict their children's use of violent video games. How
   does this story comment indirectly on those parenting choices?

2. Everyone has a birthday, but the boy gets to choose his own. Why is that fact significant in terms of the story's broader thematic concerns?

3. The fact that the man and the boy lived in the ruins of war for seven years is extraordinary. What is your response to the soldier's implied reaction, that the two of them "had lived [without] official permission to be alive" (para. 5)?

4. How do you interpret the repetition of the word *nothing* in paragraph 9?

5. Explain the different reactions the boy and the old man have toward soldiers.

6. The man is dedicated to protecting the boy from everything associated with the war. How does the boy seem to know so much about, for instance, the meaning of insignia on soldiers' uniforms?

7. The old man takes the boy into nature and declares it "Eden" (para. 43). How does this allusion to the biblical place of innocence and tranquillity function in the story?

8. Why is the boy so uncomfortable in nature?

9. The old man tells the boy that he will someday appreciate nature: Do you think he's right?

10. The boy gets to choose his birthday. What other choices does he make throughout the story? How do they collectively form his identity?

11. Why do you suppose Vonnegut chose not to name these characters?

CONNECTION TO ANOTHER SELECTION

1. Compare this story to Tobias Wolff's "Powder" (p. 56) in terms of significant moments in the maturity of young men.

POETRY

Credits, clockwise from top left: AP Photo/Ramon Espinosa; Todd-Bingham picture collection, 1837–1966 (inclusive). Manuscripts & Archives, Yale University; Henri Cartier-Bresson/Magnum Photos; Dartmouth College; Library of Congress/Getty Images.

POETRY

The Elements
of Poetry

11

Reading Poetry

Ink runs from the corners of my mouth.
There is no happiness like mine.
I have been eating poetry.
— MARK STRAND

Chris Felver/Getty Images.

READING POETRY RESPONSIVELY

Perhaps the best way to begin reading poetry responsively is not to allow
yourself to be intimidated by it. Come to it, initially at least, the way you
might listen to a song on the radio. You probably listen to a song several
times before you hear it all, before you have a sense of how it works, where
it's going, and how it gets there. You don't worry about analyzing a song
when you listen to it, even though after repeated experiences with it you
know and anticipate a favorite part and know, on some level, why it works
for you. Give yourself a chance to respond to poetry. The hardest work has
already been done by the poet, so all you need to do at the start is listen for
the pleasure produced by the poet's arrangement of words.

Try reading the following poem aloud. Read it aloud before you read
it silently. You may stumble once or twice, but you'll make sense of it if
you pay attention to its punctuation and don't stop at the end of every line
where there is no punctuation. The title gives you an initial sense of what
the poem is about.

LISA PARKER (B. 1972)

Snapping Beans 1998

For Fay Whitt

I snapped beans into the silver bowl
that sat on the splintering slats
of the porchswing between my grandma and me.
I was home for the weekend,
from school, from the North,   5
Grandma hummed "What A Friend We Have In Jesus"
as the sun rose, pushing its pink spikes
through the slant of cornstalks,
through the fly-eyed mesh of the screen.
We didn't speak until the sun overcame   10
the feathered tips of the cornfield
and Grandma stopped humming. I could feel
the soft gray of her stare
against the side of my face
when she asked, *How's school a-goin'?*   15
I wanted to tell her about my classes,
the revelations by book and lecture,
as real as any shout of faith
and potent as a swig of strychnine.
She reached the leather of her hand   20
over the bowl and cupped
my quivering chin; the slick smooth of her palm
held my face the way she held tomatoes
under the spigot, careful not to drop them,
and I wanted to tell her   25
about the nights I cried into the familiar
heartsick panels of the quilt she made me,
wishing myself home on the evening star.
I wanted to tell her
the evening star was a planet,   30
that my friends wore noserings and wrote poetry
about sex, about alcoholism, about Buddha.
I wanted to tell her how my stomach burned
acidic holes at the thought of speaking in class,
speaking in an accent, speaking out of turn,   35
how I was tearing, splitting myself apart
with the slow-simmering guilt of being happy
despite it all.
I said, *School's fine.*
We snapped beans into the silver bowl between us   40

and when a hickory leaf, still summer green,
skidded onto the porchfront,
Grandma said,
It's funny how things blow loose like that.

CONSIDERATIONS FOR CRITICAL THINKING AND WRITING

1. FIRST RESPONSE. Describe the speaker's feelings about starting a life at college. How do those feelings compare with your own experiences?
2. How does the grandmother's world differ from the speaker's at school? What details especially reveal those differences?
3. Discuss the significance of the grandmother's response to the hickory leaf in line 44. How do you read the last line?

The next poem creates a different kind of mood. Think about the title, "Those Winter Sundays," before you begin reading the poem. What associations do you have with winter Sundays? What emotions does the phrase evoke in you?

ROBERT HAYDEN (1913–1980)

Those Winter Sundays   1962

Sundays too my father got up early
and put his clothes on in the blueblack cold,
then with cracked hands that ached
from labor in the weekday weather made
banked fires blaze. No one ever thanked him.   5

I'd wake and hear the cold splintering, breaking.
When the rooms were warm, he'd call,
and slowly I would rise and dress,
fearing the chronic angers of that house,

Speaking indifferently to him,   10
who had driven out the cold
and polished my good shoes as well.
What did I know, what did I know
of love's austere and lonely offices?

Does the poem match the feelings you have about winter Sundays? Either way, your response can be useful in reading the poem. For most of us, Sundays are days at home; they might be cozy and pleasant experiences or they might be dull and depressing. Whatever they are, Sundays are more evocative than, say, Tuesdays. Hayden uses that response to call forth a sense of missed opportunity in the poem. The person who reflects on those winter Sundays didn't know until much later how much he had to thank his father for "love's austere and lonely offices." This is a poem about a cold past and a present reverence for his father — elements brought together by the phrase "Winter Sundays." *His* father? You may have noticed that the poem doesn't use a masculine pronoun; hence the voice could be a woman's. Does the gender of the voice make any difference to your reading? Would it make any difference about which details are included or what language is used?

What is most important about your initial readings of a poem is that you ask questions. If you read responsively, you'll find yourself asking all kinds of questions about the words, descriptions, sounds, and structure of a poem. The specifics of those questions will be generated by the particular poem. We don't, for example, ask how humor is achieved in "Those Winter Sundays" because there is none, but it is worth asking what kind of tone is established by the description of "the chronic angers of that house." The remaining chapters in this part of the book will help you formulate and answer questions about a variety of specific elements in poetry, such as speaker, image, metaphor, symbol, rhyme, and rhythm. For the moment, however, read the following poem several times and note your response at different points in the poem. Then write down a half-dozen or so questions about what produces your response to the poem. To answer questions, it's best to know first what the questions are, and that's what the rest of this chapter is about.

JOHN UPDIKE (1932–2009)

Dog's Death   1969

She must have been kicked unseen or brushed by a car.
Too young to know much, she was beginning to learn
To use the newspapers spread on the kitchen floor
And to win, wetting there, the words, "Good dog! Good dog!"

We thought her shy malaise was a shot reaction.   5
The autopsy disclosed a rupture in her liver.
As we teased her with play, blood was filling her skin
And her heart was learning to lie down forever.

Monday morning, as the children were noisily fed
And sent to school, she crawled beneath the youngest's bed.   10
We found her twisted and limp but still alive.
In the car to the vet's, on my lap, she tried

To bite my hand and died. I stroked her warm fur
And my wife called in a voice imperious with tears.
Though surrounded by love that would have upheld her,   15
Nevertheless she sank and, stiffening, disappeared.

Back home, we found that in the night her frame,
Drawing near to dissolution, had endured the shame
Of diarrhoea and had dragged across the floor
To a newspaper carelessly left there. *Good dog.*   20

Here's a simple question to get started with your own questions: What would the poem's effect have been if Updike had titled it "Good Dog" instead of "Dog's Death"?

THE PLEASURE OF WORDS

The impulse to create and appreciate poetry is as basic to human experience as language itself. Although no one can point to the precise origins of poetry, it is one of the most ancient of the arts, because it has existed ever since human beings discovered pleasure in language. The tribal ceremonies of peoples without written languages suggest that the earliest primitive cultures incorporated rhythmic patterns of words into their rituals. These chants, very likely accompanied by the music of a simple beat and the dance of a measured step, expressed what people regarded as significant and memorable in their lives. They echoed the concerns of the chanters and the listeners by chronicling acts of bravery, fearsome foes, natural disasters, mysterious events, births, deaths, and whatever else brought people pain or pleasure, bewilderment or revelation. Later cultures, such as the ancient Greeks, made poetry an integral part of religion.

Thus, from its very beginnings, poetry has been associated with what has mattered most to people. These concerns — whether natural or supernatural — can, of course, be expressed without vivid images, rhythmic patterns, and pleasing sounds, but human beings have always sensed a magic in words that goes beyond rational, logical understanding. Poetry is not simply a method of communication; it is a unique experience in itself.

What is special about poetry? What makes it valuable? Why should we read it? How is reading it different from reading prose? To begin with, poetry pervades our world in a variety of forms, ranging from advertising jingles to song lyrics. These may seem to be a long way from the chants heard around a primitive campfire, but they serve some of the same purposes. Like poems printed in a magazine or book, primitive chants, catchy jingles, and popular songs attempt to stir the imagination through the carefully measured use of words.

Although reading poetry usually makes more demands than does the kind of reading we use to skim a magazine or newspaper, the appreciation of poetry comes naturally enough to anyone who enjoys playing with words. Play is an important element of poetry. Consider, for example, how the following words appeal to the children who gleefully chant them in playgrounds:

I scream, you scream
We all scream
For ice cream.

These lines are an exuberant evocation of the joy of ice cream. Indeed, chanting the words turns out to be as pleasurable as eating ice cream. In poetry, the expression of the idea is as important as the idea expressed.

But is "I scream . . ." poetry? Some poets and literary critics would say that it certainly is one kind of poem because the children who chant it experience some of the pleasures of poetry in its measured beat and repeated sounds. However, other poets and critics would define poetry more narrowly and insist, for a variety of reasons, that this isn't true poetry but merely **doggerel**, a term used for lines whose subject matter is trite and whose rhythm and sounds are monotonously heavy-handed.

Although probably no one would argue that "I scream . . ." is a great poem, it does contain some poetic elements that appeal, at the very least, to children. Does that make it poetry? The answer depends on one's definition, but poetry has a way of breaking loose from definitions. Because there are nearly as many definitions of poetry as there are poets, Edwin Arlington Robinson's succinct observations are useful: "[P]oetry has two outstanding characteristics. One is that it is undefinable. The other is that it is eventually unmistakable."

This comment places more emphasis on how a poem affects a reader than on how a poem is defined. By characterizing poetry as "undefinable," Robinson acknowledges that it can include many different purposes, subjects, emotions, styles, and forms. What effect does the following poem have on you?

GREGORY CORSO (1930–2001)

I am 25   1955

With a love a madness for Shelley
Chatterton   Rimbaud
and the needy-yap of my youth
      has gone from ear to ear:
    I HATE OLD POETMEN!   5
Especially old poetmen who retract
who consult other old poetmen
who speak their youth in whispers,
saying:—I did those then
      but that was then   10
      that was then—
O I would quiet old men
say to them:—I am your friend
      what you once were, thru me
      you'll be again—   15
The at night in the confidence of their homes
rip out their apology-tongues
      and steal their poems.

A SAMPLE CLOSE READING

"I am 25"

After you've read a poem two or three times, a deeper, closer reading — line by line, word by word, syllable by syllable — will help you discover even more about the poem. Ask yourself: What happens (or does not happen) in the poem? What are the poem's central ideas? How do the poem's words, images, and sounds, for example, contribute to its meaning? What is the poem's overall tone? How is the poem put together?

Before you dive into the poem, take a moment to appreciate the way it looks. Your eyes are probably drawn to the capitalized line "I HATE OLD POETMEN!" This shouted line, complete with an exclamation point, probably gives you an immediate sense of the poem's tone: it's either anger or humor. We often associate poetry with love — the opposite emotion of hatred. This poem derives its power from its antagonism, from its opposition, to some sort of poetry. How seriously are we to take this line, though? "Poetmen" — is that even a word? The speaker could have said "poets." Poetmen — an invented word, or **neologism**, he repeats twice in the next two lines — makes those poets sound silly. There is undoubtedly a violent undercurrent to the poem, but when deciding on the poem's tone, humor might be a better bet than anger initially. It could, of course, be both.

Other visual effects of the poem might strike you as well. There is a gap in the middle of the second line, creating white space on the page. There are also a few gaps on the left-hand side of the poem: some lines are indented, and not in a way that forms a pattern. There are also dashes surrounding some of the lines, and capital letters at the beginning of lines are irregularly used. It is not a tidy poem: it looks ragged; it refuses to be contained. You might begin to think that it is a poem about rebelliousness even before you really look into its content.

So let's dive in. The prominent line we lifted out is one about hatred, but the poem leads with love, then corrects itself: "With a love a madness for Shelley. . . ." Before we get to the identity of Shelley, consider what the **speaker** has done. (Note that we refer to the speaker of the poem just as we refer to the narrator of a story: it's dangerous to automatically associate these voices with the author.) The speaker corrects himself: "With a love for Shelley . . . no, that's not right: with a *madness* for Shelley. . . ." Madness is stronger than love, in a way: to love Shelley is perhaps to admire him, to appreciate him from a distance. *Madness* connotes obsession: "I cannot get enough of Shelley. I am crazy for Shelley. Love is too mild a word for what I feel for Shelley." But since the speaker started with love, he feels the need to hang onto it: he's someone who wants to get the words right, but who is also aware he makes mistakes and does not erase them. The making of poetry is a messy process, he seems to say: here's my mess.

Alright, so who are Shelley, Chatterton, and Rimbaud? Poets, of course, but more particularly poets who died young (at the ages of 29, 17, and 37, respectively). Age is on the speaker's mind: the title states his overtly, and it is a declaration of the most salient feature of his identity: I am a young poetman, he declares. Here are other young poetmen from the past, and I am mad for them, meaning I admire their vision, their work, their spirit. If we are willing to do even a little reading into the lives of Percy Shelley, Thomas Chatterton, and Arthur Rimbaud, we will learn that they all lived passionately, that they were interested in the extreme emotions associated with what might be called the life force. They were also so passionate that art was their only vehicle to express it, and like many musicians you may be familiar with, they lived fast and burned out young. Chatterton committed suicide. Rimbaud had a torrid affair with another poet, Paul Verlaine, who shot him in the wrist during a drunken lovers' quarrel. Shelley drowned under suspicious circumstances after leading a chaotic life, including the apparently suicidal drowning of his first wife who had been pregnant at the time. In summary, these models represent the kind of "madness" that the speaker feels for them. If we were to read their work, we would perhaps understand even more why the speaker of Corso's poem was "mad" for them. (See Shelley's "Ozymandias," p. 667.)

The tension in the poem is not what we might expect, that a young poet has no respect for the poetic tradition and wants to do his own thing. Quite the contrary: the poets he loves are from the eighteenth and nineteenth centuries; he is writing in 1955. He hates a certain type of old poetman, though he doesn't name them:

> Especially old poetmen who retract
> who consult other old poetmen
> who speak their youth in whispers,
> saying: — I did those then
>> but that was then
>> that was then —

These old poetmen can be understood through their actions: they retract, they consult others, they speak in whispers. They sound, in short, like librarians or cautious lawyers more than what the speaker wants a poet to be: risky, dangerous, passionate, and unapologetic about the power of youth. Why apologize for what you did when you were younger? These old poetmen pretend they are wise and no longer capable of handling the wild energies of their youth. What they really are, the speaker implies, is boring.

This 25-year-old speaker must do something, then. It is a sneaky response: he seems to repress the line that he wants to shout — I HATE OLD POETMEN! — in favor of an approach that will allow him to conquer these old poetmen without directly battling them. He begins his next sentence with an antiquated poetic word: "O." This is known as the "vocative O": it indicates that the speaker is addressing someone or something directly. The reader is thus involved: we are drawn in as we would be during an anthem ("O say can you see . . ."). The speaker is letting us in on his plan and implicating us. He writes a little poem that is parallel to the ones the old poetmen whisper. Note the similarities between what they say and what he says:

> — I did those then
> but that was then
> that was then —

> and
> — I am your friend
> what you once were, thru me
> you'll be again —

They're both surrounded by dashes; they use simple, almost monosyllabic language; and they even rhyme! This is how the speaker will get the old poetmen to take him into their confidence: by imitating them. He knows they are vain: he promises that their spirit will be reborn in him, a young poet, and they will thus be comforted and "quieted."

And here is where the speaker asserts himself: "Then at night in the confidence of their homes / rip out their apology-tongues / and steal their poems." This is violent, criminal behavior! Ripping out tongues? Stealing poems? Our young poet sounds like a burglar and a torturer rather than someone who likes to mess around with words. We must understand, though, the degree to which poetry relies on *figurative language*. Essentially, figurative language is not literal. We do not think the speaker actually wants to do bodily harm to these older poets, but rather that he wants to take away their power — their voice — and replace it with his own. "Steal" is a little more ambiguous: does he want to plagiarize their poems? Or does he want to take them away and destroy them or maybe even just hide them? He seems capable of writing poetry like theirs as he demonstrates in his short three-line *parody*, but he has no respect for them. He also seems to be having a wonderful time writing his own original poems, even inventing words like "poetmen" and "needy-yap" or spelling "thru" in an inventive way. It's a poem about rebelliousness, as we originally said: if we've been following the speaker's logic and his tone, this stealing probably doesn't involve taking someone else's work and claiming it for his own. This stealing is another enactment of power: everything in the poem suggests that's what he wants. He steals their poems not to claim them for his own, but to show that he can. He is 25; he believes that his youth implies strength, confidence, brashness, and freedom from doubt or regret. Yes, I'm stealing your poem, old poetman: what are you going to do about it?

All of this careful unpacking is what the poem demands. You could accurately say, "Gregory Corso's 'I am 25' is about a young poet who struggles to assert his voice in a world dominated by old poets." As you can see, reading a description of what happens in a poem is not the same as experiencing a poem. The exuberance of "I scream (for ice cream)" and the somewhat sinister promise of violence in "I am 25" are in the hearing or reading rather than in the retelling. A *paraphrase* is a prose restatement of the central ideas of a poem in your own language. Consider the difference between the following poem and the paraphrase that follows it. What is missing from the paraphrase?

ROBERT FRANCIS (1901–1987)

Catch   1950

Two boys uncoached are tossing a poem together,
Overhand, underhand, backhand, sleight of hand, every hand,
Teasing with attitudes, latitudes, interludes, altitudes,
High, make him fly off the ground for it, low, make him stoop,
Make him scoop it up, make him as-almost-as-possible miss it,   5
Fast, let him sting from it, now, now fool him slowly,
Anything, everything tricky, risky, nonchalant,
Anything under the sun to outwit the prosy,
Over the tree and the long sweet cadence down,
Over his head, make him scramble to pick up the meaning,   10
And now, like a posy, a pretty one plump in his hands.

Paraphrase: A poet's relationship to a reader is similar to a game of catch. The poem, like a ball, should be pitched in a variety of ways to challenge and create interest. Boredom and predictability must be avoided if the game is to be engaging and satisfying.

A paraphrase can help us achieve a clearer understanding of a poem, but, unlike a poem, it misses all the sport and fun. It is the poem that "outwit[s] the prosy" because the poem serves as an example of what it suggests poetry should be. Moreover, the two players — the poet and the reader — are "uncoached." They know how the game is played, but their expectations do not preclude spontaneity and creativity or their ability to surprise and be surprised. The solid pleasure of the workout — of reading poetry — is the satisfaction derived from exercising your imagination and intellect.

That pleasure is worth emphasizing. Poetry uses language to move and delight even when it threatens to rip out the tongues of old men. The pleasure is in having the poem work its spell on us. For that to happen, it is best to relax and enjoy poetry rather than worry about definitions of it. Pay attention to what the poet throws you. We read poems for emotional and intellectual discovery — to feel and to experience something about the world and ourselves. The ideas in poetry — what can be paraphrased in prose — are important, but the real value of a poem consists in the words that work their magic by allowing us to feel, see, and be more than we were before. Perhaps the best way to approach a poem is similar to what Francis's "Catch" implies: expect to be surprised, stay on your toes, and concentrate on the delivery.

A SAMPLE STUDENT ANALYSIS

Tossing Metaphors Together in Robert Francis's "Catch"

The following sample paper on Robert Francis's "Catch" was written in response to an assignment that asked students to discuss the use of metaphor in the poem. Notice that Chris Leggett's paper is clearly focused and well organized. His discussion of the use of metaphor in the poem stays on track from beginning to end without any detours concerning unrelated topics (for a definition of *metaphor*, see p. 1163.) His title draws on the central metaphor of the poem, and he organizes the paper around four key words used in the poem: "attitudes, latitudes, interludes, altitudes." These constitute the heart of the paper's four substantive paragraphs, and they are effectively framed by introductory and concluding paragraphs. Moreover, the transitions between paragraphs clearly indicate that the author was not merely tossing a paper together.

Chris Leggett

Professor Lyles

English 203-1

9 November 2018

Tossing Metaphors Together in Robert Francis's "Catch"

> **Exploration of the meaning of the word *catch*.**

The word *catch* is an attention getter. It usually means something is about to be hurled at someone and that he or she is expected to catch it. *Catch* can also signal a challenge to another player if the toss is purposefully difficult. Robert Francis, in his

> **Thesis statement identifying purpose of poem's metaphors.**

poem "Catch," uses the extended metaphor of two boys playing catch to explore the considerations a poet makes when "tossing a poem together" (line 1). Line 3 of "Catch" enumerates these considerations metaphorically as "attitudes, latitudes, interludes, [and] altitudes."

> **Reference to specific language in poem, around which the paper is organized.**

While regular prose is typically straightforward and easily understood, poetry usually takes great effort to understand and appreciate. To exemplify this, Francis presents the reader not with a normal game of catch with the ball flying back and forth in a repetitive and predictable fashion, but with a physically challenging game in which one must concentrate, scramble, and exert oneself to catch the ball, as one must stretch the intellect to truly grasp a poem.

> **Introductory analysis of the poem's purpose.**

The first consideration mentioned by Francis is attitude. Attitude, when applied to the game of catch, indicates the ball's pitch in flight—upward, downward, or straight. It could also describe the players' attitudes toward each other or toward the game

> **Analysis of the meaning of *attitude* in the poem.**

in general. Below this literal level lies *attitude*'s meaning in relation to poetry. Attitude in this case represents a poem's tone. A poet may "Teas[e] with attitudes" (3) by experimenting with different tones

> **Discussion of how the attitude metaphor contributes to poem's tone.**

to achieve the desired mood. The underlying tone of "Catch" is a playful one, set and reinforced by the use of a game. This playfulness is further reinforced by such words and phrases as "[t]easing" (3), "outwit" (8), and "fool him" (6).

Considered also in the metaphorical game of catch is latitude, which, when applied to the game, suggests the range the object may be thrown—how high, how low, or how far. Poetic latitude, along similar lines, concerns a poem's breadth, or the scope of topic. Taken one level further, latitude suggests freedom from normal restraints or limitations, indicating the ability to go outside the norm to find originality of expression. The entire game of catch described in Francis's poem reaches outside the normal expectations of something being merely tossed back and forth in a predictable manner. The ball is thrown in almost every conceivable fashion, "Overhand, underhand . . . every hand" (2). Other terms describing the throws— such as "tricky," "risky," "Fast," "slowly," and "Anything under the sun" (6-8)—express endless latitude for avoiding predictability in Francis's game of catch and metaphorically in writing poetry.

During a game of catch the ball may be thrown at different intervals, establishing a steady rhythm or a broken, irregular one. Other intervening features, such as the field being played on or the weather, could also affect the game. These features of the game are alluded to in the poem by the use of the word *interludes. Interlude* in the poetic sense represents the poem's form, which can similarly establish or diminish rhythm or enhance meaning. Lines 6 and 9, respectively, show a broken and a flowing rhythm. Line 6 begins rapidly as a hard toss that stings the catcher's hand is described. The rhythm of the line is immediately slowed, however, by the word "now" followed by a comma, followed by the rest of the line. In contrast, line 9 flows smoothly as the reader visualizes the ball flying over the tree and sailing downward. The words chosen for this line function perfectly. The phrase "the long sweet cadence down" establishes a sweet rhythm that reads smoothly and rolls off the tongue easily. The choice of diction not only affects the poem's rhythmic flow but also establishes through connotative language the

Analysis of the meaning of *latitude* in the poem.

Discussion of how the latitude metaphor contributes to the poem's scope and message.

Analysis of the meaning of *interlude* in the poem.

Discussion of how the interlude metaphor contributes to the poem's form and rhythm.

Leggett 3

various levels at which the poem can be understood, represented in "Catch" as altitude.

Analysis of the meaning of *altitudes* in the poem.

While *altitudes* when referring to the game of catch means how high an object is thrown, in poetry it could refer to the level of diction, lofty or down-to-earth, formal or informal. It suggests also the levels at which a poem can be comprehended, the literal as well as the interpretive. In Francis's game of catch, the ball is thrown high to make the player reach, low to "make him stoop" (4), or "Over his head [to] make him scramble" (10), implying that the player should have to exert himself to catch it. So too, then, should the reader of poetry put great effort into understanding the full meaning of a poem. Francis exemplifies this consideration in writing poetry by giving "Catch" not only an enjoyable literal meaning concerning the game of catch, but also a rich metaphorical meaning—reflecting the process of writing poetry. Francis uses several phrases and words with multiple meanings. The phrase "tossing a poem together" (1) can be understood as tossing something back and forth or the process of constructing a poem. While "prosy" (8) suggests prose itself, it also means the mundane or the ordinary. In the poem's final line the word *posy* of course represents a flower, while it is also a variant of the word *poesy*, meaning poetry, or the practice of composing poetry.

Discussion of how the altitude metaphor contributes to the poem's literal and symbolic meanings, with references to specific language.

Francis effectively describes several considerations to be taken in writing poetry in order to "outwit the prosy" (8). His use of the extended metaphor in "Catch" shows that a poem must be unique, able to be comprehended on multiple levels, and a challenge to the reader. The various rhythms in the lines of "Catch" exemplify the ideas they express. While achieving an enjoyable poem on the literal level, Francis has also achieved a rich metaphorical meaning. The poem offers a good workout both physically and intellectually.

Conclusion summarizing ideas explored in paper.

Leggett 4

Work Cited

Francis, Robert. "Catch." *Literature to Go,* edited by Michael Meyer
    and D. Quentin Miller, 4th ed., Bedford/St. Martin's, 2020,
    p. 372.

Before beginning your own writing assignment on poetry, you should review Chapter 31, "Writing about Literature," which provides a step-by-step overview of how to choose a topic, develop a thesis, and organize various types of writing assignments. If you are using outside sources in your paper, you should make sure that you are familiar with the conventional documentation procedures described in Chapter 32, "The Literary Research Paper." (p. 1132)

How does the speaker's description in Francis's "Catch" of what readers might expect from reading poetry compare with the speaker's expectations concerning fiction in the next poem by Philip Larkin?

PHILIP LARKIN (1922–1985)

A Study of Reading Habits 1964

When getting my nose in a book
Cured most things short of school,
It was worth ruining my eyes
To know I could still keep cool,
And deal out the old right hook   5
To dirty dogs twice my size.

Later, with inch-thick specs,
Evil was just my lark:
Me and my cloak and fangs
Had ripping times in the dark.   10
The women I clubbed with sex!
I broke them up like meringues.

Don't read much now: the dude
Who lets the girl down before
The hero arrives, the chap   15
Who's yellow and keeps the store,
Seem far too familiar. Get stewed:
Books are a load of crap.

In "A Study of Reading Habits," Larkin distances himself from a speaker whose sensibilities he does not wholly share. The poet — and many readers — might identify with the reading habits described by the speaker in the first twelve lines, but Larkin uses the last six lines to criticize the speaker's attitude toward life as well as reading. The speaker recalls in lines 1–6 how as a schoolboy he identified with the hero, whose virtuous strength always triumphed over "dirty dogs," and in lines 7–12 he recounts how his schoolboy fantasies were transformed by adolescence into a fascination with violence and sex. This description of early reading habits is pleasantly amusing, because many readers of popular fiction will probably recall having moved through similar stages, but at the end of the poem the speaker provides more information about himself than he intends to.

As an adult the speaker has lost interest in reading because it is no longer an escape from his own disappointed life. Instead of identifying with heroes or villains, he finds himself identifying with minor characters who are irresponsible and cowardly. Reading is now a reminder of his failures, so he turns to alcohol. His solution, to "Get stewed" because "Books are a load of crap," is obviously self-destructive. The speaker is ultimately exposed by Larkin as someone who never grew beyond fantasies. Getting drunk is consistent with the speaker's immature reading habits. Unlike the speaker, the poet understands that life is often distorted by escapist fantasies, whether through a steady diet of popular fiction or through alcohol. The speaker in this poem, then, is not Larkin but a created identity whose voice is filled with disillusionment and delusion.

The problem with Larkin's speaker is that he misreads books as well as his own life. Reading means nothing to him unless it serves as an escape from himself. It is not surprising that Larkin has him read fiction rather than poetry because poetry places an especially heavy emphasis on language. Fiction, indeed any kind of writing, including essays and drama, relies on carefully chosen and arranged words, but poetry does so to an even greater extent. Notice, for example, how Larkin's deft use of trite expressions and slang characterizes the speaker so that his language reveals nearly as much about his dreary life as what he says. Larkin's speaker would have no use for poetry.

What is "unmistakable" in poetry (to use Robinson's term again) is its intense, concentrated use of language — its emphasis on individual words to convey meanings, experiences, emotions, and effects. Poets never simply process words; they savor them. Words in poems frequently create their own tastes, textures, scents, sounds, and shapes. They often seem more sensuous than ordinary language, and readers usually sense that a word has been hefted before making its way into a poem. Although poems are crafted differently from the ways a painting, sculpture, or musical composition is created, in each form of art the creator delights in the medium. Poetry is carefully orchestrated so that the words work together as elements in a structure to sustain close, repeated readings. The words are chosen to interact with one another to create the maximum desired effect, whether the purpose is to capture a mood or feeling, create a vivid experience, express a point of view, narrate a story, or portray a character.

Here is a poem that looks quite different from most *verse*, a term used for lines composed in a measured rhythmical pattern, which are often, but not necessarily, rhymed.

ROBERT MORGAN (B. 1944)

Mountain Graveyard 1979

for the author of "Slow Owls"

Spore Prose

stone	notes
slate	tales
sacred	cedars
heart	earth
asleep	please
hated	death

Though unconventional in its appearance, this is unmistakably poetry because of its concentrated use of language. The poem demonstrates how serious play with words can lead to some remarkable discoveries. At first glance "Mountain Graveyard" may seem intimidating. What, after all, does this list of words add up to? How is it in any sense a poetic use of language? But if the words are examined closely, it is not difficult to see how they work. The wordplay here is literally in the form of a game. Morgan uses a series of *anagrams* (words made from the letters of other words, such as *read* and *dare*) to evoke feelings about death. "Mountain Graveyard" is one of several poems that Morgan has called "Spore Prose" (another anagram) because he finds in individual words the seeds of poetry. He wrote the poem in honor of the fiftieth birthday of another poet, Jonathan Williams, the author of "Slow Owls," whose title is also an anagram.

The title, "Mountain Graveyard," indicates the poem's setting, which is also the context in which the individual words in the poem interact to provide a larger meaning. Morgan's discovery of the words on the stones of a graveyard is more than just clever. The observations he makes among the silent graves go beyond the curious pleasure a reader experiences in finding that the words *sacred cedars,* referring to evergreens common in cemeteries, consist of the same letters. The surprise and delight of realizing the connection between *heart* and *earth* are tempered by the more sober recognition that everyone's story ultimately ends in the ground. The hope that the dead are merely asleep is expressed with a plea that is answered grimly by a hatred of death's finality.

Little is told in this poem. There is no way of knowing who is buried or who is looking at the graves, but the emotions of sadness, hope, and pain are unmistakable — and are conveyed in fewer than half the words of this sentence. Morgan takes words that initially appear to be a dead, prosaic list and energizes their meanings through imaginative juxtapositions.

The following poem also involves a startling discovery about words. With the peculiar title "l(a," the poem cannot be read aloud, so there is no sound, but is there sense, a **theme** — a central idea or meaning — in the poem?

E. E. CUMMINGS (1894–1962)

l(a   1958

l(a

le
af
fa
ll
s)
one
l
iness

Bettmann/Getty Images.

CONSIDERATIONS FOR CRITICAL THINKING AND WRITING

1. **FIRST RESPONSE.** Discuss the connection between what appears inside and outside the parentheses in this poem.

2. What does Cummings draw attention to by breaking up the words? How do this strategy and the poem's overall shape contribute to its theme?

3. Which seems more important in this poem — what is expressed or the way it is expressed?

Although "Mountain Graveyard" and "l(a" do not resemble the kind of verse that readers might recognize immediately as poetry on a page, both are actually a very common type of poem, called the **lyric**, usually a brief poem that expresses the personal emotions and thoughts of a single speaker. Lyrics are often written in the first person, but sometimes — as in "Mountain Graveyard" and "l(a" — no speaker is specified. Lyrics present a subjective mood, emotion, or idea. Very often they are about love or death, but almost any subject or experience that evokes some intense emotional response can be found in lyrics. In addition to brevity and emotional intensity, lyrics are also frequently characterized by their musical qualities. The word *lyric* derives from the Greek word *lyre,* meaning a musical instrument that originally accompanied the singing of a lyric. Lyric poems can be organized in a variety of ways, such as the sonnet, elegy, and ode (see Chapter 18), but it is enough to point out here that lyrics are an extremely popular kind of poetry with writers and readers.

The following anonymous lyric was found in a sixteenth-century manuscript.

ANONYMOUS

Western Wind   ca. 1500

Western wind, when wilt thou blow,
The small rain down can rain?
Christ, if my love were in my arms,
And I in my bed again!

This speaker's intense longing for his lover is characteristic of lyric poetry. He impatiently addresses the western wind that brings spring to England and could make it possible for him to be reunited with the woman he loves. We do not know the details of these lovers' lives because this poem focuses on the speaker's emotion. We do not learn why the lovers are apart or if they will be together again. We don't even know if the speaker is a man. But those issues are not really important. The poem gives us a feeling rather than a story.

A poem that tells a story is called a **narrative poem**. Narrative poetry may be short or very long. An **epic**, for example, is a long narrative poem on a serious subject chronicling heroic deeds and important events. Among the most famous epics are Homer's *Iliad* and *Odyssey,* the Old English *Beowulf,* Dante's *Divine Comedy,* and John Milton's *Paradise Lost.* More typically, however, narrative poems are considerably shorter, as is the case with the following poem, which tells the story of a child's memory of her father.

REGINA BARRECA (B. 1957)

Nighttime Fires 1986

Nicolette Theriault.

When I was five in Louisville
we drove to see nighttime fires. Piled seven of us,
all pajamas and running noses, into the Olds,
drove fast toward smoke. It was after my father
lost his job, so not getting up in the morning
gave him time: awake past midnight, he read
    old newspapers
with no news, tried crosswords until he split the
    pencil
between his teeth, mad. When he heard
the wolf whine of the siren, he woke my mother,
and she pushed and shoved   10
us all into waking. Once roused we longed for burnt wood
and a smell of flames high into the pines. My old man liked
driving to rich neighborhoods best, swearing in a good mood
as he followed fire engines that snaked like dragons
and split the silent streets. It was festival, carnival.   15

If there were a Cadillac or any car
in a curved driveway, my father smiled a smile
from a secret, brittle heart.
His face lit up in the heat given off by destruction
like something was being made, or was being set right.   20
I bent my head back to see where sparks
ate up the sky. My father who never held us
would take my hand and point to falling cinders that
covered the ground like snow, or, excited, show us
the swollen collapse of a staircase. My mother   25
watched my father, not the house. She was happy
only when we were ready to go, when it was finally over
and nothing else could burn.
Driving home, she would sleep in the front seat
as we huddled behind. I could see his quiet face in the   30
rearview mirror, eyes like hallways filled with smoke.

WHEN I WRITE "There are lots of things that are going on in the world, in your room, or in that book you didn't read for class that could set you on fire if you gave them a chance. Poetry isn't only about what you feel, it's about what you think, and about capturing the way the world exists in one particular moment." — REGINA BARRECA

This narrative poem could have been a short story if the poet had wanted to say more about the "brittle heart" of this unemployed man whose daughter so vividly remembers the desperate pleasure he took in watching fire consume other people's property. Indeed, a reading of William Faulkner's famous short story "Barn Burning" (available in *Selected Short Stories of William Faulkner,* Modern Library, 1993) suggests how such a character can be further developed and how his child responds to him. The similarities between Faulkner's angry character and the poem's father, whose "eyes [are] like hallways filled with smoke," are coincidental, but the characters' sense of "something . . . being set right" by flames is worth comparing. Although we do not know everything about this man and his family, we have a much firmer sense of their story than we do of the story of the couple in "Western Wind."

Although narrative poetry is still written, short stories and novels have largely replaced the long narrative poem. Lyric poems tend to be the predominant type of poetry today. Regardless of whether a poem is a narrative or a lyric, however, the strategies for reading it are somewhat different from those for reading prose. Try these suggestions for approaching poetry.

Suggestions for Approaching Poetry

1. Assume that it will be necessary to read a poem more than once. Give yourself a chance to become familiar with what the poem has to offer. Like a piece of music, a poem becomes more pleasurable with each encounter.

2. Pay attention to the title; it will often provide a helpful context for the poem and serve as an introduction to it. Larkin's "A Study of Reading Habits" is precisely what its title describes.

3. As you read the poem for the first time, avoid becoming entangled in words or lines that you don't understand. Instead, give yourself a chance to take in the entire poem before attempting to resolve problems encountered along the way.

4. On a second reading, identify any words or passages that you don't understand. Look up words you don't know; these might include names, places, historical and mythical references, or anything else that is unfamiliar to you.

5. Read the poem aloud (or perhaps have a friend read it to you). You'll probably discover that some puzzling passages suddenly fall into place when you hear them. You'll find that nothing helps, though, if the poem is read in an artificial, exaggerated manner. Read in as natural a voice as possible, with slight pauses at line breaks. Silent reading is preferable to imposing a te-tumpty-te-tum reading on a good poem.

6. Read the punctuation. Poems use punctuation marks — in addition to the space on the page — as signals for readers. Be especially careful not to assume that the end of a line marks the end of a sentence, unless it is concluded by punctuation.

7. Paraphrase the poem to determine whether you understand what happens in it. As you work through each line of the poem, a paraphrase will help you to see which words or passages need further attention.

8. Try to get a sense of who is speaking and what the setting or situation is. Don't assume that the speaker is the author; often it is a created character.

9. Assume that each element in the poem has a purpose. Try to explain how the elements of the poem work together.

10. Be generous. Be willing to entertain perspectives, values, experiences, and subjects that you might not agree with or approve of. Even if baseball bores you, you should be able to comprehend its imaginative use in Francis's "Catch."

11. Try developing a coherent approach to the poem that helps you to shape a discussion of the text. See Chapter 30, "Critical Strategies for Reading," (p. 1069) to review formalist, biographical, historical, psychological, feminist, and other possible critical approaches.

12. Don't expect to produce a definitive reading. Many poems do not resolve all the ideas, issues, or tensions in them, and so it is not always possible to drive their meaning into an absolute corner. Your reading will explore rather than define the poem. Poems are not trophies to be stuffed and mounted. They're usually more elusive. And don't be afraid that a close reading will damage the poem. Poems aren't hurt when we analyze them; instead, they come alive as we experience them and put into words what we discover through them.

A list of more specific questions using the literary terms and concepts discussed in the following chapters begins on page 1114. That list, like the suggestions just made, raises issues and questions that can help you read just about any poem closely. These strategies should be a useful means for getting inside poems to understand how they work. Furthermore, because reading poetry inevitably increases sensitivity to language, you're likely to find yourself a better reader of words in any form — whether in a novel, a newspaper editorial, an advertisement, a political speech, or a conversation — after having studied poetry. In short, many of the reading skills that make poetry accessible also open up the world you inhabit.

You'll probably find some poems amusing or sad, some fierce or tender, and some fascinating or dull. You may find, too, some poems that will get inside you. Their kinds of insights — the poet's and yours — are what Emily Dickinson had in mind when she defined poetry this way: "If I read a book and it makes my whole body so cold no fire can ever warm me, I know that it is poetry. If I feel physically as if the top of my head were taken off, I know that it is poetry." Dickinson's response may be more intense than most — poetry was, after all, at the center of her life — but you, too, might find yourself moved by poems in unexpected ways. In any case, as Edwin Arlington Robinson knew, poetry is, to an alert and sensitive reader, "eventually unmistakable."

POETIC DEFINITIONS OF POETRY

It is quite common for poets to try to articulate what they are doing while they are doing it — to write poetry about poetry, in other words. The term for this phenomenon is *ars poetica*, a Latin term meaning "the art of poetry." There are hundreds of examples, dating back to antiquity: Horace's "Ars Poetica" is generally considered the earliest. These poems reflect the perspective of a particular poet at a particular time: definitions of poetry, its meaning, its intent, and its ideal form change over time, and even within a time period, poets are not likely to agree. As a reader of poetry, you might concentrate on what types of poems reach you in a particularly exciting way. Do you prefer poems with vivid imagery, poems with an inventive use of language, poems with a regular meter and rhyme scheme, or poems that disregard poetical conventions? Are you more attuned to a loud voice in a poem or to a subtle metaphor? Should poetry change the world, describe the world, or just exist in the world? The following four poems are variations on the *ars poetica* genre: spend a little time appreciating them and comparing them.

Marianne Moore (1887–1972)

Poetry 1919

I, too, dislike it: there are things that are important beyond all this fiddle.
Reading it, however, with a perfect contempt for it, one discovers in
it after all, a place for the genuine.
    Hands that can grasp, eyes
    that can dilate, hair that can rise
        if it must, these things are important not because a   5

high-sounding interpretation can be put upon them but because they are
    useful. When they become so derivative as to become unintelligible,
    the same thing may be said for all of us, that we
        do not admire what
        we cannot understand: the bat   10
            holding on upside down or in quest of something to

eat, elephants pushing, a wild horse taking a roll, a tireless wolf under
    a tree, the immovable critic twitching his skin like a horse that feels a
        flea, the base-
    ball fan, the statistician—
        nor is it valid   15
            to discriminate against "business documents and

school-books"; all these phenomena are important. One must make a
        distinction
    however: when dragged into prominence by half poets, the result is not
        poetry,

nor till the poets among us can be   20
   "literalists of
     the imagination"—above
       insolence and triviality and can present

for inspection, "imaginary gardens with real toads in them," shall we have
   it. In the meantime, if you demand on the one hand,   25
    the raw material of poetry in
      all its rawness and
      that which is on the other hand
genuine, then you are interested in poetry.

BILLY COLLINS (B. 1941)

Introduction to Poetry 1988

I ask them to take a poem
and hold it up to the light
like a color slide

or press an ear against its hive.

I say drop a mouse into a poem   5
and watch him probe his way out,

or walk inside the poem's room
and feel the walls for a light switch.

I want them to water-ski
across the surface of a poem   10
waving at the author's name on the shore.

But all they want to do
is tie the poem to a chair with rope
and torture a confession out of it.

They begin beating it with a hose   15
to find out what it really means.

RUTH FORMAN (B. 1968)

Poetry Should Ride the Bus 1993

poetry should hopscotch in a polka dot dress
wheel cartwheels
n hold your hand
when you walk past the yellow crackhouse

poetry should wear bright red lipstick
n practice kisses in the mirror

Photograph by Christine
Bennett, www.cbimages.org/

for all the fine young men with fades
shootin craps around the corner

poetry should dress in fine plum linen suits
n not be so educated that it don't stop in   10
every now n then to sit on the porch
and talk about the comins and goins of the world

poetry should ride the bus
in a fat woman's Safeway bag
between the greens n chicken wings   15
to be served with tuesday's dinner

poetry should drop by a sweet potato pie
ask about the grandchildren
n sit through a whole photo album
on a orange plastic covered lazy boy with no place to go   20

poetry should sing red revolution love songs
that massage your scalp
and bring hope to your blood
when you think you're too old to fight

yeah   25
poetry should whisper electric blue magic
all the years of your life
never forgettin to look you in the soul
every once in a while
n smile   30

CHARLES BUKOWSKI (1920–1994)

a poem is a city   1962

a poem is a city filled with streets and sewers
filled with saints, heroes, beggars, madmen,
filled with banality and booze,
filled with rain and thunder and periods of
drought, a poem is a city at war,   5
a poem is a city asking a clock why,
a poem is a city burning,
a poem is a city under guns
its barbershops filled with cynical drunks,
a poem is a city where God rides naked   10
through the streets like Lady Godiva,
where dogs bark at night, and chase away
the flag; a poem is a city of poets,
most of them quite similar

and envious and bitter . . .   15
a poem is this city now,
50 miles from nowhere,
9:09 in the morning,
the taste of liquor and cigarettes,
no police, no lovers, walking the streets,   20
this poem, this city, closing its doors,
barricaded, almost empty,
mournful without tears, aging without pity,
the hardrock mountains,
the ocean like a lavender flame,   25
a moon destitute of greatness,
a small music from broken windows . . .

a poem is a city, a poem is a nation,
a poem is the world . . .
and now I stick this under glass   30
for the mad editor's scrutiny,
and night is elsewhere
and faint gray ladies stand in line,
dog follows dog to estuary,
the trumpets bring on gallows   35
as small men rant at things
they cannot do.

Considerations for Critical Thinking and Writing

1. FIRST RESPONSE. Which of the four poems most intrigues you? Why?

2. There is a recurrent idea within these poems that poetry should be treated a certain way by its readers: How would you summarize that idea? Do you agree with the poets who express it?

3. These poems rely heavily on metaphor to make their argument. Find a metaphor in each poem and discuss in detail how it works.

RECURRENT POETIC FIGURES: FIVE WAYS OF LOOKING AT ROSES

One of poetry's charms is the way it encourages us to look at something from a new perspective. Wallace Stevens's poem "Thirteen Ways of Looking at a Blackbird" (p. 668) does just that: he places the image of a blackbird in each of thirteen numbered stanzas. We may initially scrutinize the blackbird — what does it mean? — but we will probably come around to the idea that the poem is not about the blackbird: it is about the looking.

Roses have been a favored image in poetry for many centuries. They are beautiful; they are associated with a tribute of love; their beauty is ephemeral;

they have thorns on their stems that make them difficult to grab; they require special care and knowledge to reach their perfect bloom, and so forth. Dandelions have not received the same poetic attention. Maybe the American experimental writer Gertrude Stein was just tired of reading about roses when she famously (and cryptically) wrote, "A rose is a rose is a rose is a rose." Read the following five short poems to consider how much can be done with roses.

ROBERT BURNS (1759–1796)
A Red, Red Rose 1799

O my luve's like a red, red rose
That's newly sprung in June;
O my luve's like the melodie
That's sweetly played in tune.

As fair art thou, my bonny lass,   5
So deep in luve am I;
And I will luve thee still my dear,
Till a' the seas gang° dry —   *go*

Till a' the seas gang dry, my dear,
And the rocks melt wi' the sun: 10
O I will luve thee still, my dear,
While the sands o' life shall run.

And fare thee weel, my only luve,
And fare thee weel awhile!
And I will come again, my luve,   15
Though it were a thousand mile.

EDMUND WALLER (1606–1687)
Go, Lovely Rose 1645

    Go, lovely rose,
Tell her that wastes her time and me
    That now she knows,
When I resemble° her to thee,   *compare*
How sweet and fair she seems to be,   5

    Tell her that's young
And shuns to have her graces spied,
    That hadst thou sprung
In deserts where no men abide,
Thou must have uncommended died.   10

Small is the worth
Of beauty from the light retired:
    Bid her come forth,
Suffer herself to be desired,
And not blush so to be admired.   15

       Then die, that she
The common fate of all things rare
    May read in thee,
How small a part of time they share
That are so wondrous sweet and fair.   20

WILLIAM BLAKE (1757–1827)

The Sick Rose 1794

O Rose, thou art sick;
The invisible worm
That flies in the night,
In the howling storm,

Hath found out thy bed   5
Of crimson joy,
And her dark secret love
Does thy life destroy.

DOROTHY PARKER (1893–1967)

One Perfect Rose 1926

A single flow'r he sent me, since we met.
    All tenderly his messenger he chose;
Deep-hearted, pure, with scented dew still wet—
    One perfect rose.

I knew the language of the floweret;   5
    "My fragile leaves," it said, "his heart enclose."
Love long has taken for his amulet
    One perfect rose.

Why is it no one ever sent me yet
    One perfect limousine, do you suppose?   10
Ah no, it's always just my luck to get
    One perfect rose.

H. D. (HILDA DOOLITTLE) (1886–1961)

Sea Rose 1916

Rose, harsh rose,
marred and with stint of petals,
meagre flower, thin,
sparse of leaf,

more precious 5
than a wet rose
single on a stem—
you are caught in the drift.

Stunted, with small leaf,
you are flung on the sand, 10
you are lifted
in the crisp sand
that drives in the wind.

Can the spice-rose
drip such acrid fragrance 15
hardened in a leaf?

CONSIDERATIONS FOR CRITICAL THINKING AND WRITING

1. FIRST RESPONSE. Which treatment of roses is the most conventional and which one is the most surprising? What factors explain your choices?

2. What precise emotion is expressed in each poem?

3. Is there a meaningful difference between poems in which the rose is the subject and poems in which it is a tool for comparison? How would you express that difference?

POEMS FOR FURTHER STUDY

MARY OLIVER (1935–2019)

The Poet with His Face in His Hands 2005

You want to cry aloud for your
mistakes. But to tell the truth the world
doesn't need any more of that sound.

So if you're going to do it and can't
stop yourself, if your pretty mouth can't 5
hold it in, at least go by yourself across

the forty fields and the forty dark inclines
of rocks and water to the place where
the falls are flinging out their white sheets

like crazy, and there is a cave behind all that   10
jubilation and water fun and you can
stand there, under it, and roar all you

want and nothing will be disturbed; you can
drip with despair all afternoon and still,
on a green branch, its wings just lightly touched   15

by the passing foil of the water, the thrush,
puffing out its spotted breast, will sing
of the perfect, stone-hard beauty of everything.

CONSIDERATIONS FOR CRITICAL THINKING AND WRITING

1. **FIRST RESPONSE.** Describe the kind of poet the speaker characterizes. What is the speaker's attitude toward that sort of poet?

2. Explain which single phrase used by the speaker to describe the poet most reveals for you the speaker's attitude toward the poet.

3. How is nature contrasted with the poet?

CONNECTION TO ANOTHER SELECTION

1. Compare the thematic use of nature in Oliver's poem and in Robert Frost's "Design" (p. 394.)

ALBERTO RÍOS (B. 1952)

Seniors   1985

William cut a hole in his Levi's pocket
so he could flop himself out in class
behind the girls so the other guys
could see and shit what guts we all said.
All Konga wanted to do over and over   5
was the rubber band trick, but he showed
everyone how, so nobody wanted to see
anymore and one day he cried, just cried
until his parents took him away forever.
Maya had a Hotpoint refrigerator standing   10
in his living room, just for his family to show
anybody who came that they could afford it.

Me, I got a French kiss, finally, in the catholic
darkness, my tongue's farthest half vacationing

Alberto Rios.

loudly in another mouth like a man in Bermudas, 15
and my body jumped against a flagstone wall,
I could feel it through her thin, almost
nonexistent body: I had, at that moment, that moment,
a hot girl on a summer night, the best of all
the things we tried to do. Well, she 20
let me kiss her, anyway, all over.

Or it was just a flagstone wall
with a flaw in the stone, an understanding cavity
for burning young men with smooth dreams —
the true circumstance is gone, the true 25
circumstances about us all then
are gone. But when I kissed her, all water,
she would close her eyes, and they into somewhere
would disappear. Whether she was there
or not, I remember her, clearly, and she moves 30
around the room, sometimes, until I sleep.

I have lain on the desert in watch
low in the back of a pick-up truck
for nothing in particular, for stars, for
the things behind stars, and nothing comes 35
more than the moment: always now, here in a truck,
the moment again to dream of making love and sweat,
this time to a woman, or even to all of them
in some allowable way, to those boys, then,
who couldn't cry, to the girls before they were 40
women, to friends, me on my back, the sky over me
pressing its simple weight into her body
on me, into the bodies of them all, on me.

Considerations for Critical Thinking and Writing

1. **FIRST RESPONSE.** Comment on the use of slang in the poem. Does it surprise you? How does it characterize the speaker?

2. How does the language of the final stanza differ from that of the first stanza? To what purpose?

3. Write an essay that discusses the speaker's attitudes toward sex and life. How are they related?

Connection to Another Selection

1. Think about "Seniors" as a kind of love poem and compare the speaker's voice here with the one in T. S. Eliot's "The Love Song of J. Alfred Prufrock" (p. 654.) How are these two voices used to evoke different cultures? Of what value is love in these cultures?

ROBERT FROST

Design   1936

I found a dimpled spider, fat and white,
On a white heal-all,° holding up a moth
Like a white piece of rigid satin cloth —
Assorted characters of death and blight
Mixed ready to begin the morning right,   5
Like the ingredients of a witches' broth —
A snow-drop spider, a flower like a froth,
And dead wings carried like a paper kite.

What had the flower to do with being white,
The wayside blue and innocent heal-all?   10
What brought the kindred spider to that height,
Then steered the white moth thither in the night?
What but design of darkness to appall? —
If design govern in a thing so small.

2 *heal-all:*   A common flower, usually blue, once used for medicinal purposes.

CONSIDERATIONS FOR CRITICAL THINKING AND WRITING

1. **FIRST RESPONSE.** What kinds of speculations are raised in the poem's
   final two lines? Consider the meaning of the title. Is there more than
   one way to read it?

2. How does the division of the octave and sestet in this sonnet (see chapter 18) serve to organize the speaker's thoughts and feelings? What is
   the predominant rhyme? How does that rhyme relate to the poem's
   meaning?

3. Which words seem especially rich in connotative meanings? Explain
   how they function in the sonnet.

CONNECTIONS TO OTHER SELECTIONS

1. Compare the ironic tone of "Design" with the tone of Countee Cullen's
   "Yet Do I Marvel" (p. 516.) What would you have to change in Cullen's
   poem to make it more like Frost's?

2. In an essay discuss Frost's view of God in this poem and Emily Dickinson's perspective in "I know that He exists" (p. 581.)

Edgar Allan Poe (1809–1849)

Sonnet — To Science 1845

Science! true daughter of Old Time thou art!
   Who alterest all things with thy peering eyes.
Why preyest thou thus upon the poet's heart,
   Vulture, whose wings are dull realities?
How should he love thee? or how deem thee wise,   5
   Who wouldst not leave him in his wandering
To seek for treasure in the jewelled skies,
   Albeit he soared with an undaunted wing?
Hast thou not dragged Diana° from her car?   *goddess of hunting and the moon*
   And driven the Hamadryad° from the wood   *tree nymph* 10
To seek a shelter in some happier star?
   Hast thou not torn the Naiad° from her flood,   *water nymph*
The Elfin from the green grass, and from me
The summer dream beneath the tamarind tree?°   *exotic Asian tree*

Considerations for Critical Thinking and Writing

1. **First response.** How is science characterized in lines 1–4? Which words are particularly revealing?

2. Given the references to Diana, the Hamadryad, the Naiad, the Elfin, and the tamarind tree, how would you describe the poet's world compared to the scientist's?

3. How do you think a scientist might respond to this poem?

Connection to Another Selection

1. Compare the speaker's attitudes toward what Poe calls in this poem "peering eyes" with the speaker's attitude toward the readers in Billy Collins's "Introduction to Poetry" (p. 386.)

Cornelius Eady (b. 1954)

The Supremes 1991

We were born to be gray. We went to school,
Sat in rows, ate white bread,
Looked at the floor a lot. In the back
Of our small heads

A long scream. We did what we could,   5
And all we could do was

Turn on each other. How the fat kids suffered!
Not even being jolly could save them.

And then there were the anal retentives,
The terrified brown-noses, the desperately   10
Athletic or popular. This, of course,
Was training. At home

Our parents shook their heads and waited.
We learned of the industrial revolution,
The sectioning of the clock into pie slices.   15
We drank cokes and twiddled our thumbs. In the
Back of our minds

A long scream. We snapped butts in the showers,
Froze out shy girls on the dance floor,
Pin-pointed flaws like radar.   20
Slowly we understood: this was to be the world.

We were born insurance salesmen and secretaries,
Housewives and short order cooks,
Stock room boys and repairmen,
And it wouldn't be a bad life, they promised,   25
In a tone of voice that would force some of us
To reach in self-defense for wigs,
Lipstick,

Sequins.

CONSIDERATIONS FOR CRITICAL THINKING AND WRITING

1. **FIRST RESPONSE.** Who were the Supremes? Why is the title so crucial for this poem?

2. Explain how the meanings and mood of this poem would change if it ended with line 25.

3. How does the speaker's recollection of school experiences compare with your own?

CONNECTION TO ANOTHER SELECTION

1. Discuss the speakers' memories of school in "The Supremes" and in Judy Page Heitzman's "The Schoolroom on the Second Floor of the Knitting Mill" (p. 441.)

12

Word Choice, Word Order, and Tone

I still feel that a poet has a duty to words, and that words can do wonderful things. And it's too bad to just let them lie there without doing anything with and for them.
— GWENDOLYN BROOKS

WORD CHOICE

Diction

Like all good writers, poets are keenly aware of ***diction***, their choice of words. Poets, however, choose words especially carefully because the words in poems call attention to themselves. Characters, actions, settings, and symbols may appear in a poem, but in the foreground, before all else, is the poem's language. Also, poems are usually briefer than other forms of writing. A few inappropriate words in a 200-page novel (which would have about 100,000 words) create fewer problems than they would in a 100-word poem. Functioning in a compressed atmosphere, the words in a poem must convey meanings gracefully and economically. Readers therefore have to be alert to the ways in which those meanings are released.

Although poetic language is often more intensely charged than ordinary speech, the words used in poetry are not necessarily different from

397

everyday speech. Inexperienced readers may sometimes assume that language must be high-flown and out-of-date to be included in a poem: instead of reading about a boy "enjoying a swim," they expect to read about a boy "disporting with pliant arm o'er a glassy wave." During the eighteenth century this kind of *poetic diction* — the use of elevated language rather than ordinary language — was highly valued in English poetry, but since the nineteenth century poets have generally overridden the distinctions that were once made between words used in everyday speech and those used in poetry. Today all levels of diction can be found in poetry.

A poet, like any writer, has several levels of diction from which to choose; they range from formal to middle to informal. *Formal diction* consists of a dignified, impersonal, and elevated use of language. Notice, for example, the formality of Andrew Marvell's "To His Coy Mistress" (the entire poem appears on p. 409):

> Thou by the Indian Ganges' side
> Shouldst rubies find; I by the tide
> Of Humber would complain. . . .

There is nothing casual or relaxed about these lines. We will explain the allusions in this passage later in this chapter, but focus now on diction: Marvell's use of "Thou" and "Shouldst" clearly signals a formal speaker, and the structure of the lines is also stilted, with the verbs at the end of the lines instead of following their subjects directly as they would in more relaxed or spoken English.

The language in Randall Jarrett's "The Death of the Ball Turret Gunner" (p. 400) represents a less formal level of diction; the speaker uses a middle diction spoken by most educated people. Consider how Jarrett's speaker describes the battle that kills him:

> Six miles from earth, loosed from its dream of life,
> I woke to black flak and the nightmare fighters.

The words he uses to describe this scene are common, yet selected for a certain poetic effect. The word "loosed" has different connotations and sound properties (i.e. the alliteration achieved when placed near the word "life") than a more technical word like "separated." There are rhyming echoes in the second line ("black flak" and "nightmare fighters.") All of this is accomplished with language that will not send you running for a dictionary.

Informal diction is evident in Philip Larkin's "A Study of Reading Habits" (p. 377). The speaker's account of his early reading is presented *colloquially*, in a conversational manner that in this instance includes slang expressions not used by the culture at large:

> When getting my nose in a book
> Cured most things short of school,
> It was worth ruining my eyes

To know I could still keep cool,
And deal out the old right hook
To dirty dogs twice my size.

This level of diction is clearly not that of Marvell's or Olds's speakers.

Poets may also draw on another form of informal diction, called **dialect**. Dialects are spoken by definable groups of people from a particular geographic region, economic group, or social class. New England dialects are often heard in Robert Frost's poems, for example. Gwendolyn Brooks uses a black dialect in "We Real Cool" (p. 509) to characterize a group of pool players. Another form of diction related to particular groups is **jargon**, a category of language defined by a trade or profession. Sociologists, photographers, carpenters, baseball players, and dentists, for example, all use words that are specific to their fields. Sally Croft offers an appetizing dish of cookbook jargon in "Home-Baked Bread" (p. 428).

Many levels of diction are available to poets. The variety of diction to be found in poetry is enormous, and that is how it should be. No language is foreign to poetry because it is possible to imagine any human voice as the speaker of a poem. When we say a poem is formal, informal, or somewhere in between, we are making a descriptive statement rather than an evaluative one. What matters in a poem is not only which words are used but how they are used.

Denotations and Connotations

One important way that the meaning of a word is communicated in a poem is through sound: snakes *hiss*, saws *buzz*. This and other matters related to sound are discussed in Chapter 16. Individual words also convey meanings through denotations and connotations. **Denotations** are the literal, dictionary meanings of a word. For example, *bird* denotes a feathered animal with wings (other denotations for the same word include a shuttlecock, an airplane, or an odd person), but in addition to its denotative meanings, *bird* also carries **connotations** — associations and implications that go beyond a word's literal meanings. Connotations derive from how the word has been used and the associations people make with it. Therefore, the connotations of *bird* might include fragility, vulnerability, altitude, the sky, or freedom, depending on the context in which the word is used. Consider also how different the connotations are for the following types of birds: hawk, dove, penguin, pigeon, chicken, peacock, duck, crow, turkey, gull, owl, goose, coot, and vulture. These words have long been used to refer to types of people as well as birds. They are rich in connotative meanings.

Connotations derive their resonance from a person's experiences with a word. Those experiences may not always be the same, especially when the people having them are in different times and places. *Theater,* for instance, was once associated with depravity, disease, and sin, whereas today the word usually evokes some sense of high culture and perhaps visions of elegant opulence. In several ethnic communities in the United States many people would find *squid* appetizing, but elsewhere the word is likely to produce negative connotations. Readers must recognize, then, that words written in other times and places may have unexpected connotations. Annotations usually help in these matters, which is why it makes sense to pay attention to them when they are available.

Ordinarily, though, the language of poetry is accessible, even when the circumstances of the reader and the poet are different. Although connotative language may be used subtly, it mostly draws on associations experienced by many people. Poets rely on widely shared associations rather than on the idiosyncratic response that an individual might have to a word. Someone who has received a severe burn from a fireplace accident may associate the word *hearth* with intense pain instead of home and family life, but that reader must not allow a personal experience to undermine the response the poet intends to evoke. Connotative meanings are usually public meanings.

Perhaps this can be seen most clearly in advertising, where language is also used primarily to convey moods and feelings rather than information. For instance, three decades of increasing interest in nutrition and general fitness have created a collective consciousness that advertisers have capitalized on successfully. Knowing that we want to be slender or lean or slim (not *spare* or *scrawny* and certainly not *gaunt*), advertisers have created a new word to describe beers, wines, sodas, cheeses, canned fruits, and other products that tend to overload what used to be called sweatclothes and sneakers. The word is *lite*. The assumed denotative meaning of *lite* is "low in calories," but as close readers of ingredient labels know, some *lites* are heavier than regularly prepared products. There can be no doubt about the connotative meaning of *lite*, however. Whatever is *lite* cannot hurt you; less is more. Even the word is lighter than *light*; there is no unnecessary droopy *g* or plump *h*. *Lite* is a brilliantly manufactured use of connotation.

Connotative meanings are valuable because they allow poets to be economical and suggestive simultaneously. In this way emotions and attitudes are carefully woven into the texture of the poem's language. Read the following poem and pay close attention to the connotative meanings of its words.

RANDALL JARRELL (1914–1965)

The Death of the Ball Turret Gunner   1945

From my mother's sleep I fell into the State
And I hunched in its belly till my wet fur froze.
Six miles from earth, loosed from its dream of life,
I woke to black flak and the nightmare fighters.
When I died they washed me out of the turret with a hose.

The title of this poem establishes the setting and the speaker's situation. Like the setting of a short story, the setting of a poem is important when the time and place influence what happens. "The Death of the Ball Turret Gunner" is set in the midst of a war and, more specifically, in a ball turret — a Plexiglas sphere housing machine guns on the underside of a bomber. The speaker's situation obviously places him in extreme danger; indeed, his fate is announced in the title.

Although the poem is written in the first-person singular, its speaker is clearly not the poet. Jarrell uses a ***persona***, a speaker created by the poet. In this poem the persona is a disembodied voice that makes the gunner's story all the more powerful. What is his story? A paraphrase might read something like this:

> After I was born, I grew up to find myself at war, cramped into the turret of a bomber's belly some 31,000 feet above the ground. Below me were exploding shells from antiaircraft guns and attacking fighter planes. I was killed, but the bomber returned to base, where my remains were cleaned out of the turret so the next man could take my place.

This paraphrase is accurate, but its language is much less suggestive than the poem's. The first line of the poem has the speaker emerge from his "mother's sleep," the anesthetized sleep of her giving birth. The phrase also suggests the comfort, warmth, and security he knew as a child. This safety was left behind when he "fell," a verb that evokes the danger and involuntary movement associated with his subsequent "State" (*fell* also echoes, perhaps, the fall from innocence to experience related in the Bible).

Several dictionary definitions appear for the noun *state*; it can denote a territorial unit, the power and authority of a government, a person's social status, or a person's emotional or physical condition. The context provided by the rest of the poem makes clear that "State" has several denotative meanings here: because it is capitalized, it certainly refers to the violent world of a government at war, but it also refers to the gunner's vulnerable status as well as his physical and emotional condition. By having "State" carry more than one meaning, Jarrell has created an intentional ambiguity. ***Ambiguity*** allows for two or more simultaneous interpretations of a word, a phrase, an action, or a situation, all of which can be supported by the context of a work. Through his ambiguous use of "State," Jarrell connects the horrors of war not just to bombers and gunners but to the governments that control them.

Related to this ambiguity is the connotative meaning of "State" in the poem. The context demands that the word be read with a negative charge. The word is used not to indicate patriotic pride but to suggest an anonymous, impersonal "State" that kills rather than nurtures the life in its "belly." The state's "belly" is a bomber, and the gunner is "hunched" like a fetus in the cramped turret, where, in contrast to the warmth of his mother's womb, everything is frozen, even the "wet fur" of his flight jacket (newborn infants have wet fur too). The gunner is not just 31,000 feet from the ground but

"Six miles from earth." *Six miles* has roughly the same denotative meaning as 31,000 feet, but Jarrell knew that the connotative meaning of *six miles* makes the speaker's position seem even more remote and frightening.

When the gunner is born into the violent world of war, he finds himself waking up to a "nightmare" that is all too real. The poem's final line is grimly understated, but it hits the reader with the force of an exploding shell: what the State-bomber-turret gives birth to is a gruesome death that is merely one of an endless series. It may be tempting to reduce the theme of this poem to the idea that "war is hell," but Jarrell's target is more specific. He implicates the "State," which routinely executes such violence, and he does so without preaching or hysterical denunciations. Instead, his use of language conveys his theme subtly and powerfully.

WORD ORDER

Meanings in poems are conveyed not only by denotations and connotations but also by the poet's arrangement of words into phrases, clauses, and sentences to achieve particular effects. The ordering of words into meaningful verbal patterns is called **syntax**. A poet can manipulate the syntax of a line to place emphasis on a word; this is especially apparent when a poet varies normal word order. In Emily Dickinson's "A narrow Fellow in the Grass," (p. 2) for example, the speaker says about the snake that "His notice sudden is." Ordinarily, that would be expressed as "his notice is sudden." By placing the verb *is* unexpectedly at the end of the line, Dickinson creates the sense of surprise we feel when we suddenly come upon a snake. Dickinson's inversion of the standard word order also makes the final sound of the line a hissing *is*.

TONE

Tone is the writer's attitude toward the subject, the mood created by all the elements in the poem. Writing, like speech, can be characterized as serious or light, sad or happy, private or public, angry or affectionate, bitter or nostalgic, or by any other attitudes and feelings that human beings experience. In Jarrell's "The Death of the Ball Turret Gunner," the tone is clearly serious; the voice in the poem even sounds dead. Listen again to the persona's final words: "When I died they washed me out of the turret with a hose." The brutal, restrained matter-of-factness of this line is effective because the reader is called on to supply the appropriate anger and despair—a strategy that makes those emotions all the more convincing.

Consider how tone is used to convey meaning in the next poem, inspired by the poet's contemplation of mortality.

MARILYN NELSON (B. 1946)
How I Discovered Poetry   1997

It was like soul-kissing, the way the words
filled my mouth as Mrs. Purdy read from
   her desk.
All the other kids zoned an hour ahead to 3:15,
but Mrs. Purdy and I wandered lonely as clouds
   borne
by a breeze off Mount Parnassus. She must have
   seen
the darkest eyes in the room brim: The next day
she gave me a poem she'd chosen especially for me
to read to the all except for me white class.
She smiled when she told me to read it, smiled harder,
said oh yes I could. She smiled harder and harder   10
until I stood and opened my mouth to banjo playing
darkies, pickaninnies, disses and dats. When I finished
my classmates stared at the floor. We walked silent
to the buses, awed by the power of words.

WHEN I WRITE "Although I usually wind up showing my poems to my best friend, sometimes I ask other people to be first-readers because I don't want to ask too much of my friend! I recently joined a poetry group. Their suggestions are useful, mostly in helping me see what I'm really trying to get at." — MARILYN NELSON

CONSIDERATIONS FOR CRITICAL THINKING AND WRITING

1. **FIRST RESPONSE.** Trace your response to Mrs. Purdy from the beginning to the end of the poem.
2. How do you interpret the tone of the final two lines?

The next work is a ***dramatic monologue***, a type of poem in which a character — the speaker — addresses a silent audience in such a way as to reveal unintentionally some aspect of his or her temperament or personality. What tone is created by Machan's use of a persona?

KATHARYN HOWD MACHAN (B. 1952)
Hazel Tells LaVerne   1976

last night
im cleanin out my
howard johnsons ladies room
when all of a sudden
up pops this frog
musta come from the sewer
swimmin aroun an tryin ta

WHEN I WRITE "When a poem begins to find its shape and form and voice inside you, let your heart and your head join to give it the best life you can: passion! imagery! music! And if it will let you, humor: ah, the world needs all it can get."
— KATHARYN HOWD MACHAN

climb up the sida the bowl
so i goes ta flushm down
but sohelpmegod he starts talkin   10
bout a golden ball
an how i can be a princess
me a princess
well my mouth drops
all the way to the floor   15
an he says
kiss me just kiss me
once on the nose
well i screams
ya little green pervert   20
an i hitsm with my mop
an has ta flush
the toilet down three times
me
a princess   25

CONSIDERATIONS FOR CRITICAL THINKING AND WRITING

1. FIRST RESPONSE. What do you imagine the situation and setting are for this poem? Do you like this revision of the fairy tale "The Frog Prince"?

2. What creates the poem's humor? How does Hazel's use of language reveal her personality? Is her treatment of the frog consistent with her character?

3. Although it has no punctuation, this poem is easy to follow. How does the arrangement of the lines organize Hazel's speech for clarity and emphasis?

4. What is the theme? Is it conveyed through denotative or connotative language?

5. CREATIVE RESPONSE. Write what you think might be LaVerne's reply to Hazel. First, write LaVerne's response as a series of ordinary sentences, and then try editing and organizing them into poetic lines.

CONNECTION TO ANOTHER SELECTION

1. Although Robert Browning's "My Last Duchess" (p. 470) is a more complex poem than Machan's, both use dramatic monologues to reveal character. How are the strategies in each poem similar?

A SAMPLE STUDENT RESPONSE

Alex Georges

Professor Myerov

English 200

2 October 2018

Tone in Katharyn Howd Machan's "Hazel Tells LaVerne"

"Tone," Michael Meyer writes, "is the writer's attitude toward the subject, the mood created by all the elements in the poem" (402) and is used to convey meaning and character. In her dramatic monologue, "Hazel Tells LaVerne," the poet Katharyn Howd Machan reveals through the persona of Hazel—a funny, tough-talking, no-nonsense cleaning lady—a satirical revision of "The Frog Prince" fairy tale. Hazel's attitude toward the possibility of a fairy-tale romance is evident in her response to the frog prince. She has no use for him or his offers "bout a golden ball / an how i can be a princess" (lines 11-12). If Hazel is viewed by the reader as a princess, it is clear from her words and tone that she is far from a traditional one.

Machan's word choice and humorous tone also reveal much about Hazel's personality and circumstances. Through the use of slang, alternate spellings, and the omission of punctuation, we learn a great deal about the character:

well i screams

ya little green pervert

an i hitsm with my mop

an has ta flush

the toilet down three times

me

a princess (19-25)

Listening to her speak, the reader understands that Hazel, a cleaner at Howard Johnson's, does not have an extensive education. She speaks in the colloquial, running words into one another and using phrases like "ya little green pervert" (20) and "i screams" (19). The lack of complete sentences, capital letters, and punctuation adds to her informal tone. Hazel's speech defines her social status, brings out details of her personality, and gives the reader her view of herself. She is accustomed to the thankless daily grind of work and will not allow herself even a moment's fantasy of becoming a princess. It is a notion that she has to flush away—literally, has "ta flush . . . down three times." She tells LaVerne that the very idea of such fantasy is absurd to her, as she states in the final lines: "me / a princess" (24-25).

Works Cited

Machan, Katharyn Howd. "Hazel Tells LaVerne." Meyer, pp. 403-404.

Meyer, Michael and D. Quentin Miller, editors. *Literature to Go*, 4th ed.,
    Bedford/St. Martin's, 2020.

MARTÍN ESPADA (B. 1957)
Latin Night at the Pawnshop   1987

> **WHEN I WRITE** "As a poet and a reader, I am most interested in the theme of justice. I am interested in poems that address justice vividly, concretely, specifically. Poets are, as Shelley put it, the 'unacknowledged legislators of the world.' We shouldn't leave justice to the lawyers and the politicians."
> — MARTÍN ESPADA

Chelsea, Massachusetts
Christmas, 1987

The apparition of a salsa band
gleaming in the Liberty Loan
pawnshop window:

Golden trumpet,
silver trombone,
congas, maracas, tambourine,

all with price tags dangling
like the city morgue ticket
on a dead man's toe.

CONSIDERATIONS FOR CRITICAL THINKING AND WRITING

1. **FIRST RESPONSE.** What is "Latin" about this night at the pawnshop?
2. What kind of tone is created by the poet's word choice and by the poem's rhythm?
3. Does it matter that this apparition occurs on Christmas night? Why or why not?
4. What do you think is the central point of this poem? How do the speaker's attitude and tone change during the course of this next poem?

JONATHAN SWIFT (1667–1745)

The Character of Sir Robert Walpole   1731

With favour and fortune fastidiously° blest,	*proudly*
He's loud in his laugh and he's coarse in his Jest;	
Of favour and fortune unmerited vain,	
A sharper in trifles, a dupe in the main.	
Achieving of nothing, still promising wonders,	5
By dint of experience improving in Blunders;	
Oppressing true merit, exalting the base,	
And selling his Country to purchase his peace.	
A Jobber of Stocks by retailing false news,	
A prater at Court in the Stile of the Stews;	10
Of Virtue and worth by profession a giber,	
Of Juries and senates the bully and briber.	
Tho' I name not the wretch you know who I mean,	
T'is the Cur dog of Britain and spaniel of Spain.	

CONSIDERATIONS FOR CRITICAL THINKING AND WRITING

1. **FIRST RESPONSE.** When did you first become aware of the speaker's basic opinion of Sir Robert Walpole?
2. Describe the speaker's tone. How does it characterize the speaker as well as Walpole?
3. **CREATIVE RESPONSE.** In line 12 Swift claims he does not name the wretch, but of course he does, in the title. Try imitating Swift's tone and rhyme scheme and the length of the poem by writing an imitation of it about a recognizable public figure from our time. (Walpole was a powerful politician — the Chancellor of the Exchequer — and you may certainly choose a politician, but you might also think of an entertainer, sports figure, newsmaker, etc.)

DICTION AND TONE IN THREE LOVE POEMS

These three love poems share the same basic situation and theme: a male speaker addresses a female (in the first poem it is a type of female) urging that love should not be delayed because time is short. This theme is as familiar in poetry as it is in life. In Latin this tradition is known as ***carpe diem***, "seize the day." Notice how the poets' diction helps create a distinctive tone in each poem, even though the subject matter and central ideas are similar (although not identical) in all three.

ROBERT HERRICK (1591–1674)

To the Virgins, to Make Much of Time 1648

Gather ye rose-buds while ye may,
  Old Time is still a-flying;
And this same flower that smiles today,
  Tomorrow will be dying.

The glorious lamp of heaven, the sun,
  The higher he's a-getting,
The sooner will his race be run,
  And nearer he's to setting.

That age is best which is the first,
  When youth and blood are warmer;
But being spent, the worse, and worst
  Times still succeed the former.

Then be not coy, but use your time,
  And while ye may, go marry;
For having lost but once your prime,
  You may for ever tarry.

Hulton Deutsch/Getty Images.

15

CONSIDERATIONS FOR CRITICAL THINKING AND WRITING

1. **FIRST RESPONSE.** Would there be any change in meaning if the title of this poem were "To Young Women, to Make Much of Time"? Do you think the poem can apply to young men, too?

2. What do the virgins have in common with the flowers (lines 1–4) and the course of the day (5–8)?

3. How does the speaker develop his argument? What will happen to the virgins if they don't "marry"? Paraphrase the poem.

4. What is the tone of the speaker's advice?

The next poem was also written in the seventeenth century, but it includes some words that have changed in usage and meaning over the past three hundred years. The title of Andrew Marvell's "To His Coy Mistress" requires some explanation. "Mistress" does not refer to a married man's illicit lover but to a woman who is loved and courted — a sweetheart. Marvell uses "coy" to describe a woman who is reserved and shy rather than coquettish or flirtatious. Often such shifts in meanings over time are explained in the notes that accompany reprintings of poems. You should keep in mind, however, that it is helpful to have a reasonably thick dictionary available when you are reading poetry. The most thorough is the *Oxford English Dictionary* (*OED*), which provides histories of words. The *OED* is a multivolume leviathan, but there are other useful unabridged dictionaries and desk dictionaries and many are available online.

Knowing a word's original meaning can also enrich your understanding of why a contemporary poet chooses a particular word. In "Design" (p. 394), Robert Frost raises provocative questions about the nature of evil and the existence of God in his dark examination of a moth's death, all presented in unexpected images of whiteness. He ends the poem with a series of questions concerning what causes "death and blight," wondering if it is a "design of darkness to appall" or no design at all, a universe informed only by random meaninglessness. Frost's precise contemporary use of "appall" captures the sense of consternation and dismay that such a frightening contemplation of death might evoke, but a dictionary reveals some further relevant insights. The dictionary's additional information about the history of *appall* shows us why it is the perfect word to establish the overwhelming effect of the poem. The word comes from the Middle English *appallen*, meaning "to grow faint," and in Old French *apalir* means "to grow pale" or white. These meanings reinforce the powerful sense of death buried in the images of whiteness throughout the poem. Moreover, Frost's "appall" also echoes a funereal pall, or coffin, allowing the word to bear even more connotative weight. Knowing the origin of *appall* gives us the full heft of the poet's word choice.

Although some of the language in "To His Coy Mistress" requires annotations for the modern reader, this poem continues to serve as a powerful reminder that time is a formidable foe, even for lovers.

Andrew Marvell (1621–1678)

To His Coy Mistress   1681

Had we but world enough, and time,
This coyness, lady, were no crime.
We would sit down, and think which way
To walk, and pass our long love's day.
Thou by the Indian Ganges'° side   5

Michael Nicholson/Getty Images.

Shouldst rubies find; I by the tide
Of Humber° would complain.° I would   *write love songs*
Love you ten years before the Flood,
And you should, if you please, refuse
Till the conversion of the Jews.   10
My vegetable love should grow°
Vaster than empires, and more slow;
An hundred years should go to praise
Thine eyes and on thy forehead gaze,
Two hundred to adore each breast,   15
But thirty thousand to the rest:
An age at least to every part,
And the last age should show your heart.
For, lady, you deserve this state,
Nor would I love at lower rate.   20
    But at my back I always hear
Time's wingèd chariot hurrying near;
And yonder all before us lie
Deserts of vast eternity.
Thy beauty shall no more be found,   25
Nor in thy marble vault shall sound
My echoing song; then worms shall try
That long preserved virginity,
And your quaint honor turn to dust,
And into ashes all my lust.   30
The grave's a fine and private place,
But none, I think, do there embrace.
    Now, therefore, while the youthful hue
Sits on thy skin like morning dew,
And while thy willing soul transpires°   *breathes forth* 35
At every pore with instant fires,
Now let us sport us while we may,
And now, like amorous birds of prey,
Rather at once our time devour
Than languish in his slow-chapped° power.   *slow-jawed* 40
Let us roll all our strength and all
Our sweetness up into one ball,
And tear our pleasures with rough strife
Thorough° the iron gates of life.   *through*
Thus, though we cannot make our sun   45
Stand still, yet we will make him run.

---

5 *Ganges:* A river in India sacred to the Hindus.   7 *Humber:* A river that flows through Marvell's native town, Hull.   11 *My vegetable love . . . grow:* A slow, unconscious growth.

CONSIDERATIONS FOR CRITICAL THINKING AND WRITING

1. FIRST RESPONSE. Do you think this *carpe diem* poem is hopelessly dated, or does it speak to our contemporary concerns?

2. This poem is divided into a three-part argument. Briefly summarize each section: if (lines 1–20), but (21–32), therefore (33–46).

3. What is the speaker's tone in lines 1–20? How much time would he spend adoring his mistress? Is he sincere? How does he expect his mistress to respond to these lines?

4. How does the speaker's tone change beginning with line 21? What is his view of time in lines 21–32? What does this description do to the lush and leisurely sense of time in lines 1–20? How do you think his mistress would react to lines 21–32?

5. In the final lines of Herrick's "To the Virgins, to Make Much of Time" (p. 408), the speaker urges the virgins to "go marry." What does Marvell's speaker urge in lines 33–46? How is the pace of these lines (notice the verbs) different from that of the first twenty lines of the poem?

6. This poem is sometimes read as a vigorous but simple celebration of flesh. Is there more to the theme than that?

The third in this series of *carpe diem* poems is a twenty-first-century work. The language of Ann Lauinger's "Marvell Noir" is more immediately accessible than that of Marvell's "To His Coy Mistress"; an ordinary dictionary will quickly identify any words unfamiliar to a reader. But the title might require an online search or a dictionary of biography for the reference to Marvell, as well as a dictionary of allusions to provide a succinct description that explains the reference to film noir. An **allusion** is a brief cultural reference to a person, a place, a thing, an event, or an idea in history or literature. Allusive words, like connotative words, are both suggestive and economical; poets use allusions to conjure up biblical authority, scenes from Shakespeare's plays, historic figures, wars, great love stories, and anything else that might serve to deepen and enrich their own work. The title of "Marvell Noir" makes two allusions that an ordinary dictionary may not explain, because it alludes to Marvell's most famous poem, "To His Coy Mistress," and to dark crime films (*noir* is "black" in French) of the 1940s that were often filmed in black and white featuring tough-talking, cynical heroes — such as those portrayed by Humphrey Bogart — and hardened, cold women — like the characters played by Joan Crawford. Lauinger assumes that her reader will understand the allusions.

Allusions imply reading and cultural experiences shared by the poet and the reader. Literate audiences once had more in common than they do today because more people had similar economic, social, and educational backgrounds. But a judicious use of specialized dictionaries, encyclopedias, and online reference tools such as Google Search can help you decipher allusions that grow out of this body of experience. As you read more, you'll be able to make connections based on your own experiences with literature. In a sense, allusions make available what other human beings have deemed

worth remembering, and that is certainly an economical way of supple-
menting and enhancing your own experience.

Lauinger's version of the *carpe diem* theme follows. What strikes you as
particularly modern about it?

ANN LAUINGER (B. 1948)

Marvell Noir   2005

Sweetheart, if we had the time,
A week in bed would be no crime.
I'd light your Camels, pour your Jack;
You'd do shiatsu on my back.
When you got up to scramble eggs,   5
I'd write a sonnet to your legs,
And you could watch my stubble grow.
Yes, gorgeous, we'd take it slow.
I'd hear the whole sad tale again:
A roadhouse band; you can't trust men;   10
He set you up; you had to eat,
And bitter with the bittersweet
Was what they dished you; Ginger lied;
You weren't there when Sanchez died;
You didn't know the pearls were fake . . .   15
Aw, can it, sport! Make no mistake,
You're in it, doll, up to your eyeballs!
Tears? Please! You'll dilute our highballs,
And make that angel face a mess
For the nice Lieutenant. I confess   20
I'm nuts for you — but take the rap?
You must think I'm some other sap!
And, precious, I kind of wish I was.
Well, when they spring you, give a buzz;
Guess I'll get back to Archie's wife,   25
And you'll get twenty-five to life.
You'll have time then, more than enough,
To reminisce about the stuff
That dreams are made of, and the men
You suckered. Sadly, in the pen   30
Your kind of talent goes to waste.
But Irish bars are more my taste
Than iron ones: stripes ain't my style.
You're going down; I promise I'll
Come visit every other year.   35
Now kiss me, sweet — the squad car's here.

CONSIDERATIONS FOR CRITICAL THINKING AND WRITING

1. **FIRST RESPONSE.** How does Lauinger's poem evoke Marvell's *carpe diem* poem (p. 409) and the tough-guy tone of a "noir" narrative, a crime story or thriller that is especially dark?

2. Discuss the ways in which time is a central presence in the poem.

3. Explain the allusion to dreams in lines 28–29.

CONNECTION TO ANOTHER SELECTION

1. Compare the speaker's voice in this poem with that of the speaker in "To His Coy Mistress" (p. 409). What significant similarities and differences do you find?

POEMS FOR FURTHER STUDY

WALT WHITMAN (1819–1892)
The Dalliance of the Eagles 1880

Skirting the river road, (my forenoon walk, my rest,)
Skyward in air a sudden muffled sound, the dalliance of the eagles,
The rushing amorous contact high in space together,
The clinching interlocking claws, a living, fierce, gyrating wheel,
Four beating wings, two beaks, a swirling mass tight grappling,   5
In tumbling turning clustering loops, straight downward falling,
Till o'er the river pois'd, the twain yet one, a moment's lull,
A motionless still balance in the air, then parting, talons loosing,
Upward again on slow-firm pinions slanting, their separate diverse flight,
She hers, he his, pursuing.
                                                                                          10

CONSIDERATIONS FOR CRITICAL THINKING AND WRITING

1. **FIRST RESPONSE.** Why do you think Whitman chose the word *dalliance* rather than, perhaps, *mating*?

2. List the verbs in the poem and comment on their effects in evoking the scene.

KWAME DAWES (B. 1962)
History Lesson at Eight a.m. 1993

History class at eight a.m.
Who discover Jamaica, class?
Christopher Columbus

Tell me when?   5
Fourteen ninety-two
And where?

Discovery Bay
Discovery Bay

Twisting through Mount Diablo   10
Where Juan de Bolas was hiding
Musket, fife, and powder
Guerilla, revolutionary
I am traveling to Discovery Bay
Traveling to Discovery Bay

                                       15
How many ships?
Three ships
What them name?
Niña
One   20
Pinta
Two
Santa Maria
Tell me where?

Discovery Bay   25
Discovery Bay

Twisting through Fern Gully
Arawak blood was shed here
Crack their brains with musket shot
History is buried here   30
I am traveling to Discovery Bay
Traveling to Discovery Bay

Who lived here first?
Arawak and Carib
What were the Arawak?   35
Peaceful flat-head people
What were the Caribs?
Cannibals
Cannibals?
Yes, cannibals!   40
Now tell me where?

Discovery Bay
Discovery Bay

Rush past Saint Ann's Bay
Marcus was preaching from the altar
See the slave auction inna Falmouth   45

Cane field wild with fire
I am traveling to Discovery Bay
Traveling to Discovery Bay

You teach me all kind of madness
From Hawkins to Drake to Pizarro 50
From Cortés to Penn to Venables
At eight a.m. each blessed day
No wonder I can't find Discovery Bay
Was looking for the gold
And all I see is blood 55
All I see is blood
All I see is blood

CONSIDERATIONS FOR CRITICAL THINKING AND WRITING

1. FIRST RESPONSE. How does the poem function as a history lesson for the reader as well as for the children speaking in the poem?
2. How can you tell the difference between speakers in the poem?
3. What effect does repetition have throughout the poem? Does its effect change?
4. How does the blending of informal diction and dialect contribute to the poem's overall effect?

ROBERT FROST

"Out, Out —" ° 1916

The buzz-saw snarled and rattled in the yard
And made dust and dropped stove-length sticks of wood,
Sweet-scented stuff when the breeze drew across it.
And from there those that lifted eyes could count
Five mountain ranges one behind the other 5
Under the sunset far into Vermont.
And the saw snarled and rattled, snarled and rattled,
As it ran light, or had to bear a load.
And nothing happened: day was all but done.
Call it a day, I wish they might have said 10
To please the boy by giving him the half hour
That a boy counts so much when saved from work.
His sister stood beside them in her apron
To tell them "Supper." At the word, the saw,
As if to prove saws knew what supper meant, 15

"Out, Out —": From Act V, Scene v, of Shakespeare's *Macbeth*.

Leaped out at the boy's hand, or seemed to leap —
He must have given the hand. However it was,
Neither refused the meeting. But the hand!
The boy's first outcry was a rueful laugh,
As he swung toward them holding up the hand   20
Half in appeal, but half as if to keep
The life from spilling. Then the boy saw all —
Since he was old enough to know, big boy
Doing a man's work, though a child at heart —
He saw all spoiled. "Don't let him cut my hand off —   25
The doctor, when he comes. Don't let him, sister!"
So. But the hand was gone already.
The doctor put him in the dark of ether.
He lay and puffed his lips out with his breath.
And then — the watcher at his pulse took fright.   30
No one believed. They listened at his heart.
Little — less — nothing! — and that ended it.
No more to build on there. And they, since they
Were not the one dead, turned to their affairs.

CONSIDERATIONS FOR CRITICAL THINKING AND WRITING

1. FIRST RESPONSE. This narrative poem is about the accidental death of
   a Vermont boy. What is the purpose of the story? Some readers have
   argued that the final lines reveal the speaker's callousness and indifference. What do you think?

2. How does Frost's allusion to *Macbeth* contribute to the meaning of this
   poem? Does the speaker seem to agree with the view of life expressed in
   Macbeth's lines?

3. CRITICAL STRATEGIES. Read the section on Marxist criticism (p. 1077)
   How do you think a Marxist critic would interpret the family and events
   described in this poem?

ROBERT FROST

The Road Not Taken   1916

Two roads diverged in a yellow wood,
And sorry I could not travel both
And be one traveler, long I stood
And looked down one as far as I could
To where it bent in the undergrowth;   5

Then took the other, as just as fair,
And having perhaps the better claim,
Because it was grassy and wanted wear;

Though as for that the passing there
Had worn them really about the same,   10

And both that morning equally lay
In leaves no step had trodden black.
Oh, I kept the first for another day!
Yet knowing how way leads on to way,
I doubted if I should ever come back.   15

I shall be telling this with a sigh
Somewhere ages and ages hence:
Two roads diverged in a wood, and I —
I took the one less traveled by,
And that has made all the difference.   20

Considerations for Critical Thinking and Writing

1. **FIRST RESPONSE.** This poem is sometimes associated with nonconformity. Could you argue that it is instead about regret?

2. Why does the speaker project himself into the future in the final stanza?

3. What type of personality do you associate with the speaker?

4. **CONNECTION TO ANOTHER SELECTION.** Does the philosophy of the speaker of this poem match the philosophy of the preceding poem, "Out, Out," also by Frost?

ALICE JONES (B. 1949)

The Lungs 1997

In the tidal flux, the lobed pair avidly
  grasp the invisible.

Along oblique fissures, gnarled vascular roots
  anchor the puffed cushions,

soot-mottled froth, the pink segmented sponges
  that soak up the atmosphere,

then squeezed by the rising dome of the diaphragm's
  muscular bellows, exhale.

Braids of vessels and cartilage descend
  in vanishing smallness,   5

to grape clusters of alveoli, the sheerest
  of membranes, where oxygen

crosses the infinite cellular web, where air turns
  to blood, spirit to flesh,

WHEN I WRITE "The process of becoming a writer involves recognizing the desire to write, allowing ourselves to take the desire seriously, and then learning to recognize the obstacles we put in our own way." — ALICE JONES

in a molecular transubstantiation, to bring rich
    food to that red engine,

the heart, which like an equitable mother, pumps
    to each organ and appendage

according to need, so even the cells in the darkest
    corners can breathe.   10

CONSIDERATIONS FOR CRITICAL THINKING AND WRITING

1. FIRST RESPONSE. Why do you think the lines in this poem are arranged in pairs? How does the length of the sentences contribute to the poem's meaning?

2. Make a list of words and phrases from the poem that strike you as scientific, and compare those with a list of words that seem poetic. How do they compete or complement each other in terms of how they affect your reading?

3. Comment on the use of personification (see the Glossary, p. 1152) in the poem.

CONNECTION TO ANOTHER SELECTION

1. Compare the diction and the ending in "The Lungs" with those of "The Foot" (p. 502), another poem by Jones.

LOUIS SIMPSON (1923–2012)

In the Suburbs 1963

There's no way out.
You were born to waste your life.
You were born to this middleclass life

As others before you
Were born to walk in procession
To the temple, singing.

CONSIDERATIONS FOR CRITICAL THINKING AND WRITING

1. FIRST RESPONSE. Is the title of this poem especially significant? What images does it conjure up for you?

2. What does the repetition in lines 2–3 suggest?

3. Discuss the possible connotative meanings of lines 5 and 6. Who are the "others before you"?

CONNECTION TO ANOTHER SELECTION

1. Write an essay on suburban life based on this poem and Gregory Corso's "Marriage" (p. 650).

13

Images

AP Photo/Rogelio V. Solis.

I think poetry is always a kind of faith. It is the kind that I have.

— NATASHA TRETHEWEY

POETRY'S APPEAL TO THE SENSES

A poet, to borrow a phrase that Henry James used to describe fiction writers, is one on whom nothing is lost. Poets take in the world and give us impressions of what they experience through images. An *image* is language that addresses the senses. The most common images in poetry are visual; they provide verbal pictures of the poets' encounters — real or imagined — with the world. But poets also create images that appeal to our other senses. Li Ho arouses several senses in this excerpt from "A Beautiful Girl Combs Her Hair":

> Awake at dawn
> she's dreaming
> by cool silk curtains
>
> fragrance of spilling hair
> half sandalwood, half aloes
>
> windlass creaking at the well
> singing jade

These vivid images deftly blend textures, fragrances, and sounds that tease out the sensuousness of the moment. Images give us the physical world to experience in our imaginations. Some poems, like the following one, are written to do just that; they make no comment about what they describe.

WILLIAM CARLOS WILLIAMS (1883–1963)

Poem 1934

As the cat
climbed over
the top of

the jamcloset   5
first the right
forefoot

carefully
then the hind
stepped down

into the pit of   10
the empty
flowerpot

    This poem defies paraphrase because it is all an image of agile movement. No statement is made about the movement; the title, "Poem" — really no title — signals Williams's refusal to comment on the movements. To impose a meaning on the poem, we'd probably have to knock over the flowerpot.

    We experience the image in Williams's "Poem" more clearly because of how the sentence is organized into lines and groups of lines, or stanzas. Consider how differently the sentence is read if it is arranged as prose:

> As the cat climbed over the top of the jamcloset, first the right forefoot carefully then the hind stepped down into the pit of the empty flowerpot.

The poem's line and stanza division transforms what is essentially an awkward prose sentence into a rhythmic verbal picture. Especially when the poem is read aloud, this line and stanza division allows us to feel the image we see. Even the lack of a period at the end suggests that the cat is only pausing.

    Images frequently do more than offer only sensory impressions, however. They also convey emotions and moods, as in the following poem's view of Civil War troops moving across a river.

WALT WHITMAN (1819–1892)

Cavalry Crossing a Ford 1865

A line in long array where they wind betwixt green islands,
They take a serpentine course, their arms flash in the sun — hark to the
    musical clank,
Behold the silvery river, in it the splashing horses loitering stop to drink,
Behold the brown-faced men, each group, each person, a picture, the
    negligent rest on the saddles,
Some emerge on the opposite bank, others are just entering the ford — while,
Scarlet and blue and snowy white,
The guidon flags flutter gaily in the wind.

CONSIDERATIONS FOR CRITICAL THINKING AND WRITING

1. FIRST RESPONSE. Do the colors and sounds establish the mood of this poem? What is the mood?
2. How would the poem's mood have been changed if Whitman had used "look" or "see" instead of "behold" (lines 3–4)?
3. Where is the speaker as he observes this troop movement?
4. Does "serpentine" in line 2 have an evil connotation in this poem? Explain your answer.

Whitman seems to capture momentarily all of the troop's actions, and through carefully chosen, suggestive details — really very few — he succeeds in making "each group, each person, a picture." Specific details, even when few are provided, give us the impression that we see the entire picture; it is as if those are the details we would remember if we had viewed the scene ourselves. Notice, too, that the movement of the "line in long array" is emphasized by the continuous winding syntax of the poem's lengthy lines.

Movement is also central to the next poem, in which action and motion are created through carefully chosen verbs.

DAVID SOLWAY (B. 1941)

Windsurfing 1993

It rides upon the wrinkled hide
of water, like the upturned hull
of a small canoe or kayak
waiting to be righted — yet its law
is opposite to that of boats,
it floats upon its breastbone and

> WHEN I READ "The good poet always generates a sense of lexical surprise, an openness toward the unexpected, a feeling of novelty and delight."
> — DAVID SOLWAY

5

brings whatever spine there is to light.
A thin shaft is slotted into place.
Then a puffed right-angle of wind
pushes it forward, out into the bay,   10

where suddenly it glitters into speed,
tilts, knifes up, and for the moment's
nothing but a slim projectile
of cambered fiberglass,
peeling the crests.   15

            The man's
clamped to the mast, taut as a guywire.
Part of the sleek apparatus
he controls, immaculate nerve
of balance, plunge and curvet,   20
he clinches all component movements
into single motion.
It bucks, stalls, shudders, yaws, and dips
its hissing sides beneath the surface
that sustains it, tensing   25
into muscle that nude ellipse
of lunging appetite and power.

And now the mechanism's wholly
dolphin, springing toward its prey
of spume and beaded sunlight,   30
tossing spray, and hits the vertex
of the wide, salt glare of distance,
and reverses.

            Back it comes through
a screen of particles,   35
scalloped out of water, shimmer
and reflection, the wind snapping
and lashing it homeward,
shearing the curve of the wave,
breaking the spell of the caught breath   40
and articulate play of sinew, to enter
the haven of the breakwater
and settle in a rush of silence.

Now the crossing drifts
in the husk of its wake   45
and nothing's the same again
as, gliding elegantly on a film of water,
the man guides
his brash, obedient legend
into shore.

                                                                            50

CONSIDERATIONS FOR CRITICAL THINKING AND WRITING

1. FIRST RESPONSE. Draw a circle around the verbs that seem especially
   effective in conveying a strong sense of motion, and explain why they
   are effective.

2. How is the man made to seem to be one with his board and sail?

3. How does the rhythm of the poem change beginning with line 45?

"Windsurfing" is awash with images of speed, fluidity, and power. Even
the calming aftermath of the breakwater is described as a "rush of silence,"
adding to the sense of motion that is detailed and expanded throughout the
poem.

MATTHEW ARNOLD   (1822–1888)

Dover Beach   1867

The sea is calm tonight.
The tide is full, the moon lies fair
Upon the straits; — on the French coast the light
Gleams and is gone; the cliffs of England stand,
Glimmering and vast, out in the tranquil bay.   5
Come to the window, sweet is the night-air!
Only, from the long line of spray
Where the sea meets the moon-blanched land,
Listen! you hear the grating roar
Of pebbles which the waves draw back, and fling,   10
At their return, up the high strand,
Begin, and cease, and then again begin,
With tremulous cadence slow, and bring
The eternal note of sadness in.

Sophocles long ago   15
Heard it on the Aegean, and it brought
Into his mind the turbid ebb and flow

Of human misery°; we
Find also in the sound a thought,
Hearing it by this distant northern sea.   20

The Sea of Faith
Was once, too, at the full, and round earth's shore
Lay like the folds of a bright girdle furled.
But now I only hear
Its melancholy, long, withdrawing roar,   25
Retreating, to the breath
Of the night-wind, down the vast edges drear
And naked shingles° of the world.   *pebble beaches*
Ah, love, let us be true
To one another! for the world, which seems   30
To lie before us like a land of dreams,
So various, so beautiful, so new,
Hath really neither joy, nor love, nor light,
Nor certitude, nor peace, nor help for pain;
And we are here as on a darkling plain   35
Swept with confused alarms of struggle and flight,
Where ignorant armies clash by night.

15–18 Sophocles . . . misery: In Antigone (lines 656–77), Sophocles likens the disasters
that beset the house of Oedipus to a "mounting tide."

CONSIDERATIONS FOR CRITICAL THINKING AND WRITING

1. FIRST RESPONSE. Discuss what you consider to be this poem's central
   point. How do the speaker's descriptions of the ocean work toward making that point?

2. Contrast the images in lines 4–8 and 9–13. How do they reveal the
   speaker's mood? To whom is he speaking?

3. What is the cause of the "sadness" in line 14? What is the speaker's
   response to the ebbing "Sea of Faith"? Is there anything to replace his
   sense of loss?

4. What details of the beach seem related to the ideas in the poem? How is
   the sea used differently in lines 1–14 and 21–28?

5. Describe the differences in tone between lines 1–8 and 35–37. What has
   caused the change?

6. CRITICAL STRATEGIES. Read the section on mythological strategies
   (pp. 1081–83) in Chapter 30, "Critical Strategies for Reading," and discuss how you think a mythological critic might make use of the allusion
   to Sophocles in this poem.

CONNECTION TO ANOTHER SELECTION

1. Compare ocean imagery in this poem to the imagery found in Alfred,
   Lord Tennyson's "Break, Break, Break" (p. 487).

POEMS FOR FURTHER STUDY

ADELAIDE CRAPSEY (1878–1914)

November Night   1913

Listen . . .

With faint dry sound,
Like steps of passing ghosts,
The leaves, frost-crisp'd, break from the trees
And fall.

CONSIDERATIONS FOR CRITICAL THINKING AND WRITING

1. FIRST RESPONSE. Which senses are evoked in the poem? What sort of tone do the words produce?

2. Explain whether or not you think "November Night" has a theme.

CONNECTION TO ANOTHER SELECTION

1. Compare the use of images and their effects in this poem and in E. E. Cummings's "l(a" (p. 380).

RUTH FAINLIGHT (B. 1931)

Crocuses   2006

Pale, bare, tender stems rising
from the muddy winter-faded grass,

shivering petals the almost luminous
blue and mauve of bruises on the naked

bodies of men, women, children
herded into a forest clearing

before the shouted order, crack of gunfire,
final screams and prayers and moans.

CONSIDERATIONS FOR CRITICAL THINKING AND WRITING

1. FIRST RESPONSE. Comment on Fainlight's choice of title. What effect does it have on your reading of the poem?

2. Trace your response to each image in the poem and describe the poem's tone as it moves from line to line.

3. CREATIVE RESPONSE. Try writing an eight-line poem in the style of Fainlight's based on images that gradually but radically shift in tone.

WILLIAM BLAKE (1757–1827)

London 1794

I wander through each chartered° street,   *defined by law*
Near where the chartered Thames does flow,
And mark in every face I meet
Marks of weakness, marks of woe.

In every cry of every man,   5
In every Infant's cry of fear,
In every voice, in every ban,
The mind-forged manacles I hear.

How the Chimney-sweeper's cry
Every black'ning Church appalls;   10
And the hapless Soldier's sigh
Runs in blood down Palace walls.

But most through midnight streets I hear
How the youthful Harlot's curse
Blasts the new-born Infant's tear,   15
And blights with plagues the Marriage hearse.

CONSIDERATIONS FOR CRITICAL THINKING AND WRITING

1. FIRST RESPONSE. What feelings do the visual images in this poem suggest to you?
2. What is the predominant sound heard in the poem?
3. What is the meaning of line 8? What is the cause of the problems that the speaker sees and hears in London? Does the speaker suggest additional causes?
4. The image in lines 11 and 12 cannot be read literally. Comment on its effectiveness.
5. How does Blake's use of denotative and connotative language enrich this poem's meaning?
6. An earlier version of Blake's last stanza appeared this way:

   > But most the midnight harlot's curse
   > From every dismal street I hear,
   > Weaves around the marriage hearse
   > And blasts the new-born infant's tear.

   Examine carefully the differences between the two versions. How do Blake's revisions affect his picture of London life? Which version do you think is more effective? Why?

KWAME DAWES (B. 1962)

The Habits of Love 1998

Since his wife Loretta's death, Monty collects
the burn-stained clicking carcasses of bulbs,
storing them in cotton stuffed into plastic
pastel-colored party cups. He shelves

them in the tinderbox-shed in the backyard,   5
visiting them each week as a ritual
for the dead. He tries not to discard
the multiples, but relishes the collapsed oval

of one he found glowing in an open field,
the sun humming in the shattered filament,   10
as if the earth fed power to make light bleed
through, so a man would stare in wonderment.

It is still the cherished one, despite the hundreds
he has gathered in the gloomy innards
of his shed. Esther has seen but not said
a thing; so grand his pain, so hard, so hard.   15

CONSIDERATIONS FOR CRITICAL THINKING AND WRITING

1. **FIRST RESPONSE.** Look closely at the image Dawes creates in the first stanza. How does it evoke a stronger image than if he had said, "Monty collects used light bulbs"?

2. How does the image of the one glowing bulb Monty found in a field — an effect produced by a trick of sunlight — deepen the poem's visual appeal?

3. Identify all the adjectives in the poem. How does that list of words alone suggest the poem's dominant emotion?

CHARLES SIMIC (B. 1938)

Fork 1969

This strange thing must have crept
Right out of hell.
It resembles a bird's foot.
Worn around the cannibal's neck.

As you hold it in your hand,
As you stab with it into a piece of meat,   5
It is possible to imagine the rest of the bird:
Its head which like your fist
Is large, bald, beakless, and blind.

CONSIDERATIONS FOR CRITICAL THINKING AND WRITING

1. FIRST RESPONSE. How is the speaker's tone revealed by the images that describe the fork?
2. Explain how the final two lines broaden the poem's themes.

SALLY CROFT (1935–2006)

Home-Baked Bread 1981

Nothing gives a household a greater sense of stability and common comfort than the aroma of cooling bread. Begin, if you like, with a loaf of whole wheat, which requires neither sifting nor kneading, and go on from there to more cunning triumphs. — The Joy of Cooking

What is it she is not saying?
Cunning triumphs. It rings
of insinuation. Step into my kitchen,
I have prepared a cunning triumph
for you. Spices and herbs   5
sealed in this porcelain jar,
a treasure of my great-aunt
who sat up past midnight
in her Massachusetts bedroom
when the moon was dark. Come,   10
rest your feet. I'll make
you tea with honey and slices

of warm bread spread with peach butter.
I picked the fruit this morning
still fresh with dew. The fragrance   15
is seductive? I hoped you would say that.
See how the heat rises
when the bread opens. Come,

we'll eat together, the small flakes
have scarcely any flavor. What cunning   20
triumphs we can discover in my upstairs room
where peach trees breathe their sweetness
beside the open window and
sun lies like honey on the floor.

CONSIDERATIONS FOR CRITICAL THINKING AND WRITING

1. **FIRST RESPONSE.** Why does the speaker in this poem seize on the phrase "cunning triumphs" from the *Joy of Cooking* excerpt?

2. Distinguish between the voice we hear in lines 1–3 and the second voice in lines 3–24. Who is the "you" in the poem?

3. Why is the word "insinuation" an especially appropriate choice in line 3?

4. How do the images in lines 20–24 bring together all the senses evoked in the preceding lines?

5. **CREATIVE RESPONSE.** Write a paragraph — or stanza — that describes the sensuous (and perhaps sensual) qualities of a food you enjoy.

14

Figures of Speech

Like a piece of ice on a hot stove the poem must ride on its own melting.
— ROBERT FROST

Bettmann/Getty Images.

Figures of speech are broadly defined as a way of saying one thing in terms of something else. An overeager funeral director might, for example, be described as a vulture. Although figures of speech are indirect, they are designed to clarify, not obscure, our understanding of what they describe. Poets frequently use them because, as Emily Dickinson said, the poet's work is to "tell all the Truth but tell it slant" to capture the reader's interest and imagination. But figures of speech are not limited to poetry. Hearing them, reading them, or using them is as natural as using language itself.

Suppose that in the middle of a class discussion concerning the economic causes of World War II your history instructor introduces a series of statistics by saying, "Let's get down to brass tacks." Would anyone be likely to expect a display of brass tacks for students to examine? To interpret the statement literally would be to wholly misunderstand the instructor's point that the time has come for a close look at the economic circumstances leading to the war. A literal response transforms the statement into the sort of hilariously bizarre material often found in screwball comedies like *Arrested Development*.

The class does not look for brass tacks because, in a nutshell, they understand that the instructor is speaking figuratively. They would understand, too, that in the preceding sentence "in a nutshell" refers to brevity and conciseness rather than to the covering of a kernel of a nut. Figurative language makes its way into our everyday speech and writing as well as into literature because it is a means of achieving color, vividness, and intensity. Consider the difference, for example, between these two statements:

Literal: The diner strongly expressed anger at the waiter.
Figurative: The diner leaped from his table and roared at the waiter.

The second statement is more vivid because it creates a picture of ferocious anger by likening the diner to some kind of wild animal, such as a lion or tiger. By comparison, "strongly expressed anger" is neither especially strong nor especially expressive; it is flat. Not all figurative language avoids this kind of flatness, however. Figures of speech such as "getting down to brass tacks" and "in a nutshell" are clichés because they lack originality and freshness. Still, they suggest how these devices are commonly used to give language some color, even if that color is sometimes a bit faded.

There is nothing weak about William Shakespeare's use of figurative language in the following passage from *Macbeth*. Macbeth has just learned that his wife is dead, and he laments her loss as well as the course of his own life.

WILLIAM SHAKESPEARE (1564–1616)
From Macbeth *(Act V, Scene v)*   1605–1606

Tomorrow, and tomorrow, and tomorrow
Creeps in this petty pace from day to day
To the last syllable of recorded time;
And all our yesterdays have lighted fools
The way to dusty death. Out, out, brief candle!   5
Life's but a walking shadow, a poor player,
That struts and frets his hour upon the stage,
And then is heard no more. It is a tale
Told by an idiot, full of sound and fury,
Signifying nothing.   10

This passage might be summarized as "life has no meaning," but such a brief paraphrase does not take into account the figurative language that reveals the depth of Macbeth's despair and his view of the absolute meaninglessness of life. By comparing life to a "brief candle," Macbeth emphasizes the darkness and death that surround human beings. The light of life is too brief and unpredictable to be of any comfort. Indeed, life for Macbeth is a "walking shadow," futilely playing a role that is more farcical than dramatic, because life is, ultimately, a desperate story filled with pain and devoid of significance. What the figurative language provides, then, is the emotional force of Macbeth's assertion; his comparisons are disturbing because they are so apt.

The remainder of this chapter discusses some of the most important figures of speech used in poetry. A familiarity with them will help you to understand how poetry achieves its effects.

SIMILE AND METAPHOR

The two most common figures of speech are simile and metaphor. Both compare things that are ordinarily considered unlike each other. A *simile* makes an explicit comparison between two things by using words such as *like, as, than, appears,* or *seems:* "A sip of Mrs. Cook's coffee is like a punch in the stomach." The force of the simile is created by the differences between the two things compared. There would be no simile if the comparison were stated this way: "Mrs. Cook's coffee is as strong as the cafeteria's coffee." This is a literal comparison because Mrs. Cook's coffee is compared with something like it, another kind of coffee. Consider how simile is used in this poem.

LANGSTON HUGHES (1902–1967)

Harlem   1951

What happens to a dream deferred?

Does it dry up
like a raisin in the sun?
Or fester like a sore —
And then run?   5
Does it stink like rotten meat?
Or crust and sugar over —
like a syrupy sweet?

Maybe it just sags
like a heavy load.   10

Or does it explode?

This famous poem is a serious of somewhat elaborate similes. Their effect is cumulative: the poem asks a number of questions based on these similes and asks the reader to supply an answer. The similes are made even more complicated in that the subject is slippery: we are being asked to compare the Harlem of the title and the concept of a dream deferred to all of the images that follow. The Manhattan neighborhood known as Harlem was a mostly African American neighborhood that had fallen on hard times at the time the poem was written: despite its "renaissance" in the 1920s, Harlem had experienced damaging riots in 1935 and 1943 based on the frustrations built on poverty and the limited opportunities available to black Americans at that time. The American dream for Harlemites was deferred. What happens to that dream? Hughes asks us to consider a number of possibilities, each of which connotes something slightly different. Take a few minutes to trace through each of these and consider what makes them different. By the end of the poem, the dream, Harlem, and the poem are so heavy with the weight of these similes that they threaten to burst, to explode. We might come away from this vision covered in rotting meat or a runny sore. Also important in this list of similes are the verbs Hughes chooses: *dry up, fester, run, stink, crust and sugar over, sag, explode.* The images are not the only aspect of these similes we have to deal with: these actions are part of the comparison.

A ***metaphor***, like a simile, makes a comparison between two unlike things, but it does so implicitly, without words such as *like* or *as*: "Mrs. Cook's coffee is a punch in the stomach." Metaphor asserts the identity of dissimilar things. Macbeth tells us that life *is* a "brief candle," life *is* "a walking shadow," life *is* "a poor player," life *is* "a tale / Told by an idiot." Metaphor transforms people, places, objects, and ideas into whatever the poet imagines them to be, and if metaphors are effective, the reader's experience, understanding, and appreciation of what is described are enhanced. Metaphors are frequently more demanding than similes because they are not signaled by particular words. They are both subtle and powerful. Both similes and metaphors expand the sense of a poem economically, by compelling our minds to connect two things that are not obviously connected.

JANE KENYON (1947–1995)
The Socks 1978

While you were away
I matched your socks
and rolled them into balls.
Then I filled your drawer with
tight dark fists.

Although it would be creepy and cool to imagine the speaker dumping dozens of severed hands into her husband's sock drawer, that would clearly be a misreading of the poem's intent. We immediately understand that the speaker is saying the rolled up matched socks are *like* fists, but she goes straight to the comparison: no "like" necessary. We are left to marvel at the comparison: What's the deal with this relationship? Why such a combative metaphor? The speaker leaves it to us to speculate. We know that the speaker is quite active: "I matched . . . and rolled . . . Then I filled." The addressee hasn't done anything . . . except leave. At first the speaker's act sounds like a kindness, but the sentiment shifts at the end. The addressee might take it as a warning to expect a fight upon returning home.

Some metaphors are more subtle than others because their comparison of terms is less explicit. Notice the difference between the following two metaphors, both of which describe a shaggy derelict refusing to leave the warmth of a hotel lobby: "He was a mule standing his ground" is a quite explicit comparison. The man is a mule; X is Y. But this metaphor is much more covert: "He brayed his refusal to leave." This second version is an ***implied metaphor*** because it does not explicitly identify the man with a mule. Instead it hints at or alludes to the mule. Braying is associated with mules and is especially appropriate in this context because of the mule's reputation for stubbornness. Implied metaphors can slip by readers, but they offer the alert reader the energy and resonance of carefully chosen, highly concentrated language.

Some poets write extended comparisons in which part or all of the poem consists of a series of related metaphors or similes. Extended metaphors are more common than extended similes. In "Catch" (p. 372), Robert Francis creates an ***extended metaphor*** that compares poetry to a game of catch. The entire poem is organized around this comparison. Because these comparisons are at work throughout the entire poem, they are called ***controlling metaphors.*** Extended comparisons can serve as a poem's organizing principle; they are also a reminder that in good poems metaphor and simile are not merely decorative but inseparable from what is expressed.

Notice the controlling metaphor in this poem, published posthumously by a woman whose contemporaries identified her more as a wife and mother than as a poet. Anne Bradstreet's first volume of poetry, *The Tenth Muse,* was published by her brother-in-law in 1650 without her prior knowledge.

Anne Bradstreet (ca. 1612–1672)

The Author to Her Book   1678

Thou ill-formed offspring of my feeble brain,
Who after birth did'st by my side remain,
Till snatched from thence by friends, less wise than true,
Who thee abroad exposed to public view;
Made thee in rags, halting, to the press to trudge,   5
Where errors were not lessened, all may judge.
At thy return my blushing was not small,
My rambling brat (in print) should mother call;
I cast thee by as one unfit for light,
Thy visage was so irksome in my sight;   10
Yet being mine own, at length affection would
Thy blemishes amend, if so I could:

I washed thy face, but more defects I saw,
And rubbing off a spot, still made a flaw.
I stretched thy joints to make thee even feet,
Yet still thou run'st more hobbling than is meet;   15
In better dress to trim thee was my mind,
But nought save homespun cloth in the house I find.
In this array, 'mongst vulgars may'st thou roam;
In critics' hands beware thou dost not come;
And take thy way where yet thou are not known.   20
If for thy Father asked, say thou had'st none;
And for thy Mother, she alas is poor,
Which caused her thus to send thee out of door.

The extended metaphor likening her book to a child came naturally to
Bradstreet and allowed her to regard her work both critically and affectionately. Her conception of the book as her child creates just the right tone of
amusement, self-deprecation, and concern.

OTHER FIGURES

Perhaps the humblest figure of speech — if not one of the most familiar — is
the pun. A **pun** is a play on words that relies on a word having more than
one meaning or sounding like another word. For example, "A fad is in one
era and out the other" is the sort of pun that produces obligatory groans.
But most of us find pleasant and interesting surprises in puns. Here's one
that has a slight edge to its humor.

EDMUND CONTI (B. 1929)

Pragmatist   1985

Apocalypse soon
Coming our way
Ground zero at noon
Halve a nice day.

Grimly practical under the circumstances, the pragmatist divides the
familiar cheerful cliché by half. As simple as this poem is, its tone is mixed
because it makes us laugh and wince at the same time.

Puns can be used to achieve serious effects as well as humorous ones.
Although we may have learned to underrate puns as figures of speech, it
is a mistake to underestimate their power and the frequency with which
they appear in poetry. A close examination, for example, of Robert Frost's

"Design" (p. 394), or almost any lengthy passage from a Shakespeare play will confirm the value of puns.

Synecdoche is a figure of speech in which part of something is used to signify the whole: a neighbor is a "wagging tongue" (a gossip); a criminal is placed "behind bars" (in prison). Less typically, synecdoche refers to the whole used to signify the part: "Germany invaded Poland"; "Princeton won the fencing match." Clearly, certain individuals participated in these activities, not all of Germany or Princeton. Another related figure of speech is **metonymy**, in which something associated closely with a subject is substituted for it: "She preferred the silver screen [motion pictures] to reading." "At precisely ten o'clock the paper shufflers [office workers] stopped for coffee."

Synecdoche and metonymy may overlap and are therefore sometimes difficult to distinguish. Consider this description of a disapproving minister entering a noisy tavern: "As those pursed lips came through the swinging door, the atmosphere was suddenly soured." The pursed lips signal the presence of the minister and are therefore a synecdoche, but they additionally suggest an inhibiting sense of sin and guilt that makes the bar patrons feel uncomfortable. Hence the pursed lips are also a metonymy, as they are in this context so closely connected with religion. Although the distinction between synecdoche and metonymy can be useful, a figure of speech is usually labeled a metonymy when it overlaps categories.

Knowing the precise term for a figure of speech is, finally, less important than responding to its use in a poem. Consider how metonymy and synecdoche convey the tone and meaning of the following poem.

DYLAN THOMAS (1914–1953)
The Hand That Signed the Paper   1936

The hand that signed the paper felled a city;
Five sovereign fingers taxed the breath,
Doubled the globe of dead and halved a
     country;
These five kings did a king to death.

The mighty hand leads to a sloping shoulder,
The finger joints are cramped with chalk;
A goose's quill has put an end to murder
That put an end to talk.

Hulton Deutsch/Getty Images.

The hand that signed the treaty bred a fever,
And famine grew, and locusts came;
Great is the hand that holds dominion over
Man by a scribbled name.

10

The five kings count the dead but do not soften
The crusted wound nor stroke the brow;
A hand rules pity as a hand rules heaven;   15
Hands have no tears to flow.

The "hand" in this poem is a synecdoche for a powerful ruler because it is a part of someone used to signify the entire person. The "goose's quill" is a metonymy that also refers to the power associated with the ruler's hand. By using these figures of speech, Thomas depersonalizes and ultimately dehumanizes the ruler. The final synecdoche tells us that "Hands have no tears to flow." It makes us see the political power behind the hand as remote and inhuman. How is the meaning of the poem enlarged when the speaker says, "A hand rules pity as a hand rules heaven"?

One of the ways writers energize the abstractions, ideas, objects, and animals that constitute their created worlds is through ***personification***, the attribution of human characteristics to nonhuman things: temptation pursues the innocent; trees scream in the raging wind; mice conspire in the cupboard. We are not explicitly told that these things are people; instead, we are invited to see that they behave like people. Perhaps it is human vanity that makes personification a frequently used figure of speech. Whatever the reason, personification, a form of metaphor that connects the nonhuman with the human, makes the world understandable in human terms. Consider this concise example from William Blake's *The Marriage of Heaven and Hell,* a long poem that takes delight in attacking conventional morality: "Prudence is a rich ugly old maid courted by Incapacity." By personifying prudence, Blake transforms what is usually considered a virtue into a comic figure hardly worth emulating.

Often related to personification is another rhetorical figure called ***apostrophe***, an address either to someone who is absent and therefore cannot hear the speaker or to something nonhuman that cannot comprehend. Apostrophe provides an opportunity for the speaker of a poem to think aloud, and often the thoughts expressed are in a formal tone. John Keats, for example, begins "Ode on a Grecian Urn" (p. 531) this way: "Thou still unravished bride of quietness." Apostrophe is frequently accompanied by intense emotion that is signalled by phrasing such as "O Life." In the right hands — such as Keats's — apostrophe can provide an intense and immediate voice in a poem, but when it is overdone or extravagant it can be ludicrous. Modern poets are more wary of apostrophe than their predecessors because apostrophizing strikes many self-conscious twenty-first-century sensibilities as too theatrical. Thus modern poets tend to avoid exaggerated situations in favor of less charged though equally meditative moments, as in this next poem, with its amusing, half-serious cosmic twist.

JANICE TOWNLEY MOORE (B. 1939)

To a Wasp 1984

You must have chortled
finding that tiny hole
in the kitchen screen. Right
into my cheese cake batter
you dived,
no chance to swim ashore,
no saving spoon,
the mixer whirring
your legs, wings, stinger,   10
churning you into such
delicious death.
Never mind the bright April day.
Did you not see
rising out of cumulus clouds
That fist aimed at both of us?   15

WHEN I WRITE "I began writing poetry as a freshman in college. I wrote using poetic diction and sometimes rhyme. Then I discovered 'modern poetry.' Seeing what was published in literary magazines quickly changed my style."
— JANICE TOWNLEY MOORE

Moore's apostrophe "To a Wasp" is based on the simplest of domestic circumstances; there is almost nothing theatrical or exaggerated in the poem's tone until "That fist" in the last line, when exaggeration takes center stage. As a figure of speech, exaggeration is known as **overstatement** or **hyperbole** and adds emphasis without intending to be literally true: "The teenage boy ate everything in the house." Notice how the speaker of Andrew Marvell's "To His Coy Mistress" (p. 409) exaggerates his devotion in the following overstatement:

> An hundred years should go to praise
> Thine eyes and on thy forehead gaze,
> Two hundred to adore each breast,
> But thirty thousand to the rest:

That comes to 30,500 years. What is expressed here is heightened emotion, not deception.

The speaker also uses the opposite figure of speech, **understatement**, which says less than is intended. In the next section he sums up why he cannot take 30,500 years to express his love:

> The grave's a fine and private place,
> But none, I think, do there embrace.

The speaker is correct, of course, but by deliberately understating — saying "I think" when he is actually certain — he makes his point, that death will overtake their love, all the more emphatic. Another powerful example of understatement appears in the final line of Randall Jarrell's "The Death of the Ball Turret Gunner" (p. 400), when the disembodied voice of the machine-gunner describes his death in a bomber: "When I died they washed me out of the turret with a hose."

Paradox is a statement that initially appears to be self-contradictory but that, on closer inspection, turns out to make sense: "The pen is mightier than the sword." In a fencing match, anyone would prefer the sword, but if the goal is to win the hearts and minds of people, the art of persuasion can be more compelling than swordplay. To resolve the paradox, it is necessary to discover the sense that underlies the statement. If we see that "pen" and "sword" are used as metonymies for writing and violence, then the paradox rings true. **Oxymoron** is a condensed form of paradox in which two contradictory words are used together. Combinations such as "sweet sorrow," "silent scream," "sad joy," and "cold fire" indicate the kinds of startling effects that oxymorons can produce. Paradox is useful in poetry because it arrests a reader's attention by its seemingly stubborn refusal to make sense, and once a reader has penetrated the paradox, it is difficult to resist a perception so well earned. Good paradoxes are knotty pleasures. Here is a simple but effective one.

Tajana Kovics (b. 1985)

Text Message   2011

Because I think you're nearly perfect,
I want to love you best:
And since absence makes the heart grow fonder,
We should see each other less.

As the title suggests, the medium is part of the implicit subtext in this quatrain. Consider how the very idea of romantic love is conveyed and built on separation rather than intimacy in this witty paradox.

The following poems are rich in figurative language. As you read and study them, notice how their figures of speech vivify situations, clarify ideas, intensify emotions, and engage your imagination. Although the terms for the various figures discussed in this chapter are useful for labeling the particular devices used in poetry, they should not be allowed to get in the way of your response to a poem. Don't worry about rounding up examples of figurative language. First relax and let the figures work their effects on you. Use the terms as a means of taking you further into poetry, and they will serve your reading well.

POEMS FOR FURTHER STUDY

WILLIAM CARLOS WILLIAMS (1883–1963)
To Waken an Old Lady 1921

Old age is
a flight of small
cheeping birds
skimming
bare trees   5
above a snow glaze.
Gaining and failing
they are buffeted
by a dark wind —   10
But what?
On harsh weedstalks
the flock has rested,
the snow
is covered with broken   15
seedhusks
and the wind tempered
by a shrill
piping of plenty.

CONSIDERATIONS FOR CRITICAL THINKING AND WRITING

1. FIRST RESPONSE. Consider the images and figures of speech in this poem and explain why you think it is a positive or negative assessment of old age.
2. How does the title relate to the rest of the poem?

ERNEST SLYMAN (B. 1946)
Lightning Bugs 1988

In my backyard,
They burn peepholes in the night
And take snapshots of my house.

CONSIDERATIONS FOR CRITICAL THINKING AND WRITING

1. FIRST RESPONSE. Explain why the title is essential to this poem.
2. What makes the description of the lightning bugs effective? How do the second and third lines complement each other?
3. CREATIVE RESPONSE. As Slyman has done, take a simple, common fact of nature and make it vivid by using a figure of speech to describe it.

Martín Espada (b. 1957)

The Mexican Cabdriver's Poem for His Wife, Who Has Left Him   2000

We were sitting in traffic
on the Brooklyn Bridge,
so I asked the poets
in the backseat of my cab
to write a poem for you.   5

They asked
if you are like the moon
or the trees.

I said no,
she is like the bridge
when there is so much traffic   10
I have time
to watch the boats
on the river.

Considerations for Critical Thinking and Writing

1. FIRST RESPONSE. What do you think is the poet's attitude toward the cabdriver?

2. Explore the potential meanings of the similes concerning the moon, trees, and the bridge. How does the bridge differ from the other two?

WHEN I WRITE "Only on very rare occasions is a poem complete in a first draft. The first draft of a poem can sit for a long time waiting for its other half, or its meaning. Save everything you write, no matter how unhappy you are with it. You often won't see the beauty until later."
— JUDY PAGE HEITZMAN

Judy Page Heitzman (b. 1952)

The Schoolroom on the Second Floor of the Knitting Mill   1991

While most of us copied letters out of books,
Mrs. Lawrence carved and cleaned her nails.
Now the red and buff cardinals at my back-room window
make me miss her, her room, her hallway,
even the chimney outside
that broke up the sky.   5

In my memory it is afternoon.
Sun streams in through the door
next to the fire escape where we are lined up
getting our coats on to go out to the playground,   10
the tether ball, its towering height, the swings.
She tells me to make sure the line
does not move up over the threshold.
That would be dangerous.   15
So I stand guard at the door.
Somehow it happens
the way things seem to happen when we're not really looking,
or we are looking, just not the right way.
Kids crush up like cattle, pushing me over the line.

Judy is not a good leader is all Mrs. Lawrence says.   20
She says it quietly. Still, everybody hears.
Her arms hang down like sausages.
I hear her every time I fail.

Considerations for Critical Thinking and Writing

1. **First response.** Does your impression of Mrs. Lawrence change from the beginning to the end of the poem? How so?

2. How can line 2 be read as an implied metaphor?

3. Discuss the use of similes in the poem. How do they contribute to the poem's meaning?

Edna St. Vincent Millay (1892–1950)

Spring 1921

To what purpose, April, do you return again?
Beauty is not enough.
You can no longer quiet me with the redness
Of little leaves opening stickily.   5
I know what I know.
The sun is hot on my neck as I observe
The spikes of the crocus.
The smell of the earth is good.
It is apparent that there is no death.   10
But what does that signify?
Not only under ground are the brains of men
Eaten by maggots.
Life in itself
Is nothing,

An empty cup, a flight of uncarpeted stairs.
It is not enough that yearly, down this hill,   15
April
Comes like an idiot, babbling and strewing flowers.

CONSIDERATIONS FOR CRITICAL THINKING AND WRITING

1. FIRST RESPONSE. How do you interpret line 2, "Beauty is not enough," in the context of the rest of the poem?
2. What is the effect of personifying spring in the poem?
3. Unpack the two metaphors for life in line 15.

CONNECTION TO ANOTHER SELECTION

1. Compare the notions of natural beauty and human understanding in this poem and in Lopez's "Meditation on Beauty" (p. 628).

ROBERT PINSKY (B. 1940)

Icicles   1990

A brilliant beard of ice
Hangs from the edge of the roof
Harsh and heavy as glass.
The spikes a child breaks off

Taste of wool and the sun.
In the house, some straw for a bed,   5
Circled by a little train,
Is the tiny image of God.

The sky is a fiery blue,
And a fiery morning light
Burns on the fresh deep snow: 10
Not one track in the street.

Just as the carols tell
Everything is calm and bright:
The town lying still
Frozen silver and white.   15

Is only one child awake,
Breaking the crystal chimes —
Knocking them down with a stick,
Leaving the broken stems.
                                                                              20

CONSIDERATIONS FOR CRITICAL THINKING AND WRITING

1. FIRST RESPONSE. What did the poem make you feel upon first reading it?

2. List the things icicles are compared to throughout the poem. Do these separate comparisons work together or against one another in terms of creating a coherent picture?

3. Is the poem's mood violent or calm? Can it be both?

KAY RYAN (B. 1945)

Learning 1996

Whatever must be learned
is always on the bottom,
as with the law of drawers
and the necessary item.
It isn't pleasant,
whatever they tell children,
to turn out on the floor
the folded things in them.

CONSIDERATIONS FOR CRITICAL THINKING AND WRITING

1. FIRST RESPONSE. Why does the speaker consider learning to be unpleasant and difficult?

2. Why is unfolding what must be learned an especially apt metaphor?

Symbol, Allegory, and Irony

Angel Valentin/The New York
Times/Redux.

Poetry is serious business; literature is
the apparatus through which the world
tries to keep intact its important ideas
and feelings.
— MARY OLIVER

SYMBOL

A *symbol* is something that represents something else. An object, a person,
a place, an event, or an action can suggest more than its literal meaning.
A handshake between two world leaders might be simply a greeting, but
if it is done ceremoniously before cameras, it could be a symbolic gesture
signifying unity, issues resolved, and joint policies that will be followed. We
live surrounded by symbols. When a $100,000 Mercedes-Benz comes roar-
ing by in the fast lane, we get a quick glimpse of not only an expensive car
but also an entire lifestyle that suggests opulence, broad lawns, executive
offices, and power. One of the reasons some buyers are willing to spend
roughly the cost of five Chevrolets for a single Mercedes-Benz is that they
are aware of the car's symbolic value. A symbol is a vehicle for two things at
once: it functions as itself, and it implies meanings beyond itself.

The meanings suggested by a symbol are determined by the context in
which it appears. The Mercedes could symbolize very different things depending on where it was parked. Would an American political candidate be likely

to appear in a Detroit blue-collar neighborhood with such a car? Probably not. Although a candidate might be able to afford the car, it would be an inappropriate symbol for someone seeking votes from all of the people. As a symbol, the German-built Mercedes would backfire if voters perceived it as representing an entity partially responsible for layoffs of automobile workers or, worse, as a sign of decadence and corruption. Similarly, a huge portrait of North Korean leader Kim Jong-un conveys different meanings to residents of Pyongyang than it would to farmers in Prairie Center, Illinois. Because symbols depend on contexts for their meaning, literary artists provide those contexts so that the reader has enough information to determine the probable range of meanings suggested by a symbol.

In the following poem, the speaker describes walking at night. How is the night used symbolically?

ROBERT FROST (1874–1963)

Acquainted with the Night   1928

I have been one acquainted with the night.
I have walked out in rain —and back in rain.
I have outwalked the furthest city light.

I have looked down the saddest city lane.   5
I have passed by the watchman on his beat
And dropped my eyes, unwilling to explain.

I have stood still and stopped the sound of feet
When far away an interrupted cry
Came over houses from another street,

But not to call me back or say good-by;   10
And further still at an unearthly height
One luminary clock against the sky

Proclaimed the time was neither wrong nor right.
I have been one acquainted with the night.

In approaching this or any poem, you should read for literal meanings first and then allow the elements of the poem to invite you to symbolic readings, if they are appropriate. Here the somber tone suggests that the lines have symbolic meaning, too. The flat matter-of-factness created by the repetition of "I have" (lines 1–5, 7, 14) understates the symbolic subject matter of the poem, which is, finally, more about the "night" located in the speaker's mind or soul than it is about walking away from a city and back again. The speaker is "acquainted with the night." The importance of this phrase is emphasized by Frost's title and by the fact that he begins and ends the poem with it. Poets frequently use this kind of repetition to alert readers to details that carry more than literal meanings.

The speaker in this poem has personal knowledge of the night but does not indicate specifically what the night means. To arrive at the potential meanings of the night in this context, it is necessary to look closely at its connotations, along with the images provided in the poem. The connotative meanings of *night* suggest, for example, darkness, death, and grief. By drawing on these connotations, Frost uses a **conventional symbol** — something that is recognized by many people to represent certain ideas. Roses conventionally symbolize love or beauty; laurels, fame; spring, growth or rebirth; the moon, romance. Poets often use conventional symbols to convey tone and meaning.

Frost uses the night as a conventional symbol, but he also develops it into a **literary** or **contextual symbol** that goes beyond traditional, public meanings. A literary symbol cannot be summarized in a word or two. It tends to be as elusive as experience itself. The night cannot be reduced to or equated with darkness or death or grief, but it evokes those associations and more. Frost took what perhaps initially appears to be an overworked, conventional symbol and prevented it from becoming a cliché by deepening and extending its meaning.

The images in "Acquainted with the Night" lead to the poem's symbolic meaning. Unwilling, and perhaps unable, to explain explicitly to the watchman (and to the reader) what the night means, the speaker nevertheless conveys feelings about it. The brief images of darkness, rain, sad city lanes, the necessity for guards, the eerie sound of a distressing cry coming over rooftops, and the "luminary clock against the sky" proclaiming "the time was neither wrong nor right" all help to create a sense of anxiety in this tight-lipped speaker. Although we cannot know what unnamed personal experiences have acquainted the speaker with the night, the images suggest that whatever the night means, it is somehow associated with insomnia, loneliness, isolation, coldness, darkness, death, fear, and a sense of alienation from humanity and even time. Daylight — ordinary daytime thoughts and life itself — seems remote and unavailable in this poem. The night is literally the period from sunset to sunrise, but, more important, it is an internal state of being felt by the speaker and revealed through the images.

Frost used symbols rather than an expository essay that would explain the conditions that cause these feelings because most readers can provide their own list of sorrows and terrors that evoke similar emotions. Through symbol, the speaker's experience is compressed and simultaneously expanded by the personal darkness that each reader brings to the poem. The suggestive nature of symbols makes them valuable for poets and evocative for readers.

ALLEGORY

Unlike expansive, suggestive symbols, **allegory** is a narration or description usually restricted to a single meaning because its events, actions, characters, settings, and objects represent specific abstractions or ideas. Although the elements in an allegory may be interesting in themselves, the emphasis tends to be on what they ultimately mean. Characters may be given names such as Hope,

Pride, Youth, and Charity; they have few, if any, personal qualities beyond their abstract meanings. These personifications are a form of extended metaphor, but their meanings are severely restricted. They are not symbols because, for instance, the meaning of a character named Charity is precisely that virtue.

There is little or no room for broad speculation and exploration in allegories. If Frost had written "Acquainted with the Night" as an allegory, he might have named his speaker Loneliness and had him leave the City of Despair to walk the Streets of Emptiness, where Crime, Poverty, Fear, and other characters would define the nature of city life. The literal elements in an allegory tend to be deemphasized in favor of the message. Symbols, however, function both literally and symbolically, so that "Acquainted with the Night" is about both a walk and a sense that something is terribly wrong.

Allegory especially lends itself to **didactic poetry**, which is designed to teach an ethical, moral, or religious lesson. Many stories, poems, and plays are concerned with values, but didactic literature is specifically created to convey a message. "Acquainted with the Night" does not impart advice or offer guidance. If the poem argued that city life is self-destructive or sinful, it would be didactic; instead, it is a lyric poem that expresses the emotions and thoughts of a single speaker.

Although allegory is often enlisted in didactic causes because it can so readily communicate abstract ideas through physical representations, not all allegories teach a lesson. The following poem reveals a difficult human condition — the attempt to resolve the eternal tensions between guilt and desire in order to achieve love. Its author, James Baldwin, spent much of his career trying to redefine love; in his famous essay "Down at the Cross" he claimed he was speaking of love not in the sentimental, traditional sense of the word, but rather associating love with "quest and daring and growth."

JAMES BALDWIN (1924–1987)

Guilt, Desire and Love 1983

At the dark street corner
where Guilt and Desire
are attempting to stare
each other down
(presently, one of them
will light a cigarette
and glance in the direction
of the abandoned warehouse)
Love came slouching along,
an exploded silence
standing a little apart
but visible anyway
in the yellow, silent, steaming light,

Everett Collection Inc/Alamy Stock Photo.

while Guilt and Desire wrangled,
trying not to be overheard
by this trespasser.   15

Each time Desire looked towards Love,
hoping to find a witness,
Guilt shouted louder
and shook them hips
and the fire of the cigarette   20
threatened to burn the warehouse down.
Desire actually started across the street,
time after time,
to hear what Love might have to say,   25
but Guilt flagged down a truckload
of other people
and knelt down in the middle of the street
and, while the truckload of other people
looked away, and swore that they   30
didn't see nothing
and couldn't testify nohow,
and Love moved out of sight,
Guilt accomplished upon the standing body
of Desire   35
the momentary, inflammatory soothing
which seals their union
(for ever?)
and creates a mighty traffic problem.

The setting is important in this poem. As in Frost's poem, night is evoked: the street corner where Guilt and Desire meet is dark, and the "yellow, silent, steaming light" (line 13) that accompanies Love's entrance is more streetlight than sunlight. The cityscape is not desolate and spooky like Frost's, but rather hot and seedy. The props (if you will) of the abandoned warehouse and the lit cigarette seem like something out of a sordid movie or television show about a sinful city. Guilt and Desire are locked in a battle here, and a traditional moralist would associate Desire with sin, but Desire's goal is actually to connect with Love, who is a trespasser to their quarrel. Guilt is the most powerful of these three entities, the loudest of them (and probably the only one who speaks at all). Guilt's eventual bodily encounter with Desire is sexual, but it is not fulfilling; or if it is, that fulfilment is only "momentary." Love slinks out of sight; Desire is nearly a victim; and Guilt conquers all. The poem does not mention sin at all; in fact, if there is a lesson here, it is that guilt (which makes us associate certain human behaviors and emotions with sin) is itself a kind of sin, one that creates "a mighty traffic problem."

Modern writers generally prefer symbol over allegory because they tend to be more interested in opening up the potential meanings of an experience instead of transforming it into a closed pattern of meaning. Perhaps the major difference is that while allegory may delight a reader's imagination, symbol challenges and enriches it.

IRONY

Another important resource writers use to take readers beyond literal meanings is *irony*, a technique that reveals a discrepancy between what appears to be and what is actually true. Here is a classic example in which appearances give way to the underlying reality.

EDWIN ARLINGTON ROBINSON (1869–1935)

Richard Cory 1897

Whenever Richard Cory went down town,
We people on the pavement looked at him:
He was a gentleman from sole to crown,
Clean favored, and imperially slim.

And he was always quietly arrayed,   5
And he was always human when he talked;
But still he fluttered pulses when he said,
"Good-morning," and he glittered when he walked.

And he was rich — yes, richer than a king —
And admirably schooled in every grace: 10
In fine, we thought that he was everything
To make us wish that we were in his place.

So on we worked, and waited for the light,
And went without the meat, and cursed the bread;
And Richard Cory, one calm summer night,   15
Went home and put a bullet through his head.

Richard Cory seems to have it all. Those less fortunate, the "people on the pavement," regard him as well-bred, handsome, tasteful, and richly endowed with both money and grace. Until the final line of the poem, the reader, like the speaker, is charmed by Cory's good fortune, so quietly expressed in his decent, easy manner. That final, shocking line, however, shatters the appearances of Cory's life and reveals him to have been a desperately unhappy man. While everyone else assumes that Cory represented "everything" to which they aspire, the reality is that he could escape his miserable life only as a suicide. This discrepancy between what appears to be true and what actually exists is known as **situational irony**: what happens is entirely different from what is expected. We are not told why Cory shoots himself; instead, the irony in the poem shocks us into the recognition that appearances do not always reflect realities.

Words are also sometimes intended to be taken at other than face value. **Verbal irony** is saying something different from what is meant. If after reading "Richard Cory," you said, "That rich gentleman sure was happy," your statement would be ironic. Your tone of voice would indicate that just the opposite was meant; hence verbal irony is usually easy to detect in spoken language. In literature, however, a reader can sometimes take literally what a writer intends ironically. The remedy for this kind of misreading is to pay close attention to the poem's context. There is no formula that can detect verbal irony, but contradictory actions and statements as well as the use of understatement and overstatement can often be signals that verbal irony is present.

Consider how verbal irony is used in this poem.

KENNETH FEARING (1902–1961)

AD   1938

Wanted: Men;
Millions of men are *wanted at once* in a big new field;
New, tremendous, thrilling, great.
If you've ever been a figure in the chamber of horrors,
If you've ever escaped from a psychiatric ward,
If you thrill at the thought of throwing poison into wells, have heavenly   5
    visions of people, by the thousands, dying in flames —

You are the very man we want
We mean business and our business is *you*
Wanted: A race of brand-new men.

Apply: Middle Europe;
No skill needed;   10
No ambition required; no brains wanted and no character allowed;

Take a permanent job in the coming profession
Wages: *Death.*

This poem was written as Nazi troops stormed across Europe at the start of World War II. The advertisement suggests on the surface that killing is just an ordinary job, but the speaker indicates through understatement that there is nothing ordinary about the "business" of this "*coming profession.*" Fearing uses verbal irony to indicate how casually and mindlessly people are prepared to accept the horrors of war.

"AD" is a **satire**, an example of the literary art of ridiculing a folly or vice in an effort to expose or correct it. The object of satire is usually some human frailty; people, institutions, ideas, and things are all fair game for satirists. Fearing satirizes the insanity of a world mobilizing itself for war: his irony reveals the speaker's knowledge that there is nothing "*New, tremendous,* *thrilling*, [or] *great*" about going off to kill and be killed. The implication of the poem is that no one should respond to advertisements for war. The poem serves as a satiric corrective to those who would troop off armed with unrealistic expectations: wage war, and the wages consist of death.

   Dramatic irony is used when a writer allows a reader to know more about a situation than a character does. This creates a discrepancy between what a character says or thinks and what the reader knows to be true. Dramatic irony is often used to reveal character. In the following poem the speaker delivers a public address that ironically tells us more about him than it does about the patriotic holiday he is commemorating.

E. E. CUMMINGS (1894–1962)

next to of course god america i   1926

"next to of course god america i
love you land of the pilgrims' and so forth oh
say can you see by the dawn's early my
country 'tis of centuries come and go
and are no more what of it we should worry   5
in every language even deafanddumb
thy sons acclaim your glorious name by gorry
by jingo by gee by gosh by gum
why talk of beauty what could be more beaut-
iful than these heroic happy dead   10
who rushed like lions to the roaring slaughter
they did not stop to think they died instead
then shall the voice of liberty be mute?"

He spoke. And drank rapidly a glass of water

   This verbal debauch of chauvinistic clichés (notice the run-on phrases and lines) reveals that the speaker's relationship to God and country is not, as he claims, one of love. His public address suggests a hearty mindlessness that leads to "roaring slaughter" rather than to reverence or patriotism. Cummings allows the reader to see through the speaker's words to their dangerous emptiness. What the speaker means and what Cummings means are entirely different. Like Fearing's "AD," this poem is a satire that invites the reader's laughter and contempt in order to deflate the benighted attitudes expressed in it.

   When a writer uses God, destiny, or fate to dash the hopes and expectations of a character or humankind in general, it is called **cosmic irony**. In "Yet Do I Marvel" (p. 516), for example, Countee Cullen enumerates multiple ways in which God has tormented his human creations, and while he believes God could explain all of them, he will never understand why he was born a black poet at a time when America only paid attention to white poets. The context for understanding why he is so baffled by his condition is not explicitly stated; it must be filled in through the reader's understanding of racial discrimination. Here's a painfully terse version of cosmic irony.

STEPHEN CRANE (1871–1900)

A Man Said to the Universe 1899

A man said to the universe:
"Sir, I exist!"
"However," replied the universe,
"The fact has not created in me
A sense of obligation."

Unlike in "Yet Do I Marvel," there is the slightest bit of humor in Crane's poem, but the joke is on us.

Irony is an important technique that allows a writer to distinguish between appearances and realities. In situational irony a discrepancy exists between what we expect to happen and what actually happens; in verbal irony a discrepancy exists between what is said and what is meant; in dramatic irony a discrepancy exists between what a character believes and what the reader knows to be true; and in cosmic irony a discrepancy exists between what a character aspires to and what universal forces provide. With each form of irony, we are invited to move beyond surface appearances and sentimental assumptions to see the complexity of experience. Irony is often used in literature to reveal a writer's perspective on matters that previously seemed settled.

POEMS FOR FURTHER STUDY

CHRISTINA ROSSETTI (1830–1894)

Goblin Market 1862

Morning and evening
Maids heard the goblins cry:
"Come buy our orchard fruits,
Come buy, come buy:
Apples and quinces,
Lemons and oranges,   5
Plump unpecked cherries,
Melons and raspberries,
Bloom-down-cheeked peaches,

Swart-headed° mulberries,   10
Wild free-born cranberries,
Crabapples, dewberries,
Pineapples, blackberries,
Apricots, strawberries;—
All ripe together   15
In summer weather,—
Morns that pass by,
Fair eyes that fly;
Come buy, come buy:
Our grapes fresh from the vine,   20
Pomegranates full and fine,
Dates and sharp bullaces,
Rare pears and greengages,
Damsons° and bilberries,
Taste them and try: 25
Currants and gooseberries,
Bright-fire-like barberries,
Figs to fill your mouth,
Citrons from the South,
Sweet to tongue and sound to eye;   30
Come buy, come buy."
Evening by evening
Among the brookside rushes,
Laura bowed her head to hear,
Lizzie veiled her blushes: 35
Crouching close together
In the cooling weather,
With clasping arms and cautioning lips,
With tingling cheeks and finger tips.
"Lie close," Laura said,   40
Pricking up her golden head:
"We must not look at goblin men,
We must not buy their fruits:
Who knows upon what soil they fed
Their hungry thirsty roots?"   45
"Come buy," call the goblins
Hobbling down the glen.
"Oh," cried Lizzie, "Laura, Laura,
You should not peep at goblin men."
Lizzie covered up her eyes,   50
Covered close lest they should look;

---

10 *Swart-headed:* Black-headed.
22–24 *bullaces . . .damsons:* Bullaces, greengages, and damsons are plums.

Laura reared her glossy head,
And whispered like the restless brook:
"Look, Lizzie, look, Lizzie,
Down the glen tramp little men.   55
One hauls a basket,
One bears a plate,
One lugs a golden dish
Of many pounds' weight.
How fair the vine must grow   60
Whose grapes are so luscious;
How warm the wind must blow
Through those fruit bushes."
"No," said Lizzie: "No, no, no;
Their offers should not charm us,   65
Their evil gifts would harm us."
She thrust a dimpled finger
In each ear, shut eyes and ran:
Curious Laura chose to linger
Wondering at each merchant man.   70
One had a cat's face,
One whisked a tail,
One tramped at a rat's pace,
One crawled like a snail,
One like a wombat prowled obtuse and furry,   75
One like a ratel° tumbled hurry skurry.
She heard a voice like voice of doves
Cooing all together:
They sounded kind and full of loves
In the pleasant weather.   80

Laura stretched her gleaming neck
Like a rush-imbedded swan,
Like a lily from the beck,°
Like a moonlit poplar branch
Like a vessel at the launch   85
When its last restraint is gone.

Backwards up the mossy glen
Turned and trooped the goblin men,
With their shrill repeated cry,
"Come buy, come buy".   90
When they reached where Laura was
They stood stock still upon the moss,
Leering at each other,

---

76 *ratel:* A south African badgerlike creature.
83 *beck:* Small brook.

Brother with queer brother;   95
Signaling each other,
Brother with sly brother.
One set his basket down,
One reared his plate;
One began to weave a crown   100
Of tendrils, leaves, and rough nuts brown
(Men sell not such in any town);
One heaved the golden weight
Of dish and fruit to offer her:
"Come buy, come buy," was still their cry.   105
Laura stared but did not stir,
Longed but had no money.
The whisk-tailed merchant bade her taste
In tones as smooth as honey,
The cat-faced purr'd,   110
The rat-paced spoke a word
Of welcome, and the snail-paced even was heard;
One parrot-voiced and jolly
Cried "Pretty Goblin" still for "Pretty Polly";
One whistled like a bird.

                                                                115
But sweet-tooth Laura spoke in haste:
"Good Folk, I have no coin;
To take were to purloin:
I have no copper in my purse,
I have no silver either,   120
And all my gold is on the furze
That shakes in windy weather
Above the rusty heather."
"You have much gold upon your head."
They answered all together: 125
"Buy from us with a golden curl."
She clipped a precious golden lock,
She dropped a tear more rare than pearl,
Then sucked their fruit globes fair or red.
Sweeter than honey from the rock,   130
Stronger than man-rejoicing wine,
Clearer than water flowed that juice;
She never tasted such before,
How should it cloy with length of use?
She sucked and sucked and sucked the more   135
Fruits which that unknown orchard bore,
She sucked until her lips were sore;
Then flung the emptied rinds away
But gathered up one kernel stone,
And knew not was it night or day   140
As she turned home alone.

Lizzie met her at the gate
Full of wise upbraidings:
"Dear, you should not stay so late,
Twilight is not good for maidens;
Should not loiter in the glen
In the haunts of goblin men.   145
Do you not remember Jeanie,
How she met them in the moonlight,
Took their gifts both choice and many,
Ate their fruits and wore their flowers
Plucked from bowers   150
Where summer ripens at all hours?
But ever in the noonlight
She pined and pined away;
Sought them by night and day,
Found them no more, but dwindled and grew gray;   155
Then fell with the first snow,
While to this day no grass will grow
Where she lies low:
I planted daisies there a year ago
That never blow.°   160
                                       bloom
You should not loiter so."
"Nay, hush," said Laura:
"Nay, hush, my sister:
I ate and ate my fill,
Yet my mouth waters still: 165
Tomorrow night I will
Buy more"; and kissed her.
"Have done with sorrow;
I'll bring you plums tomorrow
Fresh on their mother twigs,   170
Cherries worth getting;
You cannot think what figs
My teeth have met in,
What melons icy-cold
Piled on a dish of gold   175
Too huge for me to hold,
What peaches with a velvet nap,
Pellucid grapes without one seed:
Odorous indeed must be the mead
Whereon they grow, and pure the wave they drink   180
With lilies at the brink,
And sugar-sweet their sap."

Golden head by golden head,
Like two pigeons in one nest
Folded in each other's wings,   185
They lay down in their curtained bed:

Like two blossoms on one stem,
Like two flakes of new-fallen snow,
Like two wands of ivory   190
Tipped with gold for awful kings.
Moon and stars gazed in at them,
Wind sang to them lullaby,
Lumbering owls forebore to fly,
Not a bat flapped to and fro   195
Round their nest:
Cheek to cheek and breast to breast
Locked together in one nest.

Early in the morning   200
When the first cock crowed his warning,
Neat like bees, as sweet and busy,
Laura rose with Lizzie:
Fetched in honey, milked the cows,
Aired and set to rights the house,   205
Kneaded cakes of whitest wheat,
Cakes for dainty mouths to eat,
Next churned butter, whipped up cream,
Fed their poultry, sat and sewed;
Talked as modest maidens should: 210
Lizzie with an open heart,
Laura in an absent dream,
One content, one sick in part;
One warbling for the mere bright day's delight,
One longing for the night.

At length slow evening came: 215
They went with pitchers to the reedy brook;
Lizzie most placid in her look,
Laura most like a leaping flame,
They drew the gurgling water from its deep.
Lizzie plucked purple and rich golden flags,   220
Then turning homeward said: "The sunset flushes
Those furthest loftiest crags;
Come, Laura, not another maiden lags.
No willful squirrel wags,
The beasts and birds are fast asleep."   225
But Laura loitered still among the rushes.
And said the bank was steep.

And said the hour was early still,
The dew not fallen, the wind not chill;
Listening ever, but not catching   230
The customary cry,
"Come buy, come buy,"

With its iterated jingle
Of sugar-baited words:
Not for all her watching
Once discerning even one goblin   235
Racing, whisking, tumbling, hobbling —
Let alone the herds
That used to tramp along the glen,
In groups or single,
Of brisk fruit-merchant men.   240
Till Lizzie urged, "O Laura, come;
I hear the fruit-call, but I dare not look:
You should not loiter longer at this brook:
Come with me home.
The stars rise, the moon bends her arc,   245
Each glow-worm winks her spark,
Let us get home before the night grows dark:
For clouds may gather
Though this is summer weather,
Put out the lights and drench us through;   250
Then if we lost our way what should we do?"

Laura turned cold as stone
To find her sister heard that cry alone,
That goblin cry,
"Come buy our fruits, come buy."   255
Must she then buy no more such dainty fruit?
Must she no more such succous pasture find,
Gone deaf and blind?
Her tree of life dropped from the root:
She said not one word in her heart's sore ache.   260
But peering through the dimness, nought discerning,
Trudged home, her pitcher dripping all the way;
So crept to bed, and lay
Silent till Lizzie slept;
Then sat up in a passionate yearning.   265
And gnashed her teeth for balked desire, and wept
As if her heart would break.

Day after day, night after night,
Laura kept watch in vain
In sullen silence of exceeding pain.   270
She never caught again the goblin cry,
"Come buy, come buy";—
She never spied the goblin men
Hawking their fruits along the glen:
But when the noon waxed bright   275
Her hair grew thin and gray;

She dwindled, as the fair full moon doth turn
To swift decay and burn
Her fire away.   280

One day remembering her kernelstone
She set it by a wall that faced the south:
Dewed it with tears, hoped for a root,
Watched for a waxing shoot,
But there came none.   285
It never saw the sun,
It never felt the trickling moisture run:
While with sunk eyes and faded mouth
She dreamed of melons, as a traveler sees
False waves in desert drouth   290
With shade of leaf-crowned trees,
And burns the thirstier in the sandful breeze.

She no more swept the house,
Tended the fowls or cows,
Fetched honey, kneaded cakes of wheat,   295
Brought water from the brook:
But sat down listless in the chimneynook
And would not eat.

Tender Lizzie could not bear
To watch her sister's cankerous care,   300
Yet not to share.
She night and morning
Caught the goblins' cry:
"Come buy our orchard fruits,
Come buy, come buy":—   305
Beside the brook, along the glen,
She heard the tramp of goblin men,
The voice and stir
Poor Laura could not hear;
Longed to buy fruit to comfort her,   310
But feared to pay too dear.
She thought of Jeanie in her grave,
Who should have been a bride;
But who for joys brides hope to have
Fell sick and died   315
In her gay prime,
In earliest winter time,
With the first glazing rime,
With the first snow-fall of crisp winter time.

Till Laura dwindling   320
Seemed knocking at Death's door.

Then Lizzie weighed no more
Better and worse;
But put a silver penny in her purse,
Kissed Laura, crossed the heath with clumps of furze
At twilight, halted by the brook: 325
And for the first time in her life
Began to listen and look.
Laughed every goblin
When they spied her peeping:
Came towards her hobbling,   330
Flying, running, leaping,
Puffing and blowing,
Chuckling, clapping, crowing,
Cluckling and gobbling,
Mopping and mowing,   335
Full of airs and graces,
Pulling wry faces,
Demure grimaces,
Cat-like and rat-like,
Ratel- and wombat-like,   340
Snail-paced in a hurry,
Parrot-voiced and whistler,
Helter skelter, hurry skurry,
Chattering like magpies,
Fluttering like pigeons,   345
Gliding like fishes,—
Hugged her and kissed her:
Squeezed and caressed her:
Stretched up their dishes,
Panniers, and plates: 350
"Look at our apples
Russet and dun,
Bob at our cherries,
Bite at our peaches,
Citrons and dates,   355
Grapes for the asking,
Pears red with basking
Out in the sun,
Plums on their twigs;
Pluck them and suck them,—   360
Pomegranates, figs."

"Good folk," said Lizzie,
Mindful of Jeanie:
"Give me much and many":
Held out her apron,   365

Tossed them her penny
"Nay, take a seat with us,
Honor and eat with us,"
They answered grinning: 370
"Our feast is but beginning.
Night yet is early,
Warm and dew-pearly,
Wakeful and starry:
Such fruits as these   375
No man can carry;
Half their bloom would fly,
Half their dew would dry,
Half their flavor would pass by.
Sit down and feast with us,   380
Be welcome guest with us,
Cheer you and rest with us."—
"Thank you, said Lizzie: "But one waits
At home alone for me:
So without further parleying,   385
If you will not sell me any
Of your fruits though much and many,
Give me back my silver penny
I tossed you for a fee."—
They began to scratch their pates,   390
No longer wagging, purring,
But visibly demurring,
Grunting and snarling.
One called her proud,
Cross-grained, uncivil;   395
Their tones waxed loud,
Their looks were evil.
Lashing their tails
They trod and hustled her,
Elbowed and jostled her,   400
Clawed with their nails,
Barking, mewing, hissing, mocking,
Tore her gown and soiled her stocking,
Twitched her hair out by the roots,
Stamped upon her tender feet,   405
Held her hands and squeezed their fruits
Against her mouth to make her eat.

White and golden Lizzie stood,
Like a lily in a flood,—
Like a rock of blue-veined stone   410
Lashed by tides obstreperously,—
Like a beacon left alone

In a hoary roaring sea,
Sending up a golden fire,—
Like a fruit-crowned orange-tree
White with blossoms honey-sweet   415
Sore beset by wasp and bee,—
Like a royal virgin town
Topped with gilded dome and spire
Close beleaguered by a fleet
Mad to tug her standard° down.   420
                                        a banner, or flag
One may lead a horse to water,
Twenty cannot make him drink.
Though the goblins cuffed and caught her,
Coaxed and fought her,
Bullied and besought her,   425
Scratched her, pinched her black as ink,
Kicked and knocked her,
Mauled and mocked her,
Lizzie uttered not a word;
Would not open lip from lip   430
Lest they should cram a mouthful in:
But laughed in heart to feel the drip
Of juice that syruped all her face,
And lodged in dimples of her chin,
And streaked her neck which quaked like curd.   435
At last the evil people,
Worn out by her resistance,
Flungback her penny, kicked their fruit
Along whichever road they took,
Not leaving root or stone or shoot;   440
Some writhed into the ground,
Some dived into the brook
With ring and ripple,
Some scudded on the gale without a sound.
Some vanished in the distance.   445

In a smart, ache, tingle,
Lizzie went her way;
Knew not was it night or day;
Sprang up the bank, tore through the furze,
Threaded copse and dingle,   450
And heard her penny jingle
Bouncing in her purse,—
Its bounce was music to her ear.
She ran and ran
As if she feared some goblin man   455
Dogged her with gibe or curse
Or something worse:

But not one goblin skurried after,
Nor was she pricked by fear;   460
The kind heart made her windy-paced
That urged her home quite out of breath with haste
And inward laughter.

She cried, "Laura," up the garden,
"Did you miss me?   465
Come and kiss me.
Never mind my bruises,
Hug me, kiss me, suck my juices
Squeezed from goblin fruits for you,
Goblin pulp and goblin dew.   470
Eat me, drink me, love me;
Laura, make much of me;
For your sake I have braved the glen
And had to do with goblin merchant men."

Laura started from her chair,   475
Flung her arms up in the air,
Clutched her hair:
"Lizzie, Lizzie, have you tasted
For my sake the fruit forbidden?
Must your light like mine be hidden,   480
Your young life like mine be wasted,
Undone in mine undoing,
And ruined in my ruin,
Thirsty, cankered, goblin-ridden?"—
She clung about her sister,   485
Kissed and kissed and kissed her:
Tears once again
Refreshed her shrunken eyes,
Dropping like rain
After long sultry drouth;   490
Shaking with anguish, fear, and pain,
She kissed and kissed her with a hungry mouth.

Her lips began to scorch,
That juice was wormwood to her tongue,
She loathed the feast: 495
Writhing as one possessed she leaped and sung,
Rent all her robe, and wrung
Her hands in lamentable haste,
And beat her breast,
Her locks streamed like the torch   500
Borne by a racer at full speed,
Or like the mane of horses in their flight,
Or like an eagle when she stems the light

Straight toward the sun,
Or like a caged thing freed,
Or like a flying flag when armies run.   505

Swift fire spread through her veins, knocked at her heart,
Met the fire smoldering there.
And overbore its lesser flame;
She gorged on bitterness without a name: 510
Ah fool, to choose such part
Of soul-consuming care!
Sense failed in the mortal strife:
Like the watch-tower of a town
Which an earthquake shatters down,   515
Like a lightning-stricken mast,
Like a wind-uprooted tree
Spun about,
Like a foam-topped waterspout
Cast down headlong in the sea,   520
She fell at last;
Pleasure past and anguish past,
Is it death or is it life?

Life out of death.
That night long Lizzie watched by her,   525
Counted her pulse's flagging stir,
Felt for her breath,
Held water to her lips, and cooled her face
With tears and fanning leaves.
But when the first birds chirped about their eaves,   530
And early reapers plodded to the place
Of golden sheaves,
And dew-wet grass
Bowed in the morning winds so brisk to pass,
And new buds with new day   535
Opened of cup-like lilies on the stream,
Laura awoke as from a dream,
Laughed in the innocent old way,
Hugged Lizzie but not twice or thrice;
Her gleaming locks showed not one thread of gray,   540
Her breath was sweet as May,
And light danced in her eyes.

Days, weeks, months, years
Afterwards, when both were wives
With children of their own;
Their mother-hearts beset with fears,   545
Their lives bound up in tender lives:
Laura would call the little ones

And tell them of her early prime,
Those pleasant days long gone   550
Of not-returning time:
Would talk about the haunted glen,
The wicked quaint fruit-merchant men,
Their fruits like honey to the throat
But poison in the blood   555
(Men sell not such in any town):
Would tell them how her sister stood
In deadly peril to do her good,
And win the fiery antidote:
Then joining hands to little hands   560
Would bid them cling together,—
"For there is no friend like a sister
In calm or stormy weather;
To cheer one on the tedious way,
To fetch one if one goes astray,   565
To lift one if one totters down,
To strengthen whilst one stands."

CONSIDERATIONS FOR CRITICAL THINKING AND WRITING

1. **FIRST RESPONSE.** This is a lengthy poem from a bygone century, and yet even readers who are not particularly fond of poetry tend to find it riveting. How does the poet sustain your interest?

2. Goblins aren't real, but Lizzie and Laura are real people. How do you interpret "goblins" symbolically? What specifically in the poem guides your response?

3. Based on the definition and example above, would you classify this poem as allegory or not?

CONNECTION TO ANOTHER SELECTION

1. Compare the treatment of desire in this poem and in James Baldwin's "Guilt, Desire and Love" (p. 448).

JANE KENYON (1947–1995)

The Thimble 1993

I found a silver thimble
on the humusy floor of the woodshed,
neither large nor small, the open end
bent oval by the wood's weight,
or because the woman who wore it   5
shaped it to fit her finger.

Its decorative border of leaves, graceful
and regular, like the edge of acanthus
on the tin ceiling at church . . .
repeating itself over our heads   10
while we speak in unison
words the wearer must have spoken.

Considerations for Critical Thinking and Writing

1. **FIRST RESPONSE.** Do you think the sound connection between "thimble" and "symbol" is coincidental?

2. How does the thimble function as a complex symbol? How does the speaker unpack its layers?

3. When does the pronoun shift from "I" to "we"? Why is this shift significant?

Kevin Pierce (b. 1958)

Proof of Origin   2005

NEWSWIRE — A U.S. judge ordered a Georgia school district to remove from textbooks stickers challenging the theory of evolution.

Though close to their hearts is the version that starts
With Adam and Eve and no clothes,
What enables their grip as the stickers they strip
Is Darwinian thumbs that oppose.

Considerations for Critical Thinking and Writing

1. **FIRST RESPONSE.** How do the rhymes contribute to the humorous tone?

2. Discuss the levels of irony in the poem.

3. How do you read the title? Can it be explained in more than one way?

Carl Sandburg (1878–1967)

A Fence   1916

Now the stone house on the lake front is finished and the workmen
        are beginning the fence.
The palings are made of iron bars with steel points that can stab the
        life out of any man who falls on them.

As a fence, it is a masterpiece, and will shut off the rabble and all
      vagabonds and hungry men and all wandering children looking
      for a place to play.
Passing through the bars and over the steel points will go nothing
      except Death and the Rain and Tomorrow.

CONSIDERATIONS FOR CRITICAL THINKING AND WRITING

1. FIRST RESPONSE. What is the effect of the capital letters in the final line?
2. Discuss the symbolic meaning of the fence and whether you think the symbolism is too spelled out or not.

CONNECTION TO ANOTHER SELECTION

1. Consider the themes in "A Fence" and Robert Frost's "Mending Wall" (p. 659). Which poem do you prefer? Why?

JULIO MARZÁN (B. 1946)

Ethnic Poetry 1994

The ethnic poet said: "The earth is maybe
a huge maraca / and the sun a trombone /
and life / is to move your ass / to slow beats."
The ethnic audience roasted a suckling pig.

The ethnic poet said: "Oh thank Goddy, Goddy /   5
I be me, my toenails curled downward /
deep, deep, deep into Mama earth."
The ethnic audience shook strands of sea shells.

The ethnic poet said: "The sun was created black /
so we should imagine light / and also dream /   10
a walrus emerging from the broken ice."
The ethnic audience beat on sealskin drums.

The ethnic poet said: "Reproductive organs /
Eagles nesting California redwoods /
Shut up and listen to my ancestors."   15
The ethnic audience ate fried bread and honey.

The ethnic poet said: "Something there is that
doesn't love a wall / That sends
the frozen-ground-swell under it."
The ethnic audience deeply understood humanity.   20

> **WHEN I WRITE** "Words you are sure convey your truest feelings or thoughts may record only sentiment, not a line of poetry, while another arrangement, different words in another tone or rhythm, unlock and reveal what you really wanted to say." — JULIO MARZÁN

Considerations for Critical Thinking and Writing

1. **FIRST RESPONSE.** What is the implicit definition of *ethnic poetry* in this poem?

2. The final stanza quotes lines from Robert Frost's "Mending Wall" (p. 659). Read the entire poem. Why do you think Marzán chooses these lines and this particular poem as one kind of ethnic poetry?

3. What is the poem's central irony? Pay particular attention to the final line. What is being satirized here?

Connection to Another Selection

1. Write an essay that discusses the speakers' ideas about what poetry should be in "Ethnic Poetry" and in Ruth Forman's "Poetry Should Ride the Bus" (p. 386).

Mark Halliday (b. 1949)

Graded Paper   1991

On the whole this is quite successful work:
your main argument about the poet's ambivalence —
how he loves the very things he attacks —
is mostly persuasive and always engaging.

At the same time,   5
                    there are spots
where your thinking becomes, for me,
alarmingly opaque, and your syntax seems to jump
backwards through unnecessary hoops,
as on p. 2 where you speak of "precognitive awareness   10
not yet disestablished by the shell that encrusts
each thing that a person actually says"
or at the top of p. 5 where your discussion of
"subverbal undertow miming the subversion of self-belief
woven counter to desire's outreach"   15
leaves me groping for firmer footholds.
(I'd have said it differently,
or rather, said something else.)
And when you say that women "could not fulfill themselves" (p. 6)
"in that era" (only forty years ago, after all!)   20
are you so sure that the situation is so different today?
Also, how does Whitman bluff his way into
your penultimate paragraph? He is the *last* poet
I would have quoted in this context!
What plausible way of behaving   25

does the passage you quote represent? Don't you think
literature should ultimately reveal possibilities for *action*?

Please notice how I've repaired your use of semicolons.

And yet, despite what may seem my cranky response,
I do admire the freshness of   30
your thinking and your style; there is
a vitality here; your sentences thrust themselves forward
with a confidence as impressive as it is cheeky. . . .
You are not
          me, finally,   35
and though this is an awkward problem, involving
the inescapable fact that you are so young, so young
it is also a delightful provocation.

CONSIDERATIONS FOR CRITICAL THINKING AND WRITING

1. **FIRST RESPONSE.** How do you characterize the grader of this paper based
   on the comments about the paper?

2. Is the speaker a man or a woman? What makes you think so? Does the
   gender of the speaker affect your reading of the poem? How?

3. Explain whether or not you think the teacher's comments on the paper are
   consistent with the grade awarded it. How do you account for the grade?

CONNECTION TO ANOTHER SELECTION

1. Compare the ways in which Halliday reveals the speaker's character
   in this poem with the strategies used by Robert Browning in "My Last
   Duchess" (below).

ROBERT BROWNING (1812–1889)
My Last Duchess   1842

Ferrara°

That's my last Duchess painted on the wall,
Looking as if she were alive. I call
That piece a wonder, now: Frà Pandolf's°
          hands
Worked busily a day, and there she stands.

Bettmann/Getty Images.

Ferrara: In the sixteenth century, the duke of this Italian city arranged to marry a second
time after the mysterious death of his very young first wife.   3 *Frà Pandolf:* A fictitious artist.

Will't please you sit and look at her? I said
"Frà Pandolf" by design, for never read
Strangers like you that pictured countenance,
The depth and passion of its earnest glance,
But to myself they turned (since none puts by
The curtain I have drawn for you, but I)   10
And seemed as they would ask me, if they durst,
How such a glance came there; so, not the first
Are you to turn and ask thus. Sir, 'twas not
Her husband's presence only, called that spot
Of joy into the Duchess' cheek: perhaps   15
Frà Pandolf chanced to say "Her mantle laps
Over my lady's wrist too much," or "Paint
Must never hope to reproduce the faint
Half-flush that dies along her throat": such stuff
Was courtesy, she thought, and cause enough   20
For calling up that spot of joy. She had
A heart — how shall I say? — too soon made glad,
Too easily impressed; she liked whate'er
She looked on, and her looks went everywhere.
Sir, 'twas all one! My favor at her breast,   25
The dropping of the daylight in the West,
The bough of cherries some officious fool
Broke in the orchard for her, the white mule
She rode with round the terrace — all and each
Would draw from her alike the approving speech,   30
Or blush, at least. She thanked men, — good! but thanked
Somehow — I know not how — as if she ranked
My gift of a nine-hundred-years-old name
With anybody's gift. Who'd stoop to blame
This sort of trifling? Even had you skill   35
In speech — which I have not — to make your will
Quite clear to such an one, and say, "Just this
Or that in you disgusts me; here you miss,
Or there exceed the mark" — and if she let
Herself be lessoned so, nor plainly set   40
Her wits to yours, forsooth, and made excuse,
— E'en then would be some stooping; and I choose
Never to stoop. Oh sir, she smiled, no doubt,
Whene'er I passed her; but who passed without
Much the same smile? This grew; I gave commands;   45
Then all smiles stopped together. There she stands
As if alive. Will't please you rise? We'll meet
The company below, then. I repeat,
The Count your master's known munificence
Is ample warrant that no just pretense   50

Of mine for dowry will be disallowed;
Though his fair daughter's self, as I avowed
At starting, is my object. Nay, we'll go
Together down, sir. Notice Neptune, though,
Taming a sea-horse, thought a rarity,   55
Which Claus of Innsbruck° cast in bronze for me!

56 *Claus of Innsbruck:* Also a fictitious artist.

CONSIDERATIONS FOR CRITICAL THINKING AND WRITING

1. FIRST RESPONSE. What do you think happened to the duchess?
2. To whom is the duke addressing his remarks about the duchess in this poem? What is ironic about the situation?
3. Why was the duke unhappy with his first wife? What does this reveal about him? What does the poem's title suggest about his attitude toward women in general?
4. What seems to be the visitor's response (lines 53–54) to the duke's account of his first wife?

CONNECTION TO ANOTHER SELECTION

1. Write an essay describing the ways in which the speakers of "My Last Duchess" and Katharyn Howd Machan's "Hazel Tells LaVerne" (p. 403) inadvertently reveal themselves.

WILLIAM BLAKE (1757–1827)

A Poison Tree 1794

I was angry with my friend:
I told my wrath, my wrath did end.
I was angry with my foe:
I told it not, my wrath did grow.

And I water'd it in fears,   5
Night & morning with my tears;
And I sunned it with smiles,
And with soft deceitful wiles.

And it grew both day and night,
Till it bore an apple bright.   10
And my foe beheld it shine,
And he knew that it was mine,

And into my garden stole,
When the night had veild the pole;
In the morning glad I see   15
My foe outstretched beneath the tree.

CONSIDERATIONS FOR CRITICAL THINKING AND WRITING

1. **FIRST RESPONSE.** Considering the "apple bright" allusion in the third stanza, how can "A Poison Tree" be read as more than a meditation on a personal relationship gone bad?

2. What is the speaker's attitude toward anger and revenge? What do you think the speaker wants the reader's attitude to be?

16

Sounds

In a poem the words should be as pleasing to the ear as the meaning is to the mind.

— MARIANNE MOORE

LISTENING TO POETRY

Poems yearn to be read aloud. Much of their energy, charm, and beauty come to life only when they are heard. Poets choose and arrange words for their sounds as well as for their meanings. Most poetry is best read with your lips, teeth, and tongue because they serve to articulate the effects that sound may have in a poem. When a voice is breathed into a good poem, there is pleasure in the reading, the saying, and the hearing.

The earliest poetry — before writing and painting — was chanted or sung. The rhythmic quality of such oral performances served two purposes: it helped the chanting bard remember the lines and it entertained audiences with patterned sounds of language, which were sometimes accompanied by musical instruments. Poetry has always been closely related to music. Indeed, as the word suggests, lyric poetry evolved from songs (see chapter 22). "Scarborough Fair", an anonymous Middle English lyric, survived as song long before it was written down, and the folk-rock duo Simon and Garfunkel put it to music in the 1960s. Had Robert Frost lived in a nonliterate society, he probably would have sung some version — a very different version to be sure — of "Acquainted with the Night" (p. 446) instead of writing it down. Even though Frost creates a speaking rather than a singing voice, the speaker's anxious tone is distinctly heard in any careful reading of the poem.

Like lyrics, early narrative poems were originally part of an anonymous oral folk tradition. A **ballad** such as "Lord Randal" (p. 606) told a story that was sung from one generation to the next until it was finally transcribed. Since the eighteenth century, this narrative form has sometimes been imitated by poets who write **literary ballads**. In considering poetry as sound, we should not forget that poetry traces its beginnings to song. See Chapter 22, "Song Lyrics as Poetry," for an in-depth examination of the relationship between these categories.

Of course, reading a poem is not the same as hearing it. Like the lyrics of a song, many poems must be heard — or at least read with listening eyes — before they can be fully understood and enjoyed. The sounds of words are a universal source of music for human beings. This has been so from ancient tribes to bards to the two-year-old child in a bakery gleefully chanting "Cuppitycake, cuppitycake!"

Listen to the sound of this poem as you read it aloud. How do the words provide, in a sense, their own musical accompaniment?

JOHN UPDIKE (1932–2009)

Player Piano   1958

My stick fingers click with a snicker
And, chuckling, they knuckle the keys;
Light-footed, my steel feelers flicker
And pluck from these keys melodies.

My paper can caper; abandon   5
Is broadcast by dint of my din,
And no man or band has a hand in
The tones I turn on from within.

At times I'm a jumble of rumbles,
At others I'm light like the moon,
But never my numb plunker fumbles,   10
Misstrums me, or tries a new tune.

The speaker in this poem is a piano that can play automatically by means of a mechanism that depresses keys in response to signals on a perforated roll. Notice how the speaker's voice approximates the sounds of a piano. In each stanza a predominant sound emerges from the carefully chosen words. How is the sound of each stanza tuned to its sense?

Like Updike's "Player Piano," this next poem also employs sounds to reinforce meanings.

EMILY DICKINSON (1830–1886)

A Bird came down the Walk —   ca. 1862

A Bird came down the Walk —
He did not know I saw —
He bit an Angleworm in halves
And ate the fellow, raw,

And then he drank a Dew   5
From a convenient Grass —
And then hopped sidewise to the Wall
To let a Beetle pass —

He glanced with rapid eyes
That hurried all around —   10
They looked like frightened Beads, I thought —
He stirred his Velvet Head

Like one in danger, Cautious,
I offered him a Crumb
And he unrolled his feathers   15
And rowed him softer home —

Than Oars divide the Ocean,
Too silver for a seam —
Or Butterflies, off Banks of Noon
Leap, plashless as they swim.   20

This description of a bird offers a close look at how differently a bird moves when it hops on the ground than when it flies in the air. On the ground the bird moves quickly, awkwardly, and irregularly as it plucks up a worm, washes it down with dew, and then hops aside to avoid a passing beetle. The speaker recounts the bird's rapid, abrupt actions from a somewhat superior, amused perspective. By describing the bird in human terms (as if, for example, it chose to eat the worm "raw"), the speaker is almost condescending. But when the attempt to offer a crumb fails and the frightened bird flies off, the speaker is left looking up instead of down at the bird.

With that shift in perspective the tone shifts from amusement to awe in response to the bird's graceful flight. The jerky movements of lines 1 to 13 give way to the smooth motion of lines 15 to 20. The pace of the first three stanzas is fast and discontinuous. We tend to pause at the end of each line, and this reinforces a sense of disconnected movements. In contrast, the final six lines are to be read as a single sentence in one flowing movement, lubricated by various sounds.

Read again the description of the bird flying away. Several *o*-sounds contribute to the image of the serene, expansive, confident flight, just as the *s*-sounds serve as smooth transitions from one line to the next. Notice how these sounds are grouped in the following vertical columns:

unrolled	softer	Too	his	Ocean	Banks
rowed	Oars	Noon	feathers	silver	plashless
home	Or		softer	seam	as
Ocean	off		Oars	Butterflies	swim

This blending of sounds (notice how "Leap, plashless" brings together the *p*- and *l*-sounds without a ripple) helps convey the bird's smooth grace in the air. Like a feathered oar, the bird moves seamlessly in its element.

The repetition of sounds in poetry is similar to the function of the tones and melodies that are repeated, with variations, in music. Just as the patterned sounds in music unify a work, so do the words in poems, which have been carefully chosen for the combinations of sounds they create. These sounds are produced in a number of ways.

The most direct way in which the sound of a word suggests its meaning is through **onomatopoeia**, which is the use of a word that resembles the sound it denotes: *quack, buzz, rattle, bang, squeak, bowwow, burp, choo-choo, ding-a-ling, sizzle.* The sound and sense of these words are closely related, but such words represent a very small percentage of the words available to us. Poets usually employ more subtle means for echoing meanings.

Onomatopoeia can consist of more than just single words. In its broadest meaning the term refers to lines or passages in which sounds help to convey meanings, as in these lines from Updike's "Player Piano":

My stick fingers click with a snicker
And, chuckling, they knuckle the keys.

The sharp, crisp sounds of these two lines approximate the sounds of a piano; the syllables seem to "click" against one another. Contrast Updike's rendition with the following lines:

My long fingers play with abandon
And, laughing, they cover the keys.

The original version is more interesting and alive because the sounds of the words are pleasurable and reinforce the meaning through a careful blending of consonants and vowels.

Alliteration is the repetition of the same consonant sounds at the beginnings of nearby words: "*d*escending *d*ewdrops," "*l*uscious *l*emons." Sometimes the term is also used to describe the consonant sounds within words: "trespasser's reproach," "wedded lady." Alliteration is based on sound rather than spelling. "Keen" and "car" alliterate, but "car" does not alliterate with "cite."

Rarely is heavy-handed alliteration effective. Used too self-consciously, it can be distracting instead of strengthening meaning or emphasizing a relation between words. Consider the relentless *h*'s in this line: "Horrendous horrors haunted Helen's happiness." Those *h*'s certainly suggest that Helen is being pursued, but they have a more comic than serious effect because they are overdone.

Assonance is the repetition of the same vowel sound in nearby words: "asl*ee*p under a tr*ee*," "t*i*me and t*i*de," "h*au*nt" and "*aw*esome," "*ea*ch evening." Both alliteration and assonance help to establish relations among words in a line or a series of lines. Whether the effect is **euphony** (lines that are musically pleasant to the ear and smooth, like the final lines of Dickinson's "A Bird came down the Walk —") or **cacophony** (lines that are discordant and difficult to pronounce, like the claim that "never my numb plunker fumbles" in Updike's "Player Piano"), the sounds of words in poetry can be as significant as the words' denotative or connotative meanings.

A SAMPLE STUDENT RESPONSE

Ryan Lee

Professor McDonough

English 211

1 December 2018

Sound in Emily Dickinson's "A Bird came down the Walk—"

In her poem "A Bird came down the Walk—" Emily Dickinson uses the sound and rhythm of each line to reflect the motion of a bird walking awkwardly—and then flying gracefully. Particularly when read aloud, the staccato phrases and stilted breaks in lines 1 through 14 create a sense of the bird's movement on land, quick and off-balanced, which helps bring the scene to life.

The first three stanzas are structured to make the bird's movement consistent. The bird hops around, eating worms while keeping guard for any threats. Vulnerable on the ground, the bird is intensely aware of danger:

He glanced with rapid eyes

That hurried all around—

They looked like frightened Beads, I thought—

He stirred his Velvet Head (9-12)

In addition to choosing words that portray the bird as cautious—it "glanced with rapid eyes" (9) that resemble "frightened Beads" (11)—Dickinson chooses to end each line abruptly. This abrupt halting of sound allows the reader to experience the bird's fear more immediately, and the effect is similar to the missing of a beat or a breath.

These halting lines stand in contrast to the smoothness of the last six lines, during which the bird takes flight. The sounds in these lines are pleasingly soft, and rich in the "s" sound. The bird

> unrolled his feathers
> And rowed him softer home—
>
> Than Oars divide the Ocean,
> Too silver for a seam— (15-18). . . .

Lee 4

Work Cited

Dickinson, Emily. "A Bird came down the Walk—." *Literature to Go*, edited by Michael Meyer and D. Quentin Miller, 4th ed., Bedford/St. Martin's, 2020, p. 476.

RHYME

Like alliteration and assonance, **rhyme** is a way of creating sound patterns. Rhyme, broadly defined, consists of two or more words or phrases that repeat the same sounds: *happy* and *snappy*. Rhyme words often have similar spellings, but that is not a requirement of rhyme; what matters is that the words sound alike: *vain* rhymes with *reign* as well as *rain*. Moreover, words may look alike but not rhyme at all. In *eye rhyme* the spellings are similar, but the pronunciations are not, as with *bough* and *cough,* or *brow* and *blow.*

Not all poems use rhyme. Many great poems have no rhymes, and many weak verses use rhyme as a substitute for poetry. These are especially apparent in commercial messages and greeting-card lines. At its worst, rhyme is merely a distracting decoration that can lead to dullness and predictability. But used skillfully, rhyme creates lines that are memorable and musical.

Here is a poem using rhyme that you might remember the next time you are in a restaurant.

RICHARD ARMOUR (1906–1989)

Going to Extremes   1954

Shake and shake
   The catsup bottle
None'll come —
   And then a lot'll.

The experience recounted in Armour's poem is common enough, but the rhyme's humor is special. The final line clicks the poem shut — an effect that is often achieved by the use of rhyme. That click provides a sense of a satisfying and fulfilled form. Rhymes have a number of uses: they can emphasize words, direct a reader's attention to relations between words, and provide an overall structure for a poem.

Rhyme is used in the following poem to imitate the sound of cascading water.

ROBERT SOUTHEY (1774–1843)

From "The Cataract of Lodore"   1820

   "How does the water
   Come down at Lodore?"

. . . .

From its sources which well
   In the tarn on the fell;
      From its fountains   5
      In the mountains,
   Its rills and its gills;
Through moss and through brake,
      It runs and it creeps
      For awhile, till it sleeps   10

In its own little lake.
And thence at departing,
Awakening and starting,
It runs through the reeds
And away it proceeds,
Through meadow and glade,   15
In sun and in shade,
And through the wood-shelter,
Among crags in its flurry,
Helter-skelter,
Hurry-scurry.   20
Here it comes sparkling,
And there it lies darkling;
Now smoking and frothing
Its tumult and wrath in,
Till in this rapid race   25
On which it is bent,
It reaches the place
Of its steep descent.

. . . .

Dividing and gliding and sliding,
And falling and brawling and sprawling,   30
And driving and riving and striving,
And sprinkling and twinkling and wrinkling,
And sounding and bounding and rounding,
And bubbling and troubling and doubling,
And grumbling and rumbling and tumbling,   35
And clattering and battering and shattering;
Retreating and beating and meeting and sheeting,
Delaying and straying and playing and spraying,
Advancing and prancing and glancing and dancing,
Recoiling, turmoiling and toiling and boiling,   40
And gleaming and streaming and steaming and beaming,
And rushing and flushing and brushing and gushing,
And flapping and rapping and clapping and slapping,
And curling and whirling and purling and twirling,
And thumping and plumping and bumping and jumping,   45
And dashing and flashing and splashing and clashing;
And so never ending, but always descending,
Sounds and motions forever and ever are blending,
All at once and all o'er, with a mighty uproar;
And this way the water comes down at Lodore.   50

This deluge of rhymes consists of "Sounds and motions forever and ever . . . blending" (line 49). The pace quickens as the water creeps from its mountain source and then descends in rushing cataracts. As the speed of the water increases, so do the number of rhymes, until they run in fours: "dashing and flashing and splashing and clashing" (line 47). Most rhymes meander through poems instead of flooding them; nevertheless, Southey's use of rhyme suggests how sounds can flow with meanings. "The Cataract of Lodore" has been criticized, however, for overusing onomatopoeia. Some readers find the poem silly; others regard it as a brilliant example of sound effects. What do you think?

A variety of types of rhyme is available to poets. The most common form, **end rhyme**, comes at the ends of lines (lines 14–17).

> It runs through the reeds
>> And away it proceeds,
> Through meadow and glade,
>> In sun and in shade.

Internal rhyme places at least one of the rhymed words within the line, as in "Dividing and gliding and sliding" (line 30) or, more subtly, in the fourth and final words of "In mist or cloud, on mast or shroud."

The rhyming of single-syllable words such as *glade* and *shade* is known as **masculine rhyme**, as we see in these lines from A. E. Housman:

> Loveliest of trees, the cherry now
> Is hung with bloom along the bough.

Rhymes using words of more than one syllable are also called masculine when the same sound occurs in a final stressed syllable, as in *defend, contend; betray, away*. A **feminine rhyme** consists of a rhymed stressed syllable followed by one or more rhymed unstressed syllables, as in *butter, clutter; gratitude, attitude; quivering, shivering*. This rhyme is evident in John Millington Synge's verse:

> Lord confound this surly sister,
> Blight her brow and blotch and blister.

All of the examples so far have been **exact rhymes** because they share the same stressed vowel sounds as well as any sounds that follow the vowel. In **near rhyme** (also called **off rhyme**, **slant rhyme**, and **approximate rhyme**), the sounds are almost but not exactly alike. There are several kinds of near rhyme. One of the most common is **consonance**, an identical consonant sound preceded by a different vowel sound: *home, same; worth, breath; trophy, daffy*. Near rhyme can also be achieved by using different vowel sounds with identical consonant sounds: *sound, sand; kind, conned; fellow, fallow*. The dissonance of *blade* and *blood* in the following lines from Wilfred Owen helps to reinforce their grim tone:

> Let the boy try along this bayonet-blade
> How cold steel is, and keen with hunger of blood.

Near rhymes greatly broaden the possibility for musical effects in English, a language that, compared with Spanish or Italian, contains few exact rhymes. Do not assume, however, that a near rhyme represents a failed attempt at exact rhyme. Near rhymes allow a musical subtlety and variety and can avoid the sometimes overpowering jingling effects that exact rhymes may create.

These basic terms hardly exhaust the ways in which the sounds in poems can be labeled and discussed, but the terms can help you to describe how poets manipulate sounds for effect. Read Gerard Manley Hopkins's "God's Grandeur" (below) aloud and try to determine how the sounds of the lines contribute to their sense.

SOUND AND MEANING

GERARD MANLEY HOPKINS (1844–1889)
God's Grandeur   1877

The world is charged with the grandeur of God.
   It will flame out, like shining from shook foil;°   *shaken gold foil*
   It gathers to a greatness, like the ooze of oil
Crushed.° Why do men then now not reck his rod?°
Generations have trod, have trod, have trod;
   And all is seared with trade; bleared, smeared with toil;   5
   And wears man's smudge and shares man's smell: the soil
Is bare now, nor can foot feel, being shod.
And for all this, nature is never spent;
   There lives the dearest freshness deep down things;
And though the last lights off the black West went   10
   Oh, morning, at the brown brink eastward, springs —
Because the Holy Ghost over the bent
   World broods with warm breast and with ah! bright wings.

The subject of this poem is announced in the title and the first line: "The world is charged with the grandeur of God." The poem is a celebration of the power and greatness of God's presence in the world, but the speaker is also perplexed and dismayed by people who refuse to recognize God's authority and grandeur as they are manifested in the creation. Instead of glorifying God, "men" have degraded the earth through meaningless toil and cut themselves off from the spiritual renewal inherent in the beauty

---

4 *Crushed:*   Olives crushed in their oil; *reck his rod:*   Obey God.

of nature. The relentless demands of commerce and industry have blinded people to the earth's natural and spiritual resources. Despite this abuse and insensitivity to God's grandeur, however, "nature is never spent"; the morning light that "springs" in the east redeems the "black West" of the night and is a sign that the spirit of the Holy Ghost is ever present in the world. This summary of the poem sketches some of the thematic significance of the lines, but it does not do justice to how they are organized around the use of sound. Hopkins's poem, unlike Southey's "The Cataract of Lodore," uses sounds in a subtle and complex way.

In the opening line Hopkins uses alliteration — a device apparent in almost every line of the poem — to connect "Go*d*" to the "worl*d*," which is "charge*d*" with his "gran*d*eur." These consonants unify the line as well. The alliteration in lines 2 and 3 suggests a harmony in the creation: the *f*'s in "*f*lame" and "*f*oil," the *sh*'s in "*sh*ining" and "*sh*ook," the *g*'s in "*g*athers" and "*g*reatness," and the visual (not alliterative) similarities of "*oo*ze of *oi*l" emphasize a world that is held together by God's will.

That harmony is abruptly interrupted by the speaker's angry question in line 4: "Why do men then now not reck his rod?" The question is as painful to the speaker as it is difficult to pronounce. The arrangement of the alliteration ("*n*ow," "*n*ot"; "*r*eck," "*r*od"), the assonance ("n*o*t," "r*o*d"; "m*e*n," "th*e*n," "r*e*ck"), and the internal rhyme ("m*en*," "th*en*") contribute to the difficulty in saying the line — a difficulty associated with human behavior. That behavior is introduced in line 5 by the repetition of "have trod" to emphasize the repeated mistakes — sins — committed by human beings. The tone is dirgelike because humanity persists in its mistaken path rather than progressing. The speaker's horror at humanity is evident in the cacophonous sounds of lines 6 to 8. Here the alliteration of "*sm*eared," "*sm*udge," and "*sm*ell" along with the internal rhymes of "s*eared*," "bl*eared*," and "sm*eared*" echo the disgust with which the speaker views humanity's "t*oil*" with the "s*oil*," an end rhyme that calls attention to our mistaken equation of nature with production rather than with spirituality.

In contrast to this cacophony, the final six lines build toward the joyful recognition of the new possibilities that accompany the rising sun. This recognition leads to the euphonic description of the "Holy Gh*o*st *o*ver" (notice the reassuring consistency of the assonance) the world. Traditionally represented as a dove, the Holy Ghost brings love and peace to the "*w*orld," and "*b*roods *w*ith *w*arm *b*reast and *w*ith ah! *b*right *w*ings." The effect of this alliteration is mellifluous: the sound bespeaks the harmony that prevails at the end of the poem resulting from the speaker's recognition that "nature is never spent" because God loves and protects the world.

The sounds of "God's Grandeur" enhance the poem's theme; more can be said about its sounds, but it is enough to point out here that for this poem the sound strongly echoes the theme in nearly every line. Here are some more poems in which sound plays a significant role.

POEMS FOR FURTHER STUDY

LEWIS CARROLL (CHARLES LUTWIDGE DODGSON/1832–1898)

Jabberwocky 1871

'Twas brillig, and the slithy toves
   Did gyre and gimble in the wabe:
All mimsy were the borogoves,
   And the mome raths outgrabe.

"Beware the Jabberwock, my son!
   The jaws that bite, the claws that catch!   5
Beware the Jubjub bird, and shun
   The frumious Bandersnatch!"

He took his vorpal sword in hand;
   Long time the manxome foe he sought —
So rested he by the Tumtum tree,   10
   And stood awhile in thought.

And, as in uffish thought he stood,
   The Jabberwock, with eyes of flame,
Came whiffling through the tulgey wood,
   And burbled as it came!   15

One, two! One, two! And through and through
   The vorpal blade went snicker-snack!
He left it dead, and with its head
   He went galumphing back.
     20

"And hast thou slain the Jabberwock?
   Come to my arms, my beamish boy!
O frabjous day! Callooh, Callay!"
   He chortled in his joy.

'Twas brillig, and the slithy toves
   Did gyre and gimble in the wabe: 25
All mimsy were the borogoves,
   And the mome raths outgrabe.

CONSIDERATIONS FOR CRITICAL THINKING AND WRITING

1. **FIRST RESPONSE.** What happens in this poem? Does it have any meaning?
2. Not all of the words used in this poem appear in dictionaries. In *Through the Looking Glass*, Humpty Dumpty explains to Alice that "'slithy' means 'lithe and slimy.' 'Lithe' is the same as 'active.' You see it's

like a portmanteau — there are two meanings packed up into one word."
Are there any other portmanteau words in the poem?

3. Which words in the poem sound especially meaningful, even if they are
devoid of any denotative meanings?

CONNECTION TO ANOTHER SELECTION

1. Compare Carroll's strategies for creating sound and meaning with those
used by Updike in "Player Piano" (p. 475).

WILLIAM HEYEN (B. 1940)

The Trains 1984

Signed by Franz Paul Stangl, Commandant,
there is in Berlin a document,
an order of transmittal from Treblinka:

248 freight cars of clothing,
400,000 gold watches,   5
25 freight cars of women's hair.

Some clothing was kept, some pulped for paper.
The finest watches were never melted down.
All the women's hair was used for mattresses, or dolls.

Would these words like to use some of that same paper?   10
One of those watches may pulse in your own wrist.
Does someone you know collect dolls, or sleep on human hair?

He is dead at last, Commandant Stangl of Treblinka,
but the camp's three syllables still sound like freight cars
straining around a curve, Treblinka,   15

Treblinka. Clothing, time in gold watches,
women's hair for mattresses and dolls' heads.
Treblinka. The trains from Treblinka.

CONSIDERATIONS FOR CRITICAL THINKING AND WRITING

1. FIRST RESPONSE. How does the sound of the word *Treblinka* inform your
understanding of the poem?

2. Why does the place name of Treblinka continue to resonate over
time? To learn more about Treblinka, search the Web, perhaps starting at ushmm.org, the site of the United States Holocaust Memorial
Museum.

3. Why do you suppose Heyen uses the word *in* instead of *on* in line 11?

4. Why is sound so important for establishing the tone of this poem? In what sense do "the camp's three syllables still sound like freight cars" (line 14)?

5. CRITICAL STRATEGIES. Read the section on reader-response strategies (pp. 1083–85) in Chapter 30, "Critical Strategies for Reading." How does this poem make you feel? Why?

ALFRED, LORD TENNYSON (1809–1892)

Break, Break, Break   1842

Break, break, break,
　　On thy cold gray stones, O Sea!
And I would that my tongue could utter
　　The thoughts that arise in me.

O, well for the fisherman's boy,
　　That he shouts with his sister at play!　　　　　　　　　　5
O, well for the sailor lad,
　　That he sings in his boat on the bay!

And the stately ships go on
　　To their haven under the hill;
But O for the touch of a vanish'd hand,　　　　　　　　　　10
　　And the sound of a voice that is still!

Break, break, break
　　At the foot of thy crags, O Sea!
But the tender grace of a day that is dead
　　Will never come back to me.　　　　　　　　　　　　　15

CONSIDERATIONS FOR CRITICAL THINKING AND WRITING

1. FIRST RESPONSE. The poem was written as an *elegy* following the death of Tennyson's friend, the poet Robert Hallum. Based on this context, what feelings does the poem evoke?

2. Which of the sound qualities of poetic language we have described can you find here? What is their effect?

3. Are the end rhymes at the end of alternating lines masculine or feminine as we describe those terms above? How does this type of rhyme intensify the feelings you associate with the poem?

4. What sound qualities of an ocean are evident in the words and rhythm of this poem?

JOHN DONNE (1572–1631)

Song 1633

Go and catch a falling star,
  Get with child a mandrake root,°
Tell me where all past years are,
  Or who cleft the Devil's foot,
Teach me to hear mermaids singing,   5
  Or to keep off envy's stinging,
        And find
        What wind
Serves to advance an honest mind.

If thou be'st borne to strange sights,   10
  Things invisible to see,
Ride ten thousand days and nights,
  Till age snow white hairs on thee,
Thou, when thou return'st, wilt tell me
  All strange wonders that befell thee,   15
        And swear
        Nowhere
Lives a woman true, and fair.

If thou findst one, let me know,
  Such a pilgrimage were sweet —   20
Yet do not, I would not go,
  Though at next door we might meet;
Though she were true, when you met her,
  And last, till you write your letter,
        Yet she   25
        Will be
False, ere I come, to two or three.

---

2 *mandrake root:* This V-shaped root resembles the lower half of the human body.

CONSIDERATIONS FOR CRITICAL THINKING AND WRITING

1. **FIRST RESPONSE.** What is the speaker's tone in this poem? What is his view of a woman's love? What does the speaker's use of hyperbole reveal about his emotional state?

2. Do you think Donne wants the speaker's argument to be taken seriously? Is there any humor in the poem?

3. Most of these lines end with masculine rhymes. What other kinds of rhymes are used for end rhymes?

KAY RYAN (B. 1945)

Dew   1996

As neatly as peas
in their green canoe,
as discretely as beads
strung in a row,
sit drops of dew
along a blade of grass.
But unattached and
subject to their weight,
they slip if they accumulate.
Down the green tongue
out of the morning sun
into the general damp,
they're gone.

Chris Felver/Getty Images.

CONSIDERATIONS FOR CRITICAL THINKING AND WRITING

1. **FIRST RESPONSE.** How does reading the poem aloud affect your understanding of Ryan's use of rhyme to create a particular tone?

2. Explain whether the images in the poem are simply descriptive or are presented as a means of producing a theme. What is the role of the title?

ANDREW HUDGINS (B. 1951)

The Ice-Cream Truck   2009

From blocks away the music floats
to my enchanted ears.
It builds. It's here! And then it fades —
and I explode in tears.

I kick the TV set, and scream,   5
sobbing to extort her,
while Mom stares at *One Life to Live*°,
and won't give me a quarter.

I pause, change tactics, snatch a coin
from the bottom of her purse,
then race to catch the ice-cream truck,   10
ignoring Mama's curse.

I stop the truck, I start to choose —
then see I won't be eating.

7 *One Life to Live:* A long-running popular daytime TV drama, or "soap opera"

I stare down at a goddamn dime, 15
and trudge home to my beating.

CONSIDERATIONS FOR CRITICAL THINKING AND WRITING

1. FIRST RESPONSE. Describe the tone of each stanza. How do the rhymes serve to establish the tone?

2. Characterize the speaker. How do you reconcile what is said in the first stanza with the description in the final stanza?

3. This poem appeared in a collection by Hudgins titled *Shut Up, You're Fine: Poems for Very, Very Bad Children*. How does that context affect your reading of it?

4. CREATIVE RESPONSE. Add a four-line stanza in Hudgins's style that rhymes and concludes back at home.

ROBERT FRANCIS (1901–1987)

The Pitcher 1953

His art is eccentricity, his aim
How not to hit the mark he seems to aim at,

His passion how to avoid the obvious,
His technique how to vary the avoidance.

The others throw to be comprehended. He 5
Throws to be a moment misunderstood.

Yet not too much. Not errant, arrant, wild,
But every seeming aberration willed.

Not to, yet still, still to communicate
Making the batter understand too late. 10

CONSIDERATIONS FOR CRITICAL THINKING AND WRITING

1. FIRST RESPONSE. Explain how each pair of lines in this poem works together to describe the pitcher's art.

2. Consider how the poem itself works the way a good pitcher does. Which lines illustrate what they describe?

3. Comment on the effects of the poem's rhymes. How are the final two lines different in their rhyme from the previous lines? How does sound echo sense in lines 9–10?

4. Write an essay that examines "The Pitcher" as an extended metaphor for talking about poetry. How well does the poem characterize strategies for writing poetry as well as pitching?

5. Write an essay that develops an extended comparison between writing or reading poetry and playing or watching another sport.

1. Write an essay comparing "The Pitcher" with another work by Francis, "Catch" (p. 372). One poem defines poetry implicitly; the other defines it explicitly. Which poem do you prefer? Why?

HELEN CHASIN (1938–2015)
The Word Plum   1968

The word *plum* is delicious

pout and push, luxury of
self-love, and savoring murmur
full in the mouth and falling
like fruit   5

taut skin
pierced, bitten, provoked into
juice, and tart flesh

question
and reply, lip and tongue   10
of pleasure.

CONSIDERATIONS FOR CRITICAL THINKING AND WRITING

1. FIRST RESPONSE. What is the effect of the repetitions of the alliteration and assonance throughout the poem? How does it contribute to the poem's meaning?

2. Which sounds in the poem are like the sounds one makes while eating a plum?

3. Discuss the title. Explain whether you think this poem is more about the word *plum* or about the plum itself. Can the two be separated in the poem?

MAJOR JACKSON (B. 1968)
Autumn Landscape   2010

Seeking what I could not name, my vespertine
spirit loitered evenings down leaf-lined
streets. Stray dogs for company, curbs were empty.
Afar dim poles resembled women. The wind pushed me
like an open hand. Flesh frothed in my head.   5
I reached for stirred shadows in windows aimed for bed.

When did I not strain for touch? I've a mind
to eat as many stars and refract their dark expanse.
My sadness brings tears, so many victims.
Close your eyes. Here comes the nightmare.   10

CONSIDERATIONS FOR CRITICAL THINKING AND WRITING

1. **FIRST RESPONSE.** What type of poem do you envision with a title like "Autumn Landscape"? In what ways does this poem depart from your expectations?

2. Which of the sound qualities described above are present in the poem? What effects do they have on your understanding of the poem's meaning or its concerns?

3. In addition to sound, what other dimensions of poetry you have studied thus far (such as diction or figurative language) are on display in this poem, and how do they function?

17

Patterns of Rhythm

I would define, in brief, the Poetry of words as the Rhythmical Creation of Beauty. Its sole arbiter is Taste.

— EDGAR ALLAN POE

Library of Congress, Prints and Photographs Division.

The rhythms of everyday life surround us in regularly recurring movements and sounds. As you read these words, your heart pulsates while somewhere else a clock ticks, a cradle rocks, a drum beats, a dancer sways, a foghorn blasts, a wave recedes, or a child skips. We may tend to overlook rhythm because it is so tightly woven into the fabric of our experience, but it is there nonetheless, one of the conditions of life. Rhythm is also one of the conditions of speech because the voice alternately rises and falls as words are stressed or unstressed and as the pace quickens or slackens. In poetry *rhythm* refers to the recurrence of stressed and unstressed sounds. Depending on how the sounds are arranged, this can result in a pace that is fast or slow, choppy or smooth.

SOME PRINCIPLES OF METER

Poets use rhythm to create pleasurable sound patterns and to reinforce meanings. "Rhythm," Edith Sitwell once observed, "might be described as, to the world of sound, what light is to the world of sight. It shapes and gives new meaning." Prose can use rhythm effectively too, but prose that does so tends to be an exception. The following exceptional lines are from a speech by Winston Churchill to the House of Commons after Allied forces lost a great battle to German forces at Dunkirk during World War II:

> We shall not flag or fail. We shall go on to the end. We shall fight in France, we shall fight on the seas and oceans, we shall fight with growing confidence and growing strength in the air, we shall defend our island, whatever the cost may be, we shall fight on the beaches, we shall fight on the landing grounds, we shall fight in the fields and in the streets, we shall fight in the hills; we shall never surrender.

The stressed repetition of "we shall" bespeaks the resolute singleness of purpose that Churchill had to convey to the British people if they were to win the war. Repetition is also one of the devices used in poetry to create rhythmic effects. In the following excerpt from "Song of the Open Road," Walt Whitman urges the pleasures of limitless freedom on his reader:

> Allons!° the road is before us!   *Let's go!*
> It is safe — I have tried it — my own feet have tried it well — be
>   not detain'd!
> Let the paper remain on the desk unwritten, and the book on the
>   shelf unopen'd!
> Let the tools remain in the workshop! Let the money remain unearn'd!
> Let the school stand! mind not the cry of the teacher!   5
> Let the preacher preach in his pulpit! Let the lawyer plead in the
>   court, and the judge expound the law.
>
> Camerado,° I give you my hand!   *friend*
> I give you my love more precious than money,
> I give you myself before preaching or law;
> Will you give me yourself? will you come travel with me?   10
> Shall we stick by each other as long as we live?

These rhythmic lines quickly move away from conventional values to the open road of shared experiences. Their recurring sounds are created not by rhyme or alliteration and assonance (see Chapter 16) but by the repetition of words and phrases.

  Although the repetition of words and phrases can be an effective means of creating rhythm in poetry, the more typical method consists of patterns of accented or unaccented syllables. Words contain syllables that are either stressed or unstressed. A **stress** (or **accent**) places more emphasis on one syllable than on another. We say "*syl*lable" not "syl*la*ble," "*em*phasis" not "em*pha*sis." We routinely stress syllables when we speak: "*Is* she con*tent* with the *con*tents of the *ye*llow *pack*age?" To distinguish between two people we might put special emphasis on a single-syllable word, saying "Is *she* content . . . ?" In this way stress can be used to emphasize a particular word in a sentence. Poets often arrange words so that the desired meaning is suggested by the rhythm; hence emphasis is controlled by the poet rather than left entirely to the reader.

When a rhythmic pattern of stresses recurs in a poem, the result is **meter**. Taken together, all the metrical elements in a poem make up what is called the poem's **prosody**. **Scansion** consists of measuring the stresses in a line to determine its metrical pattern. Several methods can be used to mark lines. One widely used system uses ´ for a stressed syllable and ˘ for an unstressed syllable. In a sense, the stress mark represents the equivalent of tapping one's foot to a beat:

> Híckŏrў, díckŏrў, dóck,
>
> Tȟe móuse răn úp tȟe clóck
>
> Tȟe clóck strŭck ońe,
>
> Aňd dowń hě ruń,
>
> Híckŏrў, díckŏrў, dóck.

In the first two lines and the final line of this familiar nursery rhyme we hear three stressed syllables. In lines 3 and 4, where the meter changes for variety, we hear just two stressed syllables. The combination of stresses provides the pleasure of the rhythm we hear.

To hear the rhythms of "Hickory, dickory, dock" does not require a formal study of meter. Nevertheless, an awareness of the basic kinds of meter that appear in English poetry can enhance your understanding of how a poem achieves its effects. Understanding the sound effects of a poem and having a vocabulary with which to discuss those effects can intensify your pleasure in poetry. Although the study of meter can be extremely technical, the terms used to describe the basic meters of English poetry are relatively easy to comprehend.

The **foot** is the metrical unit by which a line of poetry is measured. A foot usually consists of one stressed and one or two unstressed syllables. A vertical line is used to separate the feet: "Tȟe clóck | strŭck ońe" consists of two feet. A foot of poetry can be arranged in a variety of patterns; here are five of the chief ones:

Foot	Pattern	Example
iamb	˘ ´	ăwáy
trochee	´ ˘	Lóvĕly
anapest	˘ ˘ ´	uňdĕrstánd
dactyl	´ ˘ ˘	déspĕraťe
spondee	´ ´	déad sét

The most common lines in English poetry contain meters based on iambic feet. However, even lines that are predominantly iambic will often include variations to create particular effects. Other important patterns include trochaic, anapestic, and dactylic feet. The spondee is not a sustained meter but occurs for variety or emphasis.

Iambic	Whăt képt | hĭs eyés | frŏm gív | ĭng báck | thĕ gáze
Trochaic	Hé wăs | loúdĕr | thán thĕ | préachĕr
Anapestic	Ĭ ăm callĕd | tŏ thĕ frónt | ŏf thĕ roóm
Dactylic	Síng ĭt áll | mérrĭlў

These meters have different rhythms and can create different effects. Iambic and anapestic are known as **rising meters** because they move from unstressed to stressed sounds, while trochaic and dactylic are known as **falling meters**. Anapests and dactyls tend to move more lightly and rapidly than iambs or trochees. Although no single kind of meter can be considered always better than another for a given subject, it is possible to determine whether the meter of a specific poem is appropriate for its subject. A serious poem about a tragic death would most likely not be well served by lilting rhythms. Keep in mind, too, that though one or another of these four basic meters might constitute the predominant rhythm of a poem, variations can occur within lines to change the pace or call attention to a particular word.

A **line** is measured by the number of feet it contains. Here, for example, is an iambic line with three feet: "If she \| shŏuld wríte \| ă nóte." These are the names for line lengths:

monometer: one foot	pentameter: five feet
dimeter: two feet	hexameter: six feet
trimeter: three feet	heptameter: seven feet
tetrameter: four feet	octameter: eight feet

By combining the name of a line length with the name of a foot, we can describe the metrical qualities of a line concisely. Consider, for example, the pattern of feet and length of this line:

I didn't want the boy to hit the dog.

The iambic rhythm of this line falls into five feet; hence it is called **iambic pentameter**. Iambic is the most common pattern in English poetry because its rhythm appears so naturally in English speech and writing. Unrhymed iambic pentameter is called **blank verse**; Shakespeare's plays are built on such lines.

Less common than the iamb, trochee, anapest, or dactyl is the **spondee**, a two-syllable foot in which both syllables are stressed (′ ′). Note the effect of the spondaic foot at the beginning of this line:

Déad sét \| ăgaínst \| thĕ plán \| hĕ wént \| ăwáy.

Spondees can slow a rhythm and provide variety and emphasis, particularly in iambic and trochaic lines. Also less common is a ***pyrrhic*** foot, which consists of two unstressed syllables, as in Shakespeare's "A horse! A horse! My kingdom for a horse!" Pyrrhic feet are typically variants for iambic verse rather than predominant patterns in lines. A line that ends with a stressed syllable is said to have a ***masculine ending***, whereas a line that ends with an extra unstressed syllable is said to have a *feminine ending*. Consider, for example, these two lines from Timothy Steele's "Waiting for the Storm" (the entire poem appears on p. 499):

> feminine: Thĕ sánd | ăt m̆y feet | grŏw cóld | er̆,
> masculine: Thĕ damp | aír chíll | and̆ spréad.

The speed of a line is also affected by the number of pauses in it. A pause within a line is called a ***caesura*** and is indicated by a double vertical line (||). A caesura can occur anywhere within a line and need not be indicated by punctuation:

> Camerado, || I give you my hand!
> I give you my love || more precious than money.

A slight pause occurs within each of these lines and at its end. Both kinds of pauses contribute to the lines' rhythm.

When a line has a pause at its end, it is called an ***end-stopped line***. Such pauses reflect normal speech patterns and are often marked by punctuation. A line that ends without a pause and continues into the next line for its meaning is called a ***run-on line***. Running over from one line to another is also called ***enjambment***. The first and eighth lines of the following poem are run-on lines; the rest are end-stopped.

WILLIAM WORDSWORTH (1770–1850)

My Heart Leaps Up   1807

My heart leaps up when I behold
   A rainbow in the sky:
So was it when my life began;
So is it now I am a man;
So be it when I shall grow old,
   Or let me die!
The child is father of the Man;
And I could wish my days to be
Bound each to each by natural piety.

Run-on lines have a different rhythm from end-stopped lines. Lines 3 and 4 and lines 8 and 9 are iambic, but the effect of their two rhythms is very different when we read these lines aloud. The enjambment of lines 8 and 9 reinforces their meaning; just as the "days" are bound together, so are the lines.

The rhythm of a poem can be affected by several devices: the kind and number of stresses within lines, the length of lines, and the kinds of pauses that appear within lines or at their ends. In addition, as we saw in Chapter 16, the sound of a poem is affected by alliteration, assonance, rhyme, and consonance. These sounds help to create rhythms by controlling our pronunciations, as in the following lines excerpted from "An Essay on Criticism," a poem by Alexander Pope:

> Soft is the strain when Zephyr gently blows,
> And the smooth stream in smoother numbers flows;
> But when loud surges lash the sounding shore,
> The hoarse, rough verse should like the torrent roar.

These lines are effective because their rhythm and sound work with their meaning.

Suggestions for Scanning a Poem

These suggestions should help you in talking about a poem's meter.

1. After reading the poem through, read it aloud and mark the stressed syllables in each line. Then mark the unstressed syllables.

2. From your markings, identify what kind of foot is dominant (iambic, trochaic, dactylic, or anapestic) and divide the lines into feet, keeping in mind that the vertical line marking a foot may come in the middle of a word as well as at its beginning or end.

3. Determine the number of feet in each line. Remember that there may be variations; some lines may be shorter or longer than the predominant meter. What is important is the overall pattern. Do not assume that variations represent the poet's inability to fulfill the overall pattern. Notice the effects of variations and whether they emphasize words and phrases or disrupt your expectation for some other purpose.

4. Listen for pauses within lines and mark the caesuras; many times there will be no punctuation to indicate them.

5. Recognize that scansion does not always yield a definitive measurement of a line. Even experienced readers may differ over the scansion of a given line. What is important is not a precise description of the line but an awareness of how a poem's rhythms contribute to its effects.

6. If possible, attend a live poetry reading. (If not possible, find a video clip on YouTube of a poet reading his or her own poetry.) Compare the poem as it looks on the page to the way a poet interprets its meter and its rhythm.

The following poem demonstrates how you can use an understanding of meter and rhythm to gain a greater appreciation for what a poem is saying.

TIMOTHY STEELE (B. 1948)

Waiting for the Storm 1986

Bréeze sént | ă wrínk | lĭng dárk | nĕss
Acróss | thĕ bay. || Ĭ knélt
Bĕnéath | ăn úp | turnĕd bóat,
Aňd, mo | mĕnt bу mó | mĕnt, félt

Thĕ sánd | ăt mу féet | grŏw cóld | ĕr,
Thĕ damp | áir chíll | aňd spréad.
Thĕn thĕ | fírst ráin | dróps sóund | ĕd
Oň thĕ húll | ăbóve | mу héad.

   The predominant meter of this poem is iambic trimeter, but there is plenty of variation as the storm rapidly approaches and finally begins to pelt the sheltered speaker. The emphatic spondee ("Breeze sent") pushes the darkness quickly across the bay while the caesura at the end of the sentence in line 2 creates a pause that sets up a feeling of suspense and expectation that is measured in the ticking rhythm of line 4, a run-on line that brings us into the chilly sand and air of the second stanza. Perhaps the most impressive sound effect used in the poem appears in the second syllable of "sounded" in line 7. That "ed" precedes the sound of the poem's final word, "head," just as if it were the first drop of rain hitting the hull above the speaker. The visual, tactile, and auditory images make "Waiting for the Storm" an intense sensory experience.

A SAMPLE STUDENT RESPONSE

Marco Pacini
Professor Fierstein
English 201
2 November 2018

The Rhythm of Anticipation in Timothy Steele's "Waiting for the Storm"

   In his poem "Waiting for the Storm," Timothy Steele uses run-on lines, or enjambment, to create a feeling of anticipation. Every line ends unfinished or is a continuation of the previous line, so we must read on to gain completion. This open-ended rhythm mirrors the waiting experienced by the speaker of the poem.

Nearly every line of the poem leaves the reader in suspense:

> I knelt
> Beneath an upturned boat,
> And, moment by moment, felt
>
> The sand at my feet grow colder,
> The damp air chill and spread. (2-6)

Action is interrupted at every line break. We have to wait to find out where the speaker knelt and what was felt, since information is given in small increments. So, like the speaker, we must take in the details of the storm little by little, "moment by moment" (4). Even when the first drops of rain hit the hull, the poem ends before we can see or feel the storm's full force, and we are left waiting, in a continuous state of anticipation. . . .

Work Cited

Steele, Timothy. "Waiting for the Storm." *Literature to Go*, edited by
    Michael Meyer and D. Quentin Miller, 4th ed., Bedford/St. Martin's,
    2020, p. 499.

This next poem also reinforces meanings through its use of meter and rhythm.

WILLIAM BUTLER YEATS (1865–1939)
That the Night Come   1912

She lived | in storm | and strife,

Her soul | had such | a desire

For what | proud death | may bring

That it | could not | endure

The com | mon good | of life,   5

But lived | as 'twere | a king

That packed | his mar | riage day

With ban | neret | and pen | non,

Trumpet | and ket | tledrum,

And the | outrag | eous can | non,   10

To bun | dle time | away

That the | night come.

    Scansion reveals that the predominant meter here is iambic trimeter: each line contains three stressed and unstressed syllables that form a regular, predictable rhythm through line 7. That rhythm is disrupted, however, when the speaker compares the woman's longing for what death brings to a king's eager anticipation of his wedding night. The king packs the day with noisy fanfares and celebrations to fill up time and distract himself. Unable to accept "The common good of life," the woman fills her days with "storm and strife." In a determined effort "To bundle time away," she, like the king, impatiently awaits the night.

    Lines 8–10 break the regular pattern established in the first seven lines. The extra unstressed syllable in lines 8 and 10 along with the trochaic feet in lines 9 ("Trúmpet") and 10 ("And the") interrupt the basic iambic trimeter and parallel the woman's and the king's frenetic activity. These lines thus echo the inability of the woman and king to "endure" regular or normal time. The last line is the most irregular in the poem. The final two accented syllables sound like the deep resonant beats of a kettledrum or a cannon firing. The words "night come" dramatically remind us that what the woman anticipates is not a lover but the mysterious finality of death. The meter serves, then, in both its regularity and variations to reinforce the poem's meaning and tone.

The following poems are especially rich in their rhythms and sounds. As you read and study them, notice how patterns of rhythm and the sounds of words reinforce meanings and contribute to the poems' effects. And, perhaps most important, read the poems aloud so that you can hear them.

POEMS FOR FURTHER STUDY

JOHN MALONEY (B. 1947)

Good! 1999

The ball goes up off glass and rebounded
down the court, outlet flung to the quick guard
like clicking seconds: he dribbles, hounded
by hands, calls the play, stops short, looking hard
for a slant opening, fakes it twice, passes   5
into the center — he lobs to the small
forward, top of the key, a pick: asses
crash (the pick-and-roll), he cuts, bumps, the ball
reaches him as he turns, dribbles, sends it
back to the baseline, forward back to him,   10
jump — and in midair, twisting, he bends it
over a tangle of arms — SHOOTS, the rim
rattles as it jerks against the back joints,
and into the net, trippingly drop two points.

CONSIDERATIONS FOR CRITICAL THINKING AND WRITING

1. FIRST RESPONSE. Comment on the effects of the lines' rhythms.

2. Notice the precise pattern of rhyme. How is that related to the action in the poem?

ALICE JONES (B. 1949)

The Foot 1993

Our improbable support, erected
on the osseous architecture
of the calcaneus, talus, cuboid,
navicular, cuneiforms, metatarsals,
phalanges, a plethora of hinges,   5

all strung together by gliding
tendons, covered by the pearly
plantar fascia, then fat-padded
to form the sole, humble surface
of our contact with earth.   10

Here the body's broadest tendon
anchors the heel's fleshy base,
the finely wrinkled skin stretches
forward across the capillaried arch,
to the ball, a balance point.   15

A wide web of flexor tendons
and branched veins maps the dorsum,
fades into the stub-laden bone
splay, the stuffed sausage sacks
of toes, each with a tuft   20

of proximal hairs to introduce
the distal nail, whose useless
curve remembers an ancestor,
the vanished creature's wild
and necessary claw.   25

Considerations for Critical Thinking and Writing

1. **First Response.** What is the effect of the diction? What sort of tone is established by the use of anatomical terms? How do the terms affect the rhythm?

2. Jones has described the form of "The Foot" as "five stubby stanzas." Explain why the lines of this poem may or may not warrant this description of the stanzas.

3. **Critical Strategies.** Read the section on formalist strategies (pp. 1071–72) in Chapter 30, "Critical Strategies for Reading." Describe the effect of the final stanza. How would your reading be affected if the poem ended after the comma in the middle of line 22?

Robert Herrick (1591–1674)
Delight in Disorder   1648

A sweet disorder in the dress
Kindles in clothes a wantonness.
A lawn° about the shoulders thrown   *linen scarf*
Into a fine distraction;
An erring lace, which here and there   5

Enthralls the crimson stomacher,
A cuff neglectful, and thereby
Ribbons to flow confusedly;
A winning wave, deserving note,
In the tempestuous petticoat;
A careless shoestring, in whose tie
I see a wild civility;
Do more bewitch me than when art
Is too precise in every part.

10

CONSIDERATIONS FOR CRITICAL THINKING AND WRITING

1. FIRST RESPONSE. Why does the speaker in this poem value "disorder" so highly? How do the poem's organization and rhythmic order relate to its theme? Are they "precise in every part" (line 14)?

2. Which words in the poem indicate disorder? Which words indicate the speaker's response to that disorder? What are the connotative meanings of each set of words? Why are they appropriate? What do they suggest about the woman and the speaker?

3. Write a short essay in which you agree or disagree with the speaker's views on dress.

E. E. CUMMINGS (1894–1962)

O sweet spontaneous   1920

O sweet spontaneous
earth how often have
the
doting

   fingers of

5

prurient philosophers pinched
and
poked

thee
, has the naughty thumb
of science prodded
thy

10

   beauty   .how
often have religions taken
thee upon their scraggy knees
squeezing and

15

buffeting thee that thou mightest conceive
gods
    (but
true

to the incomparable
couch of death thy
rhythmic
lover

    thou answerest

them only with

    spring)

20

25

Considerations for Critical Thinking and Writing

1. **FIRST RESPONSE.** What is the controlling metaphor that Cummings uses to characterize philosophers, scientists, and theologians? How is the earth portrayed?

2. In what sense is spring the answer to the issues raised in the poem?

3. To what extent does the arrangement of lines on the page serve to establish rhythm?

Connection to Another Selection

1. Discuss the treatment of science in "O sweet spontaneous" and in Edgar Allan Poe's "Sonnet — To Science" (p. 395).

William Blake (1757–1827)
The Lamb   1789

Bettmann/Getty Images.

    Little Lamb, who made thee?
    Dost thou know who made thee?
Gave thee life, and bid thee feed
By the stream and o'er the mead;
Gave thee clothing of delight,
Softest clothing, wooly, bright;
Gave thee such a tender voice,
Making all the vales rejoice?
    Little Lamb, who made thee?
    Dost thou know who made thee?
    Little Lamb, I'll tell thee,
    Little Lamb, I'll tell thee:
He is callèd by thy name,
For he calls himself a Lamb.

10

He is meek, and he is mild;   15
He became a little child.
I a child, and thou a lamb,
We are callèd by his name.
    Little Lamb, God bless thee!
    Little Lamb, God bless thee!   20

Considerations for Critical Thinking and Writing

1. **FIRST RESPONSE.** This poem is from Blake's *Songs of Innocence*. Describe its tone. How do the meter, rhyme, and repetition help to characterize the speaker's voice?

2. Why is it significant that the animal addressed by the speaker is a lamb? What symbolic value would be lost if the animal were, for example, a doe?

3. How does the second stanza answer the question raised in the first? What is the speaker's view of the creation?

William Blake (1757–1827)

The Tyger   1794

Tyger! Tyger! burning bright
In the forests of the night,
What immortal hand or eye
Could frame thy fearful symmetry?

In what distant deeps or skies   5
Burnt the fire of thine eyes?
On what wings dare he aspire?
What the hand dare seize the fire?

And what shoulder, and what art,
Could twist the sinews of thy heart?   10
And when thy heart began to beat,
What dread hand? and what dread feet?

What the hammer? what the chain?
In what furnace was thy brain?
What the anvil? what dread grasp   15
Dare its deadly terrors clasp?

When the stars threw down their spears,
And watered heaven with their tears,
Did he smile his work to see?
Did he who made the Lamb make thee?   20

Tyger! Tyger! burning bright
In the forests of the night,

What immortal hand or eye
Dare frame thy fearful symmetry?

CONSIDERATIONS FOR CRITICAL THINKING AND WRITING

1. FIRST RESPONSE. This poem from Blake's *Songs of Experience* is often paired with "The Lamb." Describe the poem's tone. Is the speaker's voice the same here as in "The Lamb"? Which words are repeated, and how do they contribute to the tone?

2. What is revealed about the nature of the tiger by the words used to describe its creation? What do you think the tiger symbolizes?

3. Unlike in "The Lamb," more than one question is raised in "The Tyger." What are these questions? Are they answered?

4. Compare the rhythms in "The Lamb" and "The Tyger." Each basically uses a seven-syllable line, but the effects are very different. Why?

5. Using these two poems as the basis of your discussion, describe what distinguishes innocence from experience.

ROBERT FROST (1874–1963)

Stopping by Woods on a Snowy Evening   1923

Whose woods these are I think I know.
His house is in the village, though;
He will not see me stopping here
To watch his woods fill up with snow.

My little horse must think it queer   5
To stop without a farmhouse near
Between the woods and frozen lake
The darkest evening of the year.

He gives his harness bells a shake
To ask if there is some mistake.   10
The only other sound's the sweep
Of easy wind and downy flake.

The woods are lovely, dark and deep,
But I have promises to keep,
And miles to go before I sleep,   15
And miles to go before I sleep.

CONSIDERATIONS FOR CRITICAL THINKING AND WRITING

1. FIRST RESPONSE. What is the significance of the setting in this poem? How is tone conveyed by the images?

2. What does the speaker find appealing about the woods? What is the purpose of the horse in the poem?

3. Although the last two lines are identical, they are not read at the same speed. Why the difference? What is achieved by the repetition?

4. What is the poem's rhyme scheme? What is the effect of the rhyme in the final stanza?

LANGSTON HUGHES (1902–1967)

The Weary Blues 1925

Droning a drowsy syncopated tune,
Rocking back and forth to a mellow croon,
　　I heard a Negro play.
Down on Lenox Avenue° the other night
By the pale dull pallor of an old gas light　　　　　　　　　　5
　　He did a lazy sway. . . .
　　He did a lazy sway. . . .
To the tune o' those Weary Blues.
With his ebony hands on each ivory key
He made that poor piano moan with melody.　　　　　　　　10
　　O Blues!
Swaying to and fro on his rickety stool
He played that sad raggy tune like a musical fool.
　　Sweet Blues!
Coming from a black man's soul.　　　　　　　　　　　　　15
　　O Blues!
In a deep song voice with a melancholy tone
I heard that Negro sing, that old piano moan—
　　"Ain't got nobody in all this world,
　　Ain't got nobody but ma self.　　　　　　　　　　　　20
　　I's gwine to quit ma frownin'
　　And put ma troubles on the shelf."
Thump, thump, thump, went his foot on the floor.
He played a few chords then he sang some more—
　　"I got the Weary Blues　　　　　　　　　　　　　　　25
　　And I can't be satisfied.
　　Got the Weary Blues
　　And can't be satisfied—
　　I ain't happy no mo'
　　And I wish that I had died."　　　　　　　　　　　　30
And far into the night he crooned that tune.
The stars went out and so did the moon.

---

4 *Lenox Avenue:* Major Harlem thoroughfare, now known as Malcolm X Boulevard.

The singer stopped playing and went to bed
While the Weary Blues echoed through his head.
He slept like a rock or a man that's dead.   35

CONSIDERATIONS FOR CRITICAL THINKING AND WRITING

1. FIRST RESPONSE. In line 2, who is "rocking back and forth": the blues
   player or the speaker? Why does it matter?
2. What is the effect of personifying the piano?
3. There are two sets of blues lyrics within the poem: How are they different? Would the poem's overall effect change if their order were reversed?

GWENDOLYN BROOKS (1917–2000)

We Real Cool   1960

The Pool Players.

Seven at the Golden Shovel.

We real cool. We
Left school. We

Lurk late. We   5
Strike straight. We

Sing sin. We
Thin gin. We

Jazz June. We
Die soon.   10

CONSIDERATIONS FOR CRITICAL THINKING AND WRITING

1. FIRST RESPONSE. How does the speech of the pool players in this poem
   help to characterize them? What is the effect of the pronouns coming at
   the ends of the lines? How would the poem sound if the pronouns came
   at the beginnings of lines?
2. What is the author's attitude toward the players? Is there a change in
   tone in the last line?
3. How is the pool hall's name related to the rest of the poem and its
   theme?
4. Use this poem to discuss the use of enjambment in poetry more
   generally.

18

Poetic Forms

Poetry gives you permission to say any kind
of language, using any kind of grammar.
— GARY SNYDER

Poems come in a variety of shapes. Although the best poems always have their own unique qualities, many of them also conform to traditional patterns. Frequently the *form* of a poem — its overall structure or shape — follows an already established design. A poem that can be categorized by the patterns of its lines, meter, rhymes, and stanzas is considered a *fixed form* because it follows a prescribed model such as a sonnet. However, poems written in a fixed form do not always fit models precisely; writers sometimes work variations on traditional forms to create innovative effects.

Not all poets are content with variations on traditional forms. Some prefer to create their own structures and shapes. Poems that do not conform to established patterns of meter, rhyme, and stanza are called *free verse* or *open form* poetry. (See Chapter 19 for further discussion of open forms.) This kind of poetry creates its own ordering principles through the careful arrangement of words and phrases in line lengths that embody rhythms appropriate to the meaning. Modern and contemporary poets in particular have learned to use the blank space on the page as a significant functional element (for a vivid example, see E. E. Cummings's "l(a," p. 380). Good poetry of this kind is structured in ways that can be as demanding, interesting, and satisfying as fixed forms. Open and fixed forms represent different poetic styles, but they are identical in the sense that both use language in concentrated ways to convey meanings, experiences, emotions, and effects.

SOME COMMON POETIC FORMS

A familiarity with some of the most frequently used fixed forms of poetry is useful because it allows for a better understanding of how a poem works. By classifying patterns we can talk about the effects of established rhythm and rhyme and recognize how the pace and meaning of the lines can be affected by variations or deviations from the patterns. An awareness of form also allows us to anticipate how a poem is likely to proceed. As we shall see, a sonnet creates a different set of expectations in a reader from those of, say, a limerick. A reader isn't likely to find in limericks the kind of serious themes that often make their way into sonnets. The discussion that follows identifies some of the important poetic forms frequently encountered in poetry, especially (but not exclusively) poetry in the English tradition.

The shape of a fixed-form poem is often determined by the way in which the lines are organized into stanzas. A **stanza** — the Italian word for "room" — consists of a grouping of lines, set off by a space, that usually has a set pattern of meter and rhyme. This pattern is ordinarily repeated in other stanzas throughout the poem. What is usual is not obligatory, however; some poems may use a different pattern for each stanza, somewhat like paragraphs in prose.

Traditionally, though, stanzas do share a common **rhyme scheme**, the pattern of end rhymes. We can map out rhyme schemes by noting patterns of rhyme with lowercase letters: the first rhyme sound is designated *a*, the second becomes *b*, the third *c*, and so on. Using this system, we can describe the rhyme scheme in the following three-stanza poem this way: *aabb, ccdd, eeff.*

A. E. HOUSMAN (1859–1936)

Loveliest of trees, the cherry now 1896

Loveliest of trees, the cherry now	*a*
Is hung with bloom along the bough,	*a*
And stands about the woodland ride	*b*
Wearing white for Eastertide.	*b*
Now, of my threescore years and ten,	*c*
Twenty will not come again,	*c*
And take from seventy springs a score,	*d*
It only leaves me fifty more.	*d*

5

And since to look at things in bloom   *e*
Fifty springs are little room,   *e*   10
About the woodlands I will go   *f*
To see the cherry hung with snow.   *f*

CONSIDERATIONS FOR CRITICAL THINKING AND WRITING

1. FIRST RESPONSE. What is the speaker's attitude in this poem toward time and life?

2. Why is spring an appropriate season for the setting rather than, say, winter?

3. Paraphrase each stanza. How do the images in each reinforce the poem's themes?

4. Lines 1 and 12 are not intended to rhyme, but they are close. What is the effect of the near rhyme of "now" and "snow"? How does the rhyme enhance the theme?

Poets often create their own stanzaic patterns; hence there is an infinite number of kinds of stanzas. One way of talking about stanzaic forms is to describe a given stanza by how many lines it contains.

A *couplet* consists of two lines that usually rhyme and have the same meter; couplets are frequently not separated from each other by space on the page. A *heroic couplet* consists of rhymed iambic pentameter. Here is an example from Alexander Pope's "Essay on Criticism":

One science only will one genius fit;   *a*
So vast is art, so narrow human wit: *a*
Not only bounded to peculiar arts,   *b*
But oft in those confined to single parts.   *b*

A *tercet* is a three-line stanza. When all three lines rhyme, they are called a *triplet*. Two triplets make up this captivating poem.

ROBERT HERRICK (1591–1674)
Upon Julia's Clothes   1648

Whenas in silks my Julia goes,   *a*
Then, then, methinks, how sweetly flows   *a*
That liquefaction of her clothes.   *a*

Next, when I cast mine eyes, and see   *b*
That brave vibration, each way free,   *b*
O, how that glittering taketh me!   *b*

CONSIDERATIONS FOR CRITICAL THINKING AND WRITING

1. **FIRST RESPONSE.** What purpose does alliteration serve in this poem?

2. Comment on the effect of the meter. How is it related to the speaker's description of Julia's clothes?

3. Look up the word *brave* in the *Oxford English Dictionary*. Which of its meanings is appropriate to describe Julia's movement? Some readers interpret lines 4–6 to mean that Julia has no clothes on. What do you think?

Terza rima consists of an interlocking three-line rhyme scheme: *aba, bcb, cdc, ded,* and so on. Dante's *Divine Comedy* uses this pattern, as does Robert Frost's "Acquainted with the Night" (p. 446).

A **quatrain**, or four-line stanza, is the most common stanzaic form in the English language and can have various meters and rhyme schemes (if any). The most common rhyme schemes are *aabb, abba, aaba,* and *abcb.* This last pattern is especially characteristic of the popular **ballad stanza**, which consists of alternating eight- and six-syllable lines. Samuel Taylor Coleridge adopted this pattern in "The Rime of the Ancient Mariner"; here is one representative stanza:

> All in a hot and copper sky
> The bloody Sun, at noon,
> Right up above the mast did stand,
> No bigger than the Moon.

There are a number of longer stanzaic forms, and the list of types of stanzas could be extended considerably, but knowing these three most basic patterns should prove helpful to you in talking about the form of a great many poems. In addition to stanzaic forms, there are fixed forms that characterize entire poems. Lyric poems can be, for example, sonnets, villanelles, sestinas, or epigrams.

Sonnet

The **sonnet** has been a popular literary form in English since the sixteenth century, when it was adopted from the Italian *sonnetto,* meaning "little song." A sonnet consists of fourteen lines, usually written in iambic pentameter. Because the sonnet has been such a favorite form, writers have experimented with many variations on its essential structure. Nevertheless, there are two basic types of sonnets: the Italian and the English.

The **Italian sonnet** (also known as the **Petrarchan sonnet**, from the fourteenth-century Italian poet Petrarch) divides into two parts. The first eight lines (the **octave**) typically rhyme *abbaabba.* The final six lines (the **sestet**) may vary; common patterns are *cdecde, cdcdcd,* and *cdccdc.* Very often the octave presents a situation, an attitude, or a problem that the sestet comments upon or resolves, as in John Keats's "On First Looking into Chapman's Homer."

JOHN KEATS (1795–1821)

On First Looking into Chapman's Homer° 1816

Historical/Getty Images.

Much have I traveled in the realms of gold,
  And many goodly states and kingdoms
   seen;
Round many western islands have I been
Which bards in fealty to Apollo° hold.
Oft of one wide expanse had I been told
  That deep-browed Homer ruled as his
   demesne;
  Yet did I never breathe its pure serene°   *atmosphere*
Till I heard Chapman speak out loud and bold:
Then felt I like some watcher of the skies
  When a new planet swims into his ken;   10
Or like stout Cortez° when with eagle eyes
  He stared at the Pacific — and all his men
Looked at each other with a wild surmise —
  Silent, upon a peak in Darien.

Chapman's Homer: Before reading George Chapman's (ca. 1560–1634) poetic Elizabethan translations of Homer's *Iliad* and *Odyssey*, Keats had known only stilted and pedestrian eighteenth-century translations. 4 *Apollo:* Greek god of poetry. 11 *Cortez:* Vasco Núñez de Balboa, not Hernán Cortés, was the first European to sight the Pacific from Darién, a peak in Panama.

CONSIDERATIONS FOR CRITICAL THINKING AND WRITING

1. **FIRST RESPONSE.** How do the images shift from the octave to the sestet? How does the tone change? Does the meaning change as well?

2. What is the controlling metaphor of this poem?

3. What is it that the speaker discovers?

4. How does the rhythm of the lines change between the octave and the sestet? How does that change reflect the tones of both the octave and the sestet?

5. Does Keats's mistake concerning Cortés and Balboa affect your reading of the poem? Explain why or why not.

  The **English sonnet**, more commonly known as the **Shakespearean sonnet**, is organized into three quatrains and a couplet, which typically rhyme *abab cdcd efef gg.* This rhyme scheme is more suited to English poetry because English has fewer rhyming words than Italian. English sonnets, because of their four-part organization, also have more flexibility about where thematic breaks can occur. Frequently, however, the most pronounced break or turn comes with the concluding couplet.

In the following Shakespearean sonnet, the three quatrains compare the speaker's loved one to a summer's day and explain why the loved one is even more lovely. The couplet bestows eternal beauty and love upon both the loved one and the sonnet.

WILLIAM SHAKESPEARE (1564–1616)

Shall I compare thee to a summer's day? 1609

Shall I compare thee to a summer's day?
Thou art more lovely and more temperate:
Rough winds do shake the darling buds of May,
And summer's lease hath all too short a date.
Sometime too hot the eye of heaven shines,   5
And often is his gold complexion dimmed;
And every fair from fair sometime declines,
By chance, or nature's changing course, untrimmed.
But thy eternal summer shall not fade,
Nor lose possession of that fair thou ow'st°   *possess* 10
Nor shall death brag thou wand'rest in his shade,
When in eternal lines to time thou grow'st.
  So long as men can breathe or eyes can see,
  So long lives this, and this gives life to thee.

CONSIDERATIONS FOR CRITICAL THINKING AND WRITING

1. **FIRST RESPONSE.** Describe the shift in tone and subject matter that begins in line 9.

2. Why is the speaker's loved one more lovely than a summer's day? What qualities does he admire in the loved one?

3. What does the couplet say about the relation between art and love?

4. Which syllables are stressed in the final line? How do these syllables relate to the line's meaning?

Sonnets have been the vehicles for all kinds of subjects, including love, death, politics, and cosmic questions. Although most sonnets tend to treat their subjects seriously, this fixed form does not mean a fixed expression; humor is also possible in it. Compare this next Shakespearean sonnet with "Shall I compare thee to a summer's day?" They are, finally, both love poems, but their tones are markedly different.

William Shakespeare (1564–1616)

My mistress' eyes are nothing like the sun 1609

My mistress' eyes are nothing like the sun;
Coral is far more red than her lips' red;
If snow be white, why then her breasts are dun;
If hairs be wires, black wires grow on her head.
I have seen roses damasked red and white,   5
But no such roses see I in her cheeks;
And in some perfumes is there more delight
Than in the breath that from my mistress reeks.
I love to hear her speak, yet well I know
That music hath a far more pleasing sound;   10
I grant I never saw a goddess go:
My mistress, when she walks, treads on the ground.
    And yet, by heaven, I think my love as rare
    As any she,° belied with false compare.   *lady*

Considerations for Critical Thinking and Writing

1. **First response.** What does "mistress" mean in this sonnet? Write a description of this particular mistress based on the images used in the sonnet.

2. What sort of person is the speaker? Does he truly love the woman he describes?

3. In what sense are this sonnet and "Shall I compare thee to a summer's day?" about poetry as well as love?

Connection to Another Selection

1. Compare the way this speaker depicts his "mistress" to that of the speaker in Andrew Marvell's "To His Coy Mistress" (p. 409). Which speaker is more persuasive?

Countee Cullen (1903–1946)

Yet Do I Marvel 1925

I doubt not God is good, well-meaning, kind,
And did He stoop to quibble could tell why
The little buried mole continues blind,
Why flesh that mirrors Him must some day die,
Make plain the reason tortured Tantalus   5
Is baited by the fickle fruit, declare
If merely brute caprice dooms Sisyphus

To struggle up a never-ending stair.
Inscrutable His ways are, and immune
To catechism by a mind too strewn
With petty cares to slightly understand   10
What awful brain compels His awful hand.
Yet do I marvel at this curious thing:
To make a poet black, and bid him sing!

Considerations for Critical Thinking and Writing

1. **FIRST RESPONSE.** How does the speaker envision the nature of God in lines 1–8?

2. Research the Tantalus and Sisyphus allusions. Why are these Greek myths particularly relevant in the context of the poem?

3. How do you interpret the meaning of "awful" in line 12?

Connection to Another Selection

1. Compare the view of God in "Yet Do I Marvel" with the perspective offered by the speaker in Emily Dickinson's "I know that He exists" (p. 581).

Mark Jarman (b. 1952)

Unholy Sonnet   1998

Breath like a house fly batters the shut mouth.
The dream begins, turns over, and goes flat.
The virus cleans the attic and heads south.
Somebody asks, "What did you mean by that?"
But nobody says, "Nothing," in response.   5
The body turns a last cell into cancer.
The ghost abandons all of his old haunts.
Silence becomes the question and the answer.
And then — banal epiphany — and then,
Time kick starts and the deaf brain hears a voice.   10
The eyes like orphans find the world again.
Day washes down the city streets with noise.
And oxygen repaints the blood bright red.
How good it is to come back from the dead!

Considerations for Critical Thinking and Writing

1. **FIRST RESPONSE.** This poem is one of forty-eight sonnets Jarman published under the title "Unholy Sonnets," clearly an allusion to John Donne's *Holy Sonnets* from the seventeenth century. Do you see any traditional Judeo-Christian religious themes in this poem?

2. Does this Shakespearean sonnet build an argument the same way that other examples of that form do?

3. If you were asked to make a case that the underlying subject of this poem is either sleep or death, which would you choose? How different would these two interpretations be?

R. S. Gwynn (b. 1948)

Shakespearean Sonnet   2010

With a first line taken from the tv listings

A man is haunted by his father's ghost.
Boy meets girl while feuding families fight.
A Scottish king is murdered by his host.
Two couples get lost on a summer night.
A hunchback murders all who block his way.   5
A ruler's rivals plot against his life.
A fat man and a prince make rebels pay.
A noble Moor has doubts about his wife.
An English king decides to conquer France.
A duke learns that his best friend is a she.   10
A forest sets the scene for this romance.
An old man and his daughters disagree.
A Roman leader makes a big mistake.
A sexy queen is bitten by a snake.

Considerations for Critical Thinking and Writing

1. First Response. How many Shakespearean plays can you identify from the fourteen encapsulated plots that make up this poem?

2. Discuss the significance of the title.

3. Creative Response. Try your hand at creating a poem — a sonnet or another form — in whole or in part from TV listings.

Claude McKay (1889–1948)

If We Must Die   1919

If we must die, let it not be like hogs
Hunted and penned in an inglorious spot,
While round us bark the mad and hungry dogs,
Making their mock at our accursèd lot.
If we must die, O let us nobly die,   5
So that our precious blood may not be shed

In vain; then even the monsters we defy
Shall be constrained to honor us though dead!
O Kinsmen! we must meet the common foe!
Though far outnumbered let us show us brave,   10
And for their thousand blows deal one deathblow!
What though before us lies the open grave?
Like men we'll face the murderous, cowardly pack,
Pressed to the wall, dying, but fighting back!

CONSIDERATIONS FOR CRITICAL THINKING AND WRITING

1. FIRST RESPONSE. How do the poem's images influence its tone?
2. Notice that this sonnet does not specifically mention race. How does that affect your reading?
3. Describe the poem's sonnet form.

CONNECTION TO ANOTHER SELECTION

1. Compare the themes in "If We Must Die" and in Langston Hughes's "Harlem" (p. 432).

Villanelle

The **villanelle** is a fixed form consisting of nineteen lines of any length divided into six stanzas: five tercets and a concluding quatrain. The first and third lines of the initial tercet rhyme; these rhymes are repeated in each subsequent tercet (*aba*) and in the final two lines of the quatrain (*abaa*). Moreover, line 1 appears in its entirety as lines 6, 12, and 18, while line 3 appears as lines 9, 15, and 19. This form may seem to risk monotony, but in competent hands a villanelle can create haunting echoes, as in Dylan Thomas's "Do Not Go Gentle into That Good Night."

DYLAN THOMAS (1914–1953)

Do Not Go Gentle into That Good Night   1952

Do not go gentle into that good night,
Old age should burn and rave at close of day;
Rage, rage against the dying of the light.

Though wise men at their end know dark is right,
Because their words had forked no lightning they   5
Do not go gentle into that good night.

Good men, the last wave by, crying how bright
Their frail deeds might have danced in a green bay,
Rage, rage against the dying of the light.

Wild men who caught and sang the sun in flight,   10
And learn, too late, they grieved it on its way,
Do not go gentle into that good night.

Grave men, near death, who see with blinding sight
Blind eyes could blaze like meteors and be gay,
Rage, rage against the dying of the light.   15

And you, my father, there on the sad height,
Curse, bless, me now with your fierce tears, I pray.
Do not go gentle into that good night.
Rage, rage against the dying of the light.

CONSIDERATIONS FOR CRITICAL THINKING AND WRITING

1. FIRST RESPONSE. How does Thomas vary the meanings of the poem's two refrains: "Do not go gentle into that good night" and "Rage, rage against the dying of the light"?

2. Thomas's father was close to death when this poem was written. How does the tone contribute to the poem's theme?

3. How is "good" used in line 1?

4. Characterize the men who are "wise" (line 4), "Good" (7), "Wild" (10), and "Grave" (13).

5. What do figures of speech contribute to this poem?

6. Discuss this villanelle's sound effects.

Sestina

Although the **sestina** usually does not rhyme, it is perhaps an even more demanding fixed form than the villanelle. A sestina consists of thirty-nine lines of any length divided into six six-line stanzas and a three-line concluding stanza called an **envoy**. The difficulty lies in repeating the six words at the ends of the first stanza's lines at the ends of the lines in the other five six-line stanzas as well, but in a very specific order that varies from stanza to stanza. Those words must also appear in the final three lines, where they often resonate important themes. The sestina originated in the Middle Ages, but contemporary poets continue to find it a fascinating and challenging form.

FLORENCE CASSEN MAYERS (B. 1940)

All-American Sestina 1996

One nation, indivisible
two-car garage
three strikes you're out

four-minute mile
five-cent cigar   5
six-string guitar

six-pack Bud
one-day sale
five-year warranty
two-way street   10
fourscore and seven years ago
three cheers

three-star restaurant
sixty-
four-dollar question   15
one-night stand
two-pound lobster
five-star general

five-course meal
three sheets to the wind   20
two bits
six-shooter
one-armed bandit
four-poster

four-wheel drive   25
five-and-dime
hole in one
three-alarm fire
sweet sixteen

two-wheeler   30
two-tone Chevy
four rms, hi flr, w/vu
six-footer
high five
three-ring circus   35
one-room schoolhouse

two thumbs up, five-karat diamond
Fourth of July, three-piece suit
six feet under, one-horse town

Considerations for Critical Thinking and Writing

1. **FIRST RESPONSE.** Discuss the significance of the title; what is "All-American" about this sestina?

2. How is the structure of this poem different from that of a conventional sestina? (What structural requirement does Mayers add for this sestina?)

3. Do you think important themes are raised by this poem, as is traditional for a sestina? If so, what are they? If not, what is being played with by using this convention?

CONNECTION TO ANOTHER SELECTION

1. Describe and compare the strategy used to create meaning in "All-American Sestina" with that used by E. E. Cummings in "next to of course god america i" (p. 452).

JULIA ALVAREZ (B. 1950)

Bilingual Sestina   1995

Some things I have to say aren't getting said
in this snowy, blond, blue-eyed, gum-chewing English:
dawn's early light sifting through *persianas* closed
the night before by dark-skinned girls whose words
evoke *cama, aposento, sueños* in *nombres*   5
from that first world I can't translate from Spanish.

Gladys, Rosario, Altagracia — the sounds of Spanish
wash over me like warm island waters as I say
your soothing names: a child again learning the *nombres*
of things you point to in the world before English   10
turned *sol, tierra, cielo, luna* to vocabulary words —
sun, earth, sky, moon. Language closed

like the touch-sensitive *morivivi* whose leaves closed
when we kids poked them, astonished. Even Spanish
failed us back then when we saw how frail a word is   15
when faced with the thing it names. How saying
its name won't always summon up in Spanish or English
the full blown genie from the bottled *nombre*.

Gladys, I summon you back by saying your *nombre*.
Open up again the house of slatted windows closed   20
since childhood, where *palabras* left behind for English
stand dusty and awkward in neglected Spanish.
Rosario, muse of *el patio*, sing in me and through me say
that world again, begin first with those first words

you put in my mouth as you pointed to the world —   25
not Adam, not God, but a country girl numbering
the stars, the blades of grass, warming the sun by saying,
¡Qué calor! as you opened up the morning closed
inside the night until you sang in Spanish,
Estas son las mañanitas, and listening in bed, no English   30

yet in my head to confuse me with translations, no English
doubling the world with synonyms, no dizzying array of words
— the world was simple and intact in Spanish —
luna, so, casa, luz, flor, as if the *nombres*
were the outer skin of things, as if words were so close   35
one left a mist of breath on things by saying

their names, an intimacy I now yearn for in English —
words so close to what I mean that I almost hear my Spanish
heart beating, beating inside what I say *en inglés.*

CONSIDERATIONS FOR CRITICAL THINKING AND WRITING

1. FIRST RESPONSE. Of the forms we have introduced, why do you think
   a sestina is a particularly appropriate form for the poet to choose to
   express the tension between her two languages?
2. Of the six sestina words — the ones that conclude each line — one is
   varied from stanza to stanza. Write a brief essay on why the poet might
   choose to vary that one particular word.
3. How would you describe the relationship between Spanish and English
   in this poem?

Epigram

An *epigram* is a brief, pointed, and witty poem. Although most rhyme
and they are often written in couplets, epigrams take no prescribed form.
Instead, they are typically polished bits of compressed irony, satire, or paradox. Here is an epigram that defines itself.

SAMUEL TAYLOR COLERIDGE (1772–1834)
What Is an Epigram? 1802

What is an epigram? A dwarfish whole;
Its body brevity, and wit its soul.

These additional examples by David McCord and Paul Laurence
Dunbar satisfy Coleridge's definition.

DAVID McCORD (1897–1997)
Epitaph on a Waiter 1954

By and by
God caught his eye.

PAUL LAURENCE DUNBAR
(1872–1906)

Theology   1896

There is a heaven, for ever, day by day,
The upward longing of my soul doth tell
     me so.
There is a hell, I'm quite as sure; for pray,
If there were not, where would my
     neighbors go?

Library of Congress/Getty Images.

CONSIDERATIONS FOR CRITICAL THINKING AND WRITING

1. **FIRST RESPONSE.** In what sense is each of these three epigrams, as Coleridge puts it, a "dwarfish whole"?
2. Explain how all three epigrams, in addition to being witty, make a serious point.
3. **CREATIVE RESPONSE.** Try writing a few epigrams that say something memorable about whatever you choose to focus on.

Limerick

The **limerick** is always light and humorous. Its usual form consists of five predominantly anapestic lines rhyming *aabba;* lines 1, 2, and 5 contain three feet, while lines 3 and 4 contain two. Limericks have delighted everyone from schoolchildren to sophisticated adults, and they range in subject matter from the simply innocent and silly to the satiric or obscene. The sexual humor helps to explain why so many limericks are written anonymously. Here is one that is more concerned with physics than physiology.

ARTHUR HENRY REGINALD BULLER (1874–1944)

There was a young lady named Bright   1923

There was a young lady named Bright,
Whose speed was far faster than light,
    She set out one day,
    In a relative way,
And returned home the previous night.

This next one is a particularly clever definition of a limerick.

LAURENCE PERRINE (1915–1995)
The limerick's never averse 1982

The limerick's never averse
To expressing itself in a terse
   Economical style,
   And yet, all the while,
The limerick's *always* a verse.

CONSIDERATIONS FOR CRITICAL THINKING AND WRITING

1. **FIRST RESPONSE.** How does this limerick differ from others you know? How is it similar?

2. Scan Perrine's limerick. How do the lines measure up to the traditional fixed metrical pattern?

3. **CREATIVE RESPONSE.** Try writing a limerick. Use the following basic pattern.

   ᵕ ᵕ ′   ᵕ ᵕ ′   ᵕ ᵕ ′
   ᵕ ᵕ ′   ᵕ ᵕ ′   ᵕ ᵕ ′
          ᵕ ᵕ ′   ᵕ ᵕ ′
          ᵕ ᵕ ′   ᵕ ᵕ ′
   ᵕ ᵕ ′   ᵕ ᵕ ′   ᵕ ᵕ ′

You might begin with a friend's name or the name of your school or town. Your instructor is, of course, fair game, too, provided your tact matches your wit.

Haiku

Another brief fixed poetic form, borrowed from the Japanese, is the **haiku**. A haiku is usually described as consisting of seventeen syllables organized into three unrhymed lines of five, seven, and five syllables. Owing to language difference, however, English translations of haiku are often only approximated, because a Japanese haiku exists in time (Japanese syllables have duration). The number of syllables in our sense is not as significant as the duration in Japanese. These poems typically present an intense emotion or vivid image of nature, which, in the Japanese, is also designed to lead to a spiritual insight.

MATSUO BASHŌ (1644–1694)
Under cherry trees date unknown

Under cherry trees
Soup, the salad, fish and all . . .
Seasoned with petals.

CAROLYN KIZER (1925–2014)

After Bashō   1984

Tentatively, you
slip onstage this evening,
pallid, famous moon.

AMY LOWELL (1874–1925)

Last night it rained   1921

Last night it rained.
Now, in the desolate dawn,
Crying of blue jays.

GARY SNYDER (B. 1930)

A Dent in a Bucket   2004

Hammering a dent out of a bucket
   a woodpecker
      answers from the woods

CONSIDERATIONS FOR CRITICAL THINKING AND WRITING

1. FIRST RESPONSE. What different emotions do these four haiku evoke?
2. What differences and similarities are there between the effects of a haiku and those of an epigram?
3. CREATIVE RESPONSE. Compose a haiku. Try to make it as allusive and suggestive as possible.

Ghazal

The ghazal form originated in Arabic poetry in the seventh and eighth centuries. Over the next thousand years its popularity spread from the Arabian peninsula to Persia, India, and other parts of Asia, the Middle East, Africa, and Spain. Its theme, historically, deals with love: both the pain one feels upon separation and the beauty that love brings despite this pain. The form is slightly more flexible than some we have described, partly since the form evolved over centuries and was often accompanied by music, but it is always written in couplets, usually between five and fifteen in number.

Mirza Asadullah Khan Ghalib (1797–1869)
Ghazal 4   1864

Though beyond compare is the beauty of the full moon,
More beautiful is my beloved who shines like the sun at noon.

She will not let me kiss her but keeps her eyes on my heart to see:
She says to herself, "It is a good bargain if I get him for free."

As my face lights up when I set eyes upon her   5
She thinks my illness has passed, I must be better.

Let us see what lovers get from the gods they hold dear,
A soothsayer predicts this will be a lucky year.

We all know the truth about paradise, I fear,
But Ghalib, the illusion keeps the heart in good cheer.   10

Considerations for Critical Thinking and Writing

1. **First response.** The poet addresses himself in the final line ("Ghalib" was his pen name). What is the effect of this self-address?

2. Who seems to be a stronger individual in the poem: the speaker or his lover? Why?

3. Discuss the emphasis on vision or the visual in this poem.

Connection to Another Selection

1. Write an essay comparing the themes, relationships, and imagery of "Ghazal 4" and Shakespeare's "My mistress' eyes are nothing like the sun" (p. 516).

Patricia Smith (b. 1955)
Hip-Hop Ghazal   2007

Gotta love us brown girls, munching on fat, swinging blue hips,
decked out in shells and splashes, Lawdie, bringing them woo hips.

As the jukebox teases, watch my sistas throat the heartbreak,
inhaling bassline, cracking backbone and singing thru hips.

Like something boneless, we glide silent, seeping 'tween floorboards,   5
wrapping around the hims, and *ooh wee,* clinging like glue hips.

Engines grinding, rotating, smokin', gotta pull back some.
Natural minds are lost at the mere sight of ringing true hips.

Gotta love us girls, just struttin' down Manhattan streets
killing the menfolk with a dose of that stinging view. Hips.   10

Crying 'bout getting old — Patricia, you need to get up off
what God gave you. Say a prayer and start slinging. Cue hips.

Considerations for Critical Thinking and Writing

1. **FIRST RESPONSE.** This poem identifies itself as a ghazal in its title, but it also identifies the cultural context as hip-hop. Do the ghazal form and hip-hop sensibility cooperate or are they at odds with one another?

2. What effect does the repetition of "hips" at the end of more than half the lines have on the poem? How about the rhyming words that precede "hips" in each instance?

3. Is this a poem of seduction or of empowerment (or both)?

Connection to Another Selection

1. As in Ghalib's "Ghazal 4," the poem that immediately precedes it, in "Hip-Hop Ghazal" the poet names and addresses herself in the final couplet. (This feature is not strictly a rule in the ghazal form, but it is not uncommon.) Write a brief essay about the effect of this convention on your understanding of individual identity in the ghazal.

Elegy

An elegy in classical Greek and Roman literature was written in alternating hexameter and pentameter lines. Since the seventeenth century, however, the term *elegy* has been used to describe a lyric poem written to commemorate someone who is dead. The word is also used to refer to a serious meditative poem produced to express the speaker's melancholy thoughts. Elegies no longer conform to a fixed pattern of lines and stanzas, but their characteristic subject is related to death and their tone is mournfully contemplative.

Ben Jonson (1573–1637)

On My First Son   1603

Farewell, thou child of my right hand,° and joy.
My sin was too much hope of thee, loved boy;
Seven years thou wert lent to me, and I thee pay,
Exacted by thy fate, on the just day.°   *his birthday*
Oh, could I lose all father° now. For why   *fatherhood*   5

1 *child of my right hand*: This phrase translates the Hebrew name "Benjamin," Jonson's son.

Will man lament the state he should envý? —
To have so soon 'scaped world's and flesh's rage,
And, if no other misery, yet age.
Rest in soft peace, and asked, say, "Here doth lie
Ben Jonson his best piece of poetry,"
For whose sake henceforth all his vows be such   10
As what he loves may never like too much.

CONSIDERATIONS FOR CRITICAL THINKING AND WRITING

1. FIRST RESPONSE. Describe the tone of this elegy. What makes it so emotionally convincing?

2. In what sense is Jonson's son "his best piece of poetry" (line 10)?

3. Interpret the final two lines. Do they seem consistent with the rest of the poem? Why or why not?

KATE HANSON FOSTER (B. 1962)
Elegy of Color   2018

Green shutters — white house.
Paper whites in the weak western light.
Brown mouse and its brown hush
across the stairs, four daughters
brushing long brown hair. Brown   5
beer in Black Label cans, black bible
on the nightstand. Baby Jesus
on the wall — incarnadine cheeks.
Shimmering red rosary beads. Red
garnet of my claddagh ring. A leak   10
yellowing in the ceiling. The many
colors of my father singing. I was blessed
and I was blessed, like foreheads, like palm
wisps, like water my mother bought
from the church — colorless, colorless.   15

CONSIDERATIONS FOR CRITICAL THINKING AND WRITING

1. FIRST RESPONSE. If this poem did not have "elegy" in the title, would you classify it as an elegy? Why or why not?

2. The poem covers many topics. What would you identify as its central subject?

3. What is the effect of the speaker repeating the phrase "I was blessed" in lines 12 and 13?

Ode

An **ode** is characterized by a serious topic and formal tone, but no pre-scribed formal pattern describes all odes. In some odes the pattern of each stanza is repeated throughout, while in others each stanza introduces a new pattern. Odes are lengthy lyrics that often include lofty emotions conveyed by a dignified style. Typical topics include truth, art, freedom, justice, and the meaning of life. Frequently such lyrics tend to be more public than private, and their speakers often use apostrophe.

ALEXANDER POPE (1688–1744)

Ode on Solitude 1700

Happy the man, whose wish and care
A few paternal acres bound,
Content to breathe his native air,
  In his own ground.

Whose herds with milk, whose fields with bread,   5
Whose flocks supply him with attire,
Whose trees in summer yield him shade,
  In winter fire.

Blest, who can unconcernedly find
Hours, days, and years slide soft away,   10
In health of body, peace of mind,
  Quiet by day,

Sound sleep by night; study and ease,
Together mixed; sweet recreation;
And innocence, which most does please,   15
  With meditation.

Thus let me live, unseen, unknown;
Thus unlamented let me die;
Steal from the world, and not a stone
  Tell where I lie.   20

CONSIDERATIONS FOR CRITICAL THINKING AND WRITING

1. **FIRST RESPONSE.** This poem is singularly populated. What distinction does the speaker make implicitly between solitude and loneliness?

2. Explain why "Ode on Solitude" can be accurately described as an ode.

3. How does the happy contentment expressed by the language in the first stanza anticipate the resolute wish expressed in the final stanza.

JOHN KEATS (1795–1821)

Ode on a Grecian Urn 1819

I

Thou still unravished bride of quietness,
   Thou foster-child of silence and slow time,
Sylvan° historian, who canst thus express
   A flowery tale more sweetly than our rhyme:
What leaf-fringed legend haunts about thy shape   5
   Of deities or mortals, or of both,
      In Tempe or the dales of Arcady?°
What men or gods are these? What maidens loath?
   What mad pursuit? What struggle to escape?
      What pipes and timbrels? What wild ecstasy?   10

II

Heard melodies are sweet, but those unheard
   Are sweeter; therefore, ye soft pipes, play on;
Not to the sensual ear, but, more endeared,
   Pipe to the spirit ditties of no tone:
Fair youth, beneath the trees, thou canst not leave   15
   Thy song, nor ever can those trees be bare;
      Bold Lover, never, never canst thou kiss,
Though winning near the goal — yet, do not grieve;
   She cannot fade, though thou hast not thy bliss,
      For ever wilt thou love, and she be fair!   20

III

Ah, happy, happy boughs! that cannot shed
   Your leaves, nor ever bid the Spring adieu;
And, happy melodist, unwearièd,
   For ever piping songs for ever new;
More happy love! more happy, happy love!   25
   For ever warm and still to be enjoyed,
      For ever panting, and for ever young;
All breathing human passion far above,
   That leaves a heart high-sorrowful and cloyed,
      A burning forehead, and a parching tongue.   30

IV

Who are these coming to the sacrifice?
   To what green altar, O mysterious priest,

---

3 *Sylvan:* Rustic. The urn is decorated with a forest scene.   7 *Tempe, Arcady:* Beautiful rural valleys in Greece.

Lead'st thou that heifer lowing at the skies,
　　And all her silken flanks with garlands drest?
What little town by river or sea shore, 35
　　Or mountain-built with peaceful citadel,
　　　　Is emptied of this folk, this pious morn?
And, little town, thy streets for evermore
　　Will silent be; and not a soul to tell
　　　　Why thou art desolate, can e'er return. 40

V

O Attic° shape! Fair attitude! with brede°
　　Of marble men and maidens overwrought,
With forest branches and the trodden weed;
　　Thou, silent form, dost tease us out of thought
As doth eternity: Cold Pastoral! 45
　　When old age shall this generation waste,
　　　　Thou shalt remain, in midst of other woe
Than ours, a friend to man, to whom thou say'st,
　　Beauty is truth, truth beauty — that is all
　　　　Ye know on earth, and all ye need to know. 50

41 *Attic:* Possessing classic Athenian simplicity; *-brede:* Design.

CONSIDERATIONS FOR CRITICAL THINKING AND WRITING

1. FIRST RESPONSE. What does the speaker's diction reveal about his attitude toward the urn in this ode? Does his view develop or change?

2. How is the happiness in stanza 3 related to the assertion in lines 11–12 that "Heard melodies are sweet, but those unheard / Are sweeter"?

3. What is the difference between the world depicted on the urn and the speaker's world?

4. What do lines 49 and 50 suggest about the relation of art to life? Why is the urn described as a "Cold Pastoral" (line 45)?

5. Which world does the speaker seem to prefer, the urn's or his own?

6. Describe the overall tone of the poem.

CONNECTIONS TO OTHER SELECTIONS

1. Write an essay comparing the view of time in this ode with that in Marvell's "To His Coy Mistress" (p. 409). Pay particular attention to the connotative language in each poem.

2. Compare the tone and attitude toward life in this ode with those in John Keats's "When I have Fears that I May Cease to Be" (p. 663).

Parody

A *parody* is a humorous imitation of another, usually serious, work. It can take any fixed or open form because parodists imitate the tone, language, and shape of the original. While a parody may be teasingly close to a work's style, it typically deflates the subject matter to make the original seem absurd. Parody can be used as a kind of literary criticism to expose the defects in a work, but it is also very often an affectionate acknowledgment that a well-known work has become both institutionalized in our culture and fair game for some fun. Read Robert Frost's "The Road Not Taken" (p. 416) and then study this parody.

BLANCHE FARLEY (1937–2018)

The Lover Not Taken　1984

Committed to one, she wanted both
And, mulling it over, long she stood,
Alone on the road, loath
To leave, wanting to hide in the undergrowth.
This new guy, smooth as a yellow wood 　　　　　　　　5

Really turned her on. She liked his hair,
His smile. But the other, Jack, had a claim
On her already and she had to admit, he did wear
Well. In fact, to be perfectly fair,
He understood her. His long, lithe frame 　　　　　　　　10

Beside hers in the evening tenderly lay.
Still, if this blond guy dropped by someday,
Couldn't way just lead on to way?
No. For if way led on and Jack
Found out, she doubted if he would ever come back. 　　　　15

Oh, she turned with a sigh.
Somewhere ages and ages hence,
She might be telling this. "And I —"
She would say, "stood faithfully by."
But by then who would know the difference? 　　　　　　　　20

With that in mind, she took the fast way home,
The road by the pond, and phoned the blond.

WHEN I WRITE "Keep your work, even if it is unfinished or not to your liking. It can be revised or even rewritten in another form. Maybe the original idea is what will prove valuable. Most importantly, despite all else going on in your life, despite rejection or feelings of discouragement, keep writing." — BLANCHE FARLEY

CONSIDERATIONS FOR CRITICAL THINKING AND WRITING

1. **FIRST RESPONSE.** To what degree does this poem duplicate Frost's style? How does it differ?

2. Does this parody seem successful to you? Explain what you think makes a successful parody.

3. **CREATIVE RESPONSE.** Choose a poet whose work you know reasonably well or would like to know better and determine what is characteristic about his or her style. Then choose a poem to parody. It's probably best to attempt a short poem or a section of a long work. If you have difficulty selecting an author, you might consider Herrick, Blake, Keats, Dickinson, Whitman, Hughes, or Frost, as a number of their works are included in this book.

The following poem is a parody of Gwendolyn Brooks's "We Real Cool" (p. 509).

JOAN MURRAY (B. 1945)
We Old Dudes   2006

We old dudes. We
White shoes. We

Golf ball. We
Eat mall. We

Soak teeth. We
Palm Beach; We

Vote red. We
Soon dead.

> **WHEN I READ** "Reading stretches your mind and imagination. It lets you discover what you like and admire. Sometimes after I read a poem, I want to write one. It's as if someone's speaking my language, and I want to converse." — JOAN MURRAY

CONSIDERATIONS FOR CRITICAL THINKING AND WRITING

1. **FIRST RESPONSE.** Consider the poem's humor. To what extent does it make a serious point?

2. What does the reference to Palm Beach tell you about these "old dudes"?

3. **CREATIVE RESPONSE.** Write a poem similar in style that characterizes your life as a student.

CONNECTION TO ANOTHER SELECTION

1. Compare the themes of "We Old Dudes" and Brooks's "We Real Cool" (p. 509). How do the two poems speak to each other?

Picture Poem

By arranging lines into particular shapes, poets can sometimes organize typography into *picture poems* of what they describe. Words have been arranged into all kinds of shapes, from apples to light bulbs. Notice how the shape of this next poem embodies its meaning.

> **WHEN I WRITE** "I've shared my poems with a friend, who's also a poet, for decades now. He marks them up and gives them back; I do the same for him. You need a sympathetic critic who is not you, to help make your poetry as strong and clear as possible to readers who are not you." — MICHAEL MCFEE

MICHAEL MCFEE (B. 1954)

In Medias Res°   1985

His waist
like the plot
thickens, wedding
pants now breathtaking,
belt no longer the cinch   5
it once was, belly's cambium
expanding to match each birthday,
his body a wad of anonymous tissue
swung in the same centrifuge of years
that separates a house from its foundation,   10
undermining sidewalks grim with joggers
and loose-filled graves and families
and stars collapsing on themselves,
no preservation society capable
of plugging entropy's dike,   15
under his zipper's sneer
a belly hibernation-
soft, ready for
the kill.

In Medias Res: A Latin term for a story that begins "in the middle of things."

CONSIDERATIONS FOR CRITICAL THINKING AND WRITING

1. **FIRST RESPONSE.** Explain how the title is related to this poem's shape and meaning.
2. Identify the puns. How do they work in the poem?
3. What is "cambium" (line 6)? Why is the phrase "belly's cambium" especially appropriate?
4. What is the tone of this poem? Is it consistent throughout?

Perspective

ELAINE MITCHELL (1924–2012)

Form   1994

Is it a corset
or primal wave?
Don't try to force it.

Even endorse it
to shape and deceive.   5
Ouch, too tight a corset.

Take it off. No remorse. It
's an ace up your sleeve.
No need to force it.

Can you make a horse knit?   10
Who would believe?
Consider. Of course, it

might be a resource. Wit,
your grateful slave.
Form. Sometimes you force it,   15

sometimes divorce it
to make it behave.
So don't try to force it.
Respect a good corset.

CONSIDERATIONS FOR CRITICAL THINKING AND WRITING

1. **FIRST RESPONSE.** What is the speaker's attitude toward form?
2. Explain why you think the form of this poem does or does not conform to the speaker's advice.
3. Why is the metaphor of a corset an especially apt image for this poem?

19

Open Form

I'm not very good at communicating verbally. I'm somebody who listens more than talks. I like to listen and absorb. But when I need to connect with people and I need to reach out, I write.

— RUTH FORMAN

Photograph by Christine Bennett, www.cbimages.org.

Many poems, especially those written in the past century, are composed of lines that cannot be scanned for a fixed or predominant meter. Moreover, very often these poems do not rhyme. Known as *free verse* (from the French, *vers libre*), such lines can derive their rhythmic qualities from the repetition of words, phrases, or grammatical structures; the arrangement of words on the printed page; or some other means. In recent years the term *open form* has been used in place of *free verse* to avoid the erroneous suggestion that this kind of poetry lacks all discipline and shape. Robert Frost, toward the end of his decorated career as a poet, archly dismissed free verse, saying, "I'd just as soon play tennis with the net down." This oft-quoted phrase indicates a shift in literary history in the 1950s, when Frost uttered it, but it's not as though all poets started open form verse in the mid-twentieth century. Contemporary poets have a wide range of choices, and poets from earlier times did too, although in some eras (like England in the eighteenth century) poets who did not adhere to strict conventions might not have found a publisher.

Although the following poem does not use measurable meters, it does have rhythm.

WALT WHITMAN (1819–1892)

From "I Sing the Body Electric" 1855

O my body! I dare not desert the likes of you in other men and women,
      nor the likes of the parts of you,
I believe the likes of you are to stand or fall with the likes of the soul,
      (and that they are the soul,)
I believe the likes of you shall stand or fall with my poems, and that
      they are my poems.
Man's, woman's, child's, youth's, wife's, husband's, mother's, father's,
      young man's, young woman's poems.
Head, neck, hair, ears, drop and tympan of the ears. 5
Eyes, eye-fringes, iris of the eye, eyebrows, and the waking or sleeping
      of the lids,
Mouth, tongue, lips, teeth, roof of the mouth, jaws, and the jaw-hinges,
Nose, nostrils of the nose, and the partition,
Cheeks, temples, forehead, chin, throat, back of the neck, neck-slue,
Strong shoulders, manly beard, scapula, hind-shoulders, and the
      ample side-round of the chest, 10
Upper-arm, armpit, elbow-socket, lower-arm, arm-sinews, arm-bones,
Wrist and wrist-joints, hand, palm, knuckles, thumb, forefinger, finger-
      joints, finger-nails,
Broad breast-front, curling hair of the breast, breast-bone, breast-side,
Ribs, belly, backbone, joints of the backbone,
Hips, hip-sockets, hip-strength, inward and outward round, man-balls,
      man-root, 15
Strong set of thighs, well carrying the trunk above,
Leg-fibers, knee, knee-pan, upper-leg, under-leg,
Ankles, instep, foot-ball, toes, toe-joints, the heel;
All attitudes, all the shapeliness, all the belongings of my or your body
      or of any one's body, male or female,
The lung-sponges, the stomach-sac, the bowels sweet and clean, 20
The brain in its folds inside the skull-frame,
Sympathies, heart-valves, palate-valves, sexuality, maternity,
Womanhood, and all that is a woman, and the man that comes
      from woman,
The womb, the teats, nipples, breast-milk, tears, laughter, weeping, love-
      looks, love-perturbations and risings,
The voice, articulation, language, whispering, shouting aloud, 25
Food, drink, pulse, digestion, sweat, sleep, walking, swimming,
Poise on the hips, leaping, reclining, embracing, arm-curving and
      tightening,
The continual changes of the flex of the mouth, and around the eyes,
The skin, the sunburnt shade, freckles, hair,
The curious sympathy one feels when feeling with the hand the naked
      meat of the body, 30

The circling rivers the breath, and breathing it in and out,
The beauty of the waist, and thence of the hips, and thence downward
    toward the knees,
The thin red jellies within you or within me, the bones and the marrow in
    the bones,
The exquisite realization of health;
O I say these are not the parts and poems of the body only, but
    of the soul,
O I say now these are the soul!   35

CONSIDERATIONS FOR CRITICAL THINKING AND WRITING

1. FIRST RESPONSE. What informs this speaker's attitude toward the human
   body?
2. Read the poem aloud. Is it simply a tedious enumeration of body parts,
   or do the lines achieve some kind of rhythmic cadence?

A SAMPLE STUDENT RESPONSE

Bloom 1

Avery Bloom

Professor Rios

English 212

7 October 2018

The Power of Walt Whitman's Open Form Poem

"I Sing the Body Electric"

Walt Whitman's "I Sing the Body Electric" is an ode to the human
body. The poem is open form, without rhymes or consistent meter, and
instead relies almost entirely on the use of language and the structure of
lists to affect the reader. The result is a thorough inventory of parts of
the body that illustrates the beauty of the human form and its intimate
connection to the soul.

At times, Whitman lists the parts of the body with almost complete
objectivity, making it difficult to understand the poem's purpose. The poem

initially appears to do little more than recite the names of body parts: "Head, neck, hair, ears, drop and tympan of the ears" (line 5); "Mouth, tongue, lips, teeth, roof of the mouth, jaws, and the jaw-hinges" (7). There are no end rhymes, but the exhaustive and detailed list of body parts—from the brain to the "thin red jellies . . . , the bones and the marrow in the bones" (33)—offers language that has a certain rhythm. The language and rhythm of the list create a visual image full of energy and momentum that builds, emphasizing the body's functions and movements. As Michael Meyer writes, open form poems "rely on an intense use of language to establish rhythms and relations between meaning and form. [They] use the arrangement of words and phrases . . . to create unique forms" (page 541). No doubt Whitman chose the open form for this work—relying on his "intense use of language" and the rhythm of the list—because it allowed a basic structure that held together but did not restrain, and a full freedom and range of motion to create a poem that is alive with movement and electricity. . . .

Bloom 4

Works Cited

Meyer, Michael and D. Quentin Miller, editors. *Literature to Go*. 4th ed.,
    Bedford/St. Martin's, 2020.
Whitman, Walt. "From 'I Sing the Body Electric.'" Meyer and Miller,
    pp. 538-39.

Open form poetry is sometimes regarded as formless because it is unlike the strict fixed forms of a sonnet, villanelle, or sestina (which are defined in chapter 18). But even though open form poems may not employ traditional meters and rhymes, they still rely on an intense use of language to establish rhythms and relations between meaning and form. Open form poems use the arrangement of words and phrases on the printed page, pauses, line lengths, and other means to create unique forms that express their particular meaning and tone.

The excerpt from Whitman's "I Sing the Body Electric" demonstrates how rhythmic cadences can be aligned with meaning, but there is one kind of open form poetry that doesn't even look like poetry on a page. A **prose poem** is printed as prose and represents, perhaps, the most clear opposite of fixed forms. Here are two brief examples.

DAVID SHUMATE (B. 1950)

Shooting the Horse   2004

I unlatch the stall door, step inside, and stroke the silky neck of the old mare like a lover about to leave. I take an ear in hand, fold it over, and run my fingers across her muzzle. I coax her head up so I can blow into those nostrils. All part of the routine we taught each other long ago. I turn a half turn, pull a pistol from my coat, raise it to that long brow with the white blaze and place it between her sleepy eyes. I clear my throat. A sound much louder than it should be. I squeeze the trigger and the horse's feet fly out from under her as gravity gives way to a force even more austere, which we have named mercy.

CONSIDERATIONS FOR CRITICAL THINKING AND WRITING

1. **FIRST RESPONSE.** Describe the range of emotions that this poem produces for you.

2. Think of other words that could be substituted for *mercy* in the final line. How does your choice change the tone and theme of the poem?

3. Rearrange the poem so that its words, phrases, and sentences are set up to use the white space on the page to convey tone and meaning. Which version do you prefer? Why?

REGINALD SHEPHERD (1963–2008)

Self-Portrait Surviving Spring   1996

He went down to the dock to watch the boats
the short-haired boys rowed every afternoon
while gulls rowed overhead through liquid gusts
of cloud, to feed on sight, the flourishing
accomplishments of water. His own body

5

was in question, a hive of privacies and feelings
anyone could have; a wind prickled
his neck with salt from tides away, the skin's
blind babble of sensation. Then he was
asleep, then waking to a clock's alarm,   10

and then he slept again, without a sound
but soundly all the same. It never was
the same, of course, except it never changed
for him, seascapes of boys taped to his wall,
and clanging crows clapping *Wake up, it's time*   15

not to believe. He's walking past the slanted
embankments, he's running on cement,
he's catching up with them, long waves of short
-haired boys in sculls. He thinks he's catching up.
Clouds sail too slowly to be seen, white boys   20

glide out of sight too quickly to be missed.
He's scribbling down a clouded over page
just like a day, a week of gulls and crows,
rowboats. Days come and go, weeks go, years go
that way, all of them his, equally lost.   25

To make him smile what would they do (the days,
the clear indifferent weeks), what promise would
they break? Blond teams row down the sluggish river
every spring, the hydropower plant
for backdrop, and the highway, mud for boots   30

and shoots, and little seeds the gulls drop, not
particularly concerned where they might land.

Considerations for Critical Thinking and Writing

1. **FIRST RESPONSE.** Pay careful attention to the stanza breaks in this poem.
   What do they do to the poem's flow? How might this effect be related to
   the poem's theme?

2. Would it have even been possible for the poet to have written this poem
   as a sonnet? What would be gained or lost by trying?

3. What is at the center of this poem's appeal? At the very least, what are its
   unique poetic features?

Much of the poetry published today is written in open form; however,
many poets continue to take pleasure in the requirements imposed by fixed
forms. Some poets write both fixed form and open form poetry. Each kind
offers rewards to careful readers as well. Here are several more open form
poems that establish their own unique patterns.

Major Jackson (b. 1968)
The Chase 2010

"What are you thinking?" she said. "Falling pheasants."
      He said. "Please look at me." she said.
"I've seen too much." he said. "You're like a wet cave."
      She said. "You're a feast of rhythms." he said.
"I want more than thunderbolts inside." she said.
      "Wave after wave after wave." he said. "Your eyes
are stitching tighter." she said. "I am lost in a blizzard
      of feathers." he said. "You are lost." she said.

Considerations for Critical Thinking and Writing

1. **First Response.** Look again at the poem's title. Who or what is being chased?

2. The repeated phrases "he said" and "she said" are punctuated as though they are complete sentences, but they don't always follow the convention of capitalizing the first letter. How difficult is it to tell who is saying what? How does that difficulty relate to the poem's theme?

3. Some phrases seem so personal to this couple's experience and/or so abstract that we cannot know their connotations. Despite their personal nature, are you able to discern the nature of their relationship?

Natasha Trethewey (b. 1966)
On Captivity 2007

*Being all Stripped as Naked as
We were Born, and endeav-
oring to hide our Nakedness,
these Cannaballs took [our]
Books, and tearing out the
Leaves would give each of us a
Leaf to cover us . . .*
    —Jonathan Dickinson, 1699

AP Photo/Rogelio V. Solis.

At the hands now
    of their captors, those
        they've named *savages,*
    do they say the word itself
savagely — hissing

5

that first letter,
> the serpent's image,
> > releasing
> thought into speech?
For them now,

everything is flesh
> as if their thoughts, made
> > suddenly corporeal,
> reveal even more
their nakedness —

the shame of it:
> their bodies rendered
> > plain as the natives' —
> homely and pale,
their ordinary sex,

the secret illicit hairs
> that do not (cannot)
> > cover enough.
This is how they are brought,
naked as newborns,

to knowledge. Adam and Eve
> in the New World,
> > they have only the Bible
> to cover them. Think of it:
a woman holding before her

the torn leaves of *Genesis*,
> and a man covering himself
> > with the Good Book's
> frontispiece — his own name
inscribed on the page.

10

15

20

25

30

35

CONSIDERATIONS FOR CRITICAL THINKING AND WRITING

1. **FIRST RESPONSE.** Trethewey has written about the sources of her epigraph: "Because the conquerors made use of the written word to claim land [in North America] inhabited by native people, I found the detail of settlers forced to cover themselves with torn pages from books a compelling irony" (*The Best American Poetry 2008*, p. 182). How does this comment contribute to the central irony in the poem?

2. Discuss Trethewey's use of alliteration in lines 1–9.

3. In what sense are the captors "brought, / naked as newborns, / to knowledge" (lines 24–26)?

JULIO MARZÁN (B. 1946)

The Translator at the Reception for Latin American Writers 1997

Air-conditioned introductions,
then breezy Spanish conversation
fan his curiosity to know
what country I come from.
"Puerto Rico and the Bronx."   5

Spectacled downward eyes
translate disappointment
like a poison mushroom
puffed in his thoughts as if,
after investing a sizable   10
intellectual budget, transporting
a huge cast and camera crew
to film on location
Mayan pyramid grandeur,
indigenes whose ancient gods   15
and comet-tail plumage
inspire a glorious epic
of revolution across a continent,
he received a lurid script
for a social documentary   20
rife with dreary streets
and pathetic human interest,
meager in the profits of high culture.

Understandably he turns,
catches up with the hostess,   25
praising the uncommon quality
of her offerings of cheese.

CONSIDERATIONS FOR CRITICAL THINKING AND WRITING

1. **FIRST RESPONSE.** What is the speaker's attitude toward the person he meets at the reception? What lines in particular lead you to that conclusion?

2. Why is that person so disappointed about the answer, "Puerto Rico and the Bronx" (line 5)?

3. Explain lines 6–23. How do they reveal both the speaker and the person encountered at the reception?

4. Why is the setting of this poem significant?

CHARLES HARPER WEBB (B. 1952)

Descent 1998

For my son

Let
there be
amino acids,
and there were: a slop
of molecules in ancient seas,   5
building cell walls to keep their
distance, dividing, replicating, starting
to diversify, one growing oars, one rotors, one
a wiry tail, lumping into clusters — cyanobacteria, sea-
worms, medusae, trilobites, lobe-finned fish dragging onto   10
land, becoming thrinaxodon, protoceratops, growing larger —
diplodocus, gorgosaurus — dying out — apatosaurus, tyrannosaurus —
mammals evolving from shrew-like deltatheridium into hyenadon, eohippus,
mammoth, saber-tooth, dire wolf, australopithecus rising on two feet, homo erectus
tramping from Africa into Europe and Asia, thriving like a weed that will grow anywhere —   15
jungle, desert, snow-pack — the genetic rivers flowing downhill now: a husband's skull crushed
in the Alps, a Tartar raping a green-eyed girl who dies in childbirth, whose daughter falls in
love with a Viking who takes her to Istanbul, a Celt who marries a Saxon, a weaver
who abducts the daughter of a witch, a son who steals his father's gold, a girl
who loses one eye leaping from a tree, dozens who die of smallpox,   20
cholera, black plague, a knight, a prostitute, thieves, carpenters,
farmers, poachers, blacksmiths, seamstresses, peddlers of
odds and ends, an Irishman who sells his family into
servitude, a Limey who jumps ship in New York,
Jews who flee Hungary, a midwife, an X-ray   25
machine repairman, a psychologist,
a writer, all flowing down,
converging on the great
delta, the point
of all this: 30
you.

CONSIDERATIONS FOR CRITICAL THINKING AND WRITING

1. **FIRST RESPONSE.** What do you make of the shape of this poem? Given its content, why is the shape appropriate?

2. Describe the significance of the change in diction from the first half of the poem to the second half.

3. Why do you think Webb titled the poem "Descent" rather than "Ascent"?

CONNECTION TO ANOTHER SELECTION

1. Compare the themes in "Descent" with those in Robert Frost's "Design" (p. 394).

ANONYMOUS

The Frog date unknown

What a wonderful bird the frog are!
When he stand he sit almost;
When he hop he fly almost.
He ain't got no sense hardly;
He ain't got no tail hardly either.
When he sit, he sit on what he ain't got almost.

CONSIDERATIONS FOR CRITICAL THINKING AND WRITING

1. FIRST RESPONSE. How is the poem a description of the speaker as well as of a frog?

2. Though this poem is ungrammatical, it does have a patterned structure. How does the pattern of sentences create a formal structure?

DAVID HERNANDEZ (B. 1971)

All-American 2012

I'm this tiny, this statuesque, and everywhere
in between, and everywhere in between
bony and overweight, my shadow cannot hold
one shape in Omaha, in Tuscaloosa, in Aberdeen.
My skin is mocha brown, two shades darker   5
than taupe, your question is racist, nutmeg, beige,
I'm not offended by your question at all.
Penis or vagina? Yes and yes. Gay or straight?
Both boxes. Bi, not bi, who cares, stop
fixating on my sex life, Jesus never leveled   10
his eye to a bedroom's keyhole. I go to church
in Tempe, in Waco, the one with the exquisite
stained glass, the one with a white spire
like the tip of a Klansman's hood. Churches
creep me out, I never step inside one,   15
never utter hymns, Sundays I hide my flesh
with camouflage and hunt. I don't hunt
but wish every deer wore a bulletproof vest
and fired back. It's cinnamon, my skin,
it's more sandstone than any color I know.   20
I voted for Obama, McCain, Nader, I was too
apathetic to vote, too lazy to walk one block,
two blocks to the voting booth. For or against

a woman's right to choose? Yes, for and against.   25
For waterboarding, for strapping detainees
with snorkels and diving masks. Against burning
fossil fuels, let's punish all those smokestacks
for eating the ozone, bring the wrecking balls,
but build more smokestacks, we need jobs
here in Harrisburg, here in Kalamazoo. Against   30
gun control, for cotton bullets, for constructing
a better fence along the border, let's raise
concrete toward the sky, why does it need
all that space to begin with? For creating
holes in the fence, adding ladders, they're not   35
here to steal work from us, no one dreams
of crab walking for hours across a lettuce field
so someone could order the Caesar salad.
No one dreams of sliding a squeegee down
the cloud-mirrored windows of a high-rise,
but some of us do it. Some of us sell flowers.   40
Some of us cut hair. Some of us carefully
steer a mower around the cemetery grounds.
Some of us paint houses. Some of us monitor
the power grid. Some of us ring you up   45
while some of us crisscross a parking lot
to gather the shopping carts into one long,
rolling, clamorous and glittering backbone.

Considerations for Critical Thinking and Writing

1. FIRST RESPONSE. How does the arrangement of lines communicate a
   sense of energy and vitality?
2. How does the speaker characterize the United States?
3. Discuss the tone and thematic significance of the final image in lines
   46–48.

Connection to Another Selection

1. How does Hernandez's description of what is "All-American" compare
   with Julio Marzán's in "The Translator at the Reception for Latin American Writers" (p. 545)?

Found Poem

This next selection is a *found poem*, unintentional verse discovered in a
nonpoetic context, such as a conversation, news story, or an advertisement.
Found poems are playful reminders that the words in poems are very often

the language we use every day. Whether such found language should be regarded as a poem is an issue left for you to consider.

DONALD JUSTICE (1925–2004)
Order in the Streets 1969

(From instructions printed on a child's toy, Christmas 1968, as reported in the New York Times)

1. 2. 3.
Switch on.

Jeep rushes
to the scene
of riot

     5

Jeep goes
in all directions
by mystery action.

Jeep stops periodically
to turn hood over

     10

machine gun appears
with realistic
shooting noise.

After putting down riot,
jeep goes
back to the headquarters.

     15

CONSIDERATIONS FOR CRITICAL THINKING AND WRITING

1. **FIRST RESPONSE.** What is the effect of arranging these instructions in discrete lines? How are the language and meaning enhanced by this arrangement?

2. How does this poem connect upon the many riots that occurred throughout the United States during the late sixties?

3. **CREATIVE RESPONSE.** Look for phrases or sentences in ads, textbooks, labels, or directions — in anything that might inadvertently contain provocative material that would be revealed by arranging the words in verse lines. You may even discover some patterns of rhyme and rhythm. After arranging the lines, explain why you organized them as you did.

Poetry in Depth

A Study of Emily Dickinson

My business is circumference.
— EMILY DICKINSON

Todd-Bingham Picture Collection, 1837–1966 (inclusive). Manuscripts and Archives, Yale University.

In this chapter you'll find a variety of poems by Emily Dickinson so that you can study her work in some depth. While this collection is not wholly representative of her work, it does offer enough poems to suggest some of the techniques and concerns that characterize her writings. The poems speak not only to readers but also to one another. That's natural enough: the more familiar you are with a writer's work, the easier it is to perceive and enjoy the strategies and themes the poet uses. If you are asked to write about a number of poems by the same author, you may find useful the Questions for Writing about an Author in Depth (p. 579) and the sample paper on Dickinson's attitudes toward religious faith in four of her poems (pp. 580–81).

Emily E, Dickinson.

Edward and Mary Judson Hitchcock Family Papers, Amherst College Archives and Special Collections.

This daguerreotype of Emily Dickinson, taken shortly after her sixteenth birthday, and the silhouette (see p. 555), created when she was fourteen years old, are the only authenticated mechanically produced images of the poet.
Todd-Bingham Picture Collection, 1837–1966 (inclusive). Manuscripts and Archives, Yale University.

A BRIEF BIOGRAPHY

Emily Dickinson (1830–1886) grew up in a prominent and prosperous household in Amherst, Massachusetts. Along with her younger sister, Lavinia, and older brother, Austin, she experienced a quiet and reserved family life headed by her father, Edward Dickinson. In a letter to Austin at law school, she once described the atmosphere in her father's house as

(*Right*) This silhouette shows Dickinson at age fourteen.
Todd-Bingham Picture Collection, 1837–1966 (inclusive). Manuscripts and Archives, Yale University.

(*Below*) This recently discovered print of a mid-1850s daguerreotype, acquired by the scholar Philip F. Gura in 2000, may represent the poet in her twenties.
Collection of Philip F. Gura.

"pretty much all sobriety." Her mother, Emily Norcross Dickinson, was not as powerful a presence in her life; she seems not to have been as emotionally accessible as Dickinson would have liked. Her daughter is said to have characterized her as not the sort of mother "to whom you hurry when you are troubled." Both parents raised Dickinson to be a cultured Christian woman who would one day be responsible for a family of her own. Her father attempted to protect her from reading books that might "joggle" her mind, particularly her religious faith, but Dickinson's individualistic instincts and irreverent sensibilities created conflicts that did not allow her to fall into step with the conventional piety, domesticity, and social duty prescribed by her father and the orthodox Congregationalism of Amherst.

The Dickinsons were well known in Massachusetts. Emily's father was a lawyer and served as the treasurer of Amherst College (a position Austin eventually took up as well), and her grandfather was one of the college's founders. Although nineteenth-century politics, economics, and social issues do not appear in the foreground of her poetry, Dickinson lived in a family environment that was steeped in them: her father was an active town official and served in the General Court of Massachusetts, the state senate, and the U.S. House of Representatives.

Dickinson, however, withdrew not only from her father's public world but also from almost all social life in Amherst. She refused to see most people, and aside from a single year at South Hadley Female Seminary (now Mount Holyoke College), one excursion to Philadelphia and Washington, and several brief trips to Boston to see a doctor about eye problems, she lived all her life in her father's house. She dressed only in white and developed a reputation as a reclusive eccentric. Dickinson selected her own society carefully and frugally. Like her poetry, her relationship to the world was intensely reticent. Indeed, during the last twenty years of her life she rarely left the house.

Though Dickinson never married, she had significant relationships with several men who were friends, confidants, and mentors. She also enjoyed an intimate relationship with her friend Susan Huntington Gilbert, who became her sister-in-law by marrying Austin. Susan and her husband lived next door and were extremely close with Dickinson. Biographers have attempted to find in a number of her relationships the source for the passion of some of her love poems and letters. Several possibilities have been put forward as the person she addressed in three letters as "Dear Master": Benjamin Newton, a clerk in her father's office who talked about books with her; Samuel Bowles, editor of the *Springfield Republican* and friend of the family; the Reverend Charles Wadsworth, a Presbyterian preacher with a reputation for powerful sermons; and an old friend and widower, Judge Otis P. Lord. Despite these speculations, no biographer has been able to identify definitively the object of Dickinson's love. What matters, of course, is not with whom she was in love — if, in fact, there was any single person — but that she wrote about such passions so intensely and convincingly in her poetry.

Choosing to live life internally within the confines of her home, Dickinson brought her life into sharp focus, for she also chose to live within the limitless expanses of her imagination — a choice she was keenly aware of and which she described in one of her poems this way: "I dwell in Possibility —" (p. 568). Her small circle of domestic life did not impinge on her creative sensibilities. Like Henry David Thoreau, she simplified her life so that doing without was a means of being within. In a sense, she redefined the meaning of deprivation because being denied something — whether faith, love, literary recognition, or some other desire — provided a sharper, more intense understanding than she would have experienced had she achieved what she wanted: "'Heaven,'" she wrote, "is what I cannot reach!" This poem (p. 565) — along with many others, such as "Water, is taught by thirst" (p. 561) and "Success is counted sweetest / By those who ne'er succeed" (p. 561) — suggests just how persistently she saw deprivation as a way of sensitizing herself to the value of what she was missing. For Dickinson, hopeful expectation was always more satisfying than achieving a golden moment. Perhaps that's one reason she was so attracted to John Keats's poetry (see, for example, his "Ode on a Grecian Urn," p. 531).

Dickinson enjoyed reading Keats as well as other British writers from the nineteenth century: Emily and Charlotte Brontë; Robert and Elizabeth Barrett Browning; Alfred, Lord Tennyson; and George Eliot. Even so, these writers had little or no effect on the style of her writing. In her own work she was original and innovative, but she did draw on her knowledge of the Bible, classical myths, and Shakespeare for allusions and references in her poetry. She also used contemporary popular church hymns, transforming their standard rhythms into free-form hymn meters. Among American writers she appreciated Ralph Waldo Emerson and Thoreau, but she apparently felt Walt Whitman was better left unread. She once mentioned to Thomas Wentworth Higginson, a leading critic with whom she corresponded about her poetry, that as for Whitman "I never read his Book — but was told that he was disgraceful" (for the kind of Whitman poetry she had been warned against, see his "I Sing the Body Electric," p. 538). Nathaniel Hawthorne, however, intrigued her with his faith in the imagination and his dark themes: "Hawthorne appals — entices," a remark that might be used to describe her own themes and techniques.

AN INTRODUCTION TO HER WORK

Today, Dickinson is regarded as one of America's greatest poets, but when she died at the age of fifty-six after devoting most of her life to writing poetry, her nearly two thousand poems — only a dozen of which were published, anonymously, during her lifetime — were unknown except to a small number of friends and relatives. Dickinson was not recognized as a major poet until the twentieth century, when modern readers ranked her as a major new voice whose literary innovations were unmatched by any other nineteenth-century poet in the United States.

Dickinson neither completed many poems nor prepared them for publication. She wrote her drafts on scraps of paper, grocery lists, and the backs of recipes and used envelopes. Early editors of her poems took the liberty of making them more accessible to nineteenth-century readers when several volumes of selected poems were published in the 1890s. The poems were made to appear like traditional nineteenth-century verse by assigning them titles, rearranging their syntax, normalizing their grammar, and regularizing their capitalizations. Instead of dashes, editors used standard punctuation; instead of the highly elliptical telegraphic lines so characteristic of her poems, editors added articles, conjunctions, and prepositions to make them more readable and in line with conventional expectations. In addition, the poems were made more predictable by organizing them into categories such as friendship, nature, love, and death. Not until 1955, when Thomas Johnson published Dickinson's complete works in a form that attempted to be true to her manuscript versions, did readers have the opportunity to see the full range of her style and themes.

Like that of Robert Frost, Dickinson's popular reputation has sometimes relegated her to the role of a New England regionalist who writes quaint uplifting verses that touch the heart. In 1971 that image was mailed first class all over the country by the U.S. Postal Service. In addition to issuing a commemorative stamp featuring a portrait of Dickinson, the postal service affixed the stamp to a first-day-of-issue envelope that included an engraved rose and one of her poems. Here's the poem chosen from among the nearly two thousand she wrote:

If I can stop one Heart from breaking   ca. 1864

If I can stop one Heart from breaking
I shall not live in vain
If I can ease one Life the Aching
or cool one Pain

Or help one fainting Robin
Unto his Nest again
I shall not live in Vain.

This is typical not only of many nineteenth-century popular poems but also of the kind of verse that can be found in contemporary greeting cards. The speaker tells us what we imagine we should think about and makes the point simply with a sentimental image of a "fainting Robin." To point out that robins don't faint or that altruism isn't necessarily the only rule of conduct by which one should live one's life is to make trouble for this poem. Moreover, its use of language is unexceptional; the metaphors used, like that robin, are a bit weary. If this poem were characteristic of Dickinson's poetry, the U.S. Postal Service probably would not have been urged to issue a stamp in her honor, nor would you be reading her poems in this anthology or many others. Here's a poem by Dickinson that is more typical of her writing:

If I shouldn't be alive ca. 1860

If I shouldn't be alive
When the Robins come,
Give the one in Red Cravat,
A Memorial crumb.

If I couldn't thank you,
Being fast asleep,
You will know I'm trying
With my Granite lip!

     This poem is more representative of Dickinson's sensibilities and techniques. Although the first stanza sets up a rather mild concern that the speaker might not survive the winter (a not uncommon fear for those who fell prey to pneumonia, for example, during Dickinson's time), the concern can't be taken too seriously — a gentle humor lightens the poem when we realize that all robins have red cravats and are therefore the speaker's favorite. Furthermore, the euphemism that describes the speaker "Being fast asleep" in line 6 makes death seem not so threatening after all. But the sentimental expectations of the first six lines — lines that could have been written by any number of popular nineteenth-century writers — are dashed by the penultimate word of the last line. *Granite* is the perfect word here because it forces us to reread the poem and to recognize that it's not about feeding robins or offering a cosmetic treatment of death; rather, it's a bone-chilling description of a corpse's lip that evokes the cold, hard texture and grayish color of tombstones. These lips will never say "thank you" or anything else.

     Instead of the predictable rhymes and sentiments of "If I can stop one Heart from breaking," this poem is unnervingly precise in its use of language and tidily points out how much emphasis Dickinson places on an individual word. Her use of near rhyme with "asleep" and "lip" brilliantly mocks a euphemistic approach to death by its jarring dissonance. This is a better poem, not because it's grim or about death, but because it demonstrates Dickinson's skillful use of language to produce a shocking irony.

     Dickinson found irony, ambiguity, and paradox lurking in the simplest and commonest experiences. The materials and subject matter of her poetry are quite conventional. Her poems are filled with robins, bees, winter light, household items, and domestic duties. These materials represent the range of what she experienced in and around her father's house. She used them because they constituted so much of her life and, more important, because she found meanings latent in them. Though her world was simple, it was also complex in its beauties and its terrors. Her lyric poems capture impressions of particular moments, scenes, or moods, and she characteristically focuses on topics such as nature, love, immortality, death, faith, doubt, pain, and the self.

Though her materials were conventional, her treatment of them was innovative because she was willing to break whatever poetic conventions stood in the way of the intensity of her thought and images. Her conciseness, brevity, and wit are tightly packed. Typically she offers her observations via one or two images that reveal her thought in a powerful manner. She once characterized her literary art by writing, "My business is circumference." Her method is to reveal the inadequacy of declarative statements by evoking qualifications and questions with images that complicate firm assertions and affirmations. In one of her poems she describes her strategies this way: "Tell all the Truth but tell it slant — / Success in Circuit lies" (p. 571). This might well stand as a working definition of Dickinson's aesthetics.

Dickinson's poetry is challenging because it is radical and original in its rejection of most traditional nineteenth-century themes and techniques. Her poems require active engagement from the reader because she seems to leave out so much with her elliptical style and remarkable contracting metaphors. But these apparent gaps are filled with meaning if we are sensitive to her use of devices such as personification, allusion, symbolism, and startling syntax and grammar. Because her use of dashes is sometimes puzzling, it helps to read her poems aloud to hear how carefully the words are arranged. What might initially seem intimidating on a silent page can surprise the reader with meaning when heard. It's also worth keeping in mind that Dickinson was not always consistent in her views and that they can change from poem to poem, depending on how she felt at a given moment. For example, her definition of religious belief in "'Faith' is a fine invention" (p. 580) reflects an ironically detached wariness in contrast to the faith embraced in "I never saw a Moor —" (p. 581). Dickinson was less interested in absolute answers to questions than she was in examining and exploring their "circumference."

Because Dickinson's poems are all relatively brief (none is longer than fifty lines), they invite browsing and sampling, but perhaps a useful way into their highly metaphoric and witty world is this "how to" poem that reads almost like a recipe:

To make a prairie it takes a clover and one bee *(date unknown)*

To make a prairie it takes a clover and one bee,
One clover, and a bee,
And revery.
The revery alone will do,
If bees are few.

This quiet but infinite claim for a writer's imagination brings together the range of ingredients in Dickinson's world of domestic and ordinary natural details. Not surprisingly, she deletes rather than adds to the recipe, because the one essential ingredient is the writer's creative imagination. *Bon appétit.*

Success is counted sweetest   ca. 1859

Success is counted sweetest
By those who ne'er succeed.
To comprehend a nectar
Requires sorest need.

Not one of all the purple Host   5
Who took the Flag today
Can tell the definition
So clear of Victory

As he defeated — dying —
On whose forbidden ear   10
The distant strains of triumph
Burst agonized and clear!

Considerations for Critical Thinking and Writing

1. **First response.** How is *success* defined in this poem? To what extent does that definition agree with your own understanding of the word?
2. What do you think is meant by the use of *comprehend* in line 3? How can a nectar be comprehended?
3. Why do the defeated understand victory better than the victorious?
4. Discuss the effect of the poem's final line.

Connection to Another Selection

1. In an essay compare the themes of this poem with those of John Keats's "Ode on a Grecian Urn" (p. 531).

Water, is taught by thirst   ca. 1859

Water, is taught by thirst.
Land — by the Oceans passed.
Transport — by throe —
Peace — by its battles told —

Love, by Memorial Mold —
Birds, by the Snow.

CONSIDERATIONS FOR CRITICAL THINKING AND WRITING

1. FIRST RESPONSE. Which image in the poem do you find most powerful? Explain why.

2. How is the paradox of each line of the poem resolved? How is the first word of each line "taught" by the phrase that follows it?

3. CREATIVE RESPONSE. Try your hand at writing similar lines in which something is "taught."

CONNECTIONS TO OTHER SELECTIONS

1. What does this poem have in common with "Success is counted sweetest" (p. 561)? Which poem do you think is more effective? Explain why.

2. How is the crucial point of this poem related to "I like a look of Agony" (p. 565)?

Safe in their Alabaster Chambers —   1861 VERSION

Safe in their Alabaster Chambers —
Untouched by Morning —
And untouched by Noon —
Lie the meek members of the Resurrection —
Rafter of Satin — and Roof of Stone!   5

Grand go the Years — in the Crescent — above them —
Worlds scoop their arcs —
And Firmaments — row —
Diadems — drop — and Doges° — surrender —
Soundless as dots — on a Disc of Snow —   10

⁹ *Doges:* Chief magistrates of Venice from the twelfth to the sixteenth centuries.

CONSIDERATIONS FOR CRITICAL THINKING AND WRITING

1. Describe the different kinds of images used in the two second stanzas. How do those images affect the tones and meanings of those stanzas?

CONNECTION TO ANOTHER SELECTIONS

1. Compare the theme of this poem with the theme of Robert Frost's "Design" (p. 394).

Portraits are to daily faces   ca. 1860

Portraits are to daily faces
As an Evening West,
To a fine, pedantic sunshine —
In a satin Vest!

CONSIDERATIONS FOR CRITICAL THINKING AND WRITING

1. **FIRST RESPONSE.** Dickinson once described her literary art this way: "My business is circumference." Does this poem fit her characterization of her poetry?

2. How is the basic strategy of this poem similar to the following statement: "Doorknob is to door as button is to sweater"?

3. Identify the four metonymies in the poem. Pay close attention to their connotative meanings.

4. If you don't know the meaning of *pedantic* (line 3), look it up in a dictionary. How does its meaning affect your reading of *fine* (line 3)?

CONNECTIONS TO OTHER SELECTIONS

1. Compare Dickinson's view of poetry in this poem with Robert Francis's perspective in "Catch" (p. 372). What important similarities and differences do you find?

2. Write an essay describing Robert Frost's strategy in "Mending Wall" (p. 659) as the "business of circumference."

3. Compare the use of the word *fine* here with its use in "'Faith' is a fine invention" (p. 580).

Some keep the Sabbath going to Church —   ca. 1860

Some keep the Sabbath going to Church —
I keep it, staying at Home —
With a Bobolink for a Chorister —
And an Orchard, for a Dome —

Some keep the Sabbath in Surplice°   *holy robes*   5
I just wear my Wings —
And instead of tolling the Bell, for Church,
Our little Sexton — sings.

God preaches, a noted Clergyman —
And the sermon is never long,   10

So instead of getting to Heaven, at last —
I'm going, all along.

CONSIDERATIONS FOR CRITICAL THINKING AND WRITING

1. FIRST RESPONSE. What is the effect of referring to "Some" people (line 1)?
2. Characterize the speaker's tone.
3. How does the speaker distinguish himself or herself from those who go to church?
4. How might "Surplice" (line 5) be read as a pun?
5. According to the speaker, how should the Sabbath be observed?

CONNECTION TO ANOTHER SELECTION

1. Write an essay that discusses nature in this poem and in Walt Whitman's "When I Heard the Learn'd Astronomer" (p. 674).

I taste a liquor never brewed —   1861

I taste a liquor never brewed —
From Tankards scooped in Pearl —
Not all the Vats upon the Rhine
Yield such an Alcohol!

Inebriate of Air — am I —   5
And Debauchee of Dew —
Reeling — thro endless summer days —
From inns of Molten Blue —

When "Landlords" turn the drunken Bee
Out of the Foxglove's door —   10
When Butterflies — renounce their "drams" —
I shall but drink the more!

Till Seraphs° swing their snowy Hats —   *angels*
And Saints — to windows run —
To see the little Tippler   15
Leaning against the — Sun —

CONSIDERATIONS FOR CRITICAL THINKING AND WRITING

1. FIRST RESPONSE. What is the poem's central metaphor? How is it developed in each stanza?
2. Which images suggest the causes of the speaker's intoxication?
3. Characterize the speaker's relationship to nature.

CONNECTION TO ANOTHER SELECTION

1. In an essay compare this speaker's relationship with nature to that of "A narrow Fellow in the Grass" (p. 2).

"Heaven" — is what I cannot reach!   ca. 1861

"Heaven" — is what I cannot reach!
The Apple on the Tree —
Provided it do hopeless — hang —
That — "Heaven" is — to Me!

The Color, on the Cruising Cloud —   5
The interdicted Land —
Behind the Hill — the House behind —
There — Paradise — is found!

Her teasing Purples — Afternoons —
The credulous — decoy —   10
Enamored — of the Conjuror —
That spurned us — Yesterday!

CONSIDERATIONS FOR CRITICAL THINKING AND WRITING

1. FIRST RESPONSE. How does the speaker define *heaven*? How does that definition compare with conventional views of heaven?
2. Look up the myth of Tantalus and explain the allusion in line 3.
3. Given the speaker's definition of *heaven,* how do you think he or she would describe hell?

CONNECTIONS TO OTHER SELECTIONS

1. Write an essay that discusses desire in this poem and in "Water, is taught by thirst" (p. 561).
2. Discuss the speakers' attitudes toward pleasure and nature in this poem and in Reginald Shepherd's "Self-Portrait Surviving Spring" (p. 541).

I like a look of Agony   ca. 1861

I like a look of Agony,
Because I know it's true —
Men do not sham Convulsion,
Nor simulate, a Throe —

The Eyes glaze once — and that is Death —
Impossible to feign
The Beads upon the Forehead
By homely Anguish strung.

CONSIDERATIONS FOR CRITICAL THINKING AND WRITING

1. **FIRST RESPONSE.** Why does the speaker "like a look of Agony"? How do you respond to her appreciation of "Convulsion" (line 3)?

2. Discuss the image of "The Eyes glaze once —" (line 5). Why is that a particularly effective metaphor for death?

3. Characterize the speaker. One critic described the voice in this poem as "almost a hysterical shriek." Explain why you agree or disagree.

CONNECTION TO ANOTHER SELECTION

1. Write an essay on Dickinson's attitudes toward pain and deprivation, using this poem and "'Heaven' — is what I cannot reach!" (p. 565).

Wild Nights — Wild Nights!   ca. 1861

Wild Nights — Wild Nights!
Were I with thee
Wild Nights should be
Our luxury!

Futile — the Winds —   5
To a Heart in port —
Done with the Compass —
Done with the Chart!

Rowing in Eden —
Ah, the Sea!   10
Might I but moor — Tonight —
In Thee!

CONSIDERATIONS FOR CRITICAL THINKING AND WRITING

1. **FIRST RESPONSE.** Thomas Wentworth Higginson, Dickinson's mentor, once said he was afraid that some "malignant" readers might "read into [a poem like this] more than that virgin recluse ever dreamed of putting there." What do you think?

2. Look up the meaning of *luxury* in a dictionary. Why does this word work especially well here?

3. Given the imagery of the final stanza, do you think the speaker is a man or a woman? Explain why.

4. **CRITICAL STRATEGIES.** Read the section on psychological strategies (pp. 1074–76) in Chapter 30, "Critical Strategies for Reading." What do you think this poem reveals about the author's personal psychology?

CONNECTION TO ANOTHER SELECTION

1. Write an essay that compares the voice, figures of speech, and theme of this poem with those of Kwame Dawes's "The Habits of Love" (p. 427).

The Soul selects her own Society — ca. 1862

The Soul selects her own Society —
Then — shuts the Door —
To her divine Majority —
Present no more —

Unmoved — she notes the Chariots — pausing —   5
At her low Gate —
Unmoved — an Emperor be kneeling
Upon her Mat —

I've known her — from an ample nation —
Choose One —
Then — close the Valves of her attention —   10
Like Stone —

CONSIDERATIONS FOR CRITICAL THINKING AND WRITING

1. **FIRST RESPONSE.** Characterize the speaker. Is she self-reliant and self-sufficient? Cold? Angry?

2. Why do you suppose the "Soul" in this poem is female? Would it make any difference if it were male?

3. Discuss the effect of the images in the final two lines. Pay particular attention to the meanings of *Valves* in line 11.

Much Madness is divinest Sense — ca. 1862

Much Madness is divinest Sense —
To a discerning Eye —
Much Sense — the starkest Madness —

'Tis the Majority
In this, as All, prevail —
Assent — and you are sane —
Demur — you're straightway dangerous —
And handled with a Chain —

CONSIDERATIONS FOR CRITICAL THINKING AND WRITING

1. FIRST RESPONSE. Thomas Wentworth Higginson's wife once referred to Dickinson as the "partially cracked poetess of Amherst." Assuming that Dickinson had some idea of how she was regarded by "the Majority" (line 4), how might this poem be seen as an insight into her life?

2. Discuss the conflict between the individual and society in this poem. Which images are used to describe each? How do these images affect your attitudes about them?

3. Comment on the effectiveness of the poem's final line.

CONNECTION TO ANOTHER SELECTION

1. Discuss the theme of self-reliance in this poem and in "The Soul selects her own Society —" (p. 567).

I dwell in Possibility —   ca. 1862

I dwell in Possibility —
A fairer House than Prose —
More numerous of Windows —
Superior — for Doors —

Of Chambers as the Cedars —   5
Impregnable of Eye —
And for an Everlasting Roof
The Gambrels° of the Sky —   *angled roofs*

Of Visitors — the fairest —
For Occupation — This —   10
The spreading wide my narrow Hands
To gather Paradise —

CONSIDERATIONS FOR CRITICAL THINKING AND WRITING

1. FIRST RESPONSE. What distinction is made between poetry and prose in this poem? Explain why you agree or disagree with the speaker's distinctions.

2. What is the poem's central metaphor in the second and third stanzas?

3. How does the use of metaphor in this poem become a means for the speaker to envision and create a world beyond the circumstances of his or her actual life?

CONNECTION TO ANOTHER SELECTION

1. How can the speaker's sense of expansiveness in this poem be reconciled with the speaker's insistence on contraction in "The Soul selects her own Society—" (p. 567)? Are these poems contradictory? Explain why or why not.

I heard a Fly buzz — when I died — ca. 1862

I heard a Fly buzz — when I died —
The Stillness in the Room
Was like the Stillness in the Air —
Between the Heaves of Storm —

The Eyes around — had wrung them dry —   5
And Breaths were gathering firm
For that last Onset — when the King
Be witnessed — in the Room —

I willed my Keepsakes — Signed away
What portion of me be
Assignable — and then it was   10
There interposed a Fly —

With Blue — uncertain stumbling Buzz —
Between the light — and me —
And then the Windows failed — and then
I could not see to see —   15

CONSIDERATIONS FOR CRITICAL THINKING AND WRITING

1. **FIRST RESPONSE.** What was expected to happen "when the King" was "witnessed" (lines 7–8)? What happened instead?

2. Why do you think Dickinson chooses a fly rather than perhaps a bee or gnat?

3. What is the effect of the last line? Why not end the poem with "I could not see" instead of the additional "to see"?

4. Discuss the sounds in the poem. Are there any instances of onomatopoeia?

Because I could not stop for Death —   ca. 1863

Because I could not stop for Death —
He kindly stopped for me —
The Carriage held but just Ourselves —
And Immortality.

We slowly drove — He knew no haste   5
And I had put away
My labor and my leisure too,
For His Civility —

We passed the School, where Children strove
At Recess — in the Ring —   10
We passed the Fields of Gazing Grain —
We passed the Setting Sun —

Or rather — He passed Us —
The Dews drew quivering and chill —
For only Gossamer, my Gown —   15
My Tippet° — only Tulle —   *shawl*

We paused before a House that seemed
A Swelling of the Ground —
The Roof was scarcely visible —
The Cornice — in the Ground —   20

Since then — 'tis Centuries — and yet
Feels shorter than the Day
I first surmised the Horses' Heads
Were toward Eternity —

CONSIDERATIONS FOR CRITICAL THINKING AND WRITING

1. **FIRST RESPONSE.** Why couldn't the speaker "stop for Death"?

2. How is death personified in this poem? How does the speaker respond to him? Why are they accompanied by Immortality?

3. What is the significance of the things they "passed" in the third stanza?

4. What is the "House" in lines 17–20?

5. Discuss the rhythm of the lines. How, for example, is the rhythm of line 14 related to its meaning?

CONNECTIONS TO OTHER SELECTIONS

1. Compare the tone of this poem with that of Dickinson's "Apparently with no surprise" (p. 581).

2. Write an essay comparing Dickinson's view of death in this poem and in "If I shouldn't be alive" (p. 559). Which poem is more powerful for you? Explain why.

Tell all the Truth but tell it slant — ca. 1868

Tell all the Truth but tell it slant —
Success in Circuit lies
Too bright for our infirm Delight
The Truth's superb surprise

As Lightning to the Children eased
With explanation kind
The Truth must dazzle gradually
Or every man be blind —

CONSIDERATIONS FOR CRITICAL THINKING AND WRITING

1. FIRST RESPONSE. What do you think the first line means? Why should truth be told "slant" and circuitously?

2. How does the second stanza explain the first?

3. How is this poem an example of its own theme?

CONNECTIONS TO OTHER SELECTIONS

1. How does the first stanza of "I know that He exists" (p. 581) suggest an idea similar to this poem's? Why do you think the last eight lines of the former aren't similar in theme to this poem?

2. Write an essay on Dickinson's attitudes about the purpose and strategies of poetry by considering this poem as well as "Portraits are to daily faces" (p. 563).

Perspectives on Emily Dickinson

EMILY DICKINSON

A Description of Herself 1862

Mr Higginson,

Your kindness claimed earlier gratitude — but I was ill — and write today, from my pillow.

Thank you for the surgery — it was not so painful as I supposed. I bring you others° — as you ask — though they might not differ —

While my thought is undressed — I can make the distinction, but when I put them in the Gown — they look alike, and numb.

You asked how old I was? I made no verse — but one or two° — until this winter — Sir —

I had a terror — since September — I could tell to none — and so I sing, as the Boy does by the Burying Ground — because I am afraid — You inquire my Books — For Poets — I have Keats — and Mr and Mrs Browning. For Prose — Mr Ruskin — Sir Thomas Browne — and the Revelations. I went to school — but in your manner of the phrase — had no education. When a little Girl, I had a friend, who taught me Immortality — but venturing too near, himself — he never returned — Soon after, my Tutor, died — and for several years, my Lexicon — was my only companion — Then I found one more — but he was not contented I be his scholar — so he left the Land.

You ask of my Companions Hills — Sir — and the Sundown — and a Dog — large as myself, that my Father bought me — They are better than Beings — because they know — but do not tell — and the noise in the Pool, at Noon — excels my Piano. I have a Brother and Sister — My Mother does not care for thought — and Father, too busy with his Briefs — to notice what we do — He buys me many Books — but begs me not to read them — because he fears they joggle the Mind. They are religious — except me — and address an Eclipse, every morning — whom they call their "Father." But I fear my story fatigues you — I would like to learn — Could you tell me how to grow — or is it unconveyed — like Melody — or Witchcraft?

From a letter to Thomas Wentworth Higginson, April 25, 1862

others: Dickinson had sent poems to Higginson for his opinions and enclosed more with this letter. *one or two:* Actually she had written almost 300 poems.

CONSIDERATIONS FOR CRITICAL THINKING AND WRITING

1. What impression does this letter give you of Dickinson?
2. What kinds of thoughts are there in the foreground of her thinking?
3. To what extent is the style of her letter writing like that of her poetry?

THOMAS WENTWORTH HIGGINSON (1823–1911)

On Meeting Dickinson for the First Time 1870

A large county lawyer's house, brown brick, with great trees & a garden — I sent up my card. A parlor dark & cool & stiffish, a few books & engravings & an open piano. . . .

A step like a pattering child's in entry & in glided a little plain woman with two smooth bands of reddish hair & a face a little like Belle Dove's; not plainer — with no good feature — in a very plain & exquisitely clean white pique & a blue net worsted shawl. She came to me with two day lilies which she put in a sort of childlike way into my hand & said "These are my intro-duction" in a soft frightened breathless childlike voice — & added under her breath Forgive me if I am frightened; I never see strangers & hardly know what I say — but she talked soon & thenceforward continuously — & deferentially — sometimes stopping to ask me to talk instead of her — but readily recommencing . . . thoroughly ingenuous & simple . . . & saying many things which you would have thought foolish & I wise — & some things you wd. hv. liked. I add a few over the page. . . .

> "Women talk; men are silent; that is why I dread women."
> "My father only reads on Sunday — he reads *lonely* & *rigorous* books."
> "If I read a book [and] it makes my whole body so cold no fire ever can warm me I know *that* is poetry. If I feel physically as if the top of my head were taken off, I know *that* is poetry. These are the only ways I know it. Is there any other way."
> "How do most people live without any thoughts. There are many people in the world (you must have noticed them in the street) How do they live. How do they get strength to put on their clothes in the morning"
> "When I lost the use of my Eyes it was a comfort to think there were so few real *books* that I could easily find some one to read me all of them"
> "Truth is such a *rare* thing it is delightful to tell it."
> "I find ecstasy in living — the mere sense of living is joy enough"

I asked if she never felt want of employment, never going off the place & never seeing any visitor "I never thought of conceiving that I could ever have the slightest approach to such a want in all future time" (& added) "I feel that I have not expressed myself strongly enough."

From a letter to his wife, August 16, 1870

Considerations for Critical Thinking and Writing

1. How old is Dickinson when Higginson meets her? Does this description seem commensurate with her age? Explain why or why not.

2. Choose one of the quotations from Dickinson that Higginson includes and write an essay about what it reveals about her.

Mabel Loomis Todd (1856–1932)

The Character *of Amherst*   1881

I must tell you about the *character* of Amherst. It is a lady whom the people call the *Myth.* She is a sister of Mr. Dickinson, & seems to be the climax of all the family oddity. She has not been outside of her own house in fifteen years, except once to see a new church, when she crept out at night, & viewed it by moonlight. No one who calls upon her mother & sister ever see her, but she allows little children once in a great while, & one at a time, to come in, when she gives them cake or candy, or some nicety, for she is very fond of little ones. But more often she lets down the sweetmeat by a string, out of a window, to them. She dresses wholly in white, & her mind is said to be perfectly wonderful. She writes finely, but no one *ever* sees her. Her sister, who was at Mrs. Dickinson's party, invited me to come & sing to her mother sometime. . . . People tell me the *myth* will hear every note — she will be near, but unseen. . . . Isn't that like a book? So interesting.

From a letter to her parents, November 6, 1881

Considerations for Critical Thinking and Writing

1. Todd, who in the 1890s would edit Dickinson's poems and letters, had known her for only two months when she wrote this letter. How does Todd characterize Dickinson?

2. Does this description seem positive or negative to you? Explain your answer.

3. A few of Dickinson's poems, such as "Much Madness is divinest Sense —" (p. 567), suggest that she was aware of this perception of her. Refer to her poems in discussing Dickinson's response to this perception.

Richard Wilbur   (1921–2017)

On Dickinson's Sense of Privation   1960

What did Emily Dickinson do, as a poet, with her sense of privation? One thing she quite often did was to pose as the laureate and attorney of the empty-handed, and question God about the economy of His creation. Why, she asked, is a fatherly God so sparing of His presence? Why is there never a sign that prayers are heard? Why does Nature tell us no comforting news of its Maker? Why do some receive a whole loaf, while others must starve on a crumb? Where is the benevolence in shipwreck and earthquake? By asking such questions as these, she turned complaint into critique, and used her own sufferings as experiential evidence about the nature of the deity. The God who emerges from these poems is a God who does not answer, an unrevealed God whom one cannot confidently approach through Nature or through doctrine.

But there was another way in which Emily Dickinson dealt with her sentiment of lack — another emotional strategy which was both more frequent and more fruitful. I refer to her repeated assertion of the paradox that privation is more plentiful than plenty; that to renounce is to possess the more; that "The Banquet of abstemiousness / Defaces that of wine." We all know how the poet illustrated this ascetic paradox in her behavior — how in her latter years she chose to live in relative retirement, keeping the world, even in its dearest aspects, at a physical remove. She would write her friends, telling them how she missed them, then flee upstairs when they came to see her; afterward, she might send a note of apology, offering the odd explanation that "We shun because we prize." Any reader of Dickinson biographies can furnish other examples, dramatic or homely, of this prizing and shunning, this yearning and renouncing: in my own mind's eye is a picture of Emily Dickinson watching a gay circus caravan from the distance of her chamber window.

> From "Sumptuous Destitution" in *Emily Dickinson: Three Views,*
> by Richard Wilbur, Louise Bogan, and Archibald MacLeish

CONSIDERATIONS FOR CRITICAL THINKING AND WRITING

1. Which poems by Dickinson reprinted in this anthology suggest that she was "the laureate and attorney of the empty-handed"?

2. Which poems suggest that "privation is more plentiful than plenty"?

3. Of these two types of poems, which do you prefer? Write an essay that explains your preference.

SANDRA M. GILBERT (B. 1936) AND SUSAN GUBAR (B. 1944)
On Dickinson's White Dress   1979

Today a dress that the Amherst Historical Society assures us is *the* white dress Dickinson wore — or at least one of her "Uniforms of Snow" — hangs in a drycleaner's plastic bag in the closet of the Dickinson homestead. Perfectly preserved, beautifully flounced and tucked, it is larger than most readers would have expected this self-consciously small poet's dress to be, and thus reminds visiting scholars of the enduring enigma of Dickinson's central metaphor, even while it draws gasps from more practical visitors, who reflect with awe upon the difficulties of maintaining such a costume. But what exactly did the literal and figurative whiteness of this costume represent? What rewards did it offer that would cause an intelligent woman to overlook those practical difficulties? Comparing Dickinson's obsession with whiteness to [Herman] Melville's, William R. Sherwood suggests that "it reflected in her case the Christian mystery and not a Christian enigma . . . a decision to announce . . . the assumption of a worldly death that paradoxically involved regeneration." This, he adds, her gown — "a typically slant demonstration of truth" — should have revealed "to anyone with the wit to catch on."[1]

---

[1] *Circumference and Circumstance: Stages in the Mind and Art of Emily Dickinson* (New York: Columbia UP, 1968), 152, 231.

We might reasonably wonder, however, if Dickinson herself consciously intended her wardrobe to convey any one message. The range of associations her white poems imply suggests, on the contrary, that for her, as for Melville, white is the ultimate symbol of enigma, paradox, and irony, "not so much a color as the visible absence of color, and at the same time the concrete of all colors." Melville's question [in *Moby-Dick*] might, therefore, also be hers: "is it for these reasons that there is such a dumb blankness, full of meaning, in a wide landscape of snows — a colorless, all-color of atheism from which we shrink?" And his concluding speculation might be hers too, his remark "that the mystical cosmetic which produces every one of [Nature's] hues, the great principle of light, for ever remains white or colorless in itself, and if operating without medium upon matter, would touch all objects . . . with its own blank tinge." For white, in Dickinson's poetry, frequently represents both the energy (the white heat) of Romantic creativity, and the loneliness (the polar cold) of the renunciation or tribulation Romantic creativity may demand, both the white radiance of eternity — or Revelation — and the white terror of a shroud.

From *The Madwoman in the Attic: The Woman Writer
and the Nineteenth-Century Literary Imagination*

Considerations for Critical Thinking and Writing

1. What meanings do Gilbert and Gubar attribute to Dickinson's white dress?

2. Discuss the meaning of the implicit whiteness in "Safe in their Alabaster Chambers —" (p. 562). To what extent does this poem incorporate the meaning of whiteness that Gilbert and Gubar suggest?

3. What other reasons can you think of that might account for Dickinson's wearing only white?

Paula Bennett (b. 1936)

On "I heard a Fly buzz — when I died —"   1990

Dickinson's rage against death, a rage that led her at times to hate both life and death, might have been alleviated, had she been able to gather hard evidence about an afterlife. But, of course, she could not. "The *Bareheaded life* — under the grass —," she wrote to Samuel Bowles in c. 1860, "worries one like a Wasp." If death was the gate to a better life in "the childhood of the kingdom of Heaven," as the sentimentalists — and Christ — claimed, then, perhaps, there was compensation and healing for life's woes. . . . But how do we know? What can we know? In "I heard a Fly buzz — when I died," Dickinson concludes that we do not know much. . . .

Like many people in her period, Dickinson was fascinated by death-bed scenes. How, she asked various correspondents, did this or that person die? In particular, she wanted to know if their deaths revealed any information about the nature of the afterlife. In this poem, however, she imagines her own death-bed scene, and the answer she provides is grim, as grim (and, at the same time, as ironically mocking) as anything she ever wrote.

In the narrowing focus of death, the fly's insignificant buzz, magnified tenfold by the stillness in the room, is all that the speaker hears. This kind of distortion in scale is common. It is one of the "illusions" of perception. But here it is horrifying because it defeats every expectation we have. Death is supposed to be an experience of awe. It is the moment when the soul, departing the body, is taken up by God. Hence the watchers at the bedside wait for the moment when the "King" (whether God or death) "be witnessed" in the room. And hence the speaker assigns away everything but that which she expects God (her soul) or death (her body) to take.

What arrives instead, however, is neither God nor death but a fly, "[w]ith Blue — uncertain — stumbling Buzz," a fly, that is, no more secure, no more sure, than we are. Dickinson had associated flies with death once before in the exquisite lament, "How many times these low feet / staggered." In this poem, they buzz "on the / chamber window," and speckle it with dirt, reminding us that the housewife, who once protected us from such intrusions, will protect us no longer. Their presence is threatening but only in a minor way, "dull" like themselves. They are a background noise we do not have to deal with yet.

In "I heard a Fly buzz," on the other hand, there is only one fly and its buzz is not only foregrounded. Before the poem is over, the buzz takes up the entire field of perception, coming between the speaker and the "light" (of day, of life, of knowledge). It is then that the "Windows" (the eyes that are the windows of the soul as well as, metonymically, the light that passes through the panes of glass) "fail" and the speaker is left in darkness — in death, in ignorance. She cannot "see" to "see" (understand).

Given that the only sure thing we know about "life after death" is that flies — in their adult form and more particularly, as maggots — devour us, the poem is at the very least a grim joke. In projecting her death-bed scene, Dickinson confronts her ignorance and gives back the only answer human knowledge can with any certainty give. While we may hope for an afterlife, no one, not even the dying, can prove it exists.

From *Emily Dickinson: Woman Poet*

Considerations for Critical Thinking and Writing

1. According to Bennett, what is the symbolic value of the fly?

2. Does Bennett leave out any significant elements of the poem in her analysis? Explain why you think she did or did not.

3. Choose a Dickinson poem and write a detailed analysis that attempts to account for all of its major elements.

Martha Nell Smith (b. 1953)

On "Because I could not stop for Death —" 1993

That this poem begins and ends with humanity's ultimate dream of self-importance — Immortality and Eternity — could well be the joke central to its meaning, for Dickinson carefully surrounds the fantasy of living ever after with the dirty facts of life — dusty carriage rides, schoolyards, and farmers' fields. Many may contend that, like the Puritans and metaphysicals before her, Dickinson pulls the sublime down to the ridiculous but unavoidable facts of existence, thus imbues life on earth with its real import. On the other hand, Dickinson may have argued otherwise. Very late in her life, she wrote, "When Jesus tells us about his Father, we distrust him. When he shows us his Home, we turn away, but when he confides to us that he is 'acquainted with Grief,' we listen, for that is also an Acquaintance of our own." Instead of sharing their faith, Dickinson may be showing the community around her, most of whom were singing "When we all get to Heaven what a day of rejoicing that will be," how selfishly selective is their belief in a system that bolsters egocentrism by assuring believers not only that their individual identities will survive death, but also that they are one of the exclusive club of the saved. Waiting for the return of Eden or Paradise, which "is always eligible" and which she "never believed . . . to be a superhuman site," those believers may simply find themselves gathering dust. Surrounded by the faithful, Dickinson struggled with trust and doubt in Christian promises herself, but whether she believed in salvation or even in immortality is endlessly debatable. Readers can select poems and letters and construct compelling arguments to prove that she did or did not. But for every declaration evincing belief, there is one like that to Elizabeth Holland:

> The Fiction of "Santa Claus" always reminds me of the reply to my early question of "Who made the Bible" — "Holy Men moved by the Holy Ghost," and though I have now ceased my investigations, the Solution is insufficient —

What "Because I could not stop for Death —" will not allow is any hard and fast conclusion to be drawn about the matter. Once again . . . by mixing tropes and tones Dickinson underscores the importance of refusing any single-minded response to a subject and implicitly attests to the power in continually opening possibilities by repeatedly posing questions.

From *Comic Power in Emily Dickinson,* by Suzanne Juhasz, Cristanne Miller, and Martha Nell Smith

Considerations for Critical Thinking and Writing

1. In what sense, according to Smith, could a joke be central to the meaning of "Because I could not stop for Death —"(p. 570)?
2. Compare the potential joke in this poem and in "I know that He exists" (p. 581). How is your reading of each poem influenced by considering them together?

3. Read the sample paper on "Religious Faith in Four Poems by Emily Dickinson" (pp. 582–85) and write an analysis of "Because I could not stop for Death —" that supports or refutes the paper's thesis.

Questions for Writing about an Author in Depth

As you read multiple works by the same author, you're likely to be struck by the similarities and differences in those selections. You'll begin to recognize situations, events, characters, issues, perspectives, styles, and strategies — even recurring words or phrases — that provide a kind of signature, making the poems in some way identifiable with that particular writer.

The following questions can help you respond to multiple works by the same author. They should help you listen to how a writer's works can speak to one another and to you. Additional useful questions can be found elsewhere in this book. See Chapter 31, "Writing about Literature."

1. What topics reappear in the writer's work? What seem to be the major concerns of the author?

2. Does the author have a definable worldview that can be discerned from work to work? Is, for example, the writer liberal, conservative, apolitical, or religious?

3. What social values come through in the author's work? Does he or she seem to identify with a particular group or social class?

4. Is there a consistent voice or point of view from work to work? Is it a persona or the author's actual self?

5. How much of the author's own life experiences and historical moment make their way into the works?

6. Does the author experiment with style from work to work, or are the works mostly consistent with one another?

7. Can the author's work be identified with a literary tradition, such as *carpe diem* poetry, that aligns his or her work with that of other writers?

8. What is distinctive about the author's writing? Is the language innovative? Are the themes challenging? Are the voices conventional? Is the tone characteristic?

9. Could you identify another work by the same author without a name being attached to it? What are the distinctive features that allow you to do so?

10. Do any of the writer's works seem *not* to be by that writer? Why?

11. What other writers are most like this author in style and content? Why?

12. Has the writer's work evolved over time? Are there significant changes or developments? Are there new ideas and styles, or do the works remain largely the same?

13. How would you characterize the author's writing habits? Is it possible to anticipate what goes on in different works, or are you surprised by their content or style?

14. Can difficult or ambiguous passages in a work be resolved by referring to a similar passage in another work?

15. What does the writer say about his or her own work? Do you trust the teller or the tale? Which do you think is more reliable?

A SAMPLE IN-DEPTH STUDY

The following paper was written for an assignment that called for an analysis (about 750 words) on any topic that could be traced in three or four poems by Dickinson. The student, Michael Weitz, chose "'Faith' is a fine invention," "I know that He exists," "I never saw a Moor —," and "Apparently with no surprise."

Previous knowledge of a writer's work can set up useful expectations in a reader. In the case of the four Dickinson poems included in this section, religion emerges as a central topic linked to a number of issues, including faith, immortality, skepticism, and the nature of God. The student selected these poems because he noticed Dickinson's intense interest in religious faith owing to the many poems that explore a variety of religious attitudes in her work. He chose these four because they were closely related, but he might have found equally useful clusters of poems about love, nature, domestic life, or writing. What especially intrigued him was some of the information he read about Dickinson's sternly religious father and the orthodox nature of the religious values of her hometown of Amherst, Massachusetts. Because this paper was not a research paper, he did not pursue these issues beyond the level of the general remarks provided in an introduction to her poetry (though he might have). He did, however, use this biographical and historical information as a means of framing his search for poems that were related to one another. In doing so he discovered consistent concerns along with contradictory themes that became the basis of his paper.

"Faith" is a fine invention   ca. 1860

"Faith" is a fine invention
When Gentlemen can *see* —
But *Microscopes* are prudent
In an Emergency.

I know that He exists   ca. 1862

I know that He exists.
Somewhere — in Silence —
He has hid his rare life
From our gross eyes.

'Tis an instant's play.   5
'Tis a fond Ambush —
Just to make Bliss
Earn her own surprise!

But — should the play
Prove piercing earnest —
Should the glee — glaze —   10
In Death's — stiff — stare —

Would not the fun
Look too expensive!
Would not the jest —
Have crawled too far!   15

I never saw a Moor —   ca. 1865

I never saw a Moor —
I never saw the Sea —
Yet know I how the Heather looks
And what a Billow be.

I never spoke with God
Nor visited in Heaven —
Yet certain am I of the spot
As if the Checks were given —

Apparently with no surprise   ca. 1884

Apparently with no surprise
To any happy Flower
The Frost beheads it at its play —
In accidental power —
The blond Assassin passes on —
The Sun proceeds unmoved
To measure off another Day
For an Approving God.

A SAMPLE STUDENT PAPER

Religious Faith in Four Poems by Emily Dickinson

Michael Weitz

Professor Pearl

English 270

5 May 2018

Religious Faith in Four Poems by Emily Dickinson

Throughout much of her poetry, Emily Dickinson wrestles
with complex notions of God, faith, and religious devotion. She
adheres to no consistent view of religion; rather, her poetry reveals
a vision of God and faith that is constantly evolving. Dickinson's
gods range from the strict and powerful Old Testament father to
a loving spiritual guide to an irrational and ridiculous imaginary
figure. Through these varying images of God, Dickinson portrays
contrasting images of the meaning and validity of religious faith.
Her work reveals competing attitudes toward religious devotion as
conventional religious piety struggles with a more cynical perception
of God and religious worship.

Dickinson's "I never saw a Moor—" reveals a vision of
traditional religious sensibilities. Although the speaker readily
admits that "I never spoke with God / Nor visited in Heaven—"
(lines 5-6), her devout faith in a supreme being does not waver.
The poem appears to be a straightforward profession of true faith
stemming from the argument that the proof of God's existence is
the universe's existence. Dickinson's imagery therefore evolves from
the natural to the supernatural, first establishing her convictions
that moors and seas exist, in spite of her lack of personal contact
with either. This leads to the foundation of her religious faith, again
based not on physical experience but on intellectual convictions. The

---

Marginal notes:

Introduction providing overview of faith in Dickinson's work

Thesis analyzing poet's attitudes toward God and religion

Analysis of religious piety in "I never saw a Moor—" supported with textual evidence

Weitz 2

speaker professes that she believes in the existence of Heaven even without conclusive evidence: "Yet certain am I of the spot / As if the Checks were given—" (7-8). But the appearance of such idealistic views of God and faith in "I never saw a Moor—" are transformed in Dickinson's other poems into a much more skeptical vision of the validity of religious piety.

> Contrast between attitudes in "Moor" and other poems

While faith is portrayed as an authentic and deeply important quality in "I never saw a Moor—," Dickinson's "'Faith' is a fine invention" portrays faith as much less essential. Faith is defined in the poem as "a fine invention" (1), suggesting that it is created by man for man and therefore is not a crucial aspect of the natural universe. Thus the strong idealistic faith of "I never saw a Moor—" becomes discredited in the face of scientific rationalism. The speaker compares religious faith with actual microscopes, both of which are meant to enhance one's vision in some way. But "Faith" is useful only "When Gentlemen can *see*—" already (2); "In an Emergency," when one ostensibly cannot see, "*Microscopes* are prudent" (4, 3). Dickinson pits religion against science, suggesting that science, with its tangible evidence and rational attitude, is a more reliable lens through which to view the world. Faith is irreverently reduced to a mere "invention" and one that is ultimately less useful than microscopes or other scientific instruments.

> Analysis of scientific rationalism in "'Faith' is a fine invention" supported with textual evidence

Rational, scientific observations are not the only contributing factor to the portrayal of religious skepticism in Dickinson's poems; nature itself is seen to be incompatible in some ways with conventional religious ideology. In "Apparently with no surprise," the speaker recognizes the inexorable cycle of natural life and death as a morning frost kills a flower. But the tension in this poem stems not from the "happy Flower" (2) struck down by the frost's "accidental power" (4) but from the apparent indifference of the "Approving God" (8) who condones this seemingly cruel and unnecessary death.

> Analysis of God and nature in "Apparently with no surprise" supported with textual evidence

God is seen as remote and uncompromising, and it is this perceived distance between the speaker and God that reveals the increasing absurdity of traditional religious faith. The speaker understands that praying to God or believing in religion cannot change the course of nature, and as a result feels so helplessly distanced from God that religious faith becomes virtually meaningless.

Dickinson's religious skepticism becomes even more explicit in "I know that He exists," in which the speaker attempts to understand the connection between seeing God and facing death. In this poem Dickinson characterizes God as a remote and mysterious figure; the speaker mockingly asserts, "I know that He exists" (1), even though "He has hid his rare life / From our gross eyes" (3-4). The skepticism toward religious faith revealed in this poem stems from the speaker's recognition of the paradoxical quest that people undertake to know and to see God. A successful attempt to see God, to win the game of hide-and-seek that He apparently is orchestrating, results inevitably in death. With this recognition the speaker comes to view religion as an absurd and reckless game in which the prize may be "Bliss" (7) but more likely is "Death's— stiff—stare—" (12). For, to see God and to meet one's death as a result certainly suggests that the game of trying to see God (the so-called "fun" of line 13) is much "too expensive" and that religion itself is a "jest" that, like the serpent in Genesis, has "crawled too far" (14-16).

Ultimately, the vision of religious faith that Dickinson describes in her poems is one of suspicion and cynicism. She cannot reconcile the physical world to the spiritual existence that Christian doctrine teaches, and as a result the traditional perception of God becomes ludicrous. "I never saw a Moor—" does attempt to sustain a conventional vision of religious devotion, but Dickinson's poems overall are far more likely to suggest that God is elusive, indifferent,

> Analysis of characteri-zation of God in "I know that He exists" supported with textual evidence

Weitz 4

and often cruel, thus undermining the traditional vision of God as a loving father worthy of devout worship. Thus, not only religious faith but also those who are religiously faithful become targets for Dickinson's irreverent criticism of conventional belief.

> Conclusion providing well-supported final analysis of poet's views on God and faith

Weitz 5

Works Cited

Dickinson, Emily. "Apparently with no surprise." Meyer and Miller, p. 581.

---. "'Faith' is a fine invention." Meyer and Miller, p. 580.

---. "I know that He exists." Meyer and Miller, p. 581.

---. "I never saw a Moor—." Meyer and Miller, p. 581.

Meyer, Michael and D. Quentin Miller, editors. *Literature to Go.* 4th ed., Bedford/St. Martin's, 2020.

Suggested Topics for Longer Papers

1. Irony is abundant in Dickinson's poetry. Choose five poems from this chapter that strike you as especially ironic and discuss her use of irony in each. Taken individually and collectively, what do these poems suggest to you about the poet's sensibilities and her ways of looking at the world?

2. Readers have sometimes noted that Dickinson's poetry does not reflect very much of the social, political, economic, religious, and historical events of her lifetime. Using the poems in this chapter as the basis of your discussion, what can you say about the contexts in which Dickinson wrote? What kind of world do you think she inhabited, and how did she respond to it?

21

A Study of Billy Collins: The Author Reflects on Three Poems

Pako Mera/AP Images.

More interesting to me than what a poem means is how it travels. In the classroom, I like to substitute for the question, "What is the meaning of the poem?" other questions: "How does this poem go?" or "How does this poem travel through itself in search of its own ending?"

— BILLY COLLINS

Billy Collins selected the three poems presented in this chapter and provided commentaries for each so that readers of this anthology might gain a sense of how he, a former poet laureate and teacher, writes and thinks about poetry. In his perspectives on these poems, Collins explores a variety of literary elements ranging from the poems' origins, allusions, images, metaphors, symbols, and tone to his strategies for maintaining his integrity and sensitivity to both language and the reader. Be advised, however, that these discussions do not constitute CliffsNotes to the poems; Collins does not interpret a single one of them for us. Instead of "beating it with a hose / to find out what it really means," as he writes in his poem "Introduction to Poetry" (p. 386), he "hold[s] it up to the light" so that we can see more clearly how each poem works. He explains that the purpose of his discussions is to have students "see how a poem gets written from the opening lines, through the shifts and maneuvers of the body to whatever closure the poem manages to achieve . . . to make the process of writing a poem less mysterious without taking away the mystery that is at the heart of every good poem."

Along with Collins's illuminating and friendly tutorial, the chapter also provides some additional contexts, such as photos from the poet's personal collection; screen shots that offer a look at his unique — and dynamic — Web presence, including a collection of short animated films set to his work; a collection of draft manuscript pages; and an interview with Michael Meyer. Finally, we include an additional five poems by Collins without commentary so that you might use some of the insights from the first part of the chapter to analyze one or more of them.

A BRIEF BIOGRAPHY AND AN INTRODUCTION TO HIS WORK

Born in New York City in 1941, Billy Collins grew up in Queens, the only child of a nurse and an electrician. His father had hoped that he might go to the Harvard Business School, but following his own lights, after graduating from The College of the Holy Cross, he earned a Ph.D. at the University of California, Riverside, in Romantic poetry, and then began a career in the English department at Lehman College, City University of New York, where he taught writing and literature for more than thirty years. He has also tutored writers at the National University of Ireland at Galway, Sarah Lawrence University, Arizona State University, Columbia University, and Rollins College. Along the way, he wrote poems that eventually earned him a reputation among many people as the most popular living poet in America.

Among his numerous collections of poetry are *The Rain in Portugal* (2016), *Voyage* (2014), *Aimless Love* (2013), *Horoscopes for the Dead* (2011), *Ballistics* (2008), *The Trouble with Poetry* (2005), *Nine Horses* (2002), *Sailing Alone Around the Room* (2001), *Picnic, Lightning* (1998), *The Art of Drowning* (1995), *Questions About Angels* (1991), and *The Apple That Astonished Paris* (1988). Collins also edited two anthologies of contemporary poetry designed to entice high school students: *Poetry 180: A Turning Back to Poetry* (2003) and *180 More: Extraordinary Poems for Every Day* (2005). His many honors include fellowships from the New York Foundation for the Arts, the National Endowment for the Arts, and the Guggenheim Foundation. *Poetry* magazine has awarded him the Oscar Blumenthal Prize, the Bess Hokin Prize, the Frederick Bock Prize, and the Levinson Prize.

Collins characterizes himself as someone who was once a professor who wrote poems but who is now a poet who occasionally teaches. This transformation was hard earned because he didn't publish his first complete book of poems until he was in his early forties, with no expectation that twenty years later he would be named United States poet laureate (a gift

Billy Collins on his first day as a student at St. Joan of Arc School, Jackson Heights, New York, 1948.
Reprinted with permission by Chris Calhoun Agency, © Billy Collins.

of hope to writers everywhere). Just as writing poetry has been good for Billy Collins, he has been good for poetry. Both their reputations have risen simultaneously owing to his appeal to audiences that pack high school auditoriums, college halls, and public theaters all over the country. His many popular readings — including broadcasts on National Public Radio — have helped to make him a best-selling poet, a phrase that is ordinarily an oxymoron in America.

Billy Collins on his first day at The College of the Holy Cross, 1959.
Reprinted with permission by Chris Calhoun Agency, © Billy Collins.

Unlike many poetry readings, Collins's are attended by readers and fans who come to whoop, holler, and cheer after nearly every poem, as well as to laugh out loud. His audiences are clearly relieved to be in the presence of a poet who speaks to (not down to) them without a trace of pretension, superiority, or presumption. His work is welcoming and readable because he weaves observations about the commonplace materials of our lives — the notes we write in the margins of our books, the food we eat, the way we

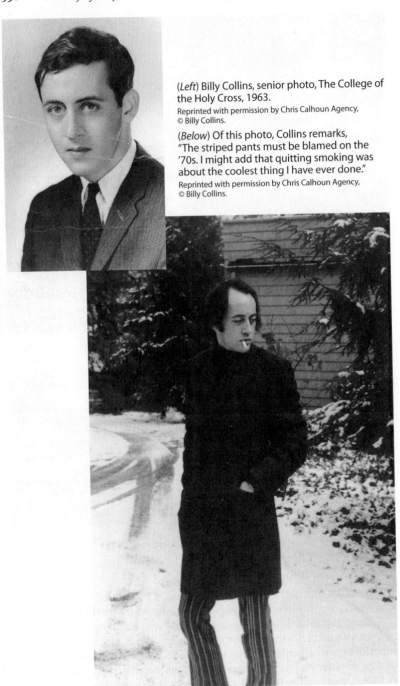

(*Left*) Billy Collins, senior photo, The College of the Holy Cross, 1963.
Reprinted with permission by Chris Calhoun Agency, © Billy Collins.

(*Below*) Of this photo, Collins remarks, "The striped pants must be blamed on the '70s. I might add that quitting smoking was about the coolest thing I have ever done."
Reprinted with permission by Chris Calhoun Agency, © Billy Collins.

(*Above*) The poet with his dog, Luke. Scarsdale, New York, 1970s.

Reprinted with permission by Chris Calhoun Agency, © Billy Collins.

(*Left*) Billy Collins, in his office at Lehman College, 1984.

Reprinted with permission by Chris Calhoun Agency, © Billy Collins.

speak, even the way we think of death — into startling, evocative insights that open our eyes wider than they were before.

To understand Collins's attraction to audiences is to better understand his appeal on the page. He wins the affection of audiences with his warmth and genial charm, an affability that makes him appear unreserved and approachable but never intrusive or over-the-top. He is a quieter, suburban version of Walt Whitman — with a dash of Emily Dickinson's reserve. He gives just enough and lets the poems do the talking so that he remains as mysteriously appealing as his poems. His persona is well crafted and serves to engage readers in the world of his art rather than in his personal life. In a parallel manner, he has often described the openings of his poems as "hospitable" — an invitation to the reader to move further into the poem without having to worry about getting lost in the kind of self-referential obscurity and opacity that sometimes characterize modern poetry.

Perhaps not surprisingly, some critics and fellow poets have objected that Collins's poems may sometimes bear up to little more than the pleasures of one reading. Collins, however, believes immediate pleasure can be a primary motivation for reading poetry, and he argues that a poem using simple language should not be considered simpleminded. In his work the ordinary, the everyday, and the familiar often become curious, unusual, and surprising the more closely the poems are read. In interviews, he has compared a first reading of his poems to a reading of the large *E* at the top of an eye chart in an optometrist's office. What starts out clear and unambiguous gradually becomes more complicated and demanding as we squint to make our way to the end. That big *E* — it might be read as "enter" — welcomes us in and gives us the confidence to enjoy the experience, but it doesn't mean that there aren't challenges ahead. The casual, "easy" read frequently becomes a thought-provoking compound of humor, irony, and unconventional wisdom. Humor is such an essential part of Collins's work that in 2004 he was the first recipient of the Poetry Foundation's Mark Twain Award for Humor in Poetry. Given this remarkable trifecta of humor, popularity, and book sales, it is hardly to be unexpected that Collins gives some of his colleagues — as Mark Twain might have put it — the "fantods," but his audiences and readers eagerly anticipate whatever poetic pleasures he will offer them next. In any case, Whitman made the point more than 150 years ago in his preface to *Leaves of Grass*: "The proof of a poet is that his country absorbs him as affectionately as he has absorbed it."

BILLY COLLINS

"How Do Poems Travel?"   2008

Asking a poet to examine his or her own work is a bit like trying to get a puppy interested in looking in a mirror. Parakeets take an interest in their own reflections but not puppies, who are too busy smelling everything and tumbling over themselves to have time for self-regard. Maybe the difficulty is that most imaginative poems issue largely from the intuitive right side of the brain, whereas literary criticism draws on the brain's more rational, analytic left side. So, writing about your own writing involves getting up, moving from one room of the brain to another, and taking all the furniture with you. When asked about the source of his work, one contemporary poet remarked that if he knew where his poems came from, he would go there and never come back. What he was implying is that much of what goes on in the creative moment takes place on a stealthy level beneath the writer's conscious awareness. If creative work did not offer access to this somewhat mysterious, less than rational region, we would all be writing annual reports or law briefs, not stories, plays, and poems.

Just because you don't know what you are doing doesn't mean you are not doing it; so let me say what I do know about the writing process. While writing a poem, I am also listening to it. As the poem gets underway, I am pushing it forward — after all, I am the one holding the pencil — but I am also ready to be pulled in the direction that the poem seems to want to go. I am willfully writing the poem, but I am also submitting to the poem's will. Emerson once compared writing poetry to ice-skating. I think he meant that both the skater on a frozen pond and the poet on the page might end up going places they didn't intend to go. And Mario Andretti, the Grand Prix driver, once remarked that "If you think everything is under control, you're just not driving fast enough."

Total control over any artistic material eliminates the possibility of surprise. I would not bother to start a poem if I already knew how it was going to end. I try to "maintain the benefits of my ignorance," as another poet put it, letting the poem work toward an understanding of itself (and of me) as I go along. In a student essay, the idea is to stick to the topic. In much imaginative poetry, the pleasure lies in finding a way to escape the initial topic, to transcend the subject and ride the poem into strange, unforeseen areas. As poet John Ashbery put it: "In the process of writing, all sorts of unexpected things happen that shift the poet away from his plan; these accidents are really what we mean whenever we talk about Poetry." Readers of poetry see only the finished product set confidently on the page; but the process of writing a poem involves uncertainty, ambiguity, improvisation, and surprise.

I think of poetry as the original travel literature in that a poem can take me to an imaginative place where I have never been. A good poem often progresses by a series of associative leaps, including sudden shifts in time and space, all of which results in a kind of mental journey. I never know the ending of the poem when I set out, but I am aware that I am moving the poem toward some destination, and when I find the ending, I recognize it right away. More interesting to me than what a poem means is how it travels. In the classroom, I like to substitute for the question, "What is the meaning of the poem?" other questions: "How does this poem go?" or "How does this poem travel through itself in search of its own ending?"

Maybe a few of my poems that follow will serve as illustrations, and I hope what I have said so far will help you articulate how poems go and how they find their endings.

BILLY COLLINS

Questions About Angels   1991

Of all the questions you might want to ask
about angels, the only one you ever hear
is how many can dance on the head of a pin.

No curiosity about how they pass the eternal time
besides circling the Throne chanting in Latin   5
or delivering a crust of bread to a hermit on earth
or guiding a boy and girl across a rickety wooden bridge.

Do they fly through God's body and come out singing?
Do they swing like children from the hinges
of the spirit world saying their names backwards and forwards?   10
Do they sit alone in little gardens changing colors?

What about their sleeping habits, the fabric of their robes,
their diet of unfiltered divine light?
What goes on inside their luminous heads? Is there a wall
these tall presences can look over and see hell?   15

If an angel fell off a cloud, would he leave a hole
in a river and would the hole float along endlessly
filled with the silent letters of every angelic word?

If an angel delivered the mail, would he arrive
in a blinding rush of wings or would he just assume   20
the appearance of the regular mailman and
whistle up the driveway reading the postcards?

No, the medieval theologians control the court.
The only question you ever hear is about
the little dance floor on the head of a pin   25
where halos are meant to converge and drift invisibly.

It is designed to make us think in millions,
billions, to make us run out of numbers and collapse
into infinity, but perhaps the answer is simply one:
one female angel dancing alone in her stocking feet,   30
a small jazz combo working in the background.

She sways like a branch in the wind, her beautiful
eyes closed, and the tall thin bassist leans over

to glance at his watch because she has been dancing
forever, and now it is very late, even for musicians.   35

BILLY COLLINS
On Writing "Questions About Angels"   2008

I find that it doesn't take much to get a poem going. A poem can start casually with something trivial and then develop significance along the way. The
first inkling may act as a keyhole that allows the poet to look into an imaginary room. When I started to write "Questions About Angels," I really had
nothing on my mind except that odd, speculative question: How many angels
can dance on the head of a pin? Seemingly unanswerable, the question originated as an attempt to mock certain medieval philosophers (notably Thomas
Aquinas) who sought to solve arcane theological mysteries through the sheer
application of reason. I had first heard the question when I was studying theology at a Jesuit college, but well before that, the phrase had made its way
into the mainstream of modern parlance. It was typical of me to want to
begin a poem with something everyone knows and then proceed from there.
The poem found a direction to go in when it occurred to me to open up the
discussion to include other questions. At that point, it was "Game on."
    My investigation really begins in the second stanza, which draws on tra-
ditional images of angels in religious art, either worshipping God or paying helpful visits to earth, assisting the poor and protecting the innocent.
Then the questions become more fanciful — off-the-wall, really: "Do they fly
through God's body and come out singing?" No doubt you could come up
with questions of your own about angel behavior; clearly, that has become
the poem's game — an open inquiry into the spirit life of these creatures.
    After the poem's most bizarre question, which involves a hole that a
fallen angel has left in a river, the interrogation descends into the everyday
with the image of an angel delivering mail, not gloriously "in a blinding rush
of wings" but just like "the regular mailman." After a reminder of the monop-
oly "the medieval theologians" seem to have on questions about angels, the
poem makes a sudden turn (one I did not see coming) by offering a simple,
irreducible answer to that unanswerable question. On the little word "but"
(line 29), the poem drops down abruptly from "billions" to "one," and the
scene shrinks from heaven to a jazz club located in eternity.
    In the process of composing a poem, the poet is mentally juggling many
concerns, one of the most dominant and persistent being how the poem is
going to find a place to end, a point where the journey of the poem was meant
to stop, a point where the poet does not want to say any more, and the reader
has heard just enough. In this case, the moment she appeared — rather miraculously, as I remember — I knew that this beautiful angel "dancing alone
in her stocking feet" was how the poem would close. She was the hidden
destination the poem was moving toward all along without my knowing it.

I had only to add the detail of the bored bassist and the odd observation that even musicians playing in eternity cannot be expected to stay awake forever.

BILLY COLLINS

Litany   2002

> *You are the bread and the knife,*
> *The crystal goblet and the wine.*
> > *— Jacques Crickillon*

You are the bread and the knife,
the crystal goblet and the wine.
You are the dew on the morning grass,
and the burning wheel of the sun.
You are the white apron of the baker,   5
and the marsh birds suddenly in flight.

However, you are not the wind in the orchard,
the plums on the counter,
or the house of cards.
And you are certainly not the pine-scented air.   10

There is no way you are the pine-scented air.
It is possible that you are the fish under the bridge,
maybe even the pigeon on the general's head,
but you are not even close
to being the field of cornflowers at dusk.   15

And a quick look in the mirror will show
that you are neither the boots in the corner
nor the boat asleep in its boathouse.

It might interest you to know,
speaking of the plentiful imagery of the world,   20
that I am the sound of rain on the roof.

I also happen to be the shooting star,
the evening paper blowing down an alley,
and the basket of chestnuts on the kitchen table.

I am also the moon in the trees   25
and the blind woman's teacup.
But don't worry, I am not the bread and the knife.
You are still the bread and the knife.
You will always be the bread and the knife,
not to mention the crystal goblet and — somehow — the wine.   30

BILLY COLLINS

On Writing "Litany"   2008

As the epigraph to this poem indicates, "Litany" was written in reaction to another poem, a love poem I came across in a literary magazine by a poet I had not heard of. What struck me about his poem was its reliance on a strategy that had its heyday in the love sonnets of the Elizabethan age, namely, the convention of flattering the beloved by comparing her to various aspects of nature. Typically, her eyes were like twin suns, her lips red as coral or rubies, her skin pure as milk, and her breath as sweet as flowers or perfume. Such exaggerations were part of the overall tendency to idealize women who were featured in the courtly love poetry of the time, each of whom was as unattainable as she was beautiful and as cruel as she was fair. It took Shakespeare to point out the ridiculousness of these hyperboles, questioning in one of his sonnets the very legitimacy of comparisons ("Shall I compare thee to a summer's day?" [p. 515]), then drenching the whole process with the cold water of realism ("My mistress' eyes are nothing like the sun" [p. 516]). You might think that would have put an end to the practice, but the habit of appealing to women's vanity through comparisons persists even in the poetry of today. That poem in the magazine prompted me to respond.

Starting with the same first two lines, "Litany" seeks to rewrite the earlier poem by offering a corrective. It aims to point out the latent silliness in such comparisons and perhaps the potential absurdity at the heart of metaphor itself. The poem even wants us to think about the kind of romantic relationships that would permit such discourse.

The poem opens by adding some new metaphors (morning dew, baker's apron, marsh birds) to the pile, but in the second stanza, the poem reverses direction by trading in flattery for a mock-serious investigation of what this woman might be and what she is not. Instead of appealing to her sense of her own beauty, the speaker is perfectly willing to insult her by bringing up her metaphoric shortcomings. By the time he informs her that "There is no way you are the pine-scented air" and "you are not even close / to being the field of cornflowers at dusk," we know that this is a different kind of love poem altogether.

The second big turn comes in the fifth stanza when the speaker unexpectedly begins comparing himself to such things as "the sound of rain on the roof." Notice that the earlier comparisons were not all positive. The "pigeon on the general's head" should remind us of an equestrian statue in a park, and we all know what pigeons like to do to statues. But the speaker is not the least bit ashamed to flatter himself with a string of appealing images including a "shooting star," a "basket of chestnuts," and "the moon in the trees." Turning attention away from the "you" of the poem to the speaker is part of the poem's impertinence — the attentive lover turns into an egomaniac — but it echoes a strategy used by Shakespeare himself. Several of his sonnets begin by being about the beloved but end by being about the poet, specifically about his power to bestow immortality on the beloved through his art. Thus, what begins as a love poem ends as a self-love poem.

The last thing to notice is that "Litany" has a circular structure: It ends by swinging back to its beginning, to the imagery of the epigraph. True to the cheekiness of the speaker, his last words are devoted to tossing the woman a bit of false reassurance that she is still and will always be "the bread and the knife." For whatever that's worth.

BILLY COLLINS

Building with Its Face Blown Off   2005

How suddenly the private
is revealed in a bombed-out city,
how the blue and white striped wallpaper

of a second story bedroom is now
exposed to the lightly falling snow   5
as if the room had answered the explosion

wearing only its striped pajamas.
Some neighbors and soldiers
poke around in the rubble below

and stare up at the hanging staircase,
the portrait of a grandfather,   10
a door dangling from a single hinge.

And the bathroom looks almost embarrassed
by its uncovered ochre walls,
the twisted mess of its plumbing,   15

the sink sinking to its knees,
the ripped shower curtain,
the torn goldfish trailing bubbles.

It's like a dollhouse view
as if a child on its knees could reach in   20
and pick up the bureau, straighten a picture.

Or it might be a room on a stage
in a play with no characters,
no dialogue or audience,

no beginning, middle and end —   25
just the broken furniture in the street,
a shoe among the cinder blocks,

a light snow still falling
on a distant steeple, and people
crossing a bridge that still stands.   30

And beyond that — crows in a tree,
the statue of a leader on a horse,
and clouds that look like smoke,

and even farther on, in another country
on a blanket under a shade tree,   35
a man pouring wine into two glasses

and a woman sliding out
the wooden pegs of a wicker hamper
filled with bread, cheese, and several kinds of olives.

Perspective

On "Building with Its Face Blown Off": Michael Meyer Interviews Billy Collins 2009

Meyer: The subject matter of your poetry is well known for being typically about the patterns and rhythms of everyday life, along with its delights, humor, ironies, and inevitable pain. "Building with Its Face Blown Off," however, explicitly concerns war and is implicitly political. What prompted this minority report in your writing?

Collins: It's true that I usually steer away from big historical subjects in my poems. I don't want to assume a level of authority beyond what a reader might trust, nor do I want to appear ridiculous by taking a firm stand against some moral horror that any other humane person would naturally oppose. A few years back, I consciously avoided joining the movement called "Poets against the War" because I thought it was as self-obviating as "Generals for the War." A direct approach to subjects as enormous as war or slavery or genocide carries the risk that the poet will be smothered under the weight of the topic. Plus, readers are already morally wired to respond in a certain way to such things. As a writer, you want to *create* an emotion, not merely activate one that already exists in the reader. And who wants to preach to the choir? I have come across few readers of poetry who are all for war; and, besides, poets have enough work to do without trying to convert the lost. William Butler Yeats put it best in his "On Being Asked for a War Poem":

> I think it better that in times like these
> A poet's mouth be silent, for in truth

> We have no gift to set a statesman right;
> He has had enough of meddling who can please
> A young girl in the indolence of her youth,
> Or an old man upon a winter's night.

Before poetry can be political, it must be personal.

That's my dim view of poems that do little more than declare that the poet, walking the moral high road, is opposed to ethically reprehensible acts. But the world does press in on us, and I was stopped in my tracks one morning when I saw in a newspaper still another photograph of a bombed-out building, which echoed all the similar images I had seen for too many decades in too many conflicts around the world in Dresden, Sarajevo, or Baghdad, wherever shells happen to fall. That photograph revealed one personal aspect of the war: the apartment of a family blown wide open for all to see. "Building with Its Face Blown Off" was my response.

Meyer: The images in the poem have a photojournalistic quality, but they are snapped through the lens of personification rather than a camera. Isn't a picture better than a thousand words?

Collins: I wanted to avoid the moralistic antiwar rhetoric that the underlying subject invites, so I stuck to the visual. A photojournalist once observed that to capture the horrors of war, you don't have to go to the front lines and photograph actual armed conflict: just take a picture of a child's shoe lying on a road. That picture would be worth many words, but as a poet I must add, maybe not quite a thousand. In this poem, I wanted to downplay the horrible violence of the destruction by treating the event as a mere social embarrassment, an invasion of domestic privacy. As Chekhov put it, if you want to get the reader emotionally involved, write cold. For the same reason, I deployed nonviolent metaphors such as the dollhouse and the theater, where the fourth wall is absent. The poem finds a way to end by withdrawing from the scene like a camera pulling back to reveal a larger world. Finally, we are looking down as from a blimp on another country, one where the absence of war provides the tranquility that allows a man and a woman to have a picnic.

A reader once complimented me for ending this poem with olives, the olive branch being a traditional symbol of peace. Another reader heard an echo of Ernest Hemingway's short story "In Another Country," which concerns World War I. Just between you and me, neither of these references had ever occurred to me; but I am always glad to take credit for such happy accidents even if it is similar to drawing a target around a bullet hole. No writer can — or should want to — have absolute control over the reactions of his readers.

Meyer: In your essay on writing "Nostalgia," you point out that "formal rules give the poet an enclosed space in which to work, and they keep the poem from descending into chaos or tantrum". How does form in "Building with Its Face Blown Off" prevent its emotions and thoughts from being reduced to a prose bumper sticker such as "War is hell"?

Collins: I hope what keeps this poem from getting carried away with its traumatic subject is its concentration on the photograph so that the poem maintains a visual, even cinematic, focus throughout. You could think of the poem as a one-minute movie — a short subject about a big topic. Another sign of apparent form here is the division of the poem into three-line stanzas, or tercets, which slow down the reader's progress through the poem. Just as readers should pause slightly at the end of every poetic line (even an unpunctuated one — the equivalent of half a comma), they should also observe a little pause between stanzas. Poetry is famous for condensing large amounts of mental and emotional material into small packages, and it also encourages us to slow down from the speed at which we usually absorb information. The stanzas give the poem a look of regularity, and some of them make visible the grammatical structure of the poem's sentences. Regular stanzas suggest that the poem comes in sections, and they remind us that poetry is a spatial arrangement of words on the page. Think of such stanzas as stones in a stream; the reader steps from one to the next to get to the other side.

Meyer: In a classroom discussion of the final two stanzas, one of my students read the couple's picnic scene as "offering an image of hope and peace in contrast to the reckless destruction that precedes it," while another student countered that the scene appeared to be a depiction of "smug indifference and apathy to suffering." Care to comment?

Collins: I find it fascinating that such contrary views of the poem's ending could exist. Probably the most vexing question in poetry studies concerns interpretation. One thing to keep in mind is that readers of poetry, students especially, are much more preoccupied with "meaning" than poets are. While I am writing, I am not thinking about the poem's meaning; I am only trying to write a good poem, which involves securing the form of the poem and getting the poem to hold together so as to stay true to itself. Thinking about what my poem means would only distract me from the real work of poetry. Neurologically speaking, I am trying to inhabit the intuitive side of the brain, not the analytical side where critical thought and "study questions" come from. "Meaning," if I think of it at all, usually comes as an afterthought.

But the question remains: How do poets react to interpretations of their work? Generally speaking, once a poem is completed and then published, it is out of the writer's hands. I'm disposed to welcome interpretations that I did not consciously intend — that doesn't mean my unconscious didn't play a role — as long as those readings do not twist the poem out of shape.

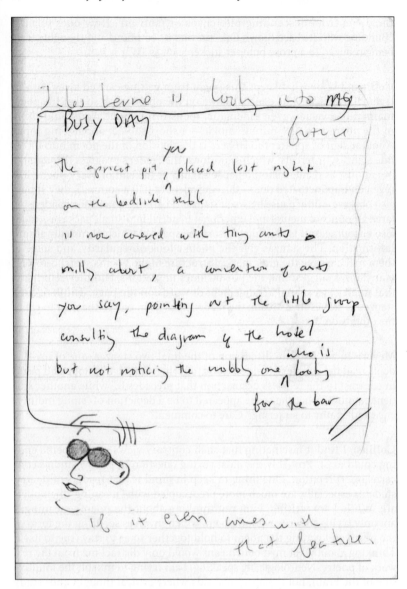

A draft of the unpublished poem "Busy Day" from an undated page of Collins's notebooks.

Billy Collins Action Poetry Web Site.
In a 2003 interview with the American Booksellers Association, Billy Collins explained that his goal as United States poet laureate was for poetry "to pop up in unexpected places, like the daily announcement in high schools and on airplanes." At the Web site for the Billy Collins Action Poetry film project (www.bcactionpoet.org), you can view artful new interpretations of the poet's work and hear them read aloud by Collins himself, in what makes for an imaginative and elegant combination of poetry and technology.
Library of Congress.

In "Building with Its Face Blown Off," I added the picnicking couple simply as a sharp contrast to the scene of destruction in the war-torn city. The man and woman are free to enjoy the luxury of each other's company, the countryside, wine, cheese, and even a choice of olives. Are they a sign of hope? Well, yes, insofar as they show us that the whole world is not at war. Smugness? Not so much to my mind, even though that strikes me as a sensible reaction. But if a reader claimed that the couple represented Adam and Eve, or more absurdly, Antony and Cleopatra, or Donny and Marie Osmond, then I would question the person's common sense or sanity. I might even ring for Security. Mainly, the couple is there simply to show us what is no longer available to the inhabitants of the beleaguered city and to give me a place to end the poem.

Suggested Topics for Longer Papers

1. Analyze the humor in the of Collins's poems included in this anthology (see also "Introduction to Poetry." What purpose does the humor serve? Does the humor appeal to you? Explain why or why not, giving examples.

2. View the poems available on the Billy Collins Action Poetry Web site (see p. 603 and bcactionpoet.org), where you can find visual interpretations of individual poems and hear Collins read the poems aloud. Choose three of the poems and write an analysis of how the visual and auditory representations affect your response to the poems' language. Explain why you think this approach enhances or diminishes — or is simply different from — reading the poem on a page.

3. Identify a theme in the three poems in this chapter and discuss whether it is consistent with Collins's commentary or whether it represents a departure.

22

Song Lyrics as Poetry

AF archive/Alamy Stock Photo.

"Anything I can sing, I call a song. Anything I can't sing, I call a poem."
— BOB DYLAN

In 2016 the Nobel Prize committee shocked the world by awarding the Nobel Prize in Literature to a singer. No one was more shocked, perhaps, than the recipient, Bob Dylan, who mysteriously did not respond to the committee's announcement for more than a week. He eventually responded, but he didn't show up to accept the award, sending another rock musician (Patti Smith) in his place to sing one of his songs, "A Hard Rain's A-Gonna Fall" (p. 613). The radical decision to award the prize to the folk-singer-turned-rock-star was surprising because literature has long been associated with written language rather than language meant to be performed live or recorded. Yet Dylan changed the direction of popular music by focusing on the artistic possibilities of lyrics, and his songs reveal a deep connection to literature proper. There are allusions in his work to countless books, from Spenser's *The Faerie Queen* to contemporary novelists such as Erica Jong. The recent study *Why Bob Dylan Matters* roots Dylan in the tradition of the ancient classics.

In 2018 Kendrick Lamar's album "DAMN" was awarded the Pulitzer Prize in music, the first time the award was given to an artist outside of the classical and jazz traditions. "Rap," according to some legends, is an acronym for Rhythm and Poetry. Whether or not that legend is factual, it is indisputable that rap lyrics are poetry (as Jay-Z argues convincingly in his book *Decoded*), and that they can be analyzed using techniques similar to the ones we introduce in this book. Like Dylan in the folk/rock world, some hip-hop artists are keen to expand the artistic boundaries of music while understanding that it can still function as entertainment. As they do so, they find new and exciting ways to manipulate language — exploiting its nuances, playing with its sound qualities, and creating metrical principles that are guided by the melodies that drive it.

Despite these relatively recent accolades for Bob Dylan and Kendrick Lamar, the connection between music and poetry is ancient. Note that the word "lyric" derives from "lyre," a stringed instrument that preceded guitars and that could be used to accompany songs. Ancient troubadours were storytellers responsible for transporting culture between lands before literature was able to be recorded, reproduced, and widely distributed. In this chapter we offer a sampling of song lyrics from a variety of traditions, but we are just scratching the surface of what could be included here. What we hope to communicate is that literature is already part of your daily life: think of how many song lyrics are permanently stored in your brain. To consider their poetic importance, all you have to do is to listen carefully and repeatedly, appreciating them not just for their catchy melodies, but for the way they do something special with language.

Anonymous

Lord Randal   1803

"O where ha' you been, Lord Randal, my son?
And where ha' you been, my handsome young man?"
"I ha' been at the greenwood; mother, mak my bed soon,
For I'm wearied wi' hunting, and fain wad lie down."

"An wha met ye there, Lord Randal, my son?   5
An wha met you there, my handsome young man?"
"O I met wi my true-love; mother, mak my bed soon,
For I'm wearied wi' hunting, and fain wad lie down."

"And what did she give you, Lord Randal, my son?
And what did she give you, my handsome young man?"   10
"Eels fried in a pan; mother, mak my bed soon,
For I'm wearied wi' hunting, and fain wad lie down."

"And wha gat your leavins, Lord Randal, my son?
And wha gat your leavins, my handsome young man?"
"My hawks and my hounds; mother, mak my bed soon,   15
For I'm wearied wi' hunting, and fain wad lie down."

"And what became of them, Lord Randal, my son?
And what became of them, my handsome young man?"
"They stretched their legs out an died; mother, mak my bed soon,
For I'm weary wi' hunting, and fain wad lie down."   20

"O I fear you are poisoned, Lord Randal, my son!
I fear you are poisoned, my handsome young man!"
"O yes, I am poisoned; mother, mak my bed soon,
For I'm sick at the heart, and I fain wad lie down."

"What d'ye leave to your mother, Lord Randal, my son?   25
What d'ye leave to your mother, my handsome young man?"
"Four and twenty milk kye; mother, mak my bed soon,
For I'm sick at the heart, and I fain wad lie down."

"What d'ye leave to your sister, Lord Randal, my son?
What d'ye leave to your sister, my handsome young man?"   30
"My gold and my silver; mother, mak my bed soon,
For I'm sick at the heart, and I fain wad lie down."

"What d'ye leave to your brother, Lord Randal, my son?
What d'ye leave to your brother, my handsome young man?"
"My house and my lands; mother, mak my bed soon,   35
For I'm sick at the heart, and I fain wad lie down."

"What d'ye leave to your true-love, Lord Randal, my son?
What d'ye leave to your true-love, my handsome young man?"
"I leave her hell and fire; mother, mak my bed soon,
For I'm sick at the heart, and I fain wad lie down."   40

CONSIDERATIONS FOR CRITICAL THINKING AND WRITING

1. **FIRST RESPONSE.** Is there any reason to believe that Lord Randal's mother suspects that her son is poisoned before she declares it in line 21?

2. Discuss the relationship between the poem's structure or form and its theme.

3. The poem's power is in the final stanza when Lord Randal declares that he leaves "hell and fire" to his "true-love." Are his words a kind of revenge curse or do you see them as just the angry ranting of a dying man?

CONNECTION TO ANOTHER SELECTION

1. Bob Dylan's "A Hard Rain's A-Gonna Fall" (p. 613) borrows its structure consciously and directly from this poem. Dylan's lyrics are considerably more complex, but do they share anything with the theme of this poem?

FREDERIC WEATHERLY (1848–1929)

Danny Boy   1910

Oh Danny boy, the pipes, the pipes are calling
From glen to glen, and down the mountain side
The summer's gone, and all the flowers are dying
'Tis you, 'tis you must go and I must bide.

But come ye back when summer's in the meadow 5
Or when the valley's hushed and white with snow
'Tis I'll be here in sunshine or in shadow
Oh Danny boy, oh Danny boy, I love you so.

And when you come, and all the flowers are dying
If I am dead, as dead I well may be 10
You'll come and find the place where I am lying
And kneel and say an "Ave" there for me.
And I shall hear, tho' soft you tread above me
And all my dreams will warm and sweeter be
If you'll not fail to tell me that you love me 15
I'll simply sleep in peace until you come to me.
I'll simply sleep in peace until you come to me.

Considerations for Critical Thinking and Writing

1. **first response.** Would you describe the poem as comforting or hope-less? Why?

2. What do you imagine the relationship between the speaker and Danny to be?

3. Do you have a sense of why Danny is leaving and the speaker must stay? Does it matter?

4. **creative response.** Write a poem from the point of view of "Danny Boy" to the speaker of this poem, imitating its poetic form, rhyme scheme, and meter, but also considering what Danny's feelings are upon leaving.

Connection to Another Selection

1. Compare the theme and context of this poem to the theme and context of "To the Virgins, To Make Much of Time" (p. 408). Would you say the poems are *essentially* similar or opposite in terms of theme?

W. C. Handy (1873–1958)

Beale Street Blues 1917

I've seen the lights of gay Broadway,
Old Market Street, down by the Frisco Bay,
I've strolled the Prado,
I've gambled on the Bourse,
The seven wonders of the world I've seen, 5
And many are the places I have been.

Take my advice folks
And see Beale Street first.

You'll see pretty browns in beautiful gowns,
You'll see tailor-mades and hand-me-downs,   10
You'll meet honest men and pick-pockets skilled,
You'll find that business never closes till somebody gets killed.

I'd rather be here than any place I know,
I'd rather be here than any place I know.
It's goin' to take the Sergeant   15
For to make me go.

Goin' to the river
Maybe, by and by,
Goin' to the river,
And there's a reason why: 20
Because the river's wet,
and Beale Street's gone dry.

You'll see Hog Nose rest'rants and Chitlin' Cafes,
You'll see jugs that tell of by-gone days,
And places, once places, now just a sham,   25
You'll see Golden Balls enough to pave the New Jerusalem.

Goin' to the river
Maybe, by and by,
Goin' to the river,
And there's a reason why: 30
Because the river's wet,
and Beale Street's gone dry.

I'd rather be here than any place I know,
I'd rather be here than any place I know.
It's goin' to take the Sergeant   35
For to make me go.

Goin' to the river
Maybe, by and by,
Goin' to the river,
And there's a reason why: 40
Because the river's wet,
and Beale Street's gone dry.

If Beale Street could talk, if Beale Street could talk
Married men would have to take their beds and walk,
Except one or two, who never drink booze,   45
And the blind man on the corner who sings the Beale Street Blues.

I'd rather be here than any place I know,
I'd rather be here than any place I know.
It's goin' to take the Sergeant
For to make me go.   50

CONSIDERATIONS FOR CRITICAL THINKING AND WRITING

1. **FIRST RESPONSE.** The speaker begins by insisting on his worldly experiences. Why is that perspective important? Do you know why he advises the reader to "see Beale Street first" (line 8)?

2. Line length and meter vary considerably between stanzas: Is there a pattern or is it irregular?

3. In the tenth stanza the speaker identifies three groups: married men, a smaller group of married men who do not drink alcohol, and the blind man on the corner who sings the Beale Street Blues. Can you tell which of these categories is closest to the speaker's sensibility?

CONNECTION TO ANOTHER SELECTION

1. Compare the poem in form and theme to Langston Hughes's "The Weary Blues" (p. 508).

WOODY GUTHRIE (1912–1967)

Gypsy Davy   1938

It was late last night when the boss came home
askin' for his lady
The only answer that he got,
"She's gone with the Gypsy Davy,
She's gone with the Gypsy Dave."

Go saddle for me a buckskin horse
And a hundred dollar saddle.
Point out to me their wagon tracks
And after them I'll travel,
After them I'll ride.   10

Well I had not rode to the midnight moon,
When I saw the campfire gleaming.
I heard the notes of the big guitar
And the voice of the gypsies singing
That song of the Gypsy Dave.   15

There in the light of the camping fire,
I saw her fair face beaming.
Her heart in tune with the big guitar
And the voice of the gypsies singing
That song of the Gypsy Dave.   20

Have you forsaken your house and home?
Have you forsaken your baby?
Have you forsaken your husband dear

Eric Schaal/Getty Images.

To go with the Gypsy Davy?
And sing with the Gypsy Davy?
The song of the Gypsy Dave?   25

Yes I've forsaken my husband dear
To go with the Gypsy Davy,
And I've forsaken my mansion high
But not my blue-eyed baby,
Not my blue-eyed baby.   30

She smiled to leave her husband dear
And go with the Gypsy Davy;
But the tears come a-trickling down her cheeks
To think of the blue-eyed baby,
Pretty little blue-eyed baby.   35

Take off, take off your buckskin gloves
Made of Spanish leather;
Give to me your lily-white hair
And we'll ride home together
We'll ride home again.   40

No, I won't take off my buckskin gloves,
They're made of Spanish leather.
I'll go my way from day to day
And sing with the Gypsy Davy
That song of the Gypsy Davy,   45
That song of the Gypsy Davy,
That song of the Gypsy Dave.

Considerations for Critical Thinking and Writing

1. **FIRST RESPONSE.** Do you feel more sympathy for "the boss" or for "his lady"? How does the poem's form condition your response?

2. The woman who has run off with Gypsy Davy feels no remorse for leaving her husband, but she sheds tears for leaving her "blue-eyed baby." Why does the poet highlight the woman's guilt about leaving her child?

3. Where is the poem detailed and where does it forsake important details? How does the contrast between details and abstraction contribute to the poem's overall effect?

Connection to Another Selection

1. Compare this poem to "Lord Randal" (p. 606) in terms of the motif of love gone wrong. Which one is more emotionally evocative? Why?

HANK WILLIAMS (1923–1953)

I'm So Lonesome I Could Cry 1949

Hear that lonesome whippoorwill
He sounds too blue to fly
The midnight train is whining low
I'm so lonesome I could cry

I've never seen a night so long   5
When time goes crawling by
The moon just went behind the clouds
To hide its face and cry

Did you ever see a robin weep
When leaves began to die?   10
Like me, he's lost the will to live
I'm so lonesome I could cry

The silence of a falling star
Lights up a purple sky
And as I wonder where you are   15
I'm so lonesome I could cry

CONSIDERATIONS FOR CRITICAL THINKING AND WRITING

1. FIRST RESPONSE. Why does the speaker describe nature and a train rather than himself as he expresses his loneliness?

2. Discuss the use of personification in the poem.

3. Is the speaker addressing the same person in the first three stanzas of the poem as the one he addresses directly in the last? Would the poem have a different effect if the pronoun in the last stanza were "he" or "she" rather than "you"?

CONNECTION TO ANOTHER SELECTION

1. Compare the way emotion is expressed in this poem and in Tennyson's "Break, Break, Break" (p. 487).

Bob Dylan (b. 1941)

A Hard Rain's A-Gonna Fall 1963

Oh, where have you been, my blue-eyed son?
Oh, where have you been, my darling young one?
I've stumbled on the side of twelve misty mountains
I've walked and I've crawled on six crooked highways
I've stepped in the middle of seven sad forests
I've been out in front of a dozen dead oceans
I've been ten thousand miles in the mouth of a graveyard
And it's a hard, and it's a hard, it's a hard, and it's a hard
And it's a hard rain's a-gonna fall

AF archive/Alamy Stock Photo.

Oh, what did you see, my blue-eyed son?   10
Oh, what did you see, my darling young one?
I saw a newborn baby with wild wolves all around it
I saw a highway of diamonds with nobody on it
I saw a black branch with blood that kept drippin'
I saw a room full of men with their hammers a-bleedin'   15
I saw a white ladder all covered with water
I saw ten thousand talkers whose tongues were all broken
I saw guns and sharp swords in the hands of young children
And it's a hard, and it's a hard, it's a hard, it's a hard
And it's a hard rain's a-gonna fall   20

And what did you hear, my blue-eyed son?
And what did you hear, my darling young one?
I heard the sound of a thunder, it roared out a warnin'
Heard the roar of a wave that could drown the whole world
Heard one hundred drummers whose hands were a-blazin'   25
Heard ten thousand whisperin' and nobody listenin'
Heard one person starve, I heard many people laughin'
Heard the song of a poet who died in the gutter
Heard the sound of a clown who cried in the alley
And it's a hard, and it's a hard, it's a hard, it's a hard   30
And it's a hard rain's a-gonna fall

Oh, who did you meet, my blue-eyed son?
Who did you meet, my darling young one?
I met a young child beside a dead pony
I met a white man who walked a black dog
I met a young woman whose body was burning   35
I met a young girl, she gave me a rainbow
I met one man who was wounded in love
I met another man who was wounded with hatred
And it's a hard, it's a hard, it's a hard, it's a hard
It's a hard rain's a-gonna fall   40

Oh, what'll you do now, my blue-eyed son?
Oh, what'll you do now, my darling young one?
I'm a-goin' back out 'fore the rain starts a-fallin'
I'll walk to the depths of the deepest black forest   45
Where the people are many and their hands are all empty
Where the pellets of poison are flooding their waters
Where the home in the valley meets the damp dirty prison
Where the executioner's face is always well hidden
Where hunger is ugly, where souls are forgotten   50
Where black is the color, where none is the number
And I'll tell it and think it and speak it and breathe it
And reflect it from the mountain so all souls can see it
Then I'll stand on the ocean until I start sinkin'
But I'll know my song well before I start singin'   55
And it's a hard, it's a hard, it's a hard, it's a hard
It's a hard rain's a-gonna fall

Considerations for Critical Thinking and Writing

1. **First Response.** The poem is full of rich but confusing imagery. Focus on the imagery in a single stanza and discuss its cumulative effect.

2. Each stanza begins and ends the same way, with a slight variation at the beginning of each. What other repetitions do you see in the poem? Why are they significant?

3. How do experience and prophecy work together in the poem? Put differently, is the "blue-eyed son" a reporter or a visionary?

Connection to Another Selection

1. Compare the role of the poet/singer in this poem and in Allen Ginsberg's "Sunflower Sutra" (p. 635).

Bob Dylan (B. 1941)

It's Alright, Ma (I'm Only Bleeding)   1965

Darkness at the break of noon
Shadows even the silver spoon
The handmade blade, the child's balloon
Eclipses both the sun and moon
To understand you know too soon   5
There is no sense in trying

Pointed threats, they bluff with scorn
Suicide remarks are torn

From the fool's gold mouthpiece the hollow horn
Plays wasted words, proves to warn   10
That he not busy being born is busy dying

Temptation's page flies out the door
You follow, find yourself at war
Watch waterfalls of pity roar
You feel to moan but unlike before   15
You discover that you'd just be one more
Person crying

So don't fear if you hear
A foreign sound to your ear
It's alright, Ma, I'm only sighing   20

As some warn victory some downfall
Private reasons great or small
Can be seen in the eyes of those that call
To make all that should be killed to crawl
While others say don't hate nothing at all   25
Except hatred

Disillusioned words like bullets bark
As human gods aim for their mark
Make everything from toy guns that spark
To flesh-colored Christs that glow in the dark   30
It's easy to see without looking too far
That not much is really sacred

While preachers preach of evil fates
Teachers teach that knowledge waits
Can lead to hundred-dollar plates   35
Goodness hides behind the gates
But even the president of the United States
Sometimes must have to stand naked

An' though the rules of the road have been lodged
It's only people's games that you got to dodge   40
And it's alright, Ma, I can make it

Advertising signs they con
You into thinking you're the one
That can do what's never been done
That can win what's never been won   45
Meantime life outside goes on
All around you

You lose yourself, you reappear
You suddenly find you got nothing to fear
Alone you stand with nobody near   50

When a trembling distant voice, unclear
Startles your sleeping ears to hear
That somebody thinks they really found you

A question in your nerves is lit
Yet you know there is no answer fit   55
To satisfy, insure you not to quit
To keep it in your mind and not forget
That it is not he or she or them or it
That you belong to

Although the masters make the rules   60
For the wise men and the fools
I got nothing, Ma, to live up to

For them that must obey authority
That they do not respect in any degree
Who despise their jobs, their destinies   65
Speak jealously of them that are free
Cultivate their flowers to be
Nothing more than something they invest in

While some on principles baptized
To strict party platform ties   70
Social clubs in drag disguise
Outsiders they can freely criticize
Tell nothing except who to idolize
And then say God bless him

While one who sings with his tongue on fire   75
Gargles in the rat race choir
Bent out of shape from society's pliers
Cares not to come up any higher
But rather get you down in the hole
That he's in   80

But I mean no harm nor put fault
On anyone that lives in a vault
But it's alright, Ma, if I can't please him

Old lady judges watch people in pairs
Limited in sex, they dare   85
To push fake morals, insult and stare
While money doesn't talk, it swears
Obscenity, who really cares
Propaganda, all is phony

While them that defend what they cannot see   90
With a killer's pride, security
It blows the minds most bitterly

For them that think death's honesty
Won't fall upon them naturally
Life sometimes must get lonely

My eyes collide head-on with stuffed
Graveyards, false gods, I scuff
At pettiness which plays so rough
Walk upside-down inside handcuffs
Kick my legs to crash it off
Say okay, I have had enough, what else can you show me?

And if my thought-dreams could be seen
They'd probably put my head in a guillotine
But it's alright, Ma, it's life, and life only

CONSIDERATIONS FOR CRITICAL THINKING AND WRITING

1. **FIRST RESPONSE.** What is the poem's rhyme scheme and how does it contribute to its overall effect?

2. Identify all the individuals and groups of people in the poem. Is the speaker allied with any of them or is he completely isolated? If you believe he is isolated, is everyone else basically in the same category? Is it him against the world, in other words?

3. Besides end rhyme, what poetic devices does Dylan employ in this poem? To what effect?

CONNECTION TO ANOTHER SELECTION

1. Compare this poem to the preceding poem by Dylan, "A Hard Rain's A-Gonna Fall" (p. 613) in terms of tone, diction, and/or theme.

JOHN LENNON (1940–1980) AND PAUL MCCARTNEY (B. 1942)
I Am the Walrus 1967

I am he
As you are he
As you are me
And we are all together

See how they run

Like pigs from a gun
See how they fly
I'm crying

Sitting on a cornflake
Waiting for the van to come   10
Corporation tee shirt
Stupid bloody Tuesday
Man, you been a naughty boy
You let your face grow long

I am the eggman (Ooh)   15
They are the eggmen, (Ooh)
I am the walrus
Goo goo g' joob

Mister city p'liceman sitting pretty
Little p'licemen in a row   20
See how they fly
Like Lucy in the sky
See how they run
I'm crying
I'm crying, I'm crying, I'm crying   25

Yellow matter custard
Dripping from a dead dog's eye
Crabalocker fishwife pornographic priestess
Boy you been a naughty girl
You let your knickers down   30

I am the eggman (Ooh)
They are the eggmen (Ooh)
I am the walrus
Goo goo g' joob

Sitting in an English   35
Garden waiting for the sun
If the sun don't come
You get a tan from standing in the English rain

I am the eggman
They are the eggmen   40
I am the walrus
Goo goo g' joob g' goo goo g' joob
Expert texpert choking smokers
Don't you think the joker laughs at you?
See how they smile   45
Like pigs in a sty, see how they snied
I'm crying

Semolina pilchards
Climbing up the Eiffel Tower
Element'ry penguin singing Hare Krishna   50
Man, you should have seen them kicking Edgar Allan Poe

I am the eggman (Ooh)
They are the eggmen (Ooh)
I am the walrus
Goo goo g' joob   55
Goo goo g' joob
G' goo goo g' joob
Goo goo g' joob, goo goo g' goo g' goo goo g' joob joob
Joob joob . . .

CONSIDERATIONS FOR CRITICAL THINKING AND WRITING

1. FIRST RESPONSE. What sound qualities do the poets employ or exploit?
2. The poem juxtaposes a number of images that do not seem to belong
   together. What is the effect of this juxtaposition on the reader?
3. How does the poem employ allusion?

CONNECTION TO ANOTHER SELECTION

1. Compare "I Am the Walrus" to Lewis Carroll's "Jabberwocky" (p. 485).
   Which one is more accessible? Why?

VAN MORRISON (B. 1945)

Astral Weeks   1968

If I ventured in the slipstream
Between the viaducts of your dream
Where immobile steel rims crack
And the ditch in the back roads stop
Could you find me?   5
Would you kiss-a my eyes?
To lay me down
In silence easy
To be born again
To be born again   10
From the far side of the ocean
If I put the wheels in motion
And I stand with my arms behind me
And I'm pushin' on the door
Could you find me?   15
Would you kiss-a my eyes?
To lay me down
In silence easy
To be born again
To be born again   20

There you go
Standin' with the look of avarice
Talkin' to Huddie Ledbetter°
Showin' pictures on the wall
Whisperin' in the hall   25
And pointin' a finger at me
There you go, there you go
Standin' in the sun darlin'
With your arms behind you
And your eyes before   30
There you go
Takin' good care of your boy
Seein' that he's got clean clothes
Puttin' on his little red shoes
I see you know he's got clean clothes   35
A-puttin' on his little red shoes
A-pointin' a finger at me
And here I am
Standing in your sad arrest
Trying to do my very best   40
Lookin' straight at you
Comin' through, darlin'
Yeah, yeah, yeah
If I ventured in the slipstream
Between the viaducts of your dreams   45
Where immobile steel rims crack
And the ditch in the back roads stop
Could you find me
Would you kiss-a my eyes
Lay me down   50
In silence easy
To be born again
To be born again
To be born again
In another world   55
In another world
In another time
Got a home on high
Ain't nothing but a stranger in this world
I'm nothing but a stranger in this world   60
I got a home on high
In another land
So far away
So far away

23 *Huddie Ledbetter:* The actual name of the folk musician known as "Lead Belly" (1888–1949).

Way up in the heaven   65
Way up in the heaven
Way up in the heaven
Way up in the heaven
In another time
In another place   70
In another time
In another place
Way up in the heaven
Way up in the heaven
We are goin' up to heaven   75
We are goin' to heaven
In another time
In another place
In another time
In another place   80
In another face

CONSIDERATIONS FOR CRITICAL THINKING AND WRITING

1. FIRST RESPONSE. The poem is challenging because of its improvised
   repetitions and its dreamlike imagery. Focusing initially on the "I" and
   "you," what separates them (literally or figuratively)? Where do they
   make progress toward reconciliation?

2. How do you interpret the references to rebirth and death in the poem?

3. How might the poem's title offer an inroad to understanding it?

JONI MITCHELL (B. 1943)
Cold Blue Steel and Sweet Fire   1972

Cold blue steel out of money
One eye for the beat police
Sweet Fire calling
"You can't deny me
Now you know what you need"   5
Underneath the jungle gym

Photo by David Gahr/Getty Images.

Hollow grey fire escape thief
Looking for sweet fire
Shadow of lady release

"Come with me   10
I know the way" she says
"It's down, down, down the dark ladder
Do you want to contact somebody first
Leave someone a letter
You can come now   15
Or you can come later"

A wristwatch, a ring, a downstairs screamer
Edgy-black cracks of the sky
"Pin cushion prick fix this poor bad dreamer"
"Money" cold shadows reply   20
Pawnshops crisscrossed and padlocked
Corridors spit on prayers and pleas
Sparks fly up from sweet fire
Black soot of lady release

"Come with me   25
I know the way" she says
"It's down, down, down the dark ladder
Do you want to contact somebody first
Does it really matter
If you come now   30
Or if you come on later?"

Red water in the bathroom sink
Fever and the scum brown bowl
Blue steel still begging
But it's indistinct   35
Someone's hi-fi drumming Jelly Roll°
Concrete concentration camp
Bashing in veins for peace
Cold Blue Steel and Sweet Fire
Fall into Lady Release   40

"Come with me
I know the way" she says
"It's down, down, down the dark ladder
Do you want to contact somebody first
I mean what does it really matter   45
You're going to come now
Or you're going to come later"

---

36 *Jelly Roll:* Jelly Roll Morton (1890–1941), popular ragtime jazz pianist and composer.
A "hi-fi" was a type of record player (short for "high fidelity.")

CONSIDERATIONS FOR CRITICAL THINKING AND WRITING

1. FIRST RESPONSE. What does the title refer to? What images in the poem lead to your interpretation?

2. How does the slight alteration of the penultimate line in each stanza help to frame its theme?

3. How does Mitchell employ end rhyme, alliteration, and assonance throughout the poem? To what effect?

CONNECTION TO ANOTHER SELECTION

1. Compare the relationship between the central figure and setting in this poem and in Robert Lowell's "Skunk Hour" (p. 664).

BRUCE SPRINGSTEEN (B. 1949)

You're Missing 2002

Shirts in the closet, shoes in the hall
Mama's in the kitchen, baby and all
Everything is everything
Everything is everything
But you're missing   5

Coffee cups on the counter, jackets on the chair
Papers on the door step, but you're not there
Everything is everything
Everything is everything
But you're missing   10

Pictures on the nightstand, TV's on the den
Your house is waiting, your house is waiting
For you to walk in, for you to walk in
But you're missing, you're missing, you're missing
When I shut out the lights, you're missing   15
When I close my eyes, you're missing
When I see the sun rise, you're missing

Children are asking if it's alright
Will you be in our arms tonight

Morning is morning, the evening falls I got   20
Too much room in my bed, too many phone calls
How's everything, everything
Everything, everything
But you're missing, you're missing

And God's drifting in heaven, devil's in the mailbox   25
I got dust on my shoes, nothing but teardrops

CONSIDERATIONS FOR CRITICAL THINKING AND WRITING

1. FIRST RESPONSE. What is the cumulative effect of all of the mundane images in the first three stanzas?

2. Characterize the use of the word *everything* in this poem. Does its meaning change as the poem progresses?

3. Discuss the contrast between the imagery of the final stanza and the rest of the poem. How does this contrast either illuminate or obscure the poem's theme?

CONNECTION TO ANOTHER SELECTION

1. This poem, "Danny Boy" (p. 607), and "I'm So Lonesome I Could Cry" (p. 612) are all about separation. Compare them in terms of the emotions they evoke in the reader.

JANELLE MONÁE (B. 1985)

Americans 2018

Hold on, don't fight your war alone
Halo around you, don't have to face it on your own
We will win this fight
All souls be brave
We'll find a way to heaven   5
We'll find a way

War is old, so is sex
Let's play god, you go next
Hands go up, men go down
Try my luck, stand my ground   10
Die in church, live in jail
Say her name, twice in hell
Uncle Sam kissed a man
Jim Crow Jesus rose again

JEP Live Music/Alamy Stock Photo.

I like my woman in the kitchen 15
I teach my children superstitions
I keep my two guns on my blue nightstand
A pretty young thang, she can wash my clothes
But she'll never ever wear my pants

I pledge allegiance to the flag 20
Learned the words from my mom and dad
Cross my heart and I hope to die
With a big old piece of American pie
Love me baby, love me for who I am
Fallen angels singing, "clap your hands" 25
Don't try to take my country, I will defend my land
I'm not crazy, baby, naw
I'm American
I'm American
I'm American 30
I'm American

Seventy-nine cent to your dollar
All that bullshit from white-collars
You see my color before my vision
Sometimes I wonder if you were blind 35
Would it help you make a better decision?

I pledge allegiance to the flag
Learned the words from my mom and dad
Cross my heart and I hope to die
With a big old piece of American pie 40
Just love me baby, love me for who I am
Fallen angels singing, "clap your hands"
Don't try to take my country, I will defend my land
I'm not crazy, baby, naw
I'm American 45
I'm American
I'm American
I'm American

Let me help you in here
Until women can get equal pay for equal work 50
This is not my America
Until same gender loving people can be who they are
This is not my America
Until black people can come home from a police stop without being
    shot in the head
This is not my America 55
Until poor whites can get a shot at being successful
This is not my America
I can't hear nobody talkin' to me

Just love me baby, love me for who I am
Fallen angels singing, "clap your hands"   60
Don't try to take my country, I will defend my land
I'm not crazy, baby, naw
I'm American (love me baby)
I'm American (love me for who I am)

Until Latinos and Latinas don't have to run from walls   65
This is not my America
But I tell you today that the devil is a liar
Because it's gon' be my America before it's all over

Please sign your name on the dotted line

CONSIDERATIONS FOR CRITICAL THINKING AND WRITING

1. FIRST RESPONSE. Where does the speaker's identity shift?

2. How are American myths and American realities treated in this poem? How can you tell which is which?

3. Locate all the Judeo-Christian religious imagery in the poem. How does it help to frame the poem's theme?

23

"I find myself absolutely fulfilled when I have written a poem, when I'm writing one. Having written one, then you fall away very rapidly from having been a poet to becoming a sort of poet in rest, which isn't the same thing at all. But I think the actual experience of writing a poem is a magnificent one."

—SYLVIA PLATH

Everett Collection Historical/Alamy Stock Photo.

This chapter is a collection of poems thematically related to the natural environment we inhabit. Though poets may have a popular (and mistaken) reputation for being somewhat ethereal in their concerns, they still breathe the same air as the rest of us. Not surprisingly, because poets instinctively draw inspiration from nature, they are often as delighted to praise its vivid joys as they are compelled to warn us when it is abused. Having neither the technical knowledge of scientists nor the political means of legislators to defend the environment, poets nevertheless lend a voice to remind us of its pleasures, importance, and urgent fragility. The celebration of nature has always, of course, been a major poetic theme, but only fairly recently has poetry treated nature as a cause célèbre. Nature has forever aroused poets to write poems and so, given the contemporary environmental issues that have descended upon us, it is only fitting that poetry is enlisted to uphold nature.

The poems in this chapter provide some relatively recent or even contemporary reflections on our relationship to nature. Though they are not representative of all the kinds of environmental poetry being written today, these thirteen poems do offer a range of voices and issues that can serve as prompts for seeing and responding to your own natural environment through poetic language. You'll find among them detailed and vivid observations of nature, as well as meditations on climate change, the sustainability of the wild, and, indeed, the future of the planet. Some of the voices are quietly thoughtful, like Wendell Berry's "The Peace of Wild Things" (p. 630), while others are ironic or funny, and a couple will emphasize the violent side of nature that the poet Alfred, Lord Tennyson famously called "red in tooth and claw." The first, "Meditation on Beauty," calls attention to the current state of ecological destruction in a subtle way. Most of the poems in this chapter explore the natural world inhabited with human beings. What is never absent, however, is the human perception that creates the poems.

J. ESTANISLAO LOPEZ (B. 1987)

Meditation on Beauty   2018

There are days I think beauty has been exhausted
but then I read about the New York subway cars that,

dumped into the ocean, have become synthetic reefs.
Coral gilds the stanchions, feathered with dim Atlantic light.

Fish glisten, darting from a window into the sea grass   5
that bends around them like green flames —

this is human-enabled grace. So maybe there's room
in the margin of error for us to save ourselves

from the trends of self-destruction.
Or maybe such beauty is just another distraction,   10

stuffing our hearts with its currency, paraded for applause.
Here, in the South, you can hear applause

coming from the ground: even the buried are divided.
At the bottom of the Gulf, dark with Mississippi silt,

rests the broken derrick of an oil rig — and isn't oil   15
also beautiful? Ancient and opaque, like an allegory

that suggests we sacrifice our most beloved. Likely
ourselves. In one photograph, a sea turtle skims its belly

across a hull, unimpressed with what's restored,
barely aware of the ocean around it growing warm.   20

CONSIDERATIONS FOR CRITICAL THINKING AND WRITING

1. FIRST RESPONSE. Where does the poem turn?
2. How does the meaning of "beauty" change throughout the poem? Is it competing with some more powerful force?
3. How would you describe the relationship between humanity and nature in this poem?

CONNECTIONS TO OTHER SELECTIONS

1. Which is more optimistic about the planet's future: this poem or the one that follows, "Optimism" by Jane Hirschfield?
2. Compare the relationship between human garbage and natural life in this poem and in Allen Ginsberg's "Sunflower Sutra" (p. 635).

JANE HIRSHFIELD (B. 1953)

Optimism   2002

More and more I have come to admire resilience.
Not the simple resistance of a pillow, whose foam returns over and
over to the same shape, but the sinuous tenacity of a tree: finding the
light newly blocked on one side,
it turns in another.
A blind intelligence, true.
But out of such persistence arose turtles, rivers, mitochondria, figs —
all this resinous, unretractable earth.

CONSIDERATIONS FOR CRITICAL THINKING AND WRITING

1. FIRST RESPONSE. How do trees inform the speaker's description of optimism?
2. Discuss the way nature is envisioned in the poem.
3. How is optimism defined by the speaker? To what extent does this definition match your own perspective?

CONNECTIONS TO OTHER SELECTIONS

1. Contrast the view of nature presented in "Optimism" with that in Emily Dickinson's "Apparently with no surprise" (p. 581) and Robert Frost's "Design" (p. 394).
2. Discuss how tone affects your reading of the themes in "Optimism" and in Wendell Berry's "The Peace of Wild Things" (p. 630). To what extent does each poem approximate your own response to nature?

WENDELL BERRY (B. 1934)

The Peace of Wild Things 1968

When despair for the world grows in me
and I wake in the night at the least sound
in fear of what my life and my children's lives may be,
I go and lie down where the wood drake
rests in his beauty on the water, and the great heron feeds.   5
I come into the peace of wild things
who do not tax their lives with forethought
of grief. I come into the presence of still water.
And I feel above me the day-blind stars
waiting with their light. For a time   10
I rest in the grace of the world, and am free.

CONSIDERATIONS FOR CRITICAL THINKING AND WRITING

1. FIRST RESPONSE. How does the diction in this poem present nature as more than simply an escape from despair and fear?

2. Consider this response by a student to Berry's poem: "The images are pleasant enough, but the overall effect seems sentimental to me." What do you think?

CONNECTION TO ANOTHER SELECTION

1. Discuss the similarities that you see in style and theme in this poem and in Mary Oliver's "Wild Geese" (p. 637). Which poem did you prefer? Why?

GAIL WHITE (B. 1945)

Dead Armadillos 2000

> WHEN I WRITE "I'm a very secretive writer. Usually no one but me sees a poem before it's published. I don't especially recommend this. I probably miss a lot of helpful advice, but I also miss a lot of aggravation."
> —GAIL WHITE

The smart armadillo stays
on the side of the road
where it was born. The dumb ones
get a sudden urge to check the pickings
across the asphalt, and nine   5
times out of ten, collide
with a ton of moving metal.
They're on my daily route — soft shells
of land crustacea, small blind knights
in armor. No one cares.   10

There is no Save the Armadillo
Society. The Sierra Club and Greenpeace
take no interest. There are too
damned many armadillos, and beauty,
like money, is worth more when it's scarce.   15
Give us time. Let enough of them
try to cross the road.
When we're down to the last half dozen,
we'll see them with the eyes of God.

CONSIDERATIONS FOR CRITICAL THINKING AND WRITING

1. **FIRST RESPONSE.** Why do you think White chooses armadillos rather than, say, foxes to make her point?

2. What keeps this poem from becoming preachy?

3. How does the poem's language reveal the speaker's character?

CONNECTION TO ANOTHER SELECTION

1. Discuss the similarities in theme in "Dead Armadillos" and Walt McDonald's "Coming Across It" (p. 632).

DAVE LUCAS (B. 1980)

November 2007

October's brief, bright gush is over.
Leaf-lisp and fetch, their cold-tea smell
raked to the curb in copper- and shale-
stained piles, or the struck-match-sweet of sulfur

becoming smoke. The overcast
sky the same slight ambergris.
Hung across it, aghast surprise
of so many clotted, orphaned nests.

WHEN I WRITE "I admire and envy writers who can keep a structured writing schedule. The lines and poems I tend to keep are those written in time stolen from other responsibilities — so that the act of writing always feels subversive, even if I'm only subverting the laundry that needs to be done." — DAVE LUCAS

CONSIDERATIONS FOR CRITICAL THINKING AND WRITING

1. **FIRST RESPONSE.** What overall impression does this poem convey about the month of November? How does it serve as a dramatic contrast to October?

2. Carefully examine the diction in each line to determine how the poem's images achieve their effects.

3. **CREATIVE RESPONSE.** Choose two consecutive months that offer striking climatic environmental changes in the region where you live and write a two-stanza poem that includes vivid diction and images.

CONNECTION TO ANOTHER SELECTION

1. Discuss the differences in the way Lucas and Edna St. Vincent Millay depict their respective months in this poem and in "Spring" (p. 442).

WALT MCDONALD (B. 1934)

Coming Across It   1988

Cans rattle in the alley, a cat
prowling, or a man down on his luck
and starving. Neon on buildings

above us blinks like those eyes
in the dark, too slow for a cat,   5
lower than a man, like fangs,

yellow gold. Crowds shove us toward
something that crouches, this blind
alley like a cave. Someone shouts

Otter, and suddenly a sharp nose   10
wedges into focus, pelt shining,
webbed mammal feet begging for room.

Like a tribe, we huddle here
in the city and call *Here, otter,*
otter, asking how far to the river,   15

the police, the safest zoo. We call it
cute, call it ugly, maybe diseased
or lonely, amazed to find something wild

in the city. We wait for someone
with a gun or net to rescue it.   20
We talk to strangers like brothers,

puzzling what should be done
with dark alleys, with garbage,
with vermin that run free at night.

We keep our eyes on it, keep calling   25
softly to calm it. But if we had
clubs, we'd kill it.

CONSIDERATIONS FOR CRITICAL THINKING AND WRITING

1. FIRST RESPONSE. How is suspense created and sustained in the poem?

2. How do these city people respond to "something wild / in the city" (lines 18–19)?

3. How is the otter described? What is the effect of repeatedly referring to the animal as "it"?

CONNECTION TO ANOTHER SELECTION

1. Discuss how the unexpected encounter between civilization and nature produces anxiety in "Coming Across It" and in Alden Nowlan's "The Bull Moose" (below).

ALDEN NOWLAN (1933–1983)

The Bull Moose   1962

Down from the purple mist of trees on the mountain,
lurching through forests of white spruce and cedar,
stumbling through tamarack swamps,
came the bull moose
to be stopped at last by a pole-fenced pasture.   5

Too tired to turn or, perhaps, aware
there was no place left to go, he stood with the cattle.
They, scenting the musk of death, seeing his great head
like the ritual mask of a blood god, moved to the other end
of the field, and waited.   10

The neighbors heard of it, and by afternoon
cars lined the road. The children teased him
with alder switches and he gazed at them
like an old, tolerant collie. The women asked
if he could have escaped from a Fair.   15

The oldest man in the parish remembered seeing
a gelded moose yoked with an ox for plowing.
The young men snickered and tried to pour beer
down his throat, while their girl friends took their pictures.

The bull moose let them stroke his tick-ravaged flanks,   20
let them pry open his jaws with bottles, let a giggling girl
plant a little purple cap
of thistles on his head.

When the wardens came, everyone agreed it was a shame
to shoot anything so shaggy and cuddlesome.   25

He looked like the kind of pet
women put to bed with their sons.

So they held their fire. But just as the sun dropped in the river
the bull moose gathered his strength
like a scaffolded king, straightened and lifted his horns   30
so that even the wardens backed away as they raised their rifles.
When he roared, people ran to their cars. All the young men
leaned on their automobile horns as he toppled.

CONSIDERATIONS FOR CRITICAL THINKING AND WRITING

1. **FIRST RESPONSE.** How does the speaker present the moose and the townspeople? How are the moose and townspeople contrasted? Discuss specific lines to support your response.

2. Explain how the symbols in this poem point to a conflict between humanity and nature. What do you think the speaker's attitude toward this conflict is?

3. **CRITICAL STRATEGIES.** Read the section on mythological criticism (pp. 1081–83) in Chapter 30, "Critical Strategies for Reading," and write an essay on "The Bull Moose" that approaches the poem from a mythological perspective.

CONNECTION TO ANOTHER SELECTION

1. In an essay compare and contrast how the animals portrayed in "The Bull Moose" and in Kay Ryan's "Turtle" (below) are used as symbols.

KAY RYAN (B. 1945)

Turtle   2010

Who would be a turtle who could help it?
A barely mobile hard roll, a four-oared helmet,
she can ill afford the chances she must take
in rowing toward the grasses that she eats.
Her track is graceless, like dragging   5
a packing case places, and almost any slope
defeats her modest hopes. Even being practical,
she's often stuck up to the axle on her way
to something edible. With everything optimal,
she skirts the ditch which would convert   10
her shell into a serving dish. She lives
below luck-level, never imagining some lottery
will change her load of pottery to wings.
Her only levity is patience,
the sport of truly chastened things.   15

CONSIDERATIONS FOR CRITICAL THINKING AND WRITING

1. FIRST RESPONSE. Explain how the poem's imagery captures what it means to be a turtle.

2. How does Ryan transform all the perceived disadvantages of being a turtle into something positive?

3. Discuss the paradox created by the diction in the final two lines.

CONNECTION TO ANOTHER SELECTION

1. Compare Ryan's "Turtle" with Emily Dickinson's "A narrow Fellow in the Grass" (p. 2). How do the poems make you feel about the respective animal in each?

ALLEN GINSBERG (1926–1997)

Sunflower Sutra   1955

I walked on the banks of the tincan banana dock and sat down under the
    huge shade of a Southern Pacific locomotive to look at the sunset
    over the box house hills and cry.
Jack Kerouac sat beside me on a busted rusty iron pole, companion, we
    thought the same thoughts of the soul, bleak and blue and sad-   5
    eyed, surrounded by the gnarled steel roots of trees of machinery.
The oily water on the river mirrored the red sky, sun sank on top of final
    Frisco peaks, no fish in that stream, no hermit in those mounts, just
    ourselves rheumy-eyed and hung-over like old bums on the river-
    bank, tired and wily.   10
Look at the Sunflower, he said, there was a dead gray shadow against the
    sky, big as a man, sitting dry on top of a pile of ancient sawdust —
— I rushed up enchanted — it was my first sunflower, memories of
    Blake — my visions — Harlem
and Hells of the Eastern rivers, bridges clanking Joes Greasy Sandwiches, 15
    dead baby carriages, black treadless tires forgotten and unretreaded,
    the poem of the riverbank, condoms & pots, steel knives, nothing
    stainless, only the dank muck and the razor-sharp artifacts passing
    into the past —
and the gray Sunflower poised against the sunset, crackly bleak and dusty   20
    with the smut and smog and smoke of olden locomotives in its eye —
corolla of bleary spikes pushed down and broken like a battered crown,
    seeds fallen out of its face, soon-to-be-toothless mouth of sunny air,
    sunrays obliterated on its hairy head like a dried wire spiderweb,
leaves stuck out like arms out of the stem, gestures from the sawdust root, 25
    broke pieces of plaster fallen out of the black twigs, a dead fly in its
    ear,

Unholy battered old thing you were, my sunflower O my soul, I loved
    you then!

The grime was no man's grime but death and human locomotives,   30
    all that dress of dust, that veil of darkened railroad skin, that smog of
    cheek, that eyelid of black mis'ry, that sooty hand or phallus or
    protuberance of artificial worse-than-dirt — industrial — modern —
    all that civilization spotting your crazy golden crown —

and those blear thoughts of death and dusty loveless eyes and ends and   35
    withered roots below, in the home-pile of sand and sawdust, rubber
    dollar bills, skin of machinery, the guts and innards of the weeping
    coughing car, the empty lonely tin-cans with their rusty tongues
    alack, what more could I name, the smoked ashes of some cock
    cigar, the cunts of wheel-barrows and the milky breasts of cars,   40
    wornout asses out of chairs & sphincters of dynamos — all these

entangled in your mummied roots — and you there standing before me in
    the sunset, all your glory in your form!

A perfect beauty of a sunflower! a perfect excellent lovely sunflower exis-
    tence! a sweet natural eye to the new hip moon, woke up alive and   45
    excited grasping in the sunset shadow sunrise golden monthly breeze!

How many flies buzzed round you innocent of your grime, while you
    cursed the heavens of the railroad and your flower soul?

Poor dead flower? when did you forget you were a flower? when did you
    look at your skin and decide you were an impotent dirty old   50
    locomotive? the ghost of a locomotive? the specter and shade of
    a once powerful mad American locomotive?

You were never no locomotive, Sunflower, you were a sunflower!

And you Locomotive, you are a locomotive, forget me not!

So I grabbed up the skeleton thick sunflower and stuck it at my side   55
    like a scepter,

and deliver my sermon to my soul, and Jack's soul too, and anyone who'll
    listen,

— We're not our skin of grime, we're not our dread bleak dusty imageless
    locomotive, we're all golden sunflowers inside, blessed by our own   60
    seed & hairy naked accomplishment-bodies growing into mad black
    formal sunflowers in the sunset, spied on by our eyes under the
    shadow of the mad locomotive riverbank sunset Frisco hilly tincan
    evening sit-down vision.

CONSIDERATIONS FOR CRITICAL THINKING AND WRITING

1. **FIRST RESPONSE.** List the images of destruction, death, and/or decay in the poem. What is their cumulative effect?

2. A "sutra" (from Buddhism and Hinduism) is a series of bits of wisdom that together impart a kind of spiritual lesson. (The word *sutra* in Sanskrit means "string" or "thread.") Are you able to summarize the spiritual lesson here?

3. What initially prevents the speaker from recognizing the sunflower's beauty? What brings about his change in perspective?

4. When the speaker plucks the sunflower from the earth to give his sermon, he is essentially killing it. Is that action ironic or does it actually support what the speaker comes to understand about the nature of the sunflower?

CONNECTION TO ANOTHER SELECTION

1. Discuss the importance of the mind, body, and soul in this poem and in Edna St. Vincent Millay's "Spring" (p. 442).

MARY OLIVER (1935–2019)

Wild Geese   1986

You do not have to be good.
You do not have to walk on your knees
for a hundred miles through the desert, repenting.
You only have to let the soft animal of your body
    love what it loves.
Tell me about despair, yours, and I will tell you mine.   5
Meanwhile the world goes on.
Meanwhile the sun and the clear pebbles of the rain
are moving across the landscapes,
over the prairies and the deep trees,
the mountains and the rivers.   10
Meanwhile the wild geese, high in the clean blue air,
are heading home again.
Whoever you are, no matter how lonely,
the world offers itself to your imagination,
calls to you like the wild geese, harsh and exciting —
over and over announcing your place   15
in the family of things.

CONSIDERATIONS FOR CRITICAL THINKING AND WRITING

1. FIRST RESPONSE. Discuss the thematic significance of the wild geese. What do they offer that the poem's first three lines do not?

2. What phrases are repeated — and to what effect?

3. How would you describe the meaning of "the family of things" (last line)?

CONNECTION TO ANOTHER SELECTION

1. Discuss the treatment of imagination in "Wild Geese" and in Emily Dickinson's "To make a prairie it takes a clover and one bee" (p. 560).

Sylvia Plath (1932–1963)

Pheasant 1962

You said you would kill it this morning.
Do not kill it. It startles me still,
The jut of that odd, dark head, pacing

Through the uncut grass on the elm's hill.   5
It is something to own a pheasant,
Or just to be visited at all.

I am not mystical: it isn't
As if I thought it had a spirit.
It is simply in its element.

That gives it a kingliness, a right.   10
The print of its big foot last winter,
The tail-track, on the snow in our court —

The wonder of it, in that pallor,
Through crosshatch of sparrow and starling.
Is it its rareness, then? It is rare.   15

But a dozen would be worth having,
A hundred, on that hill — green and red,
Crossing and recrossing: a fine thing!

It is such a good shape, so vivid.
It's a little cornucopia.   20
It unclaps, brown as a leaf, and loud,

Settles in the elm, and is easy.
It was sunning in the narcissi.
I trespass stupidly. Let be, let be.

CONSIDERATIONS FOR CRITICAL THINKING AND WRITING

1. FIRST RESPONSE. The speaker is trying to convince someone not to kill a pheasant. What is the most convincing aspect of the argument?

2. List examples of rhyme or near-rhyme in the poem and discuss their cumulative impact. Why do you think the poet chose not to adhere to a strict rhyme scheme?

3. What does the pheasant represent to the speaker? How does the speaker's diction and word choice help you understand the bird as a kind of symbol?

CONNECTION TO ANOTHER SELECTION

1. Discuss the relationship between the speaker and nature in "Pheasant" and in "Sunflower Sutra" by Allen Ginsberg (p. 635).

SUGGESTED TOPICS FOR LONGER PAPERS

1. Write an analysis of Gail White's "Dead Armadillos" (p. 630), Walt McDonald's "Coming Across It" (p. 632), and Alden Nowlan's "The Bull Moose" (p. 633) as commentaries on our civilization's problematic relationship to the wild. How does each poem add to and extend a consideration of the issue?

2. Use the Internet to find the lyrics of popular songs written within the past five years about environmental issues. Choose three and write a comparative analysis of their style and themes.

A Collection
of Poems

24

Poems for Further Reading

Chris Jackson/Getty Images.

> Now the role of poetry is not simply to hold understanding in place but to help create and hold a realm of experience. Poetry has become a kind of tool for knowing the world in a particular way.
>
> —JANE HIRSHFIELD

MARGARET ATWOOD (B. 1939)

Owl Song   1976

I am the heart of a murdered woman
who took the wrong way home
who was strangled in a vacant lot and not buried
who was shot with care beneath a tree
who was mutilated by a crisp knife.
There are many of us.   5

I grew feathers and tore my way out of her;
I am shaped like a feathered heart.
My mouth is a chisel, my hands
the crimes done by hands.   10

I sit in the forest talking of death
which is monotonous:
though there are many ways of dying
there is only one death song,
the colour of mist: 15
it says Why Why

I do not want revenge, I do not want expiation,
I only want to ask someone
how I was lost,
how I was lost   20

I am the lost heart of a murderer
who has not yet killed,
who does not yet know he wishes
to kill; who is still the same
as the others   25

I am looking for him,
he will have answers for me,
he will watch his step, he will be
cautious and violent, my claws
will grow through his hands   30
and become claws, he will not be caught.

CHARLES BAUDELAIRE (1821–1867)

A Carrion   1857

TRANSLATED FROM FRENCH BY ALLEN TATE

Remember now, my Love, what piteous thing
    We saw on a summer's gracious day:
By the roadside a hideous carrion, quivering
    On a clean bed of pebbly clay,

Her legs flexed in the air like a courtesan,   5
    Burning and sweating venomously,
Calmly exposed its belly, ironic and wan,
    Clamorous with foul ecstasy.

The sun bore down upon this rottenness
    As if to roast it with gold fire,   10
And render back to nature her own largess
    A hundredfold of her desire.

Heaven observed the vaunting carcass there
    Blooming with the richness of a flower;
And that almighty stink which corpses wear   15
    Choked you with sleepy power!

The flies swarmed on the putrid vulva, then
   A black tumbling rout would seethe
Of maggots, thick like a torrent in a glen,
   Over those rags that lived and seemed to breathe.   20

They darted down and rose up like a wave
   Or buzzed impetuously as before;
One would have thought the corpse was held a slave
   To living by the life it bore!

This world had music, its own swift emotion   25
   Like water and the wind running,
Or corn that a winnower in rhythmic motion
   Fans with fiery cunning.

All forms receded, as in a dream were still,
   Where white visions vaguely start
From the sketch of a painter's long-neglected idyl   30
   Into a perfect art!

Behind the rocks a restless bitch looked on
   Regarding us with jealous eyes,
Waiting to tear from the livid skeleton
   Her loosed morsel quick with flies.   35

And even you will come to this foul shame,
   This ultimate infection,
Star of my eyes, my being's inner flame,
   My angel and my passion!   40

Yes: such shall you be, O queen of heavenly grace,
   Beyond the last sacrament,
When through your bones the flowers and sucking grass
   Weave their rank cerement.

Speak, then, my Beauty, to this dire putrescence,   45
   To the worm, that shall kiss your proud estate,
That I have kept the divine form and the essence
   Of my festered loves inviolate!

WILLIAM BLAKE (1757–1827)

Infant Sorrow   1794

My mother groand! my father wept.
Into the dangerous world I leapt:
Helpless naked piping loud:
Like a fiend hid in a cloud.

Struggling in my father's hands:
Striving against my swaddling bands

Bound and weary I thought best
To sulk upon my mother's breast.

ANNE BRADSTREET (CA. 1612–1672)

Before the Birth of One of Her Children   1678

All things within this fading world hath end,
Adversity doth still our joys attend;
No ties so strong, no friends so dear and sweet,
But with death's parting blow is sure to meet.
The sentence past is most irrevocable,   5
A common thing, yet oh, inevitable.
How soon, my Dear, death may my steps attend,
How soon't may be thy lot to lose thy friend,
We both are ignorant, yet love bids me
These farewell lines to recommend to thee,   10
That when that knot's untied that made us one,
I may seem thine, who in effect am none.
And if I see not half my days that's due,
What nature would, God grant to yours and you;
The many faults that well you know I have   15
Let be interred in my oblivious grave;
If any worth or virtue were in me,
Let that live freshly in thy memory
And when thou feel'st no grief, as I no harms,
Yet love thy dead, who long lay in thine arms,   20
And when thy loss shall be repaid with gains
Look to my little babes, my dear remains.
And if thou love thyself, or loved'st me,
These O protect from stepdame's° injury.   *stepmother's*
And if chance to thine eyes shall bring this verse,   25
With some sad sighs honor my absent hearse;
And kiss this paper for thy love's dear sake,
Who with salt tears this last farewell did take.

EMILY BRONTË (1818–1848)

Stars   1845

Ah! why, because the dazzling sun
Restored my earth to joy
Have you departed, every one,
And left a desert sky?

All through the night, your glorious eyes   5
Were gazing down in mine,
And with a full heart's thankful sighs
I blessed that watch divine!

I was at peace, and drank your beams
As they were life to me   10
And revelled in my changeful dreams
Like petrel on the sea.

Thought followed thought — star followed star
Through boundless regions on,
While one sweet influence, near and far,   15
Thrilled through and proved us one.

Why did the morning rise to break
So great, so pure a spell,
And scorch with fire the tranquil cheek
Where your cool radiance fell?   20

Blood-red he rose, and arrow-straight
His fierce beams struck my brow:
The soul of Nature sprang elate,
But mine sank sad and low!

My lids closed down — yet through their veil
I saw him blazing still;   25
And bathe in gold the misty dale,
And flash upon the hill.

I turned me to the pillow then
To call back Night, and see
Your worlds of solemn light, again   30
Throb with my heart and me!

It would not do — the pillow glowed
And glowed both roof and floor,
And birds sang loudly in the wood,
And fresh winds shook the door.   35

The curtains waved, the wakened flies
Were murmuring round my room,
Imprisoned there, till I should rise
And give them leave to roam.
                                                     40
O Stars and Dreams and Gentle Night;
O Night and Stars return!
And hide me from the hostile light
That does not warm, but burn —

That drains the blood of suffering men;
Drinks tears, instead of dew: 45

Let me sleep through his blinding reign,
And only wake with you!

ELIZABETH BARRETT BROWNING (1806–1861)
How Do I Love Thee? Let Me Count the Ways   1850

How do I love thee? Let me count the ways.
I love thee to the depth and breadth and height
My soul can reach, when feeling out of sight
For the ends of being and ideal grace.
I love thee to the level of every day's   5
Most quiet need, by sun and candle-light.
I love thee freely, as men strive for right.
I love thee purely, as they turn from praise.
I love thee with the passion put to use
In my old griefs, and with my childhood's faith.   10
I love thee with a love I seemed to lose
With my lost saints. I love thee with the breath,
Smiles, tears, of all my life; and, if God choose,
I shall but love thee better after death.

MICHELLE CLIFF (1946–2016)
The Land of Look Behind   1985

*On the edge of each canefield or "piece" was a watch house, a tiny structure with
one entry. These were used for the babies of nursing slaves who worked in the
fields. An older woman was in charge of the infants and the mothers came there
for feeding time.*

— *tourist brochure of the Whim Great House*

A tiny structure with one entry
walls guttered with mortar
molasses   coral   sand
hold the whole thing fast.

One hundred years later   5
the cut limestone
sunned and salted
looks like new.

And feels like? And feels like?
I don't know.   10

Describe it.
Sad? Lost? Angry?
Let me get my bearings.

Outside
A tamarind tree with a dead nest in the first crotch   15
Dense mud construction.
Immense. The inhabitants long gone.
Hard brown pods crack underfoot
The soursweet flesh is dried.
Inedible.   20

Inside
One thin bench faces a blank wall.
No message from the watchwomen here.
No HELP ME carved in the mortar or the stone.
Try to capture the range —   25

What did their voices sound like?
What tongues? What words for day and night?
Hunger? Milk?
What songs devised to ease them?

Was there time to speak? To sing?   30
To the riverain goddesses
The mermaids bringing secrets
To bring down Shàngó's° wrath.

No fatting-houses here.
Nowhere to learn the secrets   35
except through some new code
in spaces they will never own.

How many voices? How many drops of milk?
How many gums daubed with rum to soothe the teething or
bring on sleep?
                                                                        40
How many breasts bore scars?
Not the sacred markings of the Carib —
but the mundane mark of the beast.

How many dropped in the field?
How many bare footfalls across the sand floor?   45
How many were buried?
I leave through the opening and take myself home.

---

33 *Shàngó:* The Yoruban god of thunder and lightning and vengeance.

GREGORY CORSO (1930–2001)

Marriage 1960

Should I get married? Should I be good?
Astound the girl next door with my velvet suit and faustus hood?
Don't take her to movies but to cemeteries
tell all about werewolf bathtubs and forked clarinets
then desire her and kiss her and all the preliminaries   5
and she going just so far and I understanding why
not getting angry saying You must feel! It's beautiful to feel!
Instead take her in my arms lean against an old crooked tomb stone
and woo her the entire night the constellations in the sky —

When she introduces me to her parents   10
back straightened, hair finally combed, strangled by a tie,
should I sit knees together on their 3rd degree sofa
and not ask Where's the bathroom?
How else to feel other than I am,
often thinking Flash Gordon soap —   15
O how terrible it must be for a young man
seated before a family and the family thinking
We never saw him before! He wants our Mary Lou!
After tea and homemade cookies they ask What do you do for a living?

Should I tell them? Would they like me then?   20
Say All right get married, we're losing a daughter
but we're gaining a son —
And should I then ask Where's the bathroom?

O God, and the wedding! All her family and her friends
and only a handful of mine all scroungy and bearded   25
just wait to get at the drinks and food —
And the priest! he looking at me as if I masturbated
asking me Do you take this woman for your lawful wedded wife?
And I trembling what to say say Pie Glue!
I kiss the bride all those corny men slapping me on the back   30
She's all yours, boy! Ha-ha-ha!
And in their eyes you could see some obscene honeymoon going on —
Then all that absurd rice and clanky cans and shoes
Niagara Falls! Hordes of us! Husbands! Wives! Flowers! Chocolates!
All streaming into cozy hotels   35
All going to do the same thing tonight
The indifferent clerk he knowing what was going to happen
The lobby zombies they knowing what
The whistling elevator man he knowing
The winking bellboy knowing   40
Everybody knowing! I'd be almost inclined not to do anything!

Stay up all night! Stare that hotel clerk in the eye!
Screaming: I deny honeymoon! I deny honeymoon!
running rampant into those almost climactic suites
yelling Radio belly! Cat shovel!   45
O I'd live in Niagara forever! in a dark cave beneath the Falls
I'd sit there the Mad Honeymooner
devising ways to break marriages, a scourge of bigamy
a saint of divorce —

But I should get married I should be good   50
How nice it'd be to come home to her
and sit by the fireplace and she in the kitchen
aproned young and lovely wanting my baby
and so happy about me she burns the roast beef
and comes crying to me and I get up from my big papa chair   55
saying Christmas teeth! Radiant brains! Apple deaf!
God what a husband I'd make! Yes, I should get married!
So much to do! like sneaking into Mr Jones' house late at night
and cover his golf clubs with 1920 Norwegian books
Like hanging a picture of Rimbaud on the lawnmower   60
like pasting Tannu Tuva postage stamps all over the picket fence
like when Mrs Kindhead comes to collect for the Community Chest
grab her and tell her There are unfavorable omens in the sky!
And when the mayor comes to get my vote tell him
When are you going to stop people killing whales!   65
And when the milkman comes leave him a note in the bottle
Penguin dust, bring me penguin dust, I want penguin dust —

Yet if I should get married and it's Connecticut and snow
and she gives birth to a child and I am sleepless, worn,
up for nights, head bowed against a quiet window, the past behind me,   70
finding myself in the most common of situations a trembling man
knowledged with responsibility not twig-smear nor Roman coin soup —
O what would that be like!
Surely I'd give it for a nipple a rubber Tacitus
For a rattle a bag of broken Bach records   75
Tack Della Francesca all over its crib
Sew the Greek alphabet on its bib
And build for its playpen a roofless Parthenon

No, I doubt I'd be that kind of father
not rural not snow no quiet window   80
but hot smelly tight New York City
seven flights up, roaches and rats in the walls
a fat Reichian wife screeching over potatoes Get a job!
And five nose running brats in love with Batman
And the neighbors all toothless and dry haired   85
like those hag masses of the 18th century

all wanting to come in and watch TV
The landlord wants his rent
Grocery store Blue Cross Gas & Electric Knights of Columbus
Impossible to lie back and dream Telephone snow, ghost parking —   90
No! I should not get married I should never get married!
But — imagine If I were married to a beautiful sophisticated woman
tall and pale wearing an elegant black dress and long black gloves
holding a cigarette holder in one hand and highball in the other
and we lived high up a penthouse with a huge window   95
from which we could see all of New York and even farther on clearer days
No, can't imagine myself married to that pleasant prison dream —

O but what about love? I forget love
not that I am incapable of love
it's just that I see love as odd as wearing shoes —   100
I never wanted to marry a girl who was like my mother
And Ingrid Bergman was always impossible
And there's maybe a girl now but she's already married
And I don't like men and —
but there's got to be somebody!   105
Because what if I'm 60 years old and not married,
all alone in a furnished room with pee stains on my underwear
and everybody else is married! All the universe married but me!

Ah, yet well I know that were a woman possible as I am possible
then marriage would be possible —   110
Like SHE in her lonely alien gaud waiting her Egyptian lover
so I wait — bereft of 2,000 years and the bath of life.

Bei Dao (b. 1949)

Notes from the City of the Sun   1983

TRANSLATED FROM CHINESE BY BONNIE S. McDOUGALL

   Life
The sun has risen too

   Love
Tranquillity. The wild geese have flown
over the virgin wasteland   5
the old tree has toppled, with a crash
acrid, salty rain drifts through the air

   Freedom
Torn scraps of paper
fluttering   10

   Child

A picture holding the whole ocean
is folded into a white crane

    Girl
A shimmering rainbow
gathers brightly colored birds' feathers   15

    Youth
Red waves
soak a solitary oar

    Art
A million scintillating suns   20
appear in a shattered mirror

    People
The moon is torn into gleaming grains of wheat
and sown in the honest sky and earth   25

    Labor
A pair of hands, encircling the earth

    Fate
A child strikes at random at a railing
The railing strikes at random at the night   30

    Faith
A flock of sheep spills into a green ditch
the shepherd boy pipes his monotonous tune

    Peace
In the land where the king is dead   35
the old rifle sprouts branches and new shoots
and becomes a cripple's cane

    Motherland
Cast on a shield of bronze
she leans against a darkening museum wall   40

    Living
A net

JOHN DONNE (1572–1631)

The Flea 1633

Mark but this flea, and mark in this,
How little that which thou deniest me is;
Me it sucked first, and now sucks thee,
And in this flea our two bloods mingled be;
Thou know'st that this cannot be said   5

A sin, or shame, or loss of maidenhead,
 Yet this enjoys before it woo,
 And pampered swells with one blood made of two,
 And this, alas, is more than we would do.°

Oh stay, three lives in one flea spare,   10
Where we almost, nay more than married are.
This flea is you and I, and this
Our marriage bed and marriage temple is;
Though parents grudge, and you, we are met,
And cloistered in these living walls of jet.   15
 Though use° make you apt to kill me,
 Let not to that, self-murder added be,
 And sacrilege, three sins in killing three.

Cruel and sudden, hast thou since
Purpled thy nail in blood of innocence?°   20
Wherein could this flea guilty be,
Except in that drop which it sucked from thee?
Yet thou triumph'st, and say st' that thou
Find'st not thy self nor me the weaker now;
'Tis true; then learn how false fears be: 25
 Just so much honor, when thou yield'st to me,
 Will waste, as this flea's death took life from thee.

9 I.e., we, alas, don't dare hope for this consummation of our love, which the flea freely accepts. The idea of swelling suggests pregnancy.
16 Habit.
20 Like Herod, Donne's mistress has slaughtered the innocents and is now clothed in imperial purple.

T. S. ELIOT (1888–1965)

The Love Song of J. Alfred Prufrock 1917

S'io credesse che mia risposta fosse
A persona che mai tornasse al mondo,
Questa fiamma staria senza più scosse.
Ma perciocchè giammai di questo fondo
Non tornò vivo alcun, s'i'odo il vero,
Senza tema d'infamia ti rispondo.°

Epigraph: *S'io credesse . . . rispondo:* Dante's *Inferno,* 27:58–63. In the Eighth Chasm of the Inferno, Dante and Virgil meet Guido da Montefeltro, one of the False Counselors, who is punished by being enveloped in an eternal flame. When Dante asks Guido to tell his life story, the spirit replies: "If I thought that my answer were to one who might ever return to the world, this flame would shake no more; but since from this depth none ever returned alive, if what I hear is true, I answer you without fear of infamy."

Let us go then, you and I,
When the evening is spread out against the sky
Like a patient etherized upon a table;
Let us go, through certain half-deserted streets,
The muttering retreats   5
Of restless nights in one-night cheap hotels
And sawdust restaurants with oyster-shells:
Streets that follow like a tedious argument
Of insidious intent
To lead you to an overwhelming question . . .   10

Oh, do not ask, "What is it?"
Let us go and make our visit.

In the room the women come and go
Talking of Michelangelo.

     The yellow fog that rubs its back upon the window panes,   15
The yellow smoke that rubs its muzzle on the window panes
Licked its tongue into the corners of the evening,
Lingered upon the pools that stand in drains,
Let fall upon its back the soot that falls from chimneys,
Slipped by the terrace, made a sudden leap,   20
And seeing that it was a soft October night,
Curled once about the house, and fell asleep.

     And indeed there will be time°
For the yellow smoke that slides along the street,
Rubbing its back upon the window panes;   25
There will be time, there will be time
To prepare a face to meet the faces that you meet;
There will be time to murder and create,
And time for all the works and days° of hands

That lift and drop a question on your plate: 30
Time for you and time for me,
And time yet for a hundred indecisions,
And for a hundred visions and revisions,
Before the taking of a toast and tea.

In the room the women come and go   35
Talking of Michelangelo.

     And indeed there will be time
To wonder, "Do I dare?" and, "Do I dare?" —

23 *there will be time:* An allusion to Ecclesiastes 3:1–8: "To everything there is a season, and a time to every purpose under heaven. . . ."   29 *works and days:* Hesiod's eighth-century B.C. poem *Works and Days* gives practical advice on how to conduct one's life in accordance with the seasons.

Time to turn back and descend the stair,
With a bald spot in the middle of my hair —   40
(They will say: "How his hair is growing thin!")
My morning coat, my collar mounting firmly to the chin,
My necktie rich and modest, but asserted by a simple pin —
(They will say: "But how his arms and legs are thin!")
Do I dare   45
Disturb the universe?
In a minute there is time
For decisions and revisions which a minute will reverse.

    For I have known them all already, known them all:
Have known the evenings, mornings, afternoons,   50
I have measured out my life with coffee spoons;
I know the voices dying with a dying fall
Beneath the music from a farther room.
    So how should I presume?

    And I have known the eyes already, known them all —   55
The eyes that fix you in a formulated phrase.
And when I am formulated, sprawling on a pin,
When I am pinned and wriggling on the wall,
Then how should I begin
To spit out all the butt-ends of my days and ways?   60
    And how should I presume?

    And I have known the arms already, known them all —
Arms that are braceleted and white and bare
(But in the lamplight, downed with light brown hair!)
    Is it perfume from a dress   65
    That makes me so digress?
Arms that lie along a table, or wrap about a shawl.
    And should I then presume?
    And how should I begin?

    Shall I say, I have gone at dusk through narrow streets,   70
And watched the smoke that rises from the pipes
Of lonely men in shirtsleeves, leaning out of windows? . . .

I should have been a pair of ragged claws
Scuttling across the floors of silent seas.

    And the afternoon, the evening, sleeps so peacefully!   75
Smoothed by long fingers,
Asleep . . . tired . . . or it malingers,
Stretched on the floor, here beside you and me.
Should I, after tea and cakes and ices,

Have the strength to force the moment to its crisis? 80
But though I have wept and fasted, wept and prayed,
Though I have seen my head (grown slightly bald) brought in upon a platter,°
I am no prophet — and here's no great matter;
I have seen the moment of my greatness flicker,
And I have seen the eternal Footman hold my coat, and snicker, 85
   And in short, I was afraid.

   And would it have been worth it, after all,
After the cups, the marmalade, the tea,
Among the porcelain, among some talk of you and me,
Would it have been worth while 90
To have bitten off the matter with a smile,
To have squeezed the universe into a ball°
To roll it toward some overwhelming question,
To say: "I am Lazarus,° come from the dead,
Come back to tell you all, I shall tell you all" — 95
If one, settling a pillow by her head,
   Should say: "That is not what I meant at all;
     That is not it, at all."

   And would it have been worth it, after all,
Would it have been worth while, 100
After the sunsets and the dooryards and the sprinkled streets,
After the novels, after the teacups, after the skirts that trail along the floor —
And this, and so much more? —
It is impossible to say just what I mean!
But as if a magic lantern threw the nerves in patterns on a screen: 105
Would it have been worth while
If one, settling a pillow or throwing off a shawl,
And turning toward the window, should say:
   "That is not it at all,
   That is not what I meant, at all." 110

No! I am not Prince Hamlet, nor was meant to be;
Am an attendant lord,° one that will do
To swell a progress,° start a scene or two,   *state procession*

---

82 *head . . . upon a platter:* At Salome's request, Herod had John the Baptist decapitated and had the severed head delivered to her on a platter (see Matt. 14:1–12 and Mark 6:17–29). 92 *squeezed the universe into a ball:* See Andrew Marvell's "To His Coy Mistress" (p. 410), lines 41–42: "Let us roll all our strength and all / Our sweetness up into one ball." 94 *Lazarus:* The brother of Mary and Martha who was raised from the dead by Jesus (John 11:1–44). In Luke 16:19–31, a rich man asks that another Lazarus return from the dead to warn the living about their treatment of the poor. 112 *attendant lord:* Like Polonius in Shakespeare's *Hamlet.*

Advise the prince: withal, an easy tool,
Deferential, glad to be of use,   115
Politic, cautious, and meticulous;
Full of high sentence, but a bit obtuse;
At times, indeed, almost ridiculous —
Almost, at times, the Fool.

I grow old . . . I grow old . . .   120
I shall wear the bottoms of my trousers rolled.

   Shall I part my hair behind? Do I dare to eat a peach?
I shall wear white flannel trousers, and walk upon the beach.
I have heard the mermaids singing, each to each.

I do not think that they will sing to me.   125

I have seen them riding seaward on the waves,
Combing the white hair of the waves blown back
When the wind blows the water white and black.

We have lingered in the chambers of the sea
By seagirls wreathed with seaweed red and brown,   130
Till human voices wake us, and we drown.

LAWRENCE FERLINGHETTI (B. 1919)

Constantly Risking Absurdity   1960

Constantly risking absurdity
           and death
    whenever he performs
          above the heads
             of his audience   5
  the poet like an acrobat
       climbs on rime
         to a high wire of his own making
and balancing on eyebeams
         above a sea of faces   10
   paces his way
      to the other side of day
  performing entrechats
       and sleight-of-foot tricks
and other high theatrics   15
      and all without mistaking
   any thing
      for what it may not be
  For he's the super realist

who must perforce perceive   20

taut truth

before the taking of each stance or step

in his supposed advance

toward that still higher perch

where Beauty stands and waits   25

with gravity

to start her death-defying leap

And he

a little charleychaplin man

who may or may not catch   30

her fair eternal form

spreadeagled in the empty air

of existence

ROBERT FROST (1874–1963)

Mending Wall   1914

Something there is that doesn't love a wall,
That sends the frozen-ground-swell under it,
And spills the upper boulders in the sun;
And makes gaps even two can pass abreast.
The work of hunters is another thing: 5
I have come after them and made repair
Where they have left not one stone on a stone,
But they would have the rabbit out of hiding,
To please the yelping dogs. The gaps I mean,
No one has seen them made or heard them made,   10
But at spring mending-time we find them there.
I let my neighbor know beyond the hill;
And on a day we meet to walk the line
And set the wall between us once again.
We keep the wall between us as we go.   15
To each the boulders that have fallen to each.
And some are loaves and some so nearly balls
We have to use a spell to make them balance:
"Stay where you are until our backs are turned!"
We wear our fingers rough with handling them.   20
Oh, just another kind of outdoor game,
One on a side. It comes to little more:
There where it is we do not need the wall:
He is all pine and I am apple orchard.
My apple trees will never get across   25
And eat the cones under his pines, I tell him.
He only says, "Good fences make good neighbors."

Spring is the mischief in me, and I wonder
If I could put a notion in his head:
"*Why* do they make good neighbors? Isn't it 30
Where there are cows? But here there are no cows.
Before I built a wall I'd ask to know
What I was walling in or walling out,
And to whom I was like to give offense.
Something there is that doesn't love a wall, 35
That wants it down." I could say "Elves" to him,
But it's not elves exactly, and I'd rather
He said it for himself. I see him there
Bringing a stone grasped firmly by the top
In each hand, like an old-stone savage armed. 40
He moves in darkness as it seems to me,
Not of woods only and the shade of trees.
He will not go behind his father's saying,
And he likes having thought of it so well
He says again, "Good fences make good neighbors." 45

LOUISE GLÜCK (B. 1943)

Celestial Music 1991

I have a friend who still believes in heaven.
Not a stupid person, yet with all she knows, she literally talks to god,
she thinks someone listens in heaven.
On earth, she's unusually competent.
Brave, too, able to face unpleasantness. 5

We found a caterpillar dying in the dirt, greedy ants crawling over it.
I'm always moved by weakness, by disaster, always eager to oppose vitality.
But timid, also, quick to shut my eyes.
Whereas my friend was able to watch, to let events play out according to
    nature. For my sake, she intervened, 10
brushing a few ants off the torn thing, and set it down across the road.

My friend says I shut my eyes to god, that nothing else explains
my aversion to reality. She says I'm like the child who buries her head in
    the pillow
so as not to see, the child who tells herself
that light causes sadness— 15
My friend is like the mother. Patient, urging me
to wake up an adult like herself, a courageous person—

In my dreams, my friend reproaches me. We're walking
on the same road, except it's winter now;

she's telling me that when you love the world you hear celestial music: 20
look up, she says. When I look up, nothing.
Only clouds, snow, a white business in the trees
like brides leaping to a great height —
Then I'm afraid for her; I see her
caught in a net deliberately cast over the earth —   25

In reality, we sit by the side of the road, watching the sun set;
from time to time, the silence pierced by a birdcall.
It's this moment we're both trying to explain, the fact
that we're at ease with death, with solitude.
My friend draws a circle in the dirt; inside, the caterpillar doesn't move.   30
She's always trying to make something whole, something beautiful, an image
capable of life apart from her.
We're very quiet. It's peaceful sitting here, not speaking, the composition
fixed, the road turning suddenly dark, the air
going cool, here and there the rocks shining and glittering —   35
it's this stillness that we both love.
The love of form is a love of endings.

SEAMUS HEANEY (1939–2013)

Personal Helicon   1917

for Michael Longley

As a child, they could not keep me from wells
And old pumps with buckets and windlasses.
I loved the dark drop, the trapped sky, the smells
Of waterweed, fungus and dank moss.

One, in a brickyard, with a rotted board top.
I savoured the rich crash when a bucket   5
Plummeted down at the end of a rope.
So deep you saw no reflection in it.

A shallow one under a dry stone ditch
Fructified like any aquarium.
When you dragged out long roots from the soft mulch   10
A white face hovered over the bottom.

Others had echoes, gave back your own call
With a clean new music in it. And one
Was scaresome, for there, out of ferns and tall   15
Foxgloves, a rat slapped across my reflection.

Now, to pry into roots, to finger slime,
To stare, big-eyed Narcissus,° into some spring
Is beneath all adult dignity. I rhyme
To see myself, to set the darkness echoing.   20

18 *Narcissus:* a Greek mythological figure who was infatuated with his own reflection in a pool of water; origin of the term *narcissism.*

BRIONNE JANAE (B. 1991)

Alternative Facts   2018

for Tamir Rice

the officer stops   parks his car
at the frost chipped curb
the officer can see the boy
and spends a few more moments
in the heat of his patrol car   he studies the boy   5
his boy sized body and childish desire
to clutch power in the untried soft
of his palm   the officer remembers himself
at this age   how eager he was to matter
the officer can see how the toy gun   10
makes the boy matter   the officer can see himself
in the boy   the officer can see the boy
his not yet manness
the memory of milk teeth
on his smooth cheeks   15
the officer can see how the boy
must've buried his face in his mother's flesh
when the world was too much
the world weary officer rubs his jaw and sighs
it reminds the officer of his own   20
cherry cheeked mother
how he ought to call
when he has finished
sending this boy
home to his own momma   25
the thought of his mother
dimples the officer's cheeks

JOHN KEATS (1795–1821)

When I have fears that I may cease to be   1818

When I have fears that I may cease to be
    Before my pen has gleaned my teeming brain,
Before high-piled books, in charactery,°   *print*
    Hold like rich garners the full ripened grain;
When I behold, upon the night's starred face,   5
    Huge cloudy symbols of a high romance,
And think that I may never live to trace
    Their shadows, with the magic hand of chance;
And when I feel, fair creature of an hour,
    That I shall never look upon thee more,   10
Never have relish in the faery° power   *magic*
    Of unreflecting love; — then on the shore
Of the wide world I stand alone, and think
Till love and fame to nothingness do sink.

PHILIP LARKIN (1922–1985)

Sad Steps°   1968

Groping back to bed after a piss
I part thick curtains, and am startled by
The rapid clouds, the moon's cleanliness.

Four o'clock: wedge-shadowed gardens lie
Under a cavernous, a wind-picked sky.   5
There's something laughable about this,

The way the moon dashes through clouds that blow
Loosely as cannon-smoke to stand apart
(Stone-coloured light sharpening the roofs below)

High and preposterous and separate —   10
Lozenge of love! Medallion of art!
O wolves of memory! Immensements! No,

One shivers slightly, looking up there.
The hardness and the brightness and the plain
Far-reaching singleness of that wide stare   15

Is a reminder of the strength and pain
Of being young; that it can't come again,
But is for others undiminished somewhere.

Cf. Sir Philip Sidney, *Astrophil and Stella* 31: "With how sad steps, O Moon, thou climb'st the skies.

EMMA LAZARUS (1849–1887)

The New Colossus 1883

Not like the brazen giant of Greek fame,
With conquering limbs astride from land to land;
Here at our sea-washed, sunset gates shall stand
A mighty woman with a torch, whose flame
Is the imprisoned lightning, and her name   5
Mother of Exiles. From her beacon-hand
Glows world-wide welcome; her mild eyes command
The air-bridged harbor that twin cities frame.
"Keep, ancient lands, your storied pomp!" cries she
With silent lips. "Give me your tired, your poor,   10
Your huddled masses yearning to breathe free,
The wretched refuse of your teeming shore.
Send these, the homeless, tempest-tost to me,
I lift my lamp beside the golden door!"

ROBERT LOWELL (1917–1977)

Skunk Hour 1960

(For Elizabeth Bishop)

Nautilus Island's° hermit
heiress still lives through winter in her Spartan cottage;
her sheep still graze above the sea.
Her son's a bishop. Her farmer
is first selectman in our village;   5
she's in her dotage.

Thirsting for
the hierarchic privacy
of Queen Victoria's century,
she buys up all   10
the eyesores facing her shore,
and lets them fall.

The season's ill —
we've lost our summer millionaire,
who seemed to leap from an L.L. Bean°   15
catalogue. His nine-knot yawl

1 *Nautilus Island's:* In Maine.
15 *L.L. Bean:* Freeport, Maine, mail-order house.

was auctioned off to lobstermen.
A red fox stain covers Blue Hill.

And now our fairy
decorator brightens his shop for fall;
his fishnet's filled with orange cork,   20
orange, his cobbler's bench and awl;
there is no money in his work,
he'd rather marry.

One dark night,
my Tudor Ford climbed the hill's skull;   25
I watched for love-cars. Lights turned down,
they lay together, hull to hull,
where the graveyard shelves on the town. . . .
My mind's not right.   30

A car radio bleats,
"Love, O careless Love. . . . " I hear
my ill-spirit sob in each blood cell,
as if my hand were at its throat. . . .
I myself am hell;   35
nobody's here —

only skunks, that search
in the moonlight for a bite to eat.
They march on their soles up Main Street:
white stripes, moonstruck eyes' red fire   40
under the chalk-dry and spar spire
of the Trinitarian Church.

I stand on top
of our back steps and breathe the rich air —
a mother skunk with her column of kittens swills the garbage pail.   45
She jabs her wedge-head in a cup
of sour cream, drops her ostrich tail,
and will not scare.

Naomi Shihab Nye (b. 1952)

To Manage   2018

She writes to me —
    I can't sleep because I'm seventeen
Sometimes I lie awake thinking
    I didn't even clean my room yet
And soon I will be twenty-five   5

And a failure
And when I am fifty — oh!
I write her back
    Slowly   slow
Clean one drawer   10
    Arrange words on a page
Let them find one another
    Find you
Trust they might know something
    You aren't living   the whole thing   15
       At once

That's what a minute   said to an hour
Without me   you are nothing

EDGAR ALLAN POE (1809–1849)

Annabel Lee 1849

It was many and many a year ago,
    In a kingdom by the sea,
That a maiden there lived whom you may know
    By the name of Annabel Lee;
And this maiden she lived with no other thought   5
    Than to love and be loved by me.

She was a child and *I* was a child,
    In this kingdom by the sea,
But we loved with a love that was more than love —
    I and my Annabel Lee —   10
With a love that the wingéd seraphs° of Heaven   *angels of the highest order*
    Coveted her and me.

And this was the reason that, long ago,
    In this kingdom by the sea,
A wind blew out of a cloud by night   15
    Chilling my Annabel Lee;
So that her highborn kinsmen came
    And bore her away from me,
To shut her up in a sepulchre
    In this kingdom by the sea.   20

The angels, not half so happy in Heaven,
    Went envying her and me:
Yes! that was the reason (as all men know,
    In this kingdom by the sea)

That the wind came out of the cloud, chilling
    And killing my Annabel Lee.   25

But our love it was stronger by far than the love
    Of those who were older than we —
    Of many far wiser than we —
And neither the angels in Heaven above
    Nor the demons down under the sea,   30
Can ever dissever my soul from the soul
    Of the beautiful Annabel Lee:

For the moon never beams without bringing me dreams
    Of the beautiful Annabel Lee;
And the stars never rise but I see the bright eyes   35
    Of the beautiful Annabel Lee;
And so, all the night-tide, I lie down by the side
Of my darling, my darling, my life and my bride,
    In her sepulchre there by the sea —
    In her tomb by the side of the sea.   40

PERCY BYSSHE SHELLEY (1792–1822)

Ozymandias°   1818

I met a traveler from an antique land
Who said: Two vast and trunkless legs of stone
Stand in the desert. . . . Near them, on the sand,
Half sunk, a shattered visage lies, whose frown,
And wrinkled lip, and sneer of cold command,
Tell that its sculptor well those passions read   5
Which yet survive, stamped on these lifeless things,
The hand that mocked them, and the heart that fed:
And on the pedestal these words appear:
"My name is Ozymandias, King of Kings:
Look on my works, ye Mighty, and despair!"   10
Nothing beside remains. Round the decay
Of that colossal wreck, boundless and bare
The lone and level sands stretch far away.

Ozymandias: Greek name for Ramses II, pharaoh of Egypt for sixty-seven years during the thirteenth century B.C. His colossal statue lies prostrate in the sands of Luxor. Napoleon's soldiers measured it (56 feet long, ear 3½ feet long, weight 1,000 tons). Its inscription, according to the Greek historian Diodorus Siculus, was "I am Ozymandias, King of Kings; if anyone wishes to know what I am and where I lie, let him surpass me in some of my exploits."

STEVIE SMITH (1902–1971)
Not Waving but Drowning 1957

Nobody heard him, the dead man,
But still he lay moaning:
I was much further out than you thought
And not waving but drowning.

Poor chap, he always loved larking   5
And now he's dead
It must have been too cold for him his heart gave way,
They said.

Oh, no no no, it was too cold always
(Still the dead one lay moaning)   10
I was much too far out all my life
And not waving but drowning.

WALLACE STEVENS (1879–1955)
Thirteen Ways of Looking at a Blackbird 1917

I

Among twenty snowy mountains,
The only moving thing
Was the eye of the blackbird.

II

I was of three minds,
Like a tree   5
In which there are three blackbirds.

III

The blackbird whirled in the autumn winds.
It was a small part of the pantomime.

IV

A man and a woman
Are one.   10
A man and a woman and a blackbird
Are one.

V

I do not know which to prefer,
The beauty of inflections
Or the beauty of innuendoes,
The blackbird whistling   15
Or just after.

VI

Icicles filled the long window
With barbaric glass.
The shadow of the blackbird
Crossed it, to and fro.   20
The mood
Traced in the shadow
An indecipherable cause.

VII

O thin men of Haddam,°
Why do you imagine golden birds?   25
Do you not see how the blackbird
Walks around the feet
Of the women about you?

VIII

I know noble accents
And lucid, inescapable rhythms;   30
But I know, too,
That the blackbird is involved
In what I know.

IX

When the blackbird flew out of sight,
It marked the edge   35
Of one of many circles.

X

At the sight of blackbirds
Flying in a green light,
Even the bawds of euphony
Would cry out sharply.   40

25 *Haddam:* small town in Connecticut

XI

He rode over Connecticut
In a glass coach.
Once, a fear pierced him,
In that he mistook   45
The shadow of his equipage
For blackbirds.

XII

The river is moving.
The blackbird must be flying.

XIII

It was evening all afternoon.   50
It was snowing
And it was going to snow.
The blackbird sat
In the cedar-limbs.

JONATHAN SWIFT (1667–1745)

A Description of the Morning   1711

Now hardly here and there an hackney-coach,
Appearing, showed the ruddy morn's approach.
Now Betty from her master's bed had flown,
And softly stole to discompose her own.
The slipshod prentice from his master's door   5
Had pared the dirt, and sprinkled round the floor.
Now Moll had whirled her mop with dextrous airs,
Prepared to scrub the entry and the stairs.
The youth with broomy stumps began to trace
The kennel-edge, where wheels had worn the place.   10
The small-coal man was heard with cadence deep,
Till drowned in shriller notes of chimney-sweep,
Duns at his lordship's gate began to meet,
And Brickdust Moll had screamed through half the street.
The turnkey now his flock returning sees,   15
Duly let out a-nights to steal for fees;
The watchful bailiffs take their silent stands,
And schoolboys lag with satchels in their hands.

ALFRED, LORD TENNYSON (1809–1892)

Ulysses°   1833

It little profits that an idle king,
By this still hearth, among these barren crags,
Matched with an agèd wife,° I mete and dole   *Penelope*
Unequal laws unto a savage race,
That hoard, and sleep, and feed, and know not me.   5
    I cannot rest from travel; I will drink
Life to the lees. All times I have enjoyed
Greatly, have suffered greatly, both with those
That loved me, and alone; on shore, and when
Through scudding drifts the rainy Hyades°   10
Vexed the dim sea. I am become a name;
For always roaming with a hungry heart
Much have I seen and known — cities of men
And manners, climates, councils, governments,
Myself not least, but honored of them all —   15
And drunk delight of battle with my peers,
Far on the ringing plains of windy Troy.
I am a part of all that I have met;
Yet all experience is an arch wherethrough
Gleams that untraveled world, whose margin fades   20
For ever and for ever when I move.
How dull it is to pause, to make an end,
To rust unburnished, not to shine in use!
As though to breathe were life. Life piled on life
Were all too little, and of one to me   25
Little remains; but every hour is saved
From that eternal silence, something more,
A bringer of new things; and vile it were
For some three suns to store and hoard myself,
And this gray spirit yearning in desire   30
To follow knowledge like a sinking star,
Beyond the utmost bound of human thought.

    This is my son, mine own Telemachus,
To whom I leave the scepter and the isle —
Well-loved of me, discerning to fulfill   35
This labor, by slow prudence to make mild
A rugged people, and through soft degrees

Ulysses: Ulysses, the hero of Homer's epic poem the *Odyssey,* is presented by Dante in *The Inferno,* XXVI, as restless after his return to Ithaca and eager for new adventures.
10 *Hyades:* Five stars in the constellation Taurus, supposed by the ancients to predict rain when they rose with the sun.

Subdue them to the useful and the good.
Most blameless is he, centered in the sphere
Of common duties, decent not to fail   40
In offices of tenderness, and pay
Meet adoration to my household gods,
When I am gone. He works his work, I mine.

   There lies the port; the vessel puffs her sail:
There gloom the dark, broad seas. My mariners,   45
Souls that have toiled, and wrought, and thought with me —
That ever with a frolic welcome took
The thunder and the sunshine, and opposed
Free hearts, free foreheads — you and I are old;
Old age hath yet his honor and his toil.   50
Death closes all; but something ere the end,
Some work of noble note, may yet be done,
Not unbecoming men that strove with Gods.
The lights begin to twinkle from the rocks;
The long day wanes; the slow moon climbs; the deep   55
Moans round with many voices. Come, my friends.
'Tis not too late to seek a newer world.
Push off, and sitting well in order smite
The sounding furrows; for my purpose holds
To sail beyond the sunset, and the baths   60
Of all the western stars, until I die.
It may be that the gulfs will wash us down;
It may be we shall touch the Happy Isles,°
And see the great Achilles,° whom we knew.
Though much is taken, much abides; and though   65
We are not now that strength which in old days
Moved earth and heaven, that which we are, we are:
One equal temper of heroic hearts,
Made weak by time and fate, but strong in will
To strive, to seek, to find, and not to yield.   70

63 *Happy Isles:* Elysium, the home after death of heroes and others favored by the gods. It was thought by the ancients to lie beyond the sunset in the uncharted Atlantic.
64 *Achilles:* The hero of Homer's *Iliad.*

NATASHA TRETHEWEY (B. 1966)

Incident   2006

We tell the story every year —
how we peered from the windows, shades drawn —
though nothing really happened,
the charred grass now green again.

We peered from the windows, shades drawn,   5
at the cross trussed like a Christmas tree,
the charred grass still green. Then
we darkened our rooms, lit the hurricane lamps.

At the cross trussed like a Christmas tree,
a few men gathered, white as angels in their gowns.
We darkened our rooms and lit hurricane lamps,   10
the wicks trembling in their fonts of oil.

It seemed the angels had gathered, white men in their gowns.
When they were done, they left quietly. No one came.
The wicks trembled all night in their fonts of oil;   15
by morning the flames had all dimmed.

When they were done, the men left quietly. No one came.
Nothing really happened.
By morning all the flames had dimmed.
We tell the story every year.   20

Phillis Wheatley (1753–1784)

To S. M.° a young African Painter, on seeing his Works   1773

TO show the lab'ring bosom's deep intent,
And thought in living characters to paint,
When first thy pencil did those beauties give,
And breathing figures learnt from thee to live,
How did those prospects give my soul delight,
A new creation rushing on my sight?   5
Still, wond'rous youth! each noble path pursue,
On deathless glories fix thine ardent view:
Still may the painter's and the poet's fire
To aid thy pencil, and thy verse conspire!
And may the charms of each seraphic theme   10
Conduct thy footsteps to immortal fame!
High to the blissful wonders of the skies
Elate thy soul, and raise thy wishful eyes.
Thrice happy, when exalted to survey
That splendid city, crown'd with endless day,   15
Whose twice six gates on radiant hinges ring:
Celestial *Salem*° blooms in endless spring.

To S.M.: Scipio Moorhead who, like Wheatley, was a slave in colonial America.
18 *Salem:* The heavenly city of Jerusalem.

Calm and serene thy moments glide along,
And may the muse inspire each future song!   20
Still, with the sweets of contemplation bless'd,
May peace with balmy wings your soul invest!
But when these shades of time are chas'd away,
And darkness ends in everlasting day,
On what seraphic pinions shall we move,   25
And view the landscapes in the realms above?
There shall thy tongue in heav'nly murmurs flow,
And there my muse with heav'nly transport glow:
No more to tell of *Damon's*° tender sighs,
Or rising radiance of *Aurora's*° eyes,   30
For nobler themes demand a nobler strain,
And purer language on th' ethereal plain.
Cease, gentle muse! the solemn gloom of night
Now seals the fair creation from my sight.

29 *Damon:* A generic name for a shepherd in a pastoral poem.
30 *Aurora:* The Roman goddess of dawn.

WALT WHITMAN (1819–1892)

When I Heard the Learn'd Astronomer   1865

When I heard the learn'd astronomer,
When the proofs, the figures, were ranged in columns before me,
When I was shown the charts and diagrams, to add, divide, and measure them,
When I sitting heard the astronomer where he lectured with much applause
    in the lecture-room,
How soon unaccountable I became tired and sick,
Till rising and gliding out I wandered off by myself,
In the mystical moist night-air, and from time to time,
Looked up in perfect silence at the stars.

WILLIAM WORDSWORTH (1770–1850)

I Wandered Lonely as a Cloud   1807

I wandered lonely as a cloud
That floats on high o'er vales and hills,
When all at once I saw a crowd,

A host, of golden daffodils;
Beside the lake, beneath the trees,
Fluttering and dancing in the breeze.   5

Continuous as the stars that shine
And twinkle on the milky way,
They stretched in never-ending line
Along the margin of a bay:
Ten thousand saw I at a glance,   10
Tossing their heads in sprightly dance.

The waves beside them danced; but they
Out-did the sparkling waves in glee:
A poet could not but be gay,
In such a jocund company: 15
I gazed — and gazed — but little thought
What wealth the show to me had brought:

For oft, when on my couch I lie
In vacant or in pensive mood,
They flash upon that inward eye   20
Which is the bliss of solitude;
And then my heart with pleasure fills,
And dances with the daffodils.

William Butler Yeats (1865–1939)

The Lake Isle of Innisfree°   1892

I will arise and go now, and go to Innisfree,
And a small cabin build there, of clay and wattles made:
Nine bean-rows will I have there, a hive for the honey-bee,
And live alone in the bee-loud glade.
And I shall have some peace there, for peace comes dropping slow,   5
Dropping from the veils of the morning to where the cricket sings;
There midnight's all a glimmer, and noon a purple glow,
And evening full of the linnet's wings.

I will arise and go now, for always night and day
I hear lake water lapping with low sounds by the shore:
While I stand on the roadway, or on the pavements grey,   10
I hear it in the deep heart's core.

The Lake Isle of Innisfree: An island in Lough (or Lake) Gill, in western Ireland.

DRAMA

The Study
of Drama

25

Reading Drama

Adger Cowans/Getty Images.

> My plays are about love, honor, duty,
> betrayal — things humans have written
> about since the beginning of time.
> — AUGUST WILSON

READING DRAMA RESPONSIVELY

The publication of a short story, novel, or poem represents for most writers the final step in a long creative process that might have begun with an idea, issue, emotion, or question that demanded expression. **Playwrights** — the *wright* refers to a craftsman, not to the word *write* — may begin a work in the same way as other writers, but rarely are they satisfied with only its publication because most **plays** are written to be performed by actors on a stage before an audience. Playwrights typically create a play keeping in mind not only readers but also actors, producers, directors, costumers, designers, technicians, and a theater full of other support staff who have a hand in presenting the play to a live audience.

Drama is literature equipped with arms, legs, tears, laughs, whispers, shouts, and gestures that are alive and immediate. Indeed, the word **drama** derives from the Greek word *dran,* meaning "to do" or "to perform." The text of many plays — the **script** — may fully come to life only when the written words are transformed into a performance. Although there are plays that do not invite production, they are relatively few. Such plays, written to be read rather than performed, are called ***closet dramas***. In this kind of work (primarily associated with nineteenth-century English literature), literary art outweighs all other considerations. The majority of playwrights, however, view the written word as the beginning of a larger creation and hope that a producer will deem their scripts worthy of production.

Given that most playwrights intend their works to be performed, it might be argued that reading a play is a poor substitute for seeing it acted on a stage — perhaps something like reading a recipe without having access to the ingredients and a kitchen. This analogy is tempting, but it overlooks the literary dimensions of a script; the words we hear on a stage were written first. Read from a page, these words can feed an imagination in ways that a recipe cannot satisfy a hungry cook. We can fill in a play's missing faces, voices, actions, and settings in much the same way that we imagine these elements in a short story or novel. Like any play director, we are free to include as many ingredients as we have an appetite for.

This imaginative collaboration with the playwright creates a mental world that can be nearly as real and vivid as a live performance. Sometimes readers find that they prefer their own reading of a play to a director's interpretation. The title character of Shakespeare's *Hamlet*, for instance, has been presented as a whining son, but you may read him as a strong prince. Rich plays often accommodate a wide range of imaginative responses to their texts. Reading, then, is an excellent way to appreciate and evaluate a production of a play. Moreover, reading is valuable in its own right because it allows us to enter the playwright's created world even when a theatrical production is unavailable.

Reading a play, however, requires more creative imagining than sitting in an audience watching actors on a stage presenting lines and actions before you. As a reader you become the play's director; you construct an interpretation based on the playwright's use of language, development of character, arrangement of incidents, description of settings, and directions for staging. Keeping track of the playwright's handling of these elements will help you to organize your response to the play. You may experience suspense, fear, horror, sympathy, or humor, but whatever experience a play evokes, ask yourself why you respond to it as you do. You may discover that your assessment of Hamlet's character is different from someone else's, but whether you find him heroic, indecisive, neurotic, or a complex of competing qualities, you'll be better equipped to articulate your interpretation of him if you pay attention to your responses and ask yourself questions as you read. Consider, for example, how his reactions might be similar to or different from your own. How does his language reveal his character? Does his behavior seem justified? How would you play the role yourself? What actor do you think might best play the Hamlet that you have created in your imagination? Why would he or she (women have also played Hamlet onstage) fill the role best?

These kinds of questions (see Questions for Responsive Reading and Writing about Fiction, p. 1106) can help you to think and talk about your responses to a play. Happily, such questions needn't — and often can't — be fully answered as you read the play. Frequently you must experience the entire play before you can determine how its elements work together. That's why reading a play can be such a satisfying experience. You wouldn't think of asking a live actor onstage to repeat her lines because you didn't quite comprehend their significance, but you can certainly reread a page in a book. Rereading allows you to replay language, characters, and incidents carefully and thoroughly to your own satisfaction.

Trifles

In the following play, Susan Glaspell skill-fully draws on many dramatic elements and creates an intense story that is as effective on the page as it is in the theater. Glaspell wrote *Trifles* in 1916 for the Provincetown Players on Cape Cod, in Massachusetts. Their performance of the work helped her develop a reputation as a writer sensitive to feminist issues. The year after *Trifles* was produced, Glaspell transformed the play into a short story titled "A Jury of Her Peers."

Provided courtesy of the Lear Center for Special Collections & Archives, Connecticut College.

Glaspell's life in the Midwest provided her with the setting for *Trifles*. Born and raised in Davenport, Iowa, she graduated from Drake University in 1899 and then worked for a short time as a reporter on the *Des Moines News*, until her short stories were accepted in magazines such as *Harper's* and *Ladies' Home Journal*. Glaspell moved to the Northeast when she was in her early thirties to continue writing fiction and drama. She published novels, some twenty plays, and more than forty short stories. *Alison's House*, based on Emily Dickinson's life, earned her a Pulitzer Prize for drama in 1931. *Trifles* and "A Jury of Her Peers" remain, however, Glaspell's best-known works.

Glaspell wrote *Trifles* to complete a bill that was to feature several one-act plays by Eugene O'Neill. In *The Road to the Temple* (1926), she recalls how the play came to her as she sat in the theater looking at a bare stage. First, "the stage became a kitchen. . . . Then the door at the back opened, and people all bundled up came in — two or three men. I wasn't sure which, but sure enough about the two women, who hung back, reluctant to enter that kitchen. When I was a newspaper reporter out in Iowa, I was sent down-state to do a murder trial, and I never forgot going to the kitchen of a woman who had been locked up in town."

Trifles is about a murder committed in a midwestern farmhouse, but the play goes beyond the kinds of questions raised by most whodunit stories.

The murder is the occasion instead of the focus. The play's major concerns are the moral, social, and psychological aspects of the assumptions and perceptions of the men and women who search for the murderer's motive. Glaspell is finally more interested in the meaning of Mrs. Wright's life than in the details of Mr. Wright's death.

As you read the play, keep track of your responses to the characters and note in the margin the moments when Glaspell reveals how men and women respond differently to the evidence before them. What do those moments suggest about the kinds of assumptions these men and women make about themselves and each other? How do their assumptions compare with your own?

Susan Glaspell (1882–1948)

Trifles 1916

CHARACTERS

George Henderson, county attorney
Henry Peters, sheriff
Lewis Hale, a neighboring farmer
Mrs. Peters
Mrs. Hale

SCENE: The kitchen in the now abandoned farmhouse of John Wright, a gloomy kitchen, and left without having been put in order — unwashed pans under the sink, a loaf of bread outside the breadbox, a dish towel on the table — other signs of incompleted work. At the rear the outer door opens and the Sheriff comes in followed by the County Attorney and Hale. The Sheriff and Hale are men in middle life, the County Attorney is a young man; all are much bundled up and go at once to the stove. They are followed by the two women — the Sheriff's wife first; she is a slight wiry woman, a thin nervous face. Mrs. Hale is larger and would ordinarily be called more comfortable looking, but she is disturbed now and looks fearfully about as she enters. The women have come in slowly, and stand close together near the door.

County Attorney (rubbing his hands): This feels good. Come up to the fire, ladies.
Mrs. Peters (after taking a step forward): I'm not — cold.
Sheriff (unbuttoning his overcoat and stepping away from the stove as if to mark the beginning of official business): Now, Mr. Hale, before we move things about, you explain to Mr. Henderson just what you saw when you came here yesterday morning.

County Attorney: By the way, has anything been moved? Are things just as you left them yesterday?

Sheriff (looking about): It's just about the same. When it dropped below zero last night I thought I'd better send Frank out this morning to make a fire for us — no use getting pneumonia with a big case on, but I told him not to touch anything except the stove — and you know Frank.

County Attorney: Somebody should have been left here yesterday.

Sheriff: Oh — yesterday. When I had to send Frank to Morris Center for that man who went crazy — I want you to know I had my hands full yesterday. I knew you could get back from Omaha by today and as long as I went over everything here myself —

County Attorney: Well, Mr. Hale, tell just what happened when you came here yesterday morning.

Hale: Harry and I had started to town with a load of potatoes. We came along the road from my place and as I got here I said, "I'm going to see if I can't get John Wright to go in with me on a party telephone." I spoke to Wright about it once before and he put me off, saying folks talked too much anyway, and all he asked was peace and quiet — I guess you know about how much he talked himself; but I thought maybe if I went to the house and talked about it before his wife, though I said to Harry that I didn't know as what his wife wanted made much difference to John —

County Attorney: Let's talk about that later, Mr. Hale. I do want to talk about that, but tell now just what happened when you got to the house.

Hale: I didn't hear or see anything; I knocked at the door, and still it was all quiet inside. I knew they must be up, it was past eight o'clock. So I knocked again, and I thought I heard somebody say, "Come in." I wasn't sure, I'm not sure yet, but I opened the door — this door *(indicating the door by which the two women are still standing)* and there in that rocker — *(pointing to it)* sat Mrs. Wright. *(They all look at the rocker.)*

County Attorney: What — was she doing?

Hale: She was rockin' back and forth. She had her apron in her hand and was kind of — pleating it.

County Attorney: And how did she — look?

Hale: Well, she looked queer.

County Attorney: How do you mean — queer?

Hale: Well, as if she didn't know what she was going to do next. And kind of done up.

County Attorney: How did she seem to feel about your coming?

Hale: Why, I don't think she minded — one way or other. She didn't pay much attention. I said, "How do, Mrs. Wright, it's cold, ain't it?" And she said, "Is it?" — and went on kind of pleating at her apron. Well, I was surprised; she didn't ask me to come up to the stove, or to set down, but just sat there, not even looking at me, so I said, "I want to see John." And then she — laughed. I guess you would call it a laugh. I thought of Harry and the team outside, so I said a little sharp: "Can't I see John?"

"No," she says, kind o' dull like. "Ain't he home?" says I. "Yes," says she, "he's home." "Then why can't I see him?" I asked her, out of patience. " 'Cause he's dead," says she. *"Dead?"* says I. She just nodded her head, not getting a bit excited, but rockin' back and forth. "Why — where is he?" says I, not knowing what to say. She just pointed upstairs — like that *(himself pointing to the room above).* I started for the stairs, with the idea of going up there. I walked from there to here — then I says, "Why, what did he die of ?" "He died of a rope round his neck," says she, and just went on pleatin' at her apron. Well, I went out and called Harry. I thought I might — need help. We went upstairs and there he was lyin' —

County Attorney: I think I'd rather have you go into that upstairs, where you can point it all out. Just go on now with the rest of the story.

Hale: Well, my first thought was to get that rope off. It looked . . . *(stops; his face twitches)* . . . but Harry, he went up to him, and he said, "No, he's dead all right, and we'd better not touch anything." So we went back downstairs. She was still sitting that same way. "Has anybody been notified?" I asked. "No," says she, unconcerned. "Who did this, Mrs. Wright?" said Harry. He said it businesslike — and she stopped pleatin' of her apron. "I don't know," she says. "You don't *know*?" says Harry. "No," says she. "Weren't you sleepin' in the bed with him?" says Harry. "Yes," says she, "but I was on the inside." "Somebody slipped a rope round his neck and strangled him and you didn't wake up?" says Harry. "I didn't wake up," she said after him. We must 'a' looked as if we didn't see how that could be, for after a minute she said, "I sleep sound." Harry was going to ask her more questions but I said maybe we ought to let her tell her story first to the coroner, or the sheriff, so Harry went fast as he could to Rivers' place, where there's a telephone.

County Attorney: And what did Mrs. Wright do when she knew that you had gone for the coroner?

Hale: She moved from the rocker to that chair over there *(pointing to a small chair in the corner)* and just sat there with her hands held together and looking down. I got a feeling that I ought to make some conversation, so I said I had come in to see if John wanted to put in a telephone, and at that she started to laugh, and then she stopped and looked at me — scared. *(The County Attorney, who has had his notebook out, makes a note.)* I dunno, maybe it wasn't scared. I wouldn't like to say it was. Soon Harry got back, and then Dr. Lloyd came and you, Mr. Peters, and so I guess that's all I know that you don't.

County Attorney *(looking around):* I guess we'll go upstairs first — and then out to the barn and around there. *(To the Sheriff.)* You're convinced that there was nothing important here — nothing that would point to any motive?

Sheriff: Nothing here but kitchen things. *(The County Attorney, after again looking around the kitchen, opens the door of a cupboard closet. He gets up on a chair and looks on a shelf. Pulls his hand away, sticky.)*

County Attorney: Here's a nice mess. *(The women draw nearer.)*

Mrs. Peters (to the other woman): Oh, her fruit; it did freeze. *(To the Lawyer.)* She worried about that when it turned so cold. She said the fire'd go out and her jars would break.

Sheriff (rises): Well, can you beat the woman! Held for murder and worryin' about her preserves.

County Attorney: I guess before we're through she may have something more serious than preserves to worry about.

Hale: Well, women are used to worrying over trifles. *(The two women move a little closer together.)*

County Attorney (with the gallantry of a young politician): And yet, for all their worries, what would we do without the ladies? *(The women do not unbend. He goes to the sink, takes a dipperful of water from the pail, and pouring it into a basin, washes his hands. Starts to wipe them on the roller towel, turns it for a cleaner place.)* Dirty towels! *(Kicks his foot against the pans under the sink.)* Not much of a housekeeper, would you say, ladies?

Mrs. Hale (stiffly): There's a great deal of work to be done on a farm.

County Attorney: To be sure. And yet *(with a little bow to her)* I know there are some Dickson county farmhouses which do not have such roller towels. *(He gives it a pull to expose its full length again.)*

Mrs. Hale: Those towels get dirty awful quick. Men's hands aren't always as clean as they might be.

County Attorney: Ah, loyal to your sex, I see. But you and Mrs. Wright were neighbors. I suppose you were friends, too.

Mrs. Hale (shaking her head): I've not seen much of her of late years. I've not been in this house — it's more than a year.

County Attorney: And why was that? You didn't like her?

Mrs. Hale: I liked her all well enough. Farmers' wives have their hands full, Mr. Henderson. And then —

County Attorney: Yes — ?

Mrs. Hale (looking about): It never seemed a very cheerful place.

County Attorney: No — it's not cheerful. I shouldn't say she had the home-making instinct.

Mrs. Hale: Well, I don't know as Wright had, either.

County Attorney: You mean that they didn't get on very well?

Mrs. Hale: No, I don't mean anything. But I don't think a place'd be any cheerfuller for John Wright's being in it.

County Attorney: I'd like to talk more of that a little later. I want to get the lay of things upstairs now. *(He goes to the left where three steps lead to a stair door.)*

Sheriff: I suppose anything Mrs. Peters does'll be all right. She was to take in some clothes for her, you know, and a few little things. We left in such a hurry yesterday.

County Attorney: Yes, but I would like to see what you take, Mrs. Peters, and keep an eye out for anything that might be of use to us.

Mrs. Peters: Yes, Mr. Henderson. *(The women listen to the men's steps on the stairs, then look about the kitchen.)*

Mrs. Hale: I'd hate to have men coming into my kitchen, snooping around and criticizing. *(She arranges the pans under sink which the lawyer had shoved out of place.)*

Mrs. Peters: Of course it's no more than their duty.

Mrs. Hale: Duty's all right, but I guess that deputy sheriff that came out to make the fire might have got a little of this on. *(Gives the roller towel a pull.)* Wish I'd thought of that sooner. Seems mean to talk about her for not having things slicked up when she had to come away in such a hurry.

Mrs. Peters (who has gone to a small table in the left rear corner of the room, and lifted one end of a towel that covers a pan): She had bread set. *(Stands still.)*

Mrs. Hale (eyes fixed on a loaf of bread beside the breadbox, which is on a low shelf at the other side of the room. Moves slowly toward it.): She was going to put this in there. *(Picks up loaf, then abruptly drops it. In a manner of returning to familiar things.)* It's a shame about her fruit. I wonder if it's all gone. *(Gets up on the chair and looks.)* I think there's some here that's all right, Mrs. Peters. Yes — here; *(holding it toward the window)* this is cherries, too. *(Looking again.)* I declare I believe that's the only one. *(Gets down, bottle in her hand. Goes to the sink and wipes it off on the outside.)* She'll feel awful bad after all her hard work in the hot weather. I remember the afternoon I put up my cherries last summer. *(She puts the bottle on the big kitchen table, center of the room. With a sigh, is about to sit down in the rocking-chair. Before she is seated realizes what chair it is; with a slow look at it, steps back. The chair which she has touched rocks back and forth.)*

Mrs. Peters: Well, I must get those things from the front room closet. *(She goes to the door at the right, but after looking into the other room, steps back.)* You coming with me, Mrs. Hale? You could help me carry them. *(They go in the other room; reappear, Mrs. Peters carrying a dress and skirt, Mrs. Hale following with a pair of shoes.)* My, it's cold in there. *(She puts the clothes on the big table, and hurries to the stove.)*

Mrs. Hale (examining the skirt): Wright was close. I think maybe that's why she kept so much to herself. She didn't even belong to the Ladies' Aid. I suppose she felt she couldn't do her part, and then you don't enjoy things when you feel shabby. I heard she used to wear pretty clothes and be lively, when she was Minnie Foster, one of the town girls singing in the choir. But that — oh, that was thirty years ago. This all you want to take in?

Mrs. Peters: She said she wanted an apron. Funny thing to want, for there isn't much to get you dirty in jail, goodness knows. But I suppose just to make her feel more natural. She said they was in the top drawer in this cupboard. Yes, here. And then her little shawl that always hung behind the door. *(Opens stair door and looks.)* Yes, here it is. *(Quickly shuts door leading upstairs.)*

Mrs. Hale (abruptly moving toward her): Mrs. Peters?

Mrs. Peters: Yes, Mrs. Hale?

Mrs. Hale: Do you think she did it?

Mrs. Peters (in a frightened voice): Oh, I don't know.

Mrs. Hale: Well, I don't think she did. Asking for an apron and her little shawl. Worrying about her fruit.

Mrs. Peters (starts to speak, glances up, where footsteps are heard in the room above. In a low voice): Mr. Peters says it looks bad for her. Mr. Henderson is awful sarcastic in a speech and he'll make fun of her sayin' she didn't wake up.

Mrs. Hale: Well, I guess John Wright didn't wake when they was slipping that rope under his neck.

Mrs. Peters: No, it's strange. It must have been done awful crafty and still. They say it was such a — funny way to kill a man, rigging it all up like that.

Mrs. Hale: That's just what Mr. Hale said. There was a gun in the house. He says that's what he can't understand.

Mrs. Peters: Mr. Henderson said coming out that what was needed for the case was a motive; something to show anger, or — sudden feeling.

Mrs. Hale (who is standing by the table): Well, I don't see any signs of anger around here. *(She puts her hand on the dish towel which lies on the table, stands looking down at table, one-half of which is clean, the other half messy.)* It's wiped to here. *(Makes a move as if to finish work, then turns and looks at loaf of bread outside the breadbox. Drops towel. In that voice of coming back to familiar things.)* Wonder how they are finding things upstairs. I hope she had it a little more red-up up there. You know, it seems kind of *sneaking.* Locking her up in town and then coming out here and trying to get her own house to turn against her!

Mrs. Peters: But, Mrs. Hale, the law is the law.

Mrs. Hale: I s'pose 'tis. *(Unbuttoning her coat.)* Better loosen up your things, Mrs. Peters. You won't feel them when you go out. *(Mrs. Peters takes off her fur tippet, goes to hang it on hook at back of room, stands looking at the under part of the small corner table.)*

Mrs. Peters: She was piecing a quilt. *(She brings the large sewing basket and they look at the bright pieces.)*

Mrs. Hale: It's a log cabin pattern. Pretty, isn't it? I wonder if she was goin' to quilt it or just knot it? *(Footsteps have been heard coming down the stairs. The Sheriff enters followed by Hale and the County Attorney.)*

Sheriff: They wonder if she was going to quilt it or just knot it! *(The men laugh, the women look abashed.)*

County Attorney (rubbing his hands over the stove): Frank's fire didn't do much up there, did it? Well, let's go out to the barn and get that cleared up. *(The men go outside.)*

Mrs. Hale (resentfully): I don't know as there's anything so strange, our takin' up our time with little things while we're waiting for them to get the evidence. *(She sits down at the big table smoothing out a block with decision.)* I don't see as it's anything to laugh about.

Mrs. Peters (apologetically): Of course they've got awful important things on their minds. *(Pulls up a chair and joins Mrs. Hale at the table.)*

Mrs. Hale (examining another block): Mrs. Peters, look at this one. Here, this is the one she was working on, and look at the sewing! All the rest of it has been so nice and even. And look at this! It's all over the place! Why, it looks as if she didn't know what she was about! *(After she has said this they look at each other, then start to glance back at the door. After an instant Mrs. Hale has pulled at a knot and ripped the sewing.)*

Mrs. Peters: Oh, what are you doing, Mrs. Hale?

Mrs. Hale (mildly): Just pulling out a stitch or two that's not sewed very good. *(Threading a needle.)* Bad sewing always made me fidgety.

Mrs. Peters (nervously): I don't think we ought to touch things.

Mrs. Hale: I'll just finish up this end. *(Suddenly stopping and leaning forward.)* Mrs. Peters?

Mrs. Peters: Yes, Mrs. Hale?

Mrs. Hale: What do you suppose she was so nervous about?

Mrs. Peters: Oh — I don't know. I don't know as she was nervous. I sometimes sew awful queer when I'm just tired. *(Mrs. Hale starts to say something, looks at Mrs. Peters, then goes on sewing.)* Well, I must get these things wrapped up. They may be through sooner than we think. *(Putting apron and other things together.)* I wonder where I can find a piece of paper, and string. *(Rises.)*

Mrs. Hale: In that cupboard, maybe.

Mrs. Peters (looking in cupboard): Why, here's a bird-cage. *(Holds it up.)* Did she have a bird, Mrs. Hale?

Mrs. Hale: Why, I don't know whether she did or not — I've not been here for so long. There was a man around last year selling canaries cheap, but I don't know as she took one; maybe she did. She used to sing real pretty herself.

Mrs. Peters (glancing around): Seems funny to think of a bird here. But she must have had one, or why would she have a cage? I wonder what happened to it?

Mrs. Hale: I s'pose maybe the cat got it.

Mrs. Peters: No, she didn't have a cat. She's got that feeling some people have about cats — being afraid of them. My cat got in her room and she was real upset and asked me to take it out.

Mrs. Hale: My sister Bessie was like that. Queer, ain't it?

Mrs. Peters (examining the cage): Why, look at this door. It's broke. One hinge is pulled apart.

Mrs. Hale (looking too): Looks as if someone must have been rough with it.

Mrs. Peters: Why, yes. *(She brings the cage forward and puts it on the table.)*

Mrs. Hale: I wish if they're going to find any evidence they'd be about it. I don't like this place.

Mrs. Peters: But I'm awful glad you came with me, Mrs. Hale. It would be lonesome for me sitting here alone.

Mrs. Hale: It would, wouldn't it? (*Dropping her sewing.*) But I tell you what I do wish, Mrs. Peters. I wish I had come over sometimes when *she* was here. I — (*looking around the room*) — wish I had.

Mrs. Peters: But of course you were awful busy, Mrs. Hale — your house and your children.

Mrs. Hale: I could've come. I stayed away because it weren't cheerful — and that's why I ought to have come. I — I've never liked this place. Maybe because it's down in a hollow and you don't see the road. I dunno what it is, but it's a lonesome place and always was. I wish I had come over to see Minnie Foster sometimes. I can see now — (*Shakes her head.*)

Mrs. Peters: Well, you mustn't reproach yourself, Mrs. Hale. Somehow we just don't see how it is with other folks until — something turns up.

Mrs. Hale: Not having children makes less work — but it makes a quiet house, and Wright out to work all day, and no company when he did come in. Did you know John Wright, Mrs. Peters?

Mrs. Peters: Not to know him; I've seen him in town. They say he was a good man.

Mrs. Hale: Yes — good; he didn't drink, and kept his word as well as most, I guess, and paid his debts. But he was a hard man, Mrs. Peters. Just to pass the time of day with him — (*Shivers.*) Like a raw wind that gets to the bone. (*Pauses, her eye falling on the cage.*) I should think she would 'a' wanted a bird. But what do you suppose went with it?

Mrs. Peters: I don't know, unless it got sick and died. (*She reaches over and swings the broken door, swings it again, both women watch it.*)

Mrs. Hale: You weren't raised round here, were you? (*Mrs. Peters shakes her head.*) You didn't know — her?

Mrs. Peters: Not till they brought her yesterday.

Mrs. Hale: She — come to think of it, she was kind of like a bird herself — real sweet and pretty, but kind of timid and — fluttery. How — she — did — change. (*Silence: then as if struck by a happy thought and relieved to get back to everyday things.*) Tell you what, Mrs. Peters, why don't you take the quilt in with you? It might take up her mind.

Mrs. Peters: Why, I think that's a real nice idea, Mrs. Hale. There couldn't possibly be any objection to it could there? Now, just what would I take? I wonder if her patches are in here — and her things. (*They look in the sewing basket.*)

Mrs. Hale: Here's some red. I expect this has got sewing things in it. (*Brings out a fancy box.*) What a pretty box. Looks like something somebody would give you. Maybe her scissors are in here. (*Opens box. Suddenly puts her hand to her nose.*) Why — (*Mrs. Peters bends nearer, then turns her face away.*) There's something wrapped up in this piece of silk.

Mrs. Peters: Why, this isn't her scissors.

Mrs. Hale (lifting the silk): Oh, Mrs. Peters — it's — (*Mrs. Peters bends closer.*)

Mrs. Peters: It's the bird.

Mrs. Hale (jumping up): But, Mrs. Peters — look at it! Its neck! Look at its neck! It's all — other side *to*.

Mrs. Peters: Somebody — wrung — its — neck. *(Their eyes meet. A look of growing comprehension, of horror. Steps are heard outside. Mrs. Hale slips box under quilt pieces, and sinks into her chair. Enter Sheriff and County Attorney. Mrs. Peters rises.)*

County Attorney (as one turning from serious things to little pleasantries): Well, ladies, have you decided whether she was going to quilt it or knot it?

Mrs. Peters: We think she was going to — knot it.

County Attorney: Well, that's interesting, I'm sure. *(Seeing the bird-cage.)* Has the bird flown?

Mrs. Hale (putting more quilt pieces over the box): We think the — cat got it.

County Attorney (preoccupied): Is there a cat? *(Mrs. Hale glances in a quick covert way at Mrs. Peters.)*

Mrs. Peters: Well, not *now.* They're superstitious, you know. They leave.

County Attorney (to Sheriff Peters, continuing an interrupted conversation): No sign at all of anyone having come from the outside. Their own rope. Now let's go up again and go over it piece by piece. *(They start upstairs.)* It would have to have been someone who knew just the — *(Mrs. Peters sits down. The two women sit there not looking at one another, but as if peering into something and at the same time holding back. When they talk now it is in the manner of feeling their way over strange ground, as if afraid of what they are saying, but as if they cannot help saying it.)*

Mrs. Hale: She liked the bird. She was going to bury it in that pretty box.

Mrs. Peters (in a whisper): When I was a girl — my kitten — there was a boy took a hatchet, and before my eyes — and before I could get there — *(Covers her face an instant.)* If they hadn't held me back I would have — *(catches herself, looks upstairs where steps are heard, falters weakly)* — hurt him.

Mrs. Hale (with a slow look around her): I wonder how it would seem never to have had any children around. *(Pause.)* No, Wright wouldn't like the bird — a thing that sang. She used to sing. He killed that, too.

Mrs. Peters (moving uneasily): We don't know who killed the bird.

Mrs. Hale: I knew John Wright.

Mrs. Peters: It was an awful thing was done in this house that night, Mrs. Hale. Killing a man while he slept, slipping a rope around his neck that choked the life out of him.

Mrs. Hale: His neck. Choked the life out of him. *(Her hand goes out and rests on the bird-cage.)*

Mrs. Peters (with rising voice): We don't know who killed him. We don't *know.*

Mrs. Hale (her own feeling not interrupted): If there'd been years and years of nothing, then a bird to sing to you, it would be awful — still, after the bird was still.

Mrs. Peters (something within her speaking): I know what stillness is. When we homesteaded in Dakota, and my first baby died — after he was two years old, and me with no other then —

Mrs. Hale (moving): How soon do you suppose they'll be through looking for the evidence?

Mrs. Peters: I know what stillness is. *(Pulling herself back.)* The law has got to punish crime, Mrs. Hale.

Mrs. Hale (not as if answering that): I wish you'd seen Minnie Foster when she wore a white dress with blue ribbons and stood up there in the choir and sang. *(A look around the room.)* Oh, I *wish* I'd come over here once in a while! That was a crime! That was a crime! Who's going to punish that?

Mrs. Peters (looking upstairs): We mustn't — take on.

Mrs. Hale: I might have known she needed help! I know how things can be — for women. I tell you, it's queer, Mrs. Peters. We live close together and we live far apart. We all go through the same things — it's all just a different kind of the same thing. *(Brushes her eyes, noticing the bottle of fruit, reaches out for it.)* If I was you I wouldn't tell her her fruit was gone. Tell her it *ain't.* Tell her it's all right. Take this in to prove it to her. She — she may never know whether it was broke or not.

Mrs. Peters (takes the bottle, looks about for something to wrap it in; takes petticoat from the clothes brought from the other room, very nervously begins winding this around the bottle. In a false voice): My, it's a good thing the men couldn't hear us. Wouldn't they just laugh! Getting all stirred up over a little thing like a — dead canary. As if that could have anything to do with — with — wouldn't they *laugh!* (The men are heard coming down stairs.)*

Mrs. Hale (under her breath): Maybe they would — maybe they wouldn't.

County Attorney: No, Peters, it's all perfectly clear except a reason for doing it. But you know juries when it comes to women. If there was some definite thing. Something to show — something to make a story about — a thing that would connect up with this strange way of doing it — *(The women's eyes meet for an instant. Enter Hale from outer door.)*

Hale: Well, I've got the team around. Pretty cold out there.

County Attorney: I'm going to stay here a while by myself. *(To the Sheriff.)* You can send Frank out for me, can't you? I want to go over everything. I'm not satisfied that we can't do better.

Sheriff: Do you want to see what Mrs. Peters is going to take in? *(The Lawyer goes to the table, picks up the apron, laughs.)*

County Attorney: Oh, I guess they're not very dangerous things the ladies have picked out. *(Moves a few things about, disturbing the quilt pieces which cover the box. Steps back.)* No, Mrs. Peters doesn't need supervising. For that matter a sheriff's wife is married to the law. Ever think of it that way, Mrs. Peters?

Mrs. Peters: Not — just that way.

Sheriff (chuckling): Married to the law. *(Moves toward the other room.)* I just want you to come in here a minute, George. We ought to take a look at these windows.

County Attorney (scoffingly): Oh, windows!

Sheriff: We'll be right out, Mr. Hale. (*Hale goes outside. The Sheriff follows the County Attorney into the other room. Then Mrs. Hale rises, hands tight together, looking intensely at Mrs. Peters, whose eyes make a slow turn, finally meeting Mrs. Hale's. A moment Mrs. Hale holds her, then her own eyes point the way to where the box is concealed. Suddenly Mrs. Peters throws back quilt pieces and tries to put the box in the bag she is wearing. It is too big. She opens box, starts to take bird out, cannot touch it, goes to pieces, stands there helpless. Sound of a knob turning in the other room. Mrs. Hale snatches the box and puts it in the pocket of her big coat. Enter County Attorney and Sheriff.*)

County Attorney (facetiously): Well, Henry, at least we found out that she was not going to quilt it. She was going to — what is it you call it, ladies?

Mrs. Hale (her hand against her pocket): We call it — knot it, Mr. Henderson.

Curtain

CONSIDERATIONS FOR CRITICAL THINKING AND WRITING

1. **FIRST RESPONSE.** Describe the setting of this play. What kind of atmosphere is established by the details in the opening scene? Does the atmosphere change through the course of the play?

2. Where are Mrs. Hale and Mrs. Peters while Mr. Hale explains to the county attorney how the murder was discovered? How does their location suggest the relationship between the men and the women in the play?

3. What kind of person was Minnie Foster before she married? How do you think her marriage affected her?

4. Characterize John Wright. Why did his wife kill him?

5. Why do the men fail to see the clues that Mrs. Hale and Mrs. Peters discover?

6. What is the significance of the birdcage and the dead bird? Why do Mrs. Hale and Mrs. Peters respond so strongly to them? How do you respond?

7. Why don't Mrs. Hale and Mrs. Peters reveal the evidence they have uncovered? What would you have done?

8. How do the men's conversations and actions reveal their attitudes toward women?

9. Why do you think Glaspell allows us only to hear about Mr. and Mrs. Wright? What is the effect of their never appearing onstage?

10. Does your impression of Mrs. Wright change during the course of the play? If so, what changes it?

11. What is the significance of the play's last line, spoken by Mrs. Hale: "We call it — knot it, Mr. Henderson"? Explain what you think the tone of Mrs. Hale's voice is when she says this line. What is she feeling? What are you feeling?

12. Explain the significance of the play's title. Do you think *Trifles* or "A Jury of Her Peers," Glaspell's title for the short story version of the

play, is more appropriate? Can you think of other titles that capture the play's central concerns?

13. If possible, find a copy of "A Jury of Her Peers" online or in the library (reprinted in *The Best Short Stories of 1917*, ed. E. J. O'Brien [Boston: Small, Maynard, 1918], pp. 256–82), and write an essay that explores the differences between the play and the short story.

14. CRITICAL STRATEGIES.   Read the section on formalist criticism (pp. 1071–72) in Chapter 30, "Critical Strategies for Reading." Several times the characters say things that they don't mean, and this creates a discrepancy between what appears to be and what is actually true. Point to instances of irony in the play and explain how they contribute to its effects and meanings. (For discussions of irony elsewhere in this book, see the Index of Terms.)

CONNECTIONS TO OTHER SELECTIONS

1. Compare and contrast how Glaspell provides background information in *Trifles* with how Sophocles does so in *Oedipus the King* (p. 716).

2. Write an essay comparing the views of marriage in *Trifles* and in Kate Chopin's short story "The Story of an Hour" (p. 15). What similarities do you find in the themes of these two works? Are there any significant differences between the works?

A SAMPLE CLOSE READING

An Annotated Section of Trifles

As you read a play for the first time, highlight lines, circle or underline words, and record your responses in the margins. These responses will allow you to retrieve initial reactions and questions that in subsequent readings you can pursue and resolve. Just as the play is likely to have layered meanings, so too will your own readings as you gradually piece together a variety of elements such as exposition, plot, and character that will lead you toward their thematic significance. The following annotations for an excerpt from *Trifles* offer an interpretation that was produced by several readings of the play. Of course, your annotations could be quite different, depending upon your own approach to the play.

The following excerpt appears about two pages into this nine-page play and is preceded by a significant amount of exposition that establishes the bleak midwestern farm setting and some details about Mrs. Wright, who is the prime suspect in the murder of her husband. Prior to this dialogue, only the male characters speak as they try to discover a motive for the crime.

County Attorney (*looking around*): I guess we'll go upstairs first—and then out to the barn and around there. (*To the Sheriff.*) You're convinced that there was nothing important here—nothing that would point to any motive?

Sheriff: Nothing here but kitchen things. (*The County Attorney, after again looking around the kitchen, opens the door of a cupboard closet. He gets up on a chair and looks on a shelf. Pulls his hand away, sticky.*)

County Attorney: Here's a nice mess. (*The women draw nearer.*)

Mrs. Peters (*to the other woman*): Oh, her fruit; it did freeze. (*To the Lawyer.*) She worried about that when it turned so cold. She said the fire'd go out and her jars would break.

Sheriff (*rises*): Well, can you beat the woman! Held for murder and worryin' about her preserves.

County Attorney: I guess before we're through she may have something more serious than preserves to worry about.

Hale: Well, women are used to worrying over trifles. (*The two women move a little closer together.*)

County Attorney (*with the gallantry of a young politician*): And yet, for all their worries, what would we do without the ladies? (*The women do not unbend. He goes to the sink, takes a dipperful of water from the pail, and pouring it into a basin, washes his hands. Starts to wipe them on the roller towel, turns it for a cleaner place.*) Dirty towels! (*Kicks his foot against the pans under the sink.*) Not much of a housekeeper, would you say, ladies?

Mrs. Hale (*stiffly*): There's a great deal of work to be done on a farm.

County Attorney: To be sure. And yet (*with a little bow to her*) I know there are some Dickson county farmhouses which do not have such roller towels. (*He gives it a pull to expose its full length again.*)

Mrs. Hale: Those towels get dirty awful quick. Men's hands aren't always as clean as they might be.

County Attorney: Ah, loyal to your sex, I see. But you and Mrs. Wright were neighbors. I suppose you were friends, too.

Mrs. Hale (*shaking her head*): I've not seen much of her of late years. I've not been in this house—it's more than a year.

County Attorney: And why was that? You didn't like her?

The Sheriff unknowingly announces a major conflict in the play that echoes the title: from a male point of view, there is nothing of any importance to be found in the kitchen—or in women's domestic lives. Mr. Hale confirms this by pronouncing such matters "trifles."

The County Attorney weighs in with his assessment of this "sticky" situation by calling it a "mess," from which he pulls away.

As the Attorney pulls away, the women move closer together (sides are slowly being drawn), and Mrs. Peters says more than she realizes when she observes, "Oh, her fruit; it did freeze." This anticipates our understanding of the cold, fruitless life that drove Mrs. Wright to murder.

The Sheriff's exasperation about women worrying about "preserves" will ironically help preserve the secret of Mrs. Wright—a woman who was beaten down by her husband but who cannot be beaten by these male authorities.

The Attorney has an eye for dirty towels but not for the real "dirt" embedded in the Wrights' domestic life.

The female characters are identified as "Mrs.," which emphasizes their roles as wives, while the men are autonomous and identified by their professions.

Mrs. Hale's comment begins a process of mitigating Mrs. Wright's murder of her husband. He—husbands, men—must share some of the guilt, too.

Mrs. Hale: I liked her all well enough. Farmers' wives have their hands full, Mr. Henderson. And then —
County Attorney: Yes — ?
Mrs. Hale (looking about): It never seemed a very cheerful place.

In contrast to men (a nice irony), farmers' wives' hands are full of responsibilities for which they receive little credit owing to the males' assumption that they fill their lives with trifles.

ELEMENTS OF DRAMA

Trifles is a **one-act play**; in other words, the entire play takes place in a single location and unfolds as one continuous action without a break. As in a short story, the characters in a one-act play are presented economically, and the action is sharply focused. In contrast, full-length plays can include many characters as well as different settings in place and time. The main divisions of a full-length play are typically **acts**; their ends are indicated by lowering a curtain, turning up the houselights, or turning down the stage lights while stage hands change the props. Playwrights frequently employ acts to accommodate changes in time, setting, characters on stage, or mood. In many full-length plays, such as Shakespeare's *Hamlet,* acts are further divided into **scenes**; according to tradition a scene changes when the location of the action changes or when a new character enters. Acts and scenes are **conventions** that are understood and accepted by audiences because they have come, through usage and time, to be recognized as familiar structural techniques, akin to chapters in a novel or stanzas in a poem.

The major convention of a one-act play is that it typically consists of only a single scene; nevertheless, one-act plays contain many of the elements of drama that characterize their full-length counterparts. One-act plays create their effects through compression. They especially lend themselves to modestly budgeted productions with limited stage facilities. However, the potential of a one-act play to move audiences and readers is not related to its length. As *Trifles* shows, one-acts represent a powerful form of dramatic literature.

The single location that composes the **setting** for *Trifles* is described at the very beginning of the play; it establishes an atmosphere that will later influence our judgment of Mrs. Wright. The "gloomy" kitchen is disordered, bare, and sparsely equipped with a stove, sink, rocker, cupboard, two tables, some chairs, three doors, and a window. These details are just enough to allow us to imagine the stark, uninviting place where Mrs. Wright spent most of her time. Moreover, "signs of incompleted work," coupled with the presence of the sheriff and county attorney, create an immediate tension by suggesting that something is terribly wrong. Before a single word is spoken, **suspense** is created as the characters enter. This suspenseful situation causes an anxious uncertainty about what will happen next.

The setting is further developed through the use of **exposition**, a device that provides the necessary background information about the characters and their circumstances. For example, we immediately learn through **dialogue** — the verbal exchanges between characters — that Mr. Henderson, the county attorney, is just back from Omaha. This detail establishes the setting as somewhere in the Midwest, where winters can be brutally cold and barren. We also find out that John Wright has been murdered and that his wife has been arrested for the crime.

Even more important, Glaspell deftly characterizes the Wrights through exposition alone. Mr. Hale's conversation with Mr. Henderson explains how Mr. Wright's body was discovered, but it also reveals that Wright was a non-communicative man, who refused to share a "party telephone" — that is, a telephone line shared by multiple customers — and who did not consider "what his wife wanted." Later Mrs. Hale adds to this characterization when she tells Mrs. Peters that though Mr. Wright was an honest, good man who paid his bills and did not drink, he was a "hard man" and "Like a raw wind that gets to the bone." Mr. Hale's description of Mrs. Wright sitting in the kitchen dazed and disoriented gives us a picture of a shattered, exhausted woman. But it is Mrs. Hale who again offers further insights when she describes how Minnie Foster, a sweet, pretty, timid young woman who sang in the choir, was changed by her marriage to Mr. Wright and by her childless, isolated life on the farm.

This information about Mr. and Mrs. Wright is worked into the dialogue throughout the play in order to suggest the nature of the **conflict** or struggle between them, a motive, and, ultimately, a justification for the murder. In the hands of a skillful playwright, exposition is not merely a mechanical device; it can provide important information while simultaneously developing characterizations and moving the action forward.

The action is shaped by the **plot**, the author's arrangement of incidents in the play that gives the story a particular focus and emphasis. Plot involves more than simply what happens; it involves how and why things happen. Glaspell begins with a discussion of the murder. Why? She could have begun with the murder itself: the distraught Mrs. Wright looping the rope around her husband's neck. The moment would be dramatic and horribly vivid. We neither see the body nor hear very much about it. When Mr. Hale describes finding Mr. Wright's body, Glaspell has the county attorney cut him off by saying, "I think I'd rather have you go into that upstairs, where you can point it all out. Just go on now with the rest of the story." It is precisely the "rest of the story" that interests Glaspell. Her arrangement of incidents prevents us from sympathizing with Mr. Wright. We are, finally, invited to see Mrs. Wright instead of her husband as the victim.

Mr. Henderson's efforts to discover a motive for the murder appear initially to be the play's focus, but the real conflicts are explored in what seems to be a **subplot**, a secondary action that reinforces or contrasts with the main plot. The discussions between Mrs. Hale and Mrs. Peters and the tensions between the men and the women turn out to be the main plot because they address the issues that Glaspell chooses to explore. Those issues are not about murder but about marriage and how men and women relate to each other.

The ***protagonist*** of *Trifles,* the central character with whom we tend to identify, is Mrs. Hale. The ***antagonist***, the character who is in some kind of opposition to the central character, is the county attorney, Mr. Henderson. These two characters embody the major conflicts presented in the play because each speaks for a different set of characters who represent disparate values. Mrs. Hale and Mr. Henderson are developed less individually than as representative types.

Mrs. Hale articulates a sensitivity to Mrs. Wright's miserable life as well as an awareness of how women are repressed in general by men; she also helps Mrs. Peters to arrive at a similar understanding. When Mrs. Hale defends Mrs. Wright's soiled towels from Mr. Henderson's criticism, Glaspell has her say more than the county attorney is capable of hearing. The ***stage directions*** — the playwright's instructions about how the actors are to move and behave — indicate that Mrs. Hale responds "stiffly" to Mr. Henderson's disparagements: "Men's hands aren't always as clean as they might be." Mrs. Hale eventually comes to see that the men are, in a sense, complicit because it was insensitivity like theirs that drove Mrs. Wright to murder.

Mr. Henderson, on the other hand, represents the law in a patriarchal, conventional society that blithely places a minimal value on the concerns of women. In his attempt to gather evidence against Mrs. Wright, he implicitly defends men's severe dominance over women. He also patronizes Mrs. Hale and Mrs. Peters. Like Sheriff Peters and Mr. Hale, he regards the women's world as nothing more than "kitchen things" and "trifles." Glaspell, however, patterns the plot so that the women see more about Mrs. Wright's motives than the men do and shows that the women have a deeper understanding of justice.

Many plays are plotted in what has come to be called a ***pyramidal pattern***, because the plot is divided into three essential parts. Such plays begin with a ***rising action***, in which complication creates conflict for the protagonist. The resulting tension builds to the second major division, known as the ***climax***, when the action reaches a final ***crisis***, a turning point that has a powerful effect on the protagonist. The third part consists of ***falling action***; here the tensions are diminished in the ***resolution*** of the plot's conflicts and complications (the resolution is also referred to as the ***conclusion*** or ***dénouement***, a French word meaning "unknotting"). These divisions may occur at different times. There are many variations to this pattern. The terms are helpful for identifying various moments and movements within a given plot, but they are less useful if seen as a means of reducing dramatic art to a formula.

Because *Trifles* is a one-act play, this pyramidal pattern is less elaborately worked out than it might be in a full-length play, but the basic elements of the pattern can still be discerned. The complication consists mostly of Mrs. Hale's refusal to assign moral or legal guilt to Mrs. Wright's murder of her husband. Mrs. Hale is able to discover the motive in the domestic details that are beneath the men's consideration. The men fail to see the significance of the fruit jars, messy kitchen, and badly sewn quilt.

At first Mrs. Peters seems to voice the attitudes associated with the men. Unlike Mrs. Hale, who is "more comfortable looking," Mrs. Peters is "a slight wiry woman" with "a thin nervous face" who sounds like her husband, the sheriff, when she insists, "the law is the law." She also defends the men's patronizing attitudes, because "they've got awful important things on their minds." But Mrs. Peters is a *foil* — a character whose behavior and values contrast with the protagonist's — only up to a point. When the most telling clue is discovered, Mrs. Peters suddenly understands, along with Mrs. Hale, the motive for the killing. Mrs. Wright's caged life was no longer tolerable to her after her husband had killed the bird (which was the one bright spot in her life and which represents her early life as the young Minnie Foster). This revelation brings about the climax, when the two women must decide whether to tell the men what they have discovered. Both women empathize with Mrs. Wright as they confront this crisis, and their sense of common experience leads them to withhold the evidence.

This resolution ends the play's immediate conflicts and complications. Presumably, without a motive the county attorney will have difficulty prosecuting Mrs. Wright — at least to the fullest extent of the law. However, the larger issues related to the *theme*, the central idea or meaning of the play, are left unresolved. The men have both missed the clues and failed to perceive the suffering that acquits Mrs. Wright in the minds of the two women. The play ends with Mrs. Hale's ironic answer to Mr. Henderson's question about quilting. When she says "knot it," she gives him part of the evidence he needs to connect Mrs. Wright's quilting with the knot used to strangle her husband. Mrs. Hale knows — and we know — that Mr. Henderson will miss the clue she offers because he is blinded by his own self-importance and assumptions.

Though brief, *Trifles* is a masterful representation of dramatic elements working together to keep both audiences and readers absorbed in its characters and situations.

Lynn Nottage (b. 1964)

POOF! 2004

Lynn Nottage wrote her first play in high school and has contributed consistently and importantly to the American theater scene ever since. She has twice won the Pulitzer Prize for Drama, in 2009 for *Ruined* and in 2017 for *Sweat* (which also won an Obie Award, which is an award given to an "off-Broadway" play that is not necessarily poised for commercial success). A native of New York City, Nottage earned her B.A. from Brown University and her Master's of Fine Arts degree from Yale. She currently teaches at Columbia University. Nottage's work is varied in terms of setting and plot, but her characters tend to be from the margins of their society, such as the working class from beleaguered Reading, Pennsylvania in *Sweat*, or women surviving a civil war in the Democratic Republic of Congo in *Ruined*. The following one-act play is considerably lighter and more humorous than some of her work, but it addresses some weighty subjects nonetheless.

CHARACTERS

Samuel, Loureen's husband
Loureen, a demure housewife, early thirties
Florence, Loureen's best friend, early thirties

TIME

The present

PLACE

Kitchen

A NOTE

Nearly half the women on death row in the United States were convicted of killing abusive husbands. Spontaneous combustion is not recognized as a capital crime.

Darkness.

Samuel (In the darkness): WHEN I COUNT TO TEN I DON' WANT TO SEE YA! I DON' WANT TO HEAR YA! ONE, TWO, THREE, FOUR—
Loureen (In the darkness): DAMN YOU TO HELL, SAMUEL!

> *(A bright flash.*
> *Lights rise. A huge pile of smoking ashes rests in the middle of the kitchen. Loureen, a demure housewife in her early thirties, stares down at the ashes incredulously. She bends and lifts a pair of spectacles from the remains. She ever so slowly backs away.)*

Samuel? Uh! *(Places the spectacles on the kitchen table)* Uh! . . . Samuel? *(Looks around)* Don't fool with me now. I'm not in the mood. *(Whispers)* Samuel? I didn't mean it really. I'll be good if you come back . . . Come on now, dinner's waiting. *(Chuckles, then stops abruptly)* Now stop your foolishness. . . And let's sit down. *(Examines the spectacles)* Uh! *(Softly)* Don't be cross with me. Sure I forgot to pick up your shirt for tomorrow. I can wash another, I'll do it right now. Right now! Sam? . . . *(Cautiously)* You hear me! *(Awaits a response)* Maybe I didn't ever intend to wash your shirt. *(Pulls back as though about to receive a blow; a moment)* Uh! *(Sits down and dials the telephone)* Florence, honey, could you come on down for a moment. There's been a . . . little . . . accident . . . Quickly please. Uh!

(Loureen hangs up the phone. She gets a broom and a dust pan. She hesitantly approaches the pile of ashes. She gets down on her hands and knees and takes a closer look. A fatuous grin spreads across her face. She is startled by a sudden knock on the door. She slowly walks across the room like a possessed child. Loureen lets in Florence, her best friend and upstairs neighbor. Florence, also a housewife in her early thirties, wears a floral housecoat and a pair of oversized slippers. Without acknowledgment Loureen proceeds to saunter back across the room.)

Florence: HEY!

Loureen (Pointing at the ashes): Uh! . . . *(She struggles to formulate words, which press at the inside of her mouth, not quite realized)* Uh! . . .

Florence: You all right? What happened? *(Sniffs the air)* Smells like you burned something? *(Stares at the huge pile of ashes)* What the devil is that?

Loureen (Hushed): Samuel . . . It's Samuel, I think.

Florence: What's he done now?

Loureen: It's him. It's him. *(Nods her head repeatedly)*

Florence: Chile, what's wrong with you? Did he finally drive you out your mind? I knew something was going to happen sooner or later.

Loureen: Dial 911, Florence!

Florence: Why? You're scaring me!

Loureen: Dial 911!

(Florence picks up the telephone and quickly dials.)

I think I killed him.

(Florence hangs up the telephone.)

Florence: What?

Loureen (Whimpers): I killed him! I killed Samuel!

Florence: Come again? . . . He's dead dead?

(Loureen wrings her hands and nods her head twice, mouthing "dead dead." Florence backs away.)

No, stop it, I don't have time for this. I'm going back upstairs. You know how Samuel hates to find me here when he gets home. You're not going to get me this time. *(Louder)* Y'all can have your little joke, I'm not part of it! *(A moment. She takes a hard look into Loureen's eyes; she squints)* Did you really do it this time?

Loureen (Hushed): I don't know how or why it happened, it just did.

Florence: Why are you whispering?

Loureen: I don't want to talk too loud — something else is liable to disappear.

Florence: Where's his body?

Loureen (Points to the pile of ashes): There! . . .

Florence: You burned him?

Loureen: I DON'T KNOW! *(Covers her mouth as if to muffle her words; hushed)* I think so.

Florence: Either you did or you didn't, what you mean you don't know? We're talking murder, Loureen, not oven settings.

Loureen: You think I'm playing?

Florence: How many times have I heard you talk about being rid of him. How many times have we sat at this very table and laughed about the many ways we could do it and how many times have you done it? None.

Loureen (Lifting the spectacles): A pair of cheap spectacles, that's all that's left. And you know how much I hate these. You ever seen him without them, no! . . . He counted to four and disappeared. I swear to God!

Florence: Don't bring the Lord into this just yet! Sit down now . . . What you got to sip on?

Loureen: I don't know whether to have a stiff shot of scotch or a glass of champagne.

(Florence takes a bottle of sherry out of the cupboard and pours them each a glass. Loureen downs hers, then holds out her glass for more.)

He was. . .

Florence: Take your time.

Loureen: Standing there.

Florence: And?

Loureen: He exploded.

Florence: Did that muthafucka hit you again?

Loureen: No . . . he exploded. Boom! Right in front of me. He was shouting like he does, being all colored, then he raised up that big crusty hand to hit me, and poof, he was gone . . . I barely got words out and I'm looking down at a pile of ash.

(Florence belts back her sherry. She wipes her forehead and pours them both another.)

Florence: Chile, I'll give you this, in terms of color you've matched my husband Edgar, the story king. He came in at six Sunday morning, talking about he'd hit someone with his car, and had spent all night trying to outrun the police. I felt sorry for him. It turns out he was playing poker with his paycheck no less. You don't want to know how I found out . . . But I did.

Loureen: You think I'm lying?

Florence: I certainly hope so, Loureen. For your sake and my heart's.

Loureen: Samuel always said if I raised my voice something horrible would happen. And it did. I'm a witch . . . the devil spawn!

Florence: You've been watching too much television.

Loureen: Never seen anything like this on television. Wish I had, then I'd know what to do . . . There's no question, I'm a witch. (*Looks at her hands with disgust*)

Florence: Chile, don't tell me you've been messing with them mojo women again? What did I tell ya.

(*Loureen, agitated, stands and sits back down.*)

Loureen: He's not coming back. Oh no, how could he? It would be a miracle! Two in one day . . . I could be canonized. Worse yet, he could be . . . All that needs to happen now is for my palms to bleed and I'll be eternally remembered as Saint Loureen, the patron of battered wives. Women from across the country will make pilgrimages to me, laying pies and pot roast at my feet and asking the good saint to make their husbands turn to dust. How often does a man like Samuel get damned to hell, and go?

(*She breaks down. Florence moves to console her friend, then realizes that Loureen is actually laughing hysterically.*)

Florence: You smoking crack?

Loureen: Do I look like I am?

Florence: Hell, I've seen old biddies creeping out of crack houses, talking about they were doing church work.

Loureen: Florence, please be helpful, I'm very close to the edge! . . . I don't know what to do next! Do I sweep him up? Do I call the police? Do I . . .

(*The phone rings.*)

Oh God.

Florence: You gonna let it ring?

(*Loureen reaches for the telephone slowly.*)

Loureen: NO! (*Holds the receiver without picking it up, paralyzed*) What if it's his mother? . . . She knows!

(*The phone continues to ring. They sit until it stops. They both breathe a sigh of relief.*)

I should be mourning, I should be praying, I should be thinking of the burial, but all that keeps popping into my mind is what will I wear on television when I share my horrible and wonderful story with a studio audience . . . (*Whimpers*) He's made me a killer, Florence, and you remember what a gentle child I was. (*Whispers*) I'm a killer, I'm a killer, I'm a killer.

Florence: I wouldn't throw that word about too lightly even in jest. Talk like that gets around.

Loureen: You think they'll lock me up? A few misplaced words and I'll probably get the death penalty, isn't that what they do with women like me, murderesses?

Florence: Folks have done time for less.

Loureen: Thank you, just what I needed to hear!

Florence: What did you expect, that I was going to throw up my arms and congratulate you? Why'd you have to go and lose your mind at this time of day, while I got a pot of rice on the stove and Edgar's about to walk in the door and wonder where his goddamn food is. *(Losing her cool)* And he's going to start in on me about all the nothing I've been doing during the day and why I can't work and then he'll mention how clean you keep your home. And I don't know how I'm going to look him in the eye without . . .

Loureen: I'm sorry, Florence. Really. It's out of my hands now.

(She takes Florence's hand and squeezes it.)

Florence (Regaining her composure): You swear on your right tit?

Loureen (Clutching both breasts:): I swear on both of them!

Florence: Both your breasts, Loureen! You know what will happen if you're lying. *(Loureen nods; hushed)* Both your breasts Loureen?

Loureen: Yeah!

Florence (Examines the pile of ashes, then shakes her head): Oh sweet, sweet Jesus. He must have done something truly terrible.

Loureen: No more than usual. I just couldn't take being hit one more time.

Florence: You've taken a thousand blows from that man, couldn't you've turned the cheek and waited. I'd have helped you pack. Like we talked about.

(A moment.)

Loureen: Uh! . . . I could blow on him and he'd disappear across the linoleum. *(Snaps her fingers)* Just like that. Should I be feeling remorse or regret or some other "R" word? I'm strangely jubilant, like on prom night when Samuel and I first made love. That's the feeling! *(The women lock eyes)* Uh!

Florence: Is it . . .

Loureen: Like a ton of bricks been lifted from my shoulders, yeah.

Florence: Really?

Loureen: Yeah!

(Florence walks to the other side of the room.)

Florence: You bitch!

Loureen: What?

Florence: We made a pact.

Loureen: I know.

Florence: You've broken it . . . We agreed that when things got real bad for both of us we'd . . . you know . . . together . . . Do I have to go back upstairs to that? . . . What next?

Loureen: I thought you'd tell me! . . . I don't know!

Florence: I don't know!

Loureen: I don't know!

(*Florence begins to walk around the room, nervously touching objects. Loureen sits, wringing her hands and mumbling softly to herself.*)

Florence: Now you got me, Loureen, I'm truly at a loss for words.

Loureen: Everybody always told me, "Keep your place, Loureen." My place, the silent spot on the couch with a wine cooler in my hand and a pleasant smile that warmed the heart. All this time I didn't know why he was so afraid for me to say anything, to speak up. Poof! . . . I've never been by myself, except for them two weeks when he won the office pool and went to Reno with his cousin Mitchell. He wouldn't tell me where he was going until I got that postcard with the cowboy smoking a hundred cigarettes . . . Didn't Sonny Larkin look good last week at Caroline's? He looked good, didn't he . . .

(*Florence nods. She nervously picks up Samuel's jacket, which is hanging on the back of the chair. She clutches it unconsciously.*)

NO! No! Don't wrinkle that, that's his favorite jacket. He'll kill me. Put it back!

(*Florence returns the jacket to its perch. Loureen begins to quiver.*)

I'm sorry. (*She grabs the jacket and wrinkles it up*) There! (*She then digs into the coat pockets and pulls out his wallet and a movie stub*) Look at that, he said he didn't go to the movies last night. Working late. (*Frantically thumbs through his wallet*) Picture of his motorcycle, Social Security card, driver's license, and look at that from our wedding. (*Smiling*) I looked good, didn't I? (*She puts the pictures back in the wallet and holds the jacket up to her face*) There were some good things. (*She then sweeps her hand over the jacket to remove the wrinkles, and folds it ever so carefully, and finally throws it in the garbage*) And out of my mouth those words made him disappear. All these years and just words, Florence. That's all they were.

Florence: I'm afraid I won't ever get those words out. I'll start resenting you, honey. I'm afraid won't anything change for me.

Loureen: I been to that place.

Florence: Yeah? But now I wish I could relax these old lines *(Touches her forehead)* for a minute maybe. Edgar has never done me the way Samuel did you, but he sure did take the better part of my life.

Loureen: Not yet, Florence.

Florence (Nods): I have the children to think of . . . right?

Loureen: You can think up a hundred things before . . .

Florence: Then come upstairs with me . . . we'll wait together for Edgar and then you can spit out your words and . . .

Loureen: I can't do that.

Florence: Yes you can. Come on now.

(Loureen shakes her head no.)

Well, I guess my mornings are not going to be any different.

Loureen: If you can say for certain, then I guess they won't be. I couldn't say that.

Florence: But you got a broom and a dust pan, you don't need anything more than that . . . He was a bastard and nobody will care that he's gone.

Loureen: Phone's gonna start ringing soon, people are gonna start asking soon, and they'll care.

Florence: What's your crime? Speaking your mind?

Loureen: Maybe I should mail him to his mother. I owe her that. I feel bad for her, she didn't understand how it was. I can't just throw him away and pretend like it didn't happen. Can I?

Florence: I didn't see anything but a pile of ash. As far as I know you got a little careless and burned a chicken.

Loureen: He was always threatening not to come back.

Florence: I heard him.

Loureen: It would've been me eventually.

Florence: Yes.

Loureen: I should call the police, or someone.

Florence: Why? What are you gonna tell them? About all those times they refused to help, about all those nights you slept in my bed 'cause you were afraid to stay down here? About the time he nearly took out your eye 'cause you flipped the television channel?

Loureen: No.

Florence: You've got it, girl!

Loureen: Good-bye to the fatty meats and the salty food. Good-bye to the bourbon and the bologna sandwiches. Good-bye to the smell of his feet, his breath and his bowel movements . . . *(A moment. She closes her eyes and, reliving a horrible memory, she shudders)* Good-bye. *(Walks over to the pile of ashes)* Samuel? . . . Just checking.

Florence: Good-bye Samuel.

(They both smile.)

Loureen: I'll let the police know that he's missing tomorrow . . .
Florence: Why not the next day?
Loureen: Chicken's warming in the oven, you're welcome to stay.
Florence: Chile, I got a pot of rice on the stove, kids are probably acting out . . . and Edgar, well . . . Listen, I'll stop in tomorrow.
Loureen: For dinner?
Florence: Edgar wouldn't stand for that. Cards maybe.
Loureen: Cards.

(*The women hug for a long moment. Florence exits. Loureen stands over the ashes for a few moments contemplating what to do. She finally decides to sweep them under the carpet, and then proceeds to set the table and sit down to eat her dinner.*)

End of play

CONSIDERATIONS FOR CRITICAL THINKING AND WRITING

1. **FIRST RESPONSE.** The play centers around the death of one of its three characters. Is it somehow funny? Why?

2. Why do you think Nottage's stage directions specify what Florence is wearing? Why doesn't she specify what Loureen is wearing?

3. How does the playwright convey the exposition? What are the important details from the past that precede the play's present action?

4. We never see Samuel or Florence's husband Edgar on stage. How are they characterized?

5. Loureen occasionally describes her fantasies of what will happen to her in the future. How do those fantasies operate to help determine the play's theme?

6. How do witchcraft, superstition, personal oaths, and pacts function within the story? How about if you contrast them with traditional religion?

7. Why does Loureen refuse to do to Edgar what she did to Samuel?

8. Loureen is consumed by guilt for most of the play. Does she get over it? What details inform your answer?

9. How does Florence's relationship with her husband Edgar compare to Loureen's relationship with Samuel? Do you agree with Florence's prediction ("won't anything change for me")?

CONNECTIONS TO OTHER SELECTIONS

1. Compare the plot, theme, and/or characters in *POOF!* with those of Susan Glaspell's *Trifles* (p. 684).

2. Compare the treatment of marriage in this play and in Henrik Ibsen's *A Doll's House* (p. 864).

26

A Study of Sophocles

Bettmann/Getty Images.

I depict men as they ought to be . . .
— SOPHOCLES

Not all things are to be discovered;
many are better concealed.
— SOPHOCLES

Sophocles lived a long, productive life (496?–406 B.C.) in Athens. During his life Athens became a dominant political and cultural power after the Persian Wars, but before he died, Sophocles witnessed the decline of Athens as a result of the Peloponnesian Wars and the city's subsequent surrender to Sparta. He saw Athenian culture reach remarkable heights as well as collapse under enormous pressures.

Sophocles embodied much of the best of Athenian culture; he enjoyed success as a statesman, general, treasurer, priest, and, of course, prize-winning dramatist. Although surviving fragments indicate that he wrote over 120 plays, only a handful remain intact. Those that survive consist of the three plays he wrote about Oedipus and his children — *Oedipus the King, Oedipus at Colonus,* and *Antigone* — and four additional tragedies: *Philoctetes, Ajax, Maidens of Trachis,* and *Electra.*

His plays won numerous prizes at festival competitions because of his careful, subtle plotting and the sense of inevitability with which their action is charged. Moreover, his development of character is richly complex. Instead of relying on the extreme situations and exaggerated actions that earlier tragedians used, Sophocles created powerfully motivated characters who even today fascinate audiences with their psychological depth.

In addition to crafting sophisticated tragedies for the Greek theater, Sophocles introduced several important innovations to the stage. Most important, he broke the tradition of using only two actors; adding a third resulted in more complicated relationships and intricate dialogue among characters. As individual actors took center stage more often, Sophocles reduced the role of the chorus (discussed on p. 712). This shift placed even more emphasis on the actors, although the chorus remained important as a means of commenting on the action and establishing its tone. Sophocles was also the first dramatist to write plays with specific actors in mind, a development that many later playwrights, including Shakespeare, exploited usefully. But without question Sophocles' greatest contribution to drama was *Oedipus the King,* which, it has been argued, is the most influential drama ever written.

Map of Ancient Greece. During Sophocles' time, the city-state of Athens (roughly in the center of this map) was the leading cultural and intellectual center of Greece — until the Peloponnesian Wars (431–404 B.C.) and Athens's defeat in 404 B.C. by the city-state of Sparta (below Athens, to the left).
Steven Wright/Shutterstock.com.

THEATRICAL CONVENTIONS OF GREEK DRAMA

Bettmann/Getty Images.

More than twenty-four hundred years have passed since 430 B.C., when Sophocles' *Oedipus the King* was probably first produced on a Greek stage. We inhabit a vastly different planet than Sophocles' audience did, yet concerns about what it means to be human in a world that frequently runs counter to our desires and aspirations have remained relatively constant. The ancient Greeks continue to speak to us. But inexperienced readers or viewers may have some initial difficulty understanding the theatrical conventions used in classical Greek tragedies such as *Oedipus the King* and *Antigone*. If Sophocles were alive today, he would very likely need some sort of assistance with the conventions of an Arthur Miller play or a television production of *The Simpsons*.

Classical Greek drama developed from religious festivals that paid homage to Dionysus, the god of wine and fertility. Most of the details of these festivals have been lost, but we do know that they included dancing and singing that celebrated legends about Dionysus. From these choral songs developed stories of both Dionysus and mortal culture-heroes. These heroes became the subject of playwrights whose works were produced in contests at the festivals. The Dionysian festivals lasted more than five hundred years, but relatively few of their plays have survived. Among the works of the three great writers of tragedy, only seven plays each by Sophocles and Aeschylus (525?–456 B.C.) and nineteen plays by Euripides (480?–406 B.C.) survive.

Plays were such important events in Greek society that they were partially funded by the state. The Greeks associated drama with religious and community values as well as entertainment. In a sense, their plays celebrate their civilization; in approving the plays, audiences applauded their own culture. The enormous popularity of the plays is indicated by the size of surviving amphitheaters. Although information about these theaters is sketchy, we do know that most of them had a common form. They were built into hillsides with rising rows of seats accommodating more than fourteen thousand people. These seats partially encircled an **orchestra** or "dancing place," where the ***chorus*** of a dozen or so men chanted lines and danced.

Tradition credits the Greek poet Thespis with adding an actor who was separate from the choral singing and dancing of early performances. A second actor was subsequently included by Aeschylus and a third, as noted earlier, by Sophocles. These additions made possible the conflicts and complicated relationships that evolved into the dramatic art we know today.

Classical Greek Theater in Delphi, Greece. This photo represents the features typical of a classical theater.
© Lukiyanova Natalia frenta/Shutterstock.

The two or three male actors who played all the roles appeared behind the orchestra in front of the *skene*, a stage building that served as dressing rooms. As Greek theater evolved, a wall of the skene came to be painted to suggest a palace or some other setting, and the roof was employed to indicate, for instance, a mountain location. Sometimes gods were lowered from the roof by mechanical devices to set matters right among the mortals below. This method of rescuing characters from complications beyond their abilities to resolve was known in Latin as ***deus ex machina*** ("god from the machine"), a term now used to describe any improbable means by which an author provides a too-easy resolution for a story.

Inevitably, the conventions of the Greek theaters affected how plays were presented. Few if any scene changes occurred because the amphitheater stage was set primarily for one location. If an important event happened somewhere else, it was reported by a minor character, such as a messenger. The chorus also provided necessary background information. In *Oedipus the King* and *Antigone,* the choruses, acting as townspeople, also assess the characters' strengths and weaknesses, praising them for their virtues, chiding them for their rashness, and giving them advice. The reactions of the chorus provide a connection between the actors and audience because the chorus is at once a participant in and an observer of the action. In addition, the chorus helps structure the action by indicating changes in scene or mood. Thus the chorus could be used in a variety of ways to shape the audience's response to the play's action and characters.

Actors in classical Greek amphitheaters faced considerable challenges. An intimate relationship with the audience was impossible because many spectators would have been too far away to see a facial expression or subtle gesture. Indeed, some in the audience would have had difficulty even hearing the voices of individual actors. To compensate for these disadvantages, actors wore large masks that extravagantly expressed the major characters' emotions or identified the roles of minor characters. The masks also allowed the two or three actors in a performance to play all the characters without confusing the audience. Each mask was fitted so that the mouthpiece amplified the actor's voice. The actors were further equipped with padded costumes and elevated shoes (*cothurni* or *buskins*) that made them appear larger than life.

As a result of these adaptive conventions, Greek plays tend to emphasize words — formal, impassioned speeches — more than physical action. We are invited to ponder actions and events rather than to see all of them enacted. Although the stark simplicity of Greek theater does not offer an audience realistic detail, the classical tragedies that have survived present characters in dramatic situations that transcend theatrical conventions. Tragedy, it seems, has always been compelling for human beings, regardless of the theatrical forms it has taken.

A Greek tragedy is typically divided into five parts: prologue, parodos, episodia, stasimon, and exodus. Understanding these terms provides a sense of the overall rhythm of a Greek play. The opening speech or dialogue is known as the ***prologue*** and usually gives the exposition necessary to follow the subsequent action. In the *parodos* the chorus makes its first entrance and gives its perspective on what the audience has learned in the prologue. Several *episodia,* or episodes, follow, in which characters engage in dialogue that frequently consists of heated debates dramatizing the play's conflicts. Following each episode is a choral ode or *stasimon,* in which the chorus responds to and interprets the preceding dialogue. The *exodus,* or last scene, follows the final episode and stasimon; in it the resolution occurs and the characters leave the stage.

The effect of alternating dialogues and choral odes has sometimes been likened to that of opera. Greek tragedies were written in verse, and the stasima were chanted or sung as the chorus moved rhythmically, so the plays have a strong musical element that is not always apparent on the printed page. If we remember their musical qualities, we are less likely to forget that no matter how terrifying or horrific the conflicts they describe, these plays are stately, measured, and dignified works that reflect a classical Greek sense of order and proportion.

TRAGEDY

Newspapers are filled with daily reports of tragedies: a child is struck and crippled by a car; an airplane plunges into a suburban neighborhood; a volcano erupts and kills thousands. These unexpected instances of suffering are commonly and accurately described as tragic, but they are not trage-dies in the literary sense of the term. A literary *tragedy* presents courageous individuals who confront powerful forces within or outside themselves with a dignity that reveals the breadth and depth of the human spirit in the face of failure, defeat, and even death.

Aristotle (384–322 B.C.), in his *Poetics*, defined *tragedy* on the basis of the plays contemporary to him. His definition has generated countless variations, qualifications, and interpretations, but we still derive our literary understanding of this term from Aristotle.

The protagonist of a Greek tragedy is someone regarded as extraordi-nary rather than typical: a great man or woman brought from happiness to agony. The character's stature is important because it makes his or her fall all the more terrifying. The protagonist also carries mythic significance for the audience. Oedipus and Antigone, for example, are not only human beings but legendary figures from a distant, revered past. Although the gods do not appear onstage in either *Oedipus the King* or *Antigone*, their power is ever present as the characters invoke their help or attempt to defy them. In addition, Greek tragedy tends to be public rather than private. The fate of the community — the state — is often linked with that of the protagonist, as when Thebes suffers a plague as a result of Oedipus's mistaken actions.

The protagonists of classical Greek tragedies (and of those of Shakespeare) are often rulers of noble birth who represent the monarchical values of their periods, but in modern tragedies the protagonists are more likely to reflect democratic values that make it possible for anyone to be a suitable subject. What is finally important is not so much the protagonist's social stature as a greatness of character that steadfastly confronts suffer-ing, whether it comes from supernatural, social, or psychological forces. Although Greek tragic heroes were aristocrats, the nobility of their charac-ters was more significant than their inherited titles and privileges.

The protagonist's eminence and determination to complete some task or goal make him or her admirable in Greek tragedy, but that does not free the protagonist from what Aristotle described as "some error or frailty" that brings about his or her misfortune. The term Aristotle used for this weak-ness is **hamartia**. This word has frequently been interpreted to mean that the protagonist's fall is the result of an internal **tragic flaw**, such as an excess of pride, ambition, passion, or some other character trait that leads directly to disaster.

Sometimes, however, misfortunes are the result not of a character flaw but of misunderstood events that overtake and thwart the protago-nist's best intentions. Thus, virtue can lead to tragedy too. *Hamartia* has also been interpreted to mean "wrong act" — a mistake based not on a personal failure but on circumstances outside the protagonist's personal-ity and control. Many readers find that a combination of these two inter-pretations sheds the most light on the causes of the tragic protagonist's fall. Both internal and external forces can lead to downfall because the protagonist's personality may determine crucial judgments that result in mistaken actions.

However the idea of tragic flaw is understood, it is best not to use it as a means of reducing the qualities of a complex character to an adjective or two that labels Oedipus as guilty of "overweening pride" (the Greek term for which is **hubris** or **hybris**) or Antigone as "fated." The protagonists of tragedies require more careful characterization than a simplistic label can provide.

Whatever the causes of the tragic protagonist's downfall, he or she accepts responsibility for it. Hence, even in his or her encounter with failure (and possibly death) the tragic protagonist displays greatness of character. Perhaps it is the witnessing of this greatness, which seems both to accept and to transcend human limitations, that makes audiences feel relief rather than hopelessness at the end of a tragedy. Aristotle described this response as a **catharsis**, or purgation of the emotions of "pity and fear." We are faced with the protagonist's misfortune, which often seems out of proportion to his or her actions, and so we are likely to feel compassionate pity. Simultaneously, we may experience fear because the failure of the protagonist, who is so great in stature and power, is a frightening reminder of our own vulnerabilities. Ultimately, however, both these negative emotions are purged because the tragic protagonist's suffering is an affirmation of human values — even if they are not always triumphant — rather than a despairing denial of them.

Nevertheless, tragedies are disturbing. Instead of coming away with the reassurance of a happy ending, we must take solace in the insight produced by the hero's suffering. And just as our expectations are changed, so are the protagonist's. Aristotle described the moment in the plot when this change occurs as a **reversal** (*peripeteia*), the point when the hero's fortunes turn in an unexpected direction. He more specifically defined this term as meaning an action performed by a character that has the opposite of its intended effect. An example cited by Aristotle is the messenger's attempts to relieve Oedipus's anxieties about his relationship to his father and mother. Instead, the messenger reveals previously unknown information that eventually results in a **recognition** (*anagnorisis*); Oedipus discovers the terrible truth that he has killed his father and married his mother.

Tragedy is typically filled with ironies because there are so many moments in the plot when what seems to be turns out to be radically different from what actually is. Because of this, a particular form of irony called **dramatic irony** is also known as **tragic irony**. In dramatic irony, the meaning of a character's words or actions is understood by the audience but not by the character. Audiences of Greek tragedy shared with the playwrights a knowledge of the stories on which many tragic plots were based. Consequently, they frequently were aware of what was going to happen before the characters were. When Oedipus declares that he will seek out the person responsible for the plague that ravishes his city, the audience already knows that the person Oedipus pursues is himself.

Oedipus the King

A familiarity with the Oedipus legend allows modern readers to appreciate the series of ironies that unfolds in Sophocles' *Oedipus the King*. As an infant, Oedipus had been abandoned by his parents, Laius and Jocasta, the king and queen of Thebes, because a prophecy warned that their son would kill his father and marry his mother. They instructed a servant to leave him on a mountain to die. The infant's feet were pierced and pinned together, but he was not left on the mountain; instead the servant, out of pity, gave him to a shepherd, who in turn presented him to the king and queen of Corinth. They named him Oedipus (for "swollen foot") and raised him as their own son.

On reaching manhood, Oedipus learned from an oracle that he would kill his father and marry his mother; to avoid this horrendous fate, he left Corinth forever. In his travels, Oedipus found his way blocked by a chariot at a crossroads; in a fit of anger, he killed the servants and their passenger. That passenger, unknown to Oedipus, was his real father. In Thebes, Oedipus successfully answered the riddle of the Sphinx, a winged lion with a woman's head. The reward for defeating this dreaded monster was both the crown and the dead king's wife. Oedipus and Jocasta had four children and prospered. But when the play begins, Oedipus's rule is troubled by a plague that threatens to destroy Thebes, and he is determined to find the cause of the plague in order to save the city again.

Oedipus the King is widely recognized as the greatest of the surviving Greek tragedies. Numerous translations are available. We have selected the highly regarded translation of *Oedipus the King* by David Grene. The play has absorbed readers for centuries because Oedipus's character — his intelligence, confidence, rashness, and suffering — represents powers and limitations that are both exhilarating and chastening. Although no reader or viewer is likely to identify with Oedipus's extreme circumstances, anyone can appreciate his heroic efforts to find the truth about himself. In that sense, he is one of us — at our best.

SOPHOCLES (496?–406 B.C.)

Oedipus the King   ca. 430 B.C.

TRANSLATED BY DAVID GRENE

CHARACTERS

Oedipus, King of Thebes
Jocasta, His Wife
Creon, His Brother-in-Law

Teiresias, an Old Blind Prophet
A Priest
First Messenger
Second Messenger
A Herdsman
Chorus of Old Men of Thebes

SCENE: In front of the palace of Oedipus at Thebes. To the right of the stage near the altar stands the Priest with a crowd of children. Oedipus emerges from the central door.

Oedipus: Children, young sons and daughters of old Cadmus,°
    why do you sit here with your suppliant crowns?
    The town is heavy with a mingled burden
    of sounds and smells, of groans and hymns and incense;
    I did not think it fit that I should hear   5
    of this from messengers but came myself, —
    I Oedipus whom all men call the Great.   *(He turns to the Priest.)*
    You're old and they are young; come, speak for them.
    What do you fear or want, that you sit here
    suppliant? Indeed I'm willing to give all   10
    that you may need; I would be very hard
    should I not pity suppliants like these.
Priest: O ruler of my country, Oedipus,
    you see our company around the altar;
    you see our ages; some of us, like these,   15
    who cannot yet fly far, and some of us
    heavy with age; these children are the chosen
    among the young, and I the priest of Zeus.
    Within the market place sit others crowned
    with suppliant garlands, at the double shrine   20
    of Pallas° and the temple where Ismenus
    gives oracles by fire. King, you yourself
    have seen our city reeling like a wreck
    already; it can scarcely lift its prow
    out of the depths, out of the bloody surf.   25
    A blight is on the fruitful plants of the earth,
    a blight is on the cattle in the fields,
    a blight is on our women that no children
    are born to them; a God that carries fire,
    a deadly pestilence, is on our town,   30
    strikes us and spares not, and the house of Cadmus
    is emptied of its people while black Death

---

1 *Cadmus:* Founder and first king of Thebes.   21 *Pallas:* Pallas Athene, goddess of wisdom and daughter of Zeus.

grows rich in groaning and in lamentation.
We have not come as suppliants to this altar
because we thought of you as of a God,   35
but rather judging you the first of men
in all the chances of this life and when
we mortals have to do with more than man.
You came and by your coming saved our city,
freed us from tribute which we paid of old   40
to the Sphinx,° cruel singer. This you did
in virtue of no knowledge we could give you,
in virtue of no teaching; it was God
that aided you, men say, and you are held
with God's assistance to have saved our lives.   45
Now Oedipus, Greatest in all men's eyes,
here falling at your feet we all entreat you,
find us some strength for rescue.
Perhaps you'll hear a wise word from some God,
perhaps you will learn something from a man   50
(for I have seen that for the skilled of practice
the outcome of their counsels live the most).
Noblest of men, go, and raise up our city,
go, — and give heed. For now this land of ours
calls you its savior since you saved it once.   55
So, let us never speak about your reign
as of a time when first our feet were set
secure on high, but later fell to ruin.
Raise up our city, save it and raise it up.
Once you have brought us luck with happy omen;   60
be no less now in fortune.
If you will rule this land, as now you rule it,
better to rule it full of men than empty.
For neither tower nor ship is anything
when empty, and none live in it together.   65

Oedipus: I pity you, children. You have come full of longing,
but I have known the story before you told it
only too well. I know you are all sick,
yet there is not one of you, sick though you are,
that is as sick as I myself.   70
Your several sorrows each have single scope
and touch but one of you. My spirit groans
for city and myself and you at once.
You have not roused me like a man from sleep;

41 *Sphinx:* A mythical creature with the body of a lion, wings of a bird, and the face of a woman. The Sphinx stumped Thebans with her riddle and killed those that could not answer it. Oedipus solved the riddle, the Sphinx killed herself, and Oedipus became king of Thebes.

know that I have given many tears to this,   75
gone many ways wandering in thought,
but as I thought I found only one remedy
and that I took. I sent Menoeceus' son
Creon, Jocasta's brother, to Apollo,°
to his Pythian temple,   80
that he might learn there by what act or word
I could save this city. As I count the days,
it vexes me what ails him; he is gone
far longer than he needed for the journey.
But when he comes, then, may I prove a villain,   85
if I shall not do all the God commands.

Priest: Thanks for your gracious words. Your servants here
  signal that Creon is this moment coming.

Oedipus: His face is bright. O holy Lord Apollo,
  grant that his news too may be bright for us   90
  and bring us safety.

Priest: It is happy news,
  I think, for else his head would not be crowned
  with sprigs of fruitful laurel.

Oedipus: We will know soon,
  he's within hail. Lord Creon, my good brother,   95
  what is the word you bring us from the God?   *(Creon enters.)*

Creon: A good word, — for things hard to bear themselves
  if in the final issue all is well
  I count complete good fortune.

Oedipus: What do you mean?
  What you have said so far   100
  leaves me uncertain whether to trust or fear.

Creon: If you will hear my news before these others
  I am ready to speak, or else to go within.

Oedipus: Speak it to all;
  the grief I bear, I bear it more for these   105
  than for my own heart.

Creon: I will tell you, then,
  what I heard from the God.
  King Phoebus° in plain words commanded us
  to drive out a pollution from our land,
  pollution grown ingrained within the land;   110
  drive it out, said the God, not cherish it,
  till it's past cure.

Oedipus: What is the rite
  of purification? How shall it be done?

---

79 *Apollo:* Oracular god of the sun, light, and truth, and son of Zeus.   108 *King Phoebus:* Apollo.

Creon: By banishing a man, or expiation
  of blood by blood, since it is murder guilt   115
  which holds our city in this destroying storm.
Oedipus: Who is this man whose fate the God pronounces?
Creon: My Lord, before you piloted the state
  we had a king called Laius.°
Oedipus: I know of him by hearsay. I have not seen him.   120
Creon: The God commanded clearly: let some one
  punish with force this dead man's murderers.
Oedipus: Where are they in the world? Where would a trace
  of this old crime be found? It would be hard
  to guess where.
Creon: The clue is in this land;   125
  that which is sought is found;
  the unheeded thing escapes:
  so said the God.
Oedipus: Was it at home,
  or in the country that death came upon him,
  or in another country travelling?   130
Creon: He went, he said himself, upon an embassy,
  but never returned when he set out from home.
Oedipus: Was there no messenger, no fellow traveller
  who knew what happened? Such a one might tell
  something of use.   135
Creon: They were all killed save one. He fled in terror
  and he could tell us nothing in clear terms
  of what he knew, nothing, but one thing only.
Oedipus: What was it?
  If we could even find a slim beginning   140
  in which to hope, we might discover much.
Creon: This man said that the robbers they encountered
  were many and the hands that did the murder
  were many; it was no man's single power.
Oedipus: How could a robber dare a deed like this   145
  were he not helped with money from the city,
  money and treachery?
Creon: That indeed was thought.
  But Laius was dead and in our trouble
  there was none to help.
Oedipus: What trouble was so great to hinder you   150
  inquiring out the murder of your king?
Creon: The riddling Sphinx induced us to neglect
  mysterious crimes and rather seek solution
  of troubles at our feet.

---

119 *Laius:* Former king of Thebes.

Oedipus: I will bring this to light again. King Phoebus   155
    fittingly took this care about the dead,
    and you too fittingly.
    And justly you will see in me an ally,
    a champion of my country and the God.
    For when I drive pollution from the land   160
    I will not serve a distant friend's advantage,
    but act in my own interest. Whoever
    he was that killed the king may readily
    wish to dispatch me with his murderous hand;
    so helping the dead king I help myself.   165
    Come, children, take your suppliant boughs and go;
    up from the altars now. Call the assembly
    and let it meet upon the understanding
    that I'll do everything. God will decide
    whether we prosper or remain in sorrow.   170
Priest: Rise, children — it was this we came to seek,
    which of himself the king now offers us.
    May Phoebus who gave us the oracle
    come to our rescue and stay the plague. *(Exeunt° all but the*
    Chorus.)

Chorus (Strophe°): What is the sweet spoken word of God   175
    from the shrine of Pytho° rich in gold
    that has come to glorious Thebes?
    I am stretched on the rack of doubt, and terror and
        trembling hold
    my heart, O Delian Healer,° and I worship full of fears
    for what doom you will bring to pass, new or renewed in the
        revolving years.
    Speak to me, immortal voice,
    child of golden Hope.

(Antistrophe°) First I call on you, Athene, deathless daughter
    of Zeus, and Artemis, Earth Upholder,
    who sits in the midst of the market place in the throne which
        men call Fame,
    and Phoebus, the Far Shooter, three averters of Fate,   185
    come to us now, if ever before, when ruin rushed upon
        the state,
    you drove destruction's flame away
    out of our land.

Exeunt: Stage direction indicating that the characters have left the stage.   *Strophe:* The song sung by the Chorus, dancing from stage right to stage left.   175 *shrine of Pytho:* Delphi, site of the oracle and shrine dedicated to Apollo.   178 *Delian Healer:* Apollo.   *Antistrophe:* The song sung after the strophe by the Chorus, dancing back from stage left to stage right.

(Strophe) Our sorrows defy number;
all the ship's timbers are rotten;   190
taking of thought is no spear for the driving away of the plague.
There are no growing children in this famous land;
there are no women bearing the pangs of childbirth.
You may see them one with another, like birds swift on the wing,
quicker than fire unmastered,   195
speeding away to the coast of the Western God.

(Antistrophe) In the unnumbered deaths
of its people the city dies;
those children that are born lie dead on the naked earth
unpitied, spreading contagion of death; and grey haired
    mothers and wives   200
everywhere stand at the altar's edge, suppliant, moaning;
the hymn to the healing God rings out but with it the wailing
    voices are blended.
From these our sufferings grant us, O golden Daughter of Zeus,
glad-faced deliverance.

(Strophe) There is no clash of brazen shields but our fight is
    with the War God,   205
a War God ringed with the cries of men, a savage God who burns us;
grant that he turn in racing course backwards out of our
    country's bounds to the great palace of Amphitrite° or where
    the waves of the Thracian sea
deny the stranger safe anchorage.
Whatsoever escapes the night   210
at last the light of day revisits;
so smite the War God, Father Zeus,
beneath your thunderbolt,
for you are the Lord of the lightning, the lightning that carries fire.

(Antistrophe) And your unconquered arrow shafts, winged by the
    golden corded bow,   215
Lycean King,° I beg to be at our side for help;
and the gleaming torches of Artemis with which she scours the
    Lycean hills,
and I call on the God with the turban of gold, who gave his name
    to this country of ours,
the Bacchic God° with the wind flushed face,
Evian One, who travel   220
with the Maenad company,°
combat the God that burns us

---

208 *Amphitrite:* Sea goddess and wife of Poseidon.   216 *Lycean King:* Apollo.
219 *Bacchic God:* Bacchus, also known as Dionysus, god of wine and wild celebration.
221 *Maenad company:* Female followers of Bacchus.

with your torch of pine;
for the God that is our enemy is a God unhonoured among
   the Gods.

(Oedipus returns.)

Oedipus: For what you ask me — if you will hear my words,   225
and hearing welcome them and fight the plague,
you will find strength and lightening of your load.

Hark to me; what I say to you, I say
as one that is a stranger to the story
as stranger to the deed. For I would not   230
be far upon the track if I alone
were tracing it without a clue. But now,
since after all was finished, I became
a citizen among you, citizens —
now I proclaim to all the men of Thebes: 235
who so among you knows the murderer
by whose hand Laius, son of Labdacus,
died — I command him to tell everything
to me, — yes, though he fears himself to take the blame
on his own head; for bitter punishment   240
he shall have none, but leave this land unharmed.
Or if he knows the murderer, another,
a foreigner, still let him speak the truth.
For I will pay him and be grateful, too.
But if you shall keep silence, if perhaps   245
some one of you, to shield a guilty friend,
or for his own sake shall reject my words —
hear what I shall do then:
I forbid that man, whoever he be, my land,
my land where I hold sovereignty and throne;   250
and I forbid any to welcome him
or cry him greeting or make him a sharer
in sacrifice or offering to the Gods,
or give him water for his hands to wash.
I command all to drive him from their homes,   255
since he is our pollution, as the oracle
of Pytho's God proclaimed him now to me.
So I stand forth a champion of the God
and of the man who died.
Upon the murderer I invoke this curse —   260
whether he is one man and all unknown,
or one of many — may he wear out his life
in misery to miserable doom!
If with my knowledge he lives at my hearth
I pray that I myself may feel my curse.   265

On you I lay my charge to fulfill all this
for me, for the God, and for this land of ours
destroyed and blighted, by the God forsaken.

Even were this no matter of God's ordinance
it would not fit you so to leave it lie,   270
unpurified, since a good man is dead
and one that was a king. Search it out.
Since I am now the holder of his office,
and have his bed and wife that once was his,
and had his line not been unfortunate   275
we would have common children — (fortune leaped
upon his head) — because of all these things,
I fight in his defence as for my father,
and I shall try all means to take the murderer
of Laius the son of Labdacus   280
the son of Polydorus and before him
of Cadmus and before him of Agenor.°
Those who do not obey me, may the Gods
grant no crops springing from the ground they plough
nor children to their women! May a fate   285
like this, or one still worse than this consume them!
For you whom these words please, the other Thebans,
may Justice as your ally and all the Gods
live with you, blessing you now and for ever!
Chorus: As you have held me to my oath, I speak: 290
    I neither killed the king nor can declare
    the killer; but since Phoebus set the quest
    it is his part to tell who the man is.
Oedipus: Right; but to put compulsion on the Gods
    against their will — no man can do that.   295
Chorus: May I then say what I think second best?
Oedipus: If there's a third best, too, spare not to tell it.
Chorus: I know that what the Lord Teiresias
    sees, is most often what the Lord Apollo
    sees. If you should inquire of this from him   300
    you might find out most clearly.
Oedipus: Even in this my actions have not been sluggard.
    On Creon's word I have sent two messengers
    and why the prophet is not here already
    I have been wondering.
Chorus: His skill apart   305
    there is besides only an old faint story.

280–282 *Labdacus, Polydorus, Cadmus, and Agenor:* Referring to the father, grandfather, great-grandfather, and great-great-grandfather of Laius.

Oedipus: What is it?
　　I look at every story.
Chorus: 　　　　　　　It was said
　　that he was killed by certain wayfarers.
Oedipus: I heard that, too, but no one saw the killer.
Chorus: Yet if he has a share of fear at all,　　　　　　310
　　his courage will not stand firm, hearing your curse.
Oedipus: The man who in the doing did not shrink
　　will fear no word.
Chorus: 　　　　　Here comes his prosecutor:
　　led by your men the godly prophet comes　　　　　315
　　in whom alone of mankind truth is native.
　　　　　　　(Enter Teiresias, led by a little boy.)
Oedipus: Teiresias, you are versed in everything,
　　things teachable and things not to be spoken,
　　things of the heaven and earth-creeping things.
　　You have no eyes but in your mind you know　　　320
　　with what a plague our city is afflicted.
　　My lord, in you alone we find a champion,
　　in you alone one that can rescue us.
　　Perhaps you have not heard the messengers,
　　but Phoebus sent in answer to our sending　　　325
　　an oracle declaring that our freedom
　　from this disease would only come when we
　　should learn the names of those who killed King Laius,
　　and kill them or expel from our country.
　　Do not begrudge us oracles from birds,°　　　　330
　　or any other way of prophecy
　　within your skill; save yourself and the city,
　　save me; redeem the debt of our pollution
　　that lies on us because of this dead man.
　　We are in your hands; pains are most nobly taken　335
　　to help another when you have means and power.
Teiresias: Alas, how terrible is wisdom when
　　it brings no profit to the man that's wise!
　　This I knew well, but had forgotten it,
　　else I would not have come here.
Oedipus: 　　　　　　　　What is this?　　340
　　How sad you are now you have come!
Teiresias: 　　　　　　　　Let me
　　go home. It will be easiest for us both
　　to bear our several destinies to the end
　　if you will follow my advice.

---

330 *oracles from birds:* Bird flight, a method by which prophets predicted the future
using the flight of birds.

Oedipus: You'd rob us
   of this your gift of prophecy? You talk 345
   as one who had no care for law nor love
   for Thebes who reared you.
Teiresias: Yes, but I see that even your own words
   miss the mark; therefore I must fear for mine.
Oedipus: For God's sake if you know of anything, 350
   do not turn from us; all of us kneel to you,
   all of us here, your suppliants.
Teiresias: All of you here know nothing. I will not
   bring to the light of day my troubles, mine —
   rather than call them yours.
Oedipus: What do you mean? 355
   You know of something but refuse to speak.
   Would you betray us and destroy the city?
Teiresias: I will not bring this pain upon us both,
   neither on you nor on myself. Why is it
   you question me and waste your labour? I 360
   will tell you nothing.
Oedipus: You would provoke a stone! Tell us, you villain,
   tell us, and do not stand there quietly
   unmoved and balking at the issue.
Teiresias: You blame my temper but you do not see 365
   your own that lives within you; it is me
   you chide.
Oedipus: Who would not feel his temper rise
   at words like these with which you shame our city?
Teiresias: Of themselves things will come, although I hide them 370
   and breathe no word of them.
Oedipus: Since they will come
   tell them to me.
Teiresias: I will say nothing further.
   Against this answer let your temper rage
   as wildly as you will.
Oedipus: Indeed I am
   so angry I shall not hold back a jot 375
   of what I think. For I would have you know
   I think you were complotter° of the deed
   and doer of the deed save in so far
   as for the actual killing. Had you had eyes
   I would have said alone you murdered him. 380
Teiresias: Yes? Then I warn you faithfully to keep
   the letter of your proclamation and
   from this day forth to speak no word of greeting

377 *complotter:* One who is part of a plot or conspiracy.

to these nor me; you are the land's pollution.
Oedipus: How shamelessly you started up this taunt!   385
How do you think you will escape?
Teiresias: I have.
I have escaped; the truth is what I cherish
and that's my strength.
Oedipus: And who has taught you truth?
Not your profession surely!
Teiresias: You have taught me,
for you have made me speak against my will.   390
Oedipus: Speak what? Tell me again that I may learn it better.
Teiresias: Did you not understand before or would you
provoke me into speaking?
Oedipus: I did not grasp it,
not so to call it known. Say it again.
Teiresias: I say you are the murderer of the king   395
whose murderer you seek.
Oedipus: Not twice you shall
say calumnies like this and stay unpunished.
Teiresias: Shall I say more to tempt your anger more?
Oedipus: As much as you desire; it will be said
in vain.
Teiresias: I say that with those you love best   400
you live in foulest shame unconsciously
and do not see where you are in calamity.
Oedipus: Do you imagine you can always talk
like this, and live to laugh at it hereafter?
Teiresias: Yes, if the truth has anything of strength.   405
Oedipus: It has, but not for you; it has no strength
for you because you are blind in mind and ears
as well as in your eyes.
Teiresias: You are a poor wretch
to taunt me with the very insults which
every one soon will heap upon yourself.   410
Oedipus: Your life is one long night so that you cannot
hurt me or any other who sees the light.
Teiresias: It is not fate that I should be your ruin,
Apollo is enough; it is his care
to work this out.
Oedipus: Was this your own design   415
or Creon's?
Teiresias: Creon is no hurt to you,
but you are to yourself.
Oedipus: Wealth, sovereignty and skill outmatching skill
for the contrivance of an envied life!
Great store of jealousy fill your treasury chests,   420

if my friend Creon, friend from the first and loyal,
thus secretly attacks me, secretly
desires to drive me out and secretly
suborns this juggling, trick devising quack,
this wily beggar who has only eyes   425
for his own gains, but blindness in his skill.
For, tell me, where have you seen clear, Teiresias,
with your prophetic eyes? When the dark singer,
the sphinx, was in your country, did you speak
word of deliverance to its citizens?   430
And yet the riddle's answer was not the province
of a chance comer. It was a prophet's task
and plainly you had no such gift of prophecy
from birds nor otherwise from any God
to glean a word of knowledge. But I came,   435
Oedipus, who knew nothing, and I stopped her.
I solved the riddle by my wit alone.
Mine was no knowledge got from birds. And now
you would expel me,
because you think that you will find a place   440
by Creon's throne. I think you will be sorry,
both you and your accomplice, for your plot
to drive me out. And did I not regard you
as an old man, some suffering would have taught you
that what was in your heart was treason.   445
Chorus: We look at this man's words and yours, my king,
and we find both have spoken them in anger.
We need no angry words but only thought
how we may best hit the God's meaning for us.
Teiresias: If you are king, at least I have the right   450
no less to speak in my defence against you.
Of that much I am master. I am no slave
of yours, but Loxias', and so I shall not
enroll myself with Creon for my patron.
Since you have taunted me with being blind,   455
here is my word for you.
You have your eyes but see not where you are
in sin, nor where you live, nor whom you live with.
Do you know who your parents are? Unknowing
you are an enemy to kith and kin   460
in death, beneath the earth, and in this life.
A deadly footed, double striking curse,
from father and mother both, shall drive you forth
out of this land, with darkness on your eyes,
that now have such straight vision. Shall there be   465
a place will not be harbour to your cries,

a corner of Cithaeron° will not ring
in echo to your cries, soon, soon, —
when you shall learn the secret of your marriage,
which steered you to a haven in this house, —   470
haven no haven, after lucky voyage?
And of the multitude of other evils
establishing a grim equality
between you and your children, you know nothing.
So, muddy with contempt my words and Creon's!   475
Misery shall grind no man as it will you.

Oedipus: Is it endurable that I should hear
such words from him? Go and a curse go with you!
Quick, home with you! Out of my house at once!

Teiresias: I would not have come either had you not called me.   480

Oedipus: I did not know then you would talk like a fool —
or it would have been long before I called you.

Teiresias: I am a fool then, as it seems to you —
but to the parents who have bred you, wise.

Oedipus: What parents? Stop! Who are they of all the world?   485

Teiresias: This day will show your birth and will destroy you.

Oedipus: How needlessly your riddles darken everything.

Teiresias: But it's in riddle answering you are strongest.

Oedipus: Yes. Taunt me where you will find me great.

Teiresias: It is this very luck that has destroyed you.

Oedipus: I do not care, if it has saved this city.   490

Teiresias: Well, I will go. Come, boy, lead me away.

Oedipus: Yes, lead him off. So long as you are here,
you'll be a stumbling block and a vexation;
once gone, you will not trouble me again.

Teiresias: I have said   495
what I came here to say not fearing your
countenance: there is no way you can hurt me.
I tell you, king, this man, this murderer
(whom you have long declared you are in search of,
indicting him in threatening proclamation   500
as murderer of Laius) — he is here.
In name he is a stranger among citizens
but soon he will be shown to be a citizen
true native Theban, and he'll have no joy
of the discovery: blindness for sight   505
and beggary for riches his exchange,
he shall go journeying to a foreign country
tapping his way before him with a stick.

---

467 *Cithaeron:* Mountain in Greece and the location where Oedipus was abandoned as a baby.

He shall be proved father and brother both
to his own children in his house; to her   510
that gave him birth, a son and husband both;
a fellow sower in his father's bed
with that same father that he murdered.
Go within, reckon that out, and if you find me
mistaken, say I have no skill in prophecy.   515
(Exeunt separately Teiresias and Oedipus.)

Chorus (Strophe): Who is the man proclaimed
by Delphi's prophetic rock
as the bloody handed murderer,
the doer of deeds that none dare name?
Now is the time for him to run   520
with a stronger foot
than Pegasus
for the child of Zeus leaps in arms upon him
with fire and the lightning bolt,
and terribly close on his heels   525
are the Fates that never miss.

(Antistrophe) Lately from snowy Parnassus°
clearly the voice flashed forth,
bidding each Theban track him down,
the unknown murderer.   530
In the savage forests he lurks and in
the caverns like
the mountain bull.
He is sad and lonely, and lonely his feet
that carry him far from the navel of earth;   535
but its prophecies, ever living,
flutter around his head.

(Strophe) The augur has spread confusion,
terrible confusion;
I do not approve what was said   540
nor can I deny it.
I do not know what to say;
I am in a flutter of foreboding;
I never heard in the present
nor past of a quarrel between   545
the sons of Labdacus and Polybus,
that I might bring as proof
in attacking the popular fame
of Oedipus, seeking
to take vengeance for undiscovered   550
death in the line of Labdacus.

527 *Parnassus:* Mountain in Greece that was sacred to Apollo.

(*Antistrophe*) Truly Zeus and Apollo are wise
and in human things all knowing;
but amongst men there is no
distinct judgment, between the prophet
and me — which of us is right.   555
One man may pass another in wisdom
but I would never agree
with those that find fault with the king
till I should see the word
proved right beyond doubt. For once   560
in visible form the Sphinx
came on him and all of us
saw his wisdom and in that test
he saved the city. So he will not be condemned by my mind.   565

                                               (Enter Creon.)

Creon: Citizens, I have come because I heard
   deadly words spread about me, that the king
   accuses me. I cannot take that from him.
   If he believes that in these present troubles
   he has been wronged by me in word or deed   570
   I do not want to live on with the burden
   of such a scandal on me. The report
   injures me doubly and most vitally —
   for I'll be called a traitor to my city
   and traitor also to my friends and you.   575
Chorus: Perhaps it was a sudden gust of anger
   that forced that insult from him, and no judgment.
Creon: But did he say that it was in compliance
   with schemes of mine that the seer told him lies?
Chorus: Yes, he said that, but why, I do not know.   580
Creon: Were his eyes straight in his head? Was his mind right
   when he accused me in this fashion?
Chorus: I do not know; I have no eyes to see
   what princes do. Here comes the king himself.   *(Enter Oedipus.)*
Oedipus: You, sir, how is it you come here? Have you so much   585
   brazen-faced daring that you venture in
   my house although you are proved manifestly
   the murderer of that man, and though you tried,
   openly, highway robbery of my crown?
   For God's sake, tell me what you saw in me,   590
   what cowardice or what stupidity,
   that made you lay a plot like this against me?
   Did you imagine I should not observe
   the crafty scheme that stole upon me or
   seeing it, take no means to counter it?
   Was it not stupid of you to make the attempt,   595

to try to hunt down royal power without
the people at your back or friends? For only
with the people at your back or money can
the hunt end in the capture of a crown.   600

Creon: Do you know what you're doing? Will you listen
   to words to answer yours, and then pass judgment?

Oedipus: You're quick to speak, but I am slow to grasp you,
   for I have found you dangerous, — and my foe.

Creon: First of all hear what I shall say to that.   605

Oedipus: At least don't tell me that you are not guilty.

Creon: If you think obstinacy without wisdom
   a valuable possession, you are wrong.

Oedipus: And you are wrong if you believe that one,
   a criminal, will not be punished only   610
   because he is my kinsman.

Creon: This is but just —
   but tell me, then, of what offense I'm guilty?

Oedipus: Did you or did you not urge me to send
   to this prophetic mumbler?

Creon: I did indeed,
   and I shall stand by what I told you.   615

Oedipus: How long ago is it since Laius. . . .

Creon: What about Laius? I don't understand.

Oedipus: Vanished — died — was murdered?

Creon: It is long,
   a long, long time to reckon.

Oedipus: Was this prophet
   in the profession then?

Creon: He was, and honoured   620
   as highly as he is today.

Oedipus: At that time did he say a word about me?

Creon: Never, at least when I was near him.

Oedipus: You never made a search for the dead man?

Creon: We searched, indeed, but never learned of anything.   625

Oedipus: Why did our wise old friend not say this then?

Creon: I don't know; and when I know nothing, I
   usually hold my tongue.

Oedipus: You know this much,
   and can declare this much if you are loyal.

Creon: What is it? If I know, I'll not deny it.   630

Oedipus: That he would not have said that I killed Laius
   had he not met you first.

Creon: You know yourself
   whether he said this, but I demand that I
   should hear as much from you as you from me.

Oedipus: Then hear, — I'll not be proved a murderer.   635
Creon: Well, then. You're married to my sister.
Oedipus: Yes,
   that I am not disposed to deny.
Creon: You rule
   this country giving her an equal share
   in the government?
Oedipus: Yes, everything she wants
   she has from me.
Creon: And I, as thirdsman to you,   640
   am rated as the equal of you two?
Oedipus: Yes, and it's there you've proved yourself false friend.
Creon: Not if you will reflect on it as I do.
   Consider, first, if you think any one
   would choose to rule and fear rather than rule   645
   and sleep untroubled by a fear if power
   were equal in both cases. I, at least,
   I was not born with such a frantic yearning
   to be a king — but to do what kings do.
   And so it is with every one who has learned   650
   wisdom and self-control. As it stands now,
   the prizes are all mine — and without fear.
   But if I were the king myself, I must
   do much that went against the grain.
   How should despotic rule seem sweeter to me   655
   than painless power and an assured authority?
   I am not so besotted yet that I
   want other honours than those that come with profit.
   Now every man's my pleasure; every man greets me;
   now those who are your suitors fawn on me, —   660
   success for them depends upon my favour.
   Why should I let all this go to win that?
   My mind would not be traitor if it's wise;
   I am no treason lover, of my nature,
   nor would I ever dare to join a plot.   665
   Prove what I say. Go to the oracle
   at Pytho and inquire about the answers,
   if they are as I told you. For the rest,
   if you discover I laid any plot
   together with the seer, kill me, I say,   670
   not only by your vote but by my own.
   But do not charge me on obscure opinion
   without some proof to back it. It's not just
   lightly to count your knaves as honest men,
   nor honest men as knaves. To throw away   675

an honest friend is, as it were, to throw
your life away, which a man loves the best.
In time you will know all with certainty;
time is the only test of honest men,
one day is space enough to know a rogue.   680
Chorus: His words are wise, king, if one fears to fall.
     Those who are quick of temper are not safe.
Oedipus: When he that plots against me secretly
     moves quickly, I must quickly counterplot.
     If I wait taking no decisive measure   685
     his business will be done, and mine be spoiled.
Creon: What do you want to do then? Banish me?
Oedipus: No, certainly; kill you, not banish you.
Creon: I do not think that you've your wits about you.
Oedipus: For my own interests, yes.
Creon: But for mine, too,   690
     you should think equally.
Oedipus: You are a rogue.
Creon: Suppose you do not understand?
Oedipus: But yet
     I must be ruler.
Creon: Not if you rule badly.
Oedipus: O, city, city!
Creon: I too have some share
     in the city; it is not yours alone.   695
Chorus: Stop, my lords! Here — and in the nick of time
     I see Jocasta coming from the house;
     with her help lay the quarrel that now stirs you.   *(Enter Jocasta.)*
Jocasta: For shame! Why have you raised this foolish squabbling
     brawl? Are you not ashamed to air your private   700
     griefs when the country's sick? Go in, you, Oedipus,
     and you, too, Creon, into the house. Don't magnify
     your nothing troubles.
Creon: Sister, Oedipus,
     your husband, thinks he has the right to do
     terrible wrongs — he has but to choose between   705
     two terrors: banishing or killing me.
Oedipus: He's right, Jocasta; for I find him plotting
     with knavish tricks against my person.
Creon: That God may never bless me! May I die
     accursed, if I have been guilty of   710
     one tittle of the charge you bring against me!
Jocasta: I beg you, Oedipus, trust him in this,
     spare him for the sake of this his oath to God,
     for my sake, and the sake of those who stand here.
Chorus: Be gracious, be merciful,   715
     we beg of you.

Oedipus: In what would you have me yield?
Chorus: He has been no silly child in the past.
　　He is strong in his oath now.
　　Spare him.
Oedipus: Do you know what you ask? 　　　　　　　　　　720
Chorus: Yes.
Oedipus: Tell me then.
Chorus: He has been your friend before all men's eyes; do not cast him
　　away dishonoured on an obscure conjecture. 　　　　725
Oedipus: I would have you know that this request of yours
　　really requests my death or banishment.
Chorus: May the Sun God, king of Gods, forbid! May I die
　　without God's
　　blessing, without friends' help, if I had any such thought. But my
　　spirit is broken by my unhappiness for my wasting country; and 　730
　　this would but add troubles amongst ourselves to the other
　　troubles.
Oedipus: Well, let him go then — if I must die ten times for it,
　　or be sent out dishonoured into exile.
　　It is your lips that prayed for him I pitied,
　　not his; wherever he is, I shall hate him.
　　　　　　　　　　　　　　　　　　　　　　735
Creon: I see you sulk in yielding and you're dangerous
　　when you are out of temper; natures like yours
　　are justly heaviest for themselves to bear.
Oedipus: Leave me alone! Take yourself off, I tell you.
Creon: I'll go, you have not known me, but they have,
　　and they have known my innocence. 　　　　*(Exit.)* 　740
Chorus: Won't you take him inside, lady?
Jocasta: Yes, when I've found out what was the matter.
Chorus: There was some misconceived suspicion of a story, and on the
　　other side the sting of injustice.
　　　　　　　　　　　　　　　　　　　　　745
Jocasta: So, on both sides?
Chorus: Yes.
Jocasta: What was the story?
Chorus: I think it best, in the interests of the country, to leave it where
　　it ended.
　　　　　　　　　　　　　　　　　　　　750
Oedipus: You see where you have ended, straight of judgment
　　although you are, by softening my anger.
Chorus: Sir, I have said before and I say again — be sure that I
　　would have been proved a madman, bankrupt in sane
　　council, if I should put you away, you who steered the
　　country I love safely when she was crazed
　　　　　　　　　　　　　　　　　　　　755
　　with troubles. God grant that now, too, you may prove a
　　fortunate guide for us.
Jocasta: Tell me, my lord, I beg of you, what was it
　　that roused your anger so?

Oedipus: Yes, I will tell you.   760
  I honour you more than I honour them.
  It was Creon and the plots he laid against me.
Jocasta: Tell me — if you can clearly tell the quarrel —
Oedipus: Creon says
  that I'm the murderer of Laius.
Jocasta: Of his own knowledge or on information?
Oedipus: He sent this rascal prophet to me, since   765
  he keeps his own mouth clean of any guilt.
Jocasta: Do not concern yourself about this matter;
  listen to me and learn that human beings
  have no part in the craft of prophecy.
  Of that I'll show you a short proof.   770
  There was an oracle once that came to Laius, —
  I will not say that it was Phoebus' own,
  but it was from his servants — and it told him
  that it was fate that he should die a victim
  at the hands of his own son, a son to be born   775
  of Laius and me. But, see now, he,
  the king, was killed by foreign highway robbers
  at a place where three roads meet — so goes the story;
  and for the son — before three days were out
  after his birth King Laius pierced his ankles   780
  and by the hands of others cast him forth
  upon a pathless hillside. So Apollo
  failed to fulfill his oracle to the son,
  that he should kill his father, and to Laius
  also proved false in that the thing he feared,   785
  death at his son's hands, never came to pass.
  So clear in this case were the oracles,
  so clear and false. Give them no heed, I say;
  what God discovers need of, easily
  he shows to us himself.
Oedipus: O dear Jocasta,   790
  as I hear this from you, there comes upon me
  a wandering of the soul — I could run mad.
Jocasta: What trouble is it, that you turn again
  and speak like this?
Oedipus: I thought I heard you say
  that Laius was killed at a crossroads.   795
Jocasta: Yes, that was how the story went and still
  that word goes round.
Oedipus: Where is this place, Jocasta,
  where he was murdered?
Jocasta: Phocis is the country
  and the road splits there, one of two roads from Delphi,
  another comes from Daulia.

Oedipus: How long ago is this?   800
Jocasta: The news came to the city just before
      you became king and all men's eyes looked to you.
      What is it, Oedipus, that's in your mind?
Oedipus: What have you designed, O Zeus, to do with me?
Jocasta: What is the thought that troubles your heart?   805
Oedipus: Don't ask me yet — tell me of Laius —
      How did he look? How old or young was he?
Jocasta: He was a tall man and his hair was grizzled
      already — nearly white — and in his form
      not unlike you.
Oedipus: O God, I think I have   810
      called curses on myself in ignorance.
Jocasta: What do you mean? I am terrified
      when I look at you.
Oedipus: I have a deadly fear
      that the old seer had eyes. You'll show me more
      if you can tell me one more thing.
Jocasta: I will.   815
      I'm frightened, — but if I can understand,
      I'll tell you all you ask.
Oedipus: How was his company?
      Had he few with him when he went this journey,
      or many servants, as would suit a prince?
Jocasta: In all there were but five, and among them   820
      a herald; and one carriage for the king.
Oedipus: It's plain — it's plain — who was it told you this?
Jocasta: The only servant that escaped safe home.
Oedipus: Is he at home now?
Jocasta: No, when he came home again
      and saw you king and Laius was dead,   825
      he came to me and touched my hand and begged
      that I should send him to the fields to be
      my shepherd and so he might see the city
      as far off as he might. So I
      sent him away. He was an honest man,   830
      as slaves go, and was worthy of far more
      than what he asked of me.
Oedipus: O, how I wish that he could come back quickly!
Jocasta: He can. Why is your heart so set on this?
Oedipus: O dear Jocasta, I am full of fears   835
      that I have spoken far too much; and therefore
      I wish to see this shepherd.
Jocasta: He will come;
      but, Oedipus, I think I'm worthy too
      to know what it is that disquiets you.

Oedipus: It shall not be kept from you, since my mind   840
    has gone so far with its forebodings. Whom
    should I confide in rather than you, who is there
    of more importance to me who have passed
    through such a fortune?
    Polybus was my father, king of Corinth,   845
    and Merope,° the Dorian, my mother.
    I was held greatest of the citizens
    in Corinth till a curious chance befell me
    as I shall tell you — curious, indeed,
    but hardly worth the store I set upon it.   850
    There was a dinner and at it a man,
    a drunken man, accused me in his drink
    of being bastard. I was furious
    but held my temper under for that day.
    Next day I went and taxed my parents with it;   855
    they took the insult very ill from him,
    the drunken fellow who had uttered it.
    So I was comforted for their part, but
    still this thing rankled always, for the story
    crept about widely. And I went at last   860
    to Pytho, though my parents did not know.
    But Phoebus sent me home again unhonoured
    in what I came to learn, but he foretold
    other and desperate horrors to befall me,
    that I was fated to lie with my mother,   865
    and show to daylight an accursed breed
    which men would not endure, and I was doomed
    to be murderer of the father that begot me.
    When I heard this I fled, and in the days
    that followed I would measure from the stars   870
    the whereabouts of Corinth — yes, I fled
    to somewhere where I should not see fulfilled
    the infamies told in that dreadful oracle.
    And as I journeyed I came to the place
    where, as you say, this king met with his death.   875
    Jocasta, I will tell you the whole truth.
    When I was near the branching of the crossroads,
    going on foot, I was encountered by
    a herald and a carriage with a man in it,
    just as you tell me. He that led the way   880
    and the old man himself wanted to thrust me
    out of the road by force. I became angry
    and struck the coachman who was pushing me.

---

846 *Polybus and Merope:* King and queen that adopted and raised Oedipus.

When the old man saw this he watched his moment,
and as I passed he struck me from his carriage   885
full on the head with his two pointed goad.
But he was paid in full and presently
my stick had struck him backwards from the car
and he rolled out of it. And then I killed them
all. If it happened there was any tie   890
of kinship twixt this man and Laius,
who is then now more miserable than I,
what man on earth so hated by the Gods,
since neither citizen nor foreigner
may welcome me at home or even greet me,   895
but drive me out of doors? And it is I,
I and no other have so cursed myself.
And I pollute the bed of him I killed
by the hands that killed him. Was I not born evil?
Am I not utterly unclean? I had to fly   900
and in my banishment not even see
my kindred nor set foot in my own country,
or otherwise my fate was to be yoked
in marriage with my mother and kill my father,
Polybus who begot me and had reared me.   905
Would not one rightly judge and say that on me
these things were sent by some malignant God?
O no, no, no — O holy majesty
of God on high, may I not see that day!
May I be gone out of men's sight before   910
I see the deadly taint of this disaster
come upon me.
Chorus: Sir, we too fear these things. But until you see this man
   face to face and hear his story, hope.
Oedipus: Yes, I have just this much of hope — to wait until the herdsman
   comes.   915
Jocasta: And when he comes, what do you want with him?
Oedipus: I'll tell you; if I find that his story is the same as yours, I at least
   will be clear of this guilt.
Jocasta: Why what so particularly did you learn from my story?
Oedipus: You said that he spoke of highway *robbers* who killed Laius. Now   920
   if he uses the same number, it was not I who killed him. One man
   cannot be the same as many. But if he speaks of a man travelling
   alone, then clearly the burden of the guilt inclines towards me.
Jocasta: Be sure, at least, that this was how he told the story. He cannot
   unsay it now, for everyone in the city heard it — not I alone. But,
   Oedipus, even if he diverges from what he said then, he shall never
   prove that the murder of Laius squares rightly with the prophecy —
   for Loxias declared that the king should be killed by his own son.

And that poor creature did not kill him surely, — for he died
himself first. So as far as prophecy goes, henceforward I shall
not look to the right hand or the left.   930
Oedipus: Right. But yet, send some one for the peasant to bring
him here; do not neglect it.
Jocasta: I will send quickly. Now let me go indoors. I will do
nothing except what pleases you.   *(Exeunt.)*
Chorus (Strophe): May destiny ever find me   935
pious in word and deed
prescribed by the laws that live on high:
laws begotten in the clear air of heaven,
whose only father is Olympus;
no mortal nature brought them to birth,   940
no forgetfulness shall lull them to sleep;
for God is great in them and grows not old.

(Antistrophe) Insolence breeds the tyrant, insolence
if it is glutted with a surfeit, unseasonable, unprofitable,
climbs to the roof-top and plunges   945
sheer down to the ruin that must be,
and there its feet are no service.
But I pray that the God may never
abolish the eager ambition that profits the state.
For I shall never cease to hold the God as our protector.   950

(Strophe) If a man walks with haughtiness
of hand or word and gives no heed
to Justice and the shrines of Gods
despises — may an evil doom
smite him for his ill-starred pride of heart!—   955
he reaps gains without justice
and will not hold from impiety
and his fingers itch for untouchable things.
When such things are done, what man shall contrive
to shield his soul from the shafts of the God?   960
When such deeds are held in honour,
why should I honour the Gods in the dance?

(Antistrophe) No longer to the holy place,
to the navel of earth I'll go
to worship, nor to Abae   965
nor to Olympia,
unless the oracles are proved to fit,
for all men's hands to point at.
O Zeus, if you are rightly called
the sovereign lord, all-mastering,   970
let this not escape you nor your ever-living power!

The oracles concerning Laius
are old and dim and men regard them not.
Apollo is nowhere clear in honour; God's service perishes.
(Enter Jocasta, carrying garlands.)

Jocasta: Princes of the land, I have had the thought to go   975
to the Gods' temples, bringing in my hand
garlands and gifts of incense, as you see.
For Oedipus excites himself too much
at every sort of trouble, not conjecturing,
like a man of sense, what will be from what was,   980
but he is always at the speaker's mercy,
when he speaks terrors. I can do no good
by my advice, and so I came as suppliant
to you, Lycaean Apollo, who are nearest.
These are the symbols of my prayer and this   985
my prayer: grant us escape free of the curse.
Now when we look to him we are all afraid;
he's pilot of our ship and he is frightened.   *(Enter Messenger.)*

Messenger: Might I learn from you, sirs, where is the house of
Oedipus? Or best of all, if you know, where is the king himself?   990

Chorus: This is his house and he is within doors. This lady is his wife
and mother of his children.

Messenger: God bless you, lady, and God bless your household!
God bless Oedipus' noble wife!

Jocasta: God bless you, sir, for your kind greeting! What do you want   995
of us that you have come here? What have you to tell us?

Messenger: Good news, lady. Good for your house and for your
husband.

Jocasta: What is your news? Who sent you to us?

Messenger: I come from Corinth and the news I bring will give you
pleasure. Perhaps a little pain too.   1000

Jocasta: What is this news of double meaning?

Messenger: The people of the Isthmus will choose Oedipus to be their
king. That is the rumour there.

Jocasta: But isn't their king still old Polybus?

Messenger: No. He is in his grave. Death has got him.   1005

Jocasta: Is that the truth? Is Oedipus' father dead?

Messenger: May I die myself if it be otherwise!

Jocasta (to a servant): Be quick and run to the King with the news!
O oracles of the Gods, where are you now? It was from this man
Oedipus fled, lest he should be his murderer! And now he is dead, in
the course of nature,   1010
and not killed by Oedipus.   *(Enter Oedipus.)*

Oedipus: Dearest Jocasta, why have you sent for me?

Jocasta: Listen to this man and when you hear reflect what is the
outcome of the holy oracles of the Gods.

Oedipus: Who is he? What is his message for me?   1015
Jocasta: He is from Corinth and he tells us that your father
    Polybus is dead and gone.
Oedipus: What's this you say, sir? Tell me yourself.
Messenger: Since this is the first matter you want clearly told:
    Polybus has gone down to death. You may be sure of it.   1020
Oedipus: By treachery or sickness?
Messenger: A small thing will put old bodies asleep.
Oedipus: So he died of sickness, it seems, — poor old man!
Messenger: Yes, and of age — the long years he had measured.
Oedipus: Ha! Ha! O dear Jocasta, why should one   1025
    look to the Pythian hearth?° Why should one look
    to the birds screaming overhead? They prophesied
    that I should kill my father! But he's dead,
    and hidden deep in earth, and I stand here
    who never laid a hand on spear against him, —   1030
    unless perhaps he died of longing for me,
    and thus I am his murderer. But they,
    the oracles, as they stand — he's taken them
    away with him, they're dead as he himself is,
    and worthless.
Jocasta: That I told you before now.   1035
Oedipus: You did, but I was misled by my fear.
Jocasta: Then lay no more of them to heart, not one.
Oedipus: But surely I must fear my mother's bed?
Jocasta: Why should man fear since chance is all in all
    for him, and he can clearly foreknow nothing?   1040
    Best to live lightly, as one can, unthinkingly.
    As to your mother's marriage bed, — don't fear it.
    Before this, in dreams too, as well as oracles,
    many a man has lain with his own mother.
    But he to whom such things are nothing bears   1045
    his life most easily.
Oedipus: All that you say would be said perfectly
    if she were dead; but since she lives I must
    still fear, although you talk so well, Jocasta.
Jocasta: Still in your father's death there's light of comfort?   1050
Oedipus: Great light of comfort; but I fear the living.
Messenger: Who is the woman that makes you afraid?
Oedipus: Merope, old man, Polybus' wife.
Messenger: What about her frightens the queen and you?
Oedipus: A terrible oracle, stranger, from the Gods.   1055
Messenger: Can it be told? Or does the sacred law
    forbid another to have knowledge of it?

1026 *Pythian hearth:* Delphi.

Oedipus: O no! Once on a time Loxias said
    that I should lie with my own mother and
    take on my hands the blood of my own father.   1060
    And so for these long years I've lived away
    from Corinth; it has been to my great happiness;
    but yet it's sweet to see the face of parents.
Messenger: This was the fear which drove you out of Corinth?
Oedipus: Old man, I did not wish to kill my father.   1065
Messenger: Why should I not free you from this fear, sir,
    since I have come to you in all goodwill?
Oedipus: You would not find me thankless if you did.
Messenger: Why, it was just for this I brought the news, —
    to earn your thanks when you had come safe home.   1070
Oedipus: No, I will never come near my parents.
Messenger: Son,
    it's very plain you don't know what you're doing.
Oedipus: What do you mean, old man? For God's sake, tell me.
Messenger: If your homecoming is checked by fears like these.
Oedipus: Yes, I'm afraid that Phoebus may prove right.   1075
Messenger: The murder and the incest?
Oedipus: Yes, old man;
    that is my constant terror.
Messenger: Do you know
    that all your fears are empty?
Oedipus: How is that,
    if they are father and mother and I their son?
Messenger: Because Polybus was no kin to you in blood.   1080
Oedipus: What, was not Polybus my father?
Messenger: No more than I but just so much.
Oedipus: How can
    my father be my father as much as one
    that's nothing to me?
Messenger: Neither he nor I
    begat you.
Oedipus: Why then did he call me son?   1085
Messenger: A gift he took you from these hands of mine.
Oedipus: Did he love so much what he took from another's hand?
Messenger: His childlessness before persuaded him.
Oedipus: Was I a child you bought or found when I
    was given to him?
Messenger: On Cithaeron's slopes   1090
    in the twisting thickets you were found.
Oedipus: And why
    were you a traveller in those parts?
Messenger: I was
    in charge of mountain flocks.

Oedipus: You were a shepherd?
A hireling vagrant?

Messenger: Yes, but at least at that time
the man that saved your life, son. 1095

Oedipus: What ailed me when you took me in your arms?

Messenger: In that your ankles should be witnesses.

Oedipus: Why do you speak of that old pain?

Messenger: I loosed you;
the tendons of your feet were pierced and fettered, —

Oedipus: My swaddling clothes brought me a rare disgrace. 1100

Messenger: So that from this you're called your present name.°

Oedipus: Was this my father's doing or my mother's?
For God's sake, tell me.

Messenger: I don't know, but he
who gave you to me has more knowledge than I.

Oedipus: You yourself did not find me then? You took me 1105
from someone else?

Messenger: Yes, from another shepherd.

Oedipus: Who was he? Do you know him well enough to tell?

Messenger: He was called Laius' man.

Oedipus: You mean the king who reigned here in the old days?

Messenger: Yes, he was that man's shepherd.

Oedipus: Is he alive 1110
still, so that I could see him?

Messenger: You who live here
would know that best.

Oedipus: Do any of you here
know of this shepherd whom he speaks about
in town or in the fields? Tell me. It's time
that this was found out once for all. 1115

Chorus: I think he is none other than the peasant
whom you have sought to see already; but
Jocasta here can tell us best of that.

Oedipus: Jocasta, do you know about this man
whom we have sent for? Is he the man he mentions? 1120

Jocasta: Why ask of whom he spoke? Don't give it heed;
nor try to keep in mind what has been said.
It will be wasted labour.

Oedipus: With such clues
I could not fail to bring my birth to light.

Jocasta: I beg you — do not hunt this out — I beg you, 1125
if you have any care for your own life.
What I am suffering is enough.

1101 *name: Oedipus* literally translates to "swollen foot."

Oedipus: Keep up
    your heart, Jocasta. Though I'm proved a slave,
    thrice slave, and though my mother is thrice slave,
    you'll not be shown to be of lowly lineage.   1130
Jocasta: O be persuaded by me, I entreat you;
    do not do this.
Oedipus: I will not be persuaded to let be
    the chance of finding out the whole thing clearly.
Jocasta: It is because I wish you well that I   1135
    give you this counsel — and it's the best counsel.
Oedipus: Then the best counsel vexes me, and has
    for some while since.
Jocasta: O Oedipus, God help you!
    God keep you from the knowledge of who you are!
Oedipus: Here, some one, go and fetch the shepherd for me;   1140
    and let her find her joy in her rich family!
Jocasta: O Oedipus, unhappy Oedipus!
    that is all I can call you, and the last thing
    that I shall ever call you.   (Exit.)
Chorus: Why has the queen gone, Oedipus, in wild   1145
    grief rushing from us? I am afraid that trouble
    will break out of this silence.
Oedipus: Break out what will! I at least shall be
    willing to see my ancestry, though humble.
    Perhaps she is ashamed of my low birth,   1150
    for she has all a woman's high-flown pride.
    But I account myself a child of Fortune,
    beneficent Fortune, and I shall not be
    dishonoured. She's the mother from whom I spring;
    the months, my brothers, marked me, now as small,   1155
    and now again as mighty. Such is my breeding,
    and I shall never prove so false to it,
    as not to find the secret of my birth.

Chorus (Strophe): If I am a prophet and wise of heart
    you shall not fail, Cithaeron,
    by the limitless sky, you shall not! —   1160
    to know at tomorrow's full moon
    that Oedipus honours you,
    as native to him and mother and nurse at once;
    and that you are honoured in dancing by us, as finding favour in   1165
        sight of our king.
    Apollo, to whom we cry, find these things pleasing!

    (Antistrophe) Who was it bore you, child? One of
    the long-lived nymphs who lay with Pan —
    the father who treads the hills?   1170

Or was she a bride of Loxias, your mother? The grassy slopes
are all of them dear to him. Or perhaps Cyllene's king
or the Bacchants' God that lives on the tops
of the hills received you a gift from some
one of the Helicon Nymphs, with whom he mostly plays?   1175

(Enter an old man, led by Oedipus' servants.)

Oedipus: If some one like myself who never met him
may make a guess, — I think this is the herdsman,
whom we were seeking. His old age is consonant
with the other. And besides, the men who bring him
I recognize as my own servants. You   1180
perhaps may better me in knowledge since
you've seen the man before.

Chorus: You can be sure
I recognize him. For if Laius
had ever an honest shepherd, this was he.

Oedipus: You, sir, from Corinth, I must ask you first,   1185
is this the man you spoke of?

Messenger: This is he
before your eyes.

Oedipus: Old man, look here at me
and tell me what I ask you. Were you ever
a servant of King Laius?

Herdsman: I was, —
no slave he bought but reared in his own house.   1190

Oedipus: What did you do as work? How did you live?

Herdsman: Most of my life was spent among the flocks.

Oedipus: In what part of the country did you live?

Herdsman: Cithaeron and the places near to it.

Oedipus: And somewhere there perhaps you knew this man?   1195

Herdsman: What was his occupation? Who?

Oedipus: This man here,
have you had any dealings with him?

Herdsman: No —
not such that I can quickly call to mind.

Messenger: That is no wonder, master. But I'll make him remember what
he does not know. For I know, that he well knows the country   1200
of Cithaeron, how he with two flocks, I with one kept company for
three years — each year half a year — from spring till autumn time
and then when winter came I drove my flocks to our fold home
again and he to Laius' steadings. Well — am I right or not in what
I said we did?   1205

Herdsman: You're right — although it's a long time ago.

Messenger: Do you remember giving me a child
to bring up as my foster child?

Herdsman: What's this?
　　Why do you ask this question?
Messenger: Look old man,
　　here he is — here's the man who was that child!　　　　　1210
Herdsman: Death take you! Won't you hold your tongue?
Oedipus: No, no,
　　do not find fault with him, old man. Your words
　　are more at fault than his.
Herdsman: O best of masters,
　　how do I give offense?
Oedipus: When you refuse
　　to speak about the child of whom he asks you.　　　　　1215
Herdsman: He speaks out of his ignorance, without meaning.
Oedipus: If you'll not talk to gratify me, you
　　will talk with pain to urge you.
Herdsman: O please, sir,
　　don't hurt an old man, sir.
Oedipus (to the servants): Here, one of you,
　　twist his hands behind him.
Herdsman: Why, God help me, why?　　　　　1220
　　What do you want to know?
Oedipus: You gave a child
　　to him, — the child he asked you of?
Herdsman: I did.
　　I wish I'd died the day I did.
Oedipus: You will
　　unless you tell me truly.
Herdsman: And I'll die
　　far worse if I should tell you.
Oedipus: This fellow　　　　　1225
　　is bent on more delays, as it would seem.
Herdsman: O no, no! I have told you that I gave it.
Oedipus: Where did you get this child from? Was it your own or
　　did you get it from another?
Herdsman: Not
　　my own at all; I had it from some one.　　　　　1230
Oedipus: One of these citizens? or from what house?
Herdsman: O master, please — I beg you, master, please
　　don't ask me more.
Oedipus: You're a dead man if I
　　ask you again.
Herdsman: It was one of the children
　　of Laius.
Oedipus: A slave? Or born in wedlock?　　　　　1235
Herdsman: O God, I am on the brink of frightful speech.

Oedipus: And I of frightful hearing. But I must hear.
Herdsman: The child was called his child; but she within,
    your wife would tell you best how all this was.
Oedipus: She gave it to you?
Herdsman: Yes, she did, my lord.   1240
Oedipus: To do what with it?
Herdsman: Make away with it.
Oedipus: She was so hard — its mother?
Herdsman: Aye, through fear
    of evil oracles.
Oedipus: Which?
Herdsman: They said that he
    should kill his parents.
Oedipus: How was it that you
    gave it away to this old man?
Herdsman: O master,   1245
    I pitied it, and thought that I could send it
    off to another country and this man
    was from another country. But he saved it
    for the most terrible troubles. If you are
    the man he says you are, you're bred to misery.   1250
Oedipus: O, O, O, they will all come,
    all come out clearly! Light of the sun, let me
    look upon you no more after today!
    I who first saw the light bred of a match
    accursed, and accursed in my living   1255
    with them I lived with, cursed in my killing.
                         (Exeunt all but the Chorus.)
Chorus (Strophe): O generations of men, how I
    count you as equal with those who live
    not at all!
    What man, what man on earth wins more   1260
    of happiness than a seeming
    and after that turning away?
    Oedipus, you are my pattern of this,
    Oedipus, you and your fate!
    Luckless Oedipus, whom of all men   1265
    I envy not at all.

    (Antistrophe) In as much as he shot his bolt
    beyond the others and won the prize
    of happiness complete —
    O Zeus — and killed and reduced to nought   1270
    the hooked taloned maid of the riddling speech,
    standing a tower against death for my land:
    hence he was called my king and hence

was honoured the highest of all
honours; and hence he ruled
in the great city of Thebes. 1275

(Strophe) But now whose tale is more miserable?
Who is there lives with a savager fate?
Whose troubles so reverse his life as his?

O Oedipus, the famous prince 1280
for whom a great haven
the same both as father and son
sufficed for generation,
how, O how, have the furrows ploughed
by your father endured to bear you, poor wretch, 1285
and hold their peace so long?

(Antistrophe) Time who sees all has found you out
against your will; judges your marriage accursed,
begetter and begot at one in it.

O child of Laius, 1290
would I had never seen you.
I weep for you and cry
a dirge of lamentation.

To speak directly, I drew my breath
from you at the first and so now I lull 1295
my mouth to sleep with your name.   *(Enter a second messenger.)*
Second Messenger: O Princes always honoured by our country,
    what deeds you'll hear of and what horrors see,
    what grief you'll feel, if you as true born Thebans
    care for the house of Labdacus's sons. 1300
    Phasis nor Ister cannot purge this house,
    I think, with all their streams, such things
    it hides, such evils shortly will bring forth
    into the light, whether they will or not;
    and troubles hurt the most 1305
    when they prove self-inflicted.
Chorus: What we had known before did not fall short
    of bitter groaning's worth; what's more to tell?
Second Messenger: Shortest to hear and tell — our glorious queen
    Jocasta's dead.
Chorus: Unhappy woman! How? 1310
Second Messenger: By her own hand. The worst of what was done
    you cannot know. You did not see the sight.
    Yet in so far as I remember it
    you'll hear the end of our unlucky queen.

When she came raging into the house she went   1315
straight to her marriage bed, tearing her hair
with both her hands, and crying upon Laius
long dead — Do you remember, Laius,
that night long past which bred a child for us
to send you to your death and leave   1320
a mother making children with her son?
And then she groaned and cursed the bed in which
she brought forth husband by her husband, children
by her own child, an infamous double bond.
How after that she died I do not know, —   1325
for Oedipus distracted us from seeing.
He burst upon us shouting and we looked
to him as he paced frantically around,
begging us always: Give me a sword, I say,
to find this wife no wife, this mother's womb,   1330
this field of double sowing whence I sprang
and where I sowed my children! As he raved
some god showed him the way — none of us there.
Bellowing terribly and led by some
invisible guide he rushed on the two doors, —   1335
wrenching the hollow bolts out of their sockets,
he charged inside. There, there, we saw his wife
hanging, the twisted rope around her neck.
When he saw her, he cried out fearfully
and cut the dangling noose. Then, as she lay,   1340
poor woman, on the ground, what happened after,
was terrible to see. He tore the brooches —
the gold chased brooches fastening her robe —
away from her and lifting them up high
dashed them on his own eyeballs, shrieking out   1345
such things as: they will never see the crime
I have committed or had done upon me!
Dark eyes, now in the days to come look on
forbidden faces, do not recognize
those whom you long for — with such imprecations   1350
he struck his eyes again and yet again
with the brooches. And the bleeding eyeballs gushed
and stained his beard — no sluggish oozing drops
but a black rain and bloody hail poured down.

So it has broken — and not on one head   1355
but troubles mixed for husband and for wife.
The fortune of the days gone by was true
good fortune — but today groans and destruction
and death and shame — of all ills can be named
not one is missing.   1360

Chorus: Is he now in any ease from pain?
Second Messenger: He shouts
    for some one to unbar the doors and show him
    to all the men of Thebes, his father's killer,
    his mother's — no I cannot say the word,
    it is unholy — for he'll cast himself,   1365
    out of the land, he says, and not remain
    to bring a curse upon his house, the curse
    he called upon it in his proclamation. But
    he wants for strength, aye, and some one to guide him;
    his sickness is too great to bear. You, too,   1370
    will be shown that. The bolts are opening.
    Soon you will see a sight to waken pity
    even in the horror of it.   *(Enter the blinded Oedipus.)*
Chorus: This is a terrible sight for men to see!
    I never found a worse!   1375
    Poor wretch, what madness came upon you!
    What evil spirit leaped upon your life
    to your ill-luck — a leap beyond man's strength!
    Indeed I pity you, but I cannot
    look at you, though there's much I want to ask   1380
    and much to learn and much to see.
    I shudder at the sight of you.
Oedipus: O, O,
    where am I going? Where is my voice
    borne on the wind to and fro?
    Spirit, how far have you sprung?   1385
Chorus: To a terrible place whereof men's ears
    may not hear, nor their eyes behold it.
Oedipus: Darkness!
    Horror of darkness enfolding, resistless, unspeakable visitant
        sped by an ill wind in haste!   1390
    madness and stabbing pain and memory
    of evil deeds I have done!
Chorus: In such misfortunes it's no wonder
    if double weighs the burden of your grief.
Oedipus: My friend,   1395
    you are the only one steadfast, the only one that attends on me;
    you still stay nursing the blind man.
    Your care is not unnoticed. I can know
    your voice, although this darkness is my world.
Chorus: Doer of dreadful deeds, how did you dare   1400
    so far to do despite to your own eyes?
    what spirit urged you to it?
Oedipus: It was Apollo, friends, Apollo,
    that brought this bitter bitterness, my sorrows to completion.

But the hand that struck me   1405
was none but my own.
Why should I see
whose vision showed me nothing sweet to see?
Chorus: These things are as you say.
Oedipus: What can I see to love?   1410
    What greeting can touch my ears with joy?
    Take me away, and haste — to a place out of the way!
    Take me away, my friends, the greatly miserable,
    the most accursed, whom God too hates
    above all men on earth!   1415
Chorus: Unhappy in your mind and your misfortune,
    would I had never known you!
Oedipus: Curse on the man who took
    the cruel bonds from off my legs, as I lay in the field.
    He stole me from death and saved me,   1420
    no kindly service.
    Had I died then
    I would not be so burdensome to friends.
Chorus: I, too, could have wished it had been so.
Oedipus: Then I would not have come   1425
    to kill my father and marry my mother infamously.
    Now I am godless and child of impurity,
    begetter in the same seed that created my wretched self.
    If there is any ill worse than ill,
    that is the lot of Oedipus.   1430
Chorus: I cannot say your remedy was good;
    you would be better dead than blind and living.
Oedipus: What I have done here was best done — don't tell me
    otherwise, do not give me further counsel.
    I do not know with what eyes I could look   1435
    upon my father when I die and go
    under the earth, nor yet my wretched mother —
    those two to whom I have done things deserving
    worse punishment than hanging. Would the sight
    of children, bred as mine are, gladden me?   1440
    No, not these eyes, never. And my city,
    its towers and sacred places of the Gods,
    of these I robbed my miserable self
    when I commanded all to drive *him* out,
    the criminal since proved by God impure   1445
    and of the race of Laius.
    To this guilt I bore witness against myself —
    with what eyes shall I look upon my people?
    No. If there were a means to choke the fountain
    of hearing I would not have stayed my hand   1450

from locking up my miserable carcase,
seeing and hearing nothing; it is sweet
to keep our thoughts out of the range of hurt.

Cithaeron, why did you receive me? why
having received me did you not kill me straight? 1455
And so I had not shown to men my birth.

O Polybus and Corinth and the house,
the old house that I used to call my father's —
what fairness you were nurse to, and what foulness
festered beneath! Now I am found to be 1460
a sinner and a son of sinners. Crossroads,
and hidden glade, oak and the narrow way
at the crossroads, that drank my father's blood
offered you by my hands, do you remember
still what I did as you looked on, and what 1465
I did when I came here? O marriage, marriage!
you bred me and again when you had bred
bred children of your child and showed to men
brides, wives and mothers and the foulest deeds
that can be in this world of ours. 1470

Come — it's unfit to say what is unfit
to do. — I beg of you in God's name hide me
somewhere outside your country, yes, or kill me,
or throw me into the sea, to be forever
out of your sight. Approach and deign to touch me 1475
for all my wretchedness, and do not fear.
No man but I can bear my evil doom.

Chorus: Here Creon comes in fit time to perform
or give advice in what you ask of us.
Creon is left sole ruler in your stead. 1480

Oedipus: Creon! Creon! What shall I say to him?
How can I justly hope that he will trust me?
In what is past I have been proved towards him
an utter liar. *(Enter Creon.)*

Creon: Oedipus, I've come
not so that I might laugh at you nor taunt you 1485
with evil of the past. But if you still
are without shame before the face of men
reverence at least the flame that gives all life,
our Lord the Sun, and do not show unveiled
to him pollution such that neither land 1490
nor holy rain nor light of day can welcome. *(To a servant)*
Be quick and take him in. It is most decent
that only kin should see and hear the troubles
of kin.

Oedipus: I beg you, since you've torn me from   1495
    my dreadful expectations and have come
    in a most noble spirit to a man
    that has used you vilely — do a thing for me.
    I shall speak for your own good, not for my own.
Creon: What do you need that you would ask of me?   1500
Oedipus: Drive me from here with all the speed you can
    to where I may not hear a human voice.
Creon: Be sure, I would have done this had not I
    wished first of all to learn from the God the course
    of action I should follow.
Oedipus: But his word   1505
    has been quite clear to let the parricide,°
    the sinner, die.
Creon: Yes, that indeed was said.
    But in the present need we had best discover
    what we should do.
Oedipus: And will you ask about
    a man so wretched?
Creon: Now even you will trust   1510
    the God.
Oedipus: So. I command you — and will beseech you —
    to her that lies inside that house give burial
    as you would have it; she is yours and rightly
    you will perform the rites for her. For me —
    never let this my father's city have me   1515
    living a dweller in it. Leave me live
    in the mountains where Cithaeron is, that's called
    my mountain, which my mother and my father
    while they were living would have made my tomb.
    So I may die by their decree who sought   1520
    indeed to kill me. Yet I know this much:
    no sickness and no other thing will kill me.
    I would not have been saved from death if not
    for some strange evil fate. Well, let my fate
    go where it will.
                    Creon, you need not care   1525
    about my sons; they're men and so wherever
    they are, they will not lack a livelihood.
    But my two girls — so sad and pitiful —
    whose table never stood apart from mine,
    and everything I touched they always shared —   1530
    O Creon, have a thought for them! And most
    I wish that you might suffer me to touch them

1506 *parricide:* One who kills his parent or another close relative.

and sorrow with them.

(Enter Antigone and Ismene, Oedipus' two daughters.)

O my lord! O true noble Creon! Can I
really be touching them, as when I saw?
What shall I say?   1535
Yes, I can hear them sobbing — my two darlings!
and Creon has had pity and has sent me
what I loved most?
Am I right?   1540

Creon: You're right: it was I gave you this
because I knew from old days how you loved them
as I see now.

Oedipus: God bless you for it, Creon,
and may God guard you better on your road
than he did me!

            O children,   1545
where are you? Come here, come to my hands,
a brother's hands which turned your father's eyes,
those bright eyes you knew once, to what you see,
a father seeing nothing, knowing nothing,
begetting you from his own source of life.   1550
I weep for you — I cannot see your faces —
I weep when I think of the bitterness
there will be in your lives, how you must live
before the world. At what assemblages
of citizens will you make one? to what   1555
gay company will you go and not come home
in tears instead of sharing in the holiday?
And when you're ripe for marriage, who will he be,
the man who'll risk to take such infamy
as shall cling to my children, to bring hurt   1560
on them and those that marry with them? What
curse is not there? "Your father killed his father
and sowed the seed where he had sprung himself
and begot you out of the womb that held him."
These insults you will hear. Then who will marry you?   1565
No one, my children; clearly you are doomed
to waste away in barrenness unmarried.
Son of Menoeceus,° since you are all the father
left these two girls, and we, their parents, both
are dead to them — do not allow them wander   1570
like beggars, poor and husbandless.
They are of your own blood.
And do not make them equal with myself

1568 *Son of Menoeceus:* Creon.

in wretchedness; for you can see them now
so young, so utterly alone, save for you only.   1575
Touch my hand, noble Creon, and say yes.
If you were older, children, and were wiser,
there's much advice I'd give you. But as it is,
let this be what you pray: give me a life
wherever there is opportunity   1580
to live, and better life than was my father's.

Creon: Your tears have had enough of scope; now go within the
   house.

Oedipus: I must obey, though bitter of heart.

Creon: In season, all is good.

Oedipus: Do you know on what conditions I obey?

Creon: You tell me them,   1585
   and I shall know them when I hear.

Oedipus: That you shall send me out
   to live away from Thebes.

Creon: That gift you must ask of the God.

Oedipus: But I'm now hated by the Gods.

Creon: So quickly you'll obtain your prayer.

Oedipus: You consent then?

Creon: What I do not mean, I do not use to say.

Oedipus: Now lead me away from here.

Creon: Let go the children, then, and come.   1590

Oedipus: Do not take them from me.

Creon: Do not seek to be master in everything,
   for the things you mastered did not follow you
      throughout your life.   *(As Creon and Oedipus go out.)*

Chorus: You that live in my ancestral Thebes, behold this Oedipus, —
   him who knew the famous riddles and was a man most masterful;
   not a citizen who did not look with envy on his lot —   1595
   see him now and see the breakers of misfortune swallow him!
   Look upon that last day always. Count no mortal happy till
   he has passed the final limit of his life secure from pain.

CONSIDERATIONS FOR CRITICAL THINKING AND WRITING

1. **FIRST RESPONSE.** How might a twenty-first-century reader identify
   with Oedipus's plight? What philosophic issues does Oedipus confront that remain relevant to humans today?

2. In the opening scene what does the priest's speech reveal about how
   Oedipus has been regarded as a ruler of Thebes?

3. What do Oedipus's confrontations with Teiresias and Creon indicate
   about his character?

4. Aristotle defined a tragic flaw as consisting of "error and frailties."
   What errors does Oedipus make? What are his frailties?

5. What causes Oedipus's downfall? Is he simply a pawn in a predetermined game played by the gods? Can he be regarded as responsible for the suffering and death in the play?

6. Locate instances of dramatic irony in the play. How do they serve as foreshadowings?

7. Describe the function of the Chorus in this play. How does the Chorus's view of life and the gods differ from Jocasta's?

8. Trace the images of vision and blindness throughout the play. How are they related to the theme? Why does Oedipus blind himself instead of joining Jocasta in suicide?

9. What is your assessment of Oedipus at the end of the play? Was he foolish? Heroic? Fated? To what extent can your emotions concerning him be described as "pity and fear"?

10. CRITICAL STRATEGIES. Read the section on psychological criticism (pp. 1074–76) in Chapter 30, "Critical Strategies for Reading." Given that the *Oedipus complex* is a well-known term used in psychoanalysis, what does it mean? Does the concept offer any insights into the conflicts dramatized in the play?

CONNECTIONS TO OTHER SELECTIONS

1. Consider the endings of *Oedipus the King* and William Shakespeare's *Othello* (p. 769). What feelings do you have about these endings? Are they irredeemably unhappy? Is there anything that suggests hope for the future at the ends of these plays?

2. Sophocles does not include violence in his plays; any bloodshed occurs offstage. Compare and contrast the effects of this strategy with the use of violence in *Othello*.

3. Write an essay explaining why *Oedipus the King* cannot be considered a realistic play in the way that Henrik Ibsen's *A Doll's House* (p. 864) can be.

27

A Study of
William Shakespeare

All the world's a stage,
And all the men and women
  merely players:
They have their exits and their
  entrances;
And one man in his time plays
  many parts . . .
  — WILLIAM SHAKESPEARE

Universal History Archive/Getty
Images.

Bettmann/Getty Images.

Shakespeare — the nearest thing
in incarnation to the eye of God.
  — SIR LAURENCE OLIVIER

Although relatively little is known about William Shakespeare's life, his writings reveal him to have been an extraordinary man. His vitality, compassion, and insights are evident in his broad range of characters, who have fascinated generations of audiences, and his powerful use of the English language, which has been celebrated since his death nearly four centuries ago. Ben Jonson, his contemporary, rightly claimed that "he was not of an age, but for all time!" Shakespeare's plays have been produced so often and his writings read so widely that quotations from them have woven their way into our everyday conversations. If you have ever experienced "fear and trembling" because there was "something in the wind" or discovered that it was "a foregone conclusion" that you would "make a virtue of necessity," then it wouldn't be quite accurate for you to say that Shakespeare "was Greek to me" because these phrases come, respectively, from his plays *Much Ado about Nothing, The Comedy of Errors, Othello, The Two Gentlemen of Verona,* and *Julius Caesar.* Many more examples could be cited, but it is enough to say that Shakespeare's art endures. His words may give us only an

"First Folio" portrait (top). The image of William Shakespeare above is a portrait included in the *First Folio,* a collected edition of Shakespeare's plays published seven years after his death.

"Chandos" portrait engraving (middle). This engraving is of an image painted during Shakespeare's lifetime known as the "Chandos portrait," rumored to have been painted by Shakespeare's friend and fellow actor Richard Burbage.

Shakespeare's signature (bottom). The signature shown here is one of the bard's six authenticated signatures in existence and is from his last will and testament.

Top image: Universal History Archive/Getty Images. *Middle image:* © National Portrait Gallery, London/Art Resource, NY. *Bottom image:* Courtesy of the National Archives, United Kingdom.

oblique glimpse of his life, but they continue to give us back the experience of our own lives.

Shakespeare was born in Stratford-on-Avon on or about April 23, 1564. His father, an important citizen who held several town offices, married a woman from a prominent family; however, when their son was only a teenager, the family's financial situation became precarious. Shakespeare probably attended the Stratford grammar school, but no records of either his schooling or his early youth exist. As limited as his education was, it is clear that he was for his time a learned man. At the age of eighteen, he struck out on his own and married the twenty-six-year-old Anne Hathaway, who gave birth to a daughter in 1583 and twins, a boy and a girl, in 1585. Before he was twenty-one, Shakespeare had a wife and three children to support.

What his life was like for the next seven years is not known, but there is firm evidence that by 1592 he was in London enjoying some success as both an actor and a playwright. By 1594 he had also established himself as a poet with two lengthy poems, *Venus and Adonis* and *The Rape of Lucrece*. But it was in the theater that he made his living and his strongest reputation. He was well connected with a successful troupe first known as the Lord Chamberlain's Men; they built the famous Globe Theatre in 1599. Later this company, because of the patronage of King James, came to be known as the King's Men. Writing plays for this company throughout his career, Shakespeare also became one of its principal shareholders, an arrangement that allowed him to prosper in London as well as in his native Stratford, where in 1597 he bought a fine house called New Place. About 1611 he retired there with his family, although he continued writing plays. He died on April 23, 1616, and was buried at Holy Trinity Church in Stratford.

The documented details of Shakespeare's life provide barely enough information for a newspaper obituary. But if his activities remain largely unknown, his writings — among them thirty-seven plays and 154 sonnets — more than compensate for that loss. Plenty of authors have produced more work, but no writer has created so much literature that has been so universally admired. Within twenty-five years Shakespeare's dramatic works included *Hamlet, Macbeth, King Lear, Othello, Julius Caesar, Richard III, Henry IV, Romeo and Juliet, Love's Labour's Lost, A Midsummer Night's Dream, The Tempest, Twelfth Night,* and *Measure for Measure.* These plays represent a broad range of characters and actions conveyed in poetic language that reveals human nature as well as the author's genius.

SHAKESPEARE'S THEATER

Drama languished in Europe after the fall of Rome during the fifth and sixth centuries. From about A.D. 400 to 900 almost no record of dramatic productions exists except for those of minstrels and other entertainers, such as acrobats and jugglers, who traveled through the countryside. The Catholic church was instrumental in suppressing drama because the theater — represented by the excesses of Roman productions — was seen as subversive. No state-sponsored festivals brought people together in huge theaters the way they had in Greek and Roman times.

In the tenth century, however, the church helped revive theater by incorporating dialogues into the Mass as a means of dramatizing portions of the Gospels. These brief dialogues developed into more elaborate mystery plays, miracle plays, and morality plays, anonymous works that were created primarily to inculcate religious principles rather than to entertain. But these works also marked the reemergence of relatively large dramatic productions. *Mystery plays* dramatize stories from the Bible, such as the Creation, the Fall of Adam and Eve, or the Crucifixion. The most highly regarded surviving example is *The Second Shepherd's Play* (ca. 1400), which dramatizes Christ's nativity. *Miracle plays* are based on the lives of saints. An extant play of the late fifteenth century, for example, is titled *Saint Mary Magdalene*. *Morality plays* present allegorical stories in which virtues and vices are personified to teach humanity how to achieve salvation. *Everyman* (ca. 1500), the most famous example, has as its central conflict every person's struggle to avoid the sins that lead to hell and practice the virtues that are rewarded in heaven.

The clergy who performed these plays gave way to trade guilds that presented them outside the church on stages featuring scenery and costumed characters. The plays' didactic content was gradually abandoned in favor of broad humor and worldly concerns. Thus by the sixteenth century religious drama had been replaced largely by secular drama.

Because theatrical productions were no longer sponsored and financed by the church or trade guilds during Shakespeare's lifetime, playwrights had to figure out ways to draw audiences willing to pay for entertainment. This necessitated some simple but important changes. Somehow, people had to be prevented from seeing a production unless they paid. Hence an enclosed space with controlled access was created. In addition, the plays had to change frequently enough to keep audiences returning, and this resulted in more experienced actors and playwrights sensitive to their audiences' tastes and interests. Plays compelling enough to attract audiences had to employ powerful writing brought to life by convincing actors in entertaining productions. Shakespeare always wrote his dramas for the stage — for audiences who would see and hear the characters. The conventions of the theater for which he wrote are important, then, for appreciating and understanding his plays. Detailed information about Elizabethan theater (theater during the reign of Elizabeth I, from 1558 to 1603) is less than abundant, but historians have been able to piece together a good sense of what theaters were like from sources such as drawings, building contracts, and stage directions.

Early performances of various kinds took place in the courtyards of inns and taverns. These secular entertainments attracted people of all classes.

To the dismay of London officials, such gatherings were also settings for the illegal activities of brawlers, thieves, and prostitutes. To avoid licensing regulations, some theaters were constructed outside the city's limits. The Globe, for instance, built by the Lord Chamberlain's Company, with which Shakespeare was closely associated, was located on the south bank of the Thames River. Regardless of the play, an Elizabethan theatergoer was likely to have an exciting time. Playwrights understood the varied nature of their audiences, so the plays appealed to a broad range of sensibilities and tastes. Philosophy and poetry rubbed shoulders with violence and sexual jokes, and somehow all were made compatible.

Physically, Elizabethan theaters resembled the courtyards where they originated, but the theaters could accommodate more people — perhaps as many as twenty-five hundred. The exterior of a theater building was many-sided or round and enclosed a yard that was only partially roofed over, to take advantage of natural light. The interior walls consisted of three galleries of seats looking onto a platform stage that extended from the rear wall. These seats were sheltered from the weather and more comfortable than the area in front of the stage, which was known as the *pit*. Here "groundlings" paid a penny to stand and watch the performance. Despite the large number of spectators, the theater created an intimate atmosphere because the audience closely surrounded the stage on three sides.

A Conjectural Reconstruction of the Globe Theatre, 1599–1613.
Drawing by C. Walter Hodges. Bettmann/Getty Images.

This arrangement produced two theatrical conventions: asides and soliloquies. An *aside* is a speech directed only to the audience. It makes the audience privy to a character's thoughts, allowing them to perceive ironies and intrigues that other characters know nothing about. In a large performing space, such as a Greek amphitheater, asides would be unconvincing because they would have to be declaimed loudly to be heard, but they were well suited to Elizabethan theaters. A *soliloquy* is a speech delivered while an actor is alone on the stage; like an aside, it reveals a character's state of mind. Hamlet's "To be or not to be" speech is the most famous example of a soliloquy.

The Elizabethan platform stage was large enough — approximately twenty-five feet deep and forty feet wide — to allow a wide variety of actions, ranging from festive banquets to bloody battles. Sections of the floor could be opened or removed to create, for instance, the gravediggers' scene in *Hamlet* or to allow characters to exit through trapdoors. At the rear of the platform an inner stage was covered by curtains that could be drawn to reveal an interior setting, such as a bedroom or tomb. The curtains were also a natural location for a character to hide in order to overhear conversations. On each side of the curtains were doors through which characters entered and exited. An upper stage could be used as a watchtower, a castle wall, or a balcony. Although most of the action occurred on the main platform stage, there were opportunities for fluid movements from one acting area to another, providing a variety of settings.

These settings were not, however, elaborately indicated by scenery or props. A scene might change when one group of characters left the stage and another entered. A table and some chairs could be carried on quickly to suggest a tavern. But the action was not interrupted for set changes. Instead, the characters' speeches often identify the location of a scene. (In modern editions of Shakespeare's plays, editors indicate in brackets the scene breaks, settings, and movements of actors not identified in the original manuscripts to help readers keep track of things.) Today's performances of the plays frequently use more elaborate settings and props. But Shakespeare's need to paint his scenery with words resulted in many poetic descriptions. Here is one of moonlight from *Merchant of Venice*:

> How sweet the moonlight sleeps upon this bank!
> Here will we sit and let the sounds of music
> Creep in our ears. Soft stillness and the night
> Become the touches of sweet harmony.

Although the settings were spare and the props mostly limited to what an actor carried onto the stage (a sword, a document, a shovel), Elizabethan costuming was an elaborate visual treat that identified the characters. Moreover, because women were not permitted to act in the theater, their roles were played by young boys dressed in female costumes. In addition, elaborate sound effects were used to create atmosphere. A flourish of trumpets might accompany the entrance of a king; small cannons might be heard during a battle;

thunder might punctuate a storm. In short, Elizabethan theater was alive with sights and sounds, but at the center of the stage was the playwright's language; that's where the magic began.

THE RANGE OF SHAKESPEARE'S DRAMA: HISTORY, COMEDY, AND TRAGEDY

Shakespeare's plays fall into three basic categories: histories, comedies, and tragedies. Broadly speaking, a history play is any drama based on historical materials. In this case, Shakespeare's *Antony and Cleopatra* and *Julius Caesar* would fit the definition, since they feature historical figures. More specifically, though, a *history play* is a British play based primarily on Raphael Holinshed's *Chronicles of England, Scotland, and Ireland* (1578). This account of British history was popular toward the end of the sixteenth century because of the patriotic pride that was produced by the British defeat of the Spanish Armada in 1588, and it was an important source for a series of plays Shakespeare wrote treating the reigns of British kings from Richard II to Henry VIII. The political subject matter of these plays both entertained audiences and instructed them in virtues and vices involved in England's past efforts to overcome civil war and disorder. Ambition, deception, and treason were of more than historical interest. Shakespeare's audiences saw these plays about the fifteenth century as ways of sorting through the meanings of both the calamities of the past and the uncertainties of the present.

Although Shakespeare used Holinshed's *Chronicles* as a source, he did not hesitate to make changes for dramatic purposes. In *1 Henry IV*, for example, he ages Henry IV to contrast him with the youthful Prince Hal, and he makes Hotspur younger than he actually was to have him serve as a foil to the prince. The serious theme of Hal's growth into the kind of man who would make an ideal king is counterweighted by Shakespeare's comic creation of Falstaff, that good-humored "huge hill of flesh" filled with delightful contradictions. Falstaff had historic antecedents, but the true source of his identity is the imagination of Shakespeare, a writer who was, after all, a dramatist first.

Comedy is a strong element in *1 Henry IV*, but the play's overall tone is serious. Falstaff 's behavior ultimately gives way to the measured march of English history. While Shakespeare encourages us to laugh at some of the participants, we are not invited to laugh at the history of English monarchies. Comedy even appears in Shakespeare's tragedies, as in Hamlet's jests with the gravediggers or in Emilia's biting remarks in *Othello*. This use of comedy is called *comic relief*, a humorous scene or incident that alleviates tension in an otherwise serious work. In many instances these moments enhance the thematic significance of the story in addition to providing laughter. When Hamlet jokes with the gravediggers, we laugh, but something hauntingly serious about the humor also intensifies our more serious emotions.

A true comedy, however, lacks a tragedy's sense that some great disaster will finally descend on the protagonist. There are conflicts and obstacles that must be confronted, but in comedy the characters delight us by overcoming whatever initially thwarts them. We can laugh at their misfortunes because we are confident that everything will turn out fine in the end. Shakespearean comedy tends to follow this general principle; it begins with problems and ends with their resolution.

Shakespeare's comedies are called ***romantic comedies*** because they typically involve lovers whose hearts are set on each other but whose lives are complicated by disapproving parents, deceptions, jealousies, illusions, confused identities, disguises, or other misunderstandings. Conflicts are present, but they are more amusing than threatening. This lightness is apparent in some of the comedies' titles: the conflict in a play such as *A Midsummer Night's Dream* is, in a sense, *Much Ado about Nothing*—*As You Like It* in a comedy. Shakespeare orchestrates the problems and confusion that typify the initial plotting of a romantic comedy into harmonious wedding arrangements in the final scenes. In these comedies life is a celebration, a feast that always satisfies, because the generosity of the humor leaves us with a revived appetite for life's surprising possibilities. Discord and misunderstanding give way to concord and love. Marriage symbolizes a pledge that life itself is renewable, so we are left with a sense of new beginnings.

Although a celebration of life, comedy is also frequently used as a vehicle for criticizing human affairs. ***Satire*** casts a critical eye on vices and follies by holding them up to ridicule—usually to point out an absurdity so that it can be avoided or corrected. In *Twelfth Night* Malvolio is satirized for his priggishness and pomposity. He thinks himself better than almost everyone around him, but Shakespeare reveals him to be comic as well as pathetic. We come to understand what Malvolio will apparently never comprehend: that no one can take him as seriously as he takes himself. Polonius is subjected to a similar kind of scrutiny in *Hamlet*.

Malvolio's ambitious efforts to attract Olivia's affections are rendered absurd by Shakespeare's use of both high and low comedy. **High comedy** consists of verbal wit, while **low comedy** is generally associated with physical action and is less intellectual. Through puns and witty exchanges, Shakespeare's high comedy displays Malvolio's inconsistencies of character. His self-importance is deflated by low comedy. We are treated to a ***farce***, a form of humor based on exaggerated, improbable incongruities, when the staid Malvolio is tricked into wearing bizarre clothing and behaving like a fool to win Olivia. Our laughter is Malvolio's pain, but though he has been "notoriously abus'd" and he vows in the final scene to be "reveng'd on the whole pack" of laughing conspirators who have tricked him, the play ends on a light note. Indeed, it concludes with a song, the last line of which reminds us of the predominant tone of the play as well as the nature of comedy: "And we'll strive to please you every day."

Tragedy, in contrast, does not promise peace and contentment. The basic characteristics of tragedy have already been outlined in the context of Greek drama (see Chapter 26). Like Greek tragic heroes, Shakespeare's protagonists are exceptional human beings whose stature makes their misfortune all the more dramatic. These characters pay a high price for their actions. Oedipus's search for the killer of Laios, Hamlet's agonized conviction that "The time is out of joint," and Othello's willingness to doubt his wife's fidelity all lead to irreversible results. Comic plots are largely free of this sense of inevitability. Instead of the festive mood that prevails once the characters in a comedy recognize their true connection to each other, tragedy gives us dark reflections that emanate from suffering. The laughter of comedy is a shared experience, a recognition of human likeness, but suffering estranges tragic heroes from the world around them.

Some of the wrenching differences between comedy and tragedy can be experienced in *Othello*. Although this play is a tragedy, Shakespeare includes in its plot many of the ingredients associated with comedy. For a time it seems possible that Othello and Desdemona will overcome the complications of a disapproving father, along with the seemingly minor deceptions, awkward misperceptions, and tender illusions that hover around them. But in *Othello* marriage is not a sign of concord displacing discord; instead, love and marriage mark the beginning of the tragic action.

Another important difference between tragedy and comedy is the way characters are presented. The tragic protagonist is portrayed as a remarkable individual whose unique qualities compel us with their power and complexity. Macbeth is not simply a murderer, nor is Othello merely a jealous husband. But despite their extreme passions, behavior, and even crimes, we identify with tragic heroes in ways that we do not with comic characters. We can laugh at pretentious fools, smug hypocrites, clumsy oafs, and thwarted lovers because we see them from a distance. They are amusing precisely because their problems are not ours; we recognize them as types instead of as ourselves (or so we think). No reader of *Twelfth Night* worries about Sir Toby Belch's excessive drinking; he is a cheerful "sot" whose passion for ale is cause for celebration rather than concern. Shakespeare's comedy is sometimes disturbing — Malvolio's character certainly is — but it is never devastating. Tragic heroes do confront devastation; they command our respect and compassion because they act in spite of terrifying risks. Their triumph is measured not by the attainment of what they seek but by the wisdom that defeat imposes on them.

A NOTE ON READING SHAKESPEARE

Readers who have had no previous experience with Shakespeare's language may find it initially daunting. They might well ask whether people ever talked the way, for example, Hamlet does in his most famous soliloquy:

To be, or not to be: that is the question:
Whether 'tis nobler in the mind to suffer
The slings and arrows of outrageous fortune,
Or to take arms against a sea of troubles,
And by opposing end them?

People did not talk like this in Elizabethan times. Hamlet speaks poetry. Shakespeare might have had him say something like this: "The most important issue one must confront is whether the pain that life inevitably creates should be passively accepted or resisted." But Shakespeare chose poetry to reveal the depth and complexity of Hamlet's experience. This heightened language is used to clarify rather than obscure his characters' thoughts. Shakespeare has Hamlet, as well as many other characters, speak in prose too, but in general his plays are written in poetry. If you keep in mind that Shakespeare's dialogue is not typically intended to imitate every-day speech, it should be easier to understand that his language is more than simply a vehicle for expressing the action of the play.

Here are a few practical suggestions to enhance your understanding of and pleasure in reading Shakespeare's plays.

1. Keep track of the characters by referring to the *dramatis personae* (characters) listed and briefly described at the beginning of each play.
2. Remember that poetic language deserves to be read slowly and carefully. A difficult passage can sometimes be better understood if it's read aloud. Don't worry if every line isn't absolutely clear to you.
3. Pay attention to the annotations, which explain unfamiliar words, phrases, and allusions in the text. These can be distracting, but they are sometimes necessary to determine the basic meaning of a passage.
4. As you read each scene, try to imagine how it would be played on a stage.
5. If you find the reading especially difficult, try listening to a recording of the play. (Many college libraries have recordings of Shakespeare's plays, and the Internet might be useful for this purpose, too.) Allowing professional actors to do the reading aloud for you can enrich your imaginative reconstruction of the action and characters. Hearing a play can help you with subsequent readings of it.
6. After reading the play, view a recording of a performance. It is important to view the performance *after* your reading, though, so that your own mental re-creation of the play is not short-circuited by a director's production.

And finally, to quote Hamlet, "Be not too tame . . . let your own discretion be your tutor." Read Shakespeare's work as best you can; it warrants such careful attention not because the language and characters are difficult to understand but because they offer so much to enjoy.

Othello, the Moor of Venice

Othello has compelled audiences since it was first produced in 1604. Its power is as simple and as complex as the elemental emotions it dramatizes; the play ebbs and flows with the emotional energy derived from the characters' struggles with love and hatred, good and evil, trust and jealousy, appearance and reality. These conflicts are played out on a domestic scale rather than on some metaphysical level. Anyone who has ever been in love will empathize with Othello and Desdemona. They embody a love story gone horribly — tragically — wrong.

Although the plot of *Othello* is filled with Iago's intrigues and a series of opaque mysteries for Othello, it moves swiftly and precisely to its catastrophic ending as the tragedy relentlessly claims its victims. On one level the plot is simple. As the Moorish general of the Venetian army, Othello chooses Cassio to serve as his lieutenant, a selection Iago resents and decides to subvert. To discredit Cassio, Iago poisons Othello's faith in his wife, Desdemona, by falsely insinuating that she and Cassio are having an affair. Through a series of cleverly demonic manipulations, Iago succeeds in convincing Othello of his wife's infidelity and his lieutenant's betrayal. Believing these lies, Othello insists on taking his revenge.

If the plot of *Othello* is relatively direct and simple in its focus on Iago's manipulation of events, the play's major characters are considerably more complex. Love and jealousy are central in *Othello*. The Moor's virtues of openness and trust cause him to experience betrayal as intensely as he does love. He is distinguished by his nobility, bravery, strength, and deep sense of honor, but he is also vulnerable to the doubts Iago raises owing to his race ("I am black") and marginal status in Venetian society.

Iago, whose motivations are much deeper and more mysterious than his maneuvering for a coveted lieutenancy, personifies a nearly inexplicable evil in the play. Just as Desdemona's nature seems to be all goodness, Iago's is malignant destruction. His profound villainy both horrifies and fascinates us: How can he be what he is? He thrives on ambition, envy, deception, jealousy, and doubt. Although he commands absolutely no respect, he holds our attention because of his cunning duplicity.

The play is finally, however, Othello's story. As we watch him be seduced by Iago's veiled hints and seeming confidences, we see how his trusting nature is inextricably related to his propensity to suspect Desdemona. Iago plays on the complexity and paradox of Othello's character and manipulates those tensions to keep him off balance and blind to the truth of Desdemona's faithfulness. Ultimately, though, Othello must take responsibility for the destruction of his love, a responsibility that is both his tragedy and redemption.

WILLIAM SHAKESPEARE (1564–1616)
Othello, the Moor of Venice   1604

THE NAMES OF THE ACTORS

Othello, the Moor
Brabantio, [a Venetian senator,] father to Desdemona
Cassio, an honorable lieutenant [to Othello]
Iago, [Othello's ancient,] a villain
Roderigo, a gulled gentleman
Duke of Venice
Senators [of Venice]
Montano, governor of Cyprus
Lodovico and Gratiano, [kinsmen to Brabantio,] two noble Venetians
Sailors
Clowns
Desdemona, wife to Othello
Emilia, wife to Iago
Bianca, a courtesan
[Messenger, Herald, Officers, Venetian Gentlemen, Musicians, Attendants

SCENE: *Venice and Cyprus]*

ACT I

SCENE I: *A street in Venice.*

Enter Roderigo and Iago.

Roderigo: Tush, never tell me! I take it much unkindly
    That thou, Iago, who hast had my purse
    As if the strings were thine, shouldst know of this.°
Iago: 'Sblood,° but you'll not hear me!
    If ever I did dream of such a matter,
    Abhor me.   5
Roderigo: Thou told'st me thou didst hold him in thy hate.
Iago: Despise me if I do not. Three great ones of the city,
    In personal suit to make me his lieutenant,
    Off-capped to him;° and, by the faith of man,   10
    I know my price; I am worth no worse a place.

Act I, Scene I.   3 *this:* i.e., Desdemona's elopement.   4 *'Sblood:* By God's blood.
10 *him:* i.e., Othello.

But he, as loving his own pride and purposes,
Evades them with a bombast circumstance.°
Horribly stuffed with epithets of war;
[And, in conclusion,]   15
Nonsuits° my mediators; for, "Certes," says he,
"I have already chose my officer."
And what was he?
Forsooth, a great arithmetician,°
One Michael Cassio, a Florentine   20
(A fellow almost damned in a fair wife°)
That never set a squadron in the field,
Nor the division of a battle knows
More than a spinster; unless the bookish theoric,
Wherein the togèd consuls can propose   25
As masterly as he. Mere prattle without practice
Is all his soldiership. But he, sir, had th' election;
And I (of whom his eyes had seen the proof
At Rhodes, at Cyprus, and on other grounds
Christian and heathen) must be belee'd and calmed°   30
By debitor and creditor; this counter-caster,°
He, in good time, must his lieutenant be,
And I — God bless the mark! — his Moorship's ancient.°
Roderigo: By heaven, I rather would have been his hangman.
Iago: Why, there's no remedy; 'tis the curse of service.   35
Preferment goes by letter and affection,°
And not by old gradation, where each second
Stood heir to th' first. Now, sir, be judge yourself,
Whether I in any just term am affined°
To love the Moor.
Roderigo: I would not follow him then.   40
Iago: O, sir, content you;
I follow him to serve my turn upon him.
We cannot all be masters, nor all masters
Cannot be truly followed. You shall mark
Many a duteous and knee-crooking knave   45
That, doting on his own obsequious bondage,
Wears out his time, much like his master's ass,
For naught but provender; and when he's old, cashiered.°
Whip me such honest knaves! Others there are
Who, trimmed° in forms and visages of duty,   50

---

13 *a bombast circumstance:* Pompous circumlocutions.   16 *Nonsuits:* Rejects.
19 *arithmetician:* Theoretician.   21 almost . . . wife: (An obscure allusion; Cassio
is unmarried, but see IV.i.114).   30 *belee'd and calmed:* Left in the lurch.   31 *counter-caster:* Bookkeeper.   33 *ancient:* Ensign.   36 *affection:* Favoritism.   39 *affined:*
Obliged.   48 *cashiered:* Turned off.   50 *trimmed:* Dressed up.

Keep yet their hearts attending on themselves;
And, throwing but shows of service on their lords,
Do well thrive by them, and when they have lined their coats,
Do themselves homage. These fellows have some soul;
And such a one do I profess myself. For, sir,   55
It is as sure as you are Roderigo,
Were I the Moor, I would not be Iago.
In following him, I follow but myself;
Heaven is my judge, not I for love and duty,
But seeming so, for my peculiar end;   60
For when my outward action doth demonstrate
The native act and figure of my heart°
In compliment extern,° 'tis not long after
But I will wear my heart upon my sleeve
For daws to peck at; I am not what I am.   65

Roderigo: What a full fortune does the thick-lips° owe°
    If he can carry 't thus!

Iago: Call up her father,
    Rouse him. Make after him, poison his delight,
    Proclaim him in the streets. Incense her kinsmen,
    And though he in a fertile climate dwell,   70
    Plague him with flies; though that his joy be joy,
    Yet throw such changes of vexation on 't
    As it may lose some color.

Roderigo: Here is her father's house. I'll call aloud.

Iago: Do, with like timorous° accent and dire yell   75
    As when, by night and negligence, the fire
    Is spied in populous cities.

Roderigo: What, ho, Brabantio! Signior Brabantio, ho!

Iago: Awake! What, ho, Brabantio! Thieves! thieves! thieves!
    Look to your house, your daughter, and your bags!   80
    Thieves! thieves!

Brabantio at a window.°

Brabantio (above): What is the reason of this terrible summons?
    What is the matter there?

Roderigo: Signior, is all your family within?

Iago: Are your doors locked?

Brabantio: Why, wherefore ask you this?   85

Iago: Zounds, sir, y' are robbed! For shame, put on your gown!
    Your heart is burst; you have lost half your soul.
    Even now, now, very now, an old black ram

---

62 *The . . . heart:* What I really believe and intend.   63 *compliment extern:* Outward appearance.   66 *thick-lips:* An Elizabethan epithet for blacks, including Moors;   *owe:* Own.   75 *timorous:* Terrifying.   *Brabantio at a window:* (added from quarto).

Is tupping your white ewe. Arise, arise!
Awake the snorting° citizens with the bell.   90
Or else the devil will make a grandsire of you.
Arise, I say!
Brabantio: What, have you lost your wits?
Roderigo: Most reverend signior, do you know my voice?
Brabantio: Not I. What are you?   95
Roderigo: My name is Roderigo.
Brabantio: The worser welcome!
I have charged thee not to haunt about my doors.
In honest plainness thou hast heard me say
My daughter is not for thee; and now, in madness,
Being full of supper and distemp'ring draughts,   100
Upon malicious knavery dost thou come
To start my quiet.
Roderigo: Sir, sir, sir —
Brabantio: But thou must needs be sure
My spirit and my place have in them power   105
To make this bitter to thee.
Roderigo: Patience, good sir.
Brabantio: What tell'st thou me of robbing? This is Venice;
My house is not a grange.°
Roderigo: Most grave Brabantio,
In simple and pure soul I come to you.
Iago: Zounds, sir, you are one of those that will not serve God if the   110
devil bid you. Because we come to do you service, and you think
we are ruffians, you'll have your daughter covered with a Barbary
horse; you'll have your nephews° neigh to you; you'll have coursers
for cousins, and gennets for germans.°
Brabantio: What profane wretch art thou?   115
Iago: I am one, sir, that comes to tell you your daughter and the
Moor are now making the beast with two backs.
Brabantio: Thou are a villain.
Iago: You are — a senator.
Brabantio: This thou shalt answer. I know thee, Roderigo.
Roderigo: Sir, I will answer anything. But I beseech you,   120
If 't be your pleasure and most wise consent,
As partly I find it is, that your fair daughter,
At this odd-even° and dull watch o' th' night,
Transported, with no worse nor better guard
But with a knave of common hire, a gondolier,   125

---

90 *snorting:* Snoring.   108 *grange:* Isolated farmhouse.   113 *nephews:* i.e., grandsons.
114 *gennets for germans:* Spanish horses for near kinsmen.   123 *odd-even:* Between
night and morning.

To the gross clasps of a lascivious Moor —
If this be known to you, and your allowance,°
We then have done you bold and saucy wrongs;
But if you know not this, my manners tell me
We have your wrong rebuke. Do not believe   130
That, from the sense° of all civility,
I thus would play and trifle with your reverence.
Your daughter, if you have not given her leave,
I say again, hath made a gross revolt,
Tying her duty, beauty, wit, and fortunes   135
In an extravagant and wheeling° stranger
Of here and everywhere. Straight satisfy yourself.
If she be in her chamber, or your house,
Let loose on me the justice of the state
For thus deluding you.
Brabantio: Strike on the tinder, ho!   140
Give me a taper! Call up all my people!
This accident° is not unlike my dream.
Belief of it oppresses me already.
Light, I say! light!   *Exit [above].*
Iago: Farewell, for I must leave you.
It seems not meet, nor wholesome to my place,   145
To be produced — as, if I stay, I shall —
Against the Moor. For I do know the state,
However this may gall him with some check,°
Cannot with safety cast° him; for he's embarked
With such loud reason to the Cyprus wars,   150
Which even now stand in act,° that for their souls
Another of his fathom° they have none
To lead their business; in which regard,
Though I do hate him as I do hell-pains,
Yet, for necessity of present life,   155
I must show out a flag and sign of love,
Which is indeed but sign. That you shall surely find him,
Lead to the Sagittary° the raisèd search;
And there will I be with him. So farewell.   *Exit.*

Enter [below] Brabantio in his nightgown,° and Servants with torches.

Brabantio: It is too true an evil. Gone she is;   160
And what's to come of my despisèd time
Is naught but bitterness. Now, Roderigo,

---

127 *allowance:* Approval.   131 *from the sense:* In violation.   136 *extravagant and wheeling:* Expatriate and roving.   142 *accident:* Occurrence.   148 *check:* Reprimand. 149 *cast:* Discharge.   151 *stand in act:* Are going on.   152 *fathom:* Capacity. 158 *Sagittary:* An inn.   *nightgown:* Dressing gown.

Where didst thou see her? — O unhappy girl! —
With the Moor, say'st thou? — Who would be a father? —
How didst thou know 'twas she! — O, she deceives me   165
Past thought! — What said she to you? — Get moe° tapers!
Raise all my kindred! — Are they married, think you?
Roderigo: Truly I think they are.
Brabantio: O heaven! How got she out? O treason of the blood!
    Fathers, from hence trust not your daughters' minds   170
    By what you see them act. Is there not charms
    By which the property° of youth and maidhood
    May be abused? Have you not read, Roderigo,
    Of some such thing?
Roderigo: Yes, sir, I have indeed.
Brabantio: Call up my brother. — O, would you had had her! —   175
    Some one way, some another. — Do you know
    Where we may apprehend her and the Moor?
Roderigo: I think I can discover him, if you please
    To get good guard and go along with me.
Brabantio: I pray you lead on. At every house I'll call;   180
    I may command at most. — Get weapons, ho!
    And raise some special officers of night. —
    On, good Roderigo; I'll deserve° your pains.   *Exeunt.*

SCENE II: *Before the lodgings of Othello.*

    Enter Othello, Iago, and Attendants with torches.

Iago: Though in the trade of war I have slain men,
    Yet do I hold it very stuff o' th' conscience
    To do no contrived murther. I lack iniquity
    Sometimes to do me service. Nine or ten times
    I had thought t' have yerked° him here under the ribs.   5
Othello: 'Tis better as it is.
Iago: Nay, but he prated,
    And spoke such scurvy and provoking terms
    Against your honor
    That with the little godliness I have
    I did full hard forbear him. But I pray you, sir,   10
    Are you fast° married? Be assured of this,
    That the magnifico° is much beloved,
    And hath in his effect a voice potential°
    As double° as the Duke's. He will divorce you,

---

166 *moe:* More.   172 *property:* Nature.   183 *deserve:* Show gratitude for.   **Scene II.**
5 *yerked:* Stabbed.   11 *fast:* Securely.   12 *magnifico:* Grandee (Brabantio).
13 *potential:* Powerful.   14 *double:* Doubly influential.

Or put upon you what restraint and grievance   15
The law, with all his might to enforce it on,
Will give him cable.

Othello: Let him do his spite.
My services which I have done the signiory°
Shall out-tongue his complaints. 'Tis yet to know° —
Which, when I know that boasting is an honor,   20
I shall promulgate — I fetch my life and being
From men of royal siege;° and my demerits°
May speak unbonneted to as proud a fortune
As this that I have reached.° For know, Iago,
But that I love the gentle Desdemona,
I would not my unhousèd° free condition   25
Put into circumscription and confine
For the sea's worth. But look what lights come yond?
Iago: Those are the raisèd father and his friends.
You were best go in.
Othello: Not I; I must be found.   30
My parts, my title, and my perfect soul°
Shall manifest me rightly. Is it they?
Iago: By Janus, I think no.

Enter Cassio, with torches, Officers.

Othello: The servants of the Duke, and my lieutenant.
The goodness of the night upon you, friends!   35
What is the news?
Cassio: The Duke does greet you, general;
And he requires your haste-post-haste appearance
Even on the instant.
Othello: What's the matter, think you?
Cassio: Something from Cyprus, as I may divine.
It is a business of some heat. The galleys   40
Have sent a dozen sequent° messengers
This very night at one another's heels,
And many of the consuls, raised and met,
Are at the Duke's already. You have been hotly called for;
When, being not at your lodging to be found,   45
The Senate hath sent about three several quests
To search you out.
Othello: 'Tis well I am found by you.
I will but spend a word here in the house,
And go with you.   *[Exit]*

---

18 *signiory:* Venetian government.   19 *yet to know:* Still not generally known.
22 *siege:* Rank; *demerits:* Deserts.   23–4 *May speak . . . reached:* Are equal, I modestly
assert, to those of Desdemona's family.   26 *unhousèd:* Unrestrained.   31 *perfect soul:*
Stainless conscience.   41 *sequent:* Consecutive.

Cassio: Ancient, what makes he here?
Iago: Faith, he to-night hath boarded a land carack.°   50
    If it prove lawful prize, he's made for ever.
Cassio: I do not understand.

Iago: He's married.
Cassio: To who?

    [Enter Othello.]

Iago: Marry, to — Come, captain, will you go?
Othello: Have with you.
Cassio: Here comes another troop to seek for you.

    Enter Brabantio, Roderigo, and others with lights and weapons.

Iago: It is Brabantio. General, be advised.   55
    He comes to bad intent.
Othello: Holla! stand there!
Roderigo: Signior, it is the Moor.
Brabantio: Down with him, thief!

    [They draw on both sides.]

Iago: You, Roderigo! Come, sir, I am for you.
Othello: Keep up° your bright swords, for the dew will rust them.
    Good signior, you shall more command with years   60
    Than with your weapons.
Brabantio: O thou foul thief, where hast thou stowed my daughter?
    Damned as thou art, thou hast enchanted her!
    For I'll refer me to all things of sense,
    If she in chains of magic were not bound,   65
    Whether a maid so tender, fair, and happy,
    So opposite to marriage that she shunned
    The wealthy curlèd darlings of our nation,
    Would ever have, t' incur a general mock,
    Run from her guardage to the sooty bosom   70
    Of such a thing as thou — to fear, not to delight.
    Judge me the world if 'tis not gross in sense°
    That thou hast practiced on her with foul charms,
    Abused her delicate youth with drugs or minerals
    That weaken motion.° I'll have't disputed on;   75
    'Tis probable, and palpable to thinking.
    I therefore apprehend and do attach° thee
    For an abuser of the world, a practicer
    Of arts inhibited and out of warrant.
    Lay hold upon him. If he do resist,   80
    Subdue him at his peril.

---

50 *carack:* Treasure ship.   59 *Keep up:* i.e., sheath.   72 *gross in sense:* Obvious.
75 *motion:* Perception.   77 *attach:* Arrest.

Othello: Hold your hands,
    Both you of my inclining and the rest.
    Were it my cue to fight, I should have known it
    Without a prompter. Where will you that I go
    To answer this your charge?
Brabantio: To prison, till fit time   85
    Of law and course of direct session°
    Call thee to answer.
Othello: What if I do obey?
    How may the Duke be therewith satisfied,
    Whose messengers are here about my side
    Upon some present business of the state   90
    To bring me to him?
Officer: 'Tis true, most worthy signior.
    The Duke's in council, and your noble self
    I am sure is sent for.
Brabantio: How? The Duke in council?
    In this time of the night? Bring him away.
    Mine's not an idle° cause. The Duke himself,   95
    Or any of my brothers of the state,
    Cannot but feel this wrong as 'twere their own;
    For if such actions may have passage free,
    Bondslaves and pagans shall our statesmen be.   *Exeunt.*

Scene III: *The Venetian Senate Chamber.*

Enter Duke and Senators, set at a table, with lights and Attendants.

Duke: There is no composition° in these news
    That gives them credit.
1. Senator: Indeed they are disproportioned.
    My letters say a hundred and seven galleys.
Duke: And mine a hundred forty.
2. Senator: And mine two hundred.
    But though they jump° not on a just account —   5
    As in these cases where the aim° reports
    'Tis oft with difference — yet do they all confirm
    A Turkish fleet, and bearing up to Cyprus.
Duke: Nay, it is possible enough to judgment.
    I do not so secure me° in the error
    But the main article° I do approve°   10
    In fearful sense.

---

86 *direct session:* Regular trial.   95 *idle:* Trifling.   **Scene III.**   1 *composition:* Consistency.   5 *jump:* Agree.   6 *aim:* Conjecture.   10 *so secure me:* Take such comfort.   11 *article:* Substance; *approve:* Accept.

Sailor (within):   What, ho! what, ho! what, ho!
Officer: A messenger from the galleys.

   Enter Sailor.

Duke: Now, what's the business?
Sailor: The Turkish preparation makes for Rhodes.
   So was I bid report here to the state   15
   By Signior Angelo.
Duke: How say you by this change?
1. Senator: This cannot be
   By no assay° of reason. 'Tis a pageant
   To keep us in false gaze.° When we consider
   Th' importancy of Cyprus to the Turk,   20
   And let ourselves again but understand
   That, as it more concerns the Turk than Rhodes,
   So may he with more facile question bear° it,
   For that it stands not in such warlike brace,°
   But altogether lacks th' abilities   25
   That Rhodes is dressed in — if we make thought of this,
   We must not think the Turk is so unskillful
   To leave that latest which concerns him first,
   Neglecting an attempt of ease and gain
   To wake and wage° a danger profitless.   30
Duke: Nay, in all confidence, he's not for Rhodes.
Officer: Here is more news.

   Enter a Messenger.

Messenger: The Ottomites, reverend and gracious,
   Steering with due course toward the isle of Rhodes,
   Have there injointed them with an after fleet.   35
1. Senator: Ay, so I thought. How many, as you guess?
Messenger: Of thirty sail; and now they do restem°
   Their backward course, bearing with frank appearance
   Their purposes toward Cyprus, Signior Montano,
   Your trusty and most valiant servitor,   40
   With his free duty recommends you thus,
   And prays you to believe him.
Duke: 'Tis certain then for Cyprus.
   Marcus Luccicos,° is not he in town?
1. Senator: He's now in Florence.   45
Duke: Write from us to him; post, post-haste dispatch.
1. Senator: Here comes Brabantio and the valiant Moor.

   Enter Brabantio, Othello, Cassio, Iago, Roderigo, and Officers.

18 *assay:* Test.   19 *in false gaze:* Looking the wrong way.   23 *with . . . bear:* More
easily capture.   24 *brace:* Posture of defense.   30 *wake and wage:* Rouse and
risk.   37 *restem:* Steer again.   44 *Marcus Luccicos:* (Presumably a Venetian envoy).

Duke: Valiant Othello, we must straight employ you
    Against the general enemy Ottoman.   *[To Brabantio.]*
    I did not see you. Welcome, gentle signior.   50
    We lacked your counsel and your help to-night.
Brabantio: So did I yours. Good your grace, pardon me.
    Neither my place, nor aught I heard of business,
    Hath raised me from my bed; nor doth the general care
    Take hold on me; for my particular grief   55
    Is of so floodgate° and o'erbearing nature
    That it engluts° and swallows other sorrows,
    And it is still itself.
Duke: Why, what's the matter?
Brabantio: My daughter! O, my daughter!
All: Dead?
Brabantio: Ay, to me.
    She is abused, stol'n from me, and corrupted   60
    By spells and medicines bought of mountebanks;
    For nature so prepost'rously to err,
    Being not deficient,° blind, or lame of sense,
    Sans witchcraft could not.
Duke: Whoe'er he be that in this foul proceeding   65
    Hath thus beguiled your daughter of herself,
    And you of her, the bloody book of law
    You shall yourself read in the bitter letter
    After your own sense; yea, though our proper° son
    Stood in your action.°
Brabantio: Humbly I thank your grace.   70
    Here is the man — this Moor, whom now, it seems,
    Your special mandate for the state affairs
    Hath hither brought.
All: We are very sorry for't.
Duke [to Othello]: What, in your own part, can you say to this?
Brabantio: Nothing, but this is so.   75
Othello: Most potent, grave, and reverend signiors,
    My very noble, and approved° good masters,
    That I have ta'en away this old man's daughter,
    It is most true; true I have married her.
    The very head and front of my offending   80
    Hath this extent, no more. Rude° am I in my speech,
    And little blessed with the soft phrase of peace;
    For since these arms of mine had seven years' pith°
    Till now some nine moons wasted, they have used

---

56 *floodgate:* Torrential.   57 *engluts:* Devours.   63 *deficient:* Feeble-minded.
69 *our proper:* My own.   70 *Stood in your action:* Were accused by you.   77 *approved:*
Tested by experience.   81 *Rude:* Unpolished.   83 *pith:* Strength.

Their dearest action in the tented field;   85
And little of this great world can I speak
More than pertains to feats of broil and battle;
And therefore little shall I grace my cause
In speaking for myself. Yet, by your gracious patience,
I will a round° unvarnished tale deliver   90
Of my whole course of love — what drugs, what charms,
What conjuration, and what mighty magic
(For such proceeding am I charged withal)
I won his daughter.
Brabantio: A maiden never bold;
Of spirit so still and quiet that her motion   95
Blushed° at herself; and she — in spite of nature,
Of years, of country, credit, everything —
To fall in love with what she feared to look on!
It is a judgment maimed and most imperfect
That will confess perfection so could err   100
Against all rules of nature, and must be driven
To find out practices° of cunning hell
Why this should be. I therefore vouch° again
That with some mixtures pow'rful o'er the blood,°
Or with some dram, conjured to this effect,   105
He wrought upon her.
Duke: To vouch this is no proof.
Without more certain and more overt test
Than these thin habits° and poor likelihoods
Of modern seeming° do prefer against him.
1. Senator: But, Othello, speak.   110
Did you by indirect and forcèd° courses
Subdue and poison this young maid's affections?
Or came it by request, and such fair question°
As soul to soul affordeth?
Othello: I do beseech you,
Send for the lady to the Sagittary   115
And let her speak of me before her father.
If you do find me foul in her report,
The trust, the office, I do hold of you
Not only take away, but let your sentence
Even fall upon my life.
Duke: Fetch Desdemona hither.   120
Othello: Ancient, conduct them; you best know the place.

Exit [Iago, with] two or three [Attendants].

---

90 *round:* Plain.   95–6 *her motion Blushed:* Her own emotions caused her to
blush.   102 *practices:* Plots.   103 *vouch:* Assert.   104 *blood:* Passions.   108 *thin
habits:* Slight appearances.   109 *modern seeming:* Everyday supposition.   111 *forcèd:*
Violent.   113 *question:* Conversation.

And till she come, as truly as to heaven
I do confess the vices of my blood,
So justly to your grave ears I'll present
How I did thrive in this fair lady's love,   125
And she in mine.
Duke: Say it, Othello.
Othello: Her father loved me, oft invited me;
Still° questioned me the story of my life
From year to year — the battles, sieges, fortunes   130
That I have passed.
I ran it through, even from my boyish days
To th' very moment that he bade me tell it.
Wherein I spoke of most disastrous chances,
Of moving accidents by flood and field;   135
Of hairbreadth scapes i' th' imminent deadly breach;
Of being taken by the insolent foe
And sold to slavery; of my redemption thence
And portance° in my travels' history;
Wherein of anters° vast and deserts idle,   140
Rough quarries, rocks, and hills whose heads touch heaven,
It was my hint° to speak — such was the process;
And of the Cannibals that each other eat,
The Anthropophagi,° and men whose heads
Do grow beneath their shoulders. This to hear   145
Would Desdemona seriously incline;
But still the house affairs would draw her thence;
Which ever as she could with haste dispatch,
She'ld come again, and with a greedy ear
Devour up my discourse. Which I observing,   150
Took once a pliant° hour, and found good means
To draw from her a prayer of earnest heart
That I would all my pilgrimage dilate,°
Whereof by parcels° she had something heard,
But not intentively.° I did consent,   155
And often did beguile her of her tears
When I did speak of some distressful stroke
That my youth suffered. My story being done,
She gave me for my pains a world of sighs.
She swore, i' faith, 'twas strange, 'twas passing strange;   160
'Twas pitiful, 'twas wondrous pitiful.
She wished she had not heard it; yet she wished
That heaven had made her such a man. She thanked me;
And bade me, if I had a friend that loved her,
I should but teach him how to tell my story,   165

---

144 *Anthropophagi:* Man-eaters.   151 *pliant:* Propitious.   153 *dilate:* Recount in
full.   154 *parcels:* Portions.   155 *intentively:* With full attention.

And that would woo her. Upon this hint° I spake.
She loved me for the dangers I had passed,
And I loved her that she did pity them.
This only is the witchcraft I have used.
Here comes the lady. Let her witness it.   170

Enter Desdemona, Iago, Attendants.

Duke: I think this tale would win my daughter too.
    Good Brabantio,
    Take up this mangled matter at the best.
    Men do their broken weapons rather use
    Than their bare hands.
Brabantio: I pray you hear her speak.   175
    If she confess that she was half the wooer,
    Destruction on my head if my bad blame
    Light on the man! Come hither, gentle mistress.
    Do you perceive in all this noble company
    Where most you owe obedience?
Desdemona: My noble father,   180
    I do perceive here a divided duty.
    To you I am bound for life and education;°
    My life and education both do learn me
    How to respect you: you are the lord of duty;
    I am hitherto your daughter. But here's my husband;   185
    And so much duty as my mother showed
    To you, preferring you before her father,
    So much I challenge° that I may profess
    Due to the Moor my lord.
Brabantio: God be with you! I have done.
    Please it your grace, on to the state affairs.   190
    I had rather to adopt a child than get° it.
    Come hither, Moor.
    I here do give thee that with all my heart
    Which, but thou hast already, with all my heart
    I would keep from thee. For your sake,° jewel,   195
    I am glad at soul I have no other child;
    For thy escape° would teach me tyranny,
    To hang clogs on them. I have done, my lord.
Duke: Let me speak like yourself° and lay a sentence°
    Which, as a grise° or step, may help these lovers   200
    [Into your favor.]

---

166 *hint:* Opportunity.   182 *education:* Upbringing.   129 *Still:* Continually.
139 *portance:* Behavior.   140 *anters:* Caves.   142 *hint:* Occasion.   188 *challenge:*
Claim the right.   191 *get:* Beget.   195 *For your sake:* Because of you.   197 *escape:*
Escapade.   199 *like yourself:* As you should; *sentence:* Maxim.   200 *grise:* Step.

When remedies are past, the griefs are ended
By seeing the worst, which late on hopes depended.
To mourn a mischief that is past and gone
Is the next way to draw new mischief on.   205
What cannot be preserved when fortune takes,
Patience her injury a mock'ry makes.
The robbed that smiles steals something from the thief;
He robs himself that spends a bootless grief.
Brabantio: So let the Turk of Cyprus us beguile: 210
We lose it not so long as we can smile.
He bears the sentence well that nothing bears
But the free comfort which from thence he hears;
But he bears both the sentence and the sorrow
That to pay grief must of poor patience borrow.   215
These sentences, to sugar, or to gall,
Being strong on both sides, are equivocal.
But words are words. I never yet did hear
That the bruisèd heart was piercèd through the ear.
Beseech you, now to the affairs of state.   220
Duke: The Turk with a most mighty preparation makes for Cyprus.
    Othello, the fortitude° of the place is best known to you; and though
    we have there a substitute of most allowed° sufficiency, yet opinion,°
    a more sovereign mistress of effects, throws a more safer voice on
    you. You must therefore be content to slubber° the gloss of your   225
    new fortunes with this more stubborn and boist'rous expedition.
Othello: The tyrant custom, most grave senators,
    Hath made the flinty and steel couch of war
    My thrice-driven bed of down. I do agnize
    A natural and prompt alacrity   230
    I find in hardness;° and do undertake
    These present wars against the Ottomites.
    Most humbly, therefore, bending to your state,
    I crave fit disposition for my wife,
    Due reference of place, and exhibition,°   235
    With such accommodation and besort°
    As levels° with her breeding.
Duke: If you please,
    Be't at her father's.
Brabantio: I will not have it so.
Othello: Nor I.

---

222 *fortitude:* Fortification. 223 *allowed:* Acknowledged; *opinion:* Public opinion.
225 *slubber:* Sully. 229–31 *agnize . . . hardness:* Recognize in myself a natural and
easy response to hardship. 235 *exhibition:* Allowance of money. 236 *besort:* Suitable company. 237 *levels:* Corresponds.

Desdemona: Nor I. I would not there reside,
　　To put my father in impatient thoughts 240
　　By being in his eye. Most gracious Duke,
　　To my unfolding lend your prosperous° ear,
　　And let me find a charter in your voice,
　　T' assist my simpleness.°
Duke: What would you, Desdemona? 245
Desdemona: That I did love the Moor to live with him,
　　My downright violence, and storm of fortunes,
　　May trumpet to the world. My heart's subdued
　　Even to the very quality of my lord.
　　I saw Othello's visage in his mind, 250
　　And to his honors and his valiant parts
　　Did I my soul and fortunes consecrate.
　　So that, dear lords, if I be left behind,
　　A moth of peace, and he go to the war,
　　The rites for which I love him are bereft me, 255
　　And I a heavy interim shall support
　　By his dear absence. Let me go with him.
Othello: Let her have your voice.
　　Vouch with me, heaven, I therefore beg it not
　　To please the palate of my appetite,
　　Not to comply with heat° — the young affects° 260
　　In me defunct — and proper satisfaction;
　　But to be free and bounteous to her mind;
　　And heaven defend your good souls that you think
　　I will your serious and great business scant 265
　　When she is with me. No, when light-winged toys
　　Of feathered Cupid seel° with wanton dullness
　　My speculative and officed instruments,°
　　That° my disports corrupt and taint my business,
　　Let housewives make a skillet of my helm, 270
　　And all indign° and base adversities
　　Make head against my estimation!°
Duke: Be it as you shall privately determine,
　　Either for her stay or going. Th' affair cries haste,
　　And speed must answer it. 275
1. Senator: You must away to-night.
Othello: 　　　　　　　　　　With all my heart.

---

242 *prosperous:* Favorable.　244 *simpleness:* Lack of skill.　261 *heat:* Passions;
young affects: Tendencies of youth.　267 *seel:* Blind.　268 *My . . . instruments:*
My perceptive and responsible faculties.　269 *That:* So that.　271 *indign:*
Unworthy.　272 *estimation:* Reputation.

Duke: At nine i' th' morning here we'll meet again.
    Othello, leave some officer behind,
    And he shall our commission bring to you,
    With such things else of quality and respect   280
    As doth import° you.
Othello: So please your grace, my ancient;
    A man he is of honesty and trust
    To his conveyance I assign my wife,
    With what else needful your good grace shall think
    To be sent after me.
Duke: Let it be so.   285
    Good night to every one.
        [To Brabantio.]   And, noble signior,
    If virtue no delighted° beauty lack,
    Your son-in-law is far more fair than black.
1. Senator: Adieu, brave Moor. Use Desdemona well.
Brabantio: Look to her, Moor, if thou hast eyes to see: 290
    She has deceived her father, and may thee.

                    Exeunt [Duke, Senators, Officers, &c.].

Othello: My life upon her faith! — Honest Iago,
    My Desdemona must I leave to thee.
    I prithee let thy wife attend on her,
    And bring them after in the best advantage.°   295
    Come, Desdemona. I have but an hour
    Of love, of worldly matters and direction,
    To spend with thee. We must obey the time.

                    Exit Moor and Desdemona.

Roderigo: Iago, —
Iago: What say'st thou, noble heart?   300
Roderigo: What will I do, think'st thou?
Iago: Why, go to bed and sleep.
Roderigo: I will incontinently° drown myself.
Iago: If thou dost, I shall never love thee after. Why, thou silly
    gentleman!   305
Roderigo: It is silliness to live when to live is torment; and then have we a
    prescription to die when death is our physician.
Iago: O villainous! I have looked upon the world for four times seven
    years; and since I could distinguish betwixt a benefit and an injury,
    I never found man that knew how to love himself. Ere I would say 310
    I would drown myself for the love of a guinea hen, I would
    change my humanity with a baboon.

---

281 *import:* Concern.   287 *delighted:* Delightful.   295 *in the best advantage:* At the
best opportunity.   303 *incontinently:* Forthwith.

Roderigo: What should I do? I confess it is my shame to be so fond, but
    it is not in my virtue to amend it.

Iago: Virtue? a fig! 'Tis in ourselves that we are thus or thus. Our   315
    bodies are our gardens, to which our wills are gardeners; so that
    if we will plant nettles or sow lettuce, set hyssop and weed up thyme,
    supply it with one gender° of herbs or distract it with many — either
    to have it sterile with idleness or manured with industry — why, the
    power and corrigible authority° of this lies in our wills. If the balance   320
    of our lives had not one scale of reason to poise° another of sensuality,
    the blood and baseness° of our natures would conduct us to most
    preposterous conclusions. But we have reason to cool our raging
    motions,° our carnal strings, our unbitted° lusts; whereof I take
    this that you call love to be a sect or scion.°   325

Roderigo: It cannot be.

Iago: It is merely a lust of the blood and a permission of the will. Come,
    be a man! Drown thyself? Drown cats and blind puppies! I have
    professed me thy friend, and I confess me knit to thy deserving
    with cables of perdurable toughness. I could never better stead   330
    thee than now. Put money in thy purse. Follow thou the wars;
    defeat thy favor° with an usurped beard. I say, put money in thy
    purse. It cannot be that Desdemona should long continue her
    love to the Moor — put money in thy purse — nor he his to her. It
    was a violent commencement in her, and thou shalt see an   335
    answerable sequestration° — put but money in thy purse. These
    Moors are changeable in their wills — fill thy purse with money.
    The food that to him now is as luscious as locusts shall be to him
    shortly as bitter as coloquintida.° She must change for youth:
    when she is sated with his body, she will find the error of her   340
    choice. [She must have change, she must.] Therefore put money in
    thy purse. If thou wilt needs damn thyself, do it a more delicate
    way than drowning. Make° all the money thou canst. If sancti-
    mony and a frail vow betwixt an erring° barbarian and a super-
    subtle Venetian be not too hard for my wits and all the tribe of   345
    hell, thou shalt enjoy her. Therefore make money. A pox of
    drowning thyself! 'Tis clean out of the way. Seek thou rather to
    be hanged in compassing thy joy than to be drowned and go
    without her.

---

318 *gender:* Species.   320 *corrigible authority:* Corrective power.   321 *poise:* Coun-
terbalance;   322 *blood and baseness:* Animal instincts.   324 *motions:* Appetites.
unbitted: Uncontrolled.   325 *sect or scion:* Offshoot, cutting.   332 *defeat thy*
favor: Spoil thy appearance.   336 *sequestration:* Estrangement.   339 *coloquintida:* A
medicine.   343 *Make:* Raise.   344 *erring:* Wandering.

Roderigo: Wilt thou be fast to my hopes, if I depend on the issue? 350
Iago: Thou art sure of me. Go, make money. I have told thee often, and
I retell thee again and again, I hate the Moor. My cause is hearted;°
thine hath no less reason. Let us be conjunctive in our revenge against
him. If thou canst cuckold him, thou dost thyself a pleasure, me a
sport. There are many events in the womb of time, which will be 355
delivered. Traverse,° go, provide thy money! We will have more of
this to-morrow. Adieu.
Roderigo: Where shall we meet i' th' morning?
Iago: At my lodging.
Roderigo: I'll be with thee betimes. 360
Iago: Go to, farewell — Do you hear, Roderigo?
Roderigo: What say you?
Iago: No more of drowning, do you hear?
[*Roderigo:* I am changed.
Iago: Go to, farewell. Put money enough in your purse.] 365
Roderigo: I'll sell all my land. *Exit.*
Iago: Thus do I ever make my fool my purse;
 For I mine own gained knowledge should profane
 If I would time expend with such a snipe°
 But for my sport and profit. I hate the Moor; 370
 And it is thought abroad that 'twixt my sheets
 H'as done my office. I know not if't be true;
 But I, for mere suspicion in that kind,
 Will do as if for surety. He holds me well;°
 The better shall my purpose work on him. 375
 Cassio's a proper man. Let me see now:
 To get his place, and to plume up° my will
 In double knavery — How, how? — Let's see: —
 After some time, to abuse Othello's ears
 That he is too familiar with his wife. 380
 He hath a person and a smooth dispose°
 To be suspected — framed to make women false.
 The Moor is of a free° and open nature
 That thinks men honest that but seem to be so;
 And will as tenderly be led by th' nose 385
 As asses are.
 I have't! It is engend'red! Hell and night
 Must bring this monstrous birth to the world's light. *Exit.*

352 *My cause is hearted:* My heart is in it. 356 *Traverse:* Forward march.
369 *snipe:* Fool. 374 *well:* In high regard. 377 *plume up:* Gratify. 381 *dispose:*
Manner. 383 *free:* Frank.

ACT II

SCENE I: *An open place in Cyprus, near the harbor.*

Enter Montano and two Gentlemen.

Montano: What from the cape can you discern at sea?
1. Gentleman: Nothing at all: it is a high-wrought flood.
  I cannot 'twixt the heaven and the main
  Descry a sail.
Montano: Methinks the wind hath spoke aloud at land;   5
  A fuller blast ne'er shook our battlements.
  If it hath ruffianed so upon the sea,
  What ribs of oak, when mountains melt on them,
  Can hold the mortise?° What shall we hear of this?

2. Gentleman: A segregation° of the Turkish fleet.   10
  For do but stand upon the foaming shore,
  The chidden billow seems to pelt the clouds;
  The wind-shaked surge, with high and monstrous mane,
  Seems to cast water on the burning Bear
  And quench the Guards° of th' ever-fixèd pole.°   15
  I never did like molestation° view
  On the enchafèd flood.
Montano: If that the Turkish fleet
  Be not ensheltered and embayed, they are drowned;
  It is impossible to bear it out.

Enter a third Gentleman.

3. Gentleman: News, lads! Our wars are done.   20
  The desperate tempest hath so banged the Turks
  That their designment halts.° A noble ship of Venice
  Hath seen a grievous wrack and sufferance°
  On most part of their fleet.
Montano: How? Is this true?
3. Gentleman: The ship is here put in,   25
  A Veronesa;° Michael Cassio,
  Lieutenant to the warlike Moor Othello,
  Is come on shore; the Moor himself at sea,
  And is in full commission here for Cyprus.
Montano: I am glad on't. 'Tis a worthy governor.   30
3. Gentleman: But this same Cassio, though he speak of comfort
  Touching the Turkish loss, yet he looks sadly

Act II, Scene I. 9 *hold the mortise:* Hold their joints together. 10 *segregation:* Scattering. 15 *Guards:* Stars near the North Star; *pole:* Polestar. 16 *molestation:* Tumult. 22 *designment halts:* Plan is crippled. 23 *sufferance:* Disaster. 26 *Veronesa:* Ship furnished by Verona.

And prays the Moor be safe, for they were parted
With foul and violent tempest.
Montano: Pray heaven he be,
For I have served him, and the man commands   35
Like a full soldier. Let's to the seaside, ho!
As well to see the vessel that's come in
As to throw out our eyes for brave Othello,
Even till we make the main and th' aerial blue
An indistinct regard.°
3. Gentleman: Come, let's do so;   40
For every minute is expectancy
Of more arrivance.

    Enter Cassio.

Cassio: Thanks, you the valiant of this warlike isle,
That so approve the Moor! O, let the heavens
Give him defense against the elements,   45
For I have lost him on a dangerous sea!
Montano: Is he well shipped?
Cassio: His bark is stoutly timbered, and his pilot
Of very expert and approved allowance;
Therefore my hopes, not surfeited to death,°   50
Stand in bold cure.°
        (Within.)   A sail, a sail, a sail!   *Enter a messenger.*
Cassio: What noise?
Messenger: The town is empty; on the brow o' th' sea
Stand ranks of people, and they cry "A sail!"
Cassio: My hopes do shape him for the governor.   55

    A shot.

2. Gentleman: They do discharge their shot of courtesy:
Our friends at least.
Cassio: I pray you sir, go forth
And give us truth who 'tis that is arrived.
2. Gentleman: I shall.   *Exit.*
Montano: But, good lieutenant, is your general wived?   60
Cassio: Most fortunately. He hath achieved a maid
That paragons° description and wild fame;
One that excels the quirks° of blazoning° pens,
And in th' essential vesture of creation
Does tire the ingener.°

---

39 *An indistinct regard:* Indistinguishable. 50 *surfeited to death:* Overindulged.
51 *in bold cure:* A good chance of fulfillment. 62 *paragons:* Surpasses.
63 *quirks:* Ingenuities; *blazoning:* Describing. 64–5 *And . . . ingener:* Merely to
describe her as God made her exhausts her praiser.

Enter Second Gentleman.

65

How now? Who has put in?

2. Gentleman: 'Tis one Iago, ancient to the general.

Cassio: H'as had most favorable and happy speed:
 Tempests themselves, high seas, and howling winds,
 The guttered° rocks and congregated sands,
 Traitors ensteeped° to clog the guiltless keel,   70
 As having sense of beauty, do omit
 Their mortal° natures, letting go safely by
 The divine Desdemona.

Montano: What is she?

Cassio: She that I spake of, our great captain's captain,
 Left in the conduct of the bold Iago,   75
 Whose footing° here anticipates our thoughts
 A se'nnight's° speed. Great Jove, Othello guard,
 And swell his sail with thine own pow'rful breath,
 That he may bless this bay with his tall ship,
 Make love's quick pants in Desdemona's arms,   80
 Give renewed fire to our extinct spirits,
 [And bring all Cyprus comfort!]

Enter Desdemona, Iago, Roderigo, and Emilia [with Attendants].

O, behold!
 The riches of the ship is come on shore!
 You men of Cyprus, let her have your knees.°
 Hail to thee, lady! and the grace of heaven,   85
 Before, behind thee, and on every hand,
 Enwheel thee round!

Desdemona: I thank you, valiant Cassio.
 What tidings can you tell me of my lord?

Cassio: He is not yet arrived; nor know I aught
 But that he's well and will be shortly here.   90

Desdemona: O but I fear! How lost you company?

Cassio: The great contention of the sea and skies
 Parted our fellowship.

  (Within.) A sail, a sail! *[A shot.]*

          But hark. A sail!

2. Gentleman: They give their greeting to the citadel;
 This likewise is a friend.

Cassio: See for the news.   95

          [Exit Gentleman.]

Good ancient, you are welcome.
 [To Emilia.]   Welcome, mistress. —

---

69 *guttered:* Jagged. 70 *ensteeped:* Submerged. 72 *mortal:* Deadly. 76 *footing:* Landing. 77 *se'nnight's:* Week's. 84 *knees:* i.e., kneeling.

Let it not gall your patience, good Iago,
That I extend my manners. 'Tis my breeding
That gives me this bold show of courtesy.

[Kisses Emilia.°]

Iago: Sir, would she give you so much of her lips   100
As of her tongue she oft bestows on me,
You would have enough.
Desdemona: Alas, she has no speech!
Iago: In faith, too much.
I find it still when I have list to sleep.
Marry, before your ladyship, I grant,   105
She puts her tongue a little in her heart
And chides with thinking.
Emilia: You have little cause to say so.
Iago: Come on, come on! You are pictures out of doors,
Bells in your parlors, wildcats in your kitchens,   110
Saints in your injuries, devils being offended,
Players in your housewifery,° and housewives° in your beds.
Desdemona: O, fie upon thee, slanderer!
Iago: Nay, it is true, or else I am a Turk:
You rise to play, and go to bed to work.   115
Emilia: You shall not write my praise.
Iago: No, let me not.
Desdemona: What wouldst thou write of me, if thou shouldst
    praise me?
Iago: O gentle lady, do not put me to't,
For I am nothing if not critical.
Desdemona: Come on, assay.° — There's one gone to the harbor?   120
Iago: Ay, madam.
Desdemona: I am not merry; but I do beguile
The thing I am by seeming otherwise. —
Come, how wouldst thou praise me?
Iago: I am about it; but indeed my invention   125
Comes from my pate as birdlime° does from frieze° —
It plucks out brains and all. But my Muse labors,
And thus she is delivered:
If she be fair and wise, fairness and wit —
The one's for use, the other useth it.   130
Desdemona: Well praised! How if she be black° and witty?
Iago: If she be black, and thereto have a wit,

Kisses Emilia: (Kissing was a common Elizabethan form of social courtesy).   112 *house-wifery:* Housekeeping; *housewives:* Hussies.   120 *assay:* Try.   126 *birdlime:* A sticky paste; *frieze:* Rough cloth.   131 *black:* Brunette.

She'll find a white that shall her blackness fit.

Desdemona: Worse and worse!

Emilia: How if fair and foolish? 135

Iago: She never yet was foolish that was fair,
     For even her folly° helped her to an heir.

Desdemona: These are old fond° paradoxes to make fools laugh i' th'
     alehouse. What miserable praise hast thou for her that's foul° and
     foolish? 140

Iago: There's none so foul, and foolish thereunto,
     But does foul pranks which fair and wise ones do.

Desdemona: O heavy ignorance! Thou praisest the worst best. But what
     praise couldst thou bestow on a deserving woman indeed — one that
     in the authority of her merit did justly put on the vouch° of very 145
     malice itself?

Iago: She that was ever fair, and never proud;
     Had tongue at will, and yet was never loud;
     Never lacked gold, and yet went never gay;
     Fled from her wish, and yet said "Now I may"; 150
     She that, being ang'red, her revenge being nigh,
     Bade her wrong stay, and her displeasure fly;
     She that in wisdom never was so frail
     To change the cod's head for the salmon's tail;°
     She that could think, and ne'er disclose her mind; 155
     See suitors following, and not look behind:
     She was a wight (if ever such wight were) —

Desdemona: To do what?

Iago: To suckle fools and chronicle small beer.°

Desdemona: O most lame and impotent conclusion! Do not learn of him, 160
     Emilia, though he be thy husband. How say you, Cassio? Is he not
     a most profane and liberal° counsellor?

Cassio: He speaks home,° madam. You may relish him more in the soldier
     than in the scholar.

Iago [aside]: He takes her by the palm. Ay, well said, whisper! With as 165
little a web as this will I ensnare as great a fly as Cassio. Ay, smile
upon her, do! I will gyve thee in thine own courtship.° — You say true;
'tis so, indeed! — If such tricks as these strip you out of your lieu-
tenantry, it had been better you had not kissed your three fingers so
oft — which now again you are most apt to play the sir° in. Very good! 170
well kissed! an excellent courtesy! 'Tis so, indeed. Yet again

---

137 *folly:* Wantonness.   138 *fond:* Foolish.   139 *foul:* Ugly.   145 *put on the vouch:* Compel the approval.   154 *To . . . tail:* i.e., to exchange the good for the poor but expensive.   159 *chronicle small beer:* Keep petty household accounts.   162 *profane and liberal:* Worldly and licentious.   163 *home:* Bluntly.   167 *gyve . . . courtship:* Manacle you by means of your courtly manners.   170 *sir:* Courtly gentleman.

your fingers to your lips? Would they were clyster pipes° for your sake!
(Trumpet within.)
The Moor! I know his trumpet.
Cassio: 'Tis truly so.   175
Desdemona: Let's meet him and receive him.
Cassio: Lo, where he comes.

Enter Othello and Attendants.

Othello: O my fair warrior!
Desdemona: My dear Othello!
Othello: It gives me wonder great as my content
   To see you here before me. O my soul's joy!   180
   If after every tempest come such calms,
   May the winds blow till they have wakened death!
   And let the laboring bark climb hills of seas
   Olympus-high, and duck again as low
   As hell's from heaven! If it were now to die,   185
   'Twere now to be most happy;° for I fear
   My soul hath her content so absolute
   That not another comfort like to this
   Succeeds in unknown fate.
Desdemona: The heavens forbid
   But that our loves and comforts should increase   190
   Even as our days do grow.
Othello: Amen to that, sweet powers!
   I cannot speak enough of this content;
   It stops me here; it is too much of joy.
   And this, and this, the greatest discords be

   They kiss.

   That e'er our hearts shall make!
Iago [aside]:   O, you are well tuned now!   195
   But I'll set down° the pegs that make this music,
   As honest as I am.
Othello: Come, let us to the castle.
   News, friends! Our wars are done; the Turks are drowned.
   How does my old acquaintance of this isle? —
   Honey, you shall be well desired° in Cyprus;   200
   I have found great love amongst them. O my sweet,
   I prattle out of fashion, and I dote
   In mine own comforts. I prithee, good Iago,
   Go to the bay and disembark my coffers.
   Bring thou the master° to the citadel;   205

---

172 *clyster pipes:* Syringes. 186 *happy:* Fortunate. 196 *set down:* Loosen.
200 *well desired:* Warmly welcomed. 205 *master:* Ship captain.

He is a good one, and his worthiness
Does challenge° much respect. — Come, Desdemona,
Once more well met at Cyprus.

               Exit Othello [with all but Iago and Roderigo].

Iago [to an Attendant, who goes out]: Do thou meet me presently at the
harbor. *[To Roderigo.]* Come hither. If thou be'st valiant (as they 210
say base men being in love have then a nobility in their natures
more than is native to them), list me. The lieutenant to-night
watches on the court of guard.° First, I must tell thee this: Desdemona
is directly in love with him.

Roderigo: With him? Why, 'tis not possible. 215

Iago: Lay thy finger thus,° and let thy soul be instructed. Mark me
with what violence she first loved the Moor, but for bragging and
telling her fantastical lies; and will she love him still for prating?
Let not thy discreet heart think it. Her eye must be fed; and what
delight shall she have to look on the devil? When the blood is made 220
dull with the act of sport, there should be, again to inflame
it and to give satiety a fresh appetite, loveliness in favor, sympathy
in years, manners, and beauties; all which the Moor is defective
in. Now for want of these required conveniences,° her delicate
tenderness will find itself abused, begin to heave the gorge,° 225
disrelish and abhor the Moor. Very nature will instruct her in it and
compel her to some second choice. Now, sir, this granted — as it is
a most pregnant° and unforced position — who stands so eminent
in the degree of this fortune as Cassio does? A knave very voluble;
no further conscionable° than in putting on the mere form of civil 230
and humane° seeming for the better compassing of his salt° and most
hidden loose affection? Why, none! why, none! A slipper° and subtle
knave; a finder-out of occasions; that has an eye can stamp and
advantages, though true advantage never counterfeit present
itself; a devilish knave! Besides, the knave is handsome, young, and 235
hath all those requisites in him that folly and green minds look after. A
pestilent complete knave! and the woman hath found him already.

Roderigo: I cannot believe that in her; she's full of most blessed
condition.°

Iago: Blessed fig's-end! The wine she drinks is made of grapes. If she had 240
been blessed, she would never have loved the Moor. Blessed
pudding! Didst thou not see her paddle with the palm of his
hand? Didst not mark that?

Roderigo: Yes, that I did; but that was but courtesy.

---

207 *challenge:* Deserve.   213 *court of guard:* Headquarters.   216 *thus:* i.e., on your
lips.   224 *conveniences:* Compatibilities.   225 *heave the gorge:* Be nauseated.
228 *pregnant:* Evident.   230 *conscionable:* Conscientious.   231 *humane:* Polite.
salt: Lecherous.   232 *slipper:* Slippery. 239 *condition:* Character.

Iago: Lechery, by this hand! an index and obscure prologue to the   245
history of lust and foul thoughts. They met so near with their lips
that their breaths embraced together. Villainous thoughts, Roderigo!
When these mutualities° so marshal the way, hard at hand comes
the master and main exercise, th' incorporate° conclusion. Pish!
But, sir, be you ruled by me: I have brought you from Venice. Watch   250
you to-night; for the command, I'll lay't upon you. Cassio knows you
not. I'll not be far from you: do you find some occasion to anger
Cassio, either by speaking too loud, or tainting° his discipline,
or from what other course you please which the time shall more
favorably minister.   255

Roderigo: Well.

Iago: Sir, he's rash and very sudden in choler,° and haply with his trun-
cheon may strike at you. Provoke him that he may; for even out of
that will I cause these of Cyprus to mutiny; whose qualification°
shall come into no true taste° again but by the displanting of Cassio.   260
So shall you have a shorter journey to your desires by the means
I shall then have to prefer° them; and the impediment most profit-
ably removed without the which there were no expectation of our
prosperity.

Roderigo: I will do this if you can bring it to any opportunity.   265

Iago: I warrant thee. Meet me by and by at the citadel; I must fetch his
necessaries ashore. Farewell.

Roderigo: Adieu.   *Exit.*

Iago: That Cassio loves her, I do well believe't;
That she loves him, 'tis apt° and of great credit.   270
The Moor, howbeit that I endure him not,
Is of a constant, loving, noble nature,
And I dare think he'll prove to Desdemona
A most dear husband. Now I do love her too;
Not out of absolute lust, though peradventure   275
I stand accountant° for as great a sin,
But partly led to diet° my revenge,
For that I do suspect the lusty Moor
Hath leaped into my seat; the thought whereof
Doth, like a poisonous mineral, gnaw my inwards;   280
And nothing can or shall content my soul
Till I am evened with him, wife for wife;
Or failing so, yet that I put the Moor
At least into a jealousy so strong
That judgment cannot cure. Which thing to do,   285

---

248 *mutualities:* Exchanges.   249 *incorporate:* Carnal.   253 *tainting:* Discrediting.
257 *sudden in choler:* Violent in anger.   259 *qualification:* Appeasement.   260 *true
taste:* Satisfactory state.   262 *prefer:* Advance.   270 *apt:* Probable.   276 *accountant:*
Accountable.   277 *diet:* Feed.

If this poor trash of Venice, whom I trash°
For° his quick hunting, stand the putting on,°
I'll have our Michael Cassio on the hip,°
Abuse him to the Moor in the rank garb°
(For I fear Cassio with my nightcap too),   290
Make the Moor thank me, love me, and reward me
For making him egregiously an ass
And practicing upon° his peace and quiet
Even to madness. 'Tis here, but yet confused:
Knavery's plain face is never seen till used.   *Exit.* 295

SCENE II: *A street in Cyprus.*

Enter Othello's Herald, with a proclamation.

Herald: It is Othello's pleasure, our noble and valiant general, that,
upon certain tidings now arrived, importing the mere perdition°
of the Turkish fleet, every man put himself into triumph; some to
dance, some to make bonfires, each man to what sport and revels
his addiction leads him. For, besides these beneficial news, it is the   5
celebration of his nuptial. So much was his pleasure should be proclaimed. All offices° are open, and there is full liberty of feasting
from the present hour of five till the bell have told eleven. Heaven
bless the isle of Cyprus and our noble general Othello!   *Exit.*

SCENE III: *The Cyprian Castle.*

Enter Othello, Desdemona, Cassio, and Attendants.

Othello: Good Michael, look you to the guard to-night.
Let's teach ourselves that honorable stop,
Not to outsport discretion.
Cassio: Iago hath direction what to do;
But not withstanding, with my personal eye   5
Will I look to't.
Othello: Iago is most honest.
Michael, good night. To-morrow with your earliest
Let me have speech with you.
        [*To Desdemona.*]   Come, my dear love.
The purchase made, the fruits are to ensue;
That profit 's yet to come 'tween me and you. —   10
Good night.

            Exit [Othello with Desdemona and Attendants].

---

286 *I trash:* I weight down (in order to keep under control).   287 *For:* In order to
develop; *stand the putting on:* Responds to my inciting.   288 *on the hip:* At my mercy.
289 *rank garb:* Gross manner.   293 *practicing upon:* Plotting against.   **Scene II.**
2 *mere perdition:* Complete destruction.   7 *offices:* Kitchens and storerooms.

Enter Iago.

Cassio: Welcome, Iago. We must to the watch.

Iago: Not this hour, lieutenant; 'tis not yet ten o' th' clock. Our general cast° us thus early for the love of his Desdemona; who let us not therefore blame. He hath not yet made wanton the night with her, and she is   15 sport for Jove.

Cassio: She's a most exquisite lady.

Iago: And, I'll warrant her, full of game.

Cassio: Indeed, she's a most fresh and delicate creature.

Iago: What an eye she has! Methinks it sounds a parley to provocation.   20

Cassio: An inviting eye; and yet methinks right modest.

Iago: And when she speaks, is it not an alarum to love?

Cassio: She is indeed perfection.

Iago: Well, happiness to their sheets! Come, lieutenant, I have a stoup° of wine, and here without are a brace of Cyprus gallants that would   25 fain have a measure to the health of black Othello.

Cassio: Not to-night, good Iago. I have very poor and unhappy brains for drinking; I could well wish courtesy would invent some other custom of entertainment.

Iago: O, they are our friends. But one cup! I'll drink for you.   30

Cassio: I have drunk but one cup to-night, and that was craftily quali-fied° too; and behold what innovation° it makes here. I am unfor-tunate in the infirmity and dare not task my weakness with any more.

Iago: What, man! 'Tis a night of revels: the gallants desire it.   35

Cassio: Where are they?

Iago: Here at the door; I pray you call them in.

Cassio: I'll do't, but it dislikes me.   *Exit.*

Iago: If I can fasten but one cup upon him
　　With that which he hath drunk to-night already,
　　He'll be as full of quarrel and offense   40
　　As my young mistress' dog. Now my sick fool Roderigo,
　　Whom love hath turned almost the wrong side out,
　　To Desdemona hath to-night caroused
　　Potations pottle-deep;° and he's to watch.   45
　　Three lads of Cyprus — noble swelling spirits,
　　That hold their honors in a wary distance,°
　　The very elements° of this warlike isle —
　　Have I to-night flustered with flowing cups,
　　And they watch too. Now, 'mongst this flock of drunkards   50
　　Am I to put our Cassio in some action
　　That may offend the isle.

Scene III.   13 *cast:* Dismissed.   24 *stoup:* Two-quart tankard.   32 *qualified:* Diluted; *innovation:* Disturbance.   45 *pottle-deep:* Bottoms up.   47 *That . . . distance:* Very sensitive about their honor.   48 *very elements:* True representatives.

Enter Cassio, Montano, and Gentlemen [; Servants following with wine].

But here they come.
If consequence do but approve my dream,
My boat sails freely, both with wind and stream.
Cassio: 'Fore God, they have given me a rouse° already.   55
Montano: Good faith, a little one; not past a pint, as I am a soldier.
Iago: Some wine, ho!
[*Sings.*]   And let me the canakin clink, clink;
                    And let me the canakin clink
                        A soldier's a man;   60
                        A life's but a span,
                    Why then, let a soldier drink.
        Some wine, boys!
Cassio: 'Fore God, an excellent song!
Iago: I learned it in England, where indeed they are most potent in   65
        potting. Your Dane, your German, and your swag-bellied
        Hollander — Drink, ho! — are nothing to your English.
Cassio: Is your Englishman so expert in his drinking?
Iago: Why, he drinks you with facility your Dane dead drunk; he sweats
        not to overthrow your Almain; he gives your Hollander a vomit ere   70
        the next pottle can be filled.
Cassio: To the health of our general!
Montano: I am for it, lieutenant, and I'll do you justice.
Iago: O sweet England!
[*Sings.*]   King Stephen was a worthy peer;   75
                        His breeches cost him but a crown;
                    He held 'em sixpence all too dear,
                        With that he called the tailor lown.°
                    He was a wight of high renown,
                        And thou art but of low degree.   80
                    'Tis pride that pulls the country down;
                        Then take thine auld cloak about thee.
        Some wine, ho!
Cassio: 'Fore God, this is a more exquisite song than the other.
Iago: Will you hear't again?   85
Cassio: No, for I hold him to be unworthy of his place that does those
        things.° Well, God's above all; and there be souls must be saved,
        and there be souls must not be saved.
Iago: It's true, good lieutenant.
Cassio: For mine own part — no offense to the general, nor any man of   90
        quality — I hope to be saved.
Iago: And so do I too, lieutenant.

55 *rouse:* Bumper.   78 *lown:* Rascal.   87 *does those things:* i.e., behaves in this fashion.   106 *just equinox:* Exact equivalent.

Cassio: Ay, but, by your leave, not before me. The lieutenant is to be
saved before the ancient. Let's have no more of this; let's to our
affairs. — God forgive us our sins! — Gentlemen, let's look to our   95
business. Do not think, gentlemen, I am drunk. This is my ancient;
this is my right hand, and this is my left. I am not drunk now. I can
stand well enough, and I speak well enough.

All: Excellent well!

Cassio: Why, very well then. You must not think then that I am drunk.   *Exit.*   100

Montano: To th' platform, masters. Come, let's set the watch.

Iago: You see this fellow that is gone before.
He's a soldier fit to stand by Caesar
And give direction; and do but see his vice.   105
'Tis to his virtue a just equinox,°
The one as long as th' other. 'Tis pity of him.
I fear the trust Othello puts him in,
On some odd time of his infirmity,
Will shake this island.

Montano: But is he often thus?   110

Iago: 'Tis evermore his prologue to his sleep:
He'll watch the horologe a double set°
If drink rock not his cradle.

Montano: It were well
The general were put in mind of it.
Perhaps he sees it not, or his good nature
Prizes the virtue that appears in Cassio   115
And looks not on his evils. Is not this true?

Enter Roderigo.

Iago [aside to him]: How now, Roderigo?
I pray you after the lieutenant, go!

                                        Exit Roderigo.

Montano: And 'tis great pity that the noble Moor   120
Should hazard such a place as his own second
With one of an ingraft° infirmity.
It were an honest action to say
So to the Moor.

Iago: Not I, for this fair island!
I do love Cassio well and would do much   125
To cure him of this evil.
          (Within.) Help! help!
                    But hark! What noise?

Enter Cassio, driving in Roderigo.

---

112 *watch . . . set:* Stay awake twice around the clock.   122 *ingraft:* i.e., ingrained.

Cassio: Zounds, you rogue! you rascal!
Montano: What's the matter, lieutenant?
Cassio: A knave to teach me my duty?
    I'll beat the knave into a twiggen° bottle.   130
Roderigo: Beat me?
Cassio: Dost thou prate, rogue? *[Strikes him.]*
Montano: Nay, good lieutenant!

                                                [Stays him.]

    I pray you, sir, hold your hand.
Cassio: Let me go, sir,
    Or I'll knock you o'er the mazzard.°
Montano: Come, come, you're drunk!
Cassio: Drunk?

    They fight.

Iago [aside to Roderigo]: Away, I say! Go out and cry a mutiny!   135

                                          Exit Roderigo.

    Nay, good lieutenant. God's will, gentlemen!
    Help, ho! — lieutenant — sir — Montano — sir —
    Help, masters! — Here's a goodly watch indeed!

    A bell rung.

    Who's that which rings the bell? Diablo, ho!
    The town will rise.° God's will, lieutenant, hold!   140
    You'll be shamed for ever.

    Enter Othello and Gentlemen with weapons.

Othello: What is the matter here?
Montano: Zounds, I bleed still. I am hurt to th' death.
    He dies!
Othello: Hold for your lives!
Iago: Hold, hold! Lieutenant — sir — Montano — gentlemen!   145
    Have you forgot all sense of place and duty?
    Hold! The general speaks to you. Hold, for shame!
Othello: Why, how now ho? From whence ariseth this?
    Are we turned Turks, and to ourselves do that
    Which heaven hath forbid the Ottomites?   150
    For Christian shame put by this barbarous brawl!
    He that stirs next to carve for° his own rage
    Holds his soul light; he dies upon his motion.
    Silence that dreadful bell! It frights the isle
    From her propriety.° What is the matter, masters?   155
    Honest Iago, that looks dead with grieving,

---

130 *twiggen:* Wicker-covered. 133 *mazzard:* Head. 140 *rise:* Grow riotous.
152 *carve for:* Indulge. 155 *propriety:* Proper self.

Speak. Who began this? On thy love, I charge thee.
Iago: I do not know. Friends all, but now, even now,
    In quarter,° and in terms like bride and groom
    Devesting them for bed; and then, but now —   160
    As if some planet had unwitted men —
    Swords out, and tilting one at other's breast
    In opposition bloody. I cannot speak
    Any beginning to this peevish odds,°
    And would in action glorious I had lost   165
    Those legs that brought me to a part of it!
Othello: How comes it, Michael, you are thus forgot?
Cassio: I pray you pardon me; I cannot speak.
Othello: Worthy Montano, you were wont to be civil;
    The gravity and stillness of your youth   170
    The world hath noted, and your name is great
    In mouths of wisest censure.° What's the matter
    That you unlace° your reputation thus
    And spend your rich opinion° for the name
    Of a night-brawler? Give me answer to it.   175
Montano: Worthy Othello, I am hurt to danger.
    Your officer, Iago, can inform you,
    While I spare speech, which something now offends° me,
    Of all that I do know; nor know I aught
    By me that's said or done amiss this night,   180
    Unless self-charity be sometimes a vice,
    And to defend ourselves it be a sin
    When violence assails us.
Othello: Now, by heaven,
    My blood° begins my safer guides to rule,
    And passion, having my best judgment collied,°   185
    Assays° to lead the way. If I once stir
    Or do but lift this arm, the best of you
    Shall sink in my rebuke. Give me to know
    How this foul rout began, who set it on;
    And he that is approved in° this offense,   190
    Though he had twinned with me, both at a birth,
    Shall lose me. What! in a town of war,
    Yet wild, the people's hearts brimful of fear,
    To manage° private and domestic quarrel?
    In night, and on the court and guard of safety?   195
    'Tis monstrous. Iago, who began't?

---

159 *quarter:* Friendliness.   164 *peevish odds:* Childish quarrel.   172 *censure:* Judgment.   173 *unlace:* Undo.   174 *rich opinion:* High reputation.   178 *offends:* Pains.   184 *blood:* Passion.   185 *collied:* Darkened.   186 *Assays:* Tries.   190 *approved in:* Proved guilty of.   194 *manage:* Carry on.

Montano: If partially affined, or leagued in office,°
    Thou dost deliver more or less than truth,
    Thou art no soldier.
Iago: Touch me not so near.
    I had rather have this tongue cut from my mouth   200
    Than it should do offense to Michael Cassio;
    Yet I persuade myself, to speak the truth
    Shall nothing wrong him. This it is, general.
    Montano and myself being in speech,
    There comes a fellow crying out for help,   205
    And Cassio following him with determined sword
    To execute° upon him. Sir, this gentleman
    Steps in to Cassio and entreats his pause.
    Myself the crying fellow did pursue,
    Lest by his clamor — as it so fell out —   210
    The town might fall in fright. He, swift of foot,
    Outran my purpose; and I returned then rather
    For that I heard the clink and fall of swords,
    And Cassio high in oath;° which till to-night
    I ne'er might say before. When I came back —   215
    For this was brief — I found them close together
    At blow and thrust, even as again they were
    When you yourself did part them.
    More of this matter cannot I report;
    But men are men; the best sometimes forget.   220
    Though Cassio did some little wrong to him,
    As men in rage strike those that wish them best,
    Yet surely Cassio I believe received
    From him that fled some strange indignity,
    Which patience could not pass.°
Othello: I know, Iago,   225
    Thy honesty and love doth mince this matter,
    Making it light to Cassio. Cassio, I love thee;
    But never more be officer of mine.

Enter Desdemona, attended.

    Look if my gentle love be not raised up!
    I'll make thee an example.
Desdemona: What's the matter?   230
Othello: All's well now, sweeting; come away to bed.
    [To Montano.]
    Sir, for your hurts, myself will be your surgeon.
    Lead him off.

---

197 *partially . . . office:* Prejudiced by comradeship or official relations.   207 *execute:* Work his will.   214 *high in oath:* Cursing.   225 *pass:* Pass over, ignore.

[Montano is led off.]

> Iago, look with care about the town
> And silence those whom this vile brawl distracted.°   235
> Come, Desdemona; 'tis the soldiers' life
> To have their balmy slumbers waked with strife.

Exit [with all but Iago and Cassio].

Iago: What, are you hurt, lieutenant?

Cassio: Ay, past all surgery.

Iago: Marry, God forbid!   240

Cassio: Reputation, reputation, reputation! O, I have lost my reputation! I have lost the immortal part of myself, and what remains is bestial. My reputation, Iago, my reputation!

Iago: As I am an honest man, I thought you had received some bodily wound. There is more sense in that than in reputation.   245
Reputation is an idle and most false imposition; oft got without merit and lost without deserving. You have lost no reputation at all unless you repute yourself such a loser. What, man! there are ways to recover° the general again. You are but now cast in his mood°—
a punishment more in policy than in malice, even so as one would   250
beat his offenseless dog to affright an imperious lion. Sue to him again, and he's yours.

Cassio: I will rather sue to be despised than to deceive so good a commander with so slight, so drunken, and so indiscreet an officer. Drunk! and speak parrot!° and squabble! swagger! swear!   255
and discourse fustian° with one's own shadow! O thou invisible spirit of wine, if thou hast no name to be known by, let us call thee devil!

Iago: What was he that you followed with your sword? What had he done to you?   260

Cassio: I know not.

Iago: Is't possible?

Cassio: I remember a mass of things, but nothing distinctly; a quarrel, but nothing wherefore. O God, that men should put an enemy in their mouths to steal away their brains! that we should with   265
joy, pleasance, revel, and applause° transform ourselves into beasts!

Iago: Why, but you are now well enough. How came you thus recovered?

Cassio: It hath pleased the devil drunkenness to give place to the devil   270
wrath. One unperfectness shows me another, to make me frankly despise myself.

---

235 *distracted:* Excited.   249 *recover:* Regain favor with. *in his mood:* Dismissed because of his anger.   255 *parrot:* Meaningless phrases.   256 *fustian:* Bombastic nonsense.   266 *applause:* Desire to please.

Iago: Come, you are too severe a moraler. As the time, the place, and
    the condition of this country stands, I could heartily wish this
    had not so befall'n; but since it is as it is, mend it for your own 275
    good.

Cassio: I will ask him for my place again: he shall tell me I am a drunk-
    ard! Had I as many mouths as Hydra,° such an answer would stop
    them all. To be now a sensible man, by and by a fool, and presently a
    beast! O strange! Every inordinate cup is unblest, and the ingredient° 280
    is a devil.

Iago: Come, come, good wine is a good familiar creature if it be well
    used. Exclaim no more against it. And, good lieutenant, I think
    you think I love you.

Cassio: I have well approved° it, sir. I drunk! 285

Iago: You or any man living may be drunk at some time, man. I'll tell you
    what you shall do. Our general's wife is now the general. I may
    say so in this respect, for that he hath devoted and given up him-
    self to the contemplation, mark, and denotement of her parts and
    graces. Confess yourself freely to her; importune her help to put 290
    you in your place again. She is of so free,° so kind, so apt, so blessed a
    disposition she holds it a vice in her goodness not to do more than
    she is requested. This broken joint between you and her husband
    entreat her to splinter;° and my fortunes against any lay° worth
    naming, this crack of your love shall grow stronger than it was 295
    before.

Cassio: You advise me well.

Iago: I protest, in the sincerity of love and honest kindness.

Cassio: I think it freely; and betimes in the morning will I beseech the
    virtuous Desdemona to undertake for me. I am desperate of my 300
    fortunes if they check me here.

Iago: You are in the right. Good night, lieutenant; I must to the watch.

Cassio: Good night, honest Iago.   *Exit Cassio.*

Iago: And what's he then that says I play the villain,
    When this advice is free I give and honest, 305
    Probal° to thinking, and indeed the course
    To win the Moor again? For 'tis most easy
    Th' inclining Desdemona to subdue°
    In an honest suit; she's framed as fruitful
    As the free elements. And then for her 310
    To win the Moor — were't to renounce his baptism,
    All seals and symbols of redeemèd sin —
    His soul is so enfettered to her love
    That she may make, unmake, do what she list,
    Even as her appetite shall play the god 315

---

278 *Hydra:* Monster with many heads. 280 *ingredient:* Contents. 285 *approved:*
Proved. 291 *free:* Bounteous. 294 *splinter:* Bind up with splints; *lay:* Wager.
306 *Probal:* Probable. 308 *subdue:* Persuade.

With his weak function. How am I then a villain
To counsel Cassio to this parallel° course,
Directly to his good? Divinity° of hell!
When devils will the blackest sins put on,°
They do suggest at first with heavenly shows,   320
As I do now. For whiles this honest fool
Plies Desdemona to repair his fortunes,
And she for him pleads strongly to the Moor,
I'll pour this pestilence into his ear,
That she repeals him° for her body's lust;   325
And by how much she strives to do him good,
She shall undo her credit with the Moor.
So will I turn her virtue into pitch,
And out of her own goodness make the net
That shall enmesh them all.

Enter Roderigo.

How, now, Roderigo?   330

Roderigo: I do follow here in the chase, not like a hound that hunts, but one that fills up the cry.° My money is almost spent; I have been to-night exceedingly well cudgelled; and I think the issue will be — I shall have so much experience for my pains; and so, with no money at all, and a little more wit, return again to Venice.   335

Iago: How poor are they that have not patience!
What wound did ever heal but by degrees?
Thou know'st we work by wit, and not by witchcraft;
And wit depends on dilatory time.
Does't not go well? Cassio hath beaten thee,
And thou by that small hurt hast cashiered Cassio.°   340
Though other things grow fair against the sun,
Yet fruits that blossom first will first be ripe.
Content thyself awhile. By the mass, 'tis morning!
Pleasure and action make the hours seem short.
Retire thee; go where thou art billeted.   345
Away, I say! Thou shalt know more hereafter.
Nay, get thee gone!   *Exit Roderigo.*
            Two things are to be done:
My wife must move for Cassio to her mistress;
I'll set her on;
Myself the while to draw the Moor apart   350
And bring him jump° when he may Cassio find
Soliciting his wife. Ay, that's the way!
Dull no device by coldness and delay.   *Exit.*

---

317 *parallel:* Corresponding.   318 *Divinity:* Theology.   319 *put on:* Incite.
325 *repeals him:* Seeks his recall.   332 *cry:* Pack.   341 *cashiered Cassio:* Maneu-
vered Cassio's discharge.   352 *jump:* At the exact moment.

ACT III

SCENE I: *Before the chamber of Othello and Desdemona.*

Enter Cassio, with Musicians and the Clown.

Cassio: Masters, play here, I will content° your pains:
   Something that's brief; and bid "Good morrow, general."

   [They play.]

Clown: Why, masters, ha' your instruments been in Naples,° that they speak
   i' th' nose thus?

Musician: How, sir, how?   5

Clown: Are these, I pray you, called wind instruments?

Musician: Ay, marry, are they, sir.

Clown: O, thereby hangs a tail.

Musician: Whereby hangs a tale, sir?

Clown: Marry, sir, by many a wind instrument that I know. But, masters,   10
   here's money for you; and the general so likes your music that
   he desires you, for love's sake, to make no more noise with it.

Musician: Well, sir, we will not.

Clown: If you have any music that may not be heard, to't again: but, as
   they say, to hear music the general does not greatly care.   15

Musician: We have none such, sir.

Clown: Then put up your pipes in your bag, for I'll away. Go, vanish
   into air, away!   *Exit Musician [with his fellows].*

Cassio: Dost thou hear, my honest friend?

Clown: No, I hear not your honest friend. I hear you.   20

Cassio: Prithee keep up thy quillets.° There's a poor piece of gold for
   thee. If the gentlewoman that attends the general's wife be stirring,
   tell her there's one Cassio entreats her a little favor of speech. Wilt
   thou do this?

Clown: She is stirring sir. If she will stir hither, I shall seem to notify   25
   unto her.

Cassio: [Do, good my friend.]   *Exit Clown.*

   Enter Iago.

                              In happy time,° Iago.

Iago: You have not been abed then?

Cassio: Why, no; the day had broke
   Before we parted. I have made bold, Iago,   30
   To send in to your wife: my suit to her
   Is that she will to virtuous Desdemona

Act III, Scene I.   1 *content:* Reward.   3 *Naples:* (Notorious for its association with
venereal disease).   21 *quillets:* Quips.   27 *In happy time:* Well met.

Procure me some access.

Iago: I'll send her to you presently;
And I'll devise a mean to draw the Moor
Out of the way, that your converse and business
May be more free.   35

Cassio: I humbly thank you for't.   *Exit [Iago].*
                          I never knew
A Florentine° more kind and honest.

Enter Emilia.

Emilia: Good morrow, good lieutenant. I am sorry
For your displeasure: but all will sure be well.
The general and his wife are talking of it,   40
And she speaks for you stoutly. The Moor replies
That he you hurt is of great fame in Cyprus
And great affinity,° and that in wholesome wisdom
He might not but refuse you; but he protests he loves you,   45
And needs no other suitor but his likings
[To take the safest occasion° by the front°]
To bring you in again.

Cassio: Yet I beseech you,
If you think fit, or that it may be done,
Give me advantage of some brief discourse   50
With Desdemona alone.

Emilia: Pray you come in.
I will bestow you where you shall have time
To speak your bosom° freely.

Cassio: I am much bound to you.   *Exeunt.*

SCENE II: *The castle.*

Enter Othello, Iago, and Gentlemen.

Othello: These letters give, Iago, to the pilot
And by him do my duties to the Senate.
That done, I will be walking on the works;°
Repair there to me.

Iago: Well, my good lord, I'll do't.

Othello: This fortification, gentlemen, shall we see't?
Gentlemen: We'll wait upon your lordship.   5
                                                        Exeunt.

---

38 *Florentine:* i.e., even a Florentine (like Cassio; Iago was a Venetian).   44 *affinity:*
Family connections.   47 *occasion:* Opportunity; *front:* Forelock.   53 *your
bosom:* Your inmost thoughts.   **Scene II.**   3 *works:* Fortifications.

SCENE III: *The castle grounds.*

> *Enter Desdemona, Cassio, and Emilia.*

Desdemona: Be thou assured, good Cassio, I will do
    All my abilities in thy behalf.
Emilia: Good madam, do. I warrant it grieves my husband
    As if the cause were his.
Desdemona: O, that's an honest fellow. Do not doubt, Cassio,   5
    But I will have my lord and you again
    As friendly as you were.
Cassio: Bounteous madam,
    Whatever shall become of Michael Cassio,
    He's never anything but your true servant.
Desdemona: I know't; I thank you. You do love my lord;   10
    You have known him long; and be you well assured
    He shall in strangeness° stand no farther off
    Than in a politic distance.°
Cassio: Ay, but, lady,
    That policy may either last so long,
    Or feed upon such nice and waterish diet,°   15
    Or breed itself so out of circumstance,
    That, I being absent, and my place supplied,
    My general will forget my love and service.
Desdemona: Do not doubt° that; before Emilia here
    I give thee warrant of thy place. Assure thee,   20
    If I do vow a friendship, I'll perform it
    To the last article. My lord shall never rest;
    I'll watch him tame° and talk him out of patience;
    His bed shall seem a school, his board a shrift;°
    I'll intermingle everything he does   25
    With Cassio's suit. Therefore be merry, Cassio,
    For thy solicitor shall rather die
    Than give thy cause away.

> *Enter Othello and Iago [at a distance].*

Emilia: Madam, here comes my lord.
Cassio: Madam, I'll take my leave.   30
Desdemona: Why, stay, and hear me speak.
Cassio: Madam, not now: I am very ill at ease,
    Unfit for mine own purposes.
Desdemona: Well, do your discretion.   *Exit Cassio.*

Scene III. 12 *strangeness:* Aloofness. 13 *Than . . . distance:* Than wise policy requires. 15 *Or . . . diet:* Or be continued for such slight reasons. 19 *doubt:* Fear. 23 *watch him tame:* Keep him awake until he gives in. 24 *shrift:* Confessional.

Iago: Ha! I like not that.
Othello: What dost thou say?   35
Iago: Nothing, my lord; or if — I know not what.
Othello: Was not that Cassio parted from my wife?
Iago: Cassio, my lord? No, sure, I cannot think it,
    That he would steal away so guilty-like,
    Seeing your coming.
Othello: I do believe 'twas he.   40
Desdemona: How now, my lord?
    I have been talking with a suitor here,
    A man that languishes in your displeasure.
Othello: Who is't you mean?
Desdemona: Why, your lieutenant, Cassio. Good my lord,   45
    If I have any grace or power to move you,
    His present° reconciliation take;
    For if he be not one that truly loves you,
    That errs in ignorance, and not in cunning,
    I have no judgment in an honest face,   50
    I prithee call him back.
Othello: Went he hence now?
Desdemona: Yes, faith; so humbled
    That he hath left part of his grief with me
    To suffer with him. Good love, call him back.
Othello: Not now, sweet Desdemon; some other time.   55
Desdemona: But shall't be shortly?
Othello: The sooner, sweet, for you.
Desdemona: Shall't be to-night at supper?
Othello: No, not to-night.
Desdemona: To-morrow dinner then?
Othello: I shall not dine at home;
    I meet the captains at the citadel.
Desdemona: Why then, to-morrow night, or Tuesday morn,   60
    On Tuesday noon or night, on Wednesday morn.
    I prithee name the time, but let it not
    Exceed three days. I' faith, he's penitent;
    And yet his trespass, in our common reason
    (Save that, they say, the wars must make example   65
    Out of her best), is not almost° a fault
    T' incur a private check.° When shall he come?
    Tell me, Othello. I wonder in my soul
    What you would ask me that I should deny
    Or stand so mamm'ring on.° What? Michael Cassio,   70

---

47 *present:* Immediate.   66 *not almost:* Hardly.   67 *a private check:* Even a private
reprimand.   70 *mamm'ring on:* Hesitating about.

That came a-wooing with you, and so many a time,
When I have spoke of you dispraisingly,
Hath ta'en your part — to have so much to do
To bring him in? By'r Lady, I could do much —

Othello: Prithee no more. Let him come when he will!   75
I will deny thee nothing.

Desdemona: Why, this is not a boon;
'Tis as I should entreat you wear your gloves,
Or feed on nourishing dishes, or keep you warm,
Or sue to you to do a peculiar profit
To your own person. Nay, when I have a suit   80
Wherein I mean to touch your love indeed,
It shall be full of poise and difficult weight,
And fearful° to be granted.

Othello: I will deny thee nothing!
Whereon I do beseech thee grant me this,
To leave me but a little to myself.   85

Desdemona: Shall I deny you? No. Farewell, my lord.

Othello: Farewell, my Desdemon: I'll come to thee straight.

Desdemona: Emilia, come. — Be as your fancies teach you;
Whate'er you be, I am obedient.   *Exit [with Emilia].*

Othello: Excellent wretch!° Perdition catch my soul   90
But I do love thee! and when I love thee not,
Chaos is come again.

Iago: My noble lord —

Othello: What dost thou say, Iago?

Iago: Did Michael Cassio, when you wooed my lady,
Know of your love?   95

Othello: He did, from first to last. Why dost thou ask?

Iago: But for a satisfaction of my thought;
No further harm.

Othello: Why of thy thought, Iago?

Iago: I did not think he had been acquainted with her.

Othello: O, yes, and went between us° very oft.   100

Iago: Indeed?

Othello: Indeed? Ay, indeed! Discern'st thou aught in that?
Is he not honest?

Iago: Honest, my lord?

Othello: Honest. Ay, honest.

Iago: My lord, for aught I know.

Othello: What dost thou think?

Iago: Think, my lord?

Othello: Think, my lord?   105

---

83 *fearful:* Dangerous.   90 *wretch:* (A term of endearment).   100 *went between us:* (i.e., as messenger).

By heaven, thou echo'st me,
As if there were some monster in thy thought
Too hideous to be shown. Thou dost mean something:
I heard thee say even now, thou lik'st not that,
When Cassio left my wife. What didst not like?   110
And when I told thee he was of my counsel
In my whole course of wooing, thou cried'st "Indeed?"
And didst contract and purse thy brow together,
As if thou then hadst shut up in thy brain
Some horrible conceit.° If thou dost love me,   115
Show me thy thought

Iago: My lord, you know I love you.

Othello: I think thou dost;
And, for I know thou'rt full of love and honesty
And weigh'st thy words before thou giv'st them breath,
Therefore these stops of thine fright me the more;   120
For such things in a false disloyal knave
Are tricks of custom; but in a man that's just
They're close dilations, working from the heart
That passion cannot rule.°

Iago: For Michael Cassio,
I dare be sworn I think that he is honest.   125

Othello: I think so too.

Iago: Men should be what they seem;
Or those that be not, would they might seem none!°

Othello: Certain, men should be what they seem.

Iago: Why then, I think Cassio's an honest man.

Othello: Nay, yet there's more in this.   130
I prithee speak to me as to thy thinkings,
As thou dost ruminate, and give thy worst of thoughts
The worst of words.

Iago: Good my lord, pardon me:
Though I am bound to every act of duty,
I am not bound to that all slaves are free to.°   135
Utter my thoughts? Why, say they are vile and false,
As where's that palace whereinto foul things
Sometimes intrude not? Who has a breast so pure
But some uncleanly apprehensions
Keep leets and law days,° and in Sessions sit   140
With meditations lawful?

---

115 *conceit:* Fancy.   123–24 *close dilations . . . rule:* Secret emotions which well up
in spite of restraint.   127 *seem none:* i.e., not pretend to be men when they are really
monsters.   135 *bound . . . free to:* Bound to tell that which even slaves are allowed to
keep to themselves.   140 *leets and law days:* Sittings of the courts.

Othello: Thou dost conspire against thy friend, Iago,
    If thou but think'st him wronged, and mak'st his ear
    A stranger to thy thoughts.
Iago: I do beseech you —
    Though I perchance am vicious in my guess   145
    (As I confess it is my nature's plague
    To spy into abuses, and oft my jealousy°
    Shapes faults that are not), that your wisdom yet
    From one that so imperfectly conjects°
    Would take no notice, nor build yourself a trouble   150
    Out of his scattering and unsure observance.
    It were not for your quiet nor your good,
    Nor for my manhood, honesty, and wisdom,
    To let you know my thoughts.
Othello: What dost thou mean?
Iago: Good name in man and woman, dear my lord,   155
    Is the immediate° jewel of their souls.
    Who steals my purse steals trash; 'tis something, nothing;
    'Twas mine, 'tis his, and has been slave to thousands;
    But he that filches from me my good name
    Robs me of that which not enriches him   160
    And makes me poor indeed.
Othello: By heaven, I'll know thy thoughts!
Iago: You cannot, if my heart were in your hand;
    Nor shall not whilst 'tis in my custody.
Othello: Ha!
Iago: O, beware, my lord, of jealousy!   165
    It is the green-eyed monster, which doth mock°
    The meat it feeds on. That cuckold lives in bliss
    Who, certain of his fate, loves not his wronger;
    But O, what damnèd minutes tells he o'er
    Who dotes, yet doubts — suspects, yet strongly loves!   170
Othello: O misery!
Iago: Poor and content is rich, and rich enough;
    But riches fineless° is as poor as winter
    To him that ever fears he shall be poor.
    Good God, the souls of all my tribe defend   175
    From jealousy!
Othello: Why, why is this?
    Think'st thou I'ld make a life of jealousy,
    To follow still the changes of the moon
    With fresh suspicions? No! To be once in doubt
    Is once to be resolved. Exchange me for a goat   180

---

147 *jealousy:* Suspicion.   149 *conjects:* Conjectures.   156 *immediate:* Nearest the heart.   166 *mock:* Play with, like a cat with a mouse.   173 *fineless:* Unlimited.

When I shall turn the business of my soul
To such exsufflicate and blown° surmises,
Matching this inference. 'Tis not to make me jealous
To say my wife is fair, feeds well, loves company,
Is free of speech, sings, plays, and dances well.   185
Where virtue is, these are more virtuous.
Nor from mine own weak merits will I draw
The smallest fear or doubt of her revolt,°
For she had eyes, and chose me. No, Iago;
I'll see before I doubt; when I doubt, prove;   190
And on the proof there is no more but this—
Away at once with love or jealousy!

Iago: I am glad of this; for now I shall have reason
To show the love and duty that I bear you
With franker spirit. Therefore, as I am bound,   195
Receive it from me. I speak not yet of proof.
Look to your wife; observe her well with Cassio;
Wear your eyes thus, not jealous nor secure:°
I would not have your free and noble nature,
Out of self-bounty,° be abused. Look to't.   200
I know our country disposition well:
In Venice they do let God see the pranks
They dare not show their husbands; their best conscience
Is not to leave't undone, but keep't unknown.

Othello: Dost thou say so?   205

Iago: She did deceive her father, marrying you;
And when she seemed to shake and fear your looks,
She loved them most.

Othello: And so she did.

Iago: Why, go to then!
She that, so young, could give out such a seeming
To seel° her father's eyes up close as oak°—   210
He thought 'twas witchcraft—but I am much to blame.
I humbly do beseech you of your pardon
For too much loving you.

Othello: I am bound to thee for ever.

Iago: I see this hath a little dashed your spirits.

Othello: Not a jot, not a jot.

Iago: I' faith, I fear it has.   215
I hope you will consider what is spoke
Comes from my love. But I do see y' are moved.

---

182 *exsufflicate and blown:* Spat out and flyblown.   188 *revolt:* Unfaithfulness.
198 *secure:* Overconfident.   200 *self-bounty:* Natural goodness.   210 *seel:* Close;
oak: Oak grain.

I am to pray you not to strain my speech
To grosser issues° nor to larger reach
Than to suspicion.   220
Othello: I will not.
Iago: Should you do so, my lord,
My speech should fall into such vile success°
As my thoughts aim not at. Cassio's my worthy friend —
My lord, I see y' are moved.
Othello: No, not much moved:
I do not think but Desdemona's honest.°   225
Iago: Long live she so! and long live you to think so!
Othello: And yet, how nature erring from itself —
Iago: Ay, there's the point! as (to be bold with you)
Not to affect many proposèd matches
Of her own clime, complexion, and degree,   230
Whereto we see in all things nature tends —
Foh! one may smell in such a will most rank,
Foul disproportions, thoughts unnatural —
But pardon me — I do not in position°
Distinctly speak of her; though I may fear   235
Her will, recoiling° to her better judgment,
May fall to match° you with her country forms,
And happily° repent.
Othello: Farewell, farewell!
If more thou dost perceive, let me know more.
Set on thy wife to observe. Leave me, Iago.   240
Iago: My lord, I take my leave.   *[Going.]*
Othello: Why did I marry? This honest creature doubtless
Sees and knows more, much more, than he unfolds.
Iago [returns]: My lord, I would I might entreat your honor
To scan this thing no further: leave it to time.   245
Although 'tis fit that Cassio have his place,
For sure he fills it up with great ability,
Yet, if you please to hold him off a while,
You shall by that perceive him and his means.
Note if your lady strain his entertainment°   250
With any strong or vehement importunity;
Much will be seen in that. In the mean time
Let me be thought too busy° in my fears
(As worthy cause I have to fear I am)

---

219 *To grosser issues:* To mean something more monstrous. 222 *vile success:* Evil outcome. 225 *honest:* Chaste. 234 *position:* Definite assertion. 236 *recoiling:* Reverting. 237 *fall to match:* Happen to compare. 238 *happily:* Haply, perhaps. 250 *strain his entertainment:* Urge his recall. 253 *busy:* Meddlesome.

And hold her free,° I do beseech your honor.   255
Othello: Fear not my government.°
Iago: I once more take my leave.   *Exit.*
Othello: This fellow's of exceeding honesty,
     And knows all qualities,° with a learned spirit
     Of° human dealings. If I do prove her haggard,°   260
     Though that her jesses° were my dear heartstrings,
     I'd whistle her off and let her down the wind
     To prey at fortune.° Haply, for I am black
     And have not those soft parts of conversation°
     That chamberers° have, or for I am declined   265
     Into the vale of years — yet that's not much —
     She's gone. I am abused, and my relief
     Must be to loathe her. O curse of marriage,
     That we can call these delicate creatures ours,
     And not their appetites! I had rather be a toad   270
     And live upon the vapor of a dungeon
     Than keep a corner in the thing I love
     For others' uses. Yet 'tis the plague of great ones;°
     Prerogatived° are they less than the base.
     'Tis destiny unshunnable, like death.   275
     Even then this forkèd plague° is fated to us
     When we do quicken.° Look where she comes.

Enter Desdemona and Emilia.

     If she be false, O, then heaven mocks itself!
     I'll not believe't.
Desdemona: How now, my dear Othello?
     Your dinner, and the generous° islanders   280
     By you invited, do attend your presence.
Othello: I am to blame.
Desdemona: Why do you speak so faintly?
     Are you not well?
Othello: I have a pain upon my forehead, here.
Desdemona: Faith, that's with watching;° 'twill away again.   285
     Let me but bind it hard, within this hour
     It will be well.

---

255 *hold her free:* Consider her guiltless.   256 *government:* Self-control.   259 *qualities:* Natures.   259–60 *learned spirit Of:* Mind informed about.   260 *haggard:* A wild hawk.   261 *jesses:* Thongs for controlling a hawk.   262–63 *whistle . . . fortune:* Turn her out and let her take care of herself.   264 *soft . . . conversation:* Ingratiating manners.   265 *chamberers:* Courtiers.   273 *great ones:* Prominent men.   274 *Prerogatived:* Privileged.   276 *forkèd plague:* i.e., horns of a cuckold.   277 *do quicken:* Are born.   280 *generous:* Noble.   285 *watching:* Working late.

Othello: Your napkin° is too little;

[*He pushes the handkerchief from him, and it falls unnoticed.*]

Let it° alone. Come, I'll go in with you.

Desdemona: I am very sorry that you are not well.   *Exit [with Othello].*

Emilia: I am glad I have found this napkin;   290
     This was her first remembrance from the Moor,
     My wayward husband hath a hundred times
     Wooed me to steal it; but she so loves the token
     (For he conjured her she should ever keep it)
     That she reserves it evermore about her   295
     To kiss and talk to. I'll have the work ta'en out°
     And give't Iago.
     What he will do with it heaven knows, not I;
     I nothing but to please his fantasy.°

     Enter Iago.

Iago: How now? What do you here alone?   300
Emilia: Do not you chide; I have a thing for you.
Iago: A thing for me? It is a common thing—
Emilia: Ha?
Iago: To have a foolish wife.
Emilia: O, is that all? What will you give me now   305
     For that same handkerchief?
Iago: What handkerchief?
Emilia: What handkerchief!
     Why, that the Moor first gave to Desdemona;
     That which so often you did bid me steal.
Iago: Hast stol'n it from her?   310
Emilia: No, faith; she let it drop by negligence,
     And to th' advantage,° I, being here, took't up.
     Look, here 'tis.
Iago: A good wench! Give it me.
Emilia: What will you do with't, that you have been so earnest
     To have me filch it?
Iago: Why, what is that to you?   315

     [*Snatches it.*]

Emilia: If it be not for some purpose of import,°
     Give't me again. Poor lady, she'll run mad
     When she shall lack it.
Iago: Be not acknown on't;° I have use for it.
     Go, leave me.   *Exit Emilia.*   320

---

287 *napkin:* Handkerchief. 288 *it:* i.e., his forehead. 296 *work ta'en out:* Pattern
copied. 299 *fantasy:* Whim. 312 *to th' advantage:* Opportunely. 316 *import:*
Importance. 319 *Be . . . on't:* Do not acknowledge it.

I will in Cassio's lodgings lose this napkin
And let him find it. Trifles light as air
Are to the jealous confirmations strong
As proofs of holy writ. This may do something.
The Moor already changes with my poison: 325
Dangerous conceits° are in their natures poisons,
Which at the first are scarce found to distaste,
But with a little act upon the blood
Burn like the mines of sulphur.

Enter Othello.

                                    I did say so.
Look where he comes! Not poppy nor mandragora,°   330
Nor all the drowsy syrups of the world,
Shall ever med'cine thee to that sweet sleep
Which thou owedst yesterday.
Othello: Ha! ha! false to me?
Iago: Why, how now, general? No more of that!
Othello: Avaunt! be gone! Thou hast set me on the rack.   335
     I swear 'tis better to be much abused
     Than but to know't a little.
Iago: How now, my lord?
Othello: What sense had I of her stol'n hours of lust?
     I saw't not, thought it not, it harmed not me;
     I slept the next night well, fed well, was free° and merry; 340
     I found not Cassio's kisses on her lips.
     He that is robbed, not wanting° what is stol'n,
     Let him not know't, and he's not robbed at all.
Iago: I am sorry to hear this.
Othello: I had been happy if the general camp,   345
     Pioneers° and all, had tasted her sweet body,
     So I had nothing known. O, now for ever
     Farewell the tranquil mind! farewell content!
     Farewell the plumèd troops, and the big° wars
     That make ambition virtue! O, farewell!   350
     Farewell the neighing steed and the shrill trump,
     The spirit-stirring drum, th' ear-piercing fife,
     The royal banner, and all quality,
     Pride, pomp, and circumstance° of glorious war!
     And O you mortal engines° whose rude throats   355
     Th' immortal Jove's dread clamors counterfeit,°
     Farewell! Othello's occupation's gone!

---

326 *conceits:* Ideas.   330 *mandragora:* A narcotic.   340 *free:* Carefree.   342 *wanting:*
Missing.   346 *Pioneers:* Sappers, laborers.   349 *big:* Stately.   354 *circumstance:*
Pageantry.   355 *mortal engines:* Deadly artillery.   356 *counterfeit:* Imitate.

Iago: Is't possible, my lord?

Othello: Villain, be sure thou prove my love a whore!
    Be sure of it; give me the ocular proof;   360
    Or, by the worth of mine eternal soul,
    Thou hadst been better have been born a dog
    Than answer my waked wrath!

Iago: Is't come to this?

Othello: Make me to see't; or at the least so prove it
    That the probation° bear no hinge nor loop   365
    To hang a doubt on — or woe upon thy life!

Iago: My noble lord —

Othello: If thou dost slander her and torture me,
    Never pray more; abandon all remorse;
    On horror's head horrors accumulate;   370
    Do deeds to make heaven weep, all earth amazed;
    For nothing canst thou to damnation add
    Greater than that.

Iago: O grace! O heaven forgive me!
    Are you a man? Have you a soul or sense? —
    God buy you! take mine office. O wretched fool,   375
    That lov'st to make thine honesty a vice!
    O monstrous world! Take note, take note, O world,
    To be direct and honest is not safe.
    I thank you for this profit;° and from hence
    I'll love no friend, sith love breeds such offense.   380

Othello: Nay, stay. Thou shouldst be honest.

Iago: I should be wise; for honesty's a fool
    And loses that it works for.

Othello: By the world,
    I think my wife be honest, and think she is not;
    I think that thou art just, and think thou art not.   385
    I'll have some proof. Her name, that was as fresh
    As Dian's visage, is now begrimed and black
    As mine own face. If there be cords, or knives,
    Poison, or fire, or suffocating streams,
    I'll not endure it. Would I were satisfied!°   390

Iago: I see, sir, you are eaten up with passion:
    I do repent me that I put it to you.
    You would be satisfied?

Othello: Would? Nay, and I will.

Iago: And may; but how? how satisfied, my lord?
    Would you, the supervisor,° grossly gape on?   395

---

365 *probation:* Proof.   379 *profit:* Profitable lesson.   390 *satisfied:* Completely informed.   395 *supervisor:* Spectator.

Behold her topped?
Othello: Death and damnation! O!
Iago: It were a tedious difficulty, I think,
      To bring them to that prospect. Damn them then,
      If ever mortal eyes do see them bolster°
      More than their own! What then? How then?   400
      What shall I say? Where's satisfaction?
      It is impossible you should see this,
      Were they as prime° as goats, as hot as monkeys,
      As salt° as wolves in pride,° and fools as gross
      As ignorance made drunk. But yet, I say,   405
      If imputation and strong circumstances
      Which lead directly to the door of truth
      Will give you satisfaction, you might have't.
Othello: Give me a living reason she's disloyal.
Iago: I do not like the office.   410
      But sith I am ent'red in this cause so far,
      Pricked to't by foolish honesty and love,
      I will go on. I lay with Cassio lately,
      And being troubled with a raging tooth,
      I could not sleep.   415
      There are a kind of men so loose of soul
      That in their sleeps will mutter their affairs.
      One of this kind is Cassio.
      In sleep I heard him say, "Sweet Desdemona,
      Let us be wary, let us hide our loves!"   420
      And then, sir, would he gripe and wring my hand,
      Cry "O sweet creature!" and then kiss me hard,
      As if he plucked up kisses by the roots
      That grew upon my lips; then laid his leg
      Over my thigh, and sighed, and kissed, and then   425
      Cried "Cursèd fate that gave thee to the Moor!"
Othello: O monstrous! monstrous!
Iago: Nay, this was but his dream.
Othello: But this denoted a foregone conclusion;°
Iago: 'Tis a shrewd doubt,° though it be but a dream.
      And this may help to thicken other proofs   430
      That do demonstrate thinly.
Othello: I'll tear her all to pieces!
Iago: Nay, yet be wise. Yet we see nothing done;
      She may be honest yet. Tell me but this —
      Have you not sometimes seen a handkerchief

---

399 *bolster:* Lie together.   403 *prime:* Lustful.   404 *salt:* Lecherous; *pride:*
Heat.   428 *foregone conclusion:* Previous experience.   429 *a shrewd doubt:* Cursedly
suspicious.

Spotted with strawberries in your wife's hand?   435
Othello: I gave her such a one; 'twas my first gift.
Iago: I know not that; but such a handkerchief —
        I am sure it was your wife's — did I to-day
        See Cassio wipe his beard with.
Othello: If it be that —
Iago: If it be that, or any that was hers,   440
        It speaks against her with the other proofs.
Othello: O, that the slave had forty thousand lives!
        One is too poor, too weak for my revenge.
        Now do I see 'tis true. Look here, Iago:
        All my fond love thus do I blow to heaven.   445
        'Tis gone.
        Arise, black vengeance, from the hollow hell!
        Yield up, O love, thy crown and hearted throne
        To tyrannous hate! Swell, bosom, with thy fraught,°
        For 'tis of aspics'° tongues!
Iago: Yet be content.   450
Othello: O, blood, blood, blood!
Iago: Patience, I say. Your mind perhaps may change.
Othello: Never, Iago. Like to the Pontic sea,°
        Whose icy current and compulsive course
        Ne'er feels retiring ebb, but keeps due on   455
        To the Propontic and the Hellespont,
        Even so my bloody thoughts, with violent pace,
        Shall ne'er look back, ne'er ebb to humble love,
        Till that a capable° and wide revenge
        Swallow them up.
        (He kneels.)   Now, by yond marble heaven,   460
        In the due reverence of a sacred vow
        I here engage my words.
Iago: Do not rise yet.
        (Iago kneels.)
        Witness, you ever-burning lights above,
        You elements that clip° us round about,
        Witness that here Iago doth give up   465
        The execution° of his wit,° hands, heart
        To wronged Othello's service! Let him command,
        And to obey shall be in me remorse,°
        What bloody business ever.

        [They rise.]

---

449 *fraught:* Burden.   450 *aspics:* Deadly poisonous snakes.   453 *Pontic sea:* Black
Sea.   459 *capable:* All-embracing.   464 *clip:* Encompass.   466 *execution:* Activities; *wit:* Mind.   468 *remorse:* Pity.

Othello: I greet thy love,
   Not with vain thanks but with acceptance bounteous,   470
   And will upon the instant put thee to't.
   Within these three days let me hear thee say
   That Cassio's not alive.
Iago: My friend is dead; 'tis done at your request.
   But let her live.   475
Othello: Damn her, lewd minx! O, damn her! damn her!
   Come, go with me apart. I will withdraw
   To furnish me with some swift means of death
   For the fair devil. Now art thou my lieutenant.
Iago: I am your own forever.   *Exeunt.*   480

SCENE IV: *The environs of the castle.*

   Enter Desdemona, Emilia, and Clown.

Desdemona: Do you know, sirrah, where Lieutenant Cassio lies?°
Clown: I dare not say he lies anywhere.
Desdemona: Why, man?
Clown: He's a soldier, and for me to say a soldier lies, 'tis stabbing.
Desdemona: Go to. Where lodges he?   5
Clown: To tell you where he lodges is to tell you where I lie.
Desdemona: Can anything be made of this?
Clown: I know not where he lodges; and for me to devise a lodging,
   and say he lies here or he lies there, were to lie in mine own throat.
Desdemona: Can you enquire him out, and be edified by report?   10
Clown: I will catechize the world for him; that is, make questions, and
   by them answer.
Desdemona: Seek him, bid him come hither. Tell him I have moved°
   my lord on his behalf and hope all will be well.
Clown: To do this is within the compass of man's wit, and therefore   15
   I'll attempt the doing of it.   *Exit.*
Desdemona: Where should I lose the handkerchief, Emilia?
Emilia: I know not, madam.
Desdemona: Believe me, I had rather have lost my purse
   Full of crusadoes;° and but my noble Moor   20
   Is true of mind, and made of no such baseness
   As jealous creatures are, it were enough
   To put him to ill thinking.
Emilia: Is he not jealous?
Desdemona: Who? he? I think the sun where he was born
   Drew all such humors° from him.

   Enter Othello.

Scene IV.   1 *lies:* Lives, lodges.   13 *moved:* Made proposals to.   20 *crusadoes:* Por-
tuguese gold coins.   25 *humors:* Inclinations.

Emilia: Look where he comes.   25
Desdemona: I will not leave him now till Cassio
    Be called to him — How is't with you, my lord?
Othello: Well, my good lady. *[Aside.]* O, hardness to dissemble! —
    How do you, Desdemona?
Desdemona: Well, my good lord.
Othello: Give me your hand. This hand is moist, my lady.   30
Desdemona: It yet hath felt no age nor known no sorrow.
Othello: This argues fruitfulness and liberal heart.
    Hot, hot, and moist. This hand of yours requires
    A sequester° from liberty, fasting and prayer,
    Much castigation, exercise devout;   35
    For here's a young and sweating devil here
    That commonly rebels. 'Tis a good hand,
    A frank one.
Desdemona: You may, indeed, say so;
    For 'twas that hand that gave away my heart.   40
Othello: A liberal hand! The hearts of old gave hands;
    But our new heraldry° is hands, not hearts.
Desdemona: I cannot speak of this. Come now, your promise!
Othello: What promise, chuck?
Desdemona: I have sent to bid Cassio come speak with you.   45
Othello: I have a salt and sorry rheum° offends me.
    Lend me thy handkerchief.
Desdemona: Here, my lord.
Othello: That which I gave you.
Desdemona: I have it not about me.
Othello: Not?
Desdemona: No, faith, my lord.
Othello: That's a fault.
    That handkerchief   50
    Did an Egyptian° to my mother give.
    She was a charmer,° and could almost read
    The thoughts of people. She told her, while she kept it,
    'Twould make her amiable° and subdue my father
    Entirely to her love; but if she lost it   55
    Or made a gift of it, my father's eye
    Should hold her loathèd, and his spirits should hunt
    After new fancies. She, dying, gave it me,
    And bid me, when my fate would have me wived,
    To give it her. I did so; and take heed on't;   60

---

34 *sequester:* Removal.   42 *heraldry:* Heraldic symbolism.   46 *salt . . . rheum:* Distressing head cold.   51 *Egyptian:* Gypsy.   52 *charmer:* Sorceress.   54 *amiable:* Lovable.

Make it a darling like your precious eye.
To lose't or give't away were such perdition°
As nothing else could match.
Desdemona: Is't possible?
Othello: 'Tis true. There's magic in the web of it.
　A sibyl that had numb'red in the world   65
　The sun to course two hundred compasses,°
　In her prophetic fury sewed the work;
　The worms were hallowed that did breed the silk;
　And it was dyed in mummy° which the skillful
　Conserved of maidens' hearts.
Desdemona: I'faith? Is't true?   70
Othello: Most veritable. Therefore look to't well.
Desdemona: Then would to God that I had never seen't!
Othello: Ha! Wherefore?
Desdemona: Why do you speak so startingly and rash?
Othello: Is't lost? Is't gone? Speak, is't out o' th' way?   75
Desdemona: Heaven bless us!
Othello: Say you?
Desdemona: It is not lost. But what an if it were?
Othello: How?
Desdemona: I say it is not lost.
Othello: Fetch't, let me see't!   80
Desdemona: Why, so I can, sir; but I will not now.
　This is a trick to put° me from my suit:
　Pray you let Cassio be received again.
Othello: Fetch me the handkerchief! My mind misgives.
Desdemona: Come, come!   85
　You'll never meet a more sufficient man.
Othello: The handkerchief!
[*Desdemona:*   I pray talk me of Cassio.
Othello: The handkerchief!]
Desdemona: A man that all his time°
　Hath founded his good fortunes on your love,
　Shared dangers with you —   90
Othello: The handkerchief!
Desdemona: I' faith, you are to blame.
Othello: Zounds!   *Exit Othello.*
Emilia: Is not this man jealous?
Desdemona: I ne'er saw this before.   95
　Sure there's some wonder in this handkerchief;
　I am most unhappy in the loss of it.

---

62 *perdition:* Disaster.   66 *compasses:* Annual rounds.   69 *mummy:* A drug made from mummies.   82 *put:* Divert.   88 *all his time:* During his whole career.

Emilia: 'Tis not a year or two shows us a man.
    They are all but stomachs, and we all but food;
    They eat us hungerly, and when they are full,   100
    They belch us.

    Enter Iago and Cassio.

                Look you — Cassio and my husband!
Iago: There is no other way; 'tis she must do't.
    And lo the happiness!° Go and importune her.
Desdemona: How now, good Cassio? What's the news with you?
Cassio: Madam, my former suit. I do beseech you   105
    That by your virtuous means I may again
    Exist, and be a member of his love
    Whom I with all the office of my heart
    Entirely honor. I would not be delayed.
    If my offense be of such mortal kind   110
    That neither service past, nor present sorrows,
    Nor purposed merit in futurity,
    Can ransom me into his love again,
    But to know so must be my benefit.
    So shall I clothe me in a forced content,   115
    And shut myself up in° some other course,
    To fortune's alms.
Desdemona: Alas, thrice-gentle Cassio!
    My advocation° is not now in tune.
    My lord is not my lord; nor should I know him,
    Were he in favor° as in humor altered.   120
    So help me every spirit sanctified
    As I have spoken for you all my best
    And stood within the blank° of his displeasure
    For my free speech! You must a while be patient.
    What I can do I will; and more I will   125
    Than for myself I dare. Let that suffice you.
Iago: Is my lord angry?
Emilia: He went hence but now,
    And certainly in strange unquietness.
Iago: Can he be angry? I have seen the cannon
    When it hath blown his ranks into the air   130
    And, like the devil, from his very arm
    Puffed his own brother — and is he angry?

---

103 *happiness:* Good luck.   116 *shut myself up in:* Confine myself to.   118 *advoca-tion:* Advocacy.   120 *favor:* Appearance.   123 *blank:* Bull's-eye of the target.

Something of moment then. I will go meet him.
There's matter in't indeed if he be angry.
Desdemona: I prithee do so.   *Exit [Iago].*
                          Something sure of state,°   135
Either from Venice or some unhatched practice°
Made demonstrable here in Cyprus to him,
Hath puddled° his clear spirit; and in such cases
Men's natures wrangle with inferior things,
Though great ones are their object. 'Tis even so;   140
For let our finger ache, and it endues°
Our other, healthful members even to a sense
Of pain. Nay, we must think men are not gods,
Nor of them look for such observancy
As fits the bridal. Beshrew me much, Emilia,   145
I was, unhandsome warrior° as I am,
Arraigning his unkindness with my soul;°
But now I find I had suborned the witness,
And he's indicted falsely.
Emilia: Pray heaven it be state matters, as you think,
And no conception nor no jealous toy°   150
Concerning you.
Desdemona: Alas the day! I never gave him cause.
Emilia: But jealous souls will not be answered so;
They are not ever jealous for the cause,
But jealous for they're jealous. It is a monster   155
Begot upon itself,° born on itself.
Desdemona: Heaven keep that monster from Othello's mind!
Emilia: Lady, amen.
Desdemona: I will go seek him. Cassio, walk here about: 160
If I do find him fit, I'll move your suit
And seek to effect it to my uttermost.
Cassio: I humbly thank your ladyship.

                              Exeunt Desdemona and Emilia.

   Enter Bianca.

Bianca: Save you, friend Cassio!
Cassio: What make you from home?
   How is't with you, my most fair Bianca?   165

---

135 *state:* Public affairs.   136 *unhatched practice:* Budding plot.   138 *puddled:*
Muddied.   141 *endues:* Brings.   146 *unhandsome warrior:* Inadequate soldier.
147 *Arraigning . . . soul:* Indicting his unkindness before the bar of my soul.
151 *toy:* Fancy.   157 *Begot upon itself:* Self-engendered.

I' faith, sweet love, I was coming to your house.
Bianca: And I was going to your lodging, Cassio.
    What, keep a week away? seven days and nights?
    Eightscore eight hours? and lovers' absent hours,
    More tedious than the dial° eightscore times?   170
    O weary reck'ning!
Cassio: Pardon me, Bianca:
    I have this while with leaden thoughts been pressed;
    But I shall in a more continuate° time
    Strike off this score of absence. Sweet Bianca,

    [Gives her Desdemona's handkerchief.]

    Take me this work out.°
Bianca: O Cassio, whence came this?   175
    This is some token from a newer friend
    To the felt absence now I feel a cause.
    Is't come to this? Well, well.
Cassio: Go to, woman!
    Throw your vile guesses in the devil's teeth,
    From whence you have them. You are jealous now   180
    That this is from some mistress, some remembrance.
    No, by my faith, Bianca.
Bianca: Why, whose is it?
Cassio: I know not, sweet; I found it in my chamber.
    I like the work° well; ere it be demanded,
    As like enough it will, I'd have it copied.   185
    Take it and do't, and leave me for this time.
Bianca: Leave you? Wherefore?
Cassio: I do attend here on the general
    And think it no addition, nor my wish,
    To have him see me womaned.
Bianca: Why, I pray you?   190
Cassio: Not that I love you not.
Bianca: But that you do not love me!
    I pray you bring me on the way a little,
    And say if I shall see you soon at night.

Cassio: 'Tis but a little way that I can bring you,
    For I attend here; but I'll see you soon.   195
Bianca: 'Tis very good. I must be circumstanced.°   *Exeunt.*

---

170 *dial:* Clock. 173 *continuate:* Uninterrupted. 175 *Take . . . out:* Copy this
embroidery for me. 184 *work:* Needlework. 196 *circumstanced:* Governed by
circumstances.

ACT IV

SCENE I: *The environs of the castle.*

Enter Othello and Iago.

Iago: Will you think so?
Othello: Think so, Iago?
Iago: What,
    To kiss in private?
Othello: An unauthorized kiss.
Iago: Or to be naked with her friend in bed
    An hour or more, not meaning any harm?
Othello: Naked in bed, Iago, and not mean harm?   5
    It is hypocrisy against the devil.°
    They that mean virtuously, and yet do so,
    The devil their virtue tempts, and they tempt heaven.
Iago: So they do nothing, 'tis a venial slip.
    But if I give my wife a handkerchief—   10
Othello: What then?
Iago: Why, then 'tis hers, my lord; and being hers,
    She may, I think, bestow't on any man.
Othello: She is protectress of her honor too;
    May she give that?   15
Iago: Her honor is an essence that's not seen;
    They have it very oft that have it not.
    But for the handkerchief—
Othello: By heaven, I would most gladly have forgot it!
    Thou said'st—O, it comes o'er my memory   20
    As doth the raven o'er the infected° house,
    Boding to all!—he had my handkerchief.
Iago: Ay, what of that?
Othello: That's not so good now.
Iago: What
    If I had said I had seen him do you wrong?
    Or heard him say—as knaves be such abroad   25
    Who having, by their own importunate suit,
    Or voluntary dotage of some mistress,
    Convincèd or supplied° them, cannot choose
    But they must blab—

Othello: Hath he said anything?
Iago: He hath, my lord; but be you well assured,   30
    No more than he'll unswear.

Act IV, Scene I.   6 *hypocrisy . . . devil:* i.e., feigned sin instead of feigned virtue.
21 *infected:* Plague-stricken.   28 *Convincèd or supplied:* Overcome or gratified.

Othello: What hath he said?
Iago: Faith, that he did — I know not what he did.
Othello: What? what?
Iago: Lie —
Othello: With her?
Iago: With her, on her; what you will.   35
Othello: Lie with her? lie on her? — We say lie on her when they
    belieher. — Lie with her! Zounds, that's fulsome. — Handkerchief —
    confessions — handkerchief! — To confess, and be hanged for
    his labor — first to be hanged, and then to confess! I tremble
    at it. Nature would not invest herself in such shadowing passion   40
    without some instruction.° It is not words that shakes me
    thus. — Pish! Noses, ears, and lips? Is't possible? — Confess? —
    Handkerchief? — O devil!

    (Falls in a trance.)

Iago: Work on,
    My med'cine, work! Thus credulous fools are caught,   45
    And many worthy and chaste dames even thus
    All guiltless, meet reproach. — What, ho! my lord!
    My lord, I say! Othello!
    Enter Cassio.   How now, Cassio?
Cassio: What's the matter?
Iago: My lord is fall'n into an epilepsy.   50
    This is his second fit; he had one yesterday.
Cassio: Rub him about the temples.
Iago: No, forbear.
    The lethargy° must have his quiet course.
    If not, he foams at mouth, and by and by
    Breaks out to savage madness. Look, he stirs.   55
    Do you withdraw yourself a little while.
    He will recover straight. When he is gone,
    I would on great occasion speak with you.   *[Exit Cassio.]*
    How is it, general? Have you not hurt your head?
Othello: Dost thou mock me?
Iago: I mock you? No, by heaven.   60
    Would you would bear your fortune like a man!
Othello: A hornèd man's° a monster and a beast.
Iago: There's many a beast then in a populous city,
    And many a civil monster.
Othello: Did he confess it?
Iago: Good sir, be a man.   65
    Think every bearded fellow that's but yoked

40–41 *Nature . . . instruction:* My natural faculties would not be so overcome by passion
without reason.   53 *lethargy:* Coma.   62 *hornèd man:* Cuckold.

May draw with you. There's millions now alive
That nightly lie in those unproper° beds
Which they dare swear peculiar:° your case is better.
O, 'tis the spite of hell, the fiend's arch-mock,   70
To lip a wanton in a secure° couch,
And to suppose her chaste! No, let me know;
And knowing what I am, I know what she shall be.
Othello: O, thou art wise! 'Tis certain.
Iago: Stand you awhile apart;
Confine yourself but in a patient list.°   75
Whilst you were here, o'erwhelmèd with your grief—
A passion most unsuiting such a man—
Cassio came hither. I shifted him away
And laid good 'scuse upon your ecstasy;°
Bade him anon return, and here speak with me;   80
The which he promised. Do but encave° yourself
And mark the fleers, the gibes, and notable scorns
That dwell in every region of his face;
For I will make him tell the tale anew—
Where, how, how oft, how long ago, and when   85
He hath, and is again to cope° your wife.
I say, but mark his gesture. Marry, patience!
Or I shall say y'are all in all in spleen,°
And nothing of a man.
Othello: Dost thou hear, Iago?
I will be found most cunning in my patience;   90
But—dost thou hear?—most bloody.
Iago: That's not amiss:
But yet keep time in all. Will you withdraw?

                                            [Othello retires.]

Now will I question Cassio of Bianca,
A huswife° that by selling her desires
Buys herself bread and clothes. It is a creature   95
That dotes on Cassio, as 'tis the strumpet's plague
To beguile many and be beguiled by one.
He, when he hears of her, cannot refrain
From the excess of laughter. Here he comes.

Enter Cassio.

As he shall smile, Othello shall go mad;   100

---

68 *unproper:* Not exclusively their own.   69 *peculiar:* Exclusively their own.
71 *secure:* Free from fear of rivalry.   75 *in a patient list:* Within the limits of self-control.   79 *ecstasy:* Trance.   81 *encave:* Conceal.   86 *cope:* Meet.   88 *all in all in spleen:* Wholly overcome by your passion.   94 *huswife:* Hussy.

And his unbookish° jealousy must conster°
    Poor Cassio's smiles, gestures, and light behavior
    Quite in the wrong. How do you now, lieutenant?
Cassio: The worser that you give me the addition°   105
    Whose want even kills me.
Iago: Ply Desdemona well, and you are sure on't.
    Now, if this suit lay in Bianca's power,
    How quickly should you speed!
Cassio: Alas, poor caitiff!°
Othello: Look how he laughs already!
Iago: I never knew a woman love man so.   110
Cassio: Alas, poor rogue! I think, i' faith, she loves me.
Othello: Now he denies it faintly, and laughs it out.
Iago: Do you hear, Cassio?
Othello: Now he importunes him
    To tell it o'er. Go to! Well said, well said!
Iago: She gives out that you shall marry her.   115
    Do you intend it?
Cassio: Ha, ha, ha!
Othello: Do you triumph, Roman? Do you triumph?
Cassio: I marry her? What, a customer?° Prithee bear some charity to
    my wit; do not think it so unwholesome. Ha, ha, ha!   120
Othello: So, so, so, so! They laugh that win!
Iago: Faith, the cry goes that you marry her.
Cassio: Prithee say true.
Iago: I am a very villain else.
Othello: Have you scored me?° Well.   125
Cassio: This is the monkey's own giving out. She is persuaded I will
    marry her out of her own love and flattery, not out of my promise.
Othello: Iago beckons° me; now he begins the story.
Cassio: She was here even now; she haunts me in every place. I was t' other
    day talking on the sea bank with certain Venetians, and thither   130
    comes the bauble,° and, by this hand, she falls me thus about my
    neck—
Othello: Crying "O dear Cassio!" as it were. His gesture imports it.
Cassio: So hangs, and lolls, and weeps upon me; so shakes and pulls me!
    Ha, ha, ha!   135
Othello: Now he tells how she plucked him to my chamber. O, I see that
    nose of yours, but not that dog I shall throw it to.
Cassio: Well, I must leave her company.

    Enter Bianca.

---

101 *unbookish:* Uninstructed; *conster:* Construe, interpret.   104 *addition:*
Title.   108 *caitiff:* Wretch.   119 *customer:* Prostitute.   125 *scored me:* Settled my
account (?).   128 *beckons:* Signals.   131 *bauble:* Plaything.

Iago: Before me! Look where she comes.

Cassio: 'Tis such another fitchew!° marry, a perfumed one. What do you   140
mean by this haunting of me?

Bianca: Let the devil and his dam haunt you! What did you mean by
that same handkerchief you gave me even now? I was a fine fool to
take it. I must take out the whole work? A likely piece of work that
you should find it in your chamber and know not who left it there!   145
This is some minx's token, and I must take out the work? There!
Give it your hobby-horse.° Wheresoever you had it, I'll take out
no work on't.

Cassio: How now, my sweet Bianca? How now? how now?

Othello: By heaven, that should be my handkerchief!   150

Bianca: An you'll come to supper to-night, you may; an you will
not, come when you are next prepared for.   *Exit.*

Iago: After her, after her!

Cassio: Faith, I must; she'll rail in the street else.

Iago: Will you sup there?   155

Cassio: Yes, I intend so.

Iago: Well, I may chance to see you; for I would very fain speak with
you.

Cassio: Prithee come. Will you?

Iago: Go to! say no more.   *Exit Cassio.*   160

Othello [comes forward]: How shall I murder him, Iago?

Iago: Did you perceive how he laughed at his vice?°

Othello: O Iago!

Iago: And did you see the handkerchief?

Othello: Was that mine?   165

Iago: Your, by this hand! And to see how he prizes° the foolish
woman your wife! She gave it him, and he hath giv'n it his
whore.

Othello: I would have him nine years a-killing — A fine woman! a fair
woman! a sweet woman!   170

Iago: Nay, you must forget that.

Othello: Ay, let her rot, and perish, and be damned to-night; for she
shall not live. No, my heart is turned to stone; I strike it, and it
hurts my hand. O, the world hath not a sweeter creature! She
might lie by an emperor's side and command him tasks.   175

Iago: Nay, that's not your way.

Othello: Hang her! I do but say what she is. So delicate with her needle!
an admirable musician! O, she will sing the savageness out of a
bear! Of so high and plenteous wit and invention° —

Iago: She's the worse for all this.   180

---

140 *fitchew:* Polecat (slang for *whore*). 147 *hobby-horse:* Harlot. 162 *vice:* i.e.,
vicious conduct. 166 *prizes:* Values. 179 *invention:* Imagination.

Othello: O, a thousand thousand times! And then, of so gentle a
    condition!°

Iago: Ay, too gentle.

Othello: Nay, that's certain. But yet the pity of it, Iago! O Iago, the pity
    of it, Iago!   185

Iago: If you are so fond over her iniquity, give her patent° to offend; for
    if it touch not you, it comes near nobody.

Othello: I will chop her into messes! Cuckold me!

Iago: O, 'tis foul in her.

Othello: With mine officer!   190

Iago: That's fouler.

Othello: Get me some poison, Iago, this night. I'll not expostulate with
    her, lest her body and beauty unprovide° my mind again. This night,
    Iago!

Iago: Do it not with poison. Strangle her in her bed, even the bed she hath 195
    contaminated.

Othello: Good, good! The justice of it pleases. Very good!

Iago: And for Cassio, let me be his undertaker;° you shall hear more by
    midnight.

Othello: Excellent good!   200

    A trumpet.

             What trumpet is that same?

Iago: I warrant something from Venice.

Enter Lodovico, Desdemona, and Attendants.

                      'Tis Lodovico.
    This comes from the Duke; and see, your wife is with him.

Lodovico: God save you, worthy general!

Othello: With all my heart, sir.

Lodovico: The Duke and senators of Venice greet you.   205

    [Gives him a letter.]

Othello: I kiss the instrument of their pleasures.

    [Opens the letter and reads.]

Desdemona: And what's the news, good cousin Lodovico?

Iago: I am very glad to see you, signior.
    Welcome to Cyprus.

Lodovico: I thank you. How does Lieutenant Cassio?

Iago: Lives, sir.   210

Desdemona: Cousin, there's fall'n between him and my lord

---

182 *condition:* Disposition.   186 *patent:* License.   193 *unprovide:* Disarm.   198 *be
his undertaker:* Undertake to deal with him.

An unkind breach; but you shall make all well.
Othello: Are you sure of that?
Desdemona: My lord?
Othello [reads]: "This fail you not to do, as you will —"   215
Lodovico: He did not call; he's busy in the paper.
    Is there division 'twixt my lord and Cassio?
Desdemona: A most unhappy one. I would do much
    T' atone° them, for the love I bear to Cassio.
Othello: Fire and brimstone!
Desdemona: My lord?
Othello: Are you wise?   220
Desdemona: What, is he angry?
Lodovico: May be the letter moved him;
    For, as I think, they do command him home,
    Deputing Cassio in his government.
Desdemona: By my troth, I am glad on't.
Othello: Indeed?
Desdemona: My lord?
Othello: I am glad to see you mad.°
Desdemona: Why, sweet Othello —   225
Othello: Devil!

    [Strikes her.]

Desdemona: I have not deserved this.
Lodovico: My lord, this would not be believed in Venice,
    Though I should swear I saw't. 'Tis very much.
    Make her amends; she weeps.
Othello: O devil, devil!   230
    If that the earth could teem° with woman's tears,
    Each drop she falls would prove a crocodile.°
    Out of my sight!
Desdemona: I will not stay to offend you.   *[Going.]*
Lodovico: Truly, an obedient lady.
    I do beseech your lordship call her back.   235
Othello: Mistress!
Desdemona: My lord?
Othello: What would you with her, sir?
Lodovico: Who? I, my lord?
Othello: Ay! You did wish that I would make her turn.
    Sir, she can turn, and turn, and yet go on   240
    And turn again; and she can weep, sir, weep;
    And she's obedient; as you say, obedient,
    Very obedient. — Proceed you in your tears. —

---

219 *atone:* Reconcile. 224 *mad:* i.e., waggish. 231 *teem:* Breed. 232 *crocodile:* (Crocodiles were supposed to shed hypocritical tears to lure men to destruction).

Concerning this, sir — O well-painted passion!° —
I am commanded home. — Get you away;   245
I'll send for you anon. — Sir, I obey the mandate
And will return to Venice. — Hence, avaunt!

                         [Exit Desdemona.]

Cassio shall have my place. And, sir, to-night
I do entreat that we may sup together.
You are welcome, sir, to Cyprus — Goats and monkeys!   *Exit.* 250
Lodovico: Is this the noble Moor whom our full Senate
    Call all in all sufficient? Is this the nature
    Whom passion could not shake? whose solid virtue
    The shot of accident nor dart of chance
    Could neither graze nor pierce?
Iago: He is much changed.   255
Lodovico: Are his wits safe? Is he not light of brain?
Iago: He's that he is; I may not breathe my censure.
    What he might be — if what he might he is not —
    I would to heaven he were!
Lodovico: What, strike his wife?
Iago: Faith, that was not so well; yet would I knew   260
    That stroke would prove the worst!
Lodovico: Is it his use?°
    Or did the letters work upon his blood
    And new-create this fault?
Iago: Alas, alas!
    It is not honesty in me to speak
    What I have seen and known. You shall observe him, 265
    And his own courses will denote him so
    That I may save my speech. Do but go after
    And mark how he continues.
Lodovico: I am sorry that I am deceived in him.   *Exeunt.*

Scene II: *Within the castle.*

    Enter Othello and Emilia.

Othello: You have seen nothing then?
Emilia: Nor ever heard, nor ever did suspect.
Othello: Yes, you have seen Cassio and she together.
Emilia: But then I saw no harm, and then I heard
    Each syllable that breath made up between them.   5
Othello: What, did they never whisper?
Emilia: Never, my lord.

244 *passion:* Grief.   261 *use:* Custom.

Othello: Nor send you out o' th' way?
Emilia: Never.
Othello: To fetch her fan, her gloves, her mask, nor nothing?
Emilia: Never, my lord.   10
Othello: That's strange.
Emilia: I durst, my lord, to wager she is honest,
    Lay down my soul at stake. If you think other,
    Remove your thought; it doth abuse your bosom.°
    If any wretch have put this in your head,   15
    Let heaven requite it with the serpent's curse!°
    For if she be not honest, chaste, and true,
    There's no man happy; the purest of their wives
    Is foul as slander.
Othello: Bid her come hither. Go.   *Exit Emilia.*
    She says enough; yet she's a simple bawd   20
    That cannot say as much. This is a subtle whore,
    A closet lock and key of villainous secrets;
    And yet she'll kneel and pray; I have seen her do't.

    Enter Desdemona and Emilia.

Desdemona: My lord, what is your will?
Othello: Pray you, chuck, come hither.
Desdemona: What is your pleasure?
Othello: Let me see your eyes.   25
    Look in my face.
Desdemona: What horrible fancy's this?
Othello [to Emilia]: Some of your function, mistress.
    Leave procreants° alone and shut the door;
    Cough or cry "hem" if anybody come.
    Your mystery, your mystery!° Nay, dispatch!   30

                    Exit Emilia.

Desdemona: Upon my knees, what doth your speech import?
    I understand a fury in your words,
    [But not the words.]
Othello: Why, what art thou?
Desdemona: Your wife, my lord; your true
    And loyal wife.
Othello: Come, swear it, damn thyself;   35
    Lest, being like one of heaven,° the devils themselves
    Should fear to seize thee. Therefore be double-damned —
    Swear thou art honest.°
Desdemona: Heaven doth truly know it.

Scene II. 14 *abuse your bosom:* Deceive your heart. 16 *serpent's curse:* (cf. Genesis 3: 14). 28 *procreants:* Mating couples. 30 *mystery:* Trade, occupation. 36 *being…heaven:* Looking like an angel. 38 *honest:* Chaste.

Othello: Heaven truly knows that thou art false as hell.
Desdemona: To whom, my lord? With whom? How am I false?   40
Othello: Ah, Desdemona! away! away! away!
Desdemona: Alas the heavy day! Why do you weep?
        Am I the motive of these tears, my lord?
        If haply you my father do suspect
        An instrument° of this your calling back,   45
        Lay not your blame on me. If you have lost him,
        Why, I have lost him too.
Othello: Had it pleased heaven
        To try me with affliction, had they rained
        All kinds of sores and shames on my bare head,
        Steeped me in poverty to the very lips,   50
        Given to captivity me and my utmost hopes,
        I should have found in some place of my soul
        A drop of patience. But, alas, to make me
        The fixèd figure for the time of scorn°
        To point his slow unmoving finger at!   55
        Yet could I bear that too; well, very well.
        But there where I have garnered up my heart,
        Where either I must live or bear no life,
        The fountain from the which my current runs
        Or else dries up — to be discarded thence,   60
        Or keep it as a cistern for foul toads
        To knot and gender in — turn thy complexion there,°
        Patience, thou young and rose-lipped cherubin!
        Ay, here look grim as hell!
Desdemona: I hope my noble lord esteems me honest.   65
Othello: O, ay; as summer flies are in the shambles,°
        That quicken° even with blowing. O thou weed,
        Who art so lovely fair, and smell'st so sweet,
        That the sense aches at thee, would thou hadst ne'er been born!
Desdemona: Alas, what ignorant sin have I committed?   70
Othello: Was this fair paper, this most goodly book,
        Made to write "whore" upon? What committed?
        Committed? O thou public commoner!°
        I should make very forges of my cheeks
        That would to cinders burn up modesty,   75
        Did I but speak thy deeds. What committed?
        Heaven stops the nose at it, and the moon winks;°
        The bawdy wind, that kisses all it meets,

---

45 *An instrument:* To be the cause.   54 *time of scorn:* Scornful world.   62 *turn thy complexion there:* Change your color at that point.   66 *shambles:* Slaughterhouse.   67 *quicken:* Come to life.   73 *commoner:* Harlot.   77 *winks:* Closes her eyes.

Is hushed within the hollow mine of earth
And will not hear it. What committed?   80
Impudent strumpet!
Desdemona: By heaven, you do me wrong!
Othello: Are not you a strumpet?
Desdemona: No, as I am a Christian!
    If to preserve this vessel for my lord
    From any other foul unlawful touch
    Be not to be a strumpet, I am none.   85
Othello: What, not a whore?
Desdemona: No, as I shall be saved!
Othello: Is't possible?
Desdemona: O, heaven forgive us!
Othello: I cry you mercy° then.
    I took you for that cunning whore of Venice
    That married with Othello. — *[Calling.]* You, mistress,   90
    That have the office opposite to Saint Peter
    And keep the gate of hell!

    Enter Emilia.

                              You, you, ay, you!
    We have done our course; there's money for your pains:
    I pray you turn the key, and keep our counsel.   *Exit.*
Emilia: Alas, what does this gentleman conceive?   95
    How do you, madam? How do you, my good lady?
Desdemona: Faith, half asleep.°
Emilia: Good madam, what's the matter with my lord?
Desdemona: With who?
Emilia: Why, with my lord, madam.   100
Desdemona: Who is thy lord?
Emilia: He that is yours, sweet lady.
Desdemona: I have none. Do not talk to me, Emilia.
    I cannot weep; nor answer have I none
    But what should go by water. Prithee to-night
    Lay on my bed my wedding sheets, remember;   105
    And call thy husband hither.
Emilia: Here's a change indeed!   *Exit.*
Desdemona: 'Tis meet I should be used so, very meet.
    How have I been behaved, that he might stick
    The small'st opinion° on my least misuse?°

    Enter Iago and Emilia.

---

88 *cry you mercy:* Beg your pardon.   97 *half asleep:* i.e., stunned.   109 *small'st opinion:* Least suspicion; *least misuse:* Slightest misconduct.

Iago: What is your pleasure, madam? How is't with you?   110
Desdemona: I cannot tell. Those that do teach young babes
     Do it with gentle means and easy tasks:
     He might have chid me so; for, in good faith,
     I am a child to chiding.
Iago: What is the matter, lady?
Emilia: Alas, Iago, my lord hath so bewhored her,   115
     Thrown such despite and heavy terms upon her
     As true hearts cannot bear.
Desdemona: Am I that name, Iago?
Iago: What name, fair lady?
Desdemona: Such as she said my lord did say I was.   120
Emilia: He called her whore. A beggar in his drink
     Could not have laid such terms upon his callet.°
Iago: Why did he so?
Desdemona: I do not know; I am sure I am none such.
Iago: Do not weep, do not weep. Alas the day!
Emilia: Hath she forsook so many noble matches,   125
     Her father and her country, and her friends,
     To be called whore? Would it not make one weep?
Desdemona: It is my wretched fortune.
Iago: Beshrew him for't!
     How comes this trick° upon him?
Desdemona: Nay, heaven doth know.
Emilia: I will be hanged if some eternal villain,   130
     Some busy and insinuating rogue,
     Some cogging, cozening° slave, to get some office,
     Have not devised this slander. I'll be hanged else.
Iago: Fie, there is no such man! It is impossible.
Desdemona: If any such there be, heaven pardon him!   135
Emilia: A halter pardon him! and hell gnaw his bones!
     Why should he call her whore? Who keeps her company?
     What place? what time? what form? what likelihood?
     The Moor 's abused by some most villainous knave,
     Some base notorious knave, some scurvy fellow.   140
     O heaven, that such companions° thou'dst unfold,°
     And put in every honest hand a whip
     To lash the rascals naked through the world
     Even from the east to th' west!
Iago: Speak within door.°
Emilia: O, fie upon them! Some such squire he was   145
     That turned your wit the seamy side without

---

122 *callet:* Whore.   129 *trick:* Freakish behavior.   132 *cogging, cozening*: Cheating, defrauding.   141 *companions:* Rogues; *unfold:* Expose.   144 *within door:* With restraint.

And made you to suspect me with the Moor.
Iago: You are a fool. Go to.
Desdemona: Alas, Iago,
  What shall I do to win my lord again?
  Good friend, go to him; for, by this light of heaven,   150
  I know not how I lost him. Here I kneel:
  If e'er my will did trespass 'gainst his love
  Either in discourse° of thought or actual deed,
  Or that mine eyes, mine ears, or any sense
  Delighted them in any other form,   155
  Or that I do not yet, and ever did,
  And ever will (though he do shake me off
  To beggarly divorcement) love him dearly,
  Comfort forswear° me! Unkindness may do much;
  And his unkindness may defeat° my life,   160
  But never taint my love. I cannot say "whore."
  It does abhor me now I speak the word;
  To do the act that might the addition earn
  Not the world's mass of vanity could make me.
Iago: I pray you be content. 'Tis but his humor.   165
  The business of the state does him offense,
  [And he does chide with you.]
Desdemona: If 'twere no other —
Iago: 'Tis but so, I warrant.

  [*Trumpets within.*]

  Hark how these instruments summon you to supper.
  The messengers of Venice stay the meat: 170
  Go in, and weep not. All things shall be well.
                              Exeunt Desdemona and Emilia.

  Enter Roderigo.

  How now, Roderigo?
Roderigo: I do not find that thou deal'st justly with me.
Iago: What in the contrary?
Roderigo: Every day thou daff'st me with some device,° Iago, and   175
  rather, as it seems to me now, keep'st from me all conveniency°
  than suppliest me with the least advantage of hope. I will indeed
  no longer endure it; nor am I yet persuaded to put up in peace
  what already I have foolishly suffered.
Iago: Will you hear me, Roderigo?   180

---

153 *discourse:* Course.   159 *Comfort forswear:* Happiness forsake.   160 *defeat:*
Destroy.   175 *thou . . . device:* You put me off with some trick.   176 *conveniency:*
Favorable opportunities.

Roderigo: Faith, I have heard too much; for your words and performances are no kin together.

Iago: You charge me most unjustly.

Roderigo: With naught but truth. I have wasted myself out of my
means. The jewels you have had from me to deliver Desdemona   185
would half have corrupted a votarist.° You have told me she hath
received them, and returned me expectations and comforts of
sudden respect° and acquaintance; but I find none.

Iago: Well, go to; very well.

Roderigo: Very well! go to! I cannot go to, man; nor 'tis not very well.   190
By this hand, I say 'tis very scurvy, and begin to find myself fopped°
in it.

Iago: Very well.

Roderigo: I tell you 'tis not very well. I will make myself known to
Desdemona. If she will return me my jewels, I will give over my   195
suit and repent my unlawful solicitation; if not, assure yourself I
will seek satisfaction of you.

Iago: You have said now.

Roderigo: Ay, and said nothing but what I protest intendment of
doing.   200

Iago: Why, now I see there's mettle in thee; and even from this instant do
build on thee a better opinion than ever before. Give me thy hand,
Roderigo. Thou has taken against me a most just exception; but yet I
protest I have dealt most directly° in thy affair.

Roderigo: It hath not appeared.   205

Iago: I grant indeed it hath not appeared, and your suspicion is not
without wit and judgment. But, Roderigo, if thou hast that in thee
indeed which I have greater reason to believe now than ever, I
mean purpose, courage, and valor, this night show it. If thou the
next night following enjoy not Desdemona, take me from this world   210
with treachery and devise engines for° my life.

Roderigo: Well, what is it? Is it within reason and compass?

Iago: Sir, there is especial commission come from Venice to depute
Cassio in Othello's place.

Roderigo: Is that true? Why, then Othello and Desdemona return again   215
to Venice.

Iago: O, no; he goes into Mauritania and takes away with him the fair
Desdemona, unless his abode be lingered here° by some
accident; wherein none can be so determinate° as the removing of
Cassio.   220

Roderigo: How do you mean removing of him?

---

186 *votarist:* Nun.   188 *sudden respect:* Immediate notice.   191 *fopped:* Duped.
204 *directly:* Straightforwardly.   210–11 *engines for:* Plots against.   218 *abode . . .
here:* Stay here be extended.   219 *determinate:* Effective.

Iago: Why, by making him uncapable of Othello's place — knocking
　　out his brains.

Roderigo: And that you would have me to do?

Iago: Ay, if you dare do yourself a profit and a right. He sups to-night 225
　　with a harlotry, and thither will I go to him. He knows not yet of his
　　honorable fortune. If you will watch his going thence, which I will
　　fashion to fall out between twelve and one, you may take him at your
　　pleasure. I will be near to second your attempt, and he shall fall
　　between us. Come, stand not amazed at it, but go along with me. 230
　　I will show you such a necessity in his death that you shall think
　　yourself bound to put it on him. It is now high supper time, and the
　　night grows to waste. About it!

Roderigo: I will hear further reason for this.

Iago: And you shall be satisfied.　　　　　　　　　　　*Exeunt.* 235

SCENE III:　*Within the castle.*

　　Enter Othello, Lodovico, Desdemona, Emilia, and Attendants.

Lodovico: I do beseech you, sir, trouble yourself no further.

Othello: O, pardon me; 'twill do me good to walk.

Lodovico: Madam, good night. I humbly thank your ladyship.

Desdemona: Your honor is most welcome.

Othello:　　　　　　　　　　　Will you walk, sir?
　　O, Desdemona —　　　　　　　　　　　　　　　　　5

Desdemona: My lord?

Othello: Get you to bed on th' instant; I will be returned forthwith.
　　Dismiss your attendant there. Look't be done.

Desdemona: I will, my lord.

　　Exit [Othello, with Lodovico and Attendants].

Emilia: How goes it now? He looks gentler than he did.　　　　10

Desdemona: He says he will return incontinent.°
　　He hath commanded me to go to bed,
　　And bade me to dismiss you.

Emilia:　　　　　　　　　Dismiss me?

Desdemona: It was his bidding; therefore, good Emilia,
　　Give me my nightly wearing, and adieu.　　　　　　　15
　　We must not now displease him.

Emilia: I would you had never seen him!

Desdemona: So would not I. My love doth so approve him
　　That even his stubbornness,° his checks,° his frowns —
　　Prithee unpin me — have grace and favor in them.　　　20

Emilia: I have laid those sheets you bade me on the bed.

Desdemona: All's one. Good faith, how foolish are our minds!

Scene III.　11 *incontinent:* At once.　19 *stubbornness:* Roughness;　*checks:* Rebukes.

If I do die before thee, prithee shroud me
In one of those same sheets.
Emilia: Come, come! You talk.
Desdemona: My mother had a maid called Barbary.   25
She was in love; and he she loved proved mad°
And did forsake her. She had a song of "Willow";
An old thing 'twas; but it expressed her fortune,
And she died singing it. That song to-night
Will not go from my mind; I have much to do   30
But to go hang my head all at one side
And sing it like poor Barbary. Prithee dispatch.
Emilia: Shall I go fetch your nightgown?°
Desdemona: No, unpin me here.
This Lodovico is a proper man.
Emilia: A very handsome man.   35
Desdemona: He speaks well.
Emilia: I know a lady in Venice would have walked barefoot to
Palestine for a touch of his nether lip.
Desdemona (sings): "The poor soul sat sighing by a sycamore tree
Sing all a green willow;   40
Her hand on her bosom, her head on her knee,
Sing willow, willow, willow.
The fresh streams ran by her and murmured her moans;
Sing willow, willow, willow;
Her salt tears fell from her, and soft'ned the stones" —   45
Lay by these.
"Sing willow, willow, willow" —
Prithee hie thee;° he'll come anon.
"Sing all a green willow must be my garland.
Let nobody blame him; his scorn I approve" —   50
Nay, that's not next. Hark! who is't that knocks?
Emilia: It's the wind.
Desdemona (sings): "I call my love false love; but what said he then?
Sing willow, willow, willow:
If I court moe women, you'll couch with moe men."   55
So get thee gone; good night. Mine eyes do itch.
Doth that bode weeping?
Emilia: 'Tis neither here nor there.
Desdemona: I have heard it said so. O, these men, these men!
Dost thou in conscience think — tell me, Emilia —
That there be women do abuse their husbands   60
In such gross kind?
Emilia: There be some such, no question.

---

26 *mad:* Wild, faithless.   33 *nightgown:* Dressing gown.   48 *hie thee:* Hurry.

Desdemona: Wouldst thou do such a deed for all the world?
Emilia: Why, would not you?
Desdemona: No, by this heavenly light!
Emilia: Nor I neither by this heavenly light.
    I might do't as well i' th' dark.   65
Desdemona: Wouldst thou do such a deed for all the world?
Emilia: The world's a huge thing; it is a great price for a small vice.
Desdemona: In troth, I think thou wouldst not.
Emilia: In troth, I think I should; and undo't when I had done it. Marry, I
    would not do such a thing for a joint-ring,° nor for measures of lawn,   70
    nor for gowns, petticoats, nor caps, nor any petty exhibition;° but,
    for all the whole world — 'Ud's pity! who would not make her husband
    a cuckold to make him a monarch? I should venture purgatory for't.
Desdemona: Beshrew me if I would do such a wrong
    For the whole world.   75
Emilia: Why, the wrong is but a wrong i' th' world; and having the world
    for your labor, 'tis a wrong in your own world, and you might quickly
    make it right.
Desdemona: I do not think there is any such woman.
Emilia: Yes, a dozen; and as many to th' vantage° as   80
    would store° the world they played for.
    But I do think it is their husbands' faults
    If wives do fall. Say that they slack their duties
    And pour our treasures into foreign laps;
    Or else break out in peevish° jealousies,   85
    Throwing restraint upon us; or say they strike us,
    Or scant our former having° in despite —
    Why, we have galls;° and though we have some grace,
    Yet have we some revenge. Let husbands know
    Their wives have sense like them. They see, and smell,   90
    And have their palates both for sweet and sour,
    As husbands have. What is it that they do
    When they change us for others? Is it sport?
    I think it is. And doth affection breed it?
    I think it doth. Is't frailty that thus errs?   95
    It is so too. And have not we affections,
    Desires for sport, and frailty, as men have?
    Then let them use us well; else let them know,
    The ills we do, their ills instruct us so.
Desdemona: Good night, good night. God me such usage° send,   100
    Not to pick bad from bad, but by bad mend!   *Exeunt.*

---

70 *joint-ring:* Ring made in separable halves.   71 *exhibition:* Gift.   80 *toth'
vantage:* Besides.   81 *store:* Populate.   85 *peevish:* Senseless.   87 *having:* Allowance.   88 *galls:* Spirits to resent.   100 *usage:* Habits.

ACT V

SCENE I: *A street in Cyprus.*

Enter Iago and Roderigo.

Iago: Here, stand behind this bulk;° straight will he come.
Wear thy good rapier bare, and put it home.
Quick, quick! Fear nothing; I'll be at thy elbow.
It makes us, or it mars us — think on that,
And fix most firm thy resolution.   5
Roderigo: Be near at hand; I may miscarry in't.
Iago: Here, at thy hand. Be bold, and take thy stand.

[Stands aside.]

Roderigo: I have no great devotion to the deed,
And yet he hath given me satisfying reasons.
'Tis but a man gone. Forth my sword! He dies!   10
Iago: I have rubbed this young quat° almost to the sense,°
And he grows angry. Now whether he kill Cassio,
Or Cassio him, or each do kill the other,
Every way makes my gain. Live Roderigo,
He calls me to a restitution large   15
Of gold and jewels that I bobbed° from him
As gifts to Desdemona.
It must not be. If Cassio do remain,
He hath a daily beauty in his life
That makes me ugly; and besides, the Moor   20
May unfold me to him; there stand I in much peril.
No, he must die. Be't so! I hear him coming.

Enter Cassio.

Roderigo: I know his gait. 'Tis he. Villain, thou diest!

[Makes a pass at Cassio.]

Cassio: That thrust had been mine enemy indeed
But that my coat° is better than thou know'st.   25
I will make proof of thine.

[Draws, and wounds Roderigo.]

Roderigo: O, I am slain!

[Iago darts from concealment behind Cassio, wounds him in the leg, and exit.]

Act V, Scene I.   1 *bulk:* Projecting shop-front.   11 *quat:* Pimple;   *sense:* Quick.
16 *bobbed:* Swindled.   25 *coat:* Undershirt of mail.

Cassio: I am maimed for ever. Help, ho! Murder! murder!

> [*Falls.*]
> *Enter Othello.*

Othello: The voice of Cassio. Iago keeps his word.
Roderigo: O, villain that I am!
Othello: It is even so.
Cassio: O, help, ho! light! a surgeon!   30
Othello: 'Tis he. O brave Iago, honest and just,
> That hast such noble sense of thy friend's wrong!
> Thou teachest me. Minion,° your dear lies dead,
> And your unblest fate hies.° Strumpet, I come.
> Forth of my heart those charms, thine eyes, are blotted.   35
> Thy bed, lust-stained, shall with lust's blood be spotted.

> > > > > > > > > > > *Exit Othello.*

> *Enter Lodovico and Gratiano.*

Cassio: What, ho? No watch? No passage?° Murder! murder!
Gratiano: 'Tis some mischance. The voice is very direful.
Cassio: O, help!
Lodovico: Hark!
Roderigo: O wretched villain!   40
Lodovico: Two or three groan. 'Tis a heavy° night.
> These may be counterfeits. Let's think't unsafe
> To come in to the cry without more help.
Roderigo: Nobody come? Then shall I bleed to death.   45
Lodovico: Hark!

> *Enter Iago, with a light.*

Gratiano: Here's one comes in his shirt, with light and weapons.
Iago: Who's there? Whose noise is this that cries on° murder?
Lodovico: We do not know.
Iago: Did not you hear a cry?
Cassio: Here, here! For heaven's sake, help me!
Iago: What's the matter?   50
Gratiano: This is Othello's ancient, as I take it.
Lodovico: The same indeed, a very valiant fellow.
Iago: What are you here that cry so grievously?
Cassio: Iago? O, I am spoiled, undone by villains!
> Give me some help.   55
Iago: O me, lieutenant! What villains have done this?
Cassio: I think that one of them is hereabout

---

33 *Minion:* Mistress.   34 *hies:* Hurries on.   37 *passage:* Passersby.   42 *heavy:*
Cloudy, dark.   48 *cries on:* Raises the cry of.

And cannot make° away.

Iago: O treacherous villains!

   [To Lodovico and Gratiano.]

What are you there? Come in, and give some help.

Roderigo: O, help me here!   60

Cassio: That's one of them.

Iago: O murd'rous slave! O villain!

   [Stabs Roderigo.]

Roderigo: O damned Iago! O inhuman dog!

Iago: Kill men i' th' dark? — Where be these bloody thieves? —
   How silent is this town! — Ho! murder! murder! —
   What may you be? Are you of good or evil?   65

Lodovico: As you shall prove us, praise us.

Iago: Signior Lodovico?

Lodovico: He, sir.

Iago: I cry you mercy. Here's Cassio hurt by villains.

Gratiano: Cassio?   70

Iago: How is't, brother?

Cassio: My leg is cut in two.

Iago: Marry,° heaven forbid!
   Light, gentlemen. I'll bind it with my shirt.

   Enter Bianca.

Bianca: What is the matter, ho? Who is't that cried?

Iago: Who is't that cried?   75

Bianca: O my dear Cassio! my sweet Cassio!
   O Cassio, Cassio, Cassio!

Iago: O notable strumpet! — Cassio, may you suspect
   Who they should be that have thus mangled you?

Cassio: No.   80

Gratiano: I am sorry to find you thus. I have been to seek you.

Iago: Lend me a garter. So. O for a chair°
   To bear him easily hence!

Bianca: Alas, he faints! O Cassio, Cassio, Cassio!

Iago: Gentlemen all, I do suspect this trash   85
   To be a party in this injury. —
   Patience a while, good Cassio. — Come, come!
   Lend me a light. Know we this face or no?
   Alas, my friend and my dear countryman
   Roderigo? No — Yes, sure. — O heaven, Roderigo!   90

---

58 *make:* Get.   73 *Marry:* (From "By Mary").   82 *chair:* Litter.

Gratiano: What, of Venice?
Iago: Even he, sir. Did you know him?
Gratiano: Know him? Ay.
Iago: Signior Gratiano? I cry your gentle pardon.
    These bloody accidents must excuse my manners
    That so neglected you.
Gratiano: I am glad to see you.   95
Iago: How do you, Cassio? — O, a chair, a chair!
Gratiano: Roderigo?
Iago: He, he, 'tis he!

    [A chair brought in.]

    O, that's well said;° the chair.
    Some good man bear him carefully from hence.   100
    I'll fetch the general's surgeon. *[To Bianca.]* For you, mistress,
    Save you your labor. — He that lies slain here, Cassio,
    Was my dear friend. What malice was between you?
Cassio: None in the world; nor do I know the man.
Iago [to Bianca]: What, look you pale? — O, bear him out o' th' air.   105

    [Cassio and Roderigo are borne off.]

    Stay you, good gentlemen. — Look you pale, mistress? —
    Do you perceive the gastness° of her eye? —
    Nay, if you stare, we shall hear more anon.
    Behold her well; I pray you look upon her.
    Do you see, gentlemen? Nay, guiltiness will speak.   110
    Though tongues were out of use.

    Enter Emilia.

Emilia: 'Las, what is the matter? What's the matter, husband?
Iago: Cassio hath here been set on in the dark
    By Roderigo, and fellows that are scaped.
    He's almost slain, and Roderigo dead.   115
Emilia: Alas, good gentlemen! alas, good Cassio!
Iago: This is the fruits of whoring. Prithee, Emilia,
    Go know of Cassio where he supped to-night.

    [To Bianca.]

    What, do you shake at that?
Bianca: He supped at my house; but I therefore shake not.   120
Iago: O, did he so? I charge you go with me.
Emilia: Fie, fie upon thee, strumpet!
Bianca: I am no strumpet, but of life as honest°
    As you that thus abuse me.
Emilia: As I? Foh! fie upon thee!

---

99 *well said:* Well done.   107 *gastness:* Terror.   123 *honest:* Chaste.

Iago: Kind gentlemen, let's go see poor Cassio dressed.   125
    [To Bianca.]

    Come, mistress, you must tell's another tale.
    Emilia, run you to the citadel
    And tell my lord and lady what hath happed.
                            [Exit Emilia.]
    Will you go on afore?   *Exeunt [all but Iago].*
               This is the night
    That either makes me or fordoes° me quite.   *[Exit.]*   130

Scene II: *A bedchamber in the castle.*

    Desdemona [asleep] in her bed. Enter Othello with a light.

Othello: It is the cause, it is the cause,° my soul.
    Let me not name it to you, you chaste stars!
    It is the cause. Yet I'll not shed her blood,
    Nor scar that whiter skin of hers than snow,
    And smooth as monumental alabaster.   5
    Yet she must die, else she'll betray more men.
    Put out the light, and then put out the light.
    If I quench thee, thou flaming minister,°
    I can again thy former light restore,
    Should I repent me; but once put out thy light,   10
    Thou cunning'st pattern of excelling nature,
    I know not where is that Promethean heat°
    That can thy light relume.° When I have plucked thy rose,
    I cannot give it vital growth again;
    It needs must wither. I'll smell thee on the tree.   15

    (He kisses her.)

    O balmy breath, that dost almost persuade
    Justice to break her sword! One more, one more!
    Be thus when thou art dead, and I will kill thee,
    And love thee after. One more, and that's the last!
    So sweet was ne'er so fatal. I must weep,   20
    But they are cruel tears. This sorrow's heavenly;
    It strikes where it doth love. She wakes.
Desdemona: Who's there? Othello?
Othello: Ay, Desdemona.
Desdemona: Will you come to bed, my lord?
Othello: Have you prayed to-night, Desdemon?
Desdemona: Ay, my lord.   25

---

130 *fordoes:* Destroys. **Scene II.** 1 *cause:* Cause of justice. 8 *minister:* Servant.
12 *Promethean heat:* Divine fire. 13 *relume:* Relight.

Othello: If you bethink yourself of any crime°
    Unreconciled as yet to heaven and grace,
    Solicit for it straight.
Desdemona: Alack, my lord, what may you mean by that?
Othello: Well, do it, and be brief; I will walk by.   30
    I would not kill thy unprepparèd spirit.
    No, heaven forfend!° I would not kill thy soul.
Desdemona: Talk you of killing?
Othello: Ay, I do.
Desdemona: Then heaven
    Have mercy on me!
Othello: Amen, with all my heart!
Desdemona: If you say so, I hope you will not kill me.   35
Othello: Hum!
Desdemona: And yet I fear you; for you're fatal then
    When your eyes roll so. Why I should fear I know not,
    Since guiltiness I know not; but yet I feel I fear.
Othello: Think on thy sins.
Desdemona: They are loves I bear to you.   40
Othello: Ay, and for that thou diest.
Desdemona: That death's unnatural that kills for loving.
    Alas, why gnaw you so your nether lip?
    Some bloody passion shakes your very frame.
    These are portents,° but yet I hope, I hope,   45
    They do not point on me.
Othello: Peace and be still!
Desdemona: I will so. What's the matter?
Othello: That handkerchief which I so loved and gave thee
    Thou gav'st to Cassio.
Desdemona: No, by my life and soul!
    Send for the man and ask him.
Othello: Sweet soul, take heed,   50
    Take heed of perjury; thou art on thy deathbed.

Desdemona: Ay, but not yet to die.
Othello: Yes, presently.°
    Therefore confess thee freely of thy sin;
    For to deny each article with oath
    Cannot remove nor choke the strong conception°   55
    That I do groan withal. Thou art to die.
Desdemona: Then Lord have mercy on me!
Othello: I say amen.
Desdemona: And have you mercy too! I never did

---

26 *crime:* Sin.   32 *forfend:* Forbid.   45 *portents:* Signs of impending violence.
52 *presently:* At once.   55 *conception:* Belief.

Offend° you in my life; never loved Cassio
But with such general warranty of heaven   60
As I might love. I never gave him token.
Othello: By heaven, I saw my handkerchief in's hand!
O perjured woman! thou dost stone my heart,°
And mak'st me call what I intend to do
A murder, which I thought a sacrifice.   65
I saw the handkerchief.
Desdemona: He found it then.
I never gave it him. Send for him hither.
Let him confess a truth.
Othello: He hath confessed.
Desdemona: What, my lord?
Othello: That he hath used thee.
Desdemona: How? Unlawfully?
Othello: Ay.   70
Desdemona: He will not say so.
Othello: No, his mouth is stopped.
Honest Iago hath ta'en order° for't.
Desdemona: O, my fear interprets. What, is he dead?
Othello: Had all his hairs been lives, my great revenge
Had stomach for them all.   75
Desdemona: Alas, he is betrayed, and I undone!
Othello: Out, strumpet! Weep'st thou for him to my face?
Desdemona: O, banish me, my lord, but kill me not!
Othello: Down, strumpet!
Desdemona: Kill me to-morrow; let me live to-night!   80
Othello: Nay, if you strive —
Desdemona: But half an hour!
Othello: Being done, there is no pause.
Desdemona: But while I say one prayer!
Othello: It is too late.

(*Smothers her.*)

[*Desdemona:* O Lord, Lord, Lord!]

Emilia at the door.

Emilia (calls within): My lord, my lord! What, ho! my lord, my lord!   85
Othello: What noise is this? Not dead? not yet quite dead?
I that am cruel am yet merciful;
I would not have thee linger in thy pain.
So, so.

---

59 *Offend:* Wrong.   63 *stone my heart:* Turn my heart to stone.   72 *ta'en order:* Taken measures.

Emilia (within): What, ho! my lord, my lord!
Othello: Who's there?   90
Emilia (within): O, good my lord, I would speak a word with you!
Othello: Yes, 'tis Emilia. — By and by.° — She's dead. —
    'Tis like she comes to speak of Cassio's death.
    The noise was high. Ha! no more moving?
    Still as the grave. — Shall she come in? Were't good! —   95
    I think she stirs again. No. — What's best to do?
    If she come in, she'll sure speak to my wife.
    My wife! my wife! what wife? I have no wife.
    O, insupportable! O heavy hour!
    Methinks it should be now a huge eclipse   100
    Of sun and moon, and that th' affrighted globe
    Should yawn° at alteration.
Emilia (within):   I do beseech you
    That I may speak with you, O good my lord!
Othello: I had forgot thee. O, come in, Emilia.
    Soft, by and by. — Let me the curtains draw. —   105

    [Closes the bed-curtains.]

    Where art thou?

    [Opens the door.]
    Enter Emilia.

              What's the matter with thee now?
Emilia: O my good lord, yonder's foul murder done!
Othello: What? Now?
Emilia: But now, my lord.
Othello: It is the very error° of the moon.   110
    She comes more nearer earth than she was wont
    And makes men mad.
Emilia: Cassio, my lord, hath killed a young Venetian
    Called Roderigo.
Othello: Roderigo killed?
    And Cassio killed?
Emilia: No, Cassio is not killed.   115
Othello: Not Cassio killed? Then murder's out of tune,
    And sweet revenge grows harsh.
Desdemona: O, falsely, falsely murdered?
Emilia: O, Lord! what cry is that?
Othello: That? What?
Emilia: Out and alas! that was my lady's voice.   120

---

92 *By and by:* Just a moment (addressed to Emilia).   102 *yawn:* Open, as in an earthquake.   110 *error:* Straying off course.

Help! help, ho! help! O lady, speak again!
Sweet Desdemona! O sweet mistress, speak!
Desdemona: A guiltless death I die.
Emilia: O, who hath done this deed?
Desdemona: Nobody — I myself. Farewell. 125
Commend° me to my kind lord. O, farewell!

(She dies.)

Othello: Why, how should she be murd'red?
Emilia: Alas, who knows?
Othello: You heard her say herself, it was not I.
Emilia: She said so. I must needs report the truth.
Othello: She's like a liar gone to burning hell! 130
'Twas I that killed her.
Emilia: O, the more angel she,
And you the blacker devil!
Othello: She turned to folly, and she was a whore.
Emilia: Thou dost belie her, and thou art a devil.
Othello: She was false as water.°
Emilia: Thou art rash as fire to say 135
That she was false. O, she was heavenly true!
Othello: Cassio did top her. Ask thy husband else.
O, I were damned beneath all depth in hell
But that I did proceed upon just grounds
To this extremity. Thy husband knew it all. 140
Emilia: My husband?
Othello: Thy husband.
Emilia: That she was false to wedlock?
Othello: Ay, with Cassio. Nay, had she been true,
If heaven would make me such another world
Of one entire and perfect chrysolite,° 145
I'ld not have sold her for it.
Emilia: My husband?
Othello: Ay 'twas he that told me on her first.
An honest man he is, and hates the slime
That sticks on filthy deeds.
Emilia: My husband? 150
Othello: What needs this iterance,° woman? I say thy husband.
Emilia: O mistress, villainy hath made mocks with love!
My husband say that she was false?
Othello: He, woman.
I say, thy husband. Dost understand the word?
My friend, thy husband; honest, honest Iago. 155

---

126 *Commend:* Remember.   135 *water:* (Which is yielding).   146 *chrysolite:* (Precious topaz).   151 *iterance:* Repetition.

Emilia: If he say so, may his pernicious soul
    Rot half a grain a day! he lies to th' heart.
    She was too fond of her most filthy bargain.
Othello: Ha!
Emilia: Do thy worst.   160
    This deed of thine is no more worthy heaven
    Than thou wast worthy her.
Othello: Peace, you were best.
Emilia: Thou hast not half the power to do me harm
    As I have to be hurt.° O gull! O dolt!
    As ignorant as dirt! thou hast done a deed —   165
    I care not for thy sword; I'll make thee known,
    Though I lost twenty lives. Help! help! Ho! help!
    The Moor hath killed my mistress! Murder! murder!

Enter Montano, Gratiano, Iago, and others.

Montano: What is the matter? How now, general?
Emilia: O, are you come, Iago? You have done well,   170
    That men must lay their murders on your neck.
Gratiano: What is the matter?
Emilia: Disprove this villain, if thou be'st a man.
    He says thou told'st him that his wife was false.
    I know thou didst not; thou'rt not such a villain.   175
    Speak, for my heart is full.
Iago: I told him what I thought, and told no more
    Than what he found himself was apt and true.
Emilia: But did you ever tell him she was false?
Iago: I did.   180
Emilia: You told a lie, an odious damnèd lie!
    Upon my soul, a lie! a wicked lie!
    She false with Cassio? Did you say with Cassio?
Iago: With Cassio, mistress. Go to, charm° your tongue.
Emilia: I will not charm my tongue; I am bound to speak: 185
    My mistress here lies murdered in her bed —
All: O heavens forfend!
Emilia: And your reports have set the murder on.
Othello: Nay, stare not, masters. It is true indeed.
Gratiano: 'Tis a strange truth.   190
Montano: O monstrous act!
Emilia: Villainy, villainy, villainy!
    I think upon't — I think I smell't! — O villainy!
    I thought so then. — I'll kill myself for grief. —
    O villainy, villainy!
Iago: What, are you mad? I charge you get you home.   195

---

164 *to be hurt:* To endure hurt.   184 *charm:* Cast a spell on.

Emilia: Good gentlemen, let me have leave to speak.
        'Tis proper I obey him, but not now.
        Perchance, Iago, I will ne'er go home.
Othello: O! O! O!   *(Falls on the bed.)*
Emilia: Nay, lay thee down and roar!
        For thou hast killed the sweetest innocent   200
        That e'er did lift up eye.
Othello: O, she was foul!

    [Rises.]

    I scarce did know you, uncle. There lies your niece,
    Whose breath, indeed, these hands have newly stopped.
    I know this act shows° horrible and grim.
Gratiano: Poor Desdemon! I am glad thy father's dead.   205
        Thy match was mortal to him, and pure grief
        Shore his old thread in twain. Did he live now,
        This sight would make him do a desperate turn;°
        Yea, curse his better angel from his side,
        And fall to reprobation.°   210
Othello: 'Tis pitiful; but yet Iago knows
        That she with Cassio hath the act of shame
        A thousand times committed. Cassio confessed it;
        And she did gratify° his amorous works
        With that recognizance° and pledge of love   215
        Which I first gave her. I saw it in his hand.
        It was a handkerchief, an antique token
        My father gave my mother.
Emilia: O God! O heavenly God!
Iago: Zounds, hold your peace!
Emilia: 'Twill out, 'twill out! I peace?   220
        No, I will speak as liberal as the north,°
        Let heaven and men and devils, let them all,
        All, all, cry shame against me, yet I'll speak.
Iago: Be wise, and get you home.
Emilia: I will not.

    [Iago draws and threatens Emilia.]

Gratiano: Fie!
        Your sword upon a woman?   225
Emilia: O thou dull Moor, that handkerchief thou speak'st of
        I found by fortune, and did give my husband;
        For often with a solemn earnestness —
        More than indeed belonged to such a trifle —

---

204 *shows:* Appears. 208 *turn:* Act. 210 *reprobation:* Rejection by God, damnation. 214 *gratify:* Reward. 215 *recognizance:* Token. 221 *liberal as the north:* Unchecked as the north wind blows.

He begged of me to steal't.

Iago:　　　　　　　　　　　　Villainous whore!　　　　　　　　　　230

Emilia: She give it Cassio? No, alas, I found it,
　　　And I did give't my husband.

Iago:　　　　　　　　　　　　Filth, thou liest!

Emilia: By heaven, I do not, I do not, gentlemen.
　　　O murd'rous coxcomb! what should such a fool
　　　Do with so good a wife?

Othello:　　　　　　　　Are there no stones° in heaven　　235
　　　But what serves for the thunder? Precious villain!

*The Moor runs at Iago [but is disarmed by Montano].
Iago kills his wife.*

Gratiano: The woman falls. Sure he hath killed his wife.

Emilia: Ay, ay. O, lay me by my mistress' side.　　　　*Exit Iago.*

Gratiano: He's gone, but his wife's killed.

Montano: 'Tis a notorious° villain. Take you this weapon,　　240
　　　Which I have here recovered from the Moor.
　　　Come, guard the door without. Let him not pass,
　　　But kill him rather. I'll after that same villain,
　　　For 'tis a damnèd slave.

Exit [Montano, with all but Othello and Emilia].

Othello:　　　　　　　　　I am not valiant neither;
　　　But every puny whipster° gets my sword.　　　　　　245
　　　But why should honor outlive honesty?
　　　Let it go all.

Emilia:　　　　　　What did thy song bode, lady?
　　　Hark, canst thou hear me? I will play the swan,
　　　And die in music. *[Sings.]* "Willow, willow, willow."
　　　Moor, she was chaste. She loved thee, cruel Moor:　　250
　　　So come my soul to bliss as I speak true.
　　　So speaking as I think, alas, I die.

(She dies.)

Othello: I have another weapon in this chamber;
　　　It is a sword of Spain, the ice brook's° temper.
　　　O, here it is. — Uncle, I must come forth.　　　　　255

Gratiano (within): If thou attempt it, it will cost thee dear.
　　　Thou hast no weapon, and perforce must suffer.

Othello: Look in upon me then and speak with me,
　　　Or, naked° as I am, I will assault thee.

[Enter Gratiano.]

---

235 *stones:* Bolts like those used for thunderbolts.　240 *notorious:* Notable.　245 *puny whipster:* Whippersnapper.　254 *ice brook:* i.e., a Spanish blade, tempered in cold running water.　259 *naked:* Disarmed.

Gratiano: What is the matter?
Othello: Behold, I have a weapon;   260
    A better never did itself sustain
    Upon a soldier's thigh. I have seen the day
    That with this little arm and this good sword
    I have made my way through more impediments
    Than twenty times your stop.° But O vain boast!   265
    Who can control his fate? 'Tis not so now.
    Be not afraid, though you do see me weaponed.
    Here is my journey's end, here is my butt,°
    And very seamark° of my utmost sail:
    Do you go back dismayed? 'Tis a lost° fear.   270
    Man but a rush° against Othello's breast,
    And he retires. Where should Othello go?
    Now, how dost thou look now? O ill-starred wench!
    Pale as thy smock! When we shall meet at compt,°
    This look of thine will hurl my soul from heaven,   275
    And fiends will snatch at it. Cold, cold, my girl?
    Even like thy chastity.
    O cursèd, cursèd slave! Whip me, ye devils,
    From the possession of this heavenly sight!
    Blow me about in winds! roast me in sulphur!   280
    Wash me in steep-down gulfs of liquid fire!
    Oh Desdemon! dead Desdemon! dead! Oh! Oh!

    Enter Lodovico, Montano, Iago [as prisoner], and Officers; Cassio in
    a chair.

Lodovico: Where is this rash and most unfortunate man?
Othello: That's he that was Othello. Here I am.
Lodovico: Where is that viper? Bring the villain forth.   285
Othello: I look down towards his feet° — but that's a fable.
    If that thou be'st a devil, I cannot kill thee.

    [Wounds Iago.]

Lodovico: Wrench his sword from him.

    [Othello is disarmed.]

Iago: I bleed, sir, but not killed.
Othello: I am not sorry neither. I'ld have thee live;
    For in my sense, 'tis happiness to die.   290
Lodovico: O thou Othello that wert once so good,
    Fall'n in the practice° of a damnèd slave,

---

265 *stop:* Power to stop. 268 *butt:* Limit. 269 *seamark:* Beacon, destination.
270 *lost:* Wasted. 271 *Man but a rush:* Wield only a reed. 274 *compt:* Final
accounting, Last Judgment. 286 *I . . . feet:* i.e., to see if they are cloven, like the Devil's.
292 *practice:* Plot.

    What shall be said to thee?
Othello: Why, anything;
    An honorable murderer, if you will;
    For naught did I in hate, but all in honor.   295
Lodovico: This wretch hath part confessed his villainy.
    Did you and he consent in° Cassio's death?
Othello: Ay.
Cassio: Dear general, I never gave you cause.
Othello: I do believe it, and I ask your pardon.   300
    Will you, I pray, demand that demi-devil
    Why he hath thus ensnared my soul and body?
Iago: Demand me nothing. What you know, you know.
    From this time forth I never will speak word.
Lodovico: What, not to pray?
Gratiano: Torments will ope your lips.   305
Othello: Well, thou dost best.
Lodovico: Sir, you shall understand what hath befall'n,
    Which, as I think, you know not. Here is a letter
    Found in the pocket of the slain Roderigo;
    And here another. The one of them imports   310
    The death of Cassio to be undertook
    By Roderigo.
Othello: O villain!
Cassio: Most heathenish and most gross!
Lodovico: Now here's another discontented paper
    Found in the pocket too; and this, it seems,
    Roderigo meant t' have sent this damnèd villain;   315
    But that, belike, Iago in the nick°
    Came in and satisfied him.
Othello: O thou pernicious caitiff! —
    How came you, Cassio, by that handkerchief
    That was my wife's?
Cassio: I found it in my chamber;   320
    And he himself confessed but even now
    That there he dropped it for a special purpose
    Which wrought to his desire.
Othello: O fool! fool! fool!
Cassio: There is besides in Roderigo's letter,
    How he upbraids Iago that he made him
    Brave me upon the watch; whereon it came   325
    That I was cast;° and even but now he spake,
    After long seeming dead — Iago hurt him,
    Iago set him on.

297 *consent in:* Agree upon.   317 *nick:* Nick of time.

Lodovico: You must forsake this room and go with us.   330
    Your power and your command is taken off,
    And Cassio rules in Cyprus. For this slave,
    If there be any cunning cruelty
    That can torment him much and hold him long,
    It shall be his. You shall close prisoner rest   335
    Till that the nature of your fault be known
    To the Venetian state. Come, bring away.
Othello: Soft you! a word or two before you go.
    I have done the state some service, and they know't.
    No more of that. I pray you, in your letters,   340
    When you shall these unlucky° deeds relate,
    Speak of me as I am. Nothing extenuate,
    Nor set down aught in malice. Then must you speak
    Of one that loved not wisely, but too well;
    Of one not easily jealous, but, being wrought,   345
    Perplexed° in the extreme; of one whose hand,
    Like the base Judean,° threw a pearl away
    Richer than all his tribe; of one whose subdued° eyes,
    Albeit unusèd to the melting mood,
    Drop tears as fast as the Arabian trees   350
    Their med'cinable gum. Set you down this.
    And say besides that in Aleppo once,
    Where a malignant and a turbaned Turk
    Beat a Venetian and traduced the state,
    I took by th' throat the circumcisèd dog   355
    And smote him — thus.
    (He stabs himself.)
Lodovico: O bloody period!°
Gratiano: All that's spoke is marred.
Othello: I kissed thee ere I killed thee. No way but this,
    Killing myself, to die upon a kiss.

    (He [falls upon the bed and] dies.)

Cassio: This did I fear, but thought he had no weapon;   360
    For he was great of heart.
Lodovico [to Iago]:   O Spartan dog,
    More fell° than anguish, hunger, or the sea!
    Look on the tragic loading of this bed.
    This is thy work. The object poisons sight;
    Let it be hid.° Gratiano, keep the house,   365
    And seize upon° the fortunes of the Moor,

---

327 *cast:* Dismissed.   341 *unlucky:* Fatal.   346 *Perplexed:* Distracted.   347 *Judean:* Judas Iscariot (?) (quarto reads "Indian").   348 *subdued:* i.e., conquered by grief.   357 *period:* Ending.   362 *fell:* Cruel.   365 *Let it be hid:* i.e., draw the bed curtains.   366 *seize upon:* Take legal possession of.

For they succeed on you. To you, lord governor,
Remains the censure° of this hellish villain,
The time, the place, the torture. O, enforce it!
Myself will straight aboard, and to the state   370
This heavy act with heavy heart relate.

Exeunt.

368 *censure:* Judicial sentence.

Considerations for Critical Thinking and Writing

1. **first response.** Characterize Othello. In what ways is he presented as having a jealous disposition as well as a noble one? Why is he so vulnerable to Iago's villainy?

2. Explain how Iago presents himself to the world. What is beneath the surface of his public identity? Why does he hate Othello so passionately? What makes Iago so effective at manipulating people? What do other characters, besides Othello, think of him?

3. Explain why you think Othello's racial background does or doesn't affect events in the play.

4. How does Othello change during the course of the play? Do you feel the same about him from beginning to end? Trace your response to his character as it develops, paying particular attention to Othello's final speech.

5. Consider how women — Desdemona, Emilia, and Bianca — are presented in the play. What characteristics do they have in common? How do they relate to the men in their lives?

6. Despite its grinding emotional impact and bleak ending, Othello does have its humorous moments. Locate a scene that includes humor and describe its tone and function in the play.

Connection to Another Selection

1. Here's a long reach but a potentially interesting one: Write an essay that considers Desdemona as a wife alongside Nora in Henrik Ibsen's *A Doll's House* (p. 864). How responsible are they to themselves and to others? Can they be discussed in the same breath, or are they from such different worlds that nothing useful can be said about comparing them? Either way, explain your response.

Suggested Topics for Longer Papers

1. Discuss Shakespeare's use of humor in *Othello*. Focus on at least one humorous scene as the basis of your discussion and characterize the tone of the humor. What generalizations can you make about the tone and purpose of the humor in the play?

2. Research how marriage was regarded in Elizabethan times and compare those attitudes and values with the treatment of marriage in *Othello*.

28

Henrik Ibsen and
Modern Drama

A play should give you something to think about. When I see a play and understand it the first time, then I know it can't be much good.

—T. S. ELIOT

MS Am 2560 (177). By permission of the Houghton Library, Harvard University.

REALISM

Realism is a literary technique that attempts to create the appearance of life as it is actually experienced. Characters in modern realistic plays (written during and after the last quarter of the nineteenth century) speak dialogue that we might hear in our daily lives. These characters are not larger than life but representative of it; they seem to speak the way we do rather than in highly poetic language, formal declarations, asides, or soliloquies. It is impossible to imagine a heroic figure such as Oedipus inhabiting a comfortably furnished living room and chatting about his wife's household budget the way Torvald Helmer does in Henrik Ibsen's *A Doll's House* (p. 864). Realism brings into focus commonplace, everyday life rather than the extraordinary kinds of events that make up Sophocles' *Oedipus the King* (p. 716) or Shakespeare's *Othello* (p. 769).

Realistic characters can certainly be heroic, but like Nora Helmer, they find that their strength and courage are tested in the context of events ordinary people might experience. Work, love, marriage, children, and death are often the focus of realistic dramas. These subjects can also constitute much of the material in nonrealistic plays, but modern realistic dramas present such material in the realm of the probable. Conflicts in realistic plays are likely to reflect problems in our own lives. Making ends meet takes precedence over saving a kingdom; middle- and lower-class individuals take center stage as primary characters in main plots rather than being secondary characters in subplots. Thus, we can see why the nineteenth-century movement toward realism paralleled the rise of a middle class eagerly seeking representations of its concerns in the theater.

Before the end of the nineteenth century, however, few attempts were made in the theater to present life as it is actually lived. The chorus's role in Sophocles' *Oedipus the King*, the allegorical figures in morality plays, the remarkable mistaken identities in Shakespeare's comedies, or the rhymed couplets spoken in seventeenth-century plays such as Molière's *Tartuffe* represent theatrical conventions rather than life. Theatergoers have understood and appreciated these conventions for centuries — and still do — but in the nineteenth century in Europe and the United States social, political, and industrial revolutions helped create an atmosphere in which some playwrights found it necessary to create works that more directly reflected their audiences' lives.

Playwrights such as Ibsen and Anton Chekhov refused to join the ranks of their romantic contemporaries, who they felt falsely idealized life. The most popular plays immediately preceding the works of these realistic writers consisted primarily of love stories and action-packed plots. Such **melodramas** offer audiences thrills and chills as well as happy endings. They typically include a virtuous individual struggling under the tyranny of a wicked oppressor, who is defeated only at the last moment. Suspense is reinforced by a series of pursuits, captures, and escapes that move the plot quickly and de-emphasize character or theme. These representations of extreme conflicts enjoyed wide popularity in the nineteenth century — indeed, they still do — because their formula was varied enough to be entertaining yet their outcomes were always comforting to the audience's sense of justice. From the realists' perspective, melodramas were merely escape fantasies that distorted life by refusing to examine the real world closely and objectively. But an indication of the popularity of such happy endings can be seen in Chekhov's farcical comedies, such as *The Proposal*, a one-act play filled with exaggerated characters and action. Despite his realist's values, Chekhov was also sometimes eager to please audiences.

Realists attempted to open their audiences' eyes; to their minds, the only genuine comfort was in knowing the truth. Many of their plays concern controversial issues of the day and focus on people who fall prey to indifferent societal institutions. English dramatist John Galsworthy (1867–1933) examined social values in *Strife* (1909) and *Justice* (1910), two plays whose titles broadly suggest the nature of his concerns. Irish-born playwright George Bernard Shaw (1856–1950) often used comedy and irony as a means of awakening his audiences to contemporary problems: *Arms and the Man* (1894) satirizes romantic attitudes toward war, and *Mrs. Warren's Profession* (1898) indicts a social and economic system that drives a woman to prostitution. Chekhov's major plays are populated by characters frustrated by their social situations and their own sensibilities; they are ordinary people who long for happiness but become entangled in everyday circumstances that limit their lives. Ibsen also took a close look at his characters' daily lives. His plays attack social conventions and challenge popular attitudes toward marriage; he stunned audiences by dramatizing the suffering of a man dying of syphilis.

With these kinds of materials, Ibsen and his contemporaries popularized the ***problem play***, a drama that represents a social issue in order to awaken the audience to it. These plays usually reject romantic plots in favor of holding up a mirror that reflects not simply what audiences want to see but what the playwright sees in them. Nineteenth-century realistic theater was no refuge from the social, economic, and psychological problems that melodrama ignored or sentimentalized.

THEATRICAL CONVENTIONS OF MODERN DRAMA

The picture-frame stage that is often used for realistic plays typically reproduces the setting of a room in some detail. (Brander Matthews, the first American drama professor, pointed out that the invention of the light bulb had much to do with other innovations in modern drama. Lighting is only one of many technological innovations that forever changed the way theater was conceived of in the modern age, which is an age defined largely by rapid technological change.) Within the stage, framed by a proscenium arch (from which the curtain hangs), scenery and props are used to create an illusion of reality. Whether the "small book-case with well-bound books" described in the opening setting of Ibsen's *A Doll's House* is only painted scenery or an actual case with books, it will probably look real to the audience. Removing the fourth wall of a room so that an audience can look in fosters the illusion that the actions onstage are real events happening before unseen spectators. The texture of Nora's life is communicated by the set as well as by what she says and does. That doesn't happen in a play like Sophocles' *Oedipus the King*. Technical effects can make us believe there is wood burning in a fireplace or snow falling outside a window. Outdoor settings are made similarly realistic by props and painted sets. In one of Chekhov's full-length plays, for example, the second act opens in a meadow with the faint outline of a city on the horizon.

In addition to lifelike sets, a particular method of acting is used to create a realistic atmosphere. Actors address each other instead of directing formal speeches toward the audience; they act within the setting, not merely before it. At the beginning of the twentieth century Konstantin Stanislavsky (1863–1938), a Russian director, teacher, and actor, developed a system of acting that was an important influence in realistic theater. He trained actors to identify with the inner emotions of the characters they played. They were encouraged to recall from their own lives emotional responses similar to those they were portraying. The goal was to present a role truthfully by first feeling and then projecting the character's situation. Among Stanislavsky's early successes in this method were the plays of Chekhov.

There are, however, degrees of realism on the stage. Tennessee Williams's *The Glass Menagerie* (1945), for example, is a partially realistic portrayal of characters whose fragile lives are founded on illusions. Williams's dialogue rings true, and individual scenes resemble the kind of real-life action we would imagine such vulnerable characters engaging in, but other elements of the play are nonrealistic. For instance, Williams uses Tom as a major character in the play as well as narrator and stage manager. Here is part of Williams's stage directions: "The narrator is an undisguised convention of the play. He takes whatever license with dramatic convention as is convenient to his purposes." Although this play can be accurately described as including realistic elements, Williams, like many other contemporary playwrights, does not attempt an absolute fidelity to reality. He uses flashbacks to present incidents that occurred before the opening scene because the past impinges so heavily on the present. Most playwrights don't attempt to duplicate reality, since that can now be done so well by movies and television.

Realism needn't lock a playwright into a futile attempt to make everything appear as it is in life. There is no way to avoid theatrical conventions: actors impersonate characters in a setting that is, after all, a stage. Indeed, even the dialogue in a realistic play is quite different from the pauses, sentence fragments, repetitions, silences, and incoherencies that characterize the way people usually speak. Realistic dialogue may seem like ordinary speech, but it, like Shakespeare's poetic language, is constructed. If we remember that realistic drama represents only the appearance of reality and that what we read on a page or see and hear onstage is the result of careful selecting, editing, and even distortion, then we are more likely to appreciate the playwright's art.

A Doll's House

Henrik Ibsen was born in Skien, Norway, to wealthy parents, who lost their money while he was a young boy. His early experiences with small-town life and genteel poverty sensitized him to the problems that he subsequently dramatized in a number of his plays. At age sixteen he was apprenticed to a druggist; he later thought about studying medicine, but by his early twenties he was earning a living writing and directing plays in various

Time Life Pictures/Getty Images.

Norwegian cities. By the time of his death he enjoyed an international reputation for his treatment of social issues related to middle-class life.

Ibsen's earliest dramatic works were historical and romantic plays, some in verse. His first truly realistic work was *The Pillars of Society* (1877), whose title ironically hints at the corruption and hypocrisy exposed in it. The realistic social-problem plays for which he is best known followed. These dramas at once fascinated and shocked international audiences. Among his most produced and admired works are *A Doll's House* (1879), *Ghosts* (1881), *An Enemy of the People* (1882), *The Wild Duck* (1884), and *Hedda Gabler* (1890). The common denominator in many of Ibsen's dramas is his interest in individuals struggling for an authentic identity in the face of tyrannical social conventions. This conflict often results in his characters' being divided between a sense of duty to themselves and their responsibility to others.

Ibsen used such external and internal conflicts to propel his plays' action. Like many of his contemporaries who wrote realistic plays, he adopted the form of the **well-made play**. A dramatic structure popularized in France by Eugène Scribe (1791–1861) and Victorien Sardou (1831–1908), the well-made play employs conventions including plenty of suspense created by meticulous plotting. Extensive exposition explains past events that ultimately lead to an inevitable climax. Tension is released when a secret that reverses the protagonist's fortunes is revealed. Ibsen, having directed a number of Scribe's plays in Norway, knew their cause-to-effect plot arrangements and used them for his own purposes in his problem plays.

A Doll's House dramatizes the tensions of a nineteenth-century middle-class marriage in which a wife struggles to step beyond the limited identity imposed on her by her husband and society. Although the Helmers' pleasant apartment seems an unlikely setting for the fierce conflicts that develop, the issues raised in the play are unmistakably real. *A Doll's House* affirms the necessity to reject hypocrisy, complacency, cowardice, and stifling conventions if life is to have dignity and meaning.

HENRIK IBSEN (1828–1906)

A Doll's House 1879

TRANSLATED BY R. FARQUHARSON SHARP

DRAMATIS PERSONAE

Torvald Helmer
Nora, his wife
Doctor Rank
Mrs. Linde
Nils Krogstad
Helmer's three small children
Anne, their nurse

A Housemaid
A Porter

SCENE: The action takes place in Helmer's house.

ACT I

SCENE: *A room furnished comfortably and tastefully, but not extravagantly. At the back, a door to the right leads to the entrance-hall, another to the left leads to Helmer's study. Between the doors stands a piano. In the middle of the left-hand wall is a door, and beyond it a window. Near the window are a round table, arm-chairs, and a small sofa. In the right-hand wall, at the farther end, another door; and on the same side, nearer the footlights, a stove, two easy chairs, and a rocking-chair; between the stove and the door, a small table. Engravings on the walls; a cabinet with china and other small objects; a small book-case with well-bound books. The floors are carpeted, and a fire burns in the stove. It is winter.*

A bell rings in the hall; shortly afterwards the door is heard to open. Enter Nora, humming a tune and in high spirits. She is in outdoor dress and carries a number of parcels; these she lays on the table to the right. She leaves the outer door open after her, and through it is seen a Porter who is carrying a Christmas Tree and a basket, which he gives to the Maid who has opened the door.

Nora: Hide the Christmas Tree carefully, Helen. Be sure the children do not see it until this evening, when it is dressed. *(To the Porter, taking out her purse.)* How much?

Porter: Sixpence.

Nora: There is a shilling. No, keep the change. *(The Porter thanks her, and goes out. Nora shuts the door. She is laughing to herself, as she takes off her hat and coat. She takes a packet of macaroons from her pocket and eats one or two; then goes cautiously to her husband's door and listens.)* Yes, he is in. *(Still humming, she goes to the table on the right.)*

Helmer (calls out from his room): Is that my little lark twittering out there?

Nora (busy opening some of the parcels): Yes, it is!

Helmer: Is it my little squirrel bustling about?

Nora: Yes!

Helmer: When did my squirrel come home?

Nora: Just now. *(Puts the bag of macaroons into her pocket and wipes her mouth.)* Come in here, Torvald, and see what I have bought.

Helmer: Don't disturb me. *(A little later, he opens the door and looks into the room, pen in hand.)* Bought, did you say? All these things? Has my little spendthrift been wasting money again?

Nora: Yes but, Torvald, this year we really can let ourselves go a little. This is the first Christmas that we have not needed to economise.

Helmer: Still, you know, we can't spend money recklessly.

Nora: Yes, Torvald, we may be a wee bit more reckless now, mayn't we? Just a tiny wee bit! You are going to have a big salary and earn lots and lots of money.

Helmer: Yes, after the New Year; but then it will be a whole quarter before the salary is due.

Nora: Pooh! we can borrow until then.

Helmer: Nora! (*Goes up to her and takes her playfully by the ear.*) The same little featherhead! Suppose, now, that I borrowed fifty pounds to-day, and you spent it all in the Christmas week, and then on New Year's Eve a slate fell on my head and killed me, and —

Nora (putting her hands over his mouth): Oh! don't say such horrid things.

Helmer: Still, suppose that happened, — what then?

Nora: If that were to happen, I don't suppose I should care whether I owed money or not.

Helmer: Yes, but what about the people who had lent it?

Nora: They? Who would bother about them? I should not know who they were.

Helmer: That is like a woman! But seriously, Nora, you know what I think about that. No debt, no borrowing. There can be no freedom or beauty about a home life that depends on borrowing and debt. We two have kept bravely on the straight road so far, and we will go on the same way for the short time longer that there need be any struggle.

Nora (moving towards the stove): As you please, Torvald.

Helmer (following her): Come, come, my little skylark must not droop her wings. What is this! Is my little squirrel out of temper? (*Taking out his purse.*) Nora, what do you think I have got here?

Nora (turning round quickly): Money!

Helmer: There you are. (*Gives her some money.*) Do you think I don't know what a lot is wanted for housekeeping at Christmas-time?

Nora (counting): Ten shillings — a pound — two pounds! Thank you, thank you, Torvald; that will keep me going for a long time.

Helmer: Indeed it must.

Nora: Yes, yes, it will. But come here and let me show you what I have bought. And all so cheap! Look, here is a new suit for Ivar, and a sword; and a horse and a trumpet for Bob; and a doll and dolly's bedstead for Emmy, — they are very plain, but anyway she will soon break them in pieces. And here are dress-lengths and handkerchiefs for the maids; old Anne ought really to have something better.

Helmer: And what is in this parcel?

Nora (crying out): No, no! you mustn't see that until this evening.

Helmer: Very well. But now tell me, you extravagant little person, what would you like for yourself?

Nora: For myself? Oh, I am sure I don't want anything.

Helmer: Yes, but you must. Tell me something reasonable that you would particularly like to have.

Nora: No, I really can't think of anything — unless, Torvald —

Helmer: Well?

Nora (playing with his coat buttons, and without raising her eyes to his): If you really want to give me something, you might — you might —

Helmer: Well, out with it!

Nora (speaking quickly): You might give me money, Torvald. Only just as much as you can afford; and then one of these days I will buy something with it.

Helmer: But, Nora —

Nora: Oh, do! dear Torvald; please, please do! Then I will wrap it up in beautiful gilt paper and hang it on the Christmas Tree. Wouldn't that be fun?

Helmer: What are little people called that are always wasting money?

Nora: Spendthrifts — I know. Let us do as you suggest, Torvald, and then I shall have time to think what I am most in want of. That is a very sensible plan, isn't it?

Helmer (smiling): Indeed it is — that is to say, if you were really to save out of the money I give you, and then really buy something for yourself. But if you spend it all on the housekeeping and any number of unnecessary things, then I merely have to pay up again.

Nora: Oh but, Torvald —

Helmer: You can't deny it, my dear little Nora. *(Puts his arm round her waist.)* It's a sweet little spendthrift, but she uses up a deal of money. One would hardly believe how expensive such little persons are!

Nora: It's a shame to say that. I do really save all I can.

Helmer (laughing): That's very true, — all you can. But you can't save anything!

Nora (smiling quietly and happily): You haven't any idea how many expenses we skylarks and squirrels have, Torvald.

Helmer: You are an odd little soul. Very like your father. You always find some new way of wheedling money out of me, and, as soon as you have got it, it seems to melt in your hands. You never know where it has gone. Still, one must take you as you are. It is in the blood; for indeed it is true that you can inherit these things, Nora.

Nora: Ah, I wish I had inherited many of papa's qualities.

Helmer: And I would not wish you to be anything but just what you are, my sweet little skylark. But, do you know, it strikes me that you are looking rather — what shall I say — rather uneasy today?

Nora: Do I?

Helmer: You do, really. Look straight at me.

Nora (looks at him): Well?

Helmer (wagging his finger at her): Hasn't Miss Sweet Tooth been breaking rules in town today?

Nora: No; what makes you think that?

Helmer: Hasn't she paid a visit to the confectioner's?

Nora: No, I assure you, Torvald —

Helmer: Not been nibbling sweets?

Nora: No, certainly not.

Helmer: Not even taken a bite at a macaroon or two?

Nora: No, Torvald, I assure you really —

Helmer: There, there, of course I was only joking.

Nora (going to the table on the right): I should not think of going against your wishes.

Helmer: No, I am sure of that; besides, you gave me your word — *(Going up to her.)* Keep your little Christmas secrets to yourself, my darling. They will all be revealed to-night when the Christmas Tree is lit, no doubt.

Nora: Did you remember to invite Doctor Rank?

Helmer: No. But there is no need; as a matter of course he will come to dinner with us. However, I will ask him when he comes in this morning. I have ordered some good wine. Nora, you can't think how I am looking forward to this evening.

Nora: So am I! And how the children will enjoy themselves, Torvald!

Helmer: It is splendid to feel that one has a perfectly safe appointment, and a big enough income. It's delightful to think of, isn't it?

Nora: It's wonderful!

Helmer: Do you remember last Christmas? For a full three weeks beforehand you shut yourself up every evening until long after midnight, making ornaments for the Christmas Tree, and all the other fine things that were to be a surprise to us. It was the dullest three weeks I ever spent!

Nora: I didn't find it dull.

Helmer (smiling): But there was precious little result, Nora.

Nora: Oh, you shouldn't tease me about that again. How could I help the cat's going in and tearing everything to pieces?

Helmer: Of course you couldn't, poor little girl. You had the best of intentions to please us all, and that's the main thing. But it is a good thing that our hard times are over.

Nora: Yes, it is really wonderful.

Helmer: This time I needn't sit here and be dull all alone, and you needn't ruin your dear eyes and your pretty little hands —

Nora (clapping her hands): No, Torvald, I needn't any longer, need I! It's wonderfully lovely to hear you say so! *(Taking his arm.)* Now I will tell you how I have been thinking we ought to arrange things, Torvald. As soon as Christmas is over — *(A bell rings in the hall.)* There's the bell. *(She tidies the room a little.)* There's some one at the door. What a nuisance!

Helmer: If it is a caller, remember I am not at home.

Maid (in the doorway): A lady to see you, ma'am, — a stranger.

Nora: Ask her to come in.

Maid (to Helmer): The doctor came at the same time, sir.

Helmer: Did he go straight into my room?
Maid: Yes, sir.

> *Helmer goes into his room. The Maid ushers in Mrs. Linde, who is in travelling dress, and shuts the door.*

Mrs. Linde (in a dejected and timid voice): How do you do, Nora?
Nora (doubtfully): How do you do —
Mrs. Linde: You don't recognise me, I suppose.
Nora: No, I don't know — yes, to be sure, I seem to — *(Suddenly.)* Yes! Christine! Is it really you?
Mrs. Linde: Yes, it is I.
Nora: Christine! To think of my not recognising you! And yet how could I — *(In a gentle voice.)* How you have altered, Christine!
Mrs. Linde: Yes, I have indeed. In nine, ten long years —
Nora: Is it so long since we met? I suppose it is. The last eight years have been a happy time for me, I can tell you. And so now you have come into the town, and have taken this long journey in winter — that was plucky of you.
Mrs. Linde: I arrived by steamer this morning.
Nora: To have some fun at Christmas-time, of course. How delightful! We will have such fun together! But take off your things. You are not cold, I hope. *(Helps her.)* Now we will sit down by the stove, and be cosy. No, take this armchair; I will sit here in the rocking-chair. *(Takes her hands.)* Now you look like your old self again; it was only the first moment — You are a little paler, Christine, and perhaps a little thinner.
Mrs. Linde: And much, much older, Nora.
Nora: Perhaps a little older; very, very little; certainly not much. *(Stops suddenly and speaks seriously.)* What a thoughtless creature I am, chattering away like this. My poor, dear Christine, do forgive me.
Mrs. Linde: What do you mean, Nora?
Nora (gently): Poor Christine, you are a widow.
Mrs. Linde: Yes; it is three years ago now.
Nora: Yes, I knew; I saw it in the papers. I assure you, Christine, I meant ever so often to write to you at the time, but I always put it off and something always prevented me.
Mrs. Linde: I quite understand, dear.
Nora: It was very bad of me, Christine. Poor thing, how you must have suffered. And he left you nothing?
Mrs. Linde: No.
Nora: And no children?
Mrs. Linde: No.
Nora: Nothing at all, then.
Mrs. Linde: Not even any sorrow or grief to live upon.
Nora (looking incredulously at her): But, Christine, is that possible?
Mrs. Linde (smiles sadly and strokes her hair): It sometimes happens, Nora.

Nora: So you are quite alone. How dreadfully sad that must be. I have three lovely children. You can't see them just now, for they are out with their nurse. But now you must tell me all about it.

Mrs. Linde: No, no; I want to hear about you.

Nora: No, you must begin. I mustn't be selfish today; today I must only think of your affairs. But there is one thing I must tell you. Do you know we have just had a great piece of good luck?

Mrs. Linde: No, what is it?

Nora: Just fancy, my husband has been made manager of the Bank!

Mrs. Linde: Your husband? What good luck!

Nora: Yes, tremendous! A barrister's profession is such an uncertain thing, especially if he won't undertake unsavoury cases; and naturally Torvald has never been willing to do that, and I quite agree with him. You may imagine how pleased we are! He is to take up his work in the Bank at the New Year, and then he will have a big salary and lots of commissions. For the future we can live quite differently — we can do just as we like. I feel so relieved and so happy, Christine! It will be splendid to have heaps of money and not need to have any anxiety, won't it?

Mrs. Linde: Yes, anyhow I think it would be delightful to have what one needs.

Nora: No, not only what one needs, but heaps and heaps of money.

Mrs. Linde (smiling): Nora, Nora, haven't you learned sense yet? In our schooldays you were a great spendthrift.

Nora (laughing): Yes, that is what Torvald says now. *(Wags her finger at her.)* But "Nora, Nora" is not so silly as you think. We have not been in a position for me to waste money. We have both had to work.

Mrs. Linde: You too?

Nora: Yes; odds and ends, needlework, crotchet-work, embroidery, and that kind of thing. *(Dropping her voice.)* And other things as well. You know Torvald left his office when we were married? There was no prospect of promotion there, and he had to try and earn more than before. But during the first year he over-worked himself dreadfully. You see, he had to make money every way he could, and he worked early and late; but he couldn't stand it, and fell dreadfully ill, and the doctors said it was necessary for him to go south.

Mrs. Linde: You spent a whole year in Italy, didn't you?

Nora: Yes. It was no easy matter to get away, I can tell you. It was just after Ivar was born; but naturally we had to go. It was a wonderfully beautiful journey, and it saved Torvald's life. But it cost a tremendous lot of money, Christine.

Mrs. Linde: So I should think.

Nora: It cost about two hundred and fifty pounds. That's a lot, isn't it?

Mrs. Linde: Yes, and in emergencies like that it is lucky to have the money.

Nora: I ought to tell you that we had it from papa.

Mrs. Linde: Oh, I see. It was just about that time that he died, wasn't it?

Nora: Yes; and, just think of it, I couldn't go and nurse him. I was expecting little Ivar's birth every day and I had my poor sick Torvald to look after.

My dear, kind father — I never saw him again, Christine. That was the saddest time I have known since our marriage.

Mrs. Linde: I know how fond you were of him. And then you went off to Italy?

Nora: Yes; you see we had money then, and the doctors insisted on our going, so we started a month later.

Mrs. Linde: And your husband came back quite well?

Nora: As sound as a bell!

Mrs. Linde: But — the doctor?

Nora: What doctor?

Mrs. Linde: I thought your maid said the gentleman who arrived here just as I did, was the doctor?

Nora: Yes, that was Doctor Rank, but he doesn't come here professionally. He is our greatest friend, and comes in at least once every day. No, Torvald has not had an hour's illness since then, and our children are strong and healthy and so am I. *(Jumps up and claps her hands.)* Christine! Christine! it's good to be alive and happy! — But how horrid of me; I am talking of nothing but my own affairs. *(Sits on a stool near her, and rests her arms on her knees.)* You mustn't be angry with me. Tell me, is it really true that you did not love your husband? Why did you marry him?

Mrs. Linde: My mother was alive then, and was bedridden and helpless, and I had to provide for my two younger brothers; so I did not think I was justified in refusing his offer.

Nora: No, perhaps you were quite right. He was rich at that time, then?

Mrs. Linde: I believe he was quite well off. But his business was a precarious one; and, when he died, it all went to pieces and there was nothing left.

Nora: And then? —

Mrs. Linde: Well, I had to turn my hand to anything I could find — first a small shop, then a small school, and so on. The last three years have seemed like one long working-day, with no rest. Now it is at an end, Nora. My poor mother needs me no more, for she is gone; and the boys do not need me either; they have got situations and can shift for themselves.

Nora: What a relief you must feel it —

Mrs. Linde: No, indeed; I only feel my life unspeakably empty. No one to live for anymore. *(Gets up restlessly.)* That was why I could not stand the life in my little backwater any longer. I hope it may be easier here to find something which will busy me and occupy my thoughts. If only I could have the good luck to get some regular work — office work of some kind —

Nora: But, Christine, that is so frightfully tiring, and you look tired out now. You had far better go away to some watering-place.

Mrs. Linde (walking to the window): I have no father to give me money for a journey, Nora.

Nora (rising): Oh, don't be angry with me!

Mrs. Linde (going up to her): It is you that must not be angry with me, dear. The worst of a position like mine is that it makes one so bitter. No one to work for, and yet obliged to be always on the lookout for chances. One must live, and so one becomes selfish. When you told me of the happy turn your fortunes have taken — you will hardly believe it — I was delighted not so much on your account as on my own.

Nora: How do you mean? — Oh, I understand. You mean that perhaps Torvald could get you something to do.

Mrs. Linde: Yes, that was what I was thinking of.

Nora: He must, Christine. Just leave it to me; I will broach the subject very cleverly — I will think of something that will please him very much. It will make me so happy to be of some use to you.

Mrs. Linde: How kind you are, Nora, to be so anxious to help me! It is doubly kind in you, for you know so little of the burdens and troubles of life.

Nora: I — ? I know so little of them?

Mrs. Linde (smiling): My dear! Small household cares and that sort of thing! — You are a child, Nora.

Nora (tosses her head and crosses the stage): You ought not to be so superior.

Mrs. Linde: No?

Nora: You are just like the others. They all think that I am incapable of anything really serious —

Mrs. Linde: Come, come —

Nora: — that I have gone through nothing in this world of cares.

Mrs. Linde: But, my dear Nora, you have just told me all your troubles.

Nora: Pooh! — those were trifles. *(Lowering her voice.)* I have not told you the important thing.

Mrs. Linde: The important thing? What do you mean?

Nora: You look down upon me altogether, Christine — but you ought not to. You are proud, aren't you, of having worked so hard and so long for your mother?

Mrs. Linde: Indeed, I don't look down on anyone. But it is true that I am both proud and glad to think that I was privileged to make the end of my mother's life almost free from care.

Nora: And you are proud to think of what you have done for your brothers?

Mrs. Linde: I think I have the right to be.

Nora: I think so, too. But now, listen to this; I too have something to be proud and glad of.

Mrs. Linde: I have no doubt you have. But what do you refer to?

Nora: Speak low. Suppose Torvald were to hear! He mustn't on any account — no one in the world must know, Christine, except you.

Mrs. Linde: But what is it?

Nora: Come here. *(Pulls her down on the sofa beside her.)* Now I will show you that I too have something to be proud and glad of. It was I who saved Torvald's life.

Mrs. Linde: "Saved"? How?

Nora: I told you about our trip to Italy. Torvald would never have recovered if he had not gone there —

Mrs. Linde: Yes, but your father gave you the necessary funds.

Nora (smiling): Yes, that is what Torvald and all the others think, but —

Mrs. Linde: But —

Nora: Papa didn't give us a shilling. It was I who procured the money.

Mrs. Linde: You? All that large sum?

Nora: Two hundred and fifty pounds. What do you think of that?

Mrs. Linde: But, Nora, how could you possibly do it? Did you win a prize in the Lottery?

Nora (contemptuously): In the Lottery? There would have been no credit in that.

Mrs. Linde: But where did you get it from, then?

Nora (humming and smiling with an air of mystery): Hm, hm! Aha!

Mrs. Linde: Because you couldn't have borrowed it.

Nora: Couldn't I? Why not?

Mrs. Linde: No, a wife cannot borrow without her husband's consent.

Nora (tossing her head): Oh, if it is a wife who has any head for business — a wife who has the wit to be a little bit clever —

Mrs. Linde: I don't understand it at all, Nora.

Nora: There is no need you should. I never said I had borrowed the money. I may have got it some other way. *(Lies back on the sofa.)* Perhaps I got it from some other admirer. When anyone is as attractive as I am —

Mrs. Linde: You are a mad creature.

Nora: Now, you know you're full of curiosity, Christine.

Mrs. Linde: Listen to me, Nora dear. Haven't you been a little bit imprudent?

Nora (sits up straight): Is it imprudent to save your husband's life?

Mrs. Linde: It seems to me imprudent, without his knowledge, to —

Nora: But it was absolutely necessary that he should not know! My goodness, can't you understand that? It was necessary he should have no idea what a dangerous condition he was in. It was to me that the doctors came and said that his life was in danger, and that the only thing to save him was to live in the south. Do you suppose I didn't try, first of all, to get what I wanted as if it were for myself? I told him how much I should love to travel abroad like other young wives; I tried tears and entreaties with him; I told him that he ought to remember the condition I was in, and that he ought to be kind and indulgent to me; I even hinted that he might raise a loan. That nearly made him angry, Christine. He said I was thoughtless, and that it was his duty as my husband not to indulge me in my whims and caprices — as I believe he called them. Very well, I thought, you must be saved — and that was how I came to devise a way out of the difficulty —

Mrs. Linde: And did your husband never get to know from your father that the money had not come from him?

Nora: No, never. Papa died just at that time. I had meant to let him into the secret and beg him never to reveal it. But he was so ill then — alas, there never was any need to tell him.

Mrs. Linde: And since then have you never told your secret to your husband?

Nora: Good Heavens, no! How could you think so? A man who has such strong opinions about these things! And besides, how painful and humiliating it would be for Torvald, with his manly independence, to know that he owed me anything! It would upset our mutual relations altogether; our beautiful happy home would no longer be what it is now.

Mrs. Linde: Do you mean never to tell him about it?

Nora (meditatively, and with a half smile): Yes — someday, perhaps, after many years, when I am no longer as nice-looking as I am now. Don't laugh at me! I mean, of course, when Torvald is no longer as devoted to me as he is now; when my dancing and dressing-up and reciting have palled on him; then it may be a good thing to have something in reserve — *(Breaking off.)* What nonsense! That time will never come. Now, what do you think of my great secret, Christine? Do you still think I am of no use? I can tell you, too, that this affair has caused me a lot of worry. It has been by no means easy for me to meet my engagements punctually. I may tell you that there is something that is called, in business, quarterly interest, and another thing called payment in installments, and it is always so dreadfully difficult to manage them. I have had to save a little here and there, where I could, you understand. I have not been able to put aside much from my housekeeping money, for Torvald must have a good table. I couldn't let my children be shabbily dressed; I have felt obliged to use up all he gave me for them, the sweet little darlings!

Mrs. Linde: So it has all had to come out of your own necessaries of life, poor Nora?

Nora: Of course. Besides, I was the one responsible for it. Whenever Torvald has given me money for new dresses and such things, I have never spent more than half of it; I have always bought the simplest and cheapest things. Thank Heaven, any clothes look well on me, and so Torvald has never noticed it. But it was often very hard on me, Christine — because it is delightful to be really well dressed, isn't it?

Mrs. Linde: Quite so.

Nora: Well, then I have found other ways of earning money. Last winter I was lucky enough to get a lot of copying to do; so I locked myself up and sat writing every evening until quite late at night. Many a time I was desperately tired; but all the same it was a tremendous pleasure to sit there working and earning money. It was like being a man.

Mrs. Linde: How much have you been able to pay off in that way?

Nora: I can't tell you exactly. You see, it is very difficult to keep an account of a business matter of that kind. I only know that I have paid every penny that I could scrape together. Many a time I was at my wits' end. *(Smiles.)* Then I used to sit here and imagine that a rich old gentleman had fallen in love with me —

Mrs. Linde: What! Who was it?

Nora: Be quiet! — that he had died; and that when his will was opened it contained, written in big letters, the instruction: "The lovely Mrs. Nora Helmer is to have all I possess paid over to her at once in cash."

Mrs. Linde: But, my dear Nora — who could the man be?

Nora: Good gracious, can't you understand? There was no old gentleman at all; it was only something that I used to sit here and imagine, when I couldn't think of any way of procuring money. But it's all the same now; the tiresome old person can stay where he is, as far as I am concerned; I don't care about him or his will either, for I am free from care now. *(Jumps up.)* My goodness, it's delightful to think of, Christine! Free from care! To be able to be free from care, quite free from care; to be able to play and romp with the children; to be able to keep the house beautifully and have everything just as Torvald likes it! And, think of it, soon the spring will come and the big blue sky! Perhaps we shall be able to take a little trip — perhaps I shall see the sea again! Oh, it's a wonderful thing to be alive and be happy. *(A bell is heard in the hall.)*

Mrs. Linde (rising): There is the bell; perhaps I had better go.

Nora: No, don't go; no one will come in here; it is sure to be for Torvald.

Servant (at the hall door): Excuse me, ma'am — there is a gentleman to see the master, and as the doctor is with him —

Nora: Who is it?

Krogstad (at the door): It is I, Mrs. Helmer *(Mrs. Linde starts, trembles, and turns to the window.)*

Nora (takes a step towards him, and speaks in a strained, low voice): You? What is it? What do you want to see my husband about?

Krogstad: Bank business — in a way. I have a small post in the Bank, and I hear your husband is to be our chief now —

Nora: Then it is —

Krogstad: Nothing but dry business matters, Mrs. Helmer; absolutely nothing else.

Nora: Be so good as to go into the study, then. *(She bows indifferently to him and shuts the door into the hall; then comes back and makes up the fire in the stove.)*

Mrs. Linde: Nora — who was that man?

Nora: A lawyer, of the name of Krogstad.

Mrs. Linde: Then it really was he.

Nora: Do you know the man?

Mrs. Linde: I used to — many years ago. At one time he was a solicitor's clerk in our town.

Nora: Yes, he was.

Mrs. Linde: He is greatly altered.

Nora: He made a very unhappy marriage.

Mrs. Linde: He is a widower now, isn't he?

Nora: With several children. There now, it is burning up. *(Shuts the door of the stove and moves the rocking-chair aside.)*

Mrs. Linde: They say he carries on various kinds of business.

Nora: Really! Perhaps he does; I don't know anything about it. But don't let us think of business; it is so tiresome.

Doctor Rank (comes out of Helmer's study. Before he shuts the door he calls to him): No, my dear fellow, I won't disturb you; I would rather go in to your wife for a little while. *(Shuts the door and sees Mrs. Linde.)* I beg your pardon; I am afraid I am disturbing you too.

Nora: No, not at all. *(Introducing him.)* Doctor Rank, Mrs. Linde.

Rank: I have often heard Mrs. Linde's name mentioned here. I think I passed you on the stairs when I arrived, Mrs. Linde?

Mrs. Linde: Yes, I go up very slowly; I can't manage stairs well.

Rank: Ah! some slight internal weakness?

Mrs. Linde: No, the fact is I have been overworking myself.

Rank: Nothing more than that? Then I suppose you have come to town to amuse yourself with our entertainments?

Mrs. Linde: I have come to look for work.

Rank: Is that a good cure for overwork?

Mrs. Linde: One must live, Doctor Rank.

Rank: Yes, the general opinion seems to be that it is necessary.

Nora: Look here, Doctor Rank — you know you want to live.

Rank: Certainly. However wretched I may feel, I want to prolong the agony as long as possible. All my patients are like that. And so are those who are morally diseased; one of them, and a bad case too, is at this very moment with Helmer —

Mrs. Linde (sadly): Ah!

Nora: Whom do you mean?

Rank: A lawyer of the name of Krogstad, a fellow you don't know at all. He suffers from a diseased moral character, Mrs. Helmer; but even he began talking of its being highly important that he should live.

Nora: Did he? What did he want to speak to Torvald about?

Rank: I have no idea; I only heard that it was something about the Bank.

Nora: I didn't know this — what's his name — Krogstad had anything to do with the Bank.

Rank: Yes, he has some sort of appointment there. *(To Mrs. Linde.)* I don't know whether you find also in your part of the world that there are certain people who go zealously snuffing about to smell out moral corruption, and, as soon as they have found some, put the person concerned into some lucrative position where they can keep their eye on him. Healthy natures are left out in the cold.

Mrs. Linde: Still I think the sick are those who most need taking care of.

Rank (shrugging his shoulders): Yes, there you are. That is the sentiment that is turning Society into a sick-house.

Nora, who has been absorbed in her thoughts, breaks out into smothered laughter and claps her hands.

Rank: Why do you laugh at that? Have you any notion what Society really is?

Nora: What do I care about tiresome Society? I am laughing at something quite different, something extremely amusing. Tell me, Doctor Rank, are all the people who are employed in the Bank dependent on Torvald now?

Rank: Is that what you find so extremely amusing?

Nora (smiling and humming): That's my affair! *(Walking about the room.)* It's perfectly glorious to think that we have — that Torvald has so much power over so many people. *(Takes the packet from her pocket.)* Doctor Rank, what do you say to a macaroon?

Rank: What, macaroons? I thought they were forbidden here.

Nora: Yes, but these are some Christine gave me.

Mrs. Linde: What! I? —

Nora: Oh, well, don't be alarmed! You couldn't know that Torvald had forbidden them. I must tell you that he is afraid they will spoil my teeth. But, bah! — once in a way — That's so, isn't it, Doctor Rank? By your leave! *(Puts a macaroon into his mouth.)* You must have one too, Christine. And I shall have one, just a little one — or at most two. *(Walking about.)* I am tremendously happy. There is just one thing in the world now that I should dearly love to do.

Rank: Well, what is that?

Nora: It's something I should dearly love to say, if Torvald could hear me.

Rank: Well, why can't you say it?

Nora: No, I daren't; it's so shocking.

Mrs. Linde: Shocking?

Rank: Well, I should not advise you to say it. Still, with us you might. What is it you would so much like to say if Torvald could hear you?

Nora: I should just love to say — Well, I'm damned!

Rank: Are you mad?

Mrs. Linde: Nora, dear —!

Rank: Say it, here he is!

Nora (hiding the packet): Hush! Hush! Hush! *(Helmer comes out of his room, with his coat over his arm and his hat in his hand.)*

Nora: Well, Torvald dear, have you got rid of him?

Helmer: Yes, he has just gone.

Nora: Let me introduce you — this is Christine, who has come to town.

Helmer: Christine —? Excuse me, but I don't know —

Nora: Mrs. Linde, dear; Christine Linde.

Helmer: Of course. A school friend of my wife's, I presume?

Mrs. Linde: Yes, we have known each other since then.

Nora: And just think, she has taken a long journey in order to see you.

Helmer: What do you mean?

Mrs. Linde: No, really, I —

Nora: Christine is tremendously clever at book-keeping, and she is frightfully anxious to work under some clever man, so as to perfect herself —

Helmer: Very sensible, Mrs. Linde.

Nora: And when she heard you had been appointed manager of the Bank — the news was telegraphed, you know — she travelled here as quick as she could. Torvald, I am sure you will be able to do something for Christine, for my sake, won't you?

Helmer: Well, it is not altogether impossible. I presume you are a widow, Mrs. Linde?

Mrs. Linde: Yes.

Helmer: And have had some experience of book-keeping?

Mrs. Linde: Yes, a fair amount.

Helmer: Ah! well, it's very likely I may be able to find something for you —

Nora (clapping her hands): What did I tell you? What did I tell you?

Helmer: You have just come at a fortunate moment, Mrs. Linde.

Mrs. Linde: How am I to thank you?

Helmer: There is no need. *(Puts on his coat.)* But to-day you must excuse me —

Rank: Wait a minute; I will come with you. *(Brings his fur coat from the hall and warms it at the fire.)*

Nora: Don't be long away, Torvald dear.

Helmer: About an hour, not more.

Nora: Are you going too, Christine?

Mrs. Linde (putting on her cloak): Yes, I must go and look for a room.

Helmer: Oh, well then, we can walk down the street together.

Nora (helping her): What a pity it is we are so short of space here; I am afraid it is impossible for us —

Mrs. Linde: Please don't think of it! Good-bye, Nora dear, and many thanks.

Nora: Good-bye for the present. Of course you will come back this evening. And you too, Dr. Rank. What do you say? If you are well enough? Oh, you must be! Wrap yourself up well. *(They go to the door all talking together. Children's voices are heard on the staircase.)*

Nora: There they are! There they are! *(She runs to open the door. The Nurse comes in with the children.)* Come in! Come in! *(Stoops and kisses them.)* Oh, you sweet blessings! Look at them, Christine! Aren't they darlings?

Rank: Don't let us stand here in the draught.

Helmer: Come along, Mrs. Linde; the place will only be bearable for a mother now!

Rank, Helmer, and Mrs. Linde go downstairs. The Nurse comes forward with the children; Nora shuts the hall door.

Nora: How fresh and well you look! Such red cheeks like apples and roses. *(The children all talk at once while she speaks to them.)* Have you had great fun? That's splendid! What, you pulled both Emmy and Bob along on the sledge? — both at once? — that was good. You are a clever boy, Ivar. Let me take her for a little, Anne. My sweet little baby doll! *(Takes the baby from the Maid and dances it up and down.)* Yes, yes, mother will dance with Bob too. What! Have you been snowballing? I wish I had been there too! No, no, I will take their things off, Anne; please let me do it, it is such fun. Go in now, you look half frozen. There is some hot coffee for you on the stove.

The Nurse goes into the room on the left. Nora takes off the children's things and throws them about, while they all talk to her at once.

Nora: Really! Did a big dog run after you? But it didn't bite you? No, dogs don't bite nice little dolly children. You mustn't look at the parcels, Ivar. What are they? Ah, I daresay you would like to know. No, no — it's something nasty! Come, let us have a game! What shall we play at? Hide and Seek? Yes, we'll play Hide and Seek. Bob shall hide first. Must I hide? Very well, I'll hide first. *(She and the children laugh and shout, and romp in and out of the room; at last Nora hides under the table, the children rush in and out for her, but do not see her; they hear her smothered laughter, run to the table, lift up the cloth and find her. Shouts of laughter. She crawls forward and pretends to frighten them. Fresh laughter. Meanwhile there has been a knock at the hall door, but none of them has noticed it. The door is half opened, and Krogstad appears. He waits a little; the game goes on.)*

Krogstad: Excuse me, Mrs. Helmer.

Nora (with a stifled cry, turns round and gets up on to her knees): Ah! what do you want?

Krogstad: Excuse me, the outer door was ajar; I suppose someone forgot to shut it.

Nora (rising): My husband is out, Mr. Krogstad.

Krogstad: I know that.

Nora: What do you want here, then?

Krogstad: A word with you.

Nora: With me? — *(To the children, gently.)* Go in to nurse. What? No, the strange man won't do mother any harm. When he has gone we will have another game. *(She takes the children into the room on the left, and shuts the door after them.)* You want to speak to me?

Krogstad: Yes, I do.

Nora: To-day? It is not the first of the month yet.

Krogstad: No, it is Christmas Eve, and it will depend on yourself what sort of a Christmas you will spend.

Nora: What do you mean? To-day it is absolutely impossible for me —

Krogstad: We won't talk about that until later on. This is something different. I presume you can give me a moment?

Nora: Yes — yes, I can — although —

Krogstad: Good. I was in Olsen's Restaurant and saw your husband going down the street —

Nora: Yes?

Krogstad: With a lady.

Nora: What then?

Krogstad: May I make so bold as to ask if it was a Mrs. Linde?

Nora: It was.

Krogstad: Just arrived in town?

Nora: Yes, to-day.

Krogstad: She is a great friend of yours, isn't she?

Nora: She is. But I don't see —

Krogstad: I knew her too, once upon a time.

Nora: I am aware of that.

Krogstad: Are you? So you know all about it; I thought as much. Then I can ask you, without beating about the bush — is Mrs. Linde to have an appointment in the Bank?

Nora: What right have you to question me, Mr. Krogstad? — You, one of my husband's subordinates! But since you ask, you shall know. Yes, Mrs. Linde *is* to have an appointment. And it was I who pleaded her cause, Mr. Krogstad, let me tell you that.

Krogstad: I was right in what I thought, then.

Nora (walking up and down the stage): Sometimes one has a tiny little bit of influence, I should hope. Because one is a woman, it does not necessarily follow that —. When anyone is in a subordinate position, Mr. Krogstad, they should really be careful to avoid offending anyone who — who —

Krogstad: Who has influence?

Nora: Exactly.

Krogstad (changing his tone): Mrs. Helmer, you will be so good as to use your influence on my behalf.

Nora: What? What do you mean?

Krogstad: You will be so kind as to see that I am allowed to keep my subordinate position in the Bank.

Nora: What do you mean by that? Who proposes to take your post away from you?

Krogstad: Oh, there is no necessity to keep up the pretence of ignorance. I can quite understand that your friend is not very anxious to expose herself to the chance of rubbing shoulders with me; and I quite understand, too, whom I have to thank for being turned off.

Nora: But I assure you —

Krogstad: Very likely; but, to come to the point, the time has come when I should advise you to use your influence to prevent that.

Nora: But, Mr. Krogstad, I *have* no influence.

Krogstad: Haven't you? I thought you said yourself just now —

Nora: Naturally I did not mean you to put that construction on it. What should make you think I have any influence of that kind with my husband?

Krogstad: Oh, I have known your husband from our student days. I don't suppose he is any more unassailable than other husbands.

Nora: If you speak slightingly of my husband, I shall turn you out of the house.

Krogstad: You are bold, Mrs. Helmer.

Nora: I am not afraid of you any longer. As soon as the New Year comes, I shall in a very short time be free of the whole thing.

Krogstad (controlling himself): Listen to me, Mrs. Helmer. If necessary, I am prepared to fight for my small post in the Bank as if I were fighting for my life.

Nora: So it seems.

Krogstad: It is not only for the sake of the money; indeed, that weighs least with me in the matter. There is another reason — well, I may as well tell you. My position is this. I daresay you know, like everybody else, that once, many years ago, I was guilty of an indiscretion.

Nora: I think I have heard something of the kind.

Krogstad: The matter never came into court; but every way seemed to be closed to me after that. So I took to the business that you know of. I had to do something; and, honestly, I don't think I've been one of the worst. But now I must cut myself free from all that. My sons are growing up; for their sake I must try and win back as much respect as I can in the town. This post in the Bank was like the first step up for me — and now your husband is going to kick me downstairs again into the mud.

Nora: But you must believe me, Mr. Krogstad; it is not in my power to help you at all.

Krogstad: Then it is because you haven't the will; but I have means to compel you.

Nora: You don't mean that you will tell my husband that I owe you money?

Krogstad: Hm! — suppose I were to tell him?

Nora: It would be perfectly infamous of you. *(Sobbing.)* To think of his learning my secret, which has been my joy and pride, in such an ugly, clumsy way — that he should learn it from you! And it would put me in a horribly disagreeable position —

Krogstad: Only disagreeable?

Nora (impetuously): Well, do it, then! — and it will be the worse for you. My husband will see for himself what a blackguard you are, and you certainly won't keep your post then.

Krogstad: I asked you if it was only a disagreeable scene at home that you were afraid of?

Nora: If my husband does get to know of it, of course he will at once pay you what is still owing, and we shall have nothing more to do with you.

Krogstad (coming a step nearer): Listen to me, Mrs. Helmer. Either you have a very bad memory or you know very little of business. I shall be obliged to remind you of a few details.

Nora: What do you mean?

Krogstad: When your husband was ill, you came to me to borrow two hundred and fifty pounds.

Nora: I didn't know anyone else to go to.

Krogstad: I promised to get you that amount —

Nora: Yes, and you did so.

Krogstad: I promised to get you that amount, on certain conditions. Your mind was so taken up with your husband's illness, and you were so anxious to get the money for your journey, that you seem to have paid no attention to the conditions of our bargain. Therefore it will not be amiss if I remind you of them. Now, I promised to get the money on the security of a bond which I drew up.

Nora: Yes, and which I signed.

Krogstad: Good. But below your signature there were a few lines constituting your father a surety for the money; those lines your father should have signed.

Nora: Should? He did sign them.

Krogstad: I had left the date blank; that is to say, your father should himself have inserted the date on which he signed the paper. Do you remember that?

Nora: Yes, I think I remember—

Krogstad: Then I gave you the bond to send by post to your father. Is that not so?

Nora: Yes.

Krogstad: And you naturally did so at once, because five or six days afterwards you brought me the bond with your father's signature. And then I gave you the money.

Nora: Well, haven't I been paying it off regularly?

Krogstad: Fairly so, yes. But—to come back to the matter in hand—that must have been a very trying time for you, Mrs. Helmer.

Nora: It was, indeed.

Krogstad: Your father was very ill, wasn't he?

Nora: He was very near his end.

Krogstad: And he died soon afterwards?

Nora: Yes.

Krogstad: Tell me, Mrs. Helmer, can you by any chance remember what day your father died?—on what day of the month, I mean.

Nora: Papa died on the 29th of September.

Krogstad: That is correct; I have ascertained it for myself. And, as that is so, there is a discrepancy (*taking a paper from his pocket*) which I cannot account for.

Nora: What discrepancy? I don't know—

Krogstad: The discrepancy consists, Mrs. Helmer, in the fact that your father signed this bond three days after his death.

Nora: What do you mean? I don't understand—

Krogstad: Your father died on the 29th of September. But, look here; your father has dated his signature the 2nd of October. It is a discrepancy, isn't it? (*Nora is silent.*) Can you explain it to me? (*Nora is still silent.*) It is a remarkable thing, too, that the words "2nd of October," as well as the year, are not written in your father's handwriting but in one that I think I know. Well, of course it can be explained; your father may have forgotten to date his signature, and someone else may have dated it haphazard before they knew of his death. There is no harm in that. It all depends on the signature of the name; and *that* is genuine, I suppose, Mrs. Helmer? It was your father himself who signed his name here?

Nora (after a short pause, throws her head up and looks defiantly at him): No, it was not. It was I that wrote papa's name.

Krogstad: Are you aware that is a dangerous confession?

Nora: In what way? You shall have your money soon.

Krogstad: Let me ask you a question; why did you not send the paper to your father?

Nora: It was impossible; papa was so ill. If I had asked him for his signature, I should have had to tell him what the money was to be used for;

and when he was so ill himself I couldn't tell him that my husband's life was in danger — it was impossible.

Krogstad: It would have been better for you if you had given up your trip abroad.

Nora: No, that was impossible. That trip was to save my husband's life; I couldn't give that up.

Krogstad: But did it never occur to you that you were committing a fraud on me?

Nora: I couldn't take that into account; I didn't trouble myself about you at all. I couldn't bear you, because you put so many heartless difficulties in my way, although you knew what a dangerous condition my husband was in.

Krogstad: Mrs. Helmer, you evidently do not realise clearly what it is that you have been guilty of. But I can assure you that my one false step, which lost me all my reputation, was nothing more or nothing worse than what you have done.

Nora: You? Do you ask me to believe that you were brave enough to run a risk to save your wife's life?

Krogstad: The law cares nothing about motives.

Nora: Then it must be a very foolish law.

Krogstad: Foolish or not, it is the law by which you will be judged, if I produce this paper in court.

Nora: I don't believe it. Is a daughter not to be allowed to spare her dying father anxiety and care? Is a wife not to be allowed to save her husband's life? I don't know much about law; but I am certain that there must be laws permitting such things as that. Have you no knowledge of such laws — you who are a lawyer? You must be a very poor lawyer, Mr. Krogstad.

Krogstad: Maybe. But matters of business — such business as you and I have had together — do you think I don't understand that? Very well. Do as you please. But let me tell you this — if I lose my position a second time, you shall lose yours with me. *(He bows, and goes out through the hall.)*

Nora (appears buried in thought for a short time, then tosses her head): Nonsense! Trying to frighten me like that! — I am not so silly as he thinks. *(Begins to busy herself putting the children's things in order.)* And yet — ? No, it's impossible! I did it for love's sake.

Children (in the doorway on the left): Mother, the stranger man has gone out through the gate.

Nora: Yes, dears, I know. But, don't tell anyone about the stranger man. Do you hear? Not even papa.

Children: No, mother; but will you come and play again?

Nora: No, no, — not now.

Children: But, mother, you promised us.

Nora: Yes, but I can't now. Run away in; I have such a lot to do. Run away in, my sweet little darlings. *(She gets them into the room by degrees and shuts the door on them; then sits down on the sofa, takes up a piece of needlework and sews a few stitches, but soon stops.)* No! *(Throws down the work, gets up, goes to the hall door and calls out.)* Helen! bring the Tree in. *(Goes to the table on the left, opens a drawer, and stops again.)* No, no! it is quite impossible!

Maid (coming in with the Tree): Where shall I put it, ma'am?

Nora: Here, in the middle of the floor.

Maid: Shall I get you anything else?

Nora: No, thank you. I have all I want.   *(Exit Maid.)*

Nora (begins dressing the tree): A candle here — and flowers here — . The horrible man! It's all nonsense — there's nothing wrong. The Tree shall be splendid! I will do everything I can think of to please you, Torvald! — I will sing for you, dance for you — *(Helmer comes in with some papers under his arm.)* Oh! are you back already?

Helmer: Yes. Has anyone been here?

Nora: Here? No.

Helmer: That is strange. I saw Krogstad going out of the gate.

Nora: Did you? Oh yes, I forgot, Krogstad was here for a moment.

Helmer: Nora, I can see from your manner that he has been here begging you to say a good word for him.

Nora: Yes.

Helmer: And you were to appear to do it of your own accord; you were to conceal from me the fact of his having been here; didn't he beg that of you too?

Nora: Yes, Torvald, but —

Helmer: Nora, Nora, and you would be a party to that sort of thing? To have any talk with a man like that, and give him any sort of promise? And to tell me a lie into the bargain?

Nora: A lie — ?

Helmer: Didn't you tell me no one had been here? *(Shakes his finger at her.)* My little song-bird must never do that again. A song-bird must have a clean beak to chirp with — no false notes! *(Puts his arm around her waist.)* That is so, isn't it? Yes, I am sure it is. *(Lets her go.)* We will say no more about it. *(Sits down by the stove.)* How warm and snug it is here! *(Turns over his papers.)*

Nora (after a short pause, during which she busies herself with the Christmas Tree): Torvald!

Helmer: Yes.

Nora: I am looking forward tremendously to the fancy-dress ball at the Stenborgs' the day after to-morrow.

Helmer: And I am tremendously curious to see what you are going to surprise me with.

Nora: It was very silly of me to want to do that.

Helmer: What do you mean?

Nora: I can't hit upon anything that will do; everything I think of seems so silly and insignificant.

Helmer: Does my little Nora acknowledge that at last?

Nora (standing behind his chair with her arms on the back of it): Are you very busy, Torvald?

Helmer: Well —

Nora: What are all those papers?

Helmer: Bank business.

Nora: Already?

Helmer: I have got authority from the retiring manager to undertake the necessary changes in the staff and in the rearrangement of the work; and I must make use of the Christmas week for that, so as to have everything in order for the new year.

Nora: Then that was why this poor Krogstad —

Helmer: Hm!

Nora (leans against the back of his chair and strokes his hair): If you hadn't been so busy I should have asked you a tremendously big favour, Torvald.

Helmer: What is that? Tell me.

Nora: There is no one has such good taste as you. And I do so want to look nice at the fancy-dress ball. Torvald, couldn't you take me in hand and decide what I shall go as, and what sort of a dress I shall wear?

Helmer: Aha! so my obstinate little woman is obliged to get someone to come to her rescue?

Nora: Yes, Torvald, I can't get along a bit without your help.

Helmer: Very well, I will think it over, we shall manage to hit upon something.

Nora: That is nice of you. *(Goes to the Christmas Tree. A short pause.)* How pretty the red flowers look —. But, tell me, was it really something very bad that this Krogstad was guilty of ?

Helmer: He forged someone's name. Have you any idea what that means?

Nora: Isn't it possible that he was driven to do it by necessity?

Helmer: Yes; or, as in so many cases, by imprudence. I am not so heartless as to condemn a man altogether because of a single false step of that kind.

Nora: No, you wouldn't, would you, Torvald?

Helmer: Many a man has been able to retrieve his character, if he has openly confessed his fault and taken his punishment.

Nora: Punishment — ?

Helmer: But Krogstad did nothing of that sort; he got himself out of it by a cunning trick, and that is why he has gone under altogether.

Nora: But do you think it would — ?

Helmer: Just think how a guilty man like that has to lie and play the hypocrite with every one, how he has to wear a mask in the presence of those near and dear to him, even before his own wife and children. And about the children — that is the most terrible part of it all, Nora.

Nora: How?

Helmer: Because such an atmosphere of lies infects and poisons the whole life of a home. Each breath the children take in such a house is full of the germs of evil.

Nora (coming nearer him): Are you sure of that?

Helmer: My dear, I have often seen it in the course of my life as a lawyer. Almost everyone who has gone to the bad early in life has had a deceitful mother.

Nora: Why do you only say — mother?

Helmer: It seems most commonly to be the mother's influence, though naturally a bad father's would have the same result. Every lawyer is familiar with the fact. This Krogstad, now, has been persistently poisoning his own children with lies and dissimulation; that is why I say he has lost all moral character. *(Holds out his hands to her.)* That is why my sweet little Nora must promise me not to plead his cause. Give me your hand on it. Come, come, what is this? Give me your hand. There now, that's settled. I assure you it would be quite impossible for me to work with him; I literally feel physically ill when I am in the company of such people.

Nora (takes her hand out of his and goes to the opposite side of the Christmas Tree): How hot it is in here; and I have such a lot to do.

Helmer (getting up and putting his papers in order): Yes, and I must try and read through some of these before dinner; and I must think about your costume, too. And it is just possible I may have something ready in gold paper to hang up on the Tree. *(Puts his hand on her head.)* My precious little singing-bird! *(He goes into his room and shuts the door after him.)*

Nora (after a pause, whispers): No, no — it isn't true. It's impossible; it must be impossible.

The Nurse opens the door on the left.

Nurse: The little ones are begging so hard to be allowed to come in to mamma.

Nora: No, no, no! Don't let them come in to me! You stay with them, Anne.

Nurse: Very well, ma'am. *(Shuts the door.)*

Nora (pale with terror): Deprave my little children? Poison my home? *(A short pause. Then she tosses her head.)* It's not true. It can't possibly be true.

ACT II

The Same Scene: *The Christmas Tree is in the corner by the piano, stripped of its ornaments and with burnt-down candle-ends on its dishevelled branches. Nora's cloak and hat are lying on the sofa. She is alone in the room, walking about uneasily. She stops by the sofa and takes up her cloak.*

Nora (drops her cloak): Someone is coming now! *(Goes to the door and listens.)* No — it is no one. Of course, no one will come to-day, Christmas Day — nor to-morrow either. But, perhaps — *(opens the door and looks out).* No, nothing in the letter-box; it is quite empty. *(Comes forward.)*

What rubbish! of course he can't be in earnest about it. Such a thing couldn't happen; it is impossible — I have three little children.

Enter the Nurse from the room on the left, carrying a big cardboard box.

Nurse: At last I have found the box with the fancy dress.

Nora: Thanks; put it on the table.

Nurse (doing so): But it is very much in want of mending.

Nora: I should like to tear it into a hundred thousand pieces.

Nurse: What an idea! It can easily be put in order — just a little patience.

Nora: Yes, I will go and get Mrs. Linde to come and help me with it.

Nurse: What, out again? In this horrible weather? You will catch cold, ma'am, and make yourself ill.

Nora: Well, worse than that might happen. How are the children?

Nurse: The poor little souls are playing with their Christmas presents, but —

Nora: Do they ask much for me?

Nurse: You see, they are so accustomed to have their mamma with them.

Nora: Yes, but, nurse, I shall not be able to be so much with them now as I was before.

Nurse: Oh well, young children easily get accustomed to anything.

Nora: Do you think so? Do you think they would forget their mother if she went away altogether?

Nurse: Good heavens! — went away altogether?

Nora: Nurse, I want you to tell me something I have often wondered about — how could you have the heart to put your own child out among strangers?

Nurse: I was obliged to, if I wanted to be little Nora's nurse.

Nora: Yes, but how could you be willing to do it?

Nurse: What, when I was going to get such a good place by it? A poor girl who has got into trouble should be glad to. Besides, that wicked man didn't do a single thing for me.

Nora: But I suppose your daughter has quite forgotten you.

Nurse: No, indeed she hasn't. She wrote to me when she was confirmed, and when she was married.

Nora (putting her arms round her neck): Dear old Anne, you were a good mother to me when I was little.

Nurse: Little Nora, poor dear, had no other mother but me.

Nora: And if my little ones had no other mother, I am sure you would — What nonsense I am talking! *(Opens the box.)* Go in to them. Now I must —. You will see to-morrow how charming I shall look.

Nurse: I am sure there will be no one at the ball so charming as you, ma'am. *(Goes into the room on the left.)*

Nora (begins to unpack the box, but soon pushes it away from her): If only I dared go out. If only no one would come. If only I could be sure nothing would happen here in the meantime. Stuff and nonsense! No one will come. Only I mustn't think about it. I will brush my muff. What lovely, lovely gloves! Out of my thoughts, out of my thoughts! One, two, three, four, five, six — *(Screams.)* Ah! there is someone coming — . *(Makes a movement towards the door, but stands irresolute.)*

Enter Mrs. Linde from the hall, where she has taken off her cloak and hat.

Nora: Oh, it's you, Christine. There is no one else out there, is there? How good of you to come!

Mrs. Linde: I heard you were up asking for me.

Nora: Yes, I was passing by. As a matter of fact, it is something you could help me with. Let us sit down here on the sofa. Look here. To-morrow evening there is to be a fancy-dress ball at the Stenborgs', who live above us; and Torvald wants me to go as a Neapolitan fisher-girl, and dance the Tarantella that I learned at Capri.

Mrs. Linde: I see; you are going to keep up the character.

Nora: Yes, Torvald wants me to. Look, here is the dress; Torvald had it made for me there, but now it is all so torn, and I haven't any idea —

Mrs. Linde: We will easily put that right. It is only some of the trimming come unsewn here and there. Needle and thread? Now then, that's all we want.

Nora: It *is* nice of you.

Mrs. Linde (sewing): So you are going to be dressed up to-morrow, Nora. I will tell you what — I shall come in for a moment and see you in your fine feathers. But I have completely forgotten to thank you for a delightful evening yesterday.

Nora (gets up, and crosses the stage): Well, I don't think yesterday was as pleasant as usual. You ought to have come to town a little earlier, Christine. Certainly Torvald does understand how to make a house dainty and attractive.

Mrs. Linde: And so do you, it seems to me; you are not your father's daughter for nothing. But tell me, is Doctor Rank always as depressed as he was yesterday?

Nora: No; yesterday it was very noticeable. I must tell you that he suffers from a very dangerous disease. He has consumption of the spine, poor creature. His father was a horrible man who committed all sorts of excesses; and that is why his son was sickly from childhood, do you understand?

Mrs. Linde (dropping her sewing): But, my dearest Nora, how do you know anything about such things?

Nora (walking about): Pooh! When you have three children, you get visits now and then from — from married women, who know something of medical matters, and they talk about one thing and another.

Mrs. Linde (goes on sewing. A short silence): Does Doctor Rank come here every day?

Nora: Every day regularly. He is Torvald's most intimate friend, and a great friend of mine too. He is just like one of the family.

Mrs. Linde: But tell me this — is he perfectly sincere? I mean, isn't he the kind of man that is very anxious to make himself agreeable?

Nora: Not in the least. What makes you think that?

Mrs. Linde: When you introduced him to me yesterday, he declared he had often heard my name mentioned in this house; but afterwards I noticed that your husband hadn't the slightest idea who I was. So how could Doctor Rank — ?

Nora: That is quite right, Christine. Torvald is so absurdly fond of me that he wants me absolutely to himself, as he says. At first he used to seem almost jealous if I mentioned any of the dear folk at home, so naturally I gave up doing so. But I often talk about such things with Doctor Rank, because he likes hearing about them.

Mrs. Linde: Listen to me, Nora. You are still very like a child in many things, and I am older than you in many ways and have a little more experience. Let me tell you this — you ought to make an end of it with Doctor Rank.

Nora: What ought I to make an end of?

Mrs. Linde: Of two things, I think. Yesterday you talked some nonsense about a rich admirer who was to leave you money —

Nora: An admirer who doesn't exist, unfortunately! But what then?

Mrs. Linde: Is Doctor Rank a man of means?

Nora: Yes, he is.

Mrs. Linde: And has no one to provide for?

Nora: No, no one; but —

Mrs. Linde: And comes here every day?

Nora: Yes, I told you so.

Mrs. Linde: But how can this well-bred man be so tactless?

Nora: I don't understand you at all.

Mrs. Linde: Don't prevaricate, Nora. Do you suppose I don't guess who lent you the two hundred and fifty pounds?

Nora: Are you out of your senses? How can you think of such a thing! A friend of ours, who comes here every day! Do you realise what a horribly painful position that would be?

Mrs. Linde: Then it really isn't he?

Nora: No, certainly not. It would never have entered into my head for a moment. Besides, he had no money to lend then; he came into his money afterwards.

Mrs. Linde: Well, I think that was lucky for you, my dear Nora.

Nora: No, it would never have come into my head to ask Doctor Rank. Although I am quite sure that if I had asked him —

Mrs. Linde: But of course you won't.

Nora: Of course not. I have no reason to think it could possibly be necessary. But I am quite sure that if I told Doctor Rank —

Mrs. Linde: Behind your husband's back?

Nora: I must make an end of it with the other one, and that will be behind his back too. I *must* make an end of it with him.

Mrs. Linde: Yes, that is what I told you yesterday, but —

Nora (walking up and down): A man can put a thing like that straight much easier than a woman —

Mrs. Linde: One's husband, yes.

Nora: Nonsense! *(Standing still.)* When you pay off a debt you get your bond back, don't you?

Mrs. Linde: Yes, as a matter of course.

Nora: And can tear it into a hundred thousand pieces, and burn it up — the nasty dirty paper!

Mrs. Linde (looks hard at her, lays down her sewing and gets up slowly): Nora, you are concealing something from me.

Nora: Do I look as if I were?

Mrs. Linde: Something has happened to you since yesterday morning. Nora, what is it?

Nora (going nearer to her): Christine! *(Listens.)* Hush! there's Torvald come home. Do you mind going in to the children for the present? Torvald can't bear to see dressmaking going on. Let Anne help you.

Mrs. Linde (gathering some of the things together): Certainly — but I am not going away from here until we have had it out with one another. *(She goes into the room on the left, as Helmer comes in from the hall.)*

Nora (going up to Helmer): I have wanted you so much, Torvald dear.

Helmer: Was that the dressmaker?

Nora: No, it was Christine; she is helping me to put my dress in order. You will see I shall look quite smart.

Helmer: Wasn't that a happy thought of mine, now?

Nora: Splendid! But don't you think it is nice of me, too, to do as you wish?

Helmer: Nice? — because you do as your husband wishes? Well, well, you little rogue, I am sure you did not mean it in that way. But I am not going to disturb you; you will want to be trying on your dress, I expect.

Nora: I suppose you are going to work.

Helmer: Yes. *(Shows her a bundle of papers.)* Look at that. I have just been into the bank. *(Turns to go into his room.)*

Nora: Torvald.

Helmer: Yes.

Nora: If your little squirrel were to ask you for something very, very prettily — ?

Helmer: What then?

Nora: Would you do it?

Helmer: I should like to hear what it is, first.

Nora: Your squirrel would run about and do all her tricks if you would be nice, and do what she wants.

Helmer: Speak plainly.

Nora: Your skylark would chirp about in every room, with her song rising and falling —

Helmer: Well, my skylark does that anyhow.

Nora: I would play the fairy and dance for you in the moonlight, Torvald.

Helmer: Nora — you surely don't mean that request you made to me this morning?

Nora (going near him): Yes, Torvald, I beg you so earnestly —

Helmer: Have you really the courage to open up that question again?

Nora: Yes, dear, you *must* do as I ask; you *must* let Krogstad keep his post in the bank.

Helmer: My dear Nora, it is his post that I have arranged Mrs. Linde shall have.

Nora: Yes, you have been awfully kind about that; but you could just as well dismiss some other clerk instead of Krogstad.

Helmer: This is simply incredible obstinacy! Because you chose to give him a thoughtless promise that you would speak for him, I am expected to —

Nora: That isn't the reason, Torvald. It is for your own sake. This fellow writes in the most scurrilous newspapers; you have told me so yourself. He can do you an unspeakable amount of harm. I am frightened to death of him —

Helmer: Ah, I understand; it is recollections of the past that scare you.

Nora: What do you mean?

Helmer: Naturally you are thinking of your father.

Nora: Yes — yes, of course. Just recall to your mind what these malicious creatures wrote in the papers about papa, and how horribly they slandered him. I believe they would have procured his dismissal if the Department had not sent you over to inquire into it, and if you had not been so kindly disposed and helpful to him.

Helmer: My little Nora, there is an important difference between your father and me. Your father's reputation as a public official was not above suspicion. Mine is, and I hope it will continue to be so, as long as I hold my office.

Nora: You never can tell what mischief these men may contrive. We ought to be so well off, so snug and happy here in our peaceful home, and have no cares — you and I and the children, Torvald! That is why I beg you so earnestly —

Helmer: And it is just by interceding for him that you make it impossible for me to keep him. It is already known at the Bank that I mean to dismiss Krogstad. Is it to get about now that the new manager has changed his mind at his wife's bidding —

Nora: And what if it did?

Helmer: Of course! — if only this obstinate little person can get her way! Do you suppose I am going to make myself ridiculous before my whole staff, to let people think that I am a man to be swayed by all sorts of outside influence? I should very soon feel the consequences of it, I can tell you! And besides, there is one thing that makes it quite impossible for me to have Krogstad in the Bank as long as I am manager.

Nora: Whatever is that?

Helmer: His moral failings I might perhaps have overlooked, if necessary —

Nora: Yes, you could — couldn't you?

Helmer: And I hear he is a good worker, too. But I knew him when we were boys. It was one of those rash friendships that so often prove an incubus in afterlife. I may as well tell you plainly, we were once on very intimate terms with one another. But this tactless fellow lays no restraint on himself when other people are present. On the contrary, he thinks it gives him the right to adopt a familiar tone with me, and every minute it is "I say, Helmer, old fellow!" and that sort of thing. I assure you it is extremely painful for me. He would make my position in the Bank intolerable.

Nora: Torvald, I don't believe you mean that.

Helmer: Don't you? Why not?

Nora: Because it is such a narrow-minded way of looking at things.

Helmer: What are you saying? Narrow-minded? Do you think I am narrow-minded?

Nora: No, just the opposite, dear — and it is exactly for that reason.

Helmer: It's the same thing. You say my point of view is narrow-minded, so I must be so too. Narrow-minded! Very well — I must put an end to this. *(Goes to the hall door and calls.)* Helen!

Nora: What are you going to do?

Helmer (looking among his papers): Settle it. *(Enter Maid.)* Look here; take this letter and go downstairs with it at once. Find a messenger and tell him to deliver it, and be quick. The address is on it, and here is the money.

Maid: Very well, sir. *(Exit with the letter.)*

Helmer (putting his papers together): Now then, little Miss Obstinate.

Nora (breathlessly): Torvald — what was that letter?

Helmer: Krogstad's dismissal.

Nora: Call her back, Torvald! There is still time. Oh Torvald, call her back! Do it for my sake — for your own sake — for the children's sake! Do you hear me, Torvald? Call her back! You don't know what that letter can bring upon us.

Helmer: It's too late.

Nora: Yes, it's too late.

Helmer: My dear Nora, I can forgive the anxiety you are in, although really it is an insult to me. It is, indeed. Isn't it an insult to think that I should be afraid of a starving quill-driver's vengeance? But I forgive you nevertheless, because it is such eloquent witness to your great love for me. *(Takes her in his arms.)* And that is as it should be, my own darling Nora. Come what will, you may be sure I shall have both courage and strength if they be needed. You will see I am man enough to take everything upon myself.

Nora (in a horror-stricken voice): What do you mean by that?

Helmer: Everything, I say —

Nora (recovering herself): You will never have to do that.

Helmer: That's right. Well, we will share it, Nora, as man and wife should. That is how it shall be. *(Caressing her.)* Are you content now? There!

there! — not these frightened dove's eyes! The whole thing is only the wildest fancy! — Now, you must go and play through the Tarantella and practise with your tambourine. I shall go into the inner office and shut the door, and I shall hear nothing; you can make as much noise as you please. *(Turns back at the door.)* And when Rank comes, tell him where he will find me. *(Nods to her, takes his papers and goes into his room, and shuts the door after him.)*

Nora *(bewildered with anxiety, stands as if rooted to the spot, and whispers):* He was capable of doing it. He will do it. He will do it in spite of everything. — No, not that! Never, never! Anything rather than that! Oh, for some help, some way out of it! *(The door-bell rings.)* Doctor Rank! Anything rather than that — anything, whatever it is! *(She puts her hands over her face, pulls herself together, goes to the door and opens it. Rank is standing without, hanging up his coat. During the following dialogue it begins to grow dark.)*

Nora: Good-day, Doctor Rank. I knew your ring. But you mustn't go in to Torvald now; I think he is busy with something.

Rank: And you?

Nora *(brings him in and shuts the door after him):* Oh, you know very well I always have time for you.

Rank: Thank you. I shall make use of as much of it as I can.

Nora: What do you mean by that? As much of it as you can?

Rank: Well, does that alarm you?

Nora: It was such a strange way of putting it. Is anything likely to happen?

Rank: Nothing but what I have long been prepared for. But I certainly didn't expect it to happen so soon.

Nora *(gripping him by the arm):* What have you found out? Doctor Rank, you must tell me.

Rank *(sitting down by the stove):* It is all up with me. And it can't be helped.

Nora *(with a sigh of relief):* Is it about yourself?

Rank: Who else? It is no use lying to one's self. I am the most wretched of all my patients, Mrs. Helmer. Lately I have been taking stock of my internal economy. Bankrupt! Probably within a month I shall lie rotting in the churchyard.

Nora: What an ugly thing to say!

Rank: The thing itself is cursedly ugly, and the worst of it is that I shall have to face so much more that is ugly before that. I shall only make one more examination of myself; when I have done that, I shall know pretty certainly when it will be that the horrors of dissolution will begin. There is something I want to tell you. Helmer's refined nature gives him an unconquerable disgust at everything that is ugly; I won't have him in my sick-room.

Nora: Oh, but, Doctor Rank —

Rank: I won't have him there. Not on any account. I bar my door to him. As soon as I am quite certain that the worst has come, I shall send you my card with a black cross on it, and then you will know that the loathsome end has begun.

Nora: You are quite absurd to-day. And I wanted you so much to be in a really good humour.

Rank: With death stalking beside me? — To have to pay this penalty for another man's sin? Is there any justice in that? And in every single family, in one way or another, some such inexorable retribution is being exacted —

Nora (putting her hands over her ears): Rubbish! Do talk of something cheerful.

Rank: Oh, it's a mere laughing matter, the whole thing. My poor innocent spine has to suffer for my father's youthful amusements.

Nora (sitting at the table on the left): I suppose you mean that he was too partial to asparagus and pâté de foie gras, don't you?

Rank: Yes, and to truffles.

Nora: Truffles, yes. And oysters too, I suppose?

Rank: Oysters, of course, that goes without saying.

Nora: And heaps of port and champagne. It is sad that all these nice things should take their revenge on our bones.

Rank: Especially that they should revenge themselves on the unlucky bones of those who have not had the satisfaction of enjoying them.

Nora: Yes, that's the saddest part of it all.

Rank (with a searching look at her): Hm! —

Nora (after a short pause): Why did you smile?

Rank: No, it was you that laughed.

Nora: No, it was you that smiled, Doctor Rank!

Rank (rising): You are a greater rascal than I thought.

Nora: I am in a silly mood to-day.

Rank: So it seems.

Nora (putting her hands on his shoulders): Dear, dear Doctor Rank, death mustn't take you away from Torvald and me.

Rank: It is a loss you would easily recover from. Those who are gone are soon forgotten.

Nora (looking at him anxiously): Do you believe that?

Rank: People form new ties, and then —

Nora: Who will form new ties?

Rank: Both you and Helmer, when I am gone. You yourself are already on the high road to it, I think. What did that Mrs. Linde want here last night?

Nora: Oho! — you don't mean to say you are jealous of poor Christine?

Rank: Yes, I am. She will be my successor in this house. When I am done for, this woman will —

Nora: Hush! don't speak so loud. She is in that room.

Rank: To-day again. There, you see.

Nora: She has only come to sew my dress for me. Bless my soul, how unreasonable you are! *(Sits down on the sofa.)* Be nice now, Doctor Rank, and to-morrow you will see how beautifully I shall dance, and you can imagine I am doing it all for you — and for Torvald too, of course.

(Takes various things out of the box.) Doctor Rank, come and sit down here, and I will show you something.

Rank (sitting down): What is it?

Nora: Just look at those!

Rank: Silk stockings.

Nora: Flesh-coloured. Aren't they lovely? It is so dark here now, but to-morrow —. No, no, no! you must only look at the feet. Oh well, you may have leave to look at the legs too.

Rank: Hm! —

Nora: Why are you looking so critical? Don't you think they will fit me?

Rank: I have no means of forming an opinion about that.

Nora (looks at him for a moment): For shame! *(Hits him lightly on the ear with the stockings.)* That's to punish you. *(Folds them up again.)*

Rank: And what other nice things am I to be allowed to see?

Nora: Not a single thing more, for being so naughty. *(She looks among the things, humming to herself.)*

Rank (after a short silence): When I am sitting here, talking to you as intimately as this, I cannot imagine for a moment what would have become of me if I had never come into this house.

Nora (smiling): I believe you do feel thoroughly at home with us.

Rank (in a lower voice, looking straight in front of him): And to be obliged to leave it all —

Nora: Nonsense, you are not going to leave it.

Rank (as before): And not be able to leave behind one the slightest token of one's gratitude, scarcely even a fleeting regret — nothing but an empty place which the first comer can fill as well as any other.

Nora: And if I asked you now for a —? No!

Rank: For what?

Nora: For a big proof of your friendship —

Rank: Yes, yes!

Nora: I mean a tremendously big favour.

Rank: Would you really make me so happy for once?

Nora: Ah, but you don't know what it is yet.

Rank: No — but tell me.

Nora: I really can't, Doctor Rank. It is something out of all reason; it means advice, and help, and a favour —

Rank: The bigger a thing it is the better. I can't conceive what it is you mean. Do tell me. Haven't I your confidence?

Nora: More than anyone else. I know you are my truest and best friend, and so I will tell you what it is. Well, Doctor Rank, it is something you must help me to prevent. You know how devotedly, how inexpressibly deeply Torvald loves me; he would never for a moment hesitate to give his life for me.

Rank (leaning towards her): Nora — do you think he is the only one —?

Nora (with a slight start): The only one —?

Rank: The only one who would gladly give his life for your sake.

Nora (sadly): Is that it?

Rank: I was determined you should know it before I went away, and there will never be a better opportunity than this. Now you know it, Nora. And now you know, too, that you can trust me as you would trust no one else.

Nora (rises, deliberately and quietly): Let me pass.

Rank (makes room for her to pass him, but sits still): Nora!

Nora (at the hall door): Helen, bring in the lamp. *(Goes over to the stove.)* Dear Doctor Rank, that was really horrid of you.

Rank: To have loved you as much as anyone else does? Was that horrid?

Nora: No, but to go and tell me so. There was really no need —

Rank: What do you mean? Did you know — ? *(Maid enters with lamp, puts it down on the table, and goes out.)* Nora — Mrs. Helmer — tell me, had you any idea of this?

Nora: Oh, how do I know whether I had or whether I hadn't? I really can't tell you — To think you could be so clumsy, Doctor Rank! We were getting on so nicely.

Rank: Well, at all events you know now that you can command me, body and soul. So won't you speak out?

Nora (looking at him): After what happened?

Rank: I beg you to let me know what it is.

Nora: I can't tell you anything now.

Rank: Yes, yes. You mustn't punish me in that way. Let me have permission to do for you whatever a man may do.

Nora: You can do nothing for me now. Besides, I really don't need any help at all. You will find that the whole thing is merely fancy on my part. It really is so — of course it is! *(Sits down in the rocking-chair, and looks at him with a smile.)* You are a nice sort of man, Doctor Rank! — don't you feel ashamed of yourself, now the lamp has come?

Rank: Not a bit. But perhaps I had better go — for ever?

Nora: No, indeed, you shall not. Of course you must come here just as before. You know very well Torvald can't do without you.

Rank: Yes, but you?

Nora: Oh, I am always tremendously pleased when you come.

Rank: It is just that, that put me on the wrong track. You are a riddle to me. I have often thought that you would almost as soon be in my company as in Helmer's.

Nora: Yes — you see there are some people one loves best, and others whom one would almost always rather have as companions.

Rank: Yes, there is something in that.

Nora: When I was at home, of course I loved papa best. But I always thought it tremendous fun if I could steal down into the maids' room, because they never moralised at all, and talked to each other about such entertaining things.

Rank: I see — it is *their* place I have taken.

Nora (jumping up and going to him): Oh, dear, nice Doctor Rank, I never meant that at all. But surely you can understand that being with Torvald is a little like being with papa —

Enter Maid from the hall.

Maid: If you please, ma'am. *(Whispers and hands her a card.)*

Nora (glancing at the card): Oh! *(Puts it in her pocket.)*

Rank: Is there anything wrong?

Nora: No, no, not in the least. It is only something — it is my new dress —

Rank: What? Your dress is lying there.

Nora: Oh, yes, that one; but this is another. I ordered it. Torvald mustn't know about it —

Rank: Oho! Then that was the great secret.

Nora: Of course. Just go in to him; he is sitting in the inner room. Keep him as long as —

Rank: Make your mind easy; I won't let him escape. *(Goes into Helmer's room.)*

Nora (to the Maid): And he is standing waiting in the kitchen?

Maid: Yes; he came up the back stairs.

Nora: But didn't you tell him no one was in?

Maid: Yes, but it was no good.

Nora: He won't go away?

Maid: No; he says he won't until he has seen you, ma'am.

Nora: Well, let him come in — but quietly. Helen, you mustn't say anything about it to anyone. It is a surprise for my husband.

Maid: Yes, ma'am, I quite understand. *(Exit.)*

Nora: This dreadful thing is going to happen! It will happen in spite of me! No, no, no, it can't happen — it shan't happen! *(She bolts the door of Helmer's room. The Maid opens the hall door for Krogstad and shuts it after him. He is wearing a fur coat, high boots and a fur cap.)*

Nora (advancing towards him): Speak low — my husband is at home.

Krogstad: No matter about that.

Nora: What do you want of me?

Krogstad: An explanation of something.

Nora: Make haste then. What is it?

Krogstad: You know, I suppose, that I have got my dismissal.

Nora: I couldn't prevent it, Mr. Krogstad. I fought as hard as I could on your side, but it was no good.

Krogstad: Does your husband love you so little, then? He knows what I can expose you to, and yet he ventures —

Nora: How can you suppose that he has any knowledge of the sort?

Krogstad: I didn't suppose so at all. It would not be the least like our dear Torvald Helmer to show so much courage —

Nora: Mr. Krogstad, a little respect for my husband, please.

Krogstad: Certainly — all the respect he deserves. But since you have kept the matter so carefully to yourself, I make bold to suppose that you have a little clearer idea, than you had yesterday, of what it actually is that you have done?

Nora: More than you could ever teach me.

Krogstad: Yes, such a bad lawyer as I am.

Nora: What is it you want of me?

Krogstad: Only to see how you were, Mrs. Helmer. I have been thinking about you all day long. A mere cashier, a quill-driver, a — well, a man like me — even he has a little of what is called feeling, you know.

Nora: Show it, then; think of my little children.

Krogstad: Have you and your husband thought of mine? But never mind about that. I only wanted to tell you that you need not take this matter too seriously. In the first place there will be no accusation made on my part.

Nora: No, of course not; I was sure of that.

Krogstad: The whole thing can be arranged amicably; there is no reason why anyone should know anything about it. It will remain a secret between us three.

Nora: My husband must never get to know anything about it.

Krogstad: How will you be able to prevent it? Am I to understand that you can pay the balance that is owing?

Nora: No, not just at present.

Krogstad: Or perhaps that you have some expedient for raising the money soon?

Nora: No expedient that I mean to make use of.

Krogstad: Well, in any case, it would have been of no use to you now. If you stood there with ever so much money in your hand, I would never part with your bond.

Nora: Tell me what purpose you mean to put it to.

Krogstad: I shall only preserve it — keep it in my possession. No one who is not concerned in the matter shall have the slightest hint of it. So that if the thought of it has driven you to any desperate resolution —

Nora: It has.

Krogstad: If you had it in your mind to run away from your home —

Nora: I had.

Krogstad: Or even something worse —

Nora: How could you know that?

Krogstad: Give up the idea.

Nora: How did you know I had thought of *that*?

Krogstad: Most of us think of that at first. I did, too — but I hadn't the courage.

Nora (faintly): No more had I.

Krogstad (in a tone of relief): No, that's it, isn't it — you hadn't the courage either?

Nora: No, I haven't — I haven't.

Krogstad: Besides, it would have been a great piece of folly. Once the first storm at home is over — . I have a letter for your husband in my pocket.

Nora: Telling him everything?

Krogstad: In as lenient a manner as I possibly could.

Nora (quickly): He mustn't get the letter. Tear it up. I will find some means of getting money.

Krogstad: Excuse me, Mrs. Helmer, but I think I told you just now —

Nora: I am not speaking of what I owe you. Tell me what sum you are asking my husband for, and I will get the money.

Krogstad: I am not asking your husband for a penny.

Nora: What do you want, then?

Krogstad: I will tell you. I want to rehabilitate myself, Mrs. Helmer; I want to get on; and in that your husband must help me. For the last year and a half I have not had a hand in anything dishonourable, and all that time I have been struggling in most restricted circumstances. I was content to work my way up step by step. Now I am turned out, and I am not going to be satisfied with merely being taken into favour again. I want to get on, I tell you. I want to get into the Bank again, in a higher position. Your husband must make a place for me —

Nora: That he will never do!

Krogstad: He will; I know him; he dare not protest. And as soon as I am in there again with him, then you will see! Within a year I shall be the manager's right hand. It will be Nils Krogstad and not Torvald Helmer who manages the Bank.

Nora: That's a thing you will never see!

Krogstad: Do you mean that you will — ?

Nora: I have courage enough for it now.

Krogstad: Oh, you can't frighten me. A fine, spoilt lady like you —

Nora: You will see, you will see.

Krogstad: Under the ice, perhaps? Down into the cold, coal-black water? And then, in the spring, to float up to the surface, all horrible and unrecognisable, with your hair fallen out —

Nora: You can't frighten me.

Krogstad: Nor you me. People don't do such things, Mrs. Helmer. Besides, what use would it be? I should have him completely in my power all the same.

Nora: Afterwards? When I am no longer —

Krogstad: Have you forgotten that it is I who have the keeping of your reputation? *(Nora stands speechlessly looking at him.)* Well, now, I have warned you. Do not do anything foolish. When Helmer has had my letter, I shall expect a message from him. And be sure you remember that it is your husband himself who has forced me into such ways as this again. I will never forgive him for that. Good-bye, Mrs. Helmer. *(Exits through the hall.)*

Nora (goes to the hall door, opens it slightly and listens): He is going. He is not putting the letter in the box. Oh no, no! that's impossible! *(Opens the door by degrees.)* What is that? He is standing outside. He is not going downstairs. Is he hesitating? Can he — ? *(A letter drops into the box; then Krogstad's footsteps are heard, till they die away as he goes downstairs. Nora utters a stifled cry, and runs across the room to the table by the sofa. A short pause.)*

Nora: In the letter-box. *(Steals across to the hall door.)* There it lies — Torvald, Torvald, there is no hope for us now!

Mrs. Linde comes in from the room on the left, carrying the dress.

Mrs. Linde: There, I can't see anything more to mend now. Would you like to try it on —?

Nora (in a hoarse whisper): Christine, come here.

Mrs. Linde (throwing the dress down on the sofa): What is the matter with you? You look so agitated!

Nora: Come here. Do you see that letter? There, look — you can see it through the glass in the letter-box.

Mrs. Linde: Yes, I see it.

Nora: That letter is from Krogstad.

Mrs. Linde: Nora — it was Krogstad who lent you the money!

Nora: Yes, and now Torvald will know all about it.

Mrs. Linde: Believe me, Nora, that's the best thing for both of you.

Nora: You don't know all. I forged a name.

Mrs. Linde: Good heavens —!

Nora: I only want to say this to you, Christine — you must be my witness.

Mrs. Linde: Your witness? What do you mean? What am I to —?

Nora: If I should go out of my mind — and it might easily happen —

Mrs. Linde: Nora!

Nora: Or if anything else should happen to me — anything, for instance, that might prevent my being here —

Mrs. Linde: Nora! Nora! you are quite out of your mind.

Nora: And if it should happen that there were some one who wanted to take all the responsibility, all the blame, you understand —

Mrs. Linde: Yes, yes — but how can you suppose —?

Nora: Then you must be my witness, that it is not true, Christine. I am not out of my mind at all! I am in my right senses now, and I tell you no one else has known anything about it; I, and I alone, did the whole thing. Remember that.

Mrs. Linde: I will, indeed. But I don't understand all this.

Nora: How should you understand it? A wonderful thing is going to happen!

Mrs. Linde: A wonderful thing?

Nora: Yes, a wonderful thing! — But it is so terrible, Christine; it *mustn't* happen, not for all the world.

Mrs. Linde: I will go at once and see Krogstad.

Nora: Don't go to him; he will do you some harm.

Mrs. Linde: There was a time when he would gladly do anything for my sake.

Nora: He?

Mrs. Linde: Where does he live?

Nora: How should I know —? Yes *(feeling in her pocket),* here is his card. But the letter, the letter —!

Helmer (calls from his room, knocking at the door): Nora!

Nora (cries out anxiously): Oh, what's that? What do you want?

Helmer: Don't be so frightened. We are not coming in; you have locked the door. Are you trying on your dress?

Nora: Yes, that's it. I look so nice, Torvald.

Mrs. Linde (who has read the card): I see he lives at the corner here.

Nora: Yes, but it's no use. It is hopeless. The letter is lying there in the box.

Mrs. Linde: And your husband keeps the key?

Nora: Yes, always.

Mrs. Linde: Krogstad must ask for his letter back unread, he must find some pretence —

Nora: But it is just at this time that Torvald generally —

Mrs. Linde: You must delay him. Go in to him in the meantime. I will come back as soon as I can. *(She goes out hurriedly through the hall door.)*

Nora (goes to Helmer's door, opens it and peeps in): Torvald!

Helmer (from the inner room): Well? May I venture at last to come into my own room again? Come along, Rank, now you will see — *(Halting in the doorway.)* But what is this?

Nora: What is what, dear?

Helmer: Rank led me to expect a splendid transformation.

Rank (in the doorway): I understood so, but evidently I was mistaken.

Nora: Yes, nobody is to have the chance of admiring me in my dress until to-morrow.

Helmer: But, my dear Nora, you look so worn out. Have you been practising too much?

Nora: No, I have not practised at all.

Helmer: But you will need to —

Nora: Yes, indeed I shall, Torvald. But I can't get on a bit without you to help me; I have absolutely forgotten the whole thing.

Helmer: Oh, we will soon work it up again.

Nora: Yes, help me, Torvald. Promise that you will! I am so nervous about it — all the people —. You must give yourself up to me entirely this evening. Not the tiniest bit of business — you mustn't even take a pen in your hand. Will you promise, Torvald dear?

Helmer: I promise. This evening I will be wholly and absolutely at your service, you helpless little mortal. Ah, by the way, first of all I will just — *(Goes towards the hall door.)*

Nora: What are you going to do there?

Helmer: Only see if any letters have come.

Nora: No, no! don't do that, Torvald!

Helmer: Why not?

Nora: Torvald, please don't. There is nothing there.

Helmer: Well, let me look. *(Turns to go to the letter-box. Nora, at the piano, plays the first bars of the Tarantella. Helmer stops in the doorway.)* Aha!

Nora: I can't dance tomorrow if I don't practise with you.

Helmer (going up to her): Are you really so afraid of it, dear?

Nora: Yes, so dreadfully afraid of it. Let me practise at once; there is time now, before we go to dinner. Sit down and play for me, Torvald dear; criticise me, and correct me as you play.

Helmer: With great pleasure, if you wish me to. *(Sits down at the piano.)*

Nora (takes out of the box a tambourine and a long variegated shawl. She hastily drapes the shawl round her. Then she springs to the front of the stage and calls out): Now play for me! I am going to dance!

Helmer plays and Nora dances. Rank stands by the piano behind Helmer, and looks on.

Helmer (as he plays): Slower, slower!

Nora: I can't do it any other way.

Helmer: Not so violently, Nora!

Nora: This is the way.

Helmer (stops playing): No, no — that is not a bit right.

Nora (laughing and swinging the tambourine): Didn't I tell you so?

Rank: Let me play for her.

Helmer (getting up): Yes, do. I can correct her better then.

Rank sits down at the piano and plays. Nora dances more and more wildly. Helmer has taken up a position beside the stove, and during her dance gives her frequent instructions. She does not seem to hear him; her hair comes down and falls over her shoulders; she pays no attention to it, but goes on dancing. Enter Mrs. Linde.

Mrs. Linde (standing as if spell-bound in the doorway): Oh! —

Nora (as she dances): Such fun, Christine!

Helmer: My dear darling Nora, you are dancing as if your life depended on it.

Nora: So it does.

Helmer: Stop, Rank; this is sheer madness. Stop, I tell you! *(Rank stops playing, and Nora suddenly stands still. Helmer goes up to her.)* I could never have believed it. You have forgotten everything I taught you.

Nora (throwing away the tambourine): There, you see.

Helmer: You will want a lot of coaching.

Nora: Yes, you see how much I need it. You must coach me up to the last minute. Promise me that, Torvald!

Helmer: You can depend on me.

Nora: You must not think of anything but me, either to-day or to-morrow; you mustn't open a single letter — not even open the letter-box —

Helmer: Ah, you are still afraid of that fellow —

Nora: Yes, indeed I am.

Helmer: Nora, I can tell from your looks that there is a letter from him lying there.

Nora: I don't know; I think there is; but you must not read anything of that kind now. Nothing horrid must come between us until this is all over.

Rank (whispers to Helmer): You mustn't contradict her.

Helmer (taking her in his arms): The child shall have her way. But to-morrow night, after you have danced —

Nora: Then you will be free. *(The Maid appears in the doorway to the right.)*

Maid: Dinner is served, ma'am.

Nora: We will have champagne, Helen.

Maid: Very good, ma'am.

[*Exit.*]

Helmer: Hullo! — are we going to have a banquet?

Nora: Yes, a champagne banquet until the small hours. (*Calls out.*) And a few macaroons, Helen — lots, just for once!

Helmer: Come, come, don't be so wild and nervous. Be my own little sky-lark, as you used.

Nora: Yes, dear, I will. But go in now and you too, Doctor Rank. Christine, you must help me to do up my hair.

Rank (whispers to Helmer as they go out): I suppose there is nothing — she is not expecting anything?

Helmer: Far from it, my dear fellow; it is simply nothing more than this childish nervousness I was telling you of. (*They go into the right-hand room.*)

Nora: Well!

Mrs. Linde: Gone out of town.

Nora: I could tell from your face.

Mrs. Linde: He is coming home to-morrow evening. I wrote a note for him.

Nora: You should have let it alone; you must prevent nothing. After all, it is splendid to be waiting for a wonderful thing to happen.

Mrs. Linde: What is it that you are waiting for?

Nora: Oh, you wouldn't understand. Go in to them, I will come in a moment. (*Mrs. Linde goes into the dining-room. Nora stands still for a little while, as if to compose herself. Then she looks at her watch.*) Five o'clock. Seven hours until midnight; and then four-and-twenty hours until the next midnight. Then the Tarantella will be over. Twenty-four and seven? Thirty-one hours to live.

Helmer (from the doorway on the right): Where's my little skylark?

Nora (going to him with her arms outstretched): Here she is!

ACT III

THE SAME SCENE: *The table has been placed in the middle of the stage, with chairs round it. A lamp is burning on the table. The door into the hall stands open. Dance music is heard in the room above. Mrs. Linde is sitting at the table idly turning over the leaves of a book; she tries to read, but does not seem able to collect her thoughts. Every now and then she listens intently for a sound at the outer door.*

Mrs. Linde (looking at her watch): Not yet — and the time is nearly up. If only he does not — . (*Listens again.*) Ah, there he is. (*Goes into the hall and opens the outer door carefully. Light footsteps are heard on the stairs. She whispers.*) Come in. There is no one here.

Krogstad (in the doorway): I found a note from you at home. What does this mean?

Mrs. Linde: It is absolutely necessary that I should have a talk with you.

Krogstad: Really? And is it absolutely necessary that it should be here?

Mrs. Linde: It is impossible where I live; there is no private entrance to my rooms. Come in; we are quite alone. The maid is asleep, and the Helmers are at the dance upstairs.

Krogstad (coming into the room): Are the Helmers really at a dance to-night?

Mrs. Linde: Yes, why not?

Krogstad: Certainly — why not?

Mrs. Linde: Now, Nils, let us have a talk.

Krogstad: Can we two have anything to talk about?

Mrs. Linde: We have a great deal to talk about.

Krogstad: I shouldn't have thought so.

Mrs. Linde: No, you have never properly understood me.

Krogstad: Was there anything else to understand except what was obvious to all the world — a heartless woman jilts a man when a more lucrative chance turns up?

Mrs. Linde: Do you believe I am as absolutely heartless as all that? And do you believe that I did it with a light heart?

Krogstad: Didn't you?

Mrs. Linde: Nils, did you really think that?

Krogstad: If it were as you say, why did you write to me as you did at the time?

Mrs. Linde: I could do nothing else. As I had to break with you, it was my duty also to put an end to all that you felt for me.

Krogstad (wringing his hands): So that was it. And all this — only for the sake of money!

Mrs. Linde: You must not forget that I had a helpless mother and two little brothers. We couldn't wait for you, Nils; your prospects seemed hopeless then.

Krogstad: That may be so, but you had no right to throw me over for anyone else's sake.

Mrs. Linde: Indeed I don't know. Many a time did I ask myself if I had the right to do it.

Krogstad (more gently): When I lost you, it was as if all the solid ground went from under my feet. Look at me now — I am a shipwrecked man clinging to a bit of wreckage.

Mrs. Linde: But help may be near.

Krogstad: It *was* near; but then you came and stood in my way.

Mrs. Linde: Unintentionally, Nils. It was only to-day that I learned it was your place I was going to take in the Bank.

Krogstad: I believe you, if you say so. But now that you know it, are you not going to give it up to me?

Mrs. Linde: No, because that would not benefit you in the least.

Krogstad: Oh, benefit, benefit — I would have done it whether or no.

Mrs. Linde: I have learned to act prudently. Life, and hard, bitter necessity have taught me that.

Krogstad: And life has taught me not to believe in fine speeches.

Mrs. Linde: Then life has taught you something very reasonable. But deeds you must believe in?

Krogstad: What do you mean by that?

Mrs. Linde: You said you were like a shipwrecked man clinging to some wreckage.

Krogstad: I had good reason to say so.

Mrs. Linde: Well, I am like a shipwrecked woman clinging to some wreckage — no one to mourn for, no one to care for.

Krogstad: It was your own choice.

Mrs. Linde: There was no other choice — then.

Krogstad: Well, what now?

Mrs. Linde: Nils, how would it be if we two shipwrecked people could join forces?

Krogstad: What are you saying?

Mrs. Linde: Two on the same piece of wreckage would stand a better chance than each on their own.

Krogstad: Christine!

Mrs. Linde: What do you suppose brought me to town?

Krogstad: Do you mean that you gave me a thought?

Mrs. Linde: I could not endure life without work. All my life, as long as I can remember, I have worked, and it has been my greatest and only pleasure. But now I am quite alone in the world — my life is so dreadfully empty and I feel so forsaken. There is not the least pleasure in working for one's self. Nils, give me someone and something to work for.

Krogstad: I don't trust that. It is nothing but a woman's overstrained sense of generosity that prompts you to make such an offer of yourself.

Mrs. Linde: Have you ever noticed anything of the sort in me?

Krogstad: Could you really do it? Tell me — do you know all about my past life?

Mrs. Linde: Yes.

Krogstad: And do you know what they think of me here?

Mrs. Linde: You seemed to me to imply that with me you might have been quite another man.

Krogstad: I am certain of it.

Mrs. Linde: Is it too late now?

Krogstad: Christine, are you saying this deliberately? Yes, I am sure you are. I see it in your face. Have you really the courage, then — ?

Mrs. Linde: I want to be a mother to someone, and your children need a mother. We two need each other. Nils, I have faith in your real character — I can dare anything together with you.

Krogstad (grasps her hands): Thanks, thanks, Christine! Now I shall find a way to clear myself in the eyes of the world. Ah, but I forgot —

Mrs. Linde (listening): Hush! The Tarantella! Go, go!

Krogstad: Why? What is it?

Mrs. Linde: Do you hear them up there? When that is over, we may expect them back.

Krogstad: Yes, yes — I will go. But it is all no use. Of course you are not aware what steps I have taken in the matter of the Helmers.

Mrs. Linde: Yes, I know all about that.

Krogstad: And in spite of that have you the courage to — ?

Mrs. Linde: I understand very well to what lengths a man like you might be driven by despair.

Krogstad: If I could only undo what I have done!

Mrs. Linde: You cannot. Your letter is lying in the letter-box now.

Krogstad: Are you sure of that?

Mrs. Linde: Quite sure, but —

Krogstad (with a searching look at her): Is that what it all means? — that you want to save your friend at any cost? Tell me frankly. Is that it?

Mrs. Linde: Nils, a woman who has once sold herself for another's sake, doesn't do it a second time.

Krogstad: I will ask for my letter back.

Mrs. Linde: No, no.

Krogstad: Yes, of course I will. I will wait here until Helmer comes; I will tell him he must give me my letter back — that it only concerns my dismissal — that he is not to read it —

Mrs. Linde: No, Nils, you must not recall your letter.

Krogstad: But, tell me, wasn't it for that very purpose that you asked me to meet you here?

Mrs. Linde: In my first moment of fright, it was. But twenty-four hours have elapsed since then, and in that time I have witnessed incredible things in this house. Helmer must know all about it. This unhappy secret must be disclosed; they must have a complete understanding between them, which is impossible with all this concealment and falsehood going on.

Krogstad: Very well, if you will take the responsibility. But there is one thing I can do in any case, and I shall do it at once.

Mrs. Linde (listening): You must be quick and go! The dance is over; we are not safe a moment longer.

Krogstad: I will wait for you below.

Mrs. Linde: Yes, do. You must see me back to my door.

Krogstad: I have never had such an amazing piece of good fortune in my life! *(Goes out through the outer door. The door between the room and the hall remains open.)*

Mrs. Linde (tidying up the room and laying her hat and cloak ready): What a difference! what a difference! Some-one to work for and live for — a home to bring comfort into. That I will do, indeed. I wish they would be quick and come — (Listens.) Ah, there they are now. I must put on my things. (Takes up her hat and cloak. Helmer's and Nora's voices are heard outside; a key is turned, and Helmer brings Nora almost by force* *into the hall. She is in an Italian costume with a large black shawl around her; he is in evening dress, and a black domino° which is flying open.)*

Nora (hanging back in the doorway, and struggling with him): No, no, no! — don't take me in. I want to go upstairs again; I don't want to leave so early.

Helmer: But, my dearest Nora —

Nora: Please, Torvald dear — please, *please* — only an hour more.

Helmer: Not a single minute, my sweet Nora. You know that was our agreement. Come along into the room; you are catching cold standing there. *(He brings her gently into the room, in spite of her resistance.)*

Mrs. Linde: Good-evening.

Nora: Christine!

Helmer: You here, so late, Mrs. Linde?

Mrs. Linde: Yes, you must excuse me; I was so anxious to see Nora in her dress.

Nora: Have you been sitting here waiting for me?

Mrs. Linde: Yes, unfortunately I came too late, you had already gone upstairs; and I thought I couldn't go away again without having seen you.

Helmer (taking off Nora's shawl): Yes, take a good look at her. I think she is worth looking at. Isn't she charming, Mrs. Linde?

Mrs. Linde: Yes, indeed she is.

Helmer: Doesn't she look remarkably pretty? Everyone thought so at the dance. But she is terribly self-willed, this sweet little person. What are we to do with her? You will hardly believe that I had almost to bring her away by force.

Nora: Torvald, you will repent not having let me stay, even if it were only for half an hour.

Helmer: Listen to her, Mrs. Linde! She had danced her Tarantella, and it had been a tremendous success, as it deserved — although possibly the performance was a trifle too realistic — a little more so, I mean, than was strictly compatible with the limitations of art. But never mind about that! The chief thing is, she had made a success — she had made a tremendous success. Do you think I was going to let her remain there after that, and spoil the effect? No, indeed! I took my charming little Capri maiden — my capricious little Capri maiden, I should say — on my arm; took one quick turn round the room; a curtsey on either side, and, as they say in novels, the beautiful apparition disappeared. An exit ought always to be effective, Mrs. Linde; but that is what I cannot make Nora understand. Pooh! this room is hot. *(Throws his domino on a chair, and opens the door of his room.)* Hullo! it's all dark in here. Oh, of course — excuse me — . *(He goes in, and lights some candles.)*

Nora (in a hurried and breathless whisper): Well?

Mrs. Linde (in a low voice): I have had a talk with him.

---

domino: A loose cloak, worn with a mask for the upper part of the face at masquerades.

Nora: Yes, and —

Mrs. Linde: Nora, you must tell your husband all about it.

Nora (in an expressionless voice): I knew it.

Mrs. Linde: You have nothing to be afraid of as far as Krogstad is concerned; but you must tell him.

Nora: I won't tell him.

Mrs. Linde: Then the letter will.

Nora: Thank you, Christine. Now I know what I must do. Hush —!

Helmer (coming in again): Well, Mrs. Linde, have you admired her?

Mrs. Linde: Yes, and now I will say good-night.

Helmer: What, already? Is this yours, this knitting?

Mrs. Linde (taking it): Yes, thank you, I had very nearly forgotten it.

Helmer: So you knit?

Mrs. Linde: Of course.

Helmer: Do you know, you ought to embroider.

Mrs. Linde: Really? Why?

Helmer: Yes, it's far more becoming. Let me show you. You hold the embroidery thus in your left hand, and use the needle with the right — like
this — with a long, easy sweep. Do you see?

Mrs. Linde: Yes, perhaps —

Helmer: But in the case of knitting — that can never be anything but
ungraceful; look here — the arms close together, the knitting-needles
going up and down — it has a sort of Chinese effect —. That was really
excellent champagne they gave us.

Mrs. Linde: Well, — good-night, Nora, and don't be self-willed any more.

Helmer: That's right, Mrs. Linde.

Mrs. Linde: Good-night, Mr. Helmer.

Helmer (accompanying her to the door): Good-night, good-night. I hope
you will get home all right. I should be very happy to — but you hav-
en't any great distance to go. Good-night, good-night. *(She goes out; he
shuts the door after her, and comes in again.)* Ah! — at last we have got
rid of her. She is a frightful bore, that woman.

Nora: Aren't you very tired, Torvald?

Helmer: No, not in the least.

Nora: Nor sleepy?

Helmer: Not a bit. On the contrary, I feel extraordinarily lively. And
you? — you really look both tired and sleepy.

Nora: Yes, I am very tired. I want to go to sleep at once.

Helmer: There, you see it was quite right of me not to let you stay there any
longer.

Nora: Everything you do is quite right, Torvald.

Helmer (kissing her on the forehead): Now my little skylark is speaking reasonably. Did you notice what good spirits Rank was in this evening?

Nora: Really? Was he? I didn't speak to him at all.

Helmer: And I very little, but I have not for a long time seen him in such
good form. *(Looks for a while at her and then goes nearer to her.)*

It is delightful to be at home by ourselves again, to be all alone with
you — you fascinating, charming little darling!

Nora: Don't look at me like that, Torvald.

Helmer: Why shouldn't I look at my dearest treasure? — at all the beauty
that is mine, all my very own?

Nora (going to the other side of the table): You mustn't say things like that to
me to-night.

Helmer (following her): You have still got the Tarantella in your blood, I see.
And it makes you more captivating than ever. Listen — the guests are
beginning to go now. *(In a lower voice.)* Nora — soon the whole house
will be quiet.

Nora: Yes, I hope so.

Helmer: Yes, my own darling Nora. Do you know, when I am out at a party
with you like this, why I speak so little to you, keep away from you, and
only send a stolen glance in your direction now and then? — do you
know why I do that? It is because I make believe to myself that we are
secretly in love, and you are my secretly promised bride, and that no
one suspects there is anything between us.

Nora: Yes, yes — I know very well your thoughts are with me all the time.

Helmer: And when we are leaving, and I am putting the shawl over your
beautiful young shoulders — on your lovely neck — then I imagine that
you are my young bride and that we have just come from the wedding,
and I am bringing you for the first time into our home — to be alone
with you for the first time — quite alone with my shy little darling!
All this evening I have longed for nothing but you. When I watched
the seductive figures of the Tarantella, my blood was on fire; I could
endure it no longer, and that was why I brought you down so early —

Nora: Go away, Torvald! You must let me go. I won't —

Helmer: What's that? You're joking, my little Nora! You won't — you won't?
Am I not your husband — ? *(A knock is heard at the outer door.)*

Nora (starting): Did you hear — ?

Helmer (going into the hall): Who is it?

Rank (outside): It is I. May I come in for a moment?

Helmer (in a fretful whisper): Oh, what does he want now? *(Aloud.)* Wait a
minute! *(Unlocks the door.)* Come, that's kind of you not to pass by our door.

Rank: I thought I heard your voice, and felt as if I should like to look in.
(With a swift glance round.) Ah, yes! — these dear familiar rooms. You
are very happy and cosy in here, you two.

Helmer: It seems to me that you looked after yourself pretty well upstairs
too.

Rank: Excellently. Why shouldn't I? Why shouldn't one enjoy everything
in this world? — at any rate as much as one can, and as long as one can.
The wine was capital —

Helmer: Especially the champagne.

Rank: So you noticed that too? It is almost incredible how much I managed
to put away!

Nora: Torvald drank a great deal of champagne to-night too.

Rank: Did he?

Nora: Yes, and he is always in such good spirits afterwards.

Rank: Well, why should one not enjoy a merry evening after a well-spent day?

Helmer: Well spent? I am afraid I can't take credit for that.

Rank (clapping him on the back): But I can, you know!

Nora: Doctor Rank, you must have been occupied with some scientific investigation to-day.

Rank: Exactly.

Helmer: Just listen! — little Nora talking about scientific investigations!

Nora: And may I congratulate you on the result?

Rank: Indeed you may.

Nora: Was it favourable, then?

Rank: The best possible, for both doctor and patient — certainty.

Nora (quickly and searchingly): Certainty?

Rank: Absolute certainty. So wasn't I entitled to make a merry evening of it after that?

Nora: Yes, you certainly were, Doctor Rank.

Helmer: I think so too, so long as you don't have to pay for it in the morning.

Rank: Oh well, one can't have anything in this life without paying for it.

Nora: Doctor Rank — are you fond of fancy-dress balls?

Rank: Yes, if there is a fine lot of pretty costumes.

Nora: Tell me — what shall we two wear at the next?

Helmer: Little featherbrain! — are you thinking of the next already?

Rank: We two? Yes, I can tell you. You shall go as a good fairy —

Helmer: Yes, but what do you suggest as an appropriate costume for that?

Rank: Let your wife go dressed just as she is in everyday life.

Helmer: That was really very prettily turned. But can't you tell us what you will be?

Rank: Yes, my dear friend, I have quite made up my mind about that.

Helmer: Well?

Rank: At the next fancy-dress ball I shall be invisible.

Helmer: That's a good joke!

Rank: There is a big black hat — have you never heard of hats that make you invisible? If you put one on, no one can see you.

Helmer (suppressing a smile): Yes, you are quite right.

Rank: But I am clean forgetting what I came for. Helmer, give me a cigar — one of the dark Havanas.

Helmer: With the greatest pleasure. *(Offers him his case.)*

Rank (takes a cigar and cuts off the end): Thanks.

Nora (striking a match): Let me give you a light.

Rank: Thank you. *(She holds the match for him to light his cigar.)* And now good-bye!

Helmer: Good-bye, good-bye, dear old man!

Nora: Sleep well, Doctor Rank.

Rank: Thank you for that wish.

Nora: Wish me the same.

Rank: You? Well, if you want me to sleep well! And thanks for the light. *(He nods to them both and goes out.)*

Helmer (in a subdued voice): He has drunk more than he ought.

Nora (absently): Maybe. *(Helmer takes a bunch of keys out of his pocket and goes into the hall.)* Torvald! what are you going to do there?

Helmer: Empty the letter-box; it is quite full; there will be no room to put the newspaper in to-morrow morning.

Nora: Are you going to work to-night?

Helmer: You know quite well I'm not. What is this? Someone has been at the lock.

Nora: At the lock — ?

Helmer: Yes, someone has. What can it mean? I should never have thought the maid —. Here is a broken hairpin. Nora, it is one of yours.

Nora (quickly): Then it must have been the children —

Helmer: Then you must get them out of those ways. There, at last I have got it open. *(Takes out the contents of the letter-box, and calls to the kitchen.)* Helen! — Helen, put out the light over the front door. *(Goes back into the room and shuts the door into the hall. He holds out his hand full of letters.)* Look at that — look what a heap of them there are. *(Turning them over.)* What on earth is that?

Nora (at the window): The letter — No! Torvald, no!

Helmer: Two cards — of Rank's.

Nora: Of Doctor Rank's?

Helmer (looking at them): Doctor Rank. They were on the top. He must have put them in when he went out.

Nora: Is there anything written on them?

Helmer: There is a black cross over the name. Look there — what an uncomfortable idea! It looks as if he were announcing his own death.

Nora: It is just what he is doing.

Helmer: What? Do you know anything about it? Has he said anything to you?

Nora: Yes. He told me that when the cards came it would be his leave-taking from us. He means to shut himself up and die.

Helmer: My poor old friend! Certainly I knew we should not have him very long with us. But so soon! And so he hides himself away like a wounded animal.

Nora: If it has to happen, it is best it should be without a word — don't you think so, Torvald?

Helmer (walking up and down): He had so grown into our lives. I can't think of him as having gone out of them. He, with his sufferings and his loneliness, was like a cloudy background to our sunlit happiness. Well, perhaps it is best so. For him, anyway. *(Standing still.)* And perhaps for us too, Nora. We two are thrown quite upon each other now. *(Puts his arms round her.)* My darling wife, I don't feel as if I could hold you tight enough. Do you know, Nora, I have often wished that you might be threatened by some great danger, so that I might risk my life's blood, and everything, for your sake.

Nora (disengages herself, and says firmly and decidedly): Now you must read your letters, Torvald.

Helmer: No, no; not to-night. I want to be with you, my darling wife.

Nora: With the thought of your friend's death —

Helmer: You are right, it has affected us both. Something ugly has come between us — the thought of the horrors of death. We must try and rid our minds of that. Until then — we will each go to our own room.

Nora (hanging on his neck): Good-night, Torvald — Good-night!

Helmer (kissing her on the forehead): Good-night, my little singing-bird. Sleep sound, Nora. Now I will read my letters through. *(He takes his letters and goes into his room, shutting the door after him.)*

Nora (gropes distractedly about, seizes Helmer's domino, throws it round her, while she says in quick, hoarse, spasmodic whispers): Never to see him again. Never! Never! *(Puts her shawl over her head.)* Never to see my children again either — never again. Never! Never! — Ah! the icy, black water — the unfathomable depths — If only it were over! He has got it now — now he is reading it. Good-bye, Torvald and my children! *(She is about to rush out through the hall, when Helmer opens his door hurriedly and stands with an open letter in his hand.)*

Helmer: Nora!

Nora: Ah! —

Helmer: What is this? Do you know what is in this letter?

Nora: Yes, I know. Let me go! Let me get out!

Helmer (holding her back): Where are you going?

Nora (trying to get free): You shan't save me, Torvald!

Helmer (reeling): True? Is this true, that I read here? Horrible! No, no — it is impossible that it can be true.

Nora: It is true. I have loved you above everything else in the world.

Helmer: Oh, don't let us have any silly excuses.

Nora (taking a step towards him): Torvald — !

Helmer: Miserable creature — what have you done?

Nora: Let me go. You shall not suffer for my sake. You shall not take it upon yourself.

Helmer: No tragedy airs, please. *(Locks the hall door.)* Here you shall stay and give me an explanation. Do you understand what you have done? Answer me! Do you understand what you have done?

Nora (looks steadily at him and says with a growing look of coldness in her face): Yes, now I am beginning to understand thoroughly.

Helmer (walking about the room): What a horrible awakening! All these eight years — she who was my joy and pride — a hypocrite, a liar — worse, worse — a criminal! The unutterable ugliness of it all! — For shame! For shame! *(Nora is silent and looks steadily at him. He stops in front of her.)* I ought to have suspected that something of the sort would happen. I ought to have foreseen it. All your father's want of principle — be silent! — all your father's want of principle has come out in you. No religion, no morality, no sense of duty — . How I am punished for having winked at what he did! I did it for your sake, and this is how you repay me.

Nora: Yes, that's just it.

Helmer: Now you have destroyed all my happiness. You have ruined all my future. It is horrible to think of! I am in the power of an unscrupulous man; he can do what he likes with me, ask anything he likes of me, give me any orders he pleases — I dare not refuse. And I must sink to such miserable depths because of a thoughtless woman!

Nora: When I am out of the way, you will be free.

Helmer: No fine speeches, please. Your father had always plenty of those ready, too. What good would it be to me if you were out of the way, as you say? Not the slightest. He can make the affair known everywhere; and if he does, I may be falsely suspected of having been a party to your criminal action. Very likely people will think I was behind it all — that it was I who prompted you! And I have to thank you for all this — you whom I have cherished during the whole of our married life. Do you understand now what it is you have done for me?

Nora (coldly and quietly): Yes.

Helmer: It is so incredible that I can't take it in. But we must come to some understanding. Take off that shawl. Take it off, I tell you. I must try and appease him some way or another. The matter must be hushed up at any cost. And as for you and me, it must appear as if everything between us were just as before — but naturally only in the eyes of the world. You will still remain in my house, that is a matter of course. But I shall not allow you to bring up the children; I dare not trust them to you. To think that I should be obliged to say so to one whom I have loved so dearly, and whom I still — . No, that is all over. From this moment happiness is not the question; all that concerns us is to save the remains, the fragments, the appearance —

A ring is heard at the front-door bell.

Helmer (with a start): What is that? So late! Can the worst — ? Can he — ? Hide yourself, Nora. Say you are ill.

Nora stands motionless. Helmer goes and unlocks the hall door.

Maid (half-dressed, comes to the door): A letter for the mistress.

Helmer: Give it to me. *(Takes the letter, and shuts the door.)* Yes, it is from him. You shall not have it; I will read it myself.

Nora: Yes, read it.

Helmer (standing by the lamp): I scarcely have the courage to do it. It may mean ruin for both of us. No, I must know. *(Tears open the letter, runs his eye over a few lines, looks at a paper enclosed, and gives a shout of joy.)* Nora! *(She looks at him questioningly.)* Nora! — No, I must read it once again — . Yes, it is true! I am saved! Nora, I am saved!

Nora: And I?

Helmer: You too, of course; we are both saved, both you and I. Look, he sends you your bond back. He says he regrets and repents — that a happy change in his life — never mind what he says! We are saved, Nora! No one can do anything to you. Oh, Nora, Nora! — no, first I must destroy these hateful things. Let me see —. *(Takes a look at the bond.)* No, no, I won't look at it. The whole thing shall be nothing but a bad dream to me. *(Tears up the bond and both letters, throws them all into the stove, and watches them burn.)* There — now it doesn't exist any longer. He says that since Christmas Eve you —. These must have been three dreadful days for you, Nora.

Nora: I have fought a hard fight these three days.

Helmer: And suffered agonies, and seen no way out but —. No, we won't call any of the horrors to mind. We will only shout with joy, and keep saying, "It's all over! It's all over!" Listen to me, Nora. You don't seem to realise that it is all over. What is this? — such a cold, set face! My poor little Nora, I quite understand; you don't feel as if you could believe that I have forgiven you. But it is true, Nora, I swear it; I have forgiven you everything. I know that what you did, you did out of love for me.

Nora: That is true.

Helmer: You have loved me as a wife ought to love her husband. Only you had not sufficient knowledge to judge of the means you used. But do you suppose you are any the less dear to me, because you don't understand how to act on your own responsibility? No, no; only lean on me; I will advise you and direct you. I should not be a man if this womanly helplessness did not just give you a double attractiveness in my eyes. You must not think anymore about the hard things I said in my first moment of consternation, when I thought everything was going to overwhelm me. I have forgiven you, Nora; I swear to you I have forgiven you.

Nora: Thank you for your forgiveness. *(She goes out through the door to the right.)*

Helmer: No, don't go —. *(Looks in.)* What are you doing in there?

Nora (from within): Taking off my fancy dress.

Helmer (standing at the open door): Yes, do. Try and calm yourself, and make your mind easy again, my frightened little singing-bird. Be at rest, and feel secure; I have broad wings to shelter you under. *(Walks up and down by the door.)* How warm and cosy our home is, Nora. Here is shelter for you; here I will protect you like a hunted dove that I have saved from a hawk's claws; I will bring peace to your poor beating heart. It will come, little by little, Nora, believe me. To-morrow morning you will look upon it all quite differently; soon everything will be just as it was before. Very soon you won't need me to assure you that I have forgiven you; you will yourself feel the certainty that I have done so. Can you suppose I should ever think of such a thing as repudiating you, or even reproaching you? You have no idea what a true man's heart is like, Nora. There is something so indescribably sweet and satisfying, to a man, in the knowledge that he has forgiven his wife — forgiven her freely, and with all his heart. It seems as if that had made her, as it were, doubly his own; he has given her a new life, so to speak; and she has in a way become both wife and child to him. So you shall be for me after this, my little scared, helpless darling. Have no anxiety about anything, Nora; only be frank and open with me, and I will serve as will and conscience both to you — . What is this? Not gone to bed? Have you changed your things?

Nora (in everyday dress): Yes, Torvald, I have changed my things now.

Helmer: But what for? — so late as this.

Nora: I shall not sleep to-night.

Helmer: But, my dear Nora —

Nora (looking at her watch): It is not so very late. Sit down here, Torvald. You and I have much to say to one another. *(She sits down at one side of the table.)*

Helmer: Nora — what is this? — this cold, set face?

Nora: Sit down. It will take some time; I have a lot to talk over with you.

Helmer (sits down at the opposite side of the table): You alarm me, Nora! — and I don't understand you.

Nora: No, that is just it. You don't understand me, and I have never understood you either — before to-night. No, you mustn't interrupt me. You must simply listen to what I say. Torvald, this is a settling of accounts.

Helmer: What do you mean by that?

Nora (after a short silence): Isn't there one thing that strikes you as strange in our sitting here like this?

Helmer: What is that?

Nora: We have been married now eight years. Does it not occur to you that this is the first time we two, you and I, husband and wife, have had a serious conversation?

Helmer: What do you mean by serious?

Nora: In all these eight years — longer than that — from the very beginning of our acquaintance, we have never exchanged a word on any serious subject.

Helmer: Was it likely that I would be continually and forever telling you about worries that you could not help me to bear?

Nora: I am not speaking about business matters. I say that we have never sat down in earnest together to try and get at the bottom of anything.

Helmer: But, dearest Nora, would it have been any good to you?

Nora: That is just it; you have never understood me. I have been greatly wronged, Torvald — first by papa and then by you.

Helmer: What! By us two — by us two, who have loved you better than anyone else in the world?

Nora (shaking her head): You have never loved me. You have only thought it pleasant to be in love with me.

Helmer: Nora, what do I hear you saying?

Nora: It is perfectly true, Torvald. When I was at home with papa, he told me his opinion about everything, and so I had the same opinions; and if I differed from him I concealed the fact, because he would not have liked it. He called me his doll-child, and he played with me just as I used to play with my dolls. And when I came to live with you —

Helmer: What sort of an expression is that to use about our marriage?

Nora (undisturbed): I mean that I was simply transferred from papa's hands into yours. You arranged everything according to your own taste, and so I got the same tastes as you — or else I pretended to, I am really not quite sure which — I think sometimes the one and sometimes the other. When I look back on it, it seems to me as if I had been living here like a poor woman — just from hand to mouth. I have existed merely to perform tricks for you, Torvald. But you would have it so. You and papa have committed a great sin against me. It is your fault that I have made nothing of my life.

Helmer: How unreasonable and how ungrateful you are, Nora! Have you not been happy here?

Nora: No, I have never been happy. I thought I was, but it has never really been so.

Helmer: Not — not happy!

Nora: No, only merry. And you have always been so kind to me. But our home has been nothing but a playroom. I have been your doll-wife, just as at home I was papa's doll-child; and here the children have been my dolls. I thought it great fun when you played with me, just as they thought it great fun when I played with them. That is what our marriage has been, Torvald.

Helmer: There is some truth in what you say — exaggerated and strained as your view of it is. But for the future it shall be different. Playtime shall be over, and lesson-time shall begin.

Nora: Whose lessons? Mine, or the children's?

Helmer: Both yours and the children's, my darling Nora.

Nora: Alas, Torvald, you are not the man to educate me into being a proper wife for you.

Helmer: And you can say that!

Nora: And I — how am I fitted to bring up the children?

Helmer: Nora!

Nora: Didn't you say so yourself a little while ago — that you dare not trust me to bring them up?

Helmer: In a moment of anger! Why do you pay any heed to that?

Nora: Indeed, you were perfectly right. I am not fit for the task. There is another task I must undertake first. I must try and educate myself — you are not the man to help me in that. I must do that for myself. And that is why I am going to leave you now.

Helmer (springing up): What do you say?

Nora: I must stand quite alone, if I am to understand myself and everything about me. It is for that reason that I cannot remain with you any longer.

Helmer: Nora, Nora!

Nora: I am going away from here now, at once. I am sure Christine will take me in for the night—

Helmer: You are out of your mind! I won't allow it! I forbid you!

Nora: It is no use forbidding me anything any longer. I will take with me what belongs to myself. I will take nothing from you, either now or later.

Helmer: What sort of madness is this!

Nora: To-morrow I shall go home—I mean, to my old home. It will be easiest for me to find something to do there.

Helmer: You blind, foolish woman!

Nora: I must try and get some sense, Torvald.

Helmer: To desert your home, your husband and your children! And you don't consider what people will say!

Nora: I cannot consider that at all. I only know that it is necessary for me.

Helmer: It's shocking. This is how you would neglect your most sacred duties.

Nora: What do you consider my most sacred duties?

Helmer: Do I need to tell you that? Are they not your duties to your husband and your children?

Nora: I have other duties just as sacred.

Helmer: That you have not. What duties could those be?

Nora: Duties to myself.

Helmer: Before all else, you are a wife and a mother.

Nora: I don't believe that any longer. I believe that before all else I am a reasonable human being, just as you are—or, at all events, that I must try and become one. I know quite well, Torvald, that most people would think you right, and that views of that kind are to be found in books; but I can no longer content myself with what most people say, or with what is found in books. I must think over things for myself and get to understand them.

Helmer: Can you not understand your place in your own home? Have you not a reliable guide in such matters as that?—have you no religion?

Nora: I am afraid, Torvald, I do not exactly know what religion is.

Helmer: What are you saying?

Nora: I know nothing but what the clergyman said, when I went to be confirmed. He told us that religion was this, and that, and the other. When I am away from all this, and am alone, I will look into that matter too. I will see if what the clergyman said is true, or at all events if it is true for me.

Helmer: This is unheard of in a girl of your age! But if religion cannot lead you aright, let me try and awaken your conscience. I suppose you have some moral sense? Or—answer me—am I to think you have none?

Nora: I assure you, Torvald, that is not an easy question to answer. I really don't know. The thing perplexes me altogether. I only know that you and I look at it in quite a different light. I am learning, too, that the law is quite another thing from what I supposed; but I find it impossible to convince myself that the law is right. According to it a woman has no right to spare her old dying father, or to save her husband's life. I can't believe that.

Helmer: You talk like a child. You don't understand the conditions of the world in which you live.

Nora: No, I don't. But now I am going to try. I am going to see if I can make out who is right, the world or I.

Helmer: You are ill, Nora; you are delirious; I almost think you are out of your mind.

Nora: I have never felt my mind so clear and certain as to-night.

Helmer: And is it with a clear and certain mind that you forsake your husband and your children?

Nora: Yes, it is.

Helmer: Then there is only one possible explanation.

Nora: What is that?

Helmer: You do not love me anymore.

Nora: No, that is just it.

Helmer: Nora! — and you can say that?

Nora: It gives me great pain, Torvald, for you have always been so kind to me, but I cannot help it. I do not love you any more.

Helmer (regaining his composure): Is that a clear and certain conviction too?

Nora: Yes, absolutely clear and certain. That is the reason why I will not stay here any longer.

Helmer: And can you tell me what I have done to forfeit your love?

Nora: Yes, indeed I can. It was to-night, when the wonderful thing did not happen; then I saw you were not the man I had thought you.

Helmer: Explain yourself better. I don't understand you.

Nora: I have waited so patiently for eight years; for, goodness knows, I knew very well that wonderful things don't happen every day. Then this horrible misfortune came upon me; and then I felt quite certain that the wonderful thing was going to happen at last. When Krogstad's letter was lying out there, never for a moment did I imagine that you would consent to accept this man's conditions. I was so absolutely certain that you would say to him: Publish the thing to the whole world. And when that was done—

Helmer: Yes, what then? — when I had exposed my wife to shame and disgrace?

Nora: When that was done, I was so absolutely certain, you would come forward and take everything upon yourself, and say: I am the guilty one.

Helmer: Nora—!

Nora: You mean that I would never have accepted such a sacrifice on your part? No, of course not. But what would my assurances have been worth against yours? That was the wonderful thing which I hoped for and feared; and it was to prevent that, that I wanted to kill myself.

Helmer: I would gladly work night and day for you, Nora — bear sorrow and want for your sake. But no man would sacrifice his honour for the one he loves.

Nora: It is a thing hundreds of thousands of women have done.

Helmer: Oh, you think and talk like a heedless child.

Nora: Maybe. But you neither think nor talk like the man I could bind myself to. As soon as your fear was over — and it was not fear for what threatened me, but for what might happen to you — when the whole thing was past, as far as you were concerned it was exactly as if nothing at all had happened. Exactly as before, I was your little skylark, your doll, which you would in future treat with doubly gentle care, because it was so brittle and fragile. *(Getting up.)* Torvald — it was then it dawned upon me that for eight years I had been living here with a strange man, and had borne him three children — . Oh, I can't bear to think of it! I could tear myself into little bits!

Helmer (sadly): I see, I see. An abyss has opened between us — there is no denying it. But, Nora, would it not be possible to fill it up?

Nora: As I am now, I am no wife for you.

Helmer: I have it in me to become a different man.

Nora: Perhaps — if your doll is taken away from you.

Helmer: But to part! — to part from you! No, no, Nora, I can't understand that idea.

Nora (going out to the right): That makes it all the more certain that it must be done. *(She comes back with her cloak and hat and a small bag which she puts on a chair by the table.)*

Helmer: Nora, Nora, not now! Wait until to-morrow.

Nora (putting on her cloak): I cannot spend the night in a strange man's room.

Helmer: But can't we live here like brother and sister — ?

Nora (putting on her hat): You know very well that would not last long. *(Puts the shawl round her.)* Good-bye, Torvald. I won't see the little ones. I know they are in better hands than mine. As I am now, I can be of no use to them.

Helmer: But some day, Nora — some day?

Nora: How can I tell? I have no idea what is going to become of me.

Helmer: But you are my wife, whatever becomes of you.

Nora: Listen, Torvald. I have heard that when a wife deserts her husband's house, as I am doing now, he is legally freed from all obligations towards her. In any case, I set you free from all your obligations. You are not to feel yourself bound in the slightest way, any more than I shall. There must be perfect freedom on both sides. See, here is your ring back. Give me mine.

Helmer: That too?

Nora: That too.

Helmer: Here it is.

Nora: That's right. Now it is all over. I have put the keys here. The maids know all about everything in the house — better than I do. To-morrow, after I have left her, Christine will come here and pack up my own things that I brought with me from home. I will have them sent after me.

Helmer: All over! All over! — Nora, shall you never think of me again?

Nora: I know I shall often think of you, the children, and this house.

Helmer: May I write to you, Nora?

Nora: No — never. You must not do that.

Helmer: But at least let me send you —

Nora: Nothing — nothing —

Helmer: Let me help you if you are in want.

Nora: No. I can receive nothing from a stranger.

Helmer: Nora — can I never be anything more than a stranger to you?

Nora (taking her bag): Ah, Torvald, the most wonderful thing of all would have to happen.

Helmer: Tell me what that would be!

Nora: Both you and I would have to be so changed that —. Oh, Torvald, I don't believe any longer in wonderful things happening.

Helmer: But I will believe in it. Tell me! So changed that —?

Nora: That our life together would be a real wedlock. Good-bye. *(She goes out through the hall.)*

Helmer (sinks down on a chair at the door and buries his face in his hands): Nora! Nora! *(Looks round, and rises.)* Empty. She is gone. *(A hope flashes across his mind.)* The most wonderful thing of all —?

The sound of a door shutting is heard from below.

CONSIDERATIONS FOR CRITICAL THINKING AND WRITING

1. **FIRST RESPONSE.** What is the significance of the play's title?

2. Nora lies several times during the play. What kinds of lies are they? Do her lies indicate that she is not to be trusted, or are they a sign of something else about her personality?

3. What kind of wife does Helmer want Nora to be? He affectionately calls her names such as "skylark" and "squirrel." What does this reveal about his attitude toward her?

4. Why is Nora "pale with terror" at the end of Act I? What is the significance of the description of the Christmas tree now "stripped of its ornaments and with burnt-down candle-ends on its dishevelled branches" that opens Act II? What other symbols are used in the play?

5. What is Doctor Rank's purpose in the play?

6. How does the relationship between Krogstad and Mrs. Linde serve to emphasize certain qualities in the Helmers' marriage?

7. Is Krogstad's decision not to expose Nora's secret convincing? Does his shift from villainy to generosity seem adequately motivated?

8. Why does Nora reject Helmer's efforts to smooth things over between them and start again? Do you have any sympathy for Helmer?

9. Would you describe the ending as essentially happy or unhappy? Is the play more like a comedy or a tragedy?

10. Ibsen believed that a "dramatist's business is not to answer questions, but only to ask them." What questions are raised in the play? Does Ibsen propose any specific answers?

11. What makes this play a work of realism? Are there any elements that seem not to be realistic?

12. CRITICAL STRATEGIES. Read the section on new historicist criticism (pp. 1077–78) in Chapter 30, "Critical Strategies for Reading," and consider the following: Ibsen once wrote a different ending for the play to head off producers who might have been tempted to change the final scene to placate the public's sense of morality. In the second conclusion, Helmer forces Nora to look in on their sleeping children. This causes her to realize that she cannot leave her family even though it means sacrificing herself. Ibsen called this version of the ending a "barbaric outrage" and didn't use it. How do you think the play reflects or refutes social values contemporary to it?

CONNECTIONS TO OTHER SELECTIONS

1. What does Nora have in common with the protagonist in Lynn Nottage's *POOF!* (p. 700)? What significant differences are there between them?

2. Explain how Torvald's attitude toward Nora is similar to the men's attitudes toward women in Susan Glaspell's *Trifles* (p. 684). Write an essay exploring how the assumptions the men make about women in both plays contribute to the plays' conflicts.

Plays for Further Reading

29

Plays for Further Reading

My plays are about love, honor, duty, betrayal — things humans have written about since the beginning of time.
—AUGUST WILSON

The past is what you remember, imagine you remember, convince yourself you remember, or pretend you remember.
—HAROLD PINTER

Adger Cowans/Getty Images.

Jones/Getty Images.

DAVID AUBURN (B. 1969)

Proof 2000

David Auburn was born in Chicago, the setting of the following play *Proof* which won the Pulitzer Prize for Drama in 2001. He was educated at the University of Chicago and at the Julliard School in New York City where he now resides. He is the author of multiple plays and screenplays, but *Proof* remains his most prominent work. It has had a long production history in many countries and was adapted as a 2005 film.

CHARACTERS

Robert, 50s
Catherine, 25
Claire, 29
Hal, 28

SETTING

The back porch of a house in Chicago.

PA Images/Alamy Stock Photo.

ACT ONE

SCENE 1

Night. Catherine sits in a chair. She is twenty-five, exhausted, haphazardly dressed. Eyes closed. Robert is standing behind her. He is Catherine's father. Rumpled academic look. Catherine does not know he is there. After a moment:

Robert: Can't sleep?

Catherine: Jesus, you scared me.

Robert: Sorry.

Catherine: What are you doing here?

Robert: I thought I'd check up on you. Why aren't you in bed?

Catherine: Your student is still here. He's up in your study.

Robert: He can let himself out.

Catherine: I might as well wait up till he's done.

Robert: He's not my student anymore. He's teaching now. Bright kid. *(Beat.)*

Catherine: What time is it?

Robert: It's almost one.

Catherine: Huh.

Robert: After midnight . . .

Catherine: So?

Robert: So: *(He indicates something on the table behind him: a bottle of champagne.)* Happy birthday.

Catherine: Dad.

Robert: Do I ever forget?

Catherine: Thank you.

Robert: Twenty-five. I can't believe it.

Catherine: Neither can I. Should we have it now?

Robert: It's up to you.

Catherine: Yes.

Robert: You want me to open it?

Catherine: Let me. Last time you opened a bottle of champagne out here you broke a window.

Robert: That was a long time ago. I resent your bringing it up.

Catherine: You're lucky you didn't lose an eye. *(She opens the bottle.)*

Robert: Twenty-five!

Catherine: I feel old.

Robert: You're a kid.

Catherine: Glasses?

Robert: Goddamn it, I forgot the glasses. Do you want me to —

Catherine: Nah. *(She drinks from the bottle. A long pull. Robert watches her.)*

Robert: I hope you like it. I wasn't sure what to get you.

Catherine: This is the worst champagne I have ever tasted.

Robert: I am proud to say I don't know anything about wines. I hate those kind of people who are always talking about "vintages."

Catherine: It's not even champagne.

Robert: The bottle was the right shape.

Catherine: "Great Lakes Vineyards." I didn't know they made wine in Wisconsin.

Robert: A girl who's drinking from the bottle shouldn't complain. Don't guzzle it. It's an elegant beverage. Sip.

Catherine: *(Offering the bottle.)* Do you —

Robert: No, go ahead.

Catherine: You sure?

Robert: Yeah. It's your birthday.

Catherine: Happy birthday to me.

Robert: What are you going to do on your birthday?

Catherine: Drink this. Have some.

Robert: No. I hope you're not spending your birthday alone.

Catherine: I'm not alone.

Robert: I don't count.

Catherine: Why not?

Robert: I'm your old man. Go out with some friends.

Catherine: Right.

Robert: Your friends aren't taking you out?

Catherine: No.

Robert: Why not?

Catherine: Because in order for your friends to take you out you generally have to have friends.

Robert: *(Dismissive.)* Oh —

Catherine: It's funny how that works.

Robert: You have friends. What about that cute blonde, what was her name?

Catherine: What?

Robert: She lives over on Ellis Avenue — you used to spend every minute together.

Catherine: Cindy Jacobsen?

Robert: Cindy Jacobsen!

Catherine: That was in third grade, Dad. Her family moved to Florida in 1983.

Robert: What about Claire?

Catherine: She's not my friend, she's my sister. And she's in New York. And I don't like her.

Robert: I thought she was coming in.

Catherine: Not till tomorrow. *(Beat.)*

Robert: My advice, if you find yourself awake late at night, is to sit down and do some mathematics.

Catherine: Oh please.

Robert: We could do some together.

Catherine: No.

Robert: Why not?

Catherine: I can't think of anything worse. You sure you don't want any?

Robert: Yeah, thanks. You used to love it.

Catherine: Not anymore.

Robert: You knew what a prime number was before you could read.

Catherine: Well now I've forgotten.

Robert: (*Hard.*) Don't waste your talent, Catherine. (*Beat.*)

Catherine: I knew you'd say something like that.

Robert: I realize you've had a difficult time.

Catherine: Thanks.

Robert: That's not an excuse. Don't be lazy.

Catherine: I haven't been lazy, I've been taking care of you.

Robert: Kid, I've seen you. You sleep till noon, you eat junk, you don't work, the dishes pile up in the sink. If you go out it's to buy magazines. You come back with a stack of magazines this high — I don't know how you read that crap. And those are the good days. Some days you don't get up, you don't get out of bed.

Catherine: Those are the good days.

Robert: Bullshit. Those days are lost. You threw them away. And you'll never know what else you threw away with them — the work you lost, the ideas you didn't have, discoveries you never made because you were moping in your bed at four in the afternoon. (*Beat.*) You know I'm right. (*Beat.*)

Catherine: I've lost a few days.

Robert: How many?

Catherine: Oh, I don't know.

Robert: I bet you do.

Catherine: What?

Robert: I bet you count.

Catherine: Knock it off.

Robert: Well do you know or don't you?

Catherine: I don't.

Robert: Of course you do. How many days have you lost?

Catherine: A month. Around a month.

Robert: Exactly.

Catherine: Goddamn it, I don't —

Robert: HOW MANY?

Catherine: Thirty-three days.

Robert: Exactly?

Catherine: I don't know.

Robert: Be precise, for Chrissake.

Catherine: I slept till noon today.

Robert: Call it thirty-three and a quarter days.

Catherine: Yes, all right.

Robert: You're kidding!

Catherine: No.

Robert: Amazing number!

Catherine: It's a depressing fucking number.

Robert: Catherine, if every day you say you've lost were a year, it would be a very interesting fucking number.

Catherine: Thirty-three and a quarter years is not interesting.

Robert: Stop it. You know exactly what I mean.

Catherine: *(Conceding.)* 1,729 weeks.

Robert: 1,729. Great number. The smallest number expressible —

Catherine: — expressible as the sum of two cubes in two different ways.

Robert: Twelve cubed plus one cubed equals 1,729.

Catherine: And ten cubed plus nine cubed. Yes, we've got it, thank you.

Robert: You see? Even your depression is mathematical. Stop moping and get to work. The kind of potential you have —

Catherine: I haven't done anything good.

Robert: You're young. You've got time.

Catherine: I do?

Robert: Yes.

Catherine: By the time you were my age you were famous.

Robert: By the time I was your age I'd already done my best work. *(Beat.)*

Catherine: What about after?

Robert: After what?

Catherine: After you got sick.

Robert: What about it?

Catherine: You couldn't work then.

Robert: No, if anything I was sharper.

Catherine: *(She can't help it; she laughs.)* Dad.

Robert: I was. Hey, it's true. The clarity — that was the amazing thing. No doubts.

Catherine: You were happy?

Robert: Yeah, I was busy.

Catherine: Not the same thing.

Robert: I don't see the difference. I knew what I wanted to do and I did it.

If I wanted to work a problem all day long, I did it.

If I wanted to look for information — secrets, complex and tantalizing messages — I could find them all around me: in the air. In a pile of fallen leaves some neighbor raked together. In box scores in the paper, written in the steam coming up off a cup of coffee. The whole world was talking to me.

If I just wanted to close my eyes, sit quietly on the porch and listen for the messages, I did that.

It was wonderful. *(Beat.)*

Catherine: How old were you? When it started.

Robert: Mid-twenties. Twenty-three, four. *(Beat.)*

Is that what you're worried about?

Catherine: I've thought about it.

Robert: Just getting a year older means nothing, Catherine.

Catherine: It's not just getting older.

Robert: It's me. *(Beat.)*

Catherine: I've thought about it.

Robert: Really?

Catherine: How could I not?

Robert: Well if that's why you're worried you're not keeping up with the medical literature. There are all kinds of factors. It's not simply something you inherit. Just because I went bughouse doesn't mean you will.

Catherine: Dad . . .

Robert: Listen to me. Life changes fast in your early twenties and it shakes you up. You're feeling down. It's been a bad week. You've had a lousy couple years, no one knows that better than me. But you're gonna be okay.

Catherine: Yeah?

Robert: Yes. I promise you. Push yourself. Don't read so many magazines. Sit down and get the machinery going and I swear to God you'll feel fine. The simple fact that we can talk about this together is a good sign.

Catherine: A good sign?

Robert: Yes!

Catherine: How could it be a good sign?

Robert: Because! Crazy people don't sit around wondering if they're nuts.

Catherine: They don't?

Robert: Of course not. They've got better things to do. Take it from me. A very good sign that you're crazy is an inability to ask the question, "Am I crazy?"

Catherine: Even if the answer is yes?

Robert: Crazy people don't ask. You see?

Catherine: Yes.

Robert: So if you're asking . . .

Catherine: I'm not.

Robert: But if you were, it would be a very good sign.

Catherine: A good sign . . .

Robert: A good sign that you're fine.

Catherine: Right.

Robert: You see? You've just gotta think these things through. Now come on, what do you say? Let's call it a night, you go up, get some sleep, and then in the morning you can —

Catherine: Wait. No.

Robert: What's the matter?

Catherine: It doesn't work.

Robert: Why not?

Catherine: It doesn't make sense.

Robert: Sure it does.

Catherine: No.

Robert: Where's the problem?

Catherine: The problem is you are crazy!

Robert: What difference does that make?

Catherine: You admitted — You just told me that you are.

Robert: So?

Catherine: You said a crazy person would never admit that.

Robert: Yeah, but it's . . . oh. I see.

Catherine: So?

Robert: It's a point.

Catherine: So how can you admit it?

Robert: Well. Because I'm also dead. *(Beat.)* Aren't I?

Catherine: You died a week ago.

Robert: Heart failure. Quick. The funeral's tomorrow.

Catherine: That's why Claire's flying in from New York.

Robert: Yes.

Catherine: You're sitting here. You're giving me advice. You brought me champagne.

Robert: Yes. *(Beat.)*

Catherine: Which means . . .

Robert: For you?

Catherine: Yes.

Robert: For you, Catherine, my daughter, who I love very much . . . It could be a bad sign. *(They sit together for a moment. Noise off. Hal enters, twenty-eight, semi-hip clothes. He carries a backpack and a jacket, folded. He lets the door go and it bangs shut. Catherine sits up with a jolt.)*

Catherine: What?

Hal: Oh, God, sorry — Did I wake you?

Catherine: What?

Hal: Were you asleep? *(Beat. Robert is gone.)*

Catherine: You scared me, for Chrissake. What are you doing?

Hal: I'm sorry. I didn't realize it had gotten so late. I'm done for the night.

Catherine: Good.

Hal: Drinking alone? *(She realizes she is holding the champagne bottle. She puts it down quickly.)*

Catherine: Yes.

Hal: Champagne, huh?

Catherine: Yes.

Hal: Celebrating?

Catherine: No. I just like champagne.

Hal: It's festive.

Catherine: What?

Hal: Festive. *(He makes an awkward "party" gesture.)*

Catherine: Do you want some?

Hal: Sure.

Catherine: *(Gives him the bottle.)* I'm done. You can take the rest with you.

Hal: Oh. No thanks.

Catherine: Take it, I'm done.

Hal: No, I shouldn't. I'm driving. *(Beat.)*
        Well. I can let myself out.

Catherine: Good.

Hal: When should I come back?

Catherine: Come back?

Hal: Yeah. I'm nowhere near finished. Maybe tomorrow?

Catherine: We have a funeral tomorrow.

Hal: God, you're right, I'm sorry. I was going to attend, if that's all right.

Catherine: Yes.

Hal: What about Sunday? Will you be around?

Catherine: You've had three days.

Hal: I'd love to get in some more time up there.

Catherine: How much longer do you need?

Hal: Another week. At least.

Catherine: Are you joking?

Hal: No. Do you know how much stuff there is?

Catherine: A week?

Hal: I know you don't need anybody in your hair right now. Look, I spent the last couple days getting everything sorted out. It's mostly notebooks. He dated them all; now that I've got them in order I don't have to work here. I could take some stuff home, read it, bring it back.

Catherine: No.

Hal: I'll be careful.

Catherine: My father wouldn't want anything moved and I don't want anything to leave this house.

Hal: Then I should work here. I'll stay out of the way.

Catherine: You're wasting your time.

Hal: Someone needs to go through your dad's papers.

Catherine: There's nothing up there. It's garbage.

Hal: There are a hundred and three notebooks.

Catherine: I've looked at those. It's gibberish.

Hal: Someone should read them.

Catherine: He was crazy.

Hal: Yes, but he wrote them.

Catherine: He was a graphomaniac, Harold. Do you know what that is?

Hal: I know. He wrote compulsively. Call me Hal.

Catherine: There's no connection between the ideas. There's no ideas. It's like a monkey at a typewriter. One hundred and three notebooks full of bullshit.

Hal: Let's make sure they're bullshit.

Catherine: I'm sure.

Hal: I'm prepared to look at every page. Are you?

Catherine: No. I'M not crazy. *(Beat.)*

Hal: Well, I'm gonna be late . . . Some friends of mine are in this band. They're playing at a bar up on Diversey. Way down the bill, they're probably going on around two, two-thirty. I said I'd be there.

Catherine: Great.

Hal: They're all in the math department. They're really good. They have this great song, you'd like it, called "i" — lowercase I. They just stand there and don't play anything for three minutes.

Catherine: "Imaginary Number."

Hal: It's a math joke.
You see why they're way down the bill.

Catherine: Long drive to see some nerds in a band.

Hal: God I hate when people say that. It is not that long a drive.

Catherine: So they are nerds.

Hal: Oh they're raging geeks. But they're geeks who, you know, can dress themselves . . . hold down a job at a major university . . . Some of them have switched from glasses to contacts. They play sports, they play in a band, they get laid surprisingly often, so in that sense they sort of make you question the whole set of terms — geek, nerd, wonk, dweeb, Dilbert, paste-eater.

Catherine: You're in this band, aren't you?

Hal: Okay, yes. I play drums. You want to come? I never sing, I swear to God.

Catherine: No thanks.

Hal: All right. Look, Catherine, Monday: What do you say?

Catherine: Don't you have a job?

Hal: Yeah, I have a full teaching load this quarter plus my own work.

Catherine: Plus band practice.

Hal: I don't have time to do this but I'm going to. If you'll let me. *(Beat.)* I loved your dad.

   I don't believe a mind like his can just shut down. He had lucid moments. He had a lucid year, a whole year four years ago.

Catherine: It wasn't a year. It was more like nine months.

Hal: A school year. He was advising students . . . I was stalled on my Ph.D. I was this close to quitting. I met with your dad and he put me on the right track with my research. I owe him.

Catherine: Sorry.

Hal: Look. Let me — You're twenty-five, right?

Catherine: How old are you?

Hal: It doesn't matter. Listen:

Catherine: Fuck you, how old are you?

Hal: I'm twenty-eight, all right? When your dad was younger than both of us he made major contributions to three fields: game theory, algebraic geometry, and nonlinear operator theory. Most of us never get our heads around one. He basically invented the mathematical techniques for studying rational behavior, and he gave the astrophysicists plenty to work over too. Okay?

Catherine: Don't lecture me.

Hal: I'm not. I'm telling you if I came up with one-tenth of the shit your dad produced I could write my own ticket to any math department in the country. *(Beat.)*

Catherine: Give me your backpack.

Hal: What?

Catherine: Give me your backpack.

Hal: Why?

Catherine: I want to look inside it.

Hal: What?

Catherine: Open it and give it to me.

Hal: Oh come on.

Catherine: You're not taking anything out of this house.

Hal: I wouldn't do that.

Catherine: You're hoping to find something upstairs that you can publish.

Hal: Sure.

Catherine: Then you can write your own ticket.

Hal: What? No! It would be under your dad's name. It would be for your dad.

Catherine: I don't believe you. You have a notebook in that backpack.

Hal: What are you talking about?

Catherine: Give it to me.

Hal: You're being a little bit paranoid.

Catherine: PARANOID?

Hal: Maybe a little.

Catherine: Fuck you, HAL. I KNOW you have one of my notebooks.

Hal: I think you should calm down and think about what you're saying.

Catherine: I'm saying you're lying to me and stealing my family's property.

Hal: And I think that sounds paranoid.

Catherine: Just because I'm paranoid doesn't mean there isn't something in that backpack.

Hal: You just said yourself there's nothing up there. Didn't you?

Catherine: I —

Hal: Didn't you say that?

Catherine: Yes.

Hal: So what would I take?
      Right? *(Beat.)*

Catherine: You're right.

Hal: Thank you.

Catherine: So you don't need to come back.

Hal: *(Sighs.)* Please. Someone should know for sure whether —

Catherine: I LIVED WITH HIM.
      I spent my life with him. I fed him. Talked to him. Tried to listen when he talked. Talked to people who weren't there . . . Watched him shuffling around like a ghost. A very smelly ghost. He was filthy. I had to make sure he bathed. My own father.

Hal: I'm sorry. I shouldn't have . . .

Catherine: After my mother died it was just me here. I tried to keep him happy no matter what idiotic project he was doing. He used to read all day. He kept demanding more and more books. I took them out of the library by the carload. We had hundreds upstairs. Then I realized he wasn't reading: He believed aliens were sending him messages through the dewey decimal numbers on the library books. He was trying to work out the code.

Hal: What kind of messages?

Catherine: Beautiful mathematics. Answers to everything. The most elegant proofs, perfect proofs, proofs like music.

Hal: Sounds good.

Catherine: Plus fashion tips, knock-knock jokes — I mean it was NUTS, okay?

Hal: He was ill. It was a tragedy.

Catherine: Later the writing phase: scribbling, nineteen, twenty hours a day
... I ordered him a case of notebooks and he used every one.
I dropped out of school ... I'm glad he's dead.

Hal: I understand why you'd feel that way.

Catherine: Fuck you.

Hal: You're right. I can't imagine dealing with that. It must have been awful.
I know you —

Catherine: You don't know me. I want to be alone. I don't want him around.

Hal: (Confused.) Him? I don't —

Catherine: You. I don't want you here.

Hal: Why?

Catherine: He's dead.

Hal: But I'm not —

Catherine: HE's dead; I don't need any protégés around.

Hal: There will be others.

Catherine: What?

Hal: You think I'm the only one? People are already working over his stuff.
Someone's gonna read those notebooks.

Catherine: I'll do it.

Hal: No, you —

Catherine: He's my father, I'll do it.

Hal: You can't.

Catherine: Why not?

Hal: You don't have the math. It's all just squiggles on a page. You wouldn't
know the good stuff from the junk.

Catherine: It's all junk.

Hal: If it's not we can't afford to miss any through carelessness.

Catherine: I know mathematics.

Hal: If there were anything up there it would be pretty high-order. It would
take a professional to recognize it.

Catherine: I think I could recognize it.

Hal: (Patient.) Cathy ...

Catherine: WHAT?

Hal: I know your dad taught you some basic stuff, but come on.

Catherine: You don't think I could do it.

Hal: I'm sorry: I know that you couldn't. *(Beat. Catherine angrily snatches
his backpack.)* Hey! Oh come on. Give me a break. *(She opens the backpack and rifles through it.)* This isn't an airport. *(Catherine removes items
one by one. A water bottle. Some workout clothes. An orange. Drumsticks.
Nothing else. She puts everything back in and gives it back. Beat.)*

Catherine: You can come tomorrow. *(Beat. They are both embarrassed.)*

Hal: The University health service is, uh, very good.
My mom died a couple years ago and I was pretty broken up. Also
my work wasn't going that well ... I went over and talked to this doctor.
I saw her for a couple months and it really helped.

Catherine: I'm fine. *(Beat.)*

Hal: Also exercise is great. I run along the lake a couple of mornings a week. It's not too cold yet. If you wanted to come sometime I could pick you up. We wouldn't have to talk . . .

Catherine: No thanks.

Hal: All right.

    I'm gonna be late for the show. I better go.

Catherine: Okay. *(Beat.)*

Hal: It's seriously like twenty minutes up to the club. We go on, we play, we're terrible but we buy everyone drinks afterward to make up for it. You're home by four, four-thirty, tops . . .

Catherine: Good night.

Hal: Good night. *(Hal starts to exit. He has forgotten his jacket.)*

Catherine: Wait, your coat.

Hal: No, you *[don't have to]* — *(She picks up his jacket. As she does a composition book that was folded up in the coat falls to the floor. Beat. Catherine picks it up, trembling with rage.)*

Catherine: I'm PARANOID?

Hal: Wait.

Catherine: You think I should go JOGGING?

Hal: Just hold on.

Catherine: Get out!

Hal: Can I please just —

Catherine: Get the fuck out of my house.

Hal: Listen to me for a minute.

Catherine: *(Waving the book.)* You stole this!

Hal: Let me explain!

Catherine: You stole it from ME, you stole it from my FATHER — *(Hal snatches the book.)*

Hal: I want to show you something, will you calm down?

Catherine: Give it back.

Hal: Just wait a minute.

Catherine: I'm calling the police. *(She picks up the phone and dials.)*

Hal: Don't. Look, I borrowed the book, all right? I'm sorry, I just picked it up before I came downstairs and thought I'd —

Catherine: *(On phone.)* Hello?

Hal: I did it for a reason.

Catherine: Hello, Police? I — Yes, I'd like to report a robbery in progress.

Hal: I noticed something — something your father wrote. All right? Not math, something he wrote. Here, let me show you.

Catherine: A ROBBERY.

Hal: Will you put the fucking phone down and listen to me?

Catherine: *(On phone.)* Yes, I'm at 5724 South —

Hal: It's about you. See? YOU. It was written about you. Here's your name: CATHY. See?

Catherine: South . . . *(She pauses. She seems to be listening.)*

Hal: *(Reads.)* "A good day. Some very good news from Catherine." I didn't
    know what that referred to, but I thought you *[might]* . . .
Catherine. When did he write this?
Hal: I think four years ago. The handwriting is steady. It must have been
    during his remission.
            There's more. *(A moment. Catherine hangs up the phone.)* "Machin-
    ery not working yet but I am patient."
            "The machinery" is what he called his mind, his ability to do
    mathematics.
Catherine: I know.
Hal: *(Reads.)* "I know I'll get there. I am an auto mechanic who after years
    of greasy work on a hopeless wreck turns the ignition and hears a faint
    cough. I am not driving yet but there's cause for optimism. Talking with
    students helps. So does being outside, eating meals in restaurants, rid-
    ing busses, all the activities of 'normal' life.
            "Most of all Cathy. The years she has lost caring for me. I almost
    wrote 'wasted.' Yet her refusal to let me be institutionalized — her keep-
    ing me at home, caring for me herself has certainly saved my life. Made
    writing this possible. Made it possible to imagine doing math again.
    Where does her strength come from? I can never repay her.
            "Today is her birthday: She is twenty-one. I'm taking her to dinner."
    Dated September fourth.
            That's tomorrow.
Catherine: It's today.
Hal: You're right. *(She takes the book.)*
            I thought you might want to see it. I shouldn't have tried to sneak
    it out. Tomorrow I was going to — it sounds stupid now. I was going to
    wrap it.
            Happy birthday. *(Hal exits. Catherine is alone. She puts her head in
    her hands. She weeps. Eventually she stops, wipes her eyes. From off: a
    police siren, drawing closer.)*
Catherine: Shit.

Fade

SCENE 2

*The next morning. Claire, stylish, attractive, drinks coffee from a mug. She
has brought bagels and fruit out to the porch on a tray. She notices the champagne bottle lying on the floor. She picks it up and sets it on a table. Catherine
enters. Her hair is wet from a shower.*

Claire: Better. Much.
Catherine: Thanks.
Claire: Feel better?
Catherine: Yeah.

938 | *Plays for Further Reading*

Act One • Scene 2

Claire: You look a million times better. Have some coffee.

Catherine: Okay.

Claire: How do you take it?

Catherine: Black.

Claire: Have a little milk. *(She pours.)* Want a banana? It's a good thing I brought food: There was nothing in the house.

Catherine: I've been meaning to go shopping.

Claire: Have a bagel.

Catherine: No. I hate breakfast. *(Beat.)*

Claire: You didn't put on the dress.

Catherine: Didn't really feel like it.

Claire: Don't you want to try it on? See if it fits?

Catherine: I'll put it on later. *(Beat.)*

Claire: If you want to dry your hair I have a hair dryer.

Catherine: Nah.

Claire: Did you use that conditioner I brought you?

Catherine: No, shit, I forgot.

Claire: It's my favorite. You'll love it, Katie. I want you to try it.

Catherine: I'll use it next time.

Claire: You'll like it. It has jojoba.

Catherine: What is "jojoba"?

Claire: It's something they put in for healthy hair.

Catherine: Hair is dead.

Claire: What?

Catherine: It's dead tissue. You can't make it "healthy."

Claire: Whatever, it's something that's good for your hair.

Catherine: What, a chemical?

Claire: No, it's organic.

Catherine: Well it can be organic and still be a chemical.

Claire: I don't know what it is.

Catherine: Haven't you ever heard of organic chemistry?

Claire: It makes my hair feel, look, and smell good. That's the extent of my information about it. You might like it if you decide to use it.

Catherine: Thanks, I'll try it.

Claire: Good. If the dress doesn't fit we can go downtown and exchange it.

Catherine: Okay.

Claire: I'll take you to lunch.

Catherine: Great.

Claire: Maybe Sunday before I go back. Do you need anything?

Catherine: Like clothes?

Claire: Or anything. While I'm here.

Catherine: Nah, I'm cool. *(Beat.)*

Claire: I thought we'd have some people over tonight. If you're feeling okay.

Catherine: I'm feeling okay, Claire, stop saying that.

Claire: You don't have any plans?

Catherine: No.

Claire: I ordered some food. Wine, beer.

Catherine: We are burying Dad this afternoon.

Claire: I think it will be all right. Anyone who's been to the funeral and wants to come over for something to eat, can. And it's the only time I can see any old Chicago friends. It'll be nice. It's a funeral but we don't have to be completely grim about it. If it's okay with you.

Catherine: Yes, sure.

Claire: It's been a stressful time. It would be good to relax in a low-key way. Mitch says hi.

Catherine: Hi, Mitch.

Claire: He's really sorry he couldn't come.

Catherine: Yeah, he's gonna miss all the fun.

Claire: He wanted to see you. He sends his love. I told him you'd see him soon enough.

We're getting married.

Catherine: No shit.

Claire: Yes! We just decided.

Catherine: Yikes.

Claire: Yes!

Catherine: When?

Claire: January.

Catherine: Huh.

Claire: We're not going to do a huge thing. His folks are gone too. Just City Hall, then a big dinner at our favorite restaurant for all our friends. And you, of course, I hope you'll be in the wedding.

Catherine: Yeah. Of course. Congratulations, Claire, I'm really happy for you.

Claire: Thanks, me too. We just decided it was time. His job is great. I just got promoted . . .

Catherine: Huh.

Claire: You will come?

Catherine: Yes, sure. January? I mean I don't have to check my calendar or anything. Sure.

Claire: That makes me very happy. *(Beat.)* How are you?

Catherine: Okay.

Claire: How are you feeling about everything?

Catherine: About "everything"?

Claire: About Dad.

Catherine: What about him?

Claire: How are you feeling about his death? Are you all right?

Catherine: Yes, I am.

Claire: Honestly?

Catherine: Yes.

Claire: I think in some ways it was the "right time." If there is ever a right time. Do you know what you want to do now?

Catherine: No.

Claire: Do you want to stay here?

Catherine: I don't know.

Claire: Do you want to go back to school?

Catherine: I haven't thought about it.

Claire: Well there's a lot to think about.
        How do you feel?

Catherine: Physically? Great. Except my hair seems kind of unhealthy, I
        wish there were something I could do about that.

Claire: Come on, Catherine.

Catherine: What is the point of all these questions? *(Beat.)*

Claire: Katie, some policemen came by while you were in the shower.

Catherine: Yeah?

Claire: They said they were "checking up" on things here. Seeing how
        everything was this morning.

Catherine: *(Neutral.)* That was nice.

Claire: They told me they responded to a call last night and came to the
        house.

Catherine: Yeah?

Claire: Did you call the police last night?

Catherine: Yeah.

Claire: Why?

Catherine: I thought the house was being robbed.

Claire: But it wasn't.

Catherine: No. I changed my mind. *(Beat.)*

Claire: First you call 911 with an emergency and then you hang up on
        them —

Catherine: I didn't really want them to come.

Claire: So why did you call?

Catherine: I was trying to get this guy out of the house.

Claire: Who?

Catherine: One of Dad's students.

Claire: Dad hasn't had any students for years.

Catherine: No, he WAS Dad's student. Now he's — he's a mathematician.

Claire: Why was he in the house in the first place?

Catherine: Well he's been coming here to look at Dad's notebooks.

Claire: In the middle of the night?

Catherine: It was late. I was waiting for him to finish and last night I
        thought he might have been stealing them.

Claire: Stealing the notebooks.

Catherine: YES. So I told him to go.

Claire: Was he stealing them?

Catherine: Yes. That's why I called the police —

Claire: What is this man's name?

Catherine: Hal. Harold. Harold Dobbs.

Claire: The police said you were the only one here.

Catherine: He left before they got here.

Claire: With the notebooks?

Catherine: No, Claire, don't be stupid, there are over a hundred notebooks. He was only stealing ONE, but he was stealing it so he could give it BACK to me, so I let him go so he could play with his band on the North Side.

Claire: His band?

Catherine: He was late. He wanted me to come with him but I was like Yeah, right. *(Beat.)*

Claire: *(Gently.)* Is "Harold Dobbs" your boyfriend?

Catherine: No!

Claire: Are you sleeping with him?

Catherine: What? Euughh! No! He's a math geek!

Claire: And he's in a band? A rock band?

Catherine: No a marching band. He plays trombone. Yes a rock band!

Claire: What is the name of his band?

Catherine: How should I know?

Claire: "Harold Dobbs" didn't tell you the name of his rock band?

Catherine: No. I don't know. Look in the paper. They were playing last night. They do a song called "Imaginary Number" that doesn't exist. *(Beat.)*

Claire: I'm sorry, I'm just trying to understand: Is "Harold Dobbs" —

Catherine: Stop saying "Harold Dobbs."

Claire: Is this . . . person . . .

Catherine: HAROLD DOBBS EXISTS.

Claire: I'm sure he does.

Catherine: He's a mathematician at the University of Chicago. Call the fucking math department.

Claire: Don't get upset. I'm just trying to understand! I mean if you found out some creepy grad student was trying to take some of Dad's papers and you called the police I'd understand, and if you were out here partying, drinking with your boyfriend, I'd understand. But the two stories don't go together.

Catherine: Because you made up the "boyfriend" story. I was here ALONE —

Claire: Harold Dobbs wasn't here?

Catherine: No, he — YES, he was here, but we weren't "partying"!

Claire: You weren't drinking with him?

Catherine: No!

Claire: *(She holds up the champagne bottle.)* This was sitting right here. Who were you drinking champagne with? *(Catherine hesitates.)*

Catherine: With no one.

Claire: Are you sure?

Catherine: Yes. *(Beat.)*

Claire: The police said you were abusive. They said you're lucky they didn't haul you in.

Catherine: These guys were assholes, Claire. They wouldn't go away. They wanted me to fill out a report . . .

Claire: Were you abusive?

Catherine: This one cop kept spitting on me when he talked. It was disgusting.

Claire: Did you use the word "dickhead"?

Catherine: Oh I don't remember.

Claire: Did you tell one cop . . . to go fuck the other cop's mother?

Catherine: NO.

Claire: That's what they said.

Catherine: Not with that phrasing.

Claire: Did you strike one of them?

Catherine: They were trying to come in the house!

Claire: Oh my God.

Catherine: I might have pushed him a little.

Claire: They said you were either drunk or disturbed.

Catherine: They wanted to come in here and SEARCH MY HOUSE—

Claire: YOU called THEM.

Catherine: Yes but I didn't actually WANT them to come. But they did come and then they started acting like they owned the place—pushing me around, calling me "girly," smirking at me, laughing: They were assholes.

Claire: These guys seemed perfectly nice. They were off-duty and they took the trouble to come back here at the end of their shift to check up on you. They were very polite.

Catherine: Well people are nicer to you. *(Beat.)*

Claire: Katie. Would you like to come to New York?

Catherine: Yes, I told you, I'll come in January.

Claire: You could come sooner. We'd love to have you. You could stay with us. It'd be fun.

Catherine: I don't want to.

Claire: Mitch has become an excellent cook. It's like his hobby now. He buys all these gadgets. Garlic press, olive oil sprayer . . . Every night there's something new. Delicious, wonderful meals. The other day he made vegetarian chili!

Catherine: What the fuck are you talking about?

Claire: Stay with us for a while. We would have so much fun.

Catherine: Thanks, I'm okay here.

Claire: Chicago is dead. New York is so much more fun, you can't believe it.

Catherine: The "fun" thing is really not where my focus is at the moment.

Claire: I think New York would be a really fun and . . . safe . . . place for you to—

Catherine: I don't need a safe place and I don't want to have any fun! I'm perfectly fine here.

Claire: You look tired. I think you could use some downtime.

Catherine: Downtime?

Claire: Katie, please. You've had a very hard time.

Catherine: I'm PERFECTLY OKAY.

Claire: I think you're upset and exhausted.

Catherine: I was FINE till you got here.

Claire: Yes, but you —

Hal: *(From off.)* Catherine?

Claire: Who is that? *(A beat. Hal enters.)*

Hal: Hey, I — *(Catherine stands and points triumphantly at him.)*

Catherine: HAROLD DOBBS!

Hal: *(Confused.)* Hi.

Catherine: OKAY? I really don't need this, Claire. I'm fine, you know, I'm totally fine, and then you swoop in here with these questions, and "Are you okay?" and your soothing tone of voice and "Oh, the poor policemen" — I think the police can handle themselves! — and bagels and bananas and jojoba and "Come to New York" and vegetarian chili, I mean it really pisses me off so just save it. *(Beat.)*

Claire: *(Smoothly, to Hal.)* I'm Claire. Catherine's sister.

Hal: Oh, hi. Hal. Nice to meet you. *(Uncomfortable beat.)* I . . . hope it's not too early. I was just going to try to get some work done before the uh — if uh, if . . .

Claire: Yes!

Catherine: Sure, okay. *(Hal exits. A moment.)*

Claire: That's Harold Dobbs?

Catherine: Yes.

Claire: He's cute.

Catherine: *(Disgusted.)* Eugh.

Claire: He's a mathematician?

Catherine: I think you owe me an apology, Claire.

Claire: We need to make some decisions. But I shouldn't have tried to start first thing in the morning. I don't want an argument. *(Beat.)* Maybe Hal would like a bagel? *(Catherine doesn't take the hint. She exits.)*

Fade

SCENE 3

Night. Inside the house a party is in progress. Loud music from a not-very-good but enthusiastic band. Catherine is alone on the porch. She wears a flattering black dress. Inside, the band finishes a number. Cheers, applause. After a moment Hal comes out. He wears a dark suit. He has taken off his tie. He is sweaty and revved-up from playing. He holds two bottles of beer. Catherine regards him. A beat.

Catherine: I feel that for a funeral reception this might have gotten a bit out of control.

Hal: Aw come on. It's great. Come on in.

Catherine: I'm okay.

Hal: We're done playing, I promise.

Catherine: No, thanks.

Hal: Do you want a beer?

Catherine: I'm okay.

Hal: I brought you one. *(Beat. She hesitates.)*

Catherine: Okay. *(She takes it, sips.)* How many people are in there?

Hal: It's down to about forty.

Catherine: Forty?

Hal: Just the hard-core partyers.

Catherine: My sister's friends.

Hal: No, mathematicians. Your sister's friends left hours ago.
    The guys were really pleased to be asked to participate. They worshiped your dad.

Catherine: It was Claire's idea.

Hal: It was good.

Catherine: *(Concedes.)* The performance of "Imaginary Number" was . . . sort of . . . moving.

Hal: Good funeral. I mean not "good," but —

Catherine: No. Yeah.

Hal: Can you believe how many people came?

Catherine: I was surprised.

Hal: I think he would have liked it. *(She looks at him.)* Sorry, it's not my place to —

Catherine: No, you're right. Everything was better than I thought. *(Beat.)*

Hal: You look great.

Catherine: *(Indicates the dress.)* Claire gave it to me.

Hal: I like it.

Catherine: It doesn't really fit.

Hal: No, Catherine, it's good. *(A moment. Noise from inside.)*

Catherine: When do you think they'll leave?

Hal: No way to know. Mathematicians are insane. I went to this conference in Toronto last fall. I'm young, right? I'm in shape, I thought I could hang with the big boys. Wrong. I've never been so exhausted in my life. Forty-eight straight hours of partying, drinking, drugs, papers, lectures . . .

Catherine: Drugs?

Hal: Yeah. Amphetamines, mostly. I mean I don't. Some of the older guys are really hooked.

Catherine: Really?

Hal: Yeah, they think they need it.

Catherine: Why?

Hal: They think math's a young man's game. Speed keeps them racing, makes them feel sharp. There's this fear that your creativity peaks around twenty-three and it's all downhill from there. Once you hit fifty it's over, you might as well teach high school.

Catherine: That's what my father thought.

Hal: I dunno. Some people stay prolific.

Catherine: Not many.

Hal: No, you're right. Really original work — it's all young guys.

Catherine: Young guys.

Hal: Young people.

Catherine: But it is men, mostly.

Hal: There are some women.

Catherine: Who?

Hal: There's a woman at Stanford, I can't remember her name.

Catherine: Sophie Germain.

Hal: Yeah? I've probably seen her at meetings, I just don't think I've met her.

Catherine: She was born in Paris in 1776. *(Beat.)*

Hal: So I've definitely never met her.

Catherine: She was trapped in her house.

> The French Revolution was going on, the Terror. She had to stay inside for safety and she passed the time reading in her father's study. The Greeks . . . Later she tried to get a real education but the schools didn't allow women. So she wrote letters. She wrote to Gauss. She used a man's name. Uh, "Antoine-August Le Blanc." She sent him some proofs involving a certain kind of prime number, important work. He was delighted to correspond with such a brilliant young man.
>
> Dad gave me a book about her.

Hal: I'm stupid. Sophie Germain, of course.

Catherine: You know her?

Hal: Germain Primes.

Catherine: Right.

Hal: They're famous. Double them and add one, and you get another prime. Like two. Two is prime, doubled plus one is five: also prime.

Catherine: Right. Or 92,305 times 2^{16998} plus one.

Hal: *(Startled.)* Right.

Catherine: That's the biggest one. The biggest one known . . . *(Beat.)*

Hal: Did he ever find out who she was? Gauss.

Catherine: Yeah. Later a mutual friend told him the brilliant young man was a woman.

> He wrote to her: "A taste for the mysteries of numbers is excessively rare, but when a person of the sex which, according to our customs and prejudices, must encounter infinitely more difficulties than men to familiarize herself with these thorny researches, succeeds nevertheless in penetrating the most obscure parts of them, then without a doubt she must have the noblest courage, quite extraordinary talents and superior genius."
>
> *(Now self-conscious.)* I memorized it . . . *(Hal stares at her. He suddenly kisses her, then stops, embarrassed. He moves away.)*

Hal: Sorry. I'm a little drunk.

Catherine: It's okay. *(Uncomfortable beat.)* I'm sorry about yesterday. I wasn't helpful. About the work you're doing. Take as long as you need upstairs.

Hal: You were fine. I was pushy.

Catherine: I was awful.

Hal: No. My timing was terrible. Anyway, you're probably right.

Catherine: What?

Hal: About it being junk.

Catherine: *(Nods.)* Yes.

Hal: I read through a lot of stuff today, just skimming. Except for the book I stole —

Catherine: Oh, God, I'm sorry about that.

Hal: No, you were right.

Catherine: I shouldn't have called the police.

Hal: It was my fault.

Catherine: No.

Hal: The point is, that book — I'm starting to think it's the only lucid one, really. And there's no math in it.

Catherine: No.

Hal: I mean, I'll keep reading, but if I don't find anything in a couple of days . . .

Catherine: Back to the drums.

Hal: Yeah.

Catherine: And your own research.

Hal: Such as it is.

Catherine: What's wrong with it?

Hal: It's not exactly setting the world on fire.

Catherine: Oh come on.

Hal: It sucks, basically.

Catherine: Harold.

Hal: My papers get turned down. For the right reasons — my stuff is trivial. The big ideas aren't there.

Catherine: It's not about big ideas. It's work. You've got to chip away at a problem.

Hal: That's not what your dad did.

Catherine: I think it was, in a way. He'd attack a question from the side, from some weird angle, sneak up on it, grind away at it. He was slogging. He was just so much faster than anyone else that from the outside it looked magical.

Hal: I don't know.

Catherine: I'm just guessing.

Hal: Plus the work was beautiful. It's streamlined: no wasted moves, like a ninety-five-mile-an-hour fastball. It's just . . . elegant.

Catherine: Yeah.

Hal: And that's what you can never duplicate. At least I can't.

     It's okay. At a certain point you realize it's not going to happen, you readjust your expectations. I enjoy teaching.

Catherine: You might come up with something.

Hal: I'm twenty-eight, remember? On the downhill slope.

Catherine: Have you tried speed? I've heard it helps.

Hal: *(Laughs.)* Yeah. *(Beat.)*

Catherine: So, Hal.

Hal: Yeah?

Catherine: What do you do for sex?

Hal: What?

Catherine: At your conferences.

Hal: Uh, I uh —

Catherine: Isn't that why people hold conferences? Travel. Room service. Tax-deductible sex in big hotel beds.

Hal: (*Laughs, nervous.*) Maybe. I don't know.

Catherine: So what do you do? All you guys. (*Beat. Is she flirting with him? Hal is not sure.*)

Hal: Well we are scientists.

Catherine: So?

Hal: So there's a lot of experimentation.

Catherine: (*Laughs.*) I see. (*Beat. Catherine goes to him. She kisses him. A longer kiss. It ends. Hal is surprised and pleased.*)

Hal: Huh.

Catherine: That was nice.

Hal: Really?

Catherine: Yes.

Hal: Again?

Catherine: Yes. (*Kiss.*)

Hal: I always liked you.

Catherine: You did?

Hal: Even before I knew you. I'd catch glimpses of you when you visited your dad's office at school. I wanted to talk to you but I thought, No, you do not flirt with your doctoral adviser's daughter.

Catherine: Especially when your adviser's crazy.

Hal: Especially then. (*Kiss.*)

Catherine: You came here once. Four years ago. Remember?

Hal: Sure. I can't believe you do. I was dropping off a draft of my thesis for your dad. Jesus I was nervous.

Catherine: You looked nervous.

Hal: I can't believe you remember that.

Catherine: I remember you. (*Kiss.*) I thought you seemed . . . not boring. (*They continue to kiss.*)

Fade

Scene 4

The next morning. Catherine alone on the porch, in a robe. Hal enters, half-dressed. He walks up behind her quietly. She hears him and turns.

Hal: How long have you been up?

Catherine: A while.

Hal: Did I oversleep?

Catherine: No. (*Beat. Morning-after awkwardness.*)

Hal: Is your sister up?

Catherine: No. She's flying home in a couple hours. I should probably wake her.

Hal: Let her sleep. She was doing some pretty serious drinking with the theoretical physicists last night.

Catherine: I'll make her some coffee when she gets up. (*Beat.*)

Hal: Sunday mornings I usually go out. Get the paper, have some breakfast.

Catherine: Okay. (*Beat.*)

Hal: Do you want to come?

Catherine: Oh. No. I ought to stick around until Claire leaves.

Hal: All right. Do you mind if I stay?

Catherine: No. You can work if you want.

Hal: (*Taken aback.*) Okay.

Catherine: Okay.

Hal: Should I?

Catherine: If you want to.

Hal: Do you want me to go?

Catherine: Do you want to go?

Hal: I want to stay here with you.

Catherine: Oh . . .

Hal: I want to spend the day with you if possible. I'd like to spend as much time with you as I can unless of course I'm coming on way too strong right now and scaring you in which case I'll begin back-pedaling immediately . . . (*She laughs. Her relief is evident; so is his. They kiss.*)
How embarrassing is it if I say last night was wonderful?

Catherine: It's only embarrassing if I don't agree.

Hal: Uh, so . . .

Catherine: Don't be embarrassed. (*They kiss. After a moment Catherine breaks off. She hesitates, making a decision. Then she takes a chain from around her neck. There is a key on the chain. She tosses it to Hal.*) Here.

Hal: What's this?

Catherine: It's a key.

Hal: Ah.

Catherine: Try it.

Hal: Where?

Catherine: Bottom drawer of the desk in my dad's office.

Hal: What's in there?

Catherine: There's one way to find out, Professor.

Hal: Now? (*Catherine shrugs. Hal laughs, unsure if this is a joke or not.*) Okay. (*He kisses her quickly then goes inside. Catherine smiles to herself. She is happy, on the edge of being giddy. Claire enters, hungover. She sits down, squinting.*)

Catherine: Good morning.

Claire: Please don't yell please.

Catherine: Are you all right?

Claire: No. *(Beat. She clutches her head.)* Those fucking physicists.

Catherine: What happened?

Claire: Thanks a lot for leaving me all alone with them.

Catherine: Where were your friends?

Claire: My stupid friends left — it was only eleven o'clock! — they all had to get home and pay their babysitters or bake bread or something. I'm left alone with these lunatics . . .

Catherine: Why did you drink so much?

Claire: I thought I could keep up with them. I thought they'd stop. They didn't. Oh God.

Catherine: Do you want some coffee?

Claire: In a minute.

    That BAND.

Catherine: Yeah.

Claire: They were terrible.

Catherine: They were okay. They had fun. I think.

Claire: Well as long as everyone had fun.

    Your dress turned out all right.

Catherine: I love it.

Claire: You do.

Catherine: Yeah, it's wonderful.

Claire: I was surprised you even wore it.

Catherine: I love it, Claire. Thanks.

Claire: *(Surprised.)* You're welcome. You're in a good mood.

Catherine: Should I not be?

Claire: Are you kidding? No. I'm thrilled.

    I'm leaving in a few hours.

Catherine: I know.

Claire: The house is a wreck. Don't clean it up yourself. I'll hire someone to come in.

Catherine: Thanks. You want your coffee?

Claire: No, thanks.

Catherine: *(Starting in.)* It's no trouble.

Claire: Hold on a sec, Katie. I just . . . *(Claire takes a breath.)*

    I'm leaving soon. I —

Catherine: You said. I know.

Claire: I'd still like you to come to New York.

Catherine: Yes: January.

Claire: I'd like you to move to New York.

Catherine: Move?

Claire: Would you think about it? For me?

    You could stay with me and Mitch at first. There's plenty of room. Then you could get your own place. I've already scouted some apartments for you, really cute places.

Catherine: What would I do in New York?

Claire: What are you doing here?

Catherine: I live here.

Claire: You could do whatever you want. You could work, you could go to school.

Catherine: I don't know, Claire. This is pretty major.

Claire: I realize that.

Catherine: I know you mean well. I'm just not sure what I want to do. I mean to be honest you were right yesterday. I do feel a little confused. I'm tired. It's been a pretty weird couple of years. I think I'd like to take some time to figure things out.

Claire: You could do that in New York.

Catherine: And I could do it here.

Claire: But it would be much easier for me to get you set up in an apartment in New York, and —

Catherine: I don't need an apartment, I'll stay in the house.

Claire: We're selling the house. *(Beat.)*

Catherine: What?

Claire: We — I'm selling it.

Catherine: WHEN?

Claire: I'm hoping to do the paperwork this week. I know it seems sudden.

Catherine: No one was here looking at the place, who are you selling it to?

Claire: The University. They've wanted the block for years.

Catherine: I LIVE HERE.

Claire: Honey, now that Dad's gone it doesn't make sense. It's in bad shape. It costs a fortune to heat. It's time to let it go. Mitch agrees, it's a very smart move. We're lucky, we have a great offer —

Catherine: Where am I supposed to live?

Claire: Come to New York.

Catherine: I can't believe this.

Claire: It'll be so good. You deserve a change. This would be a whole new adventure for you.

Catherine: Why are you doing this?

Claire: I want to help.

Catherine: By kicking me out of my house?

Claire: It was my house too.

Catherine: You haven't lived here for years.

Claire: I know that. You were on your own. I really regret that, Katie.

Catherine: Don't.

Claire: I know I let you down. I feel awful about it. Now I'm trying to help.

Catherine: You want to help now?

Claire: Yes.

Catherine: Dad is dead.

Claire: I know.

Catherine: He's dead. Now that he's dead you fly in for the weekend and decide you want to help? YOU'RE LATE. Where have you been?

Claire: I —

Catherine: Where were you five years ago? You weren't helping then.

Claire: I was working.

Catherine: I was HERE. I lived with him ALONE.

Claire: I was working fourteen-hour days. I paid every bill here. I paid off the mortgage on this three-bedroom house while I was living in a studio in Brooklyn.

Catherine: You had your life. You got to finish school.

Claire: You could have stayed in school!

Catherine: How?

Claire: I would have done anything — I told you that. I told you a million times to do anything you wanted.

Catherine: What about Dad? Someone had to take care of him.

Claire: He was ill. He should have been in a full-time professional care situation.

Catherine: He didn't belong in the nuthouse.

Claire: He might have been better off.

Catherine: How can you say that?

Claire: This is where I'm meant to feel guilty, right?

Catherine: Sure, go for it.

Claire: I'm heartless. My own father.

Catherine: He needed to be here. In his own house, near the University, near his students, near everything that made him happy.

Claire: Maybe. Or maybe some real, professional care would have done him more good than rattling around in a filthy house with YOU looking after him.

I'm sorry, Catherine, it's not your fault. It's my fault for letting you do it.

Catherine: I was right to keep him here.

Claire: No.

Catherine: What about his remission? Four years ago. He was healthy for almost a year.

Claire: And then he went right downhill again.

Catherine: He might have been worse in a hospital.

Claire: And he MIGHT have been BETTER. Did he ever do any work again?

Catherine: No.

Claire: NO.

And you might have been better.

Catherine: (*Keeping her voice under control.*) Better than what?

Claire: Living here with him didn't do you any good. You said that yourself. You had so much talent . . .

Catherine: You think I'm like Dad.

Claire: I think you have some of his talent and some of his tendency toward . . . instability. (*Beat.*)

Catherine: Claire, in addition to the "cute apartments" that you've "scouted" for me in New York, would you by any chance also have devoted some of your considerable energies toward scouting out another type of—

Claire: NO.

Catherine: — living facility for your bughouse little sister?

Claire: NO! Absolutely not. That is not what this is about.

Catherine: Don't lie to me, Claire, I'm smarter than you. *(Beat.)*

Claire: The resources . . . I've investigated —

Catherine: Oh my GOD.

Claire: — if you WANTED to, all I'm saying is the doctors in New York and the people are the BEST, and they —

Catherine: FUCK YOU.

Claire: It would be entirely up to you. You wouldn't LIVE anywhere, you can —

Catherine: I hate you.

Claire: Don't yell, please, calm down.

Catherine: I HATE YOU. I — *(Hal enters, holding a notebook. Claire and Catherine stop suddenly. Beat.)*

Claire: What are you doing here? . . . *(She looks at Catherine. Hal is nearly speechless. He stares at Catherine.)*

Hal: How long have you known about this?

Catherine: A while.

Hal: Why didn't you tell me about it?

Catherine: I wasn't sure I wanted to. *(Beat.)*

Hal: Thank you.

Catherine: You're welcome.

Claire: What's going on?

Hal: God, Catherine, thank you.

Catherine: I thought you'd like to see it.

Claire: What is it?

Hal: It's incredible.

Claire: What IS it?

Hal: Oh, uh, it's a result. A proof.

        I mean it looks like one. I mean it is one, a very long one, I haven't read it all of course, or checked it, I don't even know if I could check it, but if it IS what I think it is a proof of, it's a very . . . important . . . proof.

Claire: What does it prove?

Hal: It looks like it proves a theorem . . . a mathematical theorem about prime numbers, something mathematicians have been trying to prove since . . . since there were mathematicians, basically. Most people thought it couldn't be done.

Claire: Where did you find it?

Hal: In your father's desk. Cathy told me about it.

Claire: You know what this is?

Catherine: Sure.

Claire: Is it good?

Catherine: Yes.

Hal: It's historic. If it checks out.

Claire: What does it say?

Hal: I don't know yet. I've just read the first few pages.

Claire: But what does it mean?

Hal: It means that during a time when everyone thought your dad was crazy... or barely functioning . . . he was doing some of the most import- ant mathematics in the world. If it checks out it means you publish instantly. It means newspapers all over the world are going to want to talk to the person who found this notebook.

Claire: Cathy.

Hal: Cathy.

Catherine: I didn't find it.

Hal: Yes you did.

Catherine: No.

Claire: Well did you find it or did Hal find it?

Hal: I didn't find it.

Catherine: I didn't find it. I wrote it.

Curtain

ACT TWO

Scene 1

Robert is alone on the porch. He sits quietly, enjoying the quiet, the September afternoon. A notebook nearby, unopened. He closes his eyes, apparently dozing. It is four years earlier than the events in Act One. Catherine enters quietly. She stands behind her father for a moment.

Robert: Hello.

Catherine: How did you know I was here?

Robert: I heard you.

Catherine: I thought you were asleep.

Robert: On an afternoon like this? No.

Catherine: Do you need anything?

Robert: No.

Catherine: I'm going to the store.

Robert: What's for dinner?

Catherine: What do you want?

Robert: Not spaghetti.

Catherine: All right.

Robert: Disgusting stuff.

Catherine: That's what I was going to make.

Robert: I had a feeling. Good thing I spoke up. You make it too much.

Catherine: What do you want?

Robert: What do you have a taste for?

Catherine: Nothing.

Robert: Nothing at all?

Catherine: I don't care. I thought pasta would be easy.

Robert: Pasta, oh God don't even say the word "pasta." It sounds so hopeless, like surrender: "Pasta would be easy." Yes, yes it would. Pasta. It doesn't MEAN anything. It's just a euphemism people invented when they got sick of eating spaghetti.

Catherine: Dad, what do you want to eat?

Robert: I don't know.

Catherine: Well I don't know what to get.

Robert: I'll shop.

Catherine: No.

Robert: I'll do it.

Catherine: No, Dad, rest.

Robert: I wanted to take a walk anyway.

Catherine: Are you sure?

Robert: Yes. What about a walk to the lake? You and me.

Catherine: All right.

Robert: I would love to go to the lake. Then on the way home we'll stop at the store, see what jumps out at us.

Catherine: It's warm. It would be nice, if you're up for it.

Robert: You're damn right I'm up for it. We'll work up an appetite. Give me ten seconds, let me put this stuff away and we're out the door.

Catherine: I'm going to school. (*Beat.*)

Robert: When?

Catherine: I'm gonna start at Northwestern at the end of the month.

Robert: Northwestern?

Catherine: They were great about my credits. They're taking me in as a sophomore.

I wasn't sure when to talk to you about it.

Robert: Northwestern?

Catherine: Yes.

Robert: What's wrong with Chicago?

Catherine: You still teach there. I'm sorry, it's too weird, taking classes in your department.

Robert: It's a long drive.

Catherine: Not that long, half an hour.

Robert: Still, twice a day . . .

Catherine: Dad, I'd live there. (*Beat.*)

Robert: You'd actually want to live in Evanston?

Catherine: Yes. I'll still be close. I can come home whenever you want.

You've been well — really well — for almost seven months. I don't think you need me here every minute of the day. (*Beat.*)

Robert: This is all a done deal? You're in.

Catherine: Yes.

Robert: You're sure.

Catherine: Yes.

Robert: Who pays for it?

Catherine: They're giving me a free ride, Dad. They've been great.

Robert: On tuition, sure. What about food, books, clothes, gas, meals out — do you plan to have a social life?

Catherine: I don't know.

Robert: You gotta pay your own way on dates, at least the early dates, say the first three, otherwise they expect something.

Catherine: The money will be fine. Claire's gonna help out.

Robert: When did you talk to Claire?

Catherine: I don't know, a couple weeks ago.

Robert: You talk to her before you talk to me?

Catherine: There were a lot of details to work out. She was great, she offered to take care of all the expenses.

Robert: This is a big step. A different city —

Catherine: It's not even a long distance phone call.

Robert: It's a huge place. They're serious up there. I mean serious. Yeah the football's a disaster but the math guys don't kid around. You haven't been in school. You sure you're ready? You can get buried up there.

Catherine: I'll be all right.

Robert: You're way behind.

Catherine: I know.

Robert: A year, at least.

Catherine: Thank you, I KNOW. Look, I don't know if this is a good idea. I don't know if I can handle the work. I don't know if I can handle any of it.

Robert: For Chrissake, Catherine, you should have talked to me.

Catherine: Dad. Listen. If you ever . . . if for any reason it ever turned out that you needed me here full time again —

Robert: I WON'T. That's not *[what I'm talking about]* —

Catherine: I can always take a semester off, or —

Robert: No. Stop it. I just — the end of the MONTH? Why didn't you say something before?

Catherine: Dad, come on. It took a while to set this up, and until recently, until very recently, you weren't —

Robert: You just said yourself I've been fine.

Catherine: Yes, but I didn't know — I hoped, but I didn't know, no one knew if this would last. I told myself to wait until I was sure about you. That you were feeling okay again. Consistently okay.

Robert: So I'm to take this conversation as a vote of confidence? I'm honored.

Catherine: Take it however you want. I believed you'd get better.

Robert: Well thank you very much.

Catherine: Don't thank me. I had to. I was living with you.

Robert: All right, that's enough, Catherine. Let's stay on the subject.

Catherine: This is the subject! There were LIBRARY BOOKS stacked up to the ceiling upstairs, do you remember that? You were trying to decode MESSAGES —

Robert: The fucking books are gone, I took them back myself. Why do you bring that garbage up? *(Knocking, off. Beat. Catherine goes inside to answer the door. She returns with Hal. He carries a manila envelope. He is nervous.)*
      Mr. Dobbs.

Hal: Hi. I hope it's not a bad time.

Robert: Yes it is, actually, you couldn't have picked worse.

Hal: Oh, I, uh —

Robert: You interrupted an argument.

Hal: I'm sorry. I can come back.

Robert: It's all right. We needed a break.

Hal: Are you sure?

Robert: Yes. The argument was about dinner. We don't know what to eat. What's your suggestion? *(A beat while Hal is on the spot.)*

Hal: Uh, there's a good pasta place not too far from here.

Robert: NO!

Catherine: *(With Robert.)* That is a BRILLIANT idea.

Robert: Oh dear Jesus God no.

Catherine: *(With Robert.)* What's it called? Give me the address.

Robert: No! Sorry. Wrong answer but thank you for trying. *(Hal stands there, looking at both of them.)*

Hal: I can come back.

Robert: Stay. *(To Catherine.)* Where are you going?

Catherine: Inside.

Robert: What about dinner?

Catherine: What about him?

Robert: What are you doing here, Dobbs?

Hal: My timing sucks. I am really sorry.

Robert: Don't be silly.

Hal: I'll come to your office.

Robert: Stop. Sit down. Glad you're here. Don't let the dinner thing throw you, you'll bounce back. *(To Catherine.)* This should be easier. Let's back off the problem, let it breathe, come at it again when it's not looking.

Catherine: Fine. *(Exiting.)* Excuse me.

Robert: Sorry, I'm rude. Hal, this is my daughter Catherine.
    (To Catherine.) Don't go, have a drink with us. Catherine, Harold Dobbs.

Catherine: Hi.

Hal: Hi.

Robert: Hal is a grad student. He's doing his Ph.D., very promising stuff. Unfortunately for him his work coincided with my return to the department and he got stuck with me.

Hal: No, no, it's been — I've been very lucky.

Catherine: How long have you been at U. of C.?

Hal: Well I've been working on my thesis for —

Robert: Hal's in our "Infinite" program. As he approaches completion of his dissertation, time approaches infinity. Would you like a drink, Hal?

Hal: Yes I would.

And uh, with all due respect . . . *(He hands Robert the envelope.)*

Robert: Really? *(He opens it and looks inside.)*

You must have had an interesting few months.

Hal: *(Cheerfully.)* Worst summer of my life.

Robert: Congratulations.

Hal: It's just a draft. Based on everything we talked about last spring. *(Robert pours a drink. Hal babbles.)*

I wasn't sure if I should wait till the quarter started, or if I should give it to you now, or hold off, do another draft, but I figured fuck it I, I mean I just . . . let's just get it over with, so I thought I'd just come over and see if you were home, and —

Robert: Drink this.

Hal: Thanks. *(He drinks.)*

I decided, I don't know, if it feels done, maybe it is.

Robert: Wrong. If it feels done there are major errors.

Hal: Uh, I —

Robert: That's okay, that's good, we'll find them and fix them.

Don't worry. You're on your way to a solid career, you'll be teaching younger, more irritating versions of yourself in no time.

Hal: Thank you.

Robert: Catherine's in the math department at Northwestern, Hal. *(Catherine looks up, startled.)*

Hal: Oh, who are you working with?

Catherine: I'm just starting this fall. Undergrad.

Robert: She's starting in . . . three weeks?

Catherine: A little more. *(Beat.)*

Robert: They have some good people at Northwestern. O'Donohue. Kaminsky.

Catherine: Yes.

Robert: They will work your ass off.

Catherine: I know.

Robert: You'll have to run pretty hard to catch up.

Catherine: I think I can do it.

Robert: Of course you can. *(Beat.)*

Hal: You must be excited.

Catherine: I am.

Hal: First year of school can be great.

Catherine: Yeah?

Hal: Sure, all the new people, new places, getting out of the house.

Catherine: *(Embarrassed.)* Yes.

Hal: *(Embarrassed.)* Or, no, I —

Robert: Absolutely, getting the hell out of here, thank God, it's about time. I'll be glad to see the back of her.

Catherine: You will?

Robert: Of course. Maybe I want to have the place to myself for a while, did that ever occur to you? *(To Hal.)* It's awful the way children sentimentalize their parents. *(To Catherine.)* We could use some quiet around here.

Catherine: Oh don't worry, I'll come back. I'll be here every Sunday cooking up big vats of spaghetti to last you through the week.

Robert: And I'll drive up, strut around Evanston, embarrass you in front of your classmates.

Catherine: Good. So we'll be in touch.

Robert: Sure. And if you get stuck with a problem, give me a call.

Catherine: Okay. Same to you.

Robert: Fine. Make sure to get me your number. *(To Hal.)* I'm actually looking forward to getting some work done.

Hal: Oh, what are you working on?

Robert: Nothing. *(Beat.)*

Nothing at the moment.

Which I'm glad of, really. This is the time of year when you don't want to be tied down to anything. You want to be outside. I love Chicago in September. Perfect skies. Sailboats on the water. Cubs losing. Warm, the sun still hot . . . with the occasional blast of Arctic wind to keep you on your toes, remind you of winter. Students coming back, bookstores full, everybody busy.

I was in a bookstore yesterday. Completely full, students buying books . . . browsing . . . Students do a hell of a lot of browsing, don't they? Just browsing. You see them shuffling around with their backpacks, goofing off, taking up space. You'd call it loitering except every once in a while they pick up a book and flip the pages: "Browsing." I admire it. It's an honest way to kill an afternoon. In the back of a used bookstore, or going through a crate of somebody's old record albums — not looking for anything, just looking, what the hell, touching the old book jackets, seeing what somebody threw out, seeing what they underlined . . . maybe you find something great, like an old thriller with a painted cover from the forties, or a textbook one of your professors used when he was a student — his name is written in it very carefully . . . Yeah, I like it. I like watching the students. Wondering what they're gonna buy, what they're gonna read. What kind of ideas they'll come up with when they settle down and get to work . . .

I'm not doing much right now. It does get harder. It's a stereotype that happens to be true, unfortunately for me — unfortunately for you, for all of us.

Catherine: Maybe you'll get lucky.

Robert: Maybe I will.

Maybe you'll pick up where I left off.

Catherine: Don't hold your breath.

Robert: Don't underestimate yourself.

Catherine: Anyway. *(Beat.)*

Robert: Another drink? Cathy? Hal?

Catherine: No thanks.

Hal: Thanks, I really should get going.

Robert: Are you sure?

Hal: Yes.

Robert: I'll call you when I've looked at this. Don't think about it till then. Enjoy yourself, see some movies.

Hal: Okay.

Robert: You can come by my office in a week. Call it —

Hal: The eleventh?

Robert: Yes, we'll . . . *(Beat. He turns to Catherine. Grave:)*
I am sorry. I used to have a pretty good memory for numbers. Happy birthday.

Catherine: Thank you.

Robert: I am so sorry. I'm embarrassed.

Catherine: Dad, don't be stupid.

Robert: I didn't get you anything.

Catherine: Don't worry about it.

Robert: I'm taking you out.

Catherine: You don't have to.

Robert: We are going out. I didn't want to shop and cook. Let's go to dinner. Let's get the hell out of this neighborhood. What do you want to eat? Let's go to the North Side. Or Chinatown. Or Greektown. I don't know what's good anymore.

Catherine: Whatever you want.

Robert: Whatever you want goddamnit, Catherine, it's your birthday. *(Beat.)*

Catherine: Steak.

Robert: Steak. Yes.

Catherine: No, first beer, really cold beer. Really cheap beer.

Robert: Done.

Catherine: That Chicago beer that's watery with no flavor and you can just drink gallons of it.

Robert: They just pump the water out of Lake Michigan and bottle it.

Catherine: It's so awful.

Robert: I have a taste for it myself.

Catherine: Then the steak, grilled really black, and potatoes and creamed spinach.

Robert: I remember a place. If it's still there I think it will do the trick.

Catherine: And dessert.

Robert: That goes without saying. It's your birthday, hooray. And there's the solution to our dinner problem. Thank you for reminding me, Harold Dobbs.

Catherine: *(To Hal.)* We're being rude. Do you want to come?

Hal: Oh, no, I shouldn't.

Robert: Why not? Please, come.

Catherine: Come on. (*A tiny moment between Hal and Catherine. Hal wavers, then:*)

Hal: No, I can't, I have plans. Thank you though. Happy birthday.

Catherine: Thanks. Well. I'll let you out.

Robert: I'll see you on the eleventh, Hal.

Hal: Great.

Catherine: I'm gonna change my clothes, Dad. I'll be ready in a sec. (*Hal and Catherine exit. A moment. It's darker. Robert looks out at the evening. Eventually he picks up the notebook and a pen. He sits down. He opens to a blank page. He writes.*)

Robert: "September fourth.
      A good day . . . " (*He continues to write.*)

Fade

SCENE 2

Morning. An instant after the end of Act One: Catherine, Claire, and Hal.

Hal: You wrote this?

Catherine: Yes.

Claire: When?

Catherine: I started after I quit school. I finished a few months before Dad died.

Claire: Did he see it?

Catherine: No. He didn't know I was working on it. It wouldn't have mattered to him anyway, he was too sick.

Hal: I don't understand — you did this by yourself?

Catherine: Yes.

Claire: It's in Dad's notebook.

Catherine: I used one of his blank books. There were a bunch of them upstairs. (*Beat.*)

Claire: (*To Hal.*) Tell me exactly where you found this?

Hal: In his study.

Catherine: In his desk. I gave him the —

Claire: (*To Catherine.*) Hold on. (*To Hal.*) Where did you find it?

Hal: In the bottom drawer of the desk in the study, a locked drawer: Catherine gave me the key.

Claire: Why was the drawer locked?

Catherine: It's mine, it's the drawer I keep my private things in. I've used it for years.

Claire: (*To Hal.*) Was there anything else in the drawer?

Hal: No.

Catherine: No, that's the only —

Claire: Can I see it? (*Hal gives Claire the book. She pages through it. Beat.*) I'm sorry, I just . . . (*To Catherine.*) The book was in the . . . You told him where to find it . . . You gave him the key . . . You wrote this incredible thing and you didn't tell anyone?

Catherine: I'm telling you both now. After I dropped out of school I had nothing to do. I was depressed, really depressed, but at a certain point I decided Fuck it, I don't need them. It's just math, I can do it on my own. So I kept working here. I worked at night, after Dad had gone to sleep. It was hard but I did it. *(Beat.)*

Claire: Catherine, I'm sorry, but I just find this very hard to believe.

Catherine: Claire. I wrote. The proof.

Claire: I'm sorry, I —

Catherine: Claire . . .

Claire: This is Dad's handwriting.

Catherine: It's not.

Claire: It looks exactly like it.

Catherine: It's my writing.

Claire: I'm sorry —

Catherine: Ask *Hal:* He's been looking at Dad's writing for weeks. *(Claire gives Hal the book. He looks at it. Beat.)*

Hal: I don't know.

Catherine: Hal, come on.

Claire: What does it look like?

Hal: It looks . . . I don't know what Catherine's handwriting looks like.

Catherine: It LOOKS like THAT.

Hal: Okay. It . . . okay. *(Beat. He hands the book back.)*

Claire: I think — you know what? I think it's early, and people are tired, and not in the best state to make decisions about emotional things, so maybe we should all just take a breath . . .

Catherine: You don't believe me?

Claire: I don't know. I really don't know anything about this.

Catherine: Never mind. I don't know why I expected you to believe me about ANYTHING.

Claire: Could you tell us the proof? That would show it was yours.

Catherine: You wouldn't understand it.

Claire: Tell it to Hal.

Catherine: *(Taking the book.)* We could talk through it together. It might take a while.

Claire: *(Taking the book.)* You can't use the book.

Catherine: For God's sake, it's forty pages long. I didn't MEMORIZE it. It's not a muffin recipe. *(Beat.)* This is stupid. It's my book, my writing, my key, my drawer, my proof. Hal, tell her!

Hal: Tell her what?

Catherine: Whose book is that?

Hal: I don't know.

Catherine: What is the matter with you? You've been looking at his other stuff, you know there's nothing even remotely like this!

Hal: Look, Catherine —

Catherine: We'll go through the proof together. We'll sit down — if Claire will please let me have my book back —

Claire: *(Giving her the book.)* All right, talk him through it.

Hal: That might take days and it still wouldn't show that she wrote it.

Catherine: Why not?

Hal: Your dad might have written it and explained it to you later. I'm not saying he did, I'm just —

Catherine: Come on! He didn't do this, he couldn't have. He didn't do any mathematics at all for years. Even in the good year he couldn't work: You know that. You're supposed to be a scientist. *(Beat.)*

Hal: You're right. Okay. Here's my suggestion. I know three or four guys at the department, very sharp, disinterested people who knew your father, knew his work. Let me take this to them.

Catherine: WHAT?

Hal: I'll tell them we've found something, something potentially major, we're not sure about the authorship; I'll sit down with them. We'll go through the thing carefully —

Claire: Good.

Hal: — and figure out exactly what we've got. It would only take a couple of days, probably, and then we'd have a lot more information.

Claire: I think that's an excellent suggestion.

Catherine: You can't.

Claire: Catherine.

Catherine: No! You can't take it.

Hal: I'm not "taking" it.

Catherine: This is what you wanted.

Hal: Oh come on, Jesus.

Catherine: You don't waste any time, do you? No hesitation. You can't wait to show them your brilliant discovery.

Hal: I'm trying to determine what this is.

Catherine: I'm telling you what it is.

Hal: You don't know!

Catherine: I WROTE it.

Hal: IT'S YOUR FATHER'S HANDWRITING. *(Beat. Pained.)*

At least it looks an awful lot like the writing in the other books. Maybe your writing looks exactly like his, I don't know.

Catherine: *(Softly.)* It does look like his.

I didn't show this to anyone else. I could have. I wanted you to be the first to see it. I didn't know I wanted that until last night. It's ME. I trusted you.

Hal: I know.

Catherine: Was I wrong?

Hal: No. I —

Catherine: I should have known she wouldn't believe me but why don't you?

Hal: This is one of his notebooks. The exact same kind he used.

Catherine: I told you. I just used one of his blank books. There were extras.

Hal: There aren't any extra books in the study.

Catherine: There were when I started writing the proof. I bought them for him. He used the rest up later.

Hal: And the writing.

Catherine: You want to test the handwriting?

Hal: No. It doesn't matter. He could have dictated it to you, for Chrissake. It still doesn't make sense.

Catherine: Why not?

Hal: I'm a mathematician.

Catherine: Yes.

Hal: I know how hard it would be to come up with something like this. I mean it's impossible. You'd have to be . . . you'd have to be your dad, basically. Your dad at the peak of his powers.

Catherine: I'm a mathematician too.

Hal: Not like your dad.

Catherine: Oh he's the only one who could have done this?

Hal: The only one I know.

Catherine: Are you sure?

Hal: Your father was the most —

Catherine: Just because you and the rest of the geeks worshiped him doesn't mean he wrote this proof, Hal!

Hal: He was the best. My generation hasn't produced anything like him. He revolutionized the field twice before he was twenty-two. I'm sorry, Catherine, but you took some classes at Northwestern for a few months.

Catherine: My education wasn't at Northwestern. It was living in this house for twenty-five years.

Hal: Even so, it doesn't matter. This is too advanced. I don't even understand most of it.

Catherine: You think it's too advanced.

Hal: Yes.

Catherine: It's too advanced for YOU.

Hal: You could not have done this work.

Catherine: But what if I did?

Hal: Well what if?

Catherine: It would be a real disaster for you, wouldn't it? And for the other geeks who barely finished their Ph.D.s, who are marking time doing lame research, bragging about the conferences they go to — WOW — playing in an awful band, and whining that they're intellectually past it at twenty-eight, BECAUSE THEY ARE. *(Beat. Hal hesitates, then abruptly exits. Beat. Catherine is furious and so upset she looks dazed.)*

Claire: Katie.

Let's go inside.

Katie? *(Catherine opens the book and tries to rip out the pages, destroy it. Claire goes to take it from her. They struggle. Catherine gets the book away. They stand apart, breathing hard. After a moment, Catherine throws the book to the floor. She exits.)*

Fade

SCENE 3

The next day. The porch is empty. Knocking, off. No one appears. After a
moment Hal comes around the side of the porch and knocks on the back door.

Hal: Catherine? *(Claire enters.)*
       I thought you were leaving.
Claire: I had to delay my flight. *(Beat.)*
Hal: Is Catherine here?
Claire: I don't think this is a good time, Hal.
Hal: Could I see her?
Claire: Not now.
Hal: What's the matter?
Claire: She's sleeping.
Hal: Can I wait here until she gets up?
Claire: She's been sleeping since yesterday. She won't get up. She won't eat,
    won't talk to me. I couldn't go home. I'm going to wait until she seems
    okay to travel.
Hal: Jesus, I'm sorry.
Claire: Yes.
Hal: I'd like to talk to her.
Claire: I don't think that's a good idea.
Hal: Has she said anything?
Claire: About you? No.
Hal: Yesterday . . . I know I didn't do what she wanted.
Claire: Neither of us did.
Hal: I didn't know what to say. I feel awful.
Claire: Why did you sleep with her? *(Beat.)*
Hal: I'm sorry, that's none of your business.
Claire: Bullshit. I have to take care of her. It's a little bit harder with you
    jerking her around.
Hal: I wasn't jerking her around. It just happened.
Claire: Your timing was not great.
Hal: It wasn't my timing, it was both of our —
Claire: Why'd you do it? You know what she's like. She's fragile and you
    took advantage of her.
Hal: No. It's what we both wanted. I didn't mean to hurt her.
Claire: You did.
Hal: I'd like to talk to Catherine, please.
Claire: You can't.
Hal: Are you taking her away?
Claire: Yes.
Hal: To New York.
Claire: Yes.
Hal: Just going to drag her to New York.
Claire: If I have to.

Hal: Don't you think she should have some say in whether or not she goes?

Claire: If she's not going to speak, what else can I do?

Hal: Let me try. Let me talk to her.

Claire: Hal, give up. This has nothing to do with you.

Hal: I know her. She's tougher than you think, Claire.

Claire: What?

Hal: She can handle herself. She can handle talking to me — maybe it would help. Maybe she'd like it.

Claire: Maybe she'd LIKE it? Are you out of your MIND? You're the reason she's up there right now! You have NO IDEA what she needs. You don't know her! She's my sister. Jesus, you fucking mathematicians: You DON'T THINK. You don't know what you're doing. You stagger around creating these catastrophes and it's people like ME who end up flying in to clean them up. *(Beat.)*

     She needs to get out of Chicago, out of this house. I'll give you my number in New York. You can call her once she's settled there. That's it, that's the deal.

Hal: Okay. *(Beat. Hal doesn't move.)*

Claire: I don't mean to be rude but I have a lot to do.

Hal: There's one more thing. You're not going to like it

Claire: Sure, take the notebook.

Hal: *(Startled.)* I —

Claire: Hold on a sec, I'll get it for you. *(She goes inside and returns with the notebook. She gives it to Hal.)*

Hal: I thought this would be harder.

Claire: Don't worry, I understand. It's very sweet you want to see Catherine but of course you'd like to see the notebook too.

Hal: *(Huffy.)* It's — No, it's my responsibility — as a professional I can't turn my back on the necessity of the —

Claire: Relax. I don't care. Take it. What would I do with it?

Hal: You sure?

Claire: Yes, of course.

Hal: You trust me with this?

Claire: Yes.

Hal: You just said I don't know what I'm doing.

Claire: I think you're a little bit of an idiot but you're not dishonest. Someone needs to figure out what's in there. I can't do it. It should be done here, at Chicago: my father would like that. When you decide what we've got let me know what the family should do.

Hal: Thanks.

Claire: Don't thank me, it's by far the most convenient option available. I put my card in there, call me whenever you want.

Hal: Okay. *(Hal starts to exit. Claire hesitates, then:)*

Claire: Hal.

Hal: Yeah?

Claire: Can you tell me about it? The proof. I'm just curious.

Hal: It would take some time. How much math have you got? *(Beat.)*

Claire: I'm a currency analyst. It helps to be very quick with numbers. I am. I probably inherited about one-one-thousandth of my father's ability. It's enough. Catherine got more, I'm not sure how much.

Fade

SCENE 4

Winter. About three and a half years earlier. Robert is on the porch. He wears a T-shirt. He writes in a notebook. After a moment we hear Catherine's voice from off.

Catherine: Dad? *(Catherine enters wearing a parka. She sees her father and stops.)* What are you doing out here?

Robert: Working.

Catherine: It's December. It's thirty degrees.

Robert: I know. *(Catherine stares at him, baffled.)*

Catherine: Don't you need a coat?

Robert: Don't you think I can make that assessment for myself?

Catherine: Aren't you cold?

Robert: Of course I am! I'm freezing my ass off!

Catherine: So what are you doing out here?

Robert: Thinking! Writing!

Catherine: You're gonna freeze.

Robert: It's too hot in the house. The radiators dry out the air. Also the clanking — I can't concentrate. If the house weren't so old we'd have central air heating but we don't so I have to come out here to get any work done.

Catherine: I'll turn off the radiators. They won't make any noise. Come inside, it isn't safe.

Robert: I'm okay.

Catherine: I've been calling. Didn't you hear the phone?

Robert: It's a distraction.

Catherine: I didn't know what was going on. I had to drive all the way down here.

Robert: I can see that.

Catherine: I had to skip class. *(She brings him a coat and he puts it on.)* Why don't you answer the phone?

Robert: Well I'm sorry, Catherine, but it's question of priorities and work takes priority, you know that.

Catherine: You're working?

Robert: Goddamnit I am working! I say "I" — the machinery. The machinery is working. Catherine, it's on full blast. All the cylinders are firing, I'm on fire. That's why I came out here, to cool off. I haven't felt like this for years.

Catherine: You're kidding.

Robert: No!

Catherine: I don't believe it.

Robert: I don't believe it either! But it's true. It started about a week ago. I woke up, came downstairs, made a cup of coffee and before I could pour in the milk it was like someone turned the LIGHT on in my head.

Catherine: Really?

Robert: Not the light, the whole POWER GRID. I LIT UP and it's like no time has passed since I was twenty-one.

Catherine: You're kidding!

Robert: No! I'm back! I'm back in touch with the source — the font, the — whatever the source of my creativity was all those years ago I'm in contact with it again. I'm SITTING on it. It's a geyser and I'm shooting right up into the air on top of it.

Catherine: My God.

Robert: I'm not talking about divine inspiration. It's not funneling down into my head and onto the page. It'll take work to shape these things; I'm not saying it won't be a tremendous amount of work. It will be a tremendous amount of work. It's not going to be easy. But the raw material is there. It's like I've been driving in traffic and now the lanes are opening up before me and I can accelerate. I see whole landscapes — places for the work to go, new techniques, revolutionary possibilities. I'm going to get whole branches of the profession talking to each other. I — I'm sorry, I'm being rude, how's school?

Catherine: *(Taken aback.)* Fine. —

Robert: You're working hard?

Catherine: Sure.

Robert: Faculty treating you all right?

Catherine: Yes. Dad —

Robert: Made any friends?

Catherine: Of course. I —

Robert: Dating?

Catherine: Dad, hold on.

Robert: No details necessary if you don't want to provide them. I'm just interested.

Catherine: School's great. I want to talk about what you're doing.

Robert: Great, let's talk.

Catherine: This work.

Robert: Yes.

Catherine: *(Indicating the notebook.)* Is it here?

Robert: Part of it, yes.

Catherine: Can I see it?

Robert: It's all at a very early stage.

Catherine: I don't mind.

Robert: Nothing's actually complete, to be honest. It's all in progress. I think we're talking years.

Catherine: That's okay. I don't care. Just let me see anything.

Robert: You really want to?

Catherine: Yes.

Robert: You're genuinely interested.

Catherine: Dad, of course!

Robert: Of course. It's your field.

Catherine: Yes.

Robert: You know how happy that makes me. *(Beat.)*

Catherine: Yes.

Robert: I think there's enough here to keep me working the rest of my life.

Not just me.

I was starting to imagine I was finished, Catherine. Really finished. Don't get me wrong, I was grateful I could go to my office, have a life, but secretly I was terrified I'd never work again. Did you know that?

Catherine: I wondered.

Robert: I was absolutely fucking terrified.

Then I remembered something and a part of the terror went away. I remembered you.

Your creative years were just beginning. You'd get your degree, do your own work. You were just getting started.

If you hadn't gone into math that would have been all right. Claire's done well for herself. I'm satisfied with her.

I'm proud of you.

I don't mean to embarrass you. It's part of the reason we have children. We hope they'll survive us, accomplish what we can't.

Now that I'm back in the game I admit I've got another idea, a better one.

Catherine: What?

Robert: I know you've got your own work. I don't want you to neglect that. You can't neglect it. But I could probably use some help. Work with me. If you want to, if you can work it out with your class schedule and everything else, I could help you with that, make some calls, talk to your teachers . . .

I'm getting ahead of myself.

Well, Jesus, look, enough bullshit, you asked to see something. Let's start with this. I've roughed something out. General outline for a proof. Major result. Important. It's not finished but you can see where it's going. Let's see: *(He selects a notebook.)* Here. *(He gives it to Catherine. She opens it and reads.)* It's very rough. *(After a long moment Catherine closes the notebook. A beat.)*

Catherine: Dad. Let's go inside.

Robert: The gaps might make it hard to follow. We can talk it through.

Catherine: You're cold. Let's go in.

Robert: Maybe we could work on this together. This might be a great place to start. What about it? What do you think? Let's talk it through.

Catherine: Not now. I'm cold too. It's really freezing out here. Let's go inside.

Robert: I'm telling you it's stifling in there, goddamn it. The radiators. Look, read out the first couple of lines. That's how we start: You read, and we go line by line, out loud, through the argument. See if there's a better way, a shorter way. Let's collaborate.

Catherine: No. Come on.

Robert: I've been waiting years for this. This is something I want to do. Come on, let's do some work together.

Catherine: We can't do it out here. It's freezing cold. I'm taking you in.

Robert: Not until we talk about the proof.

Catherine: No.

Robert: GODDAMNIT CATHERINE Open the goddamn book and read me the lines. *(Beat. Catherine opens the book. She reads slowly, without inflection.)*

Catherine: "Let x equal the quantity of all quantities of x. Let x equal the cold. It is cold in December. The months of cold equal November through February. There are four months of cold, and four of heat, leaving four months of indeterminate temperature. In February it snows. In March the Lake is a lake of ice. In September the students come back and the bookstores are full. Let x equal the month of full bookstores. The number of books approaches infinity as the number of months of cold approaches four. I will never be as cold now as I will in the future. The future of cold is infinite. The future of heat is the future of cold. The bookstores are infinite and so are never full except in September . . ." *(She stops reading and slowly closes the book. Robert is shivering uncontrollably.)* It's all right. We'll go inside.

Robert: I'm cold.

Catherine: We'll warm you up. *(Catherine puts her arms around him and helps him to his feet.)*

Robert: Don't leave. Please.

Catherine: I won't.

      Let's go inside.

Fade

SCENE 5

The present. A week after the events in Scene 3. Claire on the porch. Coffee in takeout cups. Claire takes a plane ticket out of her purse, checks the itinerary. A moment. Catherine enters with bags for travel. Claire gives her a cup of coffee. Catherine drinks in silence. Beat.

Catherine: Good coffee.

Claire: It's all right, isn't it?

      We have a place where we buy all our coffee. They roast it themselves, they have an old roaster down in the basement. You can smell it on the street. Some mornings you can smell it from our place, four stories up. It's wonderful. "Manhattan's Best": Some magazine wrote it up. Who knows. But it is very good.

Catherine: Sounds good.

Claire: You'll like it.

Catherine: Good. *(Beat.)*

Claire: You look nice.

Catherine: Thanks, so do you. *(Beat.)*

Claire: It's bright.

Catherine: Yes.

Claire: It's one of the things I do miss. All the space, the light. You could sit out here all morning.

Catherine: It's not that warm.

Claire: Are you cold?

Catherine: Not really. I just —

Claire: It has gotten chilly. I'm sorry. Do you want to go in?

Catherine: I'm okay.

Claire: I just thought it might be nice to have a quick cup of coffee out here.

Catherine: No, it is.

Claire: Plus the kitchen's all put away. If you're cold —

Catherine: I'm not. Not really.

Claire: Want your jacket?

Catherine: Yeah, okay. *(Claire gives it to her. Catherine puts it on.)* Thanks.

Claire: It's that time of year.

Catherine: Yes.
    You can feel it coming. *(Beat. Catherine stares out at the yard.)*

Claire: Honey, there's no hurry.

Catherine: I know.

Claire: If you want to hang out, be alone for a while —

Catherine: No. It's no big deal.

Claire: We don't have to leave for twenty minutes or so.

Catherine: I know. Thanks, Claire.

Claire: You're all packed.

Catherine: Yes.

Claire: If you missed anything it doesn't really matter. The movers will send us everything next month. *(Catherine doesn't move. Beat.)*
    I know this is hard.

Catherine: It's fine.

Claire: This is the right decision.

Catherine: I know.

Claire: I want to do everything I can to make this a smooth transition for you. So does Mitch.

Catherine: Good.

Claire: The actual departure is the hardest part. Once we get there we can relax. Enjoy ourselves.

Catherine: I know. *(Beat.)*

Claire: You'll love New York.

Catherine: I can't wait.

Claire: You'll love it. It's the most exciting city.

Catherine: I know.

Claire: It's not like Chicago, it's really alive.

Catherine: I've read about that.

Claire: I think you'll truly feel at home there.

Catherine: You know what I'm looking forward to?

Claire: What?

Catherine: Seeing Broadway musicals. *(Beat.)*

Claire: Mitch can get us tickets to whatever you'd like.

Catherine: And Rockefeller Center in winter — all the skaters.

Claire: Well, you —

Catherine: Also, the many fine museums! *(Beat.)*

Claire: I know how hard this is for you.

Catherine: Listening to you say how hard it is for me is what's hard for me.

Claire: Once you're there you'll see all the possibilities that are available.

Catherine: Restraints, lithium, electroshock.

Claire: SCHOOLS. In the New York area alone there's NYU, Columbia —

Catherine: Bright college days! Football games, road trips, necking on the "quad."

Claire: Or if that's not what you want we can help you find a job. Mitch has terrific contacts all over town.

Catherine: Does he know anyone in the phone sex industry?

Claire: I want to make this as easy a transition as I can.

Catherine: It's going to be easy, Claire, it's gonna be so fucking easy you won't believe it.

Claire: Thank you.

Catherine: I'm going to sit quietly on the plane to New York. And live quietly in a cute apartment. And answer Doctor Von Heimlich's questions very politely.

Claire: You can see any doctor you like, or you can see no doctor.

Catherine: I would like to see a doctor called Doctor Von Heimlich: Please find one. And I would like him to wear a monocle. And I'd like him to have a very soft, very well-upholstered couch, so that I'll be perfectly comfortable while I'm blaming everything on you. *(Claire's patience is exhausted.)*

Claire: Don't come.

Catherine: No, I'm coming.

Claire: Stay here, see how you do.

Catherine: I could.

Claire: You can't take care of yourself for five days.

Catherine: Bullshit!

Claire: You slept all week. I had to cancel my flight. I missed a week of work — I was this close to taking you to the hospital! I couldn't believe it when you finally dragged yourself up.

Catherine: I was tired!

Claire: You were completely out of it, Catherine, you weren't speaking!

Catherine: I didn't want to talk to you. *(Beat.)*

Claire: Stay here if you hate me so much.

Catherine: And do what?

Claire: You're the genius, figure it out. *(Claire is upset, near tears. She digs in her bag, pulls out a plane ticket, throws it on the table. She exits. Catherine is alone. She can't quite bring herself to leave the porch. A moment. Hal enters — not through the house, from the side. He is badly dressed and looks very tired. He is breathless from running.)*

Hal: You're still here. *(Catherine is surprised. She doesn't speak.)* I saw Claire leaving out front. I wasn't sure if you — *(He holds up the notebook.)* This fucking thing . . . checks out.

     I have been over it, twice, with two different sets of guys, old geeks and young geeks. It is weird. I don't know where the techniques came from. Some of the moves are very hard to follow. But we can't find anything wrong with it! There might be something wrong with it but we can't find it. I have not slept. *(He catches his breath.)* It works. I thought you might want to know.

Catherine: I already knew. *(Beat.)*

Hal: I had to swear these guys to secrecy. They were jumping out of their skins. See, one email and it's all over. I threatened them. I think we're safe, they're physical cowards. *(Beat.)* I had to see you.

Catherine: I'm leaving.

Hal: I know. Just wait for a minute, please?

Catherine: What do you want? You have the book. She told me you came by for it and she gave it to you. You can do whatever you want with it. Publish it.

Hal: Catherine.

Catherine: Get Claire's permission and publish it. She doesn't care. She doesn't know anything about it anyway.

Hal: I don't want Claire's permission.

Catherine: You want mine? Publish. Go for it. Have a press conference. Tell the world what my father discovered.

Hal: I don't want to.

Catherine: Or fuck my father, pass it off as your own work. Who cares? Write your own ticket to any math department in the country.

Hal: I don't think your father wrote it. *(Beat.)*

Catherine: You thought so last week.

Hal: That was last week. I spent this week reading the proof.

     I think I understand it, more or less. It uses a lot of newer mathematical techniques, things that were developed in the last decade. Elliptic Curves. Modular Forms. I think I learned more mathematics this week than I did in four years of grad school.

Catherine: So?

Hal: So the proof is very . . . hip.

Catherine: Get some sleep, Hal.

Hal: What was your father doing the last ten years? He wasn't well, was he?

Catherine: Are you done?

Hal: I don't think he would have been able to master those new techniques.

Catherine: But he was a genius.

Hal: But he was nuts.

Catherine: So he read about them later.

Hal: Maybe. The books he would have needed are upstairs. *(Beat.)* Your dad dated everything. Even his most incoherent entries he dated. There are no dates in this.

Catherine: The handwriting —

Hal: — looks like your dad's. Parents and children sometimes have similar handwriting, especially if they've spent a lot of time together. *(Beat.)*

Catherine: Interesting theory.

Hal: I like it.

Catherine: I like it too. It's what I told you last week.

Hal: I know.

Catherine: You blew it.

Hal: I —

Catherine: It's too bad, the rest of it was really good. All of it: "I loved your dad." "I always liked you." "I'd like to spend every minute with you . . . " It's killer stuff. You got laid AND you got the notebook! You're a genius!

Hal: I don't expect you to be happy with me. I just wanted . . . I don't know. I was hoping to discuss some of this with you before you left. Purely professional. I don't expect anything else.

Catherine: Forget it.

Hal: I mean we have questions. Working on this must have been amazing. I'd love just to hear you talk about some of this.

Catherine: No.

Hal: You'll have to deal with it eventually, you know. You can't ignore it, you'll have to get it published. You'll have to talk to someone.

Take it, at least. Then I'll go. Here.

Catherine: I don't want it.

Hal: Come on, Catherine. I'm trying to correct things.

Catherine: You CAN'T. Do you hear me?

You think you've figured something out? You run over here so pleased with yourself because you changed your mind. Now you're certain. You're so . . . sloppy. You don't know anything. The book, the math, the dates, the writing, all that stuff you decided with your buddies, it's just evidence. It doesn't finish the job. It doesn't prove anything.

Hal: Okay, what would?

Catherine: NOTHING.

You should have trusted me. *(Beat.)*

Hal: I know. *(Beat. Catherine gathers her things.)*

So Claire sold the house?

Catherine: Yes.

Hal: Stay in Chicago. You're an adult.

Catherine: She wants me in New York. She wants to look after me.

Hal: Do you need looking after?

Catherine: She thinks I do.

Hal: You looked after your dad for five years.

Catherine: So maybe it's my turn.

    I kick and scream but I don't know. Being taken care of, it doesn't sound so bad. I'm tired.

    And the house is a wreck, let's face it. It was my dad's house.

    I don't think I should spend another winter here.

Hal: There is nothing wrong with you.

Catherine: I think I'm like my dad.

Hal: I think you are too.

Catherine: I'm . . . afraid I'm like my dad.

Hal: You're not him.

Catherine: Maybe I will be.

Hal: Maybe. Maybe you'll be better. *(Pause. He offers her the book. This time she takes it. She looks down at the book, runs her fingers over the cover.)*

Catherine: It didn't feel "amazing" or — what word did you use?

Hal: Yeah, amazing.

Catherine: Yeah. It was just connecting the dots.

    Some nights I could connect three or four. Some nights they'd be really far apart, I'd have no idea how to get to the next one, if there was a next one.

Hal: He really never knew?

Catherine: No. I worked after midnight. He was usually in bed.

Hal: Every night?

Catherine: No. When I got stuck I watched TV. Sometimes if he couldn't sleep he'd come downstairs, sit with me. We'd talk. Not about math, he couldn't. About the movie we were watching. I'd explain the stories.

    Or about fixing the heat. Decide we didn't want to. We liked the radiators even though they clanked in the middle of the night, make the air dry.

    Or we'd plan breakfast, talk about what we were gonna eat together in the morning.

    Those nights were usually pretty good.

    I know . . . it works . . . But all I can see are the compromises, the approximations, places where it's stitched together. It's lumpy. Dad's stuff was way more elegant. When he was young. *(Beat.)*

Hal: Talk me through it? Whatever's bothering you. Maybe you'll improve it.

Catherine: I don't know . . .

Hal: Pick anything. Give it a shot? Maybe you'll discover something elegant. *(A moment. Hal sits next to her. Eventually she opens the book, turns the pages slowly, locates a section. She looks at him.)*

Catherine: Here: *(She begins to speak.)*

Curtain

Author's Note: For the Manhattan Theatre Club and Broadway productions, I wrote the following material for Catherine to speak during the final fade out, directly following her "Here:"

Catherine: I've got Eberhart's Conjecture setting up this section, qn as the nth prime, all that stuff, b's a positive not divisible by p . . . You know it. Pretty basic number theory. It just seems wrong to be using it to get to the Gauss. I'd like to go around, but when you eliminate it you get contradictions, or everything goes to zero. Unless . . .

Considerations for Critical Thinking and Writing

1. FIRST RESPONSE. How many ways can the title be read? How do the different meanings of the word *proof* help you articulate the play's theme?

2. The shock of the first scene, of course, is that Robert is actually dead and the Robert we see on the stage is a figment of Catherine's imagination. How does this revelation change the way you approach Catherine's character throughout the play?

3. What other important background information, or exposition, is provided in Act One, Scene 1?

4. Both Claire and Hal are unsympathetic characters in some ways. Summarize their negative qualities as a way of responding to this question: Are they equally culpable in terms of worsening Catherine's plight?

5. How does Catherine's retelling of the story of Sophie Germain in Act One, Scene 3 advance the play's theme?

6. The characters in this play drink fairly constantly. Is alcohol just a prop or is its presence integral to the play?

7. Act Two, Scene 1 abruptly shifts to a period four years before the action in Act One, and the next scene shifts back abruptly to the time of Act One. In what other ways does the play focus on the importance and meaning of time?

8. How does the play comment on the theme of responsibility to self vs. responsibility to others?

9. Do you think Catherine's mental struggles are hereditary or the result of her circumstances? Try to find places where the play suggests one or the other.

Connections to Another Selection

1. How do *Proof* and *How I Learned to Drive* (p. 976) comment on the influence of family over the fate of young women in the contemporary era?

How I Learned To Drive

Paula Vogel (b. 1951) is an important contemporary American playwright and professor of creative writing who has undoubtedly influenced the trajectory of American drama. Born in Washington, D.C., she was educated at Bryn Mawr, Catholic University of America, and Cornell, and she has taught at Brown and Yale universities. Her plays do not shy away from provocative, controversial, or uncomfortable topics such as her 1992 play *The Baltimore Waltz* which confronts AIDS, the disease that claimed her brother. The following play, *How I Learned to Drive*, won the Pulitzer Prize for Drama in 1997 and takes on troubling subjects: incest and child sexual abuse.

PAULA VOGEL (B. 1951)

How I Learned to Drive   1997

CHARACTERS

Walter McBride/Getty Images.

Li'l Bit, A woman who ages forty-something
    to eleven years old.
Peck, Attractive man in his forties. Despite a
    few problems, he should be played by an
    actor one might cast in the role of Atticus in *To Kill a Mockingbird*.
The Greek Chorus, If possible, these three
    members should be able to sing three-
    part harmony.
Male Greek Chorus, Plays Grandfather, Waiter, High School Boys. Thirties–
    forties.
Female Greek Chorus, Plays Mother, Aunt Mary, High School Girls. Thirty–fifty.
Teenage Greek Chorus, Plays Grandmother, High School Girls, and the voice
    of eleven-year-old Li'l Bit. Note on the casting of this actor: I would
    strongly recommend casting a young woman who is "of legal age," that
    is, twenty–one to twenty–five years old, who can look as close to eleven as
    possible. The contrast with the other cast members will help. If the actor is
    too young, the audience may feel uncomfortable.

(*As the house lights dim, a Voice announces:*)

SAFETY FIRST — YOU AND DRIVER EDUCATION.

(*Then the sound of a key turning the ignition of a car. Li'l Bit steps into a spotlight on the stage; "well-endowed," she is a softer-looking woman in the present time than she was at seventeen.*)

Li'l Bit: Sometimes to tell a secret, you first have to teach a lesson. We're going to start our lesson tonight on an early, warm summer evening.

In a parking lot overlooking the Beltsville Agricultural Farms in suburban Maryland.

Less than a mile away, the crumbling concrete of U.S. One wends its way past one-room revival churches, the porno drive-in, and boarded up motels with For Sale signs tumbling down.

Like I said, it's a warm summer evening.

Here on the land the Department of Agriculture owns, the smell of sleeping farm animals is thick on the air. The smells of clover and hay mix in with the smells of the leather dashboard. You can still imagine how Maryland used to be, before the malls took over. This countryside was once dotted with farmhouses — from their porches you could have witnessed the Civil War raging in the front fields.

Oh yes. There's a moon over Maryland tonight, that spills into the car where I sit beside a man old enough to be — did I mention how still the night is? Damp soil and tranquil air. It's the kind of night that makes a middle-aged man with a mortgage feel like a country boy again.

It's 1969. And I am very old, very cynical of the world, and I know it all. In short, I am seventeen years old, parking off a dark lane with a married man on an early summer night.

(*Lights up on two chairs facing front — or a Buick Riviera, if you will. Waiting patiently, with a smile on his face, Peck sits sniffing the night air. Li'l Bit climbs in beside him, seventeen years old and tense. Throughout the following, the two sit facing directly front. They do not touch. Their bodies remain passive. Only their facial expressions emote.*)

Peck: Ummm. I love the smell of your hair.
Li'l Bit: Uh-huh.
Peck: Oh, Lord. Ummmm. (*Beat.*) A man could die happy like this.
Li'l Bit: Well, *don't.*
Peck: What shampoo is this?
Li'l Bit: Herbal Essence.
Peck: Herbal Essence. I'm gonna buy me some. Herbal Essence. And when I'm all alone in the house, I'm going to get into the bathtub, and uncap the bottle and —
Li'l Bit: — Be good.
Peck: What?
Li'l Bit: Stop being . . . bad.
Peck: What did you think I was going to say? What do you think I'm going to do with the shampoo?
Li'l Bit: I don't want to know. I don't want to hear it.
Peck: I'm going to wash my hair. That's all.
Li'l Bit: Oh.
Peck: What did you think I was going to do?
Li'l Bit: Nothing . . . I don't know. Something . . . nasty.

Peck: With shampoo? Lord, gal — your mind!

Li'l Bit: And whose fault is it?

Peck: Not mine. I've got the mind of a boy scout.

Li'l Bit: Right. A horny boy scout.

Peck: Boy scouts are always horny. What do you think the first Merit Badge is for?

Li'l Bit: There. You're going to be nasty again.

Peck: Oh, no. I'm good. Very good.

Li'l Bit: It's getting late.

Peck: Don't change the subject. I was talking about how good I am. (*Beat.*) Are you ever gonna let me show you how good I am?

Li'l Bit: Don't go over the line now.

Peck: I won't. I'm not gonna do anything you don't want me to do.

Li'l Bit: That's right.

Peck: And I've been good all week.

Li'l Bit: You have?

Peck: Yes. All week. Not a single drink.

Li'l Bit: Good boy.

Peck: Do I get a reward? For not drinking?

Li'l Bit: A small one. It's getting late.

Peck: Just let me undo you. I'll do you back up.

Li'l Bit: All right. But be quick about it.

(*Peck pantomimes undoing Li'l Bit's brassiere with one hand.*)

You know, that's amazing. The way you can undo the hooks through my blouse with one hand.

Peck: Years of practice.

Li'l Bit: You would make an incredible brain surgeon with that dexterity.

Peck: I'll bet Clyde — what's the name of the boy taking you to the prom?

Li'l Bit: Claude Souders.

Peck: Claude Souders. I'll bet it takes him two hands, lights on, and you helping him on to get to first base.

Li'l Bit: Maybe.

(*Beat.*)

Peck: Can I . . . kiss them? Please?

Li'l Bit: I don't know.

Peck: Don't make a grown man beg.

Li'l Bit: Just one kiss.

Peck: I'm going to lift your blouse.

Li'l Bit: It's a little cold.

(*Peck laughs gently.*)

Peck: That's not why you're shivering.

(*They sit, perfectly still, for a long moment of silence. Peck makes gentle, concentric circles with his thumbs in the air in front of him.*)

How does that feel?

(*Li'l Bit closes her eyes, carefully keeps her voice calm:*)

Li'l Bit: It's . . . okay.

(*Sacred music, organ music or a boy's choir swells beneath the following.*)

Peck: I tell you, you can keep all the cathedrals of Europe. Just give me a second with these — these celestial orbs —

(*Peck bows his head as if praying. But he is kissing her nipple. Li'l Bit, eyes still closed, rears back her head on the leather Buick car seat.*)

Li'l Bit: Uncle Peck — we've got to go. I've got graduation rehearsal at school tomorrow morning. And you should get on home to Aunt Mary —
Peck: — All right, Li'l Bit.
Li'l Bit: — *Don't* call me that no more. (*Calmer.*) Any more. I'm a big girl now, Uncle Peck. As you know.

(*Li'l Bit pantomimes refastening her bra behind her back.*)

Peck: That you are. Going on eighteen. Kittens will turn into cats. (*Sighs.*) I live all week long for these few minutes with you — you know that?
Li'l Bit: I'll drive.

(*A Voice cuts in with:*)

Idling in the Neutral Gear.

(*Sound of car revving cuts off the sacred music; Li'l Bit, now an adult, rises out of the car and comes to us.*)

Li'l Bit: In most families, relatives get names like "Junior," or "Brother," or "Bubba." In my family, if we call someone "Big Papa," it's not because he's tall. In my family, folks tend to get nicknamed for their genitalia. Uncle Peck, for example. My mama's adage was "the titless wonder," and my cousin Bobby got branded for life as "B.B."

(*In unison with Greek Chorus:*)

Li'l Bit: For blue balls.	Greek Chorus: For blue balls.

Female Greek Chorus (as Mother): And of course, we were so excited to have a baby girl that when the nurse brought you in and said, "It's a girl! It's a baby girl!" I just had to see for myself. So we whipped your diapers down and parted your chubby little legs — and right between your legs there was —

(*Peck has come over during the above and chimes along:*)

Peck: Just a little bit.	Greek Chorus: Just a little bit.

Female Greek Chorus (as Mother): And when you were born, you were so tiny that you fit in Uncle Peck's outstretched hand.

(*Peck stretches his hand out.*)

Peck: Now that's a fact. I held you, one day old, right in this hand.

(*A traffic signal is projected of a bicycle in a circle with a diagonal red slash.*)

Li'l Bit: Even with my family background, I was sixteen or so before I realized that pedophilia did not mean people who loved to bicycle. . . .

(*A Voice intrudes:*)

DRIVING IN FIRST GEAR.

Li'l Bit: 1969. A typical family dinner.

Female Greek Chorus (as Mother): Look, Grandma. Li'l Bit's getting to be as big in the bust as you are.

Li'l Bit: Mother! Could we please change the subject?

Teenage Greek Chorus (as Grandmother): Well, I hope you are buying her some decent bras. I never had a decent bra, growing up in the Depression, and now my shoulders are just crippled — crippled from the weight hanging on my shoulders — the dents from my bra straps are big enough to put your finger in. — Here, let me show you —

(*As Grandmother starts to open her blouse:*)

Li'l Bit: Grandma! Please don't undress at the dinner table.

Peck: I thought the entertainment came *after* the dinner.

Li'l Bit (to the audience): This is how it always starts. My grandfather, Big Papa, will chime in next with —

Male Greek Chorus (as Grandfather): Yup. If Li'l Bit gets any bigger, we're gonna haveta buy her a wheelbarrow to carry in front of her —

Li'l Bit: — Damn it —

Peck: — How about those Redskins on Sunday, Big Papa?

Li'l Bit (to the audience): The only sport Big Papa followed was chasing Grandma around the house —

Male Greek Chorus (as Grandfather): — Or we could write to Kate Smith. Ask her for somma her used brassieres she don't want anymore — she could maybe give to Li'l Bit here —

Li'l Bit: — I can't stand it. I can't.

Peck: Now, honey, that's just their way —

Female Greek Chorus (as Mother): I tell you, Grandma, Li'l Bit's at that age. She's so sensitive, you can't say boo —

Li'l Bit: I'd like some privacy, that's all. Okay? Some goddamn privacy —

Peck: — Well, at least she didn't use the savior's name —

Li'l Bit (to the audience): And Big Papa wouldn't let a dead dog lie. No sirree.

Male Greek Chorus (as Grandfather): Well, she'd better stop being so sensitive. 'Cause five minutes before Li'l Bit turns the corner, her tits turn first —

Li'l Bit (starting to rise from the table): — That's it. That's it.

Peck: Li'l Bit, you can't let him get to you. Then he wins.

Li'l Bit: I hate him. *Hate* him.

Peck: That's fine. But hate him and eat a good dinner at the same time.

(*Li'l Bit calms down and sits with perfect dignity.*)

Li'l Bit: The gumbo is really good, Grandma.

Male Greek Chorus (as Grandfather): A'course, Li'l Bit's got a big surprise coming for her when she goes to that fancy college this fall —

Peck: Big Papa — let it go.

Male Greek Chorus (as Grandfather): What does she need a college degree for? She's got all the credentials she'll need on her chest —

Li'l Bit: — Maybe I want to learn things. Read. Rise above my cracker° background —

Peck: — Whoa, now, Li'l Bit —

Male Greek Chorus (as Grandfather): What kind of things do you want to read?

Li'l Bit: There's a whole semester course, for example, on Shakespeare —

(*Greek Chorus, as Grandfather, laughs until he weeps.*)

Male Greek Chorus (as Grandfather): Shakespeare. That's a good one. Shakespeare is really going to help you in life.

Peck: I think it's wonderful. And on scholarship!

Male Greek Chorus (as Grandfather): How is Shakespeare going to help her lie on her back in the dark?

(*Li'l Bit is on her feet.*)

Li'l Bit: You're getting old, Big Papa. You are going to die — very very soon. Maybe even *tonight.* And when you get to heaven, God's going to be a beautiful black woman in a long white robe. She's gonna look at your chart and say: Uh-oh. Fornication. Dog-ugly mean with blood relatives. Oh. Uh-oh. Voted for George Wallace. Well, one last chance: If you can name the play, all will be forgiven. And then she'll quote: "The quality of mercy is not strained." Your answer? Oh, too bad — *Merchant of Venice:* Act IV, Scene iii. And then she'll send your ass to fry in hell with all the other crackers. Excuse me, please.

(*To the audience.*) And as I left the house, I would always hear Big Papa say:

Male Greek Chorus (as Grandfather): Lucy, your daughter's got a mouth on her. Well, no sense in wasting good gumbo. Pass me her plate, Mama.

Li'l Bit: And Aunt Mary would come up to Uncle Peck:

Female Greek Chorus (as Aunt Mary): Peck, go after her, will you? You're the only one she'll listen to when she gets like this.

Peck: She just needs to cool off.

Female Greek Chorus (as Aunt Mary): Please, honey — Grandma's been on her feet cooking all day.

Peck: All right.

---

cracker: A derogatory term for a poor, southern, white person.

Li'l Bit: And as he left the room, Aunt Mary would say:

Female Greek Chorus (as Aunt Mary): Peck's so good with them when they get to be this age.

(*Li'l Bit has stormed to another part of the stage, her back turned, weeping with a teenage fury. Peck, cautiously, as if stalking a deer, comes to her. She turns away even more. He waits a bit.*)

Peck: I don't suppose you're talking to family. (*No response.*) Does it help that I'm in-law?

Li'l Bit: Don't you dare make fun of this.

Peck: I'm not. There's nothing funny about this. (*Beat.*) Although I'll bet when Big Papa is about to meet his maker, he'll remember *The Merchant of Venice*.

Li'l Bit: I've got to get away from here.

Peck: You're going away. Soon. Here, take this.

(*Peck hands her his folded handkerchief. Li'l Bit uses it, noisily. Hands it back. Without her seeing, he reverently puts it back.*)

Li'l Bit: I hate this family.

Peck: Your grandfather's ignorant. And you're right — he's going to die soon. But he's family. Family is . . . family.

Li'l Bit: Grown-ups are always saying that. Family.

Peck: Well, when you get a little older, you'll see what we're saying.

Li'l Bit: Uh-huh. So family is another acquired taste, like French kissing?

Peck: Come again?

Li'l Bit: You know, at first it really grosses you out, but in time you grow to like it?

Peck: Girl, you are . . . a handful.

Li'l Bit: Uncle Peck — you have the keys to your car?

Peck: Where do you want to go?

Li'l Bit: Just up the road.

Peck: I'll come with you.

Li'l Bit: No — please? I just need to . . . to drive for a little bit. Alone.

(*Peck tosses her the keys.*)

Peck: When can I see you alone again?

Li'l Bit: Tonight.

(*Li'l Bit crosses to center stage while the lights dim around her. A Voice directs:*)

Shifting Forward from First to Second Gear.

Li'l Bit: There were a lot of rumors about why I got kicked out of that fancy school in 1970. Some say I got caught with a man in my room. Some say as a kid on scholarship I fooled around with a rich man's daughter. (*Li'l Bit smiles innocently at the audience.*) I'm not talking.

But the real truth was I had a constant companion in my dorm room — who was less than discreet. Canadian V.O. A fifth a day.

1970. A Nixon recession. I slept on the floors of friends who were out of work themselves. Took factory work when I could find it. A string of dead-end jobs that didn't last very long.

What I did, most nights, was cruise the Beltway and the back roads of Maryland, where there was still country, past the battlefields and farm houses. Racing in a 1965 Mustang — and as long as I had gasoline for my car and whiskey for me, the nights would pass. Full tanked, I would speed past the churches and the trees on the bend, thinking just one notch of the steering wheel would be all it would take, and yet some . . . reflex took over. My hands on the wheel in the nine and three o'clock position — I never so much as got a ticket. He taught me well.

(*A Voice announces:*)

You and the Reverse Gear.

Li'l Bit: Back up. 1968. On the Eastern Shore. A celebration dinner.

(*Li'l Bit joins Peck at a table in a restaurant.*)

Peck: Feeling better, missy?

Li'l Bit: The bathroom's really amazing here, Uncle Peck! They have these little soaps — instead of borax or something — and they're in the shape of shells.

Peck: I'll have to take a trip to the gentleman's room just to see.

Li'l Bit: How did you know about this place?

Peck: This inn is famous on the Eastern Shore — it's been open since the seventeenth century. And I know how you like history. . . .

(*Li'l Bit is shy and pleased.*)

Li'l Bit: It's great.

Peck: And you've just done your first, legal, long-distance drive. You must be hungry.

Li'l Bit: I'm starved.

Peck: I would suggest a dozen oysters to start, and the crab imperial. . . . (*Li'l Bit is genuinely agog.*) You might be interested to know the town history. When the British sailed up this very river in the dead of night — see outside where I'm pointing? — they were going to bombard the heck out of this town. But the town fathers were ready for them. They crept up all the trees with lanterns so that the British would think they saw the town lights and they aimed their cannons too high. And that's why the inn is still here for business today.

Li'l Bit: That's a great story.

Peck (casually): Would you like to start with a cocktail?

Li'l Bit: You're not . . . you're not going to start drinking, are you, Uncle Peck?

Peck: Not me. I told you, as long as you're with me, I'll never drink. I asked you if *you'd* like a cocktail before dinner. It's nice to have a little something with the oysters.

Li'l Bit: But . . . I'm not . . . legal. We could get arrested. Uncle Peck, they'll never believe I'm twenty-one!

Peck: So? Today we celebrate your driver's license — on the first try. This establishment reminds me a lot of places back home.

Li'l Bit: What does that mean?

Peck: In South Carolina, like here on the Eastern Shore, they're . . . (*Searches for the right euphemism.*) . . . "European." Not so puritanical. And very understanding if gentlemen wish to escort very attractive young ladies who might want a before-dinner cocktail. If you want one, I'll order one.

Li'l Bit: Well — sure. Just . . . one.

(*The Female Greek Chorus appears in a spot.*)

Female Greek Chorus (as Mother): A Mother's Guide to Social Drinking:

A lady never gets sloppy — she may, however, get tipsy and a little gay.

Never drink on an empty stomach. Avail yourself of the bread basket and generous portions of butter. *Slather* the butter on your bread.

Sip your drink, slowly, let the beverage linger in your mouth — interspersed with interesting, fascinating conversation. Sip, never . . . slurp or gulp. Your glass should always be three-quarters full when his glass is empty.

Stay away from *ladies'* drinks: drinks like pink ladies, sloe gin fizzes, piña coladas, mai tais, planter's punch, white Russians, black Russians, red Russians, melon balls, blue balls, hummingbirds, hemorrhages, and hurricanes. In short, avoid anything with sugar, or anything with an umbrella. Get your vitamin C from *fruit*. Don't order anything with Voodoo or Vixen in the title or sexual positions in the name like Dead Man Screw or the Missionary. (*She sort of titters.*)

Believe me, they are lethal. . . . I think you were conceived after one of those.

Drink, instead, like a man: straight up or on the rocks, with plenty of water in between.

Oh, yes. And never mix your drinks. Stay with one all night long, like the man you came in with: bourbon, gin, or tequila till dawn, damn the torpedoes, full speed ahead!

(*As the Female Greek Chorus retreats, the Male Greek Chorus approaches the table as a Waiter.*)

Male Greek Chorus (as Waiter): I hope you all are having a pleasant evening. Is there something I can bring you, sir, before you order?

(*Li'l Bit waits in anxious fear. Carefully, Uncle Peck says with command:*)

Peck: I'll have a plain iced tea. The lady would like a drink, I believe.

(*The Male Greek Chorus does a double take; there is a moment when Uncle Peck and he are in silent communication.*)

Male Greek Chorus (as Waiter): Very good. What would the . . . lady like?
Li'l Bit (a bit flushed): Is there . . . is there any sugar in a martini?
Peck: None that I know of.
Li'l Bit: That's what I'd like then — a dry martini. And could we maybe have
some bread?
Peck: A drink fit for a woman of the world. — Please bring the lady a dry
martini, be generous with the olives, straight up.

(*The Male Greek Chorus anticipates a large tip.*)

Male Greek Chorus (as Waiter): Right away. Very good, sir.

(*The Male Greek Chorus returns with an empty martini glass which he puts
in front of Li'l Bit.*)

Peck: Your glass is empty. Another martini, madam?
Li'l Bit: Yes, thank you.

(*Peck signals the Male Greek Chorus, who nods.*)

So why did you leave South Carolina, Uncle Peck?
Peck: I was stationed in D.C. after the war, and decided to stay. Go North,
Young Man, someone might have said.
Li'l Bit: What did you do in the service anyway?
Peck (suddenly taciturn): I . . . I did just this and that. Nothing heroic or
spectacular.
Li'l Bit: But did you see fighting? Or go to Europe?
Peck: I served in the Pacific Theater. It's really nothing interesting to talk
about.
Li'l Bit: It is to me. (*The Waiter has brought another empty glass.*) Oh, goody.
I love the color of the swizzle sticks. What were we talking about?
Peck: Swizzle sticks.
Li'l Bit: Do you ever think of going back?
Peck: To the Marines?
Li'l Bit: No — to South Carolina.
Peck: Well, we do go back. To visit.
Li'l Bit: No, I mean to live.
Peck: Not very likely. I think it's better if my mother doesn't have a daily
reminder of her disappointment.
Li'l Bit: Are these floorboards slanted?
Peck: Yes, the floor is very slanted. I think this is the original floor.
Li'l Bit: Oh, good.

(*The Female Greek Chorus as Mother enters swaying a little, a little past
tipsy.*)

Female Greek Chorus (as Mother): Don't leave your drink unattended when
you visit the ladies' room. There is such a thing as white slavery; the
modus operandi is to spike an unsuspecting young girl's drink with a
"mickey" when she's left the room to powder her nose.

But if you feel you have had more than your sufficiency in liquor, do go to the ladies' room — often. Pop your head out of doors for a refreshing breath of the night air. If you must, wet your face and head with tap water. Don't be afraid to dunk your head if necessary. A wet woman is still less conspicuous than a drunk woman.

(*The Female Greek Chorus stumbles a little; conspiratorially.*) When in the course of human events it becomes necessary, go to a corner stall and insert the index and middle finger down the throat almost to the epiglottis. Divulge your stomach contents by such persuasion, and then wait a few moments before rejoining your beau waiting for you at your table.

Oh, no. Don't be shy or embarrassed. In the very best of establishments, there's always one or two debutantes crouched in the corner stalls, their beaded purses tossed willy-nilly, sounding like cats in heat, heaving up the contents of their stomachs.

(*The Female Greek Chorus begins to wander off.*)

I wonder what is it they do in the men's rooms. . . .

Li'l Bit: So why is your mother disappointed in you, Uncle Peck?
Peck: Every mother in Horry County has Great Expectations.
Li'l Bit: — Could I have another mar-ti-ni, please?
Peck: I think this is your last one.

(*Peck signals the Waiter. The Waiter looks at Li'l Bit and shakes his head no. Peck raises his eyebrow, raises his finger to indicate one more, and then rubs his fingers together. It looks like a secret code. The Waiter sighs, shakes his head sadly, and brings over another empty martini glass. He glares at Peck.*)

Li'l Bit: The name of the county where you grew up is "Horry"? (*Li'l Bit, plastered, begins to laugh. Then she stops.*) I think your mother should be proud of you.

(*Peck signals for the check.*)

Peck: Well, missy, she wanted me to do — to *be* everything my father was not. She wanted me to amount to something.
Li'l Bit: But you have! You've amounted a lot. . . .
Peck: I'm just a very ordinary man.

(*The Waiter has brought the check and waits. Peck draws out a large bill and hands it to the Waiter. Li'l Bit is in the soppy stage.*)

Li'l Bit: I'll bet your mother loves you, Uncle Peck.

(*Peck freezes a bit. To Male Greek Chorus as Waiter:*)

Peck: Thank you. The service was exceptional. Please keep the change.
Male Greek Chorus (*as Waiter, in a tone that could freeze*): Thank you, sir. Will you be needing any help?
Peck: I think we can manage, thank you.

(*Just then, the Female Greek Chorus as Mother lurches on stage; the Male Greek Chorus as Waiter escorts her off as she delivers:*)

Female Greek Chorus (as Mother): Thanks to judicious planning and several trips to the ladies' loo, your mother once out-drank an entire regiment of British officers on a good-will visit to Washington! Every last man of them! Milquetoasts! How'd they ever kick Hitler's cahones, huh? No match for an American lady — I could drink every man in here under the table.

> (*She delivers one last crucial hint before she is gently "bounced."*)
> As a last resort, when going out for an evening on the town, be sure to wear a skin-tight girdle — so tight that only a surgical knife or acetylene torch can get it off you — so that if you do pass out in the arms of your escort, he'll end up with rubber burns on his fingers before he can steal your virtue —

(*A Voice punctures the interlude with:*)

Vehicle Failure.

> Even with careful maintenance and preventive operation of your automobile, it is all too common for us to experience an unexpected breakdown. If you are driving at any speed when a breakdown occurs, you must slow down and guide the automobile to the side of the road.

(*Peck is slowly propping up Li'l Bit as they work their way to his car in the parking lot of the inn.*)

Peck: How are you doing, missy?

Li'l Bit: It's so far to the car, Uncle Peck. Like the lanterns in the trees the British fired on. . . .

(*Li'l Bit stumbles. Peck swoops her up in his arms.*)

Peck: Okay, I think we're going to take a more direct route.

(*Li'l Bit closes her eyes.*)

> Dizzy?

(*She nods her head.*)

> Don't look at the ground. Almost there — do you feel sick to your stomach?

(*Li'l Bit nods. They reach the "car." Peck gently deposits her on the front seat.*)

> Just settle here a little while until things stop spinning.

(*Li'l Bit opens her eyes.*)

Li'l Bit: What are we doing?

Peck: We're just going to sit here until your tummy settles down.

Li'l Bit: It's such nice upholst'ry —

Peck: Think you can go for a ride, now?

Li'l Bit: Where are you taking me?

Peck: Home.

Li'l Bit: You're not taking me — upstairs? There's no room at the inn? (*Li'l Bit giggles.*)

Peck: Do you want to go upstairs?

(*Li'l Bit doesn't answer.*)

    Or home?

Li'l Bit: — This isn't right, Uncle Peck.

Peck: What isn't right?

Li'l Bit: What we're doing. It's wrong. It's very wrong.

Peck: What are we doing?

(*Li'l Bit does not answer.*)

    We're just going out to dinner.

Li'l Bit: You know. It's not nice to Aunt Mary.

Peck: You let me be the judge of what's nice and not nice to my wife.

(*Beat.*)

Li'l Bit: Now you're mad.

Peck: I'm not mad. It's just that I thought you . . . understood me, Li'l Bit. I think you're the only one who does.

Li'l Bit: Someone will get hurt.

Peck: Have I forced you to do anything?

(*There is a long pause as Li'l Bit tries to get sober enough to think this through.*)

Li'l Bit: . . . I guess not.

Peck: We are just enjoying each other's company. I've told you, nothing is going to happen between us until you want it to. Do you know that?

Li'l Bit: Yes.

Peck: Nothing is going to happen until you want it. (*A second more, with Peck staring ahead at the river while seated at the wheel of his car. Then, softly:*) Do you want something to happen?

(*Peck reaches over and strokes her face, very gently. Li'l Bit softens, reaches for him, and buries her head in his neck. Then she kisses him. Then she moves away, dizzy again.*)

Li'l Bit: . . . I don't know.

(*Peck smiles; this has been good news for him — it hasn't been a "no."*)

Peck: Then I'll wait. I'm a very patient man. I've been waiting for a long time. I don't mind waiting.

Li'l Bit: Someone is going to get hurt.

Peck: No one is going to get hurt. (*Li'l Bit closes her eyes.*) Are you feeling sick?

Li'l Bit: Sleepy.

(*Carefully, Peck props Li'l Bit up on the seat.*)

Peck: Stay here a second.

Li'l Bit: Where're you going?

Peck: I'm getting something from the back seat.

Li'l Bit (scared; too loud): What? What are you going to do?

(*Peck reappears in the front seat with a lap rug.*)

Peck: Shhh. (*Peck covers Li'l Bit. She calms down.*) There. Think you can sleep?

(*Li'l Bit nods. She slides over to rest on his shoulder. With a look of happiness, Peck turns the ignition key. Beat. Peck leaves Li'l Bit sleeping in the car and strolls down to the audience. Wagner's Flying Dutchman comes up faintly.*)
(*A Voice interjects:*)

Idling in the Neutral Gear.

Teenage Greek Chorus: Uncle Peck Teaches Cousin Bobby How to Fish.

Peck: I get back once or twice a year — supposedly to visit Mama and the family, but the real truth is to fish. I miss this the most of all. There's a smell in the Low Country — where the swamp and fresh inlet join the saltwater — a scent of sand and cypress, that I haven't found anywhere yet.

I don't say this very often up North because it will just play into the stereotype everyone has, but I will tell you: I didn't wear shoes in the summertime until I was sixteen. It's unnatural down here to pen up your feet in leather. Go ahead — take 'em off. Let yourself breathe — it really will make you feel better.

We're going to aim for some pompano today — and I have to tell you, they're a very shy, mercurial fish. Takes patience, and psychology. You have to believe it doesn't matter if you catch one or not.

Sky's pretty spectacular — there's some beer in the cooler next to the crab salad I packed, so help yourself if you get hungry. Are you hungry? Thirsty? Holler if you are.

Okay. You don't want to lean over the bridge like that — pompano feed in shallow water, and you don't want to get too close — they're frisky and shy little things — wait, check your line. Yep, something's been munching while we were talking.

Okay, look: We take the sand flea and you take the hook like this — right through his little sand flea rump. Sand fleas should always keep their backs to the wall. Okay. Cast it in, like I showed you. That's great! I can taste that pompano now, sautéed with some pecans and butter, a little bourbon — now — let it lie on the bottom — now, reel, jerk, reel, jerk —

Look — look at your line. There's something calling, all right. Okay, tip the rod up — not too sharp — hook it — all right, now easy, reel and then rest — let it play. And reel — play it out, that's right — really good! I can't believe it! It's a pompano. — Good work! Way to go! You are an official fisherman now. Pompano are hard to catch. We are going to have a delicious little —

What? Well, I don't know how much pain a fish feels — you can't think of that. Oh, no, don't cry, come on now, it's just a fish — the other guys are going to see you. — No, no, you're just real sensitive, and I think that's wonderful at your age — look, do you want me to cut it free? You do?

Okay, hand me those pliers — look — I'm cutting the hook — okay? And we're just going to drop it in — no I'm not mad. It's just for fun, okay? There — it's going to swim back to its lady friend and tell her what a terrible day it had and she's going to stroke him with her fins until he feels better, and then they'll do something alone together that will make them both feel good and sleepy. . . .

(*Peck bends down, very earnest.*) I don't want you to feel ashamed about crying. I'm not going to tell anyone, okay? I can keep secrets. You know, men cry all the time. They just don't tell anybody, and they don't let anybody catch them. There's nothing you could do that would make me feel ashamed of you. Do you know that? Okay. (*Peck straightens up, smiles.*)

Do you want to pack up and call it a day? I tell you what — I think I can still remember — there's a really neat tree house where I used to stay for days. I think it's still here — it was the last time I looked. But it's a secret place — you can't tell anybody we've gone there — least of all your mom or your sisters. — This is something special just between you and me. Sound good? We'll climb up there and have a beer and some crab salad — okay, B.B.? Bobby? Robert. . . .

(*Li'l Bit sits at a kitchen table with the two Female Greek Chorus members.*)

Li'l Bit (to the audience): Three women, three generations, sit at the kitchen table.

On Men, Sex, and Women: Part I:

Female Greek Chorus (as Mother): Men only want one thing.

Li'l Bit (wide-eyed): But what? What is it they want?

Female Greek Chorus (as Mother): And once they have it, they lose all interest. So Don't Give It to Them.

Teenage Greek Chorus (as Grandmother): I never had the luxury of the rhythm method. Your grandfather is just a big bull. A big bull. Every morning, every evening.

Female Greek Chorus (as Mother, whispers to Li'l Bit): And he used to come home for lunch every day.

Li'l Bit: My god, Grandma!

Teenage Greek Chorus (as Grandmother): Your grandfather only cares that I do two things: have the table set and the bed turned down.

Female Greek Chorus (as Mother): And in all that time, Mother, you never have experienced — ?

Li'l Bit (to the audience): — Now my grandmother believed in all the sacraments of the church, to the day she died. She believed in Santa Claus and the Easter Bunny until she was fifteen. But she didn't believe in —

Teenage Greek Chorus (as Grandmother): — Orgasm! That's just something you and Mary have made up! I don't believe you.

Female Greek Chorus (as Mother): Mother, it happens to women all the time —

Teenage Greek Chorus (as Grandmother): — Oh, now you're going to tell me about the G force!

Li'l Bit: No, Grandma, I think that's astronauts —

Female Greek Chorus (as Mother): Well, Mama, after all, you were a child bride when Big Papa came and got you — you were a married woman and you still believed in Santa Claus.

Teenage Greek Chorus (as Grandmother): It was legal, what Daddy and I did! I was fourteen and in those days, fourteen was a grown-up woman —

(*Big Papa shuffles in the kitchen for a cookie.*)

Male Greek Chorus (as Grandfather): — Oh, now we're off on Grandma and the Rape of the Sa-bean Women!

Teenage Greek Chorus (as Grandmother): Well, you were the one in such a big hurry —

Male Greek Chorus (as Grandfather to Li'l Bit): — I picked your grandmother out of that herd of sisters just like a lion chooses the gazelle — the plump, slow, flaky gazelle dawdling at the edge of the herd — your sisters were too smart and too fast and too scrawny —

Li'l Bit (to the audience): — The family story is that when Big Papa came for Grandma, my Aunt Lily was waiting for him with a broom — and she beat him over the head all the way down the stairs as he was carrying out Grandma's hope chest —

Male Greek Chorus (as Grandfather): — And they were *mean*. 'Specially Lily.

Female Greek Chorus (as Mother): Well, you were robbing the baby of the family!

Teenage Greek Chorus (as Grandmother): I still keep a broom handy in the kitchen! And I know how to use it! So get your hand out of the cookie jar and don't you spoil your appetite for dinner — out of the kitchen!

(*Male Greek Chorus as Grandfather leaves chuckling with a cookie.*)

Female Greek Chorus (as Mother): Just one thing a married woman needs to know how to use — the rolling pin or the broom. I prefer a heavy, cast-iron fry pan — they're great on a man's head, no matter how thick the skull is.

Teenage Greek Chorus (as Grandmother): Yes, sir, your father is ruled by only two bosses! Mr. Gut and Mr. Peter! And sometimes, first thing in the morning, Mr. Sphincter Muscle!

Female Greek Chorus (as Mother): It's true. Men are like children. Just like little boys.

Teenage Greek Chorus (as Grandmother): Men are bulls! Big bulls!

(*The Greek Chorus is getting aroused.*)

Female Greek Chorus (as Mother): They'd still be crouched on their haunches over a fire in a cave if we hadn't cleaned them up!

Teenage Greek Chorus (as Grandmother; flushed): Coming in smelling of sweat—

Female Greek Chorus (as Mother): —Looking at those naughty pictures like boys in a dime store with a dollar in their pockets!

Teenage Greek Chorus (as Grandmother; raucous): No matter to them what they smell like! They've got to have it, right then, on the spot, right there! Nasty!—

Female Greek Chorus (as Mother): —Vulgar!

Teenage Greek Chorus (as Grandmother): Primitive!—

Female Greek Chorus (as Mother): —Hot!—

Li'l Bit: And just about then, Big Papa would shuffle in with—

Male Greek Chorus (as Grandfather): —What are you all cackling about in here?

Teenage Greek Chorus (as Grandmother): Stay out of the kitchen! This is just for girls!

(*As Grandfather leaves:*)

Male Greek Chorus (as Grandfather): Lucy, you'd better not be filling Mama's head with sex! Every time you and Mary come over and start in about sex, when I ask a simple question like, "What time is dinner going to be ready?," Mama snaps my head off!

Teenage Greek Chorus (as Grandmother): Dinner will be ready when I'm good and ready! Stay out of this kitchen!

(*Li'l Bit steps out.*)

(*A Voice directs:*)

WHEN MAKING A LEFT TURN, YOU MUST DOWNSHIFT WHILE GOING FORWARD.

Li'l Bit: 1979. A long bus trip to Upstate New York. I settled in to read, when a young man sat beside me.

Male Greek Chorus (as Young Man; voice cracking): "What are you reading?"

Li'l Bit: He asked. His voice broke into that miserable equivalent of vocal acne, not quite falsetto and not tenor, either. I glanced a side view. He was appealing in an odd way, huge ears at a defiant angle springing forward at ninety degrees. He must have been shaving, because his face, with a peach sheen, was speckled with nicks and styptic. "I have a class tomorrow," I told him.

Male Greek Chorus (as Young Man): "You're taking a class?"

Li'l Bit: "I'm teaching a class." He concentrated on lowering his voice.

Male Greek Chorus (as Young Man): "I'm a senior. Walt Whitman High."

Li'l Bit: The light was fading outside, so perhaps he was — with a very high voice.

I felt his "interest" quicken. Five steps ahead of the hopes in his head, I slowed down, waited, pretended surprise, acted at listening, all the while knowing we would get off the bus, he would just then seem to think to ask me to dinner, he would chivalrously insist on walking me home, he would continue to converse in the street until I would casually invite him up to my room — and — I was only into the second moment of conversation and I could see the whole evening before me.

And dramaturgically speaking, after the faltering and slightly comical "first act," there was the very briefest of intermissions, and an extremely capable and forceful and *sustained* second act. And after the second act climax and a gentle denouement — before the post-play discussion — I lay on my back in the dark and I thought about you, Uncle Peck. Oh. Oh — this is the allure. Being older. Being the first. Being the translator, the teacher, the epicure, the already jaded. This is how the giver gets taken.

(*Li'l Bit changes her tone.*) On Men, Sex, and Women: Part II:

(*Li'l Bit steps back into the scene as a fifteen-year-old, gawky and quiet, as the gazelle at the edge of the herd.*)

Teenage Greek Chorus (as Grandmother, to Li'l Bit): You're being mighty quiet, missy. Cat Got Your Tongue?

Li'l Bit: I'm just listening. Just thinking.

Teenage Greek Chorus (as Grandmother): Oh, yes, Little Miss Radar Ears? Soaking it all in? Little Miss Sponge? Penny for your thoughts?

(*Li'l Bit hesitates to ask but she really wants to know.*)

Li'l Bit: Does it — when you do it — you know, theoretically when I do it and I haven't done it before — I mean — does it hurt?

Female Greek Chorus (as Mother): Does what hurt, honey?

Li'l Bit: When a . . . when a girl does it for the first time — with a man — does it hurt?

Teenage Greek Chorus (as Grandmother; horrified): That's what you're thinking about?

Female Greek Chorus (as Mother; calm): Well, just a little bit. Like a pinch. And there's a little blood.

Teenage Greek Chorus (as Grandmother): Don't tell her that! She's too young to be thinking those things!

Female Greek Chorus (as Mother): Well, if she doesn't find out from me, where is she going to find out? In the street?

Teenage Greek Chorus (as Grandmother): Tell her it hurts! It's agony! You think you're going to die! Especially if you do it before marriage!

Female Greek Chorus (as Mother): Mama! I'm going to tell her the truth! Unlike you, you left me and Mary completely in the dark with fairy tales and told us to go to the priest! What does an eighty-year-old priest know about lovemaking with girls!

Li'l Bit (getting upset): It's not fair!

Female Greek Chorus (as Mother): Now, see, she's getting upset — you're scaring her.

Teenage Greek Chorus (as Grandmother): Good! Let her be good and scared! It hurts! You bleed like a stuck pig! And you lay there and say, "Why, O Lord, have you forsaken me?!"

Li'l Bit: It's not fair! Why does everything have to hurt for girls? Why is there always blood?

Female Greek Chorus (as Mother): It's not a lot of blood — and it feels wonderful after the pain subsides. . . .

Teenage Greek Chorus (as Grandmother): You're encouraging her to just go out and find out with the first drugstore joe who buys her a milkshake!

Female Greek Chorus (as Mother): Don't be scared. It won't hurt you — if the man you go to bed with really loves you. It's important that he loves you.

Teenage Greek Chorus (as Grandmother): — Why don't you just go out and rent a motel room for her, Lucy?

Female Greek Chorus (as Mother): I believe in telling my daughter the truth! We have a very close relationship! I want her to be able to ask me anything — I'm not scaring her with stories about Eve's sin and snakes crawling on their bellies for eternity and women bearing children in mortal pain —

Teenage Greek Chorus (as Grandmother): — If she stops and thinks before she takes her knickers off, maybe someone in this family will finish high school!

(*Li'l Bit knows what is about to happen and starts to retreat from the scene at this point.*)

Female Greek Chorus (as Mother): Mother! If you and Daddy had helped me — I wouldn't have had to marry that — that no-good-son-of-a —

Teenage Greek Chorus (as Grandmother): — He was good enough for you on a full moon! I hold you responsible!

Female Greek Chorus (as Mother): — You could have helped me! You could have told me something about the facts of life!

Teenage Greek Chorus (as Grandmother): — I told you what my mother told me! A girl with her skirt up can outrun a man with his pants down!

(*The Male Greek Chorus enters the fray; Li'l Bit edges farther downstage.*)

Female Greek Chorus (as Mother): And when I turned to you for a little help, all I got afterwards was —

Male Greek Chorus (as Grandfather): You Made Your Bed; Now Lie On It!

(*The Greek Chorus freezes, mouths open, argumentatively.*)

Li'l Bit (to the audience): Oh, please! I still can't bear to listen to it, after all these years —

(*The Male Greek Chorus "unfreezes," but out of his open mouth, as if to his surprise, comes a bass refrain from a Motown song.*)

Male Greek Chorus: "Do-Bee-Do-Wah!"

(*The Female Greek Chorus member is also surprised; but she, too, unfreezes.*)

Female Greek Chorus: "Shoo-doo-be-doo-be-doo; shoo-doo-be-doo-be-doo."

(*The Male and Female Greek Chorus members continue with their harmony, until the Teenage member of the Chorus starts in with Motown lyrics such as "Dedicated to the One I Love," or "In the Still of the Night," or "Hold Me"—any Sam Cooke will do. The three modulate down into three-part harmony, softly, until they are submerged by the actual recording playing over the radio in the car in which Uncle Peck sits in the driver's seat, waiting. Li'l Bit sits in the passenger's seat.*)

Li'l Bit: Ahh. That's better.

(*Uncle Peck reaches over and turns the volume down; to Li'l Bit:*)

Peck: How can you hear yourself think?

(*Li'l Bit does not answer.*)

(*A Voice insinuates itself in the pause:*)

Before You Drive.

> Always check under your car for obstructions — broken bottles, fallen tree branches, and the bodies of small children. Each year hundreds of children are crushed beneath the wheels of unwary drivers in their own driveways. Children depend on you to watch them.

(*Pause.*)

(*The Voice continues:*)

You and the Reverse Gear.

(*In the following section, it would be nice to have slides of erotic photographs of women and cars: women posed over the hood; women draped along the sideboards; women with water hoses spraying the car; and the actress playing Li'l Bit with a Bel Air or any 1950s car one can find for the finale.*)

Li'l Bit: 1967. In a parking lot of the Beltsville Agricultural Farms. The Initiation into a Boy's First Love.

Peck (with a soft look on his face): Of course, my favorite car will always be the '56 Bel Air Sports Coupe. Chevy sold more '55s, but the '56!—a V-8 with Corvette option, 225 horsepower; went from zero to sixty miles per hour in 8.9 seconds.

Li'l Bit (to the audience): Long after a mother's tits, but before a woman's breasts:

Peck: Super-Turbo-Fire! What a Power Pack—mechanical lifters, twin four-barrel carbs, lightweight valves, dual exhausts—

Li'l Bit (to the audience): After the milk but before the beer:

Peck: A specific intake manifold, higher-lift camshaft, and the tightest squeeze Chevy had ever made —

Li'l Bit (to the audience): Long after he's squeezed down the birth canal but before he's pushed his way back in: The boy falls in love with the thing that bears his weight with speed.

Peck: I want you to know your automobile inside and out. — Are you there? Li'l Bit?

(Slides end here.)

Li'l Bit: — What?

Peck: You're drifting. I need you to concentrate.

Li'l Bit: Sorry.

Peck: Okay. Get into the driver's seat. (*Li'l Bit does.*) Okay. Now. Show me what you're going to do before you start the car.

(Li'l Bit sits, with her hands in her lap. She starts to giggle.)

Li'l Bit: I don't know, Uncle Peck.

Peck: Now, come on. What's the first thing you're going to adjust?

Li'l Bit: My bra strap? —

Peck: — Li'l Bit. What's the most important thing to have control of on the inside of the car?

Li'l Bit: That's easy. The radio. I tune the radio from Mama's old fart tunes to —

(Li'l Bit turns the radio up so we can hear a 1960s tune. With surprising firmness, Peck commands:)

Peck: — Radio off. Right now. (*Li'l Bit turns the radio off.*) When you are driving your car, with your license, you can fiddle with the stations all you want. But when you are driving with a learner's permit in my car, I want all your attention to be on the road.

Li'l Bit: Yes, sir.

Peck: Okay. Now the seat — forward and up. (*Li'l Bit pushes it forward.*) Do you want a cushion?

Li'l Bit: No — I'm good.

Peck: You should be able to reach all the switches and controls. Your feet should be able to push the accelerator, brake and clutch all the way down. Can you do that?

Li'l Bit: Yes.

Peck: Okay, the side mirrors. You want to be able to see just a bit of the right side of the car in the right mirror — can you?

Li'l Bit: Turn it out more.

Peck: Okay. How's that?

Li'l Bit: A little more. . . . Okay, that's good.

Peck: Now the left — again, you want to be able to see behind you — but the left lane — adjust it until you feel comfortable. (*Li'l Bit does so.*) Next. I want you to check the rearview mirror. Angle it so you have a clear vision of the back. (*Li'l Bit does so.*) Okay. Lock your door. Make sure all the doors are locked.

Li'l Bit: (making a joke of it): But then I'm locked in with you.

Peck: Don't fool.

Li'l Bit: All right. We're locked in.

Peck: We'll deal with the air vents and defroster later. I'm teaching you on a manual — once you learn manual, you can drive anything. I want you to be able to drive any car, any machine. Manual gives you *control*. In ice, if your brakes fail, if you need more power — okay? It's a little harder at first, but then it becomes like breathing. Now. Put your hands on the wheel. I never want to see you driving with one hand. Always two hands. (*Li'l Bit hesitates.*) What? What is it now?

Li'l Bit: If I put my hands on the wheel — how do I defend myself?

Peck (softly): Now listen. Listen up close. We're not going to fool around with this. This is serious business. I will never touch you when you are driving a car. Understand?

Li'l Bit: Okay.

Peck: Hands on the nine o'clock and three o'clock position gives you maximum control and turn.

(*Peck goes silent for a while. Li'l Bit waits for more instruction.*)

Okay. Just relax and listen to me, Li'l Bit, okay? I want you to lift your hands for a second and look at them.

(*Li'l Bit feels a bit silly, but does it.*)

Those are your two hands. When you are driving, your life is in your own two hands. Understand?

(*Li'l Bit nods.*)

I don't have any sons. You're the nearest to a son I'll ever have — and I want to give you something. Something that really matters to me.

There's something about driving — when you're in control of the car, just you and the machine and the road — that nobody can take from you. A power. I feel more myself in my car than anywhere else. And that's what I want to give to you.

There's a lot of assholes out there. Crazy men, arrogant idiots, drunks, angry kids, geezers who are blind — and you have to be ready for them. I want to teach you to drive like a man.

Li'l Bit: What does that mean?

Peck: Men are taught to drive with confidence — with aggression. The road belongs to them. They drive defensively — always looking out for the other guy. Women tend to be polite — to hesitate. And that can be fatal.

You're going to learn to think what the other guy is going to do before he does it. If there's an accident, and ten cars pile up, and people get killed, you're the one who's gonna steer through it, put your foot on the gas if you have to, and be the only one to walk away. I don't know how long you or I are going to live, but we're for damned sure not going to die in a car.

So if you're going to drive with me, I want you to take this very seriously.

Li'l Bit: I will, Uncle Peck. I want you to teach me to drive.

Peck: Good. You're going to pass your test on the first try. Perfect score. Before the next four weeks are over, you're going to know this baby inside and out. Treat her with respect.

Li'l Bit: Why is it a "she"?

Peck: Good question. It doesn't have to be a "she" — but when you close your eyes and think of someone who responds to your touch — someone who performs just for you and gives you what you ask for — I guess I always see a "she." You can call her what you like.

Li'l Bit (to the audience): I closed my eyes — and decided not to change the gender.

(*A Voice:*)

Defensive driving involves defending yourself from hazardous and sudden changes in your automotive environment. By thinking ahead, the defensive driver can adjust to weather, road conditions, and road kill. Good defensive driving involves mental and physical preparation. Are you prepared?

(*Another Voice chimes in:*)

You and the Reverse Gear.

Li'l Bit: 1966. The Anthropology of the Female Body in Ninth Grade — Or A Walk Down Mammary Lane.

(*Throughout the following, there is occasional rhythmic beeping, like a transmitter signaling. Li'l Bit is aware of it, but can't figure out where it is coming from. No one else seems to hear it.*)

Male Greek Chorus: In the hallway of Francis Scott Key Middle School.

(*A bell rings; the Greek Chorus is changing classes and meets in the hall, conspiratorially.*)

Teenage Greek Chorus: She's coming!

(*Li'l Bit enters the scene; the Male Greek Chorus member has a sudden, violent sneezing and lethal allergy attack.*)

Female Greek Chorus: Jerome? Jerome? Are you all right?

Male Greek Chorus: I — don't — know. I can't breathe — get Li'l Bit —

Teenage Greek Chorus: — He needs oxygen! —

Female Greek Chorus: — Can you help us here?

Li'l Bit: What's wrong? Do you want me to get the school nurse —

(*The Male Greek Chorus member wheezes, grabs his throat and sniffs at Li'l Bit's chest, which is beeping away.*)

Male Greek Chorus: No — it's okay — I only get this way when I'm around an allergy trigger —

Li'l Bit: Golly. What are you allergic to?

Male Greek Chorus (with a sudden grab of her breast): Foam rubber.

(*The Greek Chorus members break up with hilarity; Jerome leaps away from Li'l Bit's kicking rage with agility; as he retreats:*)

Li'l Bit: Jerome! Creep! Cretin! Cro-Magnon!
Teenage Greek Chorus: Rage is not attractive in a girl.
Female Greek Chorus: Really. Get a Sense of Humor.

(*A Voice echoes:*)

> Good defensive driving involves mental and physical preparation. Were You Prepared?

Female Greek Chorus: Gym Class: In the showers.

(*The sudden sound of water; the Female Greek Chorus members and Li'l Bit, while fully clothed, drape towels across their fronts, miming nudity. They stand, hesitate, at an imaginary shower's edge.*)

Li'l Bit: Water looks hot.
Female Greek Chorus: Yesss. . . .

(*Female Greek Chorus members are not going to make the first move. One dips a tentative toe under the water, clutching the towel around her.*)

Li'l Bit: Well, I guess we'd better shower and get out of here.
Female Greek Chorus: Yep. You go ahead. I'm still cooling off.
Li'l Bit: Okay. — Sally? Are you gonna shower?
Teenage Greek Chorus: After you —

(*Li'l Bit takes a deep breath for courage, drops the towel and plunges in: The two Female Greek Chorus members look at Li'l Bit in the all together, laugh, gasp and high-five each other.*)

Teenage Greek Chorus: Oh my god! Can you believe —
Female Greek Chorus: Told you! It's not foam rubber! I win! Jerome owes me fifty cents!

(*A Voice editorializes:*)

WERE YOU PREPARED?

(*Li'l Bit tries to cover up; she is exposed, as suddenly 1960s Motown fills the room and we segue into:*)

Female Greek Chorus: The Sock Hop.

(*Li'l Bit stands up against the wall with her female classmates. Teenage Greek Chorus is mesmerized by the music and just sways alone, lip-synching the lyrics.*)

Li'l Bit: I don't know. Maybe it's just me — but — do you ever feel like you're just a walking Mary Jane joke?
Female Greek Chorus: I don't know what you mean.
Li'l Bit: You haven't heard the Mary Jane jokes? (*Female Greek Chorus member shakes her head no.*) Okay. "Little Mary Jane is walking through the

woods, when all of a sudden this man who was hiding behind a tree *jumps* out, *rips* open Mary Jane's blouse, and *plunges* his hands on her breasts. And Little Mary Jane just laughed and laughed because she knew her money was in her shoes."

(*Li'l Bit laughs; the Female Greek Chorus does not.*)

Female Greek Chorus: You're weird.

(*In another space, in a strange light, Uncle Peck stands and stares at Li'l Bit's body. He is setting up a tripod, but he just stands, appreciative, watching her.*)

Li'l Bit: Well, don't you ever feel . . . self-conscious? Like you're being looked at all the time?

Female Greek Chorus: That's not a problem for me. — Oh — look — Greg's coming over to ask you to dance.

(*Teenage Creek Chorus becomes attentive, flustered. Male Greek Chorus member, as Greg, bends slightly as a very short young man, whose head is at Li'l Bit's chest level. Ardent, sincere, and socially inept, Greg will become a successful gynecologist.*)

Teenage Greek Chorus (softly): Hi, Greg.

(*Greg does not hear. He is intent on only one thing.*)

Male Greek Chorus (as Greg, to Li'l Bit): Good evening. Would you care to dance?

Li'l Bit (gently): Thank you very much, Greg — but I'm going to sit this one out.

Male Greek Chorus (as Greg): Oh. Okay. I'll try my luck later.

(*He disappears.*)

Teenage Greek Chorus: Oohhh.

(*Li'l Bit relaxes. Then she tenses, aware of Peck's gaze.*)

Female Greek Chorus: Take pity on him. Someone should.

Li'l Bit: But he's so short.

Teenage Greek Chorus: He can't help it.

Li'l Bit: But his head comes up to (*Li'l Bit gestures*) here. And I think he asks me on the fast dances so he can watch me — you know — jiggle.

Female Greek Chorus: I wish I had your problems.

(*The tune changes; Greg is across the room in a flash.*)

Male Greek Chorus (as Greg): Evening again. May I ask you for the honor of a spin on the floor?

Li'l Bit: I'm . . . very complimented, Greg. But I . . . I just don't do fast dances.

Male Greek Chorus (as Greg): Oh. No problem. That's okay.

(*He disappears. Teenage Greek Chorus watches him go.*)

Teenage Greek Chorus: That is just so — *sad.*

(*Li'l Bit becomes aware of Peck waiting.*)

Female Greek Chorus: You know, you should take it as a compliment that the guys want to watch you jiggle. They're guys. That's what they're supposed to do.

Li'l Bit: I guess you're right. But sometimes I feel like these alien life forces, these two mounds of flesh have grafted themselves onto my chest, and they're using me until they can "propagate" and take over the world and they'll just keep growing, with a mind of their own until I collapse under their weight and they suck all the nourishment out of my body and I finally just waste away while they get bigger and bigger and — (*Li'l Bit's classmates are just staring at her in disbelief.*)

Female Greek Chorus: — You are the strangest girl I have ever met.

(*Li'l Bit's trying to joke but feels on the verge of tears.*)

Li'l Bit: Or maybe someone's implanted radio transmitters in my chest at a frequency I can't hear, that girls can't detect, but they're sending out these signals to men who get mesmerized, like sirens, calling them to dash themselves on these "rocks" —

(*Just then, the music segues into a slow dance, perhaps a Beach Boys tune like "Little Surfer," but over the music there's a rhythmic, hypnotic beeping transmitted, which both Greg and Peck hear. Li'l Bit hears it too, and in horror she stares at her chest. She, too, is almost hypnotized. In a trance, Greg responds to the signals and is called to her side — actually, her front. Like a zombie, he stands in front of her, his eyes planted on her two orbs.*)

Male Greek Chorus (as Greg): This one's a slow dance. I hope your dance card isn't . . . filled?

(*Li'l Bit is aware of Peck; but the signals are calling her to him. The signals are no longer transmitters, but an electromagnetic force, pulling Li'l Bit to his side, where he again waits for her to join him. She must get away from the dance floor.*)

Li'l Bit: Greg — you really are a nice boy. But I don't like to dance.

Male Greek Chorus (as Greg): That's okay. We don't have to move or anything. I could just hold you and we could just *sway* a little —

Li'l Bit: — No! I'm sorry — but I think I have to leave; I hear someone calling me —

(*Li'l Bit starts across the dance floor, leaving Greg behind. The beeping stops. The lights change, although the music does not. As Li'l Bit talks to the audience, she continues to change and prepare for the coming session. She should be wearing a tight tank top or a sheer blouse and very tight pants. To the audience:*)

In every man's home some small room, some zone in his house, is set aside. It might be the attic, or the study, or a den. And there's an invisible sign as if from the old treehouse: Girls Keep Out. Here, away from female eyes, lace doilies and crochet, he keeps his manly toys: the Vargas pinups, the tackle. A scent of tobacco and WD-40. (*She inhales deeply.*) A dash of his Bay Rum. Ahhh . . . (*Li'l Bit savors it for just a moment more.*) Here he keeps his secrets: a violin or saxophone, drum set or darkroom, and the stacks of *Playboy*. (*In a whisper.*) Here, in my aunt's home, it was the basement. Uncle Peck's turf.

(*A Voice commands:*)

You and the Reverse Gear.

Li'l Bit: 1965. The Photo Shoot.

(*Li'l Bit steps into the scene as a nervous but curious thirteen-year-old. Music, from the previous scene, continues to play, changing into something like Roy Orbison later — something seductive with a beat. Peck fiddles, all business, with his camera. As in the driving lesson, he is all competency and concentration. Li'l Bit stands awkwardly. He looks through the Leica camera on the tripod, adjusts the back lighting, etc.*)

Peck: Are you cold? The lights should heat up some in a few minutes —
Li'l Bit: — Aunt Mary is?
Peck: At the National Theatre matinee. With your mother. We have time.
Li'l Bit: But — what if —
Peck: — And so what if they return? I told them you and I were going to be working with my camera. They won't come down.

(*Li'l Bit is quiet, apprehensive.*)

Look, are you sure you want to do this?
Li'l Bit: I said I'd do it. But —
Peck: — I know. You've drawn the line.
Li'l Bit (reassured): That's right. No frontal nudity.
Peck: Good heavens, girl, where did you pick that up?
Li'l Bit (defensive): I read.

(*Peck tries not to laugh.*)

Peck: And I read *Playboy* for the interviews. Okay. Let's try some different music.

(*Peck goes to an expensive reel-to-reel and forwards. Something like "Sweet Dreams" begins to play.*)

Li'l Bit: I didn't know you listened to this.
Peck: I'm not dead, you know, I try to keep up. Do you like this song?

(*Li'l Bit nods with pleasure.*)

Good. Now listen — at professional photo shoots, they always play music for the models. Okay? I want you to just enjoy the music. Listen to it with your body, and just — respond.

Li'l Bit: Respond to the music with my . . . body?

Peck: Right. Almost like dancing. Here — let's get you on the stool, first.
  (*Peck comes over and helps her up.*)

Li'l Bit: But nothing showing —

(*Peck firmly, with his large capable hands, brushes back her hair, angles her face. Li'l Bit turns to him like a plant to the sun.*)

Peck: Nothing showing. Just a peek.

(*He holds her by the shoulders, looking at her critically. Then he unbuttons her blouse to the midpoint, and runs his hands over the flesh of her exposed sternum, arranging the fabric, just touching her. Deliberately, calmly. Asexually. Li'l Bit quiets, sits perfectly still, and closes her eyes.*)

   Okay?

Li'l Bit: Yes.

(*Peck goes back to his camera.*)

Peck: I'm going to keep talking to you. Listen without responding to what I'm saying; you want to *listen* to the music. Sway, move just your torso or your head — I've got to check the light meter.

Li'l Bit: But — you'll be watching.

Peck: No — I'm not here — just my voice. Pretend you're in your room all alone on a Friday night with your mirror — and the music feels good — just move for me, Li'l Bit —

(*Li'l Bit closes her eyes. At first self-conscious; then she gets more into the music and begins to sway. We hear the camera start to whir. Throughout the shoot, there can be a slide montage of actual shots of the actor playing Li'l Bit — interspersed with other models à la Playboy, Calvin Klein, and Victoriana/Lewis Carroll's Alice Liddell.*)

   That's it. That looks great. Okay. Just keep doing that. Lift your head up a bit more, good, good, just keep moving, that a girl — you're a very beautiful young woman. Do you know that?

(*Li'l Bit looks up, blushes. Peck shoots the camera. The audience should see this shot on the screen.*)

Li'l Bit: No. I don't know that.

Peck: Listen to the music.

(*Li'l Bit closes her eyes again.*)

   Well you are. For a thirteen-year-old, you have a body a twenty-year-old woman would die for.

Li'l Bit: The boys in school don't think so.

Peck: The boys in school are little Neanderthals in short pants. You're ten years ahead of them in maturity; it's gonna take a while for them to catch up.

(*Peck clicks another shot; we see a faint smile on Li'l Bit on the screen.*)

   Girls turn into women long before boys turn into men.

Li'l Bit: Why is that?

Peck: I don't know, Li'l Bit. But it's a blessing for men.

(*Li'l Bit turns silent.*)

Keep moving. Try arching your back on the stool, hands behind you, and throw your head back.

(*The slide shows a Playboy model in this pose.*)

Oohh, great. That one was great. Turn your head away, same position. (*Whir.*) Beautiful.

(*Li'l Bit looks at him a bit defiantly.*)

Li'l Bit: I think Aunt Mary is beautiful.

(*Peck stands still.*)

Peck: My wife is a very beautiful woman. Her beauty doesn't cancel yours out. (*More casually; he returns to the camera.*) All the women in your family are beautiful. In fact, I think all women are. You're not listening to the music. (*Peck shoots some more film in silence.*) All right, turn your head to the left. Good. Now take the back of your right hand and put it on your right cheek — your elbow angled up — now slowly, slowly, stroke your cheek, draw back your hair with the back of your hand. (*Another classic Playboy or Vargas.*) Good. One hand above and behind your head; stretch your body; smile. (*Another pose.*) Li'l Bit. I want you to think of something that makes you laugh —

Li'l Bit: I can't think of anything.

Peck: Okay. Think of Big Papa chasing Grandma around the living room.

(*Li'l Bit lifts her head and laughs. Click. We should see this shot.*)

Good. Both hands behind your head. Great! Hold that. (*From behind his camera.*) You're doing great work. If we keep this up, in five years we'll have a really professional portfolio.

(*Li'l Bit stops.*)

Li'l Bit: What do you mean in five years?

Peck: You can't submit work to *Playboy* until you're eighteen. —

(*Peck continues to shoot; he knows he's made a mistake.*)

Li'l Bit: — Wait a minute. You're joking, aren't you, Uncle Peck?

Peck: Heck, no. You can't get into *Playboy* unless you're the very best. And you are the very best.

Li'l Bit: I would never do that!

(*Peck stops shooting. He turns off the music.*)

Peck: Why? There's nothing wrong with *Playboy* — it's a very classy maga —

Li'l Bit (more upset): But I thought you said I should go to college!

Peck: Wait — Li'l Bit — it's nothing like that. Very respectable women model for *Playboy* — actresses with major careers — women in college — there's an Ivy League issue every —

Li'l Bit: — I'm never doing anything like that! You'd show other people these — other *men* — what I'm doing. — Why would you do that?! Any *boy* around here could just pick up, just go into The Stop & Go and *buy* — Why would you ever want to — to share —

Peck: — Whoa, whoa. Just stop a second and listen to me. Li'l Bit. Listen. There's nothing wrong in what we're doing. I'm very proud of you. I think you have a wonderful body and an even more wonderful mind. And of course I want other people to *appreciate* it. It's not anything shameful.

Li'l Bit (hurt): But this is something — that I'm only doing for you. This is something — that you said was just between us.

Peck: It is. And if that's how you feel, five years from now, it will remain that way. Okay? I know you're not going to do anything you don't feel like doing. (*He walks back to the camera.*) Do you want to stop now? I've got just a few more shots on this roll —

Li'l Bit: I don't want anyone seeing this.

Peck: I swear to you. No one will. I'll treasure this — that you're doing this only for me.

(*Li'l Bit, still shaken, sits on the stool. She closes her eyes.*)

Li'l Bit? Open your eyes and look at me.

(*Li'l Bit shakes her head no.*)

Come on. Just open your eyes, honey.

Li'l Bit: If I look at you — if I look at the camera:

You're gonna know what I'm thinking. You'll see right through me —

Peck: — No, I won't. I want you to look at me. All right, then. I just want you to listen. Li'l Bit.

(*She waits.*)

I love you.

(*Li'l Bit opens her eyes; she is startled. Peck captures the shot. On the screen we see right through her. Peck says softly.*)

Do you know that?

(*Li'l Bit nods her head yes.*)

I have loved you every day since the day you were born.

Li'l Bit: Yes.

(*Li'l Bit and Peck just look at each other. Beat. Beneath the shot of herself on the screen, Li'l Bit, still looking at her uncle, begins to unbutton her blouse.*

A neutral Voice cuts off the above scene with:)

IMPLIED CONSENT.

As an individual operating a motor vehicle in the state of Maryland, you must abide by "Implied Consent." If you do not consent to take the blood alcohol content test, there may be severe penalties: a suspension of license, a fine, community service, and a possible jail sentence.

(*The Voice shifts tone:*)

IDLING IN THE NEUTRAL GEAR.

Male Greek Chorus (announcing): Aunt Mary on behalf of her husband.

(*Female Greek Chorus checks her appearance, and with dignity comes to the front of the stage and sits down to talk to the audience.*)

Female Greek Chorus (as Aunt Mary): My husband was such a good man — is. Is such a good man. Every night, he does the dishes. The second he comes home, he's taking out the garbage, or doing yard work, lifting the heavy things I can't. Everyone in the neighborhood borrows Peck — it's true — women with husbands of their own, men who just don't have Peck's abilities — there's always a knock on our door for a jump start on cold mornings, when anyone needs a ride, or help shoveling the sidewalk — I look out, and there Peck is, without a coat, pitching in.

I know I'm lucky. The man works from dawn to dusk. And the overtime he does every year — my poor sister. She sits every Christmas when I come to dinner with a new stole, or diamonds, or with the tickets to Bermuda.

I know he has troubles. And we don't talk about them. I wonder, sometimes, what happened to him during the war. The men who fought World War II didn't have "rap sessions" to talk about their feelings. Men in his generation were expected to be quiet about it and get on with their lives. And sometimes I can feel him just fighting the trouble — whatever has burrowed deeper than the scar tissue — and we don't talk about it. I know he's having a bad spell because he comes looking for me in the house, and just hangs around me until it passes. And I keep my banter light — I discuss a new recipe, or sales, or gossip — because I think domesticity can be a balm for men when they're lost. We sit in the house and listen to the peace of the clock ticking in his well-ordered living room, until it passes.

(*Sharply.*) I'm not a fool. I know what's going on. I wish you could feel how hard Peck fights against it — he's swimming against the tide, and what he needs is to see me on the shore, believing in him, knowing he won't go under, he won't give up —

And I want to say this about my niece. She's a sly one, that one is. She knows exactly what she's doing; she's twisted Peck around her little finger and thinks it's all a big secret. Yet another one who's borrowing my husband until it doesn't suit her anymore.

Well. I'm counting the days until she goes away to school. And she manipulates someone else. And then he'll come back again, and sit in the kitchen while I bake, or beside me on the sofa when I sew in the evenings. I'm a very patient woman. But I'd like my husband back.

I am counting the days.

(*A Voice repeats:*)

You and the Reverse Gear.

Male Greek Chorus: Li'l Bit's Thirteenth Christmas. Uncle Peck Does the Dishes. Christmas 1964.

(*Peck stands in a dress shirt and tie, nice pants, with an apron. He is washing dishes. He's in a mood we haven't seen. Quiet, brooding. Li'l Bit watches him a moment before seeking him out.*)

Li'l Bit: Uncle Peck?

(*He does not answer. He continues to work on the pots.*)

I didn't know where you'd gone to.

(*He nods. She takes this as a sign to come in.*)

Don't you want to sit with us for a while?
Peck: No. I'd rather do the dishes.

(*Pause. Li'l Bit watches him.*)

Li'l Bit: You're the only man I know who does dishes.

(*Peck says nothing.*)

I think it's really nice.
Peck: My wife has been on her feet all day. So's your grandmother and your mother.
Li'l Bit: I know. (*Beat.*) Do you want some help?
Peck: No. (*He softens a bit towards her.*) You can help by just talking to me.
Li'l Bit: Big Papa never does the dishes. I think it's nice.
Peck: I think men should be nice to women. Women are always working for us. There's nothing particularly manly in wolfing down food and then sitting around in a stupor while the women clean up.
Li'l Bit: That looks like a really neat camera that Aunt Mary got you.
Peck: It is. It's a very nice one.

(*Pause, as Peck works on the dishes and some demon that Li'l Bit intuits.*)

Li'l Bit: Did Big Papa hurt your feelings?
Peck (tired): What? Oh, no — it doesn't hurt me. Family is family. I'd rather have him picking on me than — I don't pay him any mind, Li'l Bit.
Li'l Bit: Are you angry with us?
Peck: No, Li'l Bit. I'm not angry.

(*Another pause.*)

Li'l Bit: We missed you at Thanksgiving. . . . I did. I missed you.

Peck: Well, there were . . . "things" going on. I didn't want to spoil anyone's Thanksgiving.

Li'l Bit: Uncle Peck? (*Very carefully.*) Please don't drink anymore tonight.

Peck: I'm not . . . overdoing it.

Li'l Bit: I know. (*Beat.*) Why do you drink so much?

(*Peck stops and thinks, carefully.*)

Peck: Well, Li'l Bit — let me explain it this way. There are some people who have a . . . a "fire" in the belly. I think they go to work on Wall Street or they run for office. And then there are people who have a "fire" in their heads — and they become writers or scientists or historians. (*He smiles a little at her.*) You. You've got a "fire" in the head. And then there are people like me.

Li'l Bit: Where do you have . . . a fire?

Peck: I have a fire in my heart. And sometimes the drinking helps.

Li'l Bit: There's got to be other things that can help.

Peck: I suppose there are.

Li'l Bit: Does it help — to talk to me?

Peck: Yes. It does. (*Quiet.*) I don't get to see you very much.

Li'l Bit: I know. (*Li'l Bit thinks.*) You could talk to me more.

Peck: Oh?

Li'l Bit: I could make a deal with you, Uncle Peck.

Peck: I'm listening.

Li'l Bit: We could meet and talk — once a week. You could just store up whatever's bothering you during the week — and then we could talk.

Peck: Would you like that?

Li'l Bit: As long as you don't drink. I'd meet you somewhere for lunch or for a walk — on the weekends — as long as you stop drinking. And we could talk about whatever you want.

Peck: You would do that for me?

Li'l Bit: I don't think I'd want Mom to know. Or Aunt Mary. I wouldn't want them to think —

Peck: — No. It would just be us talking.

Li'l Bit: I'll tell Mom I'm going to a girlfriend's. To study. Mom doesn't get home until six, so you can call me after school and tell me where to meet you.

Peck: You get home at four?

Li'l Bit: We can meet once a week. But only in public. You've got to let me — draw the line. And once it's drawn, you mustn't cross it.

Peck: Understood.

Li'l Bit: Would that help?

(*Peck is very moved.*)

Peck: Yes. Very much.

Li'l Bit: I'm going to join the others in the living room now. (*Li'l Bit turns to go.*)

Peck: Merry Christmas, Li'l Bit.

(*Li'l Bit bestows a very warm smile on him.*)

Li'l Bit: Merry Christmas, Uncle Peck.

(*A Voice dictates:*)

SHIFTING FORWARD FROM SECOND TO THIRD GEAR.

(*The Male and Female Greek Chorus members come forward.*)

Male Greek Chorus: 1969. Days and Gifts: A Countdown:

Female Greek Chorus: A note. "September 3, 1969. Li'l Bit: You've only been away two days and it feels like months. Hope your dorm room is cozy. I'm sending you this tape cassette — it's a new model — so you'll have some music in your room. Also that music you're reading about for class — *Carmina Burana.* Hope you enjoy. Only ninety days to go! — Peck."

Male Greek Chorus: September 22. A bouquet of roses. A note: "Miss you like crazy. Sixty-nine days . . . "

Teenage Greek Chorus: September 25. A box of chocolates. A card: "Don't worry about the weight gain. You still look great. Got a post office box — write to me there. Sixty-six days. — Love, your candy man."

Male Greek Chorus: October 16. A note: "Am trying to get through the Jane Austen you're reading — *Emma* — here's a book in return: *Liaisons Dangereuses.* Hope you're saving time for me." Scrawled in the margin the number: "47."

Female Greek Chorus: November 16. "Sixteen days to go! — Hope you like the perfume. — Having a hard time reaching you on the dorm phone. You must be in the library a lot. Won't you think about me getting you your own phone so we can talk?"

Teenage Greek Chorus: November 18. "Li'l Bit — got a package returned to the P.O. Box. Have you changed dorms? Call me at work or write to the P.O. Am still on the wagon. Waiting to see you. Only two weeks more!"

Male Greek Chorus: November 23. A letter. "Li'l Bit. So disappointed you couldn't come home for the turkey. Sending you some money for a nice dinner out — nine days and counting!"

Greek Chorus (in unison): November 25th. A letter:

Li'l Bit: "Dear Uncle Peck: I am sending this to you at work. Don't come up next weekend for my birthday. I will not be here — "

(*A Voice directs:*)

SHIFTING FORWARD FROM THIRD TO FOURTH GEAR.

Male Greek Chorus: December 10, 1969. A hotel room. Philadelphia. There is no moon tonight.

(*Peck sits on the side of the bed while Li'l Bit paces. He can't believe she's in his room, but there's a desperate edge to his happiness. Li'l Bit is furious, edgy. There is a bottle of champagne in an ice bucket in a very nice hotel room.*)

Peck: Why don't you sit?

Li'l Bit: I don't want to. — What's the champagne for?

Peck: I thought we might toast your birthday —

Li'l Bit: — I am so pissed off at you, Uncle Peck.

Peck: Why?

Li'l Bit: I mean, are you crazy?

Peck: What did I do?

Li'l Bit: You scared the holy crap out of me — sending me that stuff in the mail —

Peck: — They were gifts! I just wanted to give you some little perks your first semester —

Li'l Bit: — Well, what the hell were those numbers all about! Forty-four days to go — only two more weeks. — And then just numbers — 69 — 68 — 67 — like some serial killer!

Peck: Li'l Bit! Whoa! This is me you're talking to — I was just trying to pick up your spirits, trying to celebrate your birthday.

Li'l Bit: My *eighteenth* birthday. I'm not a child, Uncle Peck. You were counting down to my eighteenth birthday.

Peck: So?

Li'l Bit: So? So statutory rape is not in effect when a young woman turns eighteen. And you and I both know it.

(*Peck is walking on ice.*)

Peck: I think you misunderstand.

Li'l Bit: I think I understand all too well. I know what you want to do five steps ahead of you doing it. Defensive Driving 101.

Peck: Then why did you suggest we meet here instead of the restaurant?

Li'l Bit: I don't want to have this conversation in public.

Peck: Fine. Fine. We have a lot to talk about.

Li'l Bit: Yeah. We do.

(*Li'l Bit doesn't want to do what she has to do.*) Could I . . . have some of that champagne?

Peck: Of course, madam! (*Peck makes a big show of it.*) Let me do the honors. I wasn't sure which you might prefer — Taittingers or Veuve Clicquot — so I thought we'd start out with an old standard — Perrier Jouet. (*The bottle is popped.*)

Quick — Li'l Bit — your glass! (*Uncle Peck fills Li'l Bit's glass. He puts the bottle back in the ice and goes for a can of ginger ale.*) Let me get some of this ginger ale — my bubbly — and toast you.

(*He turns and sees that Li'l Bit has not waited for him.*)

Li'l Bit: Oh — sorry, Uncle Peck. Let me have another.

(*Peck fills her glass and reaches for his ginger ale; she stops him.*)

Uncle Peck — maybe you should join me in the champagne.

Peck: You want me — to drink?

Li'l Bit: It's not polite to let a lady drink alone.

Peck: Well, missy, if you insist. . . . (*Peck hesitates.*) — Just one. It's been a while. (*Peck fills another flute for himself.*) There. I'd like to propose a toast to you and your birthday! (*Peck sips it tentatively.*) I'm not used to this anymore.

Li'l Bit: You don't have anywhere to go tonight, do you?

(*Peck hopes this is a good sign.*)

Peck: I'm all yours. — God, it's good to see you! I've gotten so used to . . . to . . . talking to you in my head. I'm used to seeing you every week — there's so much — I don't quite know where to begin. How's school, Li'l Bit?

Li'l Bit: I — it's hard. Uncle Peck. Harder than I thought it would be. I'm in the middle of exams and papers and — I don't know.

Peck: You'll pull through. You always do.

Li'l Bit: Maybe. I . . . might be flunking out.

Peck: You always think the worst, Li'l Bit, but when the going gets tough —

(*Li'l Bit shrugs and pours herself another glass.*)

— Hey, honey, go easy on that stuff, okay?

Li'l Bit: Is it very expensive?

Peck: Only the best for you. But the cost doesn't matter — champagne should be "sipped."

(*Li'l Bit is quiet.*)

Look — if you're in trouble in school — you can always come back home for a while.

Li'l Bit: No — (*Li'l Bit tries not to be so harsh.*) — Thanks, Uncle Peck, but I'll figure some way out of this.

Peck: You're supposed to get in scrapes, your first year away from home.

Li'l Bit: Right. How's Aunt Mary?

Peck: She's fine. (*Pause.*) Well — how about the new car?

Li'l Bit: It's real nice. What is it, again?

Peck: It's a Cadillac El Dorado.

Li'l Bit: Oh. Well, I'm real happy for you, Uncle Peck.

Peck: I got it for you.

Li'l Bit: What?

Peck: I always wanted to get a Cadillac — but I thought, Peck, wait until Li'l Bit's old enough — and thought maybe you'd like to drive it, too.

Li'l Bit (confused): Why would I want to drive your car?

Peck: Just because it's the best — I want you to have the best.

(*They are running out of "gas"; small talk.*)

Li'l Bit: Listen, Uncle Peck, I don't know how to begin this, but —	*Peck:* I have been thinking of how to say this in my head, over and over —

Peck: Sorry.

Li'l Bit: You first.

Peck: Well, your going away — has just made me realize how much I miss you. Talking to you and being alone with you. I've really come to depend on you, Li'l Bit. And it's been so hard to get in touch with you lately — the distance and — and you're never in when I call — I guess you've been living in the library —

Li'l Bit: — No — the problem is, I haven't been in the library —

Peck: — Well, it doesn't matter — I hope you've been missing me as much.

Li'l Bit: Uncle Peck — I've been thinking a lot about this — and I came here tonight to tell you that — I'm not doing very well. I'm getting very confused — I can't concentrate on my work — and now that I'm away — I've been going over and over it in my mind — and I don't want us to "see" each other anymore. Other than with the rest of the family.

Peck (quiet): Are you seeing other men?

Li'l Bit (getting agitated): I — no, that's not the reason — I — well, yes, I am seeing other — listen, it's not really anybody's business!

Peck: Are you in love with anyone else?

Li'l Bit: That's not what this is about.

Peck: Li'l Bit — you're scared. Your mother and your grandparents have filled your head with all kinds of nonsense about men — I hear them working on you all the time — and you're scared. It won't hurt you — if the man you go to bed with really loves you. (*Li'l Bit is scared. She starts to tremble.*) And I have loved you since the day I held you in my hand. And I think everyone's just gotten you frightened to death about something that is just like breathing —

Li'l Bit: Oh, my god — (*She takes a breath.*) I can't see you anymore, Uncle Peck.

(*Peck downs the rest of his champagne.*)

Peck: Li'l Bit. Listen. Listen. Open your eyes and look at me. Come on. Just open your eyes, honey. (*Li'l Bit, eyes squeezed shut, refuses.*) All right then. I just want you to listen. Li'l Bit — I'm going to ask you just this once. Of your own free will. Just lie down on the bed with me — our clothes on — just lie down with me, a man and a woman . . . and let's . . . hold one another. Nothing else. Before you say anything else. I want the chance to . . . hold you. Because sometimes the body knows things that the mind isn't listening to . . . and after I've held you, then I want you to tell me what you feel.

Li'l Bit: You'll just . . . hold me?

Peck: Yes. And then you can tell me what you're feeling.

(*Li'l Bit — half wanting to run, half wanting to get it over with, half wanting to be held by him:*)

Li'l Bit: Yes. All right. Just hold. Nothing else.

(*Peck lies down on the bed and holds his arms out to her. Li'l Bit lies beside him, putting her head on his chest. He looks as if he's trying to soak her into his pores by osmosis. He strokes her hair, and she lies very still. The Male*

Greek Chorus member and the Female Greek Chorus member as Aunt Mary come into the room.)

Male Greek Chorus: Recipe for a Southern Boy:

Female Greek Chorus (as Aunt Mary): A drawl of molasses in the way he speaks.

Male Greek Chorus: A gumbo of red and brown mixed in the cream of his skin.

(While Peck lies, his eyes closed, Li'l Bit rises in the bed and responds to her aunt.)

Li'l Bit: Warm brown eyes —

Female Greek Chorus (as Aunt Mary): Bedroom eyes —

Male Greek Chorus: A dash of Southern Baptist Fire and Brimstone —

Li'l Bit: A curl of Elvis on his forehead —

Female Greek Chorus (as Aunt Mary): A splash of Bay Rum —

Male Greek Chorus: A closely shaven beard that he razors just for you —

Female Greek Chorus (as Aunt Mary): Large hands — rough hands —

Li'l Bit: Warm hands —

Male Greek Chorus: The steel of the military in his walk —

Li'l Bit: The slouch of the fishing skiff in his walk —

Male Greek Chorus: Neatly pressed khakis —

Female Greek Chorus (as Aunt Mary): And under the wide leather of the belt —

Li'l Bit: Sweat of cypress and sand —

Male Greek Chorus: Neatly pressed khakis —

Li'l Bit: His heart beating Dixie —

Female Greek Chorus (as Aunt Mary): The whisper of the zipper — you could reach out with your hand and —

Li'l Bit: His mouth —

Female Greek Chorus (as Aunt Mary): You could just reach out and —

Li'l Bit: Hold him in your hand —

Female Greek Chorus (as Aunt Mary): And his mouth —

(Li'l Bit rises above her uncle and looks at his mouth; she starts to lower herself to kiss him — and wrenches herself free. She gets up from the bed.)

Li'l Bit: — I've got to get back.

Peck: Wait — Li'l Bit. Did you . . . feel nothing?

Li'l Bit (lying): No. Nothing.

Peck: Do you — do you think of me?

(The Greek Chorus whispers:)

Female Greek Chorus: Khakis —

Male Greek Chorus: Bay Rum —

Female Greek Chorus: The whisper of the —

Li'l Bit: — No.

(Peck, in a rush, trembling, gets something out of his pocket.)

Peck: I'm forty-five. That's not old for a man. And I haven't been able to do anything else but think of you. I can't concentrate on my work — Li'l Bit. You've got to — I want you to think about what I am about to ask you.

Li'l Bit: I'm listening.

(*Peck opens a small ring box.*)

Peck: I want you to be my wife.

Li'l Bit: This isn't happening.

Peck: I'll tell Mary I want a divorce. We're not blood-related. It would be legal —

Li'l Bit: — What have you been thinking! You are married to my aunt, Uncle Peck. She's my family. You have — you have gone way over the line. Family is family.
(*Quickly, Li'l Bit flies through the room, gets her coat.*) I'm leaving. Now. I am not seeing you. Again.

(*Peck lies down on the bed for a moment, trying to absorb the terrible news. For a moment, he almost curls into a fetal position.*)

I'm not coming home for Christmas. You should go home to Aunt Mary. Go home now, Uncle Peck.

(*Peck gets control, and sits, rigid.*)

Uncle Peck? — I'm sorry but I have to go.

(*Pause.*)

Are you all right?

(*With a discipline that comes from being told that boys don't cry, Peck stands upright.*)

Peck: I'm fine. I just think — I need a real drink.

(*The Male Greek Chorus has become a bartender. At a small counter, he is lining up shots for Peck. As Li'l Bit narrates, we see Peck sitting, carefully and calmly downing shot glasses.*)

Li'l Bit (to the audience): I never saw him again. I stayed away from Christmas and Thanksgiving for years after.
It took my uncle seven years to drink himself to death. First he lost his job, then his wife, and finally his driver's license. He retreated to his house, and had his bottles delivered.

(*Peck stands, and puts his hands in front of him — almost like Superman flying.*)

One night he tried to go downstairs to the basement — and he flew down the steep basement stairs. My aunt came by weekly to put food on the porch, and she noticed the mail and the papers stacked up, uncollected.
They found him at the bottom of the stairs. Just steps away from his dark room.

Now that I'm old enough, there are some questions I would have liked to have asked him. Who did it to you, Uncle Peck? How old were you? Were you eleven?

(*Peck moves to the driver's seat of the car and waits.*)

Sometimes I think of my uncle as a kind of Flying Dutchman. In the opera, the Dutchman is doomed to wander the sea; but every seven years he can come ashore, and if he finds a maiden who will love him of her own free will — he will be released.

And I see Uncle Peck in my mind, in his Chevy '56, a spirit driving up and down the back roads of Carolina — looking for a young girl who, of her own free will, will love him. Release him.

(*A Voice states:*)

You and the Reverse Gear.

Li'l Bit: The summer of 1962. On Men, Sex, and Women: Part III:

(*Li'l Bit steps, as an eleven-year-old, into:*)

Female Greek Chorus (as Mother): It is out of the question. End of Discussion.

Li'l Bit: But why?

Female Greek Chorus (as Mother): Li'l Bit — we are not discussing this. I said no.

Li'l Bit: But I could spend an extra week at the beach! You're not telling me why!

Female Greek Chorus (as Mother): Your uncle pays entirely too much attention to you.

Li'l Bit: He listens to me when I talk. And — and he talks to me. He teaches me about things. Mama — he knows an awful lot.

Female Greek Chorus (as Mother): He's a small town hick who's learned how to mix drinks from Hugh Hefner.°

Li'l Bit: Who's Hugh Hefner?

(*Beat.*)

Female Greek Chorus (as Mother): I am not letting an eleven-year-old girl spend seven hours alone in the car with a man. . . . I don't like the way your uncle looks at you.

Li'l Bit: For god's sake, mother! Just because you've gone through a bad time with my father — you think every man is evil!

Female Greek Chorus (as Mother): Oh no, Li'l Bit — not all men. . . . We . . . we just haven't been very lucky with the men in our family.

Li'l Bit: Just because you lost your husband — I still deserve a chance at having a father! Someone! A man who will look out for me! Don't I get a chance?

Female Greek Chorus (as Mother): I will feel terrible if something happens.

Hugh Hefner: (1926–2017) was the founder and editor-in-chief of *Playboy* magazine.

Li'l Bit: Mother! It's in your head! Nothing will happen! I can take care of myself. And I can certainly handle Uncle Peck.

Female Greek Chorus (as Mother): All right. But I'm warning you — if anything happens, I hold you responsible.

(*Li'l Bit moves out of this scene and toward the car.*)

Li'l Bit: 1962. On the Back Roads of Carolina: The First Driving Lesson.

(*The Teenage Greek Chorus member stands apart on stage. She will speak all of Li'l Bit's lines. Li'l Bit sits beside Peck in the front seat. She looks at him closely, remembering.*)

Peck: Li'l Bit? Are you getting tired?

Teenage Greek Chorus: A little.

Peck: It's a long drive. But we're making really good time. We can take the back road from here and see . . . a little scenery. Say — I've got an idea — (*Peck checks his rearview mirror.*)

Teenage Greek Chorus: Are we stopping, Uncle Peck?

Peck: There's no traffic here. Do you want to drive?

Teenage Greek Chorus: I can't drive.

Peck: It's easy. I'll show you how. I started driving when I was your age. Don't you want to? —

Teenage Greek Chorus: — But it's against the law at my age!

Peck: And that's why you can't tell anyone I'm letting you do this —

Teenage Greek Chorus: — But — I can't reach the pedals.

Peck: You can sit in my lap and steer. I'll push the pedals for you. Did your father ever let you drive his car?

Teenage Greek Chorus: No way.

Peck: Want to try?

Teenage Greek Chorus: Okay. (*Li'l Bit moves into Peck's lap. She leans against him, closing her eyes.*)

Peck: You're just a little thing, aren't you? Okay — now think of the wheel as a big clock — I want you to put your right hand on the clock where three o'clock would be; and your left hand on the nine —

(*Li'l Bit puts one hand to Peck's face, to stroke him. Then, she takes the wheel.*)

Teenage Greek Chorus: Am I doing it right?

Peck: That's right. Now, whatever you do, don't let go of the wheel. You tell me whether to go faster or slower —

Teenage Greek Chorus: Not so fast, Uncle Peck!

Peck: Li'l Bit — I need you to watch the road —

(*Peck puts his hands on Li'l Bit's breasts. She relaxes against him, silent, accepting his touch.*)

Teenage Greek Chorus: Uncle Peck — what are you doing?

Peck: Keep driving. (*He slips his hands under her blouse.*)

Teenage Greek Chorus: Uncle Peck — please don't do this —

Peck: — Just a moment longer . . . (*Peck tenses against Li'l Bit.*)

Teenage Greek Chorus (trying not to cry): This isn't happening.

(*Peck tenses more, sharply. He buries his face in Li'l Bit's neck, and moans softly. The Teenage Greek Chorus exits, and Li'l Bit steps out of the car. Peck, too, disappears.*)

(*A Voice reflects:*)

Driving in Today's World.

Li'l Bit: That day was the last day I lived in my body. I retreated above the neck, and I've lived inside the "fire" in my head ever since.

And now that seems like a long, long time ago. When we were both very young.

And before you know it, I'll be thirty-five. That's getting up there for a woman. And I find myself believing in things that a younger self vowed never to believe in. Things like family and forgiveness.

I know I'm lucky. Although I still have never known what it feels like to jog or dance. Anything that . . . "jiggles." I do like to watch people on the dance floor, or out on the running paths, just jiggling away. And I say — good for them. (*Li'l Bit moves to the car with pleasure.*)

The nearest sensation I feel — of flight in the body — I guess I feel when I'm driving. On a day like today. It's five A.M. The radio says it's going to be clear and crisp. I've got five hundred miles of highway ahead of me — and some back roads too. I filled the tank last night, and had the oil checked. Checked the tires, too. You've got to treat her . . . with respect.

First thing I do is: Check under the car. To see if any two-year-olds or household cats have crawled beneath, and strategically placed their skulls behind my back tires. (*Li'l Bit crouches.*)

Nope. Then I get in the car. (*Li'l Bit does so.*)

I lock the doors. And turn the key. Then I adjust the most important control on the dashboard — the radio — (*Li'l Bit turns the radio on: We hear all of the Greek Chorus overlapping, and static:*)

Female Greek Chorus (overlapping): — "You were so tiny you fit in his hand — "

Male Greek Chorus (overlapping): — "How is Shakespeare gonna help her lie on her back in the — "

Teenage Greek Chorus (overlapping): — "Am I doing it right?"

(*Li'l Bit fine-tunes the radio station. A song like "Dedicated to the One I Love" or Orbison's "Sweet Dreams" comes on, and cuts off the Greek Chorus.*)

Li'l Bit: Ahh . . . (*Beat.*) I adjust my seat. Fasten my seat belt. Then I check the right side mirror — check the left side. (*She does.*) Finally, I adjust the rearview mirror.

(*As Li'l Bit adjusts the rearview mirror, a faint light strikes the spirit of Uncle Peck, who is sitting in the back seat of the car. She sees him in the mirror. She smiles at him, and he nods at her. They are happy to be going for a long ride together. Li'l Bit slips the car into first gear; to the audience:*)

And then — I floor it.

(*Sound of a car taking off. Blackout.*)

CONSIDERATIONS FOR CRITICAL THINKING AND WRITING

1. **FIRST RESPONSE:** How does driving act as a metaphor for the play's broader concerns?

2. List all of the ways gender roles are taught or reinforced in the play. How does this list enable you to comment on the play's theme insofar as it has to do with the performance of gender roles?

3. How do the male Greek chorus, female Greek chorus, and teenage Greek chorus function in the play?

4. Uncle Peck is obviously a disturbed and destructive human being. Does the play attempt to balance this depiction in any way?

5. Why is music integral to the play? How would it be different if there were no music?

6. What is the effect of the play moving back and forth in time?

7. Comment on the way the play relies on the audience's imagination in addition to the spectacle that is on stage.

8. Near the play's conclusion, what does Li'l Bit mean when she says she no longer lives in her body but rather "inside the 'fire' in [her] head"? What is the relationship between body and mind throughout the play?

CONNECTIONS TO OTHER SELECTIONS

1. How are gender roles taught or reinforced in this play and in Ibsen's *A Doll's House* (p. 864)? Do the plays share the same theme with regard to gender roles?

2. Compare the way this play and David Auburn's *Proof* (p. 925) approach memory and the passage of time.

The Importance of Being Earnest   1854–1900

Oscar Wilde is most remembered as a playwright, but he was also a poet, essayist, and fiction writer. Born in Ireland, Wilde was educated at Trinity College in Dublin and moved to England on a scholarship to Oxford University. There he learned a great deal about aesthetics, becoming part of a movement that advocated "art for art's sake": the belief that art did not have to justify its existence, that it was inherently valuable. He remained in England for much of his life, becoming an integral part of the London theater scene. He was a notable public personality, known for his wit and eccentric sense of fashion nearly as much as for his writing. In 1884 he married Constance Mary Lloyd, and the couple had two children while enjoying his extreme success during the 1890s. Wilde was a complicated soul living in conservative times, though. The final five years of his life were plagued by scandal and tragedy after he was arrested and put on trial for "gross indecency" following an affair with a young man, Lord Alfred Douglas. Wilde was convicted and sentenced to two years hard labor. The final three years of his life were spent in obscurity. He died in Paris following complications from an ear infection.

The solitary tragedy of his final days is at odds with a body of work that is brilliant and effervescent. It is clear from even the first dialogue exchange in *The Importance of Being Earnest* — considered Wilde's masterwork — that he was delighted with language and that he found human society silly and yet not meaningless. He subtitled the play "A Trivial Comedy for Serious People." Wilde's play, published just fifteen years after the other classic modern drama included here (*A Doll's House*, chapter 28), is the polar opposite of Ibsen's moody play, and in fact it is the funniest play in this volume. (It may be the funniest play anywhere!) Tragedies are often regarded as the best plays, but that assessment may reveal a bias based on the essential gloominess of critics who tend to want literature to be heavy, anchored by the weight of dark ideas about humanity. Perhaps knowing this bias, Wilde advertises his play as "trivial." Yet what could be more a more serious and mysterious subject than human identity? As you read *The Importance of Being Earnest*, try to ponder life's great questions with a smile on your face.

Oscar Wilde (1854–1900)

The Importance of Being Earnest   1895

THE PERSONS OF THE PLAY

John Worthing, J.P., of the Manor House, Woolton,
     Hertfordshire
Algernon Moncrieff, his friend
Rev. Canon Chasuble, D.D., rector of Woolton
Merriman, butler to Mr. Worthing
Lane, Mr. Moncrieff's manservant
Lady Bracknell
Hon. Gwendolen Fairfax, her daughter
Cecily Cardew, John Worthing's ward
Miss Prism, her governess

GL Archive/Alamy Stock Photo.

THE SCENES OF THE PLAY

ACT I: *Algernon Moncrieff's Flat in Half Moon Street, W.*
ACT II: *The Garden at the Manor House, Woolton*
ACT III: *Morning Room at the Manor House, Woolton*

ACT I

(Scene: Morning room in Algernon's flat in Half Moon Street. The room is luxuriously and artistically furnished. The sound of a piano is heard in the adjoining room. Lane is arranging afternoon tea on the table, and after the music has ceased, Algernon enters.)

Algernon: Did you hear what I was playing, Lane?

Lane: I didn't think it polite to listen, sir.

Algernon: I'm sorry for that, for your sake. I don't play accurately — anyone can play accurately — but I play with wonderful expression. As far as the piano is concerned, sentiment is my forte. I keep science for Life.

Lane: Yes, sir.

Algernon: And, speaking of the science of Life, have you got the cucumber sandwiches cut for Lady Bracknell?

Lane: Yes, sir. *(Hands them on a salver.)*

Algernon (inspects them, takes two, and sits down on the sofa): Oh! — by the way, Lane, I see from your book that on Thursday night, when Lord Shoreham and Mr. Worthing were dining with me, eight bottles of champagne are entered as having been consumed.

Lane: Yes, sir; eight bottles and a pint.

Algernon: Why is it that at a bachelor's establishment the servants invariably drink the champagne? I ask merely for information.

Lane: I attribute it to the superior quality of the wine, sir. I have often observed that in married households the champagne is rarely of a first-rate brand.

Algernon: Good heavens! Is marriage so demoralizing as that?

Lane: I believe it *is* a very pleasant state, sir. I have had very little experience of it myself up to the present. I have only been married once. That was in consequence of a misunderstanding between myself and a young person.

Algernon (languidly): I don't know that I am much interested in your family life, Lane.

Lane: No, sir; it is not a very interesting subject. I never think of it myself.

Algernon: Very natural, I am sure. That will do, Lane, thank you.

Lane: Thank you, sir. *(Lane goes out.)*

Algernon: Lane's views on marriage seem somewhat lax. Really, if the lower orders don't set us a good example, what on earth is the use of them? They seem, as a class, to have absolutely no sense of moral responsibility.

(*Enter Lane.*)

Lane: Mr. Ernest Worthing.

(*Enter Jack. Lane goes out.*)

Algernon: How are you, my dear Ernest? What brings you up to town?

Jack: Oh, pleasure, pleasure! What else should bring one anywhere? Eating as usual, I see, Algy!

Algernon (stiffly): I believe it is customary in good society to take some slight refreshment at five o'clock. Where have you been since last Thursday?

Jack (sitting down on the sofa): In the country.

Algernon: What on earth do you do there?

Jack (pulling off his gloves): When one is in town one amuses oneself. When one is in the country one amuses other people. It is excessively boring.

Algernon: And who are the people you amuse?

Jack (airily): Oh, neighbors, neighbors.

Algernon: Got nice neighbors in your part of Shropshire?

Jack: Perfectly horrid! Never speak to one of them.

Algernon: How immensely you must amuse them! (*Goes over and takes sandwich.*) By the way, Shropshire is your county, is it not?

Jack: Eh? Shropshire? Yes, of course. Hallo! Why all these cups? Why cucumber sandwiches? Why such reckless extravagance in one so young? Who is coming to tea?

Algernon: Oh! merely Aunt Augusta and Gwendolen.

Jack: How perfectly delightful!

Algernon: Yes, that is all very well; but I am afraid Aunt Augusta won't quite approve of your being here.

Jack: May I ask why?

Algernon: My dear fellow, the way you flirt with Gwendolen is perfectly disgraceful. It is almost as bad as the way Gwendolen flirts with you.

Jack: I am in love with Gwendolen. I have come up to town expressly to propose to her.

Algernon: I thought you had come up for pleasure? — I call that business.

Jack: How utterly unromantic you are!

Algernon: I really don't see anything romantic in proposing. It is very romantic to be in love. But there is nothing romantic about a definite proposal. Why, one may be accepted. One usually is, I believe. Then the excitement is all over. The very essence of romance is uncertainty. If ever I get married, I'll certainly try to forget the fact.

Jack: I have no doubt about that, dear Algy. The Divorce Court was specially invented for people whose memories are so curiously constituted.

Algernon: Oh! there is no use speculating on that subject. Divorces are made in heaven — (*Jack puts out his hand to take a sandwich. Algernon at once interferes.*) Please don't touch the cucumber sandwiches. They are ordered specially for Aunt Augusta. (*Takes one and eats it.*)

Jack: Well, you have been eating them all the time.

Algernon: That is quite a different matter. She is my aunt. (*Takes plate from below.*) Have some bread and butter. The bread and butter is for Gwendolen. Gwendolen is devoted to bread and butter.

Jack (*advancing to table and helping himself*): And very good bread and butter it is too.

Algernon: Well, my dear fellow, you need not eat as if you were going to eat it all. You behave as if you were married to her already. You are not married to her already, and I don't think you ever will be.

Jack: Why on earth do you say that?

Algernon: Well, in the first place, girls never marry the men they flirt with. Girls don't think it right.

Jack: Oh, that is nonsense!

Algernon: It isn't. It is a great truth. It accounts for the extraordinary number of bachelors that one sees all over the place. In the second place, I don't give my consent.

Jack: Your consent!

Algernon: My dear fellow, Gwendolen is my first cousin. And before I allow you to marry her, you will have to clear up the whole question of Cecily. (*Rings bell.*)

Jack: Cecily! What on earth do you mean? What do you mean, Algy, by Cecily? I don't know anyone of the name of Cecily.

(*Enter Lane.*)

Algernon: Bring me that cigarette case Mr. Worthing left in the smoking room the last time he dined here.

Lane: Yes, sir. (*Lane goes out.*)

Jack: Do you mean to say you have had my cigarette case all this time? I wish to goodness you had let me know. I have been writing frantic letters to Scotland Yard about it. I was very nearly offering a large reward.

Algernon: Well, I wish you would offer one. I happen to be more than usually hard up.

Jack: There is no good offering a large reward now that the thing is found.

(*Enter Lane with the cigarette case on a salver. Algernon takes it at once. Lane goes out.*)

Algernon: I think that is rather mean of you, Ernest, I must say. (*Opens case and examines it.*) However, it makes no matter, for, now that I look at the inscription inside, I find that the thing isn't yours after all.

Jack: Of course it's mine. (*Moving to him.*) You have seen me with it a hundred times, and you have no right whatsoever to read what is written inside. It is a very ungentlemanly thing to read a private cigarette case.

Algernon: Oh! it is absurd to have a hard-and-fast rule about what one should read and what one shouldn't. More than half of modern culture depends on what one shouldn't read.

Jack: I am quite aware of the fact, and I don't propose to discuss modern culture. It isn't the sort of thing one should talk of in private. I simply want my cigarette case back.

Algernon: Yes; but this isn't your cigarette case. This cigarette case is a present from someone of the name of Cecily, and you said you didn't know anyone of that name.

Jack: Well, if you want to know, Cecily happens to be my aunt.

Algernon: Your aunt!

Jack: Yes. Charming old lady she is, too. Lives at Tunbridge Wells. Just give it back to me, Algy.

Algernon (retreating to back of sofa): But why does she call herself little Cecily if she is your aunt and lives at Tunbridge Wells? (*Reading.*) "From little Cecily with her fondest love."

Jack (moving to sofa and kneeling upon it): My dear fellow, what on earth is there in that? Some aunts are tall, some aunts are not tall. That is a matter that surely an aunt may be allowed to decide for herself. You seem to think that every aunt should be exactly like your aunt! That is absurd! For heaven's sake give me back my cigarette case.

(*Follows Algernon round the room.*)

Algernon: Yes. But why does your aunt call you her uncle? "From little Cecily, with her fondest love to her dear Uncle jack." There is no objection, I admit, to an aunt being a small aunt, but why an aunt, no matter what her size may be, should call her own nephew her uncle, I can't quite make out. Besides, your name isn't Jack at all; it is Ernest.

Jack: It isn't Ernest; it's Jack.

Algernon: You have always told me it was Ernest. I have introduced you to everyone as Ernest. You answer to the name of Ernest. You look as if your name was Ernest. You are the most earnest looking person I ever saw in my life. It is perfectly absurd your saying that your name isn't Ernest. It's on your cards. Here is one of them (*taking it from case*) "Mr. Ernest Worthing, B.4, The Albany." I'll keep this as a proof that your name is Ernest if ever you attempt to deny it to me, or to Gwendolen, or to anyone else.   (*Puts the card in his pocket.*)

Jack: Well, my name is Ernest in town and Jack in the country, and the cigarette case was given to me in the country.

Algernon: Yes, but that does not account for the fact that your small Aunt Cecily, who lives at Tunbridge Wells, calls you her dear uncle. Come, old boy, you had much better have the thing out at once.

Jack: My dear Algy, you talk exactly as if you were a dentist. It is very vulgar to talk like a dentist when one isn't a dentist. It produces a false impression.

Algernon: Well, that is exactly what dentists always do. Now, go on! Tell me the whole thing. I may mention that I have always suspected you of being a confirmed and secret Bunburyist; and I am quite sure of it now.

Jack: Bunburyist? What on earth do you mean by a Bunburyist?

Algernon: I'll reveal to you the meaning of that incomparable expression as soon as you are kind enough to inform me why you are Ernest in town and Jack in the country.

Jack: Well, produce my cigarette case first.

Algernon: Here it is. (*Hands cigarette case.*) Now produce your explanation, and pray make it improbable. (*Sits on sofa.*)

Jack: My dear fellow, there is nothing improbable about my explanation at all. In fact it's perfectly ordinary. Old Mr. Thomas Cardew, who adopted me when I was a little boy, made me in his will guardian to his granddaughter, Miss Cecily Cardew. Cecily, who addresses me as her uncle from motives of respect that you could not possibly appreciate, lives at my place in the country under the charge of her admirable governess, Miss Prism.

Algernon: Where is that place in the country, by the way?

Jack: That is nothing to you, dear boy. You are not going to be invited — I may tell you candidly that the place is not in Shropshire.

Algernon: I suspected that, my dear fellow! I have Bunburyed all over Shropshire on two separate occasions. Now, go on. Why are you Ernest in town and Jack in the country?

Jack: My dear Algy, I don't know whether you will be able to understand my real motives. You are hardly serious enough. When one is placed in the position of guardian, one has to adopt a very high moral tone on all subjects. It's one's duty to do so. And as a high moral tone can hardly be said to conduce very much to either one's health or one's happiness, in order to get up to town I have always pretended to have a younger brother of the name of Ernest, who lives in the Albany, and gets into the most dreadful scrapes. That, my dear Algy, is the whole truth pure and simple.

Algernon: The truth is rarely pure and never simple. Modern life would be very tedious if it were either and modern literature a complete impossibility!

Jack: That wouldn't be at all a bad thing.

Algernon: Literary criticism is not your forte, my dear fellow. Don't try it. You should leave that to people who haven't been at a university. They do it so well in the daily papers. What you really are is a Bunburyist. I was quite right in saying you were a Bunburyist. You are one of the most advanced Bunburyists I know.

Jack: What on earth do you mean?

Algernon: You have invented a very useful younger brother called Ernest, in order that you may be able to come up to town as often as you like. I have invented an invaluable permanent invalid called Bunbury, in order that I may be able to go down into the country whenever I choose. Bunbury is perfectly invaluable. If it wasn't for Bunbury's extraordinary bad health, for instance, I wouldn't be able to dine with you at Willis's tonight, for I have been really engaged to Aunt Augusta for more than a week.

Jack: I haven't asked you to dine with me anywhere tonight.

Algernon: I know. You are absurdly careless about sending out invitations. It is very foolish of you. Nothing annoys people so much as not receiving invitations.

Jack: You had much better dine with your Aunt Augusta.

Algernon: I haven't the smallest intention of doing anything of the kind. To begin with, I dined there on Monday, and once a week is quite enough to dine with one's own relations. In the second place, whenever I do dine there I am always treated as a member of the family, and sent down with° either no woman at all, or two. In the third place, I know perfectly well whom she will place me next to, tonight. She will place me next Mary Farquhar, who always flirts with her own husband across the dinner table. That is not very pleasant. Indeed, it is not even decent — and that sort of thing is enormously on the increase. The amount of women in London who flirt with their own husbands is perfectly scandalous. It looks so bad. It is simply washing one's clean linen in public. Besides, now that I know you to be a confirmed Bunburyist I naturally want to talk to you about Bunburying. I want to tell you the rules.

Jack: I'm not a Bunburyist at all. If Gwendolen accepts me, I am going to kill my brother, indeed I think I'll kill him in any case. Cecily is a little too much interested in him. It is rather a bore. So I am going to get rid of Ernest. And I strongly advise you to do the same with Mr. — with your invalid friend who has the absurd name.

Algernon: Nothing will induce me to part with Bunbury, and if you ever get married, which seems to me extremely problematic, you will be very glad to know Bunbury. A man who marries without knowing Bunbury has a very tedious time of it.

Jack: That is nonsense. If I marry a charming girl like Gwendolen, and she is the only girl I ever saw in my life that I would marry, I certainly won't want to know Bunbury.

Algernon: Then your wife will. You don't seem to realize, that in married life three is company and two is none.

Jack (sententiously): That, my dear young friend, is the theory that the corrupt French drama has been propounding for the last fifty years.

Algernon: Yes; and that the happy English home has proved in half the time.

Jack: For heaven's sake, don't try to be cynical. It's perfectly easy to be cynical.

Algernon: My dear fellow, it isn't easy to be anything nowadays. There's such a lot of beastly competition about. (*The sound of an electric bell is heard.*) Ah! that must be Aunt Augusta. Only relatives, or creditors, ever ring in that Wagnerian° manner. Now, if I get her out of the way for ten minutes, so that you can have an opportunity for proposing to Gwendolen, may I dine with you tonight at Willis's?

---

sent down with: Assigned a woman to escort into the dining room for dinner.

Wagnerian: Referring to the operas of Richard Wagner (1813–1883), whose music was popularly thought to be loud.

Jack: I suppose so, if you want to.

Algernon: Yes, but you must be serious about it. I hate people who are not serious about meals. It is so shallow of them.

(*Enter Lane.*)

Lane: Lady Bracknell and Miss Fairfax.

(*Algernon goes forward to meet them. Enter Lady Bracknell and Gwendolen.*)

Lady Bracknell: Good afternoon, dear Algernon, I hope you are behaving very well.

Algernon: I'm feeling very well, Aunt Augusta.

Lady Bracknell: That's not quite the same thing. In fact the two things rarely go together.

(*Sees Jack and bows to him with icy coldness.*)

Algernon (to Gwendolen): Dear me, you are smart!

Gwendolen: I am always smart! Aren't I, Mr. Worthing?

Jack: You're quite perfect, Miss Fairfax.

Gwendolen: Oh! I hope I am not that. It would leave no room for developments, and I intend to develop in many directions.

(*Gwendolen and Jack sit down together in the corner.*)

Lady Bracknell: I'm sorry if we are a little late Algernon, but I was obliged to call on dear Lady Harbury. I hadn't been there since her poor husband's death. I never saw a woman so altered; she looks quite twenty years younger. And now I'll have a cup of tea, and one of those nice cucumber sandwiches you promised me.

Algernon: Certainly, Aunt Augusta.   (*Goes over to tea table.*)

Lady Bracknell: Won't you come and sit here, Gwendolen?

Gwendolen: Thanks, Mama, I'm quite comfortable where I am.

Algernon (picking up empty plate in horror): Good heavens! Lane! Why are there no cucumber sandwiches? I ordered them specially.

Lane (gravely): There were no cucumbers in the market this morning, sir. I went down twice.

Algernon: No cucumbers?

Lane: No, sir. Not even for ready money.

Algernon: That will do, Lane, thank you.

Lane: Thank you, sir.   (*Goes out.*)

Algernon: I am greatly distressed, Aunt Augusta, about there being no cucumbers, not even for ready money.

Lady Bracknell: It really makes no matter, Algernon. I had some crumpets with Lady Harbury, who seems to me to be living entirely for pleasure now.

Algernon: I hear her hair has turned quite gold from grief.

Lady Bracknell: It certainly has changed its color. From what cause I, of course, cannot say. (*Algernon crosses and hands tea.*) Thank you. I've quite a treat for you tonight, Algernon. I am going to send you down with Mary Farquhar. She is such a nice woman, and so attentive to her husband. It's delightful to watch them.

Algernon: I am afraid, Aunt Augusta, I shall have to give up the pleasure of dining with you tonight after all.

Lady Bracknell (frowning): I hope not, Algernon. It would put my table completely out. Your uncle would have to dine upstairs. Fortunately he is accustomed to that.

Algernon: It is a great bore, and, I need hardly say, a terrible disappointment to me, but the fact is I have just had a telegram to say that my poor friend Bunbury is very ill again. (*Exchanges glances with Jack.*) They seem to think I should be with him.

Lady Bracknell: It is very strange. This Mr. Bunbury seems to suffer from curiously bad health.

Algernon: Yes; poor Bunbury is a dreadful invalid.

Lady Bracknell: Well, I must say, Algernon, that I think it is high time that Mr. Bunbury made up his mind whether he was going to live or to die. This shilly-shallying with the question is absurd. Nor do I in any way approve of the modern sympathy with invalids. I consider it morbid. Illness of any kind is hardly a thing to be encouraged in others. Health is the primary duty of life. I am always telling that to your poor uncle, but he never seems to take much notice — as far as any improvement in his ailments goes. I should be much obliged if you would ask Mr. Bunbury, from me, to be kind enough not to have a relapse on Saturday, for I rely on you to arrange my music for me. It is my last reception, and one wants something that will encourage conversation, particularly at the end of the season when everyone has practically said whatever they had to say, which, in most cases, was probably not much.

Algernon: I'll speak to Bunbury, Aunt Augusta, if he is still conscious, and I think I can promise you he'll be all right by Saturday. Of course the music is a great difficulty. You see, if one plays good music, people don't listen, and if one plays bad music people don't talk. But I'll run over the program I've drawn out, if you will kindly come into the next room for a moment.

Lady Bracknell: Thank you, Algernon. It is very thoughtful of you. (*Rising, and following Algernon.*) I'm sure the program will be delightful, after a few expurgations. French songs I cannot possibly allow. People always seem to think that they are improper, and either look shocked, which is vulgar, or laugh, which is worse. But German sounds a thoroughly respectable language, and indeed, I believe is so. Gwendolen, you will accompany me.

Gwendolen: Certainly, Mama.

(*Lady Bracknell and Algernon go into the music room. Gwendolen remains behind.*)

Jack: Charming day it has been, Miss Fairfax.

Gwendolen: Pray don't talk to me about the weather, Mr. Worthing. Whenever people talk to me about the weather, I always feel quite certain that they mean something else. And that makes me so nervous.

Jack: I do mean something else.

Gwendolen: I thought so. In fact, I am never wrong.

Jack: And I would like to be allowed to take advantage of Lady Bracknell's temporary absence—

Gwendolen: I would certainly advise you to do so. Mama has a way of coming back suddenly into a room that I have often had to speak to her about.

Jack (nervously): Miss Fairfax, ever since I met you I have admired you more than any girl—I have ever met since—I met you.

Gwendolen: Yes, I am quite aware of the fact. And I often wish that in public, at any rate, you had been more demonstrative. For me you have always had an irresistible fascination. Even before I met you I was far from indifferent to you. (*Jack looks at her in amazement.*) We live, as I hope you know, Mr. Worthing, in an age of ideals. The fact is constantly mentioned in the more expensive monthly magazines, and has reached the provincial pulpits I am told: And my ideal has always been to love someone of the name of Ernest. There is something in that name that inspires absolute confidence. The moment Algernon first mentioned to me that he had a friend called Ernest, I knew I was destined to love you.

Jack: You really love me, Gwendolen?

Gwendolen: Passionately!

Jack: Darling! You don't know how happy you've made me.

Gwendolen: My own Ernest!

Jack: But you don't mean to say that you couldn't love me if my name wasn't Ernest?

Gwendolen: But your name is Ernest.

Jack: Yes, I know it is. But supposing it was something else? Do you mean to say you couldn't love me then?

Gwendolen (glibly): Ah! that is clearly a metaphysical speculation, and like most metaphysical speculations has very little reference at all to the actual facts of real life, as we know them.

Jack: Personally, darling, to speak quite candidly, I don't much care about the name of Ernest—I don't think the name suits me at all.

Gwendolen: It suits you perfectly. It is a divine name. It has a music of its own. It produces vibrations.

Jack: Well, really, Gwendolen, I must say that I think there are lots of other much nicer names. I think Jack, for instance, a charming name.

Gwendolen: Jack?—No, there is very little music in the name Jack, if any at all, indeed. It does not thrill. It produces absolutely no vibrations—I have known several Jacks, and they all, without exception, were more than usually plain. Besides, Jack is a notorious domesticity for John!

And I pity any woman who is married to a man called John. She would probably never be allowed to know the entrancing pleasure of a single moment's solitude. The only really safe name is Ernest.

Jack: Gwendolen, I must get christened at once — I mean we must get married at once. There is no time to be lost.

Gwendolen: Married, Mr. Worthing?

Jack (astounded): Well — surely. You know that I love you, and you led me to believe, Miss Fairfax, that you were not absolutely indifferent to me.

Gwendolen: I adore you. But you haven't proposed to me yet. Nothing has been said at all about marriage. The subject has not even been touched on.

Jack: Well — may I propose to you now?

Gwendolen: I think it would be an admirable opportunity. And to spare you any possible disappointment, Mr. Worthing, I think it only fair to tell you quite frankly beforehand that I am fully determined to accept you.

Jack: Gwendolen!

Gwendolen: Yes, Mr. Worthing, what have you got to say to me?

Jack: You know what I have got to say to you.

Gwendolen: Yes, but you don't say it.

Jack: Gwendolen, will you marry me?   (*Goes on his knees.*)

Gwendolen: Of course I will, darling. How long you have been about it! I am afraid you have had very little experience in how to propose.

Jack: My own one, I have never loved anyone in the world but you.

Gwendolen: Yes, but men often propose for practice. I know my brother Gerald does. All my girlfriends tell me so. What wonderfully blue eyes you have, Ernest! They are quite, quite blue. I hope you will always look at me just like that, especially when there are other people present.

(*Enter Lady Bracknell.*)

Lady Bracknell: Mr. Worthing! Rise, sir, from this semirecumbent posture. It is most indecorous.

Gwendolen: Mama! (*He tries to rise; she restrains him.*) I must beg you to retire. This is no place for you. Besides, Mr. Worthing has not quite finished yet.

Lady Bracknell: Finished what, may I ask?

Gwendolen: I am engaged to Mr. Worthing, Mama.   (*They rise together.*)

Lady Bracknell: Pardon me, you are not engaged to anyone. When you do become engaged to someone, I, or your father, should his health permit him, will inform you of the fact. An engagement should come on a young girl as a surprise, pleasant or unpleasant, as the case may be. It is hardly a matter that she could be allowed to arrange for herself — And now I have a few questions to put to you, Mr. Worthing. While I am making these inquiries, you, Gwendolen, will wait for me below in the carriage.

Gwendolen (reproachfully): Mama!

Lady Bracknell: In the carriage, Gwendolen! (*Gwendolen goes to the door. She and Jack blow kisses to each other behind Lady Bracknell's back. Lady Bracknell looks vaguely about as if she could not understand what the noise was. Finally turns round.*) Gwendolen, the carriage!

Gwendolen: Yes, Mama. (*Goes out, looking back at Jack.*)

Lady Bracknell (sitting down): You can take a seat, Mr. Worthing. (*Looks in her pocket for notebook and pencil.*)

Jack: Thank you, Lady Bracknell, I prefer standing.

Lady Bracknell (pencil and notebook in hand): I feel bound to tell you that you are not down on my list of eligible young men, although I have the same list as the dear Duchess of Bolton has. We work together, in fact. However, I am quite ready to enter your name, should your answers be what a really affectionate mother requires. Do you smoke?

Jack: Well, yes, I must admit I smoke.

Lady Bracknell: I am glad to hear it. A man should always have an occupation of some kind. There are far too many idle men in London as it is. How old are you?

Jack: Twenty-nine.

Lady Bracknell: A very good age to be married at. I have always been of opinion that a man who desires to get married should know either everything or nothing. Which do you know?

Jack (after some hesitation): I know nothing, Lady Bracknell.

Lady Bracknell: I am pleased to hear it. I do not approve of anything that tampers with natural ignorance. Ignorance is like a delicate exotic fruit; touch it and the bloom is gone. The whole theory of modern education is radically unsound. Fortunately in England, at any rate, education produces no effect whatsoever. If it did, it would prove a serious danger to the upper classes, and probably lead to acts of violence in Grosvenor Square. What is your income?

Jack: Between seven and eight thousand a year.

Lady Bracknell (makes a note in her book): In land, or in investments?

Jack: In investments, chiefly.

Lady Bracknell: That is satisfactory. What between the duties expected of one during one's lifetime, and the duties exacted from one after one's death, land has ceased to be either a profit or a pleasure. It gives one position, and prevents one from keeping it up. That's all that can be said about land.

Jack: I have a country house with some land, of course, attached to it, about fifteen hundred acres, I believe; but I don't depend on that for my real income. In fact, as far as I can make out, the poachers are the only people who make anything out of it.

Lady Bracknell: A country house! How many bedrooms? Well, that point can be cleared up afterwards. You have a town house, I hope? A girl with a simple, unspoiled nature, like Gwendolen, could hardly be expected to reside in the country.

Jack: Well, I own a house in Belgrave Square, but it is let by the year to Lady Bloxham. Of course, I can get it back whenever I like, at six months' notice.

Lady Bracknell: Lady Bloxham? I don't know her.

Jack: Oh, she goes about very little. She is a lady considerably advanced in years.

Lady Bracknell: Ah, nowadays that is no guarantee of respectability of character. What number in Belgrave Square?

Jack: 149.

Lady Bracknell (shaking her head): The unfashionable side. I thought there was something. However, that could easily be altered.

Jack: Do you mean the fashion, or the side?

Lady Bracknell (sternly): Both, if necessary, I presume. What are your politics?

Jack: Well, I am afraid I really have none. I am a Liberal Unionist.

Lady Bracknell: Oh, they count as Tories. They dine with us. Or come in the evening, at any rate. Now to minor matters. Are your parents living?

Jack: I have lost both my parents.

Lady Bracknell: Both? To lose one parent may be regarded as a misfortune — to lose *both* seems like carelessness. Who was your father? He was evidently a man of some wealth. Was he born in what the Radical papers call the purple of commerce, or did he rise from the ranks of the aristocracy?

Jack: I am afraid I really don't know. The fact is, Lady Bracknell, I said I had lost my parents. It would be nearer the truth to say that my parents seem to have lost me — I don't actually know who I am by birth. I was — well, I was found.

Lady Bracknell: Found!

Jack: The late Mr. Thomas Cardew, an old gentleman of a very charitable and kindly disposition, found me, and gave me the name of Worthing, because he happened to have a first-class ticket for Worthing in his pocket at the time. Worthing is a place in Sussex. It is a seaside resort.

Lady Bracknell: Where did the charitable gentleman who had a first-class ticket for this seaside resort find you?

Jack (gravely): In a handbag.

Lady Bracknell: A handbag?

Jack (very seriously): Yes, Lady Bracknell. I was in a handbag — a somewhat large, black leather handbag, with handles to it — an ordinary handbag in fact.

Lady Bracknell: In what locality did this Mr. James, or Thomas, Cardew come across this ordinary handbag?

Jack: In the cloakroom at Victoria Station. It was given to him in mistake for his own.

Lady Bracknell: The cloakroom at Victoria Station?

Jack: Yes. The Brighton line.

Lady Bracknell: The line is immaterial. Mr. Worthing, I confess I feel somewhat bewildered by what you have just told me. To be born, or at any rate bred, in a handbag, whether it had handles or not, seems to me to display a contempt for the ordinary decencies of family life that reminds one of the worst excesses of the French Revolution. And I presume you know what that unfortunate movement led to? As for the particular locality in which the handbag was found, a cloakroom at a railway station might serve to conceal a social indiscretion — has probably, indeed, been used for that purpose before now — but it could hardly be regarded as an assured basis for a recognized position in good society.

Jack: May I ask you then what you would advise me to do? I need hardly say I would do anything in the world to ensure Gwendolen's happiness.

Lady Bracknell: I would strongly advise you, Mr. Worthing, to try and acquire some relations as soon as possible, and to make a definite effort to produce at any rate one parent of either sex, before the season is quite over.

Jack: Well, I don't see how I could possibly manage to do that. I can produce the handbag at any moment. It is in my dressing room at home. I really think that should satisfy you, Lady Bracknell.

Lady Bracknell: Me, sir! What has it to do with me? You can hardly imagine that I and Lord Bracknell would dream of allowing our only daughter — a girl brought up with the utmost care — to marry into a cloakroom, and form an alliance with a parcel? Good morning, Mr. Worthing!

(*Lady Bracknell sweeps out in majestic indignation.*)

Jack: Good morning! (*Algernon, from the other room, strikes up the Wedding March. Jack looks perfectly furious, and goes to the door.*) For goodness' sake don't play that ghastly tune, Algy! How idiotic you are!

(*The music stops, and Algernon enters cheerily.*)

Algernon: Didn't it go off all right, old boy? You don't mean to say Gwendolen refused you? I know it is a way she has. She is always refusing people. I think it is most ill-natured of her.

Jack: Oh, Gwendolen is as right as a trivet. As far as she is concerned, we are engaged. Her mother is perfectly unbearable. Never met such a Gorgon° — I don't really know what a Gorgon is like, but I am quite sure that Lady Bracknell is one. In any case, she is a monster, without being a myth, which is rather unfair. I beg your pardon, Algy, I suppose I shouldn't talk about your own aunt in that way before you.

Algernon: My dear boy, I love hearing my relations abused. It is the only thing that makes me put up with them at all. Relations are simply a tedious pack of people, who haven't got the remotest knowledge of how to live, nor the smallest instinct about when to die.

Jack: Oh, that is nonsense!

Algernon: It isn't!

Jack: Well, I won't argue about the matter. You always want to argue about things.

Gorgon: In Greek myth, one of three very ugly sisters who had, among other characteristics, serpents for hair.

Algernon: That is exactly what things were originally made for.

Jack: Upon my word, if I thought that, I'd shoot myself — (*A pause.*) You don't think there is any chance of Gwendolen becoming like her mother in about a hundred and fifty years, do you, Algy?

Algernon: All women become like their mothers. That is their tragedy. No man does. That's his.

Jack: Is that clever?

Algernon: It is perfectly phrased! and quite as true as any observation in civilized life should be.

Jack: I am sick to death of cleverness. Everybody is clever nowadays. You can't go anywhere without meeting clever people. The thing has become an absolute public nuisance. I wish to goodness we had a few fools left.

Algernon: We have.

Jack: I should extremely like to meet them. What do they talk about?

Algernon: The fools? Oh! about the clever people, of course.

Jack: What fools!

Algernon: By the way, did you tell Gwendolen the truth about your being Ernest in town, and Jack in the country?

Jack (in a very patronizing manner): My dear fellow, the truth isn't quite the sort of thing one tells to a nice sweet refined girl. What extraordinary ideas you have about the way to behave to a woman!

Algernon: The only way to behave to a woman is to make love to her if she is pretty, and to someone else if she is plain.

Jack: Oh, that is nonsense.

Algernon: What about your brother? What about the profligate Ernest?

Jack: Oh, before the end of the week I shall have got rid of him. I'll say he died in Paris of apoplexy. Lots of people die of apoplexy, quite suddenly, don't they?

Algernon: Yes, but it's hereditary, my dear fellow. It's a sort of thing that runs in families. You had much better say a severe chill.

Jack: You are sure a severe chill isn't hereditary, or anything of that kind?

Algernon: Of course it isn't!

Jack: Very well, then. My poor brother Ernest is carried off suddenly in Paris, by a severe chill. That gets rid of him.

Algernon: But I thought you said that — Miss Cardew was a little too much interested in your poor brother Ernest? Won't she feel his loss a good deal?

Jack: Oh, that is all right. Cecily is not a silly romantic girl, I am glad to say. She has got a capital appetite, goes on long walks, and pays no attention at all to her lessons.

Algernon: I would rather like to see Cecily.

Jack: I will take very good care you never do. She is excessively pretty, and she is only just eighteen.

Algernon: Have you told Gwendolen yet that you have an excessively pretty ward who is only just eighteen?

Jack: Oh! one doesn't blurt these things out to people. Cecily and Gwendolen are perfectly certain to be extremely great friends. I'll bet you anything you like that half an hour after they have met, they will be calling each other sister.

Algernon: Women only do that when they have called each other a lot of other things first. Now, my dear boy, if we want to get a good table at Willis's, we really must go and dress. Do you know it is nearly seven?

Jack (irritably): Oh! it always is nearly seven.

Algernon: Well, I'm hungry.

Jack: I never knew you when you weren't —

Algernon: What shall we do after dinner? Go to a theater?

Jack: Oh, no! I loathe listening.

Algernon: Well, let us go to the Club?

Jack: Oh, no! I hate talking.

Algernon: Well, we might trot round to the Empire° at ten?

Jack: Oh, no! I can't bear looking at things. It is so silly.

Algernon: Well, what shall we do?

Jack: Nothing!

Algernon: It is awfully hard work doing nothing. However, I don't mind hard work where there is no definite object of any kind.

(*Enter Lane.*)

Lane: Miss Fairfax.

(*Enter Gwendolen. Lane goes out.*)

Algernon: Gwendolen, upon my word!

Gwendolen: Algy, kindly turn your back. I have something very particular to say to Mr. Worthing.

Algernon: Really, Gwendolen, I don't think I can allow this at all.

Gwendolen: Algy, you always adopt a strictly immoral attitude towards life. You are not quite old enough to do that.

(*Algernon retires to the fireplace.*)

Jack: My own darling!

Gwendolen: Ernest, we may never be married. From the expression on Mama's face I fear we never shall. Few parents nowadays pay any regard to what their children say to them. The old-fashioned respect for the young is fast dying out. Whatever influence I ever had over Mama, I lost at the age of three. But although she may prevent us from becoming man and wife, and I may marry someone else, and marry often, nothing that she can possibly do can alter my eternal devotion to you.

Jack: Dear Gwendolen!

Gwendolen: The story of your romantic origin, as related to me by Mama, with unpleasing comments, has naturally stirred the deeper fibers of my nature. Your Christian name has an irresistible fascination. The simplicity of your character makes you exquisitely incomprehensible

---

Empire: Empire Theatre, a London music hall that was also a rendezvous for prostitutes.

to me. Your town address at the Albany I have. What is your address in the country?

Jack: The Manor House, Woolton, Hertfordshire.

(*Algernon, who has been carefully listening, smiles to himself, and writes the address on his shirt cuff. Then picks up the Railway Guide.*)

Gwendolen: There is a good postal service, I suppose? It may be necessary to do something desperate. That of course will require serious consideration. I will communicate with you daily.

Jack: My own one!

Gwendolen: How long do you remain in town?

Jack: Till Monday.

Gwendolen: Good! Algy, you may turn round now.

Algernon: Thanks, I've turned round already.

Gwendolen: You may also ring the bell.

Jack: You will let me see you to your carriage, my own darling?

Gwendolen: Certainly.

Jack (to Lane, who now enters): I will see Miss Fairfax out.

Lane: Yes, sir.   (*Jack and Gwendolen go off.*)

(*Lane presents several letters on a salver to Algernon. It is to be surmised that they are bills, as Algernon, after looking at the envelopes, tears them up.*)

Algernon: A glass of sherry, Lane.

Lane: Yes, sir.

Algernon: Tomorrow, Lane, I'm going Bunburying.

Lane: Yes, sir.

Algernon: I shall probably not be back till Monday. You can put up my dress clothes, my smoking jacket, and all the Bunbury suits —

Lane: Yes, sir. (*Handing sherry.*)

Algernon: I hope tomorrow will be a fine day, Lane.

Lane: It never is, sir.

Algernon: Lane, you're a perfect pessimist.

Lane: I do my best to give satisfaction, sir.

(*Enter Jack. Lane goes off.*)

Jack: There's a sensible, intellectual girl! the only girl I ever cared for in my life. (*Algernon is laughing immoderately.*) What on earth are you so amused at?

Algernon: Oh, I'm a little anxious about poor Bunbury, that is all.

Jack: If you don't take care, your friend Bunbury will get you into a serious scrape some day.

Algernon: I love scrapes. They are the only things that are never serious.

Jack: Oh, that's nonsense, Algy. You never talk anything but nonsense.

Algernon: Nobody ever does.

(*Jack looks indignantly at him, and leaves the room. Algernon lights a cigarette, reads his shirt cuff, and smiles.*)

ACT II

(*Scene: Garden at the Manor House. A flight of gray stone steps leads up to the house. The garden, an old-fashioned one, full of roses. Time of year, July. Basket chairs, and a table covered with books, are set under a large yew tree. Miss Prism discovered seated at the table. Cecily is at the back watering flowers.*)

Miss Prism (calling): Cecily, Cecily! Surely such a utilitarian occupation as the watering of flowers is rather Moulton's duty than yours? Especially at a moment when intellectual pleasures await you. Your German grammar is on the table. Pray open it at page fifteen. We will repeat yesterday's lesson.

Cecily (coming over very slowly): But I don't like German. It isn't at all a becoming language. I know perfectly well that I look quite plain after my German lesson.

Miss Prism: Child, you know how anxious your guardian is that you should improve yourself in every way. He laid particular stress on your German, as he was leaving for town yesterday. Indeed, he always lays stress on your German when he is leaving for town.

Cecily: Dear Uncle Jack is so very serious! Sometimes he is so serious that I think he cannot be quite well.

Miss Prism (drawing herself up): Your guardian enjoys the best of health, and his gravity of demeanor is especially to be commended in one so comparatively young as he is. I know no one who has a higher sense of duty and responsibility.

Cecily: I suppose that is why he often looks a little bored when we three are together.

Miss Prism: Cecily! I am surprised at you. Mr. Worthing has many troubles in his life. Idle merriment and triviality would be out of place in his conversation. You must remember his constant anxiety about that unfortunate young man his brother.

Cecily: I wish Uncle Jack would allow that unfortunate young man, his brother, to come down here sometimes. We might have a good influence over him, Miss Prism. I am sure you certainly would. You know German, and geology, and things of that kind influence a man very much.

(*Cecily begins to write in her diary.*)

Miss Prism (shaking her head): I do not think that even I could produce any effect on a character that according to his own brother's admission is irretrievably weak and vacillating. Indeed I am not sure that I would desire to reclaim him. I am not in favor of this modern mania for turning bad people into good people at a moment's notice. As a man sows so let him reap. You must put away your diary, Cecily. I really don't see why you should keep a diary at all.

Cecily: I keep a diary in order to enter the wonderful secrets of my life. If I didn't write them down I should probably forget all about them.

Miss Prism: Memory, my dear Cecily, is the diary that we all carry about with us.

Cecily: Yes, but it usually chronicles the things that have never happened, and couldn't possibly have happened. I believe that Memory is responsible for nearly all the three-volume novels that Mudie sends us.

Miss Prism: Do not speak slightingly of the three-volume novel, Cecily. I wrote one myself in earlier days.

Cecily: Did you really, Miss Prism? How wonderfully clever you are! I hope it did not end happily? I don't like novels that end happily. They depress me so much.

Miss Prism: The good ended happily, and the bad unhappily. That is what Fiction means.

Cecily: I suppose so. But it seems very unfair. And was your novel ever published?

Miss Prism: Alas! no. The manuscript unfortunately was abandoned. I use the word in the sense of lost or mislaid. To your work, child, these speculations are profitless.

Cecily (smiling): But I see dear Dr. Chasuble coming up through the garden.

Miss Prism (rising and advancing): Dr. Chasuble! This is indeed a pleasure.

(*Enter Canon Chasuble.*)

Chasuble: And how are we this morning? Miss Prism, you are, I trust, well?

Cecily: Miss Prism has just been complaining of a slight headache. I think it would do her so much good to have a short stroll with you in the park, Dr. Chasuble.

Miss Prism: Cecily, I have not mentioned anything about a headache.

Cecily: No, dear Miss Prism, I know that, but I felt instinctively that you had a headache. Indeed I was thinking about that, and not about my German lesson, when the Rector came in.

Chasuble: I hope, Cecily, you are not inattentive.

Cecily: Oh, I am afraid I am.

Chasuble: That is strange. Were I fortunate enough to be Miss Prism's pupil, I would hang upon her lips. (*Miss Prism glares.*) I spoke metaphorically. — My metaphor was drawn from bees. Ahem! Mr. Worthing, I suppose, has not returned from town yet?

Miss Prism: We do not expect him till Monday afternoon.

Chasuble: Ah yes, he usually likes to spend his Sunday in London. He is not one of those whose sole aim is enjoyment, as, by all accounts, that unfortunate young man his brother seems to be. But I must not disturb Egeria° and her pupil any longer.

Miss Prism: Egeria? My name is Laetitia, Doctor.

Chasuble (bowing): A classical allusion merely, drawn from the Pagan authors. I shall see you both no doubt at Evensong?

Miss Prism: I think, dear Doctor, I will have a stroll with you. I find I have a headache after all, and a walk might do it good.

Egeria: Roman goddess of water.

Chasuble: With pleasure, Miss Prism, with pleasure. We might go as far as the schools and back.

Miss Prism: That would be delightful. Cecily, you will read your Political Economy in my absence. The chapter on the Fall of the Rupee° you may omit. It is somewhat too sensational. Even these metallic problems have their melodramatic side.

(Goes down the garden with Dr. Chasuble.)

Cecily (picks up books and throws them back on table): Horrid Political Economy! Horrid Geography! Horrid, horrid German!

(*Enter Merriman with a card on a salver.*)

Merriman: Mr. Ernest Worthing has just driven over from the station. He has brought his luggage with him.

Cecily (takes the card and reads it): "Mr. Ernest Worthing, B.4, The Albany, W." Uncle Jack's brother! Did you tell him Mr. Worthing was in town?

Merriman: Yes, Miss. He seemed very much disappointed. I mentioned that you and Miss Prism were in the garden. He said he was anxious to speak to you privately for a moment.

Cecily: Ask Mr. Ernest Worthing to come here. I suppose you had better talk to the housekeeper about a room for him.

Merriman: Yes, Miss. (*Merriman goes off.*)

Cecily: I have never met any really wicked person before. I feel rather frightened. I am so afraid he will look just like everyone else.

(*Enter Algernon, very gay and debonair.*)

He does!

Algernon (raising his hat): You are my little cousin Cecily, I'm sure.

Cecily: You are under some strange mistake. I am not little. In fact, I believe I am more than usually tall for my age. (*Algernon is rather taken aback.*) But I am your cousin Cecily. You, I see from your card, are Uncle Jack's brother, my cousin Ernest, my wicked cousin Ernest.

Algernon: Oh! I am not really wicked at all, Cousin Cecily. You mustn't think that I am wicked.

Cecily: If you are not, then you have certainly been deceiving us all in a very inexcusable manner. I hope you have not been leading a double life, pretending to be wicked and being really good all the time. That would be hypocrisy.

Algernon (looks at her in amazement): Oh! Of course I have been rather reckless.

Cecily: I am glad to hear it.

Algernon: In fact, now you mention the subject, I have been very bad in my own small way.

Fall of the Rupee: Reference to the Indian rupee, whose steady deflation between 1873 and 1893 caused the Indian government finally to close the mints.

Cecily: I don't think you should be so proud of that, though I am sure it must have been very pleasant.

Algernon: It is much pleasanter being here with you.

Cecily: I can't understand how you are here at all. Uncle Jack won't be back till Monday afternoon.

Algernon: That is a great disappointment. I am obliged to go up by the first train on Monday morning. I have a business appointment that I am anxious — to miss.

Cecily: Couldn't you miss it anywhere but in London?

Algernon: No: the appointment is in London.

Cecily: Well, I know, of course, how important it is not to keep a business engagement, if one wants to retain any sense of the beauty of life, but still I think you had better wait till Uncle Jack arrives. I know he wants to speak to you about your emigrating.

Algernon: About my what?

Cecily: Your emigrating. He has gone up to buy your outfit.

Algernon: I certainly wouldn't let Jack buy my outfit. He has no taste in neckties at all.

Cecily: I don't think you will require neckties. Uncle Jack is sending you to Australia.

Algernon: Australia! I'd sooner die.

Cecily: Well, he said at dinner on Wednesday night, that you would have to choose between this world, the next world, and Australia.

Algernon: Oh, well! The accounts I have received of Australia and the next world are not particularly encouraging. This world is good enough for me, Cousin Cecily.

Cecily: Yes, but are you good enough for it?

Algernon: I'm afraid I'm not that. That is why I want you to reform me. You might make that your mission, if you don't mind, Cousin Cecily.

Cecily: I'm afraid I've no time, this afternoon.

Algernon: Well, would you mind my reforming myself this afternoon?

Cecily: It is rather quixotic° of you. But I think you should try.

Algernon: I will. I feel better already.

Cecily: You are looking a little worse.

Algernon: That is because I am hungry.

Cecily: How thoughtless of me. I should have remembered that when one is going to lead an entirely new life, one requires regular and wholesome meals. Won't you come in?

Algernon: Thank you. Might I have a buttonhole° first? I never have any appetite unless I have a buttonhole first.

Cecily: A Maréchal Niel?°

Algernon: No, I'd sooner have a pink rose.

---

quixotic: Foolishly impractical, from the idealistic hero of Cervantes's *Don Quixote.*
buttonhole: Boutonniere. *Maréchal Niel:* A yellow rose.

Cecily: Why?
> (*Cuts a flower.*)

Algernon: Because you are like a pink rose, Cousin Cecily.

Cecily: I don't think it can be right for you to talk to me like that. Miss Prism never says such things to me.

Algernon: Then Miss Prism is a shortsighted old lady. (*Cecily puts the rose in his buttonhole.*) You are the prettiest girl I ever saw.

Cecily: Miss Prism says that all good looks are a snare.

Algernon: They are a snare that every sensible man would like to be caught in.

Cecily: Oh! I don't think I would care to catch a sensible man. I shouldn't know what to talk to him about.

> (*They pass into the house. Miss Prism and Dr. Chasuble return.*)

Miss Prism: You are too much alone, dear Dr. Chasuble. You should get married. A misanthrope I can understand — a womanthrope, never!

Chasuble (with a scholar's shudder): Believe me, I do not deserve so neologistic a phrase. The precept as well as the practice of the Primitive Church was distinctly against matrimony.

Miss Prism (sententiously): That is obviously the reason why the Primitive Church has not lasted up to the present day. And you do not seem to realize, dear Doctor, that by persistently remaining single, a man converts himself into a permanent public temptation. Men should be more careful; this very celibacy leads weaker vessels astray.

Chasuble: But is a man not equally attractive when married?

Miss Prism: No married man is ever attractive except to his wife.

Chasuble: And often, I've been told, not even to her.

Miss Prism: That depends on the intellectual sympathies of the woman. Maturity can always be depended on. Ripeness can be trusted. Young women are green. (*Dr. Chasuble starts.*) I spoke horticulturally. My metaphor was drawn from fruits. But where is Cecily?

Chasuble: Perhaps she followed us to the schools.

(*Enter Jack slowly from the back of the garden. He is dressed in the deepest mourning, with crepe hatband and black gloves.*)

Miss Prism: Mr. Worthing!

Chasuble: Mr. Worthing?

Miss Prism: This is indeed a surprise. We did not look for you till Monday afternoon.

Jack (shakes Miss Prism's hand in a tragic manner): I have returned sooner than I expected. Dr. Chasuble, I hope you are well?

Chasuble: Dear Mr. Worthing, I trust this garb of woe does not betoken some terrible calamity?

Jack: My brother.

Miss Prism: More shameful debts and extravagance?

Chasuble: Still leading his life of pleasure?

Jack (shaking his head): Dead!

Chasuble: Your brother Ernest dead?

Jack: Quite dead.

Miss Prism: What a lesson for him! I trust he will profit by it.

Chasuble: Mr. Worthing, I offer you my sincere condolence. You have at least the consolation of knowing that you were always the most generous and forgiving of brothers.

Jack: Poor Ernest! He had many faults, but it is a sad, sad blow.

Chasuble: Very sad indeed. Were you with him at the end?

Jack: No. He died abroad, in Paris, in fact. I had a telegram last night from the manager of the Grand Hotel.

Chasuble: Was the cause of death mentioned?

Jack: A severe chill, it seems.

Miss Prism: As a man sows, so shall he reap.

Chasuble (raising his hand): Charity, dear Miss Prism, charity! None of us are perfect. I myself am peculiarly susceptible to drafts. Will the interment take place here?

Jack: No. He seemed to have expressed a desire to be buried in Paris.

Chasuble: In Paris! (*Shakes his head.*) I fear that hardly points to any very serious state of mind at the last. You would no doubt wish me to make some slight allusion to this tragic domestic affliction next Sunday. (*Jack presses his hand convulsively.*) My sermon on the meaning of the manna in the wilderness can be adapted to almost any occasion, joyful, or, as in the present case, distressing. (*All sigh.*) I have preached it at harvest celebrations, christenings, confirmations, on days of humiliation and festal days. The last time I delivered it was in the Cathedral, as a charity sermon on behalf of the Society for the Prevention of Discontent among the Upper Orders. The Bishop, who was present, was much struck by some of the analogies I drew.

Jack: Ah! that reminds me, you mentioned christenings I think, Dr. Chasuble? I suppose you know how to christen all right? (*Dr. Chasuble looks astounded.*) I mean, of course, you are continually christening, aren't you?

Miss Prism: It is, I regret to say, one of the Rector's most constant duties in this parish. I have often spoken to the poorer classes on the subject. But they don't seem to know what thrift is.

Chasuble: But is there any particular infant in whom you are interested, Mr. Worthing? Your brother was, I believe, unmarried, was he not?

Jack: Oh yes.

Miss Prism (bitterly): People who live entirely for pleasure usually are.

Jack: But it is not for any child, dear Doctor. I am very fond of children. No! the fact is, I would like to be christened myself, this afternoon, if you have nothing better to do.

Chasuble: But surely, Mr. Worthing, you have been christened already?

Jack: I don't remember anything about it.

Chasuble: But have you any grave doubts on the subject?

Jack: I certainly intend to have. Of course I don't know if the thing would bother you in any way, or if you think I am a little too old now.

Chasuble: Not at all. The sprinkling, and, indeed, the immersion of adults is a perfectly canonical practice.

Jack: Immersion!

Chasuble: You need have no apprehensions. Sprinkling is all that is necessary, or indeed I think advisable. Our weather is so changeable. At what hour would you wish the ceremony performed?

Jack: Oh, I might trot round about five if that would suit you.

Chasuble: Perfectly, perfectly! In fact I have two similar ceremonies to perform at that time. A case of twins that occurred recently in one of the outlying cottages on your own estate. Poor Jenkins the carter, a most hardworking man.

Jack: Oh! I don't see much fun in being christened along with other babies. It would be childish. Would half-past five do?

Chasuble: Admirably! Admirably! (*Takes out watch.*) And now, dear Mr. Worthing, I will not intrude any longer into a house of sorrow. I would merely beg you not to be too much bowed down by grief. What seem to us bitter trials are often blessings in disguise.

Miss Prism: This seems to me a blessing of an extremely obvious kind.

(*Enter Cecily from the house.*)

Cecily: Uncle Jack! Oh, I am pleased to see you back. But what horrid clothes you have got on! Do go and change them.

Miss Prism: Cecily!

Chasuble: My child! my child!

(*Cecily goes towards Jack; he kisses her brow in a melancholy manner.*)

Cecily: What is the matter, Uncle Jack? Do look happy! You look as if you had toothache, and I have got such a surprise for you. Who do you think is in the dining room? Your brother!

Jack: Who?

Cecily: Your brother Ernest. He arrived about half an hour ago.

Jack: What nonsense! I haven't got a brother.

Cecily: Oh, don't say that. However badly he may have behaved to you in the past he is still your brother. You couldn't be so heartless as to disown him. I'll tell him to come out. And you will shake hands with him, won't you, Uncle Jack? (*Runs back into the house.*)

Chasuble: These are very joyful tidings.

Miss Prism: After we had all been resigned to his loss, his sudden return seems to me peculiarly distressing.

Jack: My brother is in the dining room? I don't know what it all means. I think it is perfectly absurd.

(*Enter Algernon and Cecily hand in hand. They come slowly up to Jack.*)

Jack: Good heavens! (*Motions Algernon away.*)

Algernon: Brother John, I have come down from town to tell you that I am very sorry for all the trouble I have given you, and that I intend to lead a better life in the future.

(*Jack glares at him and does not take his hand.*)

Cecily: Uncle Jack, you are not going to refuse your own brother's hand?

Jack: Nothing will induce me to take his hand. I think his coming down here disgraceful. He knows perfectly well why.

Cecily: Uncle Jack, do be nice. There is some good in everyone. Ernest has just been telling me about his poor invalid friend Mr. Bunbury whom he goes to visit so often. And surely there must be much good in one who is kind to an invalid, and leaves the pleasures of London to sit by a bed of pain.

Jack: Oh! he has been talking about Bunbury has he?

Cecily: Yes, he has told me all about poor Mr. Bunbury, and his terrible state of health.

Jack: Bunbury! Well, I won't have him talk to you about Bunbury or about anything else. It is enough to drive one perfectly frantic.

Algernon: Of course I admit that the faults were all on my side. But I must say that I think that Brother John's coldness to me is peculiarly painful. I expected a more enthusiastic welcome, especially considering it is the first time I have come here.

Cecily: Uncle Jack, if you don't shake hands with Ernest I will never forgive you.

Jack: Never forgive me?

Cecily: Never, never, never!

Jack: Well, this is the last time I shall ever do it.

(*Shakes hands with Algernon and glares.*)

Chasuble: It's pleasant, is it not, to see so perfect a reconciliation? I think we might leave the two brothers together.

Miss Prism: Cecily, you will come with us.

Cecily: Certainly, Miss Prism. My little task of reconciliation is over.

Chasuble: You have done a beautiful action today, dear child.

Miss Prism: We must not be premature in our judgments.

Cecily: I feel very happy.   (*They all go off.*)

Jack: You young scoundrel, Algy, you must get out of this place as soon as possible. I don't allow any Bunburying here.

(*Enter Merriman.*)

Merriman: I have put Mr. Ernest's things in the room next to yours, sir. I suppose that is all right?

Jack: What?

Merriman: Mr. Ernest's luggage, sir. I have unpacked it and put it in the room next to your own.

Jack: His luggage?

Merriman: Yes, sir. Three portmanteaus, a dressing case, two hatboxes, and a large luncheon basket.

Algernon: I am afraid 1 can't stay more than a week this time.

Jack: Merriman, order the dog cart at once. Mr. Ernest has been suddenly called back to town.

Merriman: Yes, sir. *(Goes back into the house.)*

Algernon: What a fearful liar you are, Jack. I have not been called back to town at all.

Jack: Yes, you have.

Algernon: I haven't heard anyone call me.

Jack: Your duty as a gentleman calls you back.

Algernon: My duty as a gentleman has never interfered with my pleasures in the smallest degree.

Jack: I can quite understand that.

Algernon: Well, Cecily is a darling.

Jack: You are not to talk of Miss Cardew like that. I don't like it.

Algernon: Well, I don't like your clothes. You look perfectly ridiculous in them. Why on earth don't you go up and change? It is perfectly childish to be in deep mourning for a man who is actually staying for a whole week in your house as a guest. I call it grotesque.

Jack: You are certainly not staying with me for a whole week as a guest or anything else. You have got to leave — by the four-five train.

Algernon: I certainly won't leave you so long as you are in mourning. It would be most unfriendly. If I were in mourning you would stay with me, I suppose. I should think it very unkind if you didn't.

Jack: Well, will you go if I change my clothes?

Algernon: Yes, if you are not too long. I never saw anybody take so long to dress, and with such little result.

Jack: Well, at any rate, that is better than being always overdressed as you are.

Algernon: If I am occasionally a little overdressed, I make up for it by being always immensely overeducated.

Jack: Your vanity is ridiculous, your conduct an outrage, and your presence in my garden utterly absurd. However, you have got to catch the four-five, and I hope you will have a pleasant journey back to town. This Bunburying, as you call it, has not been a great success for you.

(Goes into the house.)

Algernon: I think it has been a great success. I'm in love with Cecily, and that is everything.

(Enter Cecily at the back of the garden. She picks up the can and begins to water the flowers.)

But I must see her before I go, and make arrangements for another Bunbury. Ah, there she is.

Cecily: Oh, I merely came back to water the roses. I thought you were with Uncle Jack.

Algernon: He's gone to order the dog cart for me.

Cecily: Oh, is he going to take you for a nice drive?

Algernon: He's going to send me away.

Cecily: Then have we got to part?

Algernon: I am afraid so. It's a very painful parting.

Cecily: It is always painful to part from people whom one has known for a very brief space of time. The absence of old friends one can endure with equanimity. But even a momentary separation from anyone to whom one has just been introduced is almost unbearable.

Algernon: Thank you.

(*Enter Merriman.*)

Merriman: The dog cart is at the door, sir.

(*Algernon looks appealingly at Cecily.*)

Cecily: It can wait, Merriman — for — five minutes.

Merriman: Yes, miss.   (*Exit Merriman.*)

Algernon: I hope, Cecily, I shall not offend you if I state quite frankly and openly that you seem to me to be in every way the visible personification of absolute perfection.

Cecily: I think your frankness does you great credit, Ernest. If you will allow me I will copy your remarks into my diary.

(*Goes over to table and begins writing in diary.*)

Algernon: Do you really keep a diary? I'd give anything to look at it. May I?

Cecily: Oh no. (*Puts her hand over it.*) You see, it is simply a very young girl's record of her own thoughts and impressions, and consequently meant for publication. When it appears in volume form I hope you will order a copy. But pray, Ernest, don't stop. I delight in taking down from dictation. I have reached "absolute perfection." You can go on. I am quite ready for more.

Algernon (somewhat taken aback): Ahem! Ahem!

Cecily: Oh, don't cough, Ernest. When one is dictating one should speak fluently and not cough. Besides, I don't know how to spell a cough.

(*Writes as Algernon speaks.*)

Algernon (speaking very rapidly): Cecily, ever since I first looked upon your wonderful and incomparable beauty, I have dared to love you wildly, passionately, devotedly, hopelessly.

Cecily: I don't think that you should tell me that you love me wildly, passionately, devotedly, hopelessly. Hopelessly doesn't seem to make much sense, does it?

Algernon: Cecily!

(*Enter Merriman.*)

Merriman: The dog cart is waiting, sir.

Algernon: Tell it to come round next week, at the same hour.

Merriman (looks at Cecily, who makes no sign): Yes, sir.

(*Merriman retires.*)

Cecily: Uncle Jack would be very much annoyed if he knew you were staying on till next week, at the same hour.

Algernon: Oh, I don't care about Jack. I don't care for anybody in the whole world but you. I love you, Cecily. You will marry me, won't you?

Cecily: You silly boy! Of course. Why, we have been engaged for the last three months.

Algernon: For the last three months?

Cecily: Yes, it will be exactly three months on Thursday.

Algernon: But how did we become engaged?

Cecily: Well, ever since dear Uncle Jack first confessed to us that he had a younger brother who was very wicked and bad, you of course have formed the chief topic of conversation between myself and Miss Prism. And of course a man who is much talked about is always very attractive. One feels there must be something in him after all. I daresay it was foolish of me, but I fell in love with you, Ernest.

Algernon: Darling! And when was the engagement actually settled?

Cecily: On the 14th of February last. Worn out by your entire ignorance of my existence, I determined to end the matter one way or the other, and after a long struggle with myself I accepted you under this dear old tree here. The next day I bought this little ring in your name, and this is the little bangle with the true lovers' knot I promised you always to wear.

Algernon: Did I give you this? It's very pretty, isn't it?

Cecily: Yes, you've wonderfully good taste, Ernest. It's the excuse I've always given for your leading such a bad life. And this is the box in which I keep all your dear letters.

(*Kneels at table, opens box, and produces letters tied up with blue ribbon.*)

Algernon: My letters! But my own sweet Cecily, I have never written you any letters.

Cecily: You need hardly remind me of that, Ernest. I remember only too well that I was forced to write your letters for you. I wrote always three times a week, and sometimes oftener.

Algernon: Oh, do let me read them, Cecily!

Cecily: Oh, I couldn't possibly. They would make you far too conceited. (*Replaces box.*) The three you wrote me after I had broken off the engagement are so beautiful, and so badly spelled, that even now I can hardly read them without crying a little.

Algernon: But was our engagement ever broken off?

Cecily: Of course it was. On the 22nd of last March. You can see the entry if you like. (*Shows diary.*) "Today I broke off my engagement with Ernest. I feel it is better to do so. The weather still continues charming."

Algernon: But why on earth did you break it off? What had I done? I had done nothing at all. Cecily, I am very much hurt indeed to hear you broke it off. Particularly when the weather was so charming.

Cecily: It would hardly have been a really serious engagement if it hadn't been broken off at least once. But I forgave you before the week was out.

Algernon (crossing to her, and kneeling): What a perfect angel you are, Cecily.

Cecily: You dear romantic boy. (*He kisses her; she puts her fingers through his hair.*) I hope your hair curls naturally, does it?

Algernon: Yes, darling, with a little help from others.

Cecily: I am so glad.

Algernon: You'll never break off our engagement again, Cecily?

Cecily: I don't think I could break it off now that I have actually met you. Besides, of course, there is the question of your name.

Algernon (nervously): Yes, of course.

Cecily: You must not laugh at me, darling, but it had always been a girl-ish dream of mine to love someone whose name was Ernest. (*Algernon rises, Cecily also.*) There is something in that name that seems to inspire absolute confidence. I pity any poor married woman whose husband is not called Ernest.

Algernon: But, my dear child, do you mean to say you could not love me if I had some other name?

Cecily: But what name?

Algernon: Oh, any name you like — Algernon — for instance —

Cecily: But I don't like the name of Algernon.

Algernon: Well, my own dear, sweet, loving little darling, I really can't see why you should object to the name of Algernon. It is not at all a bad name. In fact, it is rather an aristocratic name. Half of the chaps who get into the Bankruptcy Court are called Algernon. But seriously, Cecily — (*moving to her*) — if my name was Algy, couldn't you love me?

Cecily (rising): I might respect you, Ernest, I might admire your character, but I fear that I should not be able to give you my undivided attention.

Algernon: Ahem! Cecily! (*Picking up hat.*) Your Rector here is, I suppose, thoroughly experienced in the practice of all the rites and ceremonials of the Church?

Cecily: Oh yes. Dr. Chasuble is a most learned man. He has never written a single book, so you can imagine how much he knows.

Algernon: I must see him at once on a most important christening — I mean on most important business.

Cecily: Oh!

Algernon: I shan't be away more than half an hour.

Cecily: Considering that we have been engaged since February the 14th, and that I only met you today for the first time, I think it is rather hard that you should leave me for so long a period as half an hour. Couldn't you make it twenty minutes?

Algernon: I'll be back in no time.

(*Kisses her and rushes down the garden.*)

Cecily: What an impetuous boy he is! I like his hair so much. I must enter his proposal in my diary.

(*Enter Merriman.*)

Merriman: A Miss Fairfax has just called to see Mr. Worthing. On very important business Miss Fairfax states.

Cecily: Isn't Mr. Worthing in his library?

Merriman: Mr. Worthing went over in the direction of the Rectory some time ago.

Cecily: Pray ask the lady to come out here; Mr. Worthing is sure to be back soon. And you can bring tea.

Merriman: Yes, miss.   (*Goes out.*)

Cecily: Miss Fairfax! I suppose one of the many good elderly women who are associated with Uncle Jack in some of his philanthropic work in London. I don't quite like women who are interested in philanthropic work. I think it is so forward of them.

(*Enter Merriman.*)

Merriman: Miss Fairfax.

(*Enter Gwendolen. Exit Merriman.*)

Cecily (advancing to meet her): Pray let me introduce myself to you. My name is Cecily Cardew.

Gwendolen: Cecily Cardew? (*Moving to her and shaking hands.*) What a very sweet name! Something tells me that we are going to be great friends. I like you already more than I can say. My first impressions of people are never wrong.

Cecily: How nice of you to like me so much after we have known each other such a comparatively short time. Pray sit down.

Gwendolen (still standing up): I may call you Cecily, may I not?

Cecily: With pleasure!

Gwendolen: And you will always call me Gwendolen, won't you?

Cecily: If you wish.

Gwendolen: Then that is all quite settled, is it not?

Cecily: I hope so.

(*A pause. They both sit down together.*)

Gwendolen: Perhaps this might be a favorable opportunity for my mentioning who I am. My father is Lord Bracknell. You have never heard of Papa, I suppose?

Cecily: I don't think so.

Gwendolen: Outside the family circle, Papa, I am glad to say, is entirely unknown. I think that is quite as it should be. The home seems to me to be the proper sphere for the man. And certainly once a man begins to neglect his domestic duties he becomes painfully effeminate, does he not? And I don't like that. It makes men so very attractive. Cecily, Mama, whose views on education are remarkably strict, has brought me up to be extremely shortsighted; it is part of her system, so do you mind my looking at you through my glasses?

Cecily: Oh! not at all, Gwendolen. I am very fond of being looked at.

Gwendolen (after examining Cecily carefully through a lorgnette): You are here on a short visit I suppose?

Cecily: Oh no! I live here.

Gwendolen (severely): Really? Your mother, no doubt, or some female relative of advanced years, resides here also?

Cecily: Oh no! I have no mother, nor, in fact, any relations.

Gwendolen: Indeed?

Cecily: My dear guardian, with the assistance of Miss Prism, has the arduous task of looking after me.

Gwendolen: Your guardian?

Cecily: Yes, I am Mr. Worthing's ward.

Gwendolen: Oh! It is strange he never mentioned to me that he had a ward. How secretive of him! He grows more interesting hourly. I am not sure, however, that the news inspires me with feelings of unmixed delight. (*Rising and going to her.*) I am very fond of you, Cecily; I have liked you ever since I met you! But I am bound to state that now that I know that you are Mr. Worthing's ward, I cannot help expressing a wish you were — well just a little older than you seem to be — and not quite so very alluring in appearance. In fact, if I may speak candidly —

Cecily: Pray do! I think that whenever one has anything unpleasant to say, one should always be quite candid.

Gwendolen: Well, to speak with perfect candor, Cecily, I wish that you were fully forty-two, and more than usually plain for your age. Ernest has a strong upright nature. He is the very soul of truth and honor. Disloyalty would be as impossible to him as deception. But even men of the noblest possible moral character are extremely susceptible to the influence of the physical charms of others. Modern, no less than Ancient History, supplies us with many most painful examples of what I refer to. If it were not so, indeed, History would be quite unreadable.

Cecily: I beg your pardon, Gwendolen, did you say Ernest?

Gwendolen: Yes.

Cecily: Oh, but it is not Mr. Ernest Worthing who is my guardian. It is his brother — his elder brother.

Gwendolen (sitting down again): Ernest never mentioned to me that he had a brother.

Cecily: I am sorry to say they have not been on good terms for a long time.

Gwendolen: Ah! that accounts for it. And now that I think of it I have never heard any man mention his brother. The subject seems distasteful to most men. Cecily, you have lifted a load from my mind. I was growing almost anxious. It would have been terrible if any cloud had come across a friendship like ours, would it not? Of course you are quite, quite sure that it is not Mr. Ernest Worthing who is your guardian?

Cecily: Quite sure. (*A pause.*) In fact, I am going to be his.

Gwendolen (inquiringly): I beg your pardon?

Cecily (rather shy and confidingly): Dearest Gwendolen, there is no reason why I should make a secret of it to you. Our little county newspaper is sure to chronicle the fact next week. Mr. Ernest Worthing and I are engaged to be married.

Gwendolen (quite politely, rising): My darling Cecily, I think there must be some slight error. Mr. Ernest Worthing is engaged to me. The announcement will appear in the Morning Post on Saturday at the latest.

Cecily (very politely, rising): I am afraid you must be under some misconception. Ernest proposed to me exactly ten minutes ago. (*Shows diary.*)

Gwendolen (examines diary through her lorgnette carefully): It is certainly very curious, for he asked me to be his wife yesterday afternoon at 5:30. If you would care to verify the incident, pray do so. (*Produces diary of her own.*) I never travel without my diary. One should always have something sensational to read in the train. I am so sorry, dear Cecily, if it is any disappointment to you, but I am afraid *I* have the prior claim.

Cecily: It would distress me more than I can tell you, dear Gwendolen, if it caused you any mental or physical anguish, but I feel bound to point out that since Ernest proposed to you he clearly has changed his mind.

Gwendolen (meditatively): If the poor fellow has been entrapped into any foolish promise I shall consider it my duty to rescue him at once, and with a firm hand.

Cecily (thoughtfully and sadly): Whatever unfortunate entanglement my dear boy may have got into, I will never reproach him with it after we are married.

Gwendolen: Do you allude to me, Miss Cardew, as an entanglement? You are presumptuous. On an occasion of this kind it becomes more than a moral duty to speak one's mind. It becomes a pleasure.

Cecily: Do you suggest, Miss Fairfax, that I entrapped Ernest into an engagement? How dare you? This is no time for wearing the shallow mask of manners. When I see a spade I call it a spade.

Gwendolen (satirically): I am glad to say that I have never seen a spade. It is obvious that our social spheres have been widely different.

(*Enter Merriman, followed by the Footman. He carries a salver, tablecloth, and plate stand. Cecily is about to retort. The presence of the servants exercises a restraining influence, under which both girls chafe.*)

Merriman: Shall I lay tea here as usual, miss?

Cecily (sternly, in a calm voice): Yes, as usual.

(*Merriman begins to clear table and lay cloth. A long pause. Cecily and Gwendolen glare at each other.*)

Gwendolen: Are there many interesting walks in the vicinity, Miss Cardew?

Cecily: Oh! Yes! a great many. From the top of one of the hills quite close one can see five counties.

Gwendolen: Five counties! I don't think I should like that. I hate crowds.

Cecily (sweetly): I suppose that is why you live in town?

(*Gwendolen bites her lip, and beats her foot nervously with her parasol.*)

Gwendolen (looking round): Quite a well-kept garden this is, Miss Cardew.

Cecily: So glad you like it, Miss Fairfax.

Gwendolen: I had no idea there were any flowers in the country.

Cecily: Oh, flowers are as common here, Miss Fairfax, as people are in London.

Gwendolen: Personally I cannot understand how anybody manages to exist in the country, if anybody who is anybody does. The country always bores me to death.

Cecily: Ah! This is what the newspapers call agricultural depression, is it not? I believe the aristocracy are suffering very much from it just at present. It is almost an epidemic amongst them, I have been told. May I offer you some tea, Miss Fairfax?

Gwendolen (with elaborate politeness): Thank you. (*Aside.*) Detestable girl! But I require tea!

Cecily (sweetly): Sugar?

Gwendolen (superciliously): No, thank you. Sugar is not fashionable anymore.

(*Cecily looks angrily at her, takes up the tongs, and puts four lumps of sugar into the cup.*)

Cecily (severely): Cake or bread and butter?

Gwendolen (in a bored manner): Bread and butter, please. Cake is rarely seen at the best houses nowadays.

Cecily (cuts a very large slice of cake, and puts it on the tray): Hand that to Miss Fairfax.

(*Merriman does so, and goes out with Footman. Gwendolen drinks the tea and makes a grimace. Puts down cup at once, reaches out her hand to the bread and butter, looks at it, and finds it is cake. Rises in indignation.*)

Gwendolen: You have filled my tea with lumps of sugar, and though I asked most distinctly for bread and butter, you have given me cake. I am known for the gentleness of my disposition, and the extraordinary sweetness of my nature, but I warn you, Miss Cardew, you may go too far.

Cecily (rising): To save my poor, innocent, trusting boy from the machinations of any other girl there are no lengths to which I would not go.

Gwendolen: From the moment I saw you I distrusted you. I felt that you were false and deceitful. I am never deceived in such matters. My first impressions of people are invariably right.

Cecily: It seems to me, Miss Fairfax, that I am trespassing on your valuable time. No doubt you have many other calls of a similar character to make in the neighborhood.

(*Enter Jack.*)

Gwendolen (catching sight of him): Ernest! My own Ernest!

Jack: Gwendolen! Darling! *(Offers to kiss her.)*

Gwendolen (drawing back): A moment! May I ask if you are engaged to be married to this young lady? *(Points to Cecily.)*

Jack (laughing): To dear little Cecily! Of course not! What could have put such an idea into your pretty little head?

Gwendolen: Thank you. You may! *(Offers her cheek.)*

Cecily (very sweetly): I knew there must be some misunderstanding, Miss Fairfax. The gentleman whose arm is at present round your waist is my dear guardian, Mr. John Worthing.

Gwendolen: I beg your pardon?

Cecily: This is Uncle Jack.

Gwendolen (receding): Jack! Oh!

(Enter Algernon.)

Cecily: Here is Ernest.

Algernon (goes straight over to Cecily without noticing anyone else): My own love! *(Offers to kiss her.)*

Cecily (drawing back): A moment, Ernest! May I ask you — are you engaged to be married to this young lady?

Algernon (looking round): To what young lady? Good heavens! Gwendolen!

Cecily: Yes! to good heavens, Gwendolen, I mean to Gwendolen.

Algernon (laughing): Of course not! What could have put such an idea into your pretty little head?

Cecily: Thank you. *(Presenting her cheek to be kissed.)* You may.

(Algernon kisses her.)

Gwendolen: I felt there was some slight error, Miss Cardew. The gentleman who is now embracing you is my cousin, Mr. Algernon Moncrieff.

Cecily (breaking away from Algernon): Algernon Moncrieff! Oh!

(The two girls move towards each other and put their arms round each other's waists as if for protection.)

Cecily: Are you called Algernon?

Algernon: I cannot deny it.

Cecily: Oh!

Gwendolen: Is your name really John?

Jack (standing rather proudly): I could deny it if I liked. I could deny anything if I liked. But my name certainly is John. It has been John for years.

Cecily (to Gwendolen): A gross deception has been practiced on both of us.

Gwendolen: My poor wounded Cecily!

Cecily: My sweet wronged Gwendolen!

Gwendolen (slowly and seriously): You will call me sister, will you not?

(They embrace. Jack and Algernon groan and walk up and down.)

Cecily (rather brightly): There is just one question I would like to be allowed to ask my guardian.

Gwendolen: An admirable idea! Mr. Worthing, there is just one question I would like to be permitted to put to you. Where is your brother Ernest? We are both engaged to be married to your brother Ernest, so it is a matter of some importance to us to know where your brother Ernest is at present.

Jack (slowly and hesitatingly): Gwendolen — Cecily — it is very painful for me to be forced to speak the truth. It is the first time in my life that I have ever been reduced to such a painful position, and I am really quite inexperienced in doing anything of the kind. However I will tell you quite frankly that I have no brother Ernest. I have no brother at all. I never had a brother in my life, and I certainly have not the smallest intention of ever having one in the future.

Cecily (surprised): No brother at all?

Jack (cheerily): None!

Gwendolen (severely): Had you never a brother of any kind?

Jack (pleasantly): Never. Not even of any kind.

Gwendolen: I am afraid it is quite clear, Cecily, that neither of us is engaged to be married to anyone.

Cecily: It is not a very pleasant position for a young girl suddenly to find herself in. Is it?

Gwendolen: Let us go into the house. They will hardly venture to come after us there.

Cecily: No, men are so cowardly, aren't they?

                       (*They retire into the house with scornful looks.*)

Jack: This ghastly state of things is what you call Bunburying, I suppose?

Algernon: Yes, and a perfectly wonderful Bunbury it is. The most wonderful Bunbury I have ever had in my life.

Jack: Well, you've no right whatsoever to Bunbury here.

Algernon: That is absurd. One has a right to Bunbury anywhere one chooses. Every serious Bunburyist knows that.

Jack: Serious Bunburyist! Good heavens!

Algernon: Well, one must be serious about something, if one wants to have any amusement in life. I happen to be serious about Bunburying. What on earth you are serious about I haven't got the remotest idea. About everything, I should fancy. You have such an absolutely trivial nature.

Jack: Well, the only small satisfaction I have in the whole of this wretched business is that your friend Bunbury is quite exploded. You won't be able to run down to the country quite so often as you used to do, dear Algy. And a very good thing too.

Algernon: Your brother is a little off color, isn't he, dear Jack? You won't be able to disappear to London quite so frequently as your wicked custom was. And not a bad thing either.

Jack: As for your conduct towards Miss Cardew, I must say that your taking in a sweet, simple, innocent girl like that is quite inexcusable. To say nothing of the fact that she is my ward.

Algernon: I can see no possible defense at all for your deceiving a brilliant, clever, thoroughly experienced young lady like Miss Fairfax. To say nothing of the fact that she is my cousin.

Jack: I wanted to be engaged to Gwendolen, that is all. I love her.

Algernon: Well, I simply wanted to be engaged to Cecily. I adore her.

Jack: There is certainly no chance of your marrying Miss Cardew.

Algernon: I don't think there is much likelihood, Jack, of you and Miss Fairfax being united.

Jack: Well, that is no business of yours.

Algernon: If it was my business, I wouldn't talk about it. (*Begins to eat muffins.*) It is very vulgar to talk about one's business. Only people like stockbrokers do that, and then merely at dinner parties.

Jack: How you can sit there, calmly eating muffins when we are in this horrible trouble, I can't make out. You seem to me to be perfectly heartless.

Algernon: Well, I can't eat muffins in an agitated manner. The butter would probably get on my cuffs. One should always eat muffins quite calmly. It is the only way to eat them.

Jack: I say it's perfectly heartless your eating muffins at all, under the circumstances.

Algernon: When I am in trouble, eating is the only thing that consoles me. Indeed, when I am in really great trouble, as anyone who knows me intimately will tell you, I refuse everything except food and drink. At the present moment I am eating muffins because I am unhappy. Besides, I am particularly fond of muffins.   (*Rising.*)

Jack (rising): Well, that is no reason why you should eat them all in that greedy way.

(*Takes muffins from Algernon.*)

Algernon (offering tea cake): I wish you would have tea cake instead. I don't like tea cake.

Jack: Good heavens! I suppose a man may eat his own muffins in his own garden.

Algernon: But you have just said it was perfectly heartless to eat muffins.

Jack: I said it was perfectly heartless of you, under the circumstances. That is a very different thing.

Algernon: That may be, but the muffins are the same. (*He seizes the muffin dish from Jack.*)

Jack: Algy, I wish to goodness you would go.

Algernon: You can't possibly ask me to go without having some dinner. It's absurd. I never go without my dinner. No one ever does, except vegetarians and people like that. Besides I have just made arrangements with Dr. Chasuble to be christened at a quarter to six under the name of Ernest.

Jack: My dear fellow, the sooner you give up that nonsense the better. I made arrangements this morning with Dr. Chasuble to be christened myself at 5:30, and I naturally will take the name of Ernest. Gwendolen would wish it. We can't both be christened Ernest. It's absurd. Besides, I have a perfect right to be christened if I like. There is no evidence at all that I ever have been christened by anybody. I should think it extremely probable I never was, and so does Dr. Chasuble. It is entirely different in your case. You have been christened already.

Algernon: Yes, but I have not been christened for years.

Jack: Yes, but you have been christened. That is the important thing.

Algernon: Quite so. So I know my constitution can stand it. If you are not quite sure about your ever having been christened, I must say I think it rather dangerous your venturing on it now. It might make you very unwell. You can hardly have forgotten that someone very closely connected with you was very nearly carried off this week in Paris by a severe chill.

Jack: Yes, but you said yourself that a severe chill was not hereditary.

Algernon: It usen't to be, I know — but I daresay it is now. Science is always making wonderful improvements in things.

Jack (picking up the muffin dish): Oh, that is nonsense; you are always talking nonsense.

Algernon: Jack, you are at the muffins again! I wish you wouldn't. There are only two left. (*Takes them.*) I told you I was particularly fond of muffins.

Jack: But I hate tea cake.

Algernon: Why on earth then do you allow tea cake to be served up for your guests? What ideas you have of hospitality!

Jack: Algernon! I have already told you to go. I don't want you here. Why don't you go!

Algernon: I haven't quite finished my tea yet! and there is still one muffin left.

(*Jack groans, and sinks into a chair. Algernon still continues eating.*)

ACT III

(*Scene: Morning room at the Manor House. Gwendolen and Cecily are at the window, looking out into the garden.*)

Gwendolen: The fact that they did not follow us at once into the house, as anyone else would have done, seems to me to show that they have some sense of shame left.

Cecily: They have been eating muffins. That looks like repentance.

Gwendolen (after a pause): They don't seem to notice us at all. Couldn't you cough?

Cecily: But I haven't got a cough.

Gwendolen: They're looking at us. What effrontery!

Cecily: They're approaching. That's very forward of them.

Gwendolen: Let us preserve a dignified silence.

Cecily: Certainly. It's the only thing to do now.

(*Enter Jack followed by Algernon. They whistle some dreadful popular air from a British opera.*)

Gwendolen: This dignified silence seems to produce an unpleasant effect.

Cecily: A most distasteful one.

Gwendolen: But we will not be the first to speak.

Cecily: Certainly not.

Gwendolen: Mr. Worthing, I have something very particular to ask you. Much depends on your reply.

Cecily: Gwendolen, your common sense is invaluable. Mr. Moncrieff, kindly answer me the following question. Why did you pretend to be my guardian's brother?

Algernon: In order that I might have an opportunity of meeting you.

Cecily (to Gwendolen): That certainly seems a satisfactory explanation, does it not?

Gwendolen: Yes, dear, if you can believe him.

Cecily: I don't. But that does not affect the wonderful beauty of his answer.

Gwendolen: True. In matters of grave importance, style, not sincerity is the vital thing. Mr. Worthing, what explanation can you offer to me for pretending to have a brother? Was it in order that you might have an opportunity of coming up to town to see me as often as possible?

Jack: Can you doubt it, Miss Fairfax?

Gwendolen: I have the gravest doubts upon the subject. But I intend to crush them. This is not the moment for German skepticism. (*Moving to Cecily.*) Their explanations appear to be quite satisfactory, especially Mr. Worthing's. That seems to me to have the stamp of truth upon it.

Cecily: I am more than content with what Mr. Moncrieff said. His voice alone inspires one with absolute credulity.

Gwendolen: Then you think we should forgive them?

Cecily: Yes. I mean no.

Gwendolen: True! I had forgotten. There are principles at stake that one cannot surrender. Which of us should tell them? The task is not a pleasant one.

Cecily: Could we not both speak at the same time?

Gwendolen: An excellent idea! I nearly always speak at the same time as other people. Will you take the time from me?

Cecily: Certainly.

(*Gwendolen beats time with uplifted finger.*)

Gwendolen and Cecily (speaking together): Your Christian names are still an insuperable barrier. That is all!

Jack and Algernon (speaking together): Our Christian names! Is that all? But we are going to be christened this afternoon.

Gwendolen (to Jack): For my sake you are prepared to do this terrible thing?

Jack: I am!

Cecily (to Algernon): To please me you are ready to face this fearful ordeal?

Algernon: I am!

Gwendolen: How absurd to talk of the equality of the sexes! Where questions of self-sacrifice are concerned, men are infinitely beyond us.

Jack: We are! (*Clasps hands with Algernon.*)

Cecily: They have moments of physical courage of which we women know absolutely nothing.

Gwendolen (to Jack): Darling!

Algernon (to Cecily): Darling!

(*They fall into each other's arms.*)

(*Enter Merriman. When he enters he coughs loudly, seeing the situation.*)

Merriman: Ahem! Ahem! Lady Bracknell!

Jack: Good heavens!

(*Enter Lady Bracknell. The couples separate, in alarm. Exit Merriman.*)

Lady Bracknell: Gwendolen! What does this mean?

Gwendolen: Merely that I am engaged to be married to Mr. Worthing, Mama.

Lady Bracknell: Come here. Sit down. Sit down immediately. Hesitation of any kind is a sign of mental decay in the young, of physical weakness in the old. (*Turns to Jack.*) Apprised, sir, of my daughter's sudden flight by her trusty maid, whose confidence I purchased by means of a small coin, I followed her at once by a luggage train. Her unhappy father is, I am glad to say, under the impression that she is attending a more than usually lengthy lecture by the University Extension Scheme on the influence of a permanent income on thought. I do not propose to undeceive him. Indeed I have never undeceived him on any question. I would consider it wrong. But of course, you will clearly understand that all communication between yourself and my daughter must cease immediately from this moment. On this point, as indeed on all points, I am firm.

Jack: I am engaged to be married to Gwendolen, Lady Bracknell!

Lady Bracknell: You are nothing of the kind, sir. And now, as regards Algernon! — Algernon!

Algernon: Yes, Aunt Augusta.

Lady Bracknell: May I ask if it is in this house that your invalid friend Mr. Bunbury resides?

Algernon (stammering): Oh! No! Bunbury doesn't live here. Bunbury is somewhere else at present. In fact, Bunbury is dead.

Lady Bracknell: Dead! When did Mr. Bunbury die? His death must have been extremely sudden.

Algernon (airily): Oh! I killed Bunbury this afternoon. I mean poor Bunbury died this afternoon.

Lady Bracknell: What did he die of?

Algernon: Bunbury? Oh, he was quite exploded.

Lady Bracknell: Exploded! Was he the victim of a revolutionary outrage? I was not aware that Mr. Bunbury was interested in social legislation. If so, he is well punished for his morbidity.

Algernon: My dear Aunt Augusta, I mean he was found out! The doctors found out that Bunbury could not live, that is what I mean — so Bunbury died.

Lady Bracknell: He seems to have had great confidence in the opinion of his physicians. I am glad, however, that he made up his mind at the last to some definite course of action, and acted under proper medical advice. And now that we have finally got rid of this Mr. Bunbury, may I ask, Mr. Worthing, who is that young person whose hand my nephew Algernon is now holding in what seems to me a peculiarly unnecessary manner?

Jack: That lady is Miss Cecily Cardew, my ward.

(*Lady Bracknell bows coldly to Cecily.*)

Algernon: I am engaged to be married to Cecily, Aunt Augusta.

Lady Bracknell: I beg your pardon?

Cecily: Mr. Moncrieff and I are engaged to be married, Lady Bracknell.

Lady Bracknell (with a shiver, crossing to the sofa and sitting down): I do not know whether there is anything peculiarly exciting in the air of this particular part of Hertfordshire, but the number of engagements that go on seems to me considerably above the proper average that statistics have laid down for our guidance. I think some preliminary inquiry on my part would not be out of place. Mr. Worthing, is Miss Cardew at all connected with any of the larger railway stations in London? I merely desire information. Until yesterday I had no idea that there were any families or persons whose origin was a Terminus.

(*Jack looks perfectly furious, but restrains himself.*)

Jack (in a clear, cold voice): Miss Cardew is the granddaughter of the late Mr. Thomas Cardew of 149, Belgrave Square, S.W.; Gervase Park, Dorking, Surrey; and the Sporran, Fifeshire, N.B.

Lady Bracknell: That sounds not unsatisfactory. Three addresses always inspire confidence, even in tradesmen. But what proof have I of their authenticity?

Jack: I have carefully preserved the Court Guides of the period. They are open to your inspection, Lady Bracknell.

Lady Bracknell (grimly): I have known strange errors in that publication.

Jack: Miss Cardew's family solicitors are Messrs. Markby, Markby, and Markby.

Lady Bracknell: Markby, Markby, and Markby? A firm of the very highest position in their profession. Indeed I am told that one of the

Mr. Markbys is occasionally to be seen at dinner parties. So far I am satisfied.

Jack (very irritably): How extremely kind of you, Lady Bracknell! I have also in my possession, you will be pleased to hear, certificates of Miss Cardew's birth, baptism, whooping cough, registration, vaccination, confirmation, and the measles; both the German and the English variety.

Lady Bracknell: Ah! A life crowded with incident I see; though perhaps somewhat too exciting for a young girl. I am not myself in favor of premature experiences. (*Rises, looks at her watch.*) Gwendolen! the time approaches for our departure. We have not a moment to lose. As a matter of form, Mr. Worthing, I had better ask you if Miss Cardew has any little fortune?

Jack: Oh! about a hundred and thirty thousand pounds in the Funds. That is all. Good-bye, Lady Bracknell. So pleased to have seen you.

Lady Bracknell (sitting down again): A moment, Mr. Worthing. A hundred and thirty thousand pounds! And in the Funds! Miss Cardew seems to me a most attractive young lady, now that I look at her. Few girls of the present day have any really solid qualities, any of the qualities that last, and improve with time. We live, I regret to say, in an age of surfaces. (*To Cecily.*) Come over here, dear. (*Cecily goes across.*) Pretty child! your dress is sadly simple, and your hair seems almost as Nature might have left it. But we can soon alter all that. A thoroughly experienced French maid produces a really marvelous result in a very brief space of time: I remember recommending one to young Lady Lancing, and after three months her own husband did not know her.

Jack (aside): And after six months nobody knew her.

Lady Bracknell (glares at Jack for a few moments. Then bends, with a practiced smile, to Cecily): Kindly turn round, sweet child. (*Cecily turns completely round.*) No, the side view is what I want. (*Cecily presents her profile.*) Yes, quite as I expected. There are distinct social possibilities in your profile. The two weak points in our age are its want of principle and its want of profile. The chin a little higher, dear. Style largely depends on the way the chin is worn. They are worn very high, just at present. Algernon!

Algernon: Yes, Aunt Augusta!

Lady Bracknell: There are distinct social possibilities in Miss Cardew's profile.

Algernon: Cecily is the sweetest, dearest, prettiest girl in the whole world. And I don't care twopence about social possibilities.

Lady Bracknell: Never speak disrespectfully of Society, Algernon. Only people who can't get into it do that. (*To Cecily.*) Dear child, of course you know that Algernon has nothing but his debts to depend upon. But I do not approve of mercenary marriages. When I married Lord Bracknell I had no fortune of any kind. But I never dreamed for a moment of allowing that to stand in my way. Well, I suppose I must give my consent.

Algernon: Thank you, Aunt Augusta.

Lady Bracknell: Cecily, you may kiss me!

Cecily (kisses her): Thank you, Lady Bracknell.

Lady Bracknell: You may also address me as Aunt Augusta for the future.

Cecily: Thank you, Aunt Augusta.

Lady Bracknell: The marriage, I think, had better take place quite soon.

Algernon: Thank you, Aunt Augusta.

Cecily: Thank you, Aunt Augusta.

Lady Bracknell: To speak frankly, I am not in favor of long engagements. They give people the opportunity of finding out each other's character before marriage, which I think is never advisable.

Jack: I beg your pardon for interrupting you, Lady Bracknell, but this engagement is quite out of the question. I am Miss Cardew's guardian, and she cannot marry without my consent until she comes of age. That consent I absolutely decline to give.

Lady Bracknell: Upon what grounds may I ask? Algernon is an extremely, I may almost say an ostentatiously, eligible young man. He has nothing, but he looks everything. What more can one desire?

Jack: It pains me very much to have to speak frankly to you, Lady Bracknell, about your nephew, but the fact is that I do not approve at all of his moral character. I suspect him of being untruthful.

(Algernon and Cecily look at him in indignant amazement.)

Lady Bracknell: Untruthful! My nephew Algernon? Impossible! He is an Oxonian.°

Jack: I fear there can be no possible doubt about the matter. This afternoon, during my temporary absence in London on an important question of romance, he obtained admission to my house by means of the false pretense of being my brother. Under an assumed name he drank, I've just been informed by my butler, an entire pint bottle of my Perrier-Jouêt, Brut, '89; a wine I was specially reserving for myself. Continuing his disgraceful deception, he succeeded in the course of the afternoon in alienating the affections of my only ward. He subsequently stayed to tea, and devoured every single muffin. And what makes his conduct all the more heartless is, that he was perfectly well aware from the first that I have no brother, that I never had a brother, and that I don't intend to have a brother, not even of any kind. I distinctly told him so myself yesterday afternoon.

Lady Bracknell: Ahem! Mr. Worthing, after careful consideration I have decided entirely to overlook my nephew's conduct to you.

Jack: That is very generous of you, Lady Bracknell. My own decision, however, is unalterable. I decline to give my consent.

Lady Bracknell (to Cecily): Come here, sweet child. *(Cecily goes over.)* How old are you, dear?

Cecily: Well, I am really only eighteen, but I always admit to twenty when I go to evening parties.

Oxonian: Educated at Oxford University.

Lady Bracknell: You are perfectly right in making some slight alteration. Indeed, no woman should ever be quite accurate about her age. It looks so calculating — (*In a meditative manner.*) Eighteen but admitting to twenty at evening parties. Well, it will not be very long before you are of age and free from the restraints of tutelage. So I don't think your guardian's consent is, after all, a matter of any importance.

Jack: Pray excuse me, Lady Bracknell, for interrupting you again, but it is only fair to tell you that according to the terms of her grandfather's will Miss Cardew does not come legally of age till she is thirty-five.

Lady Bracknell: That does not seem to me to be a grave objection. Thirty-five is a very attractive age. London society is full of women of the very highest birth who have, of their own free choice, remained thirty-five for years. Lady Dumbleton is an instance in point. To my own knowledge she has been thirty-five ever since she arrived at the age of forty, which was many years ago now. I see no reason why our dear Cecily should not be even still more attractive at the age you mention than she is at present. There will be a large accumulation of property.

Cecily: Algy, could you wait for me till I was thirty-five?

Algernon: Of course I could, Cecily. You know I could.

Cecily: Yes, I felt it instinctively, but I couldn't wait all that time. I hate waiting even five minutes for anybody. It always makes me rather cross. I am not punctual myself, I know, but I do like punctuality in others, and waiting, even to be married, is quite out of the question.

Algernon: Then what is to be done, Cecily?

Cecily: I don't know, Mr. Moncrieff.

Lady Bracknell: My dear Mr. Worthing, as Miss Cardew states positively that she cannot wait till she is thirty-five — a remark which I am bound to say seems to me to show a somewhat impatient nature — I would beg of you to reconsider your decision.

Jack: But my dear Lady Bracknell, the matter is entirely in your own hands. The moment you consent to my marriage with Gwendolen, I will most gladly allow your nephew to form an alliance with my ward.

Lady Bracknell (rising and drawing herself up): You must be quite aware that what you propose is out of the question.

Jack: Then a passionate celibacy is all that any of us can look forward to.

Lady Bracknell: That is not the destiny I propose for Gwendolen. Algernon, of course, can choose for himself. (*Pulls out her watch.*) Come, dear; (*Gwendolen rises*) we have already missed five, if not six, trains. To miss any more might expose us to comment on the platform.

(*Enter Dr. Chasuble.*)

Chasuble: Everything is quite ready for the christenings.

Lady Bracknell: The christenings, sir! Is not that somewhat premature?

Chasuble (looking rather puzzled, and pointing to Jack and Algernon): Both these gentlemen have expressed a desire for immediate baptism.

Lady Bracknell: At their age? The idea is grotesque and irreligious! Algernon, I forbid you to be baptized. I will not hear of such excesses. Lord

Bracknell would be highly displeased if he learned that that was the way in which you wasted your time and money.

Chasuble: Am I to understand then that there are to be no christenings at all this afternoon?

Jack: I don't think that, as things are now, it would be of much practical value to either of us, Dr. Chasuble.

Chasuble: I am grieved to hear such sentiments from you, Mr. Worthing. They savor of the heretical views of the Anabaptists,° views that I have completely refuted in four of my unpublished sermons. However, as your present mood seems to be one peculiarly secular, I will return to the church at once. Indeed, I have just been informed by the pew opener that for the last hour and a half Miss Prism has been waiting for me in the vestry.

Lady Bracknell (starting): Miss Prism! Did I hear you mention a Miss Prism?

Chasuble: Yes, Lady Bracknell. I am on my way to join her.

Lady Bracknell: Pray allow me to detain you for a moment. This matter may prove to be one of vital importance to Lord Bracknell and myself. Is this Miss Prism a female of repellent aspect, remotely connected with education?

Chasuble (somewhat indignantly): She is the most cultivated of ladies, and the very picture of respectability.

Lady Bracknell: It is obviously the same person. May I ask what position she holds in your household?

Chasuble (severely): I am a celibate, madam.

Jack (interposing): Miss Prism, Lady Bracknell, has been for the last three years Miss Cardew's esteemed governess and valued companion.

Lady Bracknell: In spite of what I hear of her, I must see her at once. Let her be sent for.

Chasuble (looking off): She approaches; she is nigh.

(*Enter Miss Prism hurriedly.*)

Miss Prism: I was told you expected me in the vestry, dear Canon. I have been waiting for you there for an hour and three-quarters.

(*Catches sight of Lady Bracknell who has fixed her with a stony glare. Miss Prism grows pale and quails. She looks anxiously round as if desirous to escape.*)

Lady Bracknell (in a severe, judicial voice): Prism! (*Miss Prism bows her head in shame.*) Come here, Prism! (*Miss Prism approaches in a humble manner.*) Prism! Where is that baby? (*General consternation. The Canon starts back in horror. Algernon and Jack pretend to be anxious to*

Anabaptists: A religious sect founded in the sixteenth century and advocating adult baptism and church membership for adults only.

shield Cecily and Gwendolen from hearing the details of a terrible public scandal.) Twenty-eight years ago, Prism, you left Lord Bracknell's house, Number 104, Upper Grosvenor Street, in charge of a perambulator that contained a baby, of the male sex. You never returned. A few weeks later, through the elaborate investigations of the Metropolitan police, the perambulator was discovered at midnight, standing by itself in a remote corner of Bayswater. It contained the manuscript of a three-volume novel of more than usually revolting sentimentality. (*Miss Prism starts in involuntary indignation.*) But the baby was not there! (*Everyone looks at Miss Prism.*) Prism! Where is that baby?   (*A pause.*)

Miss Prism: Lady Bracknell, I admit with shame that I do not know. I only wish I did. The plain facts of the case are these. On the morning of the day you mention, a day that is forever branded on my memory, I prepared as usual to take the baby out in its perambulator. I had also with me a somewhat old, but capacious handbag in which I had intended to place the manuscript of a work of fiction that I had written during my few unoccupied hours. In a moment of mental abstraction, for which I never can forgive myself, I deposited the manuscript in the bassinette, and placed the baby in the handbag.

Jack (who has been listening attentively): But where did you deposit the handbag?

Miss Prism: Do not ask me, Mr. Worthing.

Jack: Miss Prism, this is a matter of no small importance to me. I insist on knowing where you deposited the handbag that contained that infant.

Miss Prism: I left it in the cloakroom of one of the larger railway stations in London.

Jack: What railway station?

Miss Prism (quite crushed): Victoria. The Brighton line.   (*Sinks into a chair.*)

Jack: I must retire to my room for a moment. Gwendolen, wait here for me.

Gwendolen: If you are not too long, I will wait here for you all my life.

(*Exit Jack in great excitement.*)

Chasuble: What do you think this means, Lady Bracknell?

Lady Bracknell: I dare not even suspect, Dr. Chasuble. I need hardly tell you that in families of high position strange coincidences are not supposed to occur. They are hardly considered the thing.

(*Noises heard overhead as if someone was throwing trunks about. Everyone looks up.*)

Cecily: Uncle Jack seems strangely agitated.

Chasuble: Your guardian has a very emotional nature.

Lady Bracknell: This noise is extremely unpleasant. It sounds as if he was having an argument. I dislike arguments of any kind. They are always vulgar, and often convincing.

Chasuble (looking up): It has stopped now.

(*The noise is redoubled.*)

Lady Bracknell: I wish he would arrive at some conclusion.

Gwendolen: This suspense is terrible. I hope it will last.

(*Enter Jack with a handbag of black leather in his hand.*)

Jack (rushing over to Miss Prism): Is this the handbag, Miss Prism? Examine it carefully before you speak. The happiness of more than one life depends on your answer.

Miss Prism (calmly): It seems to be mine. Yes, here is the injury it received through the upsetting of a Gower Street omnibus in younger and happier days. Here is the stain on the lining caused by the explosion of a temperance beverage, an incident that occurred at Leamington. And here, on the lock, are my initials. I had forgotten that in an extravagant mood I had had them placed there. The bag is undoubtedly mine. I am delighted to have it so unexpectedly restored to me. It has been a great inconvenience being without it all these years.

Jack (in a pathetic voice): Miss Prism, more is restored to you than this handbag. I was the baby you placed in it.

Miss Prism (amazed): You?

Jack (embracing her): Yes — mother!

Miss Prism (recoiling in indignant astonishment): Mr. Worthing! I am unmarried!

Jack: Unmarried! I do not deny that is a serious blow. But after all, who has the right to cast a stone against one who has suffered? Cannot repentance wipe out an act of folly? Why should there be one law for men, and another for women? Mother, I forgive you. (*Tries to embrace her again.*)

Miss Prism (still more indignant): Mr. Worthing, there is some error. (*Pointing to Lady Bracknell.*) There is the lady who can tell you who you really are.

Jack (after a pause): Lady Bracknell, I hate to seem inquisitive, but would you kindly inform me who I am?

Lady Bracknell: I am afraid that the news I have to give you will not altogether please you. You are the son of my poor sister, Mrs. Moncrieff, and consequently Algernon's elder brother.

Jack: Algy's elder brother! Then I have a brother after all. I knew I had a brother! I always said I had a brother! Cecily, — how could you have ever doubted that I had a brother. (*Seizes hold of Algernon.*) Dr. Chasuble, my unfortunate brother. Miss Prism, my unfortunate brother. Gwendolen, my unfortunate brother. Algy, you young scoundrel, you will have to treat me with more respect in the future. You have never behaved to me like a brother in all your life.

Algernon: Well, not till today, old boy, I admit. I did my best, however, though I was out of practice. (*Shakes hands.*)

Gwendolen (to Jack): My own! But what own are you? What is your Christian name, now that you have become someone else?

Jack: Good heavens! — I had quite forgotten that point. Your decision on the subject of my name is irrevocable, I suppose?

Gwendolen: I never change, except in my affections.

Cecily: What a noble nature you have, Gwendolen!

Jack: Then the question had better be cleared up at once. Aunt Augusta, a moment. At the time when Miss Prism left me in the handbag, had I been christened already?

Lady Bracknell: Every luxury that money could buy, including christening, had been lavished upon you by your fond and doting parents.

Jack: Then I was christened! That is settled. Now, what name was I given? Let me know the worst.

Lady Bracknell: Being the eldest son you were naturally christened after your father.

Jack (irritably): Yes, but what was my father's Christian name?

Lady Bracknell (meditatively): I cannot at the present moment recall what the General's Christian name was. But I have no doubt he had one. He was eccentric, I admit. But only in later years. And that was the result of the Indian climate, and marriage, and indigestion, and other things of that kind.

Jack: Algy! Can't you recollect what our father's Christian name was?

Algernon: My dear boy, we were never even on speaking terms. He died before I was a year old.

Jack: His name would appear in the Army Lists of the period, I suppose, Aunt Augusta?

Lady Bracknell: The General was essentially a man of peace, except in his domestic life. But I have no doubt his name would appear in any military directory.

Jack: The Army Lists of the last forty years are here. These delightful records should have been my constant study. (*Rushes to bookcase and tears the books out.*) M. Generals — Mallam, Maxbohm, Magley, what ghastly names they have — Markby, Migsby, Mobbs, Moncrieff! Lieutenant 1840, Captain, Lieutenant-Colonel, Colonel, General 1869, Christian names, Ernest John. (*Puts book very quietly down and speaks quite calmly.*) I always told you, Gwendolen, my name was Ernest, didn't I? Well, it is Ernest after all. I mean it naturally is Ernest.

Lady Bracknell: Yes, I remember now that the General was called Ernest. I knew I had some particular reason for disliking the name.

Gwendolen: Ernest! My own Ernest! I felt from the first that you could have no other name!

Jack: Gwendolen, it is a terrible thing for a man to find out suddenly that all his life he has been speaking nothing but the truth. Can you forgive me?

Gwendolen: I can. For I feel that you are sure to change.

Jack: My own one!

Chasuble (to Miss Prism): Laetitia! (*Embraces her.*)

Miss Prism (enthusiastically): Frederick! At last!

Algernon: Cecily! (*Embraces her.*) At last!
Jack: Gwendolen! (*Embraces her.*) At last!
Lady Bracknell: My nephew, you seem to be displaying signs of triviality.
Jack: On the contrary, Aunt Augusta, I've now realized for the first time in my life the vital Importance of Being Earnest.

CONSIDERATIONS FOR CRITICAL THINKING AND WRITING

1. FIRST RESPONSE. Discuss the pun on the word *earnest*. Are these characters earnest about anything? If so, what?

2. One simplistic definition of a dramatic comedy is that it ends with the main characters getting married. How does Wilde play with that convention? What attitudes toward marriage are expressed in *The Importance of Being Earnest*, and which ones are we meant to take seriously? What sense do you make of the speed at which characters fall in and out of love?

3. Early in the play Jack suggest that an aunt's height is a characteristic she "may be allowed to decide for herself." Height is not a characteristic we can decide for ourselves. What does this play suggest about an individual's ability to make any decisions about identity?

4. What is "Bunburying" and how does it help frame the play's themes?

5. Algernon and Jack make a number of pronouncements about modern literature. List those pronouncements: Do they apply to this play as well? Are we meant to take them at face value?

6. What does the play suggest about the relationship between a romantic couple and society more generally? Is a romantic relationship entirely a private affair or does it depend largely on a social context?

7. What role does social class play in *The Importance of Being Earnest*? You might consider the role of the servants (Lane, Moulton, and Merriman) as well as Lady Bracknell's questions about Jack's suitability as a husband to Gwendolen.

8. The title contains a pun that is sustained throughout the play. List some other instances of puns or wordplay: What is their relationship to the play's broader concerns?

9. As it continues, the play pits men against women. How are the sexes depicted? And how would you describe the relationship between them?

10. Jack and Algernon are both liars and scoundrels. Do you feel differently about each of them? If so, why?

CONNECTION TO ANOTHER SELECTION

1. Compare the depiction of marriage and gender roles in this play and in Henrik Ibsen's *A Doll's House* (p. 864).

Strategies for Reading and Writing

Credits, clockwise from top left: Everett Collection/Newscom.; Beth Gwinn/Michael Ochs Archives/Getty Images; Anthony Barboza/Getty Images; Eamonn McCabe/Getty Images.

30

Critical Strategies
for Reading

Great literature is simply language
charged with meaning to the utmost
possible degree.
— EZRA POUND

Courtesy of George
Eastman House,
International Museum
of Photography and
Film; Digital positive
from the original
gelatin silver negative
in the George Eastman
Museum's collection.

The answers you get from literature
depend upon the questions you pose.
— MARGARET ATWOOD

© Kathy deWitt/Alamy.

CRITICAL THINKING

Maybe this has happened to you: the assignment is to write an analysis of some aspect of a work — let's say, Nathaniel Hawthorne's *The Scarlet Letter* — that interests you and takes into account critical sources that comment on and interpret the work. You cheerfully begin research through your library's website but quickly find yourself bewildered by several seemingly unrelated articles. The first traces the thematic significance of images of light and darkness in the novel; the second makes a case for Hester Prynne as a liberated woman; the third argues that Arthur Dimmesdale's guilt is a projection of Hawthorne's own emotions; and the fourth analyzes the introduction, "The Custom-House," as an attack on bourgeois values. These disparate treatments may seem random and capricious — a confirmation of your worst suspicions that interpretations of literature are hit-or-miss excursions into areas that you know little about or didn't know even existed.

But if you understand that the four articles are written from four different perspectives — formalist, feminist, psychological, and Marxist — and that the purpose of each is to enhance your understanding of the novel by discussing a particular element of it, then you can see that the articles' varying strategies represent potentially interesting ways of opening up the text that might otherwise never have occurred to you. There are many ways to approach a text, and a useful first step is to develop a sense of direction, an understanding of how a perspective — your own or a critic's — shapes a discussion of a text.

This chapter offers an introduction to critical approaches to literature by outlining a variety of strategies for reading fiction, poetry, or drama. These strategies include approaches that have long been practiced by readers who have used, for example, the insights gleaned from biography and history to illuminate literary works as well as more recent approaches, such as those used by critics who rely on theories related to specialized contextual categories like gender, reader-response, and deconstruction. Each of these perspectives is sensitive to point of view, symbol, tone, irony, and other literary elements that you have been studying, but each also casts those elements in a special light. The formalist approach emphasizes how the elements within a work achieve their effects, whereas biographical and psychological approaches lead outward from the work to consider the author's life and other writings. Even broader approaches, such as historical and cultural perspectives, connect the work to historic and social phenomena that frame literary production. Mythological readings represent the broadest approach because they link an individual work to narrative structures and tropes that have repeated across multiple cultures and time periods.

Any given strategy raises its own types of questions and issues while seeking particular kinds of evidence to illustrate its concerns. An awareness of the assumptions and methods that inform an approach can help you to understand better the validity and value of a given critic's strategy for making sense of a work. More important, such an understanding can widen and deepen the responses of your own reading.

The critical thinking that goes into understanding a professional critic's approach to a work is not foreign to you because you have already used essentially the same kind of thinking to understand the work itself. You have developed skills to produce a literary ***analysis*** that describes how a character, symbol, or rhyme scheme supports a theme. These same skills are also useful for reading literary criticism because they allow you to keep track of how the parts of a critical approach create a particular reading of a literary work. When you analyze a story, poem, or play by closely examining how its various elements relate to the whole, your ***interpretation*** — your articulation of what the work means to you as supported by an analysis of its elements — necessarily involves choosing what you focus on in the work. The same is true of professional critics.

The following overview of critical strategies for reading is neither exhaustive in the types of critical approaches covered nor complete in its presentation of the complexities inherent in them, but it should help you to develop an appreciation of the intriguing possibilities that attend literary interpretation. The emphasis in this chapter is on ways of thinking about literature rather than on daunting lists of terms, names, and movements. Although a working knowledge of critical schools may be valuable and necessary for a fully informed use of a given critical approach, the aim here is more modest and practical. This chapter is no substitute for the shelves of literary criticism that can be found in your library or for the databases that can be accessed on its website, but it does suggest how different perspectives produce different readings of texts.

The summaries of critical approaches that follow are descriptive, not evaluative. Each approach has its advantages and limitations. In practice, many critical approaches overlap and complement each other, but those matters are best left to further study. Like literary artists, critics have their personal values, tastes, and styles. The appropriateness of a specific critical approach will depend, at least in part, on the nature of the literary work under discussion as well as on your own sensibilities and experience. However, any approach, if it is to enhance understanding, requires sensitivity, tact, and an awareness of the various literary elements of the text, including, of course, its use of language.

Successful critical approaches avoid eccentric decodings that reveal so-called hidden meanings that are not only hidden but totally absent from the text. Literary criticism attempts, like any valid hypothesis, to account for phenomena within a text without distorting or misrepresenting what it describes.

FORMALIST STRATEGIES

Formalist critics focus on the formal elements of a work — its language, structure, tone, and the conventions of its genre. The word *form* at the root of formalism is key: each work of literature is a unique object, but one that helps us to understand the form it has taken, or the way it was formed. A formalist reads literature as an independent work of art rather than as a reflection of the author's state of mind or as a representation of a moment in history. Historic influences on a work, an author's intentions, or anything else outside the work are generally not treated by formalists. (This is particularly true of the most famous modern formalists, known as the **New Critics**, who dominated American criticism from the 1940s through the 1960s.) Instead, formalists offer intense examinations of the relationship between form and meaning within a work, emphasizing the subtle complexity of how a work is arranged. This kind of close reading pays special attention to what are often described as *intrinsic* matters in a literary work, such as diction, irony, paradox, metaphor, and symbol, as well as larger elements, such as plot, characterization, and narrative technique. Formalists examine how these elements work together to give a coherent shape (or "unity") to a work while contributing to its meaning. The answers to the questions formalists raise about how the shape and effect of a work are related come from the work itself. Other kinds of information that go beyond the text — biography, history, politics, economics, and so on — are typically regarded by formalists as *extrinsic* matters, which are considerably less important than what goes on within the autonomous text.

For an example of a work in which the shape of the plot serves as the major organizing principle, let's examine Kate Chopin's "The Story of an Hour" (p. 15), a two-page short story that takes only a few minutes to read. A first reading probably results in surprise at the story's ending: a grieving wife "afflicted with a heart trouble" suddenly dies of a heart attack, not because she's learned that her kind and loving husband has been killed in a terrible train accident but because she discovers that he is alive, and thus still in her life. Clearly, we are witnessing an ironic situation since there is such a powerful incongruity between what is expected to happen and what actually happens. A likely formalist strategy for analyzing this story would be to raise questions about the ironic ending. Is this merely a trick ending, or is it a carefully wrought culmination of other elements in the story resulting in an interesting and challenging theme? Formalists value such complexities over simple surprise effects.

A second, closer reading indicates that Chopin's third-person narrator presents the story in a manner similar to Josephine's gentle attempts to break the news about Brently Mallard's death. The story is told in "veiled hints that [reveal] in half concealing." But unlike Josephine, who tries to protect her sister's fragile heart from stress, the narrator seeks to reveal Mrs. Mallard's complex heart. A formalist would look back over the story for signs of the ending in the imagery. Although Mrs. Mallard grieves immediately and unreservedly when she hears about the train disaster, she soon begins to feel a different emotion as she looks out the window at "the tops of trees . . . all aquiver with the new spring life." This symbolic evocation of renewal and rebirth — along with "the delicious breath of rain," the sounds of life in the street, and the birds singing — causes her to feel, in spite of her own efforts to repress her thoughts and emotions, "free, free, free!" She feels alive with a sense of possibility, with a "clear and exalted perception" that she "would live for herself" instead of for and through her husband.

It is ironic that this ecstatic "self-assertion" is interpreted by Josephine as grief, but the crowning irony for this "goddess of Victory" is the doctors' assumption that she dies of joy rather than of the shock of having to abandon her newly discovered self once she realizes her husband is still alive. In the course of an hour, Mrs. Mallard's life is irretrievably changed: her husband's assumed accidental death frees her, but the fact that he lives combined with all the expectations imposed on her by his continued life kill her. She does, indeed, die of a broken heart, but only Chopin's readers know the real ironic meaning of that explanation.

Although this brief discussion of some of the formal elements of Chopin's story does not describe all there is to say about how they produce an effect and create meaning, it does suggest the kinds of questions, issues, and evidence that a formalist strategy might raise in providing a close reading of the text itself.

BIOGRAPHICAL STRATEGIES

Knowledge of an author's life can help readers understand his or her work more fully. Events in a work might follow actual events in a writer's life just as characters might be based on people known by the author. Relevant facts about an author's life can make clearer the source of his or her convictions and how his or her own experiences inform the major concerns showcased in a given work. Biographical details might also help to fill in some of the context for the author's motivation for writing about a certain subject, or for writing about it a certain way. The aim of a biographical critic would not be to equate the author and a character in a story, or voice in a poem. The *biographer* might want to solidify such connections between author and creation, but the *critic* would use those connections to frame an interpretive response.

Some formalist critics — some New Critics, for example — argue that interpretation should be based exclusively on internal evidence rather than on any biographical information outside the work. They argue that it is not possible to determine an author's intention and that the work must stand by itself. Although this is a useful caveat for keeping the work in focus, a reader who finds biography relevant would argue that biography can at the very least serve to narrow the scope of possible interpretations.

However, it is also worth noting that biographical information can complicate a work. Chopin's "The Story of an Hour" presents a repressed wife's momentary discovery of what freedom from her husband might mean to her. She awakens to a new sense of herself when she learns of her husband's death, only to collapse of a heart attack when she sees that he is alive. Readers might be tempted to interpret this story as Chopin's fictionalized commentary about her own marriage because her husband died twelve years before she wrote the story and seven years before she began writing fiction seriously. Biographers seem to agree, however, that Chopin's marriage was evidently satisfying to her and that she was not oppressed by her husband and did not feel oppressed.

Moreover, consider this diary entry from only one month after Chopin wrote the story (quoted by Per Seyersted in *Kate Chopin: A Critical Biography*):

> If it were possible for my husband and my mother to come back to earth, I feel that I would unhesitatingly give up everything that has come into my life since they left it and join my existence again with theirs. To do that, I would have to forget the past ten years of my growth — my real growth. But I would take back a little wisdom with me; it would be the spirit of perfect acquiescence.

This passage raises provocative questions instead of resolving them. How does that "spirit of perfect acquiescence" relate to Mrs. Mallard's insistence that she "would live for herself"? Why would Chopin be willing to "forget the past ten years of . . . growth" given her protagonist's desire for "self-assertion"? Although these and other questions raised by the diary entry cannot be answered here, this kind of biographical perspective certainly adds to the possibilities of interpretation. Critics should always be cautious about assuming that a character is automatically a stand-in for the author. The narrator of a short story, speaker of a poem, or protagonist of a play might in fact be a character far removed from the author's sensibility, even a character that the author has created in order to critique that character's thoughts, words, or behavior. There might be a literary reason for having created that character, such as to engage in a debate with another character in order to advance a work's theme. Unless you are thoroughly familiar with an author's biography, we would caution against taking the biographical details you know as the defining factors in an interpretation. These details are better thought of as signposts than treasure maps.

Psychological Strategies

Given the enormous influence that Sigmund Freud's psychoanalytic theories have had on twentieth-century interpretations of human behavior, it is nearly inevitable that most people have some familiarity with his ideas concerning dreams, unconscious desires, and sexual repression, as well as his terms for different aspects of the psyche — the id, ego, and superego. Certainly an enormous number of twentieth-century European and American authors knew Freud's theories, and that awareness is evident in many literary works, even if authors did not agree with Freud or with the other theorists he influenced. But a critic using Freud's theories would not even necessarily need to know how much an author engaged with those theories: the works themselves can be used to illustrate or dispute the validity of Freud's theories. Psychological approaches to literature often draw on Freud's theories or other psychoanalytic theories to understand more fully the text, the writer, and the reader. Critics use such approaches to explore the motivations of characters and the symbolic meanings of events, while biographers speculate about a writer's own motivations — conscious or unconscious — in a literary work. Psychological approaches can also be used to describe and analyze a reader's responses to a text.

Although it is not feasible to explain psychoanalytic terms and concepts in so brief a space as this, it is possible to suggest the nature of a psychological approach. It is a strategy based heavily on the idea of the existence of a human unconscious — those impulses, desires, and feelings that a person is unaware of but that influence emotions and behavior.

Central to a number of psychoanalytic critical readings is Freud's concept of what he called the **Oedipus complex**, a term derived from Sophocles' tragedy *Oedipus the King* (p. 716). This complex is predicated on a boy's unconscious rivalry with his father for his mother's love and his desire to eliminate his father in order to take his father's place with his mother. The female version of the psychological conflict is known as the **Electra complex**, a term used to describe a daughter's unconscious rivalry with her mother for her father's affection. The name comes from a Greek legend about Electra, who avenged the death of her father, Agamemnon, by plotting the death of her mother. In *The Interpretation of Dreams*, Freud explains why *Oedipus the King* "moves a modern audience no less than it did the contemporary Greek one." What unites their powerful attraction to the play is an unconscious response:

> There must be something which makes a voice within us ready to recognize the compelling force of destiny in the *Oedipus*. . . . His destiny moves us only because it might have been ours — because the oracle laid the same curse upon us before our birth as upon him. It is the fate of all of us, perhaps, to direct our first sexual impulse towards our mother and our first hatred and our first murderous wish against our father. Our dreams convince us that this is so. King Oedipus, who slew his father Laios and married his mother Iokaste, merely shows us the fulfillment of our own childhood wishes . . . and we shrink back from him with the whole force of the repression by which those wishes have since that time been held down within us.

In this passage Freud interprets the unconscious motives of Sophocles in writing the play, Oedipus in acting within it, and the audience in responding to it. Although the Oedipus complex is, of course, not relevant to all psychological interpretations of literature, interpretations involving this complex do offer a useful example of how psychoanalytic critics might approach a text.

The situation in which Mrs. Mallard finds herself in Chopin's "The Story of an Hour" is not related to an Oedipus complex, but it is clear that news of her husband's death has released powerful unconscious desires for freedom that she had previously suppressed. As she grieved, "something" was "coming to her and she was waiting for it, fearfully." What comes to her is what she senses about the life outside her window; that's the stimulus, but the true source of what was to "possess her," which she strove to "beat . . . back with her [conscious] will," is her desperate desire for the autonomy and fulfillment she had been unable to admit did not exist in her marriage. A psychological approach to her story amounts to a case study in the destructive nature of self-repression. Moreover, the story might reflect Chopin's own views of her marriage despite her conscious statements about her loving husband, for to admit her true feelings to herself or to her public might not be possible.

One key motif to pay attention to if you are interested in psychological interpretations of literature is the presence of dreams or dream-imagery in literature. Although there has been a great deal of debate over the centuries about what dreams "mean" — ranging from prophecy, to random spasms of our brains, to the field of our unconscious desires — they are potent repositories of meaning in literary contexts. At the end of "The Love Song of J. Alfred Prufrock" (p. 654), T. S. Eliot's speaker concludes with surreal, dream-like, underwater imagery which will last "Till human voices wake us, and we drown." The juxtaposition of irrational images, whether or not framed as an actual dream, will alert the psychoanalytic critic to the possibility that we are witnessing the border between rational and irrational urges, or between the conscious and unconscious mind. Humans can't always articulate what they desire or fear; dreams can sometimes provide a key.

Historical Strategies

Historians sometimes use literature as a window onto the past because literature frequently provides the nuances of a historic period that cannot be readily perceived through other sources. Another way of approaching the relationship between literature and history, however, is to use history as a means of understanding a literary work more clearly. The approach assumes that the writing contemporary to an author is an important element of the history that helps to shape a work. There are many ways to talk about the historical and cultural dimensions of a work. Such readings treat a literary text as a document reflecting, producing, or being produced by the social conditions of its time, giving equal focus to the social milieu and the work itself. The general impulse to view literature through a historical lens provides context for meaning. There are more refined or more ideological versions of historical approaches, too: Marxist criticism, new historicist criticism, and cultural criticism.

A work of literature may transcend time to the extent that it addresses the concerns of readers over a span of decades or centuries, but it remains for the historical critic a part of the past in which it was composed, a past that can reveal more fully a work's language, ideas, and purposes. When using a historical approach, critics move beyond both the facts of an author's personal life and the text itself to the social and intellectual currents in which the author composed the work. They place the work in the context of its time, and sometimes they make connections with other literary or artistic works that may have influenced the author. The basic strategy of these critics is to illuminate the historical background in order to shed light on some aspect of the work itself.

To return to our recurrent example: the repression expressed in the lines on Mrs. Mallard's face is more distinctly seen if Chopin's "The Story of an Hour" is placed in the context of "the Woman Question" as it continued to develop in the 1890s. Mrs. Mallard's impulse toward "self-assertion" runs parallel with a growing women's movement away from the role of long-suffering and unfulfilled housewife. This desire was widely regarded by traditionalists as a form of dangerous selfishness that was considered as unnatural as it was immoral. It is no wonder that Chopin raises the question of whether Mrs. Mallard's sense of freedom owing to her husband's death isn't a selfish, "monstrous joy." Mrs. Mallard, however, dismisses this question as "trivial" in the face of her new perception of life, a dismissal that Chopin endorses by way of the story's ironic ending. This is not to conclude simply that Mrs. Mallard was representative of all American women at the time of its publication, but rather that her internal struggle connected to a broader social context, one which would have been more immediately apparent to Chopin's readers in 1894 than it is to readers in the twenty-first century. That is why a historical reconstruction of the limitations placed on married women helps to explain the pressures, tensions, and momentary release that Mrs. Mallard experiences.

Marxist Criticism

Marxist readings developed from the heightened interest in radical reform during the 1930s, when many critics sought to understand literature in terms of proletarian social and economic goals, based largely on the writings of Karl Marx. **Marxist critics** focus on the ideological content of a work — its explicit and implicit assumptions and values about matters such as culture, race, class, and power. Marxist studies typically aim at revealing and clarifying ideological issues and also correcting social injustices. Some Marxist critics have used literature to describe the competing socioeconomic interests that too often pit wealth and capitalist power against socialist morality and justice. They argue that criticism, like literature, is essentially political because it either challenges or supports economic inequality or oppression. Even if criticism attempts to ignore class conflicts, it is politicized, according to Marxists, because it accepts the status quo.

It is not surprising that Marxist critics pay more attention to the content and themes of literature than to its form. A Marxist reading of Chopin's "The Story of an Hour" might draw on evidence made available in a book by Charlotte Perkins Gilman titled *Women and Economics: A Study of the Economic Relation between Men and Women as a Factor in Social Evolution* (1898) published only a few years after Chopin's story. An examination of this study could help explain how some of the "repression" Mrs. Mallard experiences was generated by the socioeconomic structure contemporary to her and how Chopin challenges the validity of that structure by having Mrs. Mallard resist it with her very life. A Marxist reading would see the protagonist's conflict as not only an individual issue but part of a larger class struggle.

New Historicist Criticism

Since the 1960s a development in historical approaches to literature known as **new historicism** has emphasized the interaction between the historic context of a work and a modern reader's understanding and interpretation of the work. In contrast to many traditional historical frameworks for reading literature, however, new historicists attempt to describe the culture of a period by reading many different kinds of texts that earlier critics might have previously left for economists, sociologists, and anthropologists. New historicists attempt to read a period in all its dimensions, including political, economic, social, and aesthetic concerns. These considerations could be used to explain the pressures that destroy Mrs. Mallard. A new historicist might examine the story and the public attitudes toward women contemporary to "The Story of an Hour" as well as documents such as suffragist tracts and medical diagnoses to explore how the same forces — expectations about how women are supposed to feel, think, and behave — shape different kinds of texts and how these texts influence each other. A new historicist might, for example, scrutinize medical records for evidence of "nervousness" and "hysteria" as common diagnoses for women who led lives regarded as too independent by their contemporaries.

Without an awareness of just how selfish and self-destructive Mrs. Mallard's impulses would have been in the eyes of some of her contemporaries, readers in the twenty-first century might miss the pervasive pressures embedded not only in her marriage but in the social fabric surrounding her. Her death is made more understandable by such an awareness. The doctors who diagnose her as suffering from "the joy that kills" are not merely insensitive or stupid; they represent a contrasting set of assumptions and values that are as historic and real as Mrs. Mallard's yearnings.

New historicist criticism acknowledges more fully than traditional historical approaches the competing nature of readings of the past and thereby tends to offer new emphases and perspectives. New historicism reminds us that there is not only one historic context for "The Story of an Hour." Those doctors reveal additional dimensions of late-nineteenth-century social attitudes that warrant our attention, whether we agree with them or not. By emphasizing that historical perceptions are governed, at least in part, by our own concerns and preoccupations, new historicists sensitize us to the fact that the history on which we choose to focus is reconstructed by concerns that have come to the foreground in our own present moment. This reconstructed history affects our reading of texts.

Cultural Criticism

Cultural critics, like new historicists, focus on the historical contexts of a literary work, but they pay particular attention to popular manifestations of social, political, and economic contexts. Popular culture — mass-produced and consumed cultural artifacts, today ranging from advertising to popular fiction to television to rock music — and "high" culture are given equal emphasis. A cultural critic attempting to interpret Ralph Ellison's short story "King of the Bingo Game" might be less interested in the Great Depression as a global phenomenon than in the type of movie the protagonist watches before playing bingo. The critic might note that in 1934 Hollywood adopted a widespread set of guidelines that essentially amounted to censorship known as the "Hays Code." This code turned movies into escapist fantasies that upheld moral behavior: sex and violence were largely removed from the silver screen. The sexual desire the protagonist feels and the violence he experiences are thus in sharp contrast to the type of movie he is watching that day. Adding the "low" art of everyday life to "high" art opens up previously unexpected and unexplored areas of criticism. Cultural critics use widely eclectic strategies drawn from new historicism, psychology, gender studies, and deconstructionism (to name only a handful of approaches) to analyze not only literary texts but radio talk shows, comic strips, calendar art, commercials, travel guides, and baseball cards. Because all human activity falls within the ken of cultural criticism, nothing is too minor or major, obscure or pervasive, to escape the range of its analytic vision.

A cultural critic's approach to Chopin's "The Story of an Hour" might emphasize how the story reflects the potential dangers and horrors of train travel in the 1890s or it might examine how heart disease was often misdiagnosed by physicians or used as a metaphor in Mrs. Mallard's culture for a variety of emotional conditions. Each of these perspectives can serve to create a wider and more informed understanding of the story.

GENDER STRATEGIES

Gender critics explore how ideas about how traditionally masculine and feminine behavior can be regarded as socially constructed by particular cultures. According to some critics, sex is determined by simple biological and anatomical categories of male or female, and gender is determined by a culture's values. Thus, ideas about gender and what constitutes masculine and feminine behavior are created by cultural institutions and conditioning. A gender critic might, for example, focus on Chopin's characterization of an emotionally sensitive Mrs. Mallard and a rational, composed husband in "The Story of an Hour" as a manifestation of socially constructed gender identity in the 1890s. *Gender criticism* expands categories and definitions of what is masculine or feminine and tends to regard sexuality as more complex than merely masculine or feminine, heterosexual or homosexual. Gender criticism, therefore, has come to include LGBTQ+ criticism as well as feminist criticism.

Feminist Criticism

Like Marxist critics, *feminist critics* reading "The Story of an Hour" would also be interested in a text like Charlotte Perkins Gilman's *Women and Economics: A Study of the Economic Relation between Men and Women as a Factor in Social Evolution* (1898) because they seek to correct or supplement what they regard as a predominantly male-dominated critical perspective with a feminist consciousness. Like other forms of sociological criticism, feminist criticism places literature in a social context, and, like those of Marxist criticism, its analyses often have sociopolitical purposes — explaining, for example, how images of women in literature reflect the patriarchal social forces that have impeded women's efforts to achieve full equality with men. Consequently, feminist critics' approach to literature employs a broad range of disciplines, including history, sociology, psychology, and linguistics, to provide a perspective sensitive to feminist issues.

A feminist approach to Chopin's "The Story of an Hour" might explore the psychological stress created by the expectations that marriage imposes on Mrs. Mallard, expectations that literally and figuratively break her heart. Given that her husband is kind and loving, the issue is not her being married to Brently but her being married at all. Chopin presents marriage as an institution that creates in both men and women the assumed "right to impose a private will upon a fellow-creature." That "right," however, might be interpreted, especially from a feminist perspective, as primarily imposed on women by men. A feminist critic might note, for instance, that the protagonist is introduced as "Mrs. Mallard" (we learn that her first name is Louise only later); she is defined by her marital status and her husband's name, a name whose origin from the Old French is related to the word *masle*, which means "male." The appropriateness of her name points up the fact that her emotions and the cause of her death are interpreted in male terms by the doctors. The value of a feminist perspective on this work can be readily discerned if a reader imagines Mrs. Mallard's story being told from the point of view of one of the doctors who diagnoses the cause of her death as a weak heart rather than as a fierce struggle.

LGBTQ+ Criticism

LGBTQ+ critics focus on a variety of issues, including how individuals from nonnormative or nonbinary gender and sexual identifications are represented in literature, how they read literature, and whether sexuality and gender are culturally constructed or innate. The emergence of "queer theory" in the 1990s served to destabilize the dominant ideology that normalizes heterosexuality and considers other sexualities deviant. These critics have produced new readings of works by established canonical writers in which underlying homosexual concerns, desires, motifs, or motivations are lifted out and examined as revealing components of these texts. A reading of "The Story of an Hour" for example, might consider whether Mrs. Mallard's ecstatic feeling of relief — produced by the belief that her marriage is over due to the presumed death of her husband — isn't also a rejection of her heterosexual identity. Perhaps her glimpse of future freedom, evoked by feminine images of a newly discovered nature "all aquiver with the new spring life," embraces a repressed new sexual identity that "was too subtle and elusive to name" but that was "approaching to possess her" no matter how much she "was striving to beat it back with her will."

A queer theorist such as Eve Kosofsky Sedgwick would interrogate any simplistic assumptions about Mrs. Mallard's sexuality. A superficial reading of "The Story of an Hour" might point to the fact that Mrs. Mallard initially displays her grief by embracing a woman, her sister Josephine: "She wept at once, with sudden, wild abandonment, in her sister's arms." One might be tempted to read into this brief gesture a lifetime of latent homosexual longing, especially given the term "wild abandonment." But such a reading is potentially reductive, and assumes that sexual desire must be placed in one of two categories (homosexual or heterosexual). Upon closer examination, the evidence for Mrs. Mallard's lesbian tendencies is thin given the fact that she is weeping here rather than experiencing sexual pleasure. Contemporary queer theorists tend to see sexuality and sexual desire as fluid, and sometimes difficult to label. A more nuanced queer reading might look at Mrs. Mallard's autoerotic identity. Focusing on her body, such a critic would concentrate on the scenes when Mrs. Mallard is alone. She anticipates "something coming to her . . . too subtle and elusive to name . . . creeping out of the sky." On the surface this feeling is merely relief, but a LGBTQ+ critic might focus on her body's reaction to it: "her bosom rose and fell tumultuously . . . a little whispered word escaped her slightly parted lips. . . . Her pulses beat fast, and the coursing blood warmed and relaxed every inch of her body." These descriptions sound unabashedly sexual, and Mrs. Mallard seems to gradually embrace the idea that she can achieve bodily ecstasy when alone: following the quotations above, she throws open her arms, comments on the freedom of her body (as well as her soul), and locks her bedroom door. Her sister desperately calls through the keyhole, alarmed by the clearly transgressive behavior going on inside: "open the door — you will make yourself ill. What are you doing, Louise?" What she is doing is private and clearly involves a feeling of bodily ecstasy. This critic might move in a number of directions from this initial observation — to discuss the effects of a repressive culture, for instance, or to examine the fact that Mrs. Mallard's feeling of freedom can only take place behind a locked door, which is nearly a closet, the central metaphor for the repression of one's natural sexual desires. Although non-normative gender or sexuality readings often raise significant interpretive controversies among critics, they have opened up provocative discussions of texts that might otherwise seem completely unconcerned with sexual desire.

MYTHOLOGICAL STRATEGIES

Mythological approaches to literature attempt to identify what elements in a work create deep universal responses in readers. Whereas psychological critics interpret the symbolic meanings of characters and actions in order to understand more fully the unconscious dimensions of an author's mind, a character's motivation, or a reader's response, *mythological critics* (also frequently referred to as *archetypal critics*) interpret the hopes, fears, and expectations of entire cultures based on the stories they tell and the symbols they employ repeatedly.

In this context myth is not to be understood simply as referring to stories about imaginary gods who perform astonishing feats in the causes of love, jealousy, or hatred. Nor are myths to be judged as merely erroneous, primitive accounts of how nature runs its course and humanity conducts its affairs. Instead, literary critics use myths or archetypes as a strategy for understanding how human beings try to account for their lives symbolically. Myths can be a window into a culture's deepest perceptions about itself because they attempt to explain what otherwise seems unexplainable: a people's origin, purpose, and destiny.

All human beings have a need to make sense of their lives, whether they are concerned about their natural surroundings, the seasons, sexuality, birth, death, or the very meaning of existence. Myths help people organize their experiences; these systems of belief (less formally held than religious or political tenets but no less important) embody a culture's assumptions and values. What is important to the mythological critic is not the validity or truth of those assumptions and values; what matters is that they reveal common human concerns.

It is not surprising that although the details of mythic stories vary enormously, the essential patterns are often similar because these myths attempt to explain universal experiences. There are, for example, numerous myths that redeem humanity from permanent death through a hero's resurrection or rebirth. The resurrection of Jesus symbolizes for Christians the ultimate defeat of death and coincides with the rebirth of nature's fertility in spring. Features of this rebirth parallel the Greek myths of Adonis and Hyacinth, who die but are subsequently transformed into living flowers; there are also similarities that connect these stories to the reincarnation of the Indian Buddha or the rebirth of the Egyptian Osiris. Important differences exist among these stories, but each reflects a basic human need to limit the power of death and to hope for eternal life.

Mythological critics look for underlying, recurrent patterns in literature that reveal universal meanings and basic human experiences for readers regardless of when or where they live. The characters, images, and themes that symbolically embody these meanings and experiences are called *archetypes*. This term designates universal symbols that evoke deep and perhaps unconscious responses in a reader because archetypes bring with them hopes and fears that have always defined humanity. Surely one of the most powerfully compelling archetypes is the death and rebirth theme that relates the human life cycle to the cycle of the seasons. Many others could be cited and would be exhausted only after all human concerns were cataloged, but a few examples can suggest some of the range of plots, images, and characters addressed.

Among the most common literary archetypes are stories of quests, initiations, scapegoats, meditative withdrawals, descents to the underworld, and heavenly ascents. These stories are often filled with archetypal images — bodies of water that may symbolize the unconscious or eternity or baptismal rebirth; rising suns, suggesting reawakening and enlightenment; setting suns, pointing toward death; colors such as green, evocative of growth and fertility, or black, indicating chaos, evil, and death. Along the way are earth mothers, fatal women, wise old men, desert places, and paradisal gardens. No doubt your own reading has introduced you to any number of archetypal plots, images, and characters.

Mythological critics attempt to explain how archetypes are embodied in literary works. Employing various disciplines, these critics articulate the power a literary work has over us. Some critics are deeply grounded in classical literature, whereas others are more conversant with philology, anthropology, psychology, folklore, or cultural history. Whatever their emphases, however, mythological critics examine the elements of a work in order to make larger connections that explain the work's lasting appeal.

These kinds of archetypal patterns exist potentially in any literary period. Consider how in Chopin's "The Story of an Hour" Mrs. Mallard's life parallels the end of winter and the earth's renewal in spring. When she feels a surge of new life after grieving over her husband's death, her own sensibilities are closely aligned with the "new spring life" that is "all aquiver" outside her window. Although she initially tries to resist that renewal by "beat[ing] it back with her will," she cannot control the life force that surges within her and all around her. When she finally gives herself to the energy and life she experiences, she feels triumphant — like a "goddess of Victory." But this victory is short lived when she learns that her husband is still alive and with him all the obligations that made her marriage feel like a wasteland. Her death is an ironic version of a rebirth ritual. The coming of spring is an ironic contrast to her own discovery that she can no longer live a repressed, circumscribed life with her husband. Death turns out to be preferable to the living death that her marriage means to her. Although spring will go on, this "goddess of Victory" is defeated by a devastating social contract. The old, corrupt order continues, and that for Chopin is a cruel irony that mythological critics would see as an unnatural disruption of the nature of things.

READER-RESPONSE STRATEGIES

Reader-response criticism, as its name implies, emphasizes the reader's experience over the work itself. This approach to literature describes what goes on in the reader's mind during the process of reading a text and also the way communities of readers cooperate to advance an interpretation. In a sense, all critical approaches (especially psychological and mythological criticism) concern themselves with a reader's response to literature, but there is a stronger emphasis in reader-response criticism on the reader's active construction of the text's meaning. Although many critical theories inform reader-response criticism, all **reader-response critics** aim to describe the reader's experience of a work: in effect we get a reading of the reader, who comes to the work with certain expectations and assumptions, which are either met or not met. Hence the consciousness of the reader — produced by reading the work — is the subject matter of reader-response critics. Just as writing is a creative act, reading is too, since it also leads to the production of a text.

Reader-response critics do not assume that a literary work is a finished product with fixed formal properties, as, for example, formalist critics do. Instead, the literary work is seen as an evolving creation of the reader as he or she processes characters, plots, images, and other elements while reading, and also how reading communities (such as your class) are vital in directing the trajectory of interpretation. Some reader-response critics argue that this act of creative reading is, to a degree, controlled by the text, but it can produce many interpretations of the same text by different readers. There is no single definitive reading of a work, because the crucial assumption is that readers create rather than discover meanings in texts. Readers who have gone back to works they had read earlier in their lives often find that a later reading draws very different responses from them. What earlier seemed unimportant is now crucial; what at first seemed central is now barely worth noting. The reason, put simply, is that two different people have read the same text. Reader-response critics are not after the "correct" reading of the text or what the author presumably intended; instead they are interested in the reader's experience with the text.

Reader-response criticism calls attention to how we read and to what influences our readings. It does not attempt to define what a literary work means on the page but rather what it does to an informed reader, a reader who understands the language and conventions used in a given work. Reader-response criticism is not a rationale for mistaken or bizarre readings of works but an exploration of the possibilities for a plurality of readings shaped by readers' experiences with the text. This kind of strategy can help us understand how our responses are shaped by both the text and ourselves.

Chopin's "The Story of an Hour" illustrates how reader-response critical strategies read the reader. Chopin doesn't say that Mrs. Mallard's marriage is repressive; instead, that troubling fact dawns on the reader at the same time that the recognition forces its way into Mrs. Mallard's consciousness. Her surprise is also the reader's because although she remains in the midst of intense grief, she is on the threshold of a startling discovery about the new possibilities life offers. How the reader responds to that discovery, however, is not entirely controlled by Chopin. One reader, perhaps someone who has recently lost a spouse, might find Mrs. Mallard's "joy" indeed "monstrous" and selfish. Certainly that's how Mrs. Mallard's doctors — the seemingly authoritative diagnosticians in the story — would very likely read her. But for other readers Mrs. Mallard's feelings require no justification. Such readers might find Chopin's ending to the story more ironic than she seems to have intended because Mrs. Mallard's death could be read as Chopin's inability to envision a protagonist who has the strength of her convictions. In contrast, a reader in 1894 might have seen the ending as Mrs. Mallard's only escape from the repressive marriage her husband's assumed death suddenly allowed her to see. A reader in our times probably would argue that it was the marriage that should have died rather than Mrs. Mallard, that she had other alternatives, not just obligations (as the doctors would have insisted), to consider.

By imagining different readers, we can imagine a variety of responses to the story that are influenced by the readers' own impressions, memories, or experiences with marriage. Such imagining suggests the ways in which reader-response criticism opens up texts to a number of interpretations. As one final example, consider how readers' responses to "The Story of an Hour" would be affected if it were printed in two different magazines, read in the context of either *Ms.* or *Good Housekeeping.* What assumptions and beliefs would each magazine's readership be likely to bring to the story? How do you think the respective experiences and values of each magazine's readers would influence their readings? For a sample reader-response student paper on "The Story of an Hour," see page 19.

DECONSTRUCTIONIST STRATEGIES

Deconstructionist critics insist that literary works do not yield fixed, single meanings. They argue that there can be no absolute knowledge about anything because language is unstable across different contexts and time periods, and thus can never say what we intend it to mean. Anything we write conveys meanings we did not intend, so the deconstructionist argument goes. Language is not a precise instrument but a power domain whose meanings are caught in an endless web of possibilities that cannot be untangled. Accordingly, any idea or statement that insists on being understood separately can ultimately be "deconstructed" to reveal its relations and connections to contradictory and opposite meanings.

Unlike other forms of criticism, **deconstructionism** seeks to destabilize meanings instead of establishing them. In contrast to formalists such as the New Critics, who closely examine a work in order to call attention to how its various components interact to establish a unified whole, deconstructionists try to show how a close examination of the language in a text inevitably reveals conflicting, contradictory impulses that "deconstruct" or break down its apparent unity.

Although deconstructionists and New Critics both examine the language of a text closely, deconstructionists focus on the gaps and ambiguities that reveal a text's instability and indeterminacy, whereas New Critics look for patterns that explain how the text's fixed meaning is structured. Deconstructionists painstakingly examine the competing meanings within the text rather than attempting to resolve them into a unified whole.

The questions deconstructionists ask are aimed at discovering and describing how a variety of possible readings are generated by the elements of a text. In contrast to a New Critic's concerns about the ultimate meaning of a work, a deconstructionist is primarily interested in how the use of language — diction, tone, metaphor, symbol, and so on — yields only provisional, not definitive, meanings.

Deconstructionists look for ways to question and extend the meanings of a text. A deconstructionist might find, for example, the ironic ending of Chopin's "The Story of an Hour" less tidy and conclusive than would a New Critic, who might attribute Mrs. Mallard's death to her sense of lost personal freedom. A deconstructionist might use the story's ending to suggest that the narrative shares the doctors' inability to imagine a life for Mrs. Mallard apart from her husband. As difficult as it is controversial, deconstructionism is not easily summarized or paraphrased. The final sentence contains a number of phrases that are ambiguous: to whom are the doctors speaking? What does joy kill? Since language itself is unstable, its contradictions are of great interest to deconstructionists who like to examine its slippages and who like to show how the texts it produces are also unstable. Here's a thought that might delight a deconstructionist: how do we know that Mrs. Mallard is dead? Who says so? The story has already proven that Brentley Mallard was presumed dead because of a story told by Josephine and Richards; who's to say that Mrs. Mallard is not also alive but only presumed dead because the doctors said so? Why trust them? The story does not end with a dead body, but with another story.

The following lists of questions for the critical approaches covered in this chapter should be useful for discovering arguments you might make about a short story, poem, or play. As we stress above, we are only introducing these fields, and the questions that follow are designed to sharpen your sense of what these critical strategies entail, and also invite you to consider how the "meaning" of a text might look different based on the way you approach it, or the lens through which you view it.

FORMALIST QUESTIONS

1. How do various elements of the work — plot, character, point of view, setting, tone, diction, images, symbol, and so on — reinforce its meanings?

2. How are the elements related to the whole?

3. What is the work's major organizing principle? How is its structure unified?

4. What issues does the work raise? How does the work's structure resolve those issues?

BIOGRAPHICAL QUESTIONS

1. Are facts about the writer's life relevant to your understanding of the work?

2. Are characters and incidents in the work versions of the writer's own experiences? Are they treated factually or imaginatively?

3. How do you think the writer's values are reflected in the work?

PSYCHOLOGICAL QUESTIONS

1. How does the work reflect the author's personal psychology?

2. What do the characters' emotions and behavior reveal about their psychological states? What types of personalities are they?

3. Are psychological matters such as repression, dreams, and desire presented consciously or unconsciously by the author?

HISTORICAL QUESTIONS

1. How does the work reflect the period in which it is written?
2. What literary or historical influences helped to shape the form and content of the work?
3. How important is the historical context to interpreting the work?

MARXIST QUESTIONS

1. How are class differences presented in the work? Are characters aware or unaware of the economic and social forces that affect their lives?
2. How do economic conditions determine the characters' lives?
3. What ideological values are explicit or implicit?
4. Does the work challenge or affirm the social order it describes?

NEW HISTORICIST QUESTIONS

1. What kinds of documents outside the work seem especially relevant for shedding light on the work?
2. How are social values contemporary to the work reflected or refuted in the work?
3. How does your own historical moment affect your reading of the work and its historical reconstruction?

CULTURAL STUDIES QUESTIONS

1. What does the work reveal about the cultural behavior contemporary to it?
2. How does popular culture contemporary to the work reflect or challenge the values implicit or explicit in the work?
3. What kinds of cultural documents contemporary to the work add to your reading of it?
4. How do your own cultural assumptions affect your reading of the work and the culture contemporary to it?

GENDER STUDIES QUESTIONS

1. How are the lives of men and women portrayed in the work? Do the men and women in the work accept or reject these roles?
2. Are the form and content of the work influenced by the author's gender?
3. What attitudes are explicit or implicit concerning sexual relationships? Are these relationships sources of conflict? Do they provide resolutions to conflicts?
4. Does the work challenge or affirm traditional ideas about men and women and same-sex relationships?
5. Are gender and/or sexuality presented as fixed or fluid?

MYTHOLOGICAL QUESTIONS

1. How does the story resemble other stories in plot, character, setting, or use of symbols?
2. Are archetypes presented, such as quests, initiations, scapegoats, or withdrawals and returns?
3. Does the protagonist undergo any kind of transformation such as a movement from innocence to experience that seems archetypal?
4. Do any specific allusions to myths shed light on the text?

READER-RESPONSE QUESTIONS

1. What is your initial reaction to the work?
2. How do your own experiences and expectations affect your reading and interpretation?
3. What is the work's original or intended audience? To what extent are you similar to or different from that audience?
4. Do you respond in the same way to the work after more than one reading?
5. What kind of interpretive community are you a part of? Is your reading of a text conditioned by the readings offered by your peers, by professional literary critics, by your instructor, and so on?

DECONSTRUCTIONIST QUESTIONS

1. How are contradictory and opposing meanings expressed in the work?
2. How does meaning break down or deconstruct itself in the language of the text?
3. Would you say that ultimate definitive meanings are impossible to determine and establish in the text? Why? How does that affect your interpretation?
4. How are implicit ideological values revealed in the work?

These questions will not apply to all texts; and they are not mutually exclusive. They can be combined to explore a text from several critical perspectives or contexts simultaneously. A feminist approach to Kate Chopin's "The Story of an Hour" could also use Marxist concerns about class to make observations about the oppression of women's lives in the historical context of the nineteenth century. Your use of these questions should allow you to discover significant issues from which you can develop an argumentative essay that is organized around clearly defined terms, relevant evidence, and a persuasive analysis in response to your instructor's directions.

31

Writing about Literature

Writing permits me to experience life as any number of strange creations.

— ALICE WALKER

Anthony Barboza/Getty Images.

There's no question about it: writing about literature is a different experience than reading it. Reading, as you no doubt realize by now, is not a passive activity, and yet when we pick up a book, it does feel that someone else has done the hard labor and we're enjoying the fruits of it. Writing is, of course, work, but it is also a pleasure when it goes well — when ideas feel solid and the writing is fluid. You can experience that pleasure as well, if you approach writing as an intellectual and emotional opportunity rather than a chore. When Alice Walker speaks of "strange creations," she's referring to possibilities. Writing allows her to reframe reality, sensation, and perception. This idea does not apply only to fiction, poetry, and drama. The writing you will complete in response to the works in this book also has the capacity to liberate your mind and to demonstrate your intellectual power.

Just as reading literature requires an imaginative, conscious response, so does writing about literature. Composing an essay is not just recording your interpretive response to a work because the act of writing can change your response as you explore, clarify, and discover relationships you hadn't previously considered or recognized. Most writers discover new ideas and connections as they move through the process of rereading and annotating the text, taking notes, generating ideas, developing a thesis, and organizing an argumentative essay. (These activities are detailed later in this chapter.) To become more conscious of the writing process, first consider the ideas we articulate in the sections below, then study the following questions specifically aimed at sharpening your response to reading and writing about literature. Finally, examine the case studies of students' papers that take you through writing a first response to reading, brainstorming for a paper topic, writing a first draft, revising, and writing the final paper.

WHY AM I BEING ASKED TO DO THIS?

The vast majority of college literature courses require that students write formal essays about the literature they study. You might be wondering why you are being asked to write about literature. You might be in awe of the writers you have read, and you think there is no point trying to write like they do because they are professionals with abundant gifts and talents. Why not allow stories, poems, and plays to speak for themselves? Isn't it presumptuous to interpret Hemingway, Dickinson, or Shakespeare? These writers do, of course, speak for themselves, but they do so indirectly. Literary criticism seeks not to replace the text by explaining it but to enhance our readings of works by calling attention to elements that we might have overlooked or only vaguely sensed.

Your instructor probably isn't asking you to write *like* the authors in this book (although an imitation exercise might be a valuable means to understanding an author's technique), but rather to write *about* them, or put succinctly, to interpret their work. The questions that follow most of the selections in this anthology are designed to initiate this type of interpretation, and your class discussions extend and complicate such individual interpretations. A formal essay gives you the chance to develop a yet more sophisticated interpretation and to revise it so that it becomes full and persuasive. Through this process you will work toward mastery of a skill. You'll improve your ability to analyze works of literature and to develop a critical argument that showcases your analysis. But you will also increase your confidence as someone who can communicate clearly and think critically. Those broader competencies will invariably serve you well in social contexts, in your career, and in your quest to become a more impressive human. (Note that the study of literature is part of an academic branch called the *humanities*.)

Composition and rhetoric is a subfield of English that studies the type of writing assigned to you in this course. It is a vast field, and since there have been so many people working in it for so long, there are bound to be disagreements about the best way to teach students to write. You have probably noticed that your teachers from an early age right up through your professors in college have laid down rules that might seem to contradict each other. If your eighth-grade teacher forbade you to use "I" in your formal essays and warned that he would take ten points off your grade if you did so, what do you do in college when your professor encourages you to use "I"? One of your teachers taught you how to perfect the five-paragraph essay and the other asked you in a comment why your essay was only five paragraphs long when you clearly had more to say, especially in paragraph three which was three pages long and contained four paragraphs, worth of ideas. It might be tempting to throw up your hands and to conclude that academic writing is arbitrary, but a critical thinker might instead conclude that writing is a situational activity, dependent on a series of codes that is always shifting. Your teacher who hammered home the virtues of a five-paragraph essay might have been preparing you to develop into a writer who would realize when five paragraphs were too few, or too many, for the task at hand. Think about the various conventions that shape the writing you already do on a daily basis. What if all of your messages were as long and as stiff-sounding as the essay you wrote to get into college? (Conversely, where would you be if your college essay resembled any one of your messages?) Strong writers adapt to the various demands of the writing situations they find themselves in. There is a set of conventions for e-mails and office memos and another set of conventions for formal essays assigned in your literature class. This chapter will offer some broad outlines about those conventions, but it can only do so much. Your instructor will invariably want something specific from your writing that we can't anticipate here, and your instructor is your most important audience because he or she is in a position to give you feedback designed to improve your writing.

That last point is crucial. Rhetoric and composition instructors may not agree on all methods instructors use to teach writing, but they all agree on this point: the only way to improve as a writer is to write, to receive feedback on that writing, and to write more, absorbing that feedback while accepting ever more challenging writing assignments. All writers receive feedback, even the ones represented in this book who you might consider to be literary geniuses. Their work is a form of art, but that doesn't mean they weren't subjected to a lengthy editorial process, or that they didn't show an early draft to a spouse or friend before going public with it. The same might be true for you if you end up in a business setting; you might hear from your boss, "Thanks for the info, Jones, but your e-mails are way too long: cut them in half or no one's going to read them." In this class the feedback you receive from your instructor might critique your writing on multiple levels, from comma usage to the organization of your entire essay. All of this feedback is designed not simply to "correct" your writing, but to help you develop your strength and flexibility as a writer. Writing about literature is a particularly good workout because you are responding to literature, the most sophisticated form of language. The acts of reading and interpreting literature encourage you to pay especially careful attention to the way language works, to its patterns, to its possibilities. Your own writing will invariably improve as you immerse yourself in it.

FROM READING AND DISCUSSION TO WRITING

Introductory literature courses typically include three components — reading, discussion, and writing. Students usually find the readings a pleasure, the class discussions a revelation, and the writing assignments — at least initially — a little intimidating. Writing an analysis of the contrast between darkness and light in James Baldwin's "Sonny's Blues" (p. 76), for example, may seem considerably more daunting than making a case for animal rights or analyzing a campus newspaper editorial that debates the legalization of marijuana. Literary topics are not, however, all that different from the kinds of papers assigned in standard composition courses; many of the same skills are required for both. Regardless of the type of paper you're composing, you must eventually develop a structured argument with a clear thesis and support it with evidence in language that is clear and persuasive. Note the word *eventually*. Writing is a process, sometimes a long and messy one, and with practice you will develop effective strategies to produce drafts that will *eventually* lead to a polished, organized essay. More than anything, writing requires patience and faith in the process.

Whether the subject matter is a marketing survey, a political issue, or a literary work, writing is a method of communicating information and perceptions. Writing teaches. But before writing becomes an instrument for informing the reader, it serves as a means of learning for the writer. An essay is a process of discovery as well as a record of what has been discovered. One of the chief benefits of writing is that we frequently realize what we want to say only after trying out ideas on a page and seeing our thoughts take shape in language.

In terms of the assignments you will complete for this course, writing about a literary work encourages us to be better readers because it requires a close examination of the elements of a short story, poem, or play. To determine how plot, character, setting, point of view, metaphor, tone, irony, or any number of other literary elements function in a work, we must study them in relation to one another as well as separately. Speed-reading won't do. To read a text accurately and validly — neither ignoring nor distorting significant details — we must return to the work repeatedly to test our responses and interpretations. By paying attention to details and being sensitive to the author's use of language, we develop a clearer understanding of how the work conveys its effects and meanings, and we become literary critics.

Due to the connotations of the word "critical," a common misunderstanding about the purpose of literary criticism is that it restricts itself to finding faults in a work. Although a critical essay may point out limitations and flaws, most criticism — and certainly the kind of essay usually written in an introductory literature course — is designed to explain, analyze, and reveal the complexities of a work. Such sensitive consideration increases our appreciation of the writer's achievement and significantly adds to our enjoyment of a short story, poem, or play. In short, the purpose and value of writing about literature are that doing so leads to greater understanding and pleasure.

You will develop good writing habits over time, and/or you will improve on the good ones you have already developed. Regardless of your specific composition methods, there are three basic phases of the process to understand: **prewriting, writing,** and **revising**. There is not necessarily a clean break between these phases, though: you might find yourself revising even as you prewrite, for example, or writing more after you've revised your first draft. In general, though, there are distinct principles for these three stages that you should keep in mind as you approach your paper as a series of drafts. What we offer below are some tried-and-true methods: you may have developed others that work better for you, or your instructor might have more specific guidance, but these are also available.

PREWRITING

Annotating the Text and Journal Note Taking

We emphasize the value of critical reading above, and this type of reading is intertwined with prewriting. As you read, get in the habit of annotating your texts. Whether you write marginal notes, highlight, underline, or draw boxes and circles around important words and phrases, you'll eventually develop a system that allows you to retrieve significant ideas and elements from the text. Another way to record your impressions of a work — as with any other experience — is to keep a journal. By writing down your reactions to characters, images, language, actions, and other matters in a reading journal, you can often determine why you like or dislike a work or feel sympathetic or antagonistic to an author or discover paths into a work that might have eluded you if you hadn't preserved your impressions. Your journal notes and annotations may take whatever form you find useful; full sentences and grammatical correctness are not essential (unless your instructor deems them important and requires that you hand them in), though fuller thoughts might allow you to make better sense of your own reflections than incomplete thoughts might. The point is simply to put in writing ideas that you can retrieve when you need them for class discussion or a writing assignment. Far from making extra work, this process saves you considerable time when you get to the writing phase.

Taking notes will preserve your initial reactions to the work. First impressions are often valid. Your response to a peculiar character in a story, a striking phrase in a poem, or a subtle bit of stage business in a play might lead to larger perceptions. The student paper on John Updike's "A & P" (p. 138) later in this chapter, for example, began with the student writing "how come?" next to the story's title in her textbook. She thought it strange that the title didn't refer to a character or to the story's conflict. That brief annotated response eventually led her to examine the significance of the setting, which became the central focus of her paper.

Prewriting activities should not interfere with your initial encounter with a text, though: you would do well to keep your pen tucked behind your ear as you first read a text so that you can get a sense of its unique characteristics, its concerns, its possible meaning, or its pleasures and delights. You should take detailed notes only after you've read through the work. If you write too many notes during the first reading, you're likely to disrupt your response. Moreover, until you have a sense of the entire work, it will be difficult to determine how connections can be made among its various elements. In addition to recording your first impressions and noting significant passages, characters, actions, and so on, you should consult the Questions for Responsive Reading and Writing about Fiction (p. 1106), Poetry (p. 1114), and Drama (p. 1126). These questions can assist you in getting inside a work as well as organizing your notes.

Inevitably, you will take more notes than you finally use in the paper. Note taking is a form of thinking aloud, but because your ideas are on paper (or on a laptop, phone, or tablet), you don't have to worry about forgetting them. As you develop a better sense of a potential topic, your notes will become more focused and detailed.

Choosing a Topic

If your instructor assigns a topic or list of approved topics, some of your work is already completed. If that is the case, you also have the assurance that a specified topic will be manageable within the suggested number of pages. Unless you ask your instructor for permission to write on a different or related topic, be certain to address yourself to the assignment. There is room even in an assigned topic to develop your own approach. Assigned topics do not relieve you of thinking about an aspect of a work, but they do focus your thinking.

Other assignments might be left open so that you can engage your particular point of view more thoroughly. Before you start considering a topic, you should have a sense of how long the paper will be because the assigned length can help to determine the extent to which you should develop your topic. Ideally, the paper's length should be based on how much space you deem necessary to present your discussion clearly and convincingly, but if you have any doubts and no specific guidelines have been indicated, ask. The question is important; a topic that might be appropriate for a three-page paper could be too narrow for ten pages.

Once you have a firm sense of the scope of what you are expected to write, you can begin to decide on your topic. If you have a choice, it's generally best to write about a topic that you feel strongly about. If you're not fascinated by the rebellious act of tearing wallpaper off a wall in Gilman's "The Yellow Wallpaper" (p. 117), maybe you can explain why the act of destroying a room's décor is so boring to you as an act of defiance. Choose a work that has moved you so that you have something to say about it. The student who wrote "John Updike's 'A & P' as a State of Mind" (p. 1109) was initially attracted to the story's title because she had once worked in a similar store. After reading the story, she became fascinated with its setting because Updike's descriptions seemed so accurate. When a writer is engaged in a topic, the paper has a better chance of being interesting to a reader.

After you have settled on a particular work, your notes and annotations of the text should prove useful for generating a topic. The paper on "A & P" developed naturally from the notes the student jotted down about the setting and antagonist. You are likely to find when you review your notes that your thoughts have clustered into one or more topics. Perhaps there are patterns of imagery that seem to make a point about life. There may be scenes that are ironically paired or secondary characters who reveal certain qualities about the protagonist. Your notes and annotations on such aspects can lead you to a particular effect or impression.

More Focused Prewriting

When you are satisfied that you have something interesting to say about a work and that your notes have led you to a focused topic, you are moving in the direction of formulating a *thesis statement*, the central idea of the paper. Whereas the topic indicates what the paper focuses on (the setting in "A & P"), the thesis explains what you have to say about the topic (because the intolerant setting of "A & P" is the antagonist in the story, it is crucial to our understanding of Sammy's decision to quit his job). The thesis is a statement that will probably not fully emerge until the revision stage of your drafting process rather than during prewriting, but you should be aware during prewriting that you are eventually moving in the direction of an *argument*, which is the formal, structured analysis you are building; the thesis is the argument's distilled statement.

An intermediate step between deciding on a topic and formulating a thesis statement is to generate a *working thesis* that will direct your thinking. One simple first step to generate a working thesis about a literary work is to ask the question "why?" Why do these images appear in the poem? Why do the main characters in Wilde's *The Importance of Being Earnest* lie so much? Why does Hemingway choose the Midwest as the setting of "Soldier's Home"? Your responses to these kinds of questions can lead to a working thesis.

Writers sometimes use *freewriting* to help themselves explore possible answers to such questions. It can be an effective way of generating ideas. Freewriting is nonstop writing without concern for mechanics or editing of any kind. (The equivalent in fiction is *stream of consciousness.*) Freewriting for ten minutes or so on a question will result in fragments and repetitions, but it can also produce some ideas. A freewriting sentence that a student writer might generate in response to Updike's "A & P" could look like this: "Sammy's job like mine at the Cheesecake Factory both of us wear stupid uniforms and have to deal with obnoxious customers and incompetent bosses but he doesn't get to move around like I do." There's not much in

that sentence that would end up in a final draft, especially the personal connection to the character in the story, but the writer is conditioning herself to
think about elements of the story that might be relevant: Sammy's uniform
and lack of mobility could become important points for analysis.

ARGUING ABOUT LITERATURE

Most writing assignments in a literature course require you to persuade
readers that your thesis is reasonable and to support it with evidence. In
developing a thesis, you are expected not merely to present information
but to argue an interpretive point. An argumentative essay is your interpretation of a work arranged in a persuasive way. Arguing about literature
doesn't mean that you're engaged in an angry, antagonistic dispute. Instead,
argumentation requires that you present your interpretation of a work (or
an aspect of it) by supporting your discussion with clearly defined terms,
ample evidence, and a detailed analysis of relevant portions of the text.

One way to come up with persuasive answers is to generate good questions that will lead you further into the text and to critical issues related
to it. Notice how the Perspectives, Critical Case Studies, and Cultural Case
Studies in this anthology raise significant questions and issues about texts
from a variety of points of view, or contexts. Moreover, the Critical Strategies for Reading summarized in Chapter 30 can be a resource for raising
questions that can be shaped into an argument.

WRITING

Writing a First Draft

Writing is a process, as we have said, but it is not the same process for every
writer. You may be the type of writer who needs a formal outline with head-
ings and subheadings before you can begin a draft, or you may find such
methods constraining. Whether you have started with freewriting, outlining, or some other prewriting method, you should have some sense of how
your paper will be organized — or at least, what you need to cover — as you
write your first draft. The working thesis you generate during prewriting,
even if it is still somewhat tentative, should help you decide what information will need to be included and provide you with a sense of direction.

At this stage it is crucial to be flexible rather than to adhere too closely
to whatever methods you used during the prewriting stage. By using the first
draft as a means of thinking about what you want to say, you will very likely
discover more than your notes originally suggested. Once again, writing is a
process, and computers have made it easy to generate words without making a lifetime commitment to them. You do not need to get bogged down
with sentence-level perfection at this early stage. Concentrate on what you

are saying. Good writing most often occurs when you are in hot pursuit of an idea rather than in a nervous search for errors. You can improve on each draft paragraph by paragraph, sentence by sentence, and even word by word, but *at this stage* you should give yourself permission to generate the raw material you will *eventually* shape into something coherent and eloquent.

Once you have a first draft on your computer, you can delete material that is unrelated to your working thesis and add material necessary to illustrate your points and make your paper convincing. (Some writers find it useful to create a separate file of deleted items that they may want to resurrect at a later stage.) The student who wrote "John Updike's 'A & P' as a State of Mind" (p. 1109) wisely dropped a paragraph that questioned whether Sammy displays chauvinistic attitudes toward women. Although this is an interesting issue, it has nothing to do with her argument and eventual thesis, which explains how the setting influences Sammy's decision to quit his job. Instead of including that paragraph, she added one that described Lengel's crabbed response to the girls so that she could lead up to the A & P "policy" he enforces.

Textual Evidence: Using Quotations, Summarizing, and Paraphrasing

We have been referring to your essay as an "argument," and we have tried to make it clear that you are not necessarily disagreeing with someone's interpretation. You might think of your role more as building a courtroom case. In order to do so, you have to stick to provable facts, or evidence. Each academic discipline approaches evidence slightly differently, but all of them require it. In your chemistry class, evidence might take the form of the results of lab work; in history, you might have to produce a primary document to argue, for instance, that a certain party was responsible for catalyzing a certain war. In the study of literature, the hardest evidence you have access to is a direct quotation from the text. Examining the language of a text is the best way to show that you are immersed in it, and that you are willing to look at it closely.

And yet, there are times when you might find it useful to broadly summarize a work of literature, or even to paraphrase segments of it. As an analogy, imagine a work of literature as a forest. Think of how different that forest would appear if you were (1) flying over it in a helicopter, or (2) strolling through it, or (3) kneeling down with a magnifying glass to examine an ant colony in a rotting stump. The third encounter with the forest provides the most substantial evidence, like the quotation from a work of literature, but you are not in a position to describe the entire forest from that vantage point. You want to develop a sense of when each perspective might be most useful.

As you are introducing the primary text you are analyzing, you would do well to provide a bit of summary to orient the reader — the helicopter perspective in our analogy above. It might be jarring to provide direct evidence in the form of a quotation without any summary. Imagine a paper that starts like this: "Sammy says, 'She had sort of oaky hair that the sun and salt had bleached.'" That might be useful information to the author's argument, but the reader is likely to wonder, for starters, "Who is Sammy?" It might be more advantageous to think about an accurate summary of the story that also introduces your topic, like this sentence: "John Updike's 'A & P' is a story about Sammy, a teenaged grocery store clerk who is so upset by the way his boss treats three female customers that he quits his job." That's an accurate summary of the story's main plot, but it may or may not be detailed enough for your purposes. Do you need Sammy's boss's name in this summary? The age of the three female customers is not specified; should it be? Do we need to know that it is a story written from the first-person point of view? Does the fact that Sammy is keenly aware of class differences between himself and "Queenie" and the other girls matter enough to mention it in the summary?

These questions are a way of pointing out that summaries actually involve interpretation. If you and your classmates were all to summarize any work of literature you have read this semester, even if all of them are technically accurate and factual, what chance would there be that any two of them would be worded exactly the same way? Think of a summary, then, as a necessary way to frame your analysis, but also as an opportunity to begin to focus in on your perspective or context. Let's say you are writing about gender discrimination in "A & P." Your one-sentence summary might look like this: "John Updike's 'A & P' is the story of three teenaged girls who are shamed by a grocery store manager for dressing in a supposedly inappropriate manner." This is also an accurate summary of the story, and Sammy is nowhere in sight. He will probably become part of the author's argument, but this author's initial focus is clearly on the way the girls are treated rather than on Sammy's reaction to that treatment. When you summarize, you are making decisions, sometimes unconsciously, about how you have read and understood a text. You will gradually develop a sense of how much summary you need to make your point. We can distinguish between necessary and unnecessary summary in the abstract, but there is no firm rule dividing these categories. The examples above are one-sentence summaries. Depending on the length of your essay, the difficulty and length of the text under consideration, and a number of other factors, you might decide you need a fuller summary to situate the reader. Imagine that reader as someone who is familiar with the work you are writing about, but who needs a little reminder about it. That reader is not in your head, but he or she is also not someone who has never read a work of literature: you probably wouldn't need to say, "John Updike was an author (which is a name for someone who writes for a living) of a short story (which is a literary prose genre of imaginative writing that combines such elements as character, plot, theme, and imagery to form a certain effect on the reader) titled 'A & P' about Sammy (which is a nickname for Samuel . . .)." We're being a little facetious here, but hopefully you get the point: a summary can swell or shrink according to your needs. You are the author, and you are in control of its level of detail.

Just make sure it is accurate: if you were to say, "John Updike's 'A & P' is a story set in Malaysia in the 1980s," you would be writing fiction rather than summarizing it.

Paraphrase is related to summary, but it tends to be focused more narrowly. The common understanding of paraphrasing is restatement, usually concise restatement. You'll want to make sure to paraphrase in a way that is both accurate and that does not risk triteness. Take Hamlet's famous "To be, or not to be" soliloquy. You could paraphrase it this way: "Hamlet is basically saying, 'You only live once, so go for it.'" To do so would be to significantly cheapen one of the more nuanced speeches in literature, though, and to reduce it to a pair of clichés. Like summary, paraphrase is an opportunity to interpret and frame a segment of the literary work you are analyzing. This segment might be important to your essay, but you might not need to spend as much time on it as you would spend on the passages, lines, or sentences that are really crucial to your argument. That's where the analysis of direct quotations comes in.

Quotations can be a valuable means of marshaling evidence to illustrate and support your ideas. A strategic use of quoted material will make your points clearer and more convincing. A key component to the use of direct quotation, though, is that you are charged with *working with* the language of the text. Some developing writers assume that placing a quotation in an essay is the final step, but it is really the first step. You can't expect these quotations to speak for themselves: again, you are in the business of interpreting them. You might even have to break down a quotation into smaller units, calling attention to individual words or phrases in order to look at them carefully. Imagine the essay we describe above in which the author is writing about gender discrimination in Updike's "A & P." The author might say, "A significant sentence is this one: 'Queenie's blush is no sunburn now, and the plump one in plaid, that I liked better from the back — a really sweet can — pipes up, 'We weren't doing any shopping.'" If the author moves on to the next point from there and leaves it at "significant," the reader is likely to ask, "What's significant about it?" Imagine the analysis that could and should follow this incorporated quotation, something like this: "It is important to note not only that Sammy is focused on the girls' bodies, from Queenie's blush to what he deems the most attractive features of the nameless 'plump one in plaid,' but also that he is as guilty as Lengel is of treating them like objects. The rear end of the 'plump one' becomes a commodity like anything else in the grocery store, a crassly-described 'can.' In this way Sammy demonstrates how conditioned he has become by the materialistic sexist society he lives in." The quotation only becomes evidence when it is closely examined.

Here are some guidelines that should help you incorporate quotations effectively.

1. It is possible for you to include quotations at the beginning or the end of a paragraph, but we would recommend that you attempt to include them in the middle of a paragraph. The basic reason is that

each paragraph is an idea-unit that helps you to further your argument; therefore, it's best to have your voice at the beginning and end of each paragraph. This method allows you to introduce the point you are making or claim you are stating, then to include the quotation in order to illustrate that point, and finally to interpret the language of the quotation as we demonstrate above.

2. Brief quotations (four lines or fewer of prose or three lines or fewer of poetry) should be carefully introduced and integrated into the text of your paper with quotation marks around them:

> According to the narrator, Bertha "had a reputation for strictness." He tells us that she always "wore dark clothes, dressed her hair simply, and expected contrition and obedience from her pupils."

For brief poetry quotations, use a slash to indicate a division between lines:

> The concluding lines of Blake's "The Tyger" pose a disturbing question: "What immortal hand or eye / Dare frame thy fearful symmetry?"

Lengthy quotations should be separated from the text of your paper. More than three lines of poetry or more than four lines of prose should be double spaced and indented one inch from the left margin, with the right margin the same as for the text. If you are quoting something of this length (called "block quotation format"), do *not* use quotation marks for the passage; the indentation indicates that the passage is a quotation. Lengthy quotations should not be used in place of your own writing. Use them only if an extended reproduction of the work's language is absolutely necessary.

3. If any words are added to a quotation, use brackets to distinguish your addition from the original source:

> "He [Young Goodman Brown] is portrayed as self-righteous and disillusioned."

Any words inside quotation marks and not in brackets must be precisely those of the author. Brackets can also be used to change the grammatical structure of a quotation so that it fits into your sentence:

> Smith argues that Chekhov "present[s] the narrator in an ambivalent light."

If you drop any words from the source, use ellipses to indicate the omission:

> "Early to bed . . . makes a man healthy, wealthy, and wise."

Use a single line of spaced periods to indicate the omission of a line or more of poetry or more than one paragraph of prose:

Nothing would sleep in that cellar, dank as a ditch,

Bulbs broke out of boxes hunting for chinks in the dark,

. . . .

Nothing would give up life:

Even the dirt kept breathing a small breath.

4. You will be able to punctuate quoted material accurately and confidently if you observe these conventions.

   Place commas and periods inside quotation marks:

"Even the dirt," Roethke insists, "kept breathing a small breath."

Even though a comma does not appear after "dirt" in the original quotation, it is placed inside the quotation mark. The exception to this rule occurs when a parenthetical reference to a source follows the quotation:

"Even the dirt," Roethke insists, "kept breathing a small breath" (11).

Punctuation marks other than commas or periods go outside the quotation marks unless they are part of the material quoted:

What does Roethke mean when he writes that "the dirt kept breathing a small breath"?

Yeats asked, "How can we know the dancer from the dance?"

In the first quotation, there is no question mark in Roethke's original poem; in the second quotation, there is a question mark in Yeats's poem.

There is no formula about when to summarize, paraphrase, or analyze direct quotations as evidence. All three methods, though, are ways to demonstrate your engagement with the primary text. The body of your argument is based on this engagement. Consider these methods as different tools in your toolbox, each of which is designed for a different job. With practice, you'll develop a sense of proportion that will become almost instinctive, but as you start out it is good to be aware of everything you can use and to be conscious of your decisions. Feedback from readers is one of the best ways to fine-tune those decisions.

Writing the Introduction and Conclusion

After you have clearly and adequately developed the body of your paper, pay particular attention to the introductory and concluding paragraphs. It's not a bad idea to write the introduction — at least the final version of it — last, after you know precisely what you are introducing, though some writers are not comfortable composing their argument until they have an introduction in place. Regardless of when you write your introductory paragraph during the writing progress, be aware of the special status of the introduction and the conclusion. Because the introductory paragraph is crucial for generating interest in the topic, it should engage the reader and provide a sense of what the paper is about. There is no formula for writing effective introductory paragraphs because each writing situation is different — depending on the audience, topic, and approach — but if you pay attention to the introductions of the essays you read (including the student examples throughout this book), you will notice the way introductions provide focus. The introductory paragraph to "John Updike's 'A & P' as a State of Mind" (p. 1109), for example, is a straightforward explanation of why the story's setting is important for understanding Updike's treatment of the antagonist. The rest of the paper then offers evidence to support this point.

The general expectation for an academic analytical essay is that the *thesis statement* will make its appearance at the end of the introductory paragraph. We mentioned the working thesis earlier when we discussed prewriting. Through the writing process it will evolve into the thesis statement, which is the aspect of your paper that will be scrutinized the most, and yet less experienced writers are often confused about what it is. As you move toward completing your first full draft, scrutinize your working thesis carefully and work patiently to make sure it covers the breadth of your argument. There are many burdens on the thesis: it should be a complete sentence (though sometimes it may require more than one sentence) that establishes your interpretation of a text in clear, unambiguous language. It is more than a statement of your topic: it also involves your approach to that topic, the interpretation that emerges from that approach, and the *conclusion* to your argument. We'll restate that point because it's crucial, and because it might seem paradoxical: *even though it appears in your introduction, the thesis is a kind of conclusion.* Many readers lose patience with a statement like this one in place of a true thesis: "In this paper I will examine Wilde's use of puns in *The Importance of Being Earnest*." That is the promise of a thesis: stay tuned for my thesis, which will show up at some point over the next five pages! Your reader will invariably reply, "What did you learn when you examined that text?" The answer to that question is closer to your true thesis, which might look like this: "Puns in *The Importance of Being Earnest*, far more than a cheap form of humor, intensify the play's concerns with the instability of identity and the hypocritical nature of many revered social conventions." Now we know where we're going. The thesis may be revised as you get further into the topic and discover what you want to say about it, but once the thesis is established, it will serve as a guide for you and your reader.

Concluding paragraphs also demand special attention because they leave the reader with a final impression of the author's confidence, authority, and intellectual passion. The conclusion should provide a sense of closure instead of starting a new topic or ending abruptly. In the final paragraph about the significance of the setting in "A & P," the student brings together the reasons Sammy quit his job by referring to his refusal to accept Lengel's store policies. Simultaneously, she also explains the significance of Sammy ringing up the "No Sale" mentioned in her introductory paragraph. Thus, we are brought back to where we began, but we now have a greater understanding of why Sammy quits his job. Though they have something in common, the introduction and conclusion of a paper are not exactly the same: the conclusion reflects the journey that has taken place between them. Of course, the body of your paper is the substance of your presentation, but first and last impressions have a powerful impact on readers.

REVISING AND EDITING

College students are sometimes known for procrastination and other, shall we say, emerging time management skills, but we urge you to be kind to yourself (and to your instructor) by following a drafting schedule that is not so hectic. Put some distance — a day or so if you can — between yourself and each draft of your paper. The phrase that seemed just right on Wednesday may appear all wrong on Friday. You'll have a better chance of detecting lumbering sentences and thin paragraphs if you plan ahead and give yourself the time to read your paper from a fresh perspective. Through the process of revision, you can transform a competent paper into an excellent one.

Begin by asking yourself if your approach to the topic requires any rethinking. One strategy is to identify the most interesting point in your essay. (If you can't find an interesting point, you have some work to do.) One of the most common issues for writers at your stage of development is not believing in your ability to generate a good, original idea. The consequence of this circumstance is usually that the writer begins to say something interesting, then immediately pulls back, like checking your swing in baseball. Readers would rather see you follow through with those ideas or develop them by delving deeper into the text. There is always room for development, and you would do well to create space for that development by deleting the parts of the argument that are not relevant to the thesis. This is often the most difficult aspect of writing, especially if you are overly focused on the number of words or pages specified in the assignment. You are likely to want to hold onto the words you have generated, but if they are not the best words to develop your thesis, they are not as valuable as you imagine them to be. Now that you have a draft in place, though, you have more freedom to concentrate on developing the important ideas and diminishing the parts of your paper that might be weighing it down.

If your thesis fails to capture what you've identified as the most interesting point in your paper, you should see an opportunity to revise. It is possible to revise your paper in order to conform to your uninteresting thesis, but it is preferable (and ultimately easier) to change your thesis to accommodate the paper's most important analysis. The thesis is meant to be malleable. Recall that we emphasized the word *eventually* when we introduced the idea of the thesis above. Your entire paper will change with each draft, and your thesis is especially susceptible to change.

The following checklist offers questions to ask about your paper as you revise and edit it. Most of these questions will be familiar to you; however, if you need help with any of them, ask your instructor or review the appropriate section in a composition handbook.

Questions for Writing: A Revision Checklist

1. Is the topic manageable? Is it too narrow or too broad?

2. Is the thesis clear? Is it based on a careful reading of the work and on your smartest, most passionate idea in response to that work?

3. Is the paper logically organized? Does it have a firm sense of direction?

4. Is your argument persuasive? Could anyone dispute it? (Note that if an argument is *completely* indisputable, that might mean that you aren't really saying anything interpretive.)

5. Should any material be deleted? Do any important points require further illustration or evidence?

6. Does the opening paragraph introduce the topic in an interesting manner indicating a context or critical framework that leads to your thesis?

7. Is each paragraph developed, unified, and coherent? Are any notably short or long? If so, do they truly represent a single idea-unit or should they be broken up and/or combined with the paragraphs around them?

(continued)

8. Are there transitions linking the paragraphs? (This question is directly related to question #3 about organization.)

9. Does the concluding paragraph provide a sense of closure?

10. Is the tone appropriate for an academic essay? Is it, for example, flippant or pretentious?

11. Is the title engaging and suggestive?

12. Is every sentence clear, concise, and complete?

13. Are simple, complex, and compound sentences used for variety?

14. Have technical terms been used correctly? Are you certain of the meanings of all the words in the paper? Are they spelled correctly?

15. Have you documented any information borrowed from books, articles, or other sources? Have you achieved your desired balance between quoting, summarizing, and paraphrasing secondary material?

16. Have you used a standard format for citing sources (see p. 1139)?

17. Have you followed your instructor's guidelines for the manuscript format of the final draft?

18. Have you carefully proofread the final draft?

WRITING ABOUT FICTION, POETRY, AND DRAMA

Writing about each of the genres of imaginative literature that comprise this book involves a series of closely related but significantly different set of conventions. Even the way we refer to the different genres involves a slightly different vocabulary. For example, the person who tells the story in a work of short fiction is a narrator, but that voice in a poem is a speaker. In poetry we cite lines while in plays we often refer to acts and scenes. A character in a play or story might become a persona in a poem, and so forth. Although the three genres share certain elements — you can find metaphors in plays, stories, and poems — the emphasis is likely to be different. With these differences in mind, we have included sections below that apply the principles of writing about literature in general to each genre specifically.

WRITING ABOUT FICTION

Writing about fiction is sometimes less intimidating to students than writing about poetry or drama, but it comes with a unique set of challenges. First and foremost, stories center around plots that tend to bewitch the reader and to obscure the story's other elements. You might find yourself recalling a story by saying, "Oh, that's the one about the guy who works in the grocery store," but as you know, plot is only one element. Most poems are only a page or two long, meaning you can see them all at once and visually compare their elements, whereas fiction tests your power of memory. Plays consist mostly of dialogue, whereas fiction tends to intersperse dialogue and description, sometimes demanding that your imagination make great leaps over time and space. In short, fiction often creates its own world, and its expansiveness is sometimes hard to gather in.

Given the fact that fiction tends to swell over time and space and focuses on the endlessly fascinating subject of human behavior, it is probably best to begin broadly and work toward narrowing down your topic. In writing about poetry, you might start with a single feature of language, like rhythm; in writing about fiction, you will probably be drawn initially toward a character. Fiction offers a wider variety of entry points. We'd suggest that you try to determine what you find unique, fascinating, noteworthy, or perhaps just recognizable within a given story as a way of figuring out where you want to begin.

Questions for Responsive Reading and Writing about Fiction

The following questions can help you consider important elements of fiction that reveal your responses to a story's effects and meanings. The questions are general, so they will not always be relevant to a particular story. Many of them, however, should prove useful for thinking, talking, and writing about a work of fiction. Note that these are just initial ways of approaching a story as a way of generating ideas: you will probably end up combining elements or developing a context that will expand your sense of how to frame one or more of them. If you are uncertain about the meaning of a term used in a question, consult the Glossary of Literary Terms beginning on page 1152 of this book. You should also find useful the discussion of various critical approaches to literature and possible contexts in Chapter 30, "Critical Strategies for Reading."

PLOT

1. Does the plot conform to a formula? Is it like those of any other stories you have read? Did you find it predictable?

(continued)

2. What is the source and nature of the conflict for the protagonist? Was your major interest in the story based on what happens next or on some other concern? What does the title reveal now that you've finished the story?

3. Is the story told chronologically? If not, in what order are its events told, and what is the effect of that order on your response to the action?

4. What does the exposition reveal? Does the author employ flashbacks? Did you see any foreshadowing? Where is the climax?

5. Is the conflict resolved at the end? Would you characterize the ending as happy, unhappy, or somewhere in between?

6. Is the plot unified? How is each incident somehow related to some other element in the story?

CHARACTER

1. Do you identify with the protagonist? Who (or what) is the antagonist?

2. Did your response to any characters change as you read? What do you think caused the change? Do any characters change and develop in the course of the story? How?

3. Are round, flat, or stock characters used? Is their behavior motivated and plausible?

4. How does the author reveal characters? Are they directly described or indirectly presented through gestures, dialogue, interior monologue, etc.?

5. What is the purpose of the minor characters? Are they individualized, or do they primarily represent ideas or attitudes?

SETTING

1. Is the setting important in shaping your response? If it were changed, would your response to the story's action and meaning be significantly different?

2. Is the setting used symbolically? Are the time, place, and atmosphere related to the theme?

3. Is the setting used as an antagonist?

(continued)

Point of View

1. Who tells the story? Is it a first-person or third-person narrator? Is it a major or minor character or one who does not participate in the action at all? How much does the narrator know? Does the point of view change at all in the course of the story?

2. Is the narrator reliable and objective? Does the narrator appear too innocent, emotional, or self-deluded to be trusted?

3. Does the author directly comment on the action?

4. If it were told from a different point of view, how would your response to the story change? Would anything be lost?

Symbolism

1. Did you notice any potentially significant symbols in the story? Are they actions, characters, settings, objects, or words?

2. How do the symbols contribute to your understanding of the story?

Theme

1. Did you find a theme? If so, what is it?

2. Is the theme stated directly, or is it developed implicitly through the plot, characters, or some other element?

3. Is the theme a confirmation of conventional values, or does it challenge them?

Style, Tone, and Irony

1. Do you think the style is consistent and appropriate throughout the story? Do all the characters use the same kind of language, or did you hear different voices?

2. Would you describe the level of diction as formal or informal? Are the sentences short and simple, long and complex, or some combination?

3. How does the author's use of language contribute to the tone of the story? Did it seem, for example, intense, relaxed, sentimental, nostalgic, humorous, angry, sad, or remote?

4. Does the author's use of language bear close scrutiny so that you feel and experience more with each reading?

A SAMPLE STUDENT ESSAY

John Updike's "A & P" as a State of Mind

Nancy Lager's paper analyzes the setting in John Updike's "A & P" (the entire story appears on p. 138). The assignment simply asked for an essay of approximately 750 words on a short story written in the twentieth century. The approach was left to the student.

The idea for this essay began with Lager asking herself why Updike used "A & P" as the title. The initial answer to the question was that "the setting is important in this story." This answer was the rough beginning of a tentative thesis. What still had to be explained, though, was how the setting is important. To determine the significance of the setting, Lager jotted down some notes based on the passages she underlined and her marginal notations:

A & P

"usual traffic"

lights and tile

"electric eye"

shoppers like "sheep," "houseslaves," "pigs"

"Alexandrov and Petrooshki" — Russia

New England Town	*Lengel*
typical: bank, church, etc.	"manager"
traditional	"doesn't miss that much"
conservative	(like lady shopper)
proper	Sunday school
near Salem — witch trials	"It's our policy"
puritanical	spokesman for A & P values
intolerant	

From these notes Lager saw that Lengel serves as the voice of the A & P. He is, in a sense, a personification of the intolerant atmosphere of the setting. This insight led to another version of her thesis statement: "The setting of 'A & P' is the antagonist of the story." That explained at least some of the setting's importance. By seeing Lengel as a spokesman for A & P policies, Lager could view him as a voice that articulates the morally smug atmosphere created by the setting. Finally, she considered why it is significant that the setting is the antagonist, and this generated her last thesis: "Because the intolerant setting of 'A & P' is the antagonist in the story, it is crucial to our understanding of Sammy's decision to quit his job." This thesis sentence does not appear precisely in these words in the essay, but it is the backbone of the introductory paragraph.

The remaining paragraphs consist of details that describe the A & P in the second paragraph, the New England town in the third, Lengel in the fourth, and Sammy's reasons for quitting in the concluding paragraph. Paragraphs 2, 3, and 4 are largely based on Lager's notes, which she used as an outline once her thesis was established. The essay is sharply focused, well organized, and generally well written. In addition, it suggests a number of useful guidelines for analytic papers:

1. Only the points related to the thesis are included. In another type of paper the role of the girls in the bathing suits, for example, might have been considerably more prominent.
2. The analysis keeps the setting in focus while at the same time indicating how it is significant in the major incident in the story — Sammy's quitting.
3. The title is a useful lead in to the paper; it provides a sense of what the topic is. In addition, the title is drawn from a sentence (the final one of the first paragraph) that clearly explains its meaning.
4. The introductory paragraph is direct and clearly indicates that the paper will argue that the setting serves as the antagonist of the story.
5. Brief quotations are deftly incorporated into the text of the paper to illustrate points. We are told what we need to know about the story as evidence is provided to support ideas. There is no unnecessary plot summary. Even though "A & P" is only a few pages in length and is an assigned topic, page numbers are included after quoted phrases. If the story were longer, page numbers would be especially helpful for the reader.
6. The paragraphs are well developed, unified, and coherent. They flow naturally from one to another. Notice, for example, the smooth transition worked into the final sentence of the third paragraph and the first sentence of the fourth paragraph.
7. Lager makes excellent use of her careful reading and notes by finding revealing connections among the details she has observed. The store's "electric eye," for instance, is related to the woman's and Lengel's watchfulness.
8. As Lager describes events, she uses the present tense. This decision (which is standard when writing about literature) avoids awkward tense shifts and lends an immediacy to the discussion.
9. The concluding paragraph establishes the significance of why the setting should be seen as the antagonist and provides a sense of closure by

referring again to Sammy's "No Sale," which has been mentioned at the end of the first paragraph.

10. In short, Lager has demonstrated that she has read the work closely, has understood the relation of the setting to the major action, and has argued her thesis convincingly by using evidence from the story.

Lager 1

Nancy Lager

Professor Taylor

English 102-12

2 February 2018

John Updike's "A & P" as a State of Mind

The setting of John Updike's "A & P" is crucial to our understanding of Sammy's decision to quit his job. Although Sammy is the central character in the story and we learn that he is a principled, good-natured nineteen-year-old with a sense of humor, Updike seems to invest as much effort in describing the setting as he does in Sammy. The setting is the antagonist and plays a role that is as important as Sammy's. The title, after all, is not "Youthful Rebellion" or "Sammy Quits" but "A & P." Even though Sammy knows that his quitting will make life more difficult for him, he instinctively insists on rejecting what the A & P comes to represent in the story. When he rings up a "No Sale" and "saunter[s]" (144) out of the store, he leaves behind not only a job but the rigid state of mind associated with the A & P.

Sammy's descriptions of the A & P present a setting that is ugly, monotonous, and rigidly regulated. The fluorescent light is as blandly cool as the "checker-board green-and-cream rubber-tile floor" (141). We can see the uniformity Sammy describes because we have all been in chain stores. The "usual traffic" moves in one direction (except for the swimsuited girls, who move against it), and everything is neatly ordered and categorized in tidy aisles. The dehumanizing routine of this environment is suggested by Sammy's offhand references to the typical shoppers as "sheep" (141), "houseslaves" (141), and "pigs" (144). They seem to pace through the store in a stupor; as Sammy tells us, not even dynamite could move them.

The A & P is appropriately located "right in the middle" (142) of a proper, conservative, traditional New England town north of Boston. This location, coupled with the fact that the town is only five miles from Salem, the site of the famous seventeenth-century witch trials, suggests a narrow, intolerant social atmosphere in which there is no room for stepping beyond the boundaries of what is regarded as normal and proper. The importance of this setting can be appreciated even more if we imagine the action taking place in, say, a mellow suburb of southern California. In this prim New England setting, the girls in their bathing suits are bound to offend somebody's sense of propriety.

As soon as Lengel sees the girls, the inevitable conflict begins. He embodies the dull conformity represented by the A & P. As "manager" (142), he is both the guardian and enforcer of "policy" (143). When he gives the girls "that sad Sunday-school-superintendent stare" (143), we know we are in the presence of the A & P version of a dreary bureaucrat who "doesn't miss that much" (142). He is as unsympathetic and unpleasant as the woman "with rouge on her cheekbones and no eyebrows" (140) who pounces on Sammy for ringing up her "HiHo crackers" twice. Like the "electric eye" (144) in the doorway, her vigilant eyes allow nothing to escape their notice. For Sammy the logical extension of Lengel's "policy" is the half-serious notion that one day the A & P might be known as the "Great Alexandrov and Petrooshki Tea Company" (142). Sammy's connection between what he regards as mindless "policy" (143) and Soviet oppression is obviously an exaggeration, but the reader is invited to entertain the similarities anyway.

The reason Sammy quits his job has less to do with defending the girls than with his own sense of what it means to be a decent human being. His decision is not an easy one. He doesn't want to make trouble or disappoint his parents, and he knows his independence and self-reliance (the other side of New England tradition) will make life more complex for him.

Lager 2

In spite of his own hesitations, he finds himself blurting out "Fiddle-de-doo" (144) to Lengel's policies and in doing so knows that his grandmother "would have been pleased" (144). Sammy's "No Sale" rejects the crabbed perspective on life that Lengel represents as manager of the A & P. This gesture is more than just a negative, however, for as he punches in that last entry on the cash register, "the machine whirs 'pee-pul' " (144). His decision to quit his job at the A & P is an expression of his refusal to regard policies as more important than people.

Lager 4

Work Cited

Updike, John. "A & P." *Literature to Go*, edited by Michael Meyer and
D. Quentin Miller, 4th ed., Bedford/St. Martin's, 2020,
pp. 138–143.

WRITING ABOUT POETRY

Writing about poetry can be a rigorous means of developing and testing your initial response to a poem. Anyone who has been asked to write several pages about a fourteen-line poem knows how intellectually challenging this exercise is, because it means paying close attention to language. Such scrutiny of words, however, sensitizes you not only to the poet's use of language but also to your own use of language. At first you may feel intimidated by having to compose a paper that is longer than the poem you're writing about, but once you start writing — often the hardest part of the process — you will realize that you have plenty to say. Keep in mind that there is not a single hidden meaning to any poem: it is not like algebra where you are solving for *x*. Even Carl Sandburg once confessed, "I've written some poetry I don't understand myself." Because language is not stable, poems are not codes to be cracked. Don't worry about "the right answer": your role is to develop an interesting thesis and to present it clearly and persuasively.

An interesting thesis will come to you if you read and reread, take notes, annotate the text, and generate ideas. Although it requires energy to read closely and to write convincingly about the charged language found in poetry, there is nothing mysterious about such reading and writing. This section provides a set of Questions for Responsive Reading and Writing designed to sharpen your reading and writing about poetry. After reading a poem, use the questions to help you think, talk, and write about any poem. Before you do, though, be sure that you have read the poem several times without worrying actively about interpretation. With poetry, as with all literature, it's important to allow yourself the pleasure of enjoying whatever makes itself apparent to you. On subsequent readings, use the questions to understand and appreciate how the poem works; remember to keep in mind that not all questions will necessarily be relevant to a particular poem.

Following these questions is a sample paper that offers a clear and well-developed thesis concerning John Donne's "Death Be Not Proud."

Questions for Responsive Reading and Writing about Poetry

The following questions can help you respond to important elements that reveal a poem's effects and meanings. The questions are general, so not all of them will necessarily be relevant to a particular poem. Many, however, should prove useful for thinking, talking, and writing about each poem in this collection. If you are uncertain about the meaning of a term used in a question, consult the Glossary of Literary Terms beginning on page 1152.

Before addressing these questions, read the poem you are studying in its entirety. Don't worry about interpretation on a first reading; allow yourself the pleasure of enjoying whatever makes itself apparent to you. Then on subsequent readings, use the questions to understand and appreciate how the poem works.

1. Who is the speaker? Is it possible to determine the speaker's age, gender, sensibilities, level of awareness, and values?

2. Is the speaker addressing anyone in particular?

(continued)

3. How do you respond to the speaker? Favorably? Negatively? What is the situation? Are there any special circumstances that inform what the speaker says?

4. Is there a specific setting of time and place?

5. Does reading the poem aloud help you understand it?

6. Does a paraphrase reveal the basic purpose of the poem?

7. What does the title emphasize?

8. Is the theme presented directly or indirectly?

9. Do any allusions enrich the poem's meaning?

10. How does the diction reveal meaning? Are any words repeated? Do any carry evocative connotative meanings? Are there any puns or other forms of verbal wit?

11. Are figures of speech used? How does the figurative language contribute to the poem's vividness and meaning?

12. Do any objects, persons, places, events, or actions have allegorical or symbolic meanings? What other details in the poem support your interpretation?

13. Is irony used? Are there any examples of situational irony, verbal irony, or dramatic irony? Is understatement or paradox used?

14. What is the tone of the poem? Is the tone consistent?

15. Does the poem use onomatopoeia, assonance, consonance, or alliteration? How do these sounds affect you?

16. What sounds are repeated? If there are rhymes, what is their effect? Do they seem forced or natural? Is there a rhyme scheme? Do the rhymes contribute to the poem's meaning?

17. Do the lines have a regular meter? What is the predominant meter? Are there significant variations? Does the rhythm seem appropriate for the poem's tone?

18. Does the poem's form — its overall structure — follow an established pattern? Do you think the form is a suitable vehicle for the poem's meaning and effects?

(continued)

19. Is the language of the poem intense and concentrated? Do you think it warrants more than one or two close readings?

20. Did you respond positively to the poem? What, specifically, pleased or displeased you about what was expressed and how it was expressed?

21. Is there a particular critical approach or context that seems especially appropriate for this poem? (See Chapter 30, "Critical Strategies for Reading.")

22. What kinds of evidence from the poem are you focusing on to support your interpretation? Does your interpretation leave out any important elements that might undercut or qualify your interpretation?

THE ELEMENTS TOGETHER

The elements of poetry that you have studied in Chapters 11–19 of this book offer a vocabulary and a series of perspectives that open up avenues of inquiry into a poem. As you have learned, there are many potential routes that you can take. By asking questions about the speaker, diction, figurative language, sounds, rhythm, tone, or theme, you clarify your understanding while simultaneously sensitizing yourself to elements and issues especially relevant to the poem under consideration. This process of careful, informed reading allows you to see how the various elements of the poem reinforce its meanings. A poem's elements do not exist in isolation, however. They work together to create a complete experience for the reader.

This section shows you how one student, Rose Bostwick, moves through the stages of writing about how a poem's elements combine for a final effect. Included here are Rose's annotated version of the poem, her first response, her informal outline, and the final draft of an explication of John Donne's "Death Be Not Proud." After reviewing the elements of poetry covered in Chapters 11–19, Rose read the poem several times, paying careful attention to diction, figurative language, irony, symbol, rhythm, sound, and so on. Her final paper is more concerned with the overall effect of the combination of elements than with a line-by-line breakdown, and her annotated version of the poem details her attention to that task. As you read and reread "Death Be Not Proud," keep notes on how *you* think the elements of this poem work together and to what overall effect.

JOHN DONNE (1572–1631)

John Donne, now regarded as a major poet of the early seventeenth century, wrote love poems at the beginning of his career but shifted to religious themes after converting from Catholicism to Anglicanism in the early 1590s. Although trained in law, he was also ordained a priest and became dean of St. Paul's Cathedral in London in 1621. The following poem, from "Holy Sonnets," reflects both his religious faith and his ability to create elegant arguments in verse.

© Michael Nicholson/Getty Images.

Death Be Not Proud   1611

Death be not proud, though some have callèd thee
Mighty and dreadful, for thou art not so;
For those whom thou think'st thou dost overthrow
Die not, poor Death, nor yet canst thou kill me.
From rest and sleep, which but thy pictures° be,   *images*   5
Much pleasure; then from thee much more must flow,
And soonest our best men with thee do go,
Rest of their bones, and soul's delivery.°   *deliverance*
Thou art slave to Fate, Chance, kings, and desperate men,
And dost with Poison, War, and Sickness dwell;   10
And poppy or charms can make us sleep as well,
And better than thy stroke; why swell'st° thou then?   *swell with pride*
One short sleep past, we wake eternally
And death shall be no more; Death, thou shalt die.

CONSIDERATIONS FOR CRITICAL THINKING AND WRITING

1. FIRST RESPONSE. Why doesn't the speaker fear death? Explain why you find the argument convincing or not.

2. How does the speaker compare death with rest and sleep in lines 5–8? What is the point of this comparison?

3. Discuss the poem's rhythm by examining the breaks and end-stopped lines. How does the poem's rhythm contribute to its meaning?

4. What are the signs that this poem is structured as a sonnet?

A SAMPLE CLOSE READING

An Annotated Version of "Death Be Not Proud"

As she read the poem closely several times, Rose annotated it with impressions and ideas that would lead to insights on which her analysis would be built. Her close examination of the poem's elements allowed her to understand how its parts contribute to its overall effect; her annotations provide a useful map of her thinking.

Speaker scolds Death.

Death Be Not Proud   1611

In formal diction, speaker personifies and rebukes Death for undeserved pride.

Death be not proud, though some have callèd thee

Mighty and dreadful, for thou art not so;

Most lines are iambic pentameter, but first two begin with stressed syllables for emphasis.

For those whom thou think'st thou dost overthrow

Die not, poor Death, nor yet canst thou kill me.

Death cannot kill speaker, who even taunts Death.

From rest and sleep, which but thy pictures° be,   *images* 5

Much pleasure; then from thee much more must flow,

Death is only like sleep rather than something eternal.

And soonest our best men with thee do go,

Rest of their bones, and soul's delivery.°   *deliverance*

Thou art slave to Fate, Chance, kings, and desperate men,

And dost with Poison, War, and Sickness dwell;   10

And poppy or charms can make us sleep as well,

And better than thy stroke; why swell'st° thou then?   *swell with pride*

Each quatrain (4-line stanza) develops the argument that Death is ultimately weak and cannot be justly proud or rightly feared, building toward the conclusion of final two lines.

Rather than a power, Death is a slave to other forces.

One short sleep past, we wake eternally

And death shall be no more; Death, thou shalt die.

Argument in the couplet climaxes with allusion to humanity's resurrection and death of Death itself. In addition to Christianity, does sonnet form finally control Death too?

A SAMPLE FIRST RESPONSE

After Rose carefully read "Death Be Not Proud" and had a sense of how the elements work, she took the first step toward a formal explication by writing informally about the relevant elements and addressing the question *Why doesn't the speaker fear death? Explain why you find the argument convincing or not.* Note that at this point, she was not as concerned with textual evidence and detail as she would need to be in her final paper.

I've read the poem "Death Be Not Proud" by John Donne a few times now, and I have a sense of how it works. The poem is a sonnet, and each of the three quatrains presents a piece of the argument that Death should not be proud, because it is not really all-powerful, and may even be a source of pleasure. As a reader, I resist this seeming paradox at first, but I know it must be a trick, a riddle of some sort that the poem will proceed to untangle. I think one of the reasons the poem comes off as such a powerful statement is that Donne at first seems to be playful and paradoxical in his characterizations of Death. He's almost teasing Death. But beneath the teasing tone you feel the strong foundation of the real reason Death should not be proud—Donne's faith in the immortality of the soul. The poem begins to feel more solemn as it progresses, as the hints at the idea of immortality become more clearly articulated.

Donne utilizes two literary conventions to increase the effect of this poem: he uses the convention of personifying death, so that he can address it directly, and he uses the metaphor of death as a kind of sleep. These two things determine the tone and the progression from playful to solemn in the poem.

The last clause of the poem (line 14) plays with the paradoxical-seeming character of what he's been declaring. Ironically, it seems the only thing susceptible to death is death itself. Or, when death becomes powerless is when it only has power over itself.

ORGANIZING YOUR THOUGHTS

Showing in a paper how different elements of a particular poem work together is often quite challenging. While you may have a clear intuitive sense of what elements are important to the poem and how they complement one another, it is important to organize your thoughts in such a way as to make the relationships clear to your audience. The simplest way is to go line by line, but that can quickly become rote for writer and reader. Because you will want to organize your paper in the way that best serves your thesis, it may help to write an informal outline that charts how you think the argument moves. You may find, for example, that the argument is not persuasive if you start with the final lines and go back to the beginning of the poem or passage. However you decide to organize your argument, keep in mind that a unifying idea will run throughout the entire paper and that your thesis will express that idea concisely.

A SAMPLE INFORMAL OUTLINE

In her informal outline (following), Rose discovers that her argument works best if she begins at the beginning. Note that, though her later paper concerns itself with how several elements of poetry contribute to the poem's theme and message, her informal outline concerns itself much more with what that message is and how it develops as the poem progresses. She will fill in the details later.

Working Thesis: From the very first word, addressing "Death" directly, Donne uses the literary conventions of personifying death and comparing it to sleep to begin an argument that Death should not be proud of its might or dreadfulness. But these two elements of his argument come to be seen as the superficial points when the true reason for death's powerlessness becomes clear. The Christian belief in the immortality of the soul is the reason for death's powerlessness and likeness to sleep.

Body of essay: Show how argument proceeds by quatrains from playful address to Death, and statement that Death is much like sleep, its "picture," to statement that Death is "slave" to other forces (and so should not be proud of being the mightiest), to the couplet, which articulates clearly the idea of immortality and gives the final paradox, "Death, thou shalt die."

Conclusion: Donne's faith in the immortality of the soul enables him to "prove" in this argument that Death is truly like its metaphorical representation, sleep. Faith allows him to derive a source for this conventional trope, and it allows him to state his truth in paradoxes. He relies on the conventional idea that death is an end, and a conqueror, and the only all-powerful force, to make the paradoxes that lend his argument the force of mystery — the mystery of faith.

THE ELEMENTS AND THEME

As you create an informal outline, your understanding of the poem will grow, change, and finally, solidify. You will develop a much clearer sense of what the poem's elements combine to create, and you will have chosen a scheme for organizing your argument. The next step before drafting is to generate a working thesis, which will not only keep your paper focused but will also help you center your thoughts. For papers that discuss how the elements of poetry come together, the thesis is a single and concise statement of what the elements combine to create — the idea around which all the elements revolve.

Once you understand how all of the elements of the poem fit together and have articulated your understanding in the thesis statement, the next step is to flesh out your argument. By including quotations from the poem to illustrate the points you will be making, you will better explain exactly how each element relates to the others and, more specifically, to your thesis.

A SAMPLE EXPLICATION

The Use of Conventional Metaphors for Death in John Donne's "Death Be Not Proud"

In Rose's final draft, she focuses on the use of metaphor in "Death Be Not Proud." Her essay provides a coherent reading that relates each line of the poem to the speaker's intense awareness of death. Although the essay discusses each stanza in order, the introductory paragraph provides a brief overview explaining how the poem's metaphor and arguments contribute to its total meaning. In addition, Rose does not hesitate to discuss a line out of sequence when it can be usefully connected to another phrase. She also works quotations into her sentences to support her points. When she adds something to a quotation to clarify it, she encloses her words in brackets so that they will not be mistaken for the poet's, and she uses a slash to indicate line divisions: "soonest . . . with thee do go, / [for] Rest of their bones, and soul's delivery." Finally, Rose is sure to cite the line numbers for any direct quotations from the poem. As you read through her final draft, remember that the word *explication* comes from the Latin *explicare*, "to unfold." How successful do you think Rose is at unfolding this poem to reveal how its elements — here ranging from metaphor, structure, meter, personification, paradox, and irony to theme — contribute to its meaning?

Rose Bostwick

English 101

Professor Hart

24 February 2019

The Use of Conventional Metaphors for Death

in John Donne's "Death Be Not Proud"

Thesis providing interpretation of the poem's use of metaphor and how it contributes to the poem's central argument

In the sonnet that begins "Death be not proud . . ." John Donne argues that death is not "mighty and dreadful" but is more like its metaphorical representation, sleep. Death, Donne puts forth, is even a source of pleasure and rest. The poet builds this argument on two foundations. One is made up of the metaphors and literary conventions for death: death is compared with sleep and is often personified so that it can be addressed directly. The poem is an address to death that at first seems paradoxical and somewhat playful, but which then rises in all the emotion of faith as it reveals the second foundation of the argument—the Christian belief in the immortality of the soul. Seen against the backdrop of this belief, death loses its powerful threat and is seen as only a metaphorical sleep, or rest.

Discussion of how form and meter contribute to the poem's central argument

The poem is an ironic argument that proceeds according to the structure of the sonnet form. Each quatrain contains a new development or aspect of the argument, and the final couplet serves as a conclusion. The metrical scheme is mainly iambic pentameter, but in several places in the poem, the stress pattern is altered for emphasis. For example, the first foot of the poem is inverted, so that "Death," the first word, receives the stress. This announces to us right away that death is being personified and addressed. This inversion also serves to begin the poem energetically and forcefully. The second line behaves in the same way. The first syllable of "Mighty" receives the stress, emphasizing the meaning of the word and its assumed relation to death.

Discussion of how personification contributes to the poem's central argument

This first quatrain offers the first paradox and sets up the argument that death has been conventionally personified with the

wrong attributes, might and dreadfulness. The poet tells death not
to be proud, "though some have callèd thee / Mighty and dreadful,"
because, he says, death is "not so" (lines 1-2). Donne will turn this
conventional characterization of death on its head with the paradox
of the third and fourth lines: he says the people overthrown by
death (as if by a conqueror) "Die not, poor death, nor yet canst thou
kill me." These lines establish the paradox of death not being able to
cause death.

The next quatrain will not begin to answer the question of
why this paradox is so, but will posit another slight paradox—the
idea of death as pleasurable. In lines 5-8, Donne uses the literary
convention of describing death as a metaphorical sleep, or rest, to
construct the argument that death must give pleasure: "From rest
and sleep, which but thy pictures be, / Much pleasure; then from
thee much more must flow" (5-6). At this point, the argument seems
almost playful, but is carefully hinting at the solemnity of the
deeper foundation of the belief in immortality. The metaphor of sleep
for death includes the idea of waking; one doesn't sleep forever.
The next two lines put forth the idea that death is pleasurable
enough to be desired by "our best men" who "soonest . . . with thee
do go, / [for] Rest of their bones, and soul's delivery" (7-8). This
last line comes closer to announcing the true reason for death's
powerlessness and pleasure: it is the way to the "soul's delivery"
from the body and life on earth, and implicitly, into another,
better realm.

A new reason for death's powerlessness arises in the next four
lines. The poet says to death:

> Thou art slave to Fate, Chance, kings, and desperate men,
> And dost with Poison, War, and Sickness dwell;
> And poppy or charms can make us sleep as well,
> And better than thy stroke; why swell'st thou then? (9-12)

Discussion of how metaphor of sleep and idea of immortality support the poem's central argument

Donne argues here that there are forces more powerful than
death that actually control it. Fate and chance determine when
death occurs, and to whom it comes. Kings, with the powers of law
and war, can summon death and throw it on whom they wish. And
desperate men, murderers or suicides, can also summon death with
the strength of their emotions. In lines 11 and 12, Donne again uses
the metaphor of death as a kind of sleep, but says that drugs or
"charms" give one a better sleep than death. And he asks playfully
why death should be so proud, after all these illustrations of its
weakness have been given: "why swell'st thou then?" (12).

Finally, with the last couplet, Donne reveals the true, deeper
reason behind his argument that death should not be proud of its
power. These lines also offer an explanation of the metaphor for
death of sleep, or rest: "One short sleep past, we wake eternally /
And death shall be no more; Death, thou shalt die" (13-14). After
death, the soul lives on, according to Christian theology and belief.
In the Christian heaven, where the soul is immortal, death will
no longer exist, and so this last paradox, "Death, thou shalt die,"
becomes true. Again in this line, a significant inversion of metrical
stress occurs. "Death," in the second clause, receives the stress,
recalling the first line, emphasizing that it is an address and giving
the clause a forceful sense of finality. His belief in the immortality
of the soul enables Donne to "prove" in this argument that death
is in actuality like its metaphorical representation, sleep. His faith
allows him to derive a source for this conventional metaphor and to
"disprove" the metaphor of death as an all-powerful conqueror. His
Christian beliefs also allow him to state his truth in paradoxes, the
mysteries that are justified by the mystery of faith.

Margin notes:

Discussion of how language and tone contribute to the poem's central argument

Discussion of function of religious faith in the poem and how word order and meter create emphasis

Conclusion supporting thesis in context of poet's beliefs

Work Cited

Donne, John. "Death Be Not Proud." *Literature to Go*, edited by Michael
   Meyer and D. Quentin Miller, 4th ed., Bedford/St. Martin's, 2020,
   p. 1117.

WRITING ABOUT DRAMA

Because dramatic literature is written to be performed, writing about reading a play may seem twice removed from what playwrights intend the experience of drama to be: a live audience responding to live actors. Although
reading a play creates distance between yourself and a performance of
it, reading a play can actually bring you closer to understanding that the
literary dimension of a script is what supports a stage production of any
play. Writing about that script — examining carefully how the language of
the stage directions, setting, exposition, dialogue, plot, and other dramatic
elements serve to produce effects and meanings — can enhance an imaginative re-creation of a performance. In a sense, writing about a play gauges
your own interpretative response as an audience member. The difference, of
course, is that instead of applauding, you are typing.

  Composing an essay about drama records more than your response to a
play; writing also helps you explore, clarify, and discover dimensions of the
play you may not have perceived by simply watching a performance of it.
Writing is work, as we've suggested, but it's the kind of work that brings you
closer to your own imagination as well as to the play. That process is more
accessible if you read carefully, take notes, and annotate the text to generate ideas as we discuss earlier in this chapter. The following section offers
a set of questions to help you read and write about drama and includes a
sample paper that argues for a feminist reading of Susan Glaspell's *Trifles*
(pp. 683–694).

Questions for Responsive Reading and Writing about Drama

The questions in this section can help you consider important elements that reveal a play's effects and meanings. These questions are general and will not, therefore, always be relevant to a particular play. Many of them, however, should prove to be useful for thinking, talking, and writing about drama. If you are uncertain about the meaning of a term used in a question, consult the Glossary of Literary Terms beginning on page 1152.

1. Did you enjoy the play? What, specifically, pleased or displeased you about what was expressed and how it was expressed?

2. What is the significance of the play's title? How does it suggest the author's overall emphasis?

3. What information do the stage directions provide about the characters, action, and setting? Are these directions primarily descriptive, or are they also interpretive?

4. How is the exposition presented? What does it reveal? How does the playwright's choice *not* to dramatize certain events on stage help to determine what the focus of the play is?

5. In what ways is the setting important? Would the play be altered significantly if the setting were changed?

6. Are there instances of foreshadowing that suggest what is to come? Are flashbacks used to dramatize what has already happened?

7. What is the major conflict the protagonist faces? What complications constitute the rising action? Where is the climax? Is the conflict resolved?

8. Are one or more subplots used to qualify or complicate the main plot? Is the plot unified so that each incident somehow has a function that relates it to some other element in the play?

9. Does the author purposely avoid a pyramidal plot structure of rising action, climax, and falling action? Is the plot experimental? Is the plot logically and chronologically organized, or is it fantastical or absurd? What effects are produced by the plot? How does it reflect the author's view of life?

10. Who is the protagonist? Who (or what) is the antagonist?

(continued)

11. By what means does the playwright reveal character? What do the characters' names, physical qualities, actions, and words convey about them? What do the characters reveal about each other?

12. What is the purpose of the minor characters? Are they individualized, or do they primarily represent ideas or attitudes? Are any character foils used?

13. Do the characters all use the same kind of language, or is their speech differentiated? Is it formal or informal? How do the characters' diction and manner of speaking serve to characterize them?

14. Does your response to the characters change in the course of the play? What causes the change?

15. Are words and images repeated in the play so that they take on special meanings? Which speeches seem particularly important? Why?

16. How does the playwright's use of language contribute to the tone of the play? Is the dialogue, for example, predominantly light, humorous, relaxed, sentimental, sad, angry, intense, or violent?

17. Are any symbols used in the play? Which actions, characters, settings, objects, or words convey more than their literal meanings?

18. Are any unfamiliar theatrical conventions used that present problems in understanding the play? How does knowing more about the nature of the theater from which the play originated help to resolve these problems?

19. Is the theme stated directly, or is it developed implicitly through the plot, characters, or some other element? Does the theme confirm or challenge most people's values?

20. How does the play reflect the values of the society in which it is set and in which it was written?

21. How does the play reflect or challenge your own values?

22. Is there a sound recording, film, or online source for the play available in your library or media center? How does this version compare with your own reading?

(continued)

23. How would you produce the play on a stage? Consider scenery, costumes, casting, and characterizations. What would you emphasize most in your production?

24. Is there a particular critical approach or context that seems especially appropriate for this play? (See Chapter 30, "Critical Strategies for Reading," which begins on p. 1069.)

A SAMPLE STUDENT PAPER

The Feminist Evidence in Susan Glaspell's Trifles

The following paper was written in response to an assignment that required an analysis — about 750 words — of an assigned play. Chris Duffy's paper argues that although *Trifles* was written a century ago, it should be seen as a feminist play because its treatment of the tensions between men and women deliberately reveals the oppressiveness that women have had to cope with in their everyday lives. The paper discusses a number of the play's elements, but the discussion is unified through its focus on how the women characters are bound together by a set of common concerns. Notice that page numbers are provided to document quoted passages.

Duffy 1

Chris Duffy

Professor Barrina-Barrou

English 109-2

6 March 2019

The Feminist Evidence in Susan Glaspell's *Trifles*

Despite its early publication date, Susan Glaspell's *Trifles*

General thesis statement

(1916) can be regarded as a work of feminist literature. The play depicts the life of a woman who has been suppressed, oppressed, and subjugated by a patronizing, patriarchal husband. Mrs. Wright is eventually driven to kill her "hard" (691) husband who has stifled

Duffy 2

every last twitch of her identity. *Trifles* dramatizes the hypocrisy and ingrained discrimination of male-dominated society while simultaneously speaking to the dangers for women who succumb to such hierarchies. Because Mrs. Wright follows the role mapped by her husband and is directed by society's patriarchal expectations, her identity is lost somewhere along the way. However, Mrs. Hale and Mrs. Peters quietly insist on preserving their own identities by protecting Mrs. Wright from the men who seek to convict her of murder.

More specific thesis offering analysis, with supporting evidence

Mrs. Wright is described as someone who used to have a flair for life. Her neighbor, Mrs. Hale, comments that the last time Mrs. Wright appeared happy and vivacious was before she was married or, more important, when she was Minnie Foster and not Mrs. Wright. Mrs. Hale laments, "I heard she used to wear pretty clothes and be lively, when she was Minnie Foster, one of the town girls singing in the choir" (693). But after thirty years of marriage, Mrs. Wright is now worried about her canned preserves freezing and being without an apron while she is in jail. This subservient image was so accepted in society that Mrs. Peters, the sheriff's wife, speculates that Mrs. Wright must want her apron in order to "feel more natural" (688). Any other roles would be considered uncharacteristic.

Analysis of Mrs. Wright through perspectives of female characters

This wifely role is predicated on the supposition that women have no ability to make complicated decisions, to think critically, or to rely on themselves. As the title suggests, the men in this story think of homemaking as much less important than a husband's breadwinning role. Mr. Hale remarks, "Well, women are used to worrying over trifles" (687), and Sheriff Peters assumes the insignificance of "kitchen things" (686). Hence, women are forced into a domestic, secondary role, like it or not, and are not even respected for that. Mr. Hale, Sheriff Peters, and the county attorney all dismiss the dialogue between Mrs. Peters and Mrs. Hale as

Analysis of role of women through perspectives of male characters feminine chitchat. Further, the county attorney allows the women to leave the Wrights' house unsupervised because he sees Mrs. Peters as merely an extension of her husband.

Even so, the domestic system the men have set up for their wives and their disregard for them after the rules and boundaries have been laid down prove to be the men's downfall. The evidence that Mrs. Wright killed her husband is woven into Mrs. Hale's and Mrs. Peters's conversations about Mrs. Wright's sewing and her pet bird. The knots in her quilt match those in the rope used to strangle Mr. Wright, and the bird, the last symbol of Mrs. Wright's vitality to be taken by her husband, is found dead. Unable to play the role of subservient wife anymore, Mrs. Wright is foreign to herself and therefore lives a lie. As Mrs. Hale proclaims, "Why, it looks as if she didn't know what she was about!" (690).

Mrs. Hale, however, does ultimately understand what Mrs. Wright is about. She comprehends the desperation, loneliness, and pain that Mrs. Wright experienced, and she instinctively knows that the roles Mrs. Wright played—even that of murderer—are scripted by the male-dominated circumstances of her life. As Mrs. Hale shrewdly and covertly observes in the context of a discussion about housecleaning with the county attorney: "Men's hands aren't always as clean as they might be" (687). In fact, even Mrs. Hale feels some guilt for not having made an effort to visit Mrs. Wright over the years to help relieve the monotony of Mrs. Wright's life with her husband:

> I might have known she needed help! I know how things can be—for women. I tell you, it's queer, Mrs. Peters. We live close together and we live far apart. We all go through the same things—it's all just a different kind of the same thing. (693)

Mrs. Hale cannot help identifying with her neighbor.

Discussion of Mrs. Hale's identification with Mrs. Wright

Duffy 4

In contrast, Mrs. Peters is initially reluctant to support Mrs. Wright. Not only is she married to the sheriff, but, as the county attorney puts it, "a sheriff's wife is married to the law" (693) as well. She reminds Mrs. Hale that "the law has got to punish crime" (693), even if it means revealing the existence of the dead bird and exposing the motive that could convict Mrs. Wright of murdering her husband. But finally Mrs. Peters also becomes complicit in keeping information from her husband and other men. She too—owing to the loss of her first child—understands what loss means and what Mrs. Hale means when she says that women "all go through the same things" (693).

> Discussion of Mrs. Peters's identification with Mrs. Wright

The women in *Trifles* cannot, as the play reveals, be trifled with. Although Glaspell wrote the play one hundred years ago, it continues to be relevant to contemporary relationships between men and women. Its essentially feminist perspective provides a convincing case for the necessity of women to move beyond destructive stereotypes and oppressive assumptions in order to be true to their own significant—not trifling—experiences.

> Conclusion summarizing analysis

Duffy 5

Work Cited

Glaspell, Susan. Trifles. *Literature to Go*, edited by Michael Meyer and
D. Quentin Miller, 4th ed., Bedford/St. Martin's, 2020, pp. 683–694.

32

The Literary
Research Paper

Library of Congress.

"Research is formalized curiosity. It is
poking and prying with a purpose."
— ZORA NEALE HURSTON

A close reading of a primary source such as a short story, poem, or play
can give insights into a work's themes and effects, but sometimes you will
want to know more. A published commentary by a critic who knows the
work well and is familiar with the author's life and times or other contexts
for interpretation can provide insights that otherwise may not be available.
Such writings — known as *secondary sources* — are, of course, not a substitute
for the work itself, but they often can explore interpretations that you might
not have considered if you had not encountered them. The way to encounter
these published commentaries is through research.

Students sometimes tense up when they are asked to write a research
paper. It might seem like research just adds another demand to this challenging business of interpreting literature, but if you regard research as
exploration, or as "poking and prying with a purpose" as Zora Neale
Hurston says, it might become less daunting and more exciting. The literary criticism you will discover is really just an advanced version of what

you've been learning to do in this course. These published essays are models as well as sources. They will allow you to ponder interpretations you had not considered, or they might provide a perspective that you resist as you become more convinced of the validity of your own interpretation. Another way to think about these sources is as a conversation, and you have the opportunity to raise your hand and offer your own opinion, just as you do during class discussion. A research paper is really just a more formal, more sophisticated version of these discussions. It's an even better version because you are more in control of the conversation: you can "call on" the critics who help articulate what you want to say.

There is no question that a research paper requires more time than a paper that only requires you to interpret a literary text. It is important to budget your time wisely so that you aren't spending too much of it on one stage of the process at the expense of another. For most writers at your level of development, the phase of locating and assessing the value of sources takes more time than anticipated. That's because it's an unfamiliar process. As you become more used to it, this phase of the process will go more quickly, but it's still important to reserve plenty of time so that you can experience the pleasures of discovery. You will get better results if you approach your research by wondering "What can I learn?" rather than focusing on the research simply as a requirement. After you have adjusted to the challenges of locating and assessing the value of sources, perhaps the next most important quality for writing a research paper is the ability to organize material. A bit of planning should help, just as prewriting strategies pave the way for smoother writing and revising. You already know the challenges of writing an interpretive essay. The research essay just adds three basic components to that process: locating valuable secondary sources, positioning those sources comfortably within your essay, and documenting those sources.

FINDING SOURCES

Whether your college library is large or small, its reference librarians can usually help you locate secondary sources about a particular work or author. Unless you choose a very recently published story, poem, play, or essay about which little or nothing has been written, you should be able to access sources, probably more than you would guess. Your college or university library is designed to give you access to excellent, useful information. The problem many students face is that too much information is available. If you were writing an essay on *Othello* and military history and you typed "William Shakespeare" into a search engine, you would come up with tens of thousands of sources and you would have countless hours of work ahead of you sifting through them to find a useful one. Part of the art of finding sources is knowing the right way to limit your search, just as the way to knowledge is through asking the right questions.

The image of a library as a cold, dusty space where severe-looking women shush you whenever you whisper is antiquated, and was probably never completely accurate. Libraries are some of the most exciting spaces that have adapted to and even helped to create our so-called Information Age. Just as students are sometimes intimidated by the very word *research*, they can also cower at the door of their college library, daunted by the sheer amount of wisdom it seems to contain or unsure where to start sifting through it. Your library, though, is a resource that was designed for you. Think of the offices on campus that exist to ensure your success: the registrar, financial aid, admissions, counseling . . . the list is long. All of these offices employ people whose job is to help you access their services, and you have no doubt learned the value of communicating with them. If you're feeling uncertain about how to go about your research, your reference librarians are there to help you to get started. They are trained professionals who tend to love the very challenge that you might find mysterious: locating sources.

In addition to being valuable human resources, librarians have also worked hard to design a web site that helps you navigate their holdings, many of which are electronic as opposed to print sources. Libraries increasingly provide online databases that you can access from home. This can be an efficient way to locate sources on your own schedule. There also might be a way to contact your reference librarians through that web site with questions. As we suggest above, these employees of your college or university are funded through your tuition dollars: you should become comfortable asking them questions just as you would ask your professor to clarify something she said in class, or to guide you if you are having trouble with a writing assignment. Like your professors, research librarians are teachers who are eager to help you.

Some of the articles you locate through your library's databases are also available on the Internet, but know from the outset that the open Internet does not discriminate between a valid work of literary criticism and a blog post or tweet. In addition to the many electronic databases available, including your library's computerized holdings, the Internet also connects millions of sites with primary sources (the full texts of stories, poems, plays, and essays) and secondary sources (biography or criticism). If you have not had practice with academic research on the Web, it is a good idea to get guidance from your instructor or a librarian, and to use your library's home page as a starting point. Browsing on the Internet can be absorbing as well as informative, and you are undoubtedly comfortable with the ease of Googling a term and finding what you were looking for on the first page of hits. Literary research isn't quite the same process, though. You're not simply looking for information; you're encountering a range of perspectives that might fall outside the algorithms used by Internet search engines. Your library's databases are adept at organizing these sources for your discovery. Some common databases useful for this type of research are the MLA International Bibliography, JSTOR, Project Muse, and Academic Search Premier.

We cannot anticipate your library's holdings, though: an important early step for your research is to familiarize yourself with them. You should also note the difference between databases that link to a full-text article or e-book and those that do not. If there is a link to full-text source, you automatically have access to it with a click of your mouse. If not, your library may or may not have access to that article or book. Part of the challenge is finding the sources that will be useful to you, but finding them isn't always the same as being able to get your hands on them. We can't stress enough the value of familiarizing yourself with what your library offers and what its limitations are. The same can be said for the Internet: its powers and reach are not limitless, and it may not provide what you're looking for, or it may not present it when you approach it in customary ways.

EVALUATING SOURCES AND TAKING NOTES

If your instructor specifies the minimum number of sources you need for your research paper, you might be focused on that number. But the number of sources you find is not as important as the usefulness of those sources for your purposes. If you were to locate seventeen articles and two books on your topic, would you just choose the first three you found to fulfill the requirement? What if one of those three was a Wikipedia entry and another was Shmoop? Finding sources is only the first step: evaluating them is the second.

By "evaluate," we mean that you should assess the sources you find for reliability and the quality of their evidence. It is not always immediately clear, but there are some attributes that distinguish reliable sources from their counterparts. Shmoop and Wikipedia entries, for instance, generally are not attributed to an author, which is a sign that they are not the kind of source considered valid for a research paper. A popular magazine article, though it might be useful to your argument, will probably not be as suitable to the rhetorical purpose of your paper as an article in a scholarly journal will be. You should approach secondary sources just as you approach primary sources: as texts to be analyzed and interpreted. You should be able to summarize them, appreciate their rhetorical purpose, and quote from them, similar to the way you would position yourself in relation to one of your primary texts.

Just as you are being asked to document your sources in a Works Cited page or bibliography, the sources you find that cite other sources indicate their academic substance. Sources that are well documented with primary and secondary materials usually indicate that the author has done his or her homework. Books printed by university presses and established trade presses tend to be preferable to books privately printed. As with articles in scholarly journals, books printed by university presses are subject to a lengthy process of peer review, meaning that experts in the field have attested to their value and importance. In some ways, these experts have done the work of evaluation for you. This is not to say that all scholarly articles or books published by university presses are equally valuable, or readable, or useful to your argument, but rather to suggest that they are substantial and that they are taken seriously as part of an established field of study.

Citations are another key. If you find six articles on a subject that all refer to a single article, it is probably important for you to locate that article. Its author is likely to be considered an expert or an important voice in that field. In academia this is referred to as an "impact factor," meaning that certain articles or critics have had a profound effect, or impact, on the way a work has been read, and other critics are compelled to contend in some ways with that important source. If every article you read about your topic says something like, "According to Rowson . . . ," you would do well to find Rowson's text, and you can assume it is worth consulting.

Finally, think about when your source was published. This is not to suggest that the most recent articles or books are automatically the most valuable ones, but rather to consider their ongoing importance. A book published in 1957 isn't likely to be the most current work available on the text you are writing about, though it may have had a large impact on the way the source has been interpreted since 1957. A recently published source can help you locate important sources that preceded it. These sources can be helpful in both finding and evaluating sources that you can use. Also, if you are using one of the more recent critical strategies described in Chapter 30, a book published in 1957 would not be as useful. What we have come to understand as gender-based approaches to criticism, for example, would not have been available to a 1957 critic.

As you prepare a list of reliable sources relevant to your topic, record the necessary bibliographic information so that it will be available when you make up the list of works cited for your paper. It is good practice to keep a record of all of the sources you consult initially. You may not know which sources you will ultimately use, so it is wise to play it safe and record all of them. You don't want to create an extra step for yourself later on in the process by forcing yourself to track down a source a second time. For a book, include the author, editor, and/or translator, complete title, publisher, and date of publication. For an article, include the author, complete title of the article, name of periodical, volume number, date of issue, and page numbers. For an Internet source, include the author, complete title, database title, periodical or site name, date of posting of the site (or last update), name of the institution or organization, date when you accessed the source, and its URL beginning with www (no need to include http://).

We will give specific information about how to organize these sources into a Works Cited on pages 1139–51, but for now you can just have them as a list. Note that some online articles help you by linking to citation information. Once you have assembled a collection of sources that you may cite, you will need to take notes on your readings. Be sure to keep track of where the information comes from by writing the author's name and page number. If you use more than one work by the same author, include a brief title as well as the author's name.

DEVELOPING A DRAFT, INTEGRATING SOURCES, AND ORGANIZING THE PAPER

Chapter 31 describes the writing process for a standard literary analysis without research. The research paper adds the steps we describe above: locating, evaluating, and documenting sources. The other step is to integrate this work into your argument. There is no real formula for how much of the content of your research paper should be devoted to your analysis and how much to the sources you will incorporate. Your instructor's assignment may dictate this proportion, or you might consult directly with your instructor if you are unclear about this balance. In most cases, your essay will be constructed primarily of your ideas, and the sources you incorporate will help frame or support them. The key is to allow the secondary sources to contribute to rather than to inhibit the flow of your paper. It is generally evident when a writer has tacked on a quotation or two from outside sources just to fulfill the requirement of a research paper. You should think carefully about what benefits you gain by including the voice of another critic at a certain point in your paper. Are you using that source to give substance to what you are saying? Are you resisting or disagreeing with the critic? Is the source a stepping stone to help you advance a point that is key to your argument? All of these are valid reasons for bringing a secondary source into your paper, but you should be aware of how you are positioning the critical source within your argument.

Just as you might strategically summarize a story prior to quoting from it, you should consider whether it is necessary to do the same as you introduce a source. Chances are that the critical essay you've read is complex and lengthier than the essay you are writing. It is advantageous to give your reader a sense of the overall argument, not just to lift out a sentence from the essay that might not make sense without context. While taking notes on your sources, you would do well to summarize each article in a few sentences. (In fact, your instructor might require a formal version of such summaries, known as an annotated bibliography.) Even if this is not a requirement, you may be able to use your summary in the body of the paper, or it may serve as a reminder to you of the source's value to your argument.

It is an open question as to whether the location and evaluation of sources should be done during the prewriting, writing, or revision stage of your process. If you have already selected a topic and begun to gather ideas in writing, your search for valid sources will be more efficient because you will have a clearer idea of exactly what you want to say. If you wait until too late in the drafting process to conduct research, your argument may not be as flexible in terms of allowing these sources to work their way into your essay. It is best to think of the process as a fluid one in which your research and your writing cooperate instead of being two separate activities. You do not want your research to box you into a corner and limit what you want to say, nor do you want to write your paper completely and then go searching for sources that might be employed to chime in after your thesis is complete.

DOCUMENTING SOURCES AND AVOIDING PLAGIARISM

You must acknowledge the use of a source when you (1) quote someone's exact words, (2) summarize or borrow someone's opinions or ideas, or (3) use information and facts that are not considered to be common knowledge. The purpose of this documentation is to acknowledge your sources, to demonstrate that you are familiar with what others have thought about the topic, and to provide your reader access to the same sources. If your paper is not adequately documented, it will be vulnerable to a charge of *plagiarism* — the presentation of someone else's work as your own. Academic plagiarism is a serious offense that your instructor and your college or university strongly discourages. It is a form of theft and it is antithetical to the hard work expected of you on the path to becoming a better writer and critical thinker. Conscious plagiarism is easy to avoid; honesty takes care of that for most people. However, there is an unconscious form of plagiarism that is often inadvertent yet just as problematic. To paraphrase a writer's ideas without attribution or to alter some of that author's language and claim it as your own is in the same category as including the author's language without citing it.

Let's look more closely at what constitutes plagiarism. Consider the following passage quoted from John Gassner's introduction to *Four Great Plays by Henrik Ibsen* (Bantam Books, 1959), p. viii:

Today it seems incredible that *A Doll's House* should have created the furor it did. In exploding Victorian ideals of feminine dependency the play seemed revolutionary in 1879. When its heroine Nora left her home in search of self-development it seemed as if the sanctity of marriage had been flouted by a playwright treading the stage with cloven-feet.

Now read this plagiarized version:

A Doll's House created a furor in 1879 by blowing up Victorian ideals about a woman's place in the world. Nora's search for self-fulfillment outside her home appeared to be an attack on the sanctity of marriage by a cloven-footed playwright.

Though the writer has shortened the passage and made some changes in the wording, this paragraph is basically the same as Gassner's. Indeed, several of his phrases are lifted almost intact. Even if a parenthetical reference had been included at the end of the passage and the source included in the Works Cited, the language of this passage would still be plagiarism because it is presented as the writer's own. Both language and ideas must be acknowledged.

Here is an adequately documented version of the passage:

John Gassner has observed how difficult it is for today's readers to comprehend the intense reaction against *A Doll's House* in 1879. When Victorian audiences watched Nora walk out of her stifling marriage, they assumed that Ibsen was expressing a devilish contempt for the "sanctity of marriage" (viii).

This passage makes absolutely clear that the observation is Gassner's, and it is written in the student's own language with the exception of one quoted phrase. Had Gassner not been named in the passage, the parenthetical reference would have included his name: (Gassner viii).

Some mention should be made of the notion of common knowledge before we turn to the standard format for documenting sources. Observations and facts that are widely known and routinely included in many of your sources do not require documentation. It is not necessary to cite a source for the fact that Alfred, Lord Tennyson was born in 1809 or that Ernest Hemingway lived for a time in Paris. Sometimes it will be difficult for you to determine what common knowledge is for a topic that you know little about. If you are in doubt, the best strategy is to supply a reference.

For most college essays, instructors require a citation method detailed in the Modern Language Association's *MLA Handbook,* Eighth Edition (2016). This style employs parenthetical references within the text of the paper; these are keyed to an alphabetical list of Works Cited at the end of the paper. This method is designed to be less distracting for the reader than traditional methods that employ footnotes or endnotes. (An excellent web site that describes the MLA style and other citation methods is the Online Writing Lab from Purdue University, commonly known as the Purdue OWL [www.owl.purdue.edu]). Unless you are instructed to follow the footnote or endnote style for documentation, use the parenthetical method explained in the next section.

The List of Works Cited

Items in the list of works cited are arranged alphabetically according to the author's last name and indented a half inch after the first line. This allows the reader to locate quickly the complete bibliographic information for the author's name cited within the parenthetical reference in the text. The following are common entries for literature papers and should be used as models. The student essays throughout this book also follow this style and you can use them as models, though many of them are not research papers and only cite this anthology as their single source. If some of your sources are of a different nature (such as films or music), consult the *MLA Handbook, Eighth Edition* (MLA, 2016); or, for the latest updates, check MLA's Web site at style.mla.org.

The following entries include examples to follow when citing electronic sources. For electronic sources, include as many of the following elements as apply and as are available:

- Author's name
- Title of work (if it's a book, italicized; if it's a short work, such as an article or poem, use quotation marks)
- Title of the site (or of the publication, if you're citing an online periodical, for example), italicized
- Sponsor or publisher of the site (if not named as the author)
- Date of publication or last update
- Date you accessed the source
- URL

A BOOK BY ONE AUTHOR

Hendrickson, Robert. *The Literary Life and Other Curiosities*. Viking Press, 1981.

AN ONLINE BOOK

Frost, Robert. *A Boy's Will*. Henry Holt, 1915. *Bartleby.com: Great Books Online*, 1999, www.bartleby.com/117/.

PART OF AN ONLINE BOOK

Frost, Robert. "Into My Own." *A Boy's Will*. Henry Holt, 1915. *Bartleby.com: Great Books Online*, 1999, www.bartleby.com/117/1.html.

Notice that the author's name is in reverse order (last name first, separated by a comma). This information, along with the full title, publisher, and date, should be taken from the title and copyright pages of the book. The title is italicized and is also followed by a period. Use the publication date on the title page; if none appears there, use the copyright date (after ©) on the back of the title page.

A BOOK BY TWO AUTHORS

Horton, Rod W., and Herbert W. Edwards. *Backgrounds of American Literary Thought*. 3rd ed., Prentice-Hall, 1974.

Only the first author's name is given in reverse order. The edition number appears after the title.

A BOOK WITH MORE THAN TWO AUTHORS

Gates, Henry Louis, Jr., et al., editors. *The Norton Anthology of African American Literature*. 3rd ed., W.W. Norton, 2014.

(Note: The abbreviation *et al.* means "and others.")

A WORK IN A COLLECTION BY THE SAME AUTHOR

O'Connor, Flannery. "Greenleaf." *The Complete Stories*, by Flannery O'Connor, Farrar, Straus Giroux, 1971, pp. 311–34.

Page numbers are given because the reference is to only a single story in the collection.

A WORK IN A COLLECTION BY DIFFERENT WRITERS

Frost, Robert. "Design." *Literature to Go*, edited by Michael Meyer and D. Quentin Miller, 4th ed., Bedford/St. Martin's, 2020, p. 394.

Packer, ZZ. "Drinking Coffee Elsewhere." *Literature to Go*, edited by Michael Meyer and D. Quentin Miller, 4th ed., Bedford/St. Martin's, 2020, pp. 335–50.

The titles of poems and short stories are enclosed in quotation marks; plays and novels are italicized.

CROSS-REFERENCE TO A COLLECTION

When citing more than one work from the same collection, use a cross-reference to avoid repeating the same bibliographic information that appears in the main entry for the collection.

Frost, Robert. "Design." Meyer and Miller, p. 394.

Meyer, Michael and D. Quentin Miller, editors. *Literature to Go*, 4th ed., Bedford/ St. Martin's, 2020.

O'Connor, Flannery. "Revelation." Meyer and Miller, pp. 266–82.

Packer, ZZ. "Drinking Coffee Elsewhere." Meyer and Miller, pp. 335–50.

A TRANSLATED BOOK

Grass, Günter. *The Tin Drum*. Translated by Ralph Manheim, Pantheon Books, 1962.

AN INTRODUCTION, PREFACE, FOREWORD, OR AFTERWORD

Johnson, Thomas H. Introduction. *Final Harvest: Emily Dickinson's Poems*, by Emily
    Dickinson, Little, Brown, 1961, pp. vii–xiv.

This cites the introduction by Johnson. Notice that a colon is used between
the book's main title and subtitle. To cite a poem in this book, use this
method:

Dickinson, Emily. "A Tooth upon Our Peace." *Final Harvest: Emily Dickinson's
    Poems*, edited by Thomas H. Johnson, Little, Brown, 1961, p. 110.

AN ENTRY IN AN ENCYCLOPEDIA

Robinson, Lisa Clayton. "Harlem Writers Guild." *Africana: The Encyclopedia of the
    African and African American Experience*. 2nd ed., Oxford UP, 2005.

AN ARTICLE IN A MAGAZINE

Morrow, Lance. "Scribble, Scribble, Eh, Mr. Toad?" *Time*, 24 Feb. 1986, p. 84.

AN ARTICLE FROM AN ONLINE MAGAZINE

Wasserman, Elizabeth. "The Byron Complex." *TheAtlantic.com*, 1 Oct. 2002, www
    .theatlantic.com/entertainment/archive/2002/10/the-byron-
    complex/378504/.

The citation for an unsigned article would begin with the title and be alpha-
betized by the first word of the title other than "a," "an," or "the."

AN ARTICLE IN A SCHOLARLY JOURNAL WITH CONTINUOUS
PAGINATION BEYOND A SINGLE ISSUE

Fuqua, Amy. "'The Furrow of His Brow': Providence and Pragmatism in Toni
    Morrison's *Paradise*." *Midwest Quarterly*, vol. 54, no. 1, Autumn 2012,
    pp. 38–52.

Regardless of whether the journal uses continuous pagination or separate pagination for each issue, it is necessary to include the volume number and the issue number for every entry. If a journal does not offer an issue number, use only the volume number, as in the next entry. If a journal uses *only* issue numbers, use that in place of the volume number.

AN ARTICLE IN A SCHOLARLY JOURNAL WITH SEPARATE
PAGINATION FOR EACH ISSUE

Updike, John. "The Cultural Situation of the American Writer." *American Studies*
International*, vol. 15, 1977, pp. 19–28.

In the following citation, noting the winter issue helps a reader find the correct article among all of the articles published by the online journal in 2004.

AN ARTICLE FROM AN ONLINE SCHOLARLY JOURNAL

Mamet, David. "Secret Names." *Threepenny Review*, Vol. 96, Winter 2004, www
.threepennyreview.com/samples/mamet_w04.html.

AN ARTICLE IN A NEWSPAPER

The following citation indicates that the article appears on page 1 of section 7 and continues onto another page.

Ziegler, Philip. "The Lure of Gossip, the Rules of History." *The New York Times*,
23 Feb. 1986, sec. 7, pp. 1+.

AN ARTICLE FROM AN ONLINE NEWSPAPER

Brantley, Ben. "Souls Lost and Doomed Enliven London Stages." *The New York*
Times, 4 Feb. 2004, www.nytimes.com/2004/02/04/theater/critic-s-
notebook-souls-lost-and-doomed-enliven-london-stages.html.

A LECTURE

Tilton, Robert. "The Beginnings of American Studies." English 270 class lecture,
University of Connecticut, Storrs, 12 Mar. 2016.

LETTER, E-MAIL, OR INTERVIEW

Vellenga, Carolyn. Letter to the author, 9 Oct. 2018.

Harter, Stephen P. E-mail to the author, 28 Dec. 2017.

McConagha, Bill. Personal interview, 9 May 2016.

Following are additional examples for citing electronic sources.

WORK FROM A SUBSCRIPTION SERVICE

Libraries pay for access to databases such as *LexisNexis, ProQuest,* and *Expanded Academic Premier.* When you retrieve an article or other work from a subscription database, cite your source based on these models:

Macari, Anne Marie. "Lyric Impulse in a Time of Extinction." *American Poetry Review*, vol. 44, no. 4, July/Aug. 2015, pp. 11–14. General OneFile, go.galegroup.com.

Vendler, Helen Hennessey. "The Passion of Emily Dickinson." *New Republic,* 3 Aug. 1992, pp. 34–38. *Expanded Academic ASAP*, go.galegroup.com.

A DOCUMENT FROM A WEB SITE

When citing sources from the Internet, include as much publication information as possible (see guidelines on p. 1140). In some cases, as in the following example, a date of publication for the document "Dickens in America" is not available. The entry provides the author, title of document, title of site, access date, and URL:

Perdue, David. "Dickens in America." David Perdue's Charles Dickens Page, 13 Apr. 2016, charlesdickenspage.com/america.html.

AN ENTIRE WEB SITE

Perdue, David. David Perdue's Charles Dickens Page, 13 Apr. 2016, charlesdickenspage .com.

AN ONLINE POSTING

Bedford English. "Stacey Cochran explores Reflective Writing in the classroom and as a writer: http://ow.ly/YkjVB." Facebook, 15 Feb. 2016, www.facebook.com /BedfordEnglish/posts/10153415001259607.

Parenthetical References

A list of works cited is not an adequate indication of how you have used sources in your paper. You must also provide the precise location of quotations and other information by using parenthetical references within the text of the paper. You do this by citing the author's name (or the source's title if the work is anonymous) and the page number:

Collins points out that "Nabokov was misunderstood by early reviewers of his work" (28).

or

Nabokov's first critics misinterpreted his stories (Collins 28).

Either way a reader will find the complete bibliographic entry in the list of works cited under Collins's name and know that the information cited in the paper appears on page 28. Notice that the end punctuation comes after the parentheses.

If you have listed more than one work by the same author, you would add a brief title to the parenthetical reference to distinguish between them. You could also include the full title in your text:

Nabokov's first critics misinterpreted his stories (Collins, "Early Reviews" 28).

or

Collins points out in "Early Reviews of Nabokov's Fiction" that Nabokov's early work was misinterpreted by reviewers (28).

For electronic sources, provide the author's name. Unless your online source is a stable, paginated document (such as a pdf file), do not include page numbers in your parenthetical references. The following example shows an in-text citation to William Faulkner's acceptance speech for the Nobel Prize for Literature, found at the Nobel web site.

William Faulkner believed that it was his duty as a writer to "help man endure by lifting his heart" (Faulkner).

This reference would appear in the works cited list as follows:

Faulkner, William. "Banquet Speech: The Nobel Prize in Literature." Nobelprize.org, 10 Dec. 1950, nobelprize.org/nobel_prizes/literature/laureates/1949 /faulkner-speech.html.

There can be many variations on what is included in a parenthetical reference, depending on the nature of the entry in the list of works cited. But the general principle is simple enough: provide enough parenthetical information for a reader to find the work in "Works Cited." Examine the sample research paper for more examples of works cited and strategies for including parenthetical references. If you are puzzled by a given situation, refer to the *MLA Handbook*.

A SAMPLE STUDENT RESEARCH PAPER

How William Faulkner's Narrator Cultivates a Rose for Emily

The following research paper by Tony Groulx follows the format described in the *MLA Handbook,* Eighth Edition (2016). This format is discussed in the preceding section on documentation. Though the sample paper is short, it illustrates many of the techniques and strategies useful for writing an essay that includes secondary sources. (Faulkner's "A Rose for Emily" is reprinted on p. 40.)

Tony Groulx

Professor Hugo

English 109-3

4 February 2019

How William Faulkner's Narrator Cultivates a Rose for Emily

William Faulkner's "A Rose for Emily" is an absorbing mystery story whose chilling ending contains a gruesome surprise. When we discover, along with the narrator and townspeople, what was left of Homer Barron's body, we may be surprised or not, depending on how carefully we have been reading the story and keeping track of details such as Emily Grierson's purchase of rat poison and Homer's disappearance. Probably most readers anticipate finding Homer's body at the end of the story because Faulkner carefully prepares the groundwork for the discovery as the townspeople force their way into that mysterious upstairs room where a "thin, acrid pall as of the tomb seemed to lie everywhere" (46). But very few readers, if any, are prepared for the story's final paragraph, when we realize that the strand of "iron-gray hair" (the last three words of the story) on the second pillow indicates that Emily has slept with Homer since she murdered him. This last paragraph produces the real horror in the story and an extraordinary revelation about Emily's character.

References to text of the story

The final paragraph seems like the right place to begin a discussion of this story because the surprise ending not only creates a powerful emotional effect in us but also raises an important question about what we are to think of Emily. Is this isolated, eccentric woman simply mad? All the circumstantial evidence indicates that she is a murderer and necrophiliac, and yet Faulkner titles the story "A Rose for Emily," as if she is due some kind of tribute. The title somehow qualifies the gasp of horror that the story leads up to in the final paragraph. Why would anyone offer this woman a "rose"? What's behind the title?

> Faulkner was once directly asked the meaning of the title and replied: Oh it's simply the poor woman had had no life at all. Her father had kept her more or less locked up and then she had a lover who was about to quit her, she had to murder him. It was just "A Rose for Emily"—that's all. (qtd. in Gwynn and Blotner 87–88)

Reference to secondary source (Gwynn and Blotner)

This reply explains some of Emily's motivation for murdering Homer, but it doesn't actually address the purpose and meaning of the title. If Emily killed Homer out of a kind of emotional necessity—out of a fear of abandonment—how does that explain the fact that the title seems to suggest that the story is a way of paying respect to Emily? The question remains.

Whatever respect the story creates for Emily cannot be the result of her actions. Surely there can be no convincing excuse made for murder and necrophilia; there is nothing to praise about what she does. Instead, the tribute comes in the form of how her story is told rather than what we are told about her. To do this Faulkner uses a narrator who tells Emily's story in such a way as to maximize our sympathy for her. The grim information about Emily's "iron-gray hair" on the pillow is withheld until the very end and not only to produce a surprise but to permit the reader to develop a sympathetic understanding of her before we are shocked and disgusted by her necrophilia.

Significantly, the narrator begins the story with Emily's death rather than Homer's. Though a number of studies discuss the story's narrator (see, for example, Curry; Kempton; Sullivan; and Watkins), Terry Heller's is one of the most comprehensive in its focus on the narrator's effects on the readers' response to Emily. As Heller points out, before we learn of Emily's bizarre behavior we see her as a sympathetic—if antiquated—figure in a town whose life and concerns have passed her by; hence, "we are disposed to see Emily as victimized" (306). Her refusal to pay her taxes is an index to her isolation and eccentricity, but this incident also suggests a degree of dignity and power lacking in the town officials who fail to collect her taxes. Her encounters with the officials of Jefferson—whether in the form of the sneaking aldermen who try to cover up the smell around her house or the druggist who unsuccessfully tries to get her to conform to the law when she buys arsenic—place her in an admirable light because her willfulness is based on her personal strength. Moreover, it is relatively easy to side with Emily when the townspeople are described as taking pleasure in her being reduced to poverty as a result of her father's death because "now she too would know the old thrill and the old despair of a penny more or less"

Reference to secondary sources (Curry; Kempton; Sullivan; Watkins) with signal phrase for Heller

Reference to secondary source (Heller) with signal phrase ("As Heller points out . . .")

(Faulkner 43). The narrator's account of their pettiness, jealousy, and inability to make sense of Emily causes the reader to sympathize with Emily's eccentricities before we must judge her murderous behavior. We admire her for taking life on her own terms, and the narrator makes sure this response is in place prior to our realization that she also takes life.

Reference to text of the story

We don't really know much about Emily because the narrator arranges the details of her life so that it's difficult to know what she's been up to. We learn, for example, about the smell around the house before she buys the poison and Homer disappears, so that the cause-and-effect relationship among these events is a bit slippery (for a detailed reconstruction of the chronology, see McGlynn; Nebecker), but the effect is to suspend judgment of Emily. By the time we realize what she has done, we are already inclined to see her as outside community values almost out of necessity. That's not to say that the murdering of Homer is justified by the narrator, but it is to say that her life maintains its private—though no longer secret—dignity. Despite the final revelation, Emily remains "dear, inescapable, impervious, tranquil, and perverse" (Faulkner 46).

Reference to secondary sources (McGlynn and Nebecker)

Reference to text of the story

The narrator's "rose" to Emily is his recognition that Emily is all these things—including "perverse." She evokes "a sort of respectful affection for a fallen monument" (Faulkner 40). She is, to be sure, "fallen," but she is also somehow central—a "monument"—to the life of the community. Faulkner does not offer a definitive reading of Emily, but he does have the narrator pay tribute to her by attempting to provide a complex set of contexts for her actions—contexts that include a repressive father, resistance to a changing South and impinging North, the passage of time and its influence on the present, and relations between men and women as well as relations between generations. Robert Crosman discusses the narrator's efforts to understand Emily:

> The narrator is himself a "reader" of Emily's story, trying to put together from fragments a complete picture, trying to find the meaning of her life in its impact upon an audience, the citizens of Jefferson, of which he is a member. (212)

The narrator refuses to dismiss Emily as simply mad or to treat her life as merely a grotesque, sensational horror story. Instead, his narrative method brings us into her life before we too hastily reject her, and in doing so it offers us a complex imaginative treatment of fierce determination and strength coupled with illusions and shocking eccentricities. The narrator's rose for Emily is paying her the tribute of placing that "long strand of iron-gray hair" in the context of her entire life.

Reference to secondary source (Crosman)

Works Cited

Crosman, Robert. "How Readers Make Meaning." *College Literature*, vol. 9, no. 3, 1982, pp. 207–15.

Curry, Renee R. "Gender and Authorial Limitation in Faulkner's 'A Rose for Emily.'" *Mississippi Quarterly*, vol. 47, no. 3, 1994, pp. 391–402. *Expanded Academic ASAP*, connection.ebscohost.com/c/literary-criticism /9502231814/gender-authorial-limitation-faulkners-rose-emily.

Faulkner, William. "A Rose for Emily." *Literature to Go*, edited by Michael Meyer and D. Quentin Miller, 4th ed., Bedford/St. Martin's, 2020, pp. 40–47.

Gwynn, Frederick, and Joseph Blotner, editors. *Faulkner in the University: Class Conferences at the University of Virginia, 1957–58*. U of Virginia P, 1959.

Heller, Terry. "The Telltale Hair: A Critical Study of William Faulkner's 'A Rose for Emily.'" *Arizona Quarterly*, vol. 28, no. 4, 1972, pp. 301–18.

Kempton, K. P. *The Short Story*. Harvard UP, 1954, pp. 104–06.

McGlynn, Paul D. "The Chronology of 'A Rose for Emily.'" *Studies in Short Fiction*, vol. 6, no. 4, 1969, pp. 461–62.

Nebecker, Helen E. "Chronology Revised." *Studies in Short Fiction*, vol. 8, no. 4, 1971, pp. 471–73.

Sullivan, Ruth. "The Narrator in 'A Rose for Emily.'" *Journal of Narrative Technique*, vol. 1, no. 3, 1971, pp. 159–78.

Watkins, F. C. "The Structure of 'A Rose for Emily.'" *Modern Language Notes*, vol. 69, no. 6, 1954, pp. 508–10.

Glossary of Literary Terms

Accent The emphasis, or stress, given a syllable in pronunciation. We say "*syl*-lable" not "syl*lable*," "*em*phasis" not "em*phasis*." Accents can also be used to emphasize a particular word in a sentence: *Is* she con*tent* with the *con*tents of the *yel*low *pack*age? See also METER.

Act A major division in the action of a play. The ends of acts are typically indicated by lowering the curtain or turning up the houselights. Playwrights frequently employ acts to accommodate changes in time, setting, characters onstage, or mood. In many full-length plays, acts are further divided into scenes, which often mark a point in the action when the location changes or when a new character enters. See also SCENE.

Allegory A narration or description usually restricted to a single meaning because its events, actions, characters, settings, and objects represent specific abstractions or ideas. Although the elements in an allegory may be interesting in themselves, the emphasis tends to be on what they ultimately mean. Characters may be given names such as Hope, Pride, Youth, and Charity; they have few if any personal qualities beyond their abstract meanings. These personifications are not symbols because, for instance, the meaning of a character named Charity is precisely that virtue. See also SYMBOL.

Alliteration The repetition of the same consonant sounds in a sequence of words, usually at the beginning of a word or stressed syllable: "*d*escending *d*ew *d*rops"; "*l*uscious *l*emons." Alliteration is based on the sounds of letters, rather than the spelling of words; for example, "*k*een" and "*c*ar" alliterate, but "*c*ar" and "*c*ite" do not. Used sparingly, alliteration can intensify ideas by emphasizing key words, but when used too self-consciously, it can be distracting, even ridiculous, rather than effective. See also ASSONANCE, CONSONANCE.

Allusion A brief reference to a person, place, thing, event, or idea in history or literature. Allusions conjure up biblical authority, scenes from Shakespeare's plays, historic figures, wars, great love stories, and anything else that might enrich an author's work. Allusions imply reading and cultural experiences shared by the writer and reader, functioning as a kind of shorthand whereby the recalling of something outside the work supplies an emotional or intellectual context, such as a poem about current racial struggles calling up the memory of Abraham Lincoln.

Ambiguity Allows for two or more simultaneous interpretations of a word, phrase, action, or situation, all of which can be supported by the context of a work. Deliberate ambiguity can contribute to the effectiveness and richness of a work, for example, in the open-ended conclusion to Hawthorne's

1152

"Young Goodman Brown." However, unintentional ambiguity obscures meaning and can confuse readers.

Anagram A word or phrase made from the letters of another word or phrase, as *heart* is an anagram of *earth*. Anagrams have often been considered merely an exercise of one's ingenuity, but sometimes writers use anagrams to conceal proper names or veiled messages, or to suggest important connections between words, as in *hated* and *death*.

Antagonist The character, force, or collection of forces in fiction or drama that opposes the protagonist and gives rise to the conflict of the story; an opponent of the protagonist, such as Claudius in Shakespeare's play *Hamlet*. See also CHARACTER, CONFLICT.

Antihero A protagonist who has the opposite of most of the traditional attributes of a hero. He or she may be bewildered, ineffectual, deluded, or merely pathetic. Often what antiheroes learn, if they learn anything at all, is that the world isolates them in an existence devoid of God and absolute values. Yossarian from Joseph Heller's *Catch-22* is an example of an antihero. See also CHARACTER.

Apostrophe An address, either to someone who is absent and therefore cannot hear the speaker or to something nonhuman that cannot comprehend. Apostrophe often provides a speaker the opportunity to think aloud.

Approximate rhyme See RHYME.

Archetype A term used to describe universal symbols that evoke deep and sometimes unconscious responses in a reader. In literature, characters, images, and themes that symbolically embody universal meanings and basic human experiences, regardless of when or where they live, are considered archetypes. Common literary archetypes include stories of quests, initiations, scapegoats, descents to the underworld, and ascents to heaven. See also MYTHOLOGICAL CRITICISM.

Aside In drama, a speech directed to the audience that supposedly is not audible to the other characters onstage at the time. When Hamlet first appears onstage, for example, his aside "A little more than kin, and less than kind!" gives the audience a strong sense of his alienation from King Claudius. See also SOLILOQUY.

Assonance The repetition of internal vowel sounds in nearby words that do not end the same, for example, "asl*ee*p under a tr*ee*," or "*ea*ch *e*vening." Similar endings result in rhyme, as in "asl*ee*p in the d*ee*p." Assonance is a strong means of emphasizing important words in a line. See also ALLITERATION, CONSONANCE.

Ballad Traditionally, a ballad is a song, transmitted orally from generation to generation that tells a story and that eventually is written down. As such, ballads usually cannot be traced to a particular author or group of authors. Typically, ballads are dramatic, condensed, and impersonal narratives, such as "Lord Randal." A **literary ballad** is a narrative poem that is written in deliberate imitation of the language, form, and spirit of the traditional ballad, such as Keats's "La Belle Dame sans Merci." See also BALLAD STANZA, QUATRAIN.

Ballad stanza A four-line stanza, known as a quatrain, consisting of alternating eight- and six-syllable lines. Usually only the second and fourth lines rhyme (an *abcb* pattern). Coleridge adopted the ballad stanza in "The Rime of the Ancient Mariner."

All in a hot and copper sky
The bloody Sun, at noon,
Right up above the mast did stand,
No bigger than the Moon.

See also BALLAD, QUATRAIN.

Blank verse Unrhymed iambic pentameter. Blank verse is the English verse form closest to the natural rhythms of English speech and therefore is the most common pattern found in traditional English narrative and dramatic poetry from Shakespeare to the early twentieth century. Shakespeare's plays use blank verse extensively. See also IAMBIC PENTAMETER.

Cacophony Language that is discordant and difficult to pronounce, such as this line from John Updike's "Player Piano": "never my numb plunker fumbles." Cacophony ("bad sound") may be unintentional in the writer's sense of music, or it may be used consciously for deliberate dramatic effect. See also EUPHONY.

Caesura A pause within a line of poetry that contributes to the rhythm of the line. A caesura can occur anywhere within a line and need not be indicated by punctuation. In scanning a line, caesuras are indicated by a double vertical line (‖). See also METER, RHYTHM, SCANSION.

Carpe diem The Latin phrase meaning "seize the day." This is a very common literary theme, especially in lyric poetry, which emphasizes that life is short, time is fleeting, and that one should make the most of present pleasures. Robert Herrick's poem "To the Virgins, to Make Much of Time" employs the *carpe diem* theme.

Catharsis Meaning "purgation," *catharsis* describes the release of the emotions of pity and fear by the audience at the end of a tragedy. In his *Poetics,* Aristotle discusses the importance of catharsis. The audience faces the misfortunes of the protagonist, which elicit pity and compassion. Simultaneously, the audience also confronts the failure of the protagonist, thus receiving a frightening reminder of human limitations and frailties. Ultimately, however, both these negative emotions are purged because the tragic protagonist's suffering is an affirmation of human values rather than a despairing denial of them. See also TRAGEDY.

Character, characterization A character is a person presented in a dramatic or narrative work, and characterization is the process by which a writer makes that character seem real to the reader. A **hero** or **heroine**, often called the protagonist, is the central character who engages the reader's interest and empathy. The antagonist is the character, force, or collection of forces that stands directly opposed to the protagonist and gives rise to the conflict of the story. A **static character** does not change throughout the work, and the reader's knowledge of that character does not grow, whereas a **dynamic character** undergoes some kind of change because of the action in the plot. **Flat characters** embody one or two qualities, ideas, or traits that can be readily described in a brief summary. They are not psychologically complex characters and therefore are readily accessible to readers. Some flat characters are recognized as

stock characters; they embody stereotypes such as the "dumb blonde" or the "mean stepfather." They become types rather than individuals. **Round characters** are more complex than flat or stock characters, and often display the inconsistencies and internal conflicts found in most real people. They are more fully developed, and therefore are harder to summarize. Authors have two major methods of presenting characters: **showing** and **telling**. **Showing** allows the author to present a character talking and acting, and lets the reader infer what kind of person the character is. In **telling**, the author intervenes to describe and sometimes evaluate the character for the reader. Characters can be convincing whether they are presented by showing or by telling, as long as their actions are motivated. **Motivated action** by the characters occurs when the reader or audience is offered reasons for how the characters behave, what they say, and the decisions they make. **Plausible action** is action by a character in a story that seems reasonable, given the motivations presented. See also PLOT.

Chorus In Greek tragedies (especially those of Aeschylus and Sophocles), a group of people who serve mainly as commentators on the characters and events. They add to the audience's understanding of the play by expressing traditional moral, religious, and social attitudes. The role of the chorus in dramatic works evolved through the sixteenth century, and the chorus occasionally is still used by contemporary playwrights such as Paula Vogel in *How I Learned to Drive.* See also DRAMA.

Climax See PLOT.

Closet drama A play that is written to be read rather than performed onstage. In this kind of drama, literary art outweighs all other considerations. See also DRAMA.

Colloquial Refers to a type of informal diction that reflects casual, conversational language and often includes slang expressions. See also DICTION.

Comedy A work intended to interest, involve, and amuse the reader or audience, in which no terrible disaster occurs and that ends happily for the main characters. **High comedy** refers to verbal wit, such as puns, whereas **low comedy** is generally associated with physical action and is less intellectual. **Romantic comedy** involves a love affair that meets with various obstacles (like disapproving parents, mistaken identities, deceptions, or other sorts of misunderstandings) but overcomes them to end in a blissful union. Shakespeare's comedies, such as *A Midsummer Night's Dream,* are considered romantic comedies.

Comic relief A humorous scene or incident that alleviates tension in an otherwise serious work. In many instances these moments enhance the thematic significance of the story in addition to providing laughter. When Hamlet jokes with the gravediggers, we laugh, but something hauntingly serious about the humor also intensifies our more serious emotions.

Conflict The struggle within the plot between opposing forces. The protagonist engages in the conflict with the antagonist, which may take the form of a character, society, nature, or an aspect of the protagonist's personality. See also CHARACTER, PLOT.

Connotation Associations and implications that go beyond the literal meaning of a word, which derive from how the word has been commonly used and the associations people make with it. For example, the word *eagle* connotes ideas of liberty and freedom that have little to do with the word's literal meaning. See also DENOTATION.

Consonance A common type of near rhyme that consists of identical consonant sounds preceded by different vowel sounds: *home, same; worth, breath.* See also RHYME.

Contextual symbol See SYMBOL.

Controlling metaphor See METAPHOR.

Convention A characteristic of a literary genre (often unrealistic) that is understood and accepted by audiences because it has come, through usage and time, to be recognized as a familiar technique. For example, the division of a play into acts and scenes is a dramatic convention, as are SOLILOQUIES and ASIDES. FLASHBACKS and FORESHADOWING are examples of literary conventions.

Conventional symbol See SYMBOL.

Cosmic irony See IRONY.

Couplet Two consecutive lines of poetry that usually rhyme and have the same meter. A **heroic couplet** is a couplet written in rhymed iambic pentameter.

Crisis A turning point in the action of a story that has a powerful effect on the protagonist. Opposing forces come together decisively to lead to the climax of the plot. See also PLOT.

Cultural criticism An approach to literature that focuses on the historical as well as social, political, and economic contexts of a work. Popular culture — mass-produced and mass-consumed cultural artifacts ranging from advertising to popular fiction to television to rock music — is given equal emphasis with "high culture." **Cultural critics** use widely eclectic strategies such as new historicism, psychology, gender studies, and deconstructionism to analyze not only literary texts but everything from radio talk shows, comic strips, calendar art, and commercials, to travel guides and baseball cards. See also MARXIST CRITICISM.

Deconstructionism An approach to literature that suggests that literary works do not yield fixed, single meanings, because language can never say exactly what we intend it to mean. Deconstructionism seeks to destabilize meaning by examining the gaps and ambiguities of the language of a text. Deconstructionists pay close attention to language in order to discover and describe how a variety of possible readings are generated by the elements of a text. See also NEW CRITICISM.

Denotation The dictionary meaning of a word. See also CONNOTATION.

Dénouement A French term meaning "unraveling" or "unknotting," used to describe the resolution of the plot following the climax. See also PLOT, RESOLUTION.

Dialect A type of informal diction. Dialects are spoken by definable groups of people from a particular geographic region, economic group, or social class. Writers use dialect to contrast and express differences in educational, class, social, and regional backgrounds of their characters. See also DICTION.

Dialogue The verbal exchanges between characters. Dialogue makes the characters seem real to the reader or audience by revealing firsthand their thoughts, responses, and emotional states. See also DICTION.

Diction A writer's choice of words, phrases, sentence structures, and figurative language, which combine to help create meaning. **Formal diction** consists of a dignified, impersonal, and elevated use of language; it follows the rules of syntax exactly and is often characterized by complex words and lofty tone. **Middle diction** maintains correct language usage, but is less elevated than formal diction; it reflects the way most educated people speak. **Informal diction** represents the plain language of everyday use, and often includes idiomatic expressions, slang, contractions, and many simple, common words. **Poetic diction** refers to the way poets sometimes employ an elevated diction that deviates significantly from the common speech and writing of their time, choosing words for their supposedly inherent poetic qualities. Since the eighteenth century, however, poets have been incorporating all kinds of diction in their work and so there is no longer an automatic distinction between the language of a poet and the language of everyday speech. See also DIALECT.

Didactic poetry Poetry designed to teach an ethical, moral, or religious lesson. Michael Wigglesworth's Puritan poem *Day of Doom* is an example of didactic poetry.

Doggerel A derogatory term used to describe poetry whose subject is trite and whose rhythm and sounds are monotonously heavy-handed.

Drama Derived from the Greek word *dram,* meaning "to do" or "to perform," the term *drama* may refer to a single play, a group of plays ("Jacobean drama"), or to all plays ("world drama"). Drama is designed for performance in a theater; actors take on the roles of characters, perform indicated actions, and speak the dialogue written in the script. **Play** is a general term for a work of dramatic literature, and a **playwright** is a writer who makes plays.

Dramatic irony See IRONY.

Dramatic monologue A type of lyric poem in which a character (the speaker) addresses a distinct but silent audience imagined to be present in the poem in such a way as to reveal a dramatic situation, and often unintentionally, some aspect of his or her temperament or personality. See also LYRIC.

Dynamic character See CHARACTER.

Editorial omniscience See NARRATOR.

Electra complex The female version of the Oedipus complex. *Electra complex* is a term used to describe the psychological conflict of a daughter's unconscious rivalry with her mother for her father's attention. The name comes from the Greek legend of Electra, who avenged the death of her father, Agamemnon, by plotting the death of her mother. See also OEDIPUS COMPLEX.

Elegy A mournful, contemplative lyric poem written to commemorate someone who is dead, often ending in a consolation. Tennyson's *In Memoriam,* written on the death of Arthur Hallam, is an elegy. *Elegy* may also refer to a serious meditative poem produced to express the speaker's melancholy thoughts, such as Thomas Gray's "Elegy Written in a Country Churchyard." See also LYRIC.

End rhyme See RHYME.

End-stopped line A poetic line that has a pause at the end. End-stopped lines reflect normal speech patterns and are often marked by punctuation. The first line of Keats's "Endymion" is an example of an end-stopped line; the natural pause coincides with the end of the line, and is marked by a period:

A thing of beauty is a joy forever.

English sonnet See SONNET.

Enjambment In poetry, when one line ends without a pause and continues into the next line for its meaning. This is also called a **run-on line**. The transition between the first two lines of Wordsworth's poem "My Heart Leaps Up" demonstrates enjambment:

My heart leaps up when I behold
  A rainbow in the sky:

Envoy See SESTINA.

Epic A long narrative poem, told in a formal, elevated style, that focuses on a serious subject and chronicles heroic deeds and events important to a culture or nation. Milton's *Paradise Lost,* which attempts to "justify the ways of God to man," is an epic. See also NARRATIVE POEM.

Epigram A brief, pointed, and witty poem that usually makes a satiric or humorous point. Epigrams are most often written in couplets, but take no prescribed form.

Euphony *Euphony* ("good sound") refers to language that is smooth and musically pleasant to the ear. See also CACOPHONY.

Exact rhyme See RHYME.

Exposition A narrative device, often used at the beginning of a work, that provides necessary background information about the characters and their circumstances. Exposition explains what has gone on before, the relationships between characters, the development of a theme, and the introduction of a conflict. See also FLASHBACK.

Extended metaphor See METAPHOR.

Eye rhyme See RHYME.

Falling action See PLOT.

Falling meter See METER.

Farce A form of humor based on exaggerated, improbable incongruities. Farce involves rapid shifts in action and emotion, as well as slapstick comedy and extravagant dialogue. Malvolio, in Shakespeare's *Twelfth Night,* is a farcical character.

Feminine rhyme See RHYME.

Feminist criticism An approach to literature that seeks to correct or supplement what may be regarded as a predominantly male critical perspective with a feminist consciousness. Feminist criticism places literature in a social context and uses a broad range of disciplines, including history, sociology, psychology, and linguistics, to provide a perspective sensitive to feminist issues. Feminist theories also attempt to understand representation from a woman's point of view and to explain women's writing strategies as specific to their social conditions. See also GENDER CRITICISM.

Figures of speech Ways of using language that deviate from the literal, denotative meanings of words in order to suggest additional meanings or effects. Figures of speech say one thing in terms of something else, such as when an eager funeral director is described as a vulture. See also METAPHOR, SIMILE.

First-person narrator See NARRATOR.

Fixed form A poem that may be categorized by the pattern of its lines, meter, rhythm, or stanzas. A sonnet is a fixed form of poetry because by definition it must have fourteen lines. Other fixed forms include limerick, sestina, and villanelle. However, poems written in a fixed form may not always fit into categories precisely, because writers sometimes vary traditional forms to create innovative effects. See also OPEN FORM.

Flashback A narrated scene that marks a break in the narrative in order to inform the reader or audience member about events that took place before the opening scene of a work. See also EXPOSITION.

Flat character See CHARACTER.

Foil A character in a work whose behavior and values contrast with those of another character in order to highlight the distinctive temperament of that character (usually the protagonist). In Shakespeare's *Hamlet,* Laertes acts as a foil to Hamlet, because his willingness to act underscores Hamlet's inability to do so.

Foot The metrical unit by which a line of poetry is measured. A foot usually consists of one stressed and one or two unstressed syllables. An *iambic foot,* which consists of one unstressed syllable followed by one stressed syllable ("away"), is the most common metrical foot in English poetry. A *trochaic foot* consists of one stressed syllable followed by an unstressed syllable ("lovely"). An *anapestic foot* is two unstressed syllables followed by one stressed one ("understand"). A *dactylic foot* is one stressed syllable followed by two unstressed ones ("desperate"). A *spondee* is a foot consisting of two stressed syllables ("dead set"), but is not a sustained metrical foot and is used mainly for variety or emphasis. See also IAMBIC PENTAMETER, LINE, METER.

Foreshadowing The introduction early in a story of verbal and dramatic hints that suggest what is to come later.

Form The overall structure or shape of a work, which frequently follows an established design. Forms may refer to a literary type (narrative form, short story form) or to patterns of meter, lines, and rhymes (stanza form, verse form). See also FIXED FORM, OPEN FORM.

Formal diction See DICTION.

Formalist criticism An approach to literature that focuses on the formal elements of a work, such as its language, structure, and tone. Formalist critics offer intense examinations of the relationship between form and meaning in a work, emphasizing the subtle complexity in how a work is arranged.

Formalists pay special attention to diction, irony, paradox, metaphor, and symbol, as well as larger elements such as plot, characterization, and narrative technique. Formalist critics read literature as an independent work of art rather than as a reflection of the author's state of mind or as a representation of a moment in history. Therefore, anything outside of the work, including historical influences and authorial intent, is generally not examined by formalist critics. See also NEW CRITICISM.

Formula fiction Often characterized as "escape literature," formula fiction follows a pattern of conventional reader expectations. Romance novels, westerns, science fiction, and detective stories are all examples of formula fiction; while the details of individual stories vary, the basic ingredients of each kind of story are the same. Formula fiction offers happy endings (the hero "gets the girl," the detective cracks the case), entertains wide audiences, and sells tremendously well.

Found poem An unintentional poem discovered in a nonpoetic context, such as a conversation, news story, or advertisement. Found poems serve as reminders that everyday language often contains what can be considered poetry, or that poetry is definable as any text read as a poem.

Free verse Also called OPEN FORM poetry, *free verse* refers to poems characterized by their nonconformity to established patterns of meter, rhyme, and stanza. Free verse uses elements such as speech patterns, grammar, emphasis, and breath pauses to decide line breaks, and usually does not rhyme. See OPEN FORM.

Gender criticism An approach to literature that explores how ideas about men and women — what is masculine and feminine — can be regarded as socially constructed by particular cultures. Gender criticism expands categories and definitions of what is masculine or feminine and tends to regard sexuality as more complex than merely masculine or feminine, heterosexual or homosexual. See also FEMINIST CRITICISM, LGBTQ+ CRITICISM.

Haiku A style of lyric poetry borrowed from the Japanese that typically presents an intense emotion or vivid image of nature, which traditionally, is designed to lead to a spiritual insight. Haiku is traditionally a fixed poetic form, consisting of seventeen syllables organized into three unrhymed lines of five, seven, and five syllables. Today, however, many poets vary the syllabic count in their haiku. See also FIXED FORM.

Hamartia A term coined by Aristotle to describe "some error or frailty" that brings about misfortune for a tragic hero. The concept of *hamartia* is closely related to that of the tragic flaw: both lead to the downfall of the protagonist in a tragedy. *Hamartia* may be interpreted as an internal weakness in a character (like greed or passion or hubris); however, it may also refer to a mistake that a character makes that is based not on a personal failure, but on circumstances outside the protagonist's personality and control. See also TRAGEDY.

Hero, heroine See CHARACTER.

Heroic couplet See COUPLET.

High comedy See COMEDY.

Hubris or hybris Excessive pride or self-confidence that leads a protagonist to disregard a divine warning or to violate an important moral law. In tragedies, hubris is a very common form of *hamartia*. See also HAMARTIA, TRAGEDY.

Hyperbole A boldly exaggerated statement that adds emphasis without intending to be literally true, as in the statement "He ate everything in the house." Hyperbole (also called **overstatement**) may be used for serious, comic, or ironic effect. See also FIGURES OF SPEECH.

Iambic pentameter A metrical pattern in poetry that consists of five iambic feet per line. (An iamb, or iambic foot, consists of one unstressed syllable followed by a stressed syllable.) See also FOOT, METER.

Image A word, phrase, or figure of speech (especially a SIMILE or a METAPHOR) that addresses the senses, suggesting mental pictures of sights, sounds, smells, tastes, feelings, or actions. Images offer sensory impressions to the reader and also convey emotions and moods through their verbal pictures. See also FIGURES OF SPEECH.

Implied metaphor See METAPHOR.

In medias res See PLOT.

Informal diction See DICTION.

Internal rhyme See RHYME.

Irony A literary device that uses contradictory statements or situations to reveal a reality different from what appears to be true. It is ironic for a firehouse to burn down or for a police station to be burglarized. **Verbal irony** is a figure of speech that occurs when a person says one thing but means the opposite. **Sarcasm** is a strong form of verbal irony that is calculated to hurt someone through, for example, false praise. **Dramatic irony** creates a discrepancy between what a character believes or says and what the reader or audience member knows to be true. **Tragic irony** is a form of dramatic irony found in tragedies such as *Oedipus the King,* in which Oedipus searches for the person responsible for the plague that ravishes his city and ironically ends up hunting himself. **Situational irony** exists when there is an incongruity between what is expected to happen and what actually happens due to forces beyond human comprehension or control. The suicide of the seemingly successful main character in Edwin Arlington Robinson's poem "Richard Cory" is an example of situational irony. **Cosmic irony** occurs when a writer uses God, destiny, or fate to dash the hopes and expectations of a character or of humankind in general. In cosmic irony, a discrepancy exists between what a character aspires to and what universal forces provide. Stephen Crane's poem "A Man Said to the Universe" is a good example of cosmic irony, because the universe acknowledges no obligation to the man's assertion of his own existence.

Italian sonnet See SONNET.

LGBTQ+ criticism A mode of literary criticism that seeks to explore nonnormative or nonbinary sexualities and/or gender identities as they are represented in literature. See also GENDER CRITICISM.

Limerick A light, humorous style of fixed form poetry. Its usual form consists of five lines with the rhyme scheme *aabba;* lines 1, 2, and 5 contain three feet, while lines 3 and 4 usually contain two feet. Limericks range in subject matter from the silly to the obscene, and since Edward Lear popularized them in the nineteenth century, children and adults have enjoyed these comic poems. See also FIXED FORM.

Limited omniscient narrator See NARRATOR.

Line A sequence of words printed as a separate entity on the page. In poetry, lines are usually measured by the number of feet they contain. The names for various line lengths are as follows:

monometer: one foot	pentameter: five feet
dimeter: two feet	hexameter: six feet
trimeter: three feet	heptameter: seven feet
tetrameter: four feet	octameter: eight feet

The number of feet in a line, coupled with the name of the foot, describes the metrical qualities of that line. See also END-STOPPED LINE, ENJAMBMENT, FOOT, METER.

Literary ballad See BALLAD.

Literary symbol See SYMBOL.

Low comedy See COMEDY.

Lyric A type of brief poem that expresses the personal emotions and thoughts of a single speaker. It is important to realize, however, that although the lyric is uttered in the first person, the speaker is not necessarily the poet. There are many varieties of lyric poetry, including the DRAMATIC MONOLOGUE, ELEGY, HAIKU, ODE, and SONNET forms.

Marxist criticism An approach to literature that focuses on the ideological content of a work — its explicit and implicit assumptions and values about matters such as culture, race, class, and power. Marxist criticism, based largely on the writings of Karl Marx, typically aims at not only revealing and clarifying ideological issues but also correcting social injustices. Some Marxist critics use literature to describe the competing socioeconomic interests that too often advance capitalist interests such as money and power rather than socialist interests such as morality and justice. They argue that literature and literary criticism are essentially political because they either challenge or support economic oppression. Because of this strong emphasis on the political aspects of texts, Marxist criticism focuses more on the content and themes of literature than on its form. See also CULTURAL CRITICISM.

Masculine rhyme See RHYME.

Melodrama A term applied to any literary work that relies on implausible events and sensational action for its effect. The conflicts in melodramas typically arise out of plot rather than characterization; often a virtuous individual must somehow confront and overcome a wicked oppressor. Usually, a melodramatic story ends happily, with the protagonist defeating the antagonist at the last possible moment. Thus, melodramas entertain the reader or audience with exciting action while still conforming to a traditional sense of justice.

Metaphor   A metaphor is a figure of speech that makes a comparison between two unlike things, without using the word *like* or *as*. Metaphors assert the identity of dissimilar things, as when Macbeth asserts that life *is* a "brief candle." Metaphors can be subtle and powerful, and can transform people, places, objects, and ideas into whatever the writer imagines them to be. An **implied metaphor** is a more subtle comparison; the terms being compared are not so specifically explained. For example, to describe a stubborn man unwilling to leave, one could say that he was "a mule standing his ground." This is a fairly explicit metaphor; the man is being compared to a mule. But to say that the man "brayed his refusal to leave" is to create an implied metaphor, because the subject (the man) is never overtly identified as a mule. Braying is associated with the mule, a notoriously stubborn creature, and so the comparison between the stubborn man and the mule is sustained. Implied metaphors can slip by inattentive readers who are not sensitive to such carefully chosen, highly concentrated language. An **extended metaphor** is a sustained comparison in which part or all of a poem consists of a series of related metaphors. Robert Francis's poem "Catch" relies on an extended metaphor that compares poetry to playing catch. A **controlling metaphor** runs through an entire work and determines the form or nature of that work. The controlling metaphor in Anne Bradstreet's poem "The Author to Her Book" likens her book to a child. **Synecdoche** is a kind of metaphor in which a part of something is used to signify the whole, as when a gossip is called a "wagging tongue," or when ten ships are called "ten sails." Sometimes, synecdoche refers to the whole being used to signify the part, as in the phrase "Boston won the baseball game." Clearly, the entire city of Boston did not participate in the game; the whole of Boston is being used to signify the individuals who played and won the game. **Metonymy** is a type of metaphor in which something closely associated with a subject is substituted for it. In this way, we speak of the "silver screen" to mean motion pictures, "the crown" to stand for the monarch, "the White House" to stand for the activities of the president. See also FIGURES OF SPEECH, PERSONIFICATION, SIMILE.

Meter   When a rhythmic pattern of stresses recurs in a poem, it is called *meter*. Metrical patterns are determined by the type and number of feet in a line of verse; combining the name of a line length with the name of a foot concisely describes the meter of the line. **Rising meter** refers to metrical feet that move from unstressed to stressed sounds, such as the iambic foot and the anapestic foot. **Falling meter** refers to metrical feet that move from stressed to unstressed sounds, such as the trochaic foot and the dactylic foot. See also ACCENT, FOOT, IAMBIC PENTAMETER, LINE.

Metonymy   See METAPHOR.

Middle diction   See DICTION.

Motivated action   See CHARACTER.

Mythological criticism   An approach to literature that seeks to identify what in a work creates deep universal responses in readers, by paying close attention to the hopes, fears, and expectations of entire cultures. Mythological critics (sometimes called *archetypal critics*) look for underlying, recurrent patterns in literature that reveal universal meanings and basic human experiences for readers regardless of when and where they live. These critics attempt to explain how archetypes (the characters, images, and themes that symbolically embody universal meanings and experiences) are embodied in literary works in order to make larger connections that explain a particular work's lasting appeal. Mythological critics may specialize in areas such as classical literature, philology, anthropology, psychology, and cultural history, but they all emphasize the assumptions and values of various cultures. See also ARCHETYPE.

Naive narrator See NARRATOR.

Narrative poem A poem that tells a story. A narrative poem may be short or long, and the story it relates may be simple or complex. See also BALLAD, EPIC.

Narrator The voice of the person telling the story, not to be confused with the author's voice. With a **first-person narrator**, the *I* in the story presents the point of view of only one character. The reader is restricted to the perceptions, thoughts, and feelings of that single character. For example, in ZZ Packer's "Drinking Coffee Elsewhere," Dina is the first-person narrator of the story. First-person narrators can play either a major or a minor role in the story they are telling. An **unreliable narrator** reveals an interpretation of events that is somehow different from the author's own interpretation of those events. Often, the unreliable narrator's perception of plot, characters, and setting becomes the actual subject of the story, as in "Drinking Coffee Elsewhere." Narrators can be unreliable for a number of reasons: they might lack full self-knowledge (like Packer's Dina), they might be inexperienced, they might even be insane (like the narrator of Charlotte Perkins Gilman's "The Yellow Wallpaper"). **Naive narrators** are usually characterized by youthful innocence, such as Mark Twain's Huck Finn or J. D. Salinger's Holden Caulfield. An **omniscient narrator** is an all-knowing narrator who is not a character in the story and who can move from place to place and pass back and forth through time, slipping into and out of characters as no human being possibly could in real life. Omniscient narrators can report the thoughts and feelings of the characters, as well as their words and actions. The narrator of Ursula K. Le Guin's story "The Ones Who Walk Away from Omelas" is an omniscient narrator. **Editorial omniscience** refers to an intrusion by the narrator in order to evaluate a character for a reader, as when the narrator of Le Guin's story asks the reader questions about the scene she describes. Narration that allows the characters' actions and thoughts to speak for themselves is called **neutral omniscience**. Most modern writers use neutral omniscience so that readers can reach their own conclusions. **Limited omniscience** occurs when an author restricts a narrator to the single perspective of either a major or minor character. The way people, places, and events appear to that character is the way they appear to the reader. Sometimes a limited omniscient narrator can see into more than one character, particularly in a work that focuses on two characters alternately from one chapter to the next. Short stories, however, are frequently limited to a single character's point of view. See also PERSONA, POINT OF VIEW, STREAM-OF-CONSCIOUSNESS TECHNIQUE.

Near rhyme See RHYME.

Neutral omniscience See NARRATOR.

New Criticism An approach to literature made popular between the 1940s and the 1960s that evolved out of formalist criticism. New Critics suggest that detailed analysis of the language of a literary text can uncover important layers of meaning in that work. New Criticism consciously downplays the historical influences, authorial intentions, and social contexts that surround texts in order to focus on explication — extremely close textual analysis. Critics such as John Crowe Ransom, I. A. Richards, and Robert Penn Warren are commonly associated with New Criticism. See also FORMALIST CRITICISM.

New historicism An approach to literature that emphasizes the interaction between the historic context of the work and a modern reader's understanding and interpretation of the work. New historicists attempt to describe the culture of a period by reading many different kinds of texts and paying close attention to many different dimensions of a culture, including political, economic, social, and aesthetic concerns. They regard texts not simply as a reflection of the culture that produced them but also as contributing to that culture by playing an active role in the social and political conflicts of an age. New historicism acknowledges and then explores various versions of "history," sensitizing us to the fact that the history on which we choose to focus is colored by being reconstructed from our present circumstances.

Objective point of view SEE POINT OF VIEW.

Octave A poetic stanza of eight lines, usually forming one part of a Petrarchan sonnet. See also SONNET, STANZA.

Ode A relatively lengthy lyric poem that often expresses lofty emotions in a dignified style. Odes are characterized by a serious topic, such as truth, art, freedom, justice, or the meaning of life; their tone tends to be formal. There is no prescribed pattern that defines an ode; some odes repeat the same pattern in each stanza, while others introduce a new pattern in each stanza. See also LYRIC.

Oedipus complex A Freudian term derived from Sophocles' tragedy *Oedipus the King*. It describes a psychological complex that is predicated on a boy's unconscious rivalry with his father for his mother's love and his desire to eliminate his father in order to take his father's place with his mother. The female equivalent of this complex is called the **Electra complex**. See also ELECTRA COMPLEX.

Off rhyme See RHYME.

Omniscient narrator See NARRATOR.

One-act play A play that takes place in a single location and unfolds as one continuous action. The characters in a one-act play are presented economically and the action is sharply focused. See also DRAMA.

Onomatopoeia A term referring to the use of a word that resembles the sound it denotes. *Buzz, rattle, bang,* and *sizzle* all reflect onomatopoeia. Onomatopoeia can also consist of more than one word; writers sometimes create lines or whole passages in which the sound of the words helps to convey their meanings.

Open form Sometimes called **free verse**, open form poetry does not conform to established patterns of METER, RHYME, and STANZA. Such poetry derives its rhythmic qualities from the repetition of words, phrases, or grammatical structures, the arrangement of words on the printed page, or by some other means. The poet E. E. Cummings wrote open form poetry; his poems do not have measurable meters, but they do have rhythm. See also FIXED FORM.

Overstatement See HYPERBOLE.

Oxymoron A condensed form of paradox in which two contradictory words are used together, as in "sweet sorrow" or "original copy." See also PARADOX.

Paradox A statement that initially appears to be contradictory but then, on closer inspection, turns out to make sense. For example, John Donne ends his sonnet "Death, Be Not Proud" with the paradoxical statement "Death, thou shalt die." To solve the paradox, it is necessary to discover the sense that underlies the statement. Paradox is useful in poetry because it arrests a reader's attention by its seemingly stubborn refusal to make sense.

Paraphrase A prose restatement of the central ideas of a literary work, in one's own language.

Parody A humorous imitation of another, usually serious, work. It can take any fixed or open form, because parodists imitate the tone, language, and shape of the original in order to deflate the subject matter, making the original work seem absurd. Anthony Hecht's poem "Dover Bitch" is a famous parody of Matthew Arnold's well-known "Dover Beach." Parody may also be used as a form of literary criticism to expose the defects in a work. But sometimes parody becomes an affectionate acknowledgment that a well-known work has become both institutionalized in our culture and fair game for some fun. For example, Peter De Vries's "To His Importunate Mistress" gently mocks Andrew Marvell's "To His Coy Mistress."

Persona Literally, a *persona* is a mask. In literature, a persona is a speaker created by a writer to tell a story or to speak in a poem. A persona is not a character in a story or narrative, nor does a persona necessarily directly reflect the author's personal voice. A persona is a separate self, created by and distinct from the author, through which he or she speaks. See also NARRATOR.

Personification A form of metaphor in which human characteristics are attributed to nonhuman things. Personification offers the writer a way to give the world life and motion by assigning familiar human behaviors and emotions to animals, inanimate objects, and abstract ideas. For example, in Keats's "Ode on a Grecian Urn," the speaker refers to the urn as an "unravished bride of quietness," or in Langston Hughes's "The Weary Blues," the player makes "the piano moan." See also METAPHOR.

Petrarchan sonnet See SONNET.

Picture poem A type of open form poetry in which the poet arranges the lines of the poem so as to create a particular shape on the page. The shape of the poem embodies its subject; the poem becomes a picture of what the poem is describing. Michael McFee's "In Medias Res" is an example of a picture poem. See also OPEN FORM.

Plausible action See CHARACTER.

Play See DRAMA.

Playwright See DRAMA.

Plot An author's selection and arrangement of incidents in a story to shape the action and give the story a particular focus. Discussions of plot include not just what happens, but also how and why things happen the way they do. Stories that are written in a **pyramidal pattern** divide the plot into three essential parts. The first part is the **rising action**, in which complication creates some sort of conflict for the protagonist. The second part is the **climax**, the moment of greatest emotional tension in a narrative, usually marking a turning point in the plot at which the **rising action** reverses to become the falling action. The third part, the **falling action** (or RESOLUTION), is characterized by diminishing tensions and the resolution of the plot's conflicts and complications. *In medias res* is a term used to describe the common strategy of beginning a story in the middle of the action. In this type of plot, we enter the story on the verge of some important moment. See also CHARACTER, CRISIS, RESOLUTION, SUBPLOT.

Poetic diction See DICTION.

Point of view Refers to who tells us a story and how it is told. What we know and how we feel about the events in a work are shaped by the author's choice of point of view. The teller of the story, the narrator, inevitably affects our understanding of the characters' actions by filtering what is told through his or her own perspective. The various points of view that writers draw upon can be grouped into two broad categories: (1) the third-person narrator uses *he, she,* or *they* to tell the story and does not participate in the action; and (2) the first-person narrator uses *I* and is a major or minor participant in the action. In addition, a second-person narrator, *you,* is also possible, but is rarely used because of the awkwardness of thrusting the reader into the story, as in "You are minding your own business on a park bench when a drunk steps out and demands your lunch bag." An **objective point of view** employs a third-person narrator who does not see into the mind of any character. From this detached and impersonal perspective, the narrator reports action and dialogue without telling us directly what the characters think and feel. Since no analysis or interpretation is provided by the narrator, this point of view places a premium on dialogue, actions, and details to reveal character to the reader. See also NARRATOR, STREAM-OF-CONSCIOUSNESS TECHNIQUE.

Problem play Popularized by Henrik Ibsen, a problem play is a type of drama that presents a social issue in order to awaken the audience to it. These plays usually reject romantic plots in favor of holding up a mirror that reflects not simply what the audience wants to see but what the playwright sees in them. Often, a problem play will propose a solution to the problem that does not coincide with prevailing opinion. The term is also used to refer to certain Shakespeare plays that do not fit the categories of tragedy, comedy, or romance. See also DRAMA.

Prologue The opening speech or dialogue of a play, especially a classic Greek play, that usually gives the exposition necessary to follow the subsequent action. Today the term also refers to the introduction to any literary work. See also DRAMA, EXPOSITION.

Prose poem A kind of open form poetry that is printed as prose and represents the most clear opposite of fixed form poetry. Prose poems are densely compact and often make use of striking imagery and figures of speech. See also FIXED FORM, OPEN FORM.

Prosody The overall metrical structure of a poem. See also METER.

Protagonist The main character of a narrative; its central character who engages the reader's interest and empathy. See also CHARACTER.

Pun A play on words that relies on a word's having more than one meaning or sounding like another word. Shakespeare and other writers use puns extensively, for serious and comic purposes; in *Romeo and Juliet* (III.i.101), the dying Mercutio puns, "Ask for me tomorrow and you shall find me a grave man." Puns have serious literary uses, but since the eighteenth century, puns have been used almost purely for humorous effect. See also COMEDY.

Pyramidal pattern See PLOT.

Quatrain A four-line stanza. Quatrains are the most common stanzaic form in the English language; they can have various meters and rhyme schemes. See also METER, RHYME, STANZA.

Reader-response criticism An approach to literature that focuses on the process of reading rather than the work itself, by attempting to describe what goes on in the reader's mind during the reading of a text. Hence, the consciousness of the reader — produced by reading the work — is the actual subject of reader-response criticism. These critics are not after a "correct" reading of the text or what the author presumably intended; instead, they are interested in the reader's individual experience with the text, perhaps in conjunction with the responses of other similar readers, referred to as an "interpretive community." Thus, there is no single definitive reading of a work, because readers create rather than discover absolute meanings in texts. However, this approach is not a rationale for mistaken or bizarre readings, but an exploration of the possibilities for a plurality of readings. This kind of strategy calls attention to how we read and what influences our readings, and what that reveals about ourselves.

Recognition The moment in a story when previously unknown or withheld information is revealed to the protagonist, resulting in the discovery of the truth of his or her situation and, usually, a decisive change in course for that character. In *Oedipus the King,* the moment of recognition comes when Oedipus finally realizes that he has killed his father and married his mother.

Resolution The conclusion of a plot's conflicts and complications. The resolution, also known as the **falling action**, follows the climax in the plot. See also DÉNOUEMENT, PLOT.

Reversal The point in a story when the protagonist's fortunes turn in an unexpected direction. See also PLOT.

Rhyme The repetition of identical or similar concluding syllables in different words, most often at the ends of lines. Rhyme is predominantly a function of sound rather than spelling; thus, words that end with the same vowel sounds rhyme, for instance, *day, prey, bouquet, weigh,* and words with the same consonant ending rhyme, for instance *vain, feign, rein, lane.* Words do not have to be spelled the same way or look alike to rhyme. In fact, words may look alike but not rhyme at all. This is called **eye rhyme**, as with *bough* and *cough,* or *brow* and *blow.* **End rhyme** is the most common form of rhyme in poetry; the rhyme comes at the end of the lines:

> It runs through the reeds
> And away it proceeds,
> Through meadow and glade,
> In sun and in shade.

The **rhyme scheme** of a poem describes the pattern of end rhymes. Rhyme schemes are mapped out by noting patterns of rhyme with small letters: the first rhyme sound is designated *a,* the second becomes *b,* the third *c,* and so on. Thus, the rhyme scheme of the stanza above is *aabb.* **Internal rhyme** places at least one of the rhymed words within the line, as in "Dividing and gliding and sliding" or "In mist or cloud, on mast or shroud." **Masculine rhyme** describes the rhyming of single-syllable words, such as *grade* or *shade.* Masculine rhyme also occurs when rhyming words of more than one syllable, when the same sound occurs in a final stressed syllable, as in *defend* and *contend, betray* and *away.* **Feminine rhyme** consists of a rhymed stressed syllable followed by one or more identical unstressed syllables, as in *butter, clutter; gratitude, attitude; quivering, shivering.* All the examples so far have illustrated **exact rhymes,** because they share the same stressed vowel sounds as well as sharing sounds that follow the vowel. In **near rhyme** (also called **off rhyme, slant rhyme,** and **approximate rhyme**), the sounds are almost but not exactly alike. A common form of near rhyme is consonance, which consists of identical consonant sounds preceded by different vowel sounds: *home, same; worth, breath.*

Rhyme scheme See RHYME.

Rhythm A term used to refer to the recurrence of stressed and unstressed sounds in poetry. Depending on how sounds are arranged, the rhythm of a poem may be fast or slow, choppy or smooth. Poets use rhythm to create pleasurable sound patterns and to reinforce meanings. Rhythm in prose arises from pattern repetitions of sounds and pauses that create looser rhythmic effects. See also METER.

Rising action See PLOT.

Rising meter See METER.

Romantic comedy See COMEDY.

Round character See CHARACTER.

Run-on line See ENJAMBMENT.

Sarcasm See IRONY.

Satire The literary art of ridiculing a folly or vice in order to expose or correct it. The object of satire is usually some human frailty; people, institutions, ideas, and things are all fair game for satirists. Satire evokes attitudes of amusement, contempt, scorn, or indignation toward its faulty subject in the hope of somehow improving it. See also IRONY, PARODY.

Scansion The process of measuring the stresses in a line of verse in order to determine the metrical pattern of the line. See also LINE, METER.

Scene In drama, a scene is a subdivision of an act. In modern plays, scenes usually consist of units of action in which there are no changes in the setting or breaks in the continuity of time. According to traditional conventions, a scene changes when the location of the action shifts or when a new character enters. See also ACT, CONVENTION, DRAMA.

Script The written text of a play, which includes the dialogue between characters, stage directions, and often other expository information. See also DRAMA, EXPOSITION, PROLOGUE, STAGE DIRECTIONS.

Sestet A stanza consisting of exactly six lines. See also STANZA.

Sestina A type of fixed form poetry consisting of thirty-nine lines of any length divided into six sestets and a three-line concluding stanza called an *envoy*. The six words at the end of the first sestet's lines must also appear at the ends of the other five sestets, in varying order. These six words must also appear in the envoy, where they often resonate important themes. An example of this highly demanding form of poetry is Algernon Charles Swinburne's "Sestina." See also SESTET.

Setting The physical and social context in which the action of a story occurs. The major elements of setting are the time, the place, and the social environment that frames the characters. Setting can be used to evoke a mood or atmosphere that will prepare the reader for what is to come, as in Nathaniel Hawthorne's short story "Young Goodman Brown." Sometimes, writers choose a particular setting because of traditional associations with that setting that are closely related to the action of a story. For example, stories filled with adventure or romance often take place in exotic locales.

Shakespearean sonnet See SONNET.

Showing See CHARACTER.

Simile A common figure of speech that makes an explicit comparison between two things by using words such as *like, as, than, appears,* and *seems:* "A sip of Mrs. Cook's coffee is like a punch in the stomach." The effectiveness of this simile is created by the differences between the two things compared. There would be no simile if the comparison were stated this way: "Mrs. Cook's coffee is as strong as the cafeteria's coffee." This is a literal translation because Mrs. Cook's coffee is compared with something like it — another kind of coffee. See also FIGURES OF SPEECH, METAPHOR.

Situational irony See IRONY.

Slant rhyme See RHYME.

Soliloquy A dramatic convention by means of which a character, alone onstage, utters his or her thoughts aloud. Playwrights use soliloquies as a convenient way to inform the audience about a character's motivations and state of mind. Shakespeare's Hamlet delivers perhaps the best known of all soliloquies, which begins: "To be or not to be." See also ASIDE, CONVENTION.

Sonnet A fixed form of lyric poetry that consists of fourteen lines, usually written in iambic pentameter. There are two basic types of sonnets, the Italian and the English. The **Italian sonnet**, also known as the **Petrarchan sonnet**, is divided into an octave, which typically rhymes *abbaabba,* and a sestet, which may have varying rhyme schemes. Common rhyme patterns in the sestet are *cdecde, cdcdcd,* and *cdccdc.* Very often the octave presents a situation, attitude, or problem that the sestet comments upon or resolves, as in John Keats's "On First Looking into Chapman's Homer." The **English sonnet**, also known as the **Shakespearean sonnet**, is organized into three quatrains and a couplet, which typically rhyme *abab cdcd efef gg.* This rhyme scheme is more suited to English poetry because English has fewer rhyming words than Italian. English sonnets, because of their four-part organization, also have more flexibility with respect to where thematic breaks can occur. Frequently, however, the most pronounced break or turn comes with the concluding couplet, as in Shakespeare's "Shall I compare thee to a summer's day?" See also COU-PLET, IAMBIC PENTAMETER, LINE, OCTAVE, QUATRAIN, SESTET.

Speaker The voice used by an author to tell a story or speak a poem. The speaker is often a created identity, and should not automatically be equated with the author's self. See also NARRATOR, PERSONA, POINT OF VIEW.

Spondee See FOOT.

Stage directions A playwright's written instructions about how the actors are to move and behave in a play. They explain in which direction characters should move, what facial expressions they should assume, and so on. See also DRAMA, SCRIPT.

Stanza In poetry, *stanza* refers to a grouping of lines, set off by a space, that usually has a set pattern of meter and rhyme. See also LINE, METER, RHYME.

Static character See CHARACTER.

Stock character See CHARACTER.

Stream-of-consciousness technique The most intense use of a central consciousness in narration. The stream-of-consciousness technique takes a reader inside a character's mind to reveal perceptions, thoughts, and feelings on a conscious or unconscious level. This technique suggests the flow of thought as well as its content; hence, complete sentences may give way to fragments as the character's mind makes rapid associations free of conventional logic or transitions. James Joyce's novel *Ulysses* makes extensive use of this narrative technique. See also NARRATOR, POINT OF VIEW.

Stress The emphasis, or accent, given a syllable in pronunciation. See also ACCENT.

Style The distinctive and unique manner in which a writer arranges words to achieve particular effects. Style essentially combines the idea to be expressed with the individuality of the author. These arrangements include individual word choices as well as matters such as the length of sentences, their structure, tone, and use of irony. See also DICTION, IRONY, TONE.

Subplot The secondary action of a story, complete and interesting in its own right, that reinforces or contrasts with the main plot. There may be more than one subplot, and sometimes as many as three, four, or even more, running through a piece of fiction. Subplots are generally either analogous to the main plot, thereby enhancing our understanding of it, or extraneous to the main plot, to provide relief from it. See also PLOT.

Suspense The anxious anticipation of a reader or an audience as to the outcome of a story, especially concerning the character or characters with whom sympathetic attachments are formed. Suspense helps to secure and sustain the interest of the reader or audience throughout a work.

Symbol A person, object, image, word, or event that evokes a range of additional meaning beyond and usually more abstract than its literal significance. Symbols are educational devices for evoking complex ideas without having to resort to painstaking explanations that would make a story more like an essay than an experience. **Conventional symbols** have meanings that are widely recognized by a society or culture. Some conventional symbols recognizable in American culture are a soaring bird to represent freedom or sweat to represent hard work. Writers use conventional symbols to reinforce meanings. Kate Chopin, for example, emphasizes the spring setting in "The Story of an Hour" as a way of suggesting the renewed sense of life that Mrs. Mallard feels when she thinks herself free from her husband. A **literary** or **contextual symbol** can be a setting, character, action, object, name, or anything else in a work that maintains its literal significance while suggesting other meanings. Such symbols go beyond conventional symbols; they gain their symbolic meaning within the context of a specific story. For example, the white whale in Melville's *Moby-Dick* takes on multiple symbolic meanings in the work, but these meanings do not automatically carry over into other stories about whales. The meanings suggested by Melville's whale are specific to that text; therefore, it becomes a contextual symbol. See also ALLEGORY.

Synecdoche See METAPHOR.

Syntax The ordering of words into meaningful verbal patterns such as phrases, clauses, and sentences. Poets often manipulate syntax, changing conventional word order, to place certain emphasis on particular words. Emily Dickinson, for instance, writes about being surprised by a snake in her poem "A narrow Fellow in the Grass," and includes this line: "His notice sudden is." In addition to creating the alliterative hissing *s*-sounds here, Dickinson also effectively manipulates the line's syntax so that the verb *is* appears unexpectedly at the end, making the snake's hissing presence all the more "sudden."

Telling See CHARACTER.

Tercet A three-line stanza. See also STANZA, TRIPLET.

Terza rima An interlocking three-line rhyme scheme: *aba, bcb, cdc, ded,* and so on. Dante's *The Divine Comedy* and Frost's "Acquainted with the Night" are written in *terza rima*. See also RHYME, TERCET.

Theme The central meaning or dominant idea in a literary work. A theme provides a unifying point around which the plot, characters, setting, point of view, symbols, and other elements of a work are organized. It is important not to mistake the theme for the actual subject of the work; the theme refers to the abstract concept that is made concrete through the images, characterization, and action of the text. In nonfiction, however, the theme generally refers to the main topic of the discourse.

Thesis The central idea of an essay. The thesis is a complete sentence (although sometimes it may require more than one sentence) that establishes the topic of the essay in clear, unambiguous language and suggests a concluding interpretation.

Tone The author's implicit attitude toward the reader or the people, places, and events in a work as revealed by the elements of the author's style. Tone may be characterized as serious or ironic, sad or happy, private or public, angry or affectionate, bitter or nostalgic, or any other attitudes and feelings that human beings experience. See also STYLE.

Tragedy A story that presents courageous individuals who confront powerful forces within or outside themselves with a dignity that reveals the breadth and depth of the human spirit in the face of failure, defeat, and even death. Tragedies recount an individual's downfall; they usually begin high and end low. Shakespeare is known for his tragedies, including *Macbeth, King Lear, Othello,* and *Hamlet.* The revenge tragedy is a well-established type of drama that can be traced back to Greek and Roman plays, particularly through the Roman playwright Seneca (ca. 3 B.C.–A.D. 63). Revenge tragedies basically consist of a murder that has to be avenged by a relative of the victim. Typically, the victim's ghost appears to demand revenge, and invariably madness of some sort is worked into subsequent events, which ultimately end in the deaths of the murderer, the avenger, and a number of other characters. Shakespeare's *Hamlet* subscribes to the basic ingredients of revenge tragedy, but it also transcends these conventions because Hamlet contemplates not merely revenge but suicide and the meaning of life itself. A **tragic flaw** is an error or defect in the tragic hero that leads to his downfall, such as greed, pride, or ambition. This flaw may be a result of bad character, bad judgment, an inherited weakness, or any other defect of character. **Tragic irony** is a form of dramatic irony found in tragedies such as *Oedipus the King,* in which Oedipus ironically ends up hunting himself. See also COMEDY, DRAMA.

Tragic flaw See TRAGEDY.

Tragic irony See IRONY, TRAGEDY.

Triplet A tercet in which all three lines rhyme. See also TERCET.

Understatement The opposite of hyperbole, understatement (or *litotes*) refers to a figure of speech that says less than is intended. Understatement usually has an ironic effect, and sometimes may be used for comic purposes, as in Mark Twain's statement, "The reports of my death are greatly exaggerated." See also HYPERBOLE, IRONY.

Unreliable narrator See NARRATOR.

Verbal irony See IRONY.

Verse A generic term used to describe poetic lines composed in a measured rhythmical pattern that are often, but not necessarily, rhymed. See also LINE, METER, RHYME, RHYTHM.

Villanelle A type of fixed form poetry consisting of nineteen lines of any length divided into six stanzas: five tercets and a concluding quatrain. The first and third lines of the initial tercet rhyme; these rhymes are repeated in each subsequent tercet (*aba*) and in the final two lines of the quatrain (*abaa*). Line 1 appears in its entirety as lines 6, 12, and 18, while line 3 reappears as lines 9, 15, and 19. Dylan Thomas's "Do Not Go Gentle into That Good Night" is a villanelle. See also FIXED FORM, QUATRAIN, RHYME, TERCET.

Well-made play A realistic style of play that employs conventions including plenty of suspense created by meticulous plotting. Well-made plays are tightly and logically constructed, and lead to a logical resolution that is favorable to the protagonist. This dramatic structure was popularized in France by Eugène Scribe (1791–1861) and Victorien Sardou (1831–1908) and was adopted by Henrik Ibsen. See also CHARACTER, PLOT

Acknowledgments (continued from p. iv)

FICTION

James Baldwin. "Sonny's Blues," copyright © 1957 by James Baldwin, was originally published in *Partisan Review*. Copyright renewed. Collected in *Going to Meet the Man*, published by Vintage Books. Reprinted by arrangement with the James Baldwin Estate.

Dale M. Bauer. Footnotes from Charlotte Perkins Gilman, "The Yellow Wallpaper." Edited by Dale M. Bauer. Reproduced with permission of Dale M. Bauer, University of Illinois.

Ann Beattie. "Janus" from *Where You'll Find Me and Other Stories* by Ann Beattie. Copyright © 1986 by Irony & Pity, Inc. Reprinted with the permission of Scribner, a division of Simon & Schuster, Inc., and by permission of the author. All rights reserved.

T. C. Boyle. "The Hit Man" from *The Human Fly and Other Stories* by T. C. Boyle. Copyright © 2005 by T. Coraghessan Boyle. Used by permission of Viking Children's Books, an imprint of Penguin Young Readers Group, a division of Penguin Random House LLC. All rights reserved.

Raymond Carver. "Popular Mechanics" from *What We Talk about When We Talk about Love* by Raymond Carver. Copyright © 1974, 1976, 1978, 1980, 1981 by Tess Gallagher. Used by permission of Alfred A. Knopf, an imprint of the Knopf Doubleday Publishing Group, a division of Penguin Random House LLC. All rights reserved.

John Cheever. "The Enormous Radio" from *The Stories of John Cheever* by John Cheever. Copyright © 1978 by John Cheever. Used by permission of Alfred A. Knopf, an imprint of the Knopf Doubleday Publishing Group, a division of Penguin Random House LLC. All rights reserved.

Judith Ortiz Cofer. "Volar" from *The Year of Our Revolution* by Judith Ortiz Cofer. Copyright © 1998 by Arte Público Press–University of Houston. Reprinted with the permission of the publisher.

Edwidge Danticat. "The Missing Peace" from *Krik? Krak!* by Edwidge Danticat. Copyright © 1991, 1995 by Edwidge Danticat. Reprinted by permission of Soho Press, Inc. All rights reserved.

Louise Erdrich. "The Red Convertible" from *The Red Convertible: Selected and New Stories, 1978–2008* by Louise Erdrich. Copyright © 2009 by Louise Erdrich. Reprinted by permission of HarperCollins Publishers.

William Faulkner. "A Rose for Emily" from *Collected Stories of William Faulkner* by William Faulkner. Copyright © 1930 and renewed 1958 by William Faulkner. Used by permission of Random House, an imprint and division of Penguin Random House LLC, and by permission of W. W. Norton & Company, Inc. All rights reserved.

Dagoberto Gilb. "Love in L.A." from *The Magic of Blood* by Dagoberto Gilb. Copyright © 1993. Story originally published in *Buffalo*.

Ernest Hemingway. "Soldier's Home" from *In Our Time* by Ernest Hemingway. Copyright © 1925, 1930 by Charles Scribner's Sons; copyright renewed © 1953, 1958 by Ernest Hemingway. Reprinted with the permission of Scribner, a division of Simon & Schuster, Inc. All rights reserved.

Shirley Jackson. "The Lottery" from *The Lottery* by Shirley Jackson. Copyright © 1948, 1949 by Shirley Jackson. Copyright renewed 1976, 1977 by Laurence Hyman, Barry Hyman, Mrs. Sarah Webster, and Mrs. Joanne Schnurer. Reprinted by permission of Farrar, Straus & Giroux, LLC.

Claire Katz. "The Function of Violence in O'Connor's Fiction" from "Flannery O'Connor's Rage of Vision," *American Literature* 46.1 (March 1974), pp. 545–67. Copyright © 1974, Duke University Press. All rights reserved. Republished by permission of the copyright holder, Duke University Press, www .dukeupress.edu.

Jamaica Kincaid. "Girl" from *At the Bottom of the River* by Jamaica Kincaid. Copyright © 1983 by Jamaica Kincaid. Reprinted by permission of Farrar, Straus & Giroux, LLC.

Jhumpa Lahiri. "Sexy" from *Interpreter of Maladies* by Jhumpa Lahiri. Copyright © 1999 by Jhumpa Lahiri. Reprinted by permission of Houghton Mifflin Harcourt Publishing Company. All rights reserved.

Ursula K. Le Guin. "The Ones Who Walk Away from Omelas." Copyright © 1973 by Ursula K. Le Guin. First appeared in "New Dimensions 3" in 1973, and then in *The Wind's Twelve Quarters*, published by HarperCollins in 1975. Reprinted by permission of Curtis Brown, Ltd.

Maggie Mitchell. "It Would Be Different If." Originally appeared in *New South* 4.2 (2011). Copyright © 2011 by Margaret E. Mitchell. Reprinted by permission of the author.

Manuel Muñoz. "Zigzagger" from *Zigzagger* by Manuel Muñoz. Copyright © 2003 by Manuel Muñoz. Published 2003 by Northwestern University Press. All rights reserved.

Joyce Carol Oates. "Tick" from *The Assignation* by Joyce Carol Oates. Copyright © 1988 by The Ontario Review, Inc. Reprinted by permission of HarperCollins Publishers.

Flannery O'Connor. "A Good Man Is Hard to Find" and "Good Country People" from *A Good Man Is Hard to Find and Other Stories* by Flannery O'Connor. Copyright © 1953 by Flannery O'Connor, renewed 1981 by Regina O'Connor. Reprinted by permission of Houghton Mifflin Harcourt Publishing Company. All rights reserved. "Revelation" from *The Complete Stories of Flannery O'Connor* by Flannery

POETRY

Ruth Forman. "Poetry Should Ride the Bus" from *We Are the Young Magicians* (Boston: Beacon Press, 1993). Copyright © 1993 by Ruth Forman. Reprinted with the permission of the author.

Kate Hanson Foster. "Elegy of Color," *Salamander* 46 (Spring/Summer 2018), p. 34. Copyright © 2018 by Kate Hanson Foster. Reprinted by permission of the author.

Robert Francis. "Catch" and "The Pitcher," from *The Orb Weaver*. Copyright © 1960 by Robert Francis. Published by Wesleyan University Press and reprinted with permission.

Robert Frost. "Acquainted with the Night," copyright © 1928, 1969 by Henry Holt and Company. Copyright © 1956 by Robert Frost. "Design," copyright © 1928, 1939, 1967, 1969 by Henry Holt and Company. Copyright © 1936, 1942, 1956 by Robert Frost. Copyright © 1964, 1967, 1970 by Lesley Frost Ballantine. Both selections from *The Poetry of Robert Frost*, edited by Edward Connery Lathem. Reprinted by permission of Henry Holt and Company. All rights reserved.

Mirza Asadullah Khan Ghalib. "Ghazal 4" from *Celebrating the Best of Urdu Poetry*, translated by Khushwant Singh and edited by Khushwant Singh and Kamna Prasad. Copyright © 2007 by Khushwant Singh and Kamna Prasad. Reprinted by permission of Penguin Random House India.

Sandra M. Gilbert and Susan Gubar. "On Dickinson's White Dress" from *The Madwoman in the Attic*. Copyright © 1979 by Yale University Press. Reprinted by permission of Yale University Press.

Allen Ginsberg. "Sunflower Sutra" from *Collected Poems 1947–1980* by Allen Ginsberg. Copyright © 1955 by Allen Ginsberg. Reprinted by permission of HarperCollins Publishers.

Louise Glück. "Celestial Music" from *Ararat* by Louise Glück. Copyright © 1990 by Louise Glück. Reprinted by permission of HarperCollins Publishers.

Woody Guthrie. "Gypsy Davy" (Black Jack Davy), words and music adapted by Woody Guthrie. WGP/ TRO-© Copyright 1961 (Renewed) 1963 (Renewed) Woody Guthrie Publications, Inc., & Ludlow Music, Inc., New York, NY, administered by Ludlow Music, Inc.

R. S. Gwynn. "Shakespearean Sonnet." Originally appeared in *Formalist* 12.2 (2001). Copyright © 2001 by R. S. Gwynn. Reprinted by permission of the author.

Mark Halliday. "Graded Paper," *Michigan Quarterly Review*. Reprinted by permission of the author.

Robert Hayden. "Those Winter Sundays," copyright © 1966 by Robert Hayden, from *Collected Poems of Robert Hayden* by Robert Hayden, edited by Frederick Glaysher. Used by permission of Liveright Publishing Corporation.

Seamus Heaney. "Personal Helicon" from *Opened Ground: Selected Poems 1966–1996* by Seamus Heaney. Copyright © 1998 by Seamus Heaney. Reprinted by permission of Farrar, Straus & Giroux, LLC, and Faber and Faber, Ltd.

Judy Page Heitzman. "The Schoolroom on the Second Floor of the Knitting Mill." Copyright © 1991 by Judy Page Heitzman. Originally appeared in the *New Yorker*, December 2, 1992, p. 102. Reprinted by permission of the author.

David Hernandez. "All-American," *Southern Review* 48.4 (Autumn 2012). Copyright © 2012 by David Hernandez. Used by permission of the author.

William Heyen. "The Trains" from *The Host: Selected Poems 1965–1990* by William Heyen. Copyright © 1994 by Time Being Press. Reprinted by permission of the author.

Jane Hirshfield. "Optimism" from *Given Sugar, Given Salt* by Jane Hirshfield. Copyright © 2001 by Jane Hirshfield. Reprinted by permission of HarperCollins Publishers.

Andrew Hudgins. "The Ice-Cream Truck" from *Shut Up, You're Fine! Poems for Very, Very Bad Children* by Andrew Hudgins. Copyright © 2009 by Andrew Hudgins. Reprinted by permission of the author.

Langston Hughes. "Harlem [2]" and "The Weary Blues," from *The Collected Poems of Langston Hughes* by Langston Hughes, edited by Arnold Rampersad with David Roessel, Associate Editor. Copyright © 1994 by the Estate of Langston Hughes. Used by permission of Alfred A. Knopf, an imprint of the Knopf Doubleday Publishing Group, a division of Penguin Random House LLC, and by permission of Harold Ober Associates Incorporated. All rights reserved.

Major Jackson. "Autumn Landscape" and "The Chase," from *Holding Company: Poems* by Major Jackson. Copyright © 2010 by Major Jackson. Used by permission of the author and W. W. Norton & Company, Inc.

Brionne Janae. "Alternative Facts," *Salamander* 46 (Spring/Summer 2018). Copyright © 2018. Reprinted by permission of the author.

Mark Jarman. "Unholy Sonnet" ["Breath like a house fly batters the shut mouth."] from *Bone Fires: New and Selected Poems*. Copyright © 1997 by Mark Jarman. Reprinted with the permission of The Permissions Company, Inc., on behalf of Sarabande Books, www.sarabandebooks.org.

Randall Jarrell. "The Death of the Ball Turret Gunner" from *The Complete Poems* by Randall Jarrell. Copyright © 1969, renewed 1997 by Mary von S. Jarrell. Reprinted by permission of Farrar, Straus & Giroux, LLC.

Alice Jones. "The Foot" and "The Lungs," from *Anatomy* by Alice Jones (San Francisco: Bullnettle Press, 1997). Copyright © 1997 by Alice Jones. Reprinted by permission of the author.

Donald Justice. "Order in the Streets" from *Losers Weepers: Poems Found Practically Everywhere*, edited by George Hitchcock. Reprinted by permission of Jean Ross Justice.

Jane Kenyon. "The Socks" and "The Thimble," from *Collected Poems*. Copyright © 2005 by The Estate of Jane Kenyon. Reprinted with the permission of The Permissions Company, Inc., on behalf of Graywolf Press, Minneapolis, Minnesota, www.graywolfpress.org.

Carolyn Kizer. "After Bashō" from *Yin: New Poems*. Copyright © 1984 by Carolyn Kizer. Reprinted with the permission of The Permissions Company, Inc., on behalf of BOA Editions, Ltd., www.boaeditions.org.

Philip Larkin. "Sad Steps" and "A Study of Reading Habits," from *The Complete Poems of Philip Larkin* by Philip Larkin, edited by Archie Burnett. Copyright © 2012 by the Estate of Philip Larkin. Reprinted by permission of Farrar, Straus & Giroux, LLC, and Faber and Faber, Ltd.

Ann Lauinger. "Marvell Noir." First appeared in *Parnassus: Poetry in Review* 28, no. 1 & 2 (2005). Copyright © 2005 by Ann Lauinger. Reprinted by permission of the author.

John Lennon and Paul McCartney. "I Am the Walrus." Copyright © 1967 Sony/ATV Music Publishing LLC. All rights administered by Sony/ATV Music Publishing LLC, 424 Church Street, Suite 1200, Nashville, Tennessee 37219. All rights reserved. Used by permission.

J. Estanislao Lopez. "Meditation on Beauty," *New Yorker*, March 26, 2018. Copyright © 2018. Reprinted by permission of the author.

Robert Lowell. "Skunk Hour" from *Collected Poems* by Robert Lowell. Copyright © 2003 by Harriet Lowell and Sheridan Lowell. Reprinted by permission of Farrar, Straus & Giroux, LLC.

Dave Lucas. "November," originally appeared in *Shenandoah* 57.1 (Spring 2007). Copyright © 2007 by Dave Lucas. Reprinted by permission of the author.

Katharyn Howd Machan. "Hazel Tells LaVerne" from *Light Year '85*. Copyright © 1977 by Katharyn Howd Machan. Reprinted by permission of the author.

John Maloney. "Good!" from *Proposal* by John Maloney. Zoland Books, 1999. Copyright © 1999 by John Maloney. Reprinted by permission of the author.

Julio Marzán. "Ethnic Poetry." Originally appeared in *Parnassus: Poetry in Review*. "The Translator at the Reception for Latin American Writers." Reprinted by permission of the author.

Florence Cassen Mayers. "All-American Sestina," copyright © 1996 Florence Cassen Mayers, as first published in the *Atlantic Monthly*. Reprinted with permission of the author.

David McCord. "Epitaph on a Waiter" from *Odds Without Ends,* copyright © 1954 by David T. W. McCord. Reprinted by permission of the estate of David T. W. McCord.

Walt McDonald. "Coming Across It" from *Embers*, vol. 13, no. 1 (1988), p. 17. Copyright © 1988 by Walt McDonald. Reprinted with the permission of the author.

Michael McFee. "In Medias Res" from *Colander* by Michael McFee. Copyright © 1996 by Michael McFee. Reprinted by permission of Michael McFee.

Elaine Mitchell. "Form" from *Light* 9 (Spring 1994). Reprinted by permission of the Literary Estate of Elaine Mitchell.

Joni Mitchell. "Cold Blue Steel and Sweet Fire." Words and music by Joni Mitchell. Copyright © 1972 (renewed) Crazy Crow Music. All rights administered by Sony/ATV Music Publishing, 8 Music Square West, Nashville, TN 37203. All rights reserved. Used by permission of Alfred Music.

Janice Townley Moore. "To a Wasp" first appeared in *Light Year,* Bits Press. Reprinted by permission of the author.

Robert Morgan. "Mountain Graveyard" from *Sigodlin*. Copyright © 1990 by Robert Morgan. Reprinted by permission of the author.

Van Morrison. "Astral Weeks." Copyright © 1968 (renewed) WB Music Corp. (ASCAP) and Caledonia Soul Music (ASCAP). All rights administered by WB Music Corp. All rights reserved. Used by permission of Alfred Music.

Joan Murray. "We Old Dudes," copyright © 2006 by Joan Murray. First appeared in the July/August 2006 issue of *Poetry* magazine. Reprinted by permission of the author.

Marilyn Nelson. "How I Discovered Poetry" from *The Fields of Praise: New and Selected Poems* by Marilyn Nelson. Copyright © 1997 by Marilyn Nelson. Reprinted by permission of the author and Louisiana State University Press.

Alden Nowlan. "The Bull Moose" from *Alden Nowlan: Selected Poems* by Alden Nowlan. Copyright © 1967. Reprinted by permission of Claudine Nowlan.

Naomi Shihab Nye. "To Manage" from *Voices in the Air* by Naomi Shihab Nye. Copyright © 2018 by Naomi Shihab Nye. Reprinted by permission of HarperCollins Publishers.

Mary Oliver. "The Poet with His Face in His Hands" from *New and Selected Poems, Volume Two* by Mary Oliver. Copyright © 2005 by Mary Oliver. Published by Beacon Press, Boston. Reprinted by permission of the Charlotte Sheedy Literary Agency, Inc. "Wild Geese" from *Dream Work* by Mary Oliver. Copyright © 1986 by Mary Oliver. Used by permission of Grove/Atlantic, Inc. Any third-party use of this material, outside of this publication, is prohibited.

Dorothy Parker. "One Perfect Rose" from *The Portable Dorothy Parker* by Dorothy Parker, edited by Marion Meade. Copyright © 1926, renewed 1954 by Dorothy Parker. Used by permission of Viking Books, an imprint of Penguin Publishing Group, a division of Penguin Random House LLC. All rights reserved.

Lisa Parker. "Snapping Beans" from the collection *This Gone Place* by Lisa Parker. Originally appeared in *Parnassus* 23, no. 2 (1998). Reprinted by permission of the author.

Index of First Lines

Index of Authors and Titles

Index of Terms

Boldface numbers refer to the Glossary of Literary Terms.